ISBN 978-1-333-72676-8
PIBN 10539907

at each step of the long way. Of those 20,000 men, Jackson brought back to Lee on the Antietam only himself and 5000 others.[1] In the afternoon Walker came up. His two brigades had not as yet been engaged in any action. They had formed part of the rear-guard at Groveton. The two brigades numbered a little more than 3000 men when they rejoined Lee that evening. McLaws remained at Pleasant Valley until the morning of the 16th. He then crossed the Potomac by the railroad bridge, passed through Harper's Ferry, not giving his men time for rest and refreshment, and at dark encamped for a few hours on the south bank of the Potomac, close by the ford. At midnight the march was resumed, and by dawn of the 17th the command was halted close by Sharpsburg. Of the eight brigades comprised in this command, three had suffered severely at Crampton's Gap; the others had done hard duty on Maryland Heights, and in watching the outlets from Harper's Ferry. The march to Sharpsburg had been trying. Men dropped from the ranks in utter exhaustion. McLaws brought with him only 7000 men, barely half his force; of these about 3000 belonged to his own division, about 4000 to that of Anderson;[2] so that, on the morning of the 17th, Lee had, exclusive of cavalry, about 36,000 men, infantry and artillery.[3]

Meanwhile, on the afternoon of the 16th, McClellan began to move. Hooker was sent across the Antietam at a point above the extreme left of the Confederates. The passage was made without opposition. He then moved down the west bank, and came in contact with the Confederate left. Some sharp skirmishing ensued, the only result being that Hooker established himself in a position from which he could strike on the next morning; and Lee could infer from what quarter the first blow would come, and make his dispositions accordingly. Mansfield's corps followed Hooker across the Antietam during the night, and encamped a mile in the rear. McClellan's plan, if Hooker understood it rightly, was the true one. He had undertaken the offensive. The action at Turner's Gap had shown that he was in superior force. With half his strength he had forced the passage through the South Mountain, and his opponent had fallen back in full retreat. He had come up with Lee standing at bay at the farthest point to which retreat was possible. Every thing pointed to the one conclusion, that the whole Union force should be thrown at the earliest moment upon the Confederates. That this was to be done on the morning of the 17th was the decision, as understood by Hooker, to whom the initiative was assigned.[4]

Hooker opened the attack at dawn on the morning of the 17th. The onset fell upon a portion of Jackson's command, which, few in numbers, was strongly posted in a wood upon the Confederate left. This was soon swept back, with the loss of half its numbers, out of the wood, across an open field, and into another wood, where the outcropping rock gave shelter from the fierce fire poured in upon it. Lawton, who now commanded Ewell's division, called upon Hood for all the assistance which he could give. Hood threw his two strong brigades into action, and was soon followed by three brigades from Hill's division. Hooker still pressed on, meanwhile sending back for Mansfield's corps to come up to his support. This came upon the field at about 8 o'clock. While deploying his column, the veteran commander, who had joined his corps only the day before, was killed, and the command reverted to Williams. Hooker still pushed on upon the extreme left of the Confederates, and by 9 o'clock had gained an elevation which commanded the position of the enemy. He thought the battle won. The enemy, as far as he could see, were falling back in disorder, while his own troops, full of spirits, rent the sky with cheers. Just then, while looking for a point at which to post his batteries in order to sweep the retreating foe, he fell severely wounded. Having directed a telegram to his friends, announcing that he had won a great victory, and sending a message to Sumner, who was already close at hand, to hasten upon the field, he was borne half-conscious to the rear.[5]

But when Sumner came up the whole aspect of the battle had changed. Hill and Hood had sprung to the relief of Jackson. Their united force was far inferior in numbers to that of Hooker and Mansfield, but they were inordinately strong in artillery. Hill, with but 3000 infantry, had more than 80 guns at his command.[6] These, in front and upon the left, with the mounted artillery upon the right, under Stuart, were brought to bear upon Hooker's advancing corps. This was checked, then wavered, and when the enemy, with hardly half their numbers, charged from the sheltering woods, Hooker's corps broke and fled in utter rout, not to appear again upon the field. Their rout, moreover, threw into confusion a part of Mansfield's corps. The losses in Hooker's corps had been severe, but absolutely they had not been greater, and, relatively to the numbers engaged, had been less than they had inflicted. The killed and wounded had been about one sixth of the whole number, a ratio hardly one half of that of the forces which afterward bore the brunt of the fight on either side.[7]

JOSEPH K. MANSFIELD.

Sumner's large corps, more than 18,000 strong, was now thrown into action. It advanced in three columns. Sedgwick's division, on the extreme right, took the position from which Hooker had been driven so speedily that the Confederates were not aware of their signal success, but fell back to their former position before what they supposed to be merely re-enforcements brought up to support a force that had been driven back. Next on the left came the divisions of French's and Richardson's corps, pressing down toward the Confederate centre. Lee perceived that here was to be the main stress of the fight. To meet it, he ordered up every disposable man from his right. First came Walker's division, 3000 strong; then McLaws with 3000, and Anderson with 4000. So pressing seemed the emergency that Lee ventured still farther to weaken his right, detaching regiment after regiment, until D. R. Jones, who had been posted there with six brigades, had barely 2400 men with which to confront Burnside's corps of 14,000.[1] This withdrawal from the right was, however, screened from the view of the enemy by the wooded ridge along which the Confederate line was formed.

At ten it seemed that victory was secure for the Union forces. Sedgwick had gained a position a little beyond that from which Hooker had been driven an hour before, and Jackson's corps was streaming to the rear. Hood, having lost a third of his men and exhausted his ammunition, was withdrawn. Hill was sorely pressed by French and Richardson. Three of his five brigades were broken and retreating; the other two clung desperately to a sunken road which formed a natural rifle-pit. The Confederate left, worn by the fight in which it had been engaged for five hours, and pressed at every point by a superior force, was on the point of giving way. But the strong re-enforcements brought up not only restored the balance, but gave them a slight preponderance. All losses being deducted, Lee had here on his left about 24,000 men. Sumner had his own corps and half of that of Mansfield, now numbering together 22,000. The re-enforcements came up almost at the same moment. Jackson, strengthened by McLaws, advanced upon Sedgwick, who had gone considerably to the right, leaving a wide gap between himself and French. Into this gap Walker flung his division, assailing Sedgwick on the flank and threatening his rear. The combined attack was more than he could endure. The division was forced from the strip of woods which it held, and which Hooker had vainly attempted to win, across the open field, over which he had been driven for a full half mile, until they rallied behind a long line of post and rail fence. Here they re-formed, and poured in so fierce a fire that the Confederates were checked, and fell back again into the wood. Both sides now occupied here on the extreme right the positions which they had held in the morning, and the fighting in this quarter was closed. In this fierce encounter McLaws lost 1019 men and Walker 1108 out of the 6000 which they brought into the field. Jackson's loss during this final assault was nearly 1000. Sedgwick's loss was 1180, and Green's division of Mansfield's corps lost 650. Thus the Confederate loss in this final assault on the Union right was nearly double that of their opponents.[2]

[1] I accept this statement of the force brought by Jackson on the authority of the generals who commanded the divisions at Antietam: J. R. Jones, who commanded Jackson's division, says, "The old Stonewall division entered the action weary and worn, and reduced to the number of a small brigade . . . not numbering over 1600 men at the beginning of the fight."—*Lee's Rep.*, ii., 222. Early, who commanded Ewell's division, gives its losses at Antietam as 1052 "out of less than 3400, with which it went into that action."—*Ibid.*, ii., 190.

[2] *Lee's Rep.*, ii., 116, 172.

[3] From this point we take no account of the cavalry force on either side, as it was not engaged in the action of the day.

[4] "When I had left with my corps to make this attack, I had been assured that, simultaneous with my attack, there should be an attack upon the rebel army in the centre and on the left the next morning. I sent word to General McClellan when I proposed to attack, in order that he might direct the other attacks to be made at the same time. At dawn I made the attack."—*Hooker, in Com. Rep.*, 581.

[5] Hooker, in *Com. Rep.*, 581.

[6] *Lee's Rep.*, ii., 116.

[7] The completeness of the rout of Hooker's corps, after his wounding, is shown by evidence too conclusive to be questioned. Sumner says (*Com. Rep.*, 368): "On going upon the field, I found that General Hooker's corps had been dispersed and routed. I passed him some distance in the rear, where he had been carried wounded, but I saw nothing of his corps at all, as I was advancing with my command upon the field. There were some troops lying down on the left, which I took to belong to Mansfield's command. General Mansfield had been killed, and a portion of his corps also had been thrown into confusion. General Hooker's corps had been dispersed; there is no question about that. I sent one of my own staff officers to find where they were; and General Ricketts, the only officer we could find, said that he could not raise 300 men of the corps." General Meade, upon whom the command of General Hooker's men devolved, reported (*McC. Rep.*, 394): "There were but 6729 men present on the 18th; whereas, on the morning of the 22d, there were 13,093 men present for duty, showing that previous to and during the battle 6364 men were separated from their command."

[1] *Lee's Rep.*, ii., 219.

[2] The details of this action are given by McLaws and Walker in *Lee's Rep.*, 169, 205. Neither Lee nor Jackson make any separate mention of the defeat of Hooker in the morning. They

FRANCIS C. BARLOW.

French and Richardson were gaining slowly but steadily upon Hill. Colquitt's brigade had suffered severely, and fell back to the sunken road, where a vain attempt was made to rally them; they broke, and disappeared from the fight. Garland's brigade was pressing on, when an officer raised a shout, "They are flanking us!" "This cry," says Hill, "spread like an electric shock along the ranks, bringing up vivid recollections of the flank fire at South Mountain. In a moment they broke and fell to the rear." A part of it was rallied in the sunken road. Ripley's brigade had also fallen back to this road, and behind the crest of a hill which bordered it. Hill's numerous artillery had been withdrawn from his front. It had done good service in the conflict of the morning; but McClellan had posted his heavy guns near the Antietam in such a position as to command the position. "Our artillery," says Hill, "could not cope with the superior weight, caliber, range, and number of the Yankee guns. They were smashed up or withdrawn before they could be effectually turned against the massive columns of attack."[1]

Howard, who now commanded the division of Sedgwick, who, having been twice wounded, was borne from the field, was still engaged with Jackson, McLaws, and Walker, when French on the right, followed by Richardson on the left, pushed vigorously upon Hill, driving him back toward the right and rear, into and beyond the sunken road, which formed a right angle with his previous line. Kimball, of French's division, and Meagher, of Richardson's, gained the border of this natural rifle-pit at almost the same moment. Here ensued the fiercest fighting of the day. R. H. Anderson had now brought his division of 4000 men to the support of Hill, who had been farther strengthened by a number of regiments drawn from D. R. Jones, who held the extreme Confederate right, opposite Burnside, who had hardly made an attempt to cross the Antietam and take his assigned part in the action. The fight here was almost wholly with musketry, scarcely a battery being brought into action on either side. Meagher's Irish brigade suffered fearfully. Its commander was disabled by a fall from his horse. The brigade, having nearly exhausted its ammunition, was withdrawn to replenish, its place being taken by Caldwell's brigade. Both brigades moved, one to the front, the other to the rear, as steadily as though on drill. Barlow, then colonel, since major general, now dashed upon the flank of the sunken road, capturing the 300 men who still clung to it.

Anderson was wounded shortly after coming upon the field, and the command of his brigade devolved upon Pryor.[2] The ground upon which Richardson and French had been fighting was broken and irregular, intersected by numerous ravines, hills covered with corn, inclosed by stone walls, behind which the enemy could manœuvre and throw his strength, without being perceived, upon every part of the lines. More than half a score desperate attempts were made; all were repulsed, and the conclusion of each found the Union troops in possession of some additional ground and important position. Two of these repulses were given by Barlow, who, with his two regiments, the 61st and 64th New York, had won the sunken road. He fairly won his generalship upon this bloody field. Eighteen months before he had enlisted as a private. In one of the last of these, Richardson, whose services on this day were second to those of no other man, was mortally wounded, and the command of his division fell upon Hancock.

This action on the centre was fairly begun an hour before noon. By two hours after noon the Confederates here were worsted, and their force was so thoroughly shattered that it needed but a single heavy blow to shiver it to atoms, and, notwithstanding the reverse which Sedgwick had met, which was really only slight, to win a complete victory. McClellan had then at the very point where the blow should have been struck a force three-fold greater than was required to make it effectual. About noon, Franklin, with two divisions of his corps, 12,000 strong, had come up from Pleasant Valley.[1] The march had been an easy one, and these troops were perfectly fresh. McClellan had intended to keep this corps in reserve on the east side of the Antietam, to operate on either flank or on the centre, as circumstances might require. But when it came up the action was so critical that he properly abandoned this purpose, and sent the corps across the stream. The leading division, that of Smith, touched the edge of the fight somewhat sharply. It came upon the field between Sedgwick and French just at the moment when Sedgwick had been forced back. The third brigade met a force of the enemy coming out of the woods so often contested, drove them back, and attempted to enter the woods. Meeting a severe fire, it fell back, somewhat disordered, behind the crest of a hill, where it re-formed, the Confederates at the same time falling back into the shelter of the woods. Smith's second brigade was sent a little to the left to support French, and encountered a sharp fire from Hill's artillery.[2] Slocum's division of Franklin's corps followed directly after that of Smith, and the whole corps was ready for action. Franklin had given orders to advance. Had this been done, nothing in war can be more certain than that the absolute rout and capture of the Confederate army would have followed. This corps, 12,000 strong, perfectly fresh and eager for action, lay right in front of a great gap which had been left between the Confederate centre and left. On the left, Jackson, with McLaws and Walker, had left barely 8000 men; Hill, in the centre, with the remnants of his own division, of Anderson's, of the six brigades of Longstreet, including Hood's two, which returned to the field, had remaining not more than 13,000, and these were so utterly shattered and broken that, in the utmost emergency, not half that number could have been rallied for a fight. Confronting him were the divisions of Richardson, French, and Green, of Mansfield's corps, worn, exhausted, and reduced in numbers, it is true, but cheered with success, and still with quite 13,000 effective men.

Hill's condition, as told by himself and his brigade commanders, was indeed pitiable. Of his own five brigades four had been utterly routed. He had gone into action at South Mountain with 5000, and lost 2000; of the 3000 with which he entered the battle of Antietam, he could, the day after its close, muster less than 1700. In three days he had lost almost two thirds of his men. Thirty-four field-officers had gone into these two battles; when they were over, only nine were left; regiments, or the fragments of them, were commanded by lieutenants. His artillery, eighty guns and more, had been "smashed up," or withdrawn to avoid certain destruction. The Thersites of the Confederate army (saving only the point of cowardice; for, in spite of his foul pen and tongue, he was a skillful leader and desperate fighter), one can not wonder that Hill heaps invectives upon friend and foe. Reno is a "renegade Virginian," killed by "a happy shot;" the force opposed to him are always styled "Yankees," in which word he embodies the utmost of his detestation, save in one case, where, for deeper emphasis, they are denominated "the restorers of the Union." The Confederates failed of victory, he says, because McLaws and Anderson came up two hours too late; because the artillery was badly handled—"an artillery duel between the Washington artillery and the Yankee batteries was the most melancholy farce of the war;" and because "thousands of thievish poltroons had kept away from sheer cowardice; the straggler is generally a thief, and always a coward, lost to all sense of shame; he can only be kept in ranks by a strict and sanguinary discipline." Yet there is something almost sublime in the attitude of Hill at the close of the fight on his front. Two brigades had streamed to the rear in confusion, leaving a great gap, through which the enemy poured resistlessly. Rallying 150 men, Hill, musket in hand like a private, led them on.[3] He himself shall describe the closing moments of his part of the engagement: "There were no troops

were not at all aware that it was an utter rout. So closely had the advance of Sedgwick followed the retreat of Hooker that it was supposed to be a rally of the same troops with strong re-enforcements. See also McClellan's Report, and Sumner, in *Com. Rep.*, 368.

[1] D. H. Hill, in *Lee's Rep.*, II., 115.

[2] Lee's Report embodies no reports, either divisional or regimental, from Anderson's division, and its movements are barely alluded to by Hill. It was sharply engaged, losing more than 1000 men; but its efforts seem to have been desultory and ineffective.

[1] Franklin says (*Com. Rep.*, 626): "The advance of my command arrived on the battle-field of Antietam about 10 o'clock." McClellan says (*Report*, 385): "Between 12 and 1 P.M. General Franklin's corps arrived on the field of battle." From a comparison of all the indicia of time, I conclude that Franklin gives the hour correctly, and that he was actually engaged before noon.

[2] This movement of Smith's division of Franklin's corps was of considerable importance. The Confederate reports respecting it are very full, and greatly exaggerated. Thus Hill says (*Lee's Rep.*, II., 115): "Franklin's corps advanced in three parallel lines, with all the precision of a parade-day, upon my two brigades. They met with a galling fire, however, recoiled, and fell back, and finally lay down behind the crest of a hill, and kept up an irregular fire. I got a battery in position, which partly enfiladed the Yankee line, and aided materially to check its advance." Walker (*Ibid.*, II., 200) describes at length the encounter between Smith's third brigade and two regiments of his division, which were ordered by Longstreet "to charge the enemy, who was threatening his flank as if to pass through the opening between the point of timber. This order was promptly obeyed in the face of such a fire as troops have seldom encountered without running away, and with a steadiness and unfailing gallantry seldom equaled. Battery after battery, regiment after regiment, opened their fire upon them, hurling a torrent of missiles through their ranks; but nothing could arrest their prowess, and three times the enemy broke and fled before their impetuous charge. Finally they reached the fatal picket fence. To climb over it in the face of such a force, and under such a fire, would have been sheer madness to attempt, and, their ammunition being now almost exhausted, Colonel Cooke very properly gave the order to fall back, which was done in the most perfect order; after which the troops took up their former position, which they held until night."

[3] *Lee's Report*, II., 246

near to hold the centre except a few hundred rallied from various brigades. The Yankees crossed the old road which we had occupied in the morning, and occupied a corn-field and orchard in advance of it. They had now got within a few hundred yards of the hill which commanded Sharpsburg and our rear. Affairs looked very critical. I found a battery concealed in a corn-field, and ordered it to move out and open upon the Yankee columns. It moved out most gallantly, though exposed to a terrible direct and reverse fire from the long-range Yankee artillery across the Antietam. A caisson exploded, but the battery was unlimbered, and, with grape and canister, drove the Yankees back. I was now satisfied that a single regiment of fresh men could drive the whole of them in our front across the Antietam. I got up about two hundred men, who said they were willing to advance to the attack if I would lead them. We met, however, with a warm reception, and the little command was broken and dispersed. About two hundred more were gathered, and I sent them to the right to attack the Yankees in flank. They drove them back a short distance, but were in turn repulsed. These two attacks, however, had a most happy effect. The Yankees were completely deceived by their boldness, and induced to believe that there was a large force in our centre. They made no farther attempt to pierce our centre, except on a small scale."[1]

McClellan thus relates the closing operations on this part of the field: "Hancock, seeing a body of the enemy advancing to the left of his position, obtained a battery from Franklin's corps, which assisted materially in frustrating this attack. The enemy seemed at one time to be about making an attack upon this part of the line, and advanced a long column of infantry toward this division" (this must have been Hill's last 200), "but on nearing the position, General Pleasanton opening on them with sixteen guns, they halted, gave a desultory fire, and retreated, closing the operations on this part of the field." Not dreaming that the enemy who had encountered them so stubbornly, and who still showed so bold a front, was so utterly broken that a single fresh regiment would have put them to utter rout, Hancock and French desisted from the attack, and rested in the positions they had won.

Jackson's plight, had Sumner known it, was no less critical than that of Hill. Of the 5000 men whom he had brought from Harper's Ferry, 2000 had been killed or wounded in the morning's fight with Hooker. Re-enforced, he had pressed Sedgwick back for half a mile, and then fallen back himself, having not more than 7000 effective men. Sumner, in front of him, had left wellnigh 5000 of Sedgwick's division; of Hooker's routed corps at least 6000 remained with their command, and might have been rallied; of Mansfield's first division, which had withdrawn in the morning, there must have been 3000. In all, Sumner had at his hand on the extreme right twice the force of Jackson at the time when Franklin, fairly on the field, was ready and anxious to attack. Had he then thrown his fresh 12,000 between Hill and Jackson, and upon the flank of both, striking either to the right or left, one or the other of these commands must have been annihilated, even without an effort on the part of the troops with which they had already been engaged.

That this was not done was no fault of Franklin. He had made every preparation, and given orders for an assault upon the woods which had been so hotly contested all day, when Sumner came up, and, in spite of Franklin's urgency, forbade the movement. Neither is it to be charged to McClellan except in so far that he approved of Sumner's action.[2] Sumner, indeed, showed on this day a want of vigor and resource utterly at variance with the whole tenor of his military career. For six hours he seems not to have made the slightest attempt to rally the corps of Hooker and Mansfield, which had retreated hardly a mile in his rear. Among these were some of the best soldiers in the army.

McClellan's plan on the evening of the 16th, as understood by Hooker,[3] was to make a simultaneous attack upon the Confederate right, centre, and left. By the morning of the 17th he had changed his scheme, and determined "to attack the enemy's left with the corps of Hooker and Mansfield, supported by Sumner's, and, if necessary, by Franklin's, and as soon as matters looked favorably there, to move the corps of Burnside against the enemy's extreme left; and whenever either of these flank movements should be successful, to advance our centre with all their forces then disposable.[4] Now Franklin's corps was fully four hours distant, and did not commence its march until an hour, and did not reach the ground until six hours after

BURYING THE DEAD.

AT THE FENCE.

SCENES ON THE FIELD AFTER THE BATTLE.[1]

[1] These views, and those on page 408, are reproduced from Photographs by M. B. Brady, taken a day or two after the action. They are introduced as presenting the real aspect of a great battle-field. My acknowledgments are due to Mr. Brady for access to, and free use of his immense collection of scenes and portraits.

[1] D. H. Hill, in *Lee's Rep.*, ii., 116, 117.—This closing attack "on a small scale" is quite differently described by others. McClellan says: "The 7th Maine, of Franklin's corps, without any other aid, made a gallant attack against the enemy's line, and drove in the skirmishers, who were annoying our artillery and troops on the right." Hill says that "Pryor had gathered quite a respectable force behind a hill, when a Maine regiment" (he gives the number erroneously as the 21st) "came down to this hill, wholly unconscious that there were any Confederate troops near it. A shout and a volley informed them of their dangerous neighborhood. The Yankee apprehension is acute; the idea was soon taken in, and was followed by the most rapid running I ever saw."

[2] Franklin's testimony, in *Com. Rep.*, 626: "The division of General Slocum arrived on the field. I formed two brigades of it in line of battle in front of the Dunker Church, with the intention of making an attack at once upon the enemy in that wood. I was waiting for the third brigade to be a reserve for the other two, when I was informed that General Sumner had detained the brigade at his head-quarters for the protection of his right. I sent for it, and it finally arrived, and General Sumner with it. The general advised me not to make the attack, for if it failed, the right would be entirely destroyed, as there were no troops there that could be depended upon. I informed him that I thought it a very necessary thing to do, and told him that I would prefer to make the attack, unless he assumed the responsibility of forbidding it. He assumed the responsibility, and ordered me not to make it. One of General McClellan's aids was there at the time. He informed General McClellan what had been done, and the general himself came up and stated that things had gone so well (!!!?) on all the other parts of the field that he was afraid to risk the day by an attack there on the right at that time. Therefore no attack was made by that division that day." McClellan's account (*Report*, 387) is to the same effect: "General Franklin ordered two brigades of General Slocum's division, General Newton's and Colonel Torbert's, to form in column to attack the woods that had been so hotly contested by Generals Sumner and Hooker; General Bartlett's brigade was ordered to form the reserve. At this time General Sumner, having command on the right, directed farther offensive operations to be postponed, as the repulse of this, the only remaining corps available for attack, would peril the safety of the whole army."

[3] *Ante*, p. 399.

[4] *McC. Rep.*, 377.

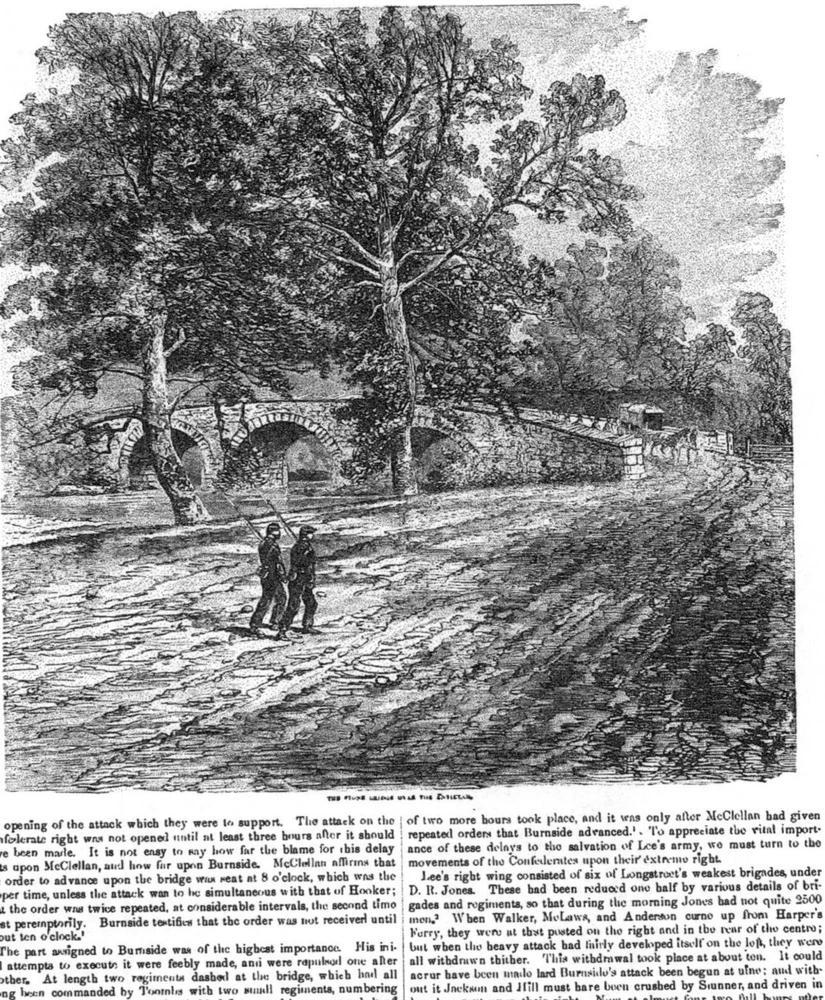

THE STONE BRIDGE OVER THE ANTIETAM.

the opening of the attack which they were to support. The attack on the Confederate right was not opened until at least three hours after it should have been made. It is not easy to say how far the blame for this delay rests upon McClellan, and how far upon Burnside. McClellan affirms that the order to advance upon the bridge was sent at 8 o'clock, which was the proper time, unless the attack was to be simultaneous with that of Hooker; that the order was twice repeated, at considerable intervals, the second time most peremptorily. Burnside testifies that the order was not received until about ten o'clock.[1]

The part assigned to Burnside was of the highest importance. His initial attempts to execute it were feebly made, and were repulsed one after another. At length two regiments dashed at the bridge, which had all along been commanded by Toombs with two small regiments, numbering together less than 500 men, hidden behind fences and in a narrow belt of woods. These had been withdrawn a little before, as well as the force which commanded the adjacent fords, so that the actual passage of the stream was made without opposition.[2] Burnside's whole corps, nearly 14,000 strong, was soon across the stream. Here an unaccountable delay of two more hours took place, and it was only after McClellan had given repeated orders that Burnside advanced.[1] To appreciate the vital importance of these delays to the salvation of Lee's army, we must turn to the movements of the Confederates upon their extreme right.

Lee's right wing consisted of six of Longstreet's weakest brigades, under D. R. Jones. These had been reduced one half by various details of brigades and regiments, so that during the morning Jones had not quite 2500 men.[2] When Walker, McLaws, and Anderson came up from Harper's Ferry, they were at first posted on the right and in the rear of the centre; but when the heavy attack had fairly developed itself on the left, they were all withdrawn thither. This withdrawal took place at about ten. It could never have been made had Burnside's attack been begun at nine; and without it Jackson and Hill must have been crushed by Sumner, and driven in hopeless rout upon their right. Now, at almost four, two full hours after the action on the right and centre had ceased, Burnside fairly began his attack. It was at first successful. The heights which command Sharpsburg were won; the Confederates were driven back through the town. Had this been done two hours before, a position would have been secured from which the whole Confederate line would have been swept by an enfilading fire of artillery. But now A. P. Hill had come up from Harper's Ferry, having marched seventeen miles that day. He brought with him tire brigades, or rather such portions of them as could endure the march. One

[1] McClellan (*Report*, 390) says: "At eight o'clock an order was sent to General Burnside to carry the bridge. After some time had elapsed, not hearing from him, I dispatched an aid to ascertain what had been done. The aid returned with information that but little progress had been made. I then sent him back with an order to General Burnside to assault the bridge at once, and carry it at all hazards. The aid returned to me a second time with the report that the bridge was still in possession of the enemy. Whereupon I directed Colonel Sackett, the Inspector General, to deliver to General Burnside my positive order to push forward his troops without a moment's delay, and, if necessary, to carry the bridge with the bayonet; and I ordered Colonel Sackett to remain with General Burnside and see that the order was executed promptly." Burnside testifies (*Com. Rep.*, 640): "On the morning of the 17th I was ordered to place the command in position to enable us to attack the enemy at the bridge as soon as I was notified to commence the attack. About ten o'clock I received an order from General McClellan to make the attack on the bridge."

[2] This withdrawal of the troops before the final attempt at crossing is expressly affirmed by D. R. Jones and Toombs (*Lee's Rep.*, ii., 219, 324). Burnside's Report, however, seems to imply, without positively affirming it, that there was a conflict here.

[1] *McCl. Rep.*, 390; Burnside, in *Com. Rep.*, 641.

[2] This number is expressly given by both Lee and Jones. The words of the latter, indeed, seem to imply that this was the entire strength of his six brigades. He says (*Lee's Rep.*, ii., 219): "My command had been further reduced on the right, leaving me for the defense of the right with only Toombs's two regiments, and Kemper's, Drayton's, and Walker's brigades. When it is known that on that morning my entire command, of six brigades, comprised only 2430 men, the enormous disparity of force with which I contended may be seen." Now, although these brigades had suffered heavily at Groveton, where two of them lost nearly 1500 men, and considerably at South Mountain, it is hardly credible that their average strength should have been reduced to 400 each—not one third of their original strength. The whole six brigades took part in the fight with Burnside.

SITE OF A BATTERY.

SCENE OF A CHARGE.

brigade was reduced to 350 men;[1] all told there were not 4000, and of these only three brigades, including the weak one, numbering all together not more than 2000 men, were brought into the fight. It was over before the others could engage. With these and Toombs's brigade, then not 1000 strong, Burnside's whole corps was driven back, just as darkness was coming on, to the Antietam, which he recrossed the next morning. A. P. Hill hardly exaggerates when he says: "The three brigades of my division actively engaged did not number over 2000 men, and these, with the help of my splendid batteries, drove back Burnside's corps of 15,000 men."[2] Hill lost 346 killed and wounded; Jones lost about 700. Burnside's loss in killed and wounded was 2173.

Porter's corps had not been brought into action at all. It was posted in the centre, between the right and left wings, to guard the trains, for the safety of which McClellan was apprehensive. Portions of it were at times detached as supports to batteries. It lost only 130. Franklin's corps can hardly be considered as engaged, although in its brief encounter it lost 438; so that 25,000 men, wellnigh a third of McClellan's force, and as many as Lee had in action at any one moment, were practically unemployed. Lee had in all, and at all times, exclusive of cavalry, something more than 40,000, of whom all but about 2000 were engaged. McClellan had 83,000, of whom 58,000 were engaged; but they were sent in by "driblets," corps after corps, at intervals of hours. What the result was has been shown; what it would have been had the assault been made in full force can hardly be a matter of doubt.[3] Had the battle of Antietam been fought on the 16th, Lee could have mustered barely 27,000 men, while McClellan had—Franklin's corps not being present—fully 70,000. The Union loss was 11,426 killed and wounded; that of the Confederates about 10,000. The disparity arises mainly from the great excess of Burnside's loss on the left. On the right and centre each side lost about equally. The entire Union loss in the series of actions in Maryland, not including missing, was 14,200; that of the Confederates about 12,500.[1]

[1] *Lee's Rep.*, ii., 263.

[2] A. P. Hill, in *Lee's Rep.*, ii., 129.—It is indeed asserted by Burnside (*Com. Rep.*, 641): "The enemy had brought away from opposite the extreme right of our army portions of their forces, and concentrated them against us." There was, indeed, time sufficient for such an operation in the interval between the cessation of the action on the right and the beginning of this on the left, had the Confederates been in a condition to make it; but I do not find in any of their reports, which fully detail the movements of every brigade, with the exception of those of Anderson's division, the least intimation of any such movement, and this division was apparently in no condition for offense.

[3] "I have always believed that, instead of sending these troops into action in driblets, as they were sent, if General McClellan had authorized me to march these 40,000 men on the left flank of the enemy, we could not have failed to throw them right back in front of the other divisions of our army on our left, Burnside's, Franklin's, and Porter's corps; and all escape for the enemy, I think, would have been impossible. Why that was not done I do not know."—Sumner, in *Com. Rep.*, 368.

[1] The Union force at Antietam is given in detail in McClellan's Report. In summing up the Confederate force we have to estimate that under Longstreet. We put down the average strength of his brigades at 1500—some were less, some greater. He had eleven brigades, and had probably lost 600 at Turner's Gap; this would give him 16,000 at Antietam. The strength present in the other commands is stated with sufficient accuracy in the various reports, as previously cited. From these data, omitting cavalry on both sides, we construct the following table:

FORCES PRESENT AT ANTIETAM.

UNION.		CONFEDERATE.	
Hooker's corps	14,856	Longstreet's division	16,000
Sumner's "	18,813	Jackson's "	5,000
Porter's "	12,930	Walker's "	3,000
Franklin's "	12,300	McLaws's "	3,000
Burnside's "	13,819	Anderson's "	4,000
Mansfield's "	10,126	D. H. Hill's "	3,000
		A. P. Hill's "	4,000
		Reserve artillery	2,000
Total force	82,844	Total force	40,000
Not engaged: Porter and Franklin	25,230	Not engaged: Part of A. P. Hill	2,000
Total engaged	57,614	Total engaged	38,000

Probably, to make the comparison entirely just, some deduction should be made from McClellan's numbers, as the Confederate commanders report usually the numbers with which "they went into the action," while the Union report gives the number "present and fit for duty;" there will always be some discrepancy between these two modes of enumeration. Lee says (*Report*, i., 35): "This great battle was fought by less than 40,000 men on our side;" which we think a true statement. D. H. Hill, indeed, asserts (*Lee's Rep.*, ii., 119): "The battle was fought with less than 30,000." Cooke (*Stonewall Jackson*, 340-342): "In General Lee's published official Report the exact numbers are given—33,000." I find in Lee's Report no such statement, but do find the one just cited. Again Cooke says: "Nor was the bulk of Jackson's corps present until four P.M., toward the end of the action. General Lee fought until late in the day with Longstreet, D. H. Hill, Ewell, and two other divisions, a force of about 25,000 men. The re-enforcements of McLaws, Anderson, and Hill increased this number to 33,000, with which force General Lee met the 87,164

—ND A BREASTWORK.

SHELTER FOR WOUNDED.

The action of Antietam was in all respects a drawn battle. The Confederates had inflicted a greater absolute loss than they had suffered; but they had suffered, in proportion to their strength, far more than they had inflicted. At the close of the fight the positions of the armies were nearly the same as at its commencement. On the extreme right and left, the Federals, after forcing back the Confederate lines, had been repelled in turn beyond the original Confederate lines; but the Confederates then fell back, so that neither side held the field of battle. In the centre the Confederate lines had been forced back a little, and here the Federals held some ground wrested from the enemy. During the night the Confederates changed ground a little, but in all essential respects their position was as advantageous as it had been in the morning. Nor did the battle decide the issue of the invasion of Maryland; that question had been decided three days before, when McClellan, forcing the passes of the South Mountain, interposed his army between Lee and his projected line of march into Pennsylvania. After the battle, Lee accomplished without hinderance just what he would have done had no action taken place. He gave up the invasion of the North, recrossed the Potomac, and awaited in Virginia the movements of his tardy opponent. But the moral effect of the battle was great. It aroused the confidence of the nation, who saw in it a sure presage of the speedy overthrow of the insurrection; and, what was more, it emboldened the President to issue his warning proclamation for the abolition of slavery. That proclamation had been written months before, though only his trusted advisers knew of it. If put forth at any time during the disastrous summer, it would have been a mockery. It would have sounded to the world like a despairing shriek for help. And so the proclamation, written and rewritten, touched and retouched, lay in his desk. How could he, without mockery, promise to "recognize and maintain" the freedom of all slaves in the insurgent states, when the victorious armies of those confederated states threatened the capital of the Union? And so, when urged to issue such a proclamation, he replied in one of the half-jesting phrases in which he was wont to couch his most serious thoughts, that it would be like "the pope's bull against the comet." But now it seemed that such a promise could be maintained. So five days after the battle of Antietam the proclamation was put forth, and the result of the contest was staked upon an issue from which a few months before the nation would have shrunk, and for which even now it was scarcely prepared. The principle upon which Mr. Lincoln acted then, before, and thereafter, was at the same time clearly expressed by himself: "My paramount object is to save the Union, and not either to save or destroy slavery. If I could save the Union without freeing any slave, I would do it; if I could save it by freeing all the slaves, I would do it; if I could save it by freeing some and leaving others alone, I would also do that. What I do about slavery and the colored race, I do because I believe it helps to save this Union; and what I forbear, I forbear because I do not believe it would help to save the Union. I shall do less whenever I believe that what I am doing hurts the cause; and I shall do more whenever I believe that doing more will help the cause."[1] The inexorable march of events had now brought things to such a state that the conflict between Slavery and the Union was irrepressible. One or the other must go down. In a few months more all men saw that, whether the Union was saved or lost, Slavery was inevitably destroyed.

The battle was over, except on the extreme right, while the sun was yet high in the heavens, and McClellan had to consider whether it should be renewed the next day. Burnside, in spite of his severe repulse, was in favor of renewing it in the morning if he could have 5000 fresh men. Franklin was of the same opinion; he was sure that he could take the hotly-contested wood, which would uncover the enemy's left. Sumner thought otherwise.[1] McClellan decided to postpone the attack. He reasoned that, "Virginia lost, Washington menaced, Maryland invaded, the national cause could afford no risks of defeat. One battle lost, and almost all would have been lost. Lee's army might then have marched as it pleased on Washington, Baltimore, Philadelphia, or New York, and nowhere east of the Alleghanies was there another organized force able to arrest its march."[2] Believing, as he and most of his generals did, that the enemy was equal or superior in numbers, he could not well have come to any other decision. But in truth his fresh troops were almost equal in number to Lee's entire remaining force, while those who were worst off were in better plight than the best of the enemy. During the morning Humphreys's and Couch's divisions, 14,000 strong, came up; Lee also received some accessions from those who had fallen out in the march from Harper's Ferry, and stood at bay all day awaiting an attack. McClellan ordered that this should be made on the morning of the 19th. But in the darkness of the night the Confederate forces slipped quietly away, and when McClellan looked for them in the morning they were safely across the Potomac, and as evening fell they encamped five miles from the river. Next morning a strong reconnoissance from Porter's corps was sent over at Shepherdstown to ascertain the position of the enemy. A. P. Hill, who brought up the Confederate rear, turned upon them and drove them back, with considerable loss.[3]

Gathering up the remnants of his army, and bringing on those who had been left behind at Harper's Ferry, and those who had fallen out on the march thence to the Antietam, numbering in all less than 40,000 effective men, Lee fell back to Martinsburg, and thence to Winchester, where he had ordered all his stragglers to rendezvous. On the 30th of September he had but 53,000 men present for duty. On that day, exclusive of 73,000 left behind for the defense of Washington, McClellan had with him 100,000 effective men.[4]

Six weeks of beautiful autumnal weather were passed in almost total inaction. McClellan, believing that his army was in no condition to provoke another battle, posted it along the eastern side of the Potomac, half near Harper's Ferry, and the remainder watching the fords above and below, for he still apprehended that Lee would attempt to recross the river. Meanwhile the old bickerings between the commander of the army in the field and the military authorities at Washington were renewed with increased pertinacity. McClellan wanted supplies, clothing, horses, and, above all, re-enforcements. The Washington authorities would not spare a man from the 73,000 lying idle in the defenses of the capital, and the clothing and horses forwarded were far less than McClellan demanded. On the 6th of October the President issued a peremptory order that the army should at once "cross the Potomac and give battle to the enemy, or drive him South." If the army crossed between the enemy and Washington, so as to cover the capital, it should receive 30,000 re-enforcements, otherwise not more than 15,000. McClellan paid no immediate attention to this order, but reiterated his demands and complaints. He assumed that he, being with the army in the field, was more competent to determine whether it was in a condition to move than was the general-in-chief in his office at Washington.[5] On the 10th, Stuart, with 1800 cavalry, crossed the Potomac above the Union positions, made a clear circuit around the Union army, and recrossed below, without having lost a man. On the 13th the President wrote to McClellan earnestly urging him to action, and indicating the true theory upon which operations should be conducted.

"You remember," he said, "my speaking to you of what I called your over-cautiousness. Are you not over-cautious when you assume that you can not do what the enemy is constantly doing? Should you not claim to be at least his equal in prowess, and act upon the claim? You say that you can not subsist your army at Winchester unless the railroad from Harper's Ferry to that point be put in working order.[6] But the enemy does now subsist his army at Winchester, at a distance nearly twice as great from railroad transportation as you would have to do. He now wagons from Culpepper Court-house, which is just about twice as far as you would have to do from Harper's Ferry. He is certainly not more than half as well provided with wagons as you are. I should certainly be pleased for you to have the advantage of the railroad from Harper's Ferry to Winchester, but it wastes all the remainder of the autumn to give it to you, and, in fact, ignores the question of time, which can not and must not be ignored. It is one of the standard maxims of war to operate upon the enemy's communications as much as possible, without exposing your own. You seem to act as if this applies against you, but can not apply in your favor. Change positions with the enemy, and think you not he would break your communications with Richmond in twenty-four hours? You dread his going into Pennsylvania. But if he does so in full force, he gives up his communications to you absolutely, and you have nothing to do but to follow and ruin him; if he does so with less than full force, fall upon and beat what is left behind all the easier. If he should move northward, I would follow him closely, holding his communications. If he should move toward Rich-

men reported by General McClellan as 'in action' on the Federal side." But McLaws and Anderson, instead of being absent until "late in the day," were hotly engaged before noon, the division of McLaws losing a larger proportion of its numbers than any other except that of D. H. Hill.

In giving their losses, the Confederate reports do not usually discriminate between the different engagements. The report by regiments (*Lee's Rep.*, ii., 107, 106) makes their entire loss 1567 killed, 8274 wounded, 10,291 in all; but this is clearly defective, as is shown by the separate reports of division commanders. Those of Longstreet, including his entire "command," are given in *Lee's Report*, p. 89; Jackson, excluding A. P. Hill's at Antietam and Shepherdstown, *Ibid.*, 105; A. P. Hill at Antietam, *Ibid.*, 131; D. H. Hill, *Ibid.*, 119. The Union loss in each engagement is given separately. The following table presents a summation:

LOSSES IN THE MARYLAND CAMPAIGN, SEPT. 14–17.

UNION.	Killed.	Wounded.	Missing.	Total.
Hooker	348	2,016	255	2,619
Sumner	860	3,801	549	5,209
Porter	21	107	2	130
Franklin	70	335	33	438
Burnside	432	1,741	120	2,293
Mansfield	274	1,384	85	1,743
Cavalry	5	32	—	37
At Antietam	2010	9,416	1043	12,469
Turner's Gap	312	1,234	22	1,568
Crampton's Gap	115	416	2	533
Total	2437	11,066	1067	14,570

CONFEDERATES.	Killed.	Wounded.	Missing.	Total.
Longstreet	964	5234	1310	7,508
Jackson	391	1809	57	2,187
A. P. Hill	63	283	—	346
D. H. Hill	464	1852	925	3,241
Reported losses	1812	9178	2292	13,282
Correcting the apportionment of killed, wounded, and missing, and adding prisoners as below, we give the following as a close approximation:				
Total	2062	10,428	4792	17,282

A large proportion of those entered as "missing" in the Confederate Reports were undoubtedly killed or wounded. D. H. Hill says (*Lee's Rep.*, ii., 118): "Doubtless a large number of the 'missing' fell into the hands of the Yankees when wounded;" and Rodes (*Ibid.*, 347): "The 'missing' are either prisoners or killed." At South Mountain they were forced to abandon their killed and severely wounded, and could only enter as such upon the lists those whose fate was known. Nearly all the killed and many of the wounded were also left behind at Antietam. It is safe to estimate that of the 2292 reported as missing, 1500 were killed or wounded; apportioning them in the usual ratio adds 250 to the killed and 1250 to the wounded, as reported, diminishing the missing by the same numbers.

McClellan puts the Confederate loss much higher. He says (*Report*, 896): "About 2700 of the enemy's dead were, under the direction of Major Davis, Assistant Inspector General, counted and buried upon the battle-field of Antietam. A portion of their dead had been previously buried by the enemy. This is conclusive evidence that the enemy sustained much greater loss than we." Accepting this, and adding the dead at South Mountain, the Confederate killed must have numbered fully 3500, which would make their total loss more than 20,000, besides prisoners, of whom there were 6000, about two thirds of whom appear to have been stragglers. We do not undertake to reconcile these conflicting accounts as to the killed, and consequently of the wounded, but adopt the Confederate statement, with the exception above noted. To the "missing," however, we add 4000 unwounded prisoners.

The method of the Confederate generals in stating the number of the "missing" is wholly inexplicable. From the 28d of August to the 17th of September they put down in all only 2378, while it is certain that they lost nearly three times that number in prisoners during the three last days of this period, and all of their reports speak of thousands of stragglers.

[1] *Ante*, p. 208. For the proclamation, see *ante*, p. 208.

[1] *Com. Rep.*, 642, 627, 869.

[2] *McC. Rep.*, 394.

[3] Hill (*Lee's Rep.*, ii., 130) gives a most exaggerated account of this engagement: "A daring charge was made, and the enemy driven pell-mell into the river. Then commenced the most terrible slaughter that this war has yet witnessed. The broad surface of the Potomac was blue with the floating bodies of our foe. But few escaped to tell the tale. By their own account they lost 3000 men killed and drowned from one brigade alone. My own loss was 30 killed and 231 wounded."

[4] See *ante*, p. 388, for Lee's force. The strength of the Army of the Potomac on the 30th of September was, according to the official report, signed by McClellan, 173,745 present for duty, of whom 73,601 were around Washington.—*Com. Rep.*, 507.

[5] *McC. Rep.*, 426.

[6] This had been destroyed by the Confederates.

mond, I would press closely to him, fight him if a favorable opportunity should present, and at least try to beat him to Richmond on the inside track. If he made a stand at Winchester, moving neither north nor south, I would fight him there, on the idea that if we can not beat him when he bears the wastage of coming to us, we never can when we bear the wastage of going to him. In coming to us he tenders to us an advantage which we must not waive. We should not so operate as merely to drive him away. As we must beat him somewhere, or fail finally, we can do it, if at all, easier near to us than far away. If we can not beat the enemy where he now is, we never can, he again being within the intrenchments of Richmond."[1]

On the 21st McClellan was convinced that his army was nearly in a condition to move. The cavalry was indeed, he thought, in numbers much inferior to that of the enemy, but in efficiency was far superior. He now asked whether the President wished him "to march on the enemy at once, or to await the arrival of new horses." The reply was that no change was intended in the order of the 6th. The President did not expect impossibilities, but the season should not be wasted in inaction. McClellan's purpose had been to cross the Potomac above Harper's Ferry, on the western side of the Blue Ridge, and move directly upon the Confederate forces, expecting that they would either give battle near Winchester or retreat toward Richmond. He believed that if he crossed below, Lee would recross into Maryland. But now the season had come when the river might be expected to rise at any hour, rendering the apprehended Confederate movement too hazardous to be ventured. McClellan therefore decided to cross on the eastern side of the Blue Ridge, thus threatening Lee's communications. He thought it possible, though not probable, that he might throw his force through some pass in the mountains, and gain the Confederate rear in the valley of the Shenandoah. Failing this, he still hoped to strike the flank of their long retreating column, separate their army, and beat it in detail, or, at all events, force them to concentrate as far back as Gordonsville, and thus leave his own army free to adopt the Fredericksburg line of advance upon Richmond, or to move by his old way of the Peninsula.[2]

The crossing of the Potomac began on the 26th of October, and continued until the 2d of November, when the whole army was over. Leaving 15,000 men at and near Harper's Ferry, the army marched more than 100,000 strong, besides 20,000 detached from the force at Washington[3] to co-operate with his movement. The weather was favorable, the roads good, and the great army moved rapidly. Keeping along the eastern foot of the Blue Ridge, Warrenton being the point of direction for the main body, its line of march for the greater part of the way being the same, but in a reverse direction, as that by which Lee had advanced upon Pope hardly three months before.

[1] *Com. Rep.*, 524.

[2] *McC. Rep.*, 428, 436. "I still considered the line of the Peninsula as the true approach to Richmond, but, for obvious reasons, did not make any proposal to return to it."—*Ibid.*, 427.

[3] According to the official return (*Com. Rep.*, 534) on the 20th of October, the Army of the Potomac numbered, "present for duty," 138,409, exclusive of 73,593 at Washington. McClellan (*Report*, 430) gives its strength at 116,000, besides some 6000 detached bodies. This discrepancy appears to be occasioned (see *McC. Rep.*, 422) by about 12,000 teamsters, officers' servants, etc., being included in the regular returns.

The Confederate army, during its two months' repose after Antietam, had been recruited to about 70,000.[1] As soon as Lee was aware of the threatening movement of McClellan, he hastened to counteract it by moving southward in the same direction. Jackson, with his own corps and Stuart's cavalry, was halted to observe, and, if occasion was given, assail the Union force upon its march, while the remainder of the army pressed up the Valley of the Shenandoah. For days the two hostile columns were moving parallel to each other, only a few miles apart, but with the Blue Mountains between them. Rapid as was the march of the Union army, that of the Confederates was still faster. Lee, in advance of his opponent, turned a spur of the Blue Ridge, passed from the valley of the Shenandoah into that of the Rappahannock, and took position at Culpepper by the time that McClellan had massed his army near Warrenton, a half score of miles to the north. But in effecting this operation he had played into his opponent's hands, and given him an opportunity to strike more favorable than he had dared to anticipate. McClellan had hoped to separate the Confederate army. Lee had himself separated it. Jackson's corps was left fully three days' rapid march behind that of Longstreet. If an attack had then been made, it could hardly have failed to result otherwise than in a serious disaster to the Confederates. McClellan resolved upon an assault. For once he seemed satisfied that he had the preponderance of force.[2]

But this intent of vigorous action came too late. The breach between McClellan and the military authorities at Washington had become too wide to be closed. His removal from the command had been resolved upon, and had been delayed only from the difficulty of deciding upon his successor. The choice finally lay between Burnside and Hooker.[3] Why Sumner, who outranked each, and had seen more service than both, was passed over, it is hard to say. But the choice now fell upon Burnside. Upon the stormy evening of the 7th of November, when McClellan had given directions for the movements of the next two days, a messenger from Washington reached the head-quarters of the army. He bore an order, couched in briefest military phrase, bearing date two days before, removing McClellan from the command of the army, and directing Burnside to assume it; and another equally curt, from Halleck to McClellan, the writing of which one may imagine to have been a pleasant task.[4]

[1] Present for duty, October 20, 67,805; November 20, 73,554.—*Ante*, p. 383.

[2] "The army was massed near Warrenton, ready to act in any required direction, perfectly in hand, and in admirable condition and spirits. I doubt whether, during the whole period that I had the honor to command the Army of the Potomac, it was in such excellent condition to fight a great battle. . . . The reports from the advance indicated the possibility of separating the two wings of the enemy's forces, and either beating Longstreet separately or forcing him to fall back at least upon Gordonsville to effect his junction with the rest of his army. . . . Had I remained in command I should have made the attempt to divide the enemy; and could he have been brought to a battle within reach of my supplies, I can not doubt that the result would have been a brilliant victory for our army."—*McC. Rep.*, 438, 439.

[3] "General Hooker came very near receiving, instead of me, the command of the Army of the Potomac."—Burnside, *in Com. Rep.*, 725.

[4] *General Orders, No.* 182.—"By direction of the President of the United States, it is ordered that Major General McClellan be relieved from the command of the Army of the Potomac, and that Major General Burnside take command of the army. By order of the Secretary of War."

Halleck to McClellan.—"GENERAL,—On the receipt of the order of the President, sent herewith, you will immediately turn over your command to Major General Burnside, and repair to Trenton, New Jersey, reporting on your arrival at that place, by telegraph, for farther orders."—*Com. Rep.*, 565.

CAVALRY RECONNOISSANCE IN VIRGINIA.

AMBROSE E. BURNSIDE.

CHAPTER XXIV.

BURNSIDE'S CAMPAIGN.—FREDERICKSBURG.

Burnside in Command.—His Plan for the Campaign.—Its Merits and Demerits.—New Organization of the Army of the Potomac.—The Movement from Warrenton to Fredericksburg.—Delay in crossing the Rappahannock.—The Pontoons.—Fredericksburg threatened with Bombardment.—The Confederate Army reaches Fredericksburg.—The Position on the Rappahannock.—Burnside's Preparations for Crossing.—The Delay opposite Fredericksburg.—Lee's Plan of Operations.—Crossing the River, and Preparations for Attack.—Burnside's final Plan for two Assaults.—Franklin's Attack upon the Left.—Meade's Advance repulsed.—Gibbon advances, and is repulsed.—The Confederate Pursuit checked by Birney.—The Moments of the Action.—The Confederate Position on the Right at Marye's Hill.—Its Strength.—Assailed by Sumner.—French and Hancock repelled.—Hooker ordered to attack.—Humphreys assaults, and is driven back.—Close of the Battle.—The Numbers engaged.—Burnside proposes to renew the Battle the next Day.—Is dissuaded by his Generals.—He recrosses the Rappahannock.—Effects of the Battle of Fredericksburg.—Condition of the Union Army.—Burnside designs a new Movement.—The proposed Cavalry Expedition.—The President forbids the Movement.—The Reasons for the Prohibition.—Franklin and Smith criticise Burnside's Plan, and propose another.—Cochrane and Newton's Interview with the President.—Burnside and Halleck.—Burnside's third Plan.—The Mud Campaign.—Burnside's Order No. 8, dismissing Hooker and others.—The President refuses to sanction the Order.—Burnside resigns, and Hooker is placed in Command.—Sumner and Franklin relieved.—Death of Sumner.—Hooker takes Command.

THE command of the Army of the Potomac was thrust into the unwilling hands of Burnside. He had twice declined it, and would have done so now had it been left to his choice;[1] but the order was peremptory, and he had no alternative but to obey. Yet, as if foreseeing the issue, he repeated to the messenger who brought the order and to members of his own staff what he had before said to the President and the Secretary of War, that he did not consider himself competent to take the command of so large an army, and, moreover, that from the place which his command had held during the campaign, he knew less than any other general of the position, numbers, and character of the several corps.[1] Still, with the knowledge then possessed by the military authorities, the choice was the wisest that could have been made. No other general had held an important separate command. His expedition to North Carolina had been successful. He had become entangled in none of the jealousies which impeded, or were thought to impede, the efficiency of the army. His personal and military character was unreproached and irreproachable. Burnside's modesty, contrasted with Hooker's vehement self-assertion, decided the question of the generalship. He was taken at the high estimate which the administration placed upon him, rather than at the low one which he placed upon himself.

Burnside was required not only to take command of the army, but to state what he proposed to do with it.[2] He had been from the first opposed to the movement made by McClellan upon Warrenton. He argued that if the army was to go to Richmond by land, the only way was that by Fredericksburg. McClellan was half convinced of the truth of this, and on the day before he was superseded gave orders which looked toward the abandonment of his present line of operations.[3] Two days after he had been placed in command, Burnside presented his plan.

Its essential features were that McClellan's design of attacking Lee should be given up, the movement toward Gordonsville abandoned, and then there should be "a rapid move of the whole force to Fredericksburg, with a view to a movement upon Richmond from that point." In favor of his plan he urged that if the Union army should move upon Culpepper and Gordonsville, and even fight a successful battle, the enemy would still have many lines of retreat, and would be able to reach Richmond with enough of force to render necessary another battle there. Should the enemy fall back without giving battle, the pursuit would be simply following up a retreating army well supplied with provisions in dépôts in its rear, while the pursuing army would have to rely for supplies upon a single long line of communication, liable to be cut at any point. But in moving by the way which he proposed, the army would cover Washington until it reached Fredericksburg, where it would be on the shortest road to Richmond, the taking of which, he thought, "should be the great object of the campaign, as the fall of that place would tend more to cripple the rebel cause than almost any other military event, except the absolute breaking up of their army." The presence of a large army on the Fredericksburg line would render it impossible for the enemy to make any successful movement upon Washington. An invasion of Pennsylvania was not to be expected at that season of the year; and, even should a lodgment be made there by any force that could be spared, its destruction would be certain soon after winter set in. "Could the army before Richmond be beaten, and their capital taken," he added, "the loss of half a dozen of our towns and cities in the interior of Pennsylvania could well be afforded."[4]

This plan was undoubtedly a judicious one upon the assumption that the capture of Richmond was the main aim of the campaign. For an advance thither by way of Gordonsville, the main base of supplies must be Alexandria, involving transportation by land of fully 150 miles by the route which must be followed. For an advance by way of Fredericksburg, Acquia Creek, on the Potomac, would be the base to which supplies could be sent by water, leaving but 75 miles of land transportation, by a line much less exposed. The advantage of the Peninsular route are still greater. The base of supplies would be at West Point, only 30 miles from Richmond. The main objection to this, that the army here would not be in a position to cover Washington, would be obviated by concentrating there a force sufficient for its defense, which the great numerical preponderance of the Union troops rendered easy. In fact, there was at this moment in and around Washington, independent of Burnside's army in the field, a force very nearly equal to the whole Confederate Army of Northern Virginia.[5]

[1] *Com. Rep.*, 645.

[1] *Com. Rep.*, 650. [2] *Ibid.*, 650. [3] *Ibid.*, 649.

[4] For the entire text of this plan, see *Com. Rep.*, 648; and for Burnside's own explanation of it, *Ibid.*, 650.

[5] The advantages of the Peninsular route, or rather a modification of it, taking the James River instead of the York as the base, were set forth six weeks later by Franklin and Smith, in a letter to the President, first made public in Swinton's *Campaigns of the Army of the Potomac*, pp. 258–265. Mr. Swinton indeed affirms (*Ibid.*, 238), upon the authority of "the corps commander then most intimate in his confidence," that "Burnside had not matured any definite plan of action, for the reason that he hoped to be able to postpone operations till the spring. He did not favor operating against Richmond by the overland route, but had his mind turned toward a repetition of McClellan's movement to the Peninsula; and in determining to march to Fredericksburg, he cherished the hope of being able to winter there upon an easy base of supplies, and in the spring embarking his army for the James River." Not only is there no trace of any such purpose to be found in Burnside's written plan, but every recommendation implies the design of moving by the overland route.

The fatal error in Burnside's plan was that it wholly misconceived the main object to be aimed at. The capture of Richmond would indeed have been in itself a great material and moral loss to the Confederacy, but it would have been of far less moment than the destruction, or even the signal defeat of the army. That army was the head and front of the offending, and at this the blow should have been aimed. The President, with a keener insight into the case than any other man had yet attained, had written, "We must beat the enemy somewhere, or fail finally. If we can not beat him where he now is, we never can, he being again within the intrenchments of Richmond." This was as true now as it was a month before. It so happened that the Confederate commander had placed his army in such a position as to invite an attack. A little more than half of it was massed at Culpepper, a little less than half was lying three days' march away in the valley of the Shenandoah. The Union army was massed only a few hours' march from the enemy, outnumbering him more than two to one. An attack in force could hardly have resulted otherwise than in a decisive victory. Burnside proposed deliberately to throw away the advantage thus thrust into his hands, and march directly away from his inferior foe, in quest of an object which, even if attained, was of wholly secondary consequence. The President, however, though with some reluctance, acceded to Burnside's plan, but with the significant intimation, "I think it will succeed if you move rapidly, otherwise not."[1] While preparing for this movement, Burnside organized his force into three "Grand Divisions"—Sumner being placed in command of the "Right," Hooker of the "Centre," and Franklin of the "Left."[2]

ROUTES TO RICHMOND.

This sketch illustrates the advantages, in point of distance, of the three proposed routes to Richmond. The first, abandoned by Burnside, assumes the basis of supply to be Alexandria. The second, proposed by him, assumes it to be at Acquia Creek. The third, that adopted by McClellan, places it at West Point.

Burnside began his movement from Warrenton to Fredericksburg on the 15th of November. He had proposed to make it by concentrating his force at Warrenton, as though he intended to attack Culpepper or Gordonsville. But Lee was not deceived. On the 17th he learned that Sumner had marched from Catlett's Station toward Falmouth, and that Federal gun-boats had entered Acquia Creek. This, he thought, "looked as if Fredericksburg was to be reoccupied," and he dispatched two divisions of infantry, with cavalry and artillery, to augment the small force which had held the town. Next day a bold dash by Stuart's cavalry upon Warrenton disclosed that the Federal army were gone, whereupon Longstreet's whole command was sent toward Fredericksburg, while Jackson was ordered from the valley to rejoin the main army.[3] Lee, having divined Burnside's movement, met it in just the manner in which one would suppose he would have done, but, as it would seem, just in the way his opponent did not anticipate. There were five conceivable things to be done: To repass down the valley of the Shenandoah and again invade Maryland, and threaten Pennsylvania; to make a demonstration upon Washington, with the intent of recalling the march to Fredericksburg; to fall back at once toward Richmond; to remain where he was, and await the issue of events; or to throw himself directly across the new line of advance proposed by Burnside. The first two movements Burnside had ruled out as impracticable or ruinous. For the third there was no immediate necessity; it could be done, if need were, afterward as well as then. Burnside seems to have supposed that Lee would choose the fourth. As it happened, he chose the fifth course, which accident enabled him to carry out under auspices far more favorable than he could have dared to anticipate.

Sumner, with the advance of the Union army, reached Falmouth, opposite Fredericksburg, on the 17th. The design was that he should cross the Rappahannock at once, and seize the heights in the rear of Fredericksburg before Lee could re-enforce the small force stationed there. The river at that point could not be forded by an army in mass, and the railroad and turnpike bridges which had spanned it were destroyed. Burnside had, as he supposed, made arrangements by which pontoons sufficient to span the stream would have been sent to him from Washington so as to meet him on his arrival. But none came for a week, during which time nothing could be done to carry out the plan of operations.[4] Sumner, indeed, who

FREDERICKSBURG, FROM FALMOUTH.

[1] *Con. Rep.*, 645.

[2] Sumner's Grand Division consisted of the 2d Corps, under Couch, lately Sumner's, and the 9th Corps, under Wilcox, formerly Burnside's. Hooker's Grand Division comprised the 3d Corps, under Stoneman, from the garrison of Washington, and the 5th Corps, formerly Fitz John Porter's, under Butterfield. Franklin's Grand Division consisted of the 1st Corps, formerly Hooker's, under Reynolds, and the 6th Corps, formerly Franklin's, under W. F. Smith. The 12th Corps, so briefly commanded by Mansfield, was left at Harper's Ferry, under Slocum. The 11th Corps, under Sigel, detached from the defenses of Washington, was near Manassas Junction, guarding the railway line. This corps did not strictly form a part of Burnside's movable army. Among the commanders of "divisions," as distinguished from the "Grand Divisions," were Birney, Doubleday, French, Gibbon, Hancock, Howard, Humphreys, Meade, Newton, Sykes.

[3] *Lee's Rep.*, i., 37.

[4] This delay, upon which so much hinged, was made the subject of strict scrutiny. Each person immediately concerned endeavored to shift from himself the burden of the responsibility. Burnside says (*Con. Rep.*, 651, 655): "My plan had been discussed by General Halleck and General Meigs at my head-quarters at Warrenton on the night of the 11th or 12th, and, after discussing it fully there, they sat down and sent telegrams to Washington, which, as I supposed, fully covered the case, and would secure the starting of the pontoons at once. I supposed, of course, that those portions of the plan which required to be attended to at Washington would have been carried out there. I understood that General Halleck was to give the necessary orders, and then the officers who should receive those orders were the ones responsible for the pontoons coming here. I could have carried out that part of the plan through officers of my own; but, having just taken the command of an army with which I was unacquainted, it was evident that it was as much as I could attend to, with the assistance of all my officers, to change its position from Warrenton to Fredericksburg."—Halleck says (*Ibid.*, 678): "On my visit to General Burnside at Warrenton on the 12th of November, in speaking about the boats and things which he required from Washington, I told him that they were all subject to his orders. To prevent the ne-

had been fired upon by a battery from across the river, and had silenced it so easily as to show that the enemy were there in only trifling force, was disposed to send a detachment by a ford which was practicable for the purpose, and gave an order to that effect. But he had received explicit orders not to cross and occupy Fredericksburg; and, "upon reflection, he concluded that he was rather too old a soldier to disobey a direct order; besides, he had had a little too much experience on the Peninsula of the consequence of getting astride a river to risk it here." So, having revoked the order, he sent a note to Burnside, asking whether he should take Fredericksburg the next morning, provided he could find, what he had already found, a practicable ford. Burnside replied in the negative; he did not think it advisable to occupy Fredericksburg until his communications were established; and Sumner coincided in this decision.[1] Hooker, who brought up the rear of the army, requested permission, on the 20th, to send a division across the Rappahannock, which should march down the south side and seize the heights behind Fredericksburg. Burnside next day refused permission. He thought that although Hooker might "beat any force of the enemy he would meet on his way, yet it would be a very hazardous movement to throw a column like that beyond the reach of its proper support;" and, moreover, a rain-storm which had set in during the night rendered the movement impossible.[2] Sumner, on the 21st, sent over a message to the corporate authorities of Fredericksburg demanding the surrender of the town, under pain of bombardment in case of refusal. The civic authorities were told by the military commander that "while the town would not be occupied for military purposes, its occupation by the enemy would be resisted." Directions were given for the removal of the people, and almost the entire population left their homes.[3] No bombardment then took place; but a fortnight later, when the movement across the river was made, Fredericksburg, which was then used by the Confederates for "military purposes," and almost the entire population having been removed in consequence of the threat, was bombarded. This was fiercely denounced as a violation of the laws of war, but without the slightest ground. The town had been formally summoned to surrender; the unarmed population had abandoned it after abundant notice; and it was used for the direct "military purpose" of "resisting the occupation by the enemy."

A fortnight passed, during which time the Union army lay upon the north bank of the Rappahannock, waiting for means to cross the stream, and for the accumulation of supplies at the Acquia Creek, and the means of transporting them from the Potomac to the Rappahannock. The Confederate army was meanwhile concentrating on the southern side to resist any advance. About this time that army was formally organized into two corps, under the immediate command of Longstreet and Jackson, who had each been raised to the rank of lieutenant general. Longstreet's corps consisted of the troops formerly belonging to his command. To Jackson was assigned, besides those which he had heretofore commanded, the division of D. H. Hill. The two corps were now of nearly equal force, that of Longstreet being perhaps slightly in excess.[4]

It was almost the middle of December. Four weeks had passed since Burnside's plan had been sanctioned by the President; but the essential thing upon which he had based the probability of success—that the movement should be rapidly made—had failed. The faultiness of the whole scheme was now apparent. Burnside had shrunk from assailing the half of Lee's force which lay directly in his front, in a position hastily taken and of no great natural strength. He was now confronted by the Confederate army, drawn up in a position almost unassailable by nature, strengthened by the labor of three unobstructed weeks, which could be assailed only by crossing a formidable stream; and even if that were passed, the enemy assailed and driven from his position, the pursuit would still encounter at every step of the way just the same obstructions which would have been met on the line which had been abandoned. If military considerations were alone in question, no farther movement would have been made, and the army would have gone into winter quarters. But public feeling demanded a movement, and Burnside, sanctioned by his generals, resolved to take the offensive. The only question was whete the intervening river should be crossed.[1]

The Rappahannock, with a general course from south to north, makes a sharp bend westward a mile above Fredericksburg, running between two lines of heights. Those on the north, known as Stafford Heights, slope steeply down to the river bank, with an elevation sufficient to command the valley across the river. On the south side, the hills just in the rear of Fredericksburg rise sharply something less than a mile from the river; then they trend away, in a semicircular form, until they sink down into the valley of the Massaponax, six miles below Fredericksburg, leaving an irregular broken valley, two miles broad at its widest point. This range of heights was mostly covered with dense woods, oaks with branches now leafless, skirted with sombre pines, rising southward by a succession of wooded ridges, each dominating the one below until lost in a wild wooded region soon to become famous under the name of the "Wilderness." Upon the crests and slopes of these wooded heights Longstreet's corps had been disposed, covering a front of about five miles. There was little need of artificial aid to the natural strength of the position; but artillery and rifle pits were dug and abatis constructed.[2] D. H. Hill's division was posted near Port Royal, twenty miles below, to prevent the Union gun-boats from ascending the river, and some skirmishing here took place.[3] The remainder of Jackson's corps was

---

cessity of the commanding officer here reporting the order for the boats there, the order was drawn up on his table and signed by me directly to General Woodbury. I saw General Woodbury on my return, and he told me that he had received the order. I told him that in all those matters he was under General Burnside's direction; I had nothing further to give him except to communicate that order to him. I gave no other order or direction in relation to the matter."—There seems to have been an unaccountable misapprehension as to the purport of the order which was addressed to General Woodbury, of the Engineer Brigade. It read: "Call upon the chief quarter-master to transport all your pontoons to Acquia Creek" (*Ibid.*, 663). Woodbury did not understand that this order demanded instant execution. "Had the emergency been made known to me in any manner," he says, "I could have disregarded the forms of service, seized teams, teamsters, and wagon-masters for instant service wherever I could find them. Then, with good roads and good weather, they might possibly have been in time. But I had no warrant for such a course, which, after all, could only have been carried out by the authority of the general-in-chief" (*Ibid.*, 665).—Quarter-master General Meigs said that the blame did not rest upon his department, "which was no more responsible for the march of a pontoon train than for the march of a battery of artillery or of a regiment of infantry. Its business was to provide material for the transportation of an army. If General Woodbury had orders from General Burnside, he was responsible for carrying them out" (*Ibid.*, 680).

[1] Sumner, in *Com. Rep.*, 657. [2] *Com. Rep.*, 654, 666. [3] *Lee's Rep.*, i., 38.

[4] Longstreet's corps, the First, consisted of the divisions of Anderson, Pickett, Ransom, Wood, and McLaws, comprising 21 brigades. Jackson's corps, the Second, consisted of the divisions of A. P. Hill, D. H. Hill, Ewell, and Taliaferro, comprising 19 brigades. The cavalry and horse artillery, under Stuart, acted somewhat independently with either corps; at the battle of Fredericksburg, mainly with Jackson.

[1] Sumner: "I was in favor of crossing the Rappahannock, because I knew that neither our government nor our people would be satisfied to have our army retire from this position or go into winter quarters until we knew the force that was on the other side of the river, and the only way of ascertaining that was by feeling them" (*Com. Rep.*, 658).

Franklin: "General Burnside called a council, in which it was the unanimous opinion, I think, of all the generals present, that if this river could be crossed, it ought to be crossed, no matter what might happen afterward. The point of crossing was not then definitely determined upon; but I thought at the time that we were to cross several miles farther down. Afterward General Burnside called us together again, and informed us that he had determined to cross at the two points at which we finally did cross. I had no objection to that, but thought they were as good as the point farther down" (*Ibid.*, 661).

Hooker: "After the pontoons arrived, it became a matter of importance to determine where and in what way we should cross the Rappahannock. The officers commanding the Grand Divisions were called together to discuss and determine that matter. General Burnside proposed that a portion of the command should cross at Fredericksburg, and a portion should cross about twelve miles below. I objected by my vote in the council to crossing two columns so far apart, and stated my preference that the whole army should cross at what is called the United States or Richards's Ford, about twelve miles above; but I was overruled" (*Ibid.*, 666).

[2] "Pits were made for the protection of the batteries; and, in addition to the natural strength of the position, ditches, stone fences, and road-cuts were found along different portions of the line, and parts were farther strengthened by rifle-trenches and abatis."—Longstreet, in *Lee's Rep.*, ii., 427.

[3] Hill always managed to say something quite out of harmony with the usual decorum of the Confederate official reports. Here, with abridgments, is his account of what took place at his extremity of the line: "Four Yankee gun-boats were then lying opposite the town of Port Royal. Rifle-pits were constructed to prevent the pirates from ascending. Hardaway opened upon the gun-boats. Finding the fire too hot for them, they fled back. Hardaway continued to pelt them, and, to stop his fire, the ruffians commenced shelling the town. A dog was killed and a negro wounded. The pirates fled down the river; but a worse fate awaited them than a distant cannonade—a section of artillery immediately on the bank gave them a parting salute. From Yankee sources we learned that the pirates lost six killed and twenty wounded. Whether they over-esti-

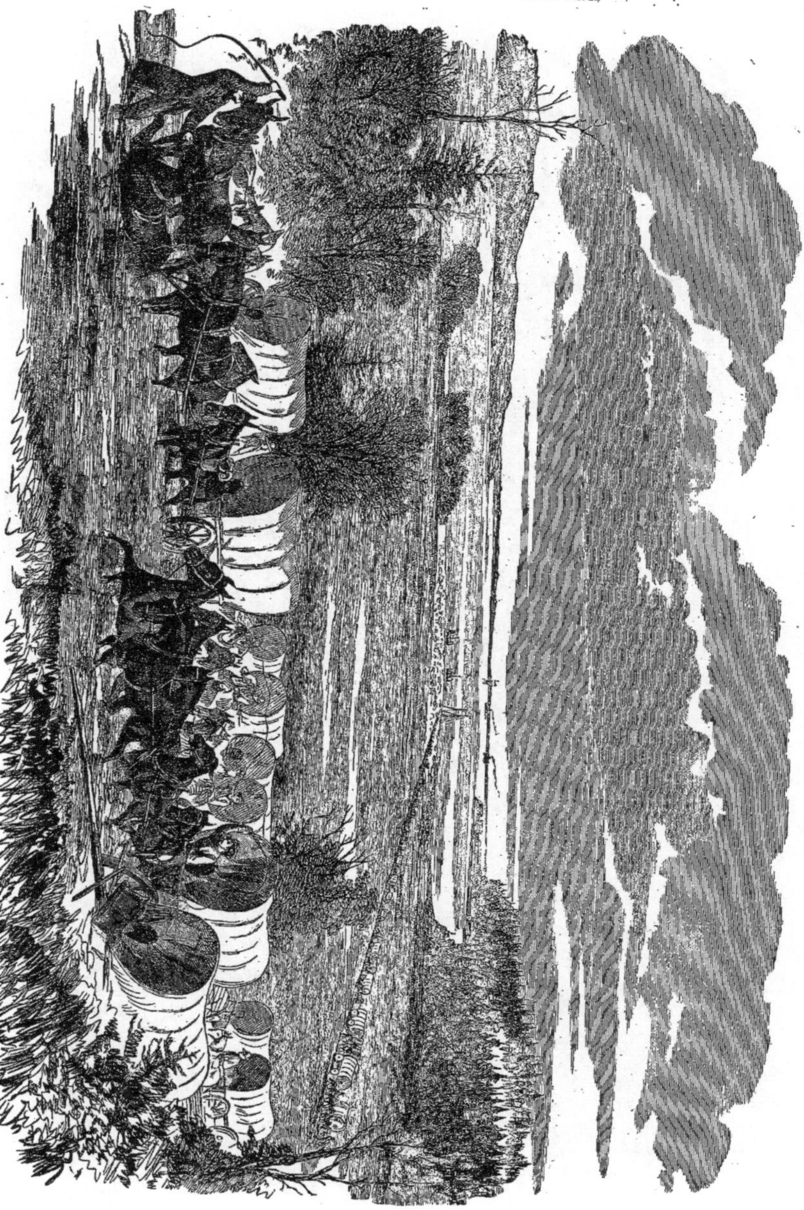

AN ARMY TRAIN.

BUILDING THE BRIDGE AT FREDERICKSBURG.

posted so as to be in a position to support either Hill or Longstreet. Two shots in immediate succession were to be the signal giving notice for the whole of the Confederate force to concentrate upon any point that should be menaced in force.

Burnside had resolved to cross at a point known by the euphoneous designation of Skinker's Neck, about twelve miles below Fredericksburg. The movements which were made for this purpose caused the enemy to concentrate much of his strength in that direction. The thought then occurred to him to detain this force there by ostentatious demonstrations, and to make the crossing at Fredericksburg. "I decided," he says, "to cross at Fredericksburg, because, in the first place, I felt satisfied that they did not expect us to cross here, but down below; and, in the next place, I felt satisfied that this was the place to fight the most decisive battle, because, if we could divide their forces by piercing their lines at one or two points, separating their left from their right, then a vigorous attack with the whole army would succeed in breaking their army in pieces."[1] No conclusion could, as matters stood, be more sound, provided that the premises upon which it was based were sure. If it was certain that Lee's left would be behind Fredericksburg, and his right a dozen miles or more away, then an adequate force flung into this great gap would divide the Confederate army, and a vigorous assault upon its left might be expected to crush it when cut off from aid from the right. To carry out this plan, it was necessary that the river should be crossed and battle be waged and won in a single day. Failing this, the rest must depend upon contingencies which no man could foresee.

The 11th of December was fixed upon as the day for crossing the river. During the previous night nearly one hundred and fifty heavy guns were placed in position upon the crest of Stafford Heights, commanding a great part of the opposite valley. The intention was to throw three bridges across at Fredericksburg, and as many more at a point two or three miles below. Sumner's Grand Division was to cross by the upper bridges, Franklin's by the lower, while Hooker's was to be held in reserve, ready, if the assault was successful, to spring upon the enemy in his retreat.[2] It was supposed that the bridges could be built in two or three hours.[3] Before dawn the pontoons were brought down to the river bank, and the work of laying the bridges was begun in the darkness. Two single shots broke the stillness which reigned through the Confederate lines. These were the signal for Longstreet's corps to concentrate upon the threatened point. Fredericksburg was held by only two regiments of sharp-shooters, who were sheltered in houses and rifle-pits, and behind walls on the river bank. In addition to the darkness of night, a dense fog filled the valley. The engineers had hardly begun to lay the bridges when they were assailed by rifle-shots at short range from the opposite shore, and driven off with severe loss. Again and again they returned, and again and again were driven off. The two or three hours had stretched to six, and the narrow stream was only half spanned, and not another length could be laid under the fierce fire. Burnside now ordered that fire should be opened upon the town from his artillery which crowned the opposite crests. Nearly one hundred and fifty heavy guns at once opened fire into the pall of mist which still shrouded the scene. After two hours a column of rising smoke indicated that a part of the town was in flames, and another attempt was made to complete the bridges. This was repelled as the former ones had been, showing that almost ten thousand shot had failed to dislodge the sharp-shooters from their coverts. When the fog lifted at noon, it was found that the elevation at which the guns were placed was so great that few of them could be sufficiently depressed to bear upon the river front of the town. The day was fast wearing away, and nothing had been accomplished. The officers reported that the bridges could not be built. Burnside said that it must be done, and some means must be found to dislodge the sharp-shooters. It was now decided that a detachment should cross in open pontoon boats and carry the town. Two regiments from Massachusetts and one from Michigan volunteered for the perilous work. They rushed down the bank and pushed the boats into the stream; a few strong strokes with the oars, and they were under shelter of the opposite bluffs, up which they dashed, and in a quarter of an hour carried the town.[4] In half an hour more the bridges were finished, and, as evening was falling, Couch's division was over and the first step in the enterprise fairly taken.[5] Franklin had indeed met with scarcely a show of opposition. His artillery covered the opposite shore, and his bridges were ready before noon; but Burnside had resolved that the attack should be made in two separate columns, and Franklin was not suffered to cross until the other bridges were completed.

It was no part of Lee's plan seriously to oppose the passage of the river by the Federal force, or even to assail it when over. He wisely chose to await its assault upon his strong position,[6] to which his opponent would

SUMNER'S GRAND DIVISION CROSSING THE RAPPAHANNOCK.

mated or under-estimated their losses I do not know; they sometimes lie on one side and sometimes on another. In a few days the pirates returned with some more of their thievish consorts. Guns were brought down to the river under cover of a dense fog, and when it lifted were opened upon them. We have learned from the same respectable Yankee source that three of the pirates were struck, one three times, and that a captain was killed, and four or five other thieves knocked on the head."—D. H. Hill, in *Lee's Rep.*, ii., 468.

[1] Burnside's Testimony, in *Com. Rep.*, 652.

[2] Hooker, in *Com. Rep.*, 667.

[3] Burnside, *Ibid.*, 656.

[4] McLaws says (*Lee's Rep.*, ii., 445) that the artillery fire was so severe that his "men could not use their rifles, and the different places occupied by them becoming untenable, the troops were withdrawn from the river bank at half past four, when the enemy crossed in boats, and, completing their bridges, passed over in force and advanced into the town."

[5] Burnside, in *Com. Rep.*, 656.

[6] Lee indeed believed that it was impossible to prevent the crossing. He says (*Rep.*, i., 39): "The plain of Fredericksburg is so completely commanded by the Stafford Heights, that no effectual opposition could be made to the construction of bridges or the passage of the river without exposing our troops to the destructive fire of the numerous batteries of the enemy. At the same time, the narrowness of the Rappahannock, its winding course and deep bed, presented opportunities for laying down bridges at points secure from the fire of our artillery. Our position was therefore selected with a view to resist the enemy's advance after crossing, and the river was guarded only by a force sufficient to impede his movements until the army could be concentrated."—Franklin, however, was confident that not only might his passage have been prevented, but that his division, when over, could have been crushed. He says (Testimony, in *Com. Rep.*, 661): "I always

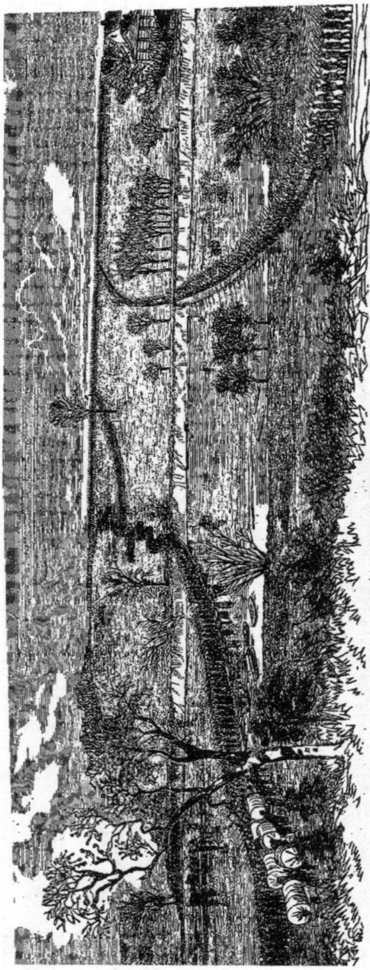

FRANKLIN'S GRAND DIVISION CROSSING THE RAPPAHANNOCK.

encountered only half of the Confederate force, and the result of the action could hardly have failed to have been different.

The whole of the 12th was most unaccountably spent in crossing the river and deciding upon the order of the attack on the next day. It was found that the extreme Confederate right was protected by a canal, all the bridges crossing which had been destroyed; there was, besides, a sluiceway and mill-pond, so that this point was unassailable; and an attack upon the right could only be made against the steep front of Marye's Hill, rising in the rear of the town and presenting a front of a mile, then sloping off sharply to a ravine traversed by a small stream; thence the heights sweep away from the river, leaving a broken plain, its edges deeply indented by wooded spurs. This plain, about two miles broad, is traversed by the Richmond and Fredericksburg Railroad, which winds around the base of the heights, occasionally cutting through the extremities of the projecting spurs. Midway between the railway and the river runs the old Richmond or Port Royal Road, often embanked and fringed with trees, affording shelter behind which the Union force could be deployed. When the final arrangements had been made on both sides, the Confederate forces, 80,000 strong, were posted along the ridge of the range of hills, their advance line in places pushed forward to the wooded base, Jackson's corps holding the right and Longstreet's the left. The Union army, 100,000 strong, was posted along the Richmond Road, from Fredericksburg down; Couch's corps, of Sumner's division, in the town; then Wilcox's corps, forming the connection with Franklin's Grand Division on the left.

The character of the ground unmistakably indicated that the main attack should be made by Franklin; for not only was the Confederate position here manifestly weaker, but the plain in front of it was spacious enough to give room to deploy his whole force; while to the right, in front of Sumner, the plain was so narrow that only a fragment of his force could at any one moment be brought into action. If he assailed the strong position before him, it must be by successive blows, not by a single attack with his whole force. Franklin understood, on the afternoon of the 12th, that Burnside intended that he should make the attack with his Grand Division, to which had been added a part of Hooker's. Hooker understood that there was to be a twofold assault, at distinct points, the main one by Sumner, on the right.[2] Burnside clearly proposed a twofold attack in force, that on the left to be the first.[3] But when, on the morning of the 13th, Franklin received his order, it was so worded as to lead him and his generals to suppose that it meant he should make merely an armed reconnoissance of the enemy's lines with but one of his eight divisions, to be supported by another, keeping the remainder in position for a different movement.[4] Franklin was also informed that a column, consisting of a division or more, detached from Sumner's corps, was to move against the heights in the rear of Fredericksburg. Thus, as the plan was framed, not more than four divisions, one quarter of the force which had crossed or was ready to cross the river, were to assail the position held by the Confederates. We can only account for this plan by supposing that Burnside thought that the enemy in his front was really in inconsiderable force, its bulk being still a score of miles away, and that not only had he crossed the Rappahannock at a point where he was not expected, but that during the eight-and-forty hours which had passed since the attempt was begun the enemy had not concentrated his strength in his front. Thus only can we explain the part assigned to Hooker, to spring upon the enemy on his retreat, and the order to Franklin to be in readiness to march down the Richmond Road, that being the direction which the retreating Confederates would naturally take. If such was his belief, he must have been confirmed in it by the trifling opposition offered to his passage of the river. There was, indeed, nothing to show the neighborhood of a great hostile army. Hardly a reply had been made to his heavy bombardment; not

---

doubted our power to cross, and I do not believe we could have crossed had the enemy chosen to prevent it; and I know, from what I have seen since and what I before suspected, that they could have prevented our crossing at those two points if they had chosen. However, the crossing was successfully made, under cover of a fog, and, as far as my wing was concerned, we got into position safely, with the loss of a very few men. Still, we were in such a position that, if the enemy had at any moment opened upon us with the guns they had bearing upon us, I think in the course of an hour our men would have been so scattered that it would have been impossible to rally them. For some unaccountable reason they did not open their batteries."

[1] "It having been definitely ascertained that the enemy had crossed the Rappahannock in large force, I was ordered to move my division at dawn on the 12th" (A. P. Hill, in *Lee's Rep.*, ii., 461).—"Just before sundown on the 12th I received an order to march that night to Fredericksburg, as the Yankees were expected to attack General Lee that day. A portion of my command was twenty-two miles from that city, and the most of them from eighteen to twenty" (D. H. Hill, *Ibid.*, 458).—"A. P. Hill moved his division at dawn on the morning of the 12th. At the same time, Taliaferro, then in command of Jackson's division, moved from his encampment. Early on the morning of the 13th, Ewell's division, ...

an enemy showed himself during that day or the next besides the few regiments which had been driven from Fredericksburg, and the scanty line of sharp-shooters, hardly more than a picket-guard, scattered along the river bank. He had indeed been informed by a German prisoner, who represented that he had been impressed into the Confederate service, of the strength of the enemy, of their positions and batteries, and that they regarded it as an impossibility that the heights could be carried; but Burnside clearly placed no faith in his story.[1]

The morning of Saturday, December 13, broke with a dense fog resting in the valley, shutting the two armies from all sight of each other. So dense was it that the Confederates could hear the word of command given to the invisible lines before them.[2] The night had been bitterly cold. Some of the Confederate pickets were frozen at their posts.[3] About ten o'clock the fog lifted, and showed Franklin's command in motion. He had placed a liberal construction upon the order to assault with at least one division, and threw forward Reynolds's entire corps, Meade's division in advance in the centre, supported by Gibbon's on the right, and Doubleday's on the left, somewhat in the rear. The Confederate horse artillery, under Stuart, was so posted across the Richmond Road as to enfilade the Union line, and Doubleday was deflected still farther to the left to dislodge them. After an hour's sharp cannonading Stuart's guns were withdrawn, and Meade opened a fierce artillery fire upon the woods in his front. The Confederate batteries making no response, Meade pushed forward right against what proved to be the centre of Jackson's position.[4]

Jackson's front line was composed of three brigades of A. P. Hill's division, posted in the woods at Hamilton's Crossing, the point which Franklin had been ordered to assail with a single division; the other three brigades formed the second line along the military road, while the divisions of D. H. Hill, Ewell, and Taliaferro were in reserve beyond the crest of the heights. A wide gap had been left between two of Hill's front brigades, just behind a strip of boggy wood which was supposed to be inaccessible.[5] By one of those accidents which sometimes change the result of a battle, Meade advanced right upon this point, and his division thrust itself like a wedge through the unguarded opening, in the face of a fierce artillery fire now opened upon his column from the hitherto silent batteries. This wedge, by sheer force of impact, forced itself between and past the Confederate brigades of Lane and Archer, sweeping back the flanks of each, and gaining the second line along the military road. A part of Gregg's brigade was thrown into confusion, but the remainder of the line stood firm, and checked the rush of Meade's column. This had pushed in so rapidly that it was separated from Gibbon's division, which was to be its immediate support; and was enveloped, for it had pierced, not shattered, the first Confederate line, whose separated portions assailed each of its flanks, while its front was headed by the second line. It was now a mere question of force. Meade's three brigades were opposed to Hill's six, and they fell back in confusion over the ground which they had gained. Meanwhile Gibbon's supporting division, after a brief delay, which to Meade seemed long,[6] came up on his right, and for a moment stemmed the Confederate advance. But in the mean while a messenger from Hill had dashed up to Early, who was in the rear, bringing tidings that "an awful gap" had been left in the front line, through which the enemy were pouring, endangering not only the infantry of that line, but all the batteries. Early sent Lawton's brigade into the fight; they rushed in with the wild "cheer peculiar to the Confederate soldier, and which is never to be mistaken for the studied hurrahs of the Yankees,"[7] closely followed by the remainder of the division. At the same time Hood, whose division of Longstreet's corps was next to Jackson, and who had received orders to co-operate with him, sent a brigade to the scene of action. This united force swept back Gibbon's division, as well as the shattered remains of Meade's.[8]

The consequences of the wording of Burnside's order, and Franklin's understanding of it, were now apparent. Franklin held his Grand Division in a position for a "rapid advance down the Richmond Road," and so, with the exception of Meade and Gibbon, it was stretched along the road, the nearest part being a full mile from the scene of conflict, and most of it much farther, for Doubleday's division, which was to have directly supported the attack, had gone so far to the left as to be beyond reach. But, fortunately, Stoneman's corps of Hooker's Grand Division had begun to cross the river opposite the place of the fight. Birney's division of that corps, which led, had been ordered to follow Meade when he advanced; but the order was countermanded, and he was directed to retire his men from a hot artillery fire which was opening upon them. He had begun to do this when he was told to push forward to aid Meade, whose division was flying back in all directions. The fugitives rushed straight through Birney's lines, closely pursued by the enemy, who dashed within fifty yards of Birney's guns. Four batteries of these opened such a furious fire of canister that the Confederates were checked; they then recoiled, falling back to their original first line on the railroad.[1] The battle on the left was now over. It had lasted about two hours, counting from the time when Meade advanced down to the moment when the Confederates recoiled from the pursuit.[2] Burnside, indeed, sent an order to Franklin directing him to attack in front, but before this was received Franklin deemed it too late to make any change in his dispositions.[3] Jackson also planned an assault under cover of darkness upon the Federal position. He proposed to attack with his artillery in advance, followed by the infantry; but his first guns had hardly moved forward a hundred yards when the Federal artillery reopened its fire, and so completely swept his front as to satisfy him that the attempt must be abandoned.[4]

In this action upon the left the Federals lost, in killed and wounded, about 3700, of which nearly 2600 fell upon the two divisions of Meade and Gibbon, and 900 upon that of Birney. The Confederates lost about 3200, of which half fell upon the division of A. P. Hill, and a fourth upon that of Ewell. In their advance the Federals captured 500 prisoners, and lost about as many in the retreat.[5]

During this action on the left, a still more fiercely contested fight was raging three miles away on the right, at the foot of Marye's Hill, directly behind Fredericksburg. The Confederate position here was of great strength.[6] "Marye's Hill, covered with their batteries, falls off abruptly toward Fredericksburg, to a stone wall which forms a terrace on the side of the hill, and the outer margin of the Telegraph Road, which winds along the foot of the hill. The road is about twenty-five feet wide, and is faced by a stone wall, about four feet high, on the city side. The road having been cut out of the side of the hill in many places, this last wall is not visible above the surface of the ground. The ground falls off rapidly to almost a level surface, which extends about a hundred and fifty yards; then, with another abrupt fall of a few feet, to another plain, which extends some two hundred yards, and then falls off abruptly into a wide ravine, which extends along the whole front of the city." This road, invisible from the direction whence the attack was to come, was precisely like the ditch of a fortress, affording perfect protection to the men posted in it. Parts of two brigades, numbering in all not 2000 men, were stationed here, and yet so small was the space that they stood four deep.[7] The line of this sunken road was continued on each side by a stone wall raised above the ground, and by rifle-pits and trenches. The crest of the hill was covered with artillery, but so narrow was the space that there was here only room for eleven guns of the Washington Artillery; these were mostly 12-pounders. Other guns, about fifty in all, of heavier calibre, were posted so as to enfilade the approaches, while the bulk of the artillery was held in reserve beyond the crest of the hills, the ammunition trains being several miles in the rear.[8] Lee, indeed, seems to have assumed that the enemy would succeed in gaining the crest of the hills, and that the battle would be fought on the plateau beyond, where his whole system of defensive works had been constructed; while Burnside supposed that these crests once gained the victory would be won.

The attack upon Marye's Hill was committed to Sumner; but, as Wilcox's corps of his Grand Division had been stretched down the river to keep up the connection with Franklin, the burden of the assault was laid upon Couch's corps. French's division was to begin the attack, followed by that of Hancock, "two of the most gallant officers in the army, and two divisions that had never turned their backs to the enemy."[9] When the fog lifted at noon, these divisions were seen formed in two columns of attack, marching straight toward the base of the heights, along two roads which here run parallel, that on the right being the "Orange Plank Road," leading westward to the "Wilderness," four months hence to become historical in connection with

[1] Hooker, in *Com. Rep.*, 667. [2] *Lee's Rep.*, ii., 428. [3] *Ibid.*, ii., 487.
[4] Reynolds, in *Com. Rep.*, 698; A. P. Hill, in *Lee's Rep.*, ii., 462. [5] *Lee's Rep.*, ii., 466.
[6] "General Gibbon's division on my right, which I understood was to have advanced simultaneously with my own, did not advance till I was driven back. It advanced until it came within short range of the enemy, when it halted. The officers could not get the men forward to a charge, and the division was held at bay there some twenty or thirty minutes, during which time my division had gone forward. That delay enabled the enemy to concentrate their force and attack me on my front and both flanks. I had penetrated the enemy's lines so far that I had no support on either flank, and was therefore forced to fall back. As I came out, Gibbon's forces advanced, and got as far probably as the railroad, which was the enemy's outer line" (Meade, in *Com. Rep.*, 691).—Gibbon says: "I saw General Meade's troops moving forward into action, and I at once sent orders to my leading brigade to advance and engage the enemy. Shortly afterward I ordered up another brigade to the support of the first. The fire was very heavy from the enemy's infantry, and I ordered up the third brigade, and directed them to take the position with the bayonet, having previously given that order to the leading brigade. But the general commanding that brigade told me that the noise and confusion was so great that it was impossible to get the men to charge, or to get them to hear any order to charge. The third brigade went in, took the position with the bayonet, and captured a considerable number of prisoners. I had just received the report of the success of the third brigade, when shortly after I saw a regiment of infantry come out on the left of my line, between myself and General Meade. No troops came up in support of my division to enable me to hold the position which I had gained" (*Ibid.*, 715).
[7] Early, in *Lee's Rep.*, ii., 470. [8] *Lee's Rep.*, ii., 428, 457.

[1] Birney, in *Com. Rep.*, 705; Reynolds, *Ibid.*, 698; Jackson, in *Lee's Rep.*, ii., 436; A. P. Hill, *Ibid.*, 464; Early, *Ibid.*, 471.
[2] The moments of the fight are best given in the dispatches of General Hardie, of Burnside's staff, who was placed at Franklin's head-quarters to report upon the operations. We give the main points of his consecutive dispatches, as contained in *Com. Rep.*, 712–714: "*December* 13, 7 40 A.M. Meade's division is to make the movement from our left; but it is just reported that the enemy's skirmishers are advancing, indicating an attack upon our position on the left.—9 A.M. Meade just moved out; Doubleday supports him. Meade's skirmishers engaged with enemy's skirmishers.—9 40. Two batteries playing upon Reynolds. They must be silenced before he can advance.—11 A.M. Meade advanced half a mile, and holds on.—12 M. Birney's division now getting into position. That done, Reynolds will order Meade to advance.—12 5 P.M. Meade's line is advancing in the direction you prescribed this morning.—1 P.M. Enemy opened a battery enfilading Meade; Reynolds has opened all his batteries upon it. Reynolds hotly engaged.—1 15 P.M. Heavy engagement of infantry; Meade is assaulting the hill.—1 25 P.M. Meade is in the Woods; seems to be able to hold on. Reynolds will push Gibbon in if necessary; the infantry firing is prolonged and quite heavy; things look well enough; men in fine spirits.—1 40 P.M. Meade having carried a portion of the enemy's position in the Woods, we have 300 prisoners; tough work; men fight well; Gibbon has advanced to Meade's right; Meade has suffered severely; Doubleday, to Meade's left, not engaged.—2 15 P.M. Gibbon and Meade driven back from the Woods; Newton gone forward; Jackson's corps of the enemy attacks on the left; Gibbon slightly wounded; Bayard mortally wounded by a shell. Things do not look so well on Reynolds's front; still we will have new troops in soon.—2 25 P.M. Franklin will do his best; new troops gone in.—3 P.M. Reynolds seems to be holding his own; things look better somewhat.—3 40 P.M. Gibbon's and Meade's divisions are badly used up, and I fear another attack can not be made this afternoon. Doubleday's division will replace Meade's as soon as it can be collected, and if it be done in time another attack will be made. The enemy are in force in the woods on our left, threatening the safety of that portion of our line. Just as soon as the left is safe, our forces here will be prepared for a front attack; but it may be too late this afternoon; indeed, we are engaged in front any how. Notwithstanding the unpleasant items I relate, the *morale* generally of the troops is good.—4 30 P.M. The enemy is still in force on our left and front. An attack on our batteries in front has been repulsed. A new attack has just opened on our left; but the left is safe, though it is too late to advance either to the left or front."
[3] *Com. Rep.*, 710. [4] Jackson, in *Lee's Rep.*, ii., 438.
[5] For detail of the losses in this action, and in that on the right, see *supra*, p. 416.
[6] This description is copied from Kershaw's Report (in *Lee's Rep.*, ii., 487). Of all the Reports on either side, this of Kershaw, who commanded here, is the only one which gives any adequate idea of the strength of the Confederate position. The existence of the sunken road, which, as it happened, was the key to the whole action here, seems never to have been known to any of the Union generals, even when they furnished their reports.
[7] *Ibid.*, 488. [8] *Ibid.*, 522, 588, 547. [9] Sumner, in *Com. Rep.*, 658.

THE ASSAULT UPON MARYE'S HILL.

the battle of Chancellorsville; the other, the "Telegraph Road," bending southwardly, and leading to Richmond, in which, hidden from view, lay the few regiments forming the advance line of the Confederate force, commanded by Cobb;[1] but he having been killed early in the day, the command was given to Kershaw, whose brigade was thrust forward into and near the sunken road.

No sooner had the Federal columns moved in dense masses out of the deep ravine, through which some suppose that the Rappahannock once flowed, and emerged upon the narrow plain at the foot of Marye's Hill, than they came within range of the Confederate artillery posted upon the crests. Every gun opened upon them with terrible effect, "making great gaps that could be seen at the distance of a mile."[2] The light guns of the Confederates, at this close range, were better than though they had been heavier, for they could be worked more rapidly. French's division, in the advance, pressed on in the face of the artillery fire, closing up the great gaps plowed through their ranks, and had crossed half of the narrow space toward the foot of the hill, when they were met by a sheet of fire full in their faces from an invisible foe. It came from the Confederate infantry hidden in the road "cut out of the side of the hill," not a man of whom was visible above the smooth slope. The heads of the advancing columns melted away before this solid wall of fire, delivered from ranks four deep,[3] like a snow-bank before a jet of steam.

French's division recoiled before this fierce fire, and streamed back over the narrow plain across which they had advanced, leaving almost half their number behind. Hancock's came close after; this, with French's remaining men, pushed straight on, disregarding the hot artillery fire from the heights; but no sooner did they come within musket-range of the sunken road than a solid sheet of lead poured upon them. The front which was to be carried was so narrow that scarcely more than a brigade could be brought upon it at once. Brigade dashed in after brigade, each taking the place of one which had been swept back so rapidly that it seemed, from the Union lines in the plain, but a single assault, lasting three hours; but, as seen from the Confederate positions on the hill, it seemed a succession of waves dashed against the rocky wall at its base. But it was not a question of numbers. Had twice as many men been brought up the result would have been the same, only the loss would have been twice as great. Nor was it a question of bravery; for never, not even when, seven months later, the Confederates in their turn dashed and were shattered against the steeps at Gettysburg, was an assault made with more desperate and unavailing valor.[4] The main stress of the assault had been borne by divisions of French and Hancock. They had pressed across the narrow plain, about 10,000 strong, and lost fully 4000 in killed and wounded.

Burnside had watched the action from the heights across the Rappahannock. Two full hours had passed, and nothing seemed gained. Assault after assault had been made by divisions which had "never turned their backs to the enemy." The regiments which he had expected to see crowning the crest had been repelled from the base. "That crest must be crossed to-night," he exclaimed, and directed Hooker to cross and attack upon the Telegraph Road—the very position against which French and Hancock had been "butting all day long." Of Hooker's six divisions, two, and these, he says, "were my favorite divisions, for the one was that which I had educated myself, and the other was that which Kearney had commanded, and of these I knew more than of any others in my command," had been sent to the left to support Franklin. Another division had been sent across to the upper end of Fredericksburg to support Howard, and still another lower down to support Sturgis, both of whom had been pushed forward to aid French and Howard. Hooker had then but two divisions left with which to act; they were that of Humphreys, composed of new men, and Sykes's regulars, who had fought at Bull Run and Cold Harbor, at Malvern and Groveton. Hooker rode forward across the river to consult with the generals who had been engaged in the attack. He saw Couch and Wilcox, French and Hancock. With a single exception, they were all of opinion that no attack could be successfully made there. Hooker examined the position himself, and sent to Burnside an aid with a message dissuading from a new assault. The messenger returned with orders that an attempt must be made. Hooker then rode back, and in person repeated his urgency

---

[1] T. R. R. Cobb, not to be confounded with Howell Cobb, once Buchanan's Secretary of the Treasury, but now also a general in the Confederate army. [2] *Lee's Rep.*, ii., 429.

[2] "I found, on my arrival, that Cobb's brigade occupied our entire front, and our troops could only get into position by doubling on them. This was accordingly done, and the formation along most of the line was consequently four deep. As an evidence of the coolness of the command, I may mention here that, notwithstanding that their fire was the most rapid and continuous that I have ever witnessed, not a man was injured by the fire of his comrades."—Kershaw, in *Lee's Rep.*, ii., 488.

[4] The Confederate reports testify abundantly to the desperate bravery with which this assault was carried on. Lee says (*Rep.*, i., 42): "Our batteries poured a rapid and destructive fire into the dense lines of the enemy as they advanced to the attack, frequently breaking their ranks, and forcing them to retreat to the shelter of the houses. Six times did the enemy, notwithstanding the havoc caused by our batteries, press on with great determination to within one hundred yards of the foot of the hill; but here, encountering the deadly fire of our infantry, his columns were broken, and fled in confusion to the town."—Ransom, whose division bore half the brunt of the fight, says (*Ibid.*, 451): "Another line was formed by the enemy, he all the while keeping up a brisk fire with sharp-shooters. This line advanced with the utmost determination, and some few of them got within fifty yards of our line; but the whole were forced to retire in wild confusion before the telling fire of our small-arms at such short range. For some minutes there was a cessation; but we were not long kept in expectancy. The enemy now seemed determined to reach our position, and formed apparently a triple line, and, almost massed, moved to the charge heroically, and met the withering fire of our artillery and small-arms with wonderful staunchness. On they came to within less than one hundred and fifty paces of our line; but nothing could live before the sheet of lead that was hurled at them from this distance. They momentarily recovered, broke, and rushed headlong from the field. A few, however, more resolute than the rest, lingered under cover of some fences and houses, and annoyed us with a scattering but well-directed fire. Nothing daunted by the fearful punishment he had received, the enemy brought out fresh and increased numbers of troops. Our men held their fire until it would be fatally effective; meanwhile the artillery was spreading fearful havoc among the enemy's ranks. Still he advanced, and received the destructive fire of our line; even more resolute than before, he seemed determined madly to press on; but his efforts could avail nothing."

FRANKLIN'S DIVISION RECROSSING THE RAPPAHANNOCK.

against an attack. But Burnside was inflexible, and insisted that it should be made.[1]

The short December day was verging to a close before Hooker was prepared to attack. He thought that the assault had not been sufficiently concentrated, and proposed to breach "a hole sufficiently large for a forlorn hope to enter." He brought forward batteries, and poured in a fire from every gun at his command. It made no more impression than if it had been poured upon "the side of a mountain of rock;" indeed, the sunken wall, which formed the real Confederate defense, could not be touched by any fire from the plain. Just at sunset Hooker ordered Humphreys's division to form in column of assault. Knapsacks, overcoats, and haversacks were thrown aside, and the men were directed "to make the assault with empty muskets, for there was no time there to load and fire." At the word, they rushed forward with loud hurrahs, charging straight for the stone wall. As it happened, the Confederate artillery, which had been posted on the crest of Marye's Hill, had exhausted its ammunition, and was passing to the rear, while other guns were coming forward to supply their places.[2] Humphreys's men thus escaped the terrible artillery fire which had staggered French and Hancock, and the head of the column gained a few yards—possibly rods—beyond the point attained by those who had gone before, and had then been hurled back by the musketry fire from the sunken road.[3] Here they met, as those who had gone before had met, the solid sheet of lead, winged with flame, poured in their faces, and turned, as they had done, from that fierce fire. Of the 4000 men whom Humphreys led up to that hidden defense, almost a half were stricken down in a quarter of an hour, for so brief had been the time between their rush and their repulse. Had Humphreys succeeded in his assault, Hooker had proposed to support him by Sykes; but the assault had signally failed; and, says Hooker, grimly, "finding that I had lost as many men as my orders required me to lose, I suspended the attack, and directed that the men should hold, for the advance line between Fredericksburg and the enemy, a ditch that runs along about midway between the enemy's lines and the city, and which would afford a shelter for the men.[4]

The Confederate army lay on their arms that night, fully expecting that the battle would be renewed the next day. The attack had been made by so small a portion of the Union force, and had been repulsed, especially on the right, by so small a part of the Confederate force, that Lee could not believe it to be the final attempt, and he resolved to await its renewal in his strong position, rather than run the risk of attacking in turn.[5] Burnside had crossed the river with 100,000 men. About 55,000 of these were with Franklin on the left; of these, about 17,000 had been fairly put into action. Against these Jackson had brought in about 20,000, being half of his own corps, and a brigade of Hood's division of Longstreet's corps. Hooker and Sumner, on the Union left, had 45,000; of these, 15,000 had been thrown

[1] Hooker, in *Com. Rep.*, 667; Burnside, *Ibid.*, 728. Both generals agree precisely as to facts. Burnside, however, considered this delay on the part of Hooker as "loss of time, and a preparation on the part of an officer for a failure, inasmuch as it was his duty to attack when ordered."

[2] *Lee's Rep.*, ii., 532.

[3] Hooker says (*Com. Rep.*, 668): "The head of General Humphreys's column advanced to within perhaps fifteen or twenty yards of the stone wall, which was the advanced position which the rebels held, and then they were thrown back as quickly as they had advanced. Probably the whole of the advance and the retiring did not occupy fifteen minutes. They left behind, as was reported to me, 1760 of their number out of about 4000."—McLaws, describing the field as it appeared after the close of the action, says (*Lee's Rep.*, ii., 447): "The body of one man, supposed to be an officer, was found within about thirty yards of the stone wall, and other single bodies were scattered at increased distances, until the main mass of the dead lay thickly strewn over the ground at something over one hundred yards off, extending to the ravine, commencing at the point where our men would allow the enemy's column to approach before opening fire, and beyond which no organized body of men was able to pass."

[4] *Com. Rep.*, 668. This ditch is what is called in the Confederate Reports a "ravine."

[5] "The attack on the 14th had been so easily repulsed, and by so small a part of our army, that it was not supposed the enemy would limit his efforts to one attempt, which, in view of the magnitude of his preparations and the extent of his forces, seemed to be comparatively insignificant. Believing, therefore, that he would attack us, it was not deemed expedient to lose the advantages of our position, and expose the troops to the fire of his inaccessible batteries beyond the river by advancing against him. But we were necessarily ignorant of the extent to which he had suffered." —*Lee's Rep.*, i., 48.

against the stone wall. Actually opposed to them were not more than 5000 of Longstreet's corps, though the whole, 40,000 strong, exclusive of Hood, could have been brought in had it been necessary; so that, in this twofold action, less than one third on either side were actually engaged.[1]

Burnside passed the night in consultation with his officers and men. Notwithstanding their dissuasion, he resolved to renew the assault next morning. Sumner, with the corps which Burnside himself had originally commanded, and which had not been seriously engaged, was to assail the heights by a direct attack, conducted just as that had been which had been so disastrously repulsed. He thought that these regiments, "coming quickly after each other, would be able to carry the stone wall and the batteries in front, forcing the enemy into their next line, and, by going in with them, they would not be able to fire upon us to any great extent." And so the order was given. With Sumner, to receive an order was to set about its execution, and before the morning lifted the columns of attack were formed. Then, when all was ready for the desperate attempt, the veteran soldier felt at liberty to remonstrate. "General," he said, "I hope you will desist from this attack. I do not know of any general officer who approves of it; and I think it will prove disastrous to the army." Burnside could not but hesitate when such advice was given by one "who was always in favor of an advance when it was possible." He kept the column formed, but suspended the order for advance until he could consult with his generals. One and all —commanders of corps and divisions on the right—were against the attempt. He sent for Franklin from the left, and his opinion was the same. So, after hours of thought, Burnside resolved that he would not venture the attack, which he himself at the time believed would have been successful, though he soon became convinced to the contrary. Night had almost come when he informed his officers that he had determined to recross the river with the bulk of the army, but to leave enough to hold Fredericksburg itself; and to protect the bridges, which were to remain, in case he should want to cross again. But upon the representations of Hooker and Butterfield—two men into whose composition entered no feeble fibre—he was convinced that even Fredericksburg could not be held; that every thing must be withdrawn across the river, and the whole enterprise abandoned as a failure.[2] Sumner alone, of all the council, was still in favor of holding on to Fredericksburg. He thought this might have been done by a single division, provided the batteries across the river were rightly posted, and so the upshot of the affair would have presented a better appearance:

[1] There is some discrepancy of statement as to the numbers of Union forces which crossed the river, the forces constituting each wing, and the numbers actually engaged. Burnside, however, testifies (in *Com. Rep.*, 656): "We had about 100,000 men on the other side of the river. Every single man of them was under artillery fire, and about half of them were at different times formed into column of attack. Every man was put in column of attack that could be got in." But a careful perusal of all the testimony shows that of the divisions formed into "columns of attack," fully a third were not fairly thrown into action.—Franklin estimated (*Com. Rep.*, 709): "The force under my command was somewhat over 40,000 men. I do not think it was over 50,000, counting Stoneman's two divisions; but I can not tell without looking at the figures. There were six divisions engaged in supporting the attack—Meade's, Doubleday's, Gibbon's, Birney's, Sickles's, and Newton's; I think the number was about 40,000." But, as has been shown, only three of these six were seriously engaged—Meade's and Gibbon's, of Reynolds's corps, which together lost fully 2500 out of the 2800 in Franklin's Grand Division, leaving only 300 for the three divisions of Doubleday, Sickles, and Newton, and of these 200 were from Doubleday's. Birney's division of Hooker's command was also engaged, losing nearly 1000 (*Ibid.*, 706). Three days before the battle Meade's and Gibbon's divisions, according to the returns of the day, numbered not quite 12,000 "present for duty," of which Meade had 6800; but he says he brought into action only 4500. Birney's numbered 7000 (*Ibid.*, 691, 702, 706); so that the estimate of 17,000 brought into action by Franklin on the left is fully equal to the truth. On the right we have seen that the three divisions of French, Hancock, and Humphreys were the only ones brought directly into the fight: the utmost strength of these divisions was 5000 each.

In placing the Confederates at 80,000 I am guided mainly by the official returns (*Ante*, p. 406), which give the numbers "present for duty" on the 20th of November, a fortnight before the battle, at 78,554; and on the 31st of December, a fortnight after the battle, at 79,092. At each date there were about 12,000 reported as "present," besides those "present for duty;" while the nominal strength, "present and absent," exceeded 150,000, being greater at the first date than the last. Of the "absent" I suppose that none could in the interval have been brought back; of those "present," but not reported as "for duty," probably a few thousand might have been available in an emergency. The Confederate Reports give the movements and losses of every brigade and regiment, so that, assuming their whole force to have been 80,000 effective men, I am able to give, without the possibility of material error, the numbers actually engaged on any part of the field.

[2] Burnside, in *Com. Rep.*, 658.

it would have been merely "a change of tactics—a drawing back a little in order to try it again."[1]

During Sunday, the 14th, and the greater part of Monday, the 15th, the two great armies lay in their positions, each expecting when the morning fog lifted to be attacked by the other. There was some firing at different points along the extended lines, but nothing which approached to an engagement. On the afternoon of the 15th a formal truce for the purpose of removing the wounded was agreed upon between Jackson and Franklin on their part of the field—the Union left and the Confederate right.[2] Opposite Fredericksburg, on the Union right, while there was no formal truce, there was little actual hostility. Each force was waiting to see what the other would do. Burnside, after some hours of deliberation, ordered, on the afternoon of the 15th, that his whole force should recross the Rappahannock. A cold rain-storm had in the mean while set in during the night, under cover of which the passage was effected without its being suspected by the enemy. Next morning, the 16th, when the fog lifted from the valley, the whole Union force was seen across the Rappahannock; the pontoons were swung back, and the river once more separated the two armies. Burnside left nothing behind save a part of the dead in front of the stone wall, some ammunition, and 9000 muskets which had fallen from the hands of his slain and wounded.[3]

The Confederates lost about 4600 men, of whom 600 were killed and 4000 wounded. The Union loss was nearly twice and a half as great: about 1500 killed and 9000 wounded. The Confederates lost also 650 prisoners, the Federals 900,[4] besides 1200 stragglers who never rejoined their commands. In the action on the left the losses were not greatly disproportionate, that of the Federals being somewhat in excess. But on the right, in front of the stone wall, the disproportion was enormous. Of the 1800 losses in Longstreet's corps, 250 occurred in holding Fredericksburg on the 11th, and as many more in Hood's division which supported Jackson, leaving but 1300 who fell in the defense of Marye's Hill.[5] The Union loss here was fully 6500, of which probably 5000 fell before the fire of the 2000 infantry who held the stone wall. These lost not more than 500, and most of these fell while getting into position; when once behind that defense they were perfectly sheltered, except when a man exposed himself accidentally to a chance shot from a skirmisher. Two thirds of the Confederate loss at Marye's Hill was sustained by regiments posted on the surrounding slopes, and partially exposed to distant artillery fire. In the final charge, when Humphreys's division dashed with unloaded muskets toward the sunken road, and were flung back in a quarter of an hour with a loss of 1700 men, it is doubtful whether the Confederates suffered the loss of a single man killed or wounded.[6]

Severe as were the casualties of the battle, they formed a small part of the injury inflicted upon the Union army. Its morale was seriously impaired. It was clear to every man, the commanding general only excepted, that the whole plan of the campaign was thwarted. Whatever might have been the chances of its success had it been promptly executed, they were all destroyed by the fatal delay of a month. Officers in their tents, and soldiers by their bivouac fires, discussed the campaign, and declared that it was not possible even to cross the Rappahannock, much less to march to Richmond. The feeling of discouragement was universal from the private up to the commander of a grand division. Burnside alone appeared ignorant of the real condition of his army. "I do not," he said, "consider the troops demoralized, or the condition of the army impaired, except so far as it has been by the loss of so many men."[7] But his officers knew otherwise. Sumner, a week after the battle, thought the army far more demoralized than was warranted by its losses. "There is a great deal too much croaking; there is not sufficient confidence," he said; but he still thought that "within a few days, with sufficient exertion, the army will again be in excellent order."[1] But this revival of confidence never came. The tone of the army was indicated by resignations among officers and desertions among privates, which increased to an alarming extent.

Burnside meanwhile determined upon another attempt, which was in effect a repetition of the one which he had first proposed, of crossing the river some miles below Fredericksburg, and thus turning the Confederate right, wholly avoiding the strong position from which he had been so disastrously hurled. Meanwhile a cavalry force of 2500 was to cross the Rappahannock by the upper fords, and gain the rear of Lee's army; they were then to separate, a part returning by different routes, while a picked body of 1000 men, with four pieces of artillery, were to press on, passing to the south of Richmond, and joining General Peck at Suffolk, where steamers were to be in waiting to bring them back to Acquia Creek. The object of this cavalry expedition was twofold: To attract the attention of the enemy from his main movement, and to "blow up the locks on the James River Canal, the iron bridge over the Nottoway, on the Richmond and Weldon Railroad," thereby seriously interrupting the Confederate communications and sources of supply.

On the 26th of December, all the preparations for this movement were made. The place of crossing had been selected, the positions for artillery to protect the passage chosen, and orders given that three days' rations should be cooked for the whole army, while ten or twelve days' supply of food, forage, and ammunition should be provided, and the whole army be in readiness to move at twelve hours' notice. On the 30th the movement had been fairly commenced, when Burnside received a telegram from the President informing him that he had good reason to order that there should be no general movement until he had been informed of it. Burnside suspended the movement, and hastened to Washington to ascertain the reason for this order.[2]

A week before, Franklin and Smith had addressed a letter to the President, declaring that in their opinion the plan of the campaign already commenced could not be successful: It was, they said, sixty-one miles to Richmond, and for the whole distance it would be necessary to keep the communications open, and these communications were liable to be broken at many points. If the railroad was rebuilt as the army advanced, the enemy would destroy it at important points. If wagon transportation was depended upon, the trains must be so large that much of the strength of the army would be required to guard them, and the troops would be so separated by the trains blocking the road that the van and the rear could not be within supporting distance. The enemy would, moreover, be able to post himself defiantly in strong positions, whence probably the whole strength of the army would not be able to drive him; and even if he were driven away, the result would not be decisive. His losses in these strong positions would be slight, while ours would be enormous. To insure a successful campaign, it was in their judgment essential that all the troops in the East should be massed; that they should approach as near as possible to Richmond without an engagement; and that the line of communication should be absolutely free from danger of interruption. These requisites could only be secured by a campaign on the James River, and they accordingly drew up the outlines of such a campaign.[3]

While the President was deliberating upon this letter, Generals Newton and Cochrane went up to Washington, and laid before him what they considered the condition of the army. They told him that it was the general opinion of officers and men that it would be a dangerous and ruinous folly to attempt to cross the Rappahannock; that they knew they could not succeed, and would therefore be deprived of a great portion of their vigor.[4] The President thereupon gave the order prohibiting any movement of which he was not previously informed. Burnside urged that the movement should be made. The President refused his assent until he had consulted with his military advisers. The general returned to his camp, whence he wrote asking for distinct authority from Halleck to cross the river. He knew, he wrote, that there was hardly an officer holding any important command who would favor the movement, but he was confident that it should be made, and he would take the responsibility of making it upon himself; but he felt that the general-in-chief should at least sanction it. Halleck replied in general terms, laying down sundry general rules which ought to govern the management of an army, and saying that while he had always favored a forward movement, he could not take the responsibility of giving any directions as to how or when it should be made. The prohibitory order appears to have been withdrawn, for Burnside resolved to make another move upon his own responsibility, and without making any reply to this letter of Halleck.[5]

This movement was to be commenced by passing the Rappahannock

[1] Sumner, *Ibid.*, 659. [2] *Lee's Rep.*, ii., 438. [3] *Lee's Rep.*, i., 43.
[4] *Ibid.*, i., 43. [5] *Ibid.*, ii., 438.
[6] The Official Reports of Losses (Union, in *Com. Rep.*, 661; Confederate, in *Lee's Rep.*, ii., 438, 439) are as follows:

UNION.

	Killed.	Wounded.	Missing.	Total.
Sumner's Grand Div.	490	4150	855	5494
Hooker's " "	327	2460	748	3548
Franklin's " "	338	2430	1581	4679
Engineers' " "	7	42	180	50
	1152	9101	3264	13771

CONFEDERATE.

	Killed.	Wounded.	Missing.	Total.
Longstreet's Corps	251	1516	127	1894
Jackson's "	344	2545	526	3415
	595	4061	653	5309

This Union Report, furnished by the Medical Inspector General soon after the battle, requires some considerable emendations. Of those set down as "missing," about 1200 returned to their commands (*Halleck's Report of Operations*), reducing the missing to 2078. The Confederates claim about 900 prisoners (*Lee's Rep.*, i., 43), leaving nearly 1200 missing to be accounted for. I have no doubt that a third of these were slain outright on the field, in addition to those reported as killed. I attribute all these to the assault on the stone wall on the right, for on the left the dead and wounded were buried or removed by truce between Franklin and Jackson. It is only by making such an addition that I can explain the great disproportion between the killed and wounded on the right, as reported. The usual ratio in a close engagement is one killed to five or six wounded; here it is put down as a little more than one to ten, while all the circumstances of the fight indicate that the killed must have borne an unusual proportion to the wounded. Moreover, the Medical Inspector says, "The return of killed may be too small." I have therefore adopted these emendations into the text, increasing the killed by 450, and diminishing the missing by 1650.

As the Confederates remained in undisturbed possession of the entire field of battle, they were able to account for every man of their army. I adopt their Official Report as accurate. In *Lee's Report*, i., 38, there is a statement of the Confederate losses, making them 458 killed and 3743 wounded; and there seems to have been published a statement purporting to be Lee's Official Report, making his entire loss only 1800 killed and wounded. I find this reproduced in several histories, notably in Pollard's *Lost Cause*, p. 346, where it appears thus: "General Lee, in his official dispatch, writes, 'Our loss during the entire operations since the movements of the enemy began amounts to about 1800 killed and wounded.'" This was published fully two years after the real official report of Lee was printed by order of the Confederate Congress. I can account for this statement only by supposing that as Lee was with Longstreet's corps during the whole action, he only referred to the casualties in that corps, not including that in Jackson's corps, which were almost twice as many.

The estimate of losses at various movements, and on the different parts of the field, has been formed from a careful analysis of the reports on both sides. The absolute loss in each army was, however, much less than the reports indicate, the proportion of those wounded so slightly as not to be disabled having been unusually large on both sides. Several of the Confederate reports note this fact. The Union Medical Inspector General says (*Com. Rep.*, 681) that, of the 9101 reported as wounded, there were only 1630 whose cases required to be treated in hospitals; these, added to the 1152 reported as killed—which he thought probably too small—amounting in all to 2782, would, he was confident, "cover the whole amount of disabling casualties occurring at the battle of Fredericksburg."

[7] Testimony in *Com. Rep.*, 656.

[1] Burnside, in *Com. Rep.*, 716–718. [2] Sumner, *Ibid.*, 660.
[3] This letter is given entire in Swinton's *Army of the Potomac*, 263–265. The arguments in its favor were, that "on the James River our troops can be concentrated more rapidly than they can be at any other point; that they can be brought to points within twenty miles of Richmond without the risk of an engagement; that the communication by the James River can be kept, by the assistance of the navy, without the slightest danger of interruption." The principal features of the proposed plan were these: Concentrate 250,000 men; land 150,000 on the north, and 100,000 on the south side of the James, as near as possible to Richmond. Let both bodies advance in the lightest marching order, pontoons being ready to make a connection at any time. It was not probable that the enemy would have sufficient force to withstand the shock of two such bodies. If he declined to fight on the river, the army on the south bank should seize the railroads running from Richmond southward, while the remainder should either attack or invest the Confederate capital.
[4] Newton's Testimony, in *Com. Rep.*, 730–740; Cochrane's, *Ibid.*, 740–746. They must also have implied, if they did not express the opinion which Newton had formed (*Ibid.*, 731), "that the dissatisfaction of the troops arose from a want of confidence in General Burnside's military capacity."
[5] Burnside, in *Com. Rep.*, 718, 719.

at fords six miles above Fredericksburg, masked by a feint at crossing some miles below the town, the feint to be made in such force that it might be converted into the real attempt, if circumstances should warrant, for there were conflicting accounts of the positions of the enemy. This required that roads should be cut through forests in both directions, and corduroyed so as to be passable for artillery and trains; sites for batteries chosen and prepared, and other arrangements made. At last a trusty spy brought information which decided Burnside to make the real attempt above Fredericksburg.

It was now the 20th of January. After the friendly storm, under whose cover the Union army had safely recrossed the Rappahannock, there had ensued five weeks of serene weather. The roads were as good as the bad Virginia roads can be. Burnside gave the final order to move in a hopeful spirit. "The commanding general," he said, "announces to the Army of the Potomac that they are about to meet the enemy once more. The late brilliant actions in North Carolina, Tennessee, and Arkansas have weakened the enemy on the Rappahannock, and the auspicious moment seems to have arrived to strike a great and mortal blow to the rebellion, and to gain that decisive victory which is due to the country." The movement had been commenced the day before. The infantry of the grand divisions of Franklin and Hooker having marched up the river by parallel roads, screened from the observation of the enemy by the intervening heights, and encamped near the fords where the crossing was to be effected, while Couch's corps moved down the river to make the proposed feint, and Sigel's reserve corps, which had in the mean while been brought up, held the communications between the two wings. But the pleasant weather, upon the continuance of which every thing depended, had come to a close. Late in the afternoon a cold, fierce storm set in. The sleet, driven by a furious gale, penetrated the clothing, and cut the faces of the men as they staggered on in their weary march. In two hours every mud-hole became a little lake, and the clayey roads, unhardened by frost, were transformed into quagmires wherein the wagons sank beyond the axles, and the mules to their bellies. It seemed as though the bottom had dropped out. The storm raged all that night and the next day. There was but one man in the army who did not perceive that the movement must be a failure. That one man was Burnside. He still hoped against hope, and resolved to struggle against fate. So all day on the 21st the army staggered on in its march through the mud. Not a gun or a wagon could be moved except by doubling or trebling the teams, and often a hundred men and more pulling at a stout rope were required to drag a pontoon-wagon through the mire. By terrible exertions some were got forward, while the roads were strewed with a chaos of confusion—shipwrecked wagons, horses and mules dead and dying, pontoons and guns immovable in the mud. Still, a formidable force of all arms was got together upon the river bank at the points where the crossing was to be essayed. But before the artillery and pontoons could be put in position, the Confederates had divined every thing, and had posted their forces so as to render the possibility of even crossing the river a matter of doubt; while, had the passage been effected, any farther advance was impossible. So thought the general officers of the army; and the opinions of some of them were expressed in such a form, that Burnside perceived that either he or they must vacate their posts. He sought direction from Halleck, but vainly. Then he recalled the troops to their former positions, and the three days' mud campaign came to an end.[1]

Burnside had for weeks been aware that his entire plan of operations was denounced by some of his leading generals. While he would not charge them with any willful disobedience of orders, he thought that they manifested a want of alacrity which seriously affected the result of the operations. He now resolved to get rid of persons whom he regarded as of no use, and to make some strong examples to the army.[2] He drew up a general order dismissing from the service Hooker, the commander of a grand division, Brooks, Newton, and Cochrane, commanding army divisions, and relieving from duty Franklin, commander of a grand division, together with Smith, Sturgis, and Ferrero, commanding army divisions, and Colonel Taylor, the acting adjutant general of Sumner's grand division.[3] This sweeping order was drawn up with the knowledge of but two men besides the general, and was ordered to be issued. But one of these confidants, "a cool, sensible man, and a firm friend" of Burnside, intimated that while the order was just and should be issued, it transcended in some points the authority of the general. He could not dismiss an officer or hang a deserter without the express approval of the President; and, moreover, by publishing the order, he would force the President to take sides in the military dispute. If he sanctioned the order, his administration would incur the hostility of many influential men, friends of the dismissed officers; if he refused to sanction it after it was issued, he would appear to be the enemy of the commanding general. Still Burnside was firmly convinced he could not retain the command unless he issued the order, with the assurance that it should be sustained. He accordingly went to Washington with the order in one hand and his resignation in the other. He told the President, "If you will say to me, 'You may take the responsibility of issuing the order, and I will sustain it,' I will take that responsibility: this is the only way in which I can retain the command of the Army of the Potomac; otherwise here is my resignation; accept it, and here is the end of the matter as far as I am concerned." The President hesitated. He must consult his advisers. "If you consult any body," replied Burnside, "you will not sanction the order." And so it proved. After deliberating for a day, the President decided to relieve Burnside from the command of the Army of the Potomac, and place Hooker in command, making also some important changes in other respects, principal among which were that Sumner and Franklin should be relieved from their commands. Burnside was satisfied with this decision. "If Hooker can gain a victory," he said to the President, "neither you nor he will be a happier man than I shall be."

Burnside then supposed that his resignation would be accepted; but the President judged otherwise. "We need you," he said, "and can not accept your resignation." The truth was, that while Burnside's own opinion had proved true, that he was not fitted for the command of so large an army, he had yet shown so much capacity for a less onerous command, and had, above all, manifested such an entire absence of all selfish purposes, that the nation could not spare him. He still wished to resign; his private affairs required his attention; and, moreover, he said, if all general officers whom it was found necessary to relieve should resign, it would be better for the President, as it would relieve him from the applications of their friends. "True," replied the President; "but there is no reason for you to resign; you can have as much time as you please for your private business, but we can not accept your resignation." Several commands were proposed to him. He could have the department of South Carolina, or the departments of South and North Carolina would be combined and given to him. He declined both, because he thought these departments were then in good hands. He would remain in the army if his services were absolutely required; but, if he staid, he wished to be employed. Then came up the question as to the form in which his retirement from the command of the Army of the Potomac should be announced. An order had been drawn up at the War Department stating simply that Burnside had been relieved at his own request. To this he objected; he did not wish to appear as having voluntarily given up his command without good reason. This order did not express the real facts of the case, and he still wished to resign. The general-in-chief and the Secretary of War urged that by so doing he would injure himself and the cause. For himself, Burnside "did not care a snap," but he did not wish to injure the cause; the Department might issue just what order it chose; he would take thirty days' leave of absence, and would then come back and go wherever ordered, even if it were to command his old army corps under Hooker. So, when the official order appeared,[1] it announced that Burnside, "at his own request," had been relieved from the command of the Army of the Potomac, and Hooker assigned to the command; that Sumner, "at his own request," had been relieved from duty in this army, and that Franklin was also relieved, but without the significant addition of "at his own request."[2]

Sumner was soon after assigned to the command of the Department of Missouri; but while on his way to the West he died at Syracuse, in New York, on the 21st of March, leaving his name honorably identified with many of the severest struggles of the war. He entered the army in 1819, and had been in active service for forty-four years. He was twice breveted for gallant and meritorious conduct in the Mexican battles; then he was placed in command of the Department of New Mexico, where he directed important military operations against the turbulent tribes of savages. The opening of the civil war found him a colonel of cavalry, but with an appointment of brigadier general to command upon the Pacific coast. From this, at his own request, he was recalled to take part in the operations of the Army of the Potomac, where his services were rewarded by promotion to the rank of major general of volunteers, and, later, of major general by brevet in the regular army.

Burnside, his thirty days' leave of absence having expired, was assigned to the command of the Department of the Ohio, his own old army corps, the 9th, going with him. Subsequently, as we shall have occasion to see, he was recalled to the Army of the Potomac, acting an important part in the closing campaign of the war.

The formal transfer of the command of the Army of the Potomac from Burnside to Hooker was made on the 26th of January. Burnside, in his farewell order, said that the short time in which he had been in command "had not been fruitful in victory," but the army had shown qualities which, under more favorable circumstances, would have accomplished great results."

[1] "Before we could get the pontoons and artillery in position, the plan had been discovered by the enemy, which rendered the crossing very precarious, and the movement of artillery on the opposite bank, even if they had been got over, would have been rendered almost impossible from the state of the roads and the whole face of the country, in consequence of the storm. But a very serious objection to attempting the crossing after this occurred was the almost universal feeling among the general officers that the crossing could not be made there. Some of them gave vent to those opinions in a very public manner, even in the presence of my own staff officers, who informed me of the fact. I telegraphed to General Halleck that I would be very glad to meet him at Acquia Creek; or, if he wished it, I would run up for an hour to Washington. He sent me word that I must be my own judge about coming up. I at once telegraphed back, 'I shall not come up.' I then determined to order the commands back to their original encampments. After doing that, I went to my adjutant general's office, and issued an order which I termed General Order No. 8. That order dismissed some officers from service, subject to the approval of the President, and relieved others from duty with the Army of the Potomac."—Burnside's Testimony, in *Com. Rep.*, 719.

[2] Testimony in *Com. Rep.*, 723.

[3] GENERAL ORDER No. 8, *Jan.* 23, 1863 (Extracts): "General Joseph E. Hooker having been guilty of unjust and unnecessary criticisms of the actions of his superior officers, and of the authorities, and having, by the general tone of his conversation, endeavored to create distrust in the minds of officers who have associated with him, and having, by omissions and otherwise, made reports and statements which were calculated to create incorrect impressions, and of habitually speaking in disparaging terms of other officers, is hereby dismissed the service of the United States as a man unfit to hold an important commission during a crisis like the present." General W. T. H. Brooks was dismissed "for complaining of the policy of the government, and for using language tending to demoralize his command." Generals John Newton and John Cochrane were also dismissed "for going to the President of the United States with criticisms upon the plans of their commanding officer." These dismissals were made subject to the approval of the President. Then followed a list of officers who were "relieved from duty," it "being evident that they can be of no farther service in this army." The names on this list were Generals Franklin, commanding a grand division; Smith, commanding an army corps; Sturgis, Ferrero, and Cochrane, commanding army divisions; and Lieutenant Colonel Taylor, adjutant general of Sumner's Corps. Cochrane's name appears in both lists, as relieved absolutely by Burnside's authority and dismissed subject to the approval of the President.

[1] Jan. 28, 1863.

[2] For the details of the transactions relating to the closing period of Burnside's command, see *Com. Rep.*, 57-60, and *Ibid.*, 716-722.

THE CAMPAIGN

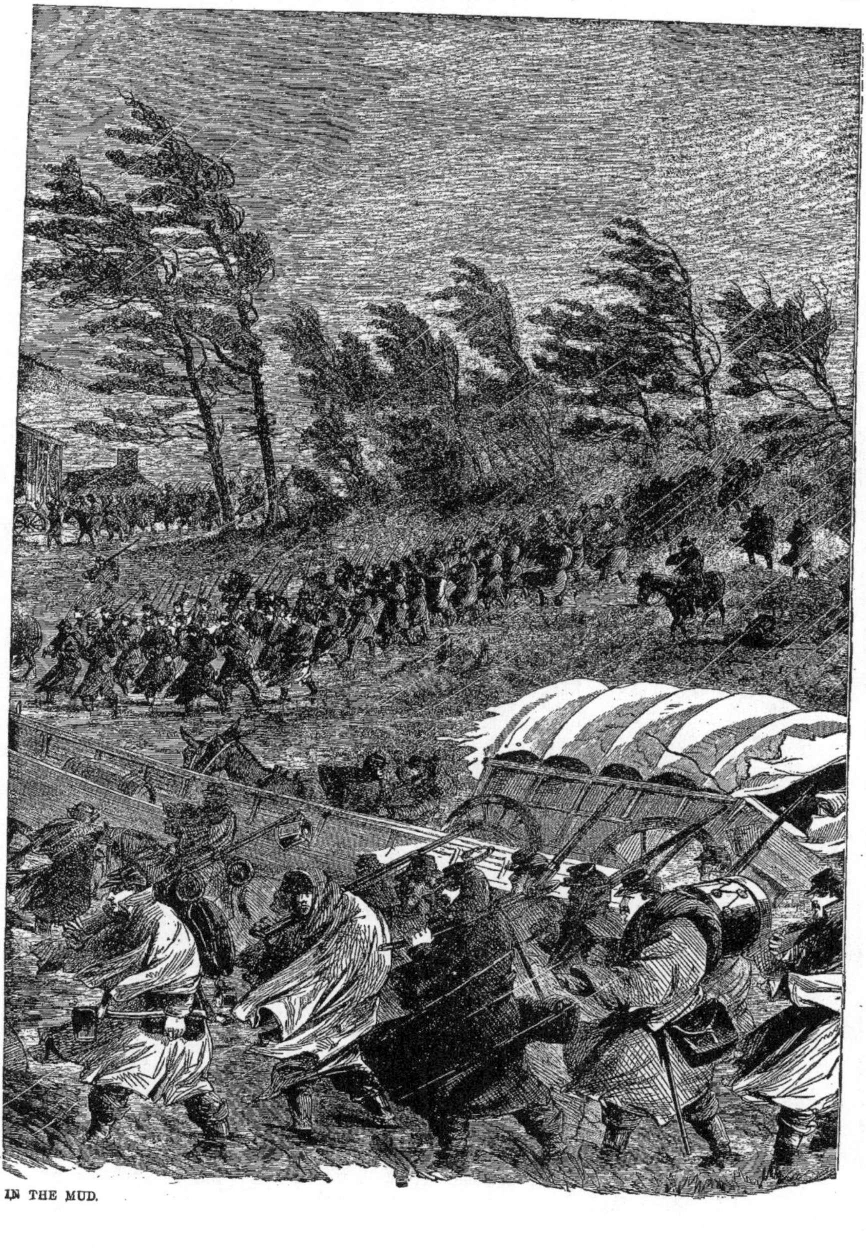

IN THE MUD.

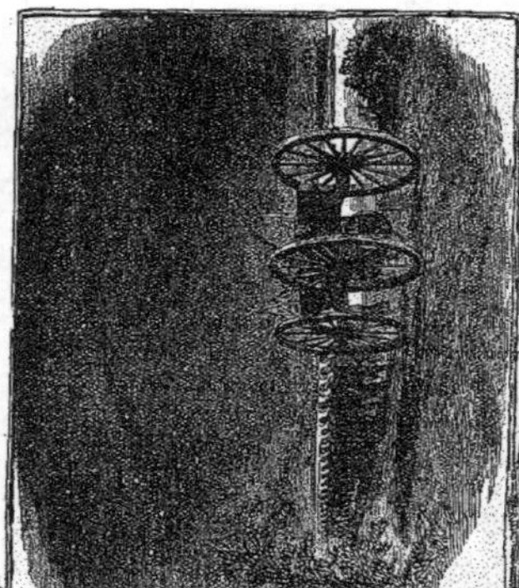

HAULING MORTARS

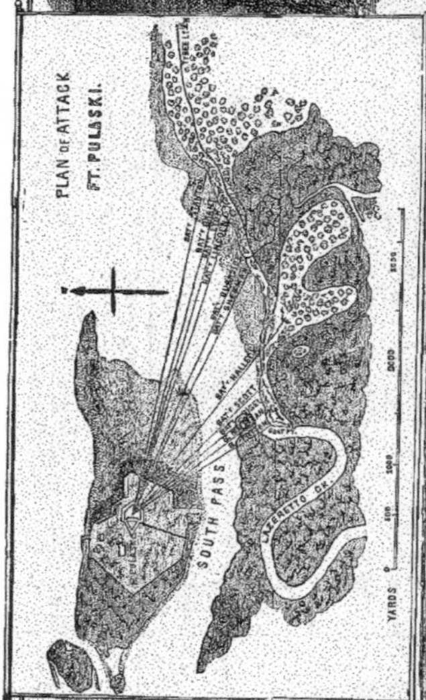

MORTAR BATTERIES ON

ATTACK UPON FORT PULASKI.

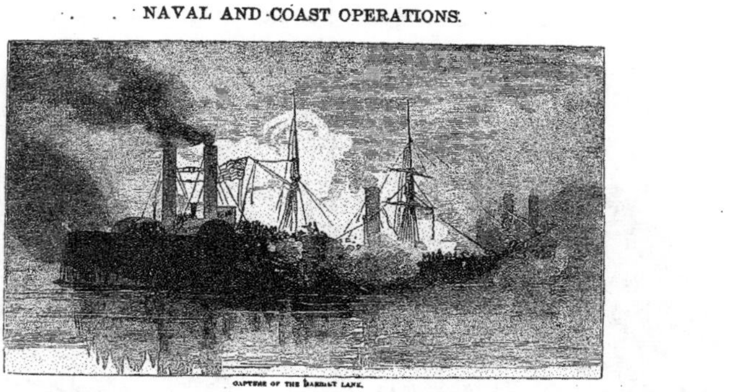

CAPTURE OF THE HARRIET LANE.

CHAPTER XXV.

NAVAL AND COAST OPERATIONS.

The Blockade.—Capture of Fort Pulaski.—Capture of Galveston.—It is retaken by the Confederates.—Loss of the Harriet Lane and Westfield.—The Confederate Cruisers.—The Florida fitted out in England.—Runs the Blockade at Mobile.—Equipped and Escapes to Sea.—The Clarence, Tacony, and Archer.—Capture and Destruction of the Florida.—The Alabama built in England.—Escapes from Liverpool.—Takes on board Armament and Crew.—Semmes assumes Command.—His previous Career.—The Cruise of the Alabama in the North Atlantic.—Cruise in the Gulf of Mexico.—Captures the Ariel.—Destroys the Hatteras.—Cruise in the South Atlantic.—At the Cape of Good Hope.—Cruise in the Indian Ocean.—Returns to Europe.—Enters the Harbor of Cherbourg.—Destroyed by the Kearsarge.—The Results of her Depredations.—Operations in North Carolina.—Burnside recalled to the Potomac.—Foster's Expedition to Tarboro and Goldsboro.

WE have already narrated the brilliant naval exploit which insured the capture of New Orleans. The farther operations of the fleet upon the Mississippi and its tributaries will be described in their appropriate place, in connection with the military operations in the West. Vessels find their natural opponents in vessels, the cases in which they can be employed in the attack upon forts and towns being exceptional. The Confederacy being wholly destitute of a force upon the ocean, and its chief sea-ports being unassailable by a fleet, the operations of the Union fleet were mainly confined to a strict blockade of the coast, and to short expeditions up the rivers. These offensive operations were of necessity on a small scale, and though not unfrequently marked by great skill and boldness, had but little influence upon the general result of the campaign of 1862. One by one, however, the minor ports along the Atlantic and Gulf of Mexico were seized, leaving to the Confederates only Wilmington, Charleston, Savannah, and Mobile, which had been rendered unassailable by a direct naval attack. These ports came to be of great importance to the Confederates, and were not captured until their armies in the field had given up, or were about to give up, the contest.

The most important of these expeditions was that which resulted in the capture of Fort Pulaski, situated on a mud island at the mouth of the Savannah River, and commanding the approach to the city of Savannah. After a series of laborious approaches, conducted at first by General T. W. Sherman, and afterward by Hunter, who succeeded him in the command of this department, Gilmore succeeded in placing batteries bearing upon the fort, but at a distance greater than a serious bombardment of a fortification had ever been attempted. There were in all eleven batteries, mounting thirty-six mortars and heavy guns, the nearest battery being 1620 yards, almost a mile, from the fort. The batteries being placed, the surrender of Pulaski was demanded on the 10th of April. Olmstead, the Confederate commander, replied that he had been placed there to defend the fort, not to surrender it. Fire was then opened, and after a bombardment of eighteen hours the walls were thoroughly breached; and the fort, having been rendered untenable, was surrendered, with forty-seven guns, a large amount of ammunition and stores, and nearly four hundred prisoners. But Hunter had not sufficient force to warrant him in making any attempt upon the immediate defenses of the town. Savannah, therefore, remained in the possession of the Confederates until captured in December, 1864, by W. T. Sherman. But the possession of Fort Pulaski by the Federals barred all direct access to Savannah by sea, and the city became of no use to the Confederates as a port by which supplies from abroad could reach them.

Galveston, in Texas, was also a port of considerable importance to the Confederates, being the main entrepôt for the commerce of a great part of the state. In May a naval force appeared at the town and demanded its surrender, but for months no effective measures were taken to enforce the demand. At last, on the 8th of October, the town surrendered, with slight attempts at resistance, to a naval force of four steam vessels under Commodore Renshaw. Banks, who had succeeded Butler in command of this department, ordered a regiment to hold Galveston; a third of it was sent, the remainder being on its way, when the Confederate General Magruder, who had just been appointed to the chief command in Texas, formed a bold plan for the recapture of Galveston, which seems to have been most negligently guarded.

The plan was carried into effect before dawn on New Year's day, 1863. Galveston stood upon a long, narrow island in the bay, connected with the main land by a bridge two miles long, built upon piles. This bridge was not destroyed, and formed a ready means of approach. The town was occupied by less than three hundred men, without artillery, the naval force being supposed to be sufficient to hold it. This consisted of eight vessels, of which only two, the Westfield and the Harriet Lane, were in serviceable condition. The former, of 1000 tons, had been one of Porter's mortar fleet in the Mississippi; the latter, of 500 tons, had been built for the revenue service, of which it was the show vessel. The three infantry companies, numbering less than three hundred men, were encamped upon a wharf, a quarter of a mile from the market-place. The Westfield and the Harriet Lane were stationed in different channels down the bay, the other vessels being opposite the town. Magruder had collected a land force of five or six regiments, and several vessels. Two of these, the Neptune and the Bayou City, were protected by cotton bales piled twenty feet high upon the low decks, so that from a distance they looked like common cotton transports: they were manned by two or three hundred sharp-shooters. Coming down the bay, they were perceived in the moonlight from the Harriet Lane, which steamed up to meet them. Meanwhile the land force of Magruder had swarmed across the long bridge, and in overwhelming numbers assailed the three Federal companies on the wharf; aided by the fire from the weak vessels, these held their ground for a while. As day was dawning, the Harriet Lane, steaming up the bay, encountered the Neptune and the Bayou City, the Confederate steamers striking the Federal vessel almost simultaneously on each side. The Neptune was disabled by the shock, and grounded in shoal water; the Bayou City, turning, ran again into the Harriet Lane and grappled with her. A sharp fire was then poured from both vessels into the Harriet Lane from riflemen thoroughly protected by the barricades of cotton bales; the men were driven from their guns, and the Lane was carried by boarding, her commander, Wainwright, being killed in the mêlée. This fine vessel fell into the hands of the Confederates almost uninjured, all her crew being made prisoners.

Meanwhile the Westfield had got under way, and was steaming up to the scene of conflict, when she grounded fast upon the bar, within full range of

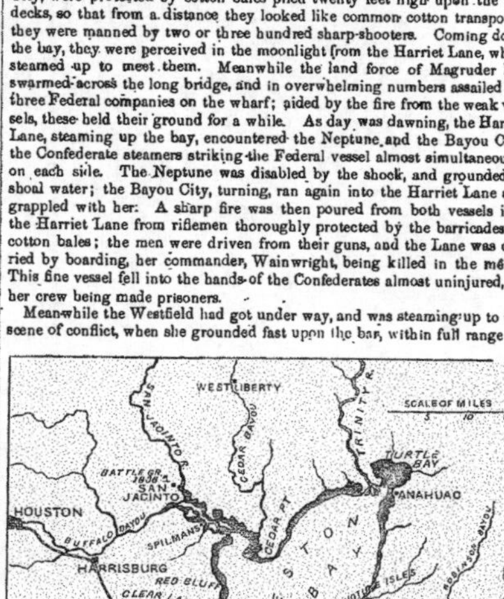

CHART OF GALVESTON BAY.

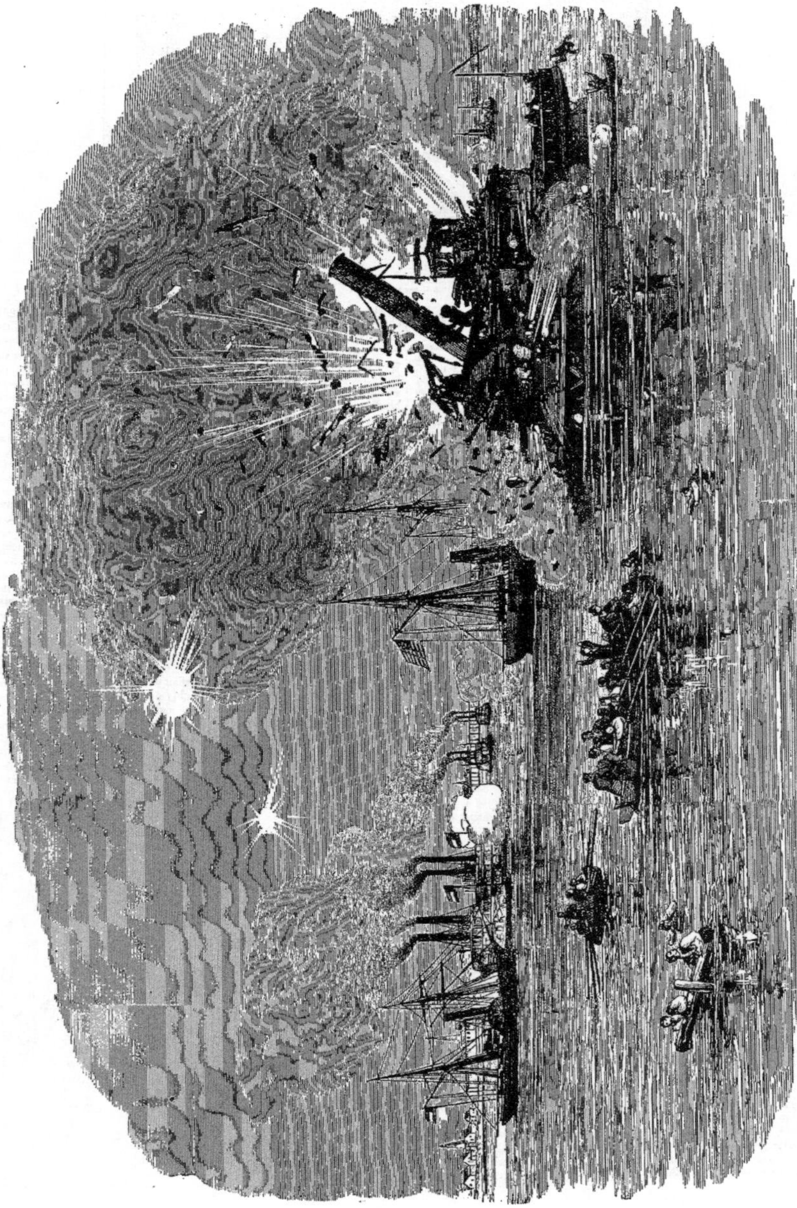

DESTRUCTION OF THE WESTFIELD.

batteries which the Confederates had established upon the shore. The other Federal gun-boats vainly endeavored to drag her off. Renshaw, perceiving that it was impossible to save his ship, resolved to destroy her, the crew to escape in boats to the transports lying hard by. A barrel of turpentine was unheaded, ready to be set ablaze as soon as the crew were free from the vessel. Nearly all had been taken to the other steamers near by, and Renshaw, who was the last to leave, was just stepping into his boat, in which were several persons, while another, loaded to the water's edge, was putting off. By some accident the turpentine was prematurely fired; the flames spread instantly to the forward magazine, and the vessel blew up, destroying the two boats and all on board.

Meanwhile an action had been going on upon the shore. The three companies of infantry, aided by the fire of the gun-boats, repelled the attack of the Confederate regiments. But the boats were at length withdrawn to attempt to aid the Westfield. The infantry, wholly destitute of artillery, and now commanded by Confederate batteries, had no alternative but to surrender at discretion.

The immediate results of this daring enterprise were that, with the loss of 26 killed and 117 wounded, the Confederates captured the Harriet Lane, wholly uninjured, two coal-barges which were lying at the wharf, destroyed the Westfield, and secured nearly 400 prisoners. But the indirect results were still more important. The whole State of Texas came into their almost undisturbed possession, and furnished many facilities for running the blockade. This was done principally by small schooners, which took out cotton and brought back munitions of war. The supplies thus acquired were of incalculable advantage to the Confederate government during the remainder of the war.

The successful career of the Sumter had demonstrated to the Confederate government the injury which might be inflicted upon the commerce of the Union by even a few vessels of a more efficient class. The resignation of more than two hundred officers of the Federal navy gave the Confederates an abundance of skillful officers; but, having no facilities at home for constructing vessels adapted for service upon the ocean, they were obliged to have recourse to foreign builders. The ship-yards of Great Britain were open to them. The first efficient cruiser which sailed under their flag was built at Birkenhead, near Liverpool, ostensibly for the Italian government.[1] In spite of the remonstrance of the American minister, she was suffered by the British government to put to sea under the British flag, bearing the name of the Oreto. After a brief detention at Nassau she was released, and, proceeding to a little island in the Bahama group, received on board her armament, which had been brought to the place of rendezvous in a British vessel, and in August, 1862, appeared off the harbor of Mobile, still carrying British colors. Commodore Preble, who commanded the blockading fleet, hesitated to fire upon her, supposing that she must be what she professed, a British man-of-war. When he discovered his mistake, it was too late; she had got beyond effective range, and steamed up the bay to Mobile. Here she remained until January, 1863, and then, her name having been changed to the Florida, she was placed under the command of John N. Maffitt, once an officer in the American navy; she escaped the blockading fleet under cover of night. The first day of her cruise she made her first prize, which was pillaged and burned. In three months the Florida captured fifteen merchantmen in the Gulf of Mexico, all of which were burned except two, which were armed, manned, and converted into Confederate privateers.

One of these, the brig Clarence, was placed under the command of Lieutenant C. W. Read, not long before a midshipman in the Federal navy, who steered northward, and made several prizes, among which was the bark Tacony, a swifter vessel than his own. Transferring his armament and crew to this, he passed up the coast as far as Massachusetts Bay, making a score of prizes. Learning that cruisers were on his track, he again shifted his guns and crew into his last prize, the Archer, burned the Tacony, and steered for Portland, Maine, where he learned that the steam revenue cutter Cushing was lying. Anchoring openly and unsuspected at the mouth of the harbor, when night fell on the 24th of June he sent two boats, fully armed, up to the city. They succeeded in capturing the Cushing and taking her out to sea. But two merchant steamers were hastily manned by volunteers, and overtook the Cushing. The captors abandoned the cutter, blew her up, and took to their boats and made for the Archer. But the pursuing steamers were too quick; they picked up the boats, overhauled the Archer, and brought her crew back to Portland as prisoners.

Meanwhile the Florida, after cruising among the West India Islands until August, steamed across the Atlantic, and on the 4th of September entered the French harbor of Brest, where she was detained a few days by the French authorities. Released from detention, she recrossed the Atlantic, cruising along the South American coast for months, but making few prizes, for the American flag had by this time been almost driven from the ocean. At length, in October, 1864, the Florida entered the Brazilian harbor of Bahia. Here she was found by the Federal steamer Wachusett, Captain Collins. Relying upon the safeguard of a neutral harbor, Morris, who now commanded the Florida, was quite at ease. Half his crew were allowed to go on shore. Collins determined to cut matters short by seizing the Florida; this was done with scarcely a show of resistance, and the Wachusett, with the prize, steamed homeward; but, coming into Hampton Roads, the Florida was run into by a United States vessel, probably designedly, and sunk. This capture was certainly made in violation of the neutral rights of Brazil. The Brazilian government put in a formal remonstrance; the

BAHIA, BRAZIL.

justice of this was conceded so far as the special act was concerned. The American government disavowed the capture, suspended Collins from command, and ordered the prisoners to be released; but at the same time took care to enter a counter complaint against the Brazilians for harboring Confederate "piratical ships." The Brazilian government protested, apparently, as a mere matter of form, and was satisfied with the course of our government; and the overthrow of the Confederate cause, which took place while negotiations were pending, removed all occasion for pressing farther the complaint against Brazil.

Of still greater importance to the Confederate cause was the Alabama, whose active career as a cruiser began some months earlier than that of the Florida. Among the great English shipbuilders was John Laird, a member of the British House of Commons. The war had just fairly commenced when he contracted with the Confederate government to build for it a steamer which should combine all the qualities of a formidable cruiser. She was to have sufficient strength, and be provided with an armament which would render her adequate to cope with any of the largest vessels in the American navy, while her speed should enable her to escape any superior enemy which she would be likely to encounter.

While this steamer, then known simply as the "290," lay upon the stocks, her destination was notorious; but the British officials would not, and the American minister could not, furnish evidence which the government judged sufficient to warrant its interference. At length, after she was launched and ready for sea, evidence was procured which eminent British counsel pronounced sufficient to require her detention.[1] For a week no action was taken by the British government. The Queen's Advocate had been seized with sudden illness, and could not attend to business, and other counsel had to be consulted. Their opinion was in favor of detention, and orders to that effect were sent by mail to Liverpool;[2] but the Confederate agents in London learned of this, and notified their friends in Liverpool by telegraph. No time was to be lost in forestalling the arrival of the order, and on the morning of the 29th of July the "290" dropped slowly down the Mersey, under pretense of a simple trial trip.[3] "To give color to this pretense, to which her even then unfinished condition lent a *primâ facie* sanction, a gay party was assembled on board." There were women, friends and acquaintances of the builder, and their accompanying gallants. Luncheon and all the appliances of naval hospitality were provided. But in the midst of the feasting, at a signal from the "290," a small steam-tug came alongside, and the astonished guests were requested to step on board. All that evening and the next day the bustle of preparation went on, and, two hours before dawn, the "290" started on her seaward voyage, bound for Nassau, in the Bahamas, as her crew supposed, but really for another port. She was away just in time, for the gold-laced custom-house officials were then coming down the river with the tardy order for her detention, and, moreover, the American steam frigate Tuscarora was hurrying—only two days too late—to the mouth of the Mersey to intercept the Confederate cruiser, as yet wholly unarmed.

The real destination of the "290" was the harbor of Porto Praya, in the Portuguese island of Terceira, where she was to meet another British vessel laden with the armament which was to form her equipment as a vessel of war. She had sailed under the command of Captain Bullock, who had superintended her construction; but when the farthermost British land was passed Bullock went ashore, and his place was taken by an Englishman,

---

[1] "Our collector at Liverpool states that he has every reason to believe that the vessel is for the Italian government."—Earl Russell to Mr. Adams, Feb. 22, 1862.

[1] "*Temple, July* 23, 1862.—I am of opinion that the Collector of Customs would be justified in detaining the vessel. Indeed, I should think it his duty to detain her; and that if, after the application which has been made to him, supported by the evidence which has been laid before me, he allows the vessel to leave Liverpool, he will incur a heavy responsibility—a responsibility in which the Board of Customs, under whose directions he appears to be acting, must take their share. It appears to be difficult to make out a stronger case of infringement of the Foreign Enlistment Act, which, if not enforced on this occasion, is little better than a dead letter. It well deserves consideration whether, if the vessel be allowed to escape, the Federal government would not have serious grounds of complaint."—R. P. COLLIER, Q. C.

[2] Diplomatic Correspondence, 1862–3, i., 168.

[3] "The Cruise of the Alabama, and the Sumter." This work is made up mainly from the journals of Semmes, and was evidently drawn up under his supervision. This has been followed almost exclusively in the following account, all quotations, unless otherwise expressly credited, being taken from it, although it has not been thought necessary, in all cases, to cite the pages. The work will be cited simply as "*Semmes.*"

RAPHAEL SEMMES.

"Captain J. Butcher, late of the Cunard service. Of the other temporary officers, three out of five were Englishmen." The crew numbered about seventy men and boys, and were shipped for a feigned voyage, the Confederate captain "trusting to the English love of adventure to induce them to re-ship when the true destination of the vessel came to be declared."[1] In nine days the "290" reached Porto Praya. Soon after arrived a British vessel, the Agrippina, with coal, ammunition, and guns, and, not long after, still another British vessel from Liverpool, having on board "a number of seamen, shipped, like those on board the "290," for a feigned voyage, in the hope of inducing them to join when the ship was fairly in commission."[2] In this vessel also came Raphael Semmes, who had been appointed to command the "290" when, under a new name, she was to appear upon the ocean as a Confederate cruiser.

Semmes, now about fifty years of age, was a native of the State of Maryland. He had entered the American navy thirty years before. At the outbreak of the war he had attained the rank of commander in the navy, was a member of the Light-house Board, and resided at Washington. He wrote to Stephens, of Georgia, indicating his willingness to fight for the South, but did not wish to thrust himself upon the new government "until his State had moved." On the 14th of February, 1861, he received a telegraphic dispatch from the Chairman of the Naval Committee at Montgomery inviting him to repair to that place. Then, and not before, he sent in his resignation

modern sailor," says Semmes, "has greatly changed in character. He now strikes for pay like a sharper." Semmes was glad to hire them upon their own terms. "I was afraid," he says, "that a large bounty in addition would be demanded of me."[1]

On the 29th of August the Alabama was fairly in trim to begin her cruise. The battle of Groveton was at that hour being fought, and the result hung in even scales. The Alabama had now assumed her true character. She was a wooden screw steam sloop, bark-rigged, of 1040 tons burden, provided with two engines of great power, pierced for twelve guns on deck, with two heavy guns amidships; her whole cost for building and equipment was a quarter of a million of dollars.[2] To man her fully required at least one hundred men; Semmes had only eighty, but he trusted that he could fill up the complement by volunteers from the prizes which he should make.[3]

The Alabama now steered straight for the great highway of commerce between Europe and America. This was reached in a week, and on the 5th of September she made her first capture. On that day the Confederate army crossed the Potomac into Maryland. "This vessel," notes Semmes in his journal, "was of course taken possession of, her crew brought on board the Alabama and placed in irons; and a quantity of rigging and small-stores transferred to the captor. Next morning the prize was fired, the Alabama having taken from her thirty-six prisoners."[4] The Alabama was now in the track of commerce, and within the next ten days captured half a score of vessels. The journal of Semmes describes the disposition made of some of them:

September 7. Captured the Starlight, from Fayal to Boston, with a number of passengers, among others some ladies. "Brought on board all the United States seamen, seven in number, including the captain, and confined them in irons." *September* 9. Several additional prizes having been made, "about 9 A.M. fired the Starlight; at 11, fired the Ocean Rover; and at 4 P.M. fired the Alert." *September* 14. "Captured a whaler, the Benjamin Tucker, from New Bedford, eight months out, with about 340 barrels of oil; crew thirty. Brought every body on board, received some soap and tobacco, and fired the ship." *September* 16. Captured another whaler; stood off to Flores; when within four or five miles, sent all the prisoners, sixty-eight in number, ashore in boats, and then, "having taken the prize some eight or ten miles distant from land, hove her to, called all hands to quarters, and made a target of her. The practice was pretty fair for green hands. At dark fired the prize." After this burst of good fortune there was a lull of a fortnight. The Alabama was crowded with prisoners taken within the last few days. "These," says Semmes, "were hard times for the prisoners, crowded together on deck, with no shelter but an extemporized tarpaulin tent between them and the pelting of the pitiless storm, which drenched the decks alternately with salt water and fresh."[5]

October passed, and at its close the Alabama, having in the mean time made twenty-seven captures, was off the American coast, hardly two hundred miles from New York. Semmes had hoped to lie off the harbor, and make some prizes at its very mouth; but his fuel was now running short, and he was obliged to run southeastward to the island where coal was to await him. On the 18th of November the Alabama made the French island of Martinique. Here she fell into sore peril, for the American steamer San Jacinto, of superior force, appeared off the harbor, and instituted a close blockade. But the Alabama managed to elude her antagonist under cover of darkness, and gained the coal rendezvous at the island of Blanquilla.

In the latter days of November the Alabama had got on board coal sufficient for nearly three weeks' steaming, and was ready for a fresh cruise. She made for the West India Islands, hoping to be able to intercept one of the treasure-ships conveying gold from the Isthmus to New York. A million of dollars in gold was a prize worth waiting for. On Sunday, December 7, a prize came within sight, though not the one which had been hoped for. A huge side-wheel steamer hove in view, pressing southward. It

HOMER C. BLAKE.

plague-stricken port, he had no alternative but to release the Ariel upon bond, and "forego the pleasure of making a bonfire of the splendid steamer that had fallen into his hands."

The Alabama was still cruising among the West India Islands, when intelligence came that Banks was about to dispatch a great naval and military expedition from New Orleans to the coast of Texas, Galveston being its immediate destination. Semmes was aware that this expedition "would be accompanied by one or more armed vessels, but the principal portion would be composed of troop-ships crowded with the enemy's soldiers; and should the Alabama but prove victorious in the fight, these transports would be of more practical importance than all the grain and oil ever carried in a merchantman's hold."[1] At noon on the 11th of January the Alabama was off Galveston, ignorant that the place had been recaptured by the Confederates, and the proposed Banks expedition delayed. Several vessels were seen lying off the bar. One of these, the gun-boat Hatteras, catching a glimpse of the Alabama on the distant horizon, stood out to reconnoitre. The Alabama edged slowly seaward, in order to draw this vessel away from her consorts, so that in case of a conflict the noise of the guns would not reach them. The rate at which the Hatteras had approached showed that she was in speed no match for the Alabama, which could thus escape if she perceived that she was overmatched in strength. Just after dark the Hatteras came within hailing distance, and from her deck came the inquiry, "What ship is that?" "Her majesty's ship Petrel. What ship is that?" was the reply from the Alabama. "I will send a boat aboard," was answered by Lieutenant Blake, the commander of the Hatteras, who gave orders accordingly, and the boat was lowered and put off. Up to this moment the commander of the Hatteras must have supposed that the Alabama was what she proclaimed herself, a British vessel, for he would have scarcely sent a boat on board what he believed to be an armed enemy. Hardly had the boat left the side of the Hatteras when a new hail, "We are the Confederate steamer Alabama," was heard, accompanied by the whizzing of a shell over the deck, followed by a full broadside. The Hatteras returned the fire, and endeavored to close, hoping to carry the enemy by boarding. But the greater speed of the Alabama enabled her to thwart the attempt, while her superior armament placed her opponent at her mercy. The only chance for the Hatteras was that a shot might strike some vulnerable point of the Alabama. In a few minutes a shell from the Alabama entered the hold of the Hatteras amidships; almost at the same instant another passed through the sick-bay, and exploded, both setting the vessel on fire, while another destroyed the steam cylinder, disabling the engine, and rendering the Hatteras wholly unmanageable. On fire in two places, utterly disabled, a mere wreck upon the water, there was nothing for Blake to do but to fire a lee gun in token of surrender, and to ask for assistance for his crew. The action had lasted only thirteen minutes, and the Hatteras was rapidly sinking. The boats from both vessels were employed in conveying the crew of the vanquished to the deck of the victor. Two minutes after the last man had left the Hatteras she went down, bow first, with her pennant at the masthead, carrying with her every thing but the living men. The Alabama suffered some injury, but not sufficient to cripple her, and had two men slightly wounded. On the Hatteras two were killed and five wounded; the boat's crew which had put off just before the action rowed back to the shore, only twenty miles distant; all the others, more than a hundred, were made prisoners, and carried to Kingston, where they were put ashore.

For two months the Alabama cruised among the West India Islands, and then, about the middle of March,[2] went southward along the coast, reaching Bahia, in Brazil, by the middle of May, making many prizes all the while. Here she found the Georgia, another Anglo-Confederate cruiser; took in coal, and, after being repeatedly warned by the Brazilian authorities that her stay was not desired, steamed away across the South Atlantic for the coast of Africa, making port near Cape Town on the 5th of August. She hovered in these waters for more than a month. Coming into the harbor of Simon's Town on the 16th of December, she found evil tidings: Vicksburg and Port Hudson had fallen; Lee, foiled at Gettysburg, had recrossed the Potomac into Virginia. "Our poor people," he writes, "seem to be terribly pressed by the Northern hordes; but we shall fight it out to the end, and the end will be what an all-wise Providence decrees." But, what was still worse for the Alabama, the Union steamer Vanderbilt, of superior force, which had been sent to look for the Alabama, was in the neighborhood. She had left the very harbor where the Alabama was, only five days before, and might return at any moment. The Confederate cruiser must go to another cruising ground. The Malay Archipelago was chosen, and, after a fortnight's run through heavy gales, the voyage of 3000 miles was accomplished early in November. But the American war-steamer Wyoming was in these waters, and the Alabama must be wary in encountering an adversary of superior force. The cruise among the intricate channels of the Indian Archipelago lasted three months. Few prizes were taken, for the American flag had almost disappeared from these waters. On the 18th of January[3] the Alabama set her head homeward, toward Great Britain, by way of the Cape of Good Hope. The Cape was reached, after a rough voyage, on the 11th of March. Here Semmes got into a controversy with the governor for a breach of neutrality in bringing a prize into that port. The case was decided against him, and, entering a protest against the "unfriendly disposition of a government from which, if it represents truly the instincts of Englishmen, the Confederates had a right to expect at least sympathy and kindness in the place of rigor and harshness,"[1] he turned the head of the Alabama toward Europe on the 25th of March. For a month not a single vessel was encountered. On the 22d of April "the guano-laden ship Rockingham was boarded, taken possession of, employed as a target, and then set fire to." Five days after, the Tycoon shared the same fate. This was the last prize taken by the Alabama. Nineteen other vessels were overhauled before the cruiser, a fortnight after, entered the French harbor of Cherbourg, but not one of them sailed under the American flag.

[1] Semmes, ii., 42. [2] 1863. [3] 1864.

The Alabama entered Cherbourg on the 11th of June,[2] and began to make some repairs, of which she stood in need after her long cruise. Three days after, the American steam-sloop Kearsarge, Captain Winslow, which had been cruising in the British Channel, looking out for several vessels apparently designed for the Confederate service, appeared off Cherbourg. The vessels were as nearly as possible equal in size and armament. Semmes, who wished to signalize himself by some exploit other than the burning of helpless merchantmen, requested Winslow to remain off the port for a day or two, when he would come out beyond neutral waters and give battle. Winslow, nowise loth to fight, complied with the request, and lay off the port. On the 19th the Alabama came out, escorted to the limit of the neutral waters by the French iron-clad Couronne. Following close after, fortunately as it happened for the Confederates, was an English steam yacht, the Deerhound, whose owner, Lancaster, wished to treat his family to the sight of a naval duel. When the neutral marine league was fairly passed, the Couronne turned back, leaving the expectant combatants to themselves. The Kearsarge edged slowly off as the Alabama advanced, wishing to make sure that the action should take place so far off shore that there should be no question about the line of national jurisdiction. The distance of seven miles from land having been gained, the Kearsarge turned, and steered straight for the enemy. The Alabama opened fire at the distance of a mile, repeating her broadsides three times. The shot passed harmlessly through the rigging of the Kearsarge, which kept head on toward the Alabama. At nine hundred yards the Kearsarge sheered round and delivered her broadside. This broadside told fearfully. Then, fearing that the Alabama would make for the shore, and take shelter in French waters, Winslow put his vessel to full speed, designing to run under the stern of the Alabama and deliver a raking fire. To counteract this, the Alabama also sheered, presenting her broadside instead of her stern. Both vessels being under full steam, the Alabama, in order to keep her broadside toward her enemy, and at the same time to avoid coming into close action, was forced to describe a series of circles around the Kearsarge, whose object was to come into close action. The Kearsarge, whose object was to gain a raking position, followed the course of the Alabama, and the combined result was that the two vessels

[1] Semmes, ii., 436. [2] 1864.

JOHN A. WINSLOW.

DESTRUCTION OF THE ALABAMA.

described a series of circles around each other; but the Kearsarge, having a slight advantage in speed, was able to diminish the orbit. The action lasted an hour. From the first the superiority of the aim of the Kearsarge had been apparent. At the seventh revolution around the shifting common axis, the Alabama perceived that victory was hopeless, and she headed for the shore, five miles distant. If she could accomplish but two of these, she would be within French waters.[1] But the attempt at retreat came too late. The Alabama was disabled, and the Kearsarge, steaming ahead, took a raking position across her bows. The white flag of surrender was raised; a boat from the Alabama came alongside, bearing an officer, who said that the Alabama had surrendered, and was fast sinking. The boats of the Kearsarge were lowered to save the drowning enemy. The British Deerhound also approached, and was requested by Winslow to aid in the rescue of those who had now become his prisoners. The Alabama was going down; the officers and crew took to the water. Forty of them, among whom was the captain, were picked up by the Deerhound and carried to England; a dozen were saved by French pilot-boats and taken to Cherbourg; seventy

[1] It has been asserted that both commanders wished to fight the action at short range. The compiler of the Confederate account says (*Semmes*, ii., 290): "Captain Semmes had great confidence in the power of his Blakeley [7-inch] rifled gun. He wished to get within easy range of his enemy, that he might try this weapon effectively; but any attempt on his part to come to closer quarters was construed by the Kearsarge as a design to bring the engagement between the ships to a hand-to-hand conflict between the men. Having the speed, she chose her distance, and made all thoughts of boarding hopeless. It was part of the plan of Captain Semmes to board, if possible, at some period of the day, supposing that he could not quickly decide the question with artillery. It was evidently Captain Winslow's determination to avoid the old-fashioned form of a naval encounter, and to fight altogether in the new style; his superior steam power gave him the option."—Captain Winslow, on the other hand, says: "It was soon apparent that Captain Semmes did not seek close action. I became then fearful lest, after some fighting, that he would again make for the shore. To defeat this, I determined to keep full speed on, and with a port helm to run under the stern of the Alabama, and rake, if he did not prevent it by sheering and keeping his broadside to us. We adopted this mode as a preventive, and, as a consequence, the Alabama was forced, with a full head of steam, into a circular track during the engagement. The effect of this manœuvre was such that, at the last of the action, when the Alabama would have made off, she was near five miles from the shore; and had the action continued from the first in parallel lines, with her head in-shore, the line of jurisdiction would no doubt have been reached. . . . . I had endeavored to close in with the Alabama, but it was not until just before the close of the action that we were in a position to use grape; this was avoided, however, by her surrender. . . . . Nearly every shot told fearfully on the Alabama, and on the seventh rotation on the circular track she winded, setting fore-trysail and two jibs, with head in-shore."—Nothing can be more clear than that neither commander expected to decide the fight by the "old-fashioned form" of boarding. Such was the character of each vessel, and the armament of the other, that long before they could have come side by side, one or both must have been disabled. Each knew the armament of the other, and each considered his own to be superior.

A NIGHT ENCAMPMENT.

were rescued by the Kearsarge. Of the crew of the Alabama seven were killed in the fight; nineteen, most of whom were wounded, went down with the vessel. On board the Kearsarge there were three wounded, one mortally.

The life of the Alabama had been two years lacking nine weeks, counting from Sunday, August 24, 1862, when she first hoisted the Confederate flag, down to Sunday, June 19, 1864, when she was sunk, leaving not a wrack behind. No one ship that ever floated ever inflicted such injury upon an enemy. In all, she had captured sixty-five vessels, burning all except the few required to save the lives of her prisoners. She had destroyed vessels and cargoes valued at ten millions of dollars, and, what was of more injury to the enemy, had well-nigh driven the American commercial flag from the ocean. She was to all intents a British vessel, built at a British dock, manned by a British crew, and sailing almost always under the British flag. Her keel was never wet in Confederate waters, and no man from her deck ever caught a glimpse of the shores claimed by the Confederates; and she rarely hoisted the Confederate flag, except when, having decoyed a prize by the show of false colors, she raised her own in the act of making a prize. Her long impunity from capture is not a matter for wonder. The whole wide ocean was her hiding-place. A hundred vessels might be in search of her, and it would be a matter of chance if one would encounter her. If heard from to-day at any point, to-morrow she would be hundreds of miles away, in what direction no man not on board of her could know. "Her stay in any neutral harbor was necessarily as short as the perching of a hawk on a bough. Like the hawk's in upper air, the Alabama's safety, as well as her business, was on the high seas."[1] At the very last, it was a mere matter of accident that the Kearsarge was at hand when the Alabama appeared at Cherbourg. No one supposed that she was then on this side of the globe. The last that had been heard of her she was in the Indian Ocean. Even at Cherbourg she might have declined to enter into combat with the Kearsarge. Safe while she remained in the neutral harbor, she might have waited her time, as she had done at Martinique, when watched by the San Jacinto, and again, fitted for sea, have crept out into the wide ocean. But Semmes wished to signalize himself by something more than the capture of defenseless merchantmen, and knowing that the ships were "equally matched,"[1] he challenged the Kearsarge to the contest. It was supposed that Semmes would soon be again at sea in command of a still more powerful vessel than the one which he had lost. This was iron-clad, and was almost completed by the builders of the Alabama; but the British government had now perceived the danger into which they were rushing by their interpretation of the neutrality laws, and took possession of the ship. Semmes, after a while, made his way to the Confederacy, and received the nominal rank of brigadier general in the army, and as such was, a year after, included in the surrender of Johnson's army.

The brilliant success which attended the early operations of Burnside at the commencement of the year has been already recorded.[2] The successive captures of Roanoke Island, Newbern, Elizabeth City, Fort Macon, and Beaufort, gave the Union forces command of the greater part of the coast of North Carolina, and of the Sound by which it is bordered. Wilmington, and the intricate approaches which lead to it, remained to the Confederates, and afforded facilities for running the blockade. It was supposed that these successes would be followed up by a march into the heart of the state, which would seize the lines of railroad connecting the far South with Richmond. But Burnside's force of 15,000 was insufficient for such an enterprise, and the exigencies of the campaign in Virginia left the Federal government no troops by which he could be re-enforced. The most that Burnside could do was to hold the points on and near the coasts which he had seized. When McClellan retreated from the Chickahominy to the James, Burnside was ordered to bring to Fortress Monroe all the troops which he could collect,[3] leaving Foster with just enough to garrison Newborn, Beaufort, and a few other points. The Confederates also brought all their available force from North Carolina to Virginia; so that, during the summer and early autumn, there was little fighting in North Carolina.

When Lee's invasion of Maryland had failed, and the Union and Confederate armies lay confronting each other on the Rappahannock, considerable re-enforcements were dispatched to Foster in North Carolina, so that he was able to assume the offensive. Early in November he pushed an expedition inland toward Tarboro, where he had learned that there were a few regiments of the enemy; but, finding that they had been largely re-enforced, he retreated. In December he planned a still more important enterprise, the main object being to reach Goldsboro, and destroy the railroads centering at that point. The Confederates meanwhile had strengthened their force in the Department of North Carolina. In November they had but 9000 men, of whom 6000 were reported as present for duty. By December these numbers were fully doubled, and Gustavus W. Smith was placed in command. After the wounding of Johnston at Fair Oaks, Smith had been placed in command of the army before Richmond. He had held it hardly for a day when he was struck down by an attack of paralysis, and Lee was appointed in his place. Foster left Newbern with his entire movable force,[4] about 10,000 strong, and encountered no serious opposition until he reached Kingston, half way between Newbern and Goldsboro. Here a sharp fight occurred,[5] the Confederates retreating. Foster pressed on toward Goldsboro,

[1] *Semmes*, ii., 280.

[1] *Ibid.*, ii., 278. [2] *Ante*, pp. 242–249. [3] July 4, 1862. [4] Dec. 11. [5] Dec. 14.

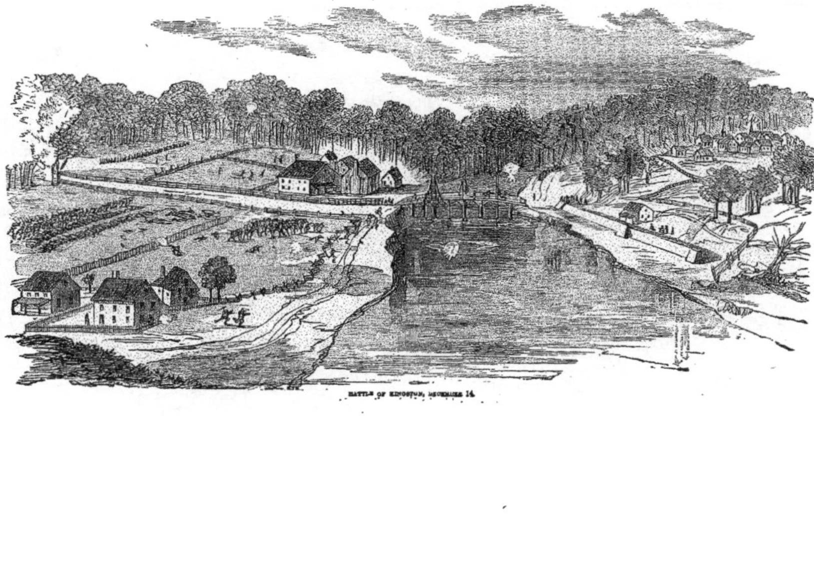

BATTLE OF KINGSTON, DECEMBER 14.

ACTION AT WHITEHALL, DECEMBER 16.

hoping to strike the railroad. On the 16th he reached Whitehall, where a brisk skirmish ensued; the Confederates were driven back, and two gun-boats which were there building were destroyed. Foster then pushed on toward Goldsboro, following the course of the Neuse, and sending detachments in various directions to destroy the railroad bridges. On the 17th another skirmish took place at a point near Goldsboro. In the mean while the Confederates had gradually concentrated a superior force at Goldsboro, and Foster found it unwise to attempt to reach this place, the point at which he had aimed. He therefore commenced a rapid retreat to Newbern, where his force arrived on the 24th, having been absent ten days, during which time it had marched nearly two hundred miles. Foster lost 90 killed and 478 wounded; the Confederates lost 71 killed, 268 wounded, besides 476 prisoners, most of whom were captured at Kingston, and immediately paroled. The expedition really accomplished nothing. The slight injury done to the railroad was soon repaired, and the communication between Richmond and the far South was hardly interrupted. With this attempt closed the active operations for 1862 in North Carolina. But in February of the ensuing year the Federal force was considerably strengthened, and Lee, perceiving that military operations on the Rappahannock would be suspended until spring, ventured to detach Longstreet, with a considerable part of his corps, from the army in Virginia, and send him to North Carolina. In March the Confederate force in this department nominally numbered 73,000 men, of whom 53,000 were reported as "present," and 45,000 "present for duty."

During the year various movements looking toward a siege of Charleston were attempted. The most important of these was an attempt on the 16th of June to take possession of James Island. The Federals were repulsed, with a loss of 700. But the siege of Charleston forms an episode so complete in itself as to require a separate chapter.

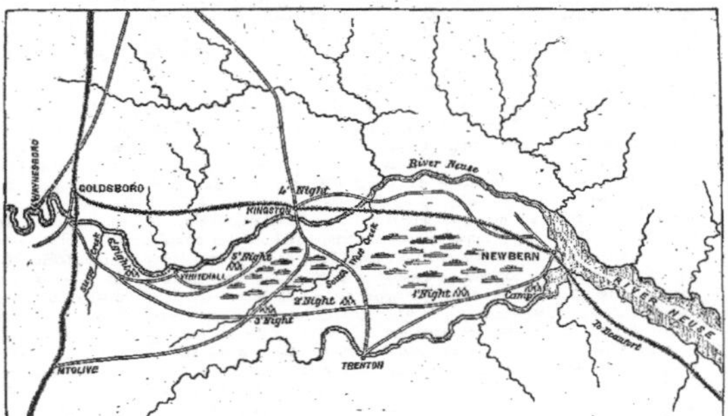

ROUTE FROM NEWBERN TO GOLDSBORO.

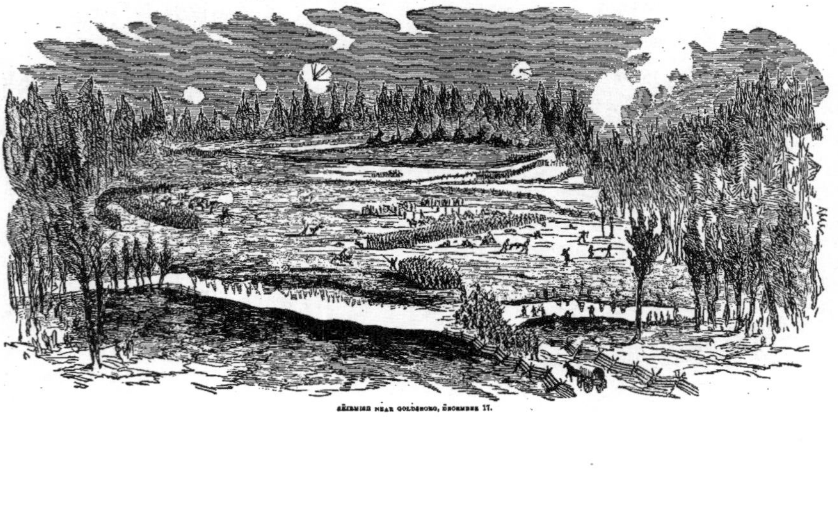

SKIRMISH NEAR GOLDSBORO, DECEMBER 17.

COURSE OF THE MISSISSIPPI FROM CAIRO TO THE GULF.

JOHN RODGERS.

CHAPTER XXVI.

THE WAR ON THE MISSISSIPPI.

The River.—Gun-boat and Mortar Fleet.—Farragut's Squadron.—A Succession of Victories.—Vicksburg becomes a Military Post.—Masked Batteries along the River Shore.—Shelling of Grand Gulf.—General Williams arrives before Vicksburg.—Farragut runs the Blockade.—Junction of the Fleets.—Bombardment of Vicksburg.—Escape of the Ram Arkansas.—Battle of Baton Rouge, and Destruction of the Arkansas.—Resumption of Operations against Vicksburg.—General Grant's Plan of the Winter Campaign.—An embarrassing Surrender.—Sherman's Defeat at Chickasaw Bayou.—McClernand in Command.—Capture of Arkansas Post.—General Grant's Army at Young's Point.—A Series of Naval Exploits.—The "pocket-full of Plans."—General Williams's Canal.—The Lake Providence Route.—The Yazoo Pass Expedition.—The "Deer-Creek Raid."—On to New Carthage.—The Transports run the Blockade.—Grierson's Raid.

"THE possession of the Mississippi," said General Sherman, in his speech at St. Louis just after the close of the war, "is the possession of America."[1] That this great river is not to the American what the Nile was to the Egyptian is owing to the greatness of America herself, who proudly refuses to be dependent upon even so important an ally; though, next to the two great oceans which skirt her continent, the river is the most important fact of her physical existence, and now (that is, in *anno Domini* 1866) has been proved to be the bond, sealed in blood, of her indissoluble union. Naturally, both in appearance and in fact, the river unites the North with the South, and, though seeming to divide between the Atlantic and the Pacific slopes, she in reality unites these also. The Algonquin Indians aptly named her *Missi Sepe*, "the Great River;" for, if the Missouri is to be considered—as it would have been but for a natural blunder on the part of the early American geographers—the parent, and not merely the tributary stream, the Mississippi is the longest river in the world. Even if we accept the more contracted limits which the geographers have given her, and date her origin from Itasca Lake, she drains a basin of more than a million of square miles—a basin which by possibility provides for a population of nearly four hundred millions, or almost one half of the present population of the entire globe. Even Aaron Burr, in his most splendid calculations respecting the destiny of this mighty garden—this granary of the world, under-estimated its gigantic possibilities. In the basin of the Mississippi the America of the future includes within its limits, as an *imperium in imperio*, a region, the population of which will outnumber the almost innumerable multitudes which have gathered about the Nile and the Ganges. For the present, however, the Englishman may well compare with the Mississippi his Thames, and the German his Rhine. Two centuries and a half go but a little way in the development of the resources of a nation, and far less than that period can be said to have been occupied in the real history of the Mississippi Valley.

The Mississippi is the most tortuous of rivers, and this circumstance, by the impediment which it offers to the current, doubtless favors navigation. Frequently the distance which has to be traversed is twelve, and sometimes even thirty times greater than it would be in a direct line. This circumstance also renders the river more capable of defensive fortification. Taken with its tributaries, the river affords nearly 17,000 miles of water which is navigable by steam. Its largest tributaries are the Missouri, Ohio, White, Arkansas, and Red Rivers. The Missouri is 3000 miles in length; it is a rapid and turbid stream, and asserts its lordship over the Mississippi by imparting to the latter a good measure of these characteristics. It enters the Mississippi a few miles above St. Louis. The Ohio, the largest eastern tributary of the Mississippi, enters the latter stream at Cairo, having previously received the waters of the Alleghany, the Kentucky, the Cumberland, and the Tennessee. From Pittsburg, where the Alleghany and Monongahela unite, to the mouth of the Ohio, is 948 miles; the river, with its tributaries, has 5000 miles of navigable waters. Within the limits of Arkansas, and not far apart, are the mouths of the White and Arkansas Rivers. The latter, much the more important tributary, is about 2000 miles long, and drains a basin of 178,000 square miles. The Red River enters the Mississippi from the west, about 200 miles above New Orleans. The greater part of its course is through fertile prairies of a reddish soil, which gives its color to the waters, and a name to the river. But for "The Raft" which obstructs its course, this river would be navigable for 400 miles from its mouth.

All of the western tributaries of the Mississippi drain the slopes of the Rocky Mountains, while its great eastern tributary, the Ohio, with *its* tributaries, drains the western slopes of the Appalachian range. Every one of these tributary and sub-tributary streams is swollen in the spring from the melting snows of the mountains. From the first of March, therefore, until the last of May—or for about ninety days—there is not simply a flood on the Mississippi, but literally an accumulation of floods. On the Missouri there is an average rise of fifteen feet, and this, added to the swollen Mississippi, makes a flood twenty-five feet in height. A second flood is heaped above this from the Ohio, below whose mouth the rise of the Mississippi is fifty feet. Above Natchez the flood begins to decline. At Baton Rouge it seldom exceeds thirty feet, and at New Orleans seldom twelve. At every flood the river overflows its banks for a distance of five hundred miles from its mouth, chiefly on the western side, inundating the country for the space of from ten to thirty miles. To guard against this, *levees* have been constructed, which confine the river within its original limits. Sometimes these levees are broken down by the violence of the current, and the consequent destruction of property is immense. To the yearly overflow of the Mississippi are to be attributed the large number of bayous in its vicinity. These vary in their extent, some of them scarcely exceeding a small river in size, while others spread out into lagoons and lakes.[1]

[1] When, at the beginning of this century, Monroe and Pinckney were negotiating with Napoleon I.—then First Consul of France—in regard to the purchase of Louisiana, Napoleon, anxious to transfer the province to the United States, lest it should fall into British possession, remarked that whatever nation held the Valley of the Mississippi would eventually be the most powerful on earth.

[1] "It is estimated that about 16,000,000 acres of the most fertile and productive lands of the states of Missouri, Arkansas, Mississippi, and Louisiana, are subject to overflow. To protect these lands from the annual devastation by the waters has been the object of incessant toil and immense outlays of capital by the inhabitants of the Valley of the Mississippi.

"So early as 1840, Congress made an appropriation for the construction of a chart of the "Hydrographical Basin of the Mississippi," which was executed by J. N. Nicollet, in the employ of the United States Topographical Bureau.

"In 1850, a corps of engineers was organized under Captain, now General A. A. Humphreys, which made a thorough survey of the Delta with special reference to the discovery of some system of works by which the country could be protected from overflow. These observations were made during and subsequent to the great flood of 1851.

"The constant increase of the volume of the flood revealed by each successive rise is ascribed by Captain Humphreys, in his Report, to the superior drainage produced by the cultivation of the country on the upper tributaries of the Mississippi, whereby the waters are thrown more rapidly into the main channel; the leveeing of the river and its tributaries in the states above Louisiana, so as to prevent the escape of the waters into the swamps and lowlands, whence it would be gradually drained to the river; the construction of cut-offs; the shortening of the channel, and more rapidly conveying the water to points below; and the lengthening of the Delta, thus extending the level mouth of the river, so that the current being retarded, the water is held back in the channel above.

"The remedies suggested are: Higher and stronger levees; prevention, by act of Congress, of the construction of additional cut-offs; formation of new outlets to the Lakes Borgne and Pontchartrain; opening of the closed bayous; enlargement of the Atchafalaya and Bayou Plaquemine, and the creation of artificial reservoirs in the swamps, to relieve the channel of the river in extreme cases.

"The early settlers, who selected the more elevated and fertile lands on the banks of the river, found little difficulty in protecting themselves from the floods. The whole country was then open to the waters, and a slight embankment, several inches high, would turn off the water, which was drained to the lowlands farther from the river. Other settlers, however, followed the pioneers; new plantations were established; and, by independent individual action, the slight embankments became linked together for many miles along both sides of the river. The waters, by reason of this confinement, rose higher every succeeding year, the embankments were enlarged, strengthened, and extended, until a line of levees, from fifteen to thirty feet wide at the base, and varying in height from five to twenty feet, stretched, with little interruption, from the lands on the coast, below New Orleans, along the channel of the river, to the boundaries of Tennessee and Missouri.

"The system, owing to its origin, was purely a selfish one. Each settler provided for his individual protection. If by a cut-off he could drain the water from his own place and throw it on the lands below, or by closing a bayou he could reclaim additional acres, the thing was done without reference to the effect it might have on the country lower down the stream. Much damage was thus done by shortening the channel of the river and by closing some of its natural outlets to the sea.

"The legislation of the states along the Mississippi has been little better than the individual action. The enactments depended more upon the comparative strength of the parties to be benefited and injured than upon any well-established plan for the control of the waters. Under authority of law, the channel of the river was shortened by the construction of cuts across the narrow necks formed by the great bends so frequent in the course of the stream. Bayous, which led from the main channel of the river to the gulf, forming independent outlets or mouths, were closed, and the water forced into one channel, which was unable to carry it to the sea.

"Before the war, therefore, the Father of Waters had become unmanageable in the hands of those who sought to control his floods. During the war, when labor that had been forced to the task day and night, and which at times was able to grapple successfully with the elements, was withdrawn, the waters swept away the levees at Morganzia, West Baton Rouge, at Chinn's and at Robertson's plantation, and at other points both above and below the mouth of the Red River, and inundated the country west of the Mississippi from Morganzia to Berwick's Bay.

"An attempt was made during last winter to rebuild these broken embankments. Under the combined efforts of the state authorities of Louisiana and the War Department at Washington, a large number of laborers were employed, and the work had been so far repaired that it was believed to be sufficiently strong to resist the pressure of the flood. Many planters and men from the North, believing that these levees would be rebuilt, engaged in the cultivation of the fertile lands in the parishes of Point Coupee, West Baton Rouge, Iberville, Lafourche, Terrebonne, and parts of others that were overflowed last year. Recent reports from Louisiana bring the sad intelligence that all these newly-constructed levees have been swept away, and that the water is rapidly filling up the swamps and spreading over the whole country, driving the homeless inhabitants before it.

"It is a grave question for the consideration of the country whether Congress should not undertake the protection of the whole Delta of the Mississippi against overflow. The present sys-

CREVASSE ON THE LOWER MISSISSIPPI.

... doubt led to their situation upon the bluffs which rise here and there along the river banks. In the development of these towns—for they could scarcely be called cities—manufactures and the arts could have but little scope. In some cases, indeed, an easy communication by railroad with the Atlantic sea-board gave them some of the characteristics of our Eastern cities. The principal towns situated upon the banks of the Mississippi are St. Louis, Cairo, Columbus, Memphis, Vicksburg, Natchez, Baton Rouge, and, near the mouth of the river, New Orleans, which alone can be said to compare in commercial importance with the great cities of the East.

All of these were in our civil war points of great military importance. Their very situation, in nearly all cases, was such as to give them many facilities for defense against a naval attack. The city of New Orleans was, however, not in itself favorably located in this respect; it was not built upon bluffs like Memphis and Vicksburg, and had to be defended against inundation by artificial levees. But the approach to the city from the Gulf was well guarded by Forts Jackson and St. Philip. With the exception of these two forts, there were no military defenses worth considering on the Mississippi at the beginning of the war, and if the nation had possessed any considerable naval strength, the entire river from Cairo to New Orleans might have been secured at the outset. But, while a navy was being provided, there were constructed at favorable points fortifications which for some time secured the greater portion of the river to the Confederacy. The two points which were the last to surrender to the national arms were Vicksburg and Port Hudson. The campaigns—naval and military—which had for their object the reduction of these two strong-holds form the main subject of this and the succeeding chapter. But, before entering directly upon these campaigns, we shall briefly review the previous naval history of the war on the Mississippi.

The importance of a navy on our Western rivers was early appreciated. A month after the capture of Fort Sumter, Commander John Rodgers was summoned to Washington, and to him was assigned the duty of creating the Western navy. In the first stages of the undertaking, the War Department, under Secretary Cameron, assumed the expense and supervision; and it was not until the autumn of 1861 that the matter was transferred to the charge of the Navy Department, where it properly belonged.

Rodgers, an officer fitly chosen to organize the armed flotilla of the West, was son of the distinguished Commodore John Rodgers, one of the fathers of the American Navy. A native of Maryland, he had entered the naval service of the United States in 1828, at an early age. He had seen much service as midshipman and lieutenant; had been for two years engaged in boat service on the coast of Florida, in the war with the Seminoles and in the Coast Survey Expedition; in 1852 had been appointed second in command of the North Pacific and Behring Straits Exploring Expedition; and, succeeding to the chief command of that expedition on account of the severe illness of Captain Ringgold, had taken his vessel, the Vincennes, farther into the Arctic region than a ship-of-war had ever before penetrated; and when the rebellion broke out he had reported for active service, and had been sent to Norfolk to attempt the rescue of the vessels there, but, arriving too late to accomplish this, had been assigned to the difficult and dangerous duty of blowing up the dry-dock. It was from Norfolk that Rodgers was, on May 16, 1861, summoned to Washington to receive orders respecting his mission to the West. Entering immediately upon this mission, he went to work heartily. He purchased steamers, which, under his supervision, were fitted, armed, and armored as gun-boats. But it was a slow and difficult undertaking, demanding much skill, and more than ordinary perseverance. The question of the comparative power of even iron-clad gun-boats as against forts was still one about which a great deal might be said on both sides. Even as we look back now and consider what the war has taught us in regard to the solution of this vexed problem, we hesitate to pronounce definitely, satisfying ourselves with the somewhat vague conclusion that the re... perseverance and courage," says Secretary Welles, "were scarcely by the heroic qualities displayed in subsequent well-fought actic decks of the gun-boats he had under so many discouragements pr

In the month of February Foote was able to bring against F seven gun-boats—the Essex, St. Louis, Carondelet, Cincinnati, T ington, and Conestoga, of which the last three were wooden. In the Cincinnati and Essex were disabled, and could not be brougl Fort Donelson a week later. In the naval action at Donelson also was absent on the Tennessee, but the two iron-clads were re the Louisville and Pittsburg. Foote declared that if the battle c been postponed one week, he could also have brought eight of hi boats into action. Besides the nine gun-boats involved in the Henry and Donelson, three others—the Benton, Mound City, and were ready for action in a few days. At Island No. 10, in Marc mortar-boats were engaged. From a letter written about this time eral Strong to Foote, it appears that the Confederates then had gun-boats independent of the five below New Madrid, and the Ma ram, at Memphis." These vessels were, however, far inferior to Foo boats, as was shown shortly afterward; yet they excited considerab hension, for Farragut's fleet had not then entered the river fror From this time additions to the gun-boat fleet of the Western na slowly made. By the close of 1862, the Tuscumbia, the Baron De K the Osage had been added, and there were in process of constructio osho, Indianola, Choctaw, and Chillicothe. The Ozark was comp 1863. Including these, the gun-boat fleet consisted of twenty vess an armament of about 170 guns, and a tonnage of nearly 10,000 ton or ten more gun-boats were added before the close of the war.[2] Of boats added to the Western fleet during the year after the fight at D the Tuscumbia was among the largest.[3] The Mound City was blow July, 1862, on the White River, and subsequently the Cairo met a fate on the Yazoo.

Next to the vessels known as gun-boats, Ellet's steam-ram fleet most important place in the Mississippi Squadron. Charles Ellet same relation to steam rams as Ericsson to the monitors. He was of Pennsylvania. As a civil engineer he had gained a reputation wl well earned. His treatise on "The Laws of Trade in Reference to of Internal Improvement," published in Philadelphia in 1837, was haustive work on the subject, and attracted considerable attention. years afterward he was chosen by the War Department to survey th Mississippi. It was an important object of his life to carry out a which he had conceived for improving the navigation of the West ers.[4] He was so impressed with this project that, in honor of it, he his son Charles *Rivers* Ellet. It is not more remarkable that De So

[1] This title remained in existence until the operation of an act of Congress of July By this act the Officers of the navy were distributed into nine grades, taking rank accor date of commission in each grade, as follows:

GRADES IN THE NAVY.	CORRESPONDING GRADES IN THE ARMY.
1. Rear Admirals.	1. Major Generals.
2. Commodores.	2. Brigadier Generals.
3. Captains.	3. Colonels.
4. Commanders.	4. Lieutenant Colonels.
5. Lieutenant Commanders.	5. Majors.
6. Lieutenants.	6. Captains.
7. Masters.	7. First Lieutenants.
8. Ensigns.	8. Second Lieutenants.
9. Midshipmen.	

In regard to the change thus introduced, Secretary Welles, in his Report for 1862, sa act of July 16, 1862, 'to Establish and Equalize the Grade of Line Officers of the Uni Navy,' does justice in conferring ranks and grades that had until that time been with as meritorious and gallant a class of officers as ever devoted their days and periled thei their country. Though the justice to which they were entitled has been long delayed, it fully and generously rendered by the present Congress, and has been and is apprecia brave men who are its recipients, and by all attached to the service, as a just recogniti worth and ability of the officers of the American Navy. . . . The commanders of rons now hold rank with those of other naval powers on the ocean, on distant service, ever they carry our flag, or appear as the representatives of their country."—Page 10.

Flag-officers Goldsborough, D...

his grave in the waters of the Mississippi, which he discovered, than that both the Ellets, father and son, perished in the attempt to secure, by their warlike invention of rams, that very navigation which the father had sought to improve by peaceful measures for so many years.[1]

After the seizure of the Norfolk Navy Yard, and when uneasiness had been aroused by the report that the Confederates were converting frigates and steamers into iron-clad rams, Ellet appreciated the threatened danger, and in a printed memorial to Congress, dated Georgetown, February 6, 1862, a month before the appearance of the Merrimac, he gave the government a warning as to the consequences which might ensue upon the appearance of these Confederate rams.[2] The government listened to this final appeal, though it was not until the appearance of the Merrimac, and the events which followed had fully vindicated Ellet's judgment, that the latter was summoned to the aid of Secretary Stanton. Foote was at this time very anxious on account of Confederate rams on the Mississippi, and he knew he had no vessels which could meet these rams on equal terms. Here was an opportunity to test Eliet'e favorite project. He was sent West by Secretary Stanton with authority to purchase and convert into rams such vessels as he should deem suited to his purposes. With a colonel's commission, he set out on the 26th of March. At Pittsburg he purchased five powerful tow-boats, the Lioness, Samson, Mingo, Fulton, and Homer. The hulls were strengthened, the bows filled with solid timber, the boilers protected by a double tier of oak twenty-four inches thick, and the pilot-house plated against musketry. At Cincinnati he purchased four side-wheel steamers of great power, as being more readily handled in the strong current of the Mississippi—the Queen of the West, Monarch, Switzerland, and Lancaster. But for Colonel Ellet's extraordinary personal influence he would never have been able to obtain men for his rams, although he had permission to recruit from the army. The project was deemed not only a visionary, but a perilous one. His brother, Alfred W. Ellet, then a captain in the Fifty-ninth Illinois, brought his own company, with another from the Sixty-third Illinois, and met the boats at Cairo. For firemen Ellet was mainly indebted to negroes.

CHARLES ELLET.

We turn now from the Mississippi squadron, which before the end of 1862 numbered about 80 vessels—gun-boats, rams, mortar-boats, and side-wheel steamers—to Farragut's fleet, which, after the fall of New Orleans, occupied the Lower Mississippi. This fleet consisted of two parts: vessels of the West Gulf squadron, and Admiral D. D. Porter's mortar flotilla.[3] At the close of 1861 the entire Gulf squadron numbered 21 vessels, with 282 guns and 1000 men. This squadron was divided into an Eastern and Western, February 21, 1862. The former was under the command of Flag-officer McKean, who was relieved June 4, 1862, by acting Rear-admiral Lardner, who was shortly succeeded by Commodore Theodorus Bailey. The limits of this eastern squadron comprised the southern and western portions of the Florida coast, commencing at Cape Canaveral and extending to Pensacola. Westward from and including Pensacola, the West Gulf squadron extended to the Rio Grande. This latter was a very important command, for two reasons: first, on account of the operations against New Orleans, which had been contemplated ever since the early autumn of 1861; and, secondly, on account of the importance of the blockade in this quarter, within the limits of which were included the ocean outlets of the Mississippi Valley. David G. Farragut, then captain, afterward admiral, vice-admiral, and finally Admiral of the United States Navy, was wisely chosen to command this de-

CHARLES RIVERS ELLET.

[1] In order that the reader may fully comprehend Mr. Eliet's connection with steam rams previous to the war, we transcribe a few paragraphs from the article in *Harper's Magazine*, already referred to:

"It was in the winter of 1854–5, at Lausanne, in Switzerland, that home of wandering savans, during the siege of Sebastopol, when the Russians spoke of sinking their splendid fleet, that Mr. Eliet first revolved in his mind the plan of protecting and strengthening war vessels, so that they might be used as rams; that thus, instead of sinking their fleet, the Russians might sink that of the allies, and raise the blockade of the harbor. In December, probably, he wrote to the Russian government, giving a detailed statement of his plan, which was thankfully received, but, in consequence of the death of the emperor soon after, was overlooked and never acted upon. In the following April (26th) he addressed a letter to the Secretary of War, through Mr. John Y. Mason, our minister at Paris, with the same propositions. These, with a reply and rejoinder from our Navy Department, were afterward published (Richmond, 1855) in pamphlet form, and circulated widely both in the South and in Europe. We were at that time slightly menaced with war with England on the Right of Search question.

"In his prefatory note, dated Richmond, December 1, 1855, Mr. Ellet says:

"'People are accustomed to regard the art of naval warfare as the art of manœuvring cannon, and throwing shot and shell. I wish them to reflect upon the power of a moving steam-boat driven against the enemy who has no means of resistance but his batteries, and to decide which is the more certain warfare. I wish, therefore, to compare the number of fighting steamers which may be sent to any port in the United States from the shores of Europe with the number of river steamers, coasting steamers, steam-tugs, and even ferry-boats, which might be found ready to meet them here.'

"This remarkable pamphlet, upon which must be based his claims to the paternity of the steam ram, is so forcible and explicit, that it should be given entire did space allow. Like all he ever wrote, it is clear, earnest, well reasoned, and nervous in style. He says:

"'My plan is simply to convert the steamer into a battering-ram, and to enable her to fight, not with her guns, but with her momentum. In short, I propose to strengthen the steamer throughout in the most substantial manner, so that she may run head on into the enemy, or burst in his ribs, or drive a hole into his hull below the water-line. A hole only two feet square, four feet under water, will sink an ordinary frigate in sixteen minutes.'

"He then minutely details the altering or building of ships for his purpose. And then he adds:

"'I have read accounts of five or six accidental collisions at sea in the last six months—sometimes by steamers running into sailing vessels, and sometimes by sailing vessels running into steamers—and in every case the vessel struck in the waist was sunk, and the vessel which ran into her was able to keep on her course. For harbor defense, however much we may continue to build and arm forts and batteries, I think we should not neglect also to build *floating batteries—rams*—great steamers, as near shot and shell proof as they can be made, with a strength of hull, speed, and power that will enable them to crush in the side of a man-of-war by simple collision.

"'To my understanding, the efficacy of the plan which I recommend is self-evident. *And I hold myself ready to carry it out in all its details whenever the day arrives that the United States is about to become engaged in a naval contest.*'

"To this letter the following remarkable answer was returned:

"'Navy Department, Washington, D. C., March 31, 1855.

"'Sir,—The receipt of your letter of the 25th ult. is acknowledged, and the Department tenders you its thanks for the views expressed therein. The suggestion to convert steamers into battering-rams, and, by the momentum, make them a means of sinking an enemy's ships, was proposed as long ago as 1832, and has been renewed many times since by various officers of the navy. No practical test has been undertaken; but with the necessary speed, strength, and weight, a large steamer on the plan proposed by you would introduce an entire change in naval warfare.

"'Very respectfully, your obedient servant,

"'Charles W. Welch, Acting Secretary of the Navy.'

"In reply to this, Mr. Ellet, on the 16th of August, sent another letter to the Navy Department, through Mr. Buchanan, then our minister in London, in which letter he still more strenuously urges the adoption of his plan. The Secretary of the Navy, J. C. Dobbin, in a very courteous reply, dismissed the subject, stating that the Department had no power, but by special vote of Congress, 'to undertake the construction of proper vessels and machinery for experimenting.'

"In the letter which elicited this last reply Mr. Ellet discusses the objections which are likely to be raised against his plan, such as that his own vessel might be sunk or hopelessly damaged in engine or vital parts by the collision or by hostile shot. With our late remarkable experience we can see that these objections fall to the ground. But from the data before him he reasoned correctly that the danger from collision would be immensely against the vessel struck; and in the danger from shot, he entered into a nice calculation of the probabilities of a vessel being struck in a vital part, between the points of extreme range and that of close contact, by which he showed that the chances were reduced to an inappreciable fraction.

"When we consider how the allied fleet bombarded the fortress of Sweaborg, defended by about 800 guns, for the space of forty-five hours, without suffering the loss of a single man by the enemy's shot, 'in consequence of the continual movement of the ships,' as the Russian general alleged, and as we also recall some very remarkable engagements of our own in the late war, we may appreciate the prevision of our advocate. The bombardment of Port Royal and the experience of blockade-runners confirm the result of his calculations.

"Among the cases of accidental collisions cited are several remarkable ones, all tending to the support of his theory. The well-known sinking of the Arctic by the Vesta, with great loss of life; the Wellington, of 131 guns, damaged by a sailing ship; the Imperatrice, steamer, sunk almost immediately by the schooner Commerce; the Victoria, ship, sunk in two minutes by a small Sardinian steamer; the brigantine Henry, run into by a diminutive steamer and lost immediately.

"In 1842, the Hudson River steamer Empire, coming into New York with a new pilot on a misty morning, ran fairly into a new wharf with the full power of the engine, forcing the bow of the boat through the timber facing of logs eighteen inches square, then through a solid stone filling eight and a half feet thick, and then through earth and rubbish seventeen feet farther, making a chasm of twelve feet wide at the logs, twenty-seven feet long, and seventeen feet deep. The only injury sustained by the boat was the breaking of one of her oblique braces and a slight leak at the stem.

"Now, if such is the effect of a frail river steamer upon an object of this sort, what must be expected of a vessel built and armed for the very purpose of a ram? There is another example, memorable for the tragical, mysterious manner in which it occurred. It may be recollected that, a few years ago, an American vessel, with an English captain, was hired, it is supposed, to run down a Russian ship of war in the Baltic. He strengthened his bows with solid timber, and followed the war vessel out of St. Petersburg, and in the gray of dawn next morning, when near the Cattegat, while his crew were asleep or below decks, he took the helm himself and ran into the Russian ship with the power of sails merely, and instantaneously sunk her with her crew of three hundred souls.

"'The practical conclusion,' says Mr. Ellet, 'to be drawn from these facts is apparent. If vessels built for ordinary commercial purposes, and propelled either by steam or sail, invariably sink the vessel they strike with their bow when running with any considerable velocity, while themselves receiving but little injury from the collision, it follows, of necessity and *à fortiori*, that a steamer expressly designed for such conflict, well fortified at the bow, strongly built throughout, divided longitudinally and centrally by a solid partition reaching from kelson to deck and from stem to stern, and transversely by other partitions, separating the hull into six or eight water-tight compartments, and horizontally by one or more partitions or floors, of which one shall be below the water-line when light—I say it follows of necessity that such a vessel, skillfully framed and properly fastened, may be driven at high speed against any ship of ordinary construction in the certainty that the ship struck will go down and the battering ship float.'

"All this, which is familiar knowledge to us in 1865, was foreseen and reasoned out in 1855. At that time Mr. Eliet was living in Richmond. His views, as set forth by his pamphlet, addresses to Congress, and by conversation and newspaper communications, were all well known. Here, indeed, is the germ of the idea wrought out but partially by the rebels after their seizure of the navy yard at Norfolk. To the suggestion that the enemy could strengthen his ships, and meet them ram with ram, it is only necessary to add that this is a fundamental condition of all civilized warfare, and will occur under every species of construction, armament, or defense."

[2] We make the following extract from this memorial:

"Steam Rams.—It is not generally known that the rebels now have five steam rams nearly ready for use. Of these, two are on the Lower Mississippi, two are at Mobile, and one is at Norfolk. The last of the five is doubtless the most formidable, being the steam frigate Merrimac, which has been so strengthened that, in the opinion of the rebels, it may be used as a ram. But we have not yet a single vessel at sea, nor, so far as I know, in course of construction, able to cope with a well-built ram. If the Merrimac is permitted to escape from the Elizabeth River, she will be almost certain to commit great depredation on our armed or unarmed vessels in Hampton Roads, and may even be expected to pass out under the guns of Fortress Monroe and prey upon our commerce in Chesapeake Bay. Indeed, if the alterations have been skillfully made, and she succeed in getting to sea, she will not only be a terrible scourge to our commerce, but may prove also to be a most dangerous visitor to our blockading squadron off the harbors of our Southern coasts.

"I have attempted to call the attention of the Navy Department and of the country so often to this subject during the last seven years that I almost hesitate to allude to it again, and would not do so here but that I think the danger from these tremendous engines is very imminent, but not at all appreciated."

[3] Farragut's fleet was constituted thus:

Steam-sloops.		*Steam-sloop.*		*Mortar Fleet.*	
Hartford	24 guns.	Sciota	4 guns.	H. Beals.	
Richmond	26 "	*Sailing-sloop.*		J. Griffith.	
Pensacola	24 "	Portsmouth	17 "	Racer.	
Brooklyn	24 "	*Mortar Fleet.*		S. Bruen.	
Mississippi	12 "	Norfolk Packet.		H. Jones.	
Colorado	28 "	Arietta.		Dan. Smith.	
Gun-boats.		Sophronia.		*Vessels accompanying Mortars.*	
Iroquois	9 "	Para.		Harriet Lane	4 guns.
Oneida	9 "	C. P. Williams.		Miami	7 "
Varuna	12 "	O. H. Lee.		Westfield	6 "
Cayuga	6 "	W. Bacon.		Clifton	6 "
Winona	4 "	T. A. Ward.		Uncas	5 "
Katahdin	4 "	A. Dugel.		Owasco	5 "
Itaska	4 "	M. Vassar.		Octorara	10 "
Kineo	4 "	C. Maugham.		Sea Foam	5 "
Wissahickon	4 "	M. J. Carlton.		A. Houghton	2 "
Pinola	4 "	S. C. Jones.		*Coast Survey Vessel.*	
Kennebec	4 "	Orvotta.		Sachem	5 "

The Octorara did not arrive until after the capture of New Orleans. Each of the mortar-boats mounted a bomb and two guns. Some of the vessels accompanying the mortars were only armed tugs.

ADMIRAL PORTER'S MORTAR FLEET.

partment. After July 11 Pensacola became the great naval dépôt for the West Gulf squadron.

Farragut sailed from Hampton Roads to take the command on February 2, 1862, and, arriving at Ship Island on the 20th, began to organize his fleet. Two months were consumed in these preparations, the greatest difficulty being encountered in landing the vessels of heavy draught. After every effort had been made, the Colorado and the Wabash could not be got over the bar. The entire fleet sent against New Orleans, including the vessels withdrawn from the blockade, consisted of 48 vessels, with about 300 guns and 20 bombs. Porter's mortar flotilla had been organized at the Brooklyn Navy Yard in the winter of 1861–2, and performed a very important part in the opening of the Mississippi. In Farragut's entire fleet there was not a single iron-clad vessel.

The most brilliant naval period of the war — if the brilliancy of naval operations depend upon their success in actual engagement with the enemy's ships and forts — is comprised within the brief space of four months, beginning February 6, and ending June 6, 1862. Yet this was far from being the period of our greatest naval strength. Very much stronger expeditions were fitted out afterward, but they failed of success, except in one or two instances.[1]

Let us review the brief, but eventful and satisfactory record of these four months. The capture of Fort Henry, February 6, was the first of a series of victories on the Western rivers that aroused the nation from a situation, if not of doubt, at least of a negative sort of confidence, to one of positive hope and courage. The capture of Donelson ten days later, though it could scarcely be called a naval victory, still derived a large measure of its importance from its bearings upon the progress of naval operations. It gave us command of the Cumberland, as the victory at Fort Henry had given us command of the Tennessee. It was followed, within the space of a fortnight, by the evacuation of Columbus and Nashville. The Confederates held New Madrid until March 14, when their communications had been cut off by General Pope. In the capture of Island No. 10, April 7, the army under Pope, and the naval squadron under Foote, had an equal share. Here there was no battle, but there were captured nearly 7000 prisoners and a large amount of war material, including 100 siege-guns. The crossing of Pope's force to the rear of the enemy, on the west side of the Mississippi, by the aid of the gun-boats, had secured the victory without the loss of a single man.

Before the close of April, Farragut, with his fleet, had steamed past Forts Jackson and St. Philip, and, arriving before New Orleans, held the city under his guns. Lovell's fleet had been disposed of in a short

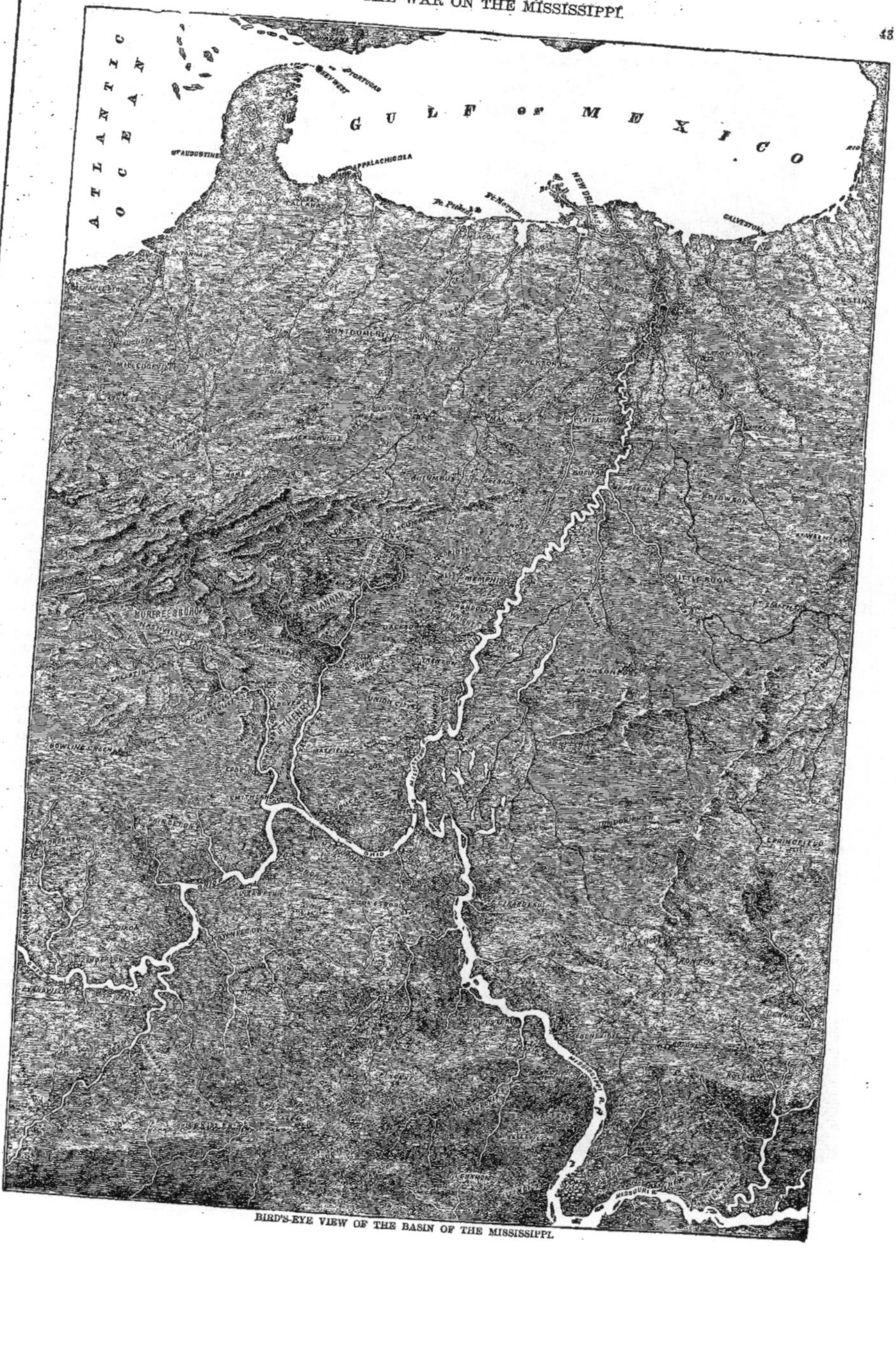

BIRD'S-EYE VIEW OF THE BASIN OF THE MISSISSIPPI.

CHARLES H. DAVIS.

was, thus far, the most substantial triumph of the war. It was to the South a greater disaster, comparatively, than the loss of New York City would have been to the North.

In the mean time, Foote was engaged in an expedition against Fort Pillow, which he had undertaken directly after the surrender of Island No. 10. But Pope's army abandoned him April 17th, to join the army moving upon Corinth, and left him helpless. Early in May, this gallant naval officer, still suffering from his wound, was, at his own request, relieved, and the command of the Mississippi squadron was assigned to Captain C. H. Davis. A little more than a year after his resignation of this command Admiral Foote died, while making preparations to depart for Charleston, to relieve Admiral Dupont. The day after Davis assumed the command—May 10—the Confederate fleet at Memphis came up the river and engaged the squadron, but withdrew, defeated, after an hour's fight, having, however, succeeded in badly crippling the Cincinnati and the Mound City. The evacuation of Corinth gave us Fort Pillow without a battle, June 4, and the next day the city of Memphis was surrendered.

But before the surrender of Memphis there was a spirited conflict with Montgomery's fleet. Davis left Fort Pillow, June 5, with a fleet of nine boats—five gun-boats, two tugs, and two of Colonel Ellet's rams, the Queen of the West and the Monarch. Montgomery, with his eight boats, had threatened to "send Lincoln's gun-boats to the bottom," and the inhabitants of Memphis gathered upon the hill-side to witness this expected catastrophe. The fight which followed has already been described in a previous chapter. It was here that Ellet redeemed all the promises which he had made for his rams. The two rams alone could have sunk the entire fleet.[1] Colonel

[1] "While the engagement," writes Captain Davis, "was going on in this manner, two vessels of the ram-fleet, under command of Colonel Ellet, steamed rapidly by us, and ran boldly into the enemy's line. Several conflicts had taken place between the rams before the flotilla (of gun-boats), led by the Benton, moving at a slower rate, could arrive at the closest quarters. In the mean time, however, the firing from the gun-boats was continuous, and exceedingly well [...]rected. The General Beauregard and the Little Rebel were struck in the boilers and blown [...]

"The ram, Queen of the West, which Colonel Ellet commanded in person, encountered [...] full power the rebel steamer General Lovell, and sunk her, but in so doing sustained pretty [...]ous damage. Up to this time the rebel fleet had maintained its position, and used its guns [...] great spirit. Those disasters compelled the remaining vessels to resort to their superiority [...] speed as the only means of safety. A running fight took place, which lasted nearly an hour, [...] carried us ten miles below the city. The attack made by the two rams under Colonel Ellet, wi[...] took place before the flotilla closed in with the enemy, was bold and successful."

[...] the effect of a blow which he had given the Lovell, and [...] was sinking the latter, received a bullet in his knee. The wound pro[...] be a dangerous one, and amputation became necessary; but the colon[...] sisted stoutly, declaring that "the life should go first." Two weeks [...] the battle he was conveyed to Cairo on one of his rams—the Switzerl[...] and died on reaching the wharf on the morning of June 21. He le[...] brother Alfred in command of the ram fleet.

After the capture of Memphis, four of the gun-boats, with an In[...] regiment under Colonel Fitch, were dispatched to the White River to [...] communication with General Curtis, who had advanced to Batesville. [...] batteries were carried at St. Charles, but the main object of the exped[...] was not accomplished, and General Curtis, in order to find a base of [...]tions, was obliged to transfer his army from Batesville to Helena, on [...] Mississippi.

Meanwhile Farragut's fleet had been advancing up the river. The [...]quois, under Commander Palmer, arrived off Baton Rouge May 7. Th[...]thorities, ordered to surrender, indulged in the same mock-heroic non[...] which the mayor and council of New Orleans had been indulging in [...] week before. They were determined that the city of Baton Rouge sh[...] not "be surrendered voluntarily to any power on earth." There wa[...] military force, the mayor added, in the city, and its possession by the Fe[...]als "must be without the consent and against the wish of the peaceabl[...] habitants." He declined to hoist the national flag because it was "offen[...] to the sensibilities of the people." Palmer, "determined to submit to [...] such nonsense," took possession of the arsenal, barracks, and other pu[...] property of the United States. No resistance was offered. In a note [...] Mayor Bryan, on the 9th, Palmer informed him that he had taken pos[...]sion of the arsenal, and hoisted over it the United States flag, and add[...] "War is a sad calamity, and often inflicts severer wounds than those u[...] the sensibilities. I therefore trust I may be spared from resorting to [...] of its dire extremities; but I warn you, Mr. Mayor, that this flag must [...]main unmolested, though I have no force on shore to protect it. The r[...] act of some individual may cause your city to pay a bitter penalty." F[...]ragut, having come up on May 10, continued the mayor in office, and enco[...]aged the employment which the latter had already made of the fore[...] corps as a police guard for the maintenance of good order. Baton Ro[...] was the first place of importance above New Orleans, from which it was [...]tant about 140 miles. It was situated on a plateau 40 or 50 feet above hi[...] water, on the east bank of the river; was the capital of Louisiana, and h[...] a population, in 1860, of 5498.

Fifteen miles above Baton Rouge is Natchez, in Mississippi. This pl[...] Palmer, with the Iroquois and other gun-boats, reached on the 12th. [...] addressed a note to the mayor, which the citizens at the landing refused [...] receive. Palmer then seized a ferry-boat which was loading with coal, [...] aboard of it a force of seamen, a few marines, and two howitzers, and s[...] the expedition across the river, with orders to see that the mayor recei[...] the note. But there was no occasion to land this force, as two members [...] the Common Council were already in waiting with the mayor's apolo[...] Mayor Hunter submitted to the necessities of the situation, if not with [...]markable grace, at least without any heroic bluster. But Natchez was

NATCHEZ UNDER THE HILL.

. by any military

eet since the cap-
ırprise, doubtless,
Farragut's squad-
rrender of Vicks-
n't know, and re-
dore Farragut or
Such, indeed, was
nilitary governor
r general in com-
is own account,
was his intention
of the city, add-
as the municipal
fenses, and none
n the 21st, gave
f Vicksburg be-
must injure or
the purpose of
mediately upon
Phillips, how-

the possession
half as large as
No. 10 could at
pened the Mis-
military force
gard's army at
educed for this
eneral Butler's

Whenever these attacks were made in the vicinity of towns, it was found necessary to retaliate by holding the inhabitants responsible; and if they were repeated, the villages or towns, as the case might be, were in some instances destroyed. Natchez, Grand Gulf, and Donaldsonville, in the course of the year, suffered severely from punishments inflicted upon them in this way. The most serious collision of this nature took place early in June, at Grand Gulf. The Confederates were just then beginning to fortify that place, and Commander Palmer, fearing that the passage down the river might be obstructed, sent down the Wissahickon and Itaska, under Commander De Camp, to reduce the newly-erected batteries. These vessels arrived off Grand Gulf on the morning of June 9, when they were attacked from the shore with rifled and other cannon. After an action of two hours, in which the gun-boats were quite roughly handled, one of them being hulled seventeen and the other twenty-five times, the batteries were silenced. On the vessels one man was killed and five wounded. Palmer then decided to bring down the rest of the squadron from below Vicksburg. His position was one of some difficulty. The batteries above him were manned by a force of 500 artillerists. Their position upon the hill seemed to protect them against serious injury, and the gun-boats had much to fear from their plunging fire. He did not dare to leave a few vessels only at Vicksburg. He expected that at any moment the iron-clad ram Arkansas might come down from the Yazoo. Fort Pillow, too, had just been evacuated; and, not aware of the destruction of the Confederate fleet at Memphis, he feared that the vessels of that fleet might, in conjunction with the Arkansas, attempt a raid against his little squadron. The fortifications of Vicksburg were daily being strengthened by the arrival of new guns and ammunition. His gunboats were "all of them in a most crippled condition;" the sick-list had largely increased; the time of the men on the Colorado had expired; he was almost out of both coal and provisions, and had little oil left for his engines. "Unless supplies come up," he writes, June 10, "we can not stay here a week longer."

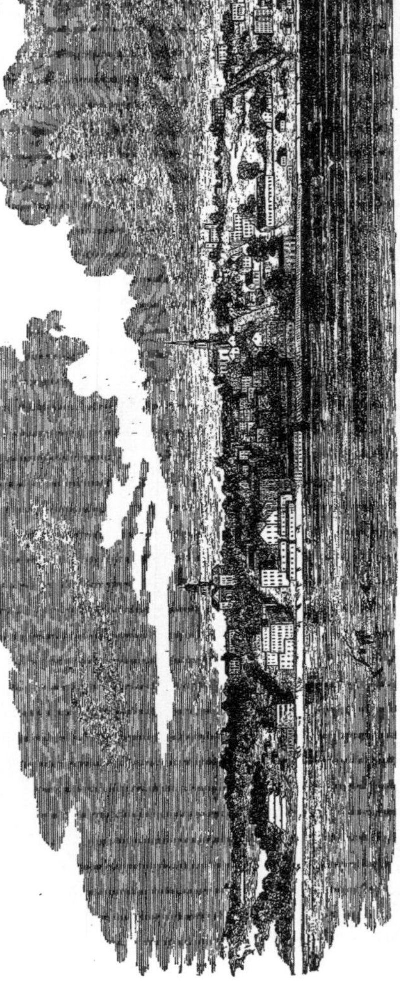

VIEW OF VICKSBURG FROM THE RIVER.

Vicksburg, which, as regards heroic and obstinate resistance to the national arms, held almost equal rank with Richmond and Charleston, lies in the State of Mississippi, on the east bank of the river, 400 miles above New Orleans, and about the same distance from Cairo. Its commercial importance is due to its location in the midst of the great cotton-growing country along the Yazoo. It is connected with Jackson, the state capital, by railroad; and from De Soto, on the opposite bank, a railroad, running to Monroe, drains the land commerce of Northern Louisiana. It is the most important, and, at the same time, the most defensible military position on the Mississippi. At the time of the capture of New Orleans, this fact was little appreciated on either side.[1] The population of Vicksburg, before the war, was, in round numbers, 5000. The town, situated on the shelving declivity of high hills, with its dwellings scattered in groups on the terraces, presents a very picturesque appearance.

On the 20th of June, a month after the first appearance of Farragut's fleet off Vicksburg, Brigadier General Thomas Williams left Baton Rouge with a large portion of the garrison which had been there posted, and in four days' time reached a position on the peninsula opposite Vicksburg. He had only four regiments and eight field-guns. The force defending Vicksburg at this time consisted of about 10,000 men.[2] General Williams immediately set about constructing a canal across the narrow neck of the peninsula, on the Louisiana side, which, if successful, would throw Vicksburg and its defenses six miles inland. Of this we shall have more to say hereafter in connection with the projects for getting a position to the rear of the city. Porter's mortar fleet of sixteen vessels had in the mean while moved up the river to Vicksburg. It was now proposed that a junction should be effected between Farragut's fleet and that under Davis's command, as preliminary to as formidable an attempt against the city as it was possible for this combined naval force to make.

In two or three instances already the national vessels had run the gauntlet of Confederate batteries on the Mississippi. The Carondelet on the 4th, and the Pittsburg on the 6th of April, had run past the enemy's fortifications on Island No. 10. In the latter part of the same month, Farragut, with nearly his entire fleet, passed Forts Jackson and St. Philip. He did not, therefore, reckon it an enterprise of very great magnitude or peril to run the Vicksburg blockade. It is not likely that he anticipated any very important results from this operation. He knew well enough that batteries could be passed with much greater ease than they could be taken. But he had been ordered by the Navy Department and the President to do something against Vicksburg, and was disposed to strike the heaviest blow possible with the force he had in hand; and on the night of the 27th of June he had every thing in readiness for the undertaking. The order was given for a movement the next morning. Porter, who had got his mortar fleet and his gun-boats in an advantageous position, and who had been for the past two days employed in ascertaining the range of the enemy's works, was to open fire upon the latter at four o'clock A.M. He was to perform a part similar to that which had been assigned him at New Orleans—that is, he was to stand still and engage the enemy's batteries, while Farragut should pass them with his fleet. This fleet of Farragut's consisted of the

---

in the vicinity of one, however, the usages of civilized warfare do not justify its destruction, unless demanded by the necessities of attack or defense.

"I can not bring myself to believe that the barbarous and cowardly policy indicated in the inclosed letter will meet with the approval of any officer of rank or standing in the United States Navy. I have, therefore, thought proper to transmit it to you under a flag of truce, with the confident expectation that you will direct those under your command to confine their offensive operations as far as possible to our troops, and forbid the wanton destruction of defenseless towns, filled with unoffending non-combatants, unless required by imperious military necessity.

"The practice of slaying women and children as an act of retaliation has happily fallen into disuse in this country with the disappearance of the Indian tribes, and I trust it will not be revived by the officers of the United States Navy, but that the demolition and pillage of the unoffending little village of Grand Gulf may be permitted to stand alone and without parallel upon record. M. LOVELL, Major General Commanding.

"Commanding Officer United States Navy, Mississippi River, near Baton Rouge."

[No. 2.]

"Baton Rouge, June 17, 1862.

"SIR,—I have to acknowledge the receipt of your communication of the 12th instant, together with its inclosure, in which you are pleased to say that vengeance will be visited upon the women and children of Rodney if our vessels are fired upon from the town. Although I find no such language contained in the letter of Lieutenant Commanding Nichols, or even any from which such inference might be drawn, still I shall meet your general remark on your own terms. You say you locate your batteries 'at such points on the river as are deemed best suited,' etc., without reference to the people of the town, and claim no immunity for your troops. Now, therefore, the violation is with you. You choose your own time and place for an attack upon our defenseless people, and should therefore see that the innocent and defenseless of your own people are out of the way before you make the attack; for rest assured that the fire will be returned, and we will not hold ourselves answerable for the death of the innocent. If we have ever fired upon your 'women and children,' it was done here at Baton Rouge, when an attempt was made to kill one of our officers, landing in a small boat manned by four boys. They were, when in the act of landing, mostly wounded by the fire of some thirty or forty horsemen, who chivalrously galloped out of the town, leaving the women and children to bear the brunt of our vengeance. At Grand Gulf, also, our transports were fired upon in passing, which caused the place to be shelled, with what effect I know not; but I do know that the fate of a town is at all times in the hands of the military commandant, who may at pleasure draw the enemy's fire upon it, and the community is made to suffer for the act of its military.

"The only instance I have known where the language of your letter could possibly apply took place at New Orleans, on the day when we passed up in front of the city, while it was still in your possession, by your soldiers firing on the crowd. I trust, however, that the time is past when women and children will be subjected by their military men to the horrors of war; it is enough for them to be subjected to the incidental inconveniences, privations, and sufferings.

"If any such things have occurred as the slaying of women and children, or innocent people, I feel well assured that it was caused by the act of your military, and much against the will of our officers; for, as Lieutenant Commanding Nichols informs the mayor, we war not against defenseless persons, but against those in open rebellion against our country, and desire to limit our punishment to them, though it may not be always in our power to do so.

"Very respectfully, your obedient servant, D. G. FARRAGUT.

"Major General MANSFIELD LOVELL."

[1] So little notion was there of any farther struggle for the possession of Vicksburg, that we find, in an intercepted letter from Mr. Davis's niece, dated May 7, 1862, and addressed to her mother in Mississippi, the following passage: "Uncle Jeff. thinks you are safe at home, as there will be no resistance at Vicksburg, and the Yankees will hardly occupy it, and, even if they did, the army would gain nothing by marching into the country, and a few soldiers would be afraid to go so far into the interior."

[2] This was Captain Craven's estimate (*Rep. Sec. Navy, Accompanying Documents*, p. 809). This estimate tallies with that given by A. S. Abrams, one of the Vicksburg garrison. (See *Abrams's Siege of Vicksburg*, pp. 6 and 7.)

three steam-sloops Brooklyn, Hartford, and Richmond, and the gun-boats Iroquois, Oneida, Wissahickon, Sciota, Winona, Pinola, and Kennebec. The fleet was to form a double line of sailing, so that the gun-boats, advancing in the order named, should form a second line, and fire between the ships. The Hartford, as occasion offered, was to fire her bow guns on the forts at the upper end of the town, while the broadside batteries of all the ships were to be particularly directed to the guns in the forts below and on the heights. "When close enough," ordered Farragut, "give them grape." Upon reaching the bend of the river, which was just above Vicksburg, the Wissahickon, Sciota, Winona, and Pinola were in any case to continue their course, but the other gun-boats were to drop down the river again if the enemy's batteries were not thoroughly silenced.

The signal to weigh anchor was given at 2 A.M. on the 28th. At four o'clock, as had been ordered, Porter opened fire from the mortars, and almost at the same moment the Confederates fired their first gun, which was returned by the leading vessels of the fleet as they came up. On Farragut's starboard quarter, Porter brought up the Octorara, Westfield, Clifton, Jackson, Harriet Lane, and Owasco, and united in the attack. By the united efforts of the fleet and the mortar flotilla the Confederate guns were soon silenced, sometimes not replying for several minutes, and then again with but a single gun. The Hartford, in its attack upon the summit batteries, succeeded better than had been expected. The passage up the river was slow, the flag-ship having but eight pounds of steam, and even stopping once in order that the vessels in its stern might close up. The Brooklyn, Kennebec, and Katahdin failed to follow the flag-ship past the batteries, and turned back. The commanders of these vessels gave various explanations of this failure, but they do not seem to have been satisfactory to the commander of the fleet. The vessels which succeeded in passing received some injury, not of a serious character, from the upper batteries, after the latter had been passed, and suffered a loss in men of fifteen killed and thirty wounded. On the vessels which failed to pass there were no casualties. General Williams, on the Louisiana side, had a battery in operation during the action, thus affording a slight support to the fleet.

PORTER'S MORTAR FLEET IN TRIM.

The whole significance of this bold affair is summed up in a few words by Admiral Farragut, namely, "that the forts can be passed; and we have done it, and can do it again as often as may be required of us." And that was all. We can do no more, he added, than silence the batteries for a time, as long as the enemy has a large force behind the hills to prevent our landing and holding the place. He said that it was impossible to take Vicksburg without an army of from 12,000 to 15,000 men. Admiral Porter, in his official report of the action on the 28th, says: "It is to be regretted that a combined attack of army and navy had not been made, by which something more substantial might have been accomplished. Such an attack, I think, would have resulted in the capture of the city. Ships and mortar vessels can keep full possession of the river and places near the water's edge, but they can not crawl up hills 800 feet high, and it is that part of Vicksburg which must be taken by the army. If it was intended merely to pass the batteries at Vicksburg, and make a junction with the fleet of Flag-officer Davis, the navy did it most gallantly and fearlessly.[1] It was as handsome a thing as has been done during the war, for the batteries to be passed extended full three miles, with a three-knot current against ships that could not make eight knots under the most favorable circumstances."

By six o'clock the batteries were passed, and Farragut met Lieutenant Colonel Charles Rivers Ellet, of the ram fleet, who had made his way down the river bank during the night, and who now offered to forward communications to Flag-officer Davis, and to General Halleck, then at Memphis. After effecting a junction with Davis, Farragut applied to Halleck for a military force to co-operate in an immediate attack on Vicksburg. Halleck's reply on the 3d of July was an utter disappointment.

In the mean while Vicksburg was subjected to a bombardment from the mortar-boats above and below. When Farragut passed the batteries there were but few guns mounted.[1] During the progress of the bombardment which followed, General Earl Van Dorn[2] was sent to Vicksburg, and placed in command over Brigadier General M. L. Smith. Soon afterward the garrison was re-enforced by Breckinridge's brigade from Beauregard's army. Van Dorn's appointment to this post, for which he certainly had no peculiar fitness, was received by the Mississippians with enthusiastic pleasure. The hope of successful resistance at this point was every day growing brighter. It was with no little pride that the citizens of Vicksburg contrasted their own position, and the fate of their city thus far, with what they naturally regarded the too facile surrender of other posts on the river. In this pride the ladies of the heroic city had their full share. On the morning of June 28, when Farragut's fleet was on its way past the city, and shells were falling like hail in the streets, crowds of these enthusiastic ladies might have been seen on the Court-house, the "Sky Parlor," and other prominent places in the city, gazing upon "the magnificent scene."[3]

While Vicksburg was being bombarded by mortars, Farragut and Davis

[1] In regard to the conduct of his own men in the bombardment, Admiral Porter says: "They know no weariness, and they really seem to take a delight in mortar-firing, which is painful even to those accustomed to it. It requires more than ordinary zeal to stand the ordeal. Though I may have been at times exacting and fault-finding with them for not conforming to the rules of the service (which requires the education of a lifetime to learn), yet I can not withhold my applause when I see these men working with such earnest and untiring devotion to their duties while under fire."—*Rep. Sec. Navy*, 1862, *Acc. Doc.*, p. 410.

[1] Abrams says only seven.—*Siege Vicks.*, p. 6. This estimate is probably considerably below the mark.

[2] "This doughty Confederate cavalier, of Rosecrans's class at West Point, has greatly astonished his old associates. West Point men of his time remember him as a small, handsome, modest youth, literally at the foot of his class. In Mexico he was on the staff of General P. F. Smith, and was very popular, for to his other qualities he added dashing bravery. His conspicuous course in the rebel interests at the breaking out of the war deceived them into thinking him a general. A good soldier he certainly was—bravo, dashing, a splendid horseman, but he lacked *head*, and was always taking his men into *culs de sacs*. He died by the hand of a man who believed he had seduced his wife."—Coppee's *Grant and his Campaigns*, p. 183.

[3] Abrams's *Siege Vicks.*, p. 7.

organized an expedition to ascend the Yazoo River. General Williams offered to send up a few sharp-shooters from his army to co-operate with the gun-boats Tyler, Carondelet, and the ram Queen of the West, which formed the naval part of the expedition. The object of the movement was to procure correct information concerning the obstructions and defenses of the river. It was known that eighty miles from the mouth there was a raft obstructing the passage with a battery near it below, and above, the new Confederate ram Arkansas, "a vessel represented to be well protected by iron, and very formidable in her battery." To find and capture this ram was the most important part of the expedition. The gun-boats, early on the morning of July 15, had scarcely passed the mouth of the Yazoo when they encountered the Arkansas coming down. This vessel, in her construction, resembled the Louisiana and Mississippi, destroyed at New Orleans. She was built at Memphis, and at the time of the capture of this place she succeeded in escaping up the Yazoo, while a consort of hers, built in the same manner, was destroyed. She was a sea-going steamer of 1200 tons. Her cut-water was a sharp, cast-iron, solid beak. She was thoroughly covered with T rail iron, with heavy bulwarks of thick timber, with cotton-pressed casemating, impervious to shot. Her port-holes were small, with heavy iron shutters; all her machinery was below the water-line, and she had a battery of ten guns.[1] She was commanded by Isaac N. Brown, and had a picked crew. The gun-boats met the ram about six miles above the mouth of the Yazoo. They were commanded, the Carondelet by Captain H. Walke, the Tyler by Captain Gwin, and the ram Queen of the West by Colonel Alfred Ellet. When the ram was discovered, the gun-boats were proceeding at intervals of a mile apart, the Queen of the West ahead, the Tyler next, and the Carondelet behind. The result of a conflict with the Arkansas was, to say the least, uncertain, and all the national vessels reversed their course, and retreated down the river, keeping up a running fight with the ram for about an hour. The firing was distinctly heard by both the squadrons in the Mississippi, and it was supposed that the gun-boats were engaging batteries. But the true cause of the firing became apparent when

MORTAR BOATS FIRING ON VICKSBURG AT NIGHT.

the Tyler was seen to proceed from the mouth of the Yazoo, with the Arkansas closely following. It was to Admiral Farragut a moment of surprise and of mortification. Had the event been anticipated, the fate of the Arkansas could have been decided in thirty minutes. As it was, the vessels of the fleet were lying with low fires, but none of them had steam, or could get it up in time for so instant an emergency, and the ram escaped without serious injury, though she received a broadside fire from all the national vessels. The Benton, it is true, got under way and pursued the ram for some distance, but at her snail's pace the pursuit seemed only less ludicrous than the situation which would have followed if she had been so unfortunate as to overtake and come into close quarters with her adversary.

DAVIS'S FLEET ON ITS WAY TO JOIN FARRAGUT'S.

Thus far the result of the ram's appearance had not been seriously disastrous. Indeed, though this was not known at the time to her opponents, she was incapable of inflicting a very severe blow. Her smoke-stack had been shivered in pieces early in the action, and for want of steam she could not be used as a ram with any effect. The Carondelet had run ashore, her wheel-ropes being shot away, and would probably have fallen a prey to the Arkansas if the latter had had leisure for improving her opportunity. The Tyler was partially injured. About thirty men on the Federal side were killed, wounded, or missing, and many of these casualties occurred among Williams's sharp-shooters, who were especially exposed. The loss on the Arkansas was ten killed and fifteen wounded.

Partly to support the few vessels of his fleet on the Lower Mississippi,

[1] *Naval Scenes on the Western Waters*, p. 59.

THE ARKANSAS RUNNING THROUGH THE UNION FLEET OFF VICKSBURG.

and partly to make another attempt against the Arkansas, Admiral Farragut determined, on the night of the 15th, to repass the Vicksburg batteries. He was supported by Davis's squadron and the mortar flotilla; but the ram, lodged under the guns of Vicksburg, was so well concealed by her situation that she escaped the destruction intended for her.

On the 22d another attack was made upon the ram, which now lay between two forts at the upper bend of the river. Farragut's fleet was four miles below, and it was understood that he would receive the ram if she should attempt to escape down the river. The attack was made by the Queen of the West, commanded by Colonel Ellet, and the Essex, under Commander W. D. Porter; but it proved a failure. The Queen of the West and the Essex passed down under cover of a fire opened upon the upper batteries by the Benton, Cincinnati, and Louisville. The Essex boldly attacked the ram, but the bow-line of the latter being let go, the current drifted her stern on, and the gun-boat, missing the Arkansas, ran ashore. There was less than a rod's distance between the two vessels, and in these close quarters the three nine-inch guns of the Essex told with serious effect upon the ram. The Queen of the West also ran at the ram, but was so severely damaged by the fire from the shore that she with difficulty escaped. "This attempt on the part of Colonel Ellet," says Farragut, "was a daring act, and one from which both Flag-officer Davis and myself tried to deter him." The Sumter, which had come down with the other vessels, on account of some misunderstanding did not join in the attack. The Essex remained aground for ten minutes, under a heavy fire, and then, getting afloat, ran down to Farragut's fleet through a storm of shot and shell, but without receiving a single blow after she left the upper forts. From the latter and from the ram she was penetrated with three projectiles, one of which went through her casemates, and, exploding inside, killed one man and wounded three of her crew. The Queen of the West steamed back, exposed to the fire from the shore and struggling against the current of the river, to Davis's squadron. She had on board two officers, four soldiers, and three negro firemen, not one of whom were injured.

Farragut had on the 20th received an order to descend the river to New Orleans. Owing to the fall in the river, this was becoming an imperative necessity. Waiting only a day or two after the engagement with the ram, and until General Williams had completed his arrangements for departure with his small force, he proceeded to obey this order. It was arranged that the Essex and Sumter, under Commander W. D. Porter, should take charge of the lower part of the river. Left in this situation, the fleet on the Mississippi, so far from being competent to make any offensive movement, was likely to have difficulty in holding its ground against the enemy, who now had, besides the Arkansas, two gun-boats on the Red River and two on the Yazoo. "I presume," says Farragut, writing from New Orleans, July 29, "Flag-officer Davis will destroy those in the Yazoo; and my gun-boats chased the Music and Webb up the Red River, but drew too much water to go far."

The situation before Vicksburg, therefore, at the beginning of August, was discouraging. There was no longer any co-operating army. Flag-officer Davis's fleet was reduced in power, both by the absence of a large number of gun-boats—undergoing repairs or engaged in special duty—and by sickness among the men.[1] The garrison of Vicksburg had been largely increased, nearly doubled, and a large number of additional guns had been mounted in the batteries. The canal, which had been finished for about ten days, had proved a failure. The bulkhead was knocked away on the 22d of July, but the Mississippi, which had so often been known to change its channel in a single night on the slightest occasion, refused by a singular caprice to take the course which General Williams had opened for it, and Vicksburg, instead of becoming an inland city, had joyful occasion for self-congratulation and for laughter at the foiled project of "the Yankees." But, although the canal failed to answer the purpose for which it had been constructed, it was of great service so long as Williams remained. It had been made a means of defense "by constructing a continued breastwork and rifle-pit on the lower border, and an angle on the upper border to enfilade the canal where it was crossed by the levee. This levee, distinguished as the *new* levee, formed in itself a convenient breastwork."[2] When Williams left, however, it was no longer safe for the ordnance, commissary, hospital, and mail boats to lie at the bank. It was also impossible to maintain communication with the vessels below Vicksburg across the neck, and the latter could no longer be used to co-operate in a bombardment from below. The Sumter and Essex must now depend upon Baton Rouge and New Orleans for their supplies. Davis found, moreover, that he would be compelled to exhaust a large measure of his force in maintaining his own connection with Cairo. He determined, therefore, to abandon his position before Vicksburg, and withdraw to the mouth of the Yazoo River. From this point there was a lull of five months in the operations against Vicksburg.

The Confederate line of defense in the West at this time ran from Vicks-

BATON ROUGE, LOUISIANA.

[1] Davis writes, July 28, just before Williams's departure, thus: "My force is also reduced by the absence of eight gun-boats, three of which are guarding important points on the river, and five of which are undergoing repairs. I have said that I am in want of 500 men to insure the efficiency of the flotilla. In this calculation I make allowance for the return to duty of many of the sick; but 600 men would not be too many to send to me. The most sickly part of the season is approaching, and the Department would be surprised to see how the most healthy men wilt and break down under the ceaseless and exhausting heat of this pernicious climate. Men who are apparently in health at the close of the day's work, sink away and die suddenly at night under the combined effects of heat and malarial poison. The enemy, however, suffers a great deal more than we do. He counts seventeen or twenty thousand men on his rolls, but can hardly muster five thousand in his ranks. To sickness are added, in his case, the want of hospital accommodations, the want of medicines, and the want of suitable food. I learn that General Williams is about to move down the river. Should it prove so, it will be very unfortunate in its results. This is one of the points at which the co-operation of the army is most essential."

[2] *Rep. Sec. Navy*, 1862, *Acc. Doc.*, p. 517.

burg southward parallel with the river, and from the same point deflected northward to the northern boundary of the State of Mississippi, and thence turned eastward, following the Virginia and East Tennessee Railroad. Morgan and Forrest had just been raiding through Kentucky and Tennessee, preparatory to Bragg's invasion. General Grant, on the northern border of Mississippi, was confronted by large Confederate armies under Brice, Lovell, and Van Dorn. As soon as General Williams left Vicksburg, Breckinridge withdrew his division in order to attack Baton Rouge, and, in co-operation with the ram Arkansas, to secure the Lower Mississippi. If the expedition could have been undertaken a few days sooner, it would have been a success so far as Baton Rouge was concerned. Breckinridge doubtless knew that a large proportion of Williams's troops were suffering from sickness. He could not have reckoned too strongly upon this element in his favor, for when Williams left Vicksburg he had scarcely well soldiers enough to take care of the sick ones.

Breckinridge's force received marching orders on the 26th of July. It was transported by railroad as far as Tangipahoa, in St. Helena Parish, Louisiana, which became the base of operations. Between forty and fifty miles from this place, at Camp Moore, on the Comite River, there was a body of Louisiana troops being fitted for active duty in the field. There were only one or two regiments here, with a battery, and a few cavalry, the whole under the command of General Ruggles. This became one of the two columns acting against Baton Rouge, and remained under Ruggles's immediate command, while the column from Vicksburg was assigned to General Charles Clarke. The latter consisted of two brigades, of four regiments, or parts of regiments, each. The troops of this column were all veterans. The design was to attack Baton Rouge from the rear, while the Arkansas, with the help of the Webb and Music from the Red River, engaged the Federal gun-boats. Several days were occupied in waiting until the ram should have recovered from the wounds inflicted upon her in her recent conflicts with the Mississippi squadron. At length Van Dorn telegraphed to Breckinridge that the ram was ready, and would be due at Baton Rouge on the morning of August 5th, which time, therefore, was fixed for the attack.

General Williams had not returned to Baton Rouge a moment too soon. He was well aware of the enemy's design, and industriously provided for the coming battle. On the river were the Essex, Cayuga, Sumter, Kineo, and Katahdin. On the land Williams had nearly 2500 men available for action. These were encamped in the rear of the city, and it was determined to meet the enemy just on the skirts of the town, and there dispute his nearer approach.

The march to Comite River from Tangipahoa, a distance of about fifty miles, was at this season very exhausting to the Confederates under Breckinridge. The heat was intense, and the men fell rapidly out of the ranks from sickness or fatigue. Almost every farm-house on the roadside was converted into a hospital. There was a brief halt at Camp Moore, and on the 4th, a little before midnight, the two columns were pushing on over a smooth sandy road that led through well-cultivated plantations to Baton Rouge. About dawn, when these columns were within three miles of the city, there occurred a strange misadventure. They were passing by a piece of woods when they were fired upon by a company of partisan rangers, who mistook them for Federal troops. Before the mistake was rectified several casualties had occurred, and the line had been thrown into confusion. General Helm, commanding one of the brigades, was disabled by the fall of his horse into a ditch, and was withdrawn from the field. It was here that Captain Alexander A. Todd, a brother-in-law of President Lincoln and an officer on General Helm's staff, met his end. He was instantly killed by a shot from the woods.[1] Order was soon restored, and the columns marched on, Clarke's to the right and Ruggles's to the left. They first appeared in the open fields bordering on the Greenwell Springs Road, toward the upper part of the city and southeast of the Arsenal. Here they attempted without success to draw out the national forces. Failing in this, they veered to the southward a little farther, and it was in the position thus taken that the battle of Baton Rouge was fought.

The streets of the city ran out to the verge of the Federal encampments. The battle-field was flat in surface, extending in the form of an arc about the city from the Arsenal grounds to those of the Capitol. Bayou Gross ran north and east of the Arsenal grounds. Within the latter were two guns, sweeping the field to the left of the Fourth Wisconsin and Ninth Connecticut, on the opposite or right bank of the bayou. In the rear of the centre of the Ninth were two guns, and on the other side of a knoll in the Government Cemetery two more. Farther to the right was the Fourteenth Maine, on the left of the Greenwell Springs Road and in rear of the Bayou Sara Road, which crosses at right angles the two main approaches to the city. In the road itself were four guns, afterward increased to six. On the right of the Greenwell Springs Road was the Twenty-first Indiana (which was under cover of a wood), with the Magnolia Cemetery in its front. To the right

[1] A Confederate, alluding to this event, says: "Captain Todd was a young gentleman of fine accomplishments, great personal daring, exceeding amiability, and the warmest home affections. But the evening before he wrote to his mother, and just before the accident he was conversing with Lieutenant L. E. Payne, ordnance officer of the brigade, communicating the messages he wished conveyed home in case of his fall. . . . Brave boy! he met his end serenely, and his body was interred by gentle and loving hands."

of Magnolia Cemetery the Sixth Michigan continued the line across a country road and another known as the Clay Cut Road, supporting two guns in the country road. The Seventh Vermont was stationed in the rear of the two latter regiments, on the right of the Catholic cemetery. The extreme right was held by the Thirtieth Massachusetts, a short distance in the rear of the Capitol, and supporting Nims's Battery. Considering that the attack was expected on the Greenwell Springs Road, this disposition of force was an admirable one, the only fault consisting in the unfortunate position of the encampments of the Fourteenth Maine and Twenty-first Indiana, which were in front of those regiments, and liable to capture in case of their retreat, an event which really did occur.[1]

The Confederates at daylight drove back the Federal pickets. General Breckinridge in person led the right wing, his young son, Cabell, acting as aid-de-camp. The full force of the first determined attack fell upon the Indiana, Maine, and Michigan regiments. The resistance was obstinate. The Federal flanks were called in to support the centre; but the enemy succeeded, after a sharp conflict, in driving in the regiments in the advanced front and capturing their encampments. The Seventh Vermont failed to give efficient support at the critical moment, and Colonel Roberts, its commander, was killed while vainly attempting to urge forward his men. "He was worthy," said General Butler, "of a better disciplined regiment and a better fate." The Indiana regiment lost all its field-officers before retreating. General Williams had just given the order for the line to fall back, when, seeing the condition of this regiment, he advanced to its front, and told the Indianians that, in the absence of their officers, he would lead them himself. Scarcely had the responding cheers died away when he fell, mortally wounded.[2] The batteries had done good execution. The soldiers, though many of them had never seen a battle before, disputed bravely every advance of

DEATH OF GENERAL THOMAS WILLIAMS.

the enemy. It had come at length to a hand-to-hand conflict, the result of which seemed to be in favor of the Confederates. As the national forces withdrew from the vicinity of Magnolia Cemetery, where had been the deadliest conflict, the gun-boats in the river opened on both of the enemy's flanks, their fire over the city being directed by a system of signals from the Capitol, instituted by Lieutenant Ransom.

In the mean time Breckinridge was listening anxiously in the intervals of conflict for the guns of the Arkansas; but he heard them not. About six miles from the city the ram had stopped in her progress down the river, unable to proceed on account of her inefficient engine machinery. She had left Brown, her former commander, sick at Vicksburg, and was now commanded by Lieutenant Stevens. Her crew numbered 180 men, well chosen; she had ten heavy guns (six 8-inch and four 50-pounders), but could not be brought into action.

Disappointed at the non-appearance of this indispensable ally, and seeing

[1] See *Weitzel's Report in Reb. Rec.*, vol. v., p. 301, *Doc.* Fletcher, an English historian of the war, says: "The position does not appear to have been well selected, as in front of the centre of the line, between the two roads, was a large cemetery, overgrown with high grass, and affording both cover for an advancing enemy, and, when occupied, a strong offensive position." This is probably true so far as the position was related to the shape which the attack finally took.

[2] The following General Order (No. 56) was issued by General Butler after the battle:

"The commanding general announces to the Army of the Gulf the sad event of the death of Brigadier General Thomas Williams, commanding Second Brigade, in camp at Baton Rouge.

"The victorious achievement—the repulse of the division of Major General Breckinridge by the troops led by General Williams, and the destruction of the mail-clad Arkansas by Captain Porter, of the Navy—is made sorrowful by the fall of our brave, gallant, and successful fellow-soldier.

"General Williams graduated at West Point in 1837; at once joined the Fourth Artillery in Florida, where he served with distinction; was thrice breveted for gallant and meritorious services in Mexico as a member of General Scott's staff. His life was that of a soldier devoted to his country's service. His country mourns in sympathy with his wife and children, now that country's core and precious charge.

"'We, his comrades in arms, who had learned to love him, weep the true friend, the gallant gentleman, the brave soldier, the accomplished officer, and the devoted Christian. All this and more went out when Williams died.' By a singular felicity, the manner of his death illustrated each of these generous qualities.

"The chivalric American gentleman, he gave up the vantage of the cover of the houses of the city, forming his lines in the open field, lest the women and children of his enemies should be hurt in the fight.

"A good general, he made his dispositions and prepared for battle at break of day, when he met his foe.

"A brave soldier, he received the death-shot leading his men.

"A patriot hero, he was fighting the battle, and died as went up the cheer of victory.

"A Christian, he sleeps in the hope of the blessed Redeemer.

"His virtues we can not exceed; his example we may emulate; and, mourning his death, we pray, 'May our last end be like his.'"

DESTRUCTION OF THE ARKANSAS.

the impossibility of attempting to fight the national infantry, artillery, and gun-boats at the same time, Breckinridge ordered the captured camps to be burned as a preliminary to withdrawal from the field. His forces found some shelter from the shells of the fleet in the woods which skirted the battle-field all around. It was not noon yet when the battle was over, and the field was left in possession of the national forces, under Colonel Cahill, who had succeeded to the command after the death of General Williams.

The enemy had suffered severe loss, especially in officers, among whom General Clarke was left in our hands mortally wounded. His dead, to the number of seventy, were left upon the field, so hasty had been his retreat. The battle-field gave striking evidence of the nature of the conflict. In front of the Indiana and Michigan regiments some of the enemy were found who had been killed with rails, which the Union soldiers, having lost their arms, had used as weapons. "In one spot," says an eye-witness, "behind a beautiful tomb, with effigies of infant children kneeling, twelve dead rebels were found in one heap."

The forces engaged in the battle, though variously estimated, were probably not very far from equal.[1] The loss on the national side was 90 killed and 250 wounded.

The morning after the battle, the Essex, accompanied by the Cayuga and Sumter, advanced up the river to where the Arkansas was lying, abandoned by her companions, the Webb and Music. There was no serious conflict. Commander W. D. Porter engaged the ram for a short time, when the latter was fired, deserted, and then blown up. Very soon the vessels of the national fleet saw floating past them the shattered fragments of their most formidable antagonist on the Mississippi. In informing the Naval Secretary of this event, Admiral Farragut said: "It is one of the happiest moments of my life that I am able to inform the Department of the destruction of the ram Arkansas, not because I held the iron-clad in such terror, but because the community did."

A few days after the battle (August 16) Baton Rouge was evacuated by the national troops, and the place was afterward held by the naval force.

Sherman had been confirmed major general of volunteers on the 1st of May, 1862. In urging this appointment, Halleck, writing from the West shortly after the battle of Shiloh, said: "It is the unanimous opinion here that Brigadier General W. T. Sherman saved the fortunes of the day on the 6th, and contributed largely to the glorious victory of the 7th." At the time when Halleck wrote thus, Grant was under a cloud; his military qualities were scarcely appreciated; he was thrust somewhat into the background, and subjected to much mortification, enjoying little of that confidence which he afterward won from the government. But in this unfortunate period of his career his rightful claims were supported heartily and in full by General Sherman.[2] Afterward when, at the very close of the war, the latter was for one single act bitterly and unjustly calumniated, he received from General Grant a full return of sympathy and support. Grant had always believed in Sherman, even when the latter had been called insane. He always gave him the most responsible position under his command. In recommending his promotion to the rank of brigadier general in the regular army in 1863, he says: "At the battle of Shiloh, on the first day, he held, with raw troops, the key-point of the landing. It is no disparagement to any other officer to say that I do not believe there was another division commander on the field who had the skill and experience to have done it. To his individual efforts I am indebted for the success of that battle."

When Halleck was called to Washington in July, 1862, to assume the duties of general-in-chief, the Department of the Mississippi was assigned to the hero of Fort Donelson.[1] There was at that time a lull in military operations, and Grant had leisure to give attention to the general administration of affairs in this department. One of the very first things which he did was to send Sherman, with his own and Hurlbut's divisions, to occupy Memphis as its military commander. Sherman assumed command of the district, superseding General Hovey, on the 21st of July, stationing his own division in Fort Pickering, Hurlbut's on the river below, and sending the other troops to Helena. He retained the mayor and other civil officers of the city in their offices, and confined the action of provost-marshal guards to persons in the military service, and to buildings and grounds used by the army. All citizens were required to yield obedience to the United States government or leave the district; if they staid, and gave aid to the enemy, they were to be treated as spies. He did not exact from all a formal oath of allegiance. He required no military passports for inland travel, but he restricted it to the five main roads leading from the city, and there was a minute inspection of all persons and property going in or out. The principal matter requiring stringent regulations was that of trade. The exportation of salt and of all war material was prohibited. All cotton bought beyond the lines and brought in had to be purchased on contracts for payment at the close of the war, because, if paid for in coin or in treasury notes, these were almost always sure to find their way into the coffers of the Confederate treasury.

As the army penetrated the southern districts along the Mississippi, the temptation to indulge in cotton speculation became a great obstruction to military discipline. But, notwithstanding this, it was found expedient to allow a partial trade in cotton, though every effort was made by General Grant to prevent this commerce from demoralizing his subordinate officers. It was manifestly the policy of the government to drain the South of its cotton. This important staple was an invaluable aid to the enemy; it was a part of his war material, since his foreign loans were based entirely upon a cotton basis. It seemed wise, therefore, to make it for the interest of Southern cotton-holders to retain the staple, instead of burning it or allowing it to pass into the hands of the Confederate government. This temptation was afforded by allowing a partial trade.[3]

[1] Whatever odds there may have been were certainly in favor of the Confederates. The wide discrepancy in the estimates given is somewhat singular. Pollard says Breckinridge had less than 3000 men, and Williams nearly 6000. Abbott, on the other hand, makes Williams's force less than 2500, and Breckinridge's 8000. The only authority for this latter estimate of the enemy's numbers is a soldier's letter published in the *Rebellion Record* (vol. v., p. 307, *Doc.*). This letter is throughout wholly unreliable. In a later statement Abbott estimates the enemy's force at 5000. Cahill makes Williams's force 2500, and that of the enemy ten regiments, or 5000 men. Weitzel estimates Breckinridge's force at 6000. Fletcher makes the numbers on both sides about 4000. It is possible that the enemy may have numbered between 3000 and 4000; Williams certainly had not 3000 men.

[2] A staff-officer of General Grant thus writes of this period: "La Fontaine truthfully says, '*Aucun chemin de fleurs ne conduit à la gloire.*' Detraction was busy with her poisonous tongue. Grant was more bitterly assailed now than at any previous time, as a 'butcher,' as 'incompetent,' and as being a 'drunkard.' Some one was disparaging Grant in Sherman's presence, when the latter broke out with, 'It won't do, sir, it won't do; Grant is a great general! He stood by me when I was crazy, and I stood by him when he was drunk, and now, sir, we stand by each other.'"

[1] It was on October 16, 1862, that General Grant was made commander of the Department of the Tennessee, this department being made to include Cairo, Forts Henry and Donelson, Northern Mississippi, and portions of Kentucky and Tennessee west of the Tennessee River.

[3] The connection of the cotton question with the Confederate conduct of the war is so important that some of its details may be interesting to the reader.

The first auction sale of confiscated cotton from Port Royal took place in New York on the 10th of June, 1862. At this sale seventy-nine bales were sold, at an average of sixty cents per pound. From this time on to the close of the war such sales were quite frequent. Before a single bale of cotton had been confiscated, however, the Confederates had contemplated the possibility of such conquests on the part of the United States government as would bring into its possession a portion of their accumulated stores. As early as February 26, 1862, a meeting of cotton and tobacco planters was held at Richmond to consider the expediency of the purchase by the Confederacy, or of a voluntary destruction of the entire tobacco and cotton crop. The *Richmond Examiner* describes the audience as "one of the largest, wealthiest, and most intellectual meetings" ever as-

COTTON HOARDS IN SOUTHERN SWAMPS.

Toward the close of October Sherman was summoned to meet Grant at Columbus for military consultation. The Department of the Mississippi had been broken up, and General Grant was at the head of the Department of the Tennessee. About this time Rosecrans assumed command of the Department of the Cumberland. Corinth and Perryville had been fought, and both battles—that of Corinth especially—had resulted in important national victories. The objective point in the campaign now contemplated by General Grant was Vicksburg.

MAP OF THE MISSISSIPPI CENTRAL RAILROAD.

During the interval of some months in which Vicksburg had been left undisturbed, the enemy had strengthened its fortifications. Several additional batteries had been erected above the town, and a strong line of defenses had been thrown up from Chickasaw Bayou to Haines's Bluff on the Yazoo River. The bluff itself had been fortified, and opposed an insuperable obstacle to the ascent of the national fleet farther up the river. Port Hudson, in the mean time, had become a strong-hold second only to Vicksburg in importance, and between these two points the Mississippi (as also the Red River) was in full possession of the Confederates, who had thus an opportunity of availing themselves, to an almost unlimited extent, of the abundant supplies to be obtained from Louisiana and Texas. After Van Dorn's defeat at Corinth, he had been superseded by John C. Pemberton, a favorite of President Davis, who, that he might outrank Van Dorn and Lovell, had been made a lieutenant general. This officer has been very severely criticised by Southern writers on the ground of his general incompetency for the position assigned him, and, in particular, for his apathy during this important period, when the opportunities for provisioning Vicksburg and increasing its efficiency as a defensive point appear to have been neglected. He made his head-quarters, it is said, at this time rather at Jackson than at Vicksburg, only paying an occasional visit to Vicksburg. He thought, probably, and with good reason, that his presence was imperatively demanded to the rear and westward of Vicksburg, to guard against

sembled in that city. The speeches made and the resolutions adopted were certainly characteristic. General T. J. Green, of North Carolina, having called the meeting to order, the Hon. C. K. Marshall arose to read the resolutions. "We have it in our power," he said, by way of preface, "to do what will have a serious influence not only within the city of Richmond, but may ameliorate the condition of the race of mankind at large."

The following is a copy of the resolutions:

"Whereas, the government of the United States have made an unprovoked, flagrant, and wicked war on the government and people of the Confederate States, and have conducted that war on principles hitherto unknown among civilized nations; and, whereas, we feel that our only safety against so ruthless and unrelenting a foe is to be found in the courage, patriotism, and self-sacrificing spirit of our people; and, whereas, no sacrifice, however enormous, is too great if it only brings us freedom from our oppressors; and, whereas, the tyrants and despots of the North have openly proclaimed their purpose to desolate our homes and appropriate our property to their own use, and have, in various instances, carried the infamous threat into practical execution by plundering our people of cotton, tobacco, rice, and other property; and, whereas, fire, when applied by heroic hands, is more formidable than the sword, therefore it is by this meeting

"*Resolved*, That as a means of national safety, dictated alike by military necessity and true patriotism, we deem it the imperative duty of this government to adopt measures for the purchase of the entire crops of cotton and tobacco now on hand, with the purpose of at once preventing the appropriation of them by the invaders of our soil and country, and making a fair and equitable compensation for the same to their owners, by such arrangements as shall enable the government to meet the debt incurred thereby without involving the public treasury in any serious liability on account of the said purchase. Certificate of government liability to be given for the entire property.

"*Resolved*, That, as the owners of these great staples, the government would hold in its hands the power of removing so great temptation from the path of the Federal army, now making its raids into our country, and robbing our citizens under the avowed pledges of supplying, by force, the markets of the world with these valuable articles of demand, which must necessarily be done, if those pledges are redeemed, by the total bankruptcy of our planting interests on the one hand, and the utter subjugation and enslavement of the people of the South on the other.

"*Resolved*, That, possessed of these products, it would become the solemn duty of the government to take immediate action through commissioners appointed for that purpose, or otherwise to take an account of such portions of said crops as are at exposed places, first furnishing the owners thereof with certificates of the amount and value of their crops as evidences of debt by the government therefor, and consign the property to the devouring flames.

"*Resolved*, That in case the owners of said staples decline to accept the terms offered by the government, a tax of —— cents per pound should be assessed and collected from such crops, and if finally lost or sacrificed, as a measure of public safety thereafter, such owners should not be allowed any compensation for the same.

"*Resolved*, That where other articles of produce or stock are exposed to the raids of the enemy, they should be removed if practicable, and if not practicable, an inventory of them should be taken, with an estimate of their value, by military authority, or a government agent, or, in the absence of either, by competent citizens, and certified to by them, and said property forthwith destroyed, and the parties thus deprived of their property should be indemnified by the government."

Mr. Marshall then made a speech on the resolutions. He alluded in terms so extravagant as to appear ludicrous, to the expedients to which the Confederates had been driven by the blockade. "Men," he said, "have seized pikes and lances, for want of proper arms, to defend their wives, and daughters, and mothers." He thought the Richmond government did not fully appreciate the exigency of the times. If it had purchased the first cotton crop the Southern navy might then have boasted of thirty such vessels as the Merrimac. The last crop was now actually rotting unbaled. They had been taught to believe that France and England wanted cotton so badly that they would come and get it. Why didn't they come? He had begun to doubt whether there were such countries as France and England. "The enemy found cotton at Ship Island; some, it is true, they found in flames, but not enough of it. At Florence they went up and took an inconsiderable quantity. No one seemed to think of setting fire to it. At Nashville they will perhaps get fifty thousand bales, and the owners, to save their property, will have to swear allegiance to that miserable tyrant, Abe Lincoln. And presently they will descend the Mississippi with perhaps fifty gun-boats, and compel the negroes to load them with cotton, and send it to Europe, and say, We have opened a cotton port—there is the evidence. I want us to do something manly—something grand. I want the Confederate government to buy all the cotton, and, if need be, destroy it. If one of those pillars which support this temple were cotton, and the other tobacco, and England, France, Russia, and the United States of America, *and ourselves* depended on them for existence, and it were necessary, I would, Samson-like, drag them down, *and let one universal ruin overwhelm civilization*. Suppose, as these resolutions propose, the government buys the cotton and tobacco crops, it is not to be expected that it will soon be able to pay for them. Hardships will be the consequence. Great numbers must suffer. A tax will have to be imposed. I will suppose that half of the cotton and tobacco crop has been burned. My cotton has been burned, and I have received seven cents a pound from the government, while my neighbor's, whose crop has not been burned, has been enhanced double in value. His small crop of cotton would be a fortune, yet who among us would hesitate to apply the torch to it sooner than it should fall into the hands of the enemy? But suppose the government were to buy the whole crop, and determine to burn it (as I want them to do), that the world may see that this little republic, as they may choose to consider us, can strike a blow that will send consternation through the world, while they are talking about conquering the republic and hanging the President. I want the government to come forward and say, Here is the money for four million bales of cotton, and give it to her commissioners, and say, Burn it. I want the government to go in search of the cotton, instead of leaving it to be captured by her [that is, the enemy's] iron-clad steamers. The government have two million of bales as a financial measure. There are some gentlemen present who raise as much as four thousand bales of cotton, and who say they will themselves burn it, indemnity or not, rather than the Yankees shall get possession of it. A lady of my acquaintance has said she will not only burn her crop, but her house itself, and take to the forest, rather than see the enemy possess it. We shall ruin our own interest by letting this crop lie here, and putting another crop upon it. Cotton, instead of being ten cents, will not command more than three cents. Suppose the blockade were opened now, we could not get it to market by August. The boats which used to transport our cotton are engaged in making war upon us, and some of them have got well peppered at Fort Donelson. They are to-day planting cotton in Texas, and next week they will begin to plant farther north. I needn't enlarge on this to planters. It is evident to them there will be two crops on the market before next January. Some will say we will force England to go to India for cotton. I will say to her, Go! England has spent three hundred and fifty million pounds, and gotten Louisiana planters to go to those distant countries, and has been obliged to give it up as a forlorn hope. But suppose England finds other cotton-fields, I'd like to know if we can't find other spinners for our crops, and be forever independent of her. To the west of us are two little countries, China and Japan. In China they desire to put all their lands in tea, but they fear to discontinue the raising of cotton. If they could get cotton elsewhere, they would put all the land in tea. Well, then, the best spinners and weavers in China can be hired for nine cents a day, and we can get them to spin and weave our cotton long before England can find other cotton-fields. China and Japan are not so distant from us as we were from England when Whitney put the first cotton-gin in operation in Savannah. I hope Congress will take up and pass these resolutions. I have great hope from this meeting. So much have these resolutions to recommend them to the people of the Southern Confederacy, that, were I addressing them to-night, I believe I could get an overwhelming vote for government buying the entire crops of cotton and tobacco, and consigning them to the flames."

Governor Moore, of Kentucky, then addressed the meeting, advocating the resolutions.

On motion of Edmund Ruffin, who fired the first gun of the war, and who blew his brains out after the defeat of the Confederacy, the resolutions were put to vote, and unanimously adopted. Henry S. Foote, the Tennessee senator in the Confederate Congress, was then called to the stand, and strongly approved of the resolutions.

About the same time, a bill was reported in the Confederate Senate to indemnify planters for property destroyed to prevent its capture. The bill, as passed, made no such provision, but made it the duty of all military commanders to destroy all cotton, tobacco, or other property that might be useful to the enemy, if the same could not be safely removed, whenever said property was, in their judgment, liable to capture. It was estimated that the amount of cotton and tobacco which would thus be destroyed would be about one twentieth of the entire crop. On the 3d of March a resolution was passed in the House advising planters to raise provisions and cattle in place of cotton and tobacco. This came before the Senate March 19, and Mr. Brown, of Mississippi, proposed a substitute, in the form of a bill to curtail the cotton crop for 1862, the amount being limited to three bales for each planter, and an additional bale per head for each hand employed in its culture, and inflicting a penalty of forty dollars for every bale raised above this quota. He thought the House measure would affect injuriously the patriotic planters, while it enriched the disloyal.

Mr. Orr, of South Carolina, thought the number of "patriotic planters" was very small. Wigfall, of Texas, was not so sure about the expediency of neglecting to raise cotton. Mr. Barnwell, of South Carolina, thought that on the cultivation of cotton, and the increase of supplies of that staple for the market, depended not only the sources of wealth, but the importance, consequence, and weight of the Confederacy with foreign nations. "We must," he said, "raise it, hold it, and fight for it." Besides, he thought the power assumed by Mr. Brown's substitute the grossest assumption of authority he had ever witnessed. Mr. Hunter, of Virginia, objected on the ground that the measure taxed the patriotism of the planters, and was an interference with state rights. Like Barnwell, he thought that reducing the supply would so advance the price that other sources of cotton would be sought. Mr. Brown urged that the main object of the United States in descending the river was to get cotton, and that there should be as little of it to be found as possible. The idea that cotton could be raised in India was "played out." He was in favor of burning all the cotton they had, and raising no more until the world was disposed to do them justice. Semmes, of Louisiana, said he had long since abandoned the idea that cotton was king. England would not interfere for it. "Rather than make war with the United States, she would convert her government into an eleemosynary for the maintenance of her hordes of starving operatives." He should vote for the resolution, to warn the people of a lengthy war, and that they must raise provisions. The resolution, being put to vote, was lost.

On the 6th of May, in answer to an inquiry made by a Southern firm whether cotton purchased on foreign account would be exempted from the order enjoining the destruction of all cotton about to fall into the enemy's hands, J. P. Benjamin, the Confederate Secretary of State, replied that if purchases of that sort were made, it must be at the risk of the purchasers.

The Charleston *Courier* of May 14 published a circular which it claimed to be "the deliberate expression of the wealthiest and most influential class of the citizens of New Orleans." For manifest reasons no signatures were attached. After a chivalric prelude, the circular goes on to urge the destruction of every bale of cotton liable to capture on the Western rivers, and the refusal to ship or sell a bale until the independence of the Confederacy was recognized. "Let the conquest of the United States," it said, "be a barren one. If we are true to ourselves there will be no trade, and the countless millions of foreign products will be without a purchaser. How long will they remain idle spectators of such a scene," etc. For copying this circular, the New Orleans *Bee* was on the 16th suppressed by General Butler. The same day, for publishing an article of similar purport, the general took possession of the New Orleans *Delta*.

The planters, for the most part, justified Mr. Orr's doubt of their patriotism. They were very reluctant to burn their cotton, and in most cases where the destruction was accomplished it was by Confederate guerrillas. Such, for instance, was the case near Memphis, where, toward the last of June, a large body of Confederate cavalry visited a number of plantations on the line of the Memphis and Charleston Railroad, burning great quantities of cotton, and arresting all persons found purchasing that staple. But, in spite of every effort made by the Confederate government, large quantities of cotton were seized by the United States at every step of the army's progress southward. A portion of the cotton found belonged to the Confederate government, and a portion to private citizens, who had in many instances secreted it against the very occasion of possible capture.

Mr. Pollard, the Southern historian, thinks it was a great mistake that the Confederate government did not, in 1861, purchase the entire cotton crop, and make it the basis of its credit. He estimates that there were at this time 3,500,000 bales of cotton in the South, which might have been secured at the rate of seven cents a pound. He enters into an indignant protest against the illicit trade in cotton indulged in by the planters: "The country had taken a solemn resolution to burn the cotton in advance of the enemy; but the conflagration of this staple soon became a rare event; instead of being committed to the flames it was spirited to Yankee markets. Nor were these operations always disguised. Some commercial houses in the Confederacy counted their gains by millions of dollars since the war, through the favor of the government in allowing them to export cotton at pleasure. . . . The cotton and sugar planters of the extreme South, who prior to the war were loudest for secession, were at the same time known to buy every article of their consumption in Yankee markets, and to cherish an ambition of shining in the society of Northern hotels. It is not surprising that many of these affected patriots have found congenial occupation in this war in planting in copartnership with the enemy, or in smuggling cotton into his lines. The North is said to have obtained in the progress of this war [Pollard is writing this in 1863], from the Southwest and Charleston, enough cotton at present prices to uphold its whole system of currency—a damning testimony to the avarice of the planter. Yet it is nothing more than a convincing proof, in general, that property, though very pretentious of patriotism, when identified with selfishness, is one of the most weak and cowardly things in revolutions, and the first to succumb under the horrors of war."—*Pollard's Second Year of the War*, p. 289.

the operations of General Grant, which were threatened in that quarter. It has been said that Pemberton was in favor of evacuating all points held by the Confederates on the water, and had even recommended the abandonment of Charleston and the destruction of its works.[1] He certainly did not act upon this theory in the Vicksburg campaign.

The first thing to be accomplished by General Grant was the expulsion of the enemy from the line of the Tallahatchie. Then, while Rosecrans occupied Bragg, Grant, with Sherman's help, proposed to take Vicksburg. The details of the campaign were admirably planned, and, so far as the principal movements were concerned, successfully carried out up to just the last point, when the whole scheme miscarried, not by reason of a great defeat, but by the disgraceful and unnecessary surrender of Holly Springs.

In the first stage of the campaign, as arranged by Grant and Sherman, three columns were to move—one, under Grant, from Jackson, in Tennessee; a second, under Sherman, from Memphis; and a third, consisting mainly of a cavalry force, under C. C. Washburne, from Helena—against Pemberton's army on the Tallahatchie, numbering 40,000 men.[2] The success of this first part of the campaign is thus concisely summed up by Sherman: "Grant moved direct on Pemberton, while I moved from Memphis, and a smaller force under General Washburne struck directly for Grenada; and the first thing Pemberton knew, the dépôt of his supplies was almost in the grasp of a small cavalry force, and he fell back in confusion, and gave us the Tallahatchie without a battle."[3]

From the vantage-ground thus gained Grant could almost see his way into Vicksburg. To him, then, Jackson seemed almost within his grasp, and thence it was but a step into the coveted strong-hold. The force sent from Helena, which had now been recalled (perhaps too soon), had swept a clear course for him to Grenada. Pemberton had fallen back to Canton, a few miles north of Jackson. On November 29th Grant reached Holly Springs; on December 3d his head-quarters were at Oxford, and his cavalry in the advance were driving Van Dorn out from Water Valley and Coffeeville. Not a score of miles from Coffeeville is Grenada; and if all holds well behind—at the dozen points in the rear where garrisons have been left to keep open communications—Jackson must fall before Christmas, and Vicksburg before New Year.

So sure was Grant of his goal, that, while at Oxford (December 8), he dispatched General Sherman, commanding the right wing of his army,[4] to undertake a co-operative expedition from Memphis against Vicksburg. Sherman was to take with him one division of his present command, and all the spare troops from Memphis and Helena. Scarcely a fortnight was allowed for the preparation of this important but ill-fated expedition. In the mean while Grant waited, or pushed on slowly, so as to give the appearance of a continuous movement. On the 14th of December he wrote to Sherman, saying that, for a week hence, his head-quarters would be at Coffeeville, and expressing particular anxiety to have the Helena cavalry back again with him—evidently not at ease about Van Dorn's movements in his rear. With one eye on Vicksburg, he was forced to cast the other suspiciously on Holly Springs, his principal dépôt of provisions and ammunition, garrisoned with little over a thousand men under Colonel R. C. Murphy. Van Dorn was leading his cavalry against this place, and Grant, knowing this, gave Murphy timely warning. The blow fell suddenly, on December 20, and found Murphy unprepared. The place was surrendered, and Grant, cut off from his base, was obliged to fall back to Grand Junction, and to give up a campaign which, but for this fatal surrender, promised a fortunate issue.

Sherman embarked from Memphis on the 20th of December,[5] the very day on which Holly Springs was surrendered. He had in his command Morgan's and the two Smiths' divisions—about 30,000 men. At Helena this army was re-enforced by over 12,000 men under General Frederick Steele, comprising the brigades of Hovey, Thayer, Blair, and Wyman.

From a letter written by Sherman to Porter (December 8), we gather a pretty definite idea of the objects which the expedition was intended to accomplish.

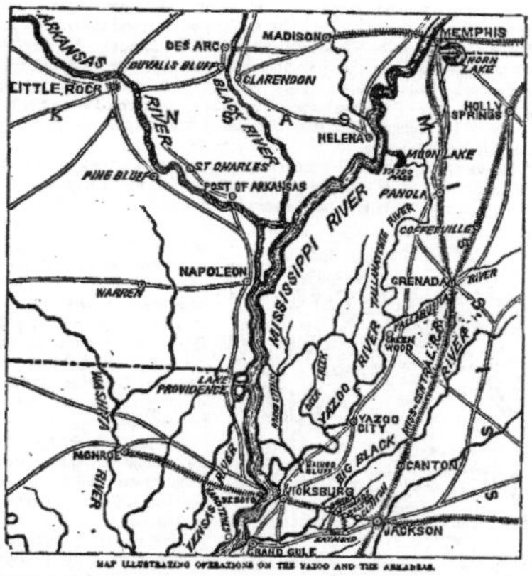

MAP ILLUSTRATING OPERATIONS ON THE YAZOO AND THE ARKANSAS.

Sherman at this time, and, indeed, up to the time of his own defeat, confidently expected that Grant would succeed on the northeast of Vicksburg—a result which, so far as he was concerned, was chiefly valuable because it would keep Pemberton on the line of the Yalabusha, and thus insure his own success on the Yazoo. "We hope," he writes, "that they (the rebels) will halt and re-form behind the Yalabusha, with Grenada as their centre. If so, General Grant can press their front, while I am ordered to take all the spare troops from Memphis and Helena, and proceed with all dispatch to Vicksburg." He intended first to break the inland communications of Vicksburg, and then to make a combined attack upon the city by land and water, Porter co-operating with the fleet. He would "cut the road to Monroe, Louisiana, to Jackson, Mississippi, and then appear up the Yazoo, threatening the Mississippi Central Road where it crosses the Big Black," thus disconcerting the enemy and throwing him on to Meridian, leaving Vicksburg an easy capture.

The want of sufficient transportation for Sherman's large force was the cause of much embarrassment in fitting out the expedition, and of great confusion and inconvenience on its route to Friar's Point. The confusion was increased by the necessary haste of the embarkation. The transports, suddenly pressed into service, were crowded so closely as to afford scarcely more than standing-room, and, of course, there were no adequate accommodations for the comfort or cleanliness of the men. The discomforts of this situation were exaggerated by the embarkation of Steele's force at Helena. The negroes along the river were greatly impressed at sight of an expedition which they confidently believed had been sent down for the express purpose of their liberation. Many of them, indeed, came upon the boats, and were taken under the protection of the flag. The fleet arrived at Milliken's Bend on Christmas-eve, and not a few of the enthusiastic soldiers expected to eat their Christmas dinner in Vicksburg.

The next day troops were landed, and destroyed the railroad leading from Vicksburg to Texas. The expedition was convoyed by Porter's gun-boats, on December 26th, to Johnston's Landing, twelve miles up the Yazoo River.[1] On the transport fleet Morgan's division led the advance, followed in order by Steele, Morgan L. Smith, and A. J. Smith.

Vicksburg itself is situated upon very high bluffs, which extend southward along the river to Warrenton, and northward till they touch the Yazoo, about fifteen miles from Haines's Bluff. Between these bluffs, upon which the Confederates were now strongly fortified, and the Yazoo is a low country, full of swamps, lagoons, sloughs, and bayous. The points of approach to the bluffs from the river are few and difficult—far more difficult than Sherman had anticipated. In this bed of mire and quicksand the national troops were landed, on the 27th, near Chickasaw Bayou, which runs from Vicksburg around the hills in the rear of the city and into the Yazoo, taking a sharp turn northward before it reaches the river.

Scarcely had Holly Springs fallen into Van Dorn's hands before Pemberton was warned of the attempt about to be made against the northern de-

---

[1] *Abrams*, p. 8.

[2] Speech at St. Louis after the war.

[3] This is Bowman's estimate.—*Sherman and his Campaigns*, p. 77.

[4] General Grant's army constituted the Thirteenth Army Corps, of which the right wing was under command of General Sherman. This right wing consisted of three divisions:

The First, commanded by A. J. Smith, and consisting of two new brigades, Burbridge's and Landrum's.

The Second, commanded by Morgan L. Smith, consisting of G. A. Smith's and David Stuart's brigades.

The Third, commanded by G. W. Morgan, comprising the new brigades of Osterhaus, Lindsay, and De Courcey.

The other brigades remained at Memphis.

[5] Before embarkation General Sherman issued the following characteristic order:

"I. The expedition now fitting out is purely of a military character, and the interests involved are of too important a character to be mixed up with personal or private business. No citizen, male or female, will be allowed to accompany it, unless employed as a part of the crew, or as servants to the transports. Female chambermaids to the boats and nurses to the sick alone will be allowed unless the wives of captains and pilots actually belonging to the boats. No laundress, officer's or soldier's wife, must pass below Helena.

"II. No person whatever, citizen, officer, or sutler, will, on any consideration, buy or deal in cotton, or other produce of the country. Should any cotton be brought on board of any transport, going or returning, the brigade quarter-master, of which the boat forms a part, will take possession of it, and invoice it to Captain A. R. Eddy, chief quarter-master at Memphis.

"III. Should any cotton or other produce be brought back to Memphis by any chartered boat, Captain Eddy will take possession of the same, and sell it for the benefit of the United States. If accompanied by its actual producer, the planter or factor, the quarter-master will furnish him with a receipt for the same, to be settled on proof of his loyalty at the close of the war.

"IV. Boats ascending the river may take cotton from the shore for bulkheads to protect their engines or crew, but on arrival at Memphis it must be turned over to the quarter-master, with a statement of the time, place, and name of its owner. The trade in cotton must await a more peaceful state of affairs.

"V. Should any citizen accompany the expedition below Helena in violation of these orders, any colonel of a regiment or captain of a battery will conscript him into the service of the United States for the unexpired term of his command. If he show a refractory spirit, unfitting him for a soldier, the commanding officer present will turn him over to the captain of the boat as a deck-hand, and compel him to work in that capacity, without wages, until the boat returns to Memphis.

"VI. Any person whatever, whether in the service of the United States or transports, found making reports for publication which might reach the enemy, giving them information, aid, or comfort, will be arrested and treated as spies."

[1] "On entering the Yazoo, the first object that attracted the attention was the ruins of a large brick house and several other buildings, which were still smoking. On inquiry, I learned that this was the celebrated plantation of the rebel General Albert Sidney Johnston, who was killed at Shiloh. It was an extensive establishment, working over three hundred negroes. It contained a large steam sugar refinery, an extensive steam saw-mill, cotton-gins, machine-shop, and a long line of negro quarters.

"The dwelling was palatial in its proportions and architecture, and the grounds around it were magnificently laid out in alcoves, with arbors, trellises, groves of evergreens, and extensive flower-beds. All was now a mass of smouldering ruins. Our gun-boats had gone up there the day before, and a small battery planted near the mansion announced itself by plugging away at one of the iron-clads, and the marines went ashore after the gun-boats had silenced the battery, and burned and destroyed every thing on the place. If any thing were wanting to complete the desolate aspect of the place, it was to be found in the sombre-hued pendent moss, peculiar to Southern forests, and which gives the trees a funereal aspect, as if they were all draped in mourning, as on almost every Southern plantation there were many deadened trees standing about in the fields, from the limbs of all of which long festoons of moss hung, swaying with a melancholy motion in every breeze."—*Missouri Democrat.*

fenses of Vicksburg. In this respect he had an overwhelming advantage over Sherman (who knew nothing of the unfavorable turn which affairs had taken in the rear of Vicksburg), and Grant's withdrawal to Grand Junction left him free to pursue his advantage without hinderance. He faced about with his army; and by the time Sherman had landed on the south bank of the Yazoo, he had not only an equal force to confront the latter, but also an impregnable line of defense, covered by abatis, constructed from the thicket in front of his works. Thousands of slaves had for months been engaged upon these fortifications.

The emergency which Sherman was about to meet was one in which neither the bravery of his Western soldiers nor his own fertile ingenuity availed him any thing. It is true, the enemy had a line of works fifteen miles in extent to defend; and, supposing that he was attacking a force much inferior to his own in point of numbers, Sherman may well be justified in the confident hope that he might, at some point in this long line, make an impression, and that, by persistent pressure, he must succeed in driving the enemy out of his fortifications.

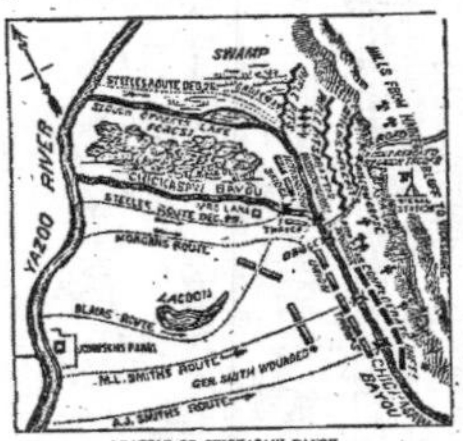

BATTLE OF CHICKASAW BAYOU.

Having debarked his troops, he pushed the enemy's pickets back toward the bluffs, and on the 28th intended to make a general assault. Chickasaw Bayou proved the chief obstacle to his plan of attack. Dividing the country in the enemy's front into nearly equal portions, it could be crossed only at two points, each completely covered by the enemy's fire. This necessitated either a division of the attacking force, or the restriction of the assault to the west side of the bayou; and, as the bayou turned westward along the base of the bluffs, it covered the enemy's entire left, and had in this section only four points at which a crossing could be effected, and even at these only in the face of rifle-pits on the table-land behind, of rifle-trenches on the hill-sides farther back, and of heavy batteries posted on the summits of the hills. Along the base of these hills, and back of the bayou, ran the road from Vicksburg to Yazoo City, serving the enemy as a covered way along which he could at leisure move his artillery and infantry, concentrating them upon any of the points which might be selected for crossing the Federal troops.

Steele advanced on the east side of the bayou, but, encountering a swamp over which there was no passage except by a long corduroy causeway, and that, too, at the risk of losing one half of his division, wisely concluded to give up the attempt. Morgan, on the other side of the bayou, advanced up to the enemy's centre as far as to the bank of the bayou in front of the bluffs, where his progress was arrested, though he held his ground during the ensuing night. Morgan L. Smith advanced simultaneously farther to the right. While reconnoitring the ground he was disabled by a bullet lodged in his hip, and Brigadier General David Stuart succeeded to the active command. Where this division reached the bayou there was a crossing by means of a narrow sand-slip, but the attempt was deemed too perilous. On the extreme right General A. J. Smith advanced, and Burbridge's brigade—arriving on the field about noon, having just returned from a raid on the Vicksburg and Shreveport Railroad—was pushed forward by Smith to the bayou, with orders to cross on rafts under cover of a heavy cannonade. Landrum's brigade occupied a high position on the main road, within three fourths of a mile of the enemy's works, and with Vicksburg in plain view on his right.

On the morning of the 29th Steele had been recalled, and held the left, supporting Morgan. The entire army lay opposite the Confederate centre and left, with the inevitable bayou on its own left and front. Nothing had been heard from Grant, but his near presence was conjectured from a signal rocket which had been seen ascending in the east the first night after landing.

Sherman determined to assault the hills in Morgan's front, while A. J. Smith should cross at the sand-spit to the right. The assault was made, and a lodgment effected on the table-land across the bayou, the heads of the supporting columns being brought well up to the enemy's works. The audacity of the troops up to this point was never surpassed. Blair's brigade, originally holding a position between Morgan and M. L. Smith, in advancing, had crossed the track of Morgan's division till it reached the extreme front on the left, in Steele's van. Here it crossed the bayou at a point where both banks were covered by tangled abatis, and the quicksand bed of the bayou was covered by water three feet deep. Through this bed Blair led his brigade across, leaving his horse floundering in the quicksands behind, and carried two lines of rifle-pits beyond, under a fire which struck down one third of his command. But, despite such instances of valor, beyond the crossing of a few regiments, and the slight foothold gained on the southern bank of the bayou, no impression was made; and so scathing was the fire from the enemy's rifle-pits, and the cross-fire from his batteries, that the advanced columns faltered and fell back, leaving many dead, wounded, and prisoners.

Still Sherman urged A. J. Smith, on the right, to push his attack across the sand-bar. The latter had already crossed the Sixth Missouri, who lay on the other side, under the bank of the bayou, with the enemy's sharp-shooters directly over their heads. They were about to make a road by undermining the bank, when the utter failure of Morgan's assault on the left led to an order for their withdrawal, which was accomplished, as the advance

POSITION OF THE SIXTH MISSOURI AFTER CROSSING THE BAYOU.

ADMIRAL PORTER'S FLEET AT THE MOUTH OF THE YAZOO.

!·been, with heavy loss. All this time Burbridge had been skirmishing oss the bayou, and Landrum pushing ahead through the abatis toward cksburg.

'he night of the 29th was spent by the troops in the position of the night ore, lying, exposed to a heavy rain, upon the miry ground, with no shel- but their blankets, and with no consolation from victory for their past or present hardship.

herman now gave up all hope of success from his present position. His resource left was an attempt to turn the enemy's line by carrying his reme right, the batteries upon Drumgould's Bluff, some miles farther up Yazoo. While his army was encamped in the swamp on the night of 29th, Sherman visited Admiral Porter on board his flag-boat, where was certed the following plan of operations: Porter was to move up the Ya- and bombard the batteries, while about 10,000 picked troops should e a determined assault, the rest of the army making a strong demonstra- on the enemy's left. If successful in carrying out this plan, the national es would have complete possession of the Yazoo River, and would hold key of Vicksburg.

teele's division, and one of Morgan L. Smith's, were accordingly em- ed on the night of the 31st. But a dense fog made it impossible for ter to advance his gun-boats, and the expedition was deferred to another t. But the next night the clear moonlight, which would last till morn- proved as unfavorable as the fog of the night before, since there would o cover of darkness for landing the troops, and the attempt to secure a

The War Department had, on December 18, 1862, issued a general order dividing the Army of the Tennessee into four separate army corps, to be

---

fested by them on all occasions. We failed in accomplishing one great purpose of our movement, the capture of Vicksburg, but we were part of a whole. Ours was but part of a combined movement, in which others were to assist. We were on time. Unforeseen contingencies must have delayed the others.

"We have destroyed the Shreveport road, we have attacked the defenses of Vicksburg, and pushed the attack as far as prudence would justify, and, having found it too strong for our single column, we have drawn off in good order and good spirits, ready for any new move. A new commander is now here to lead you. He is chosen by the President of the United States, who is charged by the Constitution to maintain and defend it, and he has the undoubted right to select his own agents. I know that all good officers and soldiers will give him the same hearty support and cheerful obedience they have hitherto given me. There are honors enough in reserve for all, and work enough too. Let each do his appropriate part, and our nation must in the end emerge from this dire conflict purified and ennobled by the fires which now test its strength and purity. All officers of the general staff not attached to my person will hereafter report in person and by letter to Major General McClernand, commanding the Army of the Mississippi, on board the steamer Tigress, at our rendezvous at Gaines's Landing, and at Montgomery Point.

"By order of Major General W. T. SHERMAN.

"J. H. HAMMOND, A. A. G."

The connection of General McClernand with this expedition against Vicksburg is chiefly worthy of note as being so characteristic of the entire want of system—and, we might add, of judgment—in the general direction of the national armies at this time, and, indeed, until Grant became lieutenant general. It appears that, independently of any consultation with Grant, of whose winter campaign Vicksburg was the objective point, McClernand had in the autumn of 1862 been intrusted by the War Department with the organization of an expedition down the Mississippi. This, we understand, was done at McClernand's own instance. There was a long correspondence between him and the Department, the latter adopting his suggestions and urging him to hasten his preparations. The President and the Secretary of War united in drafting a document ordering him to organize the troops remaining in Indiana, Iowa, and Illinois, and to forward them with all dispatch to Memphis and Cairo, that, as soon as a sufficient force, not required elsewhere, should be got together, an expedition against Vicksburg might be organized under his command. The troops, however, were "subject to the designation of the general-in-chief," and were to be

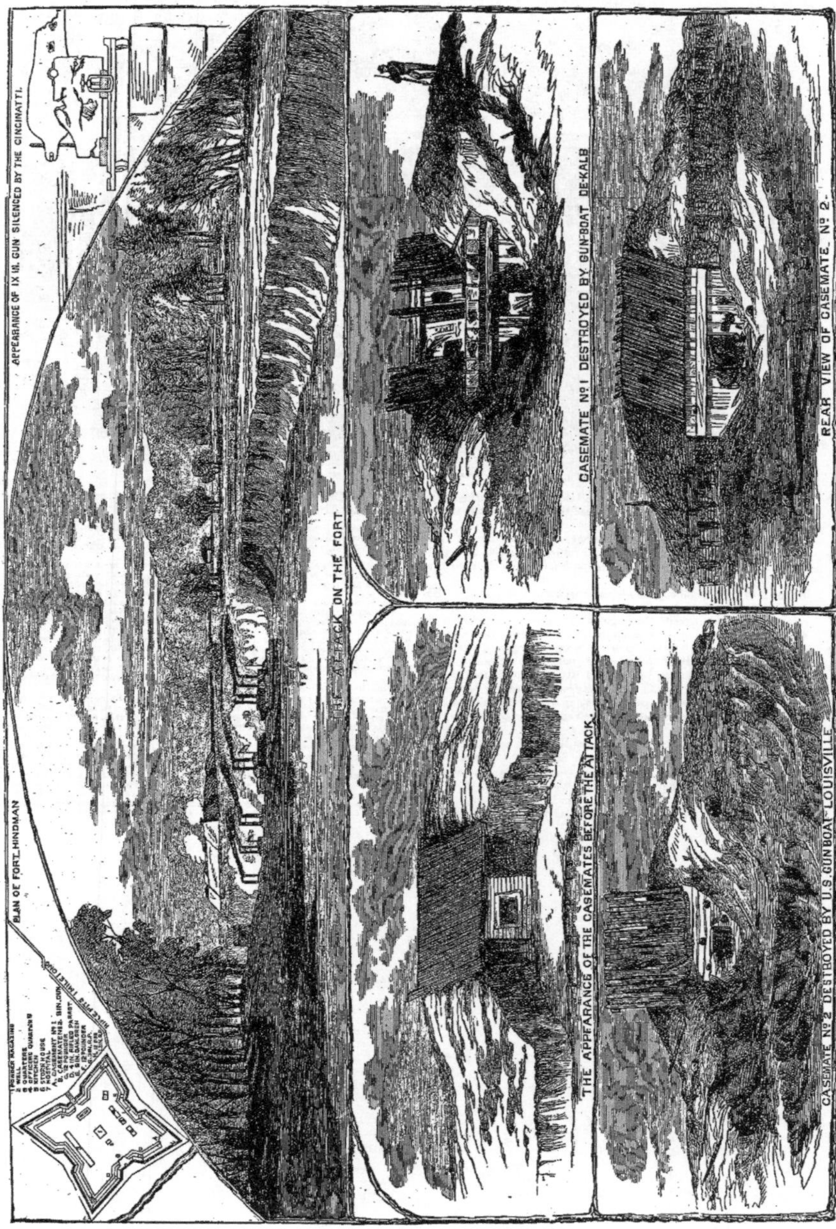

THE ATTACK ON ARKANSAS POST.

known as the Thirteenth, Fifteenth, Sixteenth, and Seventeenth, and to be commanded respectively by McClernand, Sherman, Hurlbut, and McPherson, while General Grant was to retain command of the whole. Upon assuming command of the expedition, now returned to Milliken's Bend, McClernand gave the command of his own corps to General Morgan, this command comprising the divisions of A. J. Smith and Morgan's own division, now commanded by General P. J. Osterhaus. Sherman's corps comprised also two divisions, Steele's and M. L. Smith's (now commanded by Stuart).

These two corps, with McClernand in chief command, embarked upon the same transports which had brought them from Memphis, and, under convoy of Admiral Porter's gun-boats, proceeded up the river to attack Fort Hindman, commonly known as Arkansas Post, on the north bank of the Arkansas River, fifty miles from its mouth, and a little more than twice that distance below Little Rock. Here a settlement had been made by the French in 1685. The fort was situated on the first high ground to be found in ascending the Arkansas; it had a parapet eighteen feet across, with a ditch of twenty feet wide by eight deep, strong casemates, and a cordon of rifle-pits. Its commander was General T. J. Churchill, who had under him a garrison of about 5000 men. The fort was mounted with eight guns, and its capture was an affair of no great difficulty. But Churchill had orders from Lieutenant General Holmes, the Confederate commander in Arkansas, "to hold on till help arrived, or till all were dead."

The expedition entered White River, and, after ascending it for fifteen miles, through a cut-off, moved into Arkansas River January 9, and by noon of the next day the troops were all debarked three miles below the fort. The story of the capture is soon told. The gun-boats, even while the troops were landing, had shelled the sharp-shooters out of their rifle-pits along the levee, and, moving up to the fort, opened a bombardment. By land the army was pushed up around the fort, across bayous and swamps, and during the night of the 10th slept on their arms, in readiness for the assault of the next day. The gun-boats opened again a little after noon on the 11th, and in two or three hours the guns of the fort had been completely silenced. In the mean time several brigades had charged up to within musket-range of the enemy's works, where they found partial shelter in the ravines. In this advance General Hovey was wounded, and General Thayer had a horse shot under him. General A. J. Smith pressed back the Confederate right until, as he sent word to McClernand, he could "almost shake hands with the enemy." As soon as the guns of the fort were silenced, McClernand ordered a general assault, when a white flag appeared on the ramparts, just as the Eighty-third Ohio and Sixteenth Indiana, with General Burbridge at their head, were entering the intrenchments on the east side, while Sherman's and Steele's advanced regiments were on the point of entering on the north and west, and the fort was in McClernand's hands, with 5000 prisoners, 17 guns, and 3000 small-arms. Churchill professed, even after the capture, his intention to have held out till the last man was slain, and said he was only prevented from doing so by the unauthorized display of the white flag by some of his Texan soldiers. So much the better, it would seem, for the Texans! The Confederate loss in killed was 60, and in wounded from 75 to 80. McClernand reports his own loss 129 killed, 831 wounded, and 17 missing. A few days later, the fortifications at Arkansas Post, the command of which had been assigned to General Burbridge, were dismantled and blown up. The position was of no importance, and was therefore abandoned. Before the withdrawal from Arkansas, however, an expedition under General Gorman and Lieutenant Commanding Walker was sent up the White River, and Des Arc and Duval's Bluff were captured.

Grant, having attended to the reorganization of his forces into four army corps, proceeded to Memphis, and on the 18th of January he went down the river and met Sherman, McClernand, and Porter near the mouth of the White River, returning from their successful raid into Arkansas, and, accompanying them to Helena, he consulted them in regard to further operations for the reduction of Vicksburg. Three days later, McClernand's force reached Young's Point, nine miles above Vicksburg, on the opposite bank of the river, facing the mouth of the Yazoo. For over two months—until the movement on New Carthage—Grant's army was engaged in several unsuccessful attempts at an approach to Vicksburg from above. Before entering upon a review of these experiments, let us for a moment turn our attention to the interesting exploits of some of our gun-boats during this interval.

On the 2d of February, Colonel Charles R. Ellet, with the Queen of the West, ran past the batteries, with orders to destroy the City of Vicksburg, a vessel which had, after Sherman's failure, been brought down by the enemy from the Yazoo to the front of Vicksburg. This movement had not escaped Porter's observation. It was also known to him that supplies were continually being obtained both at Vicksburg and Port Hudson by means of transports. To these transports, also, Colonel Ellet was expected to pay his regards. The Queen of the West was a wooden steamer, strengthened so as to carry an iron prow. Her armament consisted of an 80-pounder rifled Parrott gun on her main deck, one 20-pounder and three 12-pounder brass howitzers on her gun-deck. In order to protect her from the shot and shells of the batteries, she had had her steering apparatus removed and placed behind the bulwarks of her bows, and three hundred bales of cotton covered her machinery. The change in her steering apparatus proved a great inconvenience, and, after starting on her trip, it was found necessary to return it to its original position. This caused some delay, and she did not pass into full view of the batteries before sunrise, thus becoming a fair target for a hundred guns bearing upon her at once. Only three or four shots, however, struck her before she reached the City of Vicksburg, which was made fast to the river's bank at the centre of the bend. Colonel Ellet made for the steamer at once, and struck her, but the force of the blow was broken by wide guards, which overlapped the prow of the ram, and prevented the latter from reaching the hull of the Vicksburg. The current, which was very strong at this point, swung the Queen round side by side

THE QUEEN OF THE WEST AND THE VICKSBURG.

Vicksburg, says, "General Sherman's arrangement as commander of troops in the attack on Chickasaw Bluffs last December was admirable. Seeing the ground from the opposite side from the attack afterward, I saw the impossibility of making it successful."

The account of the expedition published just after its failure in the *Missouri Democrat* abounded in vituperative charges against General Sherman. It accused him of an ambition to anticipate Grant in order to gain for himself the entire glory of the capture of Vicksburg; it asserted, without any authority, that Sherman knew that McClernand was properly the commander of the expedition, and represents him as exulting in his shrewdness in "cutting that general out;" and it charges him, in effect, with the murder of 2000 soldiers for the satisfaction of his own ambition. It is, however, quite evident that the motive which led to this outburst of indignation was General Sherman's order in relation to newspaper correspondents.

LOSS OF THE QUEEN OF THE WEST.

with the enemy. At this moment Colonel Ellet fired his starboard bow gun, loaded with incendiary shells, into the Vicksburg, his own cotton bales being at the same time set on fire by shells from the batteries. It was impossible to attempt any thing farther at this point, and the Queen, without material injury, passed the lower batteries. Below Natchez she captured and burned three small steamers laden with provisions. During the night a flat-boat, with a cargo of coal, was cast loose from the fleet above, and floated down to the ram.

A week later (February 10) the Queen started upon another expedition down the river, accompanied by the De Soto as tender. The next evening she reached the mouth of Old River, into which Red River runs. On the 12th, leaving the De Soto to guard the mouth of Old River, the Queen entered the Atchafalaya, and made some captures of army wagons and provisions, and, on the way back to her anchorage of the previous night, was fired upon from the shore and her master mortally wounded. On the 12th the two steamers passed up into Red River, and, moving up to the mouth of the Black River, where they anchored for the night, they the next morning captured the Era, No. 5, a steamer of 100 tons, with fourteen Texan soldiers, $28,000 in Confederate money, and 4500 bushels of corn destined for Little Rock. The pilot of the Era was taken on board the Queen, and, either by accident or design, he grounded the steamer directly under the guns of Fort Taylor, located at a bend in the river twenty miles above the spot where the Era was captured, and where she now lay under guard. The guns of the fort opened with frightful accuracy upon the unfortunate Queen, nearly every shell striking her, and one shot pierced her smoke-pipe, filling the boat with steam. It was impossible for the Queen to reply to the shots that were crashing through her machinery. There was the greatest confusion on board; cotton-bales were tumbled into the river, and men, jumping overboard, clung to them, hoping to float down to the De Soto, a mile below; negroes, frightened to death, were plunging into the water, where, with no means of preservation within their reach, they were drowned. The De Soto endeavored to come to the rescue, but the attempt proved too perilous; and she withdrew out of range. As she floated down she picked up several of the crew. Colonel Ellet escaped in this manner. By 11 o'clock P.M. the De Soto reached the Era, and, proving unmanageable, was blown up. Upon the Era, with the Confederate ram Webb sixty miles behind him and in swift pursuit, Colonel Ellet worried his way out of Red River and up the Mississippi, past Ellis's Cliffs, where he met the Indianola, one of the finest of the national gun-boats. Just as the Era came alongside of her unlooked-for deliverer the fog lifted, and revealed her pursuer, the Webb, not far in the rear. The tables were then turned, and the Webb was pursued by the two boats, but, being a swift vessel, she escaped.

The Era was now furnished with supplies, and sent back to Admiral Porter. The Indianola[1] had set out from the mouth of the Yazoo on the night of February 13. She passed the batteries without steam, floating down with the current at the rate of about four miles an hour. Although her crew could hear the voices of the Confederate soldiers on the bank, yet she passed by unobserved until she drifted by a camp-fire on the levee, when she was discovered by a soldier, who discharged his musket at her. This was the signal for a general discharge of muskets and cannon. As the Indianola now put on steam to hasten her progress her position became known, and she was opened upon from every battery which she had now to pass; but she suffered no injury. She was commanded by Lieutenant Commander Brown. How she arrived in time to rescue the Era has been already shown.

The Queen of the West was being repaired by the enemy, and as it would be difficult to manœuvre so long a boat as the Indianola in the waters of the Red River, and no pilots could be obtained, Brown returned with his boat up the river. When he reached the mouth of the Big Black River, forty miles below Vicksburg, on the 24th, the Webb and the Queen of the West hove in sight behind him, accompanied by two cotton-clad steamers. Brown had expected another vessel to come down to assist him in meeting the emergency which now threatened, but he had been disappointed. It was now half past nine P.M., and the night was very dark. Clearing for action, Brown stood down the river to meet them. The Queen of the West led in the attack, striking through a coal-barge against the Indianola, but harmlessly; then came the Webb. "Both vessels came together, bows on," says Brown, "with a tremendous crash, which knocked nearly every one down on board both vessels, doing no damage to us, while the Webb's bow was cut in at least eight feet." Not minding the cotton-clads, which kept up an incessant fire with small-arms, Brown turned his attention to the rams, with whom he was now engaged at close quarters. From his forward guns

[1] "The Indianola was a new iron-clad gun-boat, one hundred and seventy-four feet long, fifty feet beam, ten feet from the top of her deck to the bottom of her keel, or eight feet four inches in the clear. Her sides (of wood) for five feet down were thirty-two inches thick, having beveled sticks laid outside the hull (proper), and all of oak. Outside of this was three-inch-thick plate iron. Her clamps and keelsons were as heavy as the largest ship's. Her deck was eight inches solid, with one-inch iron plate, all well bolted. Her casemate stood at an incline of twenty-six and a half degrees, and was covered with three-inch iron, as were also her ports. She had a heavy grating on top of the casemate that no shell could penetrate, and every scuttle and hatch was equally well covered. She was ironed all round, except some temporary rooms on deck, and, besides the amount of wood and iron already stated, had coal-bunkers seven feet thick alongside of her boilers, the entire machinery being in the hold. She had seven engines—two for working her side wheels, two for her propellers, two for her capstans, and one for supplying water and working the bilge and fire pumps. She had five large five-flued boilers, and made abundance of steam. Her forward casemate had two eleven-inch Dahlgren guns, and her after casemate two nine-inch. Her forward casemate was pierced for two guns in front, one on each side, and two aft, so that she could fire two guns forward, one on each side, and four at an angle sideways and astern. She had also hose for throwing scalding water from her boilers that would reach from stem to stern, and there was communication from the casemates to all parts of the vessel without the least exposure. The pilot-house was also thoroughly iron-clad, and instant communication could be had with the gunners and engineers, enabling the pilot to place the vessel in just such position as might be required for effective action."—*Appleton's Annual Cyclopædia*, 1863, p. 44.

he fired at his antagonists as opportunity offered. He received a third blow, which crushed the starboard coal-barge. Two more blows were struck without seriously damaging the Indianola. The sixth blow from the Webb crushed the starboard wheel and disabled the starboard rudder, starting a number of leaks back of the shaft. The Webb now struck a fair blow in the stern, starting the timbers of the Indianola, which let in the water in large volumes. Finally, the gun-boat, with two feet and a half of water over her floor, was run ashore. Unable longer to hold out against four vessels, mounting ten guns, and manned by over a thousand men, Brown surrendered, after a fight of an hour and a half. All his guns had been either thrown overboard or rendered useless.

THE INDIANOLA RUNNING THE VICKSBURG BATTERIES.

The enemy intended immediately to repair the Indianola, which was an important accession to his fleet. Her destruction afterward was probably the most ludicrous incident of the war. It happened in this way. Porter observed the Queen of the West on the morning of February 25th at Warrenton, seven miles below Vicksburg. He had not heard of the capture of the Indianola, and the appearance of this boat excited alarm. He had no expectation that the Queen would so soon be repaired, and began to fear (too late) for the safety of the Indianola. In a letter written by him on the 26th, he expresses his anxiety on her account. It appears that he stood in becoming awe of the Queen (whose loss he considered more to be deplored than the disaster at Galveston), but had little fear of the Webb, which really gave the death-blow to the Indianola. The latter vessel (the Indianola) Porter characterizes as weak, the only good thing about her being her battery. But a trivial instrument of war at this crisis was destined to effect more than the Queen of the West or the Indianola had been able to accomplish. Admiral Porter had observed that while the Queen and the Indianola were running past the batteries, five of the enemy's guns were burst and dismounted. He therefore tried to provoke the fire of the batteries by placing a mortar so that its fire bore upon that portion of the town where there was nothing but army supplies. For a time the mortar accomplished its object, when the enemy gave up firing.

"Finding," says the admiral, "that they could not be provoked to fire without an object, I thought of getting up an imitation monitor. Ericsson saved the country with an iron one, why could I not save it with a wooden one? An old coal-barge, picked up in the river, was the foundation to build on. It was built of old boards in twelve hours, with pork-barrels on top of each other for smoke-stacks, and two old canoes for quarter-boats; her furnaces were built of mud, and only intended to make black smoke and not steam."

Porter considered his "dummy" a very much better-looking affair, after all, than the Indianola. Well, he let slip this formidable dog of war one night (that of the 24th), hardly expecting of it such good service as it really accomplished before the enemy discovered how he had been fooled. When the dark monster, without a soul on board, was disclosed by the first dim morning light, the Confederates appear to have had no hesitation about firing. "Never," says Porter, "did the batteries of Vicksburg open with such a din; the earth fairly trembled, and the shot flew thick around the devoted monitor." Of course the "dummy" could not be sunk, for the shots went in one side and out at the other. The soldiers of Grant's army lined the banks, and "shouted and laughed like mad" to see the fun. In the very midst of this frolic the Queen of the West appeared off Warrenton, and a damper was thrown upon the jollity of the spectacle on which all eyes had been fixed, by apprehensions as to the fate of the Indianola.

In the panic occasioned by the appearance of the "dummy," the enemy had given warning to the Queen of the West, who, supposing that she was pursued by a monster gun-boat, and trembling for her life, turned and fled down the river. The sham monitor, though it deigned no reply to the Confederate guns, did pursue the Queen as rapidly as a five-knot current would allow. Dispatches had been already sent from Vicksburg ordering the Indianola to be blown up without delay, that she might be saved from the clutches of her novel antagonist. The Queen of the West took refuge in the Red River, but, having no support, was not long afterward blown up to avoid capture. The order to blow up the Indianola was obeyed, and the gun-boat was annihilated. This exploit of the "dummy,"[1] strange as it may

[1] In regard to the effects produced by Porter's "dummy," the Richmond *Examiner* of March 7, 1863, says:

"The telegraph brings us tidings of something which is tremblingly described as a 'turreted monster.' Gun-boats are deemed not more dangerous than dug-outs, but when the case is altered to an interview with a 'turreted monster,' then the brave defenders of the Father of Waters can do nothing better than make two-forty toward the mountains.

"The reported fate of the Indianola is even more disgraceful than farcical. Here was perhaps the finest iron-clad in the Western waters, captured after a heroic struggle, rapidly repaired, and destined to join the Queen of the West in a series of victories. Next we hear that she was of necessity blown up, in the true Merrimac-Mallory style, and why? Laugh and hold your sides, lest

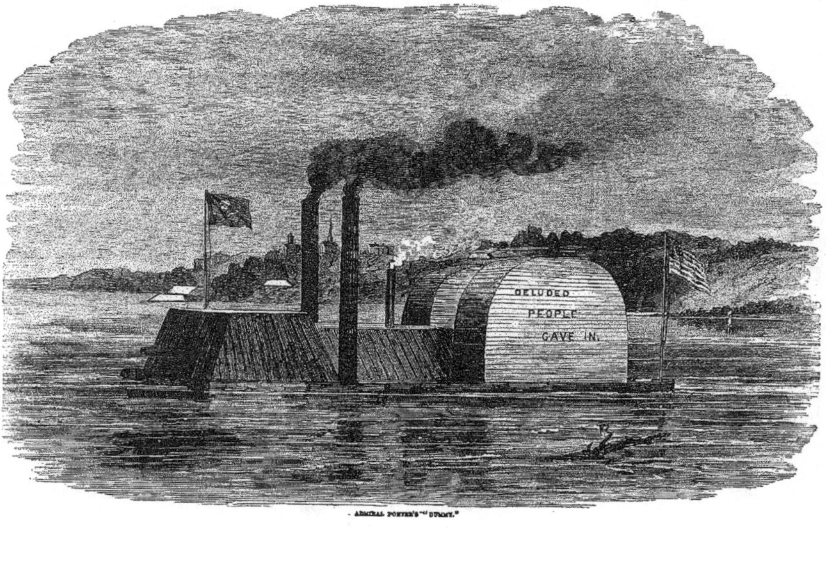

ADMIRAL PORTER'S "DUMMY."

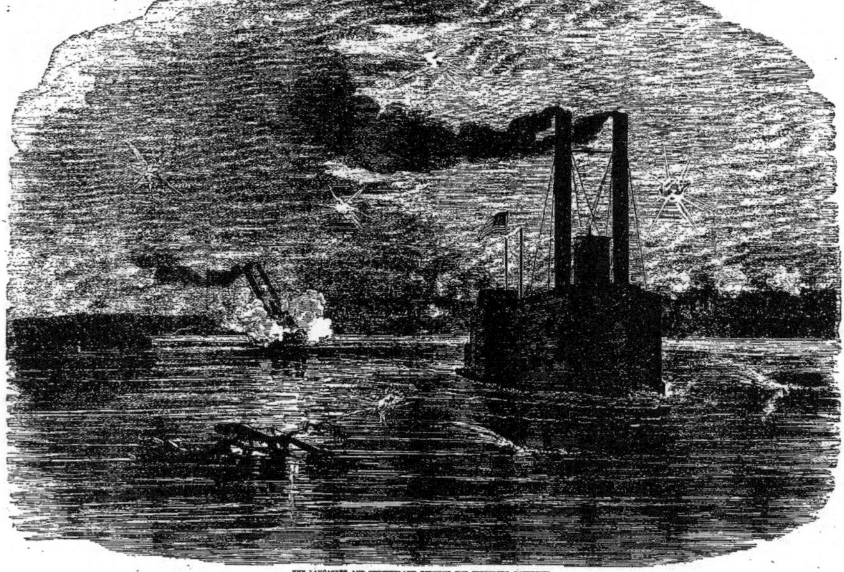

THE LANCASTER AND SWITZERLAND RUNNING THE VICKSBURG BATTERIES.

seen, broke up that naval supremacy of the river below Vicksburg which had been almost secured by the enemy. If a few more regular gun-boats had run the blockade with the same results as the Queen of the West and Indiabola, the Confederates would have soon had a powerful and almost irresistible fleet. It was certainly ingenious in Admiral Porter to send the "dummy" down instead.

Precisely a week after the victory of the "dummy" the rams Lancaster and Switzerland attempted to pass the batteries, being wanted by Admiral Farragut in the Red River. By some delay, it was daylight when they came under fire. The Lancaster was sunk, and the Switzerland, though she succeeded in passing, was badly cut up. Colonel Charles Rivers Ellet[1] commanded the latter vessel; the Switzerland was commanded by Lieutenant Colonel John A. Ellet, brother of Alfred Ellet.

The aspect of military affairs at the close of 1862 was for the nation a discouraging one. The repulse at Fredericksburg in the East had its Western counterpart in Sherman's defeat on the Yazoo. Indeed, the whole year just closed had presented no grand results in favor of the national arms except the capture of New Orleans.

The Yazoo expedition had been an experiment, and a somewhat costly one; and, following upon its failure, for several weeks, so far as Vicksburg was concerned, every operation of Grant's army was an experiment, and proved a failure. The state of the river did not allow of those brilliant operations which in the end were successful. But Grant had a large army, consisting of McClernand's command, and of his own troops brought down from Memphis. It would almost seem that it was to keep this immense force out of idleness that he embarked upon the series of adventures which preceded the advance to New Carthage in April.

you die of a surfeit of derision, oh Yankeedom! Blown up because, forsooth, a flat-boat or mud-scow, with a small house taken from the back garden of a plantation put on top of it, is floated down the river before the frightened eyes of the Partisan Rangers. A turreted monster!

"'A most unfortunate and unnecessary affair,' says the dispatch. Rather so! 'The turreted monster proved to be a flat-boat, with sundry fixtures to create deception!' Think of that! 'She passed Vicksburg on Tuesday night,' and the officers (what officers?), believing her to be a turreted monster, blew up the Indianola, but her guns fell into the enemy's hands.' That is passing odd. Her guns fell into 'the enemy's hands after she was blown up!' Incredible! Mallory and Tatnall did better than that with the Merrimac.

"'The Queen of the West,' continues the facetious dispatch, 'left in such a hurry as to forget part of her crew, who were left on shore.' Well done for the Queen of the West and her bravo officers! 'Taken altogether,' concludes the inimitable dispatch, 'it was a good joke on the Partisan Rangers, who are notoriously more cunning than brave.' Truly an excellent joke—so excellent that every man connected with this affair (if any resemblance of the truth is contained in the dispatch) should be branded with the capital letters 'T. M.,' and enrolled in a detached company, to be known by the name of 'The Turreted Monster' henceforth and forever."

[1] A few weeks afterward, at the close of the summer, Colonel Charles Rivers Ellet applied for leave of absence on account of illness, and in August retired to the home of his uncle, Dr. Ellet, at Bunker Hill, Illinois. He had been troubled with a severe attack of neuralgia in the face, for which he was in the habit of taking some opiate. On the night of October 16th he died, either from an overdose of morphine or from prostration. He was little more than twenty years old, was a man of great literary culture and refinement, and had shouldered responsibilities such as few of much riper years were called upon to bear.

POSITION OF WILLIAMS'S CANAL.

THE LAKE PROVIDENCE ROUTE.

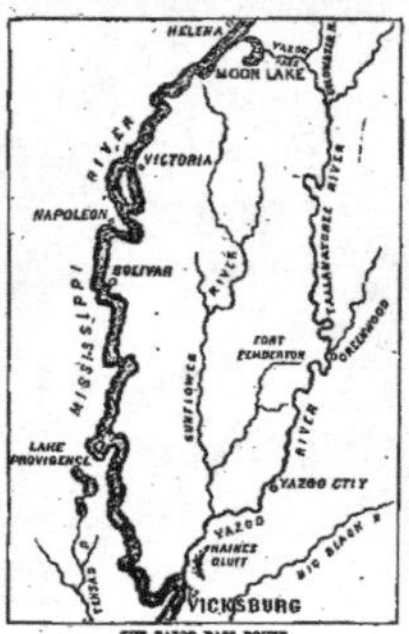

THE YAZOO PASS ROUTE.

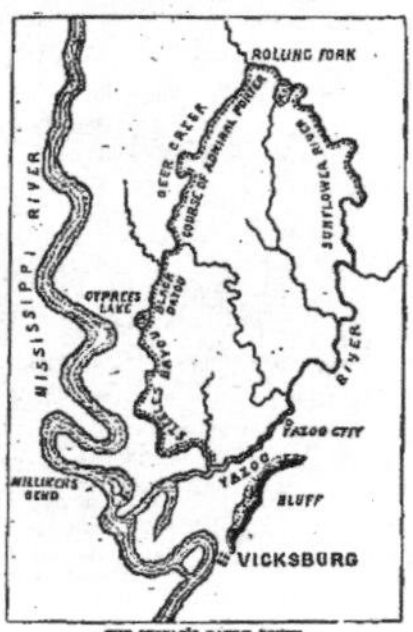

THE STEELE'S BAYOU ROUTE.

NEGROES AT WORK ON THE CANAL.

First among these was General Williams's Canal, to which allusion has already been made. Grant came down to Young's Point in person on the 2d of February, and under his superintendence the work on the canal was re-opened and vigorously prosecuted. To secure the encampment from inundation, a levee was constructed on the eastern side. The river was rising rapidly, and it proved difficult to keep the gathering flood out of the canal and the camps. While the work was still going on, on the 8th of March the levee gave way suddenly just west of the canal, and the waters with great violence rushed in, carrying away the dikes which had been built and the implements of the workmen, and, entering the camps, drove the soldiers to the refuge of the levee. The entire peninsula south of the railroad was flooded.

Failing to find a route for his transports to a point below Vicksburg by means of the canal, Grant directed his attention more prominently toward another mode of effecting this object, by a route which his engineers had pronounced practicable. By cutting a channel into Lake Providence from the Mississippi, it was thought possible that transports might be conveyed through that lake, then through the Tensas, Black, and Red Rivers into the Mississippi below Natchez. Work had been begun on the channel shortly after the work on the canal had been reopened. This Lake Providen route would have brought the army down to a point far below Vicksbur but it would have enabled Grant to co-operate with Banks at Port Hudso The channel, about a mile in length, was completed March 16th. Befo however, any thing had been fairly done in making this plan available, t promise of success by means of a similar route on the east side of the riv created a diversion. The flood, to which a path was opened by the La Providence Canal, inundated a large district of country in Louisiana, son portion of which was a fine cotton-growing region.

The plan of operations on the east of the Mississippi, by the Yazoo Pa route, had at first for its object only the destruction of the enemy's transpor on the Yazoo, and the gun-boats which were being built on that strea Eight miles below Helena (but on the opposite bank) a canal was cut in Moon Lake, from which, by Yazoo Pass and the Coldwater and Tallahatch Rivers, there was a passage into the Yazoo. The navigation by this rou proving better than was expected, Grant entertained a hope of gaining this way a foothold on the high land above Haines's Bluff. Major Gener J. B. McPherson, commanding the Seventeenth Corps, was directed to ho his men in readiness to move by this route, and he was re-enforced by o

BREAK IN THE MISSISSIPPI LEVEE, NEAR THE CANAL.

division from McClernand's and another from Sherman's corps. "But," says General Grant, "while my forces were opening one end of the pass, the enemy was diligently closing the other end, and in this way succeeded in gaining time to strongly fortify Greenwood, below the junction of the Tallahatchie and Yalabusha." The passage into the Coldwater River was an affair of great difficulty. The flood which had been occasioned by the cutting of the canal, the swift current of the stream, and the gigantic branches of the cypress and sycamore overhanging the boats and obstructing their passage, rendered the progress of the expedition very slow, the rate of speed being about one mile in four hours. The boats were greatly damaged, but the expedition succeeded in reaching the junction at Greenwood, where Fort Pemberton opposed such a resistance that it was compelled finally to withdraw. An unsuccessful attempt was made by the gun-boats to reduce the fort, which they bombarded for two days. The land about the fort was loose, and at this time flooded with water, a circumstance which debarred the army from co-operation in the attack. The Confederate force was estimated at over

IN THE SWAMPS.

BAYOU NAVIGATION.

AMONG THE BAYOUS.

McCLERNAND'S CORPS MARCHING THROUGH THE BOGS.

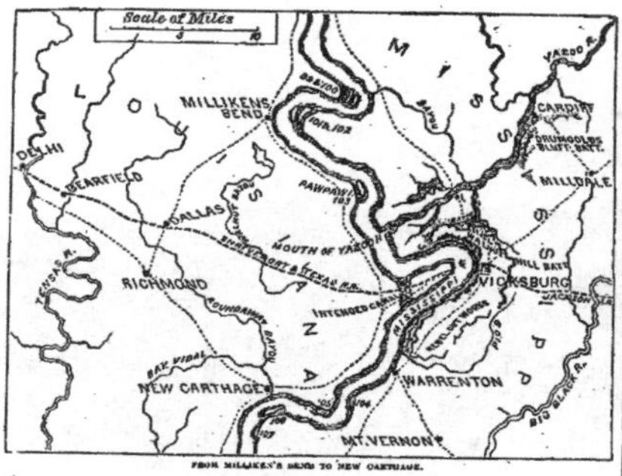

FROM MILLIKEN'S BEND TO NEW CARTHAGE.

5000 men, under the command of General Tilghman, who a year before had been captured at Fort Henry, in Kentucky.

Another plan was then attempted by which Fort Greenwood might be avoided and left in the rear. This was to be effected by a passage up the Yazoo River to Cypress Bayou (opposite the position occupied by Sherman in the attack on Chickasaw Bluffs the previous December), thence into Steele's Bayou, and through Little Black Fork into the Big Sunflower River, and turning at Rolling Fork southward into Deer Creek, which empties into the Yazoo above Haines's Bluff. The expedition, commanded by Admiral Porter, consisted of the gun-boats Pittsburg, Louisville, Mound City, Cincinnati, and Carondelet, with a number of small transports. Porter found a co-operating military force essential, and a column was sent under Sherman. "The expedition failed," says Grant, "probably more from want of knowledge as to what would be required to open this route than from any impracticability in the navigation of the streams and bayous through which it was proposed to pass. Want of this knowledge led the expedition on until difficulties were encountered, and then it would become necessary to send back to Young's Point for the means of removing them. This gave the enemy time to move forces to effectually checkmate farther progress, and the expedition was withdrawn when within a few hundred yards of free and open navigation to the Yazoo."

Grant then reverted to his original plan of moving his transports to the south of Vicksburg. His engineers had prospected a route through the bayous which ran from near Milliken's Bend on the north and New Carthage on the south, through Roundabout Bayou into Tensas River. The route was opened, and one small steamer and a number of barges were taken through the channel. But about the middle of April, the river beginning to fall rapidly, the roads became passable between Milliken's Bend and New Carthage, and communication by water was out of the question.

In the course of the Deer Creek raid a Federal soldier is reported to have been captured and taken before a Confederate officer, when the following colloquy took place: "What in the devil is Grant in here for? what does he expect to do?" "To take Vicksburg," was the reply. "Well, hasn't the old fool tried this ditching and flanking five times already?" "Yes," replied the soldier, "but he has got thirty-seven more plans in his pocket."[1] It is quite impossible to conceive what these other thirty-seven plans could have been, for certainly, with the exception of that which was next put in operation, and which resulted in the capture of Vicksburg, it seems that every possible mode of approaching, turning, or avoiding the city had been tried.

Grant's idea, from his first arrival at Young's Point, was to get his army across the river at a point below Vicksburg, having effected which, he proposed to attack the city from the rear. He was now able to set about this work in earnest. It was with this view that he had sought to open a water communication between Milliken's Bend and New Carthage. At the same time, he had determined to occupy the latter place with his troops. New Carthage was the first point below Vicksburg that could be reached by land at the stage of water then existing. On the 29th of March, McClernand, with his corps, was ordered to advance and occupy this position, to be followed by Sherman's and McPherson's corps as soon as supplies and ammunition for them could be transported. The roads, though level, were intolerably bad, and as McClernand's advance reached Smith's Plantation, two miles from New Carthage, it was found that the levee of Bayou Vidal was broken in several places, and New Carthage had been insulated. The troops were therefore compelled to take a more circuitous route by marching twelve miles around the bayou to Perkins's Plantation. Supplies of provisions, ammunition, and ordnance for the troops had to be hauled over bad roads for a distance of thirty-five miles from Millike McClernand's advance was therefore one of extreme difficulty.

[1] *Iowa Colonels and Regiments*, p. 228.

As the water fell it was found necessary to get the transports w to convey the army across the Mississippi down the river by ru Vicksburg batteries. The gun-boats selected to convoy the trans the Benton, Lafayette, Price, Louisville, Carondelet, Pittsburg, T and Mound City—all iron-clad except the Price. Three transp selected—the Forest Queen, Henry Clay, and Silver Wave—their being protected by cotton bales. They were laden with supplies night of April 16th the expedition set out. The iron-clads wer down in single file, and when abreast of the batteries were to e latter, covering the transports with the smoke of their cannonade. not opened upon the fleet until it was squarely in front of Vicks then the gun-boats responded, pouring their full broadside of tv guns into the city. Into the cloud of smoke which now rolle above the gun-boats the three transports entered. The Forest the advance, received a shot in the hull and another through t drum, which disabled her instantly. The Henry Clay, next in stopped to prevent her running into the crippled vessel, and at moment received a shell which set fire to her cotton. Her de crew launched the yawl and made for the shore, while the trans blaze of flame, floated down the river, finally disappearing below W The Forest Queen was towed down by a gun-boat, and the Silv escaped uninjured.

Succeeding in getting these two transports down, Grant ordered to be sent in the same manner. Five of these, on the 22d, suc passing the batteries with slight damage; the other was sunk just a ing the last battery.

Admiral Porter repaired the damaged transports, five of wh brought into running order, while the other two were in a fit con serve as barges. The limited number of transports in his posse Grant to extend his line of movement to Hard Times, in Louisiana, five miles from Milliken's Bend. Here, before the end of April, teenth Corps (McClernand's) was in readiness for the campaign ab undertaken across the river.

It was at this crisis that Colonel Grierson's raid was undertak directions from General Grant. The entire Confederate force in t bordering on the Mississippi was now being gathered together to blows which Grant was preparing to strike. Thus the way was ope of those bold cavalry incursions for which hitherto only the Con had distinguished themselves, but which, from this time, became a p feature in the national conduct of the war. Morgan, Forrest, and V had set the example, which was to be followed now by Colonel Gri a bold movement from La Grange, in Tennessee, through the Stat sissippi to Baton Rouge, in Louisiana.

At the outbreak of the war, Colonel Grierson, a native of Illinois, the army as an aid to General Prentiss. Subsequently colonel of t Illinois, he soon rose to the command of a brigade in Grant's arm force placed at his disposal for his celebrated raid consisted of a 1700 strong, composed of the Sixth and Seventh Illinois and Seco Cavalry.

La Grange, the starting-point of the expedition, is an inland tow fifty miles east from Memphis, on the southern border of Tennessee. son's command set out from this place on the morning of April 1 Sixth Illinois in the advance. At night the head of the column er within four miles of Ripley, the first town reached after crossing th sippi border. The route of the expedition through Mississippi, as seen from the following map, passed entirely around Pemberton's a tween the Ohio and Mobile and the New Orleans and Jackson R crossing the railroad leading east from Vicksburg a little south tur, and the New Orleans Railroad just in the rear of Natchez. Aft days of adventurous riding, and meeting only inconsiderable deta of the enemy, which were easily scattered, the command on the nigh 19th reached Mr. Wetherall's plantation, eight miles south of Ponto

GRANT'S TRANSPORTS RUNNING THE BATTERIES.

BENJAMIN H. GRIERSON.

SAVING THE BRIDGE ACROSS PEARL RIVER.

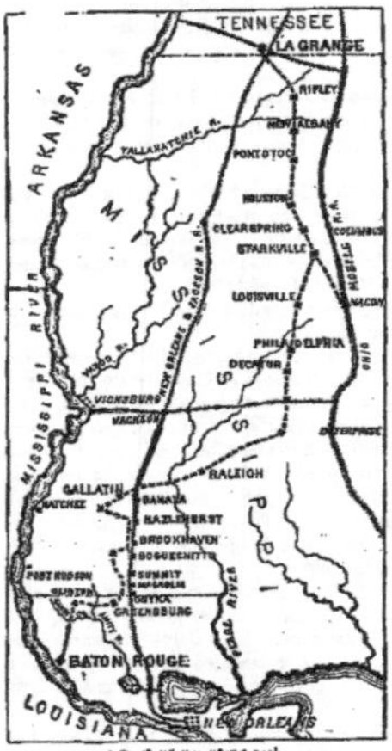

ROUTE OF GRIERSON'S RAID.

DESTROYING RAILROADS.

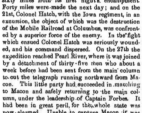

GRIERSON'S COMMAND ENTERING BATON ROUGE.

sixty miles from its first night's encampment. Forty miles were made the next day; and on the 21st, Colonel Hatch, with the Iowa regiment, in an excursion, the object of which was the destruction of the Mobile Railroad at Columbus, was confronted by a superior force of the enemy. In the fight which ensued Colonel Hatch was seriously wounded, and his command dispersed. On the 27th the expedition reached Pearl River, where it was joined by a detachment of thirty-five men who about a week before had been sent from the main column to cut the telegraph running northward from Macon. This little party had succeeded in marching to Macon and safely returning to the main column, under the leadership of Captain Forbes. It had been in great peril, for the whole state was now alarmed. Unable to capture Macon, it was misled by false information to Enterprise, where, but for the boldness of Captain Forbes, it would have fallen into the hands of three thousand Confederate soldiers. The captain, understanding his danger, tried to bluff the enemy, and succeeded. He rode boldly up to the town with a flag of truce, and demanded the instant surrender of the place to Colonel Grierson. Colonel Goodwin, commanding the Confederate force, asked an hour to consider the proposition, to which request Forbes was only too willing to accede. That hour, with rapid riding, delivered his little company from its embarrassing situation.

In the mean time, the main column, which, after Hatch's defeat, only numbered 1000 men, had been rescued from imminent peril by a deliverance still more remarkable, because it was providential rather than strategic. During the 22d and the following night, the expedition made the most difficult march of the raid. Waiting in the morning for the return of a battalion which had been detailed to destroy a large shoe factory near Starkville, it had been delayed, and toward night found itself entangled in the swamps of the Okanoxubee River, a few miles south of Louisville. The water in many places on the roads was four or five feet deep, and the tired horses, after a march already accomplished of over fifty miles, and now confronted by a waste of water, without the light of day to guide their path, were many of them drowned. Fortunately not a man was lost, and the next morning (that of the 23d) found the entire column hurrying forward to reach the bridge across Pearl River. Confederate scouts had gone before them, and if the bridge should be destroyed there was no hope of escape. It was not till late in the afternoon that Colonel Prime, with the Seventh Illinois, neared the bridge. Upon a closer approach it was discovered that the enemy's scouts were already engaged in the destruction of the bridge, stripping up the planks and hurling them into the river. The scouts were driven from the bridge, which in a few minutes more would have been rendered useless. This was near Decatur, where, on the next day, Grierson destroyed two warehouses full of commissary stores, several carloads of ammunition, and burned the railroad bridges and trestle-work, besides capturing two trains of cars

THE ADVANCE ON PORT GIBSON.

locomotives. On the morning of the 27th they reached the Pearl a point sixty miles nearer its mouth. Here again they were fortu btaining ferriage across the river.. At Gallatin, on the night of the y captured a 32-pounder rifled Parrott gun and 1400 pounds of

At Babala, on the 28th, four companies, detailed for that purpose, l the railroad dépôt and transportation. The next day, at Brook n the New Orleans and Jackson Railroad, the Seventh Illinois rough the streets, burned the railroad dépôt, cars, and bridges, and ver 200 prisoners. After farther destruction of railroads and stores Chito and Summit, Grierson's command on the 1st of May, near turned to the main road to avail itself of a bridge, its only means g an important stream. Here it fell into an ambuscade, and Lieu olonel Blackburn was severely wounded. That night it crossed ver, evading the sleeping pickets of the enemy. Finally, at noon , the raiders galloped into the streets of Baton Rouge, as dusty, d wayworn a band of heroes as ever was seen.

raid, Grierson's command, by a succession of forced marches, often lrenching rain and almost impassable swamps, sometimes without rty-eight hours, had in sixteen days traversed 800 miles of hostile destroying railroad bridges, transportation, and commissary stores, large number of prisoners, and destroying 3000 stand of arms, at nly twenty-seven men.

sult of his observations, Grierson writes:

trength of the rebels has been over-estimated. They have neither or the resources we have given them credit for. Passing through try, I found thousands of good Union men, who were ready and a return to their allegiance the moment they could do so with themselves and families. They will rally around the old flag by never our army advances. I could have brought away a thou me, who were anxious to come—men whom I found fugitives homes, hid in the swamps and forests, where they were hunted easts by conscripting officers with blood-hounds."

adred negroes followed the raiders into Baton Rouge on the cap es.

It was Grierson's raid which first demonstrated that the Confederacy was but a shell, strong at the surface by reason of organized armies, but hollow within, and destitute of resources to sustain or of strength to re cruit those armies.

The same day that Grierson entered Baton Rouge was fought and won the battle of Port Gibson, the first of a series of victorious battles in the rear of Vicksburg which in the course of two months had their crowning success in the capture of the "heroic city."

CHAPTER XXVII.

THE WAR ON THE MISSISSIPPI.—(*Continued.*)

Opening of the new Campaign against Vicksburg.—Getting into Position.—Battle of Port Gibson and Evacuation of Grand Gulf.—Feint Attack at Haines's Bluff.—General Banks's Progress in Louisiana.—Port Hudson.—Farragut runs the Blockade.—Battle at Raymond.—Capture of Jackson.—Battle of Champion Hill.—McClernand's Fight on the Black River.—Investment of Vicksburg.—First Assault, May 19th.—Second Assault, May 22d.—The Siege.—The Capitulation.—Results of the Campaign.—Capture of Port Hudson.

AT length the campaign was opened which was to result in the capture of Vicksburg. The transports had been brought down, and three corps of troops were in motion. McClernand, who had the advance, had been waiting—"impatiently waiting," according to his report, for an opportunity, had with considerable difficulty crossed the peninsula from Milliken's Bend to New Carthage. "Old roads," says he, "were repaired, new ones made, boats constructed for the transportation of men and supplies, twenty miles of levee sleeplessly guarded day and night, and every possible precaution used to prevent the rising flood from breaking through and ingulfing us." He had also to contend with Harrison's cavalry, which finally retreated to Perkins's Plantation, six miles below New Carthage. Upon McClernand's approach, New Carthage was hastily abandoned by the enemy, who, taking refuge at James's Plantation, a mile and a half below, was dislodged also from that position. The arrival of the transports at this point accelerated the movement of the corps, which advanced from New Carthage to Perkins's Plantation, General Hovey constructing on this route nearly 2000 feet of bridging out of extemporized material, thus in the short space of three days completing the military road from the river above to a point on the river forty miles below Vicksburg.

On the 22d of April Porter notified McClernand that on the following morning he would attack Grand Gulf, requesting the latter to send an infantry force to occupy the place so soon as he should succeed in silencing the enemy's guns. Osterhaus's division was detached for this purpose; but, after farther consideration, the attack was postponed. The line being now extended southward on account of the limited number of transports, McClernand advanced to Hard Times, fifteen miles below Perkins's Plantation, and seventy miles from Milliken's Bend. This position was three miles above Grand Gulf. It being desirable to get below this strong-hold, the cavalry, followed by McClernand's, and afterward by McPherson's corps, crossed Coffee Point to D'Schron's Plantation, and on to a point opposite Bruinsburg. While the cavalry were reconnoitring this route, an attack was made (April 29th) on Grand Gulf by the gun-boats, a military force 15,000 strong having embarked on transports for the purpose of effecting a landing in case the attack succeeded. Seven gun-boats participated in the attack—the Louisville,

Carondelet, Mound City, Pittsburg, Tuscumbia, Benton, and Lafayette. The three last mentioned attacked the upper and more formidable batteries. The batteries below were soon silenced, and the entire force of the bombardment was directed against the upper one, which had been hotly engaged by the Benton and Tuscumbia. Both these vessels were now suffering severely. Many on board were numbered among the killed and wounded; and, just as the Pittsburg came up to their support, a large shell passed through the Benton's pilot-house, wounding her pilot and disabling her wheel, so that she was forced to drift down and repair her injuries. In a very short time the Pittsburg had lost eight killed and sixteen wounded. The Tuscumbia, too, was being badly cut up. General Grant was watching the conflict from a tug-boat, and to him the prospect of success in this direct attack did not appear promising. The gun-boats had now fought at a disadvantage for nearly six hours in the strong currents and eddies of the stream, and were being very much crippled, while the guns of the enemy's batteries were apparently uninjured.

It was therefore determined to cross over to Bruinsburg—the landing for Port Gibson—and to turn the position at Grand Gulf. McClernand's corps was disembarked at Bruinsburg before noon on the 30th, and, after a distribution to the troops of three days' rations, which took up three or four hours, the army began its advance toward Port Gibson. McPherson's corps followed as rapidly as possible.

The march began at three o'clock P.M. Carr's division moved in the van, followed in order by Osterhaus's, Hovey's, and A. J. Smith's. There was no halting except for the preliminary packing of haversacks, and, in the case of Benton's brigade, even this had been dispensed with. This brigade, the first of Carr's division, had moved forward as soon as it was landed, and had left a detail behind to bring its supplies; not a light labor, when it is remembered that the brave fellows carried these provisions upon their backs under a broiling sun for a distance of four miles. Benton's command having gained the hills, four miles back from the river, and waited there for its rations, the whole corps was soon in motion. It marched on until midnight, when, about eight miles out from Bruinsburg, there was a smart encounter with the enemy. A fight of two or three hours ensued, in which the artillery took chief part, resulting in the withdrawal of the enemy. Farther advance was impossible, and the soldiers laid down and slept upon their arms until daylight. They had been awakened the morning before at three o'clock by the bombardment of Grand Gulf—covering the movement of the transports down the river—and for twenty-four hours had not had a moment's sleep. At dawn the march was resumed, and continued for four miles, when the enemy was encountered in his chosen position on Centre Creek, three miles west of Port Gibson.

Grant's movement had proved a complete surprise to Pemberton, who, until the last fortnight, had supposed Tullahoma, in Tennessee, to be the object of the impending campaign rather than Vicksburg. As late as April 13th, three days before the first passage of Grant's transports below Vicksburg, Pemberton telegraphed to Joe Johnston, then at Tullahoma, "I am satisfied Rosecrans will be re-enforced from Grant's army. Shall I order troops to Tullahoma?" But on the 17th the descent of the transports had apparently convinced him of his mistake, as he then telegraphed to Johnston the "return" of Grant, and the "resumption" of operations against Vicksburg. From this time he was scarcely allowed either the chance of a doubt as to Grant's real intentions, or time for preparation. And what time he had slipped leisurely away without any show of positive energy on his part. He must have known, when he saw the transports going down, that an attempt would be made by Grant to cross the river *somewhere* below Vicksburg, and that probably it would be made at Grand Gulf. Thus, on the 29th of April, he telegraphed to Johnston, "The enemy is at Hard Times in large force, with barges and transports, indicating a purpose to attack Grand Gulf, with a view to Vicksburg."

The only preparation which he had made against this contemplated attack was to send a few thousand troops, under command of General Bowen, to Grand Gulf. The attempt to occupy Grand Gulf was made, as we have seen, on the 29th; it was going on, indeed, while Pemberton was telegraphing the above dispatch to Johnston. But suddenly the attack was given up, and Bowen, leaving a small force at Grand Gulf, found it necessary, with an incompetent army, to move southward from the mouth of the Big Black, putting that river between himself and Vicksburg. Re-enforcements were on the way; but Grant was moving with precipitate rapidity, and nothing could now prevent his immediately landing two corps. On the morning of the 1st of May, Bowen found himself, with only two brigades, in a position which should have been taken ere this by the greater portion of Pemberton's army. His situation made victory for him impossible, for Grant almost inevitable. One thing, and but one, was in his favor; this was the character of the country in which he must venture battle—"a country," said Grant, "the most broken and difficult to operate in I ever saw." It is, of course, useless to speculate as to what might have happened had Pemberton appreciated the importance of the strongest possible resistance at this point; but it is none the less a damaging fact that he did *not* appreciate it. But it was too late now for Pemberton to speculate about the matter; the Vicksburg campaign was already virtually decided. Bowen, resist however bravely he might, must retreat; and Grant must advance, carrying with him the key of Vicksburg.

Bowen's resistance was as gallant and as obstinate as the circumstances of his situation allowed. His army, if it might be called an army, was posted on Centre Creek, where, out of the road leading from Bruinsburg, two others branched in opposite directions, but each conducting to Port Gibson. Upon the one rested his right, and his left upon the other. He had between five and six thousand men. Opposed to him were more than twice his own numbers, supported by a full corps, which was moving rapidly upon the field. But in such a position a small force easily opposes a very much larger one. The roads run along narrow ridges, with deep and almost impenetrable ravines on either side. Only a comparatively small army can be brought into action at one time in such a field, and it is only by long-continued fighting that the superiority in numbers is made to tell.

It was McClernand's corps which, on the national side, fought the battle of Port Gibson. Carr's division held the front, the first brigade on the right, and the second on the left. Hovey's division occupied the ridges on Carr's right. Osterhaus's confronted the enemy's left, and secured McClernand's rear. When A. J. Smith's division came up, it moved into the position first occupied by Hovey, while the latter advanced to the support of Benton's brigade (Carr's right), which had been fighting against odds for nearly two hours. Opposite the Eighteenth Indiana regiment, which was Benton's right, touching the road from Bruinsburg at Magnolia Church, was a Confederate battery, situated on an elevated position, and which was a source of great annoyance. A spirited charge was made by detachments from both Carr's and Hovey's divisions, resulting in the capture of this battery and 400 prisoners—an achievement which should be credited to both divisions. From this time the enemy was steadily though slowly driven back. Several attempts on his part, directed against McClernand's centre, had already

GENERAL LOGAN CROSSING THE BAYOU PIERRE.

failed; against Osterhaus's position on the left he still maintained his ground, until finally J. E. Smith's brigade, of McPherson's corps, came to the assistance of Osterhaus, when, by a flank movement, Bowen was driven from the field; yet, from the nature of the ground and the approach of darkness, he was able to retire in good order. The next morning Port Gibson was occupied by McPherson's corps, after bridging the Bayou Pierre, the enemy having burned the bridge in his retreat. The national loss in the battle had been 130 killed and 718 wounded; that of the enemy was in proportion probably much heavier.

On the 3d of May, as a consequence of his defeat at Port Gibson, the enemy evacuated Grand Gulf just as Admiral Porter was about to subject that position to another bombardment. As soon as the place was abandoned, Grant determined to make it his base of supplies. His forces had now advanced fifteen miles out, to Hankinson's Ferry, on the Big Black. Before any farther progress could be ventured, it was necessary to complete the arrangements occasioned by the change of base from Bruinsburg to Grand Gulf, and to wait for Sherman's corps.

This corps had been left behind until the last, as a blind to Pemberton, to prevent his sending heavy re-enforcements southward from Vicksburg to Bowen's army. Sherman, on April 28th, received an order from Grant to make a feint the next day against the Confederate batteries on the Yazoo simultaneously with the attack on Grand Gulf. The field in which this demonstration was to be made was the scene of his repulse four months before, and the associations revived were doubtless not of a pleasant character to General Sherman, who was now called upon—by a threatening advance, to be followed by a hasty retreat—to incur the popular suspicion of a second defeat. But Sherman could afford to look past disaster in the face, and to defy the popular impression which his present task must occasion, but which succeeding events would shortly dispel. So far as his own army was concerned, there would also exist, for a brief period, this unfavorable impression; but it could not last long enough to cause demoralization, or to impair the confidence of his soldiers in his military leadership. He embarked General Blair's division on ten steam-boats, and at 10 A.M. on April 29th entered the waters of the Yazoo, where he found the flag-boat Black Hawk, the iron-clads Choctaw and De Kalb, the gun-boat Tyler, and several smaller wooden boats, ready for co-operation. During that night this military and naval force lay off the mouth of Chickasaw Bayou, and early next morning got within range of the Confederate batteries. A vigorous bombardment of the latter was kept up for four hours, and, toward evening, Blair's division was disembarked in full view of the enemy, as if intending an assault. The ruse succeeded; for, although there was no road across the submerged field which lay between the river and the bluff, it seemed to the enemy, from his previous experience of Sherman's movements, more than probable that a real attack would be ventured. After the landing of the troops, the gun-boats and the batteries resumed their cannonade. The 1st of May, while the battle of Port Gibson was being fought, was occupied on the Yazoo in movements similar to those of the day before. In the midst of these movements, orders came from Grant hurrying Sherman's corps forward down the river to Grand Gulf. The force in front of the Yazoo batteries vanished as rapidly as it had appeared. Sherman, dispatching orders to Steele and Tuttle to march to Grand Gulf by way of Richmond, silently fell down to Young's Point on the night of May 1st.

At noon on May 6th Sherman's corps reached Hard Times. In the course of the next two days it had crossed the Mississippi and marched to Hankinson's Ferry, where it relieved Crocker's division, and enabled it to join McPherson's corps in the advance movement which had been ordered by Grant the day previous.

Grant's purpose had originally been to collect all his forces at Grand Gulf, accumulate a good supply of provisions and ordnance-stores before moving, and, during the time thus occupied, detach one of his corps to co-operate with General Banks in the reduction of Port Hudson; after which, by a junction of the two armies, he would have an additional force of about 12,000 men to bring against Vicksburg. But, after the advantage he had gained at the outset in defeating Bowen, he wisely deemed it not worth his while to wait for Banks, who was now west of the Mississippi, and could not be at Port Hudson before May 10th, and determined, from the foothold already acquired, to push rapidly northward to the rear of Vicksburg. He knew that Johnston would, as quickly as possible, re-enforce Pemberton, and that if he waited for the capture of Port Hudson, while the delay might bring him a few thousand more men, it would bring Pemberton a much larger force. He therefore, on the 7th, had ordered a general movement of his army against the railroad conducting from Vicksburg westward to Jackson.

Before following the course of this campaign through the battles immediately preceding the investment of Vicksburg, let us glance at General Banks's progress in Louisiana up to the commencement of operations against Port Hudson.

General Banks arrived at New Orleans December 14th, 1862, when he assumed the command of the Department of the Gulf, relieving General Butler. He brought with him a military force of about 10,000 men, and the fleet with which he sailed consisted of twenty-six steam and twenty-five sailing vessels. The entire Army of the Gulf, thus re-enforced, numbered 30,000 men, and was designated the Nineteenth Army Corps. General Banks's object was threefold—to regulate the civil government of Louisiana; to direct the military movements against the rebellion in that state and in Texas; and to co-operate in the opening of the Mississippi by the reduction of Port Hudson. This latter post, lying within his department,

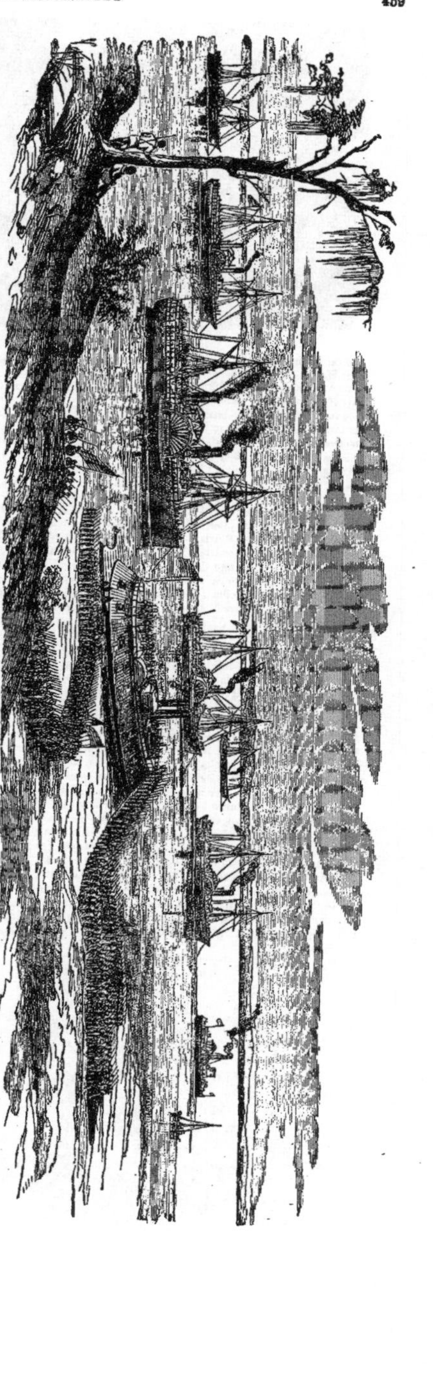

BANKS'S LANDING AT BATON ROUGE, LOUISIANA.

BURNING OF THE MISSISSIPPI.

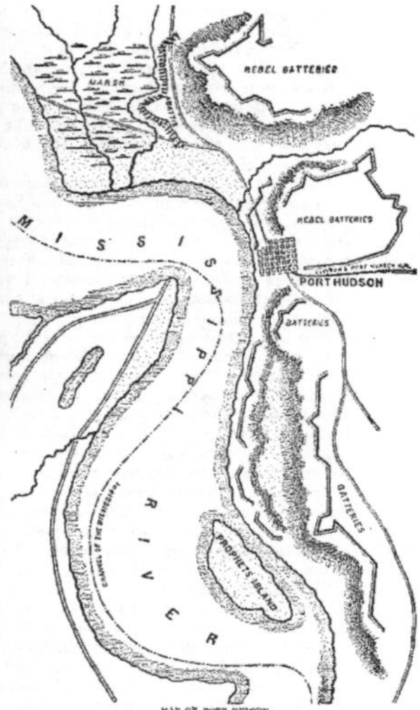

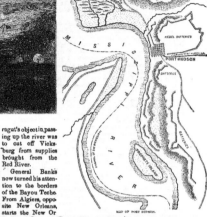

MAP OF PORT HUDSON.

was on the east bank of the Mississippi, at the terminus of the Clinton and Port Hudson Railroad, twenty-five miles above Baton Rouge.

The first notice taken of Port Hudson as a military post was in the latter part of August, 1862, when W. D. Porter, of the Essex, went up the river to reconnoitre the batteries reported to be in process of erection at this point. At that time no guns could be discovered, but earthworks were being constructed. About a week after this reconnoissance, the Anglo-American, in passing Port Hudson, was opened upon from three batteries, and received seventy-three shots.

In March, 1863, General Banks had concentrated at Baton Rouge, which he had reoccupied immediately after his arrival at New Orleans, an army of 25,000 men, and on the 13th made a strong demonstration against Port Hudson. All that was intended to be effected by this was a diversion in favor of Admiral Farragut, who, with a naval force (consisting of the Hartford, Mississippi, Richmond, and Monongahela, and the gun-boats Albatross, Genesee, Kineo, Essex, and Sachem, and six schooners), was about to run the Port Hudson batteries, which had been multiplied and strengthened during the last six months. Had Banks, instead of merely making a demonstration, invested Port Hudson, it might, according to Halleck's report, have been easily reduced; but as the garrison consisted at this time of about 18,000 men, this result would not probably have been reached.

Farragut had to pass a line of batteries commencing below the town and extending along the bluff about three and a half miles. Early on the 14th his fleet reached Prophet's Island, five miles below Port Hudson. In the afternoon the mortars and two of the gun-boats opened on the batteries, and at 9 30 P.M. the signal to advance was given. The Hartford, with the admiral on board, took the lead, with the gun-boat Albatross lashed to her side. The Richmond and the gun-boat Genesee followed; the Monongahela, with the Kineo, came next, and the Mississippi brought up the rear, the mortars still bombarding the batteries. The admiral's ship passed without difficulty, but the smoke from their fire obscured the river from the vessels following. The Richmond, receiving a shot through her steam-drum, dropped out of fire, with three of her crew killed and seven wounded. The captain of the Monongahela also dropped down the river and anchored. The gun-boat Kineo, her propeller fouled by a hawser, and with a shot through her rudder-post, followed their example. So accurate was the fire from the batteries that the destruction of the whole fleet was imminent. The Mississippi grounded, and, after destroying her engines, spiking her guns, and setting her on fire, Captain Smith, with the officers and crew, abandoned her, escaping to the shore opposite Port Hudson. The vessel soon drifted down the river, and finally exploded. Such is the story of the fleet. General Banks had a slight encounter with the enemy, and returned to Baton Rouge. Farragut's object in passing up the river was to cut off Vicksburg from supplies brought from the Red River.

General Banks now turned his attention to the borders of the Bayou Teche. From Algiers, opposite New Orleans, starts the New Orleans and Opelousas Railroad, terminating at Brashear City, eighty miles distant, where Grand Lake forms a junction with the Atchafalaya. Opposite Brashear City is Berwick, near the entrance of the Bayou Teche into the Atchafalaya. Starting from a point near Opelousas, the Teche runs southeastwardly about two hundred miles. The principal towns on its banks are Franklin, Martinsville, and Opelousas. It was up this river that, only a few weeks previous, General Weitzel had attempted to advance, but, meeting so stubborn a resistance from the Confederate General Mouton, aided by the gun-boat Cotton, had been compelled to fall back. Apprehending a second advance, however, the enemy had burned the gun-boat. The obstructions put in Weitzel's way had also been swept away by the current of the bayou. But, a few miles above Pattersonville, on the river, Fort Bisland had been constructed, and was held by several thousand Confederates.

This region was the richest in the state, and Banks devoted himself to its reclamation from the enemy. Having concentrated his forces at Brashear City, Weitzel's brigade was crossed over to Berwick on the 10th of April, followed shortly by General Emory's division. As Banks advanced up the bayou, General Dick Taylor, commanding the Confederates, retired upon Fort Bisland. On the 12th, Grover's division, embarked on transports, and accompanied by the national gun-boats Clifton, Estrella, Arizona, and Calhoun, entered Grand Lake, the object of the expedition being to get in Taylor's rear, and either to cut off his retreat if he evacuated his works, or, if he remained, to attack him, co-operating with the forces in front. On the 13th this division landed about three miles west of Franklin. The enemy, on its approach, blew up the Queen of the West, which he had only recently captured. A fight occurred at Irish Bend, where Grover landed, and the enemy retreated, destroying, as he fell back, his gun-boat Diana, and some transports at Franklin. Banks meanwhile pushing him in front, Taylor was obliged to abandon his fortified position. He was vigorously pursued; at New Iberia, on his retreat, he destroyed five transports loaded with commissary stores and ammunition, and a gun-boat not yet finished. This place was reached by Banks's army on the 17th, and a cannon foundery was taken, and two regiments sent to destroy a celebrated salt mine in the town. Already 1500 prisoners had been captured, besides a large number of horses, mules, and beeves.

Taylor retreated on Opelousas after a brief stand against Grover at Bayou Vermilion. His destruction of bridges as he fell back occasioned some delay in Banks's advance, but the latter reached Opelousas on April 20th, Taylor continuing his retreat toward Alexandria, on the Red River. The gun-boats at the same time oc-

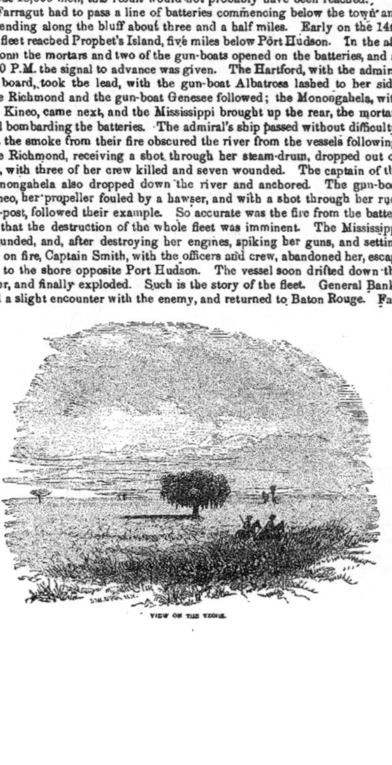

VIEW ON THE TECHE.

MAP OF THE BAYOU TECHE CAMPAIGN.

OCCUPATION OF ALEXANDRIA.

BANKS'S ARMY LEAVING SIMMSPORT.

JOHN A. LOGAN.

cupied Butte-à-la-Rose, opening the Atchafalaya to Red River, and thus establishing communication with Admiral Farragut, who held the mouth of that river. During the first week in May, while Grant was preparing for an advance from Grand Gulf, Taylor evacuated Fort De Russey and Alexandria, falling back to Shreveport, near the border of Texas, with orders from General Moore to withdraw into the latter state if pressed by General Banks. On the 6th of May Admiral Porter appeared before Alexandria with a fleet of gun-boats, and took possession of the town without opposition. Thus, after the capture of 2000 prisoners, two transports, and twenty guns, and compelling the destruction by the enemy of eight transports and three gun-boats, General Banks had conquered all of Louisiana west of New Orleans and south of the Red River, and had possession of the latter stream from its mouth to Shreveport.

He now put his army in motion against Port Hudson, sending as many as possible by water, and marching the remainder to Simmsport, where they were ferried across the Atchafalaya, and moved down the west bank of the Mississippi to a point opposite Bayou Sara, where they crossed on the night of May 23d, and the next day Port Hudson was besieged on the north, while General C. C. Augur, with 3500 men from Baton Rouge, invested it on the south. These two investing armies joined hands on the 25th, after a repulse of the enemy by Augur, and a steady advance of the right wing, under Generals Weitzel, Grover, and Dwight, resulting in the enemy's retiring within his outer line of intrenchments.

General Frank Gardner commanded the garrison at Port Hudson, which had now been very much reduced to meet the more pressing exigencies of the Vicksburg campaign. Leaving this position thus invested by an army of 12,000 men, we return to the battles around Vicksburg.

The movement ordered by General Grant on May 7th, and which had been scarcely begun before the arrival of Sherman's corps, consisted of an advance by two parallel roads up the southeast bank of the Big Black River, McPherson hugging the river closely, McClernand moving on the higher or ridge road, and Sherman following, with his corps divided on the two roads. The movements of these two corps after the battle of Port Gibson had indicated an immediate advance across Black River at Hankinson's or Hall's Ferries toward Warrenton. But their real objective was the Vicksburg and Jackson Railroad, which Grant wished to reach somewhere between Bolton and Edwards's Station. He knew what he had to apprehend from Joe Johnston's army, and that vigorous efforts would be made by the Confederate authorities of Mississippi to arouse the militia against him (Governor Pettus, indeed, had, on May 5th, called upon every man in the state to take up arms) to harass his movements. His eyes were turned now not directly upon Vicksburg—they looked eastward to Jackson. This was a point which

CROCKER'S CHARGE AT JACKSON.

railroad farther to the west.

General Grant moved with Sherman. On th
telegraphed to General Halleck that his forces
Creek, that he should communicate no longer w
fore might not be heard from for several weeks.
eral's own mind, meant "Success is certain, but n
look to the country for my soldiers' rations, and
burg to a new base of supplies on the Yazoo!"

The next day, McPherson, having nearly reac
west of Jackson and south of the railroad, met t
under Generals Gregg and Walker. A battle
Logan's division, which was in the advance, and
a strong position on a creek within three miles of
ies posted on an eminence commanding the road
moving, and with his infantry lying on the hills
and in the timber and ravines in front. Altho
enough to inflict upon Logan a loss of 69 killed a
short duration. After an unsuccessful attempt to
on Logan's left, and a furious charge for the pur
yer's battery, which was repulsed with severe loss
my was driven from the field, and Logan entered
erate loss in this battle was severe both in killed
count of desertion. The killed amounted to 103, t
to 720. The forces engaged were nearly equal.
and Walker's force as 6000. Logan's division wa
Crocker's arrived in time to accelerate the enemy'

At this stage of Grant's progress his army exte
ward toward Edwards's Station. As the enemy c
treated toward Jackson, where re-enforcements w
and where Johnston was hourly expected to take
Sherman and McClernand were ordered to move t
tory to an attack on Jackson. McPherson, on th
ton, the first important position directly west fro
stroyed the railroad and telegraph. Sherman appi
southwest by the Mississippi Springs Road, whil
Raymond, and on the 14th occupied with one div
ond Mississippi Springs, a third remaining at Ray

McPherson and Sherman were the same day
When, at about 10 A.M., the former was within tl
was met by the bulk of the enemy's forces under C
whose command, consisting of South Carolina an
rived the previous evening. At the same time, an
south of Jackson, Sherman encountered the enemy
of great strength. After some delay, caused by a h
disposed his forces for an attack. Crocker's divi
The battle here was almost an exact repetition of t
days before at Raymond, though shorter and less s
duel was followed by an impetuous charge of Cro
ravine in front, up the hill held by the Confederate
the enemy up to and out of their breastworks. Th
until they came within range of the guns defendin
ray's and Dillon's batteries were brought up and s
erates.

The resistance offered to Sherman was feeble, tl
into his interior defenses. The town was then in
the Confederates, and at 4 P.M. the flag of the Fift
ing over the Capitol, McPherson's and Sherman's
place almost simultaneously. McPherson's loss in
and 238 wounded and missing. The Confederate
and prisoners amounted to 845.

General Joe Johnston had reached Jackson on

JOHN C. PEMBERTON.

He conducted the battle of the 14th, superintended the evacuation of Jackson, and then withdrew his army northward. This general—probably the most able officer in the Confederate service—after his wound at the battle of Seven Pines, in Virginia, in May, 1862, was incapable of military service until November following, when he was assigned to the command of the West.[1] He left Richmond with his staff November 29, and on December 4 reached Chattanooga. The next day he went to Murfreesborough, but was still, on account of his wound, prevented from any other than a general supervision of Bragg's army. At this time President Davis was on a tour of inspection in the West. He visited Murfreesborough with Johnston. The next notice we have of Johnston he was with Davis (December 26, 1862) at Jackson, before the Mississippi Legislature. On this occasion the Confederate President addressed a long and eloquent speech to the Legislature. The fact that Davis belonged to Mississippi imparted an unusual interest to this address, which was also very characteristic of the man. He had left his constituency two years before to assume his present position. He alluded in eloquent terms to his political connection with the state, and to his interest in her welfare; he glanced backward to the time when he had last addressed them, and admitted that, while he then had thought war inevitable as the result of secession, the conflict had assumed proportions more gigantic than he had anticipated; this was due to a want of moderation, sagacity, and morality in the Northern people; he wondered now how it had ever been possible for the people of the South "to live for so long a time in association with such miscreants;" and loved so rotten a government. They of Mississippi knew as yet but little of the horrors of the war; but *he*, from his post at Richmond, had witnessed them in the captivity of old men, and the insults offered by "dirty Federal invaders" to delicate women, in the wanton destruction of property, and every imaginable outrage. There was a difference between the two peoples. "Our enemies," he said, "are a traditionless, homeless race;" they had, from the time of Cromwell, been disturbers of the world's peace, first in England, then in Holland, and again in England on their return; unable to let Papacy alone in the Old World, they could not let Quakers and witches alone in the New. Hence, knowing the savagery of the Yankees, it had been his chosen policy to carry on the war on the fields of the enemy—a policy which had been thwarted by the superior power of the North; and this disparity of power it was which had necessitated the rigors of conscription in the South. He appealed to the Mississippians to send every available man to the front, and alluded in complimentary terms to the bravery of the Mississippian soldiers—to the old men among them, and the gentle boys of sixteen, of whom he had heard on Virginia battle-fields. He warned them that every effort would be made by the enemy to capture Vicksburg and Port Hudson, and told them about the brilliant commanders whom he had chosen to defend these positions; then again he invoked them, by the glorious dead of Mexico, and by the still more glorious dead of the battle-fields of the Confederacy, by the desolate widows and orphans left behind, and by their maimed and wounded heroes, to rush forward and place themselves at the disposal of the state. Against the capture of New Orleans he offset the repulse formerly sustained by the enemy's fleet before Vicksburg, and his recent repulse at Fredericksburg; he referred to the smiles of the Emperor Napoleon; prophesied the conversion of the Northwest to the Confederate cause; pointed to the bright hopes of the trans-Mississippi campaign; and, as the climax of hope, mentioned the interesting fact that the gallant State of Kentucky was "still the object of the ardent wishes of General Bragg," and that he had even heard that officer, in an address to his troops, speak longingly of Kentucky and the banks of the Ohio! Such was the address of President Davis. General Johnston was then called upon for a speech. "The scar-worn hero," says a report of the proceedings, "looked a little nervous, while the house rang with loud and prolonged applause. He rose and said: 'Fellow-citizens, my only regret is that I have done so little to merit such a greeting. I promise you, however, that hereafter I shall be watchful, energetic, and indefatigable in your defense.'"

[1] The following is the order issued from the Adjutant and Inspector General's office at Richmond, November 24th, 1862:

"General J. E. Johnston, Confederate States Army, is hereby assigned to the following geographical command, to wit: Commencing with the Blue Ridge of mountains, running through the western part of North Carolina, and following the line of said mountains through the northern part of Georgia to the railroad south of Chattanooga; thence by that road to West Point, and down the west or right bank of the Chattahoochee River to the boundary of Alabama and Florida, following that boundary west to the Choctawhatchee River, and down that river to Choctawhatchee Bay—including the waters of that bay—to the Gulf of Mexico. All that portion of the country west of said line to the Mississippi River is included in the above command. General Johnston will, for the purpose of correspondence and reports, establish his head-quarters at Chattanooga, or such other place as in his judgment may best secure facilities for ready communication with the troops within the limits of his command, and will repair in person to any part of said command whenever his presence may for the time be necessary or desirable.

"By command of the Secretary of War. JOHN WITHERS, A. A. G.

"His Excellency the President, Richmond, Va."

As soon as Davis reached Richmond he was pressed to remove General Bragg and give Johnston command of the Army of Middle Tennessee. Davis referred the matter to Johnston, who (February 12, 1863) expressed his approbation of General Bragg, and his belief that the interests of the service required that the latter should not be removed. A month later, while at Mobile, on his way to Mississippi, Johnston received an order to assume command of the Army of Middle Tennessee, and to direct General Bragg to report to the War Department. When Johnston reached Tullahoma he informed the Secretary of War (March 19th) that the change could not be made, on account of the critical condition of Bragg's family. On the 10th of April he repeated this to President Davis, and added that he himself had been sick, and was not now able to serve in the field. On the 9th of May he was ordered to proceed at once to Mississippi and take chief command of the forces there. Up to this time Johnston had been physically unable to undertake any responsibility for the conduct of the war in Mississippi.

And he assumed the command too late for his assistance to be of any value. Grant's army was already within a short distance of Jackson, while Pemberton, completely deceived by the Federal demonstrations toward Warrenton, was holding the main body of his army on the west bank of the Big Black, in the vicinity of Edwards's Station, where he continued to hold it until after the capture of Jackson, making no attempt to find out the real movements of Grant, or to harass his exposed flank and rear.

This was the situation when Johnston reached Jackson, where his little army of about 6000 men was of course unable to save the place from capture. In retreating he took the Canton Road, by which alone he could preserve communication with Pemberton. Upon Grant's first landing, Johnston had urged Pemberton to attack him without delay, and with all his army. "Success," he said, "will give back what was abandoned to win it." He telegraphed on May 1st to Richmond that Pemberton was calling for re-enforcements, which could not be sent from Bragg's army without giving up Tennessee. "Could not one or two brigades be sent from the East?" A week later Johnston again begged for re-enforcements.

On the night of his arrival at Jackson, Johnston for the first time knew what had been the result of the battle at Port Gibson, and the progress of Grant's army. He urged Pemberton to immediately attack the Federal division at Clinton, and promised co-operation. But his own hands were tied the next day by Grant's advance on Jackson. After abandoning the town, he marched his army six miles the same day, and encamped for the night. He from this encampment sent a dispatch to Pemberton, informing the latter of his situation, and that re-enforcements—under General Gist from the East, and General Maxey from Port Hudson—had been ordered to assemble at some point forty or fifty miles from Jackson. The re-enforcements, he said, would, when gathered together, number from 12,000 to 13,000. As soon as these had joined the two commands under himself and Pemberton, the whole army ought to concentrate and fight a decisive battle.

This dispatch Pemberton says he did not receive until the evening of May 16th. In the mean time this general had ventured a battle on his own account. He had disobeyed Johnston's order to move toward Clinton, compliance with which would have secured the junction of the two commands on the 15th, and proceeded forthwith, against the advice of his subordinate generals, to make a movement which would render union impossible.[1] This

[1] Pemberton, upon the receipt, on the morning of the 14th, of Johnston's order, or rather suggestion, to attack Sherman at Clinton, replied that he would at once move from Edwards's Station in compliance with the order, though he considered the movement a hazardous one. Pemberton thought he ought to remain behind the Big Black, and near Vicksburg. He called a council of war, and the majority decided in favor of the movement indicated by Johnston. The others—including Generals Loring and Stevenson—preferred a movement for the purpose of cutting off Grant from his supplies by the Mississippi. Little did Loring and Stevenson know about Grant's supplies, or the facility with which the latter could feed his army, even if there were no such river as the Mississippi. Pemberton was in favor of neither movement, fearing that either would "remove him from his base," but determined finally (*i. e.*, on the afternoon of the 14th) to direct all his disposable force—about 18,000 men (probably a low estimate)—toward Raymond or Dillon's, in Grant's rear. This plan of the campaign completely ignored the existence of Johnston or his army. Johnston's plan was to attack Grant, and to attack him in such a manner as to secure, first, the co-operation of the two commands, and afterward their concentration. Johnston ignored Vicksburg; it seemed plain enough to him that if Grant could not be beaten in the field, it was not only useless to attempt the defense of Vicksburg against a siege, but involved, moreover, in the end, the capture of the besieged army. Pemberton, on the other hand, was willing to risk every thing for Vicksburg, and would risk nothing which might involve its abandonment. On

McPHERSON AND HIS CHIEF ENGINEERS.

movement led to the battle of Champion's Hill, or Baker's Creek. Johnston, in the mean while, was falling back on Canton, with his hands completely tied so far as any possible co-operation with Pemberton was concerned.¹

The capture of Jackson was followed by the destruction of the railway station, arsenals, workshops, etc., in the town. It would have been well if the work of destruction had here stopped; but some soldiers of Sherman's corps got possession of some bad rum, and burned private houses, the Roman Catholic church, the hotel, and the penitentiary.

In the mean time Pemberton was crossing the Big Black. Having remained idle while Johnston was at hand and fighting, as soon as the latter had retreated he advanced and offered battle. Grant became informed of these movements of the enemy, which were sufficiently convenient to his own purpose. He was now ready to face about toward Vicksburg with his three corps.

Early on the morning of the 16th, Sherman, who had been occupying Jackson, was ordered to join as rapidly as possible the main body of Grant's army, then in the vicinity of Bolton. Blair's division of Sherman's corps was hurried on to Edwards's Station. This division supported the left of McClernand's corps, which moved at the same time.

Three roads to the north of Raymond, leading out from the Raymond and Bolton Road, conducted to Edwards's Station, uniting two miles east of that place. The longer of these roads was a mile and a half north of Raymond, another was two miles farther north, and a third ran out from the Raymond and Bolton Road one mile south of Bolton, and was separated from the second or middle road by a distance of four miles. Upon these roads McClernand advanced on the morning of the 16th. Grant had ordered the advance on the night of the 15th to be made that morning, and McClernand, when he received the order, was ready to move. Hovey's division was at the entrance of the northern road; A. J. Smith's at that of the southern, with Blair in support; and Osterhaus's at that of the middle, supported by General Carr. Grant had already ordered on McPherson's corps, which was ready to support Hovey's division. As these columns advanced, the several divisions supporting each other, their position was one equally fitted for defense and attack.

The enemy, under General Pemberton, had taken a strong position along a ridge of hills east of Edwarde's Station, and on the right bank of Baker's Creek, his front covered by cavalry skirmishers and artillery. Early on the morning of the 16th (6 30 A.M.) Pemberton received a dispatch from General Johnston instructing him to move northward in order to effect a junction of the two commands. It was Pemberton's intention to obey this or-

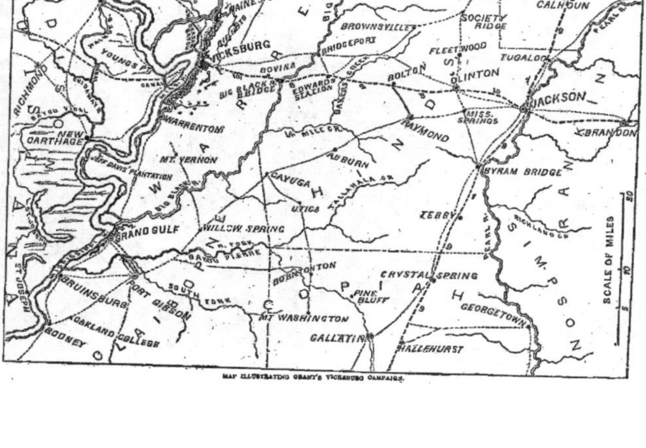

MAP ILLUSTRATING GRANT'S VICKSBURG CAMPAIGN.

¹ ... his own plan he acted without consistency. It was plainly absurd for him to refuse a battle with Johnston's co-operation, and forthwith to bring on one in which only his own command could participate.

der. His trains were ordered back to the Big Black, and the army would have followed had it not been already too late. He wrote to Johnston that he was coming in obedience to orders; but the most important part of his communication was the postscript, which told of heavy skirmishing already begun at the front. The skirmishing went on, and grew into a general engagement. The battle of Champion's Hill had to be fought, and General Pemberton could not help himself.

Five miles out from Edwarde's Station the enemy's skirmishers were first met on A. J. Smith's front. Half a mile brought the division within range of the enemy's artillery, and the advance at this point was delayed till the opposing guns were silenced. Osterhaus, in the centre, heard the firing on his left, and soon after came himself into collision with the enemy on the skirt of a thick wood, "covering," to use McClernand's phrase, "a seeming chaos of abrupt hills and yawning ravines." Soon he came upon the enemy in full force. Two hours and a half after the first skirmishing on the left, McClernand learned from Hovey that the latter "had found the enemy strongly posted in front," and that McPherson was close on his rear. McClernand had been ordered to find the enemy, but to risk an engagement only upon the assurance of certain victory. Grant was on the right, with Hovey and McPherson. He had left Clinton for the front at an early hour. When he reached the junction of the Vicksburg Railroad with the Raymond and Bolton Road, he found McPherson's advance, and his pioneer corps rebuilding a bridge which Osterhaus's cavalry had destroyed the night before. Passing on to the front, after seeing McPherson's two divisions well under way, Grant found Hovey's division ready at any moment to bring on a battle.

The top of the ridge on which the enemy rested was covered with dense forest and undergrowth. On the south side of the Vicksburg Road, which here makes a sharp turn to the left, was a precipitous height resembling in character the adjacent ridge. The country to the right of the road sloped gently through a short reach of timber, then opening into cultivated fields and into a valley of considerable extent. On the road, and into the wooded ravine on the left, lay Hovey's division disposed for attack. McPherson operated on the right of the road, threatening the enemy's rear.

McClernand, as we have seen, had been delayed, skirmishing and driving away the artillery in his front, while Grant, on the right, was waiting to hear from him. McClernand appears to have been extremely solicitous about McPherson's supporting Hovey. Grant, having already settled this matter to his own satisfaction, signified to McClernand a little after noon that he wished him to push forward with all rapidity, and that he would himself attend to Hovey and McPherson.

The Federal left had been made secure by McClernand's judicious disposition of his own and Blair's divisions. When the order came urging forward the left and centre, the right, under Hovey, had been contending for nearly two hours against superior numbers. Hovey's division bore the brunt of the whole conflict. Directly in his front was the Confederate General Stevenson's division, posted in a strong position on Champion Hill, from which the battle is named. One brigade, and then a second, of Crocker's division, was sent to re-enforce Hovey, who, after a difficult approach to the enemy's position under a galling fire, was contending against great odds, and had been borne back by the overwhelming forces of the enemy. Logan had in the mean time gained an important position on Pemberton's left flank, and Grant, appreciating the opportunity thus afforded him, again ordered Hovey's division forward, re-enforced as above stated, and this attack, with that upon the flank, finally drove the enemy from the field. Logan's movement had so far succeeded that the Confederate General Loring's division was cut off from Pemberton, and was compelled to retreat by a long detour southward, evading the Federal left, losing all its guns, and narrowly escaping capture.

Hovey's division lost in this battle 211 killed, 872 wounded, and 119 missing—a total of 1202, about one third of its entire strength. Osterhaus lost 14 killed, 76 wounded, and 20 missing. In A. J. Smith's division the loss was 24 wounded and 4 missing. This record clearly indicates that Hovey, with McPherson's assistance, had really fought and decided the battle before McClernand's other divisions had come into any very serious collision with the enemy. He had been repulsed, leaving behind eleven guns captured from the enemy; but his men, undaunted, and under cover of a heavy artillery fire, again advanced, and carried the closely-contested field.

McPherson's corps fought with equal gallantry — Stevenson's brigade, of Logan's division, making a brilliant charge on the enemy's flank, capturing seven guns and several hundred prisoners, and, gaining the Vicksburg Road, cutting off Loring.

Carr's and Osterhaus's divisions, now being well advanced on the left, were ordered to pursue the retreating enemy to the Big Black. The pursuit was continued till after dark, resulting in the capture of a large amount of munitions and stores.

Sherman's corps had no part in the battle, not coming upon the field at all. McPherson fought only two of his divisions, Ransom's brigade not having yet arrived from Milliken's Bend. The entire Federal loss in the battle was 426 killed, 1842 wounded, and 189 missing—total, 2457. The Confederate loss was not probably less in killed and wounded, besides that of some 2000 prisoners, from fifteen to twenty guns, and thousands of small-arms. Among the killed was General Lloyd Tilghman, of Fort Henry renown, now commanding one of Loring's brigades, who was shot while attempting to check the Federal pursuit.[1]

The pursuit was continued on the 17th, McClernand's corps in the advance. Sherman, having reached Bolton, was turned northward toward Bridgeport, where Blair soon joined him.

The only stand made by Pemberton's retreating and demoralized army was on the banks of the Big Black River. Here it was found by McClernand on the 17th, strongly posted on both sides of the river. At this point, on the west bank—the main position of the enemy—bluffs extend to the water's edge. On the east bank there is an open bottom a mile wide, surrounded by a stagnant bayou two or three feet in depth and from ten to twenty in width, extending in the form of a segment from the river above to the river below; behind this bayou the enemy had thrown up rifle-pits. McClernand made the most elaborate disposition of his command for an attack. Carr's division held the right, and Lawler's brigade the extreme right. After Carr's division had been delayed by the enemy's artillery for two or three hours, Lawler discovered a way of approach by which the position could be successfully assaulted. A charge was made at this point by Lawler. His brigade, coming into close quarters with the enemy, received a volley in flank, bringing down 150 men; but the charge was sustained. No shot was fired by the gallant assailants until they had crossed the bayou. They then poured in their volley, and, without reloading, swept on with fixed bayonets, and the position was abandoned by the Confederates, leaving in their works eighteen guns, 1500 prisoners, and large quantities of small-arms and commissary stores. McClernand's loss was 29 killed and 242 wounded. Those of the enemy who were not captured escaped across the river by a bridge which had been constructed of three steam-boats. This temporary bridge and the railroad bridge were burned by the fugitives, and it was impossible for the Federals to cross the river in the face of the enemy, whose sharp-shooters lined the opposite bluffs.

That night Pemberton's disordered army straggled into the streets of Vicksburg, bringing panic with its approach.[2]

[1] As to the numbers engaged on the Confederate side in the battle of Champion's Hill, we have taken Pemberton's estimate (18,000 men). This is, no doubt, below the mark. Grant estimates the enemy's numbers at 25,000. Abrams, to whom we have formerly referred, and who was well acquainted with the defense of Vicksburg, gives Pemberton a command of from 23,000 to 26,000 men, positioned as follows:

"Major General Stevenson's division, composed of the brigades commanded by Brigadier Generals Lee, Barton, and Cummings, and Colonel, now Brigadier General Reynolds; in front; General Loring's division, composed of the brigades commanded by Brigadier Generals Tilghman, Featherstone, and others, in the centre; and Bowen's division, composed of two brigades under Brigadier General Green and Colonel Cockrell. There was also one brigade commanded by Brigadier General Baldwin, detached from Major General M. L. Smith's division, Waul's legion of Texans, and Wirt Adams's cavalry regiment, the whole making an effective force of between 23,000 and 26,000 fighting men."

[2] Abrams thus describes the entrance of the Confederate army into Vicksburg:

"At about 10 o'clock on Sunday night the main body of the Confederate forces commenced entering Vicksburg, and then ensued a scene that almost beggars description. Many planters living near the city, with their families, abandoned their homes and entered our lines with the Confederate forces. We were among the troops when they entered, and never in our life beheld any thing to equal the scene. As if by magic, the stillness of the Sabbath night was broken in upon by an uproar, in which the blasphemous oath of the soldier and the cry of the child mingled, and formed a sight which the pen can not depict. It was a scene which, once beheld, can not be forgotten. There were many gentle women and tender children torn from their homes by the advance of a ruthless foe, and compelled to fly to our lines for protection; and mixed up with them, in one vast crowd, were the gallant men who had left Vicksburg three short weeks before,

COTTON BRIDGE BUILT BY McPHERSON ACROSS THE BIG BLACK.

Johnston, as soon as he learned the result of the fighting on Baker's Creek, dispatched to Pemberton: "If Haines's Bluff be untenable, Vicksburg is of no value, and can not be held. If, therefore, you are invested in Vicksburg, you must ultimately surrender. Under such circumstances, instead of losing both troops and place, you must, if possible, save the troops. If it is not too late, evacuate Vicksburg and its dependencies, and march to the northeast." But before the dispatch was received Pemberton had already shut himself up in Vicksburg, and Grant had locked him in.

Was Haines's Bluff untenable? Sherman had found it impregnable on the river side last December. But where was the Confederate army to defend this post now — this post now so absolutely necessary to General Grant?

While McClernand was crossing the Big Black on the morning of the 18th by floating bridges a short distance above the scene of the preceding day's battle, Sherman crossed the same river at Bridgeport. From that point he approached Vicksburg until within about three miles of the town, when he turned to the right and took possession of Walnut Hills and the adjacent banks of the Yazoo without resistance.

McPherson struck into and followed Sherman's course up to the point where the latter had turned eastward. McClernand advanced on the Jackson and Vicksburg Road, and thence, at St. Alban's, turned to the left into the Baldwin's Ferry Road, so as to cover the approaches to Vicksburg from the southeast.

That night Vicksburg was fairly invested. It was the night of May 18th, 1863. Precisely one year had elapsed since the first attempt had been made against Vicksburg, and since, in return to S. P. Lee's demand of surrender, the authorities of the town had replied that Mississippians did "not know, and refused to learn, how to surrender to an enemy."

Admiral Porter, in the mean time, having returned to the Yazoo, on May 16th was able to open communication with Grant's army and send it provisions; he also attacked Haines's Bluff, the evacuation of which had already begun. On the approach of the gun-boats the garrison made a precipitate retreat, leaving forts, guns, munitions, tents—every thing.[1]

The way was now open to Yazoo City and the whole valley of the Yazoo. Lieutenant Walker, with five gun-boats, was sent up the river by Admiral Porter, and, upon reaching Yazoo City (May 20th), found the Confederate navy yard there in flames and the city defenseless. There were also found two rams—the Red Republic, 310 feet long by 75 wide, and the Mobile, ready for plating—and some other vessels. In the hospital were 1500 Confederate sick and wounded.

Pemberton's army, as we have seen, began to enter Vicksburg on the night of the 17th. The eastward or land defenses of the town were not yet wholly completed, but no time was lost in repairing their defects. While Haines's Bluff was being evacuated, the Confederate troops were entering their defenses, distributed as follows: On the left was Major General M. L. Smith's division, composed of brigades under Shoup, Baldwin, Vaughan, and Buford; in the centre, Major General J. H. Forney's division, consisting of Moore's and Herbert's brigades; and on the left, Major General C. L. Stevenson's division, consisting of brigades under Barton, Cummings, Lee, and Reynolds. Bowen's division, consisting of two brigades under Green and Cockrell, was held in reserve. This army, now the garrison of Vicksburg, numbered about 25,000 effective men. Including the non-combatants, there was an accumulation of provisions sufficient to last nearly two months. The fortifications consisted of strong bastioned forts on the right, centre, and left, favorably located on high points, and without these ran an exterior line of intrenchments. The works had been admirably well planned by M. L. Smith, but the execution had been imperfect. They were neither high enough nor thick enough; the position of the guns was too much exposed, and the guns themselves, being *en barbette*, were easily dismounted. During the interval which elapsed, however, between the occupation of these intrenchments on Sunday night, and the first attempt made against them on Tuesday afternoon (the 19th), the axe and spade were diligently used, and a strong front was presented to the assailants.

McClernand's command—the left corps of the besieging army—advanced on the 19th to Two-mile Creek (so called on account of its distance from Vicksburg), after driving in the enemy's skirmishers. Overlooking this creek, a long hill ran north and south in general conformity with the Vicksburg defenses, which were in plain view on a similar range a mile westward. The intervening space between the two ranges consisted of a series of deep hollows, separated by long, narrow ridges, both the hollows and the ridges running from the enemy's works toward McClernand's position until they terminated in the valley of the creek, being covered near their termination with a thicket of trees and underbrush. McClernand had scarcely occupied the hills across Two-mile Creek, and posted his artillery, when he received an order from General Grant instructing all the corps commanders to gain as close a position to the enemy as possible, preliminary to a general assault, which was to be made at 2 o'clock P.M. A. J. Smith's division, on the right of the Vicksburg Road, and Osterhaus on the left, with Carr in reserve, by 2 o'clock had approached to within 500 yards of the enemy. General Os-

in all the pride and confidence of a just cause, and returning to it a demoralized mob and a defeated army, all caused through one man's incompetency."

[1] Admiral Porter, in his dispatch to the Secretary of War, May 20th, says:

"The works at Haines's Bluff were very formidable. There are fourteen of the heaviest kind of mounted 8- and 10-inch and 7½-inch rifled guns, with ammunition enough to last a long siege. As the gun-carriages might again fall into the hands of the enemy, I had them burned, blew up the magazine, and destroyed the works generally. I also burned up the encampments, which were permanently and remarkably well constructed, looking as though the rebels intended to stay some time. Their works and encampments covered many acres of ground; and the fortifications and rifle-pits proper of Haines's Bluff extend about a mile and a quarter. Such a network of forts I never saw."

VICKSBURG FROM THE HILLS IN THE REAR.

terhaus, who had been wounded in the fight on the Big Black, was now able to resume the command of his division.

To the right of A. J. Smith, McPherson's corps, holding the centre, advanced in like manner. The right was held by Sherman, who had on the 18th pushed forward Tuttle's division, supported by Blair's, on the northernmost approach to Vicksburg, while Steele's division, taking a blind road still farther to the right, moved toward the Mississippi. On the morning of the 19th Sherman had his right resting on the Mississippi, in plain view of Porter's fleet at the mouth of the Yazoo and at Young's Point, while his front, in sight of Vicksburg, was separated from the enemy by only 400 yards of very difficult ground, cut up by almost impracticable ravines. The Fourth Iowa Cavalry had taken possession of Haines's Bluff, and communication had been opened with Admiral Porter.

This was the situation when Grant ordered the general assault on the 19th. Sherman alone was in a position to make a determined attack; and Grant, counting on the demoralization of the enemy, hoped, by a vigorous onset against the Confederate left, to win an immediate victory. At the hour designated Blair's division moved forward, with Ewing's and Giles Smith's brigades on the right of the road, and T. K. Smith's on the left, artillery being disposed in the rear to cover the point where the road entered the Confederate intrenchments. Tuttle's division held the road, Buckland's brigade, however, being deployed to Blair's rear. The assault was not successful, though it was a most gallant affair. The line advanced across the intervening chasms, filled with standing and fallen timber, up to the trenches, and the Thirteenth Regulars (Giles Smith's left), reaching the works first, succeeded in planting its colors upon the outer slope; but this was effected at a cost of 77 out of 250 men, the commander of the regiment, Captain Washington, being mortally wounded, and five other officers more or less severely. Almost simultaneously, two other regiments (the Eighty-third Indiana and the One Hundred and Twenty-seventh Illinois) reached the same position, but, though able to hold their ground by making it fatally hazardous for any head to appear above the parapet, they could not enter the works. Other regiments on either side obtained similar positions, but night came on finding them still outside of the works, which they could only threaten but not take. Under cover of the darkness Sherman withdrew his advanced columns to a safer position.

The next two days were occupied by the Federals in perfecting their system of supplies (twenty days of marching and fighting had now been passed with but about five days' rations drawn from the commissary), opening military roads, and posting artillery in positions more commanding. The enemy, inspirited by his own success in resisting Sherman's assault, was employed meanwhile in a similar task.

On the 22d Grant determined to venture a second assault, this time engaging his whole line. He gives, in his report, four reasons for this second attempt: 1st. He hoped the assault, from the position already gained, would be successful. 2d. His present force was inadequate to maintain a complete investment of Vicksburg and at the same time attend to Johnston's army, now at Canton, and daily increasing in numbers by re-enforcements from the East. His own effective army now numbered scarcely more than 30,000 men, being but little superior in this respect to that immediately in his front. 3d. Success would close the campaign, and not only save the government from sending him large re-enforcements, but also free his own army for farther operations. 4th. Even if the attempt should prove unsuccessful, the troops, impatient now to take Vicksburg, would not work so willingly in the trenches before as after such an assault. Accordingly, the assault was made. If it had succeeded, it would have been a victory almost unparalleled in the annals of war; for success involved the forcing of a strong line of intrenchments eight and a half miles in length, by operations carried on over the most difficult ground; it involved the capture of a strong-hold defended by a garrison of 25,000 men—one third of which was fresh, and not yet dispirited by defeat—by an army of about 30,000 men, already exhausted by twenty days of rapid marching and severe fighting. It was not an

at a shoulder of the bastion.
position, half a mile to the righ
front. As Blair advanced, no
works except now and then tl
charged his piece and then di
picked skirmishers was placed.
unteer storming-party of 150 n
ditch. Meanwhile five batterie
manding the approach; but no
umn, as it came upon the crowi
ed the storming-party had reacl
ward the sally-port, followed cl
the parapet rose the enemy in
column a terrific fire, staggerin
pressed on, but vainly attempt
Still undaunted, Ewing's adv
climbed up the outer face of th
burrowing in the earth from th
meanwhile formed line in a rav
the left of the bastion, while Ki
by Ewing's brigade, kept up a
the parapet.

It had been impossible for th

THE APPROACHES TO VICKSBURG.

THE INVESTMENT OF VICKSBURG—SHERMAN'S EXTREME RIGHT ON THE MISSISSIPPI.

carried forward one of his guns by hand to the ditch, and, double-shotting it, fired into an embrasure of the work, disabling a gun in it about to be discharged, and cutting down its gunners. The works thus partially occupied by these two divisions were separated from each other by a curtain. Hovey and Osterhaus, on the left, advanced on a more extended line of attack, but, encountering an enfilading fire, were repulsed.

Thus far, the battle on the left had not in any essential feature differed from that on the right and centre. Each corps had succeeded in planting colors on the outer slopes of the enemy's bastions. Thus much had been effected, and nothing more seemed possible. The works partially carried were of no value unless the works at their left and right were also carried. Grant, who had taken a commanding position in McPherson's front, saw all this, and was almost ready to withdraw his forces, when he received a dispatch from McClernand which excited his astonishment. The dispatch informed him that McClernand had gained two of the enemy's forts, and asked for re-enforcements. It found Grant in Sherman's front. Now Grant had held a better position during the attack for observation of what was going on in McClernand's corps than McClernand himself. He had not seen any possession of forts, nor any necessity for re-enforcements. In reply to a dispatch previously received from the same source, asking for aid, he had ordered the latter to re-enforce from his left. He knew that, from the nature of the ground, "each corps had many more men than could be used in the assault. More men could only avail in case of breaking through the enemy's line or in repelling a sortie." Moreover, McArthur's division was on its way from Warrenton, and this he ordered McClernand to bring up to his aid. He showed McClernand's dispatch to General Sherman, who ordered a renewal of the attack on his front. While going back to the centre Grant received from McClernand a third dispatch, stating that the latter had gained the enemy's intrenchments *at several points*, but was brought to a stand. Grant doubted the accuracy of this information, but he could not disregard these reiterated statements, which *might*, after all, be true, and, that no possible opportunity of success should be allowed to escape through any fault of his, he ordered Quinby's division to report to McClernand, leaving McPherson with only four brigades to hold the centre. The dispatches were shown to McPherson, to satisfy him of the necessity of making a diversion in his front. At half past three a fourth dispatch was received from McClernand, still expressing a hope of forcing the enemy's line, stating that he had taken several prisoners, and that his men were still in the forts. The prisoners alluded to were probably the baker's dozen brought in by Sergeant Griffith; and the "men still in the forts" were doubtless there, but in the same condition with the eleven unfortunate braves whom Griffith had left behind. But Quinby's division did McClernand no good, and McArthur's did not get up till the next day. The only result of McClernand's illusory dispatches was a mortality list longer by half than it would have been if the troops had been withdrawn at three instead of at eight o'clock P.M. Sherman had ordered Tuttle to detail for the assault one of his brigades. Mower's was selected for this duty, but, upon advancing against the bastion, encountered a more severe fire, if possible, than that which had repulsed Ewing in the forenoon. Steele, too, renewed his attack midway between the bastion and the river. He advanced over ground exposed to a flank fire, and deeply cut by gullies and washes up to the parapet, which was found too strongly defended to be carried, and, after holding the hill-side, to which he had retreated for cover until night, he withdrew his division.

Thus ended the assault of the 22d of May, which, though it made no impression upon the Vicksburg defenses, attested the valor of the national troops. For ten hours they had fought against fortune, but had not won the battle. Repeatedly they had charged the three strong bastioned forts on the right, centre, and rear of the enemy's line, only to be swept back each time with decimated ranks. Partial successes, indeed, they had had, standing upon the very edge of victory, with their colors flaunting in the faces of the foe; but these had only excited false hopes and led to greater carnage; death had been the sole reward of their enthusiasm. McClernand's loss alone amounted to 1487 killed, wounded, and missing, making three fourths of the entire loss of this corps during the whole campaign. Nearly one half (677) of the casualties occurred in Carr's division. A. J. Smith's loss was nearly as great, amounting to 499. Sherman's corps lost about 600 men. The casualties in the three corps counted up to almost 3000, of which, therefore, nearly one third must have been in McPherson's command, which confronted the most formidable redoubt in the whole line—that commanding the main approach (by the Jackson Road) to Vicksburg.

The Confederates—mostly drawn from the Cotton States—also fought with determined bravery. Opposed to Sherman were Baldwin's and Shoup's brigades (W. L. Smith's division); Herbert's brigade (J. H. Forney's division) met the persistent attack which was made on both sides of the Jackson Road, the Third, Twenty-first, and Twenty-third Louisiana regiments especially distinguishing themselves; while farther to the right, Moore and Lee (the latter of Stevenson's division) held their ground against McClernand. Bowen's two brigades re-enforced the other commands as occasion required. The Confederate loss was upward of 1000 men. If Pemberton had not prevented sharp-shooting and artillery duels from the time of the investment—which he was probably compelled to do in order to save ammunition—the national troops would have found much greater difficulty in approaching so near the Confederate line; as it was, however, the Federal sharp-shooters had got so close that it was dangerous for the enemy's gunners to rise from cover to load their pieces; and, besides this, many of the enemy's guns were dismounted. The charges, therefore, made by the Federals in this battle met with little or no resistance from artillery.

Admiral Porter co-operated in the assault. On the evening of the 21st he was notified of the proposed attack by General Grant, and ordered to shell the water batteries before and during the first stage of the engagement. All that night he kept up a bombardment on the works and the town from six mortars which he had stationed in the river, and sent up three gun-boats to shell at the same time the water batteries. In the morning another gun-boat was added, and the four vessels crossed the river and opened on the hill batteries, which they finally silenced. The water batteries were then engaged for two hours at a distance of 440 yards. Such was the noise and smoke on the river front that Admiral Porter neither saw nor heard any thing of the battle in the rear. At 11 o'clock A.M. the spectacle presented to an occupant of Vicksburg must have been one of terrible sublimity. An unceasing storm of fire enveloped the city on all sides. The gun-boats engaged the batteries; the mortars and the Parrott guns, mounted on rafts in the river, and guns posted on the opposite peninsula, shelled the town; and Grant's army was concentrating every available gun against the forts in the rear, while his columns were forming into line for the assault. Still, though environed by this circle of fire, stores in Vicksburg were opened as usual, the streets were promenaded by women and children, and only a very few persons were injured.[1]

On the 27th of May the gun-boat Cincinnati was sunk in the attempt to silence one of the land batteries. She was abreast of the mortars, and rounding to, when a well-directed shot from a fine piece of ordnance called "Whistling Dick" entered her magazine, and she began to sink rapidly; and other shots in quick succession crashed through her iron plating. The gun-boat managed to reach the right bank of the river, and her crew was landed before she sank. She was afterward (August, 1863) raised and towed to Cairo.

After the failure of his second assault, Grant was compelled to resort to a regular siege of Vicksburg. His army was largely re-enforced.[2] McArthur was already on hand; Lauman's division and four regiments had already been ordered from Memphis; these were soon joined by Smith's and Kimball's divisions of the Sixteenth (Hurlbut's) Army Corps, which were assigned to Major General C. C. Washburne. Herron's division, from the Department of Missouri, arrived June 11th, and was put on the extreme left, Lauman's connecting it with McClernand; and, three days later, two divi-

[1] Says a citizen who occupied Vicksburg during the siege, "Such cannonading has, perhaps, scarcely ever been equaled; and the city was entirely untenable, though women and children were in the streets. It was not safe from behind or before, and every part of the city was alike within range of the Federal guns. The gun-boats withdrew after a short engagement, but the mortars kept up the shelling, and the armies continued fighting all day. . . . . It would require the pen of a poet to depict the awful sublimity of this day's work—the incessant booming of cannon and the banging of small arms, intermingled with the howling of shells and the whistling of Minié-balls, made the day most truly hideous."

[2] Grant's army, thus re-enforced, consisted of the following sixteen divisions:

1. F. Steele's,	Sherman's Corps.	9. J. A. Logan's,	McPherson's Corps.
2. F. Blair's,		10. M. M. Crocker's,	
3. J. McArthur's,		11. J. G. Lauman's,	Washburne's Command.
4. J. M. Tuttle's,		12. W. S. Smith's,	
5. P. T. Osterhaus's,	McClernand's Corps.	13. N. Kimball's,	
6. A. J. Smith's		14. F. J. Herron's,	
7. A. P. Hovey's,		15. J. Welsh's,	Parke's Corps.
8. E. A. Carr's,		16. R. B. Potter's,	

There were also belonging to Washburne's command four regiments from Memphis. The whole army numbered nearly 70,000 men.

C. C. WASHBURNE.

WILLIAM H. EMORY.

sions of the Ninth Army Corps (now belonging to Burnside's Department of the Ohio), under command of J. G. Parke, reached the field, and with Washburne's command were sent to Haines's Bluff.

On the 28th of June General McClernand's connection with Grant's army ceased, Major General Ord superseding him in command of the Thirteenth Corps. His military career had for himself been an unfortunate one. As to his bravery or his fidelity, no doubt had ever been entertained. A great favorite in the southern portion of Illinois, he was yet unpopular among his peers and superiors in the army. He had been very successful in political life, and had always identified himself with the Democratic party. At twenty years of age he took an honorable position at the bar; he established (1835) the first Democratic press in Shawneetown, Illinois, his native town; in 1836 he was elected to the State Legislature from Gallatin, his native county; in 1838 the office of lieutenant governor was tendered him, which he declined, not being of the constitutional age (thirty years); he was again in the Legislature in 1840, and during the session accepted a challenge to personal combat from Judge J. W. Smith, who had been offended by some strictures made by McClernand on the conduct of the Supreme Court, but, the judge not appearing, the duel was not fought; he was again elected in 1842, and the next year was sent as representative to Congress, being re-elected in 1844, 1846, and 1848; in 1850 he prepared and offered the first draft of the famous compromise measures of that year; the next year he retired to Jacksonville, Illinois, removing thence to Springfield in 1856, and in 1859 was elected representative in Congress from the capital district; twice he had been a presidential elector (for Van Buren and Pierce); in April, 1861, at the instance of Governor Yates, he accompanied a volunteer force to Cairo and occupied that place, and in July he resigned his seat in Congress. Such are the naked outlines of his political career. But when he entered the service of his country against the rebellion he was not without military experience, having at an early age served as a private in the Black-Hawk War until its close. It was rather to his disadvantage that he was urged forward in the first stages of the civil war by his political friends. If he could have done in his military as he had in his political life—taken his position where circumstance assigned him, and let his aspirations follow the appreciation of his military merits by his superior officers—he would then have found his true place, whether high or low. He fought well at Fort Donelson, and again at Shiloh; afterward he commanded the army corps of the reserve in Halleck's campaign against Corinth. We next hear of him in connection with the expedition against Vicksburg at the close of 1862. At that time Grant had command of the Army of the Mississippi. But Grant's time had not yet come. If the capacities for generalship which he afterward revealed had been then known, he would, at any rate, have been allowed to command his army without interference from Washington. Unhappily, this interference could not then be avoided. Grant assigned Sherman to command the Vicksburg expedition; the War Department relieved Sherman, and put McClernand in command. If any attribute was peculiarly characteristic of Grant, it was his knowledge of men. He had faith in Sherman, he had not in McClernand; but McClernand was forced upon him. It soon proved that Grant was right. McClernand, in com-

Military courtesy as well as military discipline requires absc tion; but McClernand's aspirations were disagreeably pron officious in advice and suggestions as to how the campaign c ducted. The assault of May 22d, and the false hopes enterta of his dispatches to Grant, soon brought on a crisis. In a McClernand's congratulatory order to his command, on May to an insinuation against his superior officer, and he was pro Afterward we find McClernand engaged in the advocacy o President in opposition to Lincoln. He resigned his place November, 1865.

Four days after the second assault on Vicksburg, Genera vested Port Hudson. Port Hudson is located on a bend in River, about twenty-two miles above Baton Rouge, and or forty-seven from New Orleans. Batteries had been erected on high bluffs, extending from Thompson's Creek above the t for three and a half miles. The land defenses began from Th and ran in a semicircular form for ten miles till they connect er battery. The line of investment from right to left was he brigade, and Grover's, Paine's, Augur's, and T. W. Sherman's Confederate works had been skillfully planned, consisting, lil Vicksburg, of strong redoubts commanding all the approacl and supporting each other, with rifle-pits between and in fron however, had been reduced to about 6000 men. An attem May 27th to carry the works by assault. A heavy bombar the attack, which was begun by Weitzel, Grover, and Paine 10 A.M. The left, under Augur and Sherman, did not attac or until four hours later, and thus all the value of a simultan lost. The river batteries in the mean time were engaged by —the Hartford and Albatross above, and the Richmond, Mo esee, and Essex below. The naval attack was not entirely un gun-boats compelled the enemy to abandon his southernm mounted many of his heavy guns, and even reached the lan with a fire in reverse.

But on the land side the assault was a complete failure. any want of gallantry in the troops; no men ever fougl enemy's rifle-pits were protected by impassable abatis swept The battle on the right lasted till 4 o'clock in the aftern Grover, and Paine—neither of whose commands amounted brigade—with two regiments of colored troops, crossed Sanc morning, and succeeded in driving the enemy through the w tifications. Augur and Sherman in the afternoon achieved a on the left, moving up to the fortifications until they held t parapet opposite the enemy, but, toward night, being exposed they withdrew. The position gained on the right was ma negro troops were posted on the extreme right, a position w test their steadiness and bravery. They made during the da

CUVIER GROVER.

THE ASSAULT ON PORT HUDSON, MAY 27, 1863.

PORT HUDSON FROM THE OPPOSITE BANK.

on the enemy's batteries, and, although losing heavily, they held their position with the other troops without flinching until nightfall. This was the first instance in which negro troops fought during the war. In this action General T. W. Sherman was severely wounded. The entire National loss was 1842, of whom 293 were killed. The Confederate loss was inconsiderable.

The troops now went to digging, mining, and sharp-shooting. They were mostly nine-months' men, whose time had nearly expired. In a hostile region, with a large body of Confederate cavalry in their rear, and all Louisiana left open to Dick Taylor by Banks's concentration against Port Hudson, their situation was not an enviable one, and would have been perilous if, at this time, the attention of the enemy had not been so wholly given to the more important post of Vicksburg.

After several days' bombardment a second assault was made on Port Hudson. The chief point of attack was the northeasterly corner of the enemy's line of intrenchments. The result of the assault was a nearer approach to the works, and on the left, while Grover and Weitzel made the more palpable attack on the right, General Dwight succeeded in carrying and holding an eminence which commanded a vital point in the defenses known as "the Citadel." But what had been thus gained had cost 700 more men, and no subsequent assaults were made. Among the wounded was General Paine.

On the west side of the Mississippi, Dick Taylor had had the field in Louisiana almost entirely to himself. Early in June he reoccupied Alexandria and Opelousas. Upon his advance down the Atchafalaya, apparently threatening New Orleans, the advanced federal posts were withdrawn to Brashear. To this latter point Lieutenant Colonel Stickney had been sent by General Emory from New Orleans, to take command. From mismanagement, and lack of preparation and discipline, the enemy succeeded in taking Thibodeaux, Terre Bonne, and Bayou Bœuf, capturing their garrisons, while another column, under Mouton and Green, threatened Brashear from Berwick. Brashear was surrounded and captured with 1000 prisoners, Fort Buchanan, 10 heavy guns, and thousands of liberated negroes were reduced to slavery. Ryder, who had a few weeks before needlessly burned Berwick, managed to escape with the only national gun-boat left in the bayou. The road was now open for Taylor to advance to Algiers, the western suburb of New Orleans, Lafourche having been evacuated by Stickney. But the enemy fortunately had too weak a force to attempt the recapture of New Orleans; therefore he moved northward and threatened Donaldsonville; but, even after his storming-party had entered the fort, he was repulsed by the aid of the gun-boats, with a loss of 200 killed and 124 prisoners.

In the mean time Grant's army held its ground before Vicksburg. Five days after the investment the garrison had been reduced to 14½ ounces of food per day to each man, and it is reported that Pemberton had expressed his determination never to surrender the town till the last dog had been eaten and the last man slain. The only hope of relief from the alternative of starvation or surrender was in Joe Johnston; but if Pemberton entertained any hope from this source he leaned upon a broken reed. Grant's re-enforcements enabled him to give Sherman a detached command, consisting of the forces at Haines's Bluff, a division from each of the Thirteenth, Fifteenth, and Seventeenth corps, and Lanman's division, for the especial purpose of looking after Johnston. The character of the country was also in his favor, enabling him by intrenchment to secure himself against an attack in his rear, while the Big Black formed a strong defensive line on the south, and his means of communication were beyond the enemy's reach. Johnston was also embarrassed by the frequency of straggling and desertion in his army. The evil was so great and of such extent as to cause Governor Brown, of Georgia, through which state the delinquents found their way to the East, to issue a proclamation, ordering their arrest by associations of citizens as well as by state troops.

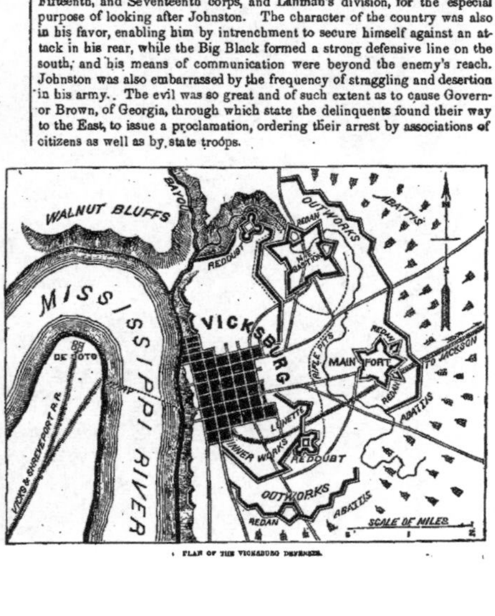

PLAN OF THE VICKSBURG DEFENSES.

ENTRANCE OF GALLERY LEADING TO THE MINE.

MINERS AT WORK UNDER THE FORT.

ıe irregularities of the ground between the two lines afforded oppor-
ies for the construction of winding covered ways leading up to the
orks of the enemy. This circumstance facilitated the construction of
s. The excavations were well guarded from the observation of even
'ederal troops. The first mine was sprung on June 25th, under a fort
site the centre, in McPherson's front, and to the left of the Jackson
l, where Logan, early in the siege, had occupied and erected a fort upon
l near the enemy, and overlooking his works. The explosion threw
ı a part of the face of the fort which had been undermined. An at-
t was made to get possession, but without success. The Confederate
ral Herbert had built a second fort in the rear, so that the explosion of
rst was of no great importance. A grandson of Henry Clay was killed
e struggle with the Federal troops on this occasion. In the same way
forts were undermined, the enemy countermining at a great disad-
ge, and often the miners and counterminers approached so nearly that
could hear each other's picks. If it had been necessary, Grant's army
l, no doubt, have dug itself into Vicksburg.

e garrison, exhausted from an insufficient supply of food, was wearied
over by uninterrupted confinement in the rifle-pits, where many, es-
g the accurate shots of Grant's sharp-shooters, fell victims to disease.
national troops, on the other hand, sheltered by the kindly covering
of woods from the burning heat of the summer sun, well supplied with food—for they had the resources of the entire West at their backs and within their command—and finding innumerable springs of the best water in the deep ravines, improved daily in health; thousands of men became available who were numbered among the non-effectives just after the assault of May 22d.

Next to the hardships endured by the brave defenders of Vicksburg were those suffered daily by the non-combatants. Starvation confronted these latter in its worst forms. All the beef in the city was exhausted before the end of June, and mule-meat was resorted to as a last expedient.[1] The poor were without money, and, but for the charity of those possessed of better means, must have starved, with flour at $1000 per barrel, meal $140 per bushel, molasses $10 per gallon, and beef at $2 50 per pound. The city looked like a pile of half-ruined buildings, so searching were the Federal shells. For safety, the inhabitants went to caves dug into the sides of the hills, and here too the missiles of death reached them, not sparing even innocent children. The spirits both of the citizens and the troops were kept up, in a measure, by the rumors continually reaching them that Johnston was about to raise the siege. Couriers frequently found their

[1] Abrams says that he "partook of mule-meat for three or four days, and found the flesh tender and nutritious, and, *under the peculiar circumstances*, a most desirable description of food."

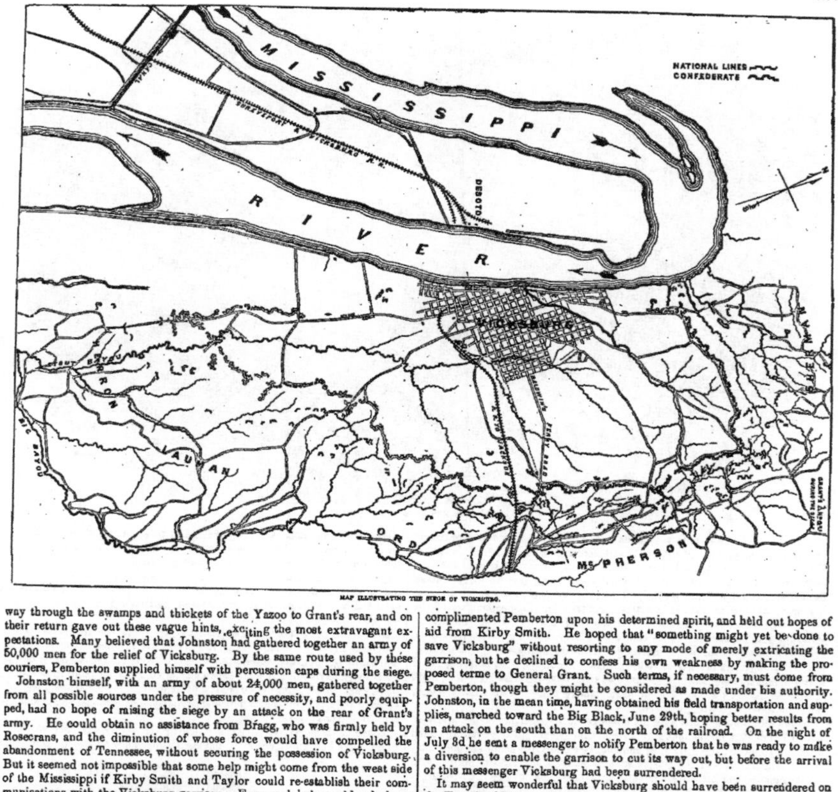

MAP ILLUSTRATING THE SIEGE OF VICKSBURG.

way through the swamps and thickets of the Yazoo to Grant's rear, and on their return gave out these vague hints, exciting the most extravagant expectations. Many believed that Johnston had gathered together an army of 50,000 men for the relief of Vicksburg. By the same route used by these couriers, Pemberton supplied himself with percussion caps during the siege.

Johnston himself, with an army of about 24,000 men, gathered together from all possible sources under the pressure of necessity, and poorly equipped, had no hope of raising the siege by an attack on the rear of Grant's army. He could obtain no assistance from Bragg, who was firmly held by Rosecrans, and the diminution of whose force would have compelled the abandonment of Tennessee, without securing the possession of Vicksburg. But it seemed not impossible that some help might come from the west side of the Mississippi if Kirby Smith and Taylor could re-establish their communications with the Vicksburg garrison. Even such help could only have protracted the campaign. But, whatever it promised, it was not to be had. An unsuccessful attempt was made, in April, by the Confederate General Marmaduke, to capture Cape Girardeau, above Cairo, which, if it had succeeded, would have somewhat seriously embarrassed General Grant's operations. General Kirby Smith's attempt to open communications with Vicksburg proved equally abortive. An attack was made early in June upon the Federal camp at Milliken's Bend. The first stage of the attack promised a favorable result to the Confederates, who succeeded in driving the small detachment of national troops from their outer line of intrenchments to the river's bank, but with the aid of a gun-boat the tide of battle was turned, and the Iowa regiments, assisted by negro troops, rallied and repulsed the assailants. After another fight at Richmond, nine miles from Milliken's Bend, in which it was defeated, Kirby Smith's army retired into the interior. His 8000 men, says Johnston, had been mismanaged, and had fallen back to Delhi. From the West no farther attempt was made for the relief of Vicksburg and Port Hudson.

A correspondence was kept up between Pemberton and Jackson during the siege. Again and again the latter professed his inability to raise the siege, or to do any thing more than co-operate with Pemberton in an attempt to extricate the garrison. To urgent appeals from the War Department at Richmond, Johnston repeatedly replied that he could effect nothing with so inadequate a command. "If I attack," he said, "there is the Big Black in my rear, cutting off my retreat." Finally, on June 21st, Pemberton wrote to Johnston recommending him to make a demonstration on the Federal right, and promised to himself move out his garrison, if possible, by the Warrenton Road and across Hankinson's Ferry. Upon mature consideration this plan was deemed impracticable. On the 22d of June, the day after he had made this bold proposition, Pemberton suggested that Johnston should make to Grant propositions to pass his army out, with all its arms and equipages. He could hold out, he said, fifteen days longer. In reply to this, Johnston complimented Pemberton upon his determined spirit, and held out hopes of aid from Kirby Smith. He hoped that "something might yet be done to save Vicksburg" without resorting to any mode of merely extricating the garrison, but he declined to confess his own weakness by making the proposed terms to General Grant. Such terms, if necessary, must come from Pemberton, though they might be considered as made under his authority. Johnston, in the mean time, having obtained his field transportation and supplies, marched toward the Big Black, June 29th, hoping better results from an attack on the south than on the north of the railroad. On the night of July 3d he sent a messenger to notify Pemberton that he was ready to make a diversion to enable the garrison to cut its way out, but before the arrival of this messenger Vicksburg had been surrendered.

It may seem wonderful that Vicksburg should have been surrendered on the Fourth of July, a "Yankee anniversary," as the enemy was now pleased to call it. Pollard, the Southern historian, takes especial umbrage at this circumstance. Surrendered it must have been, doubtless; but why, of all days of the year, on that day? The explanation must rest with General Pemberton. He knew that Grant was preparing for an overwhelming attack. This attack, he thought, would certainly be made on the 4th. The chances in such an event were wholly in Grant's favor. Of the garrison not more than 15,000 men could probably be made available for the defense of a line eight miles long, and against a brave, well-fed, and confident enemy numbering over 60,000 men. It was bad enough to surrender on the 4th of July, but it was still worse to be ingloriously beaten on that day. Moreover, it was quite natural that Pemberton should be confident of securing better terms for his army by indulging the enemy a little in this particular.

At any rate, on the morning of July 3d an unusual quiet rested upon the defenses of Vicksburg, which was soon explained by the appearance of a flag of truce upon the works in front of A. J. Smith. This flag ushered into our lines two Confederate officers, Colonel Montgomery and General Bowen, with a sealed communication from Pemberton to Grant. The letter proposed the arrangement of terms of capitulation by the appointment of commissioners, three on each side. Of course Pemberton said that he was "fully able to maintain his position for an indefinite period." General Grant replied, refusing to submit to the terms of a commission, and demanding an unconditional surrender. He, however, consented to meet Pemberton at 3 o'clock P.M., and to arrange the terms of surrender by a personal interview.

The two generals met at the appointed hour under a gigantic oak in McPherson's front. Many and various have been the accounts published of this important interview. By some Pemberton is represented as having chatted in an indifferent manner, making arrangements for the surrender of a large army and of the Mississippi River while chewing straws with marvelous *sang froid;* others report that he was stormy, irascible, and even im-

INTERVIEW BETWEEN GRANT AND PEMBERTON.

pertinent. As to General Grant's behavior there can be no doubt; of course he smoked, and equally, of course, he was cool and imperturbable. Whether Pemberton chatted or scolded is of little consequence. It is said that the latter refused to surrender unconditionally, declaring that he would rather fight it out, and that Grant replied, "Then, sir, you can continue the defense. My army has never been in a better condition for the prosecution of the siege." However this may have been, the interview ended with the understanding that Pemberton would confer with his subordinate officers, and return an answer the following morning. The oak-tree has long since disappeared through the ravages of relic-hunters. Upon the spot where it stood a monument was erected. This also was soon so much defaced that in 1866 it was displaced by a sixty-four-pounder cannon placed in an erect position, with the muzzle pointing upward.[1]

Grant, after consultation with his generals, anticipated any communication which Pemberton might make by writing him a letter on the evening of the 3d. He proposed the following scheme: Pemberton's army should be allowed to march out of the city as soon as paroled, the officers taking with them their regimental clothing, while staff, field, and cavalry officers might retain one horse each; the rank and file to be allowed all their clothing, but no other property. The necessary amount of rations could be taken from the stores in Pemberton's possession, with utensils for cooking; also thirty wagons for transportation. The sick and wounded would be subject to similar conditions as soon as they should be able to travel. If the terms were accepted, he would march in one division and take possession at 8 A.M. on the 4th.

Early the next morning Pemberton's reply was received, accepting the proposed terms in the main, but submitting that, in justice both to the honor and spirit of his army, manifested in the defense of Vicksburg, it ought to be allowed to march out with colors and arms, stacking them in front of the lines, after which Grant should take possession; that the officers should be allowed their side-arms and personal property, and that the rights and property of citizens should be respected.

Some of these requests were acceded by General Grant; others were refused. He had no objection to paying Pemberton's troops the compliment

[1] The original monument was a pyramid twenty feet high, surmounted with a fifteen-inch globe. On one of its faces was an American eagle sustaining on its wings the Goddess of Liberty. On another face was the following inscription: "To the memory of the surrender of Vicksburg by Lieutenant General J. C. Pemberton to Major General U. S. Grant, on the 3d of July, 1863."

THE OLD MONUMENT, MARKING THE SITE OF THE SURRENDER.

THE NEW VICKSBURG MONUMENT.

of allowing them to march to the front and stack their arms, provided they then marched back again, remaining as prisoners until they were paroled. The parole was insisted upon in its strictest form, to be signed in each case by the paroled soldiers individually. He refused to be bound by any stipulations as to the treatment of citizens, confining himself simply to the assurance that he did not propose to cause any of them any undue annoyance or loss. With these modifications the parley must close. If the terms were not accepted by 9 A.M. they would be regarded as refused, and hostilities would recommence. Acceptance would be indicated on Pemberton's part by the display of white flags along his lines.

These terms were promptly accepted by Pemberton. Three hours were occupied by the Confederate army in marching out and stacking their arms. In the afternoon the national troops marched in and took possession. This was the third recurrence of the national anniversary since the beginning of the war. The first saw Congress convoked to assist the executive in meeting, for the first time in our history, an aggressive enemy within our own borders. The second witnessed McClellan's return to Harrison's Landing after a most disastrous campaign. But on the third was celebrated the surrender of Vicksburg and the victory of Gettysburg, the two events which, taken together, mark the turning-point of the war against the Southern Confederacy.

By 3 o'clock P.M. the national fleet of rams, gun-boats, and transports lined the levee. Grant, with McPherson, Logan, and their several staffs, entered Vicksburg. After an active campaign of eighty days—counting from the first passage of the transports below Vicksburg—he had won the most important and stupendous victory of the war. His loss had been 8575,[1] of which 4236 fell before Vicksburg. Not more than half of the wounded had been permanently disabled. The enemy's loss before the surrender amounted to at least 10,000 killed and wounded, not counting stragglers. In addition to these, 27,000 men were captured with Vicksburg, including fifteen general officers, one hundred and twenty-eight pieces of artillery, and about eighty siege-guns, besides arms and munitions of war for an army of 60,000, together with a large amount of public property, consisting of railroads, locomotives, cars, steam-boats, cotton, etc. Much property had also been destroyed to prevent its capture.

Grant had acted at his own discretion in paroling so large a number of troops. It saved the government the expense of removing them North, which at this time would have been very difficult with the limited transportation on hand, and also of their subsistence, and it left the army free to operate against Johnston.

The enthusiasm of the national forces upon their entrance into Vicksburg surpasses description. To Pemberton's army, in addition to the distressing hardships of the siege, was added the humiliation of defeat. One of the most interesting features connected with the capture of Vicksburg was the exultation of the negroes. Crowds of them congregated upon the side-walks,

THE SURRENDER OF VICKSBURG, JULY 4, 1863.

[1] Grant sums up his loss in the series of battles about and before Vicksburg as follows:

	Killed.	Wounded.	Missing.
Port Gibson	130	718	5
Fourteen-mile Creek	4	24	—
Raymond	69	341	32
Jackson	40	240	6
Champion's Hill	426	1842	189
Big Black Bridge	29	242	2
Before Vicksburg	245	3688	303
Total	943	7095	537
Sum total			8575

FEDERAL TROOPS BEFORE JACKSON, MISSISSIPPI.

welcoming Grant's army with broad grins of satisfaction. On the next day, which was Sunday, they dressed themselves in the most extravagant style, and promenaded the streets with a more palpable expression of triumphant joy than the conquerors themselves.

When Johnston was apprised of the surrender of Vicksburg he withdrew from the Big Black to Jackson. Immediately after the capture, Grant sent the remainder of the Thirteenth and Fifteenth Corps to re-enforce the five divisions already assigned to Sherman for operations against Johnston. Sherman had constructed a line of defense in Grant's rear from Haines's Bluff to the Big Black. This line had kept Johnston from his proposed attack north of the railroad, and the surrender of Vicksburg had made a diversion on the Big Black as unnecessary as it was impracticable.

Johnston's four divisions covering Jackson on the morning of July 9th were commanded by Major Generals Loring, Walker, French, and Breckinridge, while a division of cavalry, under General Jackson, guarded the fords of Pearl River above and below the town. Sherman in the mean time had been marching his command over the intervening fifty miles in the heat and dust, and through a country almost destitute of water—so destitute, indeed, that Johnston considered a siege of Jackson impossible. His advance appeared before the enemy's intrenchments on the 9th, and on the 12th had invested the town, both flanks resting on Pearl River. While skirmishing was going on in front, the cavalry were operating on the north and south of Jackson, destroying railroads and other property.

Johnston's position was entirely untenable. Batteries posted upon the surrounding hills were within easy range, commanding the town. Sherman's army fell but little short of 50,000 men, and he had a hundred guns planted upon the hills. In this situation he only waited for his ammunition train, which arrived on the 16th. This delay gave Johnston time for retreat; to remain was certain disaster.

In a too close approach to the works on the 12th, Lauman's division suffered a severe loss—about 500 men, of whom two hundred were captured, with the colors of the Twenty-eighth, Forty-first, and Fifty-third Illinois. This unfortunate loss was the result of a misapprehension of orders. Lauman's division was under Ord's command, and held the extreme right, confronting Breckinridge. Ord, thinking the position of the division too much retired, ordered it forward, so as to connect with Hovey's. This advance was not designed to bring on an engagement, nor would it have done so but for a careless misapprehension on Lauman's part. Pugh's brigade, after crossing the New Orleans and Jackson Railroad at a point about two miles south of Jackson, and driving back the enemy's skirmishers, found itself, with less than 1000 men, confronted by a strong line of works held by two brigades of the enemy, with two full batteries, and protected by abatis in front. The intervening space was open, affording no cover to a charging column. Pugh reported this situation to Lauman; but the latter repeated the order to move forward. It was certain death to every other man in the brigade, but the order was obeyed. No other result was possible but that which followed, namely, the useless murder of half the column. Well may Lauman have wept when he looked upon the remnant of his old brigade. He was afterward relieved of his command by General Ord.[1]

Jackson was evacuated on the night of July 16th, Johnston retreating across Pearl River, burning the bridges behind him, and through Brandon toward Meridian, about 100 miles east of Jackson. The town, thus again left in possession of the national troops, was once more devoted to destruction. Sherman pursued the enemy as far as Brandon, and then returned with his army across the Big Black. The Confederate loss at Jackson, by Johnston's report, was 71 killed, 504 wounded, and about 25 missing. Desertions were frequent from his army both during the siege and in the retreat.

The navy had necessarily a less conspicuous share than the army in the capture of Vicksburg, but its co-operation had been absolutely essential to Grant's success. The gun-boats had been constantly engaged in shelling the town from below. For forty-two days the mortar-boats had also been at work without intermission, throwing shells into all parts of the city, and even reaching the works in the rear of Vicksburg, three miles distant, with a fire in reverse; thirteen guns had been transferred from the fleet to the army; the river had been patrolled from Cairo to Vicksburg, to clear out the guerrillas who had on several occasions built batteries on the shore, and attempted to sink or capture the transports conveying stores, re-enforcements, and ammunition to the besieging army; and the gun-boats, with General Ellet's marine brigade, had frustrated the schemes of Kirby Smith by their co-operation with the small force on the right bank of the Mississippi at Milliken's Bend.[2]

[1] Sherman, speaking of this affair, attributes the disaster to "misunderstanding or a misinterpretation of General Ord's minute instructions on the part of General Lauman."

[2] Immediately after the surrender Sherman penned the following impromptu, but characteristic letter to Admiral Porter:

"I can appreciate the intense satisfaction you must feel at lying before the monster that has defied us with such deep and malignant hate, and seeing your once disunited fleet again a unit; and, better still, the chain that made an inclosed sea of a link in the great river broken forever. In so magnificent a result I stop not to count who did it. It is done, and the day of the nation's birth is consecrated and baptized anew in a victory won by the united navy and army of our country. God grant that the harmony and mutual respect that exists between our respective commanders, and shared by all the true men of the joint service, may continue forever, and serve to elevate our national character, threatened with shipwreck. Thus I muse as I sit in my solitary camp out in the woods, far from the point for which we have justly striven so long and so well; and though personal curiosity would tempt me to go and see the frowning batteries and sunken pits that have defied us so long, and sent to their silent graves so many of our early comrades in the enterprise, I feel that other tasks lie before me, and time must not be lost. Without casting anchor, and despite the heat, and the dust, and the drought, I must again into the bowels of the land, to make the conquest of the land fulfill all the conditions it should in the progress of this war. Whether success attend my efforts or not, I know that Admiral Porter will ever accord to me the exhibition of a pure and unselfish zeal in the service of our country.

"Though farther apart, the navy and army will still act in concert, and I assure you I shall never reach the banks of the river or see a gun-boat but I will think of Admiral Porter, Captain

The 4th of July, 1863, also witnessed a conflict of some importance at Helena, Arkansas, on the right bank of the river, above Vicksburg. This place, since its occupation in the summer of 1862 by the advance of General Curtis's army, had rested undisturbed in the possession of the national forces, and had been of great use as a dépôt of recruits and supplies for operations farther south. It threatened also the most important points in those portions of the state occupied by the enemy.

Toward the close of the siege of Vicksburg, Lieutenant General Holmes, the Confederate commander in Arkansas, at the suggestion of Secretary Mallory, and with Kirby Smith's permission, prepared an expedition to attack Helena. He left Little Rock on the 25th of June, and made Clarendon, sixty miles east of the capital, on White River, the rendezvous for his forces. Fagan, Sterling Price, and Marmaduke were to command columns in the attacking army. It was Holmes's design to surprise the Federal force; but Price, owing to high water, was four days behindhand, and in the mean time General B. M. Prentiss, commanding at Helena, became acquainted with the enemy's intentions. The garrison numbered about 4000 men, and was intrenched behind strong earth-works, well mounted with artillery, and with their main approaches covered by abatis. Prentiss had also an important ally, upon whose presence the enemy had not calculated, in the gun-boat Tyler, commanded by J. M. Pritchett.

The town lies upon the river-flat, but near it are high commanding ridges, with ravines opening toward the river. Upon a low ridge nearer the town Fort Curtis was located, while upon the higher ridges commanding it outworks had been constructed by Brigadier General F. Salomon, to whose charge also had been assigned their defense. These outworks consisted of four strong batteries, designated from right to left by the first four letters of the alphabet in their succession. The flanks, which, being between the ridges and the river, were open, were protected by rifle-pits and batteries.

Holmes reports his total force to have been 7646, or about twice the strength of the garrison. The Missourians were under Price, Parsons, and Marmaduke, while the brigades of Fagan, McRae, and Walker consisted of troops gathered together from Arkansas. The Confederate command was not lacking in bravery, and the attack was admirably conducted, but the assailing force was too weak by half for any chance of success against a determined garrison in so strong a position. The Confederate Governor of Arkansas, Harris Flanagan, with his adjutant general, Colonel Gordon Bear, were on the field, acting as volunteer aids to General Holmes.

On the morning of July 4th Holmes's army was within a mile of the outworks. Price led the brigades of Parsons and McRae (3095 men) against Battery C on Grave-yard Hill, and succeeded, after great loss, in carrying the

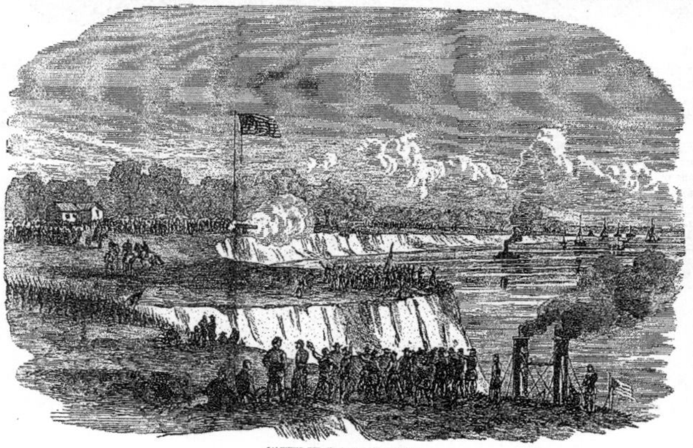

SALUTING THE FLAG AT PORT HUDSON.

work, capturing some of its guns, which were either spiked or devoid of friction-primers, and therefore useless to the captors. Price had great difficulty in bringing his own artillery over the broken country and up the hill. Meanwhile his infantry was falling under a fire from all the other works. Instead of retreating, hundreds of his command pushed forward in disorder and without support, and encountering a cross fire, until, unable to retreat, as many as had escaped death surrendered. Price reports a loss in this action of over one third of his command.

Fagan's small command of four regiments had attacked at the same time, attempting the still more difficult task of carrying Battery D on the left. The charge at this point was exceedingly gallant, but met with only partial success. The brave Arkansans rushed up the precipitous ravines, and drove the Federal sharp-shooters out of their rifle-pits; but every assault upon the fort itself only added to the useless slaughter of the assailants. A single regiment lost its colonel, lieutenant colonel, and over 100 men. The remainder withdrew to the rifle-pits already captured, where, exposed to the fire from the fort, they held their ground until 11 o'clock, when a general retreat was ordered.

Marmaduke, with 1750 men, had been ordered to take the fort on Bighton Hill (Battery A) on the north, but he failed even to make a vigorous assault, not being supported by Walker's brigade.

Holmes reports his loss in this battle as 173 killed, 687 wounded, and 776 missing. Thus, by his own admission, he lost over one fifth of his command. Prentiss says he buried nearly 300 of the enemy's killed, and took 1100 prisoners. His own loss was less than 250, all told. The gun-boat Tyler had a large share in the havoc which was made among the charging columns of the enemy.

The capture of Port Hudson and its garrison followed as the immediate and necessary consequence of the surrender of Vicksburg. In any case, Gardner could not have held out much longer. His ammunition for small-arms was almost gone, only twenty rounds remaining to each man, and the garrison was on the verge of starvation. Its mill had been fired by a shell, 2000 bushels of corn being burned with it. No meat was left, and the mules were being killed to satisfy the demand; even rats, it is reported, were eaten by the famishing soldiers. Only fifteen serviceable guns remained on the land defenses, the others having been, one after the other, disabled by the accurate fire of the Federal guns. Banks's sappers and miners had dug their way up to the works, and General Dwight had a mine ready on the left, charged with thirty barrels of powder, in such a position that its explosion would have destroyed "the Citadel," already referred to as a vital point in the enemy's defenses. The hospitals were full of the sick, and the men in the trenches were so exhausted and enfeebled that they were unfit for action. The capture of Vicksburg, however, precipitated the capitulation of Port Hudson. Grant had embarked an expedition, under General Herron, to re-enforce Banks, but scarcely were the men on board when the tidings was brought of the capture of Port Hudson, and Herron's expedition was ordered up the Yazoo.

It was on the 6th of July that the news of the victory at Vicksburg reached Port Hudson. Gardner could hardly by any possibility have misinterpreted the tremendous salute of the gun-boats, re-echoed from the land batteries, or the news shouted across his lines. He forthwith convened a council of war, and a surrender was determined upon. On the 7th he communicated with General Banks, asking the latter to give him official assurance of the news. If Vicksburg had really been surrendered, he asked for a cessation of hostilities, with a view to the consideration of terms for the capitulation of Port Hudson. Banks replied by sending Grant's own dispatch, but refusing a cessation of hostilities. Conferees were appointed on each side, and on July 8th terms of surrender were concluded upon, and the next morning formal possession was taken of the town.

Banks does not report his loss before Port Hudson, but it probably fell not far short of 3000. The enemy admitted a loss of only 610 men during the forty-five days' campaign, but this, Banks is confident, must have been too low an estimate, as he found 500 wounded in the hospitals. The number of prisoners taken was 6408, of whom 455 were officers. The captures of the whole campaign, including the trans-Mississippi operations, Banks estimates at 10,584 men, 73 guns, 6000 small-arms, three gun-boats, eight other steam-boats, besides cotton and cattle of immense value.

The capture of Port Hudson scared Dick Taylor out of the country east of the Atchafalaya, compelling him to evacuate Brashear City just one month after its capture. Both Grant and Banks now urged an immediate combined movement against Mobile, but were overruled at Washington. It seems some Texan refugees were anxious that operations should be recommenced on the line of the Red River, and Banks was advised accordingly. The history of the campaign thus opened we reserve for a subsequent chapter.

Herron, in the mean time, having transferred his troops to vessels of lighter draft, moved up the Yazoo, his transports preceded by the iron-clad De Kalb and two tin-clad gun-boats under Captain Walker. The expedition had for its object the destruction of a large number of Confederate steam-boats which had run up the Yazoo to find refuge from Porter's fleet. When nearly opposite Yazoo City the De Kalb was sunk by a torpedo. The Confederate garrison abandoned the city upon the approach of the expedition. Only one of the steam-boats was captured, the others making their escape up the river. The fugitive vessels were, however, pursued by Herron's cavalry, and all of them, to the number of twenty-two, were burned or sunk. Three hundred prisoners were captured, six heavy guns, 250 small-arms, 800 horses, and 2000 bales of cotton.

Breese, and the many elegant and accomplished gentlemen it has been my good fortune to meet on armed or unarmed decks of the Mississippi squadron."

OPENING OF THE MISSISSIPPI—ARRIVAL OF THE "IMPERIAL" AT NEW ORLEANS.

Thus ended the campaign for the possession of the Mississippi River, which now, to use the happy expression of President Lincoln, "ran unvexed to the sea." On the 16th of July, the steam-boat Imperial arrived at New Orleans from St. Louis, the first steamer which had made the trip for more than two years.

The foremost man in this campaign was General Grant, the taker of guns and armies. His name was on every tongue. The shout of joy which arose from a whole people on account of his victory was mingled with a pæan of praise to the victor. He was at once appointed to the vacant major generalship in the regular army, to date from July 4th, 1863. In the midst of these acclamations to his honor, President Lincoln addressed him a letter[1] acknowledging the inestimable service he had rendered his country, and adding a personal acknowledgment of his own error of judgment as to the propriety of re-enforcing Banks after the battle of Port Gibson instead of moving directly against Vicksburg. In this Vicksburg campaign General Grant showed his capacity for the command of a large army, and for the conduct of movements the most extensive; a remarkable boldness of conception, almost unlimited resources, and a steady persistence of purpose not to be moved by any obstacle, and not to be conquered by a succession of partial defeats. As to total defeat with such a commander, that was clearly impossible.

1 "Executive Mansion, Washington, July 13th, 1863.

"To MAJOR-GENERAL GRANT:

"MY DEAR GENERAL,—I do not remember that you and I ever met personally. I write this now as a grateful acknowledgment for *the almost inestimable service you have done the country.* I wish to say a word further: When you first reached the vicinity of Vicksburg I thought you should do what you finally did—march the troops across the neck, run the batteries with the transports, and thus go below; and I never had any faith, except a general hope that you knew better than I, that the Yazoo Pass Expedition and the like could succeed. When you got below, and took Port Gibson, Grand Gulf, and vicinity, I thought you should go down the river and join General Banks; and when you turned northward east of the Big Black, I feared it was a mistake. I now wish to make a personal acknowledgment *that you were right and I was wrong.*

"Yours, very truly, A. LINCOLN."

JOSEPH HOOKER.

CHAPTER XXVIII.

HOOKER IN COMMAND.—CHANCELLORSVILLE.

Hooker assumes Command.—Bad Condition of the Army.—Hooker's Measures of Reform.—Hooker's Plan of Operations.—Changes in the Commands.—Strength of the two Armies.—Hooker's Orders to Stoneman.—Cavalry Expedition postponed.—Hooker moves upon Chancellorsville.—The Rappahannock and Rapidan crossed.—Chancellorsville and the Wilderness.—Sedgwick crosses near Fredericksburg.—Hooker's Anticipations of Success.—Lee's Movements.—Hooker's Delay at Chancellorsville.—He advances toward Fredericksburg, then retreats.—Position of the Forces.—Lee and Jackson in Council.—A Flank Attack resolved upon.—Jackson marches.—Sickles attacks the Confederate Rear.—Jackson's March.—Lee's Operations.—Jackson routs the Federal Right.—Pleasonton checks the Confederate Advance.—Lee's Operations in Front.—The Advance of Birney.—Jackson Wounded.—Death of Jackson.—His Career.—Wishes the War to be without Quarter.—Hooker assumes a new Position.—The Union Line of Battle.—Birney's Night Attack.—*The Battle of Sunday, May 3*: Forces Present.—Stuart occupies Hazle Grove.—Assails Sickles.—Is forced back.—Sickles asks for Support.—Hooker Disabled.—Sickles falls back.—French attacks Stuart, and is repulsed.—Lee assails the Union Centre.—Unites with Stuart.—Occupies Chancellorsville.—The Federals Retreat.—Their new Position.—Sedgwick ordered up from Fredericksburg.—His dilatory Movement.—Storms the Heights and Advances.—Perilous Situation of Lee.—He sends Troops to meet Sedgwick.—The Fight at Salem Heights.—*The Battle of Monday, May 3*: Lee re-enforces McLaws.—Early retakes Fredericksburg Heights.—Howe repulses Early and McLaws.—Hooker's Orders to Sedgwick.—Sedgwick recrosses the Rappahannock.—The Council of War.—Hooker recrosses the Rappahannock.—Movements of Averill and Stoneman.—Losses at Chancellorsville.—Criticism upon Operations.—Hooker's Errors.—Lee's Errors.

FROM this survey of operations in the West we turn again to Virginia, where, at the opening of the year, the two great armies of the Union and the Confederacy lay confronting each other upon the banks of the Rappahannock.[1]

Hooker was invested with the command of the Army of the Potomac on the 26th of January. Just three days before, his predecessor had drawn up an order dismissing him from the service, and on the very day before it was doubtful whether that order should be put in force. But the transfer of command was executed with all due military courtesy. "Give," said Burnside, in his parting address to the army, "to the brave and skillful general

[1] The following are the leading authorities for Chancellorsville: Testimony before the Committee on the Conduct of the War, contained in volume i. of the second series (cited as *Com. Rep.*, ii.).—Lee's Report of Chancellorsville (cited as *Lee's Rep.*): it embraces his own report and those of nearly all of his principal commanders.—Hotchkiss and Allan, engineers in the late Confederate army, have put forth a monograph upon Chancellorsville. It is specially valuable for its elaborate maps, which clearly represent the topography of the region, and show every movement upon both sides.—Dabney's Life of Stonewall Jackson embraces some valuable information respecting the operations of that commander. The author had access to many materials which are now probably destroyed.

who has so long been identified with your organization, and who is now to command you, your full and cordial support and co-operation, and you will deserve success." Hooker, in assuming command, said that "he only gives expression to the feelings of this army when he conveys to our late commander, Major-General Burnside, the most cordial good wishes for his future."

Hooker took command with a confidence in himself which contrasted strongly with the self-distrust which had been expressed by Burnside. The position had come to him unsought, but, as he believed, not undeserved. "No being lives," he averred, "who can say that I ever expressed a desire for the position. It was conferred on me for my sword, and not for any act or word of mine indicative of a desire for it."[1] He had, indeed, grave misgivings, not as to his own capacity, but as to the state of the force placed under his command.[2] Foremost among these causes of misgiving was the hostility of Halleck, who for six months had sat, and for thrice as long was to sit, under the title of general-in-chief, as an incubus upon the Union armies. Hooker knew, or at least believed, that Halleck had been hostile to him from the first, and the sole request that he made of the President was that he would stand between him and his superior in command.[3] The condition of the army was a still more grave matter for apprehension. Burnside had received it from McClellan strong in numbers, discipline, and spirit. In three months he transmitted it to Hooker reduced in numbers and impaired in efficiency. Much of this was owing to causes over which Burnside had no control. Lincoln's policy, as finally indicated by his emancipation proclamation, was looked upon with disfavor by a very considerable part of the army. Many of the officers in high command, especially those who had belonged to the regular army, were far from hostile to slavery. McClellan, just escaped from the Chickahominy swamps, had found time six months before to present his views of the principles upon which the war should be waged. "The rebellion," he said, "has assumed the character of a war; as such it should be regarded. It should not be a war looking to the subjugation of the people of any state in any event. It should not be at all a war upon population, but against armed forces and political organizations. Neither confiscation of property, political executions of persons, territorial organizations of states, or forcible abolition of slavery, should be contemplated for a moment. Unless the principles governing the future conduct of our struggle shall be made known and approved, the effort to obtain the requisite forces will be almost hopeless. A declaration of radical views, especially upon slavery, will rapidly disintegrate our present armies."[4] McClellan gave voice to the prevailing feeling among the leading officers of the army. No inconsiderable part of the private soldiers had been drawn from a class which looked with bitter aversion upon the negro. This was especially the case with the regiments raised in the large cities of the North. To them the very name of Abolitionist was a word of reproach. But now the proclamation issued on New Year's day of 1863 had solemnly pledged the nation to the abolition of slavery as an essential feature of the future conduct of the war.

For a time it seemed that McClellan's prophecy that a declaration of radical views upon the subject of slavery would be verified by the rapid disintegration of the Army of the Potomac. Officers high in rank openly declared that they would never have embarked in the war had they anticipated this action of the government.[5] When rest came to the army after the disaster of Fredericksburg and the failure of the mud campaign, the disaffected began to show themselves and to make their influence felt. The army fell into a course of rapid depletion. Express trains, and even the mails, were burdened with civilian clothing, sent to soldiers by their friends to facilitate their escape from camp. When Hooker took command desertions numbered 200 a day. In a week the army lost as many men as were killed in any pitched battle. What with deserters and absentees, 85,000 men, almost 4000 of whom were commissioned officers, wellnigh half the nominal strength of the army, were away from the field, scattered all over the country.[6] The great body of the disaffected, whether in or out of the army, believed that the government would soon be forced to restore McClellan to the command, and practically to abandon its declared policy of emancipation. By these men the appointment of Hooker was looked upon with no favor. They could not fail to remember the unsparing terms in which he had attributed the disaster of the Peninsular campaign to the utter want of capacity of their favorite commander.[7] They looked eagerly forward to the time when he should be placed at the head of the army, and thence, as political affairs seemed to be shaping themselves, raised to the Presidency of the United States. The feeling in the army and that in the country acted and reacted upon each other, and for a time it seemed that the policy of the government would be condemned alike by citizens and soldiers.

In spite of these untoward circumstances and the grave misgivings which he felt, Hooker grasped the command with a firm hand. It was midwinter, and operations in the field must be postponed until early spring should render the roads passable. In that interval much co
Hooker set himself strenuously at work to improve the con
army. At the very outset he broke up the grand divisions, an
former organization into corps, each being placed under the c
general in whom he had confidence. Then the great evil of d
to be encountered. The loose system of furloughs was thorou
Hitherto the corps commanders had granted leaves of absence
By the new regulations no leave of absence could be granted
head-quarters to officers of high rank. In no regiment could m
field officer or two line officers be absent at the same time. N
two privates out of a hundred in any regiment could be absent
at the same time, and no man could receive a furlough unless h
record for attention to his duties. The leaves of absence being
fifteen days being the utmost limit, even these strict rules enabl
ing men who wished it to visit their homes. Disloyal officer
fully weeded out. Express trains were examined, and all citiz
found therein was burned. The police and commissariat of
ceived special attention. Comfortable winter huts were built; v
fresh bread were ordered to be issued twice a week. The g
these measures was soon apparent. Desertions ceased; absen
to their commands; the ratio of sickness sank from more than
to less than five. The cavalry, which had heretofore been sca
the grand divisions, was organized into a separate corps, and sc
a powerful arm, wanting only a fitting man to wield it; but
not, as commander of this army, to find such a leader. He di
could by giving the cavalry corps to Stoneman, with Averill
mand. Sheridan was yet to be brought from a subordinate p
West. The outpost duty had been grossly neglected; the
knew what was passing within the Union lines almost as accu
its own commanders. Hooker changed all this. The pickt
rendered impenetrable. One division lay encamped on Falmc
opposite Fredericksburg, in plain view of the enemy. The
other divisions, a score or more in number, covering a circuit
miles, lay beyond the wooded crests of Stafford. What passe
screen was hidden from the keenest view which the Confederat
could gain, saving when some ostentatious demonstration, or a
dash of pickets was made, with the object, as Hooker explained
age and stimulate in the breasts of our men, by successes how
feeling of superiority over our adversaries." Knowing, moreo
ness was the bane of all armies, every effort was made to ke
employed, and whenever the weather permitted they were eng
exercises.

As winter wore away and spring opened, the commander felt
he had at length "a living army well worthy of the republic,"
wont to express it in larger phrase, "the finest army upon the
through those winter weeks he had pondered the problem how
should strike.[1] His instructions were of the most general cha
leck wrote: "In regard to the operations of your own army,
judge when and where it can move to the greatest advantag
view always the importance of covering Washington and H
either directly or by so operating as to punish any force of th
against them."[2] Hooker had, however, caught the true idea o
be done. It was not so much to capture Richmond as to des
federate Army of Northern Virginia which lay in his front.
months before vainly sought to impress this idea upon McCle
seized upon it months later. In seeking to solve the probl
Hooker soon came to the decision that it was impossible to cro
hannock and assail the enemy directly in front. The misadven
side had demonstrated this point; and, moreover, since that luck
the Confederate position had been greatly strengthened. The
of the river in front of the Confederate lines presented, indeed,
ous difficulty, for Lee adhered to his former plan, rather invitin
cuing such an operation.[4] But his long lines of intrenchment,
a distance of twenty miles along the sides and crests of the hei
plain view. Interspersed with the infantry parapets were epa
artillery which would sweep the hill-sides and bottom-lands o

[1] "The subject of the campaign was one to which General Hooker gave much
tention. But, while getting the views of every body else, he did not give his c
intentions in regard to the proposed campaign entirely secret from every one, f
he intended to do might come to the knowledge of the enemy. When he assun
the army there was not a record or document of any kind at headquarters of the
any information at all in regard to the enemy. There was no means, no orga
apparent effort to obtain such information. We were almost as ignorant of th
immediate front as if they had been in China. An efficient organization for that
stituted, by which we were soon enabled to get correct and proper informatio
their strength and movements." (Butterfield, in *Com. Rep.*, ii., 74.)—"Knowing
of the river would be resisted, and perhaps defeated, if brought to the knowledge
had taken every precaution to keep it a profound secret. I had not even comm
Corps Commanders, or the officers of my staff." (Hooker, in *Com. Rep.*, ii., 118.)—
tion of Hooker's dispatches and orders, compared with what is now known, shows

Blacksmiths Department, Head-Quarters.

Stables and Negro Servants' Tent.

General Hooker's Tent.

HEADQUARTERS OF THE ARMY OF THE POTOMAC.

t march. Abatis of fallen timber guarded every point
able swamps at the foot of the hills, while in the rear
re covered by rifle-pits, and every little rise of ground
hments like a miniature fortress. To attack these works
eless. "Previous exposure in attempting it under Burn-
y's preparations were far less complete, had made this a
ind of every private in the ranks."[1]
l then be assailed only by turning his position either be-
ainst the former operation was the fact that the river in-
n width that it would require a thousand feet of bridging,
ins and artillery must march twenty miles over a broken
y, by roads still axle-deep with clayey mud. This march
aled from the enemy on the opposite bank, who could
ntrenchments down the river faster than the assailants
acticable roads. This movement was, then, clearly im-

to turn the Confederate right far above Fredericksburg,
ble only upon condition that the movement should be a
iles above Fredericksburg, in a straight line, but twice as
nd of the river, is Banks's Ford; seven miles farther is the
,[3] neither of them to be waded except in the dry season;
so high that the passage could be made only by bridges.
defended by works so strong and strongly held as to pre-
of carrying them. A little above the United States Ford
receives the Rapidan, an affluent almost equal to itself
mity of the Confederate lines; although small detachments
e Rapidan for some miles. If the Rappahannock should
he position, the Rapidan was still to be passed. Lee never
opponent would attempt to turn his flank by marching
er roads almost impassable, into a region where his army
what it could carry with it, crossing, also, two rivers which
ould so swell as to cut him off from his ammunition and
Yet this was the bold operation which Hooker resolved

ooker was divided into seven corps. Many changes had
principal commands. The Ninth Corps, which Burnside
from North Carolina, and which had fought under him at
and Antietam, was detached from the Army of the Poto-
be immediate command of W. F. Smith,[4] sent with its old
st. Its place was supplied by the Twelfth, under Slocum,
osted at Harper's Ferry. The Eleventh, under Sigel, which
approaches to Washington, was brought down to the main
applied for leave of absence, and, at the urgent request of
mand of this corps was given to Howard. Butterfield was
ff, and the Fifth Corps was assigned to Meade. Stoneman
e head of the cavalry, and the Third Corps was given to
ck replaced Smith in the command of the Sixth Corps.
l the First Corps, and Couch the Second. The army which
nd numbered in effective men, "present for duty," 120,000
lery, besides 13,000 cavalry.[5] The cavalry, excepting a sin-
rhaps 1000, under Pleasanton, as we shall have to show,
n an expedition in which they accomplished nothing, and
d out of the account in estimating the effective force with
ng generals encountered each other in that series of actions
battle of Chancellorsville. The Confederate force was far
months before it had numbered 80,000; but, confident in

Rep., ii., 52. [2] Ibid., 53.
[3] United States Mine Ford; sometimes called the Bark Mill Ford.
owever, Smith did not accompany the corps to the West. He remained at
mand of the corps was given to Parke.
ately official report, to which I have been able to gain access, showing the
ker's army, but scattered through the testimony given in the Report of the
nduct of the War are data which enable me to fix it without possibility of
Hooker (Com. Rep., ii., 120) gives the strength "for duty" of the Fifth, Elev-
s at 44,661—say 45,000. The Eleventh was the weakest in the army, num-
121) 11,000. There remain 34,000 for the Fifth and Twelfth. These were
ual strength, 17,000 each. The Sixth was the strongest corps; Sedgwick,
5), places it at 22,000; Hooker (Ibid., 128) says it numbered 26,288; but he
of which, by a few thousands, it is reasonable to suppose, appeared in line
rence between 22,000 and 26,000 is about the normal discrepancy between
muster-rolls as "present" and those actually at any moment "present for
o had for a time the First and the Third, as well as his own corps, the Sixth,
umbers of the two former at 35,000. Sickles (Ibid., 7) says that the strength
d, was 18,000, which would leave 17,000 for the First, that of Reynolds.
nly the Second Corps, that of Couch; of the strength of this I find no spe-
me it to have been 17,000, that being the average number of each of the

rs usually place the numbers of Lee's army at 45,000. But the official re-
) show that on the 31st of March there were present in the Army of North-
nen, of whom 60.298 were present for duty. The force was certainly not
next month, for Longstreet was detached a month before. Lee says (Rep.,
eet, with two corps, was detached for service south of the James River in
lined to suspect a clerical error here, and that for "two divisions" we should
ngstreet's Corps consisted of five divisions, those of Anderson, McLaws,
ickett. Only the first two are in any way mentioned in the Reports of the
ille, and in the list of regiments I find none belonging to the last three divi-
bney says (Stonewall Jackson, 604): "The three divisions of Hood, Pickett,
sent in Southeastern Virginia, making a demonstration against Suffolk,
n directed by the scarcity of forage and food in Spottsylvania." Dabney,
d access to authentic reports as to Jackson's force, says: "His four divisions
28,000 muskets, and an aggregate of more than 30.000 men and officers.
by 28 field batteries, containing 115 guns; besides these batteries, the army
by a reserve corps of artillery. Stuart's division of cavalry was also acting
ng the artillery and cavalry to the 28,000 muskets and more than 2000 of-
strength of Jackson up to fully 35,000. This writer, indeed, adds: "Lee
ate of about 45,000 men." But, even apart from the actual returns which
s clearly an under estimate, for Longstreet's Corps was always much stron-
on, and the divisions of Anderson and McLaws were much the largest in that
d less in the previous actions than the others. They probably numbered,
d cavalry acting with them, fully 25,000 men; so that the most reliable in-
able corroborates the accuracy of the official returns, which give Lee a little
n.

the strength of his position, and somewhat embarrassed by the scarcity of forage, Lee had sent Longstreet with half of his corps southward toward North Carolina, where offensive operations were threatened. There remained on the Rappahannock the divisions of Anderson and McLaws, and Jackson's entire corps, consisting of the divisions of A. P. Hill, D. H. Hill, Trimble (formerly that of Jackson), and Early. But D. H. Hill had been put in command of the Department of North Carolina, and his division was now under Rodes; Trimble was at home on sick-leave, and his division was commanded by Colston. Besides these, there was Stuart's cavalry, reduced to two brigades, and a strong reserve artillery. The entire effective strength of all arms was something more than 60,000 men. Anderson's and McLaws's divisions guarded the line from the United States Ford downward beyond Fredericksburg, a distance of ten miles; Early held the intrenchments at the foot of the hills opposite Franklin's Crossing; the remainder of Jackson's corps lay near Port Royal, twenty miles below Fredericksburg. Both armies had built for themselves comfortable winter huts in the wooded region on either side of the Rappahannock, which formed for the time a barrier which neither could overpass.

Hooker, having matured his plan of campaign, wished to commence its execution as early as possible. The term of enlistment of 40,000 men, a third of his army, would soon expire, and he knew that there was little use of putting troops into action just before the close of their time of service. Before the middle of April, though the roads were still too heavy for artillery and wagon trains, he thought that mounted men might move. On the 12th he ordered Stoneman to take the whole cavalry force, with the exception of a single brigade, 12,000 sabres strong, turn the hostile position on the left, throw himself between the enemy and Richmond, isolate him from his supplies, and check his retreat. Every where and all told, Stoneman could not encounter a force half equal to his own. In sharp phrases, which rang like battle orders, Hooker gave his directions to Stoneman: "Harass the enemy day and night, on the march and in the camp unceasingly. If you can not cut off from his column large slices, do not fail to take small ones. Let your watchword be Fight! and let all your orders be Fight! Keep yourself informed of the enemy's whereabouts, and attack him wherever you find him. Take the initiative in the forward movement of this grand army; bear in mind that celerity, audacity, and resolution are every thing in war." The primary object of this cavalry expedition, to which every thing was to be subservient, was to cut the enemy's communication with Richmond by the Fredericksburg route.[1] The movement was premature. The cavalry rode two days up the Rappahannock, and threw a division across, but a sudden storm swelled the capricious stream, and this division, in order to avoid being isolated, was forced to recross by swimming. The storm continued, the river became wholly impassable, and the cavalry were ordered to remain where they were.

A fortnight of genial spring weather now intervened. It seemed that the rainy season was over, the swollen river was confined within its banks, the roads grew firmer. Hooker in the mean while had matured his grand enterprise. "I concluded," he says, "to change my plan, and strike for the whole rebel army instead of forcing it back upon its line of retreat, which was as much as I could hope to accomplish in executing my first design." This plan was the one which has been already indicated. It was to ascend the Rappahannock beyond the hostile lines, throw a strong force across, which should sweep down the opposite bank, "knock away the enemy's force holding the United States and Banks's Fords by attacking them in their rear, and, as soon as these fords were opened, to re-enforce the marching column sufficiently for them to continue the march upon the rebel army until his whole force was routed, and, if successful, his retreat intercepted. Simultaneous with this movement on the right, the left were to cross the Rappahannock below Fredericksburg, and threaten the enemy in that quarter, including his dépôt of supplies, to prevent his dispatching an overwhelming force to his left."[2] How near this plan came of success, and how utterly it failed, is now to be shown.

On the 26th of April Hooker issued the orders which gave the first inti-

The foregoing was written before the appearance of Hotchkiss and Allan's work, previously noted. They give the force of each division as follows: Jackson's Corps—A. P. Hill, 11,100; D. H. Hill, 9000; Trimble, 6000; Early, 7400; in all, 33,500. Anderson and McLaws, 17,000; Artillery, 170 pieces, 5000 men; Cavalry, present, 2700—a total of 58,200. But it is expressly stated that these are the numbers of "muskets," that is, privates and non-commissioned officers. They add (page 24): "We have not the exact data on which to give the effective strength, but an addition of 4000 to the total above would be a liberal estimate." This addition to the "effective" must mean the officers, who are included in the Union returns. This statement differs only slightly from my estimate as to the total force, but makes that of Jackson larger, and those of Anderson and McLaws smaller. Anderson's division contained three more regiments than that of McLaws, and was probably the stronger by 1000. I adopt their statement, distributing the 3800 "additional," as nearly as may be, among the different organizations.

From these data is framed the following table:

FORCES AT CHANCELLORSVILLE.

Union.		Confederate.		
REYNOLDS (1st Corps). *Divisions:* Doubleday, Robinson, Wadsworth	17,000	JACKSON'S CORPS.	A. P. Hill	11,800
COUCH (2d Corps). *Divisions:* French, Gibbon, Hancock	17,000		Rodes	9,600
SICKLES (3d Corps). *Divisions:* Berry, Birney, Whipple	18,000		Colston	6,400
MEADE (5th Corps). *Divisions:* Griffin, Humphrey, Sykes	17,000		Early	7,800
SEDGWICK (6th Corps). *Divisions:* Brooks, Howe, Newton	22,000	LONGSTREET'S CORPS.	Anderson	9,500
HOWARD (11th Corps). *Divisions:* Devens, Schurz, Steinwehr	11,000		McLaws	8,500
SLOCUM (12th Corps). *Divisions:* Geary, Williams	17,000		Artillery	5,400
PLEASONTON (Cavalry)	1,000		Cavalry	3,000
Total Force	120,000		*Total Force*	62,000

[1] Hooker's Instructions, in Com. Rep., ii., 113. [2] Hooker, in Com. Rep., ii., 116.

PICKET GUARD.

mation of his plan. The corps of Meade, Slocum, and Howard were to form the main turning column. They were to march at sunrise next day, ascend the Rappahannock to Kelly's Ford, twenty-seven miles above Fredericksburg, cross the river, and move for the Rapidan, cross, and sweep down its southern bank. They were to move as lightly as possible, the men to carry eight days' rations on their persons; each corps to have but a single battery and six ambulances, the small ammunition to be carried on mule-back. Most of the artillery, and several regiments whose term was about to close, being left behind, this column marched 36,000 strong. Couch, with two of his divisions—that of Gibbon being left opposite Fredericksburg—was to follow after as far as the United States Ford, there halt in readiness to cross the moment that the hostile force guarding it should be swept away. Sedgwick, with his own corps and those of Sickles and Reynolds, were to cross the Rappahannock below Fredericksburg, and make a vigorous demonstration to distract the attention of the enemy.

The main turning column pressed rapidly up the Rappahannock, and before night of Tuesday, the 28th, reached Kelly's Ford. The stream was unfordable, but a pontoon bridge was quickly thrown over, and early on the morning of the 29th the crossing was effected. The force, separated into two columns, pressed rapidly on to the Rapidan. Slocum and Howard crossed at Germania Ford; Meade at Ely's Ford, ten miles below. The Rapidan was hardly fordable, the water reaching to the armpits of the men; but they waded through, bearing their knapsacks on their bayonets. So wholly unanticipated was this advance, that a small party of the Confederates were surprised at Germania Ford in the act of building a bridge; these were all captured. Meade swept eastward down the right bank of the Rapidan, directly toward Fredericksburg, until he came in view of the United States Ford over the Rappahannock. Two Confederate brigades which had been guarding this point fell back. As soon as Couch caught sight through the mist of the head of Meade's column, pontoon bridges were laid, his divisions passed over, and all the four corps headed straight for Chancellorsville, their appointed place of rendezvous, where they were concentrated late in the afternoon of the 30th.

Chancellorsville was a solitary brick house, with a few insignificant outbuildings, standing in a clearing on the eastern verge of a wild, wooded region known as the Wilderness. Looking eastward toward Fredericksburg,

CAVALRY CROSSING AT ELY'S FORD.

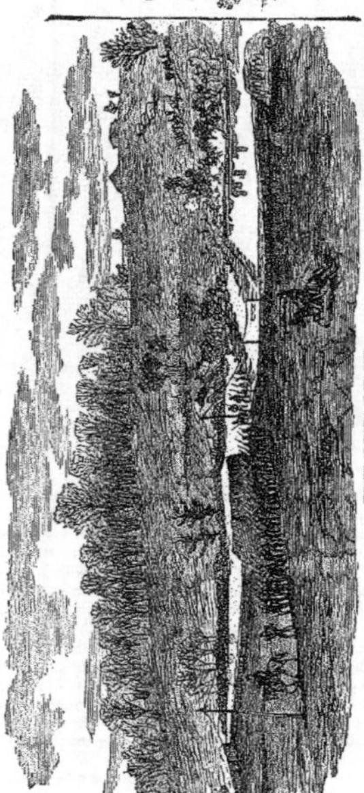

CROSSING AT UNITED STATES FORD.

eleven miles distant, are two roads; to the right the Orange plank road, to the left the turnpike. These diverge for a space, and then, converging, unite half way between Chancellorsville and Fredericksburg. Both are excellent roads; the one planked, the other macadamized. Westward from Chancellorsville they run together for a couple of miles, and then separate, the turnpike running to Culpepper, the plank road to Orange Court-house. This road is the essential feature of the military position. From the north comes in another road, which after a mile divides, sending branches to the different fords of the Rapidan and the Rappahannock. The cleared fields around Chancellorsville have a circuit of a mile; the belt of woods surrounding them eastward toward Fredericksburg, and southward toward Spottsylvania, is a mile or two in breadth. Beyond this, in both directions, lies an open cultivated country.

The Wilderness, henceforth to be historic, stretches westward from Chancellorsville. The region for a space of a dozen miles is seamed with veins of iron ore. These have been wrought for five generations. Here indeed were erected the first regular iron furnaces in North America. The forests had been cut down to furnish fuel for these furnaces. The soil being generally too poor to repay culture, the region was left to Nature, which soon covered it with a dense mass of dwarf pines, scrubby oaks, chinquapins, and the like. Every stump left by the woodman's axe sent up a cluster of sprouts in place of the parent trunk. Whortleberries and brambles of every kind, availing themselves of the temporary flood of sunshine, twined and matted themselves into thickets through which the solitary huntsman could make his way only by dragging his rifle after him. The surface was an elevated plateau, swelling every where into low hills and ridges, with swampy intervales between, along which sluggish brooks made their way toward the Rapidan on the north and the Mattapony on the south. Here and there is a little farm-house, or tavern, or church, with a small clearing around it, surrounded by the forests, like an island in the midst of waters. Four miles west of Chancellorsville, the Brock Road, leaving the turnpike, runs southeastward. Besides these, other roads, mostly mere wood-paths, penetrate the thickets. In this Wilderness, and upon its eastern and western verge, Lee, with the Confederate army of Northern Virginia, was within a year and a day thrice to encounter and foil the Union Army of the Potomac under the successive commands of Hooker, Meade, and Grant.

Hooker's turning movement, apparently the critical point of his whole plan, had been successfully performed. His wary opponent was taken by surprise. He knew nothing of it until it was practically accomplished. On the 28th, Sedgwick, with his own corps and those of Sickles and Reynolds, moved down the river, screened from the view of the enemy by the intervening heights. All that rainy night they lay upon their arms, with no camp-fires to betray their position. Before dawn, while the flanking column was crossing the river thirty miles above, the pontoons were borne silently to the river bank and swung across. When day broke, Jackson saw a great force of the enemy across the stream, holding the very ground from which they had dashed upon his lines four months and a half before. He sent the news to the commanding general. "I heard firing," said Lee to the messenger, "and was beginning to think it was time that some of you lazy young fellows were coming to tell me what it was all about. Say to General Jackson that he knows just as well what to do with the enemy as I do."[1] Noon came before Lee received tidings that Hooker had crossed the Rappahannock and was then pressing toward the Rapidan, the columns converging upon Chancellorsville. He sent a message to Anderson, who held the lines, sharply censuring him for his negligence.[2] During the night of the 29th Anderson's brigade retired from the ford to Chancellorsville, but, learning of the great force that was advancing against them, fell back the next morning six miles farther toward Fredericksburg, where they intrenched themselves. Saving some skirmishing between Pleasonton's cavalry and the retiring Confederates,[3] so slight that no Federal commander reports it, Hooker's columns reached Chancellorsville without opposition. To all human seeming, Hooker was justified in the congratulatory orders which he issued that evening. "It is with heartfelt satisfaction that the commanding general announces to the army that the operations of the last three days have determined that our enemy must either ingloriously fly, or come out from behind his intrenchments and give us battle on our own ground, where certain destruction awaits him."[4] To those around him he spoke in the same strain. "The rebel army," he said, "is now the legitimate property of the Army of the Potomac. They may as well pack up their haversacks and make for Richmond, and I shall be after them."[5] Sedgwick was ordered, should the enemy in his front show any symptoms of falling back, to pursue him with the utmost vigor along the road leading to Richmond; "pursue until you destroy or capture."[6] It was a foregone conclusion with Hooker that Lee must retreat the moment his flank was fairly turned. He hoped to force him to fall back toward Gordonsville rather than by the direct route to Richmond, for which place he would then strike, having fifty miles less to march. In anticipation of these results, he had a

[1] *Dabney*, 661.

[2] "During the forenoon of the 29th Stuart reported that the enemy had crossed the Rappahannock at Kelly's Ford on the preceding evening. Later in the day he announced that a heavy column was moving from Kelly's toward Germania Ford on the Rapidan, and another toward Ely's Ford on that river. The routes that they were pursuing, after crossing the Rapidan, converge near Chancellorsville, whence several roads lead to the rear of our position at Fredericksburg." (*Lee's Rep.*, 6.)—"I captured a courier from General Lee, with a dispatch in Lee's own handwriting. It was dated at 12 o'clock that day, and I captured it at one o'clock, only one hour from Lee's hand. It was addressed to General Anderson, and read: 'I have just received reliable intelligence that the enemy have crossed the river in force. Why have you not kept me informed? I wish to see you at my head-quarters at once.'"—Pleasonton, in *Con. Rep.*, ii., 27.

[3] "The enemy's cavalry skirmished with Anderson's rear-guard as he left Chancellorsville, but, being vigorously repulsed by Mahone's brigade, offered no farther opposition to his march."—*Lee's Rep.*, 6.

[4] Hooker's General Order, No. 47, April 30. [5] *Swinton*, 275. [6] *Con. Rep.*, ii., 103.

THE ADVANCE OF SEDGWICK'S CORPS CROSSING THE RAPPAHANNOCK.

million and a half of rations placed on board lighters, with gun-boats re to tow them down the Potomac and up the Pamunkey, so that his adv would not be impeded by want of supplies.[1]

Hooker had done much, but he left undone the one thing which needed to place his complete success beyond all reasonable doubt. On Thursday night he halted his force in the Wilderness around Chancell ville, where it was cooped up as effectually as though it had been on island, instead of pushing forward another hour's march, which would h brought it into open country beyond. To oppose this march Lee had t at hand only the single division of Anderson. McLaws and Early were on the heights at Fredericksburg, the nearest troops fully ten miles aw The bulk of Jackson's corps were twice as far off. It was not until night of the 30th was far spent that Lee was fully assured that the op tions upon his front were a feint, and that the main danger was to cc from his flank and rear. He was not minded to retreat without a strug The Union army was divided; if one half could be defeated, the wh would be neutralized, and if worst came to worst, he could retreat afte battle as well as before. Leaving Early's division and Barksdale's brig —less than 10,000 men in all—to hold the line near Fredericksburg, l began at midnight of the 30th to concentrate the remainder of his force front of Hooker. McLaws was hurried up from the extreme left, and Ja son, with the divisions of A. P. Hill, Rodes, and Colston, from the right eight o'clock on Friday morning, the first of May, the head of Jackson's c umn began to come up to Anderson, and three hours later all had arriv and formed line of battle at the very place upon which Hooker was n directing his advance.[2]

For now, as the morning was wearing away, Hooker began to prepare move out of the skirts of the Wilderness into the open space beyond. l had ordered Sickles's corps to join him, and it had come up, raising his fo to more than 60,000, a number greater by a quarter than Lee could bri against him after providing for the maintenance of the lines at Frederic burg. There were three roads centring at Chancellorsville and runni eastward. Upon each of these a column was to be pushed out. Mead corps was to lead: the divisions of Griffin and Humphreys on the left, l the river road; Sykes, to be supported by Hancock, of Couch's corps, in th centre, along the turnpike; Slocum's corps on the right, by the plank roa while French's division of Meade's corps was to strike still farther sout Two o'clock in the afternoon was assigned for the completion of these mov ments. After that time the headquarters were to be at Tabernacle Churc close by the junction of the plank road and the turnpike, half way towa Fredericksburg.[3]

Hooker was destined never, during the war, to see the spot which he ha assigned for his headquarters. The left column moved five miles down th river road, and came in sight of Banks's Ford without meeting an enem The right column marched unopposed half as far, when it was arrested b tidings from the central column. This column, Sykes leading, Hancock b hind, had pressed down the plank road, and soon came upon the enemy advance. Sykes drove them back for a space, and at noon gained the poi assigned to him. After some sharp fighting he was forced back for a littl and took up a position which he desired to hold. But orders came that b with all others, should fall back to the positions from which they had s out. Warren, who bore the order, had vainly urged that it should not l sent; Couch protested against it; Hancock thought they should advance i stead of retreating.[4]

Thus, in opposition to the opinions of every general who had felt the en my, Hooker withdrew his advancing columns, and instead of keeping up th offensive which he had assumed, threw himself upon the defensive. Wit

---

[1] *Com. Rep.*, ii., 145.

[2] "The enemy in our front, near Fredericksburg, continued inactive, and it was now appare that the main attack would be made upon our flank and rear. It was therefore determined leave sufficient troops to hold our lines, and with the main body of the army to give battle to t approaching column. Early's division of Jackson's corps, and Barksdale's brigade of McLaw division, with part of the reserve artillery under General Pendleton, were intrusted with the d fense of our position at Fredericksburg, and at midnight on the 30th General McLaws march with the rest of his command toward Fredericksburg. General Jackson followed at dawn ne morning with the remaining divisions of his corps. He reached the position occupied by Gene Anderson at eight A.M., and immediately began preparations to advance."—*Lee's Rep.*, 7.

[3] Hooker's Order, in *Com. Rep.*, ii., 124.

[4] "On gaining the ridge about one and a quarter mile from Chancellorsville, we found the en my advancing and driving back our cavalry. This small force resisted handsomely, riding up a firing almost in the faces of the Eleventh Virginia infantry, which formed the enemy's advan General Sykes moved forward in double-quick time, attacked the enemy vigorously, and drove h back with loss till he had gained the position assigned to him. This he attained at about 12 o'clo No sound yet reached us indicating that any other of our columns had encountered the advance the enemy. General Sykes bravely resolved to hold the position assigned him, which his comma had so gallantly won from the enemy, and I set out with all possible speed to report the conditi to the commanding general. From information received since the advance began, the gene decided to countermand it, and receive the enemy on the line occupied the night before."—Wa ren, in *Com. Rep.*, ii., 56.

"I was in favor of advancing, and urged it with more zeal than convincing argument. thought with our position and numbers to beat the enemy's right wing. This could be done advancing in force upon the two main roads toward Fredericksburg, each being in good suppo ing distance, at the same time throwing a heavy force on the enemy's right flank by the riv road." (Warren, in *Com. Rep.*, ii., 56.)—"The ground upon which I had posted Hancock in su port of Sykes was about one and a half mile from Chancellorsville, and commanded it. Up receiving orders from General Hooker to come in, I sent to him urging that on account of t great advantages of the position it should be held at all hazards. The reply was to return once. General Warren also went in person and urged the necessity of holding on." (Couc *Report of Chancellorsville*.)—"I have no doubt that we ought to have held our advanced positio and still kept pushing on and attempt to make a junction with General Sedgwick."—Hancock, *Com. Rep.*, ii., 66.

"At 11 o'clock the troops moved forward upon the plank and turnpike roads—Anderson, wi the brigades of Wright and Posey, leading on the former; McLaws, with his three brigades, preced by Mahone's, on the latter. Wilcox and Perry, of Anderson's division, co-operated with McLaw Jackson's troops followed Anderson on the plank road. The enemy was soon encountered both roads, and heavy skirmishing with infantry and artillery ensued, our troops pressing stead forward. A strong attack upon McLaws was repulsed with spirit by Semmes's brigade; a Wright, by direction of Anderson, diverging to the left of the plank road, marched by way of t unfinished railroad from Fredericksburg to Gordonsville, and turned the enemy's right. T whole line thereupon retreated rapidly, vigorously pursued by our troops until they arrived with about one mile of Chancellorsville."—*Lee's Rep.*, 6.

LAYING THE PONTOONS FOR SEDGWICK'S CORPS.

a force largely superior, instead of attacking, he prepared to receive the attack of the enemy. His reasons, as stated by himself, were based wholly upon the character of the region. "The ground in our vicinity," he says, "was broken, and covered with dense forests, much of which was impenetrable to infantry. The ravines to the north of the road were deep, and their general direction was at right angles to the Rappahannock, affording the enemy a formidable position behind each of them. Here was the enemy's entire army, with the exception of about 8000 men which had been left to hold the line from below Hamilton's crossing to the heights above Fredericksburg, a distance of between five and six miles. The right and central corps had proceeded but a short distance when the head of the column emerged from the heavy forest, and discovered the enemy to be advancing in line of battle. Nearly all of the Twelfth Corps had emerged from the forest at that moment, but as the passage-way through the forest was narrow, I was satisfied that I could not throw troops through it fast enough to resist the advance of General Lee, and was apprehensive of being whipped in detail. Accordingly, instructions were given for the troops in advance to return and establish themselves on the line they had just left, and to hold themselves in readiness to receive the enemy."[1] But Warren, who had scanned the ground with the eye of an engineer, thought the physical conditions favorable to the Union force. "If," he says, "the attack found the enemy in extended lines across our front, or in motion toward our right flank, it would have secured the defeat of his right wing, and consequently the retreat of the whole. The advantages of the initiative in a wooded country like this, obscuring all movements, are incalculable, and so far we had improved them."[2]

The defensive position which Hooker now assumed formed a line of nearly five miles from east to west, running mainly parallel and a little south of the united plank road and turnpike. The left, a short distance east of Chancellorsville, was bent back a little northward; the right presented a similar

[1] Hooker, in *Com. Rep.*, ii., 125.

[2] Warren, in *Com. Rep.*, ii., 56.—Hancock indeed states that Hooker too late countermanded the order for withdrawal: "General Warren, who brought the order, suggested to General Couch that he should not fall back, although the order was to that effect. But General Couch did not feel at liberty to follow that suggestion, having received peremptory orders to fall back. It appears, however, that General Warren rode off to General Hooker and explained the advantages of the position we held, and came back with an order that it should be held. But, in the mean time, the position had been abandoned, and the enemy had taken possession of it."—*Com. Rep.*, ii., 68.

MAP OF THE REGION NEAR CHANCELLORSVILLE.

curve. The general shape was nearly that of the letter C, the main front facing southward, the upper and lower curves looking west and east. The corps and divisions were somewhat broken up. The general placing in front was, Meade on the extreme left, toward Fredericksburg; Slocum in the centre; Howard on the right. The corps of Couch and Sickles were mainly in reserve, though a division of each was thrust forward into the front line, which was strengthened by abatis and breast-works. The right was weakly posted, but it was, in military phrase, flung out into the air; but as the enemy were wholly on the left, hardly reaching to the centre, it was thought that an attack was not to be looked for in that direction, and Howard gave assurance that he could hold his position against any force that could be brought against it.[2]

At nightfall Lee and Jackson, who had been engaged on different parts of the field, met upon the brow of a little hill covered by a clump of pines which had escaped the woodman's axe, whose annual shedding of leaves formed a soft carpet upon the ground. They retired apart to consult upon the situation. This was critical. They must either win a battle or retreat. Hooker having assumed the defensive, they must attack. The Confederate skirmishers which had been pushed into the belt of wood had succeeded in ascertaining that the Union lines were unassailable in front of Chancellorsville.[3] But Stuart, whose cavalry had been reconnoitring westward and northward, reported that in these directions the Federal camps were open, and that almost all of his cavalry force was absent. Jackson proposed that while a part of the Confederate force should demonstrate upon Hooker's front, the remainder should march clear around his line, and assail it upon its right flank and rear. The measure was hazardous in the extreme. The Federals, now in position, outnumbered the whole Confederate force, and this was to be divided. But it was certain that Hooker p
how small was the force remaining near Fredericksburg, a
bring up Sedgwick from the Rappahannock, increasing the d
two to one. And even if the flank attack should miscarry, t
army, then separated into three portions, would still have lin
favorable as they now had. Jackson's three divisions w
plank road westward, or the road southward through the
McLaws and Anderson had the latter route; Early could f
the others, and the three bodies could reunite and make a s
ground, or, if need were, press on to Richmond; so that, b
which must be run, of a total defeat, their position would be
it now was.[1]

This plan was settled, and the two Confederate command
rest without shelter upon the bare ground. Jackson had
nor overcoat. He declined an overcoat offered him by o
Thinking him asleep, the officer took off the cape, spread it
and fell into slumber. Jackson rose and spread the cape
and laid down again uncovered. Before dawn he was seen
over a scanty fire, almost hugging it, and shivering with cold,
ing a rough map of the region, inquiring of his chaplain, wh
thing of the country, if there were no roads by which the
might be turned. The chaplain only knew that a little beyo
forest-path, which, by various windings and turnings, struck
four miles west of Chancellorsville. The line was trace
"That is too near," said Jackson; "it goes within the lines
pickets. I wish to get well to his rear without being obser
habitant of the region was now brought up, who said that th
upon which they were, ran southward for a few miles, and
sected by the Brock road from the northwest, which struck t
so that by making a circuit of fifteen miles a point would be
miles above Hooker's extremest outposts. This was just wh
sired, and at sunrise he began the march with his three divis

SATURDAY, MAY 2.

A mile of dense forest intervened between the road and
completely hiding the march from observation. But at one
crossed a bare hill just opposite Sickles's position. For two
column, with its trains and ambulances, filed over the hill i
It was clearly a movement in force, but with what purpose w
doubt. It might be for offense upon the right, and so H
Howard to be fully prepared, to keep heavy reserves in ha
and especially to throw out pickets in his front.[4] How utt
inally this order was disregarded remains to be shown. B
which the column was observed ran here due south, straight
Union lines; this indicated that the movement was a retreat.

[1] This map shows, in a general way, the topography of the region in which Hooker proposed to operate. Though not perfectly accurate, it is the best then accessible. Of the actual character of the Wilderness he was almost wholly ignorant, and had no means of becoming acquainted with it. The essential features of the map are the relative positions of Fredericksburg and Chancellorsville, the fords by which the Rappahannock and Rapidan were to be passed, and the roads leading away from Fredericksburg by which it was supposed that the Confederate army must retreat. The roads are: (1.) The railroad to Richmond, and the Telegraph Road, running southwardly nearly parallel with it; (2.) The plank road and turnpike. These are represented on the map as one road from Fredericksburg to the point marked as the "Wilderness," where they diverge. The road from "Todd's Tavern" to the "Wilderness" shows nearly the line of Jackson's flank movement. With these exceptions, the roads laid down are mere rude country roads, hardly passable for an army with artillery and trains. In moving from near Falmouth, Meade, Slocum, and Howard crossed the Rappahannock at Kelly's Ford, north of Germania Ford, on the Rapidan; Couch, and subsequently Sickles and Reynolds, at United States Ford. Lee's chief dépôt was at Guinea's Station, on the railroad, near which Jackson's corps had its winter quarters; but they had been moved half way up to Fredericksburg, near which place McLaws and Anderson were posted. The distance between Fredericksburg and Chancellorsville is 11 miles, which will indicate the scale upon which the map is drawn.

[2] *Com. Rep.*, ii., 56.

[3] "The enemy had assumed a position of great natural strength, surrounded on all sides by a dense forest filled with a tangled undergrowth, in the midst of which breast-works of logs had been constructed, with trees felled in front so as to form an almost impenetrable abatis. His artillery swept the few narrow roads by which his position could be approached in front, and commanded the adjacent woods. Darkness was approaching before the strength and extent of his line could be ascertained; and as the nature of the country rendered it hazardous to attack by night, our troops were halted and formed in line of battle in front of Chancellorsville, at right angles with the plank road, extending on the right to the mine road, and to the left in the direction of Catharine Furnace."—*Lee's Rep.*, 8.

[1] *Dabney*, 672. [2] *Ibid.*, 675. [3] Birney, in C

[4] Hooker's Order, 9.30 A.M., in *Com. Rep.*, ii., 126.

SEDGWICK'S [illegible] LINE.

a rifled battery to a point where it could play upon this column, but the distance, a mile and a half, was too great to permit the fire to produce any serious effect. Birney's division, afterward followed by others, and Pleasonton's cavalry, were sent forward through the woods to reconnoitre. Birney passed down the blind road which Jackson had refused to take, fell upon a regiment of McLaws's division which had been placed there as a guard, and captured it. This movement of Birney's so seriously threatened Jackson's trains in the rear that two brigades were hastened back to protect them. As it happened, however, Birney did not follow after Jackson's column, and these two brigades, after seeing the trains well away, followed after, but were unable to get up in time to take part in the action of this day.[1]

Long before midday, Jackson's column—infantry and artillery, with Stuart's cavalry patroling the region between him and the enemy, in all 30,000 strong—were clear out of sight of friend and foe. The troops felt that they were upon one of those great flank marches which had more than once led them to victory, and they pressed forward with more than their wonted speed, every step for hours increasing the distance between them and Lee. Their march had been southwestwardly until they reached the Brock road; then it turned at a sharp angle to the northwest. At three o'clock they struck the plank road at the old Wilderness tavern. By this march of fifteen miles Jackson had passed clear around Hooker's position, and was in a straight line hardly six miles from the point from which he had started ten hours before. Here, like an oasis in the forest desert, was a broad clearing, which gave him ample space in which to form his corps in battle array. Barely two miles away, down the road, lay Howard's corps, forming Hooker's right. The Confederate pickets, creeping through the thickets, reported its position. Jackson from the summit of a little hill surveyed it, and made his dispositions for an assault.

His column was formed into three lines—Rodes in front, then Colston, and, last, A. P. Hill, stretching across the plank road for some distance on each side, completely overlapping the head of the Federal line, thus commanding it on front, flank, and rear.

Lee, with parts of the divisions of Anderson and McLaws,[2] not 20,000 men in all, had reserved to himself the less brilliant but not less critical task of keeping in check a force three times as strong. For a whole day the two corps would be isolated, neither being able to aid or even communicate with the other. If Hooker changed the position of his right, Jackson's meditated blow would miss its mark. If, divining the character of the movement, he should assail Anderson and McLaws either in front from Chancellorsville, or on the flank and rear by bringing Sedgwick up from Fredericksburg, their destruction was inevitable. Between Sedgwick's 30,000[3] and him lay only Early's 10,000, guarding a line of six miles. Lee confined himself during the morning to demonstrations all along Hooker's front. Early in the morning he got a few guns into a position which commanded the field in front of the Chancellorsville House, and drove all the wagons back into position. Then, at intervals, his infantry crept into the woods, delivered a yell and a volley, and disappeared, to reappear at a different point.[4] Sickles's advance was so threatening that Lee was obliged to resist it in force.[5] Sickles, with Birney's division, maintained his ground successfully, and sent back for re-enforcements; his other divisions were promised him, together with a brigade from Slocum, and one from Howard. Sickles was just about to open his attack with all this force, fully equal to the whole of Anderson's and McLaws's, when some officer came dashing up, breathless, with a report that Stuart's cavalry were moving in his rear, and might cut him off; that Jackson's infantry were very near; that the Union troops were retreating. Sickles disbelieved this story. Surely such a thing could not have happened without a serious engagement, and had there been a battle he would have heard the noise. But almost instantly an aid came up with tidings from Howard. The right flank had been turned; Howard's corps had given way, and Jackson was right on Sickles's rear. Hooker also sent word that he could not give the promised re-enforcements; he had to use them to check the enemy, who had broken through the Eleventh Corps. Sickles must withdraw his whole force, and save as many of them as he could.[6]

Jackson had struck his blow. A little after five o'clock he had formed his lines, and began to press through the dense thickets which skirted the plank road, down which, only three miles away, lay a part of Howard's corps, forming the extreme right of Hooker's army. No assault here had been dreamed of. Intrenchments had been thrown up, but they were left unguarded. The men had stacked their arms, and were scattered about cooking their suppers; ambulances, ammunition-wagons, pack-mules, and cattle were huddled together.[7] Not a picket was thrown out into the woods in front nor even up the road, where for more than two hours Jackson had been deploying his divisions, hardly three miles away. The Union right was like a militia regiment at the close of a holiday muster rather than an army in presence of an enemy.[8]

---

1 Thomas and Archer, in *Lee's Rep.*, 54–58.

2 These divisions consisted of nine brigades; but Barksdale's, of McLaws's, had been left at Marye's Heights, and Wilcox's, of Anderson's, had been sent back to Banks's Ford.

3 Reynolds's corps was withdrawn from Sedgwick that morning, and ordered to Chancellorsville, where it arrived during the night. Sedgwick had then his own corps and Gibbon's division of Couch's.

4 Warren, in *Com. Rep.*, ii., 45; Pleasonton, *Ibid.*, 27; Hooker, *Ibid.*, 127.

5 "At midday the enemy appeared in some force at the furnace. Posey's brigade was sent to dislodge him, and was soon engaged in a warm skirmish with him. The increasing numbers of the enemy made it necessary to move Wright's brigade over to the support of Posey's."—Anderson, in *Lee's Rep.*, 25.

6 Sickles, in *Com. Rep.*, ii., 6.

7 *Com. Rep.*, ii., 45, 127.

8 Devens, whose division occupied the extreme right, testifies (*Com. Rep.*, ii., 178): "About two or three o'clock in the afternoon, two soldiers, who had been sent out to observe the enemy's lines as spies from one of the other commands, came in and reported that the enemy were massing heavily on our right," and that he sent them to Howard with the tidings. But that no pickets could have been pushed out upon the road is evident. The attack which came down that road, and on both sides of it, was an utter surprise.

With a yell and a volley the Confederates dashed out of the woods into the open space occupied by this unsuspecting division. The regiments upon whom the onset first fell scattered without firing a shot, and rushed in wild confusion upon those behind them; these in turn gave way before the wild rush of their own comrades. Some of the regiments made a stand to stem the torrent; but it was vain, and the whole corps was soon streaming down the road, and through the woods toward Chancellorsville. Rodes, who commanded the front line of the Confederates, thus describes the conflict: "At once the line of battle rushed forward with a yell, and Doles at the moment debouched from the woods, and encountered a force of the enemy and a battery of two guns intrenched. Detaching two regiments to flank the position, he charged without halting, sweeping every thing before him; and pressing on to Talley's, gallantly carried the works there, and captured five guns by a similar flank movement of his command. So complete was the success of the whole manœuvre, and such was the surprise of the enemy, that scarcely any organized resistance was met with after the first volley was fired. They fled in the wildest confusion, leaving the field strewn with arms, accoutrements, clothing, caissons, and field-pieces in every direction. The larger portion of his force, as well as intrenchments, were drawn up at right angles to our line; and being thus taken in the flank and rear, they did not wait for the attack. On the next side, which had an extended line of works facing in our direction, an effort was made to check the flying columns. For a few moments they held this position; but once more my gallant troops dashed at them with a wild shout, and, firing a hasty volley, they continued their hasty flight to Chancellorsville. It was at this moment that Trimble's division, which had followed closely in my rear, headed by Colston, went over the works with my men, and from this time the two divisions were mingled in inextricable confusion. Pushing forward as rapidly as possible, the troops soon entered a second piece of woods, thickly filled with undergrowth. The right, becoming entangled in an abatis near the enemy's first line of fortifications, caused the line to halt, and such was the confusion and darkness that it was not deemed advisable to make a farther advance. I at once sent word to Lieutenant General Jackson, urging him to push forward the fresh troops of the reserve line, in order that mine might be reformed. Riding forward on the plank road, I satisfied myself that the enemy had no line of battle between our troops and the heights of Chancellorsville, and on my return informed the chief of artillery of the fact, and he opened his batteries on that point. The enemy instantly responded by a most terrific fire, which silenced our guns, but did little execution on the infantry. When the fire ceased General Hill's troops were brought up, and, as soon as a portion were deployed in my front, I commenced withdrawing my troops by order of the lieutenant general."[1]

Rodes was right. Between him and Chancellorsville, hardly half a mile away, there was no line of battle, and nothing from which to form one. Jackson was almost justified in declaring that with half an hour more of daylight he could have carried that place.[2] The check to the Confederate rush came from an unexpected quarter. When the tidings came to Sickles of the flight of Howard, Pleasonton, with two regiments of cavalry, was riding leisurely back to the rear, for in the dense forest there was nothing for cavalry to do. He found the open space which he had left a few hours before filled with fugitives, ambulances, and guns. He had with him a battery of horse artillery. The moment was critical. The enemy must be checked then and there, and to do it there was but this battery and those few horsemen. Turning to Major Keenan, he said, "You must charge into those woods with your regiment, and hold the rebels in check until I can get some of these guns into position; you must do it at any cost." "I will do it," responded Keenan, with a smile, though both knew that the order was equivalent to a death-warrant. The charge was made; a quarter of the regiment fell, their leader at their head. But ten priceless minutes were gained. Pleasonton brought up his battery at a gallop, double-shotted the guns with canister, and pointed them at the ground line of the parapet, telling the gunners to aim low. Then getting a score of guns into position out of the confused mass around, he had all double-shotted, pointed at the woods in front, and bade the gunners to await his order to fire. Hardly was this done when the whole forest, whose verge was a quarter of a mile

ALFRED PLEASONTON.

that Hooker had at hand only Berry's division of Sickles's corps, and a single brigade of Couch's, which had been held in reserve at Chancellorsville. Berry's division was the one which Hooker had commanded, and it had never failed him. He pushed this forward at double-quick to meet the enemy. It was vain to attempt to check the wild rout of the Eleventh Corps. Hooker ordered the few cavalry with him to charge the flying mass, sabre in hand. Some of the fugitives were shot down by his staff, but no human power could arrest their flight,[1] though they had already outstripped their pursuers. Berry's division, with fixed bayonets, pressed through the flying mass, hoping to regain the high ground which they had abandoned. They were too late; it was in possession of the enemy. The most that he could do was to take a stand upon a ridge, known as Fairview, upon the hither side of the forest which bounded the clearing at Chancellorsville, and thence to pour a fire of artillery and musketry up the road and into the woods.

Night was closing in. The full moon shone brightly, throwing into deep shade the forests, just bursting into leaf. The divisions of Rodes and Colston, which had chased Howard's corps two miles through the dense thickets, had fallen into inextricable confusion. Seeing no enemy before them, they had halted, and there was a lull in the contest. Jackson, who had been urging on the pursuit, ordered A. P. Hill's division to come to the front and take the place of Rodes and Colston, and, accompanied only by his staff, passed down the road to examine the position. Some of his companions remonstrated against his exposing himself. "There is no danger," he replied; "the enemy is routed. Go back and tell Hill to press on." A few minutes after a musketry fire from Berry's pickets pattered among the trees. Jackson turned back toward his own lines. Some of

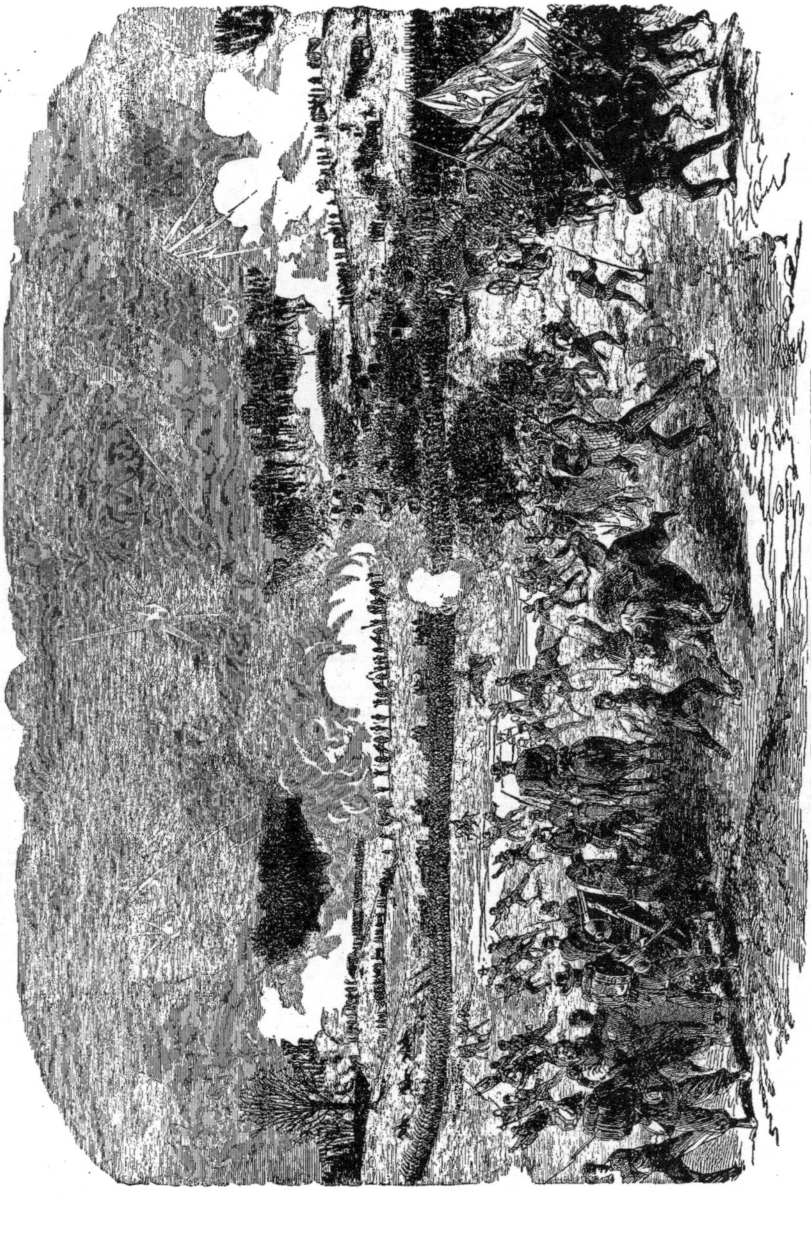

THE STAMPEDE OF THE ELEVENTH CORPS.—BERRY'S CORPS CHECKING THE PURSUIT.

NEAR CHANCELLORSVILLE, MAY 1.

wood which bordered the road. He came upon Pender's brigade lying flat to avoid the shot pouring into the gloom. "I fear," said Pender, recognizing his wounded commander, "that we can not maintain our position here." "You must hold your ground," replied Jackson, for a moment blazing into his old battle-fire. This was the last order ever given by Jackson on the field. He was soon replaced in the litter and borne back through the tangled brushwood. One of the bearers stumbled and fell. Jackson was thrown to the ground, striking heavily upon his broken arm, and bruising his side. An ambulance was soon found, in which he was borne to the rear, where the broken arm was amputated. The operation promised well. Two days later he was borne to the hospital a score of miles away. But pneumonia set in, occasioned probably by the exposure of that Friday night before his great flank march, when he had slept unsheltered upon the bare ground, aggravated perhaps by the bruise which he had received when thrown from the litter. He died on Sunday, the 10th of May. When the supreme hour approached, his mind wandered. Visions of the battle-field and of Paradise mingled together. "Order Hill to prepare for battle—pass the infantry to the front rapidly—tell—" Then a change passed over his delirium; and murmuring gently, "Let us cross over the river and rest under the shade of the trees," he fell into the sleep which knows no earthly wakening.

The military career of Thomas Jonathan Jackson as a Confederate commander lasted just two years. On the 2d of May, 1861, he was placed in command at Harper's Ferry; on the 2d of May, 1863, he received his mortal wound in the Wilderness of Virginia. His great fame was won within the last year of his life, for in May, 1862, took place his operations in the Valley of the Shenandoah, wherein, by foiling Fremont and Shields, he showed that he possessed qualities higher than those of a stubborn fighter and a daring partisan. Born of a respectable family, fallen into decay, accident gave him an appointment as cadet at West Point. Passing in due course from the Military Academy into the army, he served with credit in the war with Mexico. Soon after he left the army, and became Professor of Natural and Experimental Philosophy and Artillery Tactics in the Virginia Military Academy at Lexington. Meanwhile a great change had occurred in his moral nature—that alteration which theologians denominate "a change of heart." He embraced that form of Christianity which finds its exponents in Calvin and Edwards. Major Jackson, Professor in the Military Academy, was also Deacon Jackson of the Presbyterian Church. His ten-years' career as professor was far from brilliant. He was rather a laughing-stock to the gay youths who thronged the Academy. That he was master of the management of guns was admitted; that he understood the science which he was set to teach was possible; but he had little faculty for imparting his knowledge. There were eccentricities in his mode of life, arising, materialists would say, rather from a disordered stomach than from a disturbed brain, but still sufficiently marked to furnish occasion for men to consider him as "half-cracked." The few who knew him well, however, saw that these eccentricities were but superficial; that underlying them was a firmness and persistence of character which would enable him to run a great career if an opening to such should ever occur. Few even of these few knew the boundless ambition, and the unquestioning, almost fatalistic self-confidence which lay hidden below all the outward manifestations of his character.

When the great rebellion broke out, any one would have been justified in assuming that Jackson would have taken sides with the Union. He had been educated by the Union; he had fought with honor under the flag of the Union; all his interests, and, as might be supposed, all his feelings, were with the Union rather than with the Confederacy. His personal concern in slavery was of the slightest. The region in which he was born and where he resided was farming rather than planting. Most of the owners of slaves wrought in the fields as laboriously as their servants. Unless, as was not often the case, they reared slaves for the Southern market, they would have been richer without than with the ownership of these laborers. Society in the Valley was constructed like that of Massachusetts rather than like that of South Carolina. But somewhere and somehow Jackson, during his quiet ten years as Professor, had become imbued with the extremest Southern ideas; not merely the "State-right" doctrine that the primary allegiance of the citizen was due to his state—that to the nation being secondary and dependent—but with the extremest views of the extremest men of the extreme South. As early as 1856 he was a Disunionist.[1] He spent a part of the summer of 1860 in New England, and on his return said that he had "seen enough to justify the division that had just occurred in the Democratic party, which resulted in the defeat of Douglas and the election of Lincoln—a division which, he predicted, would render a dissolution of the Union inevitable.[3]

When the war broke out, it would have been hard to find a man so fully prepared for extremes as Jackson. The deacon who had gone round asking for subscriptions of a few dimes from negroes in aid of the Bible Society—who had, with infinite misgivings, consented, upon the representations of his pastor, to "lead in prayer" at "evening meetings"—calmly declared that no quarter should be given. It was, he said, "the true policy of the South to take no prisoners in this war."[3] He threw himself

[1] *Dabney*, 148. [3] *Ibid.*, 148.

[3] I venture this statement solely upon the assertion of Dabney, whose words I quote. This writer professes to give the substance of what was, months after, said by Jackson in justification of the ground which he had assumed. The war, he said, as reported by Dabney, "was different from all civilized wars, and therefore should not be brought under their rules. Its intention was a wholesale murder and piracy. It was the John Brown raid resumed and extended; and as Virginia had righteously put to death every one of those cut-throats upon the gallows, why were their comrades in the same crime to claim now a more honorable treatment? Such a war was an offense against humanity so monstrous that it outlawed those who shared its guilt beyond the

NEAR CHANCELLORSVILLE, MAY 1.

into the conflict with all the fervor of a firm but narrow mind, in which there was not room for doubt. In the long list of enthusiasts who have devoted themselves to a cause, there is not one whose faith was more undoubting than that of Jackson. From the moment that he took the field his hypochondria vanished. Heretofore he had timed his hours and measured his food; thenceforth the hardest lot of a soldier's life was endured without a thought. He left his home almost without warning, and never returned to it alive. He was never for a day absent from the field. The mooning professor was at once inspired with the genius of command.

In all the annals of war there can be found no general who held more absolute sway over his troops. Some have regarded him as the hand to execute what others conceived; but this certainly falls far below his military merit. Two great movements, each of which postponed for a year the issue of the war, were conceived as well as executed by him. The flank march whereby Pope was routed in the summer of 1862, and this of the spring of 1863, whereby alone, as it happened, Lee was saved from destruction at Chancellorsville, were Jackson's, both in conception and execution. The Confederates might better have lost a battle than this one man.

Hooker was greatly discouraged by the rout of Howard's corps. His first impulse was to withdraw from Chancellorsville and the road leading thence from the Wilderness; but he changed his plan during the night, and resolved to await the Confederate attack, meanwhile causing Couch to draw up an entirely new line, to which he might fall back in case of need,[1] and ordering Sedgwick up to his aid from Fredericksburg. The line of battle was necessarily somewhat contracted. What had before been the extreme Union right had been won, and was still held by the enemy. On the line now assumed, the right, instead of stretching westward parallel with the plank road, was bent sharply northward, directly across it. The position on the centre and left remained unchanged. Howard's corps, now partly reorganized, was sent to the extreme left, where no assault was anticipated. Reynolds's corps, which had come up during the night, was halted some two miles away from the actual right; Meade's was partly in reserve, and partly guarding the road leading to the river. These two corps took no part in the action which ensued.

The real line of battle for Sunday, the 3d of May, formed three sides of an irregular square. The left, facing eastward toward Fredericksburg, was held by Hancock's division of Couch's corps; the centre, facing southward, by Slocum's corps; the right, facing westward, by Sickles's corps, with French's division of Couch's corps. Sickles's extreme left, on a small plateau known as Hazle Grove, projecting southward beyond the general line, was somewhat isolated and open to assault; but it commanded the centre of the Union position. If the enemy won that, he could hold it with artillery, and pour an enfilading fire along Slocum's line. Hazle Grove was the key to every thing, and should have been held at every hazard;[2] but Hooker, knowing only of its exposure, and unaware of its vital importance, ordered Sickles to abandon it, and fall back to the line on the heights at Fairview. The movement began at daybreak, but before it was completed the battle of Sunday—the main action at Chancellorsville—was opened.

Jackson had fallen before he had accomplished half his plan. He had intended, after having driven in Hooker's right, to move still farther northward, and intrench himself at the point where the roads unite which lead from Chancellorsville to the river. He believed that he could seize and hold that point, which was vital, inasmuch as it commanded Hooker's line for supplies. "My men," he said, "sometimes fail to drive the enemy from their positions, but the enemy are never able to drive my men from theirs."[3] But the execution of this design was impossible, even had Jackson been there to attempt it, for Reynolds's corps had come up and occupied this very point.

Leaving Jackson wounded upon the battle-field, Hill had on Saturday evening pressed through the woods to the right, where Pleasonton had got his guns into position, and renewed the assault. This was repulsed, and

pals of forbearance." The war, he averred, would soon assume an internecine character; the North would arm the slaves against their masters; the Confederate States could not, and should not, submit to this, and should retaliate, rather, however, "against the instigators than the ignorant tools. But," he continued, "by the time this stern necessity had manifested itself, the Federal government might have many of our soldiers and much of our territory in their clutches, so that retaliation would be encumbered with additional difficulties. It would be better, therefore, to begin upon a plan of warfare which would place none of our citizens in their power alive;" and if, he concluded, "quarter was neither given nor asked," the Confederate soldiers "would be only the more determined, vigilant, and unconquerable;" while the Union soldiers "would be intimidated, and enlistments would be prevented" (*Dabney*, 192–194). It must be added, however, that when the murderous principle upon which Jackson wished the war to be carried on failed to meet the approval of the Confederate government, there was no general in their service who more strictly observed the amenities of warfare. When he lay wounded almost within the Union lines, he objected to being removed in case it would do him any injury. "If the enemy comes," he said, "I am not afraid of them. I have always been kind to their wounded, and I am sure they will be kind to me."—*Hotchkiss*, 124.

[1] "About midnight, or after, I was awakened by General Couch, who told me that we were ordered to withdraw, I supposed to some new position, and that the Second Corps was to form the rear-guard; but at daylight, just as the movement was about to commence, as I understood, General Couch informed me that we were going to remain there and fight a battle."—Hancock, in *Com. Rep.*, ii., 67.

[2] "I immediately"—that is, on Saturday night—"set to work, knowing the importance of this position, to fix it up for the fight of the next morning. I managed to get forty pieces in position, and I cleared out behind us the débris of the Eleventh Corps, that had gone off—the caissons, guns, ambulances, etc., all piled up in great confusion in a marsh that was there. I built three bridges across the marsh, and, with the support of Sickles's corps, we could have defeated the whole of the rebel army there that morning. At 8 o'clock I received an order to fall back in rear of the position at the Chancellorsville House. Before I left, General Sickles informed me that he also had orders to leave with his corps. I mentioned to him the importance of this position, and he agreed with me that we ought to make an effort to hold it. I feel perfectly satisfied that, had General Hooker been able to see the position that I occupied there, he would never have abandoned it; and I looked upon it as a great misfortune that he did not see that point. The rebels, having this position, could enfilade our whole line to the Chancellorsville House with their batteries at this point."—Pleasonton, in *Com. Rep.*, ii., 29.

[3] *Dabney*, 700; *Hotchkiss*, 125.

CHANCELLORSVILLE, MAY 1.

Hill was wounded. Rodes was next in rank, but Hill sent for Stuart, who was five miles away, and desired him to take command of the whole corps. When he came, Rodes yielded, not with the best grace.[1] Stuart found every thing in confusion. This was increased by a midnight attack made by Birney, who forced the Confederates back for a space through the woods, and recovered some of the guns which had been abandoned by Howard's corps in its precipitate flight. In the darkness some of the Confederate brigades fired upon each other.[2]

All that night Stuart was busy in reorganizing the shattered corps which had so unexpectedly come under his command. He was separated from Lee by six miles of dense forest. Morning was approaching before he could inform his commanding general of his position, and receive instructions. The messenger said that Jackson had urged that "the enemy should be pressed in the morning." Lee's response was, "Those people shall be pressed."

The odds on that Sunday morning were greatly in favor of Hooker. At and about Chancellorsville he still had fully 78,000 effective men. Lee proposed to press this force in its intrenchments with 30,000 less.[3] Moreover Sedgwick, with his own strong corps, and Gibbon's division of Couch's corps, quite 27,000 men in all, were near Fredericksburg, not fifteen miles away. They were confronted by Early with not more than 11,000. It was clearly possible that Sedgwick would force his way to Hooker, and, assuming that Early should escape destruction and join Lee, the Federal preponderance would be greatly increased. Taking no account of probable losses on either side, Hooker would have 95,000 men, Lee 59,000. Apart from numbers, Hooker's position was far the better. His 78,000 lay together, Lee's 48,000 were separated, and it depended upon the chances of battle whether they could be united. Hooker, moreover, was intrenched upon ground mainly of his own choosing; Lee, assuming the offensive, must assail these intrenched lines. The region was indeed a difficult one, but the physical obstacles were as great for the one side as for the other, and the one venturing the offensive must undertake to overcome them. Considering that each commander was well-informed of the force of his opponent, one can not but wonder that Lee should have ventured an attack, and that Hooker should have awaited it.

SUNDAY, MAY 3.

The action was opened at dawn by Stuart, earlier than he had intended. He had ordered his right to be swung around through the woods, from the position to which his men had fallen back during the night. This brought two of his brigades right in front of Hazle Grove, from which Sickles had withdrawn every thing except Graham's brigade, which formed his rear-guard. Stuart's direction was mistaken for an order to attack. A sharp conflict ensued, with loss on both sides; but Graham got safely off to Fairview, and Stuart took possession of Hazle Grove. A glance showed him the value of the position which had been abandoned to him. In a few minutes he occupied it with thirty guns. His whole force was then ordered to advance upon the Union lines, which, as the fog lifted, were seen crowning the Fairview ridge, a third of a mile in front. Between lay the valley of a little creek covered with a tangled forest growth, through which the attacking columns must force their way, in the face of a fierce fire of artillery and musketry. Again and again they charged down the valley, through the woods, and up the slope, and as often were thrown back in confusion, only to advance again with fresh force and unabated resolution.

Sickles, upon whom all this onset fell, first sent word to Hooker that he could hold his position so long as his ammunition lasted, and then, a little later, that he needed prompt support. This last urgent demand came in an evil time. For two hours and more the Confederate guns at Hazle Grove had been playing upon Chancellorsville. The house was riddled by shot. A ball struck a pillar of the veranda against which Hooker was leaning. He fell senseless. Those around thought him dead or dying. There was no one at hand with authority to send the re-enforcements so urgently asked by Sickles, though the two corps of Reynolds and Meade were wholly disengaged. Half of either of these sent to Sickles would have been enough to

[1] "Captain Adams, of General A. P. Hill's staff, reached me post-haste, and informed me of the sad calamities which had for the time deprived the troops of the leadership of both Jackson and Hill, and of the urgent demand for me to come and take command as quickly as possible" (Stuart, in *Lee's Rep.*, 17).—Rodes says (*Ibid.*, 112): "I yielded the command to General Stuart, not because I thought him entitled to it, belonging as he did to a different arm of the service, nor because I was unwilling to assume the responsibility of carrying on the attack, as I had already made the necessary arrangements, and they remained unchanged, but because, from the manner in which I had been informed that he had been sent for, I inferred that General Jackson or General Hill had instructed Major Pendleton to place him in command; and for the still stronger reason that I feared that the information that the command had devolved upon me, unknown except to my own immediate troops, would, in their shaken condition, be likely to increase the demoralization of the corps."

[2] "The attack was made precisely at midnight by Ward's brigade, with the remaining part of Birney's division in support. It was admirably conducted under General Birney, and was in all points successful. It was made entirely with the bayonet. We drove Jackson back to our original line, and reoccupied General Howard's rifle-pits, and recovered several pieces of artillery and some caissons which had been abandoned during the day. Jackson's force was thrown into great confusion, and his own artillery opened upon his own men" (Sickles, in *Con. Rep.*, ii., 7).—"At about midnight on Saturday, General Sickles ordered me to attack Jackson's corps with my division, driving them from the plank road and the small earthworks. At one o'clock I reported that we held the road and works, and had recaptured the artillery and caissons taken from us during the stampede of the Eleventh Corps" (Birney, *Ibid.*, 35).—"There was much confusion on the right, owing to the fact that some troops mistook friends for the enemy, and fired upon them."—Stuart, in *Lee's Rep.*, 18.

[3] Hooker had with him the corps of Reynolds, Meade, Sickles, Howard, and two divisions of Couch, numbering at the outset 81,000. Howard's corps had lost 2500, the greater part prisoners; all other losses up to this time could not have exceeded 500, leaving an effective force of 78,000. Lee's entire force, exclusive of cavalry, was 60,000. Of these, Early's division, and two brigades from Anderson and McLaws, about 11,000, were left near Fredericksburg. The entire losses on Friday and Saturday could not have exceeded 1000, leaving with Lee, near Chancellorsville, about 48,000. We take no account of the cavalry, because the character of the region prevented them from being brought into active service, on either side, in this operation.

DANIEL E. SICKLES.

have secured the victory.[1] That attack repulsed, the remainder of Hooker's unengaged force, sweeping around, would have enveloped Stuart's broken corps, and crushed it to powder. Reynolds was indeed minded to bring his corps into the fight. This seems to have been the plan of Hooker, as understood by some of his officers.[2] But if such was the purpose of Hooker, its execution was prevented by the blow which disabled him. For two eventful hours the Union army was without a commander. Hooker lay insensible for a time, then, partly recovering, mounted his horse; but pain overmastered him, and he lay upon the ground as if in a doze, the Confederate shells bursting all around him. Now and then he was partially aroused when some important dispatch required a prompt answer.[3]

Sickles's ammunition was almost exhausted. Again he sent to headquarters asking for aid, but there was no one there even to reply to his urgent demand. He withdrew his now useless artillery, and fell back with his infantry to a second line, which he resolved to hold by the bayonet. He was not followed, and, looking to his front, it seemed that the enemy was routed. They had the aspect of a disorganized crowd rather than an army. Just then French, with his division, had advanced upon the Confederate left, and driven it back.[4] Stuart concentrated all his force upon this point, and succeeded in repelling the attack, the only offensive movement made by the Union forces at Chancellorsville on that day. Had it been supported by a half, or even a quarter of Reynolds's corps, which lay idle only a few furlongs off, Stuart could not have escaped destruction.

While Stuart was thus with varying fortune pressing the attack upon the Union right, Lee, with the divisions of Anderson and McLaws, assailed the centre held by Slocum, under an enfilading fire from the batteries posted at Hazel Grove. The left, held by Hancock's division of Couch's corps, was threatened, rather than attacked,[5] for Lee was all the time edging to his left in order to make a junction with Stuart. This was effected at ten o'clock, at the very moment when the battle hung in even scales. Both sides had lost terribly. Stuart's three divisions, numbering in the morning about 27,000, had lost fully 6000 in killed and wounded, and 1500 prisoners. Sickles and French had lost well-nigh 5000 out of 22,000. The united Confederate force, 40,000 strong after all its losses, pressed on converging toward Chancellorsville. In their way lay Sickles, Fr and Slocum, with some 10,000 less. Barely two miles away on either were Reynolds, Meade, and Howard, with fully 42,000, not a regime whom were moved to the scene of conflict at the supreme moment. stress of the Confederate assault now again fell upon Sickles. His am tion exhausted, he could only hold his line with the bayonet. Five the enemy dashed upon him, five times they were thrust back. Th whole front melted away, Sickles's corps first yielding the position.[1] in obedience to orders from Couch, who had in some sort assumed t rary command, the army retreated to the line which had been trace the night before.

As a defensive position to be held against a superior force, a better hardly have been desired. It formed a sharp curve, the apex three qu of a mile back of Chancellorsville, the sides stretching back right an to the Rappahannock and Rapidan, covering the fords. Each flan covered by a little stream bordered by dense woods. An enemy co sail it only by its narrow front, and this was covered by the skirt forest, pierced with only a few rough roads. It was a position whic general might venture to hold against double his force. Hooker ha fully 70,000 men, half of whom had not been seriously engaged. Le left barely 40,000; yet, in the face of these odds, he was on the po renewing the fight, when he was arrested by ominous tidings. the fierce fight had been going on around Chancellorsville, Sedgwic marched from below Fredericksburg, stormed the heights, and was n ing to unite with Hooker.[2] Sedgwick had now his own corps, strong. These were across the river, two or three miles below Fred burg. Gibbon's division of Couch's corps, 5000 strong, which had left behind at Falmouth, opposite Fredericksburg, was also under Sedg command; thus, all told, he had 27,000. Confronting him along the h was Early, who had been left from Jackson's corps, and Barksdale's b of McLaws's, and Wilcox's of Anderson's, in all 11,000 strong. Jus four o'clock on Saturday afternoon Hooker sent an order to Sedgwick ing him to march upon Fredericksburg, capture it, and vigorously the enemy. "We know," he added, though he did not himself belie "that the enemy is flying, trying to save his trains. Two of Sickles' sions are among them." This order did not reach Sedgwick until dusk most simultaneously came another, dated three hours later, directi route which should be taken in pursuit. At this time Jackson had his blow and shattered Howard's corps. At an hour before midnig other order came to Sedgwick. Hooker, not aware that he had already ed the river, and supposing him still to be on the north bank, directed "cross the Rappahannock on the receipt of this order, take up your li march on the Chancellorsville road until you connect with the majo eral commanding, and attack and destroy any force you may fall in w the road. You will leave all your trains behind except the pack tra your ammunition, and march to be in vicinity of the general at da You will probably fall upon the rear of the force commanded by G Lee, and between you and the major general commanding he expe use him up. Be sure not to fail." This peremptory and special ord dispatched after Jackson's assault had been checked.[4] Sedgwick p corps in motion at once. The moon shone almost as brightly as day the hills, but thick fogs were gathering in the valley. The Confe were on the alert, and their skirmishers presented some annoyance. Sedgwick's march was unaccountably slow. It took the head of his c until daybreak—a space of fully six hours, to reach Fredericksburg, tance of three miles.

Two or three attempts were made to carry the heights on the Confe right, which were held by Early with the main strength of his di These attempts were repulsed with little difficulty. Gibbon, who ha crossed the river, made a demonstration against their left, but a deep the bridges over which had been removed, prevented any advance. the effect, however, of detaining there a Confederate brigade which was ing from that direction toward Marye's Hill in the centre. This hi

[1] "If Hooker had been well enough to have answered my request for re-enforcements, it would have turned the whole tide of battle. I have no doubt it would have been won in thirty minutes; at least it would have been won in an hour. It would have been won just as soon as you could have got ten thousand men from the right or the left to have repulsed that attack."—Sickles, in *Com. Rep.*, ii., 10.

[2] "We expected that Jackson's forces would assault us in the morning at Chancellorsville, and the intention was that General Sickles, with all his force, was to meet him at once; and the First Corps, Reynolds's, was also to attack him and envelop him; and, if necessary, more forces were to be drawn from the left of our line, leaving only forces enough to hold Lee's forces in check" (Warren, in *Com. Rep.*, ii., 46).—"I can not tell why the First Corps was not brought into action. I thought that the simple advance of two corps would take the enemy in flank, and would be very beneficial in its result. General Reynolds once or twice contemplated making this advance upon his own responsibility. Colonel Stone made a reconnoissance, showing it to be practicable."—Doubleday, in *Com. Rep.*, ii., 17.

[3] Pleasonton, in *Com. Rep.*, ii., 31.

[4] Sickles (in *Com. Rep.*, ii., 8) thus describes the aspect at this moment: "The enemy seemed to be satisfied with having forced me to withdraw my infantry from their front line to this second position, and the battle paused for half an hour or more. The loss inflicted upon the enemy, especially by my artillery, was most severe. Their formation for the attack was entirely broken up, and from my head-quarters they presented to the eye the appearance of a mass—a crowd without definite formation."—Stuart (in *Lee's Rep.*, 16) thus describes the situation: "In the mean time the enemy was pressing our left with infantry, and all the re-enforcements I could obtain were sent there. Colquitt's brigade of Trimble's division, ordered first to the right, was directed to the left to support Pender. Johnson's brigade, of the second line, was also engaged there, and the three lines were more or less merged into one line of battle, and reported hard pressed. Urgent requests were sent for re-enforcements, and notices that the troops were out of ammunition. I ordered that the ground must be held at all hazards, if necessary with the bayonet."—Several of the Confederate brigade commanders report how hardly they were pressed by the advance of French. Thus Pender (in *Lee's Rep.*, 52) says: "My men were about out of ammunition, broken down, and badly cut up."—Ramseur (*Ibid.*, 74) tells how he was obliged to run over the Confederate troops in his front, and how his line was "subjected to a horrible enfilade fire, by which it suffered severely." Out of 1509 men he lost 788.

[5] The left, that is of the line as actually engaged, for the Corps of Meade and Howard, forming the absolute left, were not engaged at all. Hancock says (*Com. Rep.*, ii., 68): "Although the enemy massed their infantry in the woods very near me and attempted to advance, and always

[1] "No supports coming up, and the enemy meanwhile having had time to restore ord own lines and bring up fresh reserves, I was again attacked, and, having no means of re except the bayonet, after repelling five successive attacks I again fell back to General h headquarters, which were then within easy range of the enemy's cannon, and were rap coming a pile of ruins, almost every shot telling upon the building" (Sickles, in *Com. Rep.*, Hancock, who, from his position on the left, could see something of what was going on u right, says (*Com. Rep.*, ii., 67): "The first lines finally melted away, and the whole front ed to pass out. First, the Third Corps (Sickles's) went out; then the Twelfth Corps (Sl after fighting a long time, and there was nothing left on that part of the line except my vision. I was directed to hold that position until a change of line of battle could be m was to hold it until I was notified that all the other troops had gotten off."—The Conf reports uniformly give 10 o'clock as the time when Chancellorsville was carried; the Fed ports place the time an hour later.

[2] "The troops, having become somewhat scattered by the difficulties of the ground and dor of the contest, were immediately reformed preparatory to renewing the attack. The had withdrawn to a strong position nearer the Rappahannock, which he had previously f His superiority of numbers, the unfavorable nature of the ground, which was densely and the condition of our troops after the arduous and sanguinary conflict in which they h engaged, rendered great caution necessary. Our preparations were just completed, when operations were arrested by intelligence received from Fredericksburg."—*Lee's Rep.*, 10.

[3] "It was based on a report sent in from General Sickles that the enemy was flying at t he was sent out to follow up Jackson's Corps. I was of the impression that the gene mistaken, but nevertheless felt that no harm could follow from its transmission to Genera wick."—Hooker, in *Com. Rep.*, ii., 147.

[4] Sedgwick (*Com. Rep.*, ii., 95) says that this dispatch was dated at ten minutes past 1 probably gave the hour from memory. Hooker (*Ibid.*, 129) gives its date at 9 o'clock. no doubt, however, as to the time when it was received, although Howe (*Ibid.*, 23) says "received just after dark, say 8 o'clock; but he evidently confounds it with a previous As to the character of the night, I have endeavored to reconcile statements which upon th appear wholly inconsistent. Hooker and Butterfield say expressly and in almost the sam (*Ibid.*, 76, 129): "It was a bright moonlight night, and clear, sufficiently light for staff to write dispatches by moonlight." Howe says (*Ibid.*, 22): "It was bright starlight, so could see what was in the advance." Sedgwick, on the other hand, says (*Ibid.*, 100): "In

held by only two brigades—that of Barksdale occupying the stone wall at its base, from which it had so disastrously repulsed Burnside a few weeks before. The morning was wearing away, and nothing had been effected. At length Sedgwick, urged by Warren, resolved to assail Marye's Hill in front. At 11 o'clock, just as the fight at Chancellorsville was closing, he formed two strong columns, which dashed at the wall. The enemy reserved their fire until the nearest column, led by Colonel Johns, was within a few score yards; they then poured in a solid sheet of musketry. The column faltered and fell back. In a couple of minutes it rallied, and pressed fifty yards nearer. Again it met the sheet of fire, and again broke. It seemed that the tragedy of December was to be re-enacted. But Johns, though wounded, rallied his men for a third charge. This time they did not stop; they rushed over and around the wall, and in fifteen minutes from their first advance carried it, killing or capturing its defenders. Johns was again wounded and borne from the field. Colonel Spear, who led the other column, was killed. Other regiments now swarmed up the height from both sides. The Confederates made a fierce fight, but it was vain. Early fell back southward along the telegraph road. Sedgwick's corps thus stood directly between Early and Lee, with only two brigades in his front. This little force retreated sullenly along the plank road, closely followed by Sedgwick.

Such were the tidings which reached Lee at Chancellorsville. His situation was full of peril. Sedgwick might overwhelm Early, and then the Confederate lines of communication would be cut, or he might press straight on to Chancellorsville, and fall upon Lee's rear. This corps must be defeated at every cost, or all was lost. Four brigades of McLaws and Anderson, which had suffered least in the fight of the morning, were sent back to check the Federal advance. They came up with the retreating regiments at Salem Church, midway between Chancellorsville and Fredericksburg. Here a brief stand had been made upon a low wooded ridge. This was carried by the divisions of Brooke and Newton, for Howe had been posted in the rear to keep Early in check, and Gibbon had been left behind to occupy Fredericksburg. The Confederate re-enforcements now pressed Brooke and Newton back through the wood with heavy loss, and were in turn checked by the artillery. Night coming on, both armies slept upon the field. All this afternoon, Hooker, with 70,000 men, lay supinely behind his intrenchments, in front of which were barely 30,000 of the enemy. He made no attempt to aid Sedgwick, who had at length, though tardily, accomplished two thirds of his march.

MONDAY, MAY 4.

No army ever found itself in a more dangerous position than that of Lee on Monday morning, the 4th of May. All counted, it now numbered less than 50,000 men. Stuart, with nearly all of Anderson, confronted Hooker at Chancellorsville. Six miles to the east was McLaws, with less than 10,000, holding Sedgwick in check. Three miles farther to the south was Early, with 8000. Sedgwick had lost heavily, but he still had quite as many as McLaws and Early together. It was hardly within the range of possibility that Hooker would not discover the situation, and either assail Stuart in front with twofold numbers, or, leaving enough to hold him fast, fall upon the rear of McLaws, who would thus be crushed between two fires. Lee's only hope lay in dislodging Sedgwick. To do this he must still farther weaken his force at Chancellorsville. Anderson's remaining three brigades were moved down, leaving only Stuart, with 20,000 men, in front of Hooker. These took position toward Sedgwick's left, threatening to cut him off from the river, while Early marched along the ridge and retook Marye's Hill, thus throwing himself in Sedgwick's rear and cutting him off from Fredericksburg, which was thereupon abandoned by Gibbon, who recrossed the river.[1] Sedgwick's position was now a defensive one, for Hooker directed him not to renew the attack upon Salem Heights. By noon Lee had about 27,000 men opposed to Sedgwick, who had about 18,000, having lost 8000 on the previous day. There was some skirmishing all through the day, but no serious attack was made until 6 o'clock, when, Anderson having united with Early, these two divisions fell upon Howe, who, with 6000 men, was on the Union left. Howe met the assault with great stubbornness, and then fell slowly back toward Banks's Ford, to a strong position which he had previously chosen. The enemy dashed furiously upon this, but were met by a galling fire and driven back, broken and apparently routed. Howe was confident that they would not venture another attack, as, indeed, they did not. Two hours after dark he was surprised to learn that Sedgwick was about to fall back to the ford. He refused to abandon his position without a positive order. The order came, and was obeyed.[2] The division marched to the ford without the slightest molestation, having occupied its strong position two hours after having repulsed the attack.

Hooker all this day lay wholly inactive with his great force of 70,000 men, within two hours' march. Between him and Sedgwick, by the road along which Meade had marched out on Thursday, there was at no time more than three brigades. Hooker's orders to Sedgwick indicate the uncertainty under which he labored all that day, even when he had resumed the command after his injury. Long before daybreak he directed Sedgwick not to resume his assault upon Salem Heights unless he himself attacked, for he hoped that the enemy would assail him; but he was too far away to give any directions; only, if Sedgwick thought best to cross the river, he could go either to Banks's Ford or Fredericksburg. At 11 o'clock in the morning he directed Sedgwick not to cross unless compelled to do so, but, if possible, to hold the position at the ford. Half an hour later, Hooker sent word that he proposed to advance upon the enemy the next day, and in that case Sedgwick's position would be as favorable as could be desired. Sedgwick had all day been doubtful whether he could maintain himself on the south side of the river; but after the repulse of the attack made upon him, he wrote that he could hold his position. But, just ten minutes before Hooker received this, he sent an order to Sedgwick to cross. He immediately countermanded the order, but, before this was received, which was just before daylight, nearly the whole corps were over, and the enemy had taken a position which commanded the bridge, and it was too late to return.[1] Sedgwick lost in all nearly 5000 in killed, wounded, and missing, the greater portion of them on Sunday, and captured nearly 1400 prisoners. The Confederates lost about 4000.[2]

But, during the night, Hooker had resolved to abandon his own position. He summoned his corps commanders to a consultation. Slocum was not present. Howard wished an advance. Sickles and Couch were in favor of withdrawing. Reynolds went to sleep, saying his opinion would be the same as that of Meade. Meade at first opposed the crossing of the river mainly on the ground that the movement could not be effected in the presence of an enemy flushed by success; he, however, ceased to press his objections upon Hooker's confident assurance that the army could be withdrawn without loss. Hooker had no doubt that he could hold his position, and perhaps force the enemy to retire; but he urged that, as he would fall back toward Richmond, he would become constantly stronger, while we were growing weaker; he could be better assailed near Washington than at Richmond. So the order to cross the river was issued, and a new line of intrenchments was thrown up close by the United States Ford to cover the passage. When Sedgwick announced that he could hold his ground, Hooker appears to have proposed to recross back again at Banks's Ford, unite with Sedgwick, and give battle. But this purpose was frustrated by Sedgwick's movement.[3]

Lee, leaving Early on the heights at Fredericksburg to prevent Sedgwick from recrossing, reunited his remaining force, now reduced to 40,000, before the position from which Hooker was preparing to retire. In the afternoon of Tuesday a fierce storm sprung up. The river rose rapidly, submerging the approaches to the bridges. One of these was taken down and used to piece out the others, over which the army retreated without being perceived by the enemy. The storm passed away during the night, and Lee had made preparations to attack the Federal works at daylight; but, upon advancing his skirmishers, he found that the great Union army was beyond the river.[4]

The cavalry movement, upon which Hooker had relied for destroying the enemy by cutting his communications, proved equally fruitless. Stoneman divided his corps. Averill, in command of one column, ascended the Rapidan some twenty miles. At Rapidan Station, on the Orange Railroad, he came up, on Friday, with W. F. Lee, with 900. He reported the next day that he had been engaged with the cavalry of the enemy, and destroying communications. His loss in this "engagement" was one man killed and two wounded. On Sunday he retraced his steps, whereupon Hooker displaced him from command, and appointed Pleasonton in his place. But meanwhile the battles had been fought and lost. Stoneman, with the main cavalry column, pushed on farther southward. Arriving at a point thirty miles northwest of Richmond, he divided his force into six bodies. "We dropped," he says, "like a shell in that region of country, intending to burst it in every direction, expecting each fragment would do as much harm and create nearly as much terror as would result from sending the whole shell. The result of this plan satisfied my most sanguine anticipations." One regiment struck the James River Canal, and attempted ineffectually to destroy the aqueduct which spans the Rivanna River. They then returned to the main body. Four others were sent in various directions to break up the railroad from Richmond to Fredericksburg, which was the primary object of the whole movement. Davis, with one regiment, reached to within seven

[1] Sedgwick appears to have supposed that Early's force were re-enforcements from Richmond. He says (*Com. Rep.*, ii., 106): "I was informed, at an early hour, that a column of the enemy, 15,000 strong, coming from the direction of Richmond, had occupied the heights of Fredericksburg, cutting off my communication with Fredericksburg."

[2] "The movement was commenced very late, and Hays's and Hoke's brigades were thrown into some confusion by coming in contact; and it becoming difficult to distinguish our troops from those of the enemy, on account of the growing darkness, they had therefore to fall back to reform" (Early, in Lee's *Rep.*, 35).—"The attack was delivered with a violence that I had never before encountered. We resisted the first attack better than I expected, and at a favorable time the left of my line was thrown back partially behind some woods. As I expected, the enemy seemed to be under the impression, from this movement, that we were giving way. They advanced until they reached a point that we should have desired above all others they should have advanced upon, and where a reserve force, which I had placed under cover, had an opportunity to get a flank fire upon them with full effect. When the fire from our new position struck them, it was but a short time before they were entirely broken, and fell back in a rout. After this repulse, the position of the Sixth Corps, in my judgment, was less liable to a serious attack than it had been at any time since it crossed the Rappahannock, and I saw no necessity for recrossing the river" (Howe, in *Com. Rep.*, 21).—"Some time after we had returned to our old camps, I met General Hooker, and spoke to him of the movements we had made and the position we held. I stated to him that after the fight of the 4th of May I could have gone with my division to the heights of Fredericksburg, and hold them. He expressed his surprise that those heights could have been held on the night of the 4th, and said, 'If I had known that you could have gone on those heights and held them, I would have re-enforced you with the whole army.' I told him that if I had not received orders to go back to Banks's Ford, I could have marched uninterruptedly to Fredericksburg Heights after 9 o'clock that night; for, after the fight we had had, the rebels abandoned the Heights, and there was nothing to be seen of them. There was a bright moon that night, and we could see an object of the size of a man or a horse at a great distance" (*Ibid.*, 25).—"The attack on Brooks was easily repulsed, chiefly by the skirmish line and the battery of the First Massachusetts. That on Howe was of a more determined character. It was gallantly resisted by our infantry by a counter-charge, while the artillery of the division played with fearful effect upon their advance. At length our line was forced back upon the left, and Howe directed his right to retire to a less advanced position. The division reformed promptly, the batteries keeping up a most effective fire. The advance of the enemy was checked, his troops were scattered and driven back with fearful loss, and the new position was easily maintained until nightfall. Several hundred prisoners, including one general officer and many others of rank, and three battle-flags, were captured from the enemy in this engagement."—Sedgwick, in *Com. Rep.*, ii., 107.

[1] Sedgwick, in *Com. Rep.*, ii., 97; Hooker, *Ibid.*, 133.

[2] Early, who encountered only Sedgwick, reports his entire loss at 1474; McLaws, 1889, the greater portion being in the action with Sedgwick; Anderson, 1445, probably half here.

[3] Butterfield, in *Com. Rep.*, ii., 77; Hooker, *Ibid.*, 135.

[4] *Lee's Rep.*, 13.

LDOUT BLA

GEORGE G. MEADE.

CHAPTER XXIX.

THE INVASION OF PENNSYLVANIA.—GETTYSBURG.

Hooker's Plans.—The President's Views.—Pleasonton's Cavalry Reconnoissance.—Lee's Plans.—Reasons for invading the North.—Elections at the North.—State of public Feeling.—Opinion of the British Minister.—Strength of the Confederate Army.—Route of Milroy.—The Advance into Pennsylvania.—Cavalry Encounters.—Hooker's Policy.—Halleck and Hooker.—Hooker resigns.—Meade appointed to the Command.—His Antecedents.—Lee's Movements.—The President calls for Militia.—The Armies concentrate toward Gettysburg.—Meade selects a Position on Pipe Creek.—Pleasonton marks Gettysburg as the Battle-field.—*Battle of July 1*: Topography of Gettysburg.—Reynolds and Hill approach.—Reynolds killed.—Howard takes Command.—Meade sends Hancock to the Field.—The Federals driven back.—Hancock decides to accept Battle.—The Position chosen.—Lee's Dilemma.—*Battle of July 2*: Meade's Line of Battle.—Sickles goes too far in advance.—Hood's Attack upon Round Top.—The Attack repulsed by Vincent.—Sickles and Hood wounded.—Birney attacked and driven back.—Crawford checks the Confederate Attack.—Humphreys assailed and falls back.—The Union Line re-formed.—The Confederates fall back.—Confederate Advantage on the Right.—The Situation at Night.—*Battle of July 3*: Lee's Plan of Attack.—Ewell forced back on the Right.—The Cannonade on the Centre.—Pickett and Pettigrew advance.—Lieutenant Haskell.—The Confederate Rout.—Cavalry Attack.—Close of the Fight.—Order for Pursuit given and countermanded.—The third of July at Gettysburg and Vicksburg.—Meade holds a Council of War.—Lee retreats to the Potomac.—Meade slowly advances.—Lee recrosses the Potomac.—Losses at Gettysburg.—Criticism on the Battle.

FROM Chancellorsville and the Wilderness both armies returned to their old positions on opposite banks of the Rappahannock.[1] Hooker meditated repeating, with some modifications, the attempt in which Burnside had failed.[2] He proposed to pass the river at Franklin's Crossing, and assail the enemy's intrenchments in front; for he could not anticipate that with their inferior force they would come out of their strong works, and meet him on

[1] For this campaign and the ensuing ones in Virginia, the full reports of the Confederate Army of Northern Virginia are wanting. If they were ever made, I have not been able to gain access to them. I presume that they were among the lost archives of the Confederacy. General Lee, a few days after the battles of Gettysburg, made a Preliminary Report, which will be found in the *Rebellion Record*, vol. vii. Some months later he made a somewhat more detailed report. This, I believe, has never been printed. For a MS. copy of it I am indebted to Mr. William Swinton. It, however, adds little to the information contained in the earlier Report. I find no reports from corps, division, and brigade commanders. The testimony given before the Congressional Committee on the Conduct of the War is the best authority upon the Union side. This (cited as *Com. Rep.*, ii.) will be found in the first volume of the second series of this Report. Not a few of the newspaper accounts of this battle, Northern and Southern, are very accurate. From these sources the following account has been mainly drawn.

[2] "As soon as I heard that General Sedgwick had recrossed the river, seeing no object in maintaining my position where it was, and believing that it would be much more to my advantage to hazard an engagement with the enemy at Franklin's Crossing, where I had elbow-room, than where I was, the army on the right was directed to recross the river."—Hooker, in *Com. Rep.*, ii., 134.

miles of Richmond, tore up a few rails, and destroyed some stores; captured a train filled with wounded, who were paroled; then, finding himself likely to be cut off, he headed southeastwardly for Williamsburg, but, discovering Confederate cavalry in his way, turned northward, crossed the Mattapony, and, following down its bank, reached the Union outposts at Gloucester Point, opposite Yorktown. Kilpatrick, with another regiment, on Monday struck the railroad still nearer Richmond, destroyed the dépôts at Hungary Station, then rode to within two miles of the city, passing through the outer line of defenses. With his small force it was useless to attempt any thing farther; so he turned eastward, passing the Chickahominy at Meadow Bridge, which he destroyed, and crossed the Mattapony without having encountered any opposition. Here he fell in with Davis, and both proceeded to Gloucester Point. Stoneman himself remained near the point where his divisions had separated, with only 700 men, which he kept as a nucleus around which the different parties could rally in case of need, having sent out three regiments to destroy the bridges in his vicinity. These reunited on Tuesday, and Stoneman set out on a rapid retreat to the Rapidan and Rappahannock, crossing the latter river at Kelly's Ford on Thursday, the 8th. The alarm caused by the "explosion of the bomb" was great, but the injury inflicted was small. In three days the railroad to Fredericksburg was in running order. Had it been known that almost the whole transportation of the road was collected at Guinea's Station, eighteen miles from Chancellorsville, where also were the main dépôts of supply, and that these were left wholly unguarded, a rapid dash made by half of the cavalry upon this point at any time during this eventful week would have changed the whole course of the campaign.[1]

The Federal loss in these operations at Chancellorsville was something more than 17,000, of whom 5000 were unwounded prisoners. They also lost 13 guns, some 20,000 muskets, and a considerable quantity of ammunition and accoutrements. The Confederate loss was about 13,000, of whom 1581 were killed, 8700 wounded, and about 3000 prisoners.[2]

Hooker issued an order congratulating his army on its achievements. "If," said he, "it has not accomplished all that was expected, the reasons are well known to the army. It is sufficient to say that they were of a character not to be foreseen or prevented. . . . . . . We have made long marches, crossed rivers, surprised the enemy in his intrenchments, and, wherever we have fought, have inflicted heavier blows than we have received . . . . . . have placed *hors de combat* 18,000 of his chosen troops, destroyed his stores and dépôts filled with vast amounts of stores, deranged his communications, captured prisoners within the fortifications of his capital, and filled his country with fear and consternation." But no dépôts were destroyed or communications deranged except by the cavalry; the stores destroyed were not sufficient to interfere with Lee's scanty accumulations, and the interruptions to communications were so slight that they were restored in two or three days. Far more truthful was Lee's statement to his army: "Under trying vicissitudes of heat and storm, you attacked the enemy, strongly intrenched in the depths of a tangled wilderness, and again on the hills of Fredericksburg, fifteen miles distant, and, by the valor that has triumphed on so many fields, forced him once more to seek safety beyond the Rappahannock."

Hooker declared that when he returned from Chancellorsville he "felt that he had fought no battle," for the reason that he could not get his men into position to do so, though he had more men than he could use;[3] that he failed in his enterprise from causes "of a character not to be foreseen or prevented by human sagacity or resources." A careful examination of all that was done, or left undone, evinces that every one of these circumstances was of a character which lay fairly within the limits of probability; and that there was not, in fact, any moment between Thursday afternoon and Tuesday morning when success was not wholly within the grasp of the Union army. The movement by which Chancellorsville was reached, and the Confederate position rendered worthless, was brilliantly conceived and admirably executed. The initial error, by which alone all else was rendered possible, was that halt at Chancellorsville. Had the march been continued for an hour longer, or even been resumed early in the following morning, the army would have got clear of the Wilderness without meeting any great opposing force, and then it would have been in a position where its great superiority of numbers would have told.[1] The rout of Howard's corps was possible only from the grossest neglect of all military precautions. Jackson, after a toilsome march of ten hours, halted for three hours in open ground not two miles from the Union lines. A single picket, sent for a mile up a broad road, would have discovered the whole movement in ample time for Hooker to have strengthened his position, or to have withdrawn from it without loss. The blame of this surprise can not, however, fairly be laid upon Hooker. He had a right to presume that whoever was in command there would have so picketed his lines as to prevent the possibility of being surprised in broad daylight. But even as it was, the disaster to the Eleventh Corps should have had no serious effect upon the general result. That was fully remedied when the pursuit was checked. On Sunday morning Hooker was in a better position than he had been on the evening before. He had lost 8000 men and had been strengthened by 17,000, and now had 78,000 to oppose to 47,000. The Confederate army was divided, and could reunite only by winning a battle or by a day's march. The only thing which could have lost the battle of that day was the abandonment of the position at Hazle Grove, for from this alone was it possible to enfilade Slocum's line. But surely it is within the limits of military forethought that a general who has occupied a position for two days and three nights should have discovered the very key to that position, when it lay within a mile of his own headquarters. The disabling of Hooker could not, indeed, have been foreseen; but such an accident might happen to any commander upon any field, and there should have been somewhere some man with authority to have, within the space of three hours, brought into action some of the more than 30,000 men within sound, and almost sight, of the battle then raging. Sedgwick's assault upon the heights of Fredericksburg was certainly dilatory. He could not, indeed, have safely executed to the letter his orders, which involved a night assault upon the heights; but they could have been more easily stormed at 5 o'clock than at 11, and this would have brought him upon Lee's rear by 9, when the action was going sorely against the Confederates. How the hours from Sunday noon till Monday night were wasted, has been shown. Hooker, indeed, reiterates that he could not assail the Confederate lines through the dense forests. But Lee broke through those very woods on Sunday, and was minded to attempt it again on Wednesday, when he found that the enemy had disappeared. The golden opportunity was lost never to be recovered, and the Confederate Army of Northern Virginia gained a new lease of life.

If final success were a certain test of the merits of a military plan, we must accord the highest success to that of Lee. But it succeeded only through a series of accidents, any one of which failing would have involved ruin; and a general, save in the direst emergency, has no right to reckon upon the favors of fortune. His first movement, that of marching with the bulk of his army to confront Hooker at Chancellorsville, was wise, for he had good reason to suppose that then and there the force of the enemy was inferior to his own. He had no means of knowing that Sickles's corps had come thither; and, at the worst, he could fall back if he found himself overmatched, and return to his former position, or retreat upon his communications, and make a stand at any favorable point. But when, on the next morning, he divided his army, sending three fifths of it a day's march away, he staked upon an unlikely chance every reasonable possibility of safety. He had no right to assume that the Union right would be surprised, or that Hooker would fail to fall with overwhelming force upon one part or the other of his divided army. So, on Sunday morning, he had no right to anticipate that an attack made by an inferior force upon lines strongly intrenched could succeed, or that his opponent would meet him with only half of his force. How hardly, and by what accidents only, the battle of Sunday morning was won, has already been shown. He tempted fortune still more desperately when, on that afternoon and the next morning, he still farther divided his force. How could he suppose that Stuart's 20,000 would for a long day hold in check Hooker's 70,000, while a great battle was being fought close by between forces so equally matched that a tenth of this idle force added to the enemy would assuredly turn the scale? To retreat promptly and rapidly upon and along the railroad was the only course which any man knowing what both commanders knew, and, still more, what we now know, would have pronounced safe for Lee, when he was startled by the tidings that Sedgwick had stormed the heights and was advancing upon his rear. Lee, reversing the words of Hooker, might have said, "We succeeded only through circumstances of a character not to be foreseen or brought about by human sagacity or resources."

[1] "General Lee had but two regiments of cavalry, under W. H. F. Lee, to oppose to the large force under Stoneman. The whole country in the rear of the Confederate army, up to the very fortifications of Richmond, was open to the invader. Nearly all the transportation of that army was collected at Guinea's Station, eighteen miles from Chancellorsville, with little or no guard, and might have been destroyed by one fourth of Stoneman's force. Such was the condition of the railroads and the scarcity of supplies in the country, that the Confederate commander could never accumulate more than a few days' rations ahead at Fredericksburg. To have interrupted his communications for any length of time would have imperiled his army or forced him to retreat." —*Hotchkiss*, 101–3. See also Hooker and Stoneman, in *Com. Rep.*, 137–40.

[2] The official report of Union losses is given by Hooker in *Com. Rep.*, ii., 148; the Confederate in *Lee's Rep.*, 131–133. In the Union report, the respective numbers of killed, wounded, and missing are not given; but Lee (*Rep.*, 15) states that he took "about 5000 prisoners, exclusive of wounded." This statement has been adopted, and an attempt has been made to apportion the missing among the several corps, but the estimate is almost wholly conjectural. The Confederate report, while giving separately the killed and wounded in every regiment, makes no mention of the missing. But in their separate reports (in *Lee's Rep.*, 27, 88, 86, 117), Anderson, McLaws, Early, and Rodes give the missing in their respective divisions. Hill and Colston do not report their missing; but, as they were in the hottest of the fight on Saturday and Sunday, it is presumed that their loss in missing was at least equal to the average of the others. From these data the following table has been constructed:

Losses at Chancellorsville.

Union.				Confederate.			
	Killed and Wounded.	Missing.	Total.		Killed and Wounded.	Missing.	Total.
First Corps (Reynolds)..	192	100	292	Early's Division........	851	500	1,351
Second Corps (Couch)...	1,525	500	2,025	A. P. Hill's Division....	2,583	500?	3,083
Third Corps (Sickles)...	3,439	600	4,039	Colston's Division	1,868	450?	2,318
Fifth Corps (Meade)	399	300	699	Rodes's Division........	2,178	713	2,891
Sixth Corps (Sedgwick) .	3,601	1000	4,601	Anderson's Division	1,180	210	1,390
Eleventh Corps (Howard)	558	2000	2,558	McLaws's Division	1,379	380	1,760
Twelfth Corps (Slocum)..	2,333	600	2,933	Artillery and Cavalry...	227		
Cavalry, etc............	150		150	Total............	10,277	2753	13,030
Total............	12,197	5000	17,197				

There is reason to suppose that the losses on each side were some hundreds greater than officially given. Thus Sedgwick reports his loss to have been 4926 (*Com. Rep.*, 107), and Sickles says (*Ibid.*, 10) that on Sunday he "lost 260 officers and about 4600 men in a couple of hours." Such of the Confederate generals as gave their losses state them considerably above those put down in the general report. In four divisions, the excess is about 400 in killed and wounded. Then, as to the missing, Sedgwick states that he made about 1400 prisoners, while in the division opposed to him the Confederate reports acknowledge only 1090, and some of these must have been captured before they encountered Sedgwick. Still we must consider the final official reports on both sides as the highest authority attainable in this case.

[3] *Com. Rep.*, ii., 142.

[1] "A mile or more in advance of the position I then had would have placed me beyond the forest, where, with my superior force, the enemy would probably have been beaten."—Hooker, in *Com. Rep.*, ii., 142.

GEORGE G. MEADE.

CHAPTER XXIX.

THE INVASION OF PENNSYLVANIA.—GETTYSBURG.

Hooker's Plans.—The President's Views.—Pleasonton's Cavalry Reconnoissance.—Lee's Plans.—Reasons for invading the North.—Elections at the North.—State of public Feeling.—Opinion of the British Minister.—Strength of the Confederate Army.—Route of Milroy.—The Advance into Pennsylvania.—Cavalry Encounters.—Hooker's Policy.—Halleck and Hooker.—Hooker resigns.—Meade appointed to the Command.—His Antecedents.—Lee's Movements.—The President calls for Militia.—The Armies concentrate toward Gettysburg.—Meade selects a Position on Pipe Creek.—Pleasonton marks Gettysburg as the Battle-field.—*Battle of July 1*: Topography of Gettysburg.—Reynolds and Hill approach.—Reynolds killed.—Howard takes Command.—Meade sends Hancock to the Field.—The Federals driven back.—Hancock decides to accept Battle.—The Position chosen.—Lee's Dilemma.—*Battle of July 2*: Meade's Line of Battle.—Sickles goes too far in advance.—Hood's Attack upon Round Top.—The Attack repulsed by Vincent.—Sickles and Hood wounded.—Birney attacked and driven back.—Crawford checks the Confederate Attack.—Humphreys assailed and falls back.—The Union Line re-formed.—The Confederates fall back.—Confederate Advantage on the Right.—The Situation at Night.—*Battle of July 3*: Lee's Plan of Attack.—Ewell forced back on the Right.—The Cannonade on the Centre.—Pickett and Pettigrew advance.—Lieutenant Haskell.—The Confederate Rout.—Cavalry Attack.—Close of the Fight.—Order for Pursuit given and countermanded.—The third of July at Gettysburg and Vicksburg.—Meade holds a Council of War.—Lee retreats to the Potomac.—Meade slowly advances.—Lee recrosses the Potomac.—Losses at Gettysburg.—Criticism on the Battle.

FROM Chancellorsville and the Wilderness both armies returned to their old positions on opposite banks of the Rappahannock.[1] Hooker meditated repeating, with some modifications, the attempt in which Burnside had failed.[2] He proposed to pass the river at Franklin's Crossing, and assail the enemy's intrenchments in front; for he could not anticipate that with their inferior force they would come out of their strong works, and meet him on

[1] For this campaign and the ensuing ones in Virginia, the full reports of the Confederate Army of Northern Virginia are wanting. If they were ever made, I have not been able to gain access to them. I presume that they were among the lost archives of the Confederacy. General Lee, a few days after the battles of Gettysburg, made a Preliminary Report, which will be found in the *Rebellion Record*, vol. vii. Some months later he made a somewhat more detailed report. This, I believe, has never been printed. For a MS. copy of it I am indebted to Mr. William Swinton. It, however, adds little to the information contained in the earlier Report. I find no reports from corps, division, and brigade commanders. The testimony given before the Congressional Committee on the Conduct of the War is the best authority upon the Union side. This (cited as *Com. Rep.*, ii.) will be found in the first volume of the second series of this Report. Not a few of the newspaper accounts of this battle, Northern and Southern, are very accurate. From these sources the following account has been mainly drawn.

[2] "As soon as I heard that General Sedgwick had recrossed the river, seeing no object in maintaining my position where it was, and believing that it would be much more to my advantage to hazard an engagement with the enemy at Franklin's Crossing, where I had elbow-room, than where I was, the army on the right was directed to recross the river."—Hooker, in *Com. Rep.*, ii., 134.

the open plain. This was an enterprise which he had before pronounced to be wholly impracticable. It is vain to inquire what had happened within the week to make the project more feasible. His army had been much reduced by the departure of the nine-months' and two-years' men. On the 13th of May he informed the President that his "marching force of infantry was cut down to 80,000 men;" he added, "I hope to commence my movement to-morrow; but this must not be spoken of to any one." Lincoln replied that he did not think any thing was to be gained by an early renewal of the attempt to cross the Rappahannock; still, if Hooker believed that he could renew the attack successfully, he would not restrain him.] Whatever the proposed movement was, it was not attempted.

The result at Chancellorsville had inspired the Confederates with the most unbounded confidence. There was a universal clamor that the invincible army of Virginia should assume the offensive, carry the war beyond the bounds of the Confederacy, and conquer a peace upon Federal soil. To do this, it was necessary that the entire force, except what was engaged upon the Mississippi, should be concentrated in Northern Virginia. Before the close of May it became evident to Hooker that some great operation was in contemplation. Longstreet's three divisions, which had been engaged south of Richmond, were brought up one by one toward the Rappahannock. During the month of April he had been besieging Peck at Suffolk. But on the 2d of May, the ominous tidings that Hooker had advanced upon Lee caused Longstreet to abandon the siege, and put his force upon the march northward. The issue at Chancellorsville caused the movement to be suspended, and the force moved slowly by separate divisions. During the first week of June the whole army was concentrated near Culpepper, with the exception of A. P. Hill's division, which was left at Fredericksburg to mask the contemplated movement. Hooker, discovering that something was in progress, sent over on the 5th of June a part of Sedgwick's corps for the purpose of observation. Hill made such a display of his troops as to convince Hooker that the force in his front was not seriously diminished. Prisoners reported that the movements were merely a change of camps. Hooker indeed suspected that the van of the Confederate column would be heading toward the Potomac, while its rear was still left at Fredericksburg. He asked permission in that case to cross the river and fall upon their rear: this was refused, Halleck deeming that it would be perilous to permit the main force of Lee to move upon the Potomac, while the Union army was attacking a part of it in an intrenched position. The President concurred in this view, couching his opinion in his own quaint language.[2] But if it was Hooker's purpose to cross at Banks's Ford or the United States Ford, instead of marching right upon the front of the Confederate intrenchments, one can hardly see how he could have failed to inflict serious damage upon their rear, which would be thus severed from the main body at Culpepper, sixty miles away. Hooker in the mean time had learned that the Confederate cavalry at least was concentrated at Culpepper, and, in order to break up their camps, sent Pleasonton with two brigades of cavalry and 3000 infantry in that direction. This force ascended the north bank of the Rappahannock on the 9th of June, and marched in two columns toward Culpepper. The columns soon found themselves in presence of the enemy in large force, both of cavalry and infantry. A succession of sharp skirmishes ensued, lasting from early morning until late in the afternoon. The loss was about equal, four or five hundred on each side; but Pleasonton, finding himself confronted by superior numbers of both arms, retreated. Lee claims to have taken 400 prisoners; Pleasonton claims to have taken 200. This movement, and subsequent reconnoissances, which showed that the enemy were moving into and down the Valley of the Shenandoah, clearly indicated that they were bent either upon interposing between Hooker's army and Washington, or crossing the Potomac and invading the North.

Lee's design was first to detach Hooker from his strong position at Fredericksburg, then to free the Valley of the Shenandoah from the Union force which had occupied it during the winter and spring, "and, if practicable, to transfer the scene of hostilities north of the Potomac." He also hoped that there would be an "opportunity to strike a blow at the army commanded by Hooker;" or, in any case, that "this army would be compelled to leave Virginia, and perhaps would draw with it troops from other quarters; and so court-martial, and sentenced to imprisonment in a fortress until tl the war. This sentence was commuted by the President to banis' the Confederacy. A great Democratic meeting was held at Alban' the leaders of the party in the State of New York inveighed bitte this proceeding; and at home Vallandigham was nominated by a as the Democratic candidate for Governor of Ohio. At the ti doubted that he would be elected. No one could dream that a s had just sent to Congress 14 Opposition and but 5 Administration tives would in a few months give a majority of a hundred thous administration; nor could any one presume that a very large por members of Congress elected as opposition would range themsel side of the administration in upholding the war. The draft, moreo was soon to go into effect, was vehemently denounced, declared tc stitutional, and threats were openly made that its enforcement wo lently resisted. There was fair occasion for the South to be pers any great success gained over the Union army would elicit suct throughout the North that the government would be compelle from the prosecution of the war. "It was hoped," says Lee, "th tion to military advantages, other results might be attained by the our army." Nor was this opinion that the people of the North w ing weary of the war confined to those whose interests and feelin strongly enlisted. The British minister at Washington had six mo shared in this opinion, and so informed his government.[1] Sin almost uninterrupted series of successes had been gained by the ates. They had defeated Burnside at Fredericksburg, and foiled Chancellorsville; Vicksburg and Charleston still held out agai Federal assaults; none of the operations on the Lower Mississip Gulf had succeeded; the capture of Galveston had given all Tex hands of the Confederates; the Alabama and the Florida had sw can commerce from the high seas. Saving the few miles occuf main armies, the Union forces actually held no part of the Conf ritory of which they had taken possession. During the first six the year 1863 it seemed as though the tide of success had fully s of the Confederacy, and it appeared that nothing but a successf of the North was wanting to secure its final triumph, recognized great powers of Europe.

The invasion once determined upon, the entire disposable strei Confederacy was placed at the disposal of Lee. Southern Virginia Carolina were almost stripped of troops, to augment the Army o Virginia. By the middle of June, when the movement toward was fairly commenced, Lee found himself in command of a for 100,000 men of all arms.[2] This was divided into three corps, c by Longstreet, A. P. Hill, and Ewell, the cavalry being under St advance of this great army was made with a deliberation in stroi with the hurried invasion of Maryland the year before.

Hooker, having learned of the advancing movement on the 121 withdrew his army from opposite Fredericksburg, and moved nc

[1] "The success of the Democratic—or, as it now styles itself, the Conservative pa so great as to manifest a change in public feeling among the most rapid and the r that has ever been witnessed even in this country. . . . The Conservative leaders persuaded that the result of the elections would be accepted by the President as t people; that he would seek to terminate the war, not to push it to extremity; that deavor to effect a reconciliation with the South, and renounce the idea of subjecting ating them." (*Dispatch of Lord Lyons*, November 17, 1862.)—The minister indeed that at that moment "the Conservative party were calling loudly for a more vigorou of the war;" but he adds, "I thought I perceived a desire to put an end to the war, ev of losing the Southern States altogether." He goes on to affirm that while they "w ble, obtain an armistice without the aid of foreign governments, they would be dispc an offer of mediation, if it appeared to be the only means of putting a stop to hostili

[2] Pollard (*Lost Cause*, 402) gives the numbers as 75,000 infantry and 15,000 cav the Confederate government never published official returns of the strength of its arm ment must be conjectural. I think it fully 10,000 too low. The captured returns t are wanting for Lee's army for the month of June, which would have given its stren movement commenced. At the close of May the numbers of this army were 88,75 of whom 68,352 were "present for duty." But it is clear that during the ensuing considerably augmented. The statement in the text is based upon the following da

I. It has been shown that after the close of the actions at Chancellorsville, Lee had clusive of 9000 wounded, 47,000 infantry and artillery, and 3000 cavalry. It may be of the wounded 6000 would in the ensuing six weeks be able to return to duty. Th him, apart from re-enforcements, 56,000 men. The re-enforcements consisted mai street's three corps, which had been sent south of Richmond, and rejoined the Arm Virginia late in May and early in June. The captured returns show that in Mar

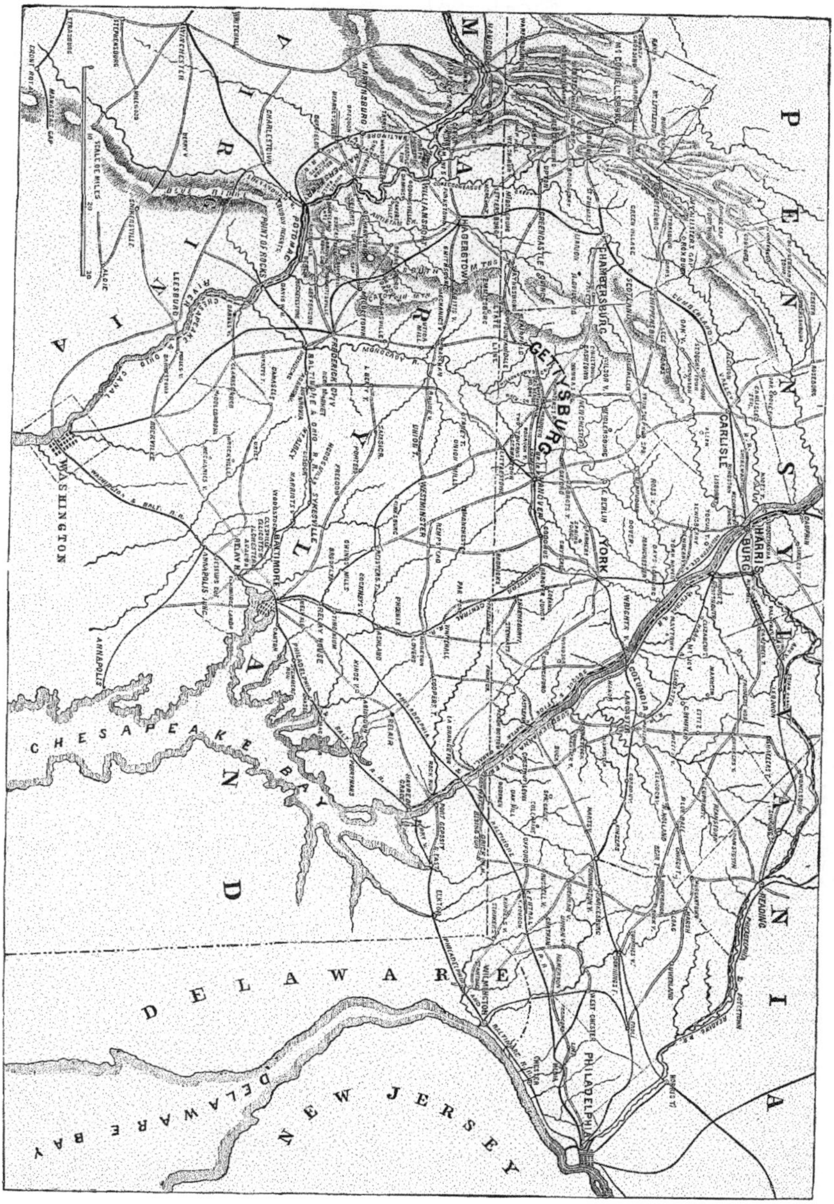
PENNSYLVANIA
MARYLAND
VIRGINIA
DELAWARE
NEW JERSEY
CHESAPEAKE BAY
DELAWARE BAY
GETTYSBURG
HARRISBURG
CARLISLE
CHAMBERSBURG
HAGERSTOWN
YORK
HANOVER
WESTMINSTER
FREDERICK CITY
BALTIMORE
WASHINGTON
PHILADELPHIA
WILMINGTON
LEESBURG
ANNAPOLIS
SCALE OF MILES

BURNING THE BRIDGE OVER THE SUSQUEHANNA, COLUMBIA, PENN.

as to cover Washington. A. P. Hill forthwith left Fredericksburg, and joined the main army at Culpepper. Lee then pushed forward his divisions one by one, and by different routes, all centring upon Winchester, the key of the lower valley of the Shenandoah. Milroy, with 7000 men, had been long lying at Winchester. On the 12th of June he began to get tidings that the enemy were pressing down upon him, in what force he could not learn; but on the next day his doubts were solved by authentic tidings that the Confederates were advancing in overwhelming force. Then was the time to retreat; but this was delayed until the 15th, when, before dawn, he destroyed what he could of his stores, spiked his guns, and started for Harper's Ferry; the Confederates having in the mean while sent a strong force, which gained his rear, while he was also attacked in front. Milroy's whole force was dispersed, and 2300 of them were captured.[1] The others made their way, utterly broken, to and across the Potomac; some of them never halted in their wild flight until they had reached Chambersburg, far into Pennsylvania. Ewell's corps, which had gone on in advance, followed on and entered Maryland, the cavalry pushing as far as Chambersburg.

Lee had supposed that this partial movement would cause Hooker to leave Virginia and cross the Potomac to defend the threatened North, rendering an attack upon Washington feasible. But Hooker was not entrapped by this manœuvre, and kept his army near the old battle-field of Manassas, effectually covering Washington. Lee now began to move the corps of Hill and Longstreet down the Valley of the Shenandoah, along the west side of the Blue Ridge, Hooker being on the east side. The cavalry of each army, sent out as feelers, came into frequent collision, sometimes in considerable force, the advantage, on the whole, being with the Federals.[2] Lee hoped by all these movements to draw Hooker farther from Washington, which had now become his base, and even to induce him to pass the Blue Ridge and venture an attack. The opportunity seemed, indeed, a favorable one. For some days the Confederate army was stretched from Culpepper a hundred miles to the Potomac. To strike that long line somewhere seemed feasible. So thought the President. "If," he wrote to Hooker, "the head of Lee's army is at Martinsburg, and the tail of it on the plank road between Fredericksburg and Chancellorsville, the animal must be very slim somewhere; could you not break him?"[3] But Hooker determined not to make the attempt. In his view, the wisest course was to move his army on a concentric but inner circle to that followed by the main body of the enemy, and thus be enabled to thwart his general design, whatever that should prove to be. Any slight advantages which he might hope to gain over portions of the hostile force would be more than counterbalanced by the necessity which would be involved of marching his army away from the point where it was most needed. Although the rear of the Confederate army was so far away from its front, it was moving to unite, and there was no probability that a Union force could strike it strongly any where without encountering a superior force. For the time the true policy was that adopted by Hooker, and thereafter for a time by Meade, to be governed in his operations by those of the main body of the hostile army.[1]

Lee having failed in finding an opportunity to strike a blow at the Union army in Virginia, or inducing Hooker to assail him upon unfavorable terms, now resolved to transform the raiding operations in Pennsylvania into a serious invasion by his whole army. Longstreet's and Hill's corps pushed rapidly to the Potomac. On the 24th and 25th, the river, now so low as to be easily fordable, was passed at Williamsport and Shepherdstown, almost within sight of the battle-field of Antietam, and the columns, uniting at Hagerstown, pressed forward toward Chambersburg. Hooker's course was now clear. On the 26th his army crossed the Potomac at Edwarde's Ferry, the point where Lee had crossed into Maryland nine months before, and headed toward Frederick City. Lee had advanced so far from the Potomac as to leave his base of communications and supply greatly exposed. Hooker's plan was in the first place to assail these rather than to precipitate a battle; for every day would weaken the invaders, while it would give him new strength. He now, more urgently than ever, urged that every soldier within reach should be added to his available army.

It so happened that there were 10,000 men at Harper's Ferry, under French, who had not long before been put in command there. The place, as we have before seen, was utterly worthless for either side. For all military purposes, these men might as well have been a thousand miles away as at Harper's Ferry. The strength of the two opposed armies was so nearly equal that 10,000 men might make the difference between victory and defeat. The force at Harper's Ferry had been in a manner placed under the command of Hooker; but, in reply to an inquiry whether there was any reason why the place should not be abandoned, and the troops there brought into use, Halleck rejoined that much expense and labor had been incurred in fortifying the works there and thereabout, and he could not approve of their abandonment except in case of absolute necessity. Hooker thereupon sent back to Halleck two dispatches at the same time. One, which was to be shown to the President and the Secretary of War, briefly reiterated his views as to the retention of Harper's Ferry; the other contained his resignation of the command of the Army of the Potomac,[2] evidently intended to be acted upon in case the former should be unavailing. Halleck replied forthwith that Hooker had been appointed to the command by the President, to whom the application for being relieved must be referred. Brief time was taken for consideration, for on that same day, already far advanced into the afternoon, Hooker's resignation had been accepted, and the command of the Army of the Potomac formally assigned to General Meade.

Viewed simply as an isolated act, this sudden resignation of Hooker at a moment when the two armies were inevitably approaching a decisive con-

[1] "In a short time the whole infantry force, amounting to more than 2300 men, with eleven stand of colors, surrendered, the cavalry alone escaping. These operations resulted in the expulsion of the enemy from the Valley, the capture of 4000 prisoners with a corresponding number of small-arms, 28 pieces of superior artillery, about 300 wagons, and as many horses. Our entire loss was 47 killed, 219 wounded, and 3 missing."—*Lee's Rep.*, *MS.*

[2] "On the 17th the enemy's cavalry encountered two brigades of ours under General Stuart, near Aldie, and was driven back with loss. The next day the engagement was renewed, the Federal cavalry being strongly supported by infantry, and General Stuart was in turn compelled to retire."—*Lee's Rep.* "On the 21st the enemy attacked with infantry and cavalry, and obliged General Stuart to fall back to the gaps of the mountains. In these engagements the cavalry sustained a loss of 510 killed, wounded, and missing."—*Ibid.*, *MS.*

[3] Lincoln to Hooker, June 14th (*Com. Rep.*, ii., 260). Two days later (*Ibid.*, 160) Lincoln recurs to the same topic: "Your idea may be right, probably is; still, it pains me to abandon the fair chance presented of breaking the enemy's lengthy and necessarily slow line, stretched now from the Rappahannock to Pennsylvania."

[1] When A. P. Hill's corps "took up its line of march, following those of Ewell and Longstreet, I was clearly of the opinion that it was my duty to be governed in my operations by those of the whole rebel army, and not a part of it, and accordingly I directed my marches with that view."—Hooker, in *Com. Rep.*, ii., 161.

[2] These dispatches both bear date June 27, 1 P.M. They were received almost at the same moment, 2.55 and 3 P.M. (See *Com. Rep.*, ii., 174, 292.)—No. 1. "I have received your telegram in regard to Harper's Ferry. I found 10,000 men here in condition to take the field. Here they are of no earthly account. They can not defend a ford of the river; and, as far as Harper's Ferry is concerned, there is nothing of it. As for the fortifications, the work of the troops, they remain when the troops are withdrawn. No enemy will ever take possession of them. This is my opinion. All the public property could have been secured to-night, and the troops marched to where they could have been of some service. Now they are but a bait for the rebels, should they return. I beg that this may be presented to the Secretary of War and his Excellency the President."—No. 2. "My original instructions require me to cover Harper's Ferry and Washington. I have now imposed upon me, in addition, an enemy in my front of more than my number. I beg to be understood that I am unable to comply with this condition with the means at my disposal, and earnestly request that I may at once be relieved from the position that I occupy."

flict would seem uncalled for and unjustifiable. The immediate occasion was not of sufficient consequence to warrant a step which involved such grave consequences. But the question now mooted as to the troops at Harper's Ferry was but the culminating point of a long course of discord. Hooker knew that Halleck had opposed and twice defeated his appointment to the command of the Army of the Potomac. He perceived, or thought he perceived, a fixed determination to thwart him in every way.[1] This ill-feeling had by this time grown to such a height, and assumed a form so personal, that it was clearly out of the question for the two men to act together in the positions which they occupied. Halleck took early occasion to vent his spite. There was an order prohibiting officers from visiting Washington without permission. Hooker, four days after his supercedure, went to the capital. He had hardly left his carriage ten minutes when he was put under arrest by order of the general-in-chief. How many opportunities were lost, and how many lives sacrificed by the personal ill feeling and professional jealousy which had sprung up among officers high in rank in the army, it would be vain to inquire.

The country and the army were astounded on the 28th of June by the announcement that the command of the Army of the Potomac had been relinquished by Hooker and was conferred upon Meade. Despite the misadventure at Chancellorsville, Hooker still retained the confidence of the soldiers who served under him. There was a kind of self-assured confidence in the man which begat confidence in others. Of Meade, who was so suddenly called upon to replace him, less had been heard than of almost any other corps commander in the army. Just a year before he had commanded a brigade at Cold Harbor. Four days later his brigade made its mark at Frazier's Farm. Glimpses were caught of him at South Mountain and Antietam. At Fredericksburg he won a partial success, but this was lost sight of in the disasters which accompanied and followed. At Chancellorsville, his corps, through no fault of his, hardly touched the fight. He had little of that imposing personal presence to which McClellan owed all, and Hooker much of power. His aspect was that of a scholar rather than of a captain. Those who knew him best could only say that wherever tried he had never been found wanting, but that he had never been subjected to a great trial. If the question had been simply whether Meade should replace Hooker, it would have been difficult to find a man to favor the change. But things had suddenly come to such a condition that a great change must be made at a critical moment. Either Halleck must be displaced as general-in-chief, or Hooker must vacate the command of the Army of the Potomac. The smaller the change at the urgent crisis involved the less of apparent peril, and so Hooker's request to be released from command was promptly granted. What special reasons fixed the choice upon Meade as his successor can only be conjectured. There were no open cliques of generals in his favor, and consequently no ostensible ones against him. Herein, perhaps, lies the secret.[2]

No man in or out of the army could have been more surprised than was Meade when the tidings came that he was appointed to the command. He took upon himself his new duties in a quiet way, which strongly contrasted with the self-distrust of Burnside and the self-assertion of Hooker. The movements planned by his predecessor were carried out by the same staff. Only that the orders were issued over a new name, the army would scarcely have known that it had a new commander. The only important changes made were that Hancock was placed in command of the Second Corps, vacated by Couch's appointment to the Department of the Susquehanna, and Sykes took the Fifth, formerly led by Meade. Reynolds retained the First Corps, Sickles the Third, Sedgwick the Sixth, Howard the Eleventh, and Slocum the Twelfth.

Lee, having crossed the Potomac, pushed rapidly forward into Pennsylvania with his whole force. Cutting loose from its supplies, his army was to live upon the country. But Lee ordered that supplies should be extorted in an orderly manner, upon formal requisitions duly made, payment being tendered in Confederate notes; if these were declined, certificates were to be given showing the amount and value of the property thus taken. If the local authorities neglected to meet these requisitions, the required supplies were to be seized. These requisitions were frequently onerous. Thus the town of York, with but 7000 inhabitants, was called upon, among other things, for 165 barrels of flour, 3500 pounds of sugar, 32,000 pounds of beef, 2000 pairs of boots or shoes, and $100,000 in cash. Probably the whole borough did not contain this amount of stores and money. At all events, only a quarter of the money could be raised.

[1] "Almost every request I made of General Halleck was refused. It was often remarked that it was of no use for me to make a request, as that of itself would be sufficient cause for General Halleck to refuse it. . . . . . . I may add as my conviction that if the general-in-chief had been in the rebel interest, it would have been impossible for him, restrained as he was by the President and the Secretary of War, to have added to the embarrassment he caused me from the moment I took command of the Army of the Potomac to the time I surrendered it."—Hooker, in *Com. Rep.*, ii., 175.

[2] "I have said that there were no "open" cliques in favor of Meade as opposed to Hooker. That there was some secret opposition to Hooker's retention of the command soon after Chancellorsville is clear. On the 14th of May the President writes to Hooker (*Com. Rep.*, ii., 160): "I have some painful intimations that some of your corps and division commanders are not giving you their entire confidence. This would be ruinous if true."—General Couch was the ranking officer of the corps commanders. But early in June he was detached from the Army of the Potomac and placed in command of the "Department of the Susquehanna," that is, of Pennsylvania. This change seems to have been quite acceptable to Hooker: "I can give a command to General Couch," telegraphed the Secretary of War to Hooker on the 9th of June; "I can spare General Couch," returned Hooker at once (*Com. Rep.*, ii., 252). Just after the battle of Gettysburg, Halleck notified Couch that Meade had the command of all the troops in the Department of the Susquehanna, and that his orders must be obeyed. To which Couch rejoined: "General Meade's wishes, instructions, and recommendations have been carried out so far as practicable. As I prominently mentioned that officer for his present position, it may be inferred that I would show no lukewarmness in carrying out his orders" (*Com. Rep.*, ii., 501).—Now, as there seems to have been no time between the resignation of Hooker and the appointment of Meade in which Couch, then in Pennsylvania, could have been consulted, it must be presumed that this "prominent mention" by Couch was made at an earlier day.

This formidable invasion aroused the most intense apprehension. Directly after the rout of Milroy at Winchester, the President issued a proclamation calling for 100,000 militia from the nearest states. Of these, Pennsylvania was to furnish 50,000, Ohio 30,000, Maryland 10,000, West Virginia 10,000. These were called out for six months, unless sooner discharged. Besides these, the Governor of New York was asked to order out 20,000. Within a few days New York sent nearly 16,000, of whom 14,000 were from the Empire City. Their absence gave opportunity for the fearful riots which ensued in the city of New York about the middle of July. In Pennsylvania, which was immediately threatened, the President's call was slightly responded to. In that state the militia system was so imperfect that there was not a brigade or regimental organization in existence. The governor called for 60,000 volunteers, who would be "mustered into the service of the state for ninety days, but would be required to serve only so much of the period of the muster as the safety of the people and the honor of the state should require." About 25,000 in all responded to these calls from Pennsylvania, but so tardily that not a man of them ever came in sight of the enemy. The Pennsylvania militia did not fire a gun to relieve their state from invasion. Some of the New York regiments came up in time to touch the van of the enemy as they halted in their advance. In New Jersey a few thousand men were raised, and a few companies actually went as far as Harrisburg. About 2000 were furnished by Delaware to guard the railroads in Maryland. The other states which were called upon did absolutely nothing. Before, indeed, any of the militia could be brought up, the battle of Gettysburg had been fought, and the crisis was past; for events had been so shaping themselves as to render a great battle inevitable. The time and place of this was determined more by accident and the physical character of the region than by any purpose on the part of either commander.

The South Mountain, a continuation of the Blue Ridge of Virginia, runs northward through a corner of Maryland far into Pennsylvania. Lee had crossed the Potomac on the west of this ridge, Hooker on the east. The line of march of the two armies was nearly parallel, the mountains between them, and each commander for a few days knew little of the movements of the other. Meade in the mean time followed out the plans conceived by Hooker. Lee, having some days the start, was considerably northward of Meade; Ewell, in the advance, was as far as Carlisle, and preparing to move toward Harrisburg, the capital of Pennsylvania, while Longstreet and Hill halted at Chambersburg. Meade had gone about half as far from the Potomac, and was in such a position that, by a rapid march to the west through the unobstructed passes of the South Mountain, which his left column had almost reached, he could throw himself right in the rear of Lee, and effectually cut him off from his supplies, wholly isolating him in a hostile country. Tidings of this movement reached Lee on the night of the 28th of June. He saw at once that the great invasion could be carried no farther, at least until he had destroyed the army which thus hung menacingly upon his flank and rear. The whole Confederate army was thereupon ordered to concentrate toward the enemy. The point of concentration was Gettysburg, beyond South Mountain. Thither Longstreet and Hill were to march eastward from Chambersburg, and Ewell southward from Carlisle.[1] Now Meade's left column, consisting of the corps of Reynolds and Howard—Sickles's corps, though not so far in advance, forming part thereof, with Buford's cavalry, had advanced farther northward than the remainder of the army, and on the 30th were close by Gettysburg. On that morning Meade learned that the enemy were moving against him. He thereupon resolved to concentrate his forces, which were now spread over many miles of country. The natural mode was to withdraw his advance, and bring up his centre and rear. His leading purposes were to compel the enemy to withdraw from the Susquehanna, and then to give or receive battle at the first favorable opportunity. The position which he selected as most likely to be the scene of conflict was on Pipe Creek, a little stream fifteen miles southeast from Gettysburg.[2]

When Lee appointed Gettysburg as the place of rendezvous for his army, he knew nothing of its supreme strategical importance. Meade, also, knew

[1] "Preparations were made for the advance upon Harrisburg; but on the night of the 29th [so printed, but it should clearly be the night of the 28th; that is, the night before the 29th] information was received that the Federal army, having crossed the Potomac, was advancing northward, and that the head of the column had reached the South Mountain. As our communications with the Potomac were thus menaced, it was resolved to prevent his farther progress in that direction by concentrating our army on the east side of the mountains. Accordingly, Longstreet and Hill were directed to proceed from Chambersburg to Gettysburg, to which point Ewell was also instructed to march from Carlisle."—*Lee's Rep.*

[2] "I determined to move my army as promptly as possible on the main line from Frederick to Harrisburg, extending my wings on both sides of that line as far as I could consistently with the safety and rapid concentration of that army, and to continue my movement until I either encountered the enemy or had reason to believe that he was about to advance upon me; my object being, at all hazards, to force him to loose his hold on the Susquehanna, and meet me in battle at some point. It was my firm determination to give battle wherever and as soon as I could possibly find the enemy, modified, of course, by such considerations as must govern every general officer. On the night of the 30th I had become satisfied that the enemy was apprised of my movements; that he had relinquished his hold on the Susquehanna; that he was concentrating his forces, and that I might expect to come in contact with him in a very short time—when and where I could not at that moment tell. I instructed my engineers to select some general ground, having reference to the existing position of the army, by which, in case the enemy should advance upon me across the South Mountain, I might be able, by rapid movement of concentration, to occupy this position, and be prepared to give him battle upon my own terms. The general line of Pipe Creek was selected, and a preliminary order issued notifying the corps commanders that such line might possibly be adopted, and directing them how they might move their corps, and what their positions should be along this line. This order was issued on the night of the 30th of June, possibly on the morning of the 1st of July; certainly before any positive information had reached me that the enemy had crossed the mountain and were in conflict with any part of my force." (Meade, in *Com. Rep.*, ii., 330.)—This statement is given in full, as it sets at rest the assertion often made that Meade proposed to retreat before the enemy, and that he was forced to fight at Gettysburg by an unauthorized attack made by Reynolds. His purpose of assuming the line of Pipe Creek was contingent upon circumstances which might or might not arise. It was, as will be seen, accident, so far as any previous purpose on the part of either commander was concerned, that made Gettysburg the scene of the conflict—the speedy occurrence of which, somewhere hard by, had become inevitable, unless, indeed, Lee should consent to retreat without having fairly attempted any thing—and this he was by no means inclined to do.

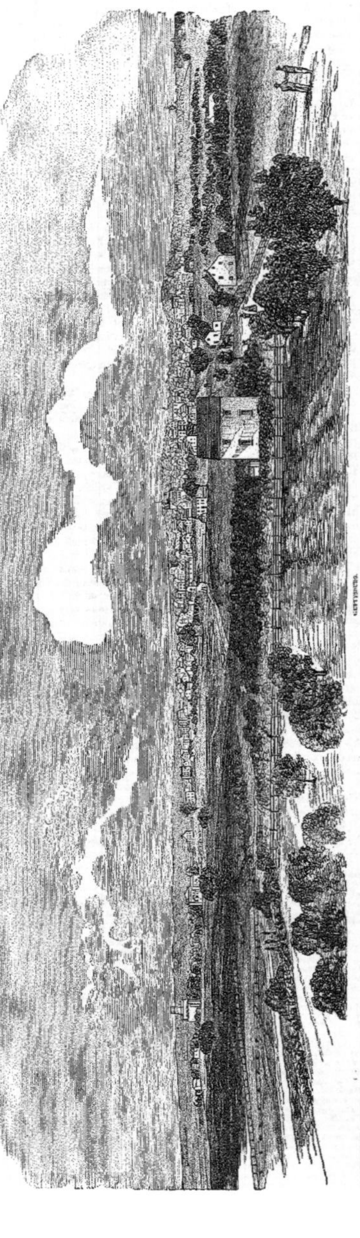

GETTYSBURG.

quite as little thereof. "It was a place," as he told the Congressional Committee on the Conduct of the War, "which I had never seen in my life, and had no more knowledge of than you have now." Yet it would seem that a glance at a map should have revealed its importance. This little town occupies, as it were, the hub of a wheel, from which roads, or spokes, radiate in every direction: northwestward toward Chambersburg; northeastward toward Harrisburg and Philadelphia; southwestward toward the Potomac; southeastward toward Baltimore. Whosoever held Gettysburg, held, if he knew it, the key to a campaign. It so chanced that one soldier had happened to study the topographical features of this region, and he had made up his mind that Gettysburg was the one spot whereat, if so it could be, to have a fight. And it so happened, also, that this man was the only one, who, as things stood, could have so ordered events that the fight should have happened just then and there. That man was Alfred Pleasonton, now commanding the cavalry corps; the man to whom primarily it was owing that the fierce rush of Jackson had been stayed at Chancellorsville. In the distribution of his troopers, he had sent the strongest division, that of Buford, to cover the left flank of the army, that is, Reynolds's column, which was nearest the enemy. His order to Buford was to hold Gettysburg to the last extremity, until the army could be concentrated there.[1] Buford reached Gettysburg early on the morning of the last day of June, in advance of the infantry of Reynolds's column, whereof the First Corps, properly his own, but now under the immediate command of Doubleday, and the Eleventh, Howard's, encamped that night four miles from Gettysburg.

WEDNESDAY, JULY 1.

On the morning of the 1st of July Buford pushed his troopers northwestward. At the same time the advance of the Confederate army was approaching from that direction. Lee had moved his force slowly from Chambersburg and Carlisle, not imagining that any considerable Union force was in the neighborhood of Gettysburg, for, as it chanced, Stuart, with his vigilant cavalry, was far away. He had been left behind in Virginia to harass the Union rear, and was then to cress into Maryland. This crossing was made far to the south of the point where Hooker went over, so that Stuart found the whole Union army between him and Lee, and he could reach Carlisle, the place appointed for rendezvous, only by making a wide circuit. When he came there on the 1st of July, he found the place evacuated, and the army on the way to Gettysburg, whither he hastened, but not in time to take any part in the action of the first two days. Reynolds set his command in motion toward Gettysburg. He had evidently discerned the supreme necessity of preventing the enemy from seizing this point.[2] No one who looked upon the ground could fail to perceive this.

The quiet town of Gettysburg nestles in a little hollow ten miles east of the South Mountain range. The surrounding country is rough and broken, granite ridges cropping up all around. This granite had been, in the formative period of the earth's history, flung up through the soft shale, which, worn away by water-currents, left exposed the bare ridges of the harder stone. The general course of these ridges is north and south; they are not continuous for any great extent; and are not unfrequently cast into irregular forms. Looking westward from the town at a distance of half a mile, one sees a long, wooded height, its centre-crowned by the buildings of a Theological Seminary, whence it receives the name of Seminary Ridge. Looking southward, at the distance of a mile, is the rounded extremity of another ridge, broken into several separate hills. Ascending the nearest of these, the ridge is seen falling away for a space, then, at the distance of three miles, rising again into a broken spur, closing in a rocky, wooded peak. This whole range bears the name of Cemetery Ridge, for upon it was the burying-ground where rest generations of the dwellers of the quiet town. But now, hard by is a great City of the Dead, made populous in three short days. This ridge, running first northward, then, with a sharp curve, eastward, then, again, bending to the south, is, in shape, not unlike a fish-hook. Each of the rugged hills which rise from the clearly-marked line of the crest bears its own name. That at the extremity of the stem of the hook is Round Top, with Little Round Top its prolongation. Cemetery Hill is at the bend; Culp's Hill forms the barb. These two ridges are now historic, for on Cemetery Ridge the Union Army took its position, the Confederate force being drawn up on Seminary Ridge. The valley between them, half a mile wide at its narrowest point, near the town, then gradually spreading southward to twice that breadth, consists of cultivated fields, interspersed with patches of woodland. In these fields and woodlands, and up the rough slopes of Cemetery Ridge, was waged for two days the mightiest conflict of the war.

On Wednesday morning, July 1, Hill, who, leading the Confederate advance, had encamped the previous night half a dozen miles west of Gettysburg, learned, to his surprise, that the town was occupied by the Union cavalry. What force of infantry lay behind he could not know. He put his divisions in motion, and sent back to urge forward Longstreet's corps, which was yet fifteen miles in the rear. Buford had meanwhile gone out two

[1] Pleasonton, in *Con. Rep.*, ii., 359.

[2] Otherwise we can not explain his conduct in acting in direct contradiction to the order which he had just received to fall back in the opposite direction to Pipe Creek. It was clearly one of those cases in which a subordinate commander was justified in disregarding a positive order, which he knew must have been given in ignorance of the real position of affairs. Sickles, later in the day, did precisely the same thing. He was some fourteen miles behind Reynolds, and had also been ordered to fall back; but, learning that an action was going on at Gettysburg, he marched directly thither. "I assumed," he says, "that this new fact [the action then going on] was not known to General Meade when the order to retreat was issued. The emergency did not admit of the delay that would have been required to communicate with General Meade, who was ten miles distant. I moved to Gettysburg on my own responsibility. As soon as I had determined to do that, I sent to General Meade informing him of what I had done, and expressed my anxiety to have his sanction of it. I received a communication from him informing me that he approved of my course."—*Con. Rep.*, ii., 296.

JOHN BUFORD.

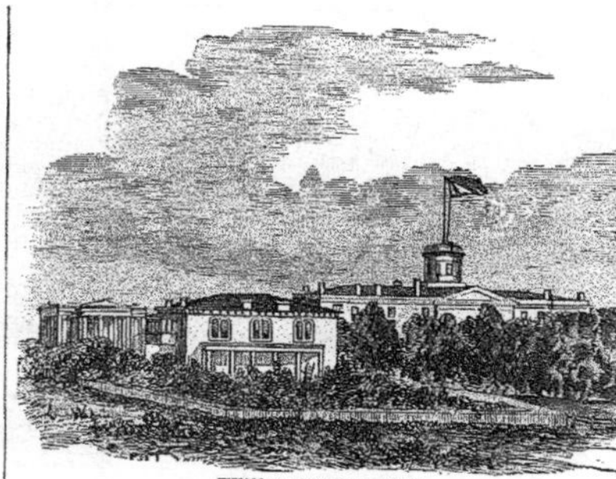

THEOLOGICAL SEMINARY, GETTYSBURG.

miles in that direction, crossing Seminary Ridge. At nine o'clock Hill's leading division, that of Heth, came upon Buford, who, knowing that Reynolds was on the march, resolved to contest the Confederate advance. Unlimbering the guns of his horse artillery, and deploying his troopers, he held the enemy briefly in check, but was soon forced back to the crest of the ridge. The sound of his guns quickened the march of Reynolds, whose leading division, under Wadsworth, 4000 strong, was now within a mile of Gettysburg. These were soon formed, under fire, in line of battle. The action had scarcely opened when Reynolds fell dead, shot through the head by a rifle-ball. There were but few men who could not have been better spared. There were not wanting those who had begun to look upon him as the most promising general in the Union army. Doubleday, who had come up, now took command; but he brought no re-enforcements to Wadsworth, for the other divisions of Reynolds's corps, and the whole of Howard's, were yet two hours' march behind. For two hours this one division maintained the fight, and then began slowly to give way. The enemy pressed on, a part of Archer's brigade so eagerly that they were isolated. Meredith swung round his "Iron Brigade," and captured 800 men, including their commander. Cutler's brigade of this division was now sorely pressed, and fell back; but two regiments of the Confederates, advancing along a deep cutting for an unfinished railway, were swept upon by a flank movement, and, shut up in this gorge, were forced to surrender. Thus far the contest had been waged between a single division on each side. The balance of success was against the Confederates. The two remaining divisions of Reynolds's corps now came up, closely followed by Howard's corps. Howard assumed command of the field.

But still heavier re-enforcements were coming up to the aid of Heth. First came Pender's division of Hill's corps, northwestward from toward Chambersburg; then from the north, Ewell from toward Carlisle, pressing down upon the Union right. They struck Robinson's division of Reynolds's corps. Their first blow was unsuccessful, and three North Carolina regiments were captured. Howard, leaving Steinwehr's division of his corps in reserve on the Cemetery Ridge behind Gettysburg, pushed Schurz and Barlow forward to meet the advance of Ewell. The roads by which the Federal troops had advanced diverge from Gettysburg like the spokes of a wheel, so that at each step the line grew thinner and thinner; while the Confederates, coming to the centre along these same spokes, were concentrating at every moment. As the afternoon wore away, Ewell's whole corps, and two thirds of that of Hill, fully 50,000 strong, were steadily pressing down upon the two corps of Reynolds and Howard, numbering at the outset not more than 21,000 men, including the division of 4000 left in reserve, which was not brought forward.[1] Howard now sent back to Sickles, a dozen miles away to the south, urging him to come up to his relief. Sickles

[1] "I do not believe that our force actually engaged, belonging to the two corps, amounted to over 14,000 men. There was a reserve of 3000 or 4000 of the Eleventh Corps, which did not join actively in the fight. It fired some shots from Cemetery Hill, but the most of them fell short into our own front line." (Doubleday, in *Com. Rep.*, ii., 309.)—Doubleday adds: "According to the reports rendered to me, we [i. e., apparently Reynolds's corps] entered the fight with 8500 men, and came out with 2450." I suspect that there is here some error in the printing of these figures; for Wadsworth states that in his division "about 4000 men went into action," and that of these, on the next morning he had but about 1600 men to answer to their names. It is hardly to be supposed that the two remaining divisions of this corps were so greatly inferior in numbers to any of the others. I think it safer, on many grounds, to estimate the six divisions of these two corps at 8500 each.

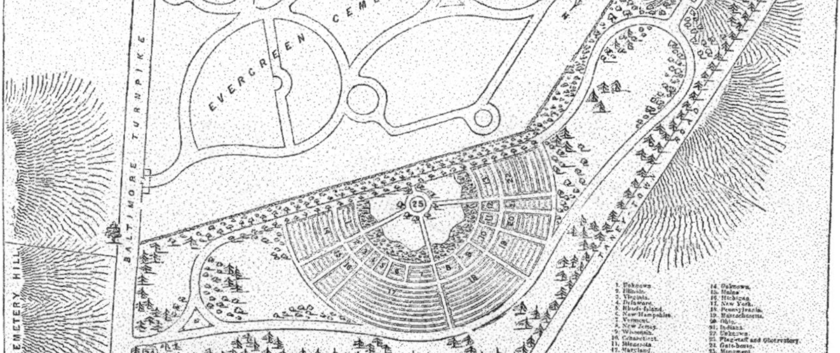

PLAN OF THE SOLDIERS' CEMETERY AT GETTYSBURG.

THE WHEAT-FIELD WHERE REYNOLDS FELL.

put his corps in motion, but a forced march only enabled him to reach Gettysburg after the action was over.

At an hour past noon, Meade, who, with his column of the centre, was at Taneytown, fourteen miles southeast of Gettysburg, learned that a fight was going on, and that Reynolds had fallen. He perceived "that the matter was being precipitated very heavily upon him." Of Gettysburg himself he knew nothing, and the first thing to be done was to ascertain whether it was a place whereat to give or receive battle. Calling to Hancock, the corps commander in whom he most confided, he ordered him to hurry to the field and take command there. Hancock was outranked by Howard, who was there, and by Sickles, who might be there; but it was no time to regard the niceties of military etiquette. Hancock sprang into an ambulance, that he might study the maps on his way, and in two hours was on the field, in time to see a lost battle, which, indeed, bore the aspect of a rout;[1] for Rodes's division of Ewell's corps had thrust itself right into a wide gap between the right of the First and the left of the Eleventh Union Corps, folding completely around the right of the First, pressing it back toward the Seminary. Here, behind a slight rail intrenchment, a stand was made long enough to permit the trains and ambulances to get off. Doubleday threw his personal guard of twoscore men into the Seminary building, whose quiet walls had never before witnessed any thing more stirring than debates upon points of theological controversy. But by this time the whole region was filled with the advancing lines of the enemy, double, sometimes triple. When the remnants of this gallant corps finally abandoned their position, they fell back to Gettysburg, right between two lines of the enemy. The Eleventh Corps at the same time was driven back to the same point, and the two retreating columns became entangled in the streets. The First Corps, being a little in advance, got well through. The Eleventh was struck heavily by Ewell's advance, and three fourths of the survivors of its two divisions engaged were made prisoners.[2] This battle cost the two Union corps not less than 10,000 men, of whom half were killed or wounded. Well-nigh half of the killed and wounded fell upon Wadsworth's division of 4000, which had for six hours withstood the enemy. The loss of the Confederates was very heavy. Wadsworth thought that his division inflicted more injury than it received.[3]

[1] "I arrived on the ground not later than half past three o'clock. I found that, practically, the fight was then over. The rear of our column, with the enemy in pursuit, was then coming through the town of Gettysburg. General Howard was on Cemetery Hill, and there had evidently been an attempt on his part to stop and form some of his troops there."—Hancock, in *Com. Rep.*, ii., 405.

[2] Lee claims to have taken here 5000 prisoners; these must have been mainly from the Eleventh, for Wadsworth says (*Com. Rep.*, ii., 413): "Very few of my division were taken prisoners; but a great many prisoners were taken on the right from the Eleventh Corps, and from one division of the First Corps that went into position on the right."

[3] "I am sure that the slaughter on the side of the enemy was greater than on our own side on the first day. I know that we almost annihilated one or two brigades that came against us." (*Com. Rep.*, ii., 416.)—More than 2000 prisoners are claimed to have been taken from the Confederates.

When Hancock rode up to Gettysburg, he bore with him the responsibility of all that was to follow; for he was charged not only to take the command of whatever force he should find there, but to decide whether that force should fall back, or whether the whole army should be brought forward and concentrated there. In a brief interval, what remained of the First and Eleventh Corps were assembled on the rocky ridge fronting Gettysburg, and presented so imposing an appearance as to cause Lee to hesitate to assail them. Looking back in the light of what is now known, the decision of the Confederate commander was most erroneous; but for one knowing only what he could then have known, it was the only safe one. Of his three corps only two had come up—Longstreet's, the strongest of all, was still behind. What part of the Union force lay upon and behind that rugged ridge he could not know. So the attack was suspended, and the Confederate army paused, waiting to see what the next day should bring forth. Hancock sent back to Meade such a report as to determine him to fight at Gettysburg, and during the night all the army was set in motion for that point. Sickles had already arrived two hours before night set in. Hancock's corps, and Slocum's, with that of Meade, now commanded by Sykes, came up in the morning. Sedgwick's did not reach the ground till afternoon, after a fatiguing march of thirty-five miles.

When the Federal army was finally posted, Slocum was on the extreme right, on Culp's Hill, the barb of the fish-hook; next was the remnant of Wadsworth's division, Howard's corps, on Cemetery Hill; then, along the stem of the hook, the corps of Hancock and Sickles, with Sykes's and Sedgwick's on the extreme left, behind the rocky rampart of the Round Tops. Reynolds's corps, to the command of which Newton had now been appointed, was in reserve behind the centre of the whole line, which was three miles in extent, measured along the ridge; but, owing to its curving form, no part of it was an hour's march from any other. As the line was intended by Meade, two thirds of the entire force could in half an hour have been concentrated upon any point; but by a misapprehension, arising from the nature of the ground, Sickles took a position considerably in advance, and upon this movement hinged the battle of the day. The bulk of the Confederate force was drawn up upon the opposite Seminary Ridge, Longstreet's corps on the right, then Hill's in the centre, that of Ewell on the extreme left, being at the foot of Culp's Hill. This line, forming an exterior curve, was fully five miles long, there being, however, an interval of a mile between Ewell's right and Hill's left. The forces were about equal, each numbering from 70,000 to 80,000 infantry and artillery.[1] The Federal po-

[1] Meade (in *Com. Rep.*, ii., 337) says: "Including all arms of the service, my strength was

MEADE'S HEADQUARTERS, CEMETERY RIDGE.

LEE'S HEADQUARTERS, SEMINARY RIDGE.

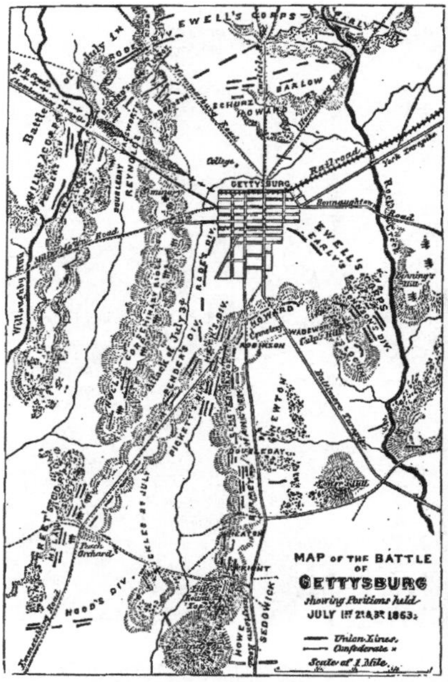

sition was very strong, its chief disadvantage being that a great portion of it was so broken and rocky as to allow not more than a third of the artillery to be brought into position. But this was counterbalanced by the advantage which it gave for infantry.

It was evident that Lee could not, for any time, retain his present position. He was far from his base of supply, and the country around would not long subsist his great army, even could he forage at will, as he had done in the fertile valley of the Cumberland; and, moreover, his foraging parties would be likely to be cut off in the mountain passes.[1] He was then shut up to a choice of one of three things. He must attack the enemy in their strong position, or he must draw them from it by continuing his march, and threatening Washington and Baltimore, or he must retreat to Virginia. The third course would be a complete abandonment of the enterprise which had been so deliberately undertaken; the second was strongly urged by Hood, but it would only be prolonging the suspense, for an action must soon take place somewhere, and the enemy would, beyond all doubt, become stronger every day.[2] He decided upon the first. The controlling reason is doubtless to be found in the temper of his army. They had won a series of great victories; among these they even counted Antietam. At Fredericksburg, with but a fraction of their available force, they had beaten Burnside, though here they had position in their favor. At Chancellorsville, with two thirds of their present numbers, they had foiled and driven off Hooker, whose force was known to be much larger than that now led by Meade. There they had successfully attacked the enemy in his intrenchments; why should they not do so now with equal success? Besides, it would seem that Lee, not without reason, greatly under-estimated the numbers in his front. The force which he had driven back the day before was certainly small, and there was nothing to indicate the great army which had been concentrated during the night, and now lay hidden behind that rocky crest.[3] So Longstreet was ordered to assail the extreme Federal left, while Ewell was at the same time to make a "demonstration on the right, to be converted into a real attack should opportunity offer."[1] The points of attack were fully five miles apart.

about 95,000." This I understand to be the entire force at the commencement of operations; but the losses on the previous day reduced this number by 10,000; the cavalry numbered about 10,000, but these took no part in the action of this day. Longstreet (see *ante*, p. 502) states that when the three Confederate corps were concentrated at Chambersburg, "the morning reports showed 67,000 bayonets," equivalent to about 75,000 officers and men; they had lost on the previous day not far from 5000. The Confederate artillery formed a separate corps, probably 5000 strong. I am not certain whether these are to be included in the 67,000 "bayonets." If they are not, then Lee's infantry and artillery would number about 75,000. Some thousands on each side were left behind with the trains. Thus, of the Confederates, Pickett's division was in the rear, and was not brought upon the field until the next day.

[1] *Lee's Rep.*

[2] "The enemy are here," said Lee to Hood, "and if we do not whip him he will whip us." Longstreet was opposed to making an attack this day; he wished to wait until Pickett's division should come up. "He did not want to walk with one boot off."—These facts were narrated after the close of the war by General Hood to General Crawford, from whom I receive them.

[3] We infer that Lee under-estimated the force of Meade, not only from the fact that he nowhere speaks of the "superior numbers of the enemy," but also from the nature of the attacks which he made on this and the following day.

Meade had intended, and so ordered, that his line should occupy the ridge directly between Cemetery Hill and Round Top; and from the point where he was, the course of this ridge was plain enough; but this crest, at its centre, where Sickles was to take position, is low, and, sinking down into a valley in front, rises at a few hundred yards into another wooded ridge, running diagonally to the one in its rear. To Sickles this seemed the position contemplated in the order, so he marched out upon it. This movement left a wide gap between him and Hancock, who was to have connected with his right. But he was also to rest his left upon Round Top. Now, as the course of this ridge is such that its extremity is a mile in advance of this hill, Sickles could only fulfill this condition by bending his left back, so that his line described two sides of a triangle. Birney's division formed the left, facing southwestward; Humphreys's division the right, facing northwestward. The Confederate right overlapped the Union left, and, swinging round to attack, completely enveloped it. At four o'clock, Meade, coming to the front, saw the perilous position in which Sickles had placed his corps, and commenced an order to withdraw, but before the sentence was completed the Confederates opened the attack, and it was thought that it was too late for any change of position. Meade determined to support Sickles, even at the hazard of disarranging all his carefully-formed plans. Troops were hurried up from every part of the field: from Slocum on the extreme right, Hancock in the centre, Sykes on the left; Sedgwick, whose corps, wearied by their long march of twenty hours, had been halted in the rear. Hood, in the mean time, had swung round his overlapping right, and penetrated the interval which separated Birney's extreme left from Little Round Top. This steep, rocky ridge, strangely enough, was not occupied. It was the key to the whole position; for, if the enemy could gain it, they could hold it, and a few guns planted there would enfilade the whole line[2] as far as Cemetery Hill. It was to Gettysburg what Hazle Grove was to Chancellorsville. They commenced scaling its rugged sides, for a time meeting no opposition except from its steep ascent. But it so happened that Warren, who, with no troops, had gone out as engineer to survey the field, reached the summit just in time to take in the peril of the situation. Hurrying back, he encountered Barnes's division of Sykes's corps marching out to the aid of Sickles. From this, Vincent's brigade and a single regiment of Ayres's were directed to scale the ridge on the side opposite to that up which the Confederates were climbing. The crest was reached from each side almost at once, the Federals a moment in advance. A fierce hand-to-hand fight ensued among the gray granite boulders piled up in wild confusion. The Confederates were flung back from the face of the hill, but, working around through the ravine at its base, some of them penetrated between the two Round Tops. Vincent's ammunition was exhausted, but the enemy were driven back by a bayonet charge, and, as darkness began to close in, this vital point was safe. Regiments from the Eastern, the Western, and the Central States were among the little band who, on this barren cliff, rendered possible the victory which was finally to crown the heights of Gettysburg.[3]

[1] *Lee's Rep.*

[2] "The enemy threw immense masses upon General Sickles's corps, which, advanced and isolated in this way, it was not in my power to support promptly. At the same time that they threw these immense masses upon General Sickles, a heavy column was thrown upon the Round Top Mountain, which was the key-point of my whole position. If they had succeeded in occupying that, it would have prevented me from holding any of the ground which I subsequently held to the last. Immediately upon the batteries opening I sent several staff officers to hurry up the column under General Sykes, of the Fifth Corps, then on its way, and which I had expected would have been there by that time. This column advanced, reached the ground in a short time, and fortunately General Sickles was enabled, by throwing a strong force upon Round Top Mountain, where a most desperate and bloody struggle ensued, to drive the enemy from it, and secure our foothold upon that important position." (Meade, in *Com. Rep.*, 332.)—"I went to what is called Bald Top, and from that point I could see the enemy's line of battle. I sent word to General Meade that we would at once have to occupy that place very strongly. He sent, as quickly as possible, a division of General Sykes's corps; but, before they arrived, the enemy's line of battle, I should think a mile and a half long, began to advance. The troops under General Sykes arrived barely in time to save Round Top Hill, and they had a very desperate fight to hold it."—Warren, *Ibid.*, 377.) See also Crawford, *Ibid.*, 470.

[3] The regiments which repelled the attack here were the 16th Michigan, the 44th and 140th New York, the 83d Pennsylvania, and the 20th Maine. Vincent was mortally wounded. Early next morning Meade telegraphed to Halleck: "I would respectfully request that Colonel Strong Vincent, 83d Pennsylvania Regiment, be made a brigadier general of volunteers for his gallant conduct on the field yesterday. He is mortally wounded, and it would gratify his friends as well as myself. It was my intention to have recommended him with others, should he live." The Secretary of War replied: "According to your request, Colonel Vincent has been appointed brigadier general for gallant conduct on the field."—*Con. Rep.*, ii., 492.

BREASTWORK IN THE WOODS.

BATTLE OF GETTYSBURG—

UNION POSITION NEAR THE CENTRE—

SUMMIT OF LITTLE ROUND TOP, JULY 3.

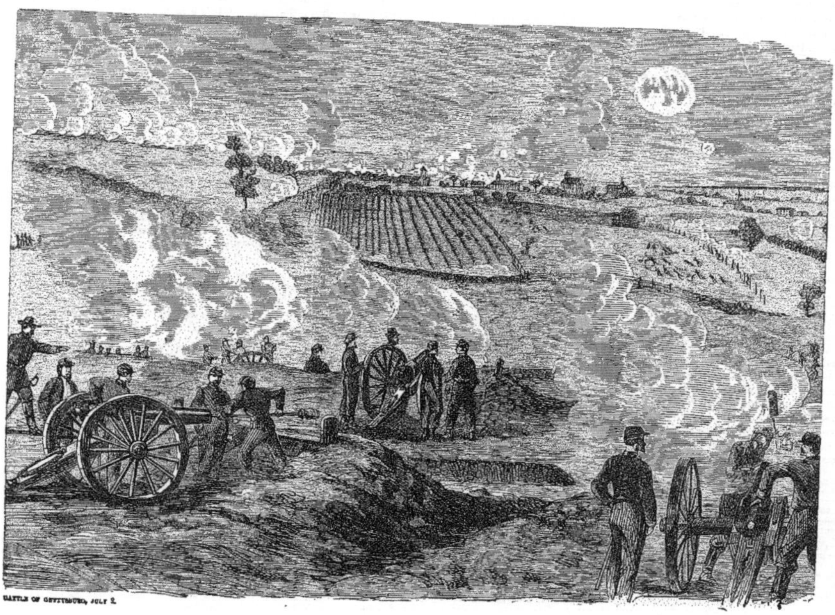

BATTLE OF GETTYSBURG, JULY 2.

Longstreet, with the remainder of Hood's division, soon joined by that of McLaws, was pressing fiercely upon Birney's division.[1] Sickles was borne from the field with his right leg shattered. Hood was also wounded, losing an arm. Birney's line was so thin that when the enemy attacked any point he was forced to draw regiments thither from other places. Caldwell and Ayres, of Sykes's corps, were sent to his support. They held the ground stubbornly, but were forced back, and their retreat soon became almost a rout.[2] Crawford, with the Pennsylvania Reserves, was now coming up. He ordered a charge with his whole division, himself leading. The color-bearer of his leading regiment had been shot down; Crawford leaned from his horse, snatched the flag, and, waving it over his head, shouting "Forward, Reserves!" dashed down the slope, and met the enemy's skirmishers advancing through the open wheat-field. They recoiled, and then fled back to their line of battle, posted behind a stone wall. Here they made a brief stand, but were driven back, with heavy loss, to a ridge in their rear. Crawford, having advanced without supports, halted, and took position behind the stone wall, the enemy holding the ridge in front and the woods on his left. It was now dusk, and the action closed upon the extreme left.

For a time Humphreys, whose division had formed Sickles's extreme right, had hardly been molested, but in front of him lay Hill's whole corps, ready to be launched upon him at any moment. When Birney found that he could no longer hold his ground, he ordered Humphreys to change front, so as to join with him upon a new line, or rather upon that from which the corps had originally advanced. Just then the enemy, who had opened a sharp artillery fire, pressed down upon his front and both flanks. Humphreys fell back deliberately, although suffering fearfully. In a few minutes he lost 2000 out of his 5000 men. By the time he reached the crest of the Cemetery Ridge the enemy were close upon him. Birney's broken force streamed beyond the crest. But the line had now been formed, patched up, indeed, by brigades from almost every corps. Some of these, as well as Birney's, had been fearfully cut up. The Confederates surged up against this line, but were encountered with a fire so fierce that they halted, then recoiled. Hancock now ordered a counter-charge. Humphreys's men, who had never broken, turned and joined in the charge. The enemy had exhausted the impulse of their onset, and were driven back to the position where they had fallen upon Sickles.

Ewell's demonstration on the right was delayed until the fight on the left was drawing to a close. Most of Slocum's corps had been brought away from Culp's Hill, and the Confederates succeeded in effecting a lodgment within the exterior intrenchments of the extreme Union right. Elsewhere the assault was repelled.

The Federal losses on this day were fully 10,000 men, of which three fifths fell upon Sickles's corps, which lost fully half its numbers.[3] The Confederate loss could not have been less, and was probably somewhat greater. The action of this day had decided nothing as to the ultimate issue. Lee indeed held the advanced line from which Sickles had been driven, but it was a line which Meade had never intended to occupy, and from which he would gladly have receded without a fight. Ewell's foothold upon the left had no significance unless it could be extended. Cemetery Ridge, from Round Top to Culp's Hill, remained intact. Still these "partial successes" encouraged Lee to hope that a stronger assault the next day might prove successful.[4]

FRIDAY, JULY 3.

Lee's general plan of attack was the same as that on the preceding day. Ewell was to press his advantage on the extreme right, while the main assault was to be upon the centre. But at daybreak Meade assumed the offensive against Ewell, and after a sharp contest, which lasted all the morning, drove him from the foothold which he had won within the Federal intrenchments on the extreme right. Now this point was fully two miles from the Seminary, where Lee had taken his post, and wholly hidden from it by the intervening heights. By some strange accident he received no tidings of the mishap which had befallen Ewell, and which, in the result, neutralized that third of the Confederate army on their left, leaving Meade at liberty to use almost his whole force, if need were, at any point. Supposing that Ewell would be able to aid by a strong demonstration, if not by a direct attack, upon the Union right, Lee resolved to assail the left centre, which held the low ridge between Cemetery Hill and Round Top.

All the morning was spent in preparation. The Confederate line along Seminary Ridge afforded an admirable position for artillery. Here, directly in front of the Union centre, at the distance of a mile, were concentrated a hundred and twenty guns. A great part of the Union line was so rugged that artillery could not be brought upon it, so that, although Meade had three hundred guns, he could reply with only about eighty at the same time. At an hour past noon the Confederates opened with all their batteries. For two hours, from a space of less than two miles, there was an incessant cannonade from two hundred guns. Upon no battle-field in the world's history had such a bombardment been witnessed. The Confederate fire told fearfully upon the Federal guns; many were disabled, but their place, as well as that of those which had expended their ammunition, was supplied by others brought up from the rear. The infantry, sheltered behind the crests, suffered little. The contest was not to be decided by artillery. At length Hunt, the chief of artillery, ordered the fire to be slowly slackened, partly "to see what the enemy were going to do, and also to make sure that there should be a sufficient supply of ammunition to meet the attack,"[1] of which this cannonade was the sure prelude.

It was now three o'clock. Lee, supposing that the Federal batteries had been silenced and the infantry disordered, now slackened his fire, and at the instant his infantry columns emerged from the woods which crown Seminary Hill and advanced down its slope. Pickett's strong division of Longstreet's corps had early that morning come upon the field. They were veteran Virginians, and had not been engaged. To them, supported by Wilcox, was assigned the right of the attacking force; Heth's division, supported by two brigades, had the left.[2] Lee had proposed to advance his artillery to the support of his infantry, but found too late that it had expended its ammunition.[3] In all, the attacking columns numbered about 18,000 men. They marched down the slope and across the plain in compact order and swiftly, but not with the fierce rush and wild yells which were wont to mark the Confederate onset. Never upon any stricken field since when, at Wagram, Massena wedged his column between the Austrian lines, was a more imposing spectacle than that now presented to friend and foe, watching from opposite crests, as this great column pressed on. All the Federal batteries from Round Top to Cemetery Hill opened upon them. Great gaps were plowed in their lines only to be closed again. At first the column headed for the left of the Union centre. Here Doubleday was posted. His division, which had suffered fearfully on the first day, had been strengthened by Stannard's Vermont brigade, and now numbered 2500 men. They were in lines five deep, and well strengthened by hasty intrenchments of rails and stones. The Confederates turned a little to their left, where Hancock's corps lay only two lines deep. In making this movement, Pickett's right wing, bending to his left, exposed his centre to a flank fire from Stannard, which threw it into some confusion,[4] and was the first of the disasters crowded into the space of a few minutes. Still the column pressed on, galled by artillery in front, and obliquely from batteries on Round Top and Cemetery Hill. Hancock's infantry withheld their fire until the enemy were within three hundred yards, and then poured in volley after volley. Pettigrew's division, on the left, first meet this sheet of flame, melted away before it like a snow-bank, and in five minutes were streaming back in wild confusion, leaving, besides their dead, a third of their numbers prisoners. Wilcox, meanwhile, had not advanced, and, Pettigrew being routed, Pickett's division was left alone, but undaunted. Their fierce onset struck first upon Webb's brigade, which, posted behind a low stone wall, occupied Gibbon's front line.[5] They broke this, and charged right among the batteries, where a fierce hand-to-hand struggle took place. The officers on each side fought pistol to pistol, the men with clubbed muskets. Gibbon, as it chanced, was a little to the right, urging the regiments there to follow Pettigrew's routed troops, and was struck down. Webb's brigade fell back from the stone wall over which the assailants were surging, but only to the second line behind the crest. Gibbon had a little before sent Lieutenant Haskell to Meade with tidings that the enemy were upon him. He was returning, and had just reached the brow of the hill, when he met Webb's brigade falling back. Without waiting to find Gibbon, Haskell rode to the left, and ordered the whole division to the right to meet the advancing foe. At that critical moment the virtual command was exercised by this young lieutenant.[6] The troops "came up helter-skelter, every body for himself, their officers among them," the only thought being to throw themselves into the breach. All that mortal men could do to win victory was done by Pickett's veterans in the five or ten immortal minutes which followed the instant when their battle-flags flaunted above the stone wall. Of his three brigade commanders, Garnet lay dead and Armistead fatally wounded within the Union lines, and Kemper was borne off to die; of fifteen field officers but one was unhurt. But all was vain; they were checked in front, and a murderous fire was poured into their flank. To advance, stand, or retreat was impossible; they flung themselves upon the ground with hands uplifted in token of surrender. Of that gallant band not one in four escaped; the others were dead or prisoners.

The few shattered remains of Pickett's and Pettigrew's commands were flying wildly to the rear, pelted by the Federal artillery and by that of the Confederates, who opened fire from all their batteries.[7] Wilcox, who had

---

[1] It must be borne in mind that a "division" in the Confederate army corresponded nearly to a "corps" in the Federal army.

[2] "I heard the cheers of the enemy, and looking in front across a low ground, I saw our men retreating in confusion; fugitives were flying across in every direction; some of them rushed through my lines. The plain in front was covered with the flying men. A wheat-field lay between two masses of wood directly in my front. The enemy in masses were coming across this field, driving every thing before them."—Crawford, in *Com. Rep.*, ii., 470.

[3] On the 10th of June this corps numbered 11,898; on the 4th of July there were but 5766, a loss of 6132. It took no active part in the action of July 3.—*Com. Rep.*, ii., 428.

[4] "In front of General Longstreet the enemy held [that is, on Thursday] a position from which, if he could be driven, it was thought that our army could be used to advantage in assailing the more elevated ground beyond, and thus enable us to reach the crest of the ridge. After a severe struggle Longstreet succeeded in getting possession of and holding the desired ground. Ewell also carried some of the strong positions which he assailed, and the result was such as to lead to the belief that he would ultimately be able to dislodge the enemy. These partial successes determined me to continue the assault the next day."—*Lee's Rep.*

[1] Hunt, in *Com. Rep.*, ii., 451.

[2] Heth's division was now commanded by Pettigrew.

[3] "The enemy's fire slackening, Longstreet ordered forward the column of attack, consisting of Pickett's and Heth's divisions in two lines; Pickett's division on the right; Wilcox's brigade marched in rear of Pickett's right to guard that flank, and Heth's was supported by Lane's and Scale's brigades, under General Trimble. . . . Our batteries, having nearly exhausted their ammunition in the protracted cannonade that preceded the advance of the infantry, were unable to reply, or render the necessary support to the attacking party. This fact was unknown to me when the assault took place."—*Lee's Rep.*, MS.

[4] "The prisoners state that what ruined them was Stannard's brigade on their flank, as they found it impossible to contend with them in that position, and they drew off all in a huddle to get away from it."—Doubleday, in *Com. Rep.*, ii., 310.

[5] Hancock in this action took charge of the whole line of battle, leaving Gibbon in command of the Second Corps.

[6] "There was one young man on my staff who has been in every battle with me, and who did more than any other one man to repulse that last assault at Gettysburg, and he did the part of a general there, yet he has been [April, 1864] only a first lieutenant until within a few weeks. I have now succeeded in getting the Governor of Wisconsin to appoint him to a colonelcy, and I have no doubt he will before long come before the Senate for a star."—Gibbon, in *Com. Rep.*, ii., 446.—He never came before the Senate for a star; among the killed at Cold Harbor not two months later we read the name of the gallant Colonel Franklin A. Haskell, 36th Wisconsin.

[7] "As soon as that attack was over, and the enemy saw that their men had given up, they opened their batteries at once, upon their own men and ours at the same time, and after that cannonade they formed another column of attack, which advanced, but more upon our left."—Hunt, in *Com. Rep.*, ii., 451.

not advanced, moved forward as if to renew the assault. But he was checked by a hot artillery fire, and never came within musket-shot of the Union line. To Stannard, who had struck the first sharp blow in this fight, it was reserved to strike the last. He launched two regiments upon the retreating force, and cut off some hundreds from its rear.

Meanwhile Ewell on the Confederate left, and Hood and McLaws upon the right, lay wholly inactive. Hood had been held in check by Kilpatrick's cavalry upon his rear, and by Crawford upon what was now his flank. The cavalry had indeed made a sharp attack upon Hood, which, though disastrous to them, had much to do with the fortune of the day. Farnsworth's brigade leaped a fence and charged up to the very muzzles of a Confederate battery, from which they were repulsed with heavy loss, their commander being among the killed.[1]

After the decisive repulse of the Confederate assault there were yet three hours of daylight. Meade rode to the left of his line and ordered Sykes to advance his corps. Crawford, who had held the position which he had won the night before, pushed a few regiments into the wood in his front. They struck Hood's foremost brigade, which broke and fled, running over another brigade which had thrown up strong intrenchments. These also fled without firing a shot, and Hood's whole division fell back a mile, leaving two or three hundred prisoners and 7000 stand of arms. Many of these had been flung away the previous day by Sickles's corps; these were piled up in heaps in order to be burnt.[2] But before the widely-scattered corps could be concentrated night was approaching, and the order for pursuit was countermanded.

Another scene in the great drama of the war was being enacted twelve hundred miles away. At the very moment when the Confederate column started upon its march to death two guns were fired from the confronting lines at Vicksburg. They were the signal that Grant and Pemberton were approaching to confer upon the terms of surrender for that strong-hold. During that hour in which two armies were struggling upon the heights of Gettysburg, those two men, seated apart in the shade of a great oak, were debating upon the conditions upon which the great Western prize should pass from the hands of those who had so long and stoutly held it into the hands of those who had so long and stoutly sought to win it. At the moment when the fragments of the Southern army streamed back in wild rout from the Northern cliffs, the great river of the West was permitted to run unvexed to the sea. The same shadow on the dial marked the time of the defeat at Gettysburg and the virtual surrender of Vicksburg.

When the Confederate army had, apparently, firmly established itself in Pennsylvania, it was thought that a favorable opportunity was presented to open negotiations with the Federal government. Alexander H. Stephens, the Vice-President, had offered to proceed to Washington as a military commissioner. On this 3d of July he set out, bearing a letter signed by Jefferson Davis as Commander-in-Chief of the Confederate forces, addressed to Abraham Lincoln as Commander-in-Chief of the army and navy of the United States. In case the President should refuse to receive a letter thus addressed, Mr. Stephens was to procure a duplicate of it, addressed to Lincoln as President of the United States, and signed by Davis as President of the Confederacy. Apparently there was no political purpose involved in this mission. Its ostensible object was to enter into stipulations by which the rigors of war might be mitigated; but it can not be doubted that it was undertaken just at this time in the confident persuasion that Lee had met with such success in the invasion of Pennsylvania as would dispose the Federal government to consent to negotiations of wider scope. But, while Stephens was awaiting permission to pass the Union lines, tidings came of the great victories at Gettysburg and Vicksburg, and the government refused to receive the commissioner, declaring that "the customary agents and channels are adequate for all needed communications and conference between the United States forces and the insurgents."

When Lee saw the remnants of Pickett and Pettigrew rushing back from their fruitless assault, he perceived that all hope of successful offensive operations had vanished. "We can not expect always to win great victories," he said. He could only hope to avoid a total rout. He contracted his lines from the right and left toward the centre, expecting and perhaps hoping to be attacked in turn.

When morning broke it became a matter of grave doubt with Meade what course to pursue. That the enemy had suffered severely was certain, but how severely could not be known. His own losses were great, and were supposed to be greater than they were. The corps commanders made hurried estimates of their remaining force. These summed up only 51,514 infantry.[3] A council of war was held, to which Meade propounded four questions: Shall the army remain at Gettysburg? If we remain, shall we resume the offensive? Shall we move upon him by way of Emmettsburg? If the enemy is retreating, shall we pursue on his direct line of retreat? The decision was to remain.[1] During the day a heavy rain set in, and at nightfall Lee, finding that an attack would not be ventured upon his position, began his retreat to the Potomac. This having been discovered on the morning of the 5th, Sedgwick's corps, which had not been engaged, was dispatched to follow him up and ascertain his whereabouts. After a march of eight miles he found their rear-guard strongly posted in the mountain passes, where a small force could hold him in check for a long time, and thought it unadvisable to pursue upon that road. Meade thereupon decided, on the 6th, to follow Lee by a flank movement, by way of Frederick and Boonesboro, involving a march of eighty miles, to Williamsport, on the Potomac, whither Lee was clearly heading. Lee, having but forty miles to march, reached the river on the 7th. But the stream which he had crossed almost dry-shod a fortnight before had been swollen by the heavy rain, and was unfordable. A bridge which he had flung across had been destroyed by a sudden cavalry dash made by French from Harper's Ferry, and Lee had no alternative but to intrench himself, with his back to the river, and await an attack.

Meade marched slowly, feeling the way with his cavalry, but on the 12th his army came in front of the Confederate lines. He had been strengthened by French with 8000 men from Harper's Ferry; Couch had sent 6000 militia, under W. F. Smith, from Carlisle, and, moreover, considerable numbers were close at hand from Baltimore and elsewhere; but these were nine months' men, just brought from North Carolina and the Peninsula, who had only one or two days more to serve. Meade judged that these would add nothing to the real strength of his army for attack, and left them behind. Still his actual numbers exceeded those of the enemy by quite a half. Meade, although he supposed the enemy to be nearly of his own strength, was disposed to attack at once, but submitted the question to his seven corps commanders. Wadsworth and Howard were in favor of attack, the other five were opposed to it until after farther examination of the position. Meade yielded his opinion, and the next day was spent in reconnoissances. The result was that in the evening an order was issued for an advance of the whole army at daylight. But when morning broke the enemy had disappeared. Lee had succeeded in patching up a bridge, and the river had fallen so that it was barely fordable at a single point. Ewell crossed by the ford, Hill and Longstreet by the bridge. The Confederate army stood once more in Virginia, and the invasion of Pennsylvania, upon which so much had been staked, was at an end.

The Federal loss at Gettysburg was 23,190, of whom 2834 were killed, 13,733 wounded, and 6643 missing. The Confederate loss was about 36,000, of whom 13,733, wounded and unwounded, remained as prisoners. The entire loss to this army during the six weeks from the middle of June, when it set forth from Culpepper to invade the North, to the close of July, when it returned to the starting-point, was about 60,000.[2]

The Confederates were slow to admit the great disaster at Gettysburg. Three weeks after the battle Alexander H. Stephens, in a speech at Charlotte, N. C., declared that "General Lee's army had whipped the enemy on their own soil, and obtained vast supplies for our own men, and was now ready to again meet the enemy on a new field. Whatever might be the movements and objects of General Lee, he had entire confidence in his ability to accomplish what he undertook. He would come out all right in the end. The loss of Vicksburg was not an occurrence to cause discouragement or gloom. It was not as severe a blow as the loss of Fort Pillow, Island No. 10, or New Orleans. The Confederacy had survived the loss of these points, and would survive the loss of Port Hudson and other places. If we were to lose Mobile, Charleston, and Richmond, it would not affect the heart of the Confederacy. After two years' war the enemy had utterly failed, and if the war continued two years longer they would fail. So far they had not broken the shell of the Confederacy."[3]

Meade, having determined "to act on the defensive, and receive the attack of the enemy, if practicable," his dispositions for the battle were to be mainly determined by the movements of the enemy. He must place his force so as to meet the assault, at whatever point it should be made, only, of course, holding the strong points of his position. It is incomprehensible, therefore, why, during all the day of July 2, the Round Tops were left wholly unguarded; for this, as Meade clearly states, was "the key-point of my whole position. If the enemy had succeeded in occupying that, it would

[1] "I have always been of the opinion," says Pleasonton (*Com. Rep.*, ii., 360), "that the demonstration of cavalry on our left materially checked the attack of the enemy on the 3d of July, for General Hood was attempting to turn our flank when he met Farnsworth's and Merritt's brigades of cavalry; and the officers reported to me that at least two divisions of infantry and a number of batteries were held back, expecting an attack from us on that flank."—Gregg, also on the right, engaged Stuart's troopers, who had now, after a wide detour, come upon the field in that quarter. In modern warfare, the great results of a campaign, when brought to an issue upon a stricken field, are decided by the shock of infantry and artillery—the hands of an army; the services of cavalry—its eyes, being mainly preliminary. If, in narrating a great campaign, the historian could detail every striking episode, he would find in this campaign nearly a score of cavalry encounters, any one of which in the earlier stages of the war would have ranked as a battle.

[2] Crawford, in *Com. Rep.*, ii., 471, and private statement.

[3] First Corps, 5000; Second, 6000; Third, 5676; Fifth, 10,000; Sixth, 12,500; Eleventh, 5500; Twelfth, 7838. These corps had marched from the Rappahanock 78,245 strong (Butterfield, in *Com. Rep.*, ii., 428), and had been re-enforced by fully 6000. This would give a loss of fully 33,000, besides that of the cavalry, which had been considerable, Buford's division having been so severely cut up on the first day that it had been sent to Westminster, twenty miles to the rear, to protect the trains and to recruit. (Pleasonton, *Ibid.*, 359.)—This estimated loss was, however, half greater than it actually proved to be. "This," says Butterfield (*Ibid.*, 427), "is always the case after a battle. A great many commanders come in and say that half their force is gone; the colonel reports that half his regiment is gone; that is reported to the brigade commander, who reports that half his brigade is gone, and so on."

[1] Birney, Sedgwick, Sykes, Hays, and Warren were for remaining for a day, and await the development of the enemy's plans; Slocum and Pleasonton were for a direct pursuit of the enemy, if he were retreating; Newton would move by way of Emmettsburg; Howard was doubtful.—See Butterfield, in *Com. Rep.*, ii., 427; Birney, *Ibid.*, 368.

[2] The statement of the Union loss and of the number of Confederate prisoners is unquestionable, being given in Meade's official report. Of the Confederate losses no reports were published, and probably none were ever rendered, for Lee, in his report, says that he is not able to give them. Recourse must therefore be had to collateral evidence. The only point absolutely fixed is the report of numbers on July 31 (*ante*, p. 383), which shows that on July 31 there were "present for duty 41,000 men." If we accept Pollard's statement that this army set out 90,000 strong, the loss would be nearly 49,000. If our estimate of 100,000 as the original strength be accepted, the loss will be 60,000. This includes not only the losses at Gettysburg, but those incurred by casualty and wastage in the march from Culpepper to Gettysburg and back, which must have amounted to many thousands. Lee especially notes that the cavalry suffered severely from toil and privation. Farther, if we accept the estimate of the forces actually present at Gettysburg, based upon Longstreet's statement (*ante*, p. 502), at 80,000, the losses of all kinds from July 1 to 31 would be 39,000, including those incurred from wastage and skirmishes on the way back from the Potomac to the Rappahannock; allowing 3000 for these, there remain 36,000 for Gettysburg and the days immediately following. Of this 14,000 prisoners, we judge from various indicia that 8000 were unwounded—1500 captured on the field on the 1st of July, 5000 on the 2d, and 1500 in the pursuit. This leaves 28,000 for killed and wounded. Apportioning these in the same ratio as in the Union loss, there will be about 5000 killed and 23,000 wounded of the Confederate army.

[3] *Richmond Dispatch*, June 25.

GETTYSBURG.

JULY 3, 1863.

have prevented me from holding any of the ground which I subsequently held to the last;" and it was only "fortunately that General Sykes was enabled, by throwing a strong force upon Round Top Mountain, where a most desperate and bloody struggle ensued, to drive the enemy from it, and secure our foothold upon that important position."[1] It was, indeed, a fortunate accident that a division of Sykes's corps, who were marching in quite a different direction, happened to be near enough to reach the summit of Round Top as the enemy were on the point of gaining it. "They arrived barely in time to save it, and they had a very desperate fight to hold it."[2] Again, if the advanced position taken by Sickles was as disadvantageous as it seemed to Meade, one may wonder why he was not withdrawn. The enemy were indeed advancing to the attack, but there was as yet some space between, and it would seem to have been easier to withdraw from an untenable position than to be driven from it.[3] It is not easy to comprehend why Sedgwick's corps, stronger by half than any other one in the army, took no active part in the action of either day,[4] or, at least, was not held in such a position that, when the enemy broke and fled at the close of the action, it could have been launched in pursuit,[5] for there was yet three hours of daylight.

But, granting that it was not advisable to pursue and assail the enemy in the position of unknown strength which he occupied on the evening of the 3d, there can be little hesitancy in condemning Meade's failure to follow when it had been ascertained that Lee was in full retreat toward the Potomac. To make a wide detour with the expectation of striking him on the flank was equivalent to declining a battle; for Lee had so far the start that he reached the river at the same time that Meade began his flank march of eighty miles. He would have crossed at once, had he been able; but the stream, swollen by rains, was not fordable, and his only bridge had been destroyed. The Confederate army was in bad plight, and looked eagerly for the falling of the waters.[6] When, upon the 12th, Meade came up with the enemy, he had every chance in his favor. He was in superior force; his army was in excellent condition and in high spirits; the enemy could not be other than wearied and disheartened. If the attack was unsuccessful, it could amount to no more than a check, for he could fall back to the South Mountain, where he would be unassailable; but if the assault was successful, the Confederates would be ruined, for they had at their back a swollen river, which they had no means of crossing. Meade was minded to fight; he had come for that purpose; but, unfortunately, he submitted the question to a council of war. He had been hardly a fortnight in command, and would not assume the responsibility of acting in opposition to the views of his corps commanders, so he yielded his opinion to theirs;[7] unwisely as it seems to us, wisely as he was himself afterward convinced.[8] When, after spending a day or two in reconnoitring, he ordered the attack to be made at daybreak on the 14th, he was too late. The enemy had crossed, and the swollen Potomac lay between. "The fruit was so ripe, so ready for plucking," said Lincoln, "that it was very hard to lose it." The President, indeed, expressed himself in terms of censure so sharp that Meade asked to be relieved from the command of the army.[9] The request was refused.

[1] Meade, in *Com. Rep.*, ii., 332.

[2] Warren, in *Com. Rep.*, ii., 377. See also Crawford, *Ibid.*, 469

[3] Sickles indeed affirms that the position which he took was a good one. He says (*Com. Rep.*, ii., 298): "I took up that line, because it enabled me to hold commanding ground, which, if the enemy had been allowed to take—as they would have taken it if I had not occupied it in force—would have rendered our position on the left untenable, and, in my judgment, would have turned the fortunes of the day hopelessly against us." But the enemy did actually take the position held for a time by Sickles at the cost of half his corps, and were only repelled from the very line which Meade had proposed to hold.

[4] "My corps did not take any important part in the battle of Gettysburg. It was frequently sent to different parts of the field to re-enforce and support other troops that were more vigorously engaged."—Sedgwick, in *Com. Rep.*, ii., 460.

[5] "I think that our lines should have advanced immediately, and I believe that we should have won a great victory. I was very confident that the attack would be made. General Meade told me before the fight that, if the enemy attacked me, he intended to put the Fifth and Sixth Corps on the enemy's flank. I therefore, when I was wounded, and lying down in my ambulance, and about leaving the field, dictated a note to General Meade, and told him if he would put in the Fifth and Sixth Corps, I believed he would win a great victory. I asked him afterward, when I returned to the army, what he had done in the premises. He said he had ordered the movement, but the troops were slow in collecting, and moved so slowly that nothing was done before night, except that some of the Pennsylvania Reserves went out and met Hood's division, and actually overthrew it. There were only two divisions of the enemy on our extreme left, opposite Round Top, and there was a gap of one mile that their assault had left; and I believe that if our whole line had advanced with spirit, it is not unlikely that we should have taken all their artillery at that point. I think that we should have pushed the enemy there, for we do not often catch them in that position; and the rule is, and it is natural, that when you defeat and repulse an enemy, you should pursue him."—Hancock, in *Com. Rep.*, ii., 408.

[6] "The Potomac was found to be so much swollen by the recent rains as to be unfordable. Our communications with the south side were thus interrupted, and it was difficult to procure either ammunition or subsistence. The enemy had not yet made his appearance, but, as he was in condition to obtain large re-enforcements, and our situation, for the reasons above mentioned, was becoming daily more embarrassing, it was deemed advisable to recross the river. Part of the pontoon bridge was recovered, and new boats built. Our preparations being completed, and the river, though still deep, being pronounced fordable, the army commenced to withdraw to the south side on the night of the 13th."—*Lee's Rep.*

[7] The objections of the council were not to fighting, but to attacking them. "We all," says Pleasonton (*Com. Rep.*, ii., 361), "wanted to fight. There was one general, General French, I think, who remarked, after General Meade declared that he would not order an attack against the vote of the council, 'Why, it does not make any difference what our opinions are. If you give the order to attack, we will fight just as well under it as if our opinions were not against it.'"

[8] Testimony, in *Com. Rep.*, ii., 336.

[9] Halleck to Meade, July 14: "I need hardly say to you that the escape of Lee's army without another battle has created great dissatisfaction in the mind of the President, and it will require an active and energetic pursuit on your part to remove the impression that it has not been sufficiently active heretofore." Meade to Halleck: "Having performed my duty conscientiously and to the best of my ability, the censure of the President is in my judgment so undeserved that I feel compelled most respectfully to ask to be immediately relieved from the command of this army." Halleck to Meade: "My telegram stating the disappointment of the President at the escape of Lee's army was not intended as a censure, but as a stimulus to an active pursuit. It is not deemed a sufficient cause for your application to be relieved."

The operations of Lee at Gettysburg can be justified, or even explained, only upon the supposition that he was wholly deceived as to the strength of the enemy in his front. He had, indeed, very good reasons to suppose himself to be in greatly superior force. On Wednesday, when he had won a decided advantage, he had clearly two to one on the field. On Thursday morning he was, after his losses, stronger by more than half, and there was nothing in the operations of that day to evince that the Federals had been greatly strengthened. He had, indeed, gained important apparent advantages at two points. Ewell had effected a lodgment within the intrenchments on the Union right. On their left, the Federals had been driven back from what seemed to be a strong part of their chosen line; and though the attack had been finally repelled, still the ground contended for had been won, and was held. Owing to two accidents—the temporary withdrawal of Slocum's corps on the right, and the advance of Sickles on the left beyond the main lines—the Confederates had seen only a force inferior to their own, and it was reasonable to infer that this formed all which could have been brought into action by the enemy. On Friday, every thing, up to the moment of the final charge, confirmed this impression. Lee was ignorant that by noon Ewell had been driven out of the intrenchments which he had won the night before. The fierce cannonade, which was opened an hour after noon, was replied to by little more than half the number of guns, and of these the fire was slackened in such a way as to indicate that the Union batteries were effectually silenced. To suppose that Lee assailed the heights of Gettysburg knowing, or imagining that they were held by an army fully equal in numbers to his own, is to attribute to him a degree of rashness which is belied by his whole military career.

Lee's attack on the last day has been subjected to grave censure. If it was made with a knowledge of the numbers opposed to him, it was wholly indefensible. But it must be judged in the light of what he knew at the time. He was under no necessity of giving or even of receiving battle. The main object of the invasion had indeed failed. There was no chance that he could seize Baltimore or Philadelphia; none, indeed, that he could hold his position in Pennsylvania. But the way of return to Virginia was open to him. He was in a position where a battle which should be less than a victory so great as to involve the destruction of the army opposed to him would have been useless, while a defeat could hardly be other than ruinous. Having decided to attack, the assault should have been made with his whole force. After all his losses he had certainly 60,000 men; his plan of attack involved the use of hardly half of these, including Ewell's proposed demonstration. The main assault was committed to only 18,000.[1] What, asked Longstreet, would have been the result if the assault had been made by 30,000 men instead of 15,000? There can be no doubt that if this attack was to be made, it should have been made by twice the force. Yet, in the light of what we now know, it was well that this was not done. If twice as many men had been sent in they must have equally failed, and with twice the loss. The Confederates only just succeeded in touching the Union line of defense, and from this they were repelled in utter rout by less than a fifth of the force which could have been brought there in another twenty minutes. Only two divisions of Hancock's corps, with a single other brigade, were really engaged.[2] The other division of that corps, together with the corps of Howard, Reynolds, and Sickles, which had been badly cut up during the two previous days, were at hand; Slocum's corps had cleared itself from Ewell at Culp's Hill, on the right, and could have been brought into action on the left; moreover, there was Sedgwick's whole corps, which had not yet even touched the fight. Meade, while holding his right and left, could easily, if need were, have brought 50,000 men to the defense of his centre. What with his artillery, which swept the approach, it is safe to say that no 50,000 or 80,000 men, if they could have been hurled at once upon the Cemetery Ridge, could ever have carried it. "The conduct of the troops," says Lee, "was all that I could desire or expect, and they deserved success so far as it can be deserved by heroic valor and fortitude. More may have been required of them than they were able to perform, but my admiration of their noble qualities, and confidence in their ability to cope successfully with the enemy, has suffered no abatement from the issue of this protracted and sanguinary conflict." This task, "more than they were able to perform," was imposed upon his votaries by Lee. Upon him, therefore, must rest the blame for the failure to execute it.

[1] It is indeed said that McLaws and Hood, with some 15,000 more, were to have taken part, and that Lee was bitterly indignant at the "slow-footed McLaws" for not coming up. But there is in his report no indication that such was any part of his plan. The wording of it, indeed, seems to exclude any such purpose, and implies that the carrying of Cemetery Heights was intrusted to Pickett and Pettigrew.

[2] "The shock of the assault fell upon the second and third divisions of the Second Corps, and these were the troops, together with the artillery of our line, which fired from Round Top to Cemetery Hill at the enemy as they advanced, whenever they had the opportunity. Those were the troops that really met the assault. No doubt there were other troops that fired a little, but these were the troops that really withstood the shock of the assault and repulsed it. The attack of the enemy was met by about six small brigades of our troops, and was finally repulsed after a very terrific contest at very close quarters."—Hancock, in *Com. Rep.*, ii., 408.

IN CAMP.

CHAPTER XXX.

MEADE'S CAMPAIGN IN VIRGINIA.

The Armies.—Meade's Advance into Virginia.—Lee's Retreat.—The Armies on the Rappahanneck.—Both Armies reduced.—Cessation of Operations.—Appeals of Davis and Lee.—Lee advances and Meade retreats.—Fight at Bristoe.—Meade falls back to Centreville.—Lee returns to the Rappahannock.—Meade slowly follows.—Stuart in Peril.—Imboden's Dash upon Charlestown.—Cavalry Fight near Warrenton.—Meade proposes to go to Fredericksburg.—Capture of Rappahannock Station.—The Mine Run Attempt.—Butler's Movement toward Richmond.—Kilpatrick and Dahlgren's Raid.—The Army in Winter-quarters.

IN a year and a week, from the beginning of the Seven Days before Richmond to the close of the battle at Gettysburg, the Union Army of the Potomac and the Confederate Army of Northern Virginia had encountered in six desperate struggles, each lasting for days. In four—on the Peninsula, at Groveton, Fredericksburg, and Chancellorsville—the Confederates won the honors and advantages of victory; in two—at Antietam and Gettysburg—they had been defeated. Besides these great conflicts, there had been many minor engagements. The losses upon each side had been singularly alike. In killed, wounded, and prisoners, each had lost about 110,000. If to these are added the scores of thousands who died from disease in pestilential camps, and upon the long and weary marches, each army lost more than its muster-rolls embraced when at the fullest.[1] During nine months they were to confront each other, neither striking or hardly attempting a blow; and then to enter upon that terrible campaign of eleven months, which resulted in the annihilation of the Confederate army, and the overthrow of the cause which it had so long and valiantly upheld. Of that nine months' indecisive campaign in Virginia I am now to write.

When Lee, after Gettysburg, had succeeded in making good his escape across the Potomac, he took up the same position which he had, after Antietam, assumed ten months before.[1] To Meade was presented the same question which had been offered to McClellan after Antietam. In what manner should he, with his superior force, assail the enemy? The decision was promptly made. It was the same to which McClellan came after long hesitation and delay. Instead of following directly upon Lee's rear, on the west side of the Blue Ridge, he would threaten his flank and menace his communications by advancing along the east side of this mountain chain. This decision was based upon the admitted impossibility of supplying his great army by the single line of railroad which traversed the Valley of the Shenandoah. Lee would be compelled, as he had before been compelled, to retreat up the valley. Meade moreover hoped, having the shorter line, to be able to throw a heavy column through some gap of the Blue Ridge, and assail the flank of Lee's long line as it passed in its retreat.[2] On the 17th and 18th the Potomac was crossed, and the army commenced its march. Some slight changes were made in the commands. Butterfield had been hurt at Gettysburg, and Humphreys was appointed chief of staff, a position which Meade had urged upon him when he took command. Sickles and Hancock had been severely wounded. French's division, from Harper's Ferry, had been added to Sickles's corps, which had suffered so terribly, and French was put at its head. Warren, who had long been chief engineer of the army, was a little after placed in command of Hancock's corps.

As soon as he discovered the Federal advance, Lee broke up his camps near Winchester, and commenced a rapid retreat up the Valley of the Shenandoah, hoping to pass from it into the Valley of the Rappahannock, and so reach the railroad leading to Richmond in advance of Meade. Thus the two armies were moving rapidly in parallel lines, but with the Blue Ridge between, shutting each from all information as to the movements and positions of the other, except such as could be gained by scouts posted at some commanding point of observation.

On the 22d, when the Union army had reached Manassas Gap, Meade learned that the enemy were marching right opposite to him. This seemed the desired opportunity to throw a column through the gap, and fall upon the centre of his line. French pushed his corps through, meeting with slight opposition, and next morning saw the Confederates drawn up at

[1] In the following table an attempt is made to give as nearly as possible in round numbers the losses in the two armies during the period of a year and a week, commencing with the battle of Mechanicsville, June 26, 1862, and ending with that of Gettysburg, July 3, 1863. The number of killed and wounded can be very closely ascertained. The errors in one case will be about balanced by contrary ones in another. The number of prisoners is much less certain. Very many prisoners claimed on both sides were also wounded, and entered on the lists as such. I have endeavored to distinguish between the wounded and unwounded prisoners, giving as "prisoners" only those not left wounded on the field. In the list of prisoners taken by the Confederates I have not included the 11,000 captured by Jackson at Harper's Ferry, for they were paroled at once, and were never actually in the hands of the enemy. I have, however, included the 2500 captured from Milroy at Winchester, for they were actually held. The "prisoners'" column is therefore to be taken merely as a rough estimate. Only the losses in the great actions have been given. Some thousands besides these fell or were captured in minor engagements, bringing the numbers fully up to those given in the text. Of the losses from disease no even approximate estimate can be formed. Fifty thousand upon each side would certainly be a moderate estimate.

Battles.	Union.		Confederate.	
	Killed and Wounded.	Prisoners.	Killed and Wounded.	Prisoners.
The Seven Days on the Peninsula	10,000	6,000	19,000	1,000
Pope's Campaign	14,000	7,000	11,000	1,000
Antietam, etc.	14,000	1,000	12,000	6,000
Fredericksburg	10,000	1,000	4,500	500
Chancellorsville	12,000	5,000	10,000	2,500
Gettysburg	16,500	5,000	25,000	8,000
Total	76,500	25,000	82,500	19,000

[1] Lee seems to have had in mind some offensive operation when he crossed the Potomac. In his report he says: "Owing to the swollen condition of the Shenandoah River, the plan of operations which had been contemplated when we recrossed the Potomac could not be put in execution, and before the waters had subsided the movements of the enemy induced me to cross the Blue Ridge, and take position south of the Rappahannock."—We can only conjecture that this contemplated plan was to march down the south side of the Potomac, and strike a blow at Washington. If this was the plan, it must have been based on the supposition that Meade would loiter upon the north bank of the Potomac, as McClellan had done after Antietam.

[2] "It was impracticable to pursue the enemy in the Valley of Virginia, because of the difficulty of supplying an army in that valley with a single-track railroad in very bad order. I therefore determined to adopt the same plan of movement as that adopted the preceding year, which was to move upon the enemy's flank through Loudon Valley."—Meade, in *Com. Rep.*, ii., 389.

ANDREW A. HUMPHREYS.

Front Royal in what seemed to be a strong line of battle. Meade now made dispositions for a fight the next day, for he believed that he had interrupted Lee's retreat, and that he would be compelled to fight in order to secure his trains. But when morning dawned the enemy had vanished. The seeming strong line of battle was but a rear-guard; the main army had been all the time swiftly marching by roads farther to the west. Lee, having thus eluded the threatened attack, pressed on, passed through a lower gap out of the Valley of the Shenandoah into that of the Rappahannock, and at length halted at Culpepper, the goal of the retreat, the point where he had six weeks before reviewed the great army with which he had set out for the invasion of the North. Meade, having missed his blow, withdrew his forces from the Manassas Gap, and marched leisurely on toward the Rappahannock.[1]

On the last day of July the Confederate Army of Northern Virginia numbered only 41,000 men "present for duty." Besides these there were 12,500 "present," a few more than the wounded whom they had brought away from Gettysburg. Through all the week during which Lee had been detained by the swollen Potomac, he had been sending his wounded across in boats, so that he had gained a full fortnight in which to transport them to Culpepper and beyond without molestation. The Union army could not have numbered less than 75,000, probably more. Meade knew that he was greatly superior, how greatly he most likely did not suspect. He wisely resolved to advance upon Lee, but unwisely consulted the authorities at Washington. The movement was forbidden. He might only "take up a threatening attitude upon the Rappahannock."[2] What any attitude upon the Rappahannock which did not involve the passage of that stream could threaten, is hard to see. Certainly not the Confederate army which lay beyond; not its communications or sources of supply; not Richmond, or any one of its connections with any part of the Confederacy.

Lee's army was strengthened from day to day. On the 31st of August it numbered 56,000 present for duty. This increase was the first, and, indeed, the only fruit of Jefferson Davis's earnest appeal, issued on the 15th of July, to those "now absent from the army without leave," in which he promised amnesty and pardon to all who should "with the least possible delay return to their posts of duty;" but this period of grace was limited to twenty days.[3] Meade's army was in the mean while considerably diminished. A division was sent to South Carolina to aid in the siege of Charleston. The draft riots in New York, which broke out the very day upon which Lee recrossed the Potomac, had indeed been suppressed, but the opposition to the draft was still so strenuous that military aid was deemed necessary to enforce it, and a large body of troops were taken from the Army of the Potomac and sent to New York for that purpose. During the first days of September Lee's force was fully equal to that of Meade. But, in the mean time, Bragg, in Tennessee, was hardly pressed by Rosecrans, and Longstreet, with his corps, was sent to his aid. Meade was soon aware of this diminution of the force opposed to him, and this time, without waiting for instructions, moved his army across the Rappahannock, and established himself at Culpepper, while Lee fell back beyond the Rapidan, and took a position strong by nature and strongly fortified.

Meade was now in a region of which he knew nothing, and could learn nothing except by sending his cavalry in every direction to reconnoitre. This took time, and he had just decided upon a plan of operations when he was told that his army must be reduced. Things had gone badly at the West. Rosecrans had been defeated at Chickamauga, and Meade must spare a quarter of his army to restore the balance in Tennessee. The corps of Slocum and Howard were chosen. Thereafter these corps ceased to form a part of the Army of the Potomac, and belong to that of the West. The command of these two corps was given to Hooker, who had never lost the confidence of the President and the Secretary of War. He had, indeed,

[1] Meade, in *Com. Rep.*, ii., 339.—Lee (*MS. Rep.*) thus describes these operations: "As the Federals continued to advance along the eastern slope of the mountains, apparently with the purpose of cutting us off from the railroad, Longstreet was ordered, on the 19th of July, to proceed to Culpepper Court-house by way of Front Royal. He succeeded in passing part of his command over the Shenandoah in time to prevent the occupation of Manassas and Chester Gaps by the enemy. As soon as a pontoon bridge could be laid down, the rest of his corps crossed, and marched through Chester Gap to Culpepper, where they arrived on the 24th. He was followed by Hill's corps. Ewell reached Front Royal the 23d, and encamped near Madison Court-house on the 29th."

[2] "Upon my arrival at the Rappahannock, which was toward the close of July, I communicated my views to the government, in which I expressed the opinion that the further pursuit of General Lee should be continued at that time, inasmuch as I believed that our relative forces were more favorable at that time than they would be at any subsequent time, if we gave him time to recuperate. It was thought proper, however, by the general-in-chief to direct me to take up a threatening attitude upon the Rappahannock, but not to advance."—Meade, in *Com. Rep.*, ii., 340.

[3] *July* 26. Lee issued the following General Order to the Army of Northern Virginia: "All officers and soldiers now absent from this army, who are able to do duty, and are not detached on special service, are ordered to return immediately. The commanding general calls upon all soldiers to return to their respective regiments at once. To remain at home in this, the hour of our country's need, is unworthy of the manhood of a Southern soldier. . . . . The commanding general appeals to the people of the states to send forth every man able to bear arms to aid the brave soldiers who have so often beaten back our foes."—The following are passages from the address of Jefferson Davis: "You know too well what the enemy mean by success. Their malignant rage aims at nothing less than the extermination of yourselves, your wives, and children. They propose, as the spoils of success, that your homes shall be partitioned among the wretches whose atrocious cruelties have stamped infamy on their government. . . . . No alternative is left you but victory or subjugation, slavery, and the utter ruin of yourselves, your families, and your country. The victory is within your reach. The men now absent from their posts would, if present in the field, suffice to create numerical equality between our force and that of the invader. . . . . . I call upon you, then, to hasten to your camps, in obedience to the dictates of honor and of duty, and summon those who have absented themselves without leave to repair without delay to their respective commands; and I do hereby declare that I grant a general pardon and amnesty to all officers and men within the Confederacy, now absent without leave, who shall, with the least possible delay, return to their posts of duty; but no excuse will be received for any delay beyond twenty days after the first publication of this proclamation in any state in which the absentee may be at the date of the publication. This amnesty shall extend to all who have been accused, or who are undergoing sentence for absence without leave or desertion, except only those who have been twice convicted of desertion."

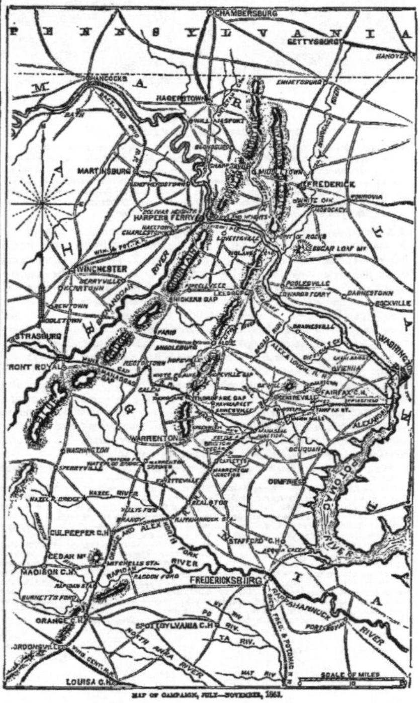

MAP OF CAMPAIGN, JULY—NOVEMBER, 1863.

CAMP AT THE FOOT OF THE BLUE RIDGE.

wished to receive the command of a corps under Meade, but one can eas understand that this proposition could not be acceptable to that gener Whatever honor Hooker lost at Chancellorsville was abundantly regair at Lookout Mountain.

The armies in Virginia, thus again brought to an equality, remained active until early in October. By that time the troops sent to New Yo had returned, diminished in number by a third; the draft also furnish some accessions, but of a character which added little real strength. St according to his own estimate, Meade had well-nigh 70,000 effective me The force of the enemy he thought to be considerably less.[2] Now occurr Meade's retreat to Centreville, which, with McClellan's flight to Malve Hill, Hooker's abandonment of Chancellorsville, and Butler's "bottling u at Bermuda Hundreds, yet to take place, must stand as the inexplicable i cidents of the war.

Early in October there appeared a very evident diminution of the Co federate forces along the Rapidan, while cavalry and some infantry we seen moving toward Meade's right flank. These operations were suscep ble of two interpretations. Lee might be falling back still farther, in whic case the movements observed on the Union right were simply a demonstr tion to throw the enemy off the track while the Confederate army was wit drawing; or it might be the purpose of Lee to gain the rear of the Unic army, and fall upon its communications, which were kept up mainly by tl single line of railroad from Alexandria southward. Meade, coming to tl front, was satisfied that the former was the design of his opponent,[3] an made preparations to throw his cavalry and two of his five infantry corp across the Rapidan. But before this was done he became satisfied that th enemy, instead of retreating, was in full advance. He could not believe tha with his inferior force Lee would venture to assail him at Culpepper, an therefore the movement must be to turn his right flank and assume a pos tion in his rear which would compel him to attack at disadvantage. H thereupon, on the morning of the 11th, withdrew his whole army across th Rappahannock. Hardly had this been done, when he learned that the Con federate force had actually moved upon Culpepper, as if with the design of offering battle in the very position which he himself had chosen. Now Meade had no desire to avoid a battle, if he could fight upon his own terms and so he directed three of his corps to recross the Rappahannock and move toward Culpepper. Hardly had this been done, when Gregg, whose caval ry had been thrown out to the right, came in with reports that he had been attacked and driven back by a heavy force of all arms, and that the whole Confederate army, after the delay of a day at Culpepper, was on the march to gain the Union rear.

The information proved true in the main. Lee, knowing how greatly the Union army had been depleted a few weeks before, but ignorant of the strong accessions which it had received within a few days, meditated a repetition of the movement by which he had a year before defeated Pope; only instead of, as Meade supposed, marching west of the Bull Run Mountains, and crossing them at Thoroughfare Gap, he designed to skirt the southern extremity of this range, and gain a position just in the Union rear, upon the railroad. Meade's communications being thus interrupted, he would be forced to attack upon the ground which the enemy should select. Lee reasoned that Meade, forced to withdraw from the Rappahannock, would not be able to resume offensive operations that season. Meade presumed that Lee's design was to occupy the strong position at Centreville, and saw nothing to be done but to retreat with all speed upon that point, hoping to reach it in advance of the enemy. But, as it happened, Lee, instead of aiming at Centreville, directed his march upon Bristoe. He moved also with much less than his wonted celerity, delaying, indeed, for a whole day, the 13th, at Warrenton, in order to supply his troops with provisions. Thus it happened that when the head of Lee's columns, moving eastward, came on the 14th near Bristoe, Meade's whole army, moving northward, had passed that point, with the exception of Warren's corps, which was bringing up the rear. Had Meade known that the army were behind instead of before him, he would, as he avers, have paused and given battle;[4] but, misinformed of the true position, he continued his retreat, crossed Bull Run, and took position at Centreville.

---

[1] "When I came to Washington, the Secretary of War informed me that he very much regretted the step that I had taken [in resigning the Command of the Army of the Potomac]; that it was the intention of the President to give me the command of all the troops I had asked for; but that fact had never been communicated to me, nor had I any intimation of it before. I inquired of the President why he had not given me a Corps in that army after he had relieved me, and he said it was for the reason that he thought it would not be agreeable to me or to General Meade. Subsequently he communicated his desire to this effect to General Meade, which was acceded to by the latter first, and afterward objected to by General Meade."—Hooker, in *Com. Rep.*, ii., 178.

[2] Meade (*Com. Rep.*, ii., 348) testified: "As near as I can judge, my army contained of efficient men, equipped and armed such as I could bring into battle, between 60,000 and 70,000 men. I think the enemy had about 60,000. I thought I was probably from 8000 to 10,000 his superior."—General Howe (*Ibid.*, 318) relates a conversation which he had with Meade at this very time. He says: "General Meade remarked that our strength was 74,000 men, and of that number he said that 68,000 were armed and in a condition to fight. Then he spoke of the strength of Lee's army. He ran over the data that he had obtained from divers and sundry sources, and made out that Lee could not have over 45,000 men. He referred to the different corps and divisions of the rebel army; to the movements that had been made, with which he seemed to be familiar; and, as I remember, he stated that Lee's army could not be over 45,000 men, showing that we had such a preponderance of force that with any thing like a fair ordinary chance we could have our own way. That was on Friday" [October 9].—This estimate of 45,000 was singularly accurate, for on the last day of September Lee's muster-rolls showed 44,367, and on the last day of October 45,614, present for duty.

[3] "I said to General Meade, 'I do not see but one thing that Lee can do with advantage with his army, and that is to throw himself suddenly upon our rear.' General Meade replied, 'Oh, he can not do that: he would not think of doing such a thing as that.'"—Howe, in *Com. Rep.*, ii., 318.—General Meade, in his testimony before the Committee on the Conduct of the War (*Report*, ii., 340–342), gives a very full account of his movements at this time, and of the reasons which governed them.

[4] "Notwithstanding my losing a day, I had moved with more celerity than the enemy, and was a little in his advance. If I had known this at the time, I would have given the enemy battle the next day in the position that I had occupied at Auburn and Greenwich."—*Com. Rep.*, ii., 341.

IN CAMP AT WARRENTON SPRINGS.

Warren had in the mean while been delayed at Auburn by a rencounter with a portion of Ewell's corps. This, after some skirmishing, drew off, and Warren followed on after the rest of the army, between which and him there was now a considerable interval. When the head of Lee's army came in the afternoon to Bristoe, they saw Sykes's corps marching out. Hill made some dispositions to assail the rear of Sykes, when he became aware of the approach of Warren from the opposite direction. Hill turned to assail Warren, while Sykes, strangely enough, kept on his retreat for a space.[1] Warren's position was perilous. His single corps was isolated from the remainder of the army, while the whole force of the enemy was coming up right upon his flank. Only a part of it was actually up, and on the next few minutes every thing depended. With quick decision, Warren sent his two leading divisions, which were a mile in advance of the other, to seize upon a deep cutting in the railroad. They dashed forward at a run, and were just in time to gain the position when Hill's advancing line of battle came up. They were received with so hot a fire that they fell back with considerable loss. Heth's division—the same which, under Pettigrew, who had been mortally wounded at Williamsport, had suffered so severely at Gettysburg—made a feeble attack upon the right flank, when it encountered Webb's division, the same which it had met on Cemetery Ridge; they again retreated in confusion. In all, the Confederates lost 400 killed and wounded and 450 prisoners—the entire Union loss being about 200. Hill had been checked, but Warren was far from being free from peril, for Ewell's corps and the remainder of Hill's were rapidly approaching, while the other Union corps, apparently ignorant of what was going on, had kept up the retreat, and were now miles away. Warren could not hope, with his single corps, long to withstand the whole Confederate army, nor while daylight lasted could he safely abandon his strong position and pursue his march. But night was approaching, and before Lee could make the necessary dispositions for attack, darkness closed in, and under its thrice welcome cover Warren marched on, and rejoined the main army at Centreville.

Had Meade on that day known the position of the enemy, he would certainly never have crossed Bull Run. He would most likely have marched back to Bristoe, before it had been abandoned by Warren, where there can be little doubt that a battle would have taken place, under such advantages that victory would have been certain.[2] But so erroneous was Meade's information that even on the next day Birney's division was ordered to march on to Fairfax Station, half way between Centreville and Washington, to hold that point against an expected attack. Had Lee really purposed to throw his army through Thoroughfare Gap, Meade should have welcomed such a movement. The Confederate army, wholly cut off from its sources of supply, would have been hemmed in between Meade's superior forces and the defenses of Washington. It could have neither food nor ammunition except what it bore with it. It could neither hold its position, nor advance nor retreat without winning a battle, against greatly superior forces. The case was widely different from what existed a year before, when Lee, fully twice as strong, had made the same flank march against Pope's disjointed and dispirited army.

After a couple of days' repose at Centreville, Meade perceived that Lee was not minded to follow him any farther, and he resolved to retrace his steps. But now a storm set in and swelled the little stream of Bull Run into a foaming torrent, which could be crossed only by pontoons. These had been left ten miles behind, and so for two days the army could not move a mile. Lee pushed a few troops as far as Bull Run, and on the 18th commenced his retreat toward the Rappahannock, marching along the railroad, which he thoroughly destroyed behind him. The next day, the Run having fallen, Meade began his advance. He moved slowly, for there was nothing to be gained by haste. More than a week was occupied in the twenty miles' march back to Warrenton, and ten more days were lost in repairing the road so that supplies could be kept up.

Besides Warren's stand at Auburn and his fight at Bristoe, there had been no fighting except by the cavalry, who were flung out from either army. On the 18th Stuart was near coming to grief hard by Catlett's Station, where he had last year performed good though accidental service by the capture of Pope's dispatch-book. He had pushed forward quite in advance of the infantry, and, coming upon the head of the leading Federal column, had fallen back toward Catlett's, where he bivouacked in a low spot among a dense pine thicket. Meantime the other Federal column had moved by a parallel road, and Stuart was hemmed in between the two, not two miles from Meade's head-quarters, and within less than a quarter of a mile from a ridge whereon Warren had pitched his camp. Stuart was hidden from observation by the thicket and by the heavy night mist, while the enemy on the hill-tops was in plain view. His destruction was inevitable should he be discovered. Sending two or three soldiers disguised in Federal uniforms to creep through the hostile lines and notify Lee of his peril, he waited till morning was beginning to dawn, and then opened a sudden artillery fire upon Warren. So unexpected was the attack that the troops upon whom

[1] "When I began the fight, the last of General Sykes's corps was moving off. I do not suppose that he got more than three or four miles away, and a part of his corps did come back just before dark. I think the orders were to concentrate at Centreville that night; but when I was engaged in battle, it seemed to me plain enough that he ought to have helped me without solicitation or orders."—Warren, in *Com. Rep.*, ii., 384.

[2] "Under the conviction that the enemy was moving on, and had moved on, I that night (of the 13th) gave orders for a further retrograde movement, until I occupied the line of Centreville and Bull Run. In performing this movement the next day, I ascertained, when too late to take advantage of it, that the enemy had not moved on the pike (leading through Thoroughfare Gap to Centreville), but that he had moved across, with the expectation of falling upon my flank and rear, and that his advance had encountered my rear-guard, under the command of General Warren, and had been severely handled."—(Meade, in *Com. Rep.*, ii., 341.)—Warren says (*Ibid.*, 387): "We lost another opportunity when the enemy attacked me at Bristoe; perhaps not at that point exactly, but during that movement we missed an opportunity that we should be very glad to have again."

DÉPÔT OF SUPPLIES ON THE RAILROAD.

it fell were thrown into momentary confusion, and moved across the crest to escape the cannonade. Stuart sprang to horse, and passing safely with all his men, rode clear around the Union rear. The scouts whom he had sent out had in the mean time succeeded in reaching Ewell, who set his column in motion, and it was the head of this which encountered Warren at Auburn.

While Meade was resting at Centreville, Imboden, with a division of Confederate cavalry, was stationed in the Valley of the Shenandoah. From Winchester, on the 16th, he made a sudden dash down to Charlestown, close by Harper's Ferry, where he captured more than 400 prisoners, and secured a large quantity of supplies, and then, upon the approach of a superior force from the Ferry, he fell back, preserving all his spoils. On the 19th Kilpatrick, with his cavalry division, having crossed Bull Run, pressed on toward Warrenton. When within a few miles of that place he encountered Hampton's troopers, who were covering the Confederate rear. Hampton fell back for a space until joined by Stuart and Fitz Lee. Kilpatrick was in turn driven back, not without confusion, losing 200 prisoners. What with Imboden's captures at Charlestown, the Confederates had made, during these five days, about 2500 prisoners, and had lost not more than a quarter as many. In killed and wounded the losses were about equal, not far from 500 on each side. Lee had, however, succeeded in his chief purpose, that of securing himself against any probable attack during the few remaining weeks of the autumn.

While, however, Meade was waiting at Warrenton for the repair of the railroad, he meditated an indirect offensive movement, being nothing other than a repetition of Burnside's, entered upon just a year before. He proposed to march rapidly to Fredericksburg, cross there and seize the heights, and thus transfer his base of operations from the Orange and Alexandria to the Fredericksburg Railroad. He argued that this movement would be a complete surprise to the enemy; that the heights of Fredericksburg could be seized before Lee could get down there; and then, he says, "if Lee followed me down there, it would be just what I wanted; if he did not, then I could take up my position there, open my communications, and then advance upon him or threaten Richmond." But Halleck refused his consent to this plan; he was opposed to any change of base—a phrase which indeed had come to have an ominous sound. If Meade chose to make any movement against Lee, he was at liberty to do so, but there must be no change of base.[1] Why, in November, Halleck should sanction the very operation which he had positively forbidden in July, is inconceivable. Lee's army was somewhat stronger now than then;[2] Meade's was considerably weaker. Then there were four months of favorable weather; now there was no likelihood of as many weeks. Then the Union army was flushed by the great victory, and the Confederate dispirited by the great defeat of Gettysburg; now the Confederates were inspirited, and the Federals dispirited by the result of the subsequent operations.

The Confederate army lay meanwhile behind the Rappahannock, widely scattered. Two brigades were on the north bank, occupying intrenchments at Rappahannock Station which had been thrown up by the Federals. On the 7th of November Meade put his army in motion. It was formed into two columns—the First, Second, and Third Corps under French; the Fifth and Sixth under Sedgwick. In the early morning Birney's division of French's corps waded across the river at Kelly's Ford, captured 500 prisoners, and prevented any supports from coming up to Rappahannock Station, where Sedgwick's corps was to cross. Sedgwick was delayed until afternoon before the works on the north bank. Russell, who led the first division, just at sunset reported that he would with his 3000 men undertake to storm the intrenchments. He charged upon them with fixed bayonets without firing a shot. He met a fire so fierce that in ten minutes his leading regiment, the Fifth Maine, lost 16 out of its 23 officers, and 123 out of 350 men; but the works were carried. At the same moment the One Hundred and Twenty-first New York and the Fifth Maine, firing but a single volley, swept through the rifle-pits and gained the pontoon bridge, cutting off the retreat of the garrison. A few escaped by swimming, but 1600 out of 2000 surrendered. This brilliant achievement redressed the balance of losses in this campaign.

It was now dark. Birney, in command of the Third Corps, sent word to French, across the river, that he would advance at daylight. He began to move, but was checked by an order from Meade. In the afternoon, having been joined by Sedgwick's corps, he advanced to Brandy Station, half way to Culpepper, whither Lee had fallen back, with some 30,000 men, being all that he could then concentrate from his widely-scattered cantonments. Birney was eager to follow, confident that he could strike a telling blow. But Meade, cautious every where except upon the actual battle-field, would not consent. He brought up his whole army to the Station, and Lee, availing himself of the hesitation, recrossed the Rapidan. Meade pushed his advance posts to Culpepper and beyond, and for nearly three weeks lay inactive.[1] It is difficult to understand why the signal advantage which had been gained was not followed up, and the whole day of the 8th wasted in uncertain movements. But the golden opportunity of falling with his whole force upon a portion of the Confederate army was lost; and when Lee had fallen back behind the Rapidan, it was hazardous to follow until the railroad could be put in thorough repair.[2]

[1] *Com. Rep.*, ii., 842.

[2] Confederate returns: July 31, 41,135; October 31, 45,614; November 20, 48,269.

[1] Birney, in *Com. Rep.*, ii., 872; Warren, *Ibid.*, 385.

[2] "I succeeded in surprising the enemy, forcing a passage [across the Rappahannock], compelling him to retreat hurriedly and rapidly to the Rapidan. The army was then moved across the Rappahannock and placed in position between the Rappahannock and the Rapidan, somewhere near its former position, but not quite so far to the front as before, because I had not my communications open. Here a farther delay was rendered necessary until the railroad could be completed from Warrenton Junction and the Rappahannock, and my communications opened."—Meade, in *Com. Rep.*, ii., 842.

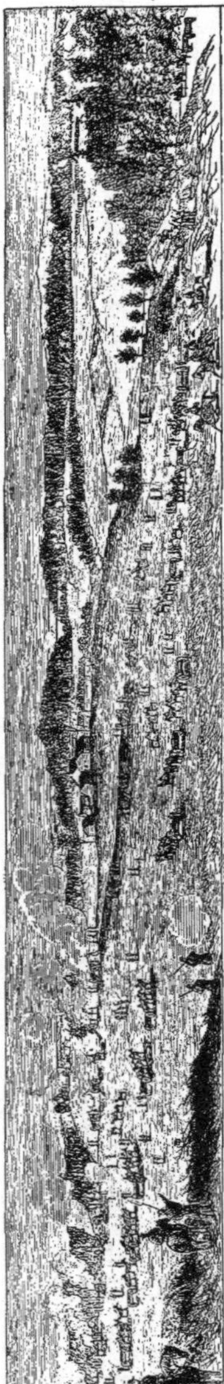

MINE RUN.—CENTRE OF CONFEDERATE POSITION.

MINE RUN.—RECROSSING AT GERMANIA FORD.

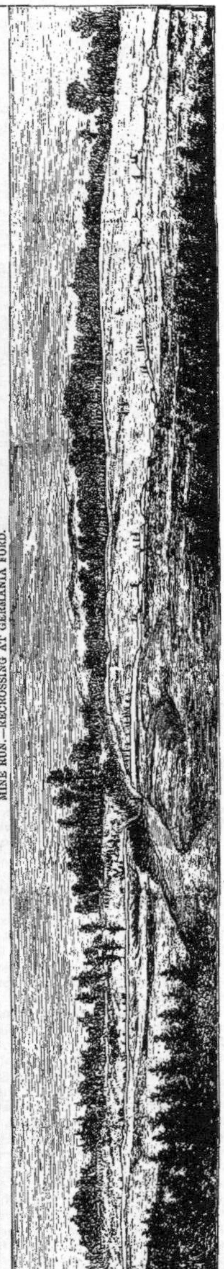

MINE RUN.—WARREN'S LAST POSITION.

As November drew near a close, Lee evidently supposed that active operations for the season were over. He therefore scattered his troops in winter quarters over a wide extent of country. Ewell's corps, on the right, rested upon Mine Run, a mere brook, with a depth of water of from a few inches to two feet, creeping through swamps and dense undergrowth. It runs along the western margin of the Wilderness, and empties into the Rapidan a dozen miles west of Chancellorsville. Along this stream intrenchments had been formed and abatis constructed. These were not very strongly held; and all the lower fords of the Rapidan were left wholly unguarded. The Confederate army was somewhat stronger than at any period since Longstreet's departure for the West. The returns of November 20 showed 56,000 men, of whom 48,000 were present for duty; but it was widely scattered. Ewell's corps was posted along Mine Run, thence stretching southward as far as Orange Court-house, a distance of fully fifteen miles. Still farther lay Hill's corps, its extremity being at Charlottesville, thirty miles farther. The distance from the extreme right to the extreme left was forty-five miles, and there was an interval of some miles between Ewell and Hill. Meade had in all about 70,000 men, closely concentrated within a few miles of Lee's right at Mine Run; of these, about 60,000 were brought forward in aid of the operation which was now to be undertaken.[1]

It seemed to Meade that by suddenly crossing the Rapidan at the fords where Hooker had before crossed, then striking the plank road and turnpike leading westward toward Orange Court-house, he would, by a rapid march of barely twenty miles, fall upon Ewell's corps, crush that before Hill could come up, and then turn upon that corps, drive it back, and thus gain an effective lodgment at Orange Court-house and Gordonsville. The movement was undoubtedly a feasible one, provided no mischance occurred, and every part of it was conducted precisely as planned; but its success depended upon the contingencies of time, space, and weather.

The 24th of November was the time set for the movement; but, as if by way of premonition, a furious storm arose, which delayed every thing for two days. On the 26th the march was begun. The several corps marched in two separate columns, by several different roads. It was supposed that all would reach their points of concentration beyond what had been ascertained to be the extremity of the Confederate intrenchments on Mine Run by noon of the 27th. Warren reached the Rapidan at Germania Ford at the time appointed; but French, who was to cross hard by, was three hours behind time, and thus the passage was delayed, for Meade would not send one corps over alone. Then, again, somebody had blundered in measuring the width of the stream; every pontoon bridge was just one boat too short, and the difficulty had to be supplied by bridging. Thus almost a day was lost in taking the first step, the passage of the Rapidan, which was not effected until the 27th. Warren then pushed on rapidly. He had, indeed, a good road from the Rapidan southward, and within an hour of the appointed time was at the point where he was to be joined by the Third Corps. But French got entangled in the labyrinth of paths, and halted four miles short of the place for junction, where he was held in check by a body of the enemy who had been pushed forward in advance of their line of intrenchments. These two corps, with the First, which was to follow, formed the left column; the right—the First and Fifth Corps—had not got within communicating distance, and till this was effected Meade would not venture an advance. Next morning this was made, but the enemy had fallen back to his intrenched position, and all that day and the next were spent in reconnoitring the position and fixing upon some point for attack. As Sunday, the 29th, drew to a close, Sedgwick, on the right, and Warren, on the left, reported that an attack was feasible on their fronts. Warren indeed, at 9 o'clock, assured Meade that he was confident that the enemy would not be found before him in the morning.[2] French was opposed to attacking on his own front, in the centre, so it was resolved to attack on the left and right, Warren being strengthened by two of French's divisions, giving him a force of 26,000. Sedgwick opened fire with his artillery, and was just about advancing to the assault, when an aid came from Warren with a dispatch stating that he had suspended his assault, finding that the enemy was in great force on his front. There had been ample time to bring up the bulk of the Confederate army, and Warren had the day before demonstrated so ostentatiously that Lee's attention was strongly directed to that part of his line, which he had strengthened by weakening the others.[3] Meade rode over to Warren's position, and was reluctantly obliged to acknowledge that he had done wisely in not making the attack. Sedgwick now reported that the enemy had strengthened himself also in his front; so the order to attack was reversed, and Birney, who had actually begun a strong demonstration upon the centre, was surprised by being ordered to fall back again. Meade was indeed half-minded to accede to Warren's suggestion—to keep on until he had passed beyond the extremity of the Confederate works, and assail them in some position where they would not have time to intrench themselves before the attack could be made. But it was now winter, and favorable weather could not be anticipated from day to day; any sudden storm would prevent the bringing forward of supplies, and of those which had been brought half were exhausted.[1] So Meade concluded that, under the circumstances, nothing more—and nothing more was equivalent to nothing at all—could be done. He withdrew his army to its former position.

With the Mine Run attempt—an enterprise which could have been successful only in case that out of a score of untoward circumstances, all of which were probable, and some of which were almost certain—the closing campaign of 1863 in Virginia came to an end, and both armies retired to winter quarters to await the opening spring.

That during the autumn and winter Richmond had been left almost wholly without troops, was ascertained from sure sources. Between October, 1863, and March, 1864, there were there at no time more than 7000 effective troops, while fully 10,000 Union prisoners were known to be confined in the military prisons. Several plans were formed of making a sudden dash upon the Confederate capital, and at all events liberating these prisoners. Early in February, General Butler, now in command at Fortress Monroe, sent a considerable body of cavalry, supported by infantry, from Yorktown toward Richmond. The cavalry reached Bottom's Bridge, on the Chickahominy, on the 7th; but tidings of the expedition had somehow preceded them, and the roads were so thoroughly obstructed as to be impassable for cavalry, and the expedition returned, having effected nothing.

At the close of the month a more formidable expedition was fitted out from the Army of the Potomac for the same purpose. Kilpatrick, with 4000 cavalry, crossed the Rapidan, and passed Spottsylvania Court-house, and pushed rapidly on toward Richmond. On the first of March he had reached within less than four miles of the city, penetrating the two outer lines of defenses; but, being stopped at the third, he fell back, and the next day, concluding that the enterprise was not feasible, retreated to Yorktown. Meanwhile, at Spottsylvania Court-house, Colonel Ulric Dahlgren, with a picked body of 400 cavalry, had been detached to the right, with the view of skirting to the south, and assailing Richmond in that direction. His guide had led him out of the way. Dahlgren, believing that this was done treacherously, hung him on the spot, and rode on his way till he reached the inner line of defenses. Here he was repulsed, as Kilpatrick had been on the other side. Endeavoring to make his way eastward, he encountered a body of militia, and was shot dead, his command dispersing, a third of them being made prisoners. The Confederates assert that on his body were found an address to his men, and orders and instructions, declaring his object to be to "destroy and burn the hateful city, and not to allow the rebel leader Davis and his traitorous crew to escape. . . . . Once in the city, it must be destroyed, and Davis and his cabinet killed." The genuineness of these papers has been strenuously denied; and, apart from the intrinsic improbability, the account given of the transaction is so suspicious as to leave little doubt that these papers were either absolute forgeries or grossly interpolated. Dahlgren's body, after having been interred, was dug up and buried again secretly, and with every indignity, as that of an outlaw.

With this unfortunate enterprise closed Meade's campaign in Virginia. On the day when Kilpatrick came within sight of Richmond, Ulysses S. Grant was commissioned Lieutenant General of the Armies of the United States. The campaign soon to be opened, lasting a year lacking a month, was conducted by Grant.

[1] Meade mentions incidentally that in the course of these operations Warren had about 25,000 or 26,000 men, and that this was "nearly half" of his whole army.—See *Com. Rep.*, ii., 345, 6.

[2] So Meade testifies (*Com. Rep.*, ii., 345, 6), and that Warren the next day wrote that he had suspended the attack which he had been directed to make, because the order had been based upon his judgment, and he found the enemy had been largely re-enforced. But Warren affirms (*Ibid.*, 386, 7): "I wish it to be distinctly understood that it was no scheme of mine at all to attack at this place. . . . . My idea was that, as we had plenty of provisions, we should keep on until we had passed their left and their intrenchments there, and attack the enemy where he had not any thing. . . . . That the plan of the fight did not depend upon any thing that I said that night is apparent from the fact that the troops on the right were already in position for the attack before I got to General Meade. I put the best face that I could on it then."

[3] "My movement had been apparent to the enemy, for I had made all the fires I could, my object being to make a demonstration as of a heavy force. The enemy saw also other troops moving, and during the night concentrated a large force there also. . . . . In one space, where there was not a gun before, we could then count seventeen guns in a commanding position." (Warren, in *Com. Rep.*, ii., 386, 7.)—Birney says (*Ibid.*, 373): "I think Warren's plan failed because it was attended with too much reconnoitring, fire-building, and delay, all of which fully advertised the movement to the watchful enemy, and prevented a surprise. When Warren was ready to attack he found the enemy ready to receive him. I think that in extending their right they had weakened their centre."

[1] Meade, in *Com. Rep.*, ii., 345.

ULRIC DAHLGREN.

WINTER QUARTERS.—ON PICKET.

CHAPTER XXXI.

THE CHATTANOOGA CAMPAIGN.

I. THE ARMY OF THE CUMBERLAND.

The Beginnings of the Army.—Rousseau's Command at Camp Joe Holt, 1861.—Creation of the Department of the Cumberland; it includes Kentucky and Tennessee; General Robert Anderson its first Commander.—General W. T. Sherman succeeds Anderson, October, 1861.—Is succeeded by Buell in November.—The Department of the Cumberland becomes the Department of the Ohio, including Ohio, Indiana, and Michigan.—Kentucky and Tennessee soon absorbed by Halleck's Department of the Missouri.—Buell's Command styled "the District of the Ohio."—Rosecrans succeeds Buell, October 30, 1862, and the Department of the Cumberland is revived.—The Fourteenth Army Corps.—General Buell's Record.—Estimate of Rosecrans's Military Career; his Disadvantages; his subordinate Commanders, Generals Thomas, McCook, Crittenden, and Stanley.—The Organization of the Army.—Deficiency in Cavalry.—The Battle of Stone River undecisive.—Fortification of Murfreesborough.—Confederate Attack on Fort Donelson.—Actions at Spring Hill and Franklin.—Capture of McMinnville.—Colonel Streight's Raid; his Capture and Escape.—Rosecrans urged to Advance.—Decision of his War Council.—Waiting for Grant.

THE campaign for the possession of Chattanooga began with Rosecrans's advance from Murfreesborough on the 24th of June, 1863, and terminated with General Bragg's defeat on the 25th of November, just five months and one day afterward. The secure tenure of Chattanooga cost two great battles, involving a loss on both sides—if we include the killed and wounded in these battles and during the siege of Knoxville—of over 50,000 men. This campaign had two well-defined periods. With the first of these, which closed when General Rosecrans was relieved of his command (October 19th, 1863), the Army of the Cumberland is alone directly connected.

The organization of this army had its beginning in a little band of Kentuckians, summoned to Camp Joe Holt, near Louisville, early in 1861. This body of volunteers was commanded by Colonel, afterward Major General Lovell H. Rousseau, who, understanding that war must for a time silence statesmanship, had left his seat in the Kentucky Senate, and rallied about him the loyalists of his State. His eloquence, courage, and patriotism found a clear and positive utterance in this unsettled period, when Kentuckians were wavering between secession and loyalty, bound on one side by the ties of kindred and association, on the other by a strong sentiment in favor of the Union. Under the influence of the words and examples of such men as Rousseau and Anderson, this sentiment became dominant over sectional interests, and was ardently espoused by the greater portion of the state. In answer to Rousseau's call, a force of nearly 2000 men was soon assembled in his encampment. At Camp Dick Robinson there was a similar force under General Nelson, and on the 15th of August, 1861, Kentucky and Tennessee were constituted a separate military district, known as the Department of the Cumberland. General Robert Anderson, the hero of Fort Sumter, was the first commander of this department, General W. T. Sherman being second in command. Sherman succeeded Anderson in October, 1861, and established his camp on Muldraugh's Hill, about 40 miles south of Louisville. Here he awaited the arrival of troops from the states north of the Ohio. These came promptly forward, so that before the close of the year there was assembled an army of 70,000 men, over 20,000 of whom were Kentuckians.

In November Sherman was succeeded by Buell. With this change of command the Department of the Cumberland became the Department of the Ohio—Indiana, Michigan, and Ohio being added to its content, while that portion of Kentucky lying west of the Cumberland River was transferred to the Department of the Missouri, then commanded by General Halleck. Subsequently (in March, 1862), Halleck's department was extended eastward to a north and south line passing through Knoxville, and was designated the Department of the Mississippi; three months later it included all of Kentucky and Tennessee, Buell's command being then known as the "District of the Ohio." When Rosecrans succeeded Buell (October 30, 1862), the title of his command was again changed, the Department of the Cumberland being revived, including all of Tennessee and Kentucky east of the Tennessee River, and such parts of Northern Alabama and Georgia as should be conquered by the United States troops. At the same time, the Department of the Tennessee, General Grant's command, comprised Cairo, Forts Henry and Donelson, and all of Kentucky and Tennessee west of the Tennessee River. Grant's troops were designated the Thirteenth, and those of Rosecrans the Fourteenth Army Corps.

The army which thus came under Rosecrans's command had an unstained record. Under Anderson and Sherman it had been but the nucleus of an army. Buell made it formidable in numbers, and perfect in organization and discipline; he created the Army of the Cumberland. Portions of it fought at Piketon, Prestonburg, Middle Creek, Pound Gap, and Mill Spring, but the whole army was engaged in battle for the first time at Shiloh, where, on the second day, it went into the fight in as perfect order as if it had fought a score of battles.

The supersedure of Buell by Rosecrans was owing to a general lack of confidence in the former commander. During the space of nearly a year he had organized and disciplined a great army, but he had done little with it; he had gained no grand, positive success. The defeat of Bragg in Kentucky would have made Buell the great military hero of 1862. But Bragg escaped, after having compelled the Federal army to abandon its advanced position—escaped without a battle, except that of Perryville, which was precipitated by General McCook's disobedience of orders. The people were disappointed. Halleck had become dissatisfied with General Buell. Nothing but Thomas's urgent remonstrance had prevented him from making a change in the command when the Federal army reached Louisville, in the fall of 1862. Thomas declined the command which was then offered him, and urged the retention of Buell. After Bragg's retreat, Buell was court-
martialed for the affair at Perryville, but was acquitted and restore
command. But scarcely had this been done when he was again r
and ordered to relieve General Banks in the Department of the Gulf.
ing that the change had been made by the President immediately
receipt of a protest from Andrew Johnson, then Military Governor
nessee, he very properly declined to accept the new appointmen
command of the Army of the Cumberland should have naturally d
upon General Thomas after Buell's removal, but it so happened that
this time it had become impossible for General Rosecrans to rem
longer in the same military department with General Grant, and
gave him the Army of the Cumberland. General Buell in some
bore a remarkable resemblance to General Thomas. In temperame
were alike. Both were cool in the presence of danger. Both were
soldiers in bearing, courage, and honor. It is impossible fairly to
Buell's military career, because it was so soon concluded. If he h
great military fault, it was an excessive regard for regularity. This
great value in the discipline of a large army, but might easily prove
pediment in the conduct of a campaign. He was a good tactician;
a general of extraordinary energy; yet he lacked dash and brillia
movement. He excited no enthusiasm, and enthusiasm is the elemen
which a volunteer army mainly lives and moves. If he lacked some
excellencies which characterized our more brilliant leaders, he was al
from many of their prominent weaknesses. He was never petulant
patient, and never lost his dignity. He was incapable of dishonor, a
charges which were made against him in 1862, impeaching his patr
were unjust, and, on the part of those who ought to have known him
were malicious.

No general could have been more widely different to Buell than h
cessor, General Rosecrans. Personally, and as regards physical te
ment, they were as far apart as the antipodes. Nature had done littl
Rosecrans for the highest requirements of generalship. He was too
ageous to avoid danger or responsibility, yet the most critical mome
battle would sometimes find him beside himself with nervous excit
To such a temperament, in any large field of human effort, the high
der of achievements is denied. Other things being equal, the best g
is he who has the most self-control at the decisive moment, whose p
are in most instant command, and to whom the hour of embarrassm
of peril comes, not fraught with confusion, but pregnant with sugge
It is in such hours that battles are lost or won—lost, in nearly eve
stance, by the over-excitable general; and, in nearly every instance, w
the cool, self-possessed commander, who, seeing only the chances of su
is blind to the tokens of possible defeat. Rosecrans fought unequally.
early campaigns in West Virginia were in every particular admirably
ducted. He very soon had the mortification of seeing other officers
had effected less, absorb his command, and other and less promising
adopted in preference to his own. After assuming command of the
of the Mississippi (June 27, 1862), he fought well at Iuka and Corinth.
had never lost a battle before he took the Army of the Cumberland.
military career had been so successful as to command popular confi
and great expectations were entertained of him, which were not fully
ized.

Rosecrans was a general of more than ordinary ability. His plans
often brilliant, and led often to successful results. Then, again, they
be elaborate to an almost absurd degree, and so faulty as to embarrass
self rather than the enemy. His strategy at one time excites our ad
tion, and at another appals us with its manifest weakness. Now w
that he is conducting a magnificent campaign, and the next mome
seems to be playing with his army. After weeks of steady and a
sleepless activity in preparing for movement, we behold him advancing
at length—after a series of manœuvres, some of them admirable, and
of them, as likely as not, desperately short-sighted—in the presence c
enemy, we find him in a state of undue excitement, without any de
plan, knowing nothing about the hostile army, and incompetent to tak
proper place as a commander on the field. Military critics will differ w
in their estimate of General Rosecrans; but he must be unjust who ca
find much in him to admire, and he must be a very partial judge i
who, after a mature consideration of Rosecrans's campaigns from No
ber, 1862, to October, 1863, can pronounce him fully equal to his duties
commander. At the same time it must be remembered that Rosecra
bored under great disadvantages, both from the difficult nature of the
try through which he moved, and from the inadequate support which
ceived from the War Department. And so much is due to accident,
favoring circumstances, in the final estimate which is made of public
that probably Rosecrans, if he had had competent subordinates, and had
numbered the enemy in his later campaigns, instead of being himsel
numbered, would to-day rank among the first generals of the war, an
faults have all been forgotten. Faults, so easily forgiven in those who
ceed (upon whatsoever their success may have depended), fall with cru
weight upon those who fail.

The army which Rosecrans received from Buell was not what it
been. The ardor with which its soldiers had enlisted had been quen
by a year of fruitless labor. Over one third of the army (33,000 men)
in hospitals, on furlough, or numbered among the deserters. Every
of Rosecrans's advance called for a strong detail of men for garrison
The cavalry arm of the service was far inferior to that of the enemy,
long lines of communication had to be guarded with extreme caution.
enemy, on the other hand, operating in a friendly country, could mak
entire force effective against Rosecrans.

Very little alteration was made in the organization of the Army of the Cumberland on the change of its commanders. Its composition remained the same. It consisted, in about equal proportions, of veterans and raw recruits—the latter, of course, destitute of discipline, and the former poorly clothed and equipped. Thomas was given an active command, and Brigadier General Gilbert was relieved, and detailed for the protection of the railroad north of Bowling Green.

Major General George H. Thomas, commanding the centre of the army, consisting of Fry's, Rousseau's, Negley's, Dumont's, and Palmer's divisions, was Rosecrans's best general. He was now forty-six years of age. He had received a thorough military education, and acquired considerable military experience in the Florida and Mexican campaigns. At the beginning of the civil war he fought in Virginia, under Patterson and Banks, and received his appointment as brigadier general of volunteers August 17, 1861, when he was removed from Virginia to General Anderson's command. Here, early in 1862, he fought the battle of Mill Spring. From March of that year until the advance upon Corinth, his division, located at Nashville, constituted the reserve of Buell's army. He was, on the 25th of April, 1862, appointed major general of volunteers. A week later his division was transferred to the Army of the Tennessee, and he was assigned by General Halleck to the command of the right wing of that army. In June his command rejoined Buell. Upon the retreat of the latter to Louisville, Thomas was appointed his second in command. After the battle of Stone River, the Army of the Cumberland, under Rosecrans, was divided into three corps—the Fourteenth, Twentieth, and Twenty-first—General Thomas commanding the Fourteenth, which consisted of five divisions, under Rousseau, Negley, J. J. Reynolds, Fry, and R. B. Mitchell.

Major General Alexander McDowell McCook, who commanded the Twentieth Corps of Rosecrans's army, was a native of Ohio, and about thirty years of age. He was a graduate of West Point, and in 1858 had been assigned to that institution as instructor in tactics and in the art of war. He was relieved from this position at the opening of the war, and appointed colonel of the First Ohio Regiment. With this regiment he fought at Bull Run. On the 3d of September, 1861, he was made a brigadier general of volunteers, and given a command in Kentucky. In his camp on Green River he organized the Second Division, with which he fought at Shiloh on the second day of that battle. In the movement on Corinth he commanded the advance of Buell's army. He fought the battle of Perryville against orders, but with determined bravery. He commanded the right wing of Rosecrans's army at Stone River, where he was driven back by the overwhelming forces of the enemy. Although a brave soldier, he was better fitted for a division than a corps commander.

The same judgment may be passed upon Major General Crittenden, commanding the Twenty-first Corps. Before the war his military education and experience had been confined to his service in the Mexican War as aide-de-camp to General Taylor. He was a Kentuckian, being the second son of Hon. John J. Crittenden. His elder brother George was in the Confederate army. He was of about the same age as General Thomas. If Generals McCook and Crittenden, who may be termed two of Rosecrans's "disadvantages," had been displaced by more competent officers, the history of the Army of the Cumberland would have been materially changed.

Major General David S. Stanley, who had been, at Rosecrans's request, transferred from the Army of the Mississippi to take the command of the cavalry of the Army of the Cumberland, was an officer whose great worth Rosecrans had already learned to appreciate. He graduated at West Point in the class of 1852, which numbered among its members McCook, Hartsuff, Slocum, and Sheridan. At the beginning of the war he was stationed at Fort Smith, in Arkansas. He fought under Lyon at Dug Springs and Wilson's Creek, and afterward joined Fremont in the movement on Springfield. He was appointed brigadier general of volunteers September 28th, 1861. Early in 1862 he joined General Pope's command, and his division was the first to occupy the trenches before New Madrid. In the advance on Corinth he commanded the Second Division of the Army of the Mississippi. In the battle of Corinth this division especially distinguished itself, holding the left centre, supporting Battery Robinette. Stanley joined Rosecrans at Nashville in November, 1862, and devoted himself to the reorganization of the cavalry of the Army of the Cumberland.

The departments of no army were ever more completely organized or more efficient in their operation than those of Rosecrans's. Take the matter of supplies for an example. No general ever was beset by greater difficulties in this respect. He was in a barren and hostile country, and the entire subsistence of his army must be transported over a distance of from one to more than two hundred miles, either by a railroad exposed at many points to interruption from the enemy's cavalry, or by the Cumberland River, which, during a considerable portion of the year, was too low for navigation. Yet the soldiers never wanted food. In other respects they were equally well provided for. To facilitate the advance of the army, a Pioneer brigade

Rosecrans. He fought stubbornly with the War Department for th
of increasing the numbers and efficiency of this arm of the servi
wanted good horses, saddles, and revolving carbines, and his import
asking for them seems to have only had the effect of vexing Genc
leck. His requests were always urgent, but respectful. "I must h
writes, January 14, 1863, "cavalry or mounted infantry. I could m
fantry had I horses and saddles. . . . . With mounted infantry I ca
the rebel cavalry to the wall, and keep the roads open in my rear.
now. . . . Will you authorize the purchase of saddles and horses fo
ing, when requisite, 5000 more infantry?" "Why," he asks, tw
later, "should the rebels command the country which, with its re
would belong to our army, because they can muster the small percen
six or eight thousand more cavalry than we?" Toward the close o
he again reminds the general-in-chief of his need. "Let it be cle
derstood," he writes, "that the enemy have five to our one, and ca
fore, command the resources of the country and the services of the
ants."[1] By this time he had gained permission to mount 5000 infan
had succeeded in mounting 2000. But he was unable to mass his
for expeditions, because they were occupied on picket duty. Gener
seau offered to raise 8000 or 10,000 infantry to increase the caval
if the government would mount and arm them, but he seems to l
ceived no assurance that this would be done until the middle of s
Of the cavalry force in hand, only forty per cent. was available f
of horses. This deficiency was repeatedly urged, but the horses w
furnished.[2]

Let us do Rosecrans ample justice in this matter. We can not o
mate his embarrassment arising from a deficient cavalry force. W
done for Grant by the gun-boats could be done for Rosecrans on
large and well-equipped force of cavalry or mounted infantry. It i
ble that his urgent representations at length opened the eyes of the

---

[1] *Report of Congressional Committee on Rosecrans's Campaigns*, p. 39.

[2] The two following letters to General Meigs and Secretary Stanton indicate Rosecr
ation in respect of cavalry:

"Murfreesborough, Ma

"GENERAL,—Your letter of the 1st instant, on the subject of cavalry horses, was yes
ceived and carefully considered. I thank you for taking pains to write so fully. I w
to you, with equal care, the true state of the case in this army, for I find you have fallen
a number of errors on the subject.

"1st. It is a fact that up to the 1st instant our total supply of cavalry horses was as

Cavalry horses on hand	6
Mounted infantry	1
Total	8
Less, at least one quarter, are not serviceable	2
Making cavalry mounted not over	6

"But when these troops are called out, we have at no time been able to turn out
5000 for active duty. The other cavalry horses, reported by Colonel Taylor, were:

Escorts and orderlies	2
Unserviceable in Nashville	
	3

"You will thus see that we have not the cavalry you suppose. We are using the m
ous and unremitting efforts to increase in care of horses and the efficiency of this arm.

"2d. But I must call your attention to the fact that this small cavalry force, effectivel
that is required for a permanent garrison of infantry equal to that of this army, have to fu
ets, scouts, and couriers for Fort Donelson, Clarksville, Nashville, Gallatin, Carthage, a
of this army from Franklin to this place, twenty-eight miles. You may thus form so
the labor imposed on our cavalry, and how our horses are worn out so rapidly.

"3d. As to the actual work of this arm, besides the routine labor, you will find it ha
pedition or fight in mass nearly every week, and as yet without a single failure.

"4th. As to expeditions, we have not a sufficiently strong cavalry force to drive that
emy to the wall, or to risk detachments for the enterprises of which you speak to the
rebels. The one which I did send out under Colonel Streight, in spite of our precau
captured by the superior cavalry force of the enemy, detached from Granger's front a
where Van Dorn has still left about four to our one.

"5th. As to forage, our want is for long forage, and is owing to the impossibility
transportation either by water or rail. You must remember we are 220 miles from o
supplies at Louisville. You may rely on it, I am fully alive to all you have suggested,
nothing which I am not fully satisfied will be an ample economy to the service. Had
alry force equal to that of the enemy, we would have commanded all the forage of the
commanded information of its inhabitants, upon whose fears we, instead of they, would th
to operate.

"As to the comparative number of cavalry in our and other armies, I am sure you ar
as to Russia at least, which has 80,000 regular cavalry, while all the outpost, picket,
duty is done by irregular cavalry. But, even were it otherwise, I know what cavalry wo
us here. I am not mistaken in saying that this great army would gain more from 10,
ive cavalry than from 20,000 infantry. W. S. ROSECRANS, Major General Comm

"Brigadier General M. C. MEIGS, Quarter-master General, U. S. Army, Washington, D. C."

"Winchester, Ju

"Hon. E. M. STANTON, Secretary of War:

"As you approve of General Rousseau's suggestions and views as to the advantage
an additional amount of force of 10,000 men to operate against the rebels from this
have sent him to Washington with letters to yourself and General Halleck, and direct
lay before you the plan which he has of obtaining from the disciplined troops recentl
out of service in the East such a mounted force as would enable us to command the cou
of us, and control its resources, cut off the enemy's means of drawing supplies from th
destroy his lines of communication, and restore law and order to the entire country from
have expelled the insurgents—a thing now impossible, because no one desires to avow
ments for fear the rebel cavalry or guerrillas will wreak vengeance on him. At the
repealing what I have so often laid before the War Department when urging the n
cavalry arms for the force we actually had in pay, but badly armed and mounted, I be
state:

"1st. An adequate cavalry force would have given us control of all Middle Tennesse
its forage, horses, cattle, and mules, and driven the enemy from it without the battle of
er, and re-established civil order.

"2d. It would save us 5000 infantry now guarding our lines of communication, and
ant expense.

"3d. We could have destroyed the enemy's lines of communication, and compelled

partment for the first time to the incalculable value of well-mounted cavalry. We find, at any rate, that after this period the Federal cavalry force was gradually increased and improved; but the change came too late to very materially assist Rosecrans, who, of all our commanders, was in most need of it.

Just before the battle of Stone River the Army of the Cumberland numbered 47,000 men, of whom little more than 3000 were cavalry. We have already, in a previous chapter, brought down the military operations of this army to the conclusion of the battle of Stone River. Before this battle Rosecrans had for some time been pressed to advance, but he found it hazardous to do so until Bragg had sent away his cavalry on distant expeditions. Yet so little were his real difficulties appreciated at Washington, that Halleck, in a long letter of instructions, had directed him to march to East Tennessee, a distance of over 240 miles, through a barren and mountainous region, and at the beginning of the most inclement season of the year. Even if the advance had been possible, Rosecrans's cavalry would have been ludicrously incompetent to protect his long line of communications, thus leaving the way open for Bragg to Nashville and the Ohio River.

The battle of Stone River was not decisive. Rosecrans inflicted upon Bragg greater damage than he received, and drove him from the field. It is a fact which can not be disputed, that the enemy had the advantage of superior numbers. The Federal army went into the battle 43,000 strong, and when it occupied Murfreesborough, January 5, numbered little more than 30,000. Neither army was in a condition, after the battle, to resume the offensive. The Army of the Cumberland had lost some of its bravest officers. Among these were its youngest brigadier general, J. W. Sill, who had been one of the first to join Sherman at Muldraugh's Hill in 1861; Colonel J. P. Garesché, chief of staff to General Rosecrans, whose head was blown away by a cannon ball while he was riding over the field in execution of a special mission for his commander; and Colonels Roberts, Milliken, Shaeffer, McKee, Reed, Forman, Jones, Hawkins, and Kell. Brigadier General James A. Garfield, the hero of Middle Creek, succeeded Garesché as Rosecrans's chief of staff. This officer's skill and bravery on the battle-field was only equaled by the talent and uncompromising patriotism which he afterward displayed in the political arena.

After its occupation by the Army of the Cumberland, Murfreesborough was fortified and made a dépôt of supplies. Here the army remained encamped for six months, while General Grant was conducting the Vicksburg campaign. The rainy season soon began, but, while interfering with offensive operations, it swelled the waters of the Cumberland, and facilitated the accumulation of supplies. The monotony of camp life was relieved only by foraging excursions and encounters with the Confederate cavalry. These were conducted at some risk. Not unfrequently the men and wagons were picked up by the enemy, who succeeded sometimes, also, in capturing and burning a transport on the river.

An attempt was made by the Confederates, early in February, to obstruct the navigation of the Cumberland by the recapture of Fort Donelson. On the third of that month, Forrest, Wheeler, and Wharton advanced upon the fort from above and below, with eleven regiments of cavalry and nine guns. The garrison defending Fort Donelson at this time consisted of nine companies of the Eighty-third Illinois, with a battalion of the Fifth Iowa cavalry, and numbered less than 800 men, under the command of Colonel A. C. Harding. The only artillery defense was a battery of four rifled pieces and a single 32-pounder siege gun. A little after noon Harding was summoned to surrender, and promptly refused. The attack was then commenced. The defense was gallantly conducted, and after repeated charges, which cost them

PACK-MULES IN THE MOUNTAINS.

upward of 1000 men, the Confederates retired. Harding's loss was 16 killed, 60 wounded, and 50 prisoners.

On the 5th of March a Federal brigade, numbering 1306 men, under Colonel John Coburn, was surrounded and captured by Forrest's and Van Dorn's cavalry near Spring Hill. The cavalry and artillery of the command escaped. The Confederate force consisted of six brigades, under Generals Van Dorn, French, Armstrong, Crosby, Martin, and Jackson.

A fortnight later, Colonel A. S. Hall, with about 1400 men, encountered the Confederate General John Morgan at Milton, twelve miles northeast of Murfreesborough. Morgan attacked with a force numbering nearly 2000 men, and, after a fight of three and a half hours, withdrew from the field, defeated. The Confederate loss was about 400. Hall lost 60, killed, wounded, and missing.

About the middle of April, Van Dorn, with 9000 men, attacked General Gordon Granger's force at Franklin, consisting of Baird's and Gilbert's divisions, 1600 men and 16 guns, and Generals Smith's and Stanley's cavalry brigades of 2700 men, with four guns. The defense was materially assisted by an uncompleted fort, mounting two siege and two rifled guns, and commanding the northern approaches to Franklin. The attack was repulsed, the enemy losing about 300 men, and General Granger 37.

McMinnville, a few miles southeast of Murfreesborough, was captured on the 21st of April by General Reynolds's division, Colonel Wilder's mounted brigade, and a cavalry force under Colonel Minty, 1700 strong. About 700 Confederates were dispersed, and a few wagons taken.

In the mean time Colonel A. D. Streight had been given the command of an independent provisional brigade, consisting of his own regiment (the Fifty-first Indiana), the Eightieth Illinois, and portions of two Ohio regiments, numbering all together about 1800 men. Colonel Streight early in April received instructions to proceed to Northern Georgia, to cut the railroads in Bragg's rear, and destroy all dépôts of supplies, manufactories of arms, clothing, etc.[1]

[1] The following is a copy of the instructions given to Colonel Streight:

"Headquarters, Department of the Cumberland, Murfreesborough, April 8, 1863.

"Colonel A. D. Streight, Fifty-first Indiana Volunteers:

"By Special Field Orders No. 94, Paragraph VIII., you have been assigned to the command of an independent provisional brigade for temporary purposes. After fitting out your command with equipments and supplies, as you have already been directed in the verbal instructions of the general commanding this department, you will proceed, by a route of which you will be advised by telegraph, to some good steamboat-landing on the Tennessee River, not far above Fort Henry, where you will embark your command and proceed up the river. At Hamburg you will communicate with Brigadier General Dodge, who will probably have a messenger there awaiting your arrival. If it should then appear unsafe to move farther up the river, you will debark at Hamburg, and without delay join the force of General Dodge, which will then be en route for Iuka, Mississippi. If, however, it should be deemed safe, you will land at Eastport and form a junction with General Dodge. From that point you will then march in conjunction with him to menace Tuscumbia; but you will not wait to join in the attack unless it should be necessary for the safety of General Dodge's command or your own, or unless some considerable advantage can be gained over the enemy without interfering with the general object of your expedition. After having marched long enough with General Dodge to create a general impression that you are a part of his expedition, you will push to the southward, and reach Russelville or Moulton. From there your route will be governed by circumstances; but you will, with all reasonable dispatch, push on to Western Georgia and cut the railroads which supply the rebel army by way of Chattanooga. To accomplish this is the chief object of your expedition, and you must not allow collateral or incidental schemes, even though promising great results, to delay you so as to endanger your return. Your quarter-master has been furnished with funds sufficient for the necessary expenses of your command. You will draw your supplies and keep your command well mounted from the country through which you pass. For all property taken for the legitimate use of your command, you will make cash payments in full to men of undoubted loyalty; give the usual conditional receipts to men whose loyalty is doubtful; *but to rebels nothing*. You are particularly commanded to restrain your command from pillage and marauding. You will destroy all dépôts of supplies for the rebel army, all manufactories of guns, ammunition, equipments, and clothing for their use, which you can, without delaying you so as to endanger your return. That you may not be trammeled with minute instructions, nothing farther will be ordered than this general outline of policy and operation. In intrusting this highly important and somewhat perilous expedition to your charge, the general commanding places great reliance upon your prudence, energy, and valor, and the well-attested bravery and endurance of the officers and men in your command." Whenever it is possible and reasonably safe, send us word of your progress. You may return by way of Northern

THE COURIER LINE.

Streight's command was of about the same strength as the column under Grierson, which was at the same time setting out from La Grange for the raid through Mississippi, described in a previous chapter. It was taken on steam-boats up the Tennessee to Eastport, Alabama, where it was joined by an infantry force under General Dodge. After the capture of Tuscumbia by Streight, the two columns separated. General Dodge made a sweeping raid through Northern Alabama, and returned to Corinth. Streight struck for Northern Georgia, intending to capture Rome and Atlanta, destroying there large manufactories and magazines. He was closely followed by Forrest and Roddy, with a superior force of Confederate cavalry. He kept up a running fight for over a hundred miles, when his command, exhausted and out of ammunition, was surrendered about fifteen miles from Rome. The privates were exchanged, but Streight and his officers were kept in close confinement in Richmond, being charged with felony for having incited slaves to rebellion. Streight finally, on February 9, 1864, with 107 other Federal officers, escaped from Libby Prison. He succeeded, with about sixty of the fugitives, in making his way into the Federal lines. He surrendered 1365, and lost in the actions with Forrest 100 men. The Confederate loss in killed and wounded he claims to have been five times as large as his own.

For six months, as already stated, Rosecrans remained in camp at Murfreesborough. The Confederate army, under Bragg, lay about thirty miles south, on a branch of the Nashville Railroad running from Wartrace to Shelbyville. In May Grant was across the Mississippi fighting Pemberton and Johnston, and before the close of the month had shut up the former in Vicksburg, while the latter was straining every nerve to gather an army sufficiently large to raise the siege. At about this time the authorities at Washington supposed that Johnston was being heavily re-enforced for this purpose from General Bragg's army. Early in June, therefore, Halleck urged Rosecrans to take advantage of Bragg's weakness and drive him into Georgia, when East Tennessee would become an easy prey to the Federal forces. But the matter was looked upon in quite a different light at Rosecrans's headquarters. There it seemed better that Bragg should stay where he was. It was not believed that he had been materially weakened: it seemed evident that the Confederate War Department was resolved upon keeping its foothold in Tennessee as well as in Mississippi.[1] Again, if Rosecrans advanced and compelled Bragg's retreat, his army, for want of an adequate cavalry force, was in no condition to pursue, and the consequence would be unfavorable to Grant, who would then have to meet the bulk of Bragg's army. At a council of war called by Rosecrans, composed of seventeen officers (corps and division commanders and generals of cavalry), it was the opinion of eleven that Bragg had not been materially weakened, the other six thinking that 10,000 men had been sent to Johnston. Only four of the seventeen thought the Army of the Cumberland could then advance with a reasonable prospect of fighting a great and successful battle, and even these were doubtful. The council unanimously agreed that an advance was unadvisable.[2]

A few days later, the Vicksburg campaign seeming so near its succes termination, and it being understood that General Burnside would co-ope by an advance into East Tennessee, the Army of the Cumberland was se motion. This advance—made under great disadvantages, which the rea has already been taught to appreciate—and the brilliant movements which General Bragg was driven from Shelbyville to Chattanooga, form subject of the next chapter.

CHAPTER XXXII.

THE CHATTANOOGA CAMPAIGN.

II. THE ADVANCE FROM MURFREESBOROUGH.

The Confederate Situation in Tennessee.—Estimate of Forces.—The Order to Advance.—Acti at Liberty and Hoover's Gaps.—Occupation of Shelbyville.—The Race for Elk River.—Br abandons Middle Tennessee.—Rosecrans brought to a Halt.

BRAGG'S army held the line of Duck River, guarding the railroad fr Nashville to Chattanooga. Polk, with 18,000 men, was strongly trenched at Shelbyville, where, by the forced labor of 3000 slaves sent fr Georgia and Alabama, a line of earth-works had been constructed five mil in extent. On his right, at Wartrace, and holding the railroad, was Harde corps, 12,000 strong, with outposts at Liberty and Hoover's Gaps, guardi the mountain approaches from the north. In the rear, eighteen miles sou of Duck River, another intrenched camp lay behind a difficult mounta range at Tullahoma. Besides Polk's and Hardee's corps north of Duck Ri er, Bragg had another, under Buckner, in East Tennessee, numbering 10,0 effective men.

The entire Confederate army of Tennessee on the 20th of June, 186 numbered 46,000 effective men.[1] Rosecrans's army at that time was n less than 60,000 strong, but this superiority of numbers was balanced by th inferiority of his cavalry, and by the necessity of a detachment of force every stage of his advance into the enemy's country. It was, therefore, th obvious policy of the Federal commander to compel Bragg to fight a battl in Tennessee. It was with this idea that Rosecrans planned his summe campaign, waiting only the assurance that the retreat of Bragg's army which must be reckoned among the things possible, would not seriously af fect the Vicksburg campaign.

The Confederate General John Morgan having been sent, with a large de tachment of cavalry, northward for an excursion into Kentucky, it seeme an opportune season for an advance against the enemy, orders for whic were issued on the 23d of June. The movement began the next day. Th direct road to Shelbyville was the easiest approach, while those farther east ward led through difficult mountain passes, strongly guarded by the enemy An advance by the former would have terminated in a battle with the ene

---

Alabama or Northern Georgia. Should you be surrounded by rebel forces and your retreat cut off, defend yourself as long as possible, and make the surrender of your command cost the enemy as many times your number as possible. A copy of the general order from the War Department in regard to paroling prisoners, together with the necessary blanks, are herewith furnished you. You are authorized to enlist all able-bodied men who desire to join the 'army of the Union.' You must return as soon as the main objects of your expedition are accomplished.

"Very respectfully, your obedient servant,

"J. A. GARFIELD, Brigadier General and Chief of Staff."

"*Additional by Telegraph.*

"April 9, 1863.

"The written instructions you have received are designed to cover the cases you allude to. It is not necessary that a manufactory be directly in the employ of the rebels to come under the rule there laid down. If it produces any considerable quantity of supplies which are likely to reach the rebel army, it is to be destroyed. Of course small mills, that can only supply the necessaries of life to the inhabitants, should not be injured. Any considerable amount of supplies likely to reach the rebel army are to be destroyed. If you dress your soldiers in the costume of the enemy, they will be liable to be treated as spies; you should not do this without the consent of the men, after they have been fully advised of the possible consequences.

"(Signed), J. A. GARFIELD, Brigadier General and Chief of Staff."

[1] This was against General Joe Johnston's advice, who said that the Confederate government must choose between Mississippi and Tennessee. He urged the retention of Tennessee, which he declared to be "the shield of the South."

[2] The following is the correspondence which passed between Rosecrans and Halleck in reference to an immediate advance:

"Murfreesborough, Tenn., June 11th, 1863.

"Your dispatch of to-day is received. You remember that I gave you, as a necessary condition of success, an adequate cavalry force. Since that time I have not lost a moment in mounting our dismounted cavalry as fast as we could get horses. Not more than three hundred remain to be mounted. The Fifth Iowa, ordered up from Donelson, arrived to-day. The First Wisconsin will be here by Saturday. My preliminary infantry movements have nearly all been completed, and I am preparing to strike a blow that will tell. But to show you how differently things are viewed here, I called on my corps and division commanders and generals of cavalry for answers in writing to the questions:

"First. From your best information, do you think the enemy materially weakened in our front? Second. Do you think this army can advance at this time with reasonable prospect of fighting a great and successful battle? Third. Do you think an advance advisable at this time? To the first, eleven answered no; six, yes, to the extent of ten thousand. To the second, four, yes, with doubts; thirteen, no. To the third, not one yes; seventeen, no.

"Not one thinks an advance advisable until Vicksburg's fate is determined. Admitting these officers to have a reasonable share of military sagacity, courage, and patriotism, you perceive that there are graver and stronger reasons than probably appear at Washington for the attitude of this army. I therefore counsel caution and patience at headquarters. Better wait a little to get all we can ready to insure the best result. If by so doing we, perforce of Providence, observe a great military maxim—not to risk two great and decisive battles at the same time—we might have cause to be thankful for it. At all events, you see that, to expect success, I must have such thorough grounds that when I say 'Forward,' my word will inspire conviction and confidence where both are now wanting. I should like to have your suggestion.

"W. S. ROSECRANS, Major General.

"To Major General H. W. HALLECK, General-in-Chief."

"Washington, June 12, 1863.

are not prepared to fight Bragg, I shall not order you to do so, for the responsibility of fightin or refusing to fight at a particular time or place must rest upon the general in immediate com mand; it can not be shared by a council of war, nor will the authorities here make you figh against your will. You ask me to counsel them to caution and patience: I have done so ver often, but after five or six months of inactivity, with your force all the time diminishing, and n hope of any immediate increase, you must not be surprised that their patience is pretty well ex hausted. If you do not deem it prudent to risk a general battle with Bragg, why can you no harass him, or make such demonstrations as to prevent his sending more re-enforcements t Johnston? I do not write this in a spirit of fault-finding, but to assure you that the prolonge inactivity of so large an army in the field is causing much complaint and dissatisfaction, not onl in Washington, but throughout the country.

"Very respectfully, your obedient servant, H. W. HALLECK, General-in-Chief.

"Major General ROSECRANS, Murfreesborough, Tennessee."

"Headquarters, Department of the Cumberland, Murfreesborough, June 21, 1863.

"GENERAL,—In your favor of the 12th instant you say you do not see how the maxim of no fighting two great battles at the same time applies to the case of this army and to Grant's. Look ing at the matter practically, we and our opposing forces are so widely separated that for Brag to materially aid Johnston he must abandon our front substantially, and then we can move to ou ultimate work with more rapidity, and less waste of material on natural obstacles. If Grant i defeated, both forces will come here, and then we ought to be near our base. The same maxin that forbids, as you take it, a single army fighting two great battles at the same time—by the way a very awkward thing to do—would forbid this nation's engaging all its forces in the great Wes at the same time, so as to leave it without a single reserve to stem the current of possible disaster This is, I think, sustained by high military and political considerations. We ought to fight here if we have a strong prospect of winning a decisive battle over the opposing force, and upon thi ground I shall act. I shall be careful not to risk our last reserve without strong grounds to ex pect success. W. S. ROSECRANS, Major General.

"Major General H. W. HALLECK, General-in-Chief."

In Rosecrans's letter (last quoted) to Halleck there is unnecessary impertinence. A single arm might easily fight two great battles at the same time. Rosecrans speaks of it as "a very awk ward thing to do," as if it were impossible.

In his testimony before the Congressional Committee on the Conduct of the War (see *Rose crans's Campaigns*, p. 27), Rosecrans says: "I felt it my duty to sacrifice all personal gratification and even to fall in the estimation, temporarily, of the country and friends who had high hope and expectations of the Army of the Cumberland, to secure General Grant, in his operations be fore Vicksburg, from the consequences of compelling Bragg to retire, when it would not be possi ble for us so to pursue as to prevent him from re-enforcing Johnston, whose relative numbers t our troops under General Grant was deemed more formidable than I subsequently learned it t have been."

[1] Estimated from official returns. The following are the returns of this army from Novembe 20, 1862, to June 20, 1863, inclusive:

	Aggregate Present and Absent.	Aggregate Present.	Present for Duty.
November 20, 1862	61,229	86,656	30,549
December 10, 1862	68,434	60,075	51,036
January, 1863	83,780	49,331	36,081
February 20, 1863	87,753	55,138	42,089
March 31, 1863	96,301	65,594	42,915
April 30, 1863	96,217	67,849	52,069
May 20, 1863	93,217	64,722	50,233
June 20, 1863	83,607	59,542	45,274

These returns show:

1. That Bragg outnumbered Rosecrans at the battle of Stone River ...

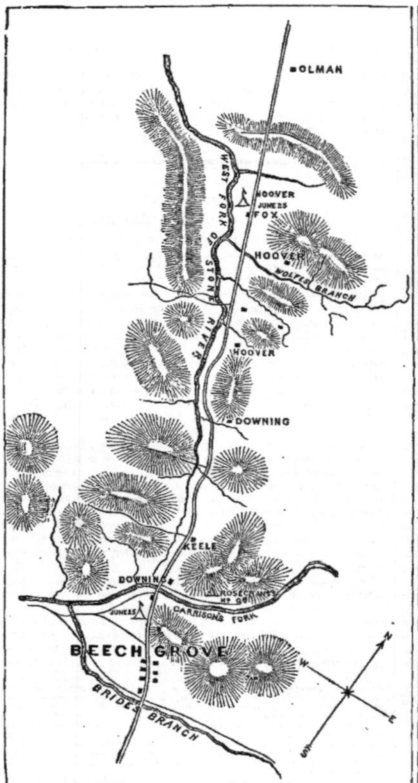

THE ADVANCE THROUGH HOOVER'S GAP.

my in his well-intrenched and chosen position—a battle which, if successful, would be gained at great sacrifice, and leave Bragg an open door for retreat. The mountain roads led to Bragg's right and rear. A strong demonstration on the Shelbyville road would compel that general to uncover the difficult approaches on his right, and once beyond these, Rosecrans, by a very rapid movement to Manchester or Winchester, would cut off retreat, and force the enemy to a battle, the conditions of which would be equal as to the field of conflict, and as to numbers much in his favor. With Morgan's command out of the way, his cavalry was able to cope with Bragg's, while he was superior in infantry by at least 20,000 men.

McCook's corps began its march early on the morning of the 24th. Phil Sheridan's division took the direct road to Shelbyville, preceded by five companies of mounted infantry. The other two divisions, under Generals Jeff C. Davis and R. W. Johnson, followed for six miles, and then turned to the left into the road to Liberty Gap. Thomas's corps, starting at the same time, moved directly on Manchester by way of Hoover's Gap. Crittenden's corps, the last to move, made a long detour to McMinnville, about forty miles southeast from Murfreesborough. Granger, commanding a reserve corps, supported McCook and Thomas. The cavalry was divided—Turchin, with one brigade, going with Crittenden, while the rest, under Stanley, were thrown out on the right flank.

For several days the weather had been clear and promising, but on the very morning of the advance from Murfreesborough it began to rain. For seventeen successive days the rain continued, swelling streams, and so badly cutting up the roads that rapid progress, the most essential element entering into the campaign, was impossible. One division occupied three days in marching twenty-one miles. Such a season at this period of the year had not been known in Tennessee for a score of years.

Both Liberty and Hoover's Gaps, about ten miles from Murfreesborough, were carried by McCook and Thomas on the 24th. The works at the entrance of Hoover's Gap, the eastern pass, were unoccupied by the enemy when Wilder's mounted infantry approached them, so sudden and unexpected was the advance, and a train of nine wagons was captured on its way to camp, with a drove of beef cattle and some prisoners. At the southern extremity of the Gap, in the vicinity of the enemy's camp at Beech Grove, there was some resistance. A miniature battle was fought between a few regiments of Wilder's brigade and a superior Confederate force, in which the Federal detachment was almost overpowered before Reynolds's division could come to its aid. The loss in Wilder's command, after two hours of fighting, was 63 killed and wounded; deserters and prisoners estimated the enemy's loss at over 500. The Confederate force defending the Gap was a part of General Pat Cleburne's division.

Another portion of Cleburne's command guarded Liberty Gap, which had in the mean time been carried by Willich's brigade of Johnson's division. Willich charged with his men, and, turning the enemy's flanks, drove him from the position, capturing his tents, baggage, and supplies. The other end of the Gap was carried with equal gallantry by Baldwin's brigade. The next day Johnson held the Gap, to keep up the delusion as to a direct advance upon Bragg's intrenchments. In the afternoon an attempt was made by the enemy to regain his lost position, and the attack was sufficiently serious to compel Johnson to send in Carlin's brigade of Davis's division. Davis was ill, but, hearing the noise of the battle, left his couch, and reached the front in time to witness the charge of Carlin's brigade and the defeat of the enemy.

Rosecrans now pushed his army on to Manchester, flanking Bragg, who immediately abandoned his useless intrenchments. These were occupied by Granger and Stanley on the 27th. Stanley, with his cavalry, had joined Granger at Christiana. Advancing on Guy's Gap, covering Shelbyville, that position was carried after a little brief skirmish. The enemy was already in retreat, and Shelbyville was captured that evening, with three guns, 500 prisoners, 3000 sacks of corn, and other supplies. The main body of Wheeler's cavalry, which had covered the retreat, escaped by swimming Duck River.

By this time all of McCook's and Thomas's corps were at Manchester. Wilder's command was ordered to Decherd to destroy the bridge over Elk River, but this was found too strongly guarded. In the race for Elk River, Bragg had come out ahead, securing his military road, which he had constructed five miles east of the railroad. Covered again by Wheeler's cavalry, he had left Tullahoma on the 30th of June, to escape the blow which Rosecrans was prepared to strike on his right flank, and succeeded in crossing the Elk at Estelle Springs without a battle. Negley's and Sheridan's divisions, with Turchin's cavalry, came up with the enemy's rear-guard, under Wheeler, July 25. Skirmishing followed, but the resistance was so stubborn that Bragg did not lose a gun. When the river, then swollen by the rains of the last nine days, was crossed by Rosecrans on the 3d, the enemy had vanished. Crittenden's corps, brought down from McMinnville, had taken possession of the road leading from Decherd by way of Tracy City to Chattanooga, thus compelling Bragg to retreat through the mountains westward. McCook had also advanced so as to keep him to the west of Winchester. But Bragg had a fair start, and these movements proved of little consequence. The Confederate army retreated across the Cumberland Mountains to Chattanooga, destroying the railroad in its rear, and crossing the Tennessee at Bridgeport.

Rosecrans was disappointed. He had hoped to fight a battle in Tennessee. He had scarcely counted upon the rapid backward movement made by Bragg. Something had been gained. He had recovered Middle Tennes-

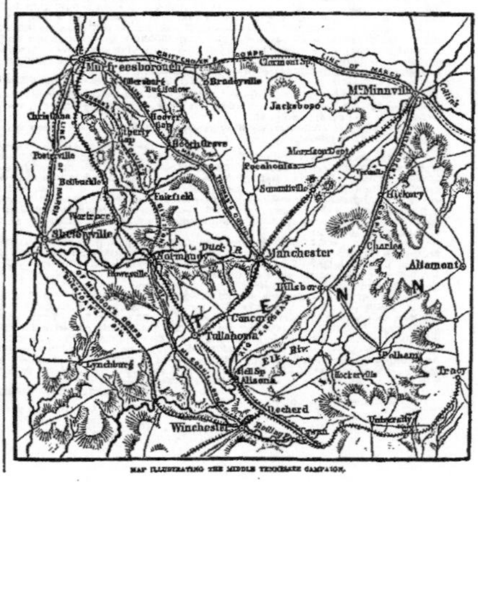

MAP ILLUSTRATING THE MIDDLE TENNESSEE CAMPAIGN.

see at a cost of less than 600 men, and had, besides causing the enemy an equal loss in killed and wounded, captured over 1600 prisoners. But Bragg had escaped. The thing which had been accomplished was not the thing which had been planned.

The worst feature of the situation in which Rosecrans found himself, after Bragg's retreat, was the impossibility of pursuit. His army occupied a line extending from McMinnville to Winchester; but his cavalry posts had followed the enemy to the Tennessee, and outposts were established from Stevenson on the right to Pelham on the left. In this position Rosecrans was brought to a halt, in order to establish his line of communications with Murfreesborough. The Middle Tennessee campaign had been concluded. The movements made by Rosecrans in this campaign were brilliant; but he had made a great mistake in too readily assuming that the enemy would fight instead of retreating. If, in place of waiting at Manchester for Crittenden, he had moved directly on Estelle Springs, Bragg must either have fought or have fallen back with an utterly demoralized army, and with great loss of artillery. If Crittenden was necessary, then he ought not, in the first instance, to have been sent so far out of the way. That which, more than any thing else, disarranged Rosecrans's plans, was the never-ceasing rain; a circumstance for which he, of course, was not accountable, and one upon which he could not have counted. Fair weather would have been the ruin of the Confederate Army of Tennessee. As it was, Rosecrans was farther than ever from his military base, and, looking forward to the next stage of his campaign, could not expect to fight a battle with the enemy under conditions as favorable as those which had just been offered him.

But Bragg's army lost by retreating. His effective force after reaching Chattanooga was only about 40,000 men, or 6000 short of his strength at Shelbyville. Two thirds of this loss is to be accounted for by straggling and desertion. His retreat, occurring at the same time with the surrender of Vicksburg and the defeat at Gettysburg, contributed much to the general despondency in the South which followed those disasters to the Confederate cause.

ROBERT B. POTTER.

CHAPTER XXXIII.

THE CHATTANOOGA CAMPAIGN.

III. THE ARMY OF THE OHIO.—RECOVERY OF EAST TENNESSEE.

Burnside's Department; its Limits; Political and Military Situation.—The Ninth Corps transferred from Newport News to the West.—Pegram's Raid; his Defeat at Somerset.—New England troops at Louisville.—The three Military Districts of Kentucky and their Commanders.—Organization of the Twenty-third Corps.—The Ninth Corps is sent to Vicksburg.—This upsets Burnside's Plan for the immediate recovery of East Tennessee.—Colonel Sanders's Expedition; he breaks the East Tennessee and Virginia Railroad, and threatens Knoxville.—John Morgan's Raid.—He starts from Sparta, June 27th.—Estimate of his Force.—Fight at Tebbs's Bend, July 4th.—Colonel Moore refuses to surrender on the Glorious Fourth; his successful Defense.—Morgan crosses Green River.—Colonel Hanson surrenders Lebanon, July 5th, after seven hours' fighting; Morgan's Brother killed.—Generals Hobson, Judah, and Shackleford in pursuit of Morgan.—Morgan crosses the Ohio into Southern Indiana.—He sweeps around Cincinnati.—His perilous Situation.—He is surrounded and captured with his Command.—His subsequent Escape.—Burnside's March across the Mountains into East Tennessee.—Difficulties of the March.—Knoxville is captured without a Battle.—Burnside's Reception by the Loyalists.—Capture of Cumberland Gap.

GENERAL BURNSIDE was assigned to the Department of the Ohio on the 15th of March, 1863. He had been relieved of the command of the Army of the Potomac on the 25th of January. The interval had been spent by the general at his home in Providence, Rhode Island. One week after his new appointment he reached Cincinnati, and there established his headquarters. General Horatio G. Wright had been the commander of the Department of the Ohio, which now comprised the states of Ohio, Indiana, Illinois, Michigan, Eastern Kentucky, and East Tennessee, as soon as the latter should be occupied. The situation, political and military, of the department required the utmost tact and sagacity on the part of its commander. The Confederate cavalry was ravaging a large portion of Kentucky, and in the more northern states there existed considerable disaffection toward the national government. Martial law had been proclaimed in Kentucky, but in Indiana, Ohio, and Illinois there was no hinderance to the most licentious freedom on the part of public speakers and of the press.

In such a state of affairs, the military force then existing was not sufficient either to meet the hostile incursions of the enemy or to silence disloyalists. Burnside, therefore, had two divisions of the Ninth Army Corps, then in camp at Newport News, under Generals Willcox and Sturgis, transferred to his department. Upon this change, Sturgis was succeeded in the command of his division by General Robert B. Potter. At this time the Confederate General Pegram, with a force of 3000 men, was marching through Central Kentucky, capturing towns and plundering citizens, and had with feeble opposition penetrated as far as Danville. Louisville was almost in danger of being captured, and Indiana open to invasion. To meet these hostile intentions of Pegram, the Ninth Corps was hurried westward, and the small detachments of Federal troops scattered over Central Kentucky were concentrated at Lebanon and Hickman's Bridge, under Generals Q. A. Gillmore and Boyle. With these latter Burnside ordered an advance against Pegram on the 28th of March. The enemy was driven rapidly southward, and at Somerset, on the 30th, Gillmore, with his cavalry, routed and drove him across the Cumberland River, inflicting upon him a loss of 500 killed, wounded, and prisoners.

The two divisions of the Ninth Corps, now commanded by General John G. Parke, who had relieved "Baldy" Smith, arrived at Louisville early in April. The corps was composed for the most part of New England troops, against whom, as Yankees *par excellence*, the Kentuckians were prejudiced. This sentiment, however, was soon overcome by the courtesy of the officers and the general good conduct of the soldiers. Kentucky was at this time divided into three military districts: the Eastern, with headquarters at Louisa, under General Julius White; the Central, under General Q. A. Gillmore, with headquarters at Lexington; and the Western, under General J. T. Boyle, with headquarters at Louisville. Gillmore, after Pegram's defeat, was relieved by General Willcox. The line held by the troops in these three districts extended from the Big Sandy to the Cumberland River. The Ninth Corps, upon its arrival, was sent to the front. It was a part of Burnside's duty to protect so much of Rosecrans's lines of communication as lay within his department. For this purpose fortified posts were established on the railroads leading to Western Kentucky and Tennessee, and the utmost precaution was used to prevent raids on the part of guerrillas and the enemy's cavalry.

On the 27th of April, in compliance with an order from Washington, all the troops in Kentucky not belonging to the Ninth began to be organized into another corps, to be designated as the Twenty-third, and to be under the command of Major General G. L. Hartsuff. This organization was completed by the 22d of May, and a plan of operations was consulted between Burnside and Rosecrans for an immediate advance, the former marching with his two corps directly into East Tennessee, while the latter moved upon Chattanooga. Preparations were made for the campaign by both armies, and on the 2d of June Burnside moved his headquarters from Cincinnati to Lexington; but, at the very last moment, the Ninth Corps was withdrawn from Burnside to re-enforce General Grant before Vicksburg, and the East Tennessee campaign was postponed.

About the middle of June Colonel H. S. Saunders led an expedition into East Tennessee, and, striking the Virginia and Tennessee Railroad at Lenoir, moved up the road, breaking up portions of it on his route. He threatened Knoxville, burned the bridge—1600 feet long—across Holston River at Strawberry Plains, captured 10 guns and 400 prisoners, and, after destroying stores of great value, returned to Lexington on the 26th.

It was at about this time that the Confederate General John Morgan was planning his grand raid into Kentucky and the states north of the Ohio. His scheme was daring, contemplating a bold march through Kentucky, breaking through Burnside's lines, now weakened by the absence of Parke's corps, then across the Ohio River and through the southern counties of Ohio and Indiana, finally sweeping down into West Virginia, or, if fortune favored, through Pennsylvania, to join General Lee's invading army.

Morgan, starting from Sparta June 27, crossed the Cumberland River near Burkesville on the 2d of July, accompanied by General Basil Duke as second in command. His force has been variously estimated, the Confederate statements putting it at 2028 men, with four guns, and the Federal officers in Kentucky at from 4000 to 5000. The truth probably lies about midway between these estimates. Pollard states the force to have been 3000 strong, in two brigades. Burnside was scarcely prepared for this sudden invasion. His best troops were away. Saunders, with his most efficient cavalry, had only just returned from an exhausting raid. Custer's troops were at a distance from the Cumberland. Morgan's command was well organized, and would have little trouble in supplying itself in the fertile valleys of the Cumberland and Ohio. Confined to no strictly-defined line of march, it easily evaded the troops first sent to intercept it, and obtained a start of two days, moving on Columbia.

MORGAN'S RAIDERS.

IMPROMPTU BARRICADE.

Passing through Columbia, Morgan attempted to cross Green River Bridge, at Tebbs's Bend, on the 4th. Guarding the river at this point were five companies of the Twenty-fifth Michigan, under Colonel Orlando H. Moore. The position was well selected for defense, and when Morgan approached, before daylight, demanding its surrender, Moore replied, "The Fourth of July is not a proper day for me to entertain such a proposition." Morgan attacked, and was driven off with a loss of nearly 50 men, among whom were some of his best officers.[1] It had been an obstinate, and at times a hand-to-hand struggle, and the 200 brave defenders of the stockade well earned the thanks which were afterward tendered them by the Kentucky Legislature. Morgan had attacked with two regiments, the rest of his force crossing the river, in the mean time, by another ford.

From the Green River Morgan swept northward, striking Lebanon the next day. The garrison at this place consisted of 400 men of the Twentieth Kentucky, under Colonel Hanson, who stood out for seven hours against Morgan's attack, placing his men in the dépôt and the neighboring houses. Surrender at length became inevitable, the enemy having charged into the town and set fire to the houses from which the garrison were firing. Here Morgan's young brother was killed while leading a charge. With the Federal cavalry now close upon him—riding swiftly on his track while he was fighting at Tebbs's Bend and Lebanon—Morgan had not time to parole his prisoners, whom he compelled to keep pace with him to Springfield, making ten miles in an hour and a half. Those who faltered were ruthlessly shot and left upon the road.

A formidable force of infantry, cavalry, and artillery, under Generals Hobson, Judah, and Shackleford, joined by Colonel Wolford, were rapidly pursuing Morgan, who was boldly advancing to the Ohio River by way of Bardstown. The experienced raider had still the best of the race, scouring the country for supplies and horses on his route, leaving behind him empty larders and stables, thus compelling his pursuers to make the most of their jaded animals. On the 7th, when the Federals reached Shepardsville, Morgan had twenty hours the start; but the exciting race was continued. Morgan, having crossed Rolling Fork, burning the bridges behind him, reached the Ohio at Brandenburg, 40 miles below Louisville, on the 8th. On board of captured steamers he ferried his command across, and his pursuers reached the southern bank just in time to witness the burning of his transports. On its swift march the Confederate command had gathered fresh accessions of force, and was now ready to fall upon the southern counties of Indiana with an army of 4000 men and 10 guns.

Taking Corydon, Greenville, and Palmyra in his way, Morgan hastened on the 9th to Salem, capturing there 350 Home Guards, breaking up the railroad, and burning the town. It was the portion of Indiana most disaffected toward the national government which Morgan was visiting with his wrath; but he had no time to distinguish friend from foe, and went on burning and ravaging. He dared not halt even to fight, and every place was secure against him which offered any serious resistance. From Salem his course veered eastward toward Lexington, which he reached on the morning of the 10th. From that point, passing northward and eastward, he menaced at once Madison and Vernon, 20 miles apart, but, finding a considerable force at the latter point, he did not venture battle, but skirmished evasively, while his men were destroying the railroads north, south, east, and west of the town. Thence he moved eastward, passing through Versailles on the 12th, seizing fresh horses as he marched, and reaching Harrison, on the Ohio border, the next day, where he gathered in his detached columns, and made a clean sweep around Cincinnati, at distances of from 7 to 18 miles. Daylight of the 14th found him 18 miles east of Cincinnati, anxiously looking for some avenue of escape.

For his position was now one of great peril. He had embarked upon a great adventure, which might have had some military consequence if he had been let alone; but, as must have been apparent to him now, it had proved little more than a bold march across one state and a portion of two others. Indeed, from a military point of view, he was more a necessity to Bragg in Tennessee than he was an injury to the Federal cause in his present position north of the Ohio. So closely had he been pursued that he had stepped lightly over the country which he had meant to crush under the heels of his horsemen. He had captured hundreds (thousands it may be, so Pollard reports) of militia, but he could do nothing with them, and their paroles placed them just where they were before. He had destroyed a large amount of property, and had broken railroad communications, but the ravages had been so slight that a single week would repair the ruin. He had only made a bold march, scarcely worthy the record which we have given it, in the event of his escape. It is the *dénouement* of the little episode which gives it any historic interest. How and where did the bold march end? is the question which the reader waits to have answered. And this was the question which Morgan was trying to answer prospectively when, on the 14th, after crossing the Miami, he moved southward to the Ohio to find a crossing for his closely-meshed command.

Generals Judah, Hobson, and Shackleford had crossed the Ohio on the 8th, following Morgan in the route which we have traced. When the raiders crossed the Miami they had only four hours the start of their pursuers. Such a disposition of the Federal forces had been made as would secure Hamilton and Cincinnati against attack. Gunboats were brought up to patrol the Ohio, and to prevent Morgan's escape southward across that river. A column under Judah moved along the river roads, while Hobson and Shackleford took those in the interior. The militia sent down by Governor Morgan, of Indiana, halted at the eastern border of their own state, but the people of Ohio, along the roads in Morgan's front, blocked up his route with fallen trees, while the Federal troops hemmed him in upon the north and in his rear. For 160 miles Morgan continued his desperate flight through Williamsburg, Winchester, Piketon, and Jackson, as if running a race with the gun-boats. But the latter, under the direction of Lieutenant Commander Fitch, had been warped over the shoals, and thus had succeeded in forcing their way up the Rapids, so that when Morgan attempted to cross the river at Buffington Island, near Pomeroy, he found the "web-footed" monsters still in his front, and was driven back in confusion, and brought face to face with his pursuers, near Chester, on the 19th. Here Shackleford met him, and soon Judah, also, was upon his flank, and Hobson upon his

[1] Moore gives the Confederate loss as 50 killed and 250 wounded.

rear. There was a good hour's fight, when Shackleford ordered a charge, and the enemy, with infantry, cavalry, and artillery attacking him upon all sides, sent in a flag of truce, and surrendered 700 men, including Dick Morgan and Basil Duke. But this was only a portion of Morgan's command. The leader himself, with the main body, had pushed up the river some 14 miles to Belleville, where he was already (about 3 P.M.) crossing his horses. Before he had got 400 men, under Colonel A. R. Johnson, across, Hobson and Shackleford were again upon him, and General Scammon's gun-boats made their appearance in his front. Here 1000 more of the raiders were surrendered.

But Morgan was not among the captured, having again disappeared with a small body of his adherents. His guns and weapons were gone, and the great raid had dwindled down into a run for dear life on Morgan's part. He fled inland to McArthur on the 21st, and thence toward Marietta, where he again made a vain attempt to cross into Virginia. Then he veered northward again to Eastport. But Shackleford, with 500 men who had volunteered to stay in the saddle without eating or drinking until Morgan should be captured, overtook the flying partisan near New Lisbon, where the latter's flight had been interrupted by an irregular force of militia and home guards. Driven to a high bluff, Morgan finally surrendered at discretion on the 27th. It was now exactly a month since he had marched from Sparta, in Tennessee. Of the command with which he first set forth, less than 400 had escaped, over 500 had been killed or wounded; the rest, with their leader, were prisoners of war.

Morgan and his officers were carried to Cincinnati, and delivered over to General Burnside. By direction of the President they were confined in Ohio penitentiaries, their heads being shaved like those of felons. Morgan, with six of his officers, managed to escape on the night of November 26 by digging their way out of their cells. Those who escaped had been confined at Columbus. Morgan, with a certain Captain Hines, took the midnight train for Cincinnati, and, just before reaching the city, put on the brakes, jumped off, and was ferried across the Ohio into Kentucky. Through Kentucky, Tennessee, and Northern Georgia, Morgan—having lost his companion by the way—proceeded to Richmond, where he was fêted and made much of. His escape from his cell, his disguise, and his flight to Virginia had been accomplished through the assistance of Confederate sympathizers outside his prison walls.

About three weeks after Morgan's capture, Burnside had at Camp Nelson, near Richmond, Kentucky, a thoroughly organized force of 20,000 men. Without waiting for the return of the Ninth Corps, he, on the 16th of August, commenced his advance to East Tennessee. Rosecrans had already driven Bragg to Chattanooga. The occupation of East Tennessee was at this time of very great importance, in order, by the destruction or possession of the railroad from Virginia, to cut off communications between Lee's a Bragg's armies. Besides, from Knoxville, Burnside could easily and effe ively co-operate with Rosecrans's next movement upon Bragg.

East Tennessee lies in the Valley of the Tennessee and Holston Rive and between the Cumberland and Blue Ridge ranges of mountains. It i mountainous district, and its inhabitants were for the most part loyal to t national government. For the latter reason, it was not advisable to occu this region before it could be permanently held. Hitherto the people h been harassed by the enemy, who had exercised his power to the utm in order to crush out and overawe the Unionists, many of whom were ready refugees.

Burnside's advance was simultaneous with Rosecrans's march from Wi chester upon Chattanooga, of which we treat in the next chapter. Conce trating his forces at Crab Orchard, he moved directly upon Knoxvil through Mount Vernon, London, Williamsburg, and thence southward in Tennessee, with Hartsuff's columns upon his right, proceeding through So erset, and Colonel Foster's cavalry upon his left. The routes taken by t several columns were those least likely to be defended by the enemy. Aft crossing the Cumberland River a force was sent, under command of Colon De Courcy, to threaten Cumberland Gap, then held by Frazier's brigade Buckner's command, while Burnside, with his main body, crossed the mou tains by the gaps farther westward. It was a most difficult route; but t troops were in light marching order, and many of them mounted, with pac mules for transportation, the few wagon trains following on the best road while the soldiers, on foot or on horseback, climbed over the mountains b comparatively unfrequented paths. During the fortnight after Burnside departure from Crab Orchard, on the 21st of August, the whole army, mul and men, were tasked to the utmost limits of endurance. Up the rugg heights the artillery was with difficulty drawn, and when the mules fail from exhaustion their places were filled by the soldiers. At length t summit was reached, and the army descended into East Tennessee, its co querors; for, surprised by the sudden and apparently formidable mov ment, General Buckner evacuated Knoxville and fell back to the Tenne see, leaving Frazier's command at Cumberland Gap without orders, witho intelligence of his retreat, and without support.

Burnside's army had moved in five columns. The first and second join at Jamestown, Tennessee, and, moving to Montgomery, were joined on t 30th by the third and fourth. The other column, composed of cavalr moved directly on Jacksborough, and thence through Wheeler's Gap Knoxville. Burnside's headquarters were established at Kingston on t 1st and at Knoxville on the 3d of September. In fourteen days he h marched his army 250 miles.

On the 5th he dispatched Shackleford to the rear of Cumberland Ga

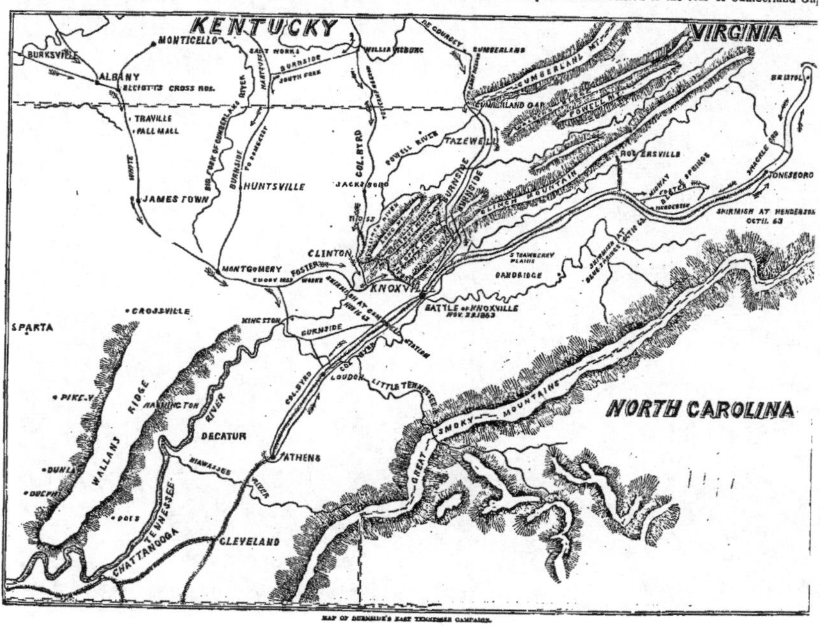

MAP OF BURNSIDE'S EAST TENNESSEE CAMPAIGN.

DRAGGING ARTILLERY OVER THE MOUNTAINS.

OCCUPATION OF CUMBERLAND GAP.

which De Courcy threatened from the north. Frazier, who occupied the Gap with four Confederate regiments, was well supplied, and confident of his ability to hold the position. But some of Shackleford's men succeeded on the 7th in creeping through the lines and burning the mill upon which the garrison depended for flour. Burnside arrived in person on the 9th, when Frazier surrendered 2000 men and 14 guns. The pursuit of a small Confederate force under Sam Jones into Virginia completed the long-sought conquest of East Tennessee. The campaign had been accomplished without a single battle.

By the Loyalists along his line of march and at Knoxville Burnside was hailed as a deliverer. His entrance into Knoxville was an ovation which might have flattered the greatest of conquerors. His wayworn troops shared the generous welcome. National flags, long concealed, came forth from the houses, and made the 3d of September seem like a 4th of July.[1] General Burnside captured at Knoxville a large quantity of ammunition, 2000 stand of small-arms, 11 guns, and 2500 prisoners.

CHAPTER XXXIV.

THE CHATTANOOGA CAMPAIGN.

IV. THE BATTLE OF CHICKAMAUGA.

Rosecrans crosses the Tennessee.—Movements of his three Corps.—Bragg retreats from Chattanooga.—Over-confidence of Rosecrans.—Why Burnside did not co-operate.—Bragg's Opportunity.—General Negley's Fight at Dug Gap discovers the Enemy.—Rosecrans alarmed.—Hurried Concentration and narrow Escape of his Army.—The Situation on the Evening of September 18.—*Battle of the 19th.*—General Thomas strikes the first Blow.—Baird's Repulse; Loss of the "Loomis" Battery.—Enemy driven, and Guns recaptured.—Confederate Attack in the Afternoon; Van Cleve driven; Hazen repulses the Enemy with Artillery.—Pat Cleburne's Night Attack.—Results of the Day's Fighting.—Council of War at the Widow Glenn's.—The Confederate General Longstreet's Arrival.—*Battle of the 20th.*—Rosecrans's Dispositions.—Bragg's Plan of Attack.—Polk's Delay.—Thomas is hard pressed, but holds his Position.—Longstreet's Attack.—Hindman breaks through the Right of the Federal Line.—How the Gap was made.—Rosecrans, McCook, and Crittenden swept from the Field.—Extent of the Disorder.—Garfield goes to Thomas.—Formation of a new Line on the Slope of Mission Ridge.—General Negley's Position.—Weakness of the new Line.—Longstreet's Assault delayed.—Granger arrives in time to meet it and to save the Day.—Withdrawal of the Army by Night to Rossville and thence to Chattanooga.—Estimate of Losses.—Review of the Campaign.

WE left Rosecrans's army at Winchester, south of Elk River, with its left and rear toward McMinnville well guarded, and its outposts advanced to Pelham and Stevenson. If its progress thus far had been difficult, it was yet mere play when compared with a farther advance across the Cumberland Mountains and the broad Tennessee to Chattanooga, whither Bragg had retreated. A direct attack upon the enemy, strongly intrenched in Chattanooga, was out of the question, even if Rosecrans's army had been a hundred thousand strong. The campaign against Bragg, therefore, necessarily involved an attack upon the railroad running southward from Chattanooga through Dalton to Atlanta. The railroad connecting Chattanooga with the East would very soon be rendered useless to the Confederates by Burnside's advance to Knoxville. The valley through which the Atlanta Road runs could be reached in two ways: westwardly, by turning the head of Sequatchie Valley, or by crossing the valley at Dunlap or Thurman's, and then moving across Walden's Ridge, crossing the Tennessee above Chattanooga; or southwardly, by moving across the Cumberland range, crossing the Tennessee below Chattanooga, and then the four ranges south of the river—Raccoon, Lookout, Mission, and Taylor's.[1] Rosecrans chose the latter, or southward route, leaving the natural valley from East Tennessee to Northern Georgia open to the co-operative movement which he expected would be undertaken by Burnside.

Upon whatsoever route Rosecrans might advance, there could be little dependence upon the country for forage, none at all for the subsistence of his soldiers. Supplies of food and ammunition sufficient for the campaign must be accumulated before moving, and must be carried with the army, thus increasing the difficulties of the march. The necessity of a long halt after Bragg's retreat was therefore inevitable; yet, strange as it may seem, General Halleck, at Washington, not appreciating Napoleon's maxim that "an army crawls upon its belly," wondered and chafed at this delay, and finally issued a peremptory order directing Rosecrans to advance, and report his progress daily to the War Department.[2] Very fortunately, Rosecrans was

---

[1] Dr. W. H. Church, of Burnside's staff, thus describes the reception of the troops on the way to and in Knoxville:

"The East Tennessee troops, of whom General Burnside had a considerable number, were kept constantly in the advance, and were received with expressions of the profoundest gratitude by the people, who are described as the most heartily and generally loyal people in the United States. There were many thrilling scenes of the meeting of our East Tennessee soldiers with their families, from whom they had been so long separated.

"The East Tennesseeans were so glad to see our soldiers that they cooked every thing they had and gave it to them freely, not asking pay, and apparently not thinking of it. Women stood by the road side with pails of water, and displayed Union flags. The wonder was where all the stars and stripes came from. Knoxville was radiant with flags. At a point on the road from Kingston to Knoxville sixty women and girls stood by the road side waving Union flags, and shouting 'Hurrah for the Union!' Old ladies rushed out of their houses and wanted to see General Burnside, and shake hands with him, and cried 'Welcome, welcome, General Burnside! welcome to East Tennessee!' A meeting of the Union citizens of Knoxville was held, and addressed by General Burnside and General Carter. It was attended by about five hundred men, and a large number of women and children. The demonstrations were not boisterous, but there was intense, quiet rejoicing. Men who had been hidden for months came in, full of gratitude for their deliverance."

[1] Or, striking farther southward, after crossing the Tennessee, there would be Sand, Lookout, and Pigeon Mountains, and Taylor's Ridge.

[2] The order was issued early in August. On the 4th Rosecrans writes:

"Your dispatch, ordering me to move forward without farther delay, reporting the movement of each corps until I cross the Tennessee, is received. As I have been determined to cross the river as soon as practicable, and have been making all preparations, and getting such information

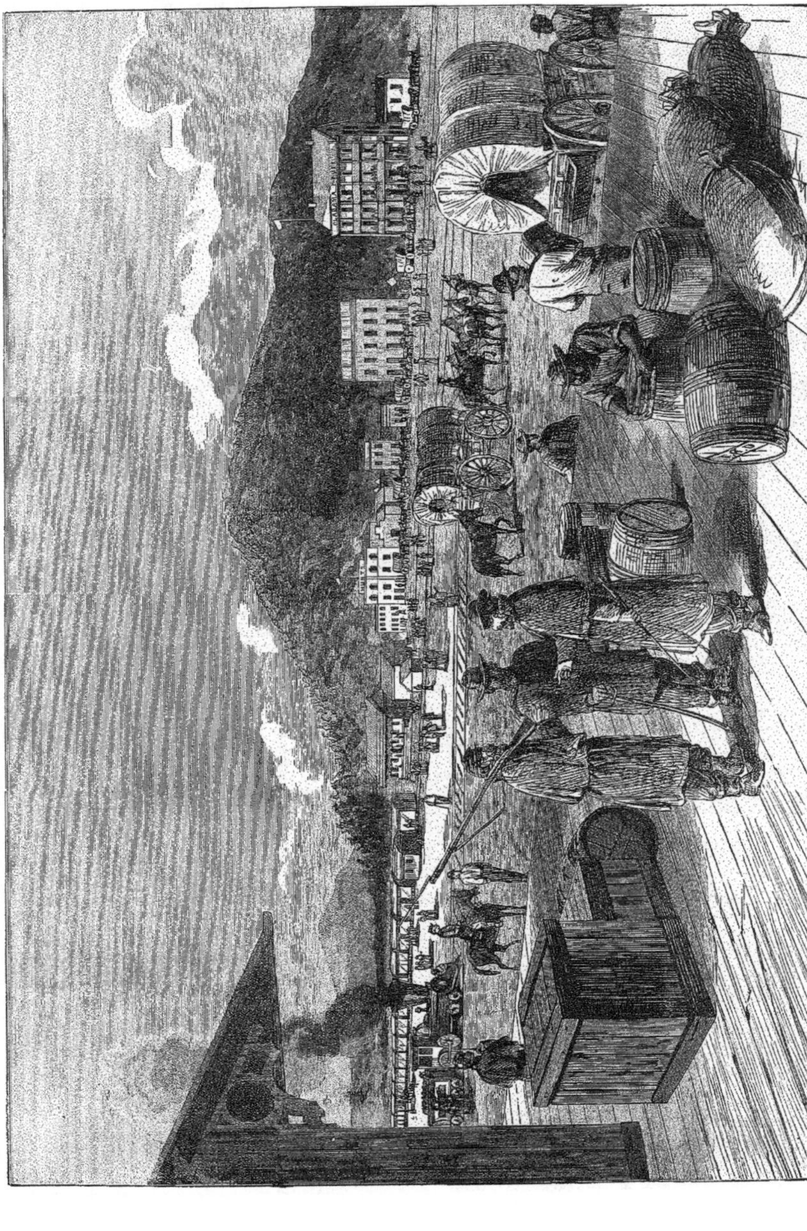

STEVENSON, ALABAMA.

nearly ready to move. He had completed the railroad from Murfreesborough to Stevenson, and thence to Bridgeport, by the 25th of July, and only waited for the opening of the road from Cowan to Tracy City. By straining to the utmost the capacities of the Stevenson Road, he had accumulated by the 8th of August a sufficient quantity of supplies to warrant his immediate advance. The enemy was in no condition to disturb his communications or to resist his advance to the Tennessee. So far, therefore, he was relieved of anxiety. While his own army covered the approaches to his rear and right, Burnside's was more than adequate to the protection of his left.

Sheridan's division had already occupied Stevenson and Bridgeport before Halleck's order was issued. The movement of the main army began on the morning of August 16th. Two of Crittenden's columns crossed the Cumberland Mountains—Palmer by Dunlap, and Wood by Thurman's—into the Sequatchie Valley, while a third, under Van Cleve, struck Pikeville at the head of the Valley. Crittenden's left, in this movement, was covered by Colonel Minty's cavalry. Thomas's and McCook's corps advanced southward to the Tennessee, occupying positions above and below Stevenson, preparatory to crossing the river. Three brigades of cavalry moved on the right, making a long detour by way of Fayetteville and Athens, to guard the river below as far as Whitesburg, about eighty miles from Stevenson.

Crittenden, upon reaching Sequatchie Valley, sent reconnoitring columns of infantry and cavalry across Walden's Ridge, Wagner's brigade and Wilder's cavalry advancing to a point opposite Chattanooga, and shelling the town on the 21st, silencing the Confederate artillery, and creating great consternation among the citizens. Another brigade (Hazen's) had also crossed the ridge farther north, at Poe's, and, with Wilder's cavalry, reconnoitred the country to Harrison's Landing, twelve miles above Chattanooga. The rest of Crittenden's command moved down the Sequatchie to the Tennessee, below Chattanooga.

On the 21st, the whole army, having crossed the Cumberland Mountains, lay upon the right bank of the Tennessee, extending over a line of 150 miles. Along this line the river flows in a southwest direction, forcing its passage through the Cumberland range, and entering Alabama at Bridgeport. The two brigades east of Walden's Ridge were prepared to enter Chattanooga in the event of its evacuation by Bragg; to force this evacuation, or to cut off the enemy from his southern communications, was the work of the main army. The preparations for crossing the river consumed ten days. During this time reconnoissances were made to discover the most available points for this purpose; the pontoons and trains were brought forward, and trestle-work and materials for improvised bridges were prepared with the utmost secrecy. The pontoons were sufficient for only two bridges, and twice that number were needed to secure rapidity of movement. The facility with which the enemy could, from the high spurs abutting on the river, overlook the whole length of the valley, prevented absolute secrecy; this, however, was of little consequence, as the intervening mountains made it impossible for Bragg to oppose any serious resistance to the movements on his left. The troops began to cross on the 29th of August, and by September 4th all were on the south side except a brigade of regulars of Baird's division, left to guard the railroad until it should be relieved by Gordon Granger's reserve corps. The crossing was conducted at four points—Shellmound, the mouth of Battle Creek, Bridgeport, and Caperton's Ferry, at the mouth of Big Crow Creek. The bridge at Bridgeport was the one mainly used for the crossing of trains. Thomas crossed one division at each of the points named; McCook crossed Woods's and Van Cleve's at Caporton'e (the lowest crossing), and Sheridan's at Bridgeport; Crittenden (except Wagner's and Hazen's brigades) crossed at Shellmound, at the mouth of Battle Creek, and at Bridgeport. An accident to the bridge at Bridgeport delayed the crossing at that point for four days. The cavalry, under General Stanley, still keeping the left, crossed with McCook at Caperton's.

The plan of Rosecrans's campaign, after crossing the Tennessee, was very simple in its idea, though attended with many difficulties in its execution. Crittenden was to threaten Chattanooga by a direct advance; Thomas was to cross Raccoon Mountain, and seize Stevens's and Cooper's Gaps, leading through Lookout Mountain into McLemore's Cove, twenty miles south of Chattanooga; McCook and Stanley, in the mean time, were to move twenty miles farther southward across the mountains to Valley Head, turning the southern extremity of Pigeon Mountain, and threatening an advance on Rome. Except in its topographical features, this plan was very similar to that adopted by Hooker in his Chancellorsville campaign. In either case the enemy was flanked by the crossing of a river and an advance upon his left and rear. Hooker thought Lee would retreat, falling back upon Richmond or Gordonsville. Rosecrans was equally confident that Bragg, abandoning Chattanooga, would fall back to Rome. Both were alike mistaken; each, finding that the enemy had indeed abandoned his position, but was ready to meet the advance squarely in front, refusing to acknowledge defeat until after the test of battle. But there were three important points of difference between the Chickamauga and Chancellorsville campaigns. Hooker was able to encounter the enemy with nearly double the force of the latter, while Rosecrans, at a greater distance from his base of supplies, accepted battle with the advantage of numerical superiority against him and in Bragg's favor. Again, Rosecrans had a more difficult country in which to ope though this was in some degree compensated by the circumstance that very obstacles in his own way afforded security to his rear. Finally sequel of the two campaigns was far different; for, although both Ho and Rosecrans each succeeded in inflicting greater injury upon the en than he suffered himself, yet the former sustained a complete defeat as garded the object of his campaign, while Rosecrans, retiring from the ba field of Chickamauga, secured Chattanooga, the professed object of his vance from Murfreesborough.

But in carrying out this comparison we are anticipating our narrat By the time the last divisions of the army had crossed the Tennessee, Th as's and McCook's corps were already far advanced. Negley's division crossed Sand Mountain into Lookout Valley, and was encamped at Brow Spring; at the foot of the mountain, on the west side, and ready to be the ascent, was Reynolds's division; Brannan's had reached the sumn Jeff Davis's division, of McCook's corps, had crossed Lookout Mountain i Wills's Valley, seizing Winston's Gap; Johnson's was across Sand Mo tain, while Sheridan had just reached the left bank of the Tennessee. the 8th all the preliminary movements of the campaign had been succ fully carried out. Their effect upon the enemy was immediate. Cha nooga was evidently no longer tenable. Bragg's effective force at this ti was about 45,000 men.[1] He could not well afford to divide this force sending a detachment of his army to fight the enemy, nor could he s in Chattanooga. The capture of Vicksburg, with its garrison, was an stance, too recent to be forgotten, of the consequence of holding a posit simply because of its strength, and in defiance of starvation. The nature the country, and the presence on his right front of Burnside's army (at Kn ville on the 3d), made a counter attack upon the Federal rear, if not imp sible, extremely hazardous. Reluctantly he abandoned Chattanooga, but the campaign for its possession. The prize must be fought for, but w Rosecrans must be left the choice of the battle-field. If the Federal ar emerged from the passes of Lookout Mountain into McLemore's Cove Wills's Valley, he would meet it there; if it drew in its left in order to cupy Chattanooga in full force, and successfully evaded battle, he would st maintain the offensive, sitting down in front of the strong-hold he had so u willingly abandoned, with his own supplies close at hand, while those of t enemy must be brought over the mountains from Murfreesborough, a hun red miles distant. His confidence in the final result was heightened by t expectation that his army, now very little inferior to that of the enem would soon be nearly doubled by re-enforcements from Mississippi and V ginia. Chattanooga was evacuated on the 7th and 8th. On the morni of the 9th Crittenden was apprised of this event by General Rosecrans, an ordered to push forward his entire command, with four days' rations, an make a vigorous pursuit. Bragg had waited at Chattanooga until Rosecrar had fully developed his movements southward. He then took position fro Lee and Gordon's Mill to Lafayette, on the road leading southward from Cha tanooga, facing the eastern slope of Pigeon Mountain. In this position h was nearer to either of Rosecrans's three corps than they were to each other

And just here Rosecrans began to base the future of his campaign upo a false calculation. His impression that Bragg's army was retreating upo Rome, demoralized and conscious of defeat, amounted to a conviction, a most to an infatuation. There was some ground for the presumption. Brag had been flanked out of Middle Tennessee. Why not out of East Tenne see and Northern Georgia? But here Rosecrans should have remembere that in the summer campaign, his strength, as compared with that of the en emy, had been much greater than it was now. Besides its additional strengt from the accession of Buckner's command, Bragg's army was now withi easier reach not only of abundant supplies, but also of extensive re-enforce ments. Under the circumstances, the greatest peril lurked in that presumj tuous confidence with which Rosecrans was now prepared to push forwar his columns.[3] There was really nothing in the way of Burnside's co-opera tion with over 20,000 effective men. There was every argument in its fa vor, and no good one against it. The moment Knoxville had been secure Burnside ought to have been ordered to Chattanooga. He could have mad

as may enable me to do so without being driven back like Hooker. I wish to know if your order is intended to take away my discretion as to the time and manner of moving my troops?"

And the following is General Halleck's reply (August 5):

"The orders for the advance of your army, and that its progress be reported daily, are peremptory."

Rosecrans appears to have received all this in good feeling. He writes (August 7):

"Your dispatch received. I can only repeat the assurance given before the issue of the order. This army shall move with all the dispatch compatible with the successful execution you wish. We are preparing every thing to bring up forage for our animals; the present rolling stock of the road will hardly suffice to keep us day by day here, but I have bought fifty more freight cars, which are arriving. Will advise you daily."

[1] The official returns from the Army of Tennessee for August 31, 1863, give: *Present for dut* 45,041; *aggregate present*, 69,027; *aggregate present and absent*, 83,273. Bragg, in his official r port of the battle of Chickamauga, says that at this time (September 8) his effective force, excl sive of cavalry, was a little over 35,000 men. He includes "two small divisions" just arrived fro Johnston's army. The estimate given in the text is no doubt correct, as the official returns of a army are always more likely to be accurate than the numbers given in the report of a battle. I includes the cavalry force and Buckner's command.

[2] Thomas was twenty-six miles from Crittenden, on his left, and the distance to McCook's corp on the right, was nearly as great. Rosecrans makes the distance "from flank to flank, by the nea est practicable roads," fifty miles.

[3] The idea that Bragg's army would make no stand on Rosecrans's present front seems also t have prevailed with General Halleck. On the 6th he had telegraphed to the latter: "There i no reason now to suppose that any of his troops have been detached, except, perhaps, a small forc at Charleston." On the 11th he gives the following instructions: "After holding the mountai passes on the west and Dalton, or some other point on the railroad, to prevent the return of Bragg army, it will be decided whether your army shall move farther south into Georgia and Alabama. So far is Halleck at this time from being aware of Rosecrans's danger, that he urges the latter t find out whether Bragg's army is re-enforcing Lee! If he had himself taken some pains to ascer tain whether Lee was re-enforcing Bragg, a mistake on Rosecrans's part which proved next to fa tal might have been avoided. As early as September 7th Rosecrans seems to have been aware o Bragg's having received re-enforcements from Johnston's army. On that day, in reply to a dis patch from Halleck (dated September 6th), inquiring about the position of Bragg and Buckne and suggesting that, in the event of their union, it would be necessary for him to unite with Burn side, he writes:

"Your dispatch of yesterday received with surprise. You have been often and fully advised the the nature of the country makes it impossible for this army to prevent Johnston from combinin with Bragg. When orders for an advance of the army were made, it must have been known tha those two rebel forces could combine against it, and to some extent choose their place of fightin us. This has doubtless been done, and Buckner, Bragg, and Johnston are all near Chattanooga The movement on East Tennessee was independent of mine. Your apprehensions are just, an the legitimate consequences of your orders. The best that can now be done is for Burnside t close his cavalry down on our left, supporting it with his infantry, and, refusing his left, threate the enemy without getting into his grasp, while we get him in our grip, and strangle him, or per ish in the attempt."

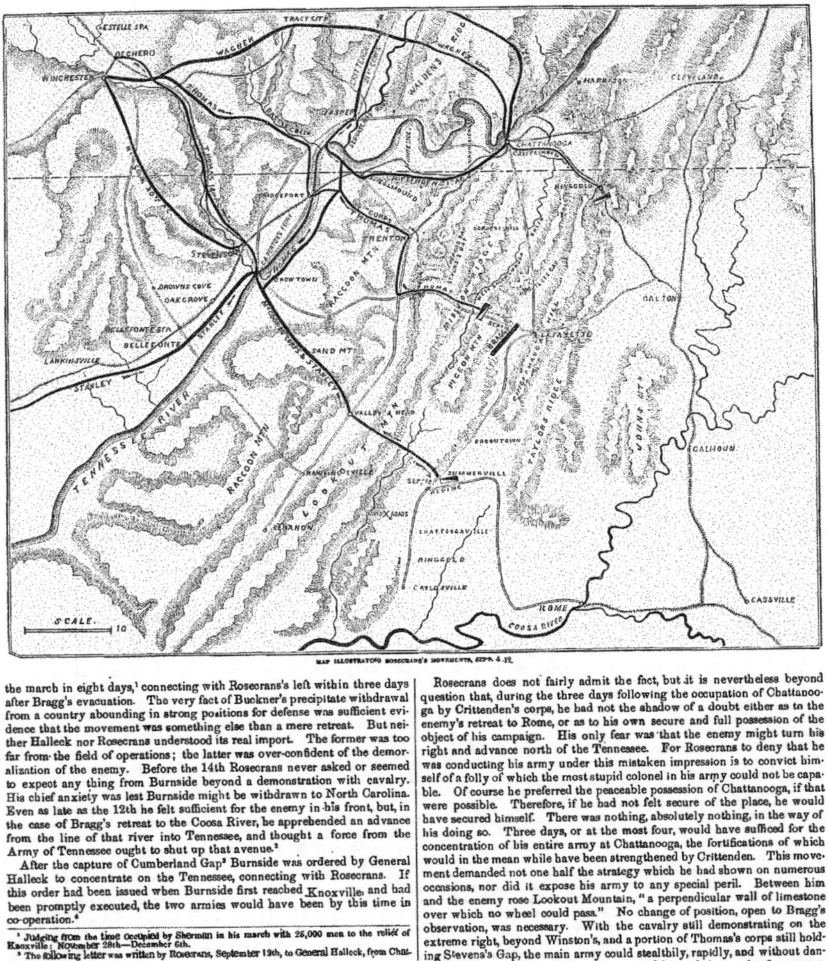

MAP ILLUSTRATING ROSECRANS'S MOVEMENTS, SEPT. 4-12.

the march in eight days,[1] connecting with Rosecrans's left within three days after Bragg's evacuation. The very fact of Buckner's precipitate withdrawal from a country abounding in strong positions for defense was sufficient evidence that the movement was something else than a mere retreat. But neither Halleck nor Rosecrans understood its real import. The former was too far from the field of operations; the latter was over-confident of the demoralization of the enemy. Before the 14th Rosecrans never asked or seemed to expect any thing from Burnside beyond a demonstration with cavalry. His chief anxiety was lest Burnside might be withdrawn to North Carolina. Even as late as the 12th he felt sufficient for the enemy in his front, but, in the case of Bragg's retreat to the Coosa River, he apprehended an advance from the line of that river into Tennessee, and thought a force from the Army of Tennessee ought to shut up that avenue.[2]

After the capture of Cumberland Gap[3] Burnside was ordered by General Halleck to concentrate on the Tennessee, connecting with Rosecrans. If this order had been issued when Burnside first reached Knoxville, and had been promptly executed, the two armies would have been by this time in co-operation.[4]

Rosecrans does not fairly admit the fact, but it is nevertheless beyond question that, during the three days following the occupation of Chattanooga by Crittenden's corps, he had not the shadow of a doubt either as to the enemy's retreat to Rome, or as to his own secure and full possession of the object of his campaign. His only fear was that the enemy might turn his right and advance north of the Tennessee. For Rosecrans to deny that he was conducting his army under this mistaken impression is to convict himself of a folly of which the most stupid colonel in his army could not be capable. Of course he preferred the peaceable possession of Chattanooga, if that were possible. Therefore, if he had not felt secure of the place, he would have secured himself. There was nothing, absolutely nothing, in the way of his doing so. Three days, or at the most four, would have sufficed for the concentration of his entire army at Chattanooga, the fortifications of which would in the mean while have been strengthened by Crittenden. This movement demanded not one half the strategy which he had shown on numerous occasions, nor did it expose his army to any special peril. Between him and the enemy rose Lookout Mountain, "a perpendicular wall of limestone over which no wheel could pass." No change of position, open to Bragg's observation, was necessary. With the cavalry still demonstrating on the extreme right, beyond Winston's, and a portion of Thomas's corps still holding Stevens's Gap, the main army could stealthily, rapidly, and without danger, in twenty-four hours' time, have passed beyond the reach of any possible interruption from the enemy. The only thing necessary was expedition.[1]

[1] Judging from the time occupied by Sherman in his march with 25,000 men to the relief of Knoxville: November 28th—December 6th.

[2] The following letter was written by Rosecrans, September 12th, to General Halleck, from Chattanooga:

"I think it would be very unwise, in the present attitude of affairs, for General Burnside to make any move in the direction of North Carolina; it would leave my left flank entirely unprotected, and open the way into Kentucky. I trust I am sufficient for the enemy now in my front; but, should he fall back to the line of the Coosa, the roads from there are short and comparatively good to the Tennessee, where it is necessary for me to cross two ranges of mountains, over very barren, rough, and difficult roads, to reach the Tennessee, and then move from thirty to fifty miles to reach the flank of a column moving from Ganter's Landing or Whitesburg on Nashville. It is desirable to have that avenue shut up. Can not you send a force from the Army of Tennessee to do it?"

[3] September 9.

[4] "The main body of General Burnside's army was now ordered to concentrate on the Tennessee River, from Loudon west, so as to connect with General Rosecrans's army, which reached Chattanooga on the 9th. . . . As the country between Dalton and the Little Tennessee was still open to the enemy, General Burnside was cautioned to move down by the north bank of the river, so as to secure its fords, and cover his own and General Rosecrans's communications from rebel raids. With our forces concentrated near Chattanooga, the enemy would be compelled to either attack us in position or to retreat farther south into Georgia. If he should attempt a flank movement on Cleveland, his own communications would be cut off and his own army destroyed. But, although repeatedly urged to effect this junction with the Army of the Cumberland, General Burnside retained most of his command in the upper valley, which was still threatened, near the Virginia line, by a small force under Sam Jones."—*Halleck's Report*, 1863. This is the statement made by General Halleck, which reflects upon Burnside. But the *ipsissima verba* of the dispatch sent to Burnside on the 11th do not indicate that the order to co-operate with Rosecrans was very explicit, or was based upon any definite idea of the enemy's movements. The dispatch reads:

"I congratulate you on your success. Hold the gaps of the North Carolina mountains, the line of the Holston River, or some point, if there be one, to prevent access from Virginia, and connect with General Rosecrans, at least with your cavalry. General Rosecrans will occupy Dalton, or some point on the railroad, to close all access from Atlanta, and also the mountain passes in the west. This being done, it will be determined whether the available force shall advance into Georgia and Alabama, or into the Valley of Virginia and North Carolina."

Two days after this dispatch was sent, it became apparent to General Halleck that troops were moving westward from Lee's army. He then instructed Burnside to move down his infantry "as rapidly as possible toward Chattanooga." But the reason given for the movement (namely, to secure against an advance of Bragg's army into Tennessee and Kentucky) gave Burnside no hint of Rosecrans's immediate danger. And, in any case, the order came too late to secure the arrival of Burnside before Longstreet could join Bragg.

The communications received all this time by Burnside directly from Rosecrans indicated that the latter, so far from being in embarrassment, was getting on swimmingly in Georgia, sweeping every thing before him. On the 10th Crittenden writes from Chattanooga:

"I am directed by the general commanding the Department of the Cumberland to inform you that I am in *full possession* of this place, having entered it yesterday, at 12 M., without resistance. The enemy has retreated in the direction of Rome, Georgia, the last of his force, cavalry, having left a few hours before my arrival. At daylight I made a rapid pursuit with my corps, and hope that he will be intercepted by the centre and right, the latter of which was at Rome. The general commanding department requests that you move down your cavalry and occupy the country recently covered by Colonel Minty, who will report particulars to you, and who has been ordered to cross the river."

[1] Rosecrans, of course, swears that this movement was impossible. He says, in his evidence before the Congressional Committee on the Conduct of the War (*Rep. Com., Rosecrans's Campaigns*, p. 31): "It has been a popular impression, possibly encouraged, if not believed, in high

JAMES S. NEGLEY.

Rosecrans's movements, more clearly than any thing else, indicate his misapprehension as to the situation of the Confederate army. On the evening of the 9th McCook was informed that Bragg was retreating southward, and ordered "to move rapidly upon Alpine and Summerville, Georgia, in pursuit, to intercept his line of retreat, and attack him in flank."[1] Thomas was at the same time ordered to move on Lafayette.[2] Crittenden was sent to Ringgold in pursuit. By this disposition of his army Rosecrans exposed each of his three corps to a separate and overwhelming attack of Bragg's army, which, instead of retreating to Rome, fronted the western slope of Pigeon Mountain, and was ready, holding a central position, to strike Thomas when he should emerge from Dug Gap on the way to Lafayette, Crittenden on his right, or McCook on his left. Rosecrans and his corps commanders had been alike misled by the reports of citizens and deserters, sent by Bragg within the Federal lines for the direct purpose of conveying an impression of his rapid retreat to Rome.[3] This ruse had been successful. Bragg fully appreciated his opportunity. Even on the 9th—the very day of the occupation of Chattanooga by the national troops, and while Rosecrans was urging a "vigorous pursuit" of the enemy by Crittenden, an advance by McCook and Stanley upon his flank and rear, and of Thomas's columns through the gaps of Pigeon Mountain upon Lafayette—Bragg was preparing to strike Thomas in McLemore's Cove, and by moving around his left, between him and Crittenden, to secure an easy victory over both, reserving for McCook's corps the final blow. Five hours after Rosecrans had telegraphed to Washington that Chattanooga was his "without a struggle," Bragg issued written orders to Hindman and Hill to move against Thomas.[1] The Confederate force thus ordered to move on Stevens's Gap outnumbered General Negley's division, holding that position, more than two to one.[2] Celerity was absolutely necessary to the accomplishment of Bragg's scheme. Either he should not disclose his position, waiting for the enemy to put himself more completely in his power before springing his trap, or, if he unmasked his force, he should strike a sudden and decisive blow. In this he was foiled by the dilatory execution or the refractoriness of his subordinate generals. Hill reported the order to move on Negley to be impracticable, "as General Cleburne was sick, and both the gaps, Dug and Catlett's, had been blocked by felling timber, which would require twenty-four hours for its removal."[3] Early on the morning of the 10th Bragg ordered General Buckner to execute with his corps the order issued to General Hill. Hindman had advanced promptly, and was at Morgan's (three or four miles from Davis's Cross-roads, but east of Pigeon Mountain), ready to move forward into the cove upon the arrival of a supporting column. Buckner joined him in the afternoon. To secure promptness of action, Bragg transferred his headquarters from Lee and Gordon's Mill to Lafayette. Polk was ordered to send Cheatham's division to cover Hindman's rear, and Cleburne, at Dug Gap, was instructed to attack in front. During the night of the 10th the obstructions were removed from the gap, and Walker's reserve corps was directed to join Cleburne in the front attack. Thus more than 25,000 men, besides cavalry, were, on the morning of the 11th, ready to spring upon Negley's division.

Negley in the mean time had advanced from Stevens's Gap to Bailey's Cross-roads, and thence, on the 10th, to Davis's, one mile west of Dug Gap. Until he had reached this latter position he was in utter ignorance of the fact that only the obstructions in the passes of Pigeon Mountain separated him from an overwhelming force of the enemy on his front and left; but then, just in time to save his division, his eyes began to be opened through information received from the citizens and his scouts.[4] He immediately urged Baird to support him, and made dispositions to meet the enemy. Baird was up by 8 A.M. on the morning of the 11th, with two brigades, and was posted in reserve at Davis's Cross-roads. Bragg's attack was fortunately delayed. At daylight on the 11th he went to Cleburne's position, and found him awaiting the opening of Hindman's guns, which were not heard until the middle of the afternoon, and Cleburne, on advancing, found that Negley had fallen back to Bailey's Cross-roads.[5] General Negley had found

military quarters, that because a portion of our command, including myself, entered Chattanooga, we had possession of it, in the sense of being so established there that we could have retained it without a battle. This is an error into which no good military mind cognizant of the facts could for a moment fall. Bragg was compelled or induced to fall back from Chattanooga by the menacing attitude of Thomas's corps at Frick's and Cooper's Gaps, twenty-six miles south, and of McCook's, with the cavalry corps, at Valley Head, forty-two miles from Chattanooga. Crittenden's corps, a part of which was employed in making the demonstration above Chattanooga, and the remainder in watching and covering the pass over the extremity of Lookout, passed into Chattanooga when Bragg fell back, and repaired at once to that point to ascertain the movement of the enemy; and all that was done was done promptly, and to that end only. And the instant these movements were discovered, and the enemy was found to have retired slowly toward Lafayette, not a moment was lost in making the necessary disposition, first, to secure our troops against being cut up in detail, and, secondly, to effect a most expeditious concentration at an eligible point between the enemy and Chattanooga, the goal of our efforts."

Now this is cool. Apart from the fact that Rosecrans does not here adduce the slightest argument to show *why* he could not on the 9th have commenced the concentration of his army at Chattanooga, or why such a movement must be discarded by any "good military mind cognizant of the facts" as impracticable, his entire statement gives a false impression of the theory upon which he conducted the campaign immediately after Bragg's abandonment of Chattanooga. He had only just ordered Crittenden to enter Chattanooga and vigorously pursue the retreating enemy, when he telegraphed to General Halleck (from Trenton, September 9th, 8 30 P.M): "Chattanooga is ours without a struggle, and East Tennessee is free. Our move on the enemy's *flank and rear* progresses, while the *tail of his retreating column will not escape unmolested.* Our troops from this side entered Chattanooga about noon. Those north of the river there are crossing." This dispatch, the instructions given to Burnside, through Crittenden, that he was in *full* possession of Chattanooga, and the tenor of all his dispatches to Halleck at this time, indicate, as clearly as words any way can, that Rosecrans believed that the campaign for Chattanooga was virtually ended, and that he did not concentrate at Chattanooga for the simple reason that he deemed it unnecessary, and hoped, through his advanced position, to prevent "the tail of Bragg's retreating column" from escaping unmolested. As to being "cognizant of the facts," it is certain that Rosecrans not only did not understand Bragg's movements, but misapprehended them, and acted upon his misapprehension. As we have said in the text, it is only under cover of his mistake that he can evade the imputation of folly. But no arguments, not even from Rosecrans himself, can make us believe that he was foolish enough to expose three corps of his army—each separated from the other by mountain barriers, and by a distance greater than that intervening between either of them and the enemy—to the danger of being cut up in detail. If we were not so compelled by all the circumstances of the case, we should still prefer to believe that it was a mistake, rather than deliberate recklessness, that led him to keep his army for even a single day in such a position. It is true that, after he found out his mistake, he succeeded in extricating his army from destruction, but, as we shall see, this was due to the dilatory movements of the enemy. And his manner of extricating it compelled him to accept the wager of a doubtful battle; whereas, if he had been less confident of the enemy's discomfiture, he might previously have evaded a battle, and, with his army strongly posted in Chattanooga, awaited re-enforcements.

[1] *McCook's Report.*

[2] Rosecrans does not publish this order, nor even allude to it in his report. But there is conclusive proof this order was given in the fact that at 8 P.M. on the 9th, General Negley (commanding the advance of Thomas's corps) received instructions to move the next day to Lafayette. Negley writes to Thomas at this date, "Your order, directing me to march to Lafayette to-morrow, has been received. I will start at 8 A.M."

[3] "Thrown off his guard by our rapid movement, apparently in retreat, when in reality we had concentrated opposite his centre, and deceived by the information from deserters and others sent into his lines, the enemy pressed on his columns to intercept us, and then exposed himself in detail."—*Bragg's Report.*

[1] The following are the orders, dated at Lee and Gordon's Mill, 11 45 P.M., September 9th:

"Major General HINDMAN, Commanding Division:

"GENERAL,—You will move with your division immediately to Davis's Cross-roads, on the road from Lafayette to Stevens's Gap. At this point you will put yourself in communication with the column of General Hill, ordered to move to the same point, and take command of the forces, or report to the officer commanding Hill's column, according to rank. If in command, you will move upon the enemy, reported to be 4000 or 5000 strong, encamped at the foot of Lookout Mountain, at Stevens's Gap. Another column of the enemy is reported to be at Cooper's Gap, number not known."

"Lieutenant General HILL, Commanding Corps:

"GENERAL,—I inclose orders given to General Hindman. General Bragg directs that you send or take, as your judgment dictates, Cleburne's division, to unite with General Hindman at Davis's Cross-roads to-morrow morning. Hindman starts at 12 o'clock to-night, and he has thirteen miles to make. The commander of the column thus united will move upon the enemy, encamped at the foot of Stevens's Gap, said to be 4000 or 5000. If unforeseen circumstances should prevent your movement, notify Hindman. A cavalry force should accompany your column. Hindman has none. Open communication with Hindman with your cavalry in advance of the junction. He marches on the road from Dr. Anderson's to Davis's Cross-roads."

[2] Negley's division numbered 5000 men. Baird's division, however, of nearly 6000 men, was moving up to his support. Brannan and Reynolds were still at Trenton, on the other side of Lookout. The two divisions ordered to move on Negley were Hindman's and Pat Cleburne's, numbering together over 11,000, with a large cavalry force, and with Bragg's whole army within easy supporting distance.

[3] *Bragg's Report.*

[4] At 8 P.M. on the 9th he writes to Thomas, "All the information I have received this evening from my scouts and others induces the belief that there is no considerable rebel force this side of Dalton." Twenty-six hours later, having discovered his danger, he writes the following dispatch to General Baird:

"Widow Davis's, September 10th, 1863—10 P.M.

"Brigadier General BAIRD:

"SIR,—There are indications of a superior force of the enemy in position near Dug Gap. Another column, estimated as a division, with twelve pieces of artillery, near Morgan's Mills, three miles to my left, in the direction of Catlett's Gap. Also a cavalry force, under Forrest, at Culp's Mills, near the road from Pond Spring to Cooper's Gap—there with the intention (as citizens and deserters report) of attacking our rear in the morning.

"My scouts all report the appearance of an offensive movement in this direction, and they confirm the reports I received this morning of a considerable force of the enemy being in the vicinity of Lafayette and Dug Gap.

"My position is somewhat advanced, and exposed to a flank approach by two roads leading from Catlett's Gap; but it is a favorable one to fight the enemy providing your division is within supporting distance, which I understood from General Thomas would be the case, and that your division would move up to Chickamauga Creek to-night. Please inform me if this will be the case.

"Have the kindness to send this information to General Thomas to-night.

"I have the honor to remain, yours very truly, JAS. S. NEGLEY, Major General."

[5] "A careful examination of the ground we occupied, which was a long, low ridge, covered with a heavy growth of small timber, descending abruptly on the north end to the Chickamauga, while the east, south, and west sides were skirted by corn-fields and commanded by high ridges, demonstrating the fact that it would be impossible to hold this or any other position south of Bailey's Cross-roads, and fight a battle, without involving the certain destruction of our trains, which, from the contour of these ridges and uneven nature of the ground, we would be obliged to park in close proximity to our position.

"The preservation of the trains, perhaps the safety of the entire command, demanded that I should retire to Bailey's Cross-roads, two miles northwest of our position, while we could get our trains under cover and fight the enemy to better advantage. I therefore directed that the trains should commence moving back slowly and in good order, and also directed General Baird to hold Widow Davis's Cross-roads until I could withdraw a portion of the second division, and take position on the north side of Chickamauga Creek, to cover the withdrawal of his two brigades and prevent the enemy from flanking us on our left.

"At 1 P.M. a heavy column of cavalry was seen moving steadily on our left flank, with the evident intention of gaining my rear. I immediately had four pieces of artillery placed in position on the ridge at John Davis's house, which commanded the valley on my left; also sent General Beatty, with one regiment and a section of artillery, to seize and hold Bailey's Cross-roads, which was reported to be in possession of the enemy's advance.

"At 2 P.M. the trains were all in motion, falling back to Bailey's Cross-roads. General Beatty and Colonel Scribner, of General Baird's division, were directed to proceed to that point without

CHATTANOOGA FROM THE NORTH BANK OF THE TENNESSEE.

his position untenable, and, after some severe fighting, retired without losing any of his artillery or transportation. His caution in observing, by means of scouts, the operations of the enemy, and his skillful disposition of his forces on the 11th, had saved his division from otherwise certain destruction. He reached Stevens's Gap with his trains at 10 o'clock P.M., and forthwith dispatched to Thomas an account of the day's operations, suggesting that the troops (Reynolds's and Brannan's divisions) moving *via* Cooper's Gap take the most direct route to Stevens's Gap, reaching that point at the earliest possible moment. He anticipated an immediate attack from the enemy; but Bragg had withdrawn his forces from the cove.

The army was still in danger. Rosecrans was as yet ignorant of the enemy's position. The weight of evidence (received through Bragg's ingenious ruse of sending deserters and citizens within the Federal lines with false information) had indicated that Bragg was moving on Rome. Information received on the 10th made it certain that the enemy had retreated by the Lafayette Road, but gave no hint of his present position. The next morning Crittenden was ordered to Ringgold, from which point he was to send a reconnoissance to Lee and Gordon's Mill. If the enemy was found in the vicinity of Lafayette, Crittenden was to support Thomas, otherwise he was to advance toward Rome.[1] In making the movement to Lee and Gordon's Mill, Crittenden drove "squads of the enemy" before him, indicating that the main body of the Confederate army was not far distant. At 3 P.M. on the 11th, Rosecrans warned Crittenden that a heavy force of the enemy was in Chattanooga Valley, and urged him to move his whole force promptly to the Rossville and Lafayette Road. This Crittenden began to do on the following morning (the 12th), moving his whole command that day to Lee and Gordon's Mill. The same day Brannan's division, of Thomas's corps, reached Negley's left, *via* Cooper's Gap, Reynolds's following close behind. In the mean while, McCook, having reached Alpine on the 10th, found "that the enemy had not retreated very far from Chattanooga."[2] He had been ordered (the day before) to move rapidly on Alpine and Summerville to intercept Bragg's line of retreat, and to attack him in flank. Finding that, after all, he was not on the enemy's flank, he communicated with Thomas, and was surprised to learn that the latter "had not reached Lafayette, as ordered." The movement to Summerville, therefore, was not made. Thomas informed McCook on the 10th that he could not reach Lafayette before the 13th. McCook, beginning to be alarmed on account of the isolated situation of his corps, on the 12th wisely returned his trains to the summit of Lookout Mountain, remaining with his command near Alpine to await the result of a cavalry reconnoissance sent out by General Stanley to ascertain the whereabouts of the enemy.

Bragg, having failed in his designs against Thomas, retired from McLemore's Cove, and sent Polk and Walker's corps in the direction of Lee and Gordon's Mill. It might not be too late for a movement northward against Crittenden. Learning from General Pegram, the Confederate cavalry commander in that direction, that this corps of the Federal army was divided, one division being at Ringgold, Bragg ordered Polk to attack this division on the morning of the 13th. His plan now was to crush Crittenden's divisions in detail, and then to turn again upon Thomas's corps in the Cove.[3] Here again he was disappointed. Polk, with double the numbers of the enemy which lay between him and Chattanooga, dispatched to Bragg (11 P.M. on the 12th) that he had taken a strong position for defense, and requesting heavy re-enforcements. He was again ordered not to delay his attack, his force already being numerically superior to the enemy, and was promised Buckner's corps the next morning. On proceeding to the front, early on the 13th, Bragg found that his orders had not been obeyed, and that Crittenden's forces were united, and on the west side of the Chickamauga.[4]

Rosecrans was at length assured from every possible source that his a was in peril, and that the theory of his movements since the occupatio Chattanooga had been founded upon a gigantic mistake.[1] He had alr (on the 11th and 12th) ordered Crittenden to Lee and Gordon's Mill, br ing in his detached forces from the east side of Chickamauga Creek,[2] directed Thomas to bring McCook and Stanley within supporting dista of his own corps. On the 13th, fully aware of his exposed situation, that, to use his own words, "it was a matter of life and death to effe concentration of his army," he began to hurry up his columns with idea of shutting off the enemy from an advance on Chattanooga by Lafayette Road. Instead of getting on the rear and flank of the enemy, task was now to get in his front.

General Thomas, when he received, during the night of Septem 12th–13th, the order brought by General Mitchell from Rosecrans to br McCook and Stanley up to his support, understood more perfectly than commander the nature of the emergency which confronted the Un army. He immediately directed McCook to move two divisions of Twentieth Corps over the mountain to the left of the Fourteenth, leav the other divisions to guard the trains. Crittenden, under instructions fr Rosecrans, on the 14th, leaving Wood's division at Lee and Gordon's M moved the remainder of his command to Mission Ridge, and sent Wild cavalry up Chickamauga Creek to connect with Thomas, whose extre left under Reynolds then touched Pond Spring.

McCook in the mean time was moving in execution of the orders wh he had received; but, unfortunately, instead of taking the mountain r direct to Stevens's Gap, he crossed Lookout Mountain, and, moving do the valley, was obliged to recross at Cooper's Gap, thus losing at least whole day at the most critical stage of the campaign.[3] This delay ca near being fatal to the army.[4] By the night of the 17th McCook's co mand was in McLemore's Cove, and the three corps of the command w within supporting distance for the first time since the crossing of the T nessee. The day previous Rosecrans was satisfied that Bragg was receivi re-enforcements from Lee's army. He had been advised by General H leck to that effect on the 15th.[5] He now calls stoutly for Burnside's assi ance. But it is already far too late for that to reach him.

From the morning of the 13th to the night of the 17th Bragg has n had five days since he abandoned his attempt against the detached corps Rosecrans's army. During this time he has been contemplating an advan around the Federal left to secure the only available approaches to Chatt nooga from McLemore's Cove. He has dispatched Wheeler's cavalry to t left to press the Federal forces in the Cove, in order to divert attention fro

---

delay, and protect the train from the attack of a large force of cavalry approaching with the view.

"At 3 o'clock the skirmishers of General Baird's division were ordered back across the creek, where they were placed in position to hold the enemy in check until I could get my artillery in position on the ridge this side. Two companies of the Nineteenth Illinois Infantry, concealed behind a stone fence, poured into the ranks of the enemy a destructive volley, killing, as I have since learned, thirty on the spot. This partially checked the enemy, who was advancing in three heavy lines. Meantime I had ten pieces of artillery planted on the ridge to the rear of Davis's house, which commanded that position, until another new line could be formed on a ridge to the rear.

"The enemy now occupied the south side of the creek with a heavy force, and opened two batteries of artillery at a distance of 400 yards. Two of his brigades were parallel to our position on the right. Buckner's corps was deployed, and moving up steadily on our left, within short range. Colonel Stanley's and a portion of General Starkweather's brigades sustained here a well-directed and terrific fire, which our troops returned with spirit and marked effect. The firing increased, and indicated an immediate general engagement along our entire front, and would have terminated in an assault from the enemy in a few moments, which would have been disastrous to us, considering the overwhelming force of the enemy and our very unfavorable position.

"By direction, General Baird deployed General Starkweather's brigade to our right, which checked the enemy's advance in that direction, and enabled Colonel Stanley to withdraw his brigade, which being done, we retired slowly and in good order to Bailey's Cross-roads, where a strong position of defense was assumed, and the troops were bivouacked for the night, with trains parked at Stevens's Gap. During the night the enemy withdrew to Dug Gap."—*General Negley's Report.*

[1] *Crittenden's Report.* [2] *McCook's Report.*

[3] His orders to Polk were explicit, and were thrice repeated, as follows:

"Lafayette, Georgia, 6 P.M., September 12th.

"Lieutenant General POLK:

"GENERAL,—I inclose you a dispatch from General Pegram. This presents you a fine opportunity of striking Crittenden in detail, and I hope you will avail yourself of it at daylight to-morrow. This division crushed, and the others are yours. We can then turn on the force in the Cove. Wheeler's cavalry will move on Wilder so as to cover your right. I shall be delighted to hear of your success.

Very truly yours, BRAXTON BRAGG.

"To attack at daylight on the 13th."

"Lafayette, Georgia, 6 P.M., September 12th, 1863.

"Lieutenant General POLK, Commanding Corps:

"GENERAL,—I inclose you a dispatch marked 'A,' and I now give you the orders of the commanding general, viz., to attack at daylight to-morrow the infantry column reported in said dispatch at three quarters of a mile beyond Peavine Church, on the road to Graysville from Lafayette.

I am, general, etc., GEORGE W. BRENT, A. A. G."

"Lafayette, Georgia, September 12th, 1863.

"Lieutenant General POLK, Commanding Corps:

"GENERAL,—The enemy is approaching from the south, and it is highly important that your attack in the morning should be quick and decided. Let no time be lost.

"I am, general, etc., GEORGE W. BRENT, A. A. G."

[4] *Bragg's Report.* It appears, however, from Crittenden's own report, that his corps had already been concentrated at Lee and Gordon's Mill on the 12th, before the order to attack had been i sued to General Polk.

[1] When was it that Rosecrans first became acquainted with the actual situation of Bragg army? This question is not answered in his report with any degree of precision. On the eve ing of the 10th he was certain that the main body of Bragg's army "retired by the Lafayette Ro but uncertain whether he had gone far." At 3 30 P.M. on the 11th, he informed Crittend that "the enemy was in heavy force in the Valley of the Chattanooga." At 3 P.M. on t 12th, he sent General R. B. Mitchell, of the cavalry corps, to General Thomas with verbal ord instructing the latter to direct McCook and Stanley to move up within supporting distance of h corps. The reason given for this movement does not imply that Rosecrans then knew that t Confederate army was near Lafayette; it was ordered "with a view of moving upon the enemy the earliest practical moment." Mitchell (probably by taking the road east of Lookout Mountai struck Negley's headquarters. The following is a copy of the letter written by Negley to Thom upon Mitchell's arrival (1 A.M. on the 13th):

"Major General THOMAS:

"GENERAL,—General Mitchell, of the cavalry corps, has just arrived from General Rosecran headquarters, having left there at 8 o'clock P.M. He brings verbal orders from General Ro crans to the following effect, which he desires me to communicate to you:

"That you order General McCook and Stanley, with his cavalry, to move at once within su porting distance of your corps, with a view of moving upon the enemy at the earliest practical moment.

"General Rosecrans complains of a want of information in regard to your movements and po tion, and of the numbers and position of the enemy.

"*Feeling confident, from the remarks that General Rosecrans made to General Mitchell, that he totally misinformed as to the character of the country in this vicinity, and of the position, force, and i tentions of the enemy,* I write you on that point, so that you can communicate with him at once.

"Also, to inform you that one of my scouts (young Bailey), who is intelligent and reliable, h just returned from the vicinity of Bird's Mills, stating that he was informed by Mr. Paine, a other citizens, that in the affair of yesterday our force was confronted by Buckner's entire co mand, two other divisions of infantry from the vicinity of Dug Gap, and a force of five or s thousand cavalry. That the enemy expected to hold us at Dug Gap, while Buckner and the ca alry could pass to our rear, and take possession of Stevens's and Cooper's Gaps. That Brecki ridge's command was on Pigeon Ridge, or at Lafayette. That Bragg was concentrating his e tire force at or near Lafayette. That the rebel cavalry west of Pigeon Ridge had passed throu Worthing Gap, and the infantry had fallen back to the top of the ridge and beyond. The smo from their line of encampment was visible this evening.

"A similar statement was made by two other citizens on hearsay. . . . . General Brannan r turned from his reconnoissance this evening. He advanced as far as Widow Davis's Cross-road He met with only a small cavalry picket, which fled at his approach. Indications were that t enemy were on and beyond Pigeon Ridge. . . . .

"I have the honor to remain yours very truly, JAS. S. NEGLEY, Major General."

The whole tenor of this letter indicates that the order brought by Mitchell was based upon accurate knowledge by Rosecrans of the enemy's position. Yet it is clear, both from this ord and from the instructions already issued to Crittenden to move to Lee and Gordon's Mill, th Rosecrans was, on the 12th, beginning to lose confidence in his scheme for striking the tail end Bragg's army, and to be alarmed for his own safety. His petulant complaint of Thomas's negl gence in forwarding information was an indication of his own fears. On the 13th the grou upon which he had stood slipped clean away from under his feet. On that day he received fro Thomas, from McCook, and from Crittenden information which only too clearly demonstrate that Bragg's entire army was concentrated at Lafayette and along the eastern slope of Pige Mountain.

[2] What is throughout this chapter called "Chickamauga Creek" is really the West Fork Chickamauga Creek.

[3] McCook probably moved upon the best instructions he had in regard to the roads. There some discrepancy, however, between his own and Rosecrans's statements. McCook says, " was my desire to join General Thomas by the mountain road, *via* Stevens's Gap; but not havi any guide, and all the citizens concurring that no such road existed, and General Thomas al stating that the route by Valley Head was the only practicable one, I determined to join him b it." Rosecrans, in his report, states that McCook was ordered to take the mountain road. Th might be explained on the supposition that McCook received an order from Rosecrans subseque to the one received from Thomas.

[4] "The tardy arrival of McCook's corps came near being fatal to us."—*Rosecrans's Testimo before the Congressional Committee.*

[5] Rosecrans thus writes to Halleck from near Gordon's Mill, 1 30 P. M., September 16: "Fro information derived from various sources from my front, I have reason to believe what you a sert in your dispatch of yesterday, 4 30 P.M., is true, and that they [*i.e.*, Longstreet's forces] ha arrived at Atlanta at last. Push Burnside down."

his real movement and Forrest's to the right to cover his advance. But he has not advanced. His forces, on the night of the 17th, lie along Peavine Creek, east of Pigeon Mountain. Nothing has been in his front between him and Chattanooga, except cavalry, with a small detachment of infantry, for the past four days. Chattanooga itself has only been held by Wagner's brigade, and all the while Bragg appears to have taken it for granted that the Federal army was concentrated in his front. He has been waiting also for Longstreet's corps, three brigades of which, under General Hood, have just arrived, and now, when Rosecrans's army *is* really concentrated in his front, he issues his orders for the crossing of Chickamauga Creek.[1] It is impossible to calculate the advantage of this delay to Rosecrans's army.

West Chickamauga Creek, which now separated the opposing armies, takes its rise from the junction of Mission Ridge with Pigeon Mountain at the southern extremity of the Cove, and runs northeastwardly down the Cove by Pond and Crawfish Springs, touching the Lafayette and Chattanooga Road at Lee and Gordon's Mill, and, after its junction with the main creek, empties into the Tennessee four miles above Chattanooga. About four and a half miles below Lee and Gordon's Mill, in a straight line, is Reed's Bridge, on one of the roads from Ringgold to Rossville. Here was the extreme right of Bragg's line on the night of the 17th. Between this point and Lee and Gordon's Mill there are several available crossings—at Alexander's Bridge, and at Byron's, Tedford's, Dalton's, and several other fords. The roads leading to these from the east were bad, both from their narrowness and from the mountainous character of the country. The stubborn resistance of Minty's and Wilder's cavalry delayed the crossing of Bragg's forces on the 18th. The right column, proceeding from Ringgold, was commanded by General Bushrod R. Johnson, and consisted of his division—made up of three improvised brigades from Mississippi—and Hood's,[2] which also consisted of three brigades. The two divisions numbered over 7000 men. Forrest's cavalry co-operated with this column, covering its front and right upon the march. At Peavine Creek, between Chickamauga Hill and Pigeon Mountain, an attempt was made by a small detachment of Minty's cavalry to resist the progress of Johnson's column, but without success. The attempt was repeated when the Confederates reached Reed's Bridge, again with insufficient force, and with no better result than before. Johnson succeeded in saving the bridge from destruction, and began to cross his command at 3 o'clock P.M., partly by the bridge, and partly by the ford above. He then swept southward in front of the points where Walker's and Buckner's corps had been ordered to cross.

Walker's corps, nearly 6000 strong, encountered stout resistance at Alexander's Bridge (about three miles south of Reed's), and, the Federal cavalry having, after a sharp skirmish, succeeded in destroying the bridge, was compelled to cross by night at Byron's Ford. One brigade was left east of the creek to guard the ordnance train, which could not cross with the troops.

Buckner's corps, 10,000 strong, started from a point near Rock Spring Church, and crossed Pigeon Mountain, following the route taken by Walker's, but, turning southward upon approaching the Chickamauga, secured the crossing at Tedford's Ford, but, waiting Walker's movements on the right, did not cross till the next morning.

Thus, before daylight on the 19th, Bragg had, including cavalry, over 15,000 men across the creek. Buckner's corps consisted of Stewart's and Preston's divisions. It was ready to cross, as was also Cheatham's division of Polk's corps. These, crossing early on the morning of the 19th, increased the force on the east of the creek by 16,000 men. Hindman's division of Polk's corps, and Breckinridge's and Cleburne's of Hill's corps, held the left, south and west of Lee and Gordon's Mill, on the opposite side of the creek, and did not cross until the afternoon and night of the 19th.

These movements indicate clearly the enemy's plan of operations. Anticipating no serious opposition on his extreme right, Bragg expected to secure the approach to Chattanooga by the Lafayette Road, and then to close down upon the Federal army and fight the battle upon a field from which, even in the improbable event of his defeat, he could fall back upon the strong-hold which a fortnight before he had been compelled to abandon on account of his weakness, but which now, with his army heavily re-enforced—nearly doubled, in fact[3]—he could easily hold against the combined armies of Burnside and Rosecrans. For Bragg to gain the front which he sought, and extend his army across the Lafayette and Dry Valley Roads and the intervening ridges, would have been to win the battle's prize before the battle itself had been fought. But here Bragg was again disappointed. His advance had been too long delayed, and his movements on the 18th had been unexpectedly retarded. And thus it happened that the battle of Chickamauga came to be fought for the very position which Bragg had hoped to gain before fighting it.

[1] The following is a copy of these orders.

"I. Johnson's column, on crossing at or near Reed's Bridge, will turn to the left by the most practicable route, and sweep up the Chickamauga toward Lee and Gordon's Mill.

"II. Walker, crossing at Alexander's Bridge, will unite in this move, and push vigorously on the enemy's flank and rear in the same direction.

"III. Buckner, crossing at Tedford's Ford, will join in the movement to the left, and press the enemy up the stream from Polk's front at Lee and Gordon's Mill.

"IV. Polk will press his forces to the front of Lee and Gordon's Mill, and, if met by too strong resistance to cross, will bear to the right, and cross at Dalton's Ford, or at Tedford's, as may be necessary, and join the attack wherever the enemy may be.

"V. Hill will cover our left flank from an advance of the enemy from the Cove, and, by pressing the cavalry in his front, ascertain if the enemy is re-enforcing at Lee and Gordon's Mill, in which event he will attack them in flank.

"VI. Wheeler's cavalry will hold the Gap in Pigeon Mountain, and cover our rear and left, and bring up the stragglers.

"VII. All teams, etc., not with the troops, should go toward Ringgold and Dalton, Georgia, beyond Taylor's Ridge. All cooking should be done at the trains; rations, when cooked, will be forwarded to the troops.

"VIII. The above movements will be executed with the utmost promptitude and perseverance."

[2] Hood did not take command of his division until it had crossed the creek.

[3] "Nearly half our army consisted of re-enforcements just before the battle."—*Bragg's Report.*

For Rosecrans's army had been, the last five days, marching for dear life, and when Bragg crossed the Chickamauga he found this army, which he had expected to strike near Lee and Gordon's Mill, upon his front and right, prepared to contest inch by inch the possession of the Lafayette and Chattanooga Road.[1] Its own celerity of movement, and Bragg's delay (in this case due to excessive caution), had again saved the Federal army.

While awaiting the arrival of McCook's corps, Thomas's and Crittenden's extended from the Dry Valley Road in front of Stevenson's Gap to Crawfish Spring, being connected at Pond Spring by Wilder's cavalry. Wood's division of Crittenden's corps still held a strong defensive position at Lee and Gordon's Mill,[2] and the river below that point was guarded by Minty's cavalry, which crossed and reconnoitred the country on the left front, occasionally meeting and skirmishing with the enemy. The gaps of Pigeon Mountain to the south were also carefully guarded by Thomas's command. As soon as McCook came up he closed in on Thomas's right, and Crittenden drew in his right upon Crawfish Spring, to give place for Thomas. Wilder's cavalry was then detached and sent to the left.

The 18th was a day of terrible anxiety to General Rosecrans. Reports at different periods of the day came in from Wood and Wilder of the enemy's advance upon the left. The Lafayette Road must be secured, if possible, at any hazard. Before night Palmer's and Van Cleve's divisions of Crittenden's corps were upon the creek to Wood's left and right, and all night long Thomas was marching by the road to Widow Glenn's, and past the slopes of Mission Ridge, toward Kelly's Farm on Chickamauga Creek, away off to the left of Crittenden; so that on the morning of the 19th the right of the army rested at Crawfish Spring, which the day before had been its left. Negley's division had been left by Thomas to guard the fords of the Upper Chickamauga in the vicinity of Crawfish Spring. Granger, with the reserve corps, was at Rossville.

The battle of the 19th was opened by General Thomas. The head of his column reached Kelly's at daylight, and went in on the left of Wilder (who had the night before been driven back to the heights east of the Widow Glenn's), Baird taking position first, then Brannan upon his left. At this point, Dan McCook, commanding a brigade of Granger's reserve corps, reported the presence of an isolated brigade of the enemy between Kelly's house and Reed's Bridge, and Brannan, with two brigades, was advanced on the road to the bridge to secure the capture of this detached force. Baird also advanced to keep in line with Brannan. These dispositions were made at 9 A.M. Soon after, Palmer's division, of Crittenden's corps, came up on Baird's right. The fight began at about ten o'clock.[3] It consisted at first of sharp skirmishing with Forrest on the Reed's Bridge Road. The movements of Johnston and Hood the night before toward Lee and Gordon's Mill had left Walker's corps in a somewhat isolated position on the Confederate right. Wilson's brigade, of this corps, after conducting the ordnance train across the creek, was called upon to support Forrest. Coming in contact with this force, Croxton's brigade, of Brannan's division, had become engaged, and drove the enemy for half a mile, when the latter was re-enforced by Ector's brigade, and it was necessary to send in Baird's division. The small force of the enemy engaged at this point was steadily pressed back until it was supported by the remainder of Walker's corps.[4] After an hour's severe fighting, Croxton's brigade had been withdrawn, and Baird and Brannan, uniting their forces, drove the enemy from their front.

In the mean time, Cheatham's division came up to Walker's support at noon, and, forming in rear of the latter, advanced upon Baird, striking him in the flank, and throwing two of his brigades into confusion. Baird was driven back before overwhelming numbers for some distance, when the fortunate arrival of Reynolds's and Johnson's divisions on his right again turned the tide of battle. These fresh divisions, advancing with Palmer's (which had been opportunely sent by Crittenden), struck Cheatham's flank, and thrust him back in disorder upon Walker's corps, Brannan's troops attacking him at the same time in front, and recapturing the artillery which Baird had lost in his retreat. While Cheatham was thus hotly engaged, and being driven in confusion, Stewart's division, of Buckner's corps, coming from the Confederate left to his support, attempted in vain to drive Thomas back from his advanced position. His three brigades—Clayton's, Brown's, and Bate's—advanced each in its turn. In one hour's fighting Clayton lost nearly 400 officers and men,[5] and, being withdrawn, Brown took his place, and gallantly charged through a dense underwood extending along his front, when he encountered a terrific fire from all arms. He was unable to use his artillery, while the batteries in his front and on his right flank poured into his ranks murderous volleys of grape and canister. Checked for a brief moment, he again pushed forward and up the slope, where the strength of the Federal position and an attack on his right compelled him to retreat, after the loss of many of his best officers and a large number of his men. Bate relieved him then, meeting the same fire which had driven back his brother commanders, but, with Clayton's support, succeeded in driving the Federal force in his front beyond the Chattanooga Road.

[1] "The enemy, whose left was at Lee and Gordon's Mill when our movement commenced, had rapidly transferred forces from his extreme right, changing his entire line, and seemed disposed to dispute, with all his ability, our effort to gain the main road to Chattanooga in his rear."—*Bragg's Report.*

[2] "A stronger position naturally than that which General Wood occupied can scarcely be imagined. The creek at Gordon's Mill bends round in the form of a semicircle, the convexity being toward the south, whence the enemy would have advanced toward General Wood. An eminence, forming what would be a diameter of the circle if completed, runs from east to west, uniting the extremities of the bend. Upon this General Wood had placed his artillery. The creek itself, of considerable depth, and with a bank several feet high upon our side of it, constituted a splendid ditch, and all along its bank lay Wood's men, behind a rude but efficient breastwork of logs and rails."—*National Account, Rebellion Record,* vii., p. 409.

[3] *Thomas's Report.*

[4] Forrest reports the capture of two batteries at an early stage of the engagement, but that he was unable to bring them off for want of horses.

[5] *General A. P. Stewart's Report.*

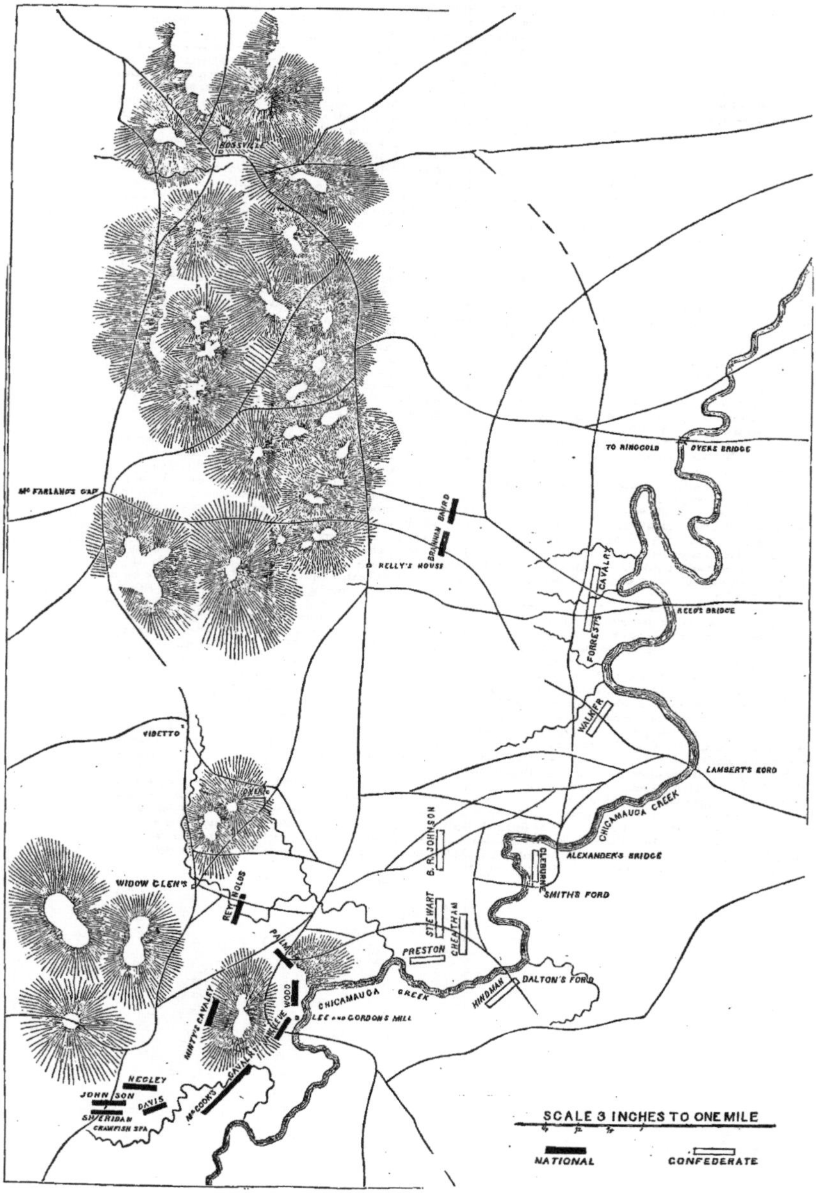
ROSSVILLE
Mc FARLAND'S GAP
KELLY'S HOUSE
BRANNAN
BAIRD
TO RINGGOLD
DYERS BRIDGE
REED'S BRIDGE
FORREST'S CAVALRY
WALKER
LAMBERT'S FORD
CHICAMAUGA CREEK
ALEXANDER'S BRIDGE
B. R. JOHNSON
CLEBURNE
SMITH'S FORD
VIDETTO
WIDOW GLEN'S
REYNOLDS
STEWART
CHEATHAM
PRESTON
HINDMAN
DALTON'S FORD
WOOD
CHICAMAUGA CREEK
LEE AND GORDONS MILL
NEGLEY
JOHNSON
SHERIDAN
CRAWFISH SPA
DAVIS
SCALE 3 INCHES TO ONE MILE
NATIONAL
CONFEDERATE

The battle had already extended far up the creek. By two o'clock Hood and Johnson had become involved in the struggle, and the entire Confederate line, as it then stood, below Lee and Gordon's Mill, had been engaged with the exception of two brigades of Preston's division (Buckner's corps), which, on rising ground, held the extreme left of Bragg's army west of the Chickamauga. On the Federal line, division after division had been sent in—Van Cleve's, of Crittenden's corps; then Davis's, of McCook's; then Wood's, from Lee and Gordon's Mill; and, finally, Sheridan's. Each in its turn had driven the enemy, and then, outflanked, had been thrust back. The arrival of Sheridan's division finally stayed the enemy's progress on the Federal right.

On the centre the Confederates had in the mean time gained considerable advantage, and the shells from their batteries almost reached the Widow Glenn's house, where Rosecrans's headquarters were. Negley's division had therefore been withdrawn from Crawfish Spring, arriving upon the field at 4 30 P.M. This division was dispatched to the centre, where it found that Van Cleve had been dislodged from the line. Negley immediately attacked, and drove the enemy steadily till night. Palmer had been endangered by the disaster to Van Cleve, but the advance of the enemy upon his flank was checked by General Hazen, who, driven back upon an elevation of ground, promptly manned twenty guns and poured a cross-fire into the enemy's charging column, which threw it back in disorder.

The attack which had for a time broken the Federal centre had begun on Reynolds's right. After Cheatham's repulse there had been a lull in the battle in front of the Federal left from 4 o'clock till about 5, during which Brannan and Baird had reorganized their commands, and had been withdrawn to a strong position on the extreme left, in which direction Thomas expected the next attack. But the enemy made his advance some distance farther to the right. Brannan's division and the greater portion of Baird's were promptly sent to Reynolds's assistance, arriving just in time to prevent disaster. Even while Van Cleve was being driven in the centre, Thomas was driving the enemy on the left.

In pursuing the enemy Thomas's lines became very much extended, and were now concentrated upon more commanding ground. It was supposed that the battle for that day was over. But Thomas had scarcely completed the disposition of his forces before he was again attacked by the enemy. Pat Cleburne's division, of Hill's corps, having crossed the river at Tedford's Ford, had reached the Confederate right soon after sunset. Passing over the line which Thomas had just driven back, and supported on his left by Cheatham, he made an unexpected charge upon Johnson and Baird's divisions, producing considerable confusion in their ranks; but order was soon restored, and the enemy repulsed.[1] In this night attack General Preston Smith, of Cheatham's division, was killed. This engagement terminated the battle of the 19th.

The battle thus far had been waged for a position. When it began in the morning neither of the two armies had formed its line, though in this respect the advantage had been with the Confederates. If Bragg had been aware of Thomas's movement made on the night of the 18th, the result of the morning's, and, probably, of the whole day's fighting would have been far different. Supposing the Federal forces to be in the neighborhood of Lee and Gordon's Mill, Bragg had moved his own too far up the creek, leaving Forrest only on his extreme right; and while he had been moving them back to the right to meet the emergencies arising out of the engagement with Thomas, Rosecrans was given time to bring up his divisions to Thomas's support. In this way Thomas's movement to the left had spoiled the enemy's preconceived plan of operations. Every assault which had been made during the day upon the vital point of the Federal line, its extreme left, had been severely repulsed. Whatever ground had been gained by Bragg had been upon the centre, where Van Cleve had been driven back so far that, until Negley's arrival, the communication was cut off between Thomas and Rosecrans's headquarters at the Widow Glenn's.[2] Earlier in the day (say at 2 o'clock P.M.) the line of each army had extended along the Lafayette and Chattanooga Road. But upon the restoration of the Federal line, after the break on its centre, the left and centre had been refused leaving

Rosecrans's headquarters had been all day at the
he could receive by a direct road communications
His immediate presence upon the field was at some
tremely necessary. If, just before noon, he had be
would have sent in supports to Thomas's right witl
Walker's corps must have been completely destroy
river. Instead of being there, he was pacing his hea
Glenn's in nervous excitement, while his aids, with ti
tressed widow, were attempting to locate the line of
the firing. The general ought to have known that
ally assist Thomas by his personal direction of the b
latter.

Leaving out the reserve corps under General Gra
crans's whole army on the field, except two brigades
the 19th. Curiously, both General Bragg and Gener
they were opposed to superior numbers on this day.
forces engaged had not been far from equal; if there
was in Rosecrans's favor. But Bragg had full 15,0
been under fire, if we include Kershaw's and Humphr
street's corps, which came up in time for the next
ridge's and Hindman's divisions were across the ri
taken no part in the battle.

A council of war was held after dark at Rosecrans's
disposition of forces and the conduct of the battle of
termined upon. That it would be a desperate conf
battle already fought had been for the road to Chatt
to secure this road would be renewed the next day
would be hard to withstand. Failing of success at
would do his best to crush the army which stood in hi

General Longstreet, in person, arrived at Bragg's he
night. To him was given the command of the left w
army, consisting of that portion of the troops which
been under Hood's command—Buckner's corps, and
divisions—with the fresh troops under Hindman and
sion of Breckinridge's division was the only change m
which had been and would still remain under the com
Bragg ordered Polk to attack the next morning at d
from his extreme right the battle should extend, divis
extreme left.

The Federal line during the night was reorganized
mained as he had already established it, with part of
reserve. It extended in a semicircular form (at least
thus characterized with sufficient accuracy for our pr
house, covering the road in front and on either fla
where it crossed the road on the south side it was ref
the refusal of the left and centre extending southw
corps closed up on Thomas, and refused its right upo
and covering the Widow Glenn's house. Wood's and
were placed in reserve, in a position to support eithe
Neither of the corps organizations was intact. Palm
Johnson, of McCook's corps, were with Thomas, while
to Thomas, was with McCook. The line extended th
Baird (his left refused to cover the road), Johnson, Pa
nan, Negley, Davis, Sheridan; with Wood and Van Cle
son's and Palmer's divisions extended from Baird's li
of Kelly's house, Reynolds's and the other divisions b
road. In the rear of Johnson and Palmer was an op
back, on the other side of the road, were dense woods.
gold to Rossville was well guarded by the cavalry and

The Confederate right wing, confronting the three
east of the Lafayette Road, consisted of four divisions
burne's, Cheatham's, and Walker's. The two latter we
street's command extended from Cleburne's position,

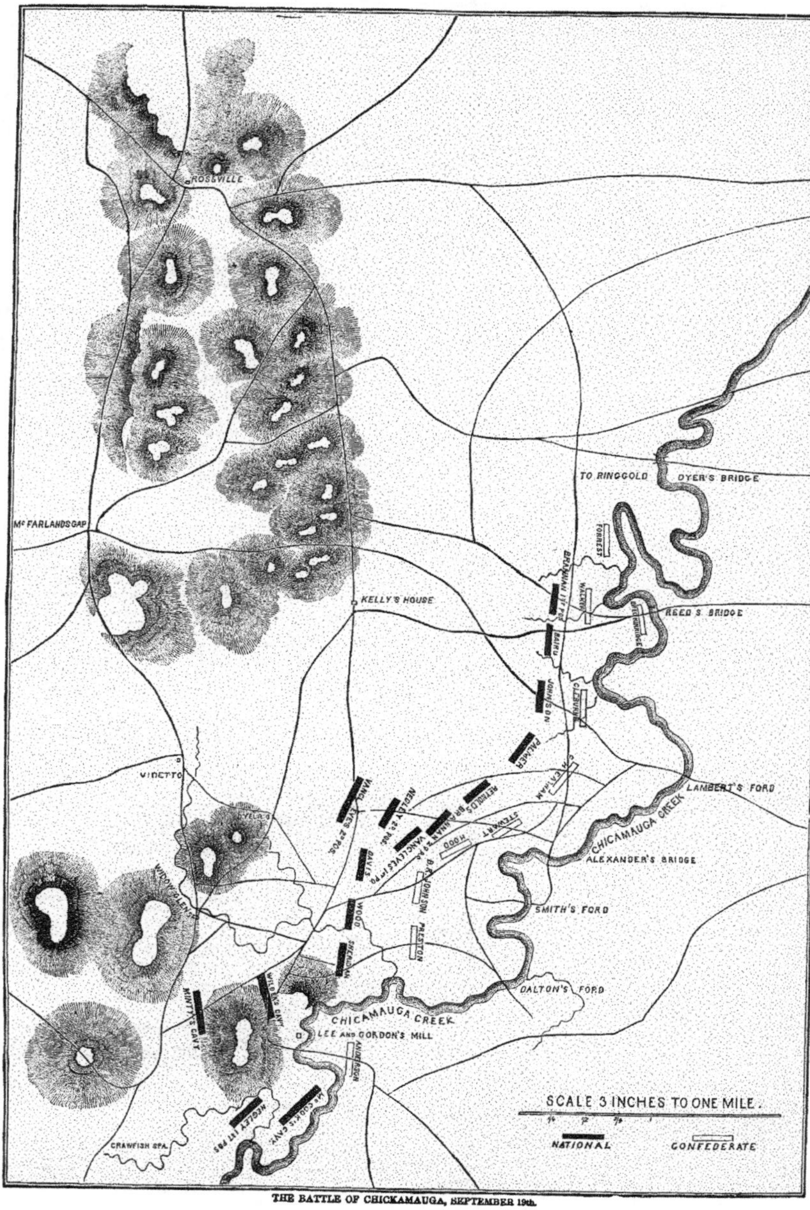

THE BATTLE OF CHICKAMAUGA, SEPTEMBER 19th.

ṗ the Federal line, pressing it back upon Longstreet—was not found easy ͻ execute.

Breckinridge opened the attack. He had not reached Cleburne's right ntil after dawn, and knew nothing of the ground. Of his three brigades lelm held the left, Stovall the centre, and Adams the right, being the exreme right of the whole line. The division extended so far to the right hat only a portion of Helm's brigade encountered the Federal line in a dicct advance westward, and thus Stovall and Adams, meeting no resistance, ushed forward, seriously threatening Thomas's flank. Baird's division did ot quite reach the Lafayette Road; Thomas had, therefore, as early as two 'clock A.M., written to Rosecrans, asking for Negley's division to supplenent his line. Rosecrans had promised that it should be sent forthwith. even o'clock came, an attack was momentarily expected, but Negley had ot arrived. The request was repeated, and was received by Rosecrans at ight o'clock. Some demonstration of the enemy in Negley's front led losecrans to retain this division until it was relieved by McCook. McCook aving been ordered to promptly relieve Negley, Rosecrans, accompanied y General Garfield, rode along his entire line. Upon returning to the ight he found Negley where he had left him, not having been relieved.

Beatty's brigade was immediately sent to Thomas, the other two being orered to follow as soon as other troops were ready to take their position. Jeatty reached Thomas in time, fortunately, to secure his line. Breckinidge's left brigade had already been severely cut up, having been exposed ͻ a front and enfilading fire from a foe concealed behind breastworks, and, fter two assaults, in which General Helm, commanding the brigade, and a irge number of his subordinate officers, had been killed, this portion of the ne was withdrawn. Stovall and Adams, however, had advanced, driving ack two lines of Baird's skirmishers. Stovall halted at the road, but Adams pressed forward, his line and Stovall's being now formed perpendiclar to the road, to conform to Baird's position. The advance now was hrough the woods west of the road. Stovall attacked the angle of the vorks, and was soon forced to retire. Adams, encountering Baird's left, ow re-enforced by Beatty and some regiments from Johnson's, Brannan's, nd Wood's divisions, was severely beaten. Adams, wounded, and a large umber of prisoners, were captured. Thus, before noon, Breckinridge had een driven from the field. To prevent a repetition of the attack at this oint, Negley was ordered to mass all the artillery which could be spared pon a position commanding the enemy's approach, but, from some misunerstanding, Negley took a very different position from that which had been ɔdicated.

Cleburne, on Breckinridge's left, had advanced against Johnson's, Palmr's, and Reynolds's divisions with no better success. Owing to Polk's utɜr neglect of his line in the morning, there was no well-arranged plan of ttack. Cleburne, in the hurry occasioned by orders to dress upon Breckinidge's left, had got into some confusion. His left, also, in advancing, conerged with Longstreet's line of advance in such a manner that part of Vood's brigade passed over some of Stewart's division, and Deshler's was ırown entirely out of line in Stuart's rear. Thus a part of Wood's brigade ıoved against that part of Thomas's line which turned westward upon the ɔad. Crossing a field bordering the road, near Poe's house, this brigade ɛceived a heavy oblique fire, and in a few minutes sustained a loss of 500 ıen, killed and wounded. Deshler might then have been sent in; but 'olk's brigade, on Wood's right, had also been repulsed, and Cleburne's hole line was withdrawn to a safe position some 400 yards in the rear. 'n the retreat General Deshler was killed, a sheli piercing "fair through is chest."[1]

In the mean time, the Federal divisions on Thomas's right have met with terrible misfortune. Upon the failure of McCook to relieve Negley in the erning, Crittenden had been ordered to do so, sending in Wood's division. ut this movement had been delayed until half past nine o'clock. McCook's ıe, holding the extreme right, was not satisfactory to Rosecrans, being too r removed from the troops on its left. After repeated orders from Roseans, this difficulty was only partially remedied. Messages still continued come from Thomas, asking for re-enforcements. Van Cleve's division as sent to his aid. Shortly after this a most unfortunate event took place. ıptain Kellogg, coming across the field to bring further tidings to Roseans that Thomas was still heavily pressed, thought he discovered a break the line on Reynolds's right. In fact there was no such break, but Bran.n's division, from its arrangement in *echelon* at this point, had occasioned e delusion. Rosecrans forthwith ordered Wood, who had relieved Neg-7, to close up and support Reynolds. Wood, misapprehending the intent the order, moved his division entirely out of line, "at double quick," and ssed to Brannan's rear. Thus a gap *was made* where previously none had isted, and through this gap the enemy advanced, throwing the entire right ng into confusion, from which it did not recover.[2]

Longstreet had waited until 11 o'clock, and then, seeing that Polk was making no serious impression upon the enemy, began the attack with the left wing. Stewart was closed up to the right, to make room for Hood in the front line. Humphreys's and Kershaw's brigades (McLaws's division), were, on their arrival, brought up as supports to Hood, whose division was made the main column of attack. Longstreet's order of battle was entirely reversed by the character which the conflict had assumed on the right. His left, instead of his right, became the movable column. Stewart's division, upon reaching the Lafayette Road, was there stationed, forming the pivot upon which Longstreet's wing turned. Hood's column was up just in time to take advantage of the break occasioned by Wood's sudden withdrawal, above alluded to, and the troops on his right and left pushed the attack with great vigor. General Hood received a severe, and it was then thought mortal wound, just after his column had penetrated the Federal lines, and General Law, commanding one of his brigades, succeeded to the command. But, notwithstanding the loss of their old commander, the troops pressed their advantage, flanking Jeff Davis on the one side, and Brannan on the other, cutting off five brigades from the right of the army, and driving them to the rear. The blow had fallen just as Rosecrans was weakening his right by sending two of Sheridan's brigades to Thomas. These brigades were recalled to oppose the enemy's advance, and Davis closed up to the left for the same purpose. But the enemy's charge could not thus be resisted. The attack now extended from beyond Brannan's right to a point west of the Dry Valley Road. The Confederates at the weak point outnumbered the Federals three to one. McCook's five brigades were driven back, with a loss of nearly half their men. The right of Brannan was driven back, and two of his batteries, moving to a new position, were taken in flank, and thrown back through two of Van Cleve's brigades, then on their way to Thomas, producing inextricable confusion. In this way these two brigades of Van Cleve, with the five already mentioned, were driven from the field on the road to Rossville. Davis and Sheridan strove in vain to make a stand. Hindman's division had advanced far to their right, making resistance useless. Johnson had advanced on Hindman's right, swelling the volume of the assaulting column. In this charge of Longstreet's command the Confederates claimed a capture of seventeen guns.

Rosecrans, McCook, and Crittenden had all been swept from the battlefield. Thomas alone was left, with one of Negley's brigades, and the divisions of Baird, Johnson, Palmer, Reynolds, and such portions of Wood's and Brannan's as had not been involved in the disaster, to withstand the entire Confederate army. Negley had taken some fifty pieces of artillery to the rear, in obedience, as he supposed, of Thomas's orders. He thus saved a large number of guns from capture, and offered a somewhat formidable resistance to the enemy's advance. But the Confederate success against McCook's line compelled him to withdraw, and he went to Rossville, where he was very efficient in the reorganization of Rosecrans's scattered troops.[1]

---

[1] *Cleburne's Report.*

[2] General Wood having claimed that he did right in moving out of line, and had no discretion do otherwise, General Rosecrans, on the 12th of January, 1864, wrote to Adjutant General omas the following letter:

'GENERAL,—The report of the general in chief shows that a letter from one of my division ɔmanders at the battle of Chickamauga, commenting on the report of his commanding general, 'been received at the War Department, and subsequently published by its authority. The genl in chief refers to that letter as a rival authority to my own, and as raising a doubt on the acscy of a point in my report. The letter, dated October 23, ult., four days after I left the comnd, is based on a quotation from my official report, to which, evidently, the writer was not at t time entitled, and which, therefore, *prima facie*, was surreptitiously obtained. It has been reꞏed and publicly used as a document disparaging my report, without having been referred to or passing through my hands, as required by military courtesy and army regulations.

'The War Department is therefore respectfully requested, as an act of justice, to cause the ve and following observations to be filed and published as an appendix to my official report of battle of Chickamauga:

'Brigadier General T. J. Wood writes and sends to the War Department a clandestine letter to ɾ, contrary to the inference drawn in my report, that he did right, under an order to 'Close up on General Reynolds and support him,' in taking his division out of the line of battle and in rear of Brannan's division, to a reserve position in rear of Reynolds. My report, dealing with facts, and avoiding personal censure, shows that General Reynolds sent me word, by Captain Kellogg, A.D.C. to General Thomas, that there were no troops on his immediate right, and that he wanted support there; that, supposing Brannan's division had been called away, I told an aid to write to General Wood an order to close up on Reynolds and support him, who wrote as follows:

"'Headquarters, September 20, 10 45 A.M.

"'Brigadier General T. J. Wood, Commanding Division, etc.:

"'The general commanding directs that you close up on Reynolds as fast as possible, and support him. Respectfully, FRANK S. BOND, Major and A.D.C.'

"Now, with this order in his hand;

"1st. When General Wood found there was no interval to close, because Brannan's troops had not left, his plain duty as a division commander was to have reported that fact to the general commanding, who was not more than six hundred yards from him, and asked further orders. His failure to do so was a grave mistake, showing want of military discretion.

"2d. When about to move, notwithstanding this, his duty, on being informed, as he was by one of his brigade commanders, that his skirmishers were engaged, and the enemy in line of battle opposite his position, General Wood was renewedly bound to have reported the facts and taken orders before leaving his position at such a critical time. But, instead of doing so, he privately withdrew his troops from the line, and let the enemy in, in the face of an order the wording of which shows that no such operation as the *opening*, but, on the contrary, the *closing* of a gap, was intended by it.

"3d. This conduct of General Wood, treated in the report with all the reserve consistent with the truth of history, contrasts most unfavorably with that of General Brannan, commanding the division next on his left, who, a little earlier in the day, when he received an order to leave his position and support the left, finding his skirmishers engaged, reported the fact to General Thomas, desiring to know if, under such circumstances, he should execute the order. He was told, 'No; stay where you are.'

"4th. It also contrasts with General Wood's own conduct and correspondence only a few days previously, when he protested against a reprimand of his corps commander for not occupying a position at Wauhatchie, lecturing his senior on the impropriety of what he termed 'blind obedience to orders,' and in upward of fifty pages of manuscript trying to prove his conduct consistent with that sound discretion which a division commander ought to exercise in removing his troops from the danger threatened by the literal execution of orders.

"The material difference of circumstances in the two cases, as appears from his own writings, being that the discretion he exercises at Wauhatchie, and the 'blind obedience' he pleads at Chickamauga, both have the effect of getting his troops out of danger.

"As the best of generals are liable to mistakes, I should have been content to leave those of General Wood to the simple historical statement of them, presuming he regretted them far more deeply than even myself. And, so feeling, I called attention to his military virtues—vigilance, discipline, providence of his commissariat, and care of his transportation. But his mean and unsoldierly defense of error shows him wrong both in head and heart.

"Respectfully, your humble servant, (Signed), W. S. ROSECRANS, Major General.

"Brigadier General L. Thomas, Adjutant General U. S. A.

"Official: R. S. THOMS, Captain, A.D.C."

[1] Both Generals Wood and Brannan, in their reports, endeavor to disparage General Negley's conduct in this connection. Brannan says:

"General Negley, so far from holding my right as he had promised, retired with extraordinary deliberation to Rossville at an early period of the day, taking with him a portion of my division, as will be seen by the report of Colonel Conwell, commanding First Brigade, leaving me open to attack from the right, as well as from the left and front (from which point the rebels attacked simultaneously on four several occasions), and my rear so far exposed that my staff officers, sent back for ammunition, were successfully cut off, and the ammunition, of such vital importance at that time, prevented from reaching me, thus necessitating the use of the bayonet as my only means of defense."

General Wood says:

"Before closing my report, I deem it my duty to bring to the notice of the commanding general certain facts which fell under my observation during the progress of the conflict on the 25th. As I was moving along the valley with my command, to the support of General Reynolds, in conformity with the order of the commanding general, I observed on my left, to the west of me, a force posted high up on the ridge. I inquired what force it was, and was informed that it was a part (a brigade, perhaps) of General Negley's division. I was informed that General Negley was with the force in person. I remember distinctly seeing a battery on the hill-side with it. At the

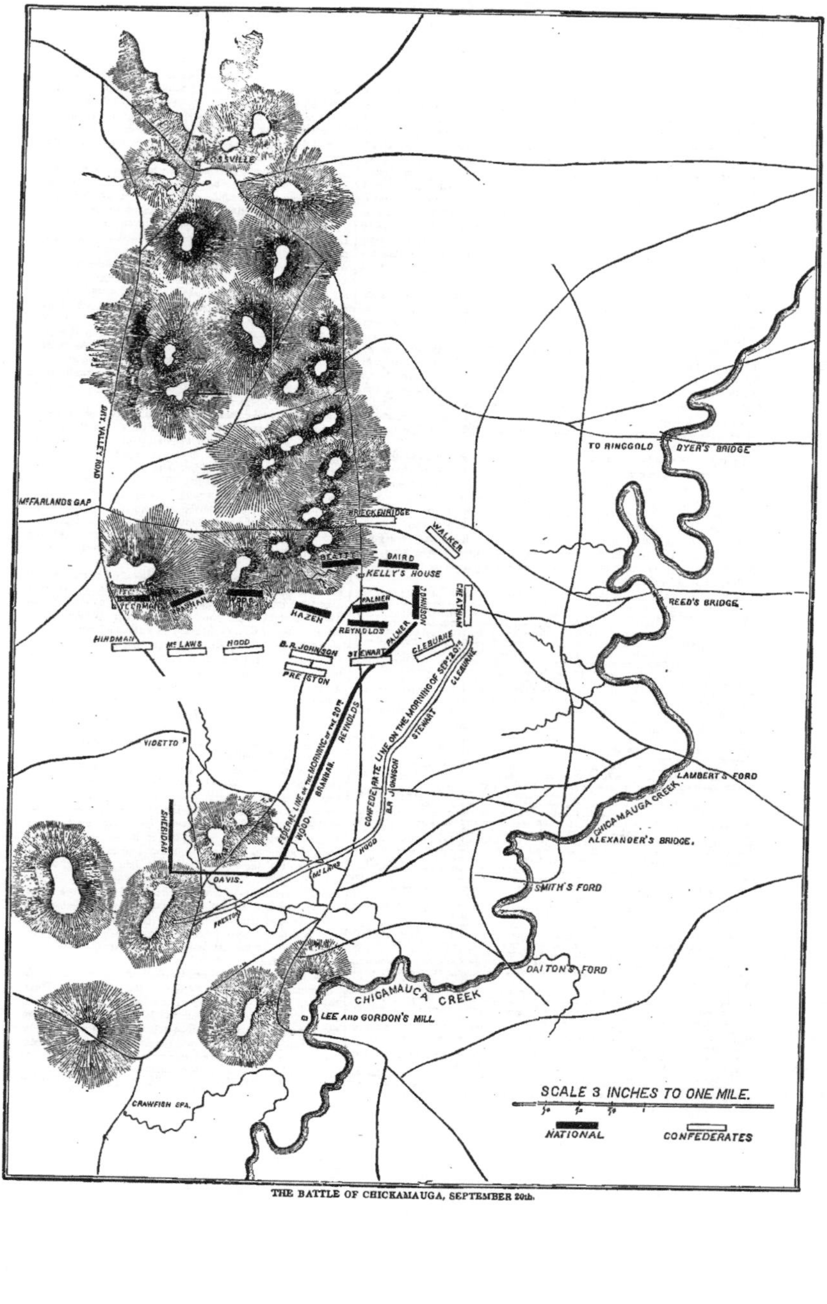

THE BATTLE OF CHICKAMAUGA, SEPTEMBER 20th.

could best provide for the safety of his army and of his trains. Finally, the two officers, before reaching Rossville, came to a point where two roads led, one to Chattanooga, and the other around to Thomas's position. Firing could be heard in the latter direction with considerable distinctness. Apart from this firing, there was no hint to guide General Rosecrans. The two officers listened most intently, and reached exactly opposite conclusions. Rosecrans had already arrived at a conviction that the entire army was defeated. He judged that the firing which he heard was scattered, and indicated disorganization. Garfield, who doubtless had a more correct ear, thought it was the firing of men who were standing their ground. He felt that Thomas was not beaten, and, as General Rosecrans was determined himself to go to Chattanooga, he asked permission to go to Thomas. This was given. Rosecrans went to Chattanooga, and telegraphed to General Halleck that his army was beaten. Garfield went to Thomas; what he found *there* we shall soon discover.

It is scarcely strange that Rosecrans should have jumped at the conclusion that Thomas was defeated. That he was not seems almost a miracle; but it was just such a miracle as had twice already during this campaign saved the army from destruction. If Longstreet had known the full extent of the disorder which his first assault had produced, he would have thrown caution to the wind, and have pursued with *abandon*. But, fortunately, he did not know. His divisions on the right had met with obstinate resistance. Hindman, instead of pursuing the advantage gained on the extreme left, was moved eastward to support Johnson. Thus time was given for the formation of a new Federal line from Thomas's right, across the commanding heights which constitute the southern spurs of Mission Ridge, east of McFarland's Gap.

Thomas, meanwhile, knew nothing of the disaster to the Federal right. Just before the repulse of the enemy on his extreme left, a little after noon, he sent to Rosecrans to hurry up Sheridan's division, which had been promised him. Captain Kellogg, his aid sent for this purpose, proceeding to the right, met a large force of the enemy in the open corn-field to the rear of Reynolds, advancing cautiously. This force was at first supposed to be Sheridan's troops, but the mistake was soon discovered, and the enemy was driven back. The gap between Reynolds and Brannan was filled, and Wood's division—so much of it as remained—was placed on the right, in prolongation of Brannan's line.

It can easily be seen that if, during the formation of this line, or previous,

time it was certainly out of reach of any fire from the enemy. This was between 11 and 12 o'clock in the day. A little later in the day, perhaps half or three quarters of an hour, when I became severely engaged, as already described, with the large hostile force that had pierced our lines and turned Brannan's right, compelling him to fall back, I looked for the force that I had seen posted on the ridge, and which, as already remarked, I had been informed was a part of General Negley's division, hoping, if I became severely pressed, it might re-enforce me, for I was resolved to check the enemy if possible. But it had entirely disappeared; whither it had gone I did not then know, but was informed later in the day it had retired to Rossville, and this information I believe was correct. By whose orders this force retired from the battle-field I do not know; but of one fact I am perfectly convinced: that there was no necessity for its retiring. It is impossible it could have been at all seriously pressed by the enemy at the time—in fact, I think it extremely doubtful whether it was engaged at all."

It is not necessary here to attempt any defense of so brave and skillful an officer as General Negley against such charges as these. We will simply quote the opinion of the Court of Inquiry called upon to investigate General Negley's conduct in the spring of 1864. The finding of this court was as follows:

"No question has any where been raised as to the conduct of General Negley on the 19th of September, the first day of the battle of Chickamauga. He commanded on that day his entire division, and it appears from the evidence that his conduct throughout was creditable.

"Early on the second day General Negley was assigned a position in the line on the right of General Brannan, from which he was relieved between 8 and 10 o'clock by Wood's division.

"He was then ordered to take a position on the extreme left; but his division having been relieved at a later hour than was expected, his reserve brigade was sent meantime in advance of the others, and became separated from him, taking a place in the line under General Baird. Subsequently another of his brigades was placed in line on the left of General Brannan, and under the command of that officer. A little later in the day, as General Negley was moving to a position on Missionary Ridge, to which he had been ordered by General Thomas, he gave up to General Brannan, on his urgent appeal for support, the largest regiment of his last brigade, retaining for himself only two weak regiments and four companies of another regiment. The point to which he was directed was in rear of the centre of the line. Here he found a battery; other batteries and parts of batteries joined him, and it appears on evidence that he had at last fifty guns under his care, with only the small infantry support above referred to, namely, two small regiments and four companies of another regiment, in all 600 or 700 men.

"The gap in the line made by the withdrawal of Wood's division, the rout of the entire right, and the unresisted advance of the enemy from that direction, as well as the advance of the enemy from the left of the line, the enemy having outflanked and driven in a portion of the left also, subjected General Negley to such hazard of losing this large park of artillery as made it expedient, in his judgment, to withdraw it to a point on the Dry Valley Road, about two or three miles from Rossville. It appears in evidence that this movement was executed in good order, and all the artillery saved.

"Here General Negley met Generals Davis and Sheridan, with portions of their command, and considerable bodies of disorganized troops from various commands. He co-operated with the division commanders above referred to in taking such measures as the exigencies of the occasion seemed to require, and toward evening retired to Rossville.

"General Negley exhibited throughout the day (the second of the battle) and the following night great activity and zeal in the discharge of his duties, and the court do not find in the evidence before them any ground of censure.

"The impression which seems to have been entertained by General Brannan that General Negley had ordered one of his brigades to the rear is not sustained by the testimony.

"It appears in the evidence that Brigadier General Wood, on one or more occasions, at the headquarters of the Army of the Cumberland, and in presence of the commander of that army and a portion of his staff, indulged in severe reflections upon the conduct of Major General Neg-

that Thomas was being hard pressed, he felt that his pres
was necessary. It was about three and a half miles fro
point where Thomas was then engaging Breckinridge.
over two thirds of this distance when the enemy made
the woods to the left. This hostile force was found to
observation, and Granger pressed on with his column, lea
this point to be taken care of by Dan McCook.

While Granger is advancing the battle has been stead
left along Thomas's line, until it has reached Reynolds's a
ions. Against these McLaws and Stewart, with a part o
ion, have been directing assaults as violent as those which
Cleburne have been making against the stronger line nor
Lafayette Road—stronger, because situated on more fave
more thoroughly fortified by breastworks. The result h
while Breckinridge and Cleburne are being driven back,
ion, though sustaining terrible loss and repeated repulse,
ing ground. It is at this point that Wood withdraws fro
and the disaster follows on the Federal right which we
scribed. Brannan now withdraws from his works, a
Thomas's line east of the Lafayette Road is refused, movi
spurs of Mission Ridge. All this has taken place as Gr
for the field. Longstreet is preparing for a fresh assault
sition with overwhelming numbers, and, when that assau
feels that, so far as he can see, there is no hope for his a
alternative to defeat.

At this critical moment clouds of dust are seen rising to
In those phantom-like columns lurk hope or disaster. S
is about to enter into the chemistry of this doubtful b
waits for the development of this approaching force for i
direction from which this force is coming gives no clew as
it is as like to prove hostile as friendly. At length long
seen emerging from the woods, crossing the Lafayette Roa
pline, their banners fluttering above, and their bayonets
sunlight. An aid has reconnoitred, and reports that it is
But *whose?* Soon this vital question was answered fro
colors—the red and blue, with the white crescent, marking
flag.

Granger had come up in time. Already Longstreet had
umns for an assault in front and on either flank. He had
ance from General Polk, but the latter had been too badly b
Thomas's right rested upon a chain of heights beginning a
a mile west of Kelly's house, and extending westward ab
ward the Dry Valley Road. These heights are covered w
have a gentle but irregular slope on the south, north, and ea
mits are a hundred feet above the level of the surrounding c
land's Gap—now the great strategic point of the battle-field
treme right. This gap is the entrance from the battle-field
Valley. The Dry Valley Road from this point to Rossvi
with the trains of the Federal army. The stand which w
Thomas, if obstinately held till nightfall, would secure th
the army to Rossville.

Granger, as he came up, was sent in on Brannan's right
ready been formed on Brannan's left. Steedman led Gran
crest of the hill, contending as be advanced against an assa
the enemy which had gained the summit of the ridge. Mo
artillery, he dislodged the enemy and drove him down th
inflicting upon him a fearful loss in killed and wounded.
fresh troops had revived the courage of the Federals at th
ery assault of the enemy from this time until nightfall w
great slaughter. The conflict here was desperate. Granger
sisted in great part of troops which had never before tasted
fought with heroic obstinacy, losing nearly half their numb
difficulty Longstreet succeeded in bringing his men to ch
they had been driven from the ridge and the gorge to the
had put in now his last division, and his troops were exha
peated assaults.

In the mean time, General Garfield, about four o'clock P.
the gauntlet of the enemy's fire on the left, reached Thom
the first official intelligence of the disaster which had bafal
the army at noon. Garfield had left the field with Rosec
seen, at the time of the disaster; as he now returned to
ridge just in rear of the point where the right had been

[1] "About 3 o'clock in the afternoon I asked the commanding general for
the right wing, but was informed by him that they had been beaten so bad
of no service to me. I had but one division [Preston's] that had not been

Thomas's line, which at the same time still retained the Lafayette Road. It was to him a glorious moment. He alone, of all the army which then held the field, had witnessed the advance of Hood's irresistible columns and the wreck of a whole line of battle; and he alone, of all those who had left the field, was permitted to witness the magnificent spectacle of Longstreet's repulse from the ridge. It was the fulfillment of the promise which his own heart had whispered to itself when he parted company with Rosecrans near Rossville.[1]

Shortly after Garfield's arrival, Thomas received a dispatch from General Rosecrans suggesting the withdrawal of the army to Rossville. Rosecrans had already learned from Garfield that Thomas was making a bold stand in the old tracks of the morning, and that the enemy was being repulsed. At half past five General Thomas ordered Reynolds to withdraw from his position. The line which had been assumed and obstinately held thus far, though strong in position, was weak in numbers. Only about twenty thousand men held the entire front from the Lafayette to the Dry Valley Road. Thomas, since noon, had been with his right. He saw that against the overwhelming numerical superiority of the enemy he could not hold out much longer. He, therefore, prepared to retire from the field. In passing from Wood's rear to Reynolds's position, to point out to the latter officer the position where he wished him to form line to cover the retirement of the divisions farther to the left, he found the enemy advancing in this direction to his rear. Upon this hostile force Reynolds was ordered to charge, and the enemy was driven beyond the left of the line. Wood, Brannan, and Granger were then withdrawn. Johnson's and Baird's divisions were attacked just as they were retiring, but they succeeded in moving from the field in order, and without serious loss.[2]

General Negley's presence at Rossville, where, with Sheridan's and Davis's assistance, he had rallied a considerable body of troops, and provided them with rations, was of very material assistance to General Thomas. But for these generals the retreat of the disorganized troops would have been continued to Chattanooga. Upon Thomas's arrival at Rossville, he posted Negley's division on the Ringgold Road; Reynolds's on Negley's right, stretching to the Dry Valley Road; Brannan's in reserve to Reynolds's right and rear; while McCook's corps extended from the Dry Valley Road nearly to Chattanooga Creek.

Bragg's army was too tired and too sadly worsted to attempt pursuit on the night of the 20th. On the 21st a few straggling blows were directed against the Federal army at Rossville. Thomas, feeling that he could not hold his position there against the Confederate army, suggested to Rosecrans that he be ordered to Chattanooga. The order was issued at 6 P.M. on the 21st, and by 7 o'clock the next morning Rosecrans's army was withdrawn to that place without opposition from the enemy.

Thus ended the battle. Though driven from the battle-field, the Federal army had succeeded in shutting the enemy out of Chattanooga. It had fought bravely, and had retired in good order, after having for two days held its position. Even the disaster upon its right on the 20th, taking from the field over 10,000 men, had not crushed its power of resistance. While it held the battle-field it repulsed every assault of the enemy, and withdrew only when its ammunition and supplies had given out, and it had become certain that its position could not be held for another day. The solitary advantage which the enemy had to show as a proof of his victory was his final possession of the battle-field. As to the numbers engaged on the Confederate side there are widely varying estimates.[3] After an investigation of the official returns of numbers from Bragg's army before the battle, of the Confederate reports of the battle (which are very minute), we j[...] that the effective force of the enemy, including re-enforcements, amou[...] to 70,000 men, of whom 55,000 infantry and cavalry were directly eng[...] on the battle-field. Rosecrans was clearly outnumbered.[1] His entire a[...] including cavalry, was not far from 60,000 strong. His force actually [...]gaged in the battle amounted to from 43,000 to 47,000 men.

The Federal army lost in the battle 1644 killed, and 9262 woun[...] Bragg reports a capture of 8000 prisoners. Halleck's report (for 1863) [...]mates Rosecrans's missing as 4945. The loss in cavalry was 500, maki[...] total Federal loss of 16,351. The Federal loss in artillery Bragg make[...] guns, and Rosecrans 36 (meaning probably the net loss, subtracting f[...] his entire loss the guns which had been captured from the enemy). [...] Confederate loss in killed and wounded largely exceeded that sustained [...] Rosecrans. Bragg reports a loss of two fifths of his command, but d[...] not give the exact figures. Halleck, in his report, says that the Confede[...] journals admitted a total loss of 18,000. This is probably not far from [...] truth.[2] Bragg lost 2003 prisoners, leaving his loss in killed and woun[...] about 16,000.

---

[1] There is a general misapprehension in regard to this ride of Garfield's to the front from Rossville, caused probably by the publication of explanatory letters from sources which *ought* to be authentic, but which are not so. Of this nature is a letter recently (during March, 1867) published in the New York *Citizen*. This letter, entitled "Rosecrans at Chickamauga—The Question Solved," is based entirely upon information given by a member of Rosecrans's staff. Now this member of Rosecrans's staff know absolutely nothing of what he relates as to this matter. He makes Rosecrans "fall in" with Garfield at or near Rossville, whereas it was at this very point that Garfield parted with Rosecrans, after having been with him all the time from the beginning of the battle on the 19th. By a still wider error he makes Rosecrans receive reports at this point that Thomas continued to hold his position. Rosecrans received no such reports. Neither Garfield nor Rosecrans had any thing to guide them in their conduct at this time save their own inferences. As to Rosecrans "knowing that the fate of our army depended upon our holding Chattanooga," it is clear that any such dependence upon Chattanooga could only follow upon the defeat of the entire army. Until this utter rout was established the case was exactly reversed: the ability to hold Chattanooga depended upon the fate of the army. Again, Rosecrans is made to send Thomas orders by Garfield "to hold his position at all hazards until nightfall, and then to retire to Rossville." Rosecrans sent *no* order to Thomas by Garfield. A dispatch was sent later in the day to Thomas, ordering the latter to retire to Rossville. Moreover, it is stated that the only way for Rosecrans to reach Thomas "was *via* Rossville, and thence out on the east side of the ridge, *it being impossible to cross the ridge at any intermediate point*." Certainly the advance of the enemy had not been continued so far as to prevent the crossing of the ridge at any point north of McFarland's Gap; and there was no other difficulty. From McFarland's Gap Rosecrans could have certainly gone on horseback to Thomas with as much ease as troops were a short time afterward brought over *precisely the same route* which he would have taken, the only difference being that the *direction* was opposite. The enemy at no time during the battle penetrated to the road which Rosecrans would have taken. But did Rosecrans *know* that this route was clear for him? We answer, no. And it is *here*, and not in the fact that there was no such route, that Rosecrans can find his only apology. From what he could see, he suspected that Thomas was also defeated. He says in his official report:

"Giving the troops direction to rally behind the ridge west of the Dry Valley Road, I passed down it, accompanied by General Garfield, Major McMichael, and Major Bond, of my staff, and a few of the escort, under a shower of grape and canister and musketry, for two or three hundred yards, and attempted to rejoin General Thomas and the troops sent to his support by passing to the rear of the broken portion of our lines, but found the routed troops far toward the left; and, hearing the enemy's advancing musketry and cheers, I became doubtful whether the left had held its ground, and started for Rossville. On consultation and further reflection, however, I determined to send General Garfield there, while I went to Chattanooga to give orders for the security of the pontoon bridges at Battle Creek and Bridgeport, and to make preliminary dispositions either to forward ammunition and supplies, should we hold our ground, or to withdraw the troops into good position."

The simple fact is that Rosecrans made a great mistake. He arrived too soon at the conviction that his whole army was defeated, and upon that conviction he went to Chattanooga, because he deemed it his duty to do so. The charge of cowardice, or of an apathetic abandonment of the field, which have been made against him, are too ridiculous to be even mentioned. Rosecrans was a general against whose bravery or patriotism there can rest no reproach.

[2] The Confederate reports indicate that the entire line was carried by assault, and that Thomas was driven. This was not the case. There was no serious assault. The enemy simply occupied a position deliberately abandoned by Thomas.

[3] Rosecrans's estimate of the numbers opposed to him seems to us to be extravagant. He says (in a letter published after the battle): "The enemy reports a loss of 18,700 killed and woun[...] and admits his loss to have been 20 per cent. of his entire command—a very large loss—w[...] gave him 93,500 at Chickamauga." But this calculation is based upon a mistake which w[...] actually *double* the enemy's numbers. Bragg distinctly states in his report that his loss amou[...] to *two fifths* (40 per cent.) of his entire command, which would give him—supposing his loss 18,[...] (Bragg, however, does not state the exact number), 46,760 instead of 93,500. Rosecrans th[...] one fifth of the numbers engaged "a very large loss." But in his official report of the battl[...] says, "I am fully satisfied that the enemy's loss largely exceeds ours." Now Rosecrans lo[...] killed and wounded 11,406, or more than one fifth of his own army.

Rosecrans (in the letter alluded to) arrives at this estimate of the enemy's numbers in ano[...] way. "Bragg," he says, "had 32,000 troops when driven from his intrenched camps at Shel[...]ville and Tullahoma, across the mountains and the Tennessee. Buckner joined with about 10,[...] troops from East Tennessee, Johnston with about 25,000, and Longstreet with about 25,000 m[...] giving again 92,000 as his whole force." This also is a gross miscalculation. Bragg's force [...] Buckner's united, on June 20th (four days before Rosecrans advanced from Murfreesboroug[...] amounted to 46,000 effectives—a larger estimate than Rosecrans gives. But we can find no [...]dence that Bragg had received 50,000 re-enforcements. At any rate, no such number was [...]gaged in the battle. From the Army of Virginia about 12,000 men were sent under Longstre[...] but Bragg reports that only 5000 of these arrived in time to participate in the battle. The [...]enforcements from other sources actually engaged were B. R. Johnson's and Walker's comman[...] or about 16,000 men. Of Bragg's own army (the Army of Tennessee, including Buckner), [...] Confederate reports indicate that there were engaged about 27,000, exclusive of cavalry. T[...] estimate would give the enemy about 47,000 infantry actually engaged at Chickamauga.

The estimate, as made up from the Confederate official reports, is the following:

LONGSTREET'S COMMAND.	
Buckner's Corps	9,207
Hindman's Division	6,122
B. R. Johnson's Division	3,683
Longstreet's Corps (proper), consisting of Hood's and McLaws's Divisions	5,000
	24,012

POLK'S COMMAND.	
Breckinridge's Division	3,769
Cleburne's Division	5,116
Walker's Corps	6,975
Cheatham's Division (approximate)	7,500
	23,360
	24,012
Total, exclusive of Cavalry	47,371

There is good reason to believe that Bragg underestimates the number of Longstreet's o[...] troops when he puts it at 5000. Longstreet had five brigades, three under Hood (Law's, Be[...]ning's, and Robertson's), and two under McLaws (Kershaw's and Humphreys's). Kershaw h[...] all the regiments which he had at Chancellorsville, and the Eighth North Carolina in additi[...] He must have had at least 2000 men. Giving Humphreys 1500 men, and Hood's three brigad[...] 3500 (a moderate estimate in either case), Longstreet's proper command (engaged) number[...] 7000. This would make the entire infantry force of the enemy, in round numbers, 50,000. T[...] cavalry force engaged probably numbered 5000, making a total of 55,000.

This army was composed of regiments from each of the eleven Confederate States, and fro[...] Kentucky. All together there were about 115 regiments and 11 battalions; and the battalio[...] would have made about four regiments of the average size. The average for each regiment w[...] little over 400 men. Forty-four regiments—a little over one third of the army—were from Te[...]nessee. Over 20 were from Alabama; 19 from Mississippi; 5 from Kentucky; 13 from Arka[...]sas, and about the same number from South Carolina; 5 from Texas; 15 or 16 from Georgi[...] 6 from Louisiana; 8 from Florida; 7 from North Carolina; and from Virginia only 2. T[...] Virginians were all in Buckner's command. B. R. Johnson's command, which Greeley (Am. Co[...]flict, vol. ii., p. 415) makes consist of Virginians, had not a Virginia regiment. Cheatham's d[...]vision consisted almost wholly of Tennesseeans. Humphreys's brigade was made up of Mississi[...]pians entirely, and Kershaw's entirely of Carolinians.

The estimate of Bragg's army which we have been considering is for the forces actually e[...]gaged. The estimate for his whole army would be largely above this. Just before his retre[...] from Chattanooga he had 45,000 effectives. His re-enforcements, and the additions made to h[...] cavalry by recruiting, before the battle, increased this force to over 70,000.

[1] The last official returns from Rosecrans's army before the battle are those of August 31s[...] C. Goddard, A. A. G. of Rosecrans's staff, quoting from these returns, gives the following as t[...] effective force of the several divisions:

Fourteenth Corps		
	Baird's	5,702
	Negley's	5,150
	Brannan's	6,015
	Reynolds's	6,615
		24,479
Twentieth Corps	Davis's	4,356
	Johnson's	5,607
	Sheridan's	4,382
		14,345

Twenty-first Corps		
	Wood's	2,564
	Palmer's	5,709
	Van Cleve's	5,208
		13,481
Granger's Reserve Corps		4,600
		13,481
		14,345
		24,479
Total		56,905

This estimate includes the entire infantry force, with the exception of Wagner's brigade left [...] Chattanooga. Goddard says: "I am morally certain that these returns, made previous to cros[...]ing the Tennessee, show a considerably larger force than took active part in the battle. Wh[...] percentage should be deducted I can not well say. . . . There was a regiment left at Crawfis[...] I think to guard the hospital. That, with the details for train guards, hospital and ambulan[...] attendance, etc., would, I think, reduce the fighting strength at least 3000 men. I made a roug[...] estimate at Crawfish, and put down our effectives at about 42,000, which was, I think, not f[...] from right."

It is probable that much more than 3000 men were detailed—it would not be unfair to s[...] 5000. Deducting this and Granger's force—which only came up at the close of the battle, a[...] after a force more than double his own had been swept from the field—and we have left 47,8[...] As the cavalry on the 19th and 20th was almost entirely detached to guard the exposed fla[...] of the army, it ought not to be estimated as a part of the force actually engaged on the fiel[...] Rosecrans's army, all told, cavalry and infantry, numbered nearly 60,000 just before the battle.

[2] The Confederate reports give the losses in all the brigades excepting those of Gist's, Ector'[...] and those of Hood, McLaws's, and Cheatham's divisions. Leaving out these 10 brigades, the l[...] in these several commands is as follows:

	Killed.	Wounded.	Missing.	Total.	Per Cent.
Wilson's Brigade	99	426	80	605	.50
Buckner's Corps	363	2576	96	2,969	.42
Breckinridge's Division	166	909	165	1,240	.33
Cleburne's Division	204	1539	6	1,749	.34
Hindman's Division	272	1456	98	1,826	.30
Liddell's Division	162	963	277	1,402	.44
B. R. Johnson's Division	168	1051	166	1,385	.42
Total	1434	8974	888	11,250	.36

Ector's loss was about the same as Wilson's. Ector and Wilson's brigades numbered togethe[...] 2400 before going into action. They lost more than half. Gist's loss is not reported, but was [...] least 400. The greater part of Cheatham's division was held in reserve on the 20th; but his lo[...] on the 19th was severe. In all he must have lost 1600 men. Thus, leaving out the casualties i[...] Longstreet's own corps, we have,

From precise data	11,250
Ector's Brigade (estimated)	600
Gist's Brigade (estimated)	400
Cheatham's Division (estimated)	1600
	13,850, or about 34 per cent.

Eighteen days after the Army of the Cumberland crossed the Tennessee it was concentrated in Chattanooga. The campaign, so far as it concerned this army alone, was over. It had been a tedious campaign of wearisome marches, terminating in a doubtful and unnecessary battle. Many mistakes had been made by both the Federal and Confederate commanders. Risks had been run on the one side which imperiled a whole army, and the disastrous results of which were only averted by delays and neglect of opportunities on the other. The battle itself was badly managed by General Rosecrans. His personal supervision of its details on the 19th would have enabled Thomas to strike blows so decisive that it is doubtful if there would have been a second day's battle. On the 20th there was, from the beginning of the fight, nothing but disorder and confusion on the right; nearly every order was either disobeyed or misunderstood. If on this day Rosecrans had devoted himself to seeing that Thomas was supported, and to such a disposition of his right as the transfer of troops to the left made necessary, there would have been no disaster, no serious loss of artillery or prisoners, and no necessity of abandoning the field to the foe. Rosecrans relied upon McCook and Crittenden to do what he ought to have known—if he knew any thing of men—would not be done by those commanders. Herein consisted his greatest blunder at Chickamauga.[1] All else—that, indeed, for which he was chiefly blamed—the historian will regard as the result of a natural mistake.

The missing, as precisely reported, we have found amounted to 882. It would be fair to suppose that the missing of Ector's and Gist's brigades and of Cheatham's division would increase this number to at least 1000. Subtracting this from the entire loss thus far estimated, we have left 12,850 as the killed and wounded, leaving out those of Longstreet's corps. Now, taking the very lowest estimate of Bragg's infantry force (as made up from official reports), it amounts to 48,000. Forty per cent. of this would give 19,200 as the number of killed and wounded in infantry alone. This would make the loss in Longstreet's corps the difference between 19,200 and 12,850, or 6350. But Bragg reports that only 5000 of Longstreet's corps took part in the battle. This estimate excludes prisoners captured from Bragg, which Rosecrans reports as 2003. We have already estimated the missing from all the other commands except Longstreet's corps as 1000; the other thousand, therefore, must have been from this corps. This would make the entire Confederate loss in infantry—killed, wounded, and missing—21,200, and Longstreet's entire loss 7350, or 2350 more men lost than, according to Bragg's report, he brought into battle.

The precise reports we are compelled to assume as correct. The error, therefore, is either in an extravagant overestimate on Bragg's part of his loss, or an equally extravagant underestimate of the number of Longstreet's corps engaged in the battle. One thing, however, is certain—namely, that the loss in Longstreet's corps was considerably above the general average. Hood's three brigades fought both days, and suffered severely on both. Kershaw's and Humphreys's brigades were engaged only on the 20th, but they sustained a fearful loss in their assaults on the afternoon of that day. It would not be extravagant, therefore, to estimate Longstreet's loss as 45 per cent. of his command. Then, supposing the entire loss of the army to have been about what Halleck says the Confederate journals stated it, 18,000, and deducting 1000 for casualties in the cavalry force, Longstreet's loss would be the difference between 17,000 and 13,850, or 3150, which would be 45 per cent. of 7000, the latter being the number which in a preceding note we gave as the probable estimate of Longstreet's force actually engaged. This calculation would decrease the percentage of loss in killed and wounded from 40 to about 30 per cent., and give Longstreet 2000 more men than Bragg gave him in his report.

The loss in some brigades of Bragg's army was almost incredible. Helm's brigade, of Breckinridge's division, went into battle with 1763 men, and came out with 432, losing over two thirds, besides its commander. Bate's brigade, of Buckner's corps, lost 608 out of 1085. Liddell's division lost 1402 out of 3175, nearly 50 per cent. In the space of a single hour, on the afternoon of the 20th, Gracie's brigade, of the same corps, lost 698 out of 2003. Another brigade (Kelly's) of this corps reports a loss of 300 out of 876. Still another reports a loss of 60 per cent. B. R. Johnson's division out of 3683 lost 1435, nearly one half. Maney's brigade, of Cheatham's division, lost half its numbers. Jackson's brigade, of the same division, lost 490 out of 1405; the loss in one of its regiments (the Fifth Georgia) was 55 per cent. Wilson's brigade lost 50 per cent., and Ector's in the same proportion.

[1] Rosecrans made no charges against McCook or Crittenden. On the contrary, in his report, he accorded them only praise. The court of inquiry which investigated Negley's conduct also considered the cases of McCook and Crittenden. We quote below the findings of the court in each case. But these opinions do not in the least affect General Rosecrans's responsibility.

Decision in McCook's Case.

"It appears from the investigation that Major General McCook commanded the Twentieth Army Corps, composed of Sheridan's, Johnson's, and Davis's divisions.

"His command on the 19th of September, 1863 (the first day of the battle of Chickamauga), consisted of Davis's and Sheridan's divisions, and of Negley's temporarily, and occupied the right of the line, Johnson's having been detached to Thomas's command. The evidence shows that General McCook did his whole duty faithfully on that day with activity and intelligence.

"Early on the 20th of September General McCook had under his command the divisions of Sheridan and Davis (the latter only 1300 to 1400 strong), and Wilder's brigade, and the senior officers of the cavalry were told they must take orders from him, though attend to their own business.

"The posting of these troops was not satisfactory to the commanding general, who in person directed several changes between 8 and 10½ o'clock P.M.

"During these changes, involving a flank movement of the whole right to the left, the enemy made a fierce attack, taking advantage of a break in the line caused by the precipitate and inopportune withdrawal of his division by Brigadier General T. J. Wood, passing through the interval, and routing the whole right and centre up to Brannan's position.

"The court deem it unnecessary to express an opinion as to the relative merits of the position taken by General McCook and that subsequently ordered to be taken by the commanding general, but it is apparent from the testimony that General McCook was not responsible for the delay in forming the new line on that occasion.

"It further appears that General McCook not only had impressed on him the vital importance of keeping well closed to the left and of maintaining a compact centre, but he was also ordered to hold the Dry Valley Road. This caused the line to be 'attenuated,' as stated in the testimony of the commanding general, who says that its length was greater than he thought it was when assumed.

"It is shown, too, that the cavalry did not obey General McCook's orders.

"The above facts, and the additional one that the small force at General McCook's disposal was inadequate to defend against greatly superior numbers the long line hastily taken under instructions, relieve General McCook entirely from the responsibility for the reverse which ensued.

"It is fully established that General McCook did every thing he could to rally and hold his troops after the line was broken, giving the necessary orders, etc., to his subordinates.

"The court are of opinion, however, that in leaving the field to go to Chattanooga, General McCook committed a mistake, but his gallant conduct in the engagements forbids the idea that he was influenced by considerations of personal safety.

"Bearing in mind that, the commanding general having previously gone to Chattanooga, it was natural for General McCook to infer that all the discomfited troops were expected to rally there, as well as to presume that a conference with the commanding general on that important subject was both desirable and necessary, the court can not regard this act of General McCook as other than an error of judgment."

Decision in Crittenden's Case.

"General Crittenden commanded the Twenty-first Army Corps, composed of Palmer's, Wood's, and Van Cleve's divisions.

"On the 19th of September, 1863 (the first day of the battle of Chickamauga), his command consisted of those divisions, except Wagner's brigade, which garrisoned Chattanooga.

"The evidence adduced respecting General Crittenden's operations on that day not only shows no cause for censure, but, on the contrary, that his whole conduct was most creditable; for by his watchfulness, and prompt and judicious support of troops engaged, serious consequences to our army were prevented, and the enemy's plans for the day disconcerted.

"Early on the morning of the 20th General Crittenden's command consisted of Wood's and Van Cleve's divisions; but as, about 8 o'clock A.M., Wood's division was detached, to take post in Thomas's line, General Crittenden is not responsible for its subsequent conduct.

"Van Cleve's division was shortly after ordered to the left, and General Crittenden was to accompany it.

"As it was moving the attack took place, and the troops were broken by our retreating artillery and infantry, as well as by the furious attack of the enemy.

"For the disaster which ensued he is in no way responsible.

"Changes were ordered to be made in the line. The break which occurred while the troops were moving by flank from the right to the left to conform to these changes was taken advantage of by the enemy, and disaster and rout ensued. It is amply proven that General Crittenden did every thing he could, by example and personal exertion, to rally and hold his troops, and to prevent the evils resulting from such a condition of affairs, but without avail.

"Believing that by his presence on the field nothing more could be effected, he left for Rossville, where he learned little else than that the commanding general had gone to Chattanooga.

"He repaired thither, where one of his brigades was stationed.

"In the opinion of the court, General Crittenden is not censurable for this act."

The battle left Rosecrans with an army in and about Chattanooga 45,000 strong. Bragg was left with an army numbering over 50,000 men, to which re-enforcements were daily being added. It was evident, therefore, that nothing farther could be accomplished by the Army of the Cumberland until it should be largely re-enforced. Rosecrans proceeded to fortify Chattanooga. Hooker's corps was sent to him from the East on the 23d of September. Other re-enforcements were on the way from Grant's army. As soon as the latter arrived Rosecrans was relieved of his command, on the 19th of October,[1] and General Grant, with the armies of the Cumberland, the Ohio, and the Tennessee, entered upon that brilliant campaign which terminated in General Bragg's utter defeat before the close of the year.[2]

CHAPTER XXXV.

THE CHATTANOOGA CAMPAIGN.

V. THE SIEGE OF KNOXVILLE.

The Campaign for Chattanooga involved the East Tennessee Problem.—Halleck's Mistake; his Contradictory Orders.—The tardy and feeble Effort toward co-operation with Rosecrans.—Plans for subsequent Movements suggested by Burnside.—Halleck still insists upon the Occupation of the Upper Valley of the Holston and Co-operation with Rosecrans at the same Time.—Why Bragg did not move on Rosecrans's Rear directly after the Battle of Chickamauga.—The Confederates occupy Lookout Mountain, abandoned by Rosecrans.—The Mistake of Rosecrans deprives him of his shortest Line of Communication.—Wheeler's Raid north of the Tennessee.—Destruction of a Federal Train.—Capture of McMinnville.—Conflict with Crook's Federal Cavalry near Farmington.—The Difficulty of supplying Chattanooga prevents the accession of Burnside's Army to the Defense of that Place.—The Campaign against Sam Jones in East Tennessee.—Longstreet crosses the Tennessee, November 14, 1863.—Burnside, in accordance with Grant's Instructions, falls back toward Knoxville.—The Battle at Campbell's Station.—Burnside's Situation after reaching Knoxville.—Longstreet, needed by Bragg, can not afford to wait, and Assaults on the 18th.—Death of General Sanders.—Defeat of Longstreet's second Assault, November 29th.—Grant sends Sherman to the Relief of Knoxville.—The Siege is raised, and Longstreet retreats eastward.

IN the campaign of General Rosecrans against Bragg, General Burnside's army had been utilized only to a very small extent. The advance upon Knoxville had been unresisted. The occupation of that point was of considerable importance. By his possession of the railroad connecting East Tennessee with Virginia, Burnside compelled the Confederate re-enforcements to Bragg's army from the east to make an extensive detour by way of Atlanta. His presence on Rosecrans's left and rear made his army a large reserve force relatively to Rosecrans; but the Army of the Ohio was too distant to answer the chief use of a reserve corps—that of active co-operation in case of necessity. The idea that Burnside's army, by remaining in the Valley of the Holston, secured the possession of East Tennessee, is simply absurd. It was security enough, doubtless, against Sam Jones's little army, or any other inconsiderable detachments which might straggle across the mountains from West Virginia. But these were only demonstrating columns sent for the purpose of keeping Burnside's army where it was. The Confederate force which was really fighting for East Tennessee was Bragg's army. The only force which actually contested Bragg's possession of this prize was the Army of the Cumberland; and it maintained the contest single-handed, while Burnside's army accomplished little beyond the illustration of General Halleck's pet theories. The enemy thoroughly understood that the defeat of General Rosecrans was the recovery not only of Chattanooga, but of all else which Bragg and Buckner had abandoned. If Rosecrans could be cut off from Chattanooga—and at one stage of the campaign this seemed likely to be accomplished—there was no alternative to Burnside's retreat but overwhelming disaster. The continued separation of the two armies was too auspicious to the Confederate government to be counted upon, and, therefore, Longstreet had been sent to Bragg.

[1] The following is a copy of General Rosecrans's order upon leaving his army:

"*General Orders, No. 242.*

"Headquarters Department of the Cumberland, Chattanooga, Tenn., October 19th, 1863.

"The general commanding announces to the officers and soldiers of the Army of the Cumberland that he leaves them, under orders from the President.

"Major General George H. Thomas, in compliance with orders, will assume the command of this army and department.

"The chiefs of all the staff departments will report to him.

"In taking leave of you, his brothers in arms—officers and soldiers—he congratulates you that your new commander comes not to you as he did, a stranger. General Thomas has been identified with this army from its first organization. He has led you often in battle. To his known prudence, dauntless courage, and true patriotism you may look with confidence that under God he will lead you to victory.

"The general commanding doubts not you will be as true to yourselves and your country in the future as you have been in the past.

"To the division and brigade commanders he tenders his cordial thanks for their valuable and hearty co-operation in all that he has undertaken.

"To the chiefs of the staff departments and their subordinates whom he leaves behind he owes a debt of gratitude for their fidelity and untiring devotion to duty.

"Companions in arms—officers and soldiers—farewell; and may God bless you!

"W. S. ROSECRANS, Major General."

[2] We have dealt thus elaborately with the history of Rosecrans's Chickamauga campaign on account of the general misapprehension which exists in regard to many of its most important features. We have endeavored to do justice to all the actors concerned. The writer has made no statement in regard to any point in dispute without substantiating it. His materials have been abundant, consisting in no small proportion of unpublished official documents. If he has erred in any important particular, it has not been from prejudice, but because the evidence before him was, after all, incomplete. Whatever mistakes may have been made on this account, time alone can correct. A fair history of any event is not often written while the historian rests under its shadow. If the present writer has failed to do justice, still justice will be done; if he has not told the exact truth, still, sooner or later, the exact truth will be told.

Burnside had received orders instructing him to co-operate with Rosecrans, but it had all the while been insisted upon that he must hold the Valley of the Holston from Rosecrans's left to the Virginia boundary, a line of nearly 200 miles. Not till it was too late did he receive an explicit order to move to Chattanooga. The first order to this effect he got on the 16th, only three days before the battle of Chickamauga. The Ninth Corps, which had been resting for the last fortnight after its struggle in Mississippi, was now ordered to move. But the necessity for haste does not seem to have been appreciated. The next night a more urgent dispatch was received from General Halleck, who wrote, "There are several reasons why you should re-enforce Rosecrans with all possible dispatch. It is believed the enemy will concentrate to give him battle. You must be there to help him." On the 21st a peremptory order came from the President, commanding Burnside to join Rosecrans without delay. By this time all the forces had been, with great deliberation, put in motion, except a small detachment of infantry and cavalry confronting the enemy on the Watauga River. With this latter force Burnside remained. Not venturing to withdraw while the enemy was in his front, he determined to wait until the next morning, and fight a battle before obeying the President's order. The next morning disclosed the fact that the enemy had retreated, burning the bridge behind him. The Federal column at this point was then started for Knoxville, where, by the 25th, the troops were all concentrated. It was then known that the battle of Chickamauga had been fought, and the emergency was past. Some correspondence followed between Halleck and Burnside, the result of which was that the command of the latter remained in East Tennessee. Burnside proposed to the general-in-chief three separate plans for the future operations of his army.

The first of these contemplated the abandonment of the railroad and East Tennessee, leaving only a small garrison at Cumberland Gap. This would leave free an army of full 20,000 men to move down the Tennessee and re-enforce Rosecrans.

The second plan suggested the movement of his main body—say 18,000 men—along the line of the railroad against Bragg's right at Cleveland, leaving garrisons at Knoxville and Loudon, also at Cumberland Gap, and at Bull's Gap and Rogersville, to cover Cumberland Gap.

The third plan proposed the movement of a force, consisting of 7000 infantry and 5000 cavalry, south of the Tennessee River, through Athens, Columbus, and Benton, past the right flank of the enemy, "down the line of the East Tennessee and Georgia Railroad to Dalton, destroying the enemy's communications, sending a cavalry force to Rome to destroy the machine works and powder-mills at that place, the main body moving on the direct road to Atlanta, the railroad centre of Georgia, and there entirely destroying the enemy's communications, breaking up the dépôts, etc., thence moving to some point on the coast where cover could be obtained." No trains were to be taken. The troops were to live upon the country. This would divert the attention of the enemy, and materially relieve Rosecrans. The chances of escape from pursuing columns of the enemy Burnside thought were in his favor.

Burnside was partial to the plan last described, which, by the way, on a miniature scale resembled Sherman's brilliant march from Atlanta to the sea, undertaken more than a year afterward. Halleck replied somewhat testily, decidedly objecting to Burnside's proposed raid. He was in favor of immediately co-operating with Rosecrans by a movement on the north side of the Tennessee. But he still insisted upon Burnside's holding the upper valley of the Holston, 200 miles away from Chattanooga.[1]

Rosecrans favored the first of the plans proposed by Burnside, but events soon occurred which made this impracticable. While the Federal commanders had been forming plans, General Bragg had not been idle. The very next day after the battle of Chickamauga, Longstreet had suggested a movement to Rosecrans's rear, above Chattanooga, to cut off his communications, and compel him to fall back to Nashville. At first Bragg seemed inclined to adopt this plan—at least Longstreet so understood. But if Bragg for a moment entertained such a scheme, he soon gave it up as impracticable.[2] But, while keeping his main army south of the Tennessee, Bragg assumed the offensive with considerable energy.

Rosecrans's most convenient line of communication with Murfreesborough was through Bridgeport, and the shortest road from Chattanooga t point lay along the south bank of the Tennessee. This route could b dered secure only by holding the point of Lookout Mountain, and Ste and Cooper's Gaps. Rosecrans, after retreating to Chattanooga, ga these important positions to the enemy. He claims that he could not held them and Chattanooga at the same time.[1] The enemy immediate cupied Lookout Mountain, and thus compelled Rosecrans to transpo supplies by the more difficult route across the mountains. But eve latter route was not left undisturbed. Bragg sent Wheeler, with a cavalry force—Wharton's, Martin's, Davidson's, and Armstrong's comn —against this line of communication. Wheeler's command crosse Tennessee above Chattanooga, and on the 2d of November reache Sequatchie Valley. Proceeding around Chattanooga on the north si Jasper and Anderson's Cross-roads, two wagon trains were captured, o them ten miles in length, consisting of from 800 to 1500 wagons, and ily loaded with ordnance and provisions. This train was destroyed, during the night Wheeler crossed the Cumberland Mountains, and the morning headed his columns toward McMinnville. Although the Fe cavalry was in close pursuit, he succeeded in capturing the place, wit fortifications, and its garrison of 587 men and 200 horses. Then he m westward to Murfreesborough. Only time was allowed for a feint on point, but the stockade guarding the railroad bridge over Stone Rive captured, and the bridge, together with the track for a distance of miles, was destroyed. On the 5th the railroad bridges and trestles bet Murfreesborough and Wartrace were destroyed, also a large quantity of s at Shelbyville. Wheeler was now ready to withdraw; but Davidson, o Duck River, did not retire with sufficient promptness, and was overtake the Federal cavalry. Rosecrans, after the battle of Chickamauga, had most of his cavalry north of the Tennessee to guard the fords of the r Those nearest Chattanooga were guarded by Colonel Miller, comman Wilder's brigade. Farther up the river were Minty's and Long's brig under the command of General Crook. Wheeler, as we have seen, wa thus prevented from crossing into Sequatchie Valley; but, as soon had crossed, the cavalry brigades along the river combined under Ge Crook's command, and pressed on in the pursuit. This force was joined by Mitchell's cavalry division. The pursuit was close, though it not prevent the enemy from doing very great injury. There were som considerable fights with the rear of Wheeler's column, but no battle u Davidson's command was engaged near Farmington. Wheeler, with M tin's division, came up just in time to relieve Davidson from his perilous uation. Both Crook and Wheeler claim each to have driven the ot Certainly Wheeler stood only long enough to secure the safety of his tra when he withdrew.

There was, apart from any interruption from the enemy, great difficu in supplying Rosecrans's army. Wheeler's movement had added to the barrassment rising from this cause. Under such circumstances, the ac tion of Burnside's army to that which was already encamped at Chattan ga was inexpedient, unless absolutely necessary.

In the mean time the enemy, under General Sam Jones, was again thr ening Burnside's left. He had advanced, by the 8th of October, as far as B Springs. Burnside had a small body of infantry at Morristown, and a c alry brigade at Bull's Gap. The Ninth Corps, re-enforced by Willct division and Shackleford's cavalry, were on the 10th led against the ene in front, while Colonel Foster's brigade of cavalry was sent *via* Rogersvill the enemy's rear, to intercept his retreat. The Confederates were driven the attack in front, but escaped Foster's blow by withdrawing during night. Shackleford pursued, driving the enemy into Virginia. Burns lost about 100 killed and wounded, and took 150 prisoners.

A week or more after the fight at Blue Springs General Grant assun command of the "Military Division of the Mississippi," which was n made to comprise the three departments of the Ohio, the Cumberland, the Tennessee. Thomas succeeded Rosecrans as commander of the Ar of the Cumberland, and McCook and Crittenden were ordered to Cincinn Sherman commanded the Army of the Tennessee, and Burnside retained present command. Hooker's corps had come from the East, and there w now four different Federal armies operating upon the soil of Tenness Halleck, after so long a time, saw the necessity of unity in the action these various commands in order to their effective co-operation, and the c trol of these four armies was therefore given to General Grant.

[1] Halleck says: "The purport of all your instructions has been that you should hold some point near the upper end of the valley, and with all your available force move to the assistance of Rosecrans. Since the battle of Chickamauga, and the wear of our force to paper, you have been repeatedly told that it would be dangerous to form a connection on the south side of the Tennessee River, and consequently that you ought to march on the north side. Rosecrans has now telegraphed to you that it is not necessary to join him at Chattanooga, but only to move down to such a position that you can go to his assistance should he require it. You are in direct communication with Rosecrans, and can learn his condition and wants sooner than I can. Distant expeditions into Georgia are not now contemplated. The object is to hold East Tennessee by forcing the enemy south of the passes, and closing the passes against his return."

[2] "The suggestion of a movement by our right, immediately after the battle to the north of the Tennessee, and thence upon Nashville, requires notice only because it will find a place among the files of the department. Such a movement was utterly impossible for want of transportation. Nearly half our army consisted of re-enforcements just before the battle, without a wagon or an artillery horse, and nearly, if not quite a third of the artillery horses on the field had been lost. The railroad bridges, too, had been destroyed to a point south of Ringgold, and in all the road from Cleveland to Knoxville. To these insurmountable difficulties were added the entire absence of means to cross the river, except by fording at a few precarious points too deep for artillery, and the well-known danger of sudden rises, by which all communication would be cut—a contingency which did actually happen a few days after the visionary scheme was proposed. But the most serious objection to the proposition was its entire want of military propriety. It abandoned to the enemy our entire line of communication, and laid open to him our dépôts of supplies, while it placed us, with a greatly inferior force, beyond a difficult, and, at times, impassable river, in a country affording no subsistence to men or animals. It also left open to the enemy, at a distance of only ten miles, our battle-field, with thousands of our wounded and his own, and all the trophies and supplies we had won. All this was to be risked and given up for what? To gain the enemy's rear, and cut him off from his dépôt of supplies by the route over the mountains, when the very movement abandoned to his unmolested use the better and more practicable route of half the length on the south side of the river. It is hardly necessary to say the proposition was not even entertained, whatever may be the inferences drawn from subsequent movements."—*Bragg's Report.*

[1] In his evidence before the Congressional Committee, Rosecrans says: "General Halleck, ic annual report, says I abandoned the passes of Lookout Mountain, leaving the public to ima that these passages were within the possible control of my army, and their abandonment not j fied as a military measure. I call the attention of the committee to the fact that one of these pa was forty-two miles south of Chattanooga, and the next nearest twenty-six miles south of C tanooga, and the nearest at the extremity of Lookout Mountain in front of our lines. This la may have been the one which gave rise to his report, and if so it ought to have been so stated. was satisfied that I could not even hold *this* pass and Chattanooga at the same time if the en did his duty, and therefore withdrew my troops from it, but established batteries on the other of the river, which rendered it practically of little, if any use to them. Subsequent events an justified the wisdom of this decision, for the enemy, with a division and a half, were unable hold it against General Hooker, and it was their attempt to cover this point which was one of causes of their being beaten so easily at Missionary Ridge."

This apology is exceedingly weak. In the first place, Rosecrans, after abandoning the p of Lookout Mountain overlooking Chattanooga and its approach *via* the south bank of the T nessee, and finding that the enemy had immediately occupied it, saw that he had made a mist in giving it up, and ordered McCook to storm and recapture the position. McCook stoutly obj ed that the thing couldn't be done, and was supported in this opinion by the judgment of some the best officers in the army. As to the other point, namely, the enemy's inability to hold same position subsequently against Hooker, the argument is no more pertinent. Hooker did and *could* not have succeeded in a direct attack upon the position, such as McCook was orde to make. He surprised the enemy by taking their works in flank. Now such a movement impossible to the enemy in the case of Rosecrans's holding the position. This is as clear as d light. For, of course, the *Federal* works would have fronted the enemy, and the entire disp tion, both of the forces holding the position as well as of the fortifications themselves, would h been altered, so that Bragg must have assaulted in front, or not at all.

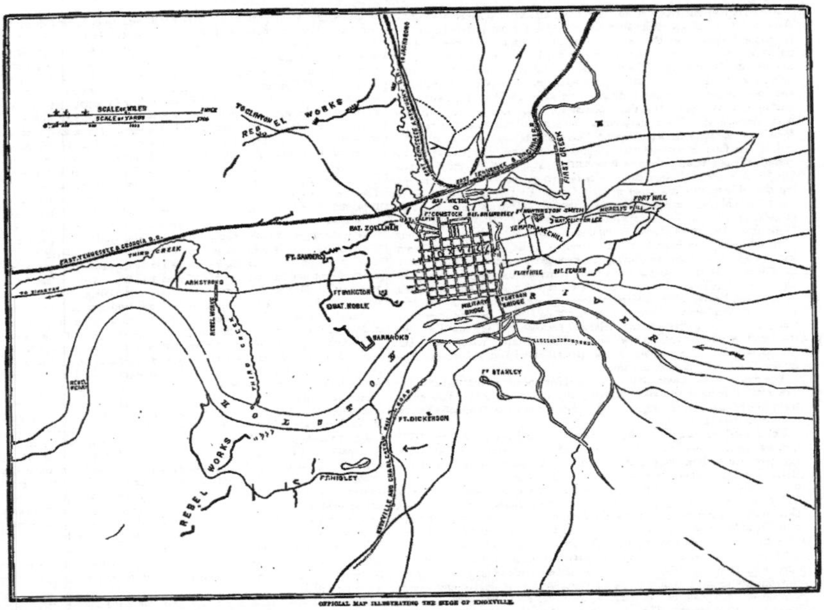

OFFICIAL MAP ILLUSTRATING THE SIEGE OF KNOXVILLE.

About the middle of October, just after Wheeler's return from Middle Tennessee, there had been indications of a movement by the enemy toward Knoxville. Bragg's right flank had begun to extend beyond Cleveland. On the 20th, Colonel Woolford, holding the Sweetwater Valley, south of the Tennessee, was attacked by a superior force of the enemy near Philadelphia, and, after several hours' fighting, finding that he was being surrounded, retired to Loudon, leaving in the enemy's hands thirty-eight wagons, six small howitzers, and between 300 and 400 prisoners. It soon became evident that Bragg was threatening Burnside with a formidable force, and the latter withdrew all his troops to the north side of the river, occupying the heights about Loudon. To this point Burnside moved his headquarters on the 28th, where he remained until the 31st, when the emergency appeared to have passed, and he returned to Knoxville. The enemy, in his operations south of the river, had captured 650 prisoners. On the 10th of November the Federal garrison at Rogersville was attacked by forces from Virginia and driven back to Morristown, with a loss of 500 prisoners, four guns, and thirty-six wagons.

Early in November, Longstreet's corps, now consisting of 12,000 men, was detached from Bragg's army, and, accompanied by 5000 cavalry under Wheeler, began to move against Burnside. Upon learning this fact, General Grant urged Burnside to concentrate his army at Kingston, where he would be in more intimate connection with the forces at Chattanooga. Burnside preferred Knoxville to Kingston. It had already been partially fortified under the superintendence of Captain O. M. Poe, who had erected two earth-works near the town. His reluctance to abandon East Tennessee was also an argument in favor of this point. About this time Charles A. Dana, Assistant Secretary of War, and Colonel Wilson, of Grant's staff, visited Knoxville. These gentlemen agreed with General Burnside, and Grant yielded the point. It seemed also to be a great advantage to Grant that Longstreet should be diverted as far as possible from Chattanooga. The movement of his corps into East Tennessee, though he had urged it at an earlier period, was at this time, it appears, opposed by Longstreet; but both Davis and Bragg insisted upon the undertaking. Longstreet was promised the support of Stevenson's and Cheatham's divisions, which would have increased his strength to over 27,000 men; but upon reaching Sweetwater (near Loudon) he discovered that they were ordered in the opposite direction. There were no indications, either, of the supplies, of which he was in pressing need, and which had been promised him. He was obliged to halt for some days at Sweetwater, losing most precious time, while he sent out his foraging expeditions in every direction to gather up corn stacked in the fields, which was then threshed and baked. His men were thinly clad; their shoes were unserviceable; they had few blankets, and no tents; but they had marched before in the same plight, and uttered no complaint.

On the morning of November 14th Longstreet's advance crossed the Tennessee at Hough's Ferry, six miles below Loudon, demonstrating against Knoxville with his cavalry at the same time. At Lenoir's General Potter was stationed, with the Ninth Corps and one division of the Twenty-third, under Brigadier-General Julius White. Longstreet did not cross the river without resistance. General White fell upon his advance in the afternoon, and drove it back for two miles to the river. Burnside would have attacked again on the morning of the 15th, but he received late at night an order from General Grant to withdraw his troops. The design was to draw Longstreet on to Knoxville. The order was promptly obeyed. "If General Grant," said Burnside, "can destroy Bragg, it is of no great consequence what becomes of ourselves. Order the troops to be ready to march in the morning." Burnside fell back to Lenoir's on the 15th, and on the night of that day prepared to continue his retreat to Campbell's Station.

The enemy endeavored by a flank movement to anticipate General Burnside in the possession of Campbell's Station, but the Federal troops reached this important position first. Here a stand was made on the 16th by Hartranft's division, while the main portion of the Federal army and the trains passed along the Loudon Road toward Knoxville. Hartranft had reached the Station a quarter of an hour before Longstreet's advance came up. He succeeded in holding his ground and covering the retreat until the army and the trains had passed the threatened point. Then Burnside, forming his army upon a low range of hills, half a mile from Campbell's, covering the approaches to Knoxville, awaited the enemy's attack. Several assaults were made upon this position, which were repulsed with great loss to the enemy. Longstreet advancing upon his rear in the afternoon, Burnside withdrew to a second position, equally strong, 1000 yards in rear of the first. The enemy repeated his attack with determination, but was finally forced to withdraw, and that night Burnside's army retired within its intrenchments at Knoxville.

In the mean time General Sanders had met the enemy's cavalry south of the Holston, on the opposite bank from Knoxville. General Parke, now Burnside's chief of staff, had been left in command of the town. A pontoon bridge was thrown across the Holston, by means of which Sanders kept up communication with the garrison defending the town. Holding this position, General Sanders successfully maintained it until Burnside's army entered Knoxville.

General Burnside held a position of great strength. His force was fully equal to that of the enemy, and the hills around Knoxville, previously fortified by General Buckner, and now connected by means of rifle-pits, formed a vast fortified camp. General Sanders's force was now drawn across the river, and covered the Loudon Road. Longstreet had already lost much time. Grant was ready to move upon Bragg, and if Longstreet would be

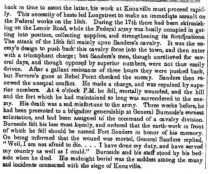

back in time to assist the latter, his work at Knoxville must proceed rapidly. This necessity of haste led Longstreet to make an immediate assault on the Federal works on the 18th. During the 17th there had been skirmishing on the Lenoir Road, while the Federal army was busily occupied in getting into position, collecting supplies, and strengthening its fortifications. The attack of the 18th fell mainly upon Sanders's cavalry. It was the enemy's design to push back this cavalry force into the town, and then enter with a triumphant charge; but Sanders's men, though unrelieved for several days, and though opposed by superior numbers, were not thus easily driven. After a gallant resistance of three hours they were pushed back, but Ferrero's guns at Rebel Point checked the enemy. Sanders then renewed the unequal conflict. He made a charge, and was repulsed by superior numbers. At 4 o'clock P.M. he fell, mortally wounded, and the hill and the fort which he had maintained so long was surrendered to the enemy. His death was a sad misfortune to the army. Three weeks before, he had been promoted to a brigadier generalship at General Burnside's earnest solicitation, and had been assigned to the command of a cavalry division. Burnside felt his loss most keenly, and ordered that the earth-work in front of which he fell should be named Fort Sanders in honor of his memory. On being informed that the wound was mortal, General Sanders replied, "Well, I am not afraid to die. . . . I have done my duty, and have served my country as well as I could." Burnside and his staff stood by his bedside when he died. His midnight burial was the saddest among the many sad incidents connected with the siege of Knoxville.

The partial success gained by Longstreet on the 18th proved of little value. To push this slight advantage against works so gallantly defended could only result in increased loss to his command, without any reasonable chance of victory. He therefore determined to reduce the garrison to surrender by famine. Burnside's army held the roads approaching Knoxville from the west; on each side of the city ran the Holston. The assault on the 18th had been on the Federal left.

Burnside was fairly besieged on the night of the 18th. The enemy had cut off communication with Cumberland Gap, and held the approaches to Knoxville on the northwest and southwest. The Federal army was supplied for three weeks; the fortifications were hourly strengthened; a *chevaux de frise* of pikes was set up in front of the rifle-pits, and the heights on the opposite side of the Holston were securely held and fortified. Burnside was urged by Grant to hold on to Knoxville. Fortunately, he was better supplied with provisions than the enemy conjectured, and had lost no time in his work upon the fortifications, which had become almost impregnable. His only hope now was Grant's speedy victory over Bragg, and the approach of a relieving force.

Grant's work, as we shall see in the next chapter, was speedily and effectually accomplished. One week after Longstreet's assault on the 18th, Bragg was defeated before Chattanooga, and Longstreet's position was rendered extremely perilous. But the latter determined to make a final effort, risking every thing upon the chances of a bold assault on Burnside's lines before a Federal force could reach his own rear. He had in the mean while

JOHN G. PARKE.

been re-enforced by two brigades of B. R. Johnson's division. The morning of the 29th of November was fixed for the assault.

The point selected for the attack was Fort Sanders, which commanded the Kingston Road, and overlooked Knoxville. The capture of this fort would be decisive, and every nerve was strained for its accomplishment. This position was held by a portion of the Ninth Corps. It was well protected by a wide ditch in front, by thickly laid abatis, and by a network of wires stretched from stump to stump.

In the gray of the morning three picked brigades of McLaws's division appeared in front of the fort, while a Georgia regiment of sharp-shooters silenced the Federal guns. Leaving the shelter of the woods, the storming column advanced up the slope. Only at the edge of the ditch did the enemy halt. Here it was found that an important feature in the assault had been forgotten. There were no means at hand for crossing this ditch. It was now the moment of glorious opportunity to the defenders of the fort, who poured a deadly fire upon the hesitating column, checking the first impetus of its assault. But, though retarded in their movement, the courage of the assailants was indomitable. They broke through the entanglement of wires, they cut their way through the abatis; the carnage made among them by musketry and artillery could not daunt their brave spirits; they filled the ditch; some of them assailed the scarp of the fort, pushing each other up to reach the parapet; a few forced their way through the embrasures. Here, with these few, a hand-to-hand conflict was waged. One officer advanced with a flag and boldly demanded the surrender of the fort, and was dragged inside a prisoner. Those who had reached the parapet were shot and hurled back into the ditch, which now writhed with its dead and wounded, while, to increase the maddening torment, hand grenades were thrown into their midst. Meanwhile, into the rear the artillery hurled its fatal missiles, until at length, entirely baffled, this column was withdrawn and another took its place, and the carnage was renewed. But no impression was made upon the garrison. After a display of courage probably unequaled by that exhibited in any assault during this war, and never surpassed in any other war, the attack was abandoned. There followed a truce, to permit the enemy to gather up his dead and wounded—over 500 all told—and here from the lips of the enemy was heard the first tidings of Grant's victory. The loss in the fort was 8 killed, 5 wounded, and about 30 captured. An assault made at the same time upon General Shackleford on the south side of the Holston had also been repulsed.

This repulse of the enemy, though it did not immediately terminate the siege, was its last important event. The day before the assault Sherman had been ordered with 25,000 men to march to the relief of Knoxville. Elliot's cavalry division were sent in the same direction. Sherman advanced along the south side of the Tennessee, cutting off Longstreet's retreat, and by the 4th of December his army was within two or three marches of Knoxville. On the 5th the enemy retired and the siege was raised. Longstreet retired up the Holston River, but there was no pursuit. He did not entirely abandon East Tennessee until the following spring, when his command rejoined the Army of Northern Virginia.[1]

[1] With the siege of Knoxville closed the active services of General Burnside in East Tennessee. The command was transferred to General Foster. The transfer was actually made on the 11th of December. Three days afterward Burnside left Knoxville, and reached his home in Providence, R. I., on the 23d. On January 28th, 1864, President Lincoln approved a resolution "that the thanks of Congress be, and they hereby are, presented to Major-General Ambrose E. Burnside, and through him to the officers and men who have fought under his command, for their gallantry, good conduct, and soldier-like endurance."

LONGSTREET'S ASSAULT ON FORT SANDERS.

LONGSTREET'S SHARPSHOOTERS ATTACKING A FEDERAL TRAIN ABOVE CHATTANOOGA.

CHAPTER XXXVI.

THE CHATTANOOGA CAMPAIGN.

VI. DEFEAT OF BRAGG:

General Grant after the Vicksburg Campaign.—He assumes Command of the Military District of the Mississippi, and of the Armies under Sherman, Thomas, Burnside, and Hooker.—His available Force for the final Struggle of the Chattanooga Campaign.—The Condition of his four Armies.—Hooker's Arrival in the West.—Chattanooga besieged by Bragg's Army.—Rosecrans's Plan for the Recovery of Lookout Valley executed by Grant.—Longstreet's Signals from Lookout Mountain interpreted by General Geary.—The Battle of Wauhatchie.—Importance of this Success.—Chattanooga relieved.—The Understanding between Grant and Burnside.—Longstreet sent against Knoxville.—Position of Bragg's Army.—Confidence of the Confederate Commander.—Grant's Plan of Attack.—Waiting for Sherman.—March of the Army of the Tennessee.—Sherman confers with Grant at Chattanooga.—Rumor of Bragg's intended Retreat.—Thomas's Reconnoissance, November 23d.—Orchard Knob carried.—Bragg strengthens his Right.—*Operations on the 24th.*—Sherman's attack on Tunnel Hill.—Hooker carries Lookout Mountain; the "Battle above the Clouds."—*Operations on the 25th.*—Bragg's altered Position.—General Corse's assault on Cleburne's Position.—Waiting for Hooker.—Thomas storms Missionary Ridge.—The Confederate Centre broken.—Hooker drives the Left.—Retreat and Pursuit.—A decisive Victory.

WE will now turn from the siege of Knoxville—an important episode in the Chattanooga campaign—to the movements of Grant's army at Chattanooga, which terminated on November 25th in the expulsion of Bragg's forces from Missionary Ridge.

Immediately after the reduction of Vicksburg, Grant dispatched expeditions in various directions in the State of Mississippi. In one of these, sent to Natchez, under General Ransom, 5000 head of cattle, which were being crossed over the Mississippi at that point for the enemy's supply, were captured. His army now became dispersed. Ord and Herron were sent to the Department of the Gulf. Steele was dispatched to Helena, to re-enforce Schofield in the Department of the Missouri. Toward the last of August General Grant proceeded upon a tour of inspection through his department. He reached New Orleans on the 2d of September. As he was returning to his hotel in that city from a review of Ord's corps, on the 4th, his horse became frightened, and, violently striking a carriage, General Grant was thrown into the street, and so severely injured in the hip that he was unable either to walk, or mount his horse without assistance, until his arrival at Chattanooga, toward the close of October. Secretary Stanton met him at Indianapolis, and both together proceeded to Louisville. Here, on the 18th, the Secretary handed him the order of the President, giving him the command of the "Military District of the Mississippi," comprising the departments of the Tennessee, the Ohio, and the Cumberland. By the same order Rosecrans was relieved of his command, being superseded by General Thomas.

This order gave Grant the military control of all the territory in possession of the government from the Mississippi River to the Alleghany Mountains, and of four large armies under Sherman (who succeeded Grant in the command of the Department and Army of the Tennessee), Thomas, Burnside, and Hooker. These armies, together, numbered probably 150,000 effective men. Two thirds of this force, or about 100,000 men, was available for the Chattanooga campaign. Deducting 20,000 for Burnside's effective command, and we have left a force 80,000 strong, which could be used directly against General Bragg. General Hooker's army was 23,000 strong, and consisted of the Eleventh and Twelfth Corps. The Army of the Cumberland, now reduced to a little over 40,000 men, had been reorganized. McCook and Crittenden had been sent to Cincinnati, and their two commands, consolidated with the reserves, now constituted the Fourth Corps, under Gordon Granger. General Palmer commanded the Fourteenth, Thomas's old corps. The remaining portion of the forces brought against Bragg were to come from the Army of the Tennessee. Of this latter army, McPherson's corps remained at Vicksburg, and, by demonstrations along the Big Black, prevented Johnston from sending farther re-enforcements to Bragg. Hurlbut's corps was retained at Memphis. Upon Sherman's taking command of the Army of the Tennessee, General Blair had been assigned to that of the Fifteenth Corps.

The transfer of General Hooker's army westward to the Tennessee was

VIEW OF CHATTANOOGA

AND THE FEDERAL ENCAMPMENT.

THE THOMAS MEDAL.

accomplished with marvelous expedition. Although accompanied by its artillery, trains, baggage, and animals, this army moved from the Rapidan, in Virginia, to Stevenson, in Alabama, a distance of 1192 miles, in seven days, crossing the Ohio twice.[1] General Hooker reached Cincinnati in person on the 29th of September, and during the first week in October his army was on Rosecrans's right flank at Stevenson. At the time of, and for a long period subsequent to Hooker's arrival, Rosecrans's army was in a state of partial siege. Bragg commanded the river road to Bridgeport, and his cavalry interrupted the communications with Bridgeport by way of Walden's Ridge, and even assailed the Nashville Railroad.[2] Rosecrans feared that the enemy would cross above Chattanooga, on his left, separating him from Burnside; but this was not his greatest danger. What Rosecrans had most reason to be apprehensive about was the subsistence of his army. To recover Lookout Valley, and the command of the river road to Bridgeport, was the important necessity of the moment. Rosecrans had already planned the movement which was to secure this road when he was relieved.

Grant met Rosecrans and Hooker at Nashville October 21st. He immediately put into execution the plan which had been adopted, and there could be no delay. The route from Stevenson over Walden's Ridge was from 60 to 70 miles in length, and the supply trains were shelled from Lookout Mountain from the very day that Rosecrans had abandoned that important position to the enemy. The roads were so bad that Wheeler's cavalry did not venture upon a raid. The animals were walking skeletons, and were dying by thousands for want of forage, and the wagons were worn out by the difficult roads. The troops were reduced to half rations. On the 19th, immediately after assuming his new command, Grant had telegraphed to Thomas to hold on to Chattanooga. Thomas replied, "I will hold the town till we starve."[3] And, as matters stood, his chance of starving was very good. Two weeks longer, and without relief from its embarrassment, the Federal army must have abandoned its position.

Grant reached Chattanooga on the 23d of October. The next day, with General Thomas and W. F. ("Baldy") Smith, chief engineer, he made a reconnoissance of Brown's Ferry (below the mouth of Lookout Creek) and of the country lying southward. It was then decided that, in accordance with the plans already formed by Rosecrans, Hooker should cross at Bridgeport, and advance to Wauhatchie in Lookout Valley, threatening the enemy's flank. This movement was open to the observation of the enemy. So also was the movement of one of Palmer's divisions down the river to a point opposite Whiteside (11 miles west of Wauhatchie), where he was to cross and move up to Hooker's support. While attention was fixed on these movements, General Smith, with 4000 men, was to move secretly, under cover of the night, across Brown's Ferry, and seize the range of steep hills at the head of Lookout Valley, three miles below Lookout Mountain. A pontoon bridge was then to be thrown across the river at Brown's Ferry, and a line of communication being thus opened between Thomas and Hooker, the latter would be enabled to advance without danger of an attack on his left flank.

This plan was successfully carried out. The position to be gained was held by a portion of Longstreet's command, which had not yet been detached from Bragg's army. The enemy's line stretched from Lookout Mountain to Missionary Ridge. But a single brigade was posted in Lookout Valley, though the Confederate pickets lined the river down to Bridgeport. The position, from the occupation of which there was especial apprehension on the part of the Federal army, was the most feebly defended of any on the Confederate line. Hooker sent Geary's division, of Slocum's corps, across on the 26th, and by the 28th this force had reached Wauhatchie. Howard, with the Eleventh Corps, held Geary's left toward Brown's Ferry. Palmer, with the Fourteenth Corps, was moving up in the rear. Smith also had accomplished the duty assigned to his command. Of the 4000 men detailed to this command, 1800, under Hazen, embarked on sixty pontoon-boats, had floated down the river from Chattanooga on the night of the 27th, past the Confederate pickets lining the left bank, and, landing at Brown's Ferry, had taken their appointed post with a loss of only four or five men wounded. The rest of Smith's force was ferried across and joined Hazen before morning. By 10 A.M. on the 28th a pontoon bridge had been thrown across the river at Brown's Ferry, and before night Howard had connected with Smith.

This movement was, however, not accomplished without a struggle. Longstreet had a signal-station on the top of Lookout Mountain, overlooking the whole field over which Howard and Geary moved. When, on the evening of the 28th, he saw, too late, the vital importance to the Federal army of the position seized by Hooker's command, he at once communicated with Bragg, explaining the altered situation, and was directed to attack and drive back Geary and Howard at all hazards. Longstreet had already seen enough from "Signal Rock" to convince him that it was useless to attack the superior numbers on his flank directly or by daylight; but, noting the situation

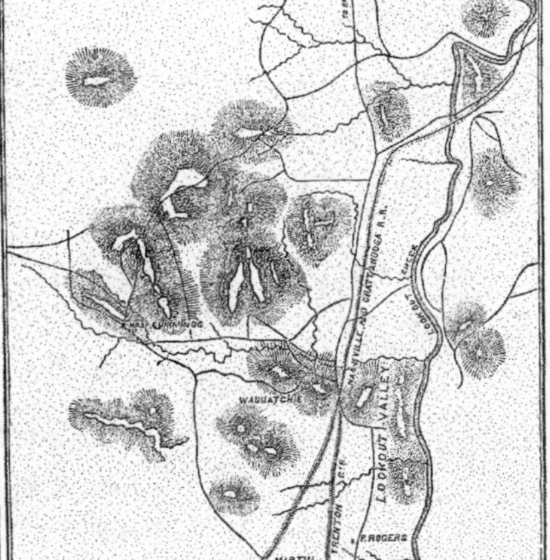

MAP ILLUSTRATING THE BATTLE OF WAUHATCHIE.

[1] *Secretary Stanton's Report*, November 2d, 1865.

[2] Rosecrans's letters to Halleck, at this time, indicate great anxiety for the safety of the Federal army. October 12th, he writes:

"Line from here to Kingston long; our side is barren mountain; rebel side has railroad. Our danger is subsistence; we can not bring up Hooker to cover our left, against a crossing above us, for want of means to transport provisions, and horse-feed. Enemy's side of Valley full of corn. Every exertion will be made to hold what we have, and gain more, after which we must put our trust in God, who never fails those who truly trust."

Again, on the 16th:

"Evidence increases that the enemy intend a desperate effort to destroy this army. They are bringing up troops to our front. They have prepared pontoons, and will probably operate on our left flank, either to cross the river and force us to quit this place and fight them, or lose our communication. They will thus separate us from Burnside. We can not feed Hooker's troops on our left, nor can we spare them from our right dépôts and communications; nor has he transportation. The rains have raised the river, and interrupted our pontoon bridge; the roads are very heavy. Our future is not bright. Had we the railroad from here to Bridgeport, the whole of Sherman's and Hooker's troops brought up, we should not, probably, outnumber the enemy. This army, with its back to the barren mountains, roads narrow and difficult, while the enemy has the railroad and the corn in his rear, is at much disadvantage. To secure this position, at least, McMinnville should be made a strong, fortified dépôt, Kingston the same, and, for ulterior operations, 20,000 or 30,000 more troops put into Tennessee, at easy points to cover the railroad, and subsist until called to the front for advance on the enemy. Additional cavalry force is indispensable to a good future for this army. Burnside must be within supporting distance of us; if we lose this point, his hold on East Tennessee is gone; if we hold it, the Rebs can not make much use of the country above, and we shall dispossess them."

[3] The accompanying illustration is a fac-simile of a medal presented to General Thomas by the State of Tennessee, after the defeat of Hood at Nashville. The resolution in favor of the presentation passed the Legislature November 2, 1865. The medal is of gold, is three inches in diameter, and was wrought by Tiffany and Co., of New York City.

GENERAL HAZEN'S BRIGADE DEFENDING THE TENNESSEE.

of Geary's weak division at Wauhatchie, holding the road leading from Kelly's Ferry up Lookout Valley, he conceived the plan of striking this force by surprise during the night. If he succeeded in routing this force—Hooker's right flank—an easy matter as it seemed to him then—he would pursue the advantage thus gained by extending his attack against Hooker's centre and left. It was an admirable conception. But there was an important element involved in its execution which Longstreet was not, and could not be aware of, namely, Geary's precise knowledge of every movement which he might order from "Signal Rock." For some months the Federal officers had been in possession of the signal code of the enemy, and every flourish of Longstreet's signal torches on the top of Lookout directing the assault, was at the same moment as significant to Geary as it was to Longstreet's commanders.

Thus, when, a little after midnight on the morning of the 29th, Law's division attacked Geary, the latter was fully prepared. Between the force at Wauhatchie and Howard's right was an interval of three miles. For three hours Geary defended his position without assistance, and repulsed every charge of the enemy, finally driving him from the field.[1] The success of the enemy at this point might have easily defeated the entire movement of Hooker. Of the two roads leading to Kelly's Ferry from Lookout Valley, Howard held one and Geary the other; the abandonment of one of these roads would have seriously imperiled the force holding the other.

A portion of Howard's command had in the mean time been engaged on Geary's left with equal success, and Longstreet was compelled to withdraw his command east of Lookout Creek. He still continued, however, to hold Lookout Mountain. Hooker's success, gained at the expense of only 437 men, recovered Lookout Valley, and gave Grant two good roads to Bridgeport from Brown's Ferry—one thirty-five miles long, running through Wauhatchie, Whiteside, and Shellmound; the other, from Brown's to Kelly's Ferry, a distance of eight miles by wagon, and thence by boat to Bridgeport. The enemy's position on Lookout commanded these roads, but the batteries which had been posted on Moccasin Point, north of the river, prevented the Confederate artillery from inflicting any serious damage to the supply trains. The siege of Chattanooga had been raised, and Bragg from this time was put upon the defensive. The only aggressive movement possible to him was that which he now attempted against Burnside with Longstreet's column; and this movement, unsuccessful in its special object, only accelerated his ruin. Longstreet's campaign against Knoxville was probably the result of President Davis's visit to Bragg's army, October 12.

[1] "For almost three hours, without assistance, he repelled the repeated attacks of vastly superior numbers, and in the end drove them ingloriously from the field. At one time they had enveloped him on three sides, under circumstances that would have dismayed any officer endowed with an iron will and the most exalted courage. Such is the character of General Geary."—*Hooker's Report.*

When Grant first heard of the proposed movement against Knoxville, he seems to have regarded it as unfavorable to the development of his own plans, and intended to immediately attack Missionary Ridge in order to detain Longstreet. But after a reconnoissance he found that such an assault did not promise success, and determined to await the arrival of Sherman's troops, now well on their way from Memphis. In the mean time he established between himself and Burnside a good understanding as to the plan

JOHN W. GEARY.

operations which he was now about to adopt.[1] He confided to him the ole scheme of his movements against Bragg, and promised to send a force the relief of Knoxville as soon as he had carried it out. Two things ke us forcibly in his correspondence with Burnside: first, the clearness his plans, which read more like a history of his brief campaign, rather n a scheme of movements contemplated; and, secondly, his confidence to their success. He almost seems to look regretfully after Longstreet's e, as if, by marching northward, it was escaping its share in the destruc- which he was preparing for Bragg's entire army.

The Confederate army was intrenched upon the western slopes of Mission- Ridge, and stretched across Chattanooga Valley to the western slopes Lookout Mountain, which, since Longstreet's departure, had been held by divisions of Walker, Stevenson, and Cheatham.[2] His line of works, elve miles in length, was occupied by less than 50,000 effective troops. army was outnumbered by Grant's in about the same proportion that it l exceeded Rosecrans's at the battle of Chickamauga Creek. Nor was this eriority in numbers balanced by superiority of position. His line, though parently strong, was too much extended for the number of its defenders, l was really very weak. If he held the two ridges, his centre must be vulnerable; the exposure of either of his flanks, by the abandonment Lookout Mountain or Missionary Ridge, must be soon followed by an en- withdrawal of his army from before Chattanooga. Yet, so confident s he of the strength of his position, that when Grant moved upon his rks he was just on the point of sending Cleburne's and Buckner's divi- ns to re-enforce Longstreet.

Grant's plan of attack was brilliant, but exceedingly simple in its general tures. It involved an assault upon the strongest points in the enemy's —its two extremes—by Hooker and Sherman, to be followed by a crush- blow from Thomas upon its centre.

But Sherman's army was not yet upon the field. It was now nearly two nths since, just after the battle of Chickamauga, Sherman had been or- ed to re-enforce Rosecrans. His corps, the Fifteenth, about 16,000 ong, consisted of four divisions, under P. J. Osterhaus, Morgan L. Smith, I. Tuttle, and Hugh Ewing.[3] Osterhaus's division had embarked for mphis on the 23d. The other divisions followed a day later. The last the fleet reached Memphis on the 4th of October. As soon as he reach- Memphis, General Sherman was ordered to proceed with his own corps, l as many troops as could be spared from the line of the Memphis and arleston Railroad, to Athens, Alabama. He was to look out for his own plies. Osterhaus by this had got as far as Corinth, and J. E. Smith was the way from Memphis. On the 11th of October the rear of the column s put in motion, and Sherman started in person for Corinth, escorted by the irteenth Regulars. At Collierville, about twenty-five miles east of Mem- s, a Confederate cavalry force was encountered, and the general, with staff, narrowly escaped capture. D. C. Anthony was defending the post h the Sixty-ninth Illinois against the enemy, who numbered about 3000 se, with eight guns, under General Chalmers. Sherman's escort joined thony, and the Confederates were repulsed. Sherman reached Corinth the 12th, and sent Blair forward with the divisions of Osterhaus and Mor- L. Smith. The railroad was repaired as the troops advanced. A Con- erate cavalry force, about 5000 strong, kept in Sherman's front. Under se circumstances, his progress was necessarily slow. Anticipating that resistance would be made to his crossing of the Tennessee, he had requested Admiral Porter to send him two gun-boats, which he found ready upon his arrival at Eastport. Blair, after considerable skirmishing, drove the enemy from his front, and occupied Tuscumbia on the 27th.

In the mean time Sherman had been notified of his appointment to the command of Grant's former department, and had made such a disposition of the troops in his rear as would secure Mississippi and West Tennessee, leaving the former under McPherson's, and the latter under Hurlbut's control. Blair was assigned to the command of the Fifteenth Corps, and General George W. Dodge was ordered to organize from the Sixteenth a select force of 8000 men, with which he was to follow Sherman eastward. Ewing, on the 27th, was ordered to cross his division at Eastport, and advance to Florence. On the same day, a messenger, having floated down the river from Chattanooga, reached Sherman with orders to stop the work on the railroad, and advance toward Bridgeport. On the 1st of November Sherman crossed the river in person, passed to the head of the column at Florence, and, leaving the rear to be brought up by Blair, marched toward the Elk River. Not having time for ferriage or bridge-building, it was necessary to advance up that stream as far as Fayetteville, where the command crossed. Here Sherman received orders to bring the Fifteenth Corps to Bridgeport, leaving Dodge's command on the railroad at Pulaski. Blair was instructed to conduct the first and second divisions, by way of Larkinsville, to Bellefonte, while Sherman took a more northern route, *via* Winchester and Decherd, reaching Bridgeport by night on the 13th of November. Telegraphing to General Grant information of his arrival and of the disposition of his divisions, he was summoned to Chattanooga. Proceeding by boat to Kelly's Ferry, he reached Grant's headquarters on the 15th. Here his part in the coming drama was explained to him, and he was shown the enemy's fortified position on Missionary Ridge; the point which he was to attack, and the details of his march across the river at Brown's Ferry, around the mountains north of the river to the mouth of Chickamauga Creek, were here determined upon. The entire movement of his corps, after crossing Brown's Ferry till it emerged upon Bragg's right flank, was so arranged as to be concealed from the enemy by covering mountains. He saw all the arrangements which had been made for him in anticipation. "Pontoons," says Sherman, in his report, "with a full supply of balks and chesses, had been prepared for the bridge over the Tennessee, and all things prearranged with a foresight that elicited my admiration. From the hills we looked down upon the amphitheatre of Chattanooga as on a map, and nothing remained but for me to put my troops in the desired position." To convince the enemy that his left was the especial point of attack, a division of Sherman's corps was to make a feint against Lookout Mountain from a point in the vicinity of Trenton. Sherman, from this visit to Chattanooga, was also enabled to understand the necessity of the utmost expedition on his part. The whole army he found "impatient for action, rendered almost acute by the natural apprehension felt for the safety of General Burnside in East Tennessee."[1]

It was expected that Sherman would be in position on the 19th, but the difficult roads delayed his movements. J. E. Smith's division was the first to cross. Morgan L. Smith's division crossed to the north bank at Brown's Ferry on the 21st. Ewing's was ready to cross, when the bridge broke, and occasioned a delay of two days. Ewing crossed on the 23d, when the bridge again broke, with Osterhaus on the south bank. It was therefore determinad to leave Osterhaus to support Hooker, while Jeff C. Davis was sent to Sherman in his place. It was evident that Sherman could not participate in the battle before the 24th.

But, in the mean while, deserters reported that Bragg was about to fall back. A letter received by flag of truce from the Confederate commander, warning General Grant to withdraw from Chattanooga whatever non-combatants still remained, seemed to corroborate these reports. Grant had no idea of suffering Bragg to retreat without a battle, and determined to attack before Sherman's arrival.

Howard's corps had been brought to Chattanooga, and this corps, with Granger's and Palmer's, was ordered to assail the enemy's centre with such vigor as to develop his lines and detain him in front. In obedience to this order, Granger and Palmer, with Howard in support, drove in the enemy's pickets on the 23d, and carried his first line of works between Chattanooga and Citico Creeks. Although Thomas's operations had been made in full view of the Confederate pickets, no attack was expected by the enemy. The Federal troops, clad in their best uniforms, and accompanied by their bands of music, thus rapidly mustering in open view, seemed to be parading for a grand review rather than for an assault upon the outposts of Missionary Ridge. The sentries occupying the advanced rifle-pits watched the display without alarm, but about noon they discovered, to their amazement, that the spectacle was one in which they were more intimately concerned as actors than as spectators. At 1 o'clock P.M. Wood's and Sheridan's divisions, of Granger's corps, advanced in front and under the guns of Fort Wood, Palmer occupying at the same time a threatening position on their right, while Howard was held in reserve on their left. Sheridan and Wood advanced at double-quick; and drove first the enemy's pickets, then their reserves, and, capturing about 200 men, including nine commissioned officers, carried Orchard Knob before the Confederates had fairly recovered from their surprise. Upon this important position Granger intrenched himself, and the advance of the troops on his left and right obliterated the front line of the Confederate works in Thomas's front. This success was won with a loss of 111 men. But the next day promised work of a more serious character.

On the 14th of November he telegraphed to Burnside:

"Your dispatch and Dana's" [in regard to the preference for Knoxville as the point to be held] st received. Being there, you can tell better how to resist Longstreet's attack than I can di- With your showing, you had better give up Kingston at the last moment, and save the productive part of your possession. Every arrangement is now made to throw Sherman's across the river just at and below the mouth of Chickamauga Creek as soon as it arrives. mas will attack on his" [the enemy's] "left at the same time, and together it is expected to y Missionary Ridge, and from there rush a force on to the railroad between Cleveland and on. Hooker will at the same time attack, and, if he can, carry Lookout Mountain. The en- now seems to be looking for an attack on his left flank. This favors us. To further confirm Sherman's advance division will march direct from Whiteside to Trenton. The remainder e force will pass over a new road just made from Whiteside to Kelly's Ferry, thus being con- d from the enemy, and leave him to suppose the whole force is going up Lookout Valley. rman's advance has only just reached Bridgeport. The rear will only reach there on the 16th. s will bring it to the 19th as the earliest day for making the combined movement as desired. rm me if you think you can sustain yourself till that time. I can hardly conceive of the en- breaking through at Kingston, and pushing for Kentucky. If they should, however, a new lem would be left for solution. Thomas has ordered a division of cavalry to the vicinity of ta. I will ascertain if they have started, and inform you. It will be entirely out of the tion to send for 10,000 men, not because they can not be spared, but how could they be fed they got one day east of here?"

n the 15th he telegraphed again as follows:

"I do not know how to impress on you the necessity of holding on to East Tennessee in strong gh terms. According to the dispatches of Mr. Dana and Colonel Wilson, it would seem that should, if pressed to do it, hold on to Knoxville, and that portion of the valley you will ssarily possess holding to that point. Should Longstreet move his whole force across the Lit- 'ennessee, an effort should be made to cut his pontoons on that stream, even if it sacrificed the cavalry of the Ohio Army. By holding on, and placing Longstreet between the Little essee and Knoxville, he should not be allowed to escape with an army capable of doing any this winter. I can hardly conceive the necessity of retreating from East Tennessee. If I t at all, it would be after losing most of the army, and then necessity would suggest the route. l not attempt to lay out a line of retreat. Kingston, looking at the map, I thought of more rtance than any one point in East Tennessee. But my attention being called more closely to can see that it might be passed by, and Knoxville, and the rich valley about it, possessed, ing that place entirely. I should not think it advisable to concentrate a force near Little essee to resist the crossing, if it would be in danger of capture; but I would harass and em- ss progress in every way possible, reflecting on the fact that the Army of the Ohio is not the army to resist the onward progress of the enemy."

[2] See map on page 565.

FIRST DIVISION, P. T. Osterhaus:	*First Brigade*, C. K. Woods. *Second Brigade*, J. A. Williamson.
COND DIVISION, Morgan L. Smith:	*First Brigade*, Giles A. Smith. *Second Brigade*, J. A. D. Lightburn.
IRD DIVISION, J. W. Tuttle:	*First Brigade*, J. A. Mower. *Second Brigade*, R. B. Buckland. *Third Brigade*, J. J. Wood.
URTH DIVISION, Hugh Ewing:	*First Brigade*, J. M. Corse. *Second Brigade*, Colonel Loomis. *Third Brigade*, J. R. Cockrell.

ttle's (Third) division was left with McPherson at Vicksburg, and its place taken by J. E. 's (of the Seventeenth Corps), which was also styled the Third Division. This division con- of three brigades, commanded by General Matthias, J. B. Raum, and J. J. Alexander.

[1] *Sherman's Report.*

LOOKOUT MOUNTAIN, FROM THE FEDERAL WORKS ON CHATTANOOGA CREEK.

It now became evident to Bragg that an attempt would be made against his right flank, with a view of severing his communication with Longstreet. To strengthen this portion of his line, Walker's division was withdrawn from the western slope of Lookout Mountain, leaving Stevenson and Cheatham to hold the left.

During the night of the 23d, Giles A. Smith's brigade, of Morgan L. Smith's division, consisting of about 3000 men, manned the boats of which the pontoon bridge was to be constructed, and, dropping down the river at midnight, captured the Confederate pickets above the North Chickamauga, and landed below the mouth of the creek. By means of these boats, and the steamer Dunbar, the rest of the division, together with John E. Smith's, were ferried across before daylight, so that on the morning of the 24th Sherman had a force of 8000 men ready to advance against the enemy's right. The whole valley between Citico and Chickamauga Creeks was an immense corn-field. Through this valley Howard moved on the forenoon of the 24th to connect with Sherman. The pontoon bridge had in the mean time been constructed, under "Baldy" Smith's immediate supervision. "I have never," says Sherman, "beheld any work done so quickly, so well; and I doubt if the history of the war can show a bridge of that extent (namely, 1350 feet) laid down so noiselessly and well in so short a time. I attribute it to the genius and intelligence of General W. F. Smith." By 1 o'clock P.M. the whole corps had crossed, and Davis's division was prepared to co-operate, as a reserve force, in the attack on Missionary Ridge.

Sherman's three divisions were now ordered to advance, M. L. Smith on the left, J. E. Smith in the centre, and Ewing on the right. A drizzling rain began to fall, and the clouds, resting upon the river, and low down upon the mountain sides, cloaked Sherman's movement. By 3 o'clock the northern spurs of the ridge were gained without loss. The enemy had not occupied these hills (north of the railroad tunnel) with any considerable force. Sherman fortified the heights gained by his troops, and brought up his artillery. He had supposed, from the map, that the ridge was continuous, but he now found that he was separated from the enemy by a deep gorge. The enemy attempted, later in the day, to regain the hill, attacking Sherman's left. The attack was repulsed, but in the fight Giles A. Smith was severely wounded, and carried to the rear.

While Sherman was thus confronting the enemy across the railroad on Missionary Ridge, Hooker had made better progress in his movement against the Confederate left on Lookout Mountain. The idea of an advance from Lookout Valley had been abandoned when Howard's corps was withdrawn from Hooker on the 22d. Indeed, Hooker, wishing to be with that portion of his command which would be in the fight, was on the point of following Howard, when he was ordered to remain and make a demonstration against Lookout Mountain, to divert the attention of the enemy from Sherman's movements. His command consisted of Geary's division of the Twelfth Corps, Osterhaus's of the Fifteenth, and Cruft's of the Fourth, with a small detachment of cavalry, making an aggregate of about 10,000 men. It was a conglomerate organization, no one of these three divisions having ever before seen either of the others. The presence of Osterhaus's division at this point led General Grant to resume his original plan, and he ordered Hooker to make a determined attack, and to carry the mountain if possible.

The enemy's pickets lined the east bank of Lookout Creek. His main force, under Cheatham, was encamped in a hollow midway up the slope of the mountain. The summit east of the palisaded crest was held by three brigades of Stevenson's division. The Confederate position was well protected by batteries and rifle-pits against an attack from the Tennessee or from the valleys on either side, and in the valleys also were strong lines of earth-works.

Geary, who had ascended Lookout Creek, supported by Whittaker's brigade of Cruft's division, crossed near Wauhatchie at 8 A.M. on the 24th, surprising and capturing the Confederate picket of 42 men on the river bank, and moved down the valley, his right keeping close up under the palisades, and thus avoiding the batteries on the crest. Osterhaus, with Cruft's other brigade (Grose's), at the same time gained a bridge on the road just below the point where the railroad to Chattanooga crosses the creek, and began to repair it. The enemy, not aware of the force marching in its rear, filed which ran diagonally across an open field covering the road which leads the mountain from Chattanooga to Summertown. Here progress was fo time interrupted. Much had been already gained. Upward of 2000 p oners had been captured, and communication was now open across Cl tanooga Creek with General Thomas. But Hooker's success thus far l been mainly the result of strategy. The enemy had been surprised.] for this, Lookout Mountain could easily have been held against Hook 10,000 men. The main object of the battle at this point had been secu All that remained was to make the victory decisive by breaking Ch ham's line on the eastern slope of the mountain, thus cutting off the l gades still holding the summit.

During the operations thus far the batteries on Moccasin Point, north the Tennessee, had been engaging the enemy's artillery on the extreme pc and highest peak of Lookout. The heavy clouds, which in the morn had enveloped the mountain's summit, and thus, to some extent, favo Hooker's movement, had gradually settled into the valley, veiling it co pletely from view. Thus the battle of the afternoon was literally "a Ba above the Clouds."

The Confederate line had been contracted in order to give it grea strength, so that there was a considerable interval between the plat which it held and the palisades. Geary, taking advantage of this interv got in upon the enemy's left flank, and an advance being made by Cruft Osterhaus in front, the entire line was carried. But it was not held by Federals undisturbed. No sooner had it been occupied by them than enemy turned upon it and made an assault. In the continual skirmishi which had been going on, Hooker's troops had now nearly exhausted th ammunition, and unless a fresh supply could be had from some source seemed probable that the position which had been gained would have to abandoned. Hooker had sent for ammunition, but it had been delay Just in time, fortunately, Carlin's brigade of Johnson's division arrived fr Thomas, having crossed Chattanooga Creek, and brought with it 120,0 rounds strapped on the backs of the men. This fresh brigade reliev Geary's exhausted troops. The enemy was repulsed, driven back from last position where he could make a stand, and hurled over the roc heights down into the valley.

By this time the darkness upon the mountain rendered farther progr extremely dangerous, and Hooker's troops encamped for the night on slope which they had so gallantly won. Lookout Mountain had been ca tured. The only drawback to the utmost completion of the victory w the fact that a route was left open for the retreat of Stevenson's briga from the crest above. Before daylight the colors of the Eighth Kentuc waved from the peak of Lookout. But the enemy had abandoned his campment, leaving behind him, in the hurry of his flight, all his camp a garrison equipage.

The morning of November 25th found Bragg's entire army stretch along Missionary Ridge from Tunnel Hill to Rossville, the valley of Chattanooga being entirely abandoned. Lieutenant General Hardee co manded the right wing, consisting of Cleburne's, Walker's, Cheatham's, a Stevenson's divisions. The left wing—consisting of Breckinridge's old vision,[1] and those of Stewart and Anderson—was under General Breck ridge. The breastworks at the foot of the rugged slope were occupied pickets, while the infantry and artillery stretched along the ridge. Wh the ascent was easy, special fortifications had been constructed to resist assailing force. The troops on Breckinridge's right had been beaten Lookout Mountain, had taken their position hurriedly, and had not yet covered from the demoralization of defeat. Breckinridge's left was refus at McFarland's Gap, occupying the breastworks in which the Federals h stood in their retreat from McLemore's Cove two months before. T point connected the old battle-field of Chickamauga with that upon whi the opposing forces were now contending.

About midnight on the 24th orders came from Grant, whose headquart were on Orchard Knob, for Sherman to attack at daylight the next mo ing. Sherman was early in the saddle. The clouds of the previous d had cleared away, and his own position, as well as that of the enemy, w fully revealed to him as he rode along from Lightburn's brigade on the

TOP OF LOOKOUT MOUNTAIN, SUNRISE, NOVEMBER 25 1863

REBEL BATTERY ON THE TOP OF LOOKOUT MOUNTAIN.

GENERAL HOOKER'S COLUMN STORMING LOOKOUT MOUNTAIN.

THE CREST OF LOOKOUT MOUNTAIN.

TO THE TOP OF THE MOUNTAIN.

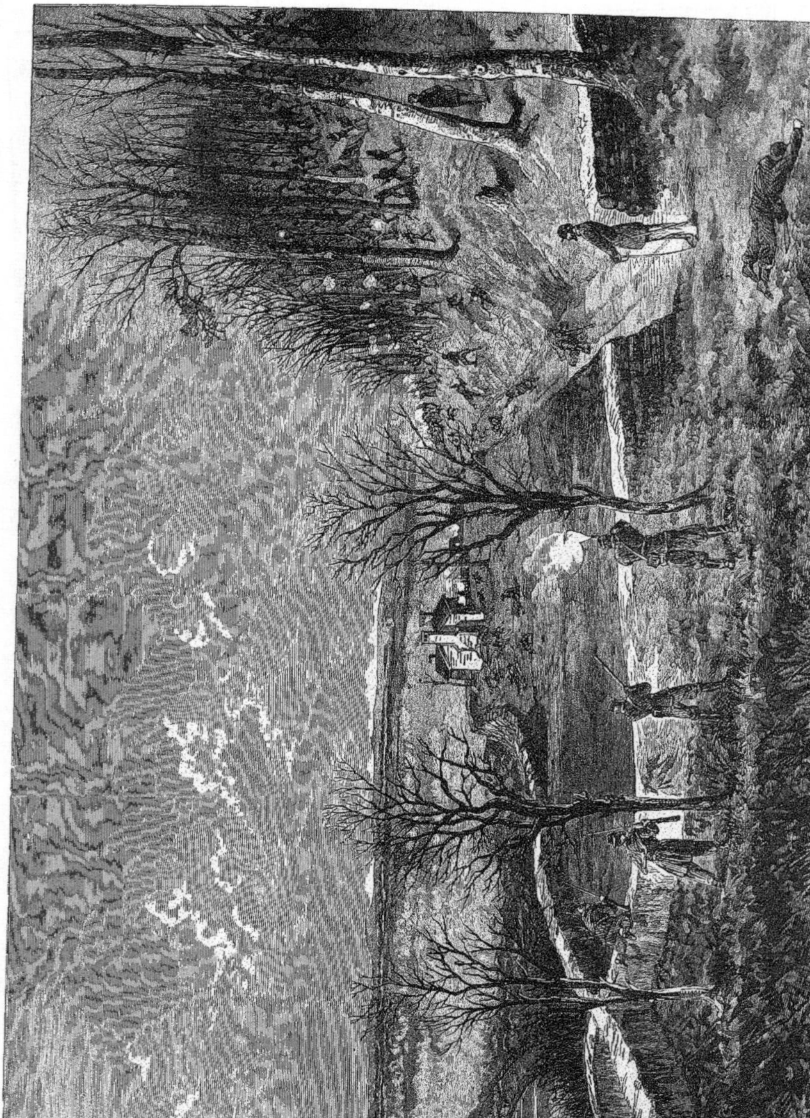

CAPTURE OF CONFEDERATE WORKS AT THE WHITE HOUSE, ON LOOKOUT MOUNTAIN.

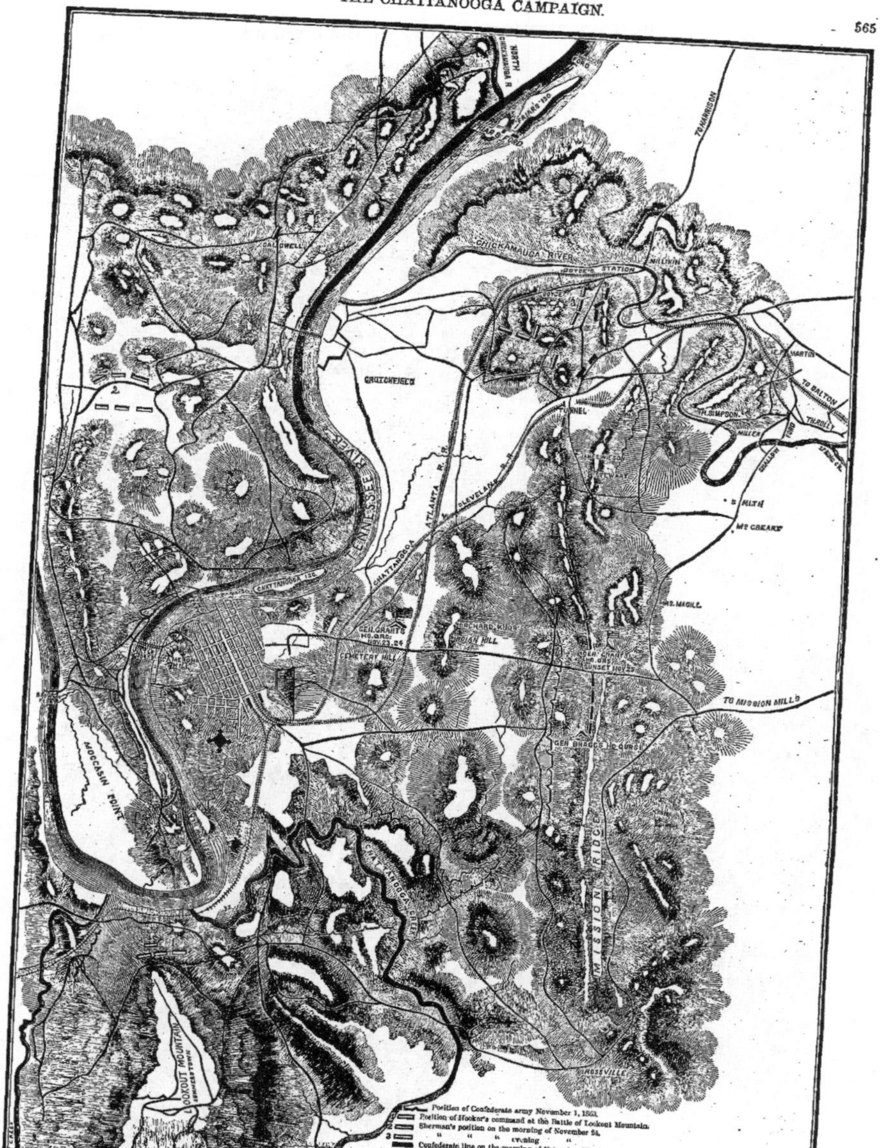

MAP ILLUSTRATING THE BATTLES ABOUT CHATTANOOGA.

THE STORMING OF MISSIONARY RIDGE.

position originally taken. Morgan L. Smith, in the mean time, had made considerable progress on the eastern slope. Loomis's brigade had got abreast of the tunnel, and, by diverting the enemy's attention, afforded some relief to General Corse. The two reserve brigades (those of John E. Smith) supporting Corse's movement had been repulsed, but the real attack was sustained. The enemy had brought to this part of the field extensive re-enforcements, and the most that Sherman could do was to maintain his position until the success of Thomas and Hooker, on the centre and right, should give him an opportunity to attack with advantage.

But the centre and right of the Federal army had been delayed. Thomas's attack was to depend upon the movements of Hooker. The latter was unexpectedly retarded in his movement from Lookout Mountain. Osterhaus's division began its march to Rossville at 10 o'clock, and the rest of Hooker's command followed, with the exception of two regiments left upon the summit of Lookout. On arriving at Chattanooga Creek it was found that the enemy had destroyed the bridge, and here Hooker was delayed for full three hours. Osterhaus was soon got across, and, pushing on to the gap in Missionary Ridge, flanked the enemy at this point, capturing artillery, ammunition, and wagons. Hooker's entire command was ready for the attack upon the enemy's left by 3 30 P.M. Craft advanced upon the ridge, Osterhaus to the east of it, and Geary, with the artillery, along the valley, against the western slope.

Thomas in the mean time had sent Baird's division to the support of Sherman, on Granger's left. This division got into position at 2 30 P.M. Thomas then assaulted the enemy's line with his whole force, driving the enemy from his rifle-pits at the foot of the hill on the centre of his line. The troops to the right of Wood advanced up to the crest, and gained the summit of the ridge, capturing large numbers of the enemy in their trenches.[1] Against Sherman, and Baird's and Wood's divisions, the enemy still held his ground; but Hooker was well up against his left, which now, attacked in front and flank, was entirely routed, leaving behind forty pieces of artillery. Here a large number of prisoners, driven by Hooker against Balmer and Johnson, were captured. Osterhaus alone took 2000 prisoners. It was not until nightfall, however, that the enemy's right was dislodged, and the entire ridge abandoned.

At daylight on the 26th Sherman and Hooker pursued the enemy's routed columns, the former by way of Chickamauga Station, the latter by Greysville and Ringgold. The rear-guard, under Gist, was overtaken and broken up, and three more guns captured. Hooker's force came upon Cleburne in a gap in Taylor's Ridge, near Ringgold, and, attacking him, was severely repulsed, losing 65 killed and 367 wounded. Finally Cleburne was flanked and driven from his strong position, leaving 130 killed and wounded on the field. There was no farther pursuit. Grose's brigade visited the battle-field of Chickamauga, and buried the remains of many of the Federal dead, which had been left by Bragg to lie mouldering where they had fallen.

Bragg attributes his defeat to a disgraceful panic on the part of his men.[2] The real causes were the weakness of his line—a weakness not of position, but of numbers—and the demoralization which had resulted from the defeat on Lookout Mountain.

The Federal losses in the battles of the 23d, 24th, 25th, and 26th were 757 killed, 4529 wounded, and 330 missing: total, 5616. The Confederate loss in killed and wounded was probably much less; but Bragg's loss in prisoners alone amounted to 6142, of whom 239 were commissioned officers; 7000 stand of small arms had also been captured by Grant's army. By these battles Bragg's army must have been diminished by at least 10,000 men. Grant probably had engaged about 65,000 men, and Bragg between 40,000 and 45,000.

General Bragg's defeat terminated the contest for Chattanooga and East Tennessee. The tidings of Grant's victory electrified the loyal portion of the country, and President Lincoln, on the 7th of December, issued a proclamation recommending the people "to assemble at their places of worship, and render special homage and gratitude to Almighty God for this great advancement of the national cause." From this time the prospects of the Southern Confederacy were indeed desperate. The resources of the Southern States were rapidly being exhausted, while the national armies were being recruited by immense numbers, at whose backs stood thousands more ready to take the field the moment their services should become necessary. Thus closed the year 1863. It had begun with the disaster at Fredericksburg, followed soon by the defeat at Chancellorsville; but the victories of Gettysburg, Vicksburg, and Missionary Ridge crowned it with imperishable glory.[1]

[1] General Thomas gives the following description of this movement:

"Our troops advancing steadily in a continuous line, the enemy, seized with panic, abandoned the works at the foot of the hill and retreated precipitately to the crest, whither they were closely followed by our troops, who, apparently inspired by the impulse of victory, carried the hill simultaneously at six different points, and so closely upon the heels of the enemy that many of them were taken prisoners in the trenches. We captured all their cannon and ammunition before they could be removed or destroyed. After halting a few moments to reorganize the troops, who had become somewhat scattered in the assault of the hill, General Sherman pushed forward in pursuit, and drove those in his front who escaped capture across Chickamauga Creek. Generals Wood and Baird, being obstinately resisted by re-enforcements from the enemy's extreme right, continued fighting until darkness set in, but steadily driving the enemy before them. In moving upon Rossville, General Hooker encountered Stewart's division and other troops. Finding his left flank threatened, Stewart attempted to escape by retreating toward Greysville; but some of his force, finding their retreat threatened in that quarter, retired in disorder toward their right, along the crest of the ridge, where they were met by another portion of General Hooker's command, and were driven by these troops in the face of Johnson's division of Palmer's corps, by whom they were nearly all made prisoners."

[2] The following is General Bragg's report of the battle:

"Headquarters Army of Tennessee, Dalton, Georgia, 30th November, 1863.

"General S. Cooper, Adjutant and Inspector General, Richmond:

"SIR,—On Monday, the 23d, the enemy advanced in heavy force, and drove in our picket line in front of Missionary Ridge, but made no farther effort.

"On Tuesday morning early they threw over the river a heavy force opposite the north end of the ridge, and just below the mouth of the Chickamauga, at the same time displaying a heavy force in our immediate front. After visiting the right, and making dispositions there for the new development in that direction, I returned toward the left, to find a heavy cannonading going on from the enemy's batteries on our forces occupying the slope of Lookout Mountain, between the crest and the river. A very heavy force soon advanced to the assault, and was met by one brigade only, Walthall's, which made a desperate resistance, but was finally compelled to yield ground. Why this command was not sustained is yet unexplained. The commander on that part of the field, Major General Stevenson, had six brigades at his disposal. Upon his urgent appeal, another brigade was dispatched in the afternoon to his support—though it appeared his own forces had not been brought into action—and I proceeded to the scene.

"Arriving just before sunset, I found that we had lost all the advantages of the position. Orders were immediately given for the ground to be disputed until we could withdraw our forces across Chattanooga Creek, and the movement was commenced. This having been successfully accomplished, our whole forces were concentrated on the ridge, and extended to the right to meet the movement in that direction.

"On Wednesday, the 25th, I again visited the extreme right, now under Lieutenant General Hardee, and threatened by a heavy force, while strong columns could be seen marching in that direction. A very heavy force in line of battle confronted our left and centre.

"On my return to this point, about 11 A.M., the enemy's forces were being moved in heavy masses from Lookout and beyond to our front, while those in front extended to our right. They formed their lines with great deliberation, just beyond the range of our guns, and in plain view of our position.

"Though greatly outnumbered, such was the strength of our position that no doubt was entertained of our ability to hold it, and every disposition was made for that purpose. During this time they had made several attempts on our extreme right, and had been handsomely repulsed, with very heavy loss, by Major General Cleburne's command, under the immediate direction of Lieutenant General Hardee. By the road across the ridge at Rossville, far to our left, a route was open to our rear. Major General Breckinridge, commanding on the left, had occupied this with two regiments and a battery. It being reported to me that a force of the enemy had moved in that direction, the general was ordered to have it reconnoitred, and to make every disposition necessary to secure his flank, which he proceeded to do.

"About half past 3 P.M., the immense force in the front of our left and centre advanced in three lines, preceded by heavy skirmishers. Our batteries opened with fine effect, and much confusion was produced before they reached musket range. In a short time the roar of musketry became very heavy, and it was soon apparent that the enemy had been repulsed in my immediate front.

"While riding along the crest congratulating the troops, intelligence reached me that our line was broken on my right, and the enemy had crowned the ridge. Assistance was promptly dispatched to that point, under Brigadier General Bate, who had so successfully maintained the ground in my front, and I proceeded to the rear of the broken line to rally our retiring troops and return them to the crest to drive the enemy back. General Bate found the disaster so great that his small force could not repair it. About this time I learned that our extreme left had also given way, and that my position was almost surrounded. Bate was immediately directed to form a second line in the rear, where, by the efforts of my staff, a nucleus of stragglers had been formed upon which to rally.

"Lieutenant General Hardee, leaving Major General Cleburne in command of the extreme right, moved toward the left when he heard the heavy firing in that direction. He reached the right of Anderson's division just in time to find it had nearly all fallen back, commencing on its right, where the enemy had first crowned the ridge. By a prompt and judicious movement, he threw a portion of Cheatham's division directly across the ridge, facing the enemy, who was now moving a strong force immediately on his left flank. By a decided stand here, the enemy was entirely checked, and that portion of our force to the right remained intact. All to the left, however, except a portion of Bate's division, was entirely routed, and in rapid flight, nearly all the artillery having been shamefully abandoned by its infantry support. Every effort which could be made by myself and staff, and by many other mounted officers, availed but little. A panic, which I had never before witnessed, seemed to have seized upon officers and men, and each seemed to be struggling for his personal safety, regardless of his duty or his character. In this distressing and alarming state of affairs, General Bate was ordered to hold his position, covering the road for the retreat of Breckinridge's command, and orders were immediately sent to Generals Hardee and Breckinridge to retire their forces upon the dépôt at Chickamauga. Fortunately, it was now near nightfall, and the country and roads in our rear were fully known to us, but equally unknown to the enemy. The routed left made its way back in great disorder, effectually covered, however, by Bate's small command, which had a sharp conflict with the enemy's advance, driving it back. After night, all being quiet, Bate retired in good order, the enemy attempting no pursuit. Lieutenant General Hardee's command, under his judicious management, retired in good order and unmolested.

"As soon as all the troops had crossed, the bridges over the Chickamauga were destroyed, to impede the enemy, though the stream was fordable in several places.

"No satisfactory excuse can possibly be given for the shameful conduct of our troops on the left in allowing their line to be penetrated. The position was one which ought to have been held by a line of skirmishers against any assaulting column; and, wherever resistance was made, the enemy fled in disorder, after suffering heavy loss. Those who reached the ridge did so in a condition of exhaustion, from the great physical exertion in climbing, which rendered them powerless, and the slightest effort would have destroyed them.

"Having secured much of our artillery, they soon availed themselves of our panic, and, turning our guns upon us, enfiladed our lines both right and left, rendering them entirely untenable. Had all parts of the line been maintained with equal gallantry and persistence, no enemy could ever have dislodged us; and but one possible reason presents itself to my mind in explanation of this bad conduct in veteran troops, who had never before failed in any duty assigned them, however difficult and hazardous. They had for two days confronted the enemy, marshaling his immense forces in plain view, and exhibiting to their sight such a superiority in numbers as may have intimidated weak minds and untried soldiers. But our veterans had so often encountered similar hosts when the strength of position was against us, and with perfect success, that not a doubt crossed my mind. As yet, I am not fully informed as to the commands which first fled, and brought this great disaster and disgrace upon our arms. Investigation will bring out the truth, however, and full justice shall be done to the good and the bad.

"After arriving at Chickamauga, and informing myself of the full condition of affairs, it was decided to put the army in motion for a point farther removed from a powerful and victorious army, that we might have some little time to replenish and recuperate for another struggle. The enemy made pursuit as far as Ringgold, but was so handsomely checked by Major General Cleburne and Brigadier General Gist, in command of their respective divisions, that he gave us but little annoyance.

"Our losses are not yet ascertained, but in killed and wounded it is known to have been very small. In prisoners and stragglers I fear it is much larger.

"The chief of artillery reports the loss of forty (40) pieces.

"I am, sir, very respectfully, your obedient servant,

"BRAXTON BRAGG, General Commanding."

President Davis also seems to have concurred with General Bragg in attributing the blame to the troops. In his message to Congress (December 7th, 1863) he says:

"After a long and severe battle, in which great carnage was inflicted on him, some of our troops inexplicably abandoned positions of great strength, and by a disorderly retreat compelled the commander to withdraw the forces elsewhere successful, and, finally, to retire with his whole army to a position some twenty or thirty miles to the rear. It is believed that if the troops who yielded to the assault had fought with the valor which they had displayed on previous occasions, and which was manifested in this battle on other parts of the lines, the enemy would have been repulsed with very great slaughter, and our country would have escaped the misfortune, and the army the mortification, of the first defeat that has resulted from misconduct by the troops."

[1] Near the close of 1863 General Grant issued the following congratulatory order to his soldiers:

"Chattanooga, December 10th, 1863.

"The general commanding takes this opportunity of returning his sincere thanks and congratulations to the brave armies of the Cumberland, the Ohio, the Tennessee, and their comrades from the Potomac, for the recent splendid and decisive successes achieved over the enemy. In a short time you have recovered from him the control of the Tennessee River from Bridgeport to Knoxville. You dislodged him from his great stronghold upon Lookout Mountain, drove him from Chattanooga Valley, wrested from his determined grasp the possession of Missionary Ridge, repelled with heavy loss to him his repeated assaults upon Knoxville, forcing him to raise the siege there, driving him at all points, utterly routed and discomfited, beyond the limits of the state. By your noble heroism and determined courage you have most effectually defeated the plans of the enemy for regaining the possession of the states of Kentucky and Tennessee. You have secured positions from which no rebellious power can drive or dislodge you. For all this the general commanding thanks you collectively and individually. The loyal people of the United States thank and bless you. Their hopes and prayers for your success against this unholy rebellion are with you daily. Their faith in you will not be in vain. Their hopes will not be blasted. Their prayers to Almighty God will be answered. You will yet go to other fields of strife; and with the invincible bravery and unflinching loyalty to justice and right which have characterized you in the past, you will prove that no enemy can withstand you, and that no defenses, however formidable, can check your onward march."

CAPTURED CONFEDERATE CANNON IN FRONT OF GENERAL THOMAS'S HEADQUARTERS.

CHAPTER XXXVII.

SHERMAN'S MERIDIAN CAMPAIGN.

Object of the Meridian Expedition.—Condition of the Confederate Commissary.—Sherman's Plan.—Co-operative Column under W. S. Smith.—Sherman starts from Vicksburg February 3d, 1864.—His third Visit to Jackson.—The Confederate Forces, under Polk, in the Department of Mississippi.—Polk retires into Alabama.—Sherman's March unopposed.—He enters Meridian on the 14th.—Defeat of Smith's Column by General Forrest.—Sherman's Return to Vicksburg.—Forrest's Raid into Tennessee.—The Fort Pillow Massacre.—Expeditions sent against General Forrest from Memphis, under Sturgis and A. J. Smith.

SINCE the capture of Vicksburg there had been no important military movements in Mississippi during 1863. About the middle of August a small force of 1600 men, sent from General Hurlbut's command, had penetrated through the northern portion of the state to Grenada, where it captured and destroyed over 50 locomotives and about 500 cars. General McPherson two months later, with about 8000 men, comprising Logan's and Tuttle's divisions, and Colonel Winslow's cavalry, pushed out from Vicksburg nearly to Canton, driving back Wirt Adams's cavalry and three brigades of Confederate infantry. Finding himself confronted by a superior force of the enemy, he retreated to Vicksburg.

After Bragg's defeat a more formidable expedition was organized by General Sherman, having for its object the completion of the work which had been begun by the reduction of Vicksburg and Port Hudson. By the capture of those strong-holds the river itself had been conquered, and Arkansas, Louisiana, and Tennessee had been cut off from any possible connection with the main theatre of the war, which was now confined to Virginia, the two Carolinas, Georgia, Northern Florida, Alabama, and Mississippi. Winter had proclaimed a truce, so far as conflicts between the main armies were concerned. But the possession by the national troops of the east bank of the Mississippi furnished a convenient basis for a winter campaign in Mississippi and Alabama. Such a campaign would be an important preparation for the advance upon Atlanta in the following spring. If the reader will examine the map he will observe that, by the successful issue of the Chattanooga campaign, the entire network of railroads north of and including the road running from Memphis eastward to Virginia, had been secured by the national government. By General Grant's victory not only had Bragg's army been defeated and driven, but had been deprived of one of the chief sources upon which it had relied for subsistence.[1] It was forced to mainly depend upon Florida for its meat, while its supply of corn was principally derived from the rich valleys of the Alabama and Tombigbee Rivers. The Confederate Army of the West was already cut off from the immense cattle-growing region west of the Mississippi, and from the corn and bacon of Tennessee. It was proposed to still farther restrict its dependencies by operations, during the winter of 1863–4, directed against the railroads leading to Atlanta from Mississippi, Alabama, and Florida. Thus the campaigns undertaken in the beginning of 1864 by Seymour in Florida, and Sherman in Mississippi, were calculated to have an important bearing upon the progress of the main Federal army southward in the spring and summer.

Probably the principal object of Sherman's expedition against the railroads west of Atlanta was to prevent the possibility of the future concentration of a Confederate army on the east bank of the Mississippi. The destruction of these railroads would render it impossible for the enemy to approach the river with artillery and trains, and the occupation of prominent points in the interior would subject any Confederate infantry column, seeking to gain a position on the river, to an attack in its rear. In this way Sherman's army would be liberated from the necessity, hitherto imposed upon it, of remaining in strong force at Vicksburg, or some other point on the Mississippi.

The plan adopted by General Sherman was the following: He was himself to move from Vicksburg with four divisions of infantry—two of McPherson's and two of Hurlbut's corps—and Colonel Winslow's cavalry brigade, and, advancing westward, was to destroy the Southern Mississippi Railroad. At Meridian, General William Sooy Smith, General Grant's chief of cavalry, was to meet him with all the cavalry of the department, having advanced along the line of the Mobile and Ohio Railroad from Memphis, destroying the road as he moved. General Smith had a long ride of 250 miles, which he was expected to accomplish in ten days, starting from Memphis on or before the 1st of February, moving by way of Pontotoc, Okalona, and Columbus, and reaching Meridian on the 10th. He was instructed to disregard all small detachments of the enemy, and to advance rapidly to his appointed destination. Simultaneously with these movements, the Eleventh Illinois and a colored regiment, with five tin-clad gun-boats, were sent up the Yazoo to create a diversion and to protect the plantations along the banks of that river; and another force, under Brigadier General Hawkins, was to patrol the country toward the Big Black, in the rear of Vicksburg, and to collect 50 skiffs, by means of which detachments of 200 or 300 men might be moved at pleasure through the labyrinth of bayous between the Yazoo and the Mississippi, for the purpose of suppressing the bands of guerrillas then infesting that region.

Sherman began his march on the 3d of February. Hurlbut moved across the Big Black by way of Messenger's Ferry, and McPherson by the railroad bridge six miles below. The two columns, with the cavalry, numbered about 25,000 men. On the 5th both columns met the enemy, Hurlbut's at Joe Davis's plantation, and McPherson's at Champion Hills, and there was skirmishing all day, with small loss on either side, but without materially impeding the progress of the troops, who the next day entered Jackson. This was the third time that Sherman's troops had entered and occupied the capital of Mississippi, and it is fair to presume that this third occupation pretty nearly completed the work of destruction so shamelessly indulged in on two previous occasions.[1]

[1] Says the Knoxville *Register* (published at Atlanta, Georgia, after the Federal occupation of East Tennessee), "If any one doubts the necessity which would compel President Davis to sacrifice Richmond, Charleston, and Mobile, all to reacquire East Tennessee, he need only ask the commissary general by what agencies and from what sources the armies of the South have been sustained during the first years of the war. East Tennessee furnished the Confederate States with 25,000,000 pounds of bacon. Last year the State of Tennessee fed the army." The Richmond *Examiner* of October 31st corroborates this testimony in the following terms: "Except what was furtively obtained from Kentucky, the whole army supply of pork came from East Tennessee, and the contiguous counties of the adjoining states. The product of corn in that region was very heavy, and no portion of the Confederacy, equal in extent, afforded as large a supply of forage and winter pasturage."

The following circular, issued in November, 1863, from the office of the chief commissary in Florida, indicates the beginning of a sad era for the armies of the Confederacy:

"Office of Chief Commissary, Quincy, Fla., November 2, 1863.

"It has been a subject of anxious consideration how I could, without injury to our cause, expose to the people throughout the state the present perilous condition of our army. To do this through the public press would point out our source of danger to our enemies. To see each one in person, or even a sufficient number to effect the object contemplated, is impossible; yet the necessity of general and immediate action is imperative to save our army, and with it our cause, from disaster. The issues of this contest are now transferred to the people at home. If they fail to do their duty and sustain the army in its present position, it must fall back. If the enemy break through our present line, the wave of desolation may roll even to the shores of the Gulf and Atlantic. In discipline, valor, and the skill of its leaders, our army has proven more than a match for the enemy. But the best-appointed army can not maintain its position without support at home. The people should never suffer it to be said that they valued their cattle and hogs, their corn and money, more than their liberties and honor, and that they had to be compelled to support an army they had sent to battle in their defense. We hope it will not become necessary to resort to impressments among a people fighting for their existence, and in defense of their homes, and country, and institutions. We prefer rather to appeal to them by every motive of duty and honor—by the love they bear their wives and daughters—by the memory of the heroic dead, and the future glory and independence of their country, to come to its rescue in this darkest hour of its peril.

"A country which can afford to send forth in its defense the flower of its youth, and the best of its manhood, can afford, and are in honor bound to sustain them at any cost and sacrifice of money and property. They have sacrificed home and ease, and suffered untold hardships, and with their lives are now defending every thing we hold most sacred. Florida has done nobly in this contest. Her sons have achieved the highest character for their state, and won imperishable honors for themselves. These brave men are now suffering for want of food. Not only the men from Florida, but the whole army of the South, are in this condition. Our honor as a people demands that we do our duty to them. They must be fed. The following extracts from official letters in my possession do but partially represent the present condition of the armies of Generals Bragg and Beauregard, and their gloomy prospect for future supplies:

"Major J. F. Cumming, who supplies General Bragg's army, writes, 'It is absolutely and vitally important that all the cattle that can possibly be brought here shall be brought as promptly as possible.' And again, on the 5th of October, he says, 'I can not too strongly urge upon you the necessity, yes, the urgent necessity, of sending forward cattle promptly. It appears that all other sources are exhausted, and that we are now dependent upon your state for beef for the very large army of General Bragg. I know you will leave no stone unturned, and I must say all is now dependent on your exertions, so far as beef is concerned. In regard to bacon, the stock is about exhausted—hence beef is our only hope. I know the prospect is very discouraging, and it only remains with those of us having charge of this important work to do all we can to exhaust our resources; and when we have done this, our country can not complain of us. If we fail to do all that can be done, and our cause shall fail, upon us will rest the responsibility; therefore let us employ every means at our command.' Again, on the 6th, he says, 'Major A. can explain to you the great and absolute necessity for prompt action in the matter; for, major, I assure you that nearly all now depends on you.' And on the 19th of October he says, 'Captain Townsend, A. C. S., having a leave of absence for thirty days from the Army of Tennessee, I have prevailed on him to see you and explain to you my straitened condition, and the imminent danger of our army suffering for the want of beef.' And on the 20th of October he wrote, 'The army to-day is on half-rations of beef, and I fear within a few days will have nothing but bread to eat. This is truly a dark hour with us, and I can not see what is to be done. All that is left for us to do is to do all we can, and then we will have a clear conscience, no matter what the world may say.'

"Major Locke, Chief Commissary of Georgia, wrote, 'I pray you, major, to put every agency in motion that you can to send cattle without a moment's delay toward the Georgia borders. The troops in Charleston are in great extremity. We look alone to you for cattle; those in Georgia are exhausted.'

"Major Guerin, Chief Commissary of South Carolina, wrote, 'We are almost entirely dependent on Florida, and it is of the last importance, at this time, that the troops here should be subsisted.' Again he says, 'As it is, our situation is full of danger from want of meat, and extraordinary efforts are required to prevent disaster.' And on the 9th of October he says, 'We have now 40,000 troops and laborers to subsist. The supply of bacon on hand in the city is 20,000 pounds, and the cattle furnished by this state is not one tenth of what is required. My anxieties and apprehensions, as you may suppose, are greatly excited.'

"Major Millen, of Savannah, on the 10th of October says, 'I assure you, major, that the stock of bacon and beef for the armies of the Confederate States is now exhausted, and we must depend entirely upon what we may gather weekly. Starvation stares the army in the face—the hand-writing is on the wall.' On the 26th of October he says, 'From the best information I have, the resources of food (meat) of both the Tennessee and Virginia armies are exhausted. The remark now applies with equal force to South Carolina and Georgia, and the army must henceforth depend upon the energy of the purchasing commissaries, through their daily or weekly collections. I have exhausted the beef cattle, and am now obliged to kill stock cattle.'

"From these you perceive that there is too much cause for the deep solicitude manifested by the writers. They should excite the fears and apprehensions of every lover of his country. Truly the responsibility upon us is great, when we are expected to feed these vast armies, whether the producers will sell to us or not. The slightest reflection would teach any one that it is impossible to provide for such armies by impressments alone. The people must cheerfully yield their supplies, or make up their minds to surrender their cause. It is their cause. It is not the cause of the government. The government is theirs. The army, the government, you and I, and every one, and every thing we have, are staked upon this contest. To fail is total and irretrievable ruin, universal confiscation of every thing, and abject and ignominious submission and slavery to the most despicable and infamous race on earth. Whoever has any other thought but to fight on, at any cost of life and property, until we achieve our independence, or all perish in the struggle, deserves to be the slave of such an enemy. But, under the guidance of Providence, our cause is safe in the hands of our army, provided we do our duty at home. But Providence will not help a people who will not help themselves. Our enemies have no hope of conquering us by arms. Their only hope is that we will be untrue to ourselves, and in the blind pursuit of gain, lose sight of our country, and thus suffer our army, and with it our cause, to perish. How stands the case? You know the resources of Tennessee are lost to us; the hog cholera and other causes have cut short the prospect in Georgia and other states. It is ascertained that the last year's crop of bacon is about exhausted, and it is certain that the crop of this will be much shorter than that of last year. Now two large armies look almost solely to Florida to supply one entire article of subsistence. The entire surplus of this year's crop of bacon throughout the Confederacy, even when husbanded with the utmost economy, will be inadequate to the demands of the government. This makes it the duty of every man to economize as much as possible—to sell not a pound to any one else while there is any danger of our army suffering, and to pledge at schedule rates his entire surplus—bacon, beef, sugar, and sirup—to the government. I solemnly believe our cause is hopeless unless our people can be brought to this point.

"I have thought it my duty to address this confidential circular to the principal men in various sections of the state, and invoke their aid and co-operation with the purchasing commissaries and government agents in their districts, in inaugurating and putting into operation some system by which our armies can be more promptly supplied, and all of our resources which are necessary secured to the government. The appeals to me are more and more urgent every day; the pressure upon our state is very great. Should she now respond to the call made upon her resources as she has upon the bloodiest battle-field of the war, the measure of her glory will be full. But if we withhold our supplies, we cripple our army, and render it impossible for them to advance after achieving the most signal victories. The people at home must put themselves upon a war footing. This they have never yet done. They must sow, and plant, and gather for the government. Then, and not till then, will the bright rays of peace break through the clouds of war which overhang us.

P. W. WHITE, Major and Chief Commissary."

[1] The Northern accounts of Sherman's march indicate its character in this respect. The following extract is taken from "A National Account," published in volume viii. of the *Rebellion Record*:

"It was the expectation, when the expedition started out, that they would draw most of their supplies, and all their forage for horses and mules, from the country. There was very little difficulty in finding enough for our purpose, even in the most barren parts of the country we passed

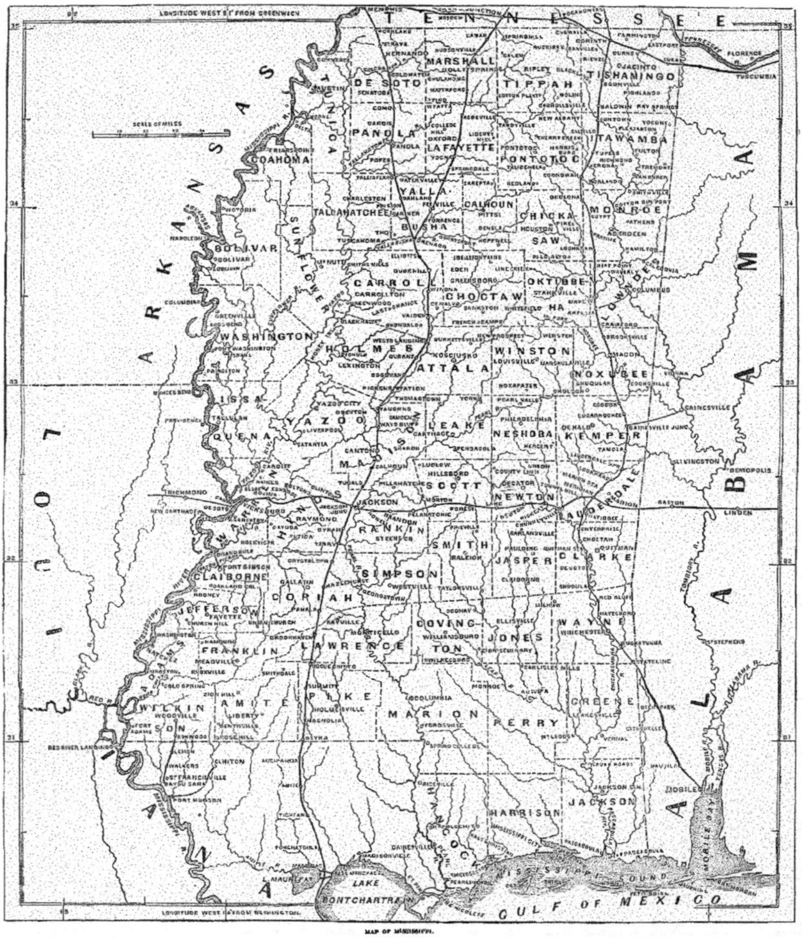

MAP OF MISSISSIPPI.

Sherman's troops marched with little other baggage than their ammunition and twenty days' provisions, and the rapidity of his movements met with very few obstacles from the enemy, who was too weak to oppose to them any formidable resistance. The entire Confederate force in the Department of Mississippi (now under General Polk's command), amounted to less than 16,000 effective men. The most which General Polk could do was to transport the supplies accumulated at the several railway stations into Alabama, behind the Tombigbee River.

Thus unopposed by the enemy, Sherman's march to Meridian was simply a promenade. He crossed the Pearl River on the pontoons which the enemy had left behind in his hurried retreat from Jackson. On his route he was joined by thousands of negroes—men, women, and children—who swelled the vast column of the march. The railroad was completely demolished along the route. On the 14th, having marched 150 miles in 11 days, Sherman entered Meridian.

But where was General Smith, due four days ago? While the enemy was giving Sherman "a wide berth," he had not been blind to the importance of cutting off the supporting column of cavalry on its way to Meridian from Memphis. In fact, it was only Smith's junction with Sherman that Polk really feared. *That* must be prevented at all hazards. The accession of this cavalry force to Sherman's army would be the preliminary to a successful advance to Selma and Montgomery, and where not? Polk, covering his infantry behind the Tombigbee, ordered his cavalry to join Forrest, to whom was assigned the difficult task of heading off Smith's column.

Associated with General Smith was General B. F. Grierson, who had become thoroughly acquainted with the country on his previous raid. The column had not left Memphis till the 11th, and thus the enemy had been given time to organize his forces for effective resistance. The Federal force numbered 7000 men, and to oppose this Forrest had at length collected to-

through. There was nothing left, however, after our passage, and in many instances the people must suffer for want of food."

This was no doubt legitimate warfare, but we question whether the same excuse may be urged for the destruction of property at Jackson, described as follows by a soldier of Sherman's army (F. McC., of the Sixteenth Iowa):

"It was truly a vivid picture of war to see the streets filled with armed men, squares of large brick buildings on fire, furniture of every description, from rocking-cradles to pianos, clothing, books—in fact, almost every article of domestic utility and ornament, piled upon the sidewalks. Women and children running hither and thither, pictures of the most abject despair. There was no protection given the town, and but little mercy shown, as this was the third time our army had been compelled to come here, and we judge General Sherman rightly concluded that he would obviate all necessity of having to come again."

W. S. SMITH.

gether about the same number at Okalona, nearly 100 miles north of Meridian. Up to this point Smith and Grierson continued their march without serious resistance. Thus far they were permitted by the enemy to revel in a carnival of devastation, destroying corn estimated by the millions of bushels (one account makes it 1,000,000 bushels, another 3,000,000), and two or three thousand bales of cotton. Either by lack of discipline, owing to the character of such a march, or on account of the sudden and formidable opposition encountered, the Federal command did not behave well when on the 22d it reached Okalona, as was its wont in the presence of the enemy. Almost the first onset of Forrest's cavalry was decisive. Six guns were lost by the Federals in the first attack. Probably even after the first reverse the Confederates would have been checked had it not been for the impediment to Smith's fighting force of the crowd of camp-followers, who gave way to panic, and fled to the rear, sweeping with them a portion of the troops coming into position. It was with great difficulty that Smith covered his retreat and saved his trains. The Fourth Missouri Cavalry, acting as rear-guard, stood well its ground, checking the enemy until nightfall. Under cover of night the Federals fell back to Okalona (the battle had been fought south of that place, on the border of the prairie country), where order was restored. Smith and Grierson, after losing over 300 men and a large number of horses, continued their retreat over the country which for ten days they had been laying waste.

This disaster, of course, forbid any farther advance on the part of Sherman, who had in the mean time been destroying the railroads centring in Meridian.[1] He then, with one of his columns, marched northward to Canton, continuing his work of destruction in that direction. Finding that the column from Memphis had been driven back, he returned to Vicksburg. His loss had been probably about 200 men. He brought away with him 1000 white and 5000 colored refugees. He had done the enemy very great injury, which, unfortunately, in a large measure, fell upon the population rather than the army; had, by the destruction of the railroads between Vicksburg and Meridian, secured the east bank of the Mississippi against any future attack on the part of the enemy—one of the chief objects of the raid—and had learned a lesson in regard to the facility of marching through the southern portion of the Confederacy, which was of the greatest value to him at a later period of the war.

It is possible that, but for the failure of Sherman's supporting cavalry column, an attempt would have been made in conjunction with Farragut's naval force against Mobile. Farragut did indeed make a strong demonstration against Mobile, assaulting Fort Powell, and losing a gun-boat in the operation. But this attack was only a feint, to divert attention from a pet project which the government was at this time nursing, and which regarded affairs on the other side of the Mississippi.

Forrest did not stop with his defeat of Smith and Grierson at Okalona. If he could meet all the cavalry of Grant's department in the open field, what was to hinder him—now that the garrisons of Tennessee were continually being weakened by the concentration of forces for the spring campaign—from moving into Western Tennessee and Kentucky? He passed over the frontier of Tennessee late in March, and his expedition throu was characterized by brutality and cowardice such as is not surpa the record of even savage warfare. It is possible that his comma infuriated by the devastation which had marked the progress of She Mississippi expedition. But this is no fair excuse for such conduct which it is now our duty to expose. Wherever Sherman's troops de from the recognized customs of war, the reader will bear us witness t have offered no excuse in their behalf. But if against them rebuke rally rises to our lips, our cheeks burn with shame for the brutal ca ties of our human nature as we follow the career of General Forres his entrance into Tennessee to the massacre at Fort Pillow.

Forrest advanced from Okalona northward by the Mobile and Ohio road. His command numbered between 5000 and 6000 men.[1] The which stood in his way, even if he looked to Cairo as his destination, d amount to more than half his own. Jackson, in Tennessee, was ca on the 23d of March. Forrest's line of march was west of the Ten River, toward the Mississippi. He captured Union City, near the no border of Tennessee, on the 24th of March. This post had been oc by Colonel Hawkins with about 500 men. Hawkins was attacked by three times that number, but easily repulsed four several charges enemy. Then a flag of truce was sent demanding a surrender, and t ing upon Colonel Hawkins the consequence of a refusal. Again wishes of the garrison the demand was complied with, although a reli force of 2000 men was within six miles of him. His conduct was pro influenced by the fear that the enemy in his front would soon be str re-enforced.[2]

The Mississippi from Paducah to Island No. 10, about 160 miles, tog with the adjacent portions of Tennessee and Kentucky, was under the mand of Brigadier General Mason Brayman. His whole force—distri at Paducah, Cairo, Columbus, Hickman, Island No. 10, and Union C amounted to 2329 men, three fourths of whom were negroes. G Hurlbut, in command of the department, had, in compliance with from the War Department, sent all his veteran regiments home on furl All his cavalry was gone save about 2000. He did not dare to leave phis exposed, and was therefore able to afford very little assistance t garrisons on the Mississippi River against which Forrest was moving. soon as Forrest approached Jackson, Grierson, with his cavalry, was se to develop his force, and soon reported that the enemy "was a littl strong for him."

From Union City Forrest moved upon Hickman, about fourteen mile tant on the Mississippi. The garrison at this point was withdrawn. enemy then advanced to Wayfield, Kentucky, which is about equally tant from Paducah, Cairo, and Columbus. He was at the centre of a ci about the edge of which General Drayman's forces were situated. The

[1] "The dépôts, store-houses, arsenals, offices, hospitals, hotels, and cantonments in the town were burned, and, during the next five days, with axes, sledges, crow-bars, clam-bars, and fire, Hurlbut's Corps destroyed on the north and east 60 miles of ties and iron, one locomotive, and eight bridges; and McPherson's Corps, on the south and west, 55 miles of railway, 63 bridges, 61,075 feet of trestle-work, 10 locomotives, 28 steam-cars, and 3 steam saw-mills. Thus was completed the destruction of railways for 100 miles from Jackson to Meridian, and for 20 miles around the latter place, in such a manner that they could not be used against us in the approaching campaigns."—Bowman's *Sherman and his Campaigns*, p. 163.

[1] Hurlbut thinks it could not have been less than 8000.—*Report on the Conduct of the War*

[2] General Hurlbut says, "Contrary to the entreaties, prayers, and advice of all his officer all his men, he did surrender his post with a relieving force within six miles of him, and su dered it, as I have no doubt, from pure cowardice."—*Report on the Conduct of the War.* It tame surrender, doubtless, but other testimony before the committee fully relieves Colonel kins of the charge of cowardice.

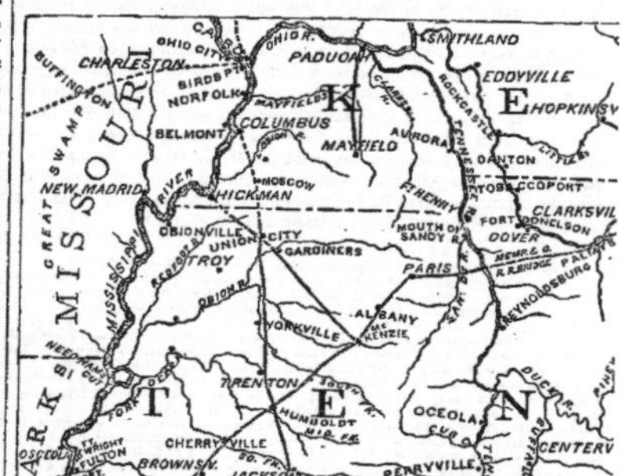

MAP ILLUSTRATING FORREST'S TENNESSEE EXPEDITION.

ter could only await attack, and send re-enforcements to such weak points in turn as the emergency might demand. "One evening," he says, "I sent 400 men to Columbus, expecting trouble there, and the next morning had them at Paducah, seventy-five miles distant."[1] No such thing as an offensive movement against Forrest could of course be contemplated, and the latter remained for three weeks subsisting upon captured stores in the very heart of a region which, almost from the beginning of the war, had been securely held by the national government. On the 25th of March an attack was made on Paducah, held by Colonel S. G. Hicks with a garrison of 650 men. The garrison retired into Fort Anderson, and there made a stand, assisted by two gun-boats, effectually repelling the enemy's assaults. Forrest then, failing to make an impression upon the defenders of the fort, demanded an unconditional surrender, closing his communication to Colonel Hicks in these words: "If you surrender you shall be treated as prisoners of war, but if I have to storm your works *you may expect no quarter.*" Hicks refused, stating, like a faithful soldier, that he had been placed there by his government to defend that post, and he should do so. Three assaults from the enemy followed, each of which was repulsed with heavy loss to the assailants. In the last, one of the Confederate general officers, General Thompson, was killed.[2] The next day Forrest retired, having suffered a loss of nearly 1500 men. The national loss was 14 killed and 46 wounded.[2] Columbus, on the Mississippi, stood out as defiantly as had Paducah, and the enemy retired without making an attack.

General Forrest appeared before Fort Pillow, 65 miles above Memphis, on the 12th of April. The garrison at this point consisted of 19 officers and 538 men, of whom 262 were negroes, commanded by Major L. F. Booth. The attack was sudden, no intimation of it being given before the pickets were driven in. Major Booth was killed early in the engagement, and Major W. F. Bradford succeeded to the command, and withdrew the forces from their outer intrenchments into the fort. The fort was situated on a high bluff, which descended precipitately to the river's edge. On either side was a ravine—the one below the fort containing several private stores and a few dwellings, constituting what is called the town. In front of the fort was an open space of level ground. The artillery defense consisted of 6 guns. The troops fought gallantly, aided by a gun-boat, and up to 2 P.M. the enemy had not gained any decisive advantage. A flag of truce was then sent in, conveying a demand for the unconditional surrender of the fort. Major Bradford asked an hour for consideration. Shortly a second flag appeared, and Bradford was allowed 20 minutes; if not out of the fort by that time an assault would be made. Bradford replied that be would not surrender. During all this time the enemy, regardless of his own flag of truce, was gaining an advantageous position for the assault. His forces were now within 100 yards of the fort, closely surrounding it. As soon as Major Bradford's reply was received, the bugle was sounded, and the Confederates, with a yell, rushed over the fortifications, raising the cry of "No quarter!" The troops composing the garrison, black and white, threw down their arms and sought to escape by running down the steep bluff on the river side, hiding behind trees, logs, bushes—any thing which could afford them cover against the maddest fiends which at that moment the sun shone upon. No wonder they fled, as it soon clearly appeared it was not a contest of men with men, but of men with brutal, fiendish murderers. The captured fort and its vicinity became at once a human shambles. Without discrimination of age or sex, and without mercy, men, women, and children were butchered until night put an end to the horrible tragedy, which was again renewed on the following morning. Not even sleep could quench the fiery hate of Forrest's men. Even the officers, with a few exceptions, assisted in the bloody carnival. It was exactly three years to a day since the attack on Fort Sumter had been made, and the same violence which had incited men to treason against their government was perhaps fitly displayed on this anniversary by the shameless massacre of United States soldiers at Fort Pillow.[3]

Forrest, in the face of his own statement that, whil[illegible]ost only 20 killed and 60 wounded, he buried 228 Federals on the e[illegible] of the assault, coolly claims that all these were killed in fair fight! After this affair the enemy retreated into Mississippi. A fortnight later General S. D. Sturgis, with 12,000 men, was sent after Forrest, but the movements of the enemy were so rapid that he easily escaped this pursuing column. Early in June Sturgis was again sent against Forrest, with instructions to find and defeat his command, in order to prevent its junction with General Johnston, then resisting General Sherman's advance in Northern Georgia. The Federal column dispatched for this purpose consisted of 9000 infantry (including most of A. J. Smith's division), and 3000 cavalry under General Grierson. The campaign was terribly mismanaged by Sturgis. After advancing through West Tennessee and Northern Mississippi to Guntown on the Mobile Railroad, Grierson's cavalry encountered Forrest, pushing his cavalry back on his infantry, which was strongly posted on a semicircular ridge, protected by a creek in front. Sturgis, with the infantry, was five or six miles behind. Getting information of Grierson's position, he pushed his command forward at double-quick, and as it was a very hot day, the troops, upon confronting the enemy, were thoroughly exhausted. To make matters still worse, the train of over 200 wagons was allowed by Sturgis to rush forward with his men, filling the road and impeding their movements. No rest was given the troops, who were immediately sent to the support of the cavalry already engaged. No attempt was made to turn the enemy's strong position, and from the attack which was made no other consequence could be expected than that which followed. Both cavalry and infantry were soon routed, and driven in disorder back upon and over the abandoned train. The pursuit was momentarily checked at Ripley, but was continued with some vigor almost to Memphis. In this expedition Sturgis lost between 3000 and 4000 men, most of whom were captured.

A month later (July 7th) another command was sent against Forrest, consisting of the same number of men, but this time under command of A. J.

[1] *Report on the Conduct of the War.*

[2] General Sherman writes to Colonel Hicks from Nashville, April 5th, 1864:

"Your defense at Paducah was exactly right. Keep cool, and give the enemy a second edition if he comes again. I want Forrest to stay just where he is, and the longer the better. Don't credit any of the foolish and exaggerated rumors that are put afloat by design. I know what Forrest has, and will attend to him in time."

[2] "The operations of the enemy at Paducah were characterized by the same bad faith and treachery that seemed to have become the settled policy of Forrest and his command. The flag of truce was taken advantage of there, as elsewhere, to secure desirable positions which the rebels were unable to obtain by fair and honorable means, and also to afford opportunities for plundering private stores as well as government property. At Paducah the rebels were guilty of acts more cowardly, if possible, than any they have practiced elsewhere. When the attack was made, the officers of the fort and of the gun-boats advised the women and children to go down to the river for the purpose of being taken across out of danger. As they were leaving the town for that purpose, the rebel sharp-shooters mingled with them, and, shielded by their presence, advanced and fired upon the gun-boats, wounding some of our officers and men. Our forces could not return the fire without endangering the lives of the women and children. The rebels also placed women in front of their lines as they moved on the fort, or were proceeding to take positions while the flag of truce was at the fort, in order to compel our men to withhold their fire out of regard for the lives of the women who were made use of in this most cowardly manner."—*Report on the Conduct of the War.*

[3] We have not described this disgraceful tragedy in its details. The following extract from the report of the Committee on the Conduct of the War will enable the reader to examine its features more minutely. All the statements made are supported by abundant and unimpeachable evidence:

"Then followed a scene of cruelty and murder without a parallel in civilized warfare, which needed but the tomahawk and scalping-knife to exceed the worst atrocities ever committed by savages. The rebels commenced an indiscriminate slaughter, sparing neither age nor sex, white nor black, soldier or civilian. The officers and men seemed to vie with each other in the devilish work; men, women, and even children, wherever found, were deliberately shot down, beaten, and hacked with sabres; some of the children, not more than ten years old, were forced to stand up and face their murderers while being shot; the sick and the wounded were butchered without mercy, the rebels even entering the hospital building and dragging them out to be shot, or killing them as they lay there unable to offer the least resistance. All over the hill-side the work of murder was going on; numbers of our men were collected together in lines or groups and deliberately shot; some were shot while in the river, while others on the bank were shot and their bodies kicked into the water, many of them still living, but unable to make any exertions to save themselves from drowning. Some of the rebels stood on the top of the hill, or a short distance down its side, and called to our soldiers to come up to them, and as they approached, shot them down in cold blood; if their guns or pistols missed fire, forcing them to stand there until they were again prepared to fire. All around were heard cries of 'No quarter!' 'No quarter!' 'Kill the damned niggers; shoot them down!' All who asked for mercy were answered by the most cruel taunts and sneers. Some were spared for a time, only to be murdered under circumstances of greater cruelty. No cruelty which the most fiendish malignity could devise was omitted by these murderers. One white soldier, who was wounded in one leg so as to be unable to walk, was made to stand up while his tormentors shot him; others who were wounded and unable to stand were held up and again shot. One negro, who had been ordered by a rebel officer to hold his horse, was killed by him when he remounted; another, a mere child, whom an officer had taken up behind him on his horse, was seen by Chalmers, who at once ordered the officer to put him down and shoot him, which was done. The huts and tents in which many of the wounded had sought shelter were set on fire, both that night and the next morning, while the wounded were still in them—those only escaping who were able to get themselves out, or who could prevail on others less injured than themselves to help them out; and even some of those thus seeking to escape the flames were met by those ruffians and brutally shot down, or had their brains beaten out. One man was deliberately fastened down to the floor of a tent, face upward, by means of nails driven through his clothing and into the boards under him, so that he could not possibly escape, and then the tent set on fire; another was nailed to the side of a building outside of the fort, and then the building set on fire and burned. The charred remains of five or six bodies were afterward found, all but one so much disfigured and consumed by the flames that they could not be identified, and the identification of that one is not absolutely certain, although there can hardly be a doubt that it was the body of Lieutenant Akerstrom, quartermaster of the Thirteenth Tennessee Cavalry, and a native Tennesseean; several witnesses who saw the remains, and who were personally acquainted with him while living, have testified that it is their firm belief that it was his body that was thus treated.

"These deeds of murder and cruelty ceased when night came on, only to be renewed the next morning, when the demons carefully sought among the dead lying about in all directions for any of the wounded yet alive, and those they found were deliberately shot. Scores of the dead and wounded were found there the day after the massacre by the men from some of our gun-boats who were permitted to go on shore and collect the wounded and bury the dead. The rebels themselves had made a pretense of burying a great many of their victims, but they had merely thrown them, without the least regard to care or decency, into the trenches and ditches about the fort, or the little hollows and ravines on the hill-side, covering them but partially with earth. Portions of heads and faces, hands and feet, were found protruding through the earth in every direction. The testimony also establishes the fact that the rebels buried some of the living with the dead, a few of whom succeeded afterward in digging themselves out, or were dug out by others, one of whom your committee found in Mound City Hospital, and there examined. And even when your committee visited the spot, two weeks afterward, although parties of men had been sent on shore from time to time to bury the bodies unburied and rebury the others, and were even then engaged in the same work, we found the evidences of this murder and cruelty still most painfully apparent; we saw bodies still unburied (at some distance from the fort) of some sick men who had been met fleeing from the hospital, and beaten down and brutally murdered, and their bodies left where they had fallen. We could still see the faces, hands, and feet of men, white and black, protruding out of the ground, whose graves had not been reached by those engaged in reinterring the victims of the massacre; and although a great deal of rain had fallen within the preceding two weeks, the ground, more especially on the side and at the foot of the bluff, where the most of the murders had been committed, was still discolored by the blood of our brave but unfortunate men, and the logs and trees showed but too plainly the evidences of the atrocities perpetrated there.

"Many other instances of equally atrocious cruelty might be enumerated, but your committee feel compelled to refrain from giving here more of the heart-sickening details, and refer to the statements contained in the voluminous testimony herewith submitted. Those statements were obtained by them from eyewitnesses and sufferers; many of them, as they were examined by your committee, were lying upon beds of pain and suffering, some so feeble that their lips could with difficulty frame the words by which they endeavored to convey some idea of the cruelties which had been inflicted on them, and which they had seen inflicted on others.

"How many of our troops thus fell victims to the malignity and barbarity of Forrest and his followers can not yet be definitely ascertained. Two officers belonging to the garrison were absent at the time of the capture and massacre. Of the remaining officers but two are known to be living, and they are wounded and now in the hospital at Mound City. One of them, Captain Potter, may even now be dead, as the surgeons, when your committee were there, expressed no hope of his recovery. Of the men, from three hundred to four hundred are known to have been killed at Fort Pillow, of whom at least three hundred were murdered in cold blood after the post was in possession of the rebels, and our men had thrown down their arms and ceased to offer resistance. Of the survivors, except the wounded in the hospital at Mound City, and the few who succeeded in making their escape unhurt, nothing definite is known; and it is to be feared that many have been murdered after being taken away from the fort.

"In reference to the fate of Major Bradford, who was in command of the fort when it was captured, and who had up to that time received no injury, there seems to be no doubt. The general understanding every where seemed to be that he had been brutally murdered the day after he was taken prisoner.

"There is some discrepancy in the testimony, but your committee do not see how the one who professed to have been an eyewitness of his death could have been mistaken. There may be some uncertainty in regard to his fate.

"When your committee arrived at Memphis, Tennessee, they found and examined a man (Mr. McLagan) who had been conscripted by some of Forrest's forces, but who, with other conscripts, had succeeded in making his escape. He testifies that while two companies of rebel troops, with Major Bradford and many other prisoners, were on their march from Brownsville to Jackson, Tennessee, Major Bradford was taken by five rebels—one an officer—led about fifty yards from the line of march, and deliberately murdered in view of all there assembled. He fell—killed instantly by three musket-balls, even while asking that his life might be spared, as he had fought them manfully, and was deserving of a better fate. The motive for the murder of Major Bradford seems to have been the simple fact that, although a native of the South, he remained loyal to his government."

THE FORT PILLOW MASSACRE.

FORREST'S RAIDERS ATTACKING IRVING PRISON.

Smith, who advanced to Tupelo, where the enemy, about 14,000 strong, was then concentrated. A battle was here fought (July 14th), in which the enemy, thrice attacking the Federal lines, was each time repulsed. It was a drawn battle, and Smith, without advancing farther, retreated to Memphis, whence he again set out with 10,000 men on the 4th of August, moving by way of Holly Springs to the Tallahatchie River. But this time Forrest was not to be found, and Smith, after remaining in this vicinity for several days, again returned to Memphis, and was sent to the Department of the Missouri.

While General Smith was looking for Forrest in Mississippi, the latter had moved upon Memphis with 3000 men. He charged into the town on the morning of August 18th. He had heard that Generals Hurlbut, Washburne, and Buckland made their quarters at the Gayoso Hotel, but, paying them a visit at that place, he found them "not at home." He captured several staff and other officers, however, and about 300 soldiers. A number of Confederate prisoners were confined in Irving Prison. Failing in an attempt to gain possession of this prison, General Forrest left the town, and beat a hasty retreat back into Mississippi.

CHAPTER XXXVIII.

THE FLORIDA EXPEDITION.

Gillmore lands 10,000 Men at Jacksonville.—Object of the Expedition in large measure Political.—Lincoln's Amnesty Proclamation.—The President's Motives.—The Enemy surprised.—Number of Confederate Troops in Florida.—The Federal Troops occupy Baldwin.—Gillmore returns to Hilton Head.—His Instructions to General Seymour disregarded by the latter.—The Battle of Olustee.—Seymour's Blunder.—Disastrous Termination of the Expedition.

WHILE Sherman was advancing upon Meridian, a force of 10,000 men was landed at Jacksonville, on the eastern coast of Florida. These were a portion of the Tenth Army Corps, under General Q. A. Gillmore, who, on the 16th of July, 1863, had succeeded General Hunter in command of the troops operating in South Carolina. The object of this Florida expedition was in large measure a political one. President Lincoln had included in his first message to the Thirty-eighth Congress (December 7th, 1863) a proclamation of amnesty, offering a free pardon to all such rebels as would take an oath to support the Federal Constitution and Union, "and abide by and faithfully support all acts of Congress passed during the existing rebellion having reference to slaves, so long and so far as not repealed, modified, or held void by Congress, or by decision of the Supreme Court." Exceptions were made in the cases of those who were or had been officers or agents of the Confederate government; of those who had left judicial stations under the United States, or seats in Congress, or had resigned commissions in the Federal army or navy to take part in the rebellion; of Confederate military and naval officers above the rank of colonel in the army or lieutenant in the navy; and of all who had in any way treated white or black soldiers otherwise than as prisoners of war. It was also proclaimed that, as soon as in any of the Confederate States "a number of persons, not less than one tenth in number of the votes cast in such state at the presidential election of 1860, each having taken the oath aforesaid, and not having since violated it, and being a qualified voter by the election law of the state existing immediately before the so-called act of secession, and excluding all others, shall re-establish a state government which shall be republican, and in nowise contravening said oath, such shall be recognized as the true government of the state; and the state shall receive thereunder the benefits of the constitutional provision which declares that 'the United States shall guarantee to every state in this Union a republican form of government, and shall protect each of them against invasion, and, on application of the Legislature or the executive (when the Legislature can not be convened), against domestic violence.'" The President entertained somewhat extravagant expectations as to the results of this proclamation. It is not necessary to say that he had no partisan motive in issuing it; he only wished to begin the reorganization of governments in the Southern States. The movement was premature; perhaps it was ill considered. If successful, some foreign complications might be avoided; but, so far as any real reconstruction was concerned, that could only come as the consequence of final victory in the war. Unfortunately, the President's too sanguine hopes conduced to the embarrassment of military operations. Expeditions were undertaken which distracted forces from vital centres, and which, contemplating nothing beyond the possession of a small slice of territory in Florida and Texas, and being undertaken with numbers only adequate to such a result, had not the remotest connection with the progress of the war from a military stand-point. The disastrous results of these expeditions are not fairly attributable to the President's plan; but, apart from their unfortunate results, no such half-military and half-political projects were in place.

The objects sought to be attained by the Florida expedition are thus stated by General Gillmore:

1. To procure an outlet for cotton, lumber, timber, etc.
2. To cut off one of the enemy's sources of commissary supplies.

S. D. STURGIS.

3. To obtain recruits for any colored regiments.

4. To inaugurate measures for the speedy restoration of Florida to her allegiance, in accordance with instructions which I had received from the President by the hands of Major John Hay, Assistant Adjutant General.[1]

The troops, consisting of twelve regiments—one half of them colored troops—under the immediate command of Brigadier General Truman Seymour, left Hilton Head on the 6th of February, and landed the next day at Jacksonville, at the mouth of St. John's River. The landing of this force was a complete surprise to the enemy. In the Confederate Departments of South Carolina, Georgia, and Florida, there were at this time about 33,000 effective troops. Of these there were about 5000 in Florida, under the command of General Finnegan. The progress of the Federal troops from Jacksonville to Baldwin, in the interior, met with no opposition. Finnegan made an attempt to stand at Camp Vinegar, seven miles west of Jacksonville, but on the approach of the Federal columns he abandoned his position, having sunk the steamer St. Mary's, and burned 270 bales of cotton. On the morning of the 9th General Gillmore reports: "We have taken, without the loss of a man, about 100 prisoners, eight pieces of artillery in serviceable order and one well supplied with ammunition, and other valuable property to a large amount." Baldwin, which the Federal troops now occupied, was eighteen miles west of Jacksonville, and was the point of junction of two railroads, one running from Fernandina, a short distance north of Jacksonville, southwestwardly to Cedar Keys, on the western coast: the other from Jacksonville, across the northern part of the state to Tallahassee, the state capital. A portion of Seymour's command, under Colonel Henry, pursued the enemy almost to Lake City.

General Gillmore had accompanied the expedition in person, and remained until the 15th, when he returned to Hilton Head. On the 11th he had instructed General Seymour not to risk a repulse by an advance on Lake City, but, if possible, to hold Sanderson (forty miles west of Jacksonville), and, at any rate, the south fork of the St. Mary's. The next day he ordered the entire force to concentrate at Baldwin. Before his departure for Hilton Head he made arrangements for the construction of fortifications at Jacksonville, Baldwin, and on the south fork of the St. Mary's. At that time it was understood that no advance should be made without farther instructions from Gillmore, nor until the defensive works were well advanced.[2]

General Gillmore was therefore astonished by receiving a communication from Seymour on the 18th (dated the 17th), stating that he intended to advance to the Suwanee River, 100 miles distant from Jacksonville, and that he was already moving his troops westward. Not being able to accumulate supplies sufficient to permit him to make the movement, Seymour declared his purpose to move without supplies, even if compelled to retrace his steps to procure them. He urged Gillmore to prevent any force re-enforcing the enemy from Georgia by a naval demonstration against Savannah. He asked, also, for a general to be sent him to command his advanced troops. General Gillmore, having no intention to occupy the western part of Florida, at once dispatched General Turner, his chief of staff, to Jacksonville to prevent the movement. Upon arriving in Florida with a letter to Seymour from Gillmore protesting against the advance of the former, Turner found that the troops were already at Olustee, and engaged with the enemy.[3]

General Seymour had begun his movement on the 18th, an[d] encounter with the enemy before reaching Lake City. On th[e] 19th he halted at Barber's, a small station on the railroad 30 Jacksonville. The Confederate General Finnegan had, in th[e] been apprized of the hostile movement, and, instead of awai[ting] Lake City, he preferred to choose his own battle-ground, an[d] Olustee, about 15 miles eastward, where his army took a stro[ng] a swamp which runs southward some distance from Ocean lake north of the railroad. His centre was protected by th[e] right rested on an earthwork protected by rifle-pits, while his ed on a slight elevation, sheltered by pines, and still farther gu[arded by cav]alry. It was a position absolutely impregnable against double which held it, and the force under General Seymour was onl[y] to that of the enemy; his only advantage was in artillery, of sixteen pieces to the enemy's four.[1]

Seymour, without knowing any thing of the enemy's posit[ion] from Barber's on the 20th, and, after a wearisome march of the sandy road, came suddenly upon the enemy's pickets near road at this point crossed the railroad to the right, to avoid t[he] the south side. There was also a swamp on the right of the tween these two swamps lay the sole approach to the enemy's action commenced about 2 o'clock P.M. The Federal troops, long march, went into battle under a great disadvantage. Th[e] pushed up so far to the front that both the gunners and ho[rses] down with such rapidity that some of the guns were abandon[ed] rendered useless. The infantry, poorly armed, were put in regiment as it arrived on the ground. There was no tactics, tion gave no opportunity for any. The road was so narrow the men had to wade knee-deep in mud and water in order t[o] tion. One regiment after another went in beyond the swa[mp] fired away its ammunition, and, exposed to a murderous fire fr[om] retired, giving place to another. The Seventh Connecticut, u[nder] Colonel J. R. Hawley (late governor of Connecticut), held the the preliminary skirmish. The field soon becomes too hot for

---

[1] The following letter was addressed to General Gillmore by President Lincoln, January 13th, 1864:

"Major General GILLMORE:

"I understand an effort is being made by some worthy gentlemen to reconstruct a legal state government in Florida. Florida is in your department, and it is not unlikely that you may be there in person. I have given Mr. Hay a commission of major, and sent him to you with some blank books and other blanks, to aid in the reconstruction. He will explain as to the manner of using the blanks, and also my general views on the subject. It is desirable for all to co-operate, but if irreconcilable differences of opinion shall arise, you are master. I wish the thing done in the most speedy way possible, so that when done it may be within the range of the late proclamation on the subject. The detail labor will of course have to be done by others, but I shall be greatly obliged if you will give it such general supervision as you can find consistent with your more strictly military duties.

A. LINCOLN."

On the 31st of January General Gillmore issued the following order:

"Headquarters Department of the South, Hilton Head, South Carolina, January 31st, 1864.

"In accordance with the provisions of the presidential proclamation of pardon and amnesty, given at Washington on the 8th day of December, in the year of our Lord 1863, and in pursuance of instructions received from the President of the United States, Major John Hay, Assistant Adjutant General, will proceed to Fernandina, Florida, and other convenient points in that state, for the purpose of extending to the citizens of the State of Florida an opportunity to avail themselves of the benefit of that proclamation, by offering for their signature the oath of allegiance therein prescribed, and by issuing to all those subscribing to said oath certificates entitling them to the benefits of the proclamation. Fugitive citizens of the State of Florida within the limits of this department will have an opportunity to subscribe to the same oath, and secure certificates in the office of the post commander at Hilton Head, South Carolina.

"By command of Major General Q. A. GILLMORE.

"E. W. SMITH, Assistant Adjutant General."

[2] *General Gillmore's Report.*

[3] The following are copies of the letters—General Seymour's announcing his movement, and General Gillmore's reply:

"Headquarters Department of the South, February 17th, 1864.

"GENERAL,—The excessive and unexpected delays experienced with regard to the locomotive, which will not be ready for two days yet, if at all, has compelled me to remain where my command could be fed. Not enough supplies could be accumulated to permit me to execute my intention of moving to the Suwanee River.

"But I now propose to go without supplies, even if compelled to retrace my steps to procure them, and with the object of so destroying the railroad near the Suwanee that there will be no danger of carrying away any portion of the track.

"All troops are therefore being moved up to Barber's, and probably by the time you receive this I shall be in motion in advance of that point.

"That a force may not be brought from Georgia (Savannah) to interfere with my movements, it is desirable that a display be made in the Savannah River; and I therefore urge that upon the reception of this, such naval force, transports, sailing vessels, etc., as can be so devoted, may rendezvous near Pulaski, and that the iron-clads in Warsaw push up with as much activity as they can exert.

"I look upon this as of great importance, and shall rely upon it as a demonstration in my favor.

"There is reason to believe that General Bardeo is in Lake City, now possibly in command, and with some force at his disposal.

"But nothing is visible this side of Sanderson. Saddles, etc., for mounting the Seventh New Hampshire as rapidly as possible, are greatly needed, and I shall send a portion of that regiment to this point as soon as it can be spared subsequent to my advance.

"I have sent for the Twenty-fourth Massachusetts entire to come to this po[st] Connecticut (eight companies) is to remain at St. Augustine, two companies to g[o]

"I shall not occupy Picolata or Magnolia at this moment: when I do, portion[s of the Twenty-]fourth Massachusetts will be sent from Jacksonville. The Fifty-fifth Massachu[setts] here for the present, or until the Twenty-fourth relieves it.

"The Second South Carolina and Third South Carolina are at Camp Shaw (la[...] instruction and organization.

"The First North Carolina will be left at Baldwin, detaching three companies

"Colonel Barton will have the Forty-seventh, Forty-eighth, and One Hundre[d] Colonel Hanlay will have the Seventh Connecticut, Seventh New Hampshire, an[d] States Colored; Colonel Montgomery the Third United States and Fifty-fourt[h] Colored; Colonel Henry the cavalry and Elder's battery, and Captain Hamilton t[...] soon as possible, Metcalf's section will be sent back. At present I should like to

"Colonel Goss is ordered to keep six companies in motion from Fernandina c[...] least five days out of seven (every seven) toward and beyond Camp Cooper.

"Nothing appears to have been done upon the locomotive while at Fernandin[a ...re]ported to me.

"The prompt use of a locomotive and a printing-press with this movement v[...] vital importance, and will continue so to be. I trust both will be economized.

"And I am, very respectfully, your obedient servant,

"T. SEYMOUR, Brigadier General [...]

"Brigadier General J. W. TURNER, Chief of Staff:

"Send me a general for the command of the advanced troops, or I shall be in [con]stant uncertainty.

"Hilton Head, South Carolina, Feb[...]

"Brigadier General T. SEYMOUR, Commanding District of Florida:

"I am just in receipt of your two letters of the sixteenth and one of the seve[nteenth ...] very much surprised at the tone of the latter, and the character of your plans a[...] You say that by the time your letter of the seventeenth should reach these he[adquarters your] forces would be in motion beyond Barber's, moving toward the Suwanee River, a[nd ...] rely upon my making a display in the Suwanee River 'with naval force, transp[orts, sailing] vessels,' and with iron-clads up from Warsaw, etc., as a demonstration in your f[avor ...] look upon as of 'great importance.' All this is upon the presumption that th[e ...] can and will be made, although contingent not only upon my power and dispositi[on, but] upon the consent of Admiral Dahlgren, with whom I can not communicate in les[s ...] You must have forgotten my last instructions, which were for the present to ho[ld ...] the St. Mary's south prong as your outposts to the westward of Jacksonville, and [Pico]lata and Magnolia on the St. John's.

"Your prospect distinctly and avowedly ignores these operations, and substitut[es ...] not only involves your command in a distant movement without provisions, far [...] from which you once withdrew on account of precisely the same necessity, but pr[...sim]ultaneous demonstration of 'great importance' to you elsewhere, over which you [...] and which requires the co-operation of the navy. It is impossible for me to dete[rmine what your] views are with respect to Florida matters, and this is the reason why I have endc[avored to make] mine known to you so fully. From your letter of the eleventh instant from Bald[win (a sin]gular letter, by the way, and which you did not modify or refer to at all when yo[u ...] me), I extract as follows:

"'I am convinced that a movement upon Lake City is not, in the present co[ndition of trans]portation, advisable, and, indeed, that what has been said of the desire of Florid[a ...] now is a delusion. This movement is in opposition to sound strategy,' etc.

"And again: 'The Union cause would have been far more benefited by Jeff [Davis having re]moved this railroad to Virginia, than by any trivial or non-strategic success you [...] all means, therefore, fall back to Jacksonville.'

"So much from your letters of the eleventh; and yet, five days later, you prop[ose to go for]ward without instructions and without provisions, with a view to destroying the [railroad which] you say it would have been better for Jeff Davis to have got; and furthermore, [you say in your] letter of the sixteenth: 'There is but little doubt in my mind (but) that the peo[ple, if] kindly treated by us, will soon be ready to return to the Union. They are hea[rtily tired of the] war.'

"As may be supposed, I am very much confused by these conflicting views, [...] into doubt as to whether my intentions with regard to Florida are fully understood[. I] therefore, reannounce them briefly.

"1st. I desire to bring Florida into the Union under the President's proclamat[ion of December] 8th, 1863, as accessory to the above.

"2d. To revive the trade on the St. John's River.

"3d. To recruit my colored regiments, and organize a regiment of Florida whi[tes ...]

"4th. To cut off in part the enemy's supplies drawn from Florida.

"After you had withdrawn your advance, it was arranged between us, at a p[...] that the places to be permanently held for the present would be the south prong o[f the St. Mary's,] Baldwin, Jacksonville, Magnolia, and Picolata, and that Henry's mounted force[s ...] moving as circumstances might justify or require. This is my plan of present [...] raid to tear up the railroad west of Lake City will be of service, but I have no int[ention to occupy] now that part of the state.

"Very respectfully, etc., Q. A. GILLMORE, Major General [...]

"ROBERT N. SCOTT, Captain of U. S. Infantry, A. D. C.

"Headquarters of the Army, Washington, March 16th, 1864."

[1] Only about half of Seymour's force was engaged, the rest being left to hold coast and St. John's River.

and the Seventh New Hampshire is brought up to its support, and this becoming confused, the Eighth United States colored regiment comes into action, some of the men with empty guns, standing its ground with heavy loss for nearly two hours. Barton's brigade of New York troops has at length formed on the right of the line, and Colonel Montgomery, with the Fifty-fourth Massachusetts and First North Carolina (colored), has got into position on the left. All the troops, black and white, fight nobly; but their loss had already been heavy, particularly in officers. Along the railroad an uninterrupted stream of wounded men flows to the rear, and hundreds more of wounded are left behind upon the field, as the line now is driven back, having lost nearly thirteen hundred men in this brief battle. The enemy has lost little over half that number, and nothing but the exhaustion of his ammunition holds him back from pursuit.

Such was the battle of Olustee, fought against orders, and upon the enemy's chosen field. General Seymour was present in the hottest of the fight, but neither his bravery nor that of his troops could avert the disaster which followed inevitably from the very conditions of the conflict. With this defeat active operations in Florida terminated, though the Federal troops continued to hold their position upon the coast.

CHAPTER XXXIX.

THE RED RIVER CAMPAIGN.

Another semi-Political Expedition.—Diplomatic Considerations.—Apprehensions of French Intervention.—Every military Motive in favor of a Campaign against Mobile.—The Government decides in favor of a Campaign in Texas.—The Sabine Pass Expedition; its Failure.—Coast Operations.—Occupation of Brazos Santiago, November 2, 1863; of Brownsville, November 6th; of Point Isabel, November 8th; of Aransas Pass, November 17th; and of Cavallo Pass, November 19th.—Mistake made in continuing a trans-Mississippi offensive Campaign.—Halleck advises a Movement on Shreveport.—Banks's Opinion of the Conditions necessary to a successful Red River Campaign.—These Requirements not met.—Halleck leaves the whole Affair to be settled between Banks, Sherman, and Steele.—Banks ought to have decided against the Movement.—Extent of his Responsibility.—Sherman meets Banks at New Orleans.—He sends A. J. Smith's Command to General Banks.—Steele not prepared.—Kirby Smith's Command.—Banks being detained at New Orleans, General Franklin is intrusted with the immediate command of the Expedition.—Franklin reaches Alexandria March 25th, 1864.—Admiral Porter's Co-operation.—Capture of Fort De Russy.—Difficulty in getting the Gun-boats over the Rapids at Alexandria.—Dépôt established at Alexandria, and Grover's Division detached to guard it.—Ellet's Marine Brigade recalled to Vicksburg.—T. K. Smith's division used for the Protection of Transports.—The Military Branch reduced by 8500 men on account of these Detachments.—Cotton Seizures.—The Army reaches Natchitoches April 2d and 3d, while the Navy proceeds to Grand Ecore.—The Difficulty of Navigation increases.—The Advance toward Mansfield.—Skirmishing with Confederate Cavalry.—The Enemy encountered beyond Pleasant Hill.—Banks arrives at the Front and ventures an Engagement.—He makes a great Mistake.—Federal Defeat at Sabine Cross-roads.—Causes of the Disaster.—A Stand made at Pleasant Grove.—Emory repulses the Enemy and covers the Retreat.—The Retreat continued to Pleasant Hill.—Battle of Pleasant Hill, April 9th.—Importance of this Conflict.—It is decided against the Confederates.—Retreat continued to Grand Ecore.—Admiral Porter's Troubles.—The Confederate Infantry charge upon the Gun-boats, and are worsted.—The Army and Fleet return to Alexandria.—On the way General Banks' defeats the Enemy at Cane River.—The Fleet can not pass the Rapids, and is relieved by Lieutenant Colonel Bailey's Dams.—The Army retreats to Simmsport.—Operations of General Steele's Co-operative Column.—Review of the military Operations in Arkansas in 1863.—Quantrell's Raid.—Capture of Little Rock by General Steele.—Steele advances upon Shreveport from the North.—A Slow Match.—Fight at Prairie d'Anne.—Steele hears of Banks's Reverse, and retreats to Little Rock.—The Political Situation in Arkansas as affected by the Campaign.

FROM the Florida expedition we turn naturally to the Red River campaign. This latter was also urged by the government without much regard to its military importance. The motives which led to its inception were more complex than those which led to the Florida expedition. In addition to political reasons, there were diplomatic considerations of still greater importance. In defiance of the Monroe Doctrine—a doctrine first promulgated in President Monroe's message of December 2, 1823, and indorsed by the whole American people, and which pronounced any interference with the affairs or destiny of any portion of the New World by the powers of the Old a hostile measure to this country, "dangerous to our peace and safety"—three European nations, France, England, and Spain, had in 1861 embarked upon an expedition against Mexico. The originally declared purposes of this joint expedition had appeared to be perfectly legitimate. The civil commotions in Mexico had endangered the liberties of foreign residents in that country, and undermined the security for its large liabilities by debt to foreign powers. The expedition proposed simply to remedy these abuses. The United States government, although its grievances were greater than those of either of the allied powers, except Great Britain, had refused to participate in the expedition, but acceded the legitimacy of its objects as openly declared. Afterward, however, the character of the movement against Mexico was essentially changed. England and Spain withdrew from the alliance, and the Emperor Napoleon entered upon the execution of a scheme which was intended to revolutionize the Mexican government, and to erect an empire upon the ruins of the republic. This was a policy hostile to this country, and, taken in connection with Louis Napoleon's expressed desire to unite with the British government in the recognition of the Confederacy, excited serious apprehension. It was deemed necessary, therefore, that the Federal government should occupy and strongly hold some point in Texas, in order to meet any emergency which might arise out of this foreign complication.

Both General Banks and General Grant, after the capture of Port Hudson and Vicksburg, were in favor of an immediate expedition against Mobile. There were good military reasons for such a movement. The full reward for the sacrifice of the army which had purchased the Mississippi could only be realized by leaving the entire trans-Mississippi region—at least all below the Arkansas River—out of the field of active military operations. The navy, with the co-operation of a few small garrisons, not amounting in the aggregate to more than 20,000 men, would have held the Mississippi against any operations of the enemy. The coast of Texas should have been occupied, and held by about 10,000 men. There should also have been an army of 20,000 men to keep down guerrillas in Missouri and Arkansas, and to prevent the enemy from advancing north of the Arkansas. Thus a Federal army, amounting in all to 50,000 men, would have maintained the defensive on and west of the Mississippi, and 50,000 men[1] would thus have been liberated for the more important, because more decisive operations in Tennessee, Georgia, and Alabama. The campaign against Mobile, if it had been undertaken immediately after the opening of the Mississippi, would have accomplished four important results:

1. It would have relieved Rosecrans—then operating against Chattanooga—more effectively than any other movement could have done.
2. It would have forestalled Sherman's Meridian raid.
3. It would have resulted in the possession of Mobile and of the fertile valleys of the Alabama and Tombigbee Rivers, upon which the Confederate Army of the West mainly relied for corn, and would have secured the Mississippi River against hostile operations from the east.
4. It would have acquired the best possible base for co-operative movements in the event either of an advance of the Federal armies southward upon Atlanta, or westward from South Carolina and Florda. Its success would have justified more formidable expeditions in the two latter states in the winter of 1863–1864, and these would in turn have materially weakened Lee's army in Virginia.

These advantages were fully appreciated by General Grant. But the government decided in favor of a trans-Mississippi campaign, the motives for which were purely of a diplomatic and political character.[2] The earliest

[1] The entire Federal force west of the Mississippi numbered at least 100,000 men.

[2] For farther illustration, we copy the correspondence on this subject between Generals Banks, Halleck, and Grant.

On the 18th of July, 1863, Banks writes to Grant:

"It is my belief that Johnston, when defeated by you . . . . will fall back upon Mobile. Such is also the expectation of the rebels. The capture of Mobile is of importance, second only in the history of the war to the opening of the Mississippi. I hope you will be able to follow him. I can aid you somewhat by land and by sea, if that should be your destination. Mobile is the last strong-hold in the West and Southwest. No pains should be spared to effect its reduction."

On the 26th of July he writes to Halleck:

"There is still strength in Mobile and in Texas which will constantly threaten Louisiana, and which ought to be destroyed without delay. The possession of Mobile and the occupation of Texas would quiet the whole of the Southwest, and every effort should be made to accomplish this. Its importance can hardly be overestimated."

And again, July 30:

"Information from Mobile leads us to believe that the force at that point is now about 5000, which is engaged industriously on the land side in strengthening the position. My belief is that Johnston's forces are moving to the East, and that the garrison of Mobile will not be strengthened, unless it be by paroled men from Vicksburg and Port Hudson; while the rebel army of the East is occupied at Charleston and at Richmond by our forces, it would be impossible for them to strengthen Mobile to any great extent. It seems to be a favorable opportunity for a movement in that direction. An attack should be made by land. Troops can be transported by the river to Mobile, with the intervention of a march of 25 miles from Portersville, on the west side of the bay and the rear of the city. We have outlines of their works, as I can estimate very well their strength. I am confident that a sudden movement, such as can be made with 15,000 or 20,000 men on this line, will reduce that position with certainty and without delay. The troops of the West need rest, and are incapable of long or rapid marches. It is therefore impracticable to attack Mobile except by the river and Mississippi Sound. A portion of General Grant's forces could be transported there with but little labor to themselves, and the place could be invested before the enemy could anticipate our movement."

On August 1 he writes:

"The possession of Mobile gives the government the control of the Alabama River and the line of railways east and west from Charleston and Savannah to Vicksburg, *via* Montgomery, and places the whole of the State of Mississippi and Southern Alabama in position to return to the Union. If the rebel government loses this position, it has no outlet to the Gulf except Galveston. The operation need not last more than 30 days, and can scarcely interfere with any other movements East or West. I understand it to meet with General Grant's approval, if it be consistent with the general plans of the government, upon which condition only I urge it."

August 10, Banks writes to Grant:

"I have the honor to inclose you some memoranda concerning Mobile. I still think it of the utmost moment that that post should be in our hands. Except for Johnston's army, we should have no difficulty. He seems to occupy a position intended to cover Mobile, and if he is in force 30,000 or 40,000 strong, as I suppose, he could embarrass the operations against that point very seriously. I am unable, however, to see how he can hold his position in the Southwest with Rosecrans's army pressing down upon the rebel centre. A line extending from Mobile to Richmond, in the present shattered condition of the rebel armies—the right, centre, and left having been disastrously defeated—it seems to me impossible that they can maintain their positions if Rosecrans, with a heavy force, pushes down upon their centre, or if Charleston shall fall into our hands through the operations of the fleet and army combined. A successful movement in either direction, from Charleston or by Rosecrans, will cut their centre, and place Bragg and Johnston with their forces between the troops under Rosecrans, your troops, and mine at New Orleans. I do not believe that that condition of things can be maintained."

Halleck, on the 12th of August, replies to Banks's dispatches in regard to Mobile:

"I fully appreciate the importance of the operation proposed by you in these dispatches, but *there are reasons other than military* why those heretofore directed should be undertaken first. On this matter we have no choice, but must carry out the views of the government."

The operations "heretofore directed" were against Texas.

On the 8th of January, 1864, Halleck writes to Grant:

"In regard to General Banks's campaign against Texas, it is proper to remark that it was undertaken *less for military reasons than as a matter of state policy. As a military measure simply, it perhaps presented less advantage than a movement on Mobile and the Alabama River, so as to threaten the enemy's interior lines, and effect a diversion in favor of our armies at Chattanooga and in East Tennessee.* But, however this may have been, it was deemed necessary, as a matter of political or state policy connected with our foreign relations, and especially with France and Mexico, that our troops should occupy and hold at least a portion of Texas. The President so considered, for reasons satisfactory to himself and to his cabinet, and it was therefore unnecessary for us to inquire whether or not the troops could have been employed elsewhere with greater military advantage."

When General Banks assumed the command of the Gulf Department, his instructions from General Halleck (dated November 9, 1862) allude to operations to be undertaken after the opening of the Mississippi in the following terms:

"The river being opened, the question arises how the troops and naval forces there can be employed to the best advantage. Two objects are suggested as worthy of your attention:

"First, on the capture of Vicksburg, to send a military force directly East to destroy the railroads at Jackson and Marion, and thus cut off all connection by rail between Northern Mississippi and Mobile and Atlanta. The latter place is now the chief military dépôt of the rebel armies in the West.

"Second, To ascend, with a naval and military force, the Red River as far as it is navigable, and thus open an outlet for the sugar and cotton of Northern Louisiana. Possibly both of these objects may be accomplished, if the circumstances should be favorable. It is also suggested that, having Red River in our possession, it would form the best base for operations in Texas."

On July 24, 1863, Halleck writes to Banks:

"I suppose the first thing done by your army, after the fall of Port Hudson, was to clean out the Teche and Atchafalaya counties. That being accomplished, your next operations must depend very much upon the then condition of affairs. Texas and Mobile will present themselves to your attention. The navy are very anxious for an attack upon the latter place, but I think Tex-

NATHANIEL P. BANKS.

instructions which General Banks received, pointing to Texas as the immediate field of operations, were issued during the last week in July, 1863, shortly after the reduction of Port Hudson. They were not definite as to the plan to be pursued, insisting only upon the occupation of some portion of Texas. Distinctly permission was given Banks to choose his own objective. The movement was again urged in a dispatch from Halleck, dated

as much the most important. It is possible that Johnston may fall back toward Mobile, but I think he will unite with Bragg. While your army is engaged in cleaning out Southwestern Louisiana, every preparation should be made for an expedition into Texas. Should Johnston be driven from Mississippi, General Grant can send you considerable re-enforcements."

July 31, 1863, he writes:

"It is important that we immediately occupy some point or points in Texas. Whether the movement should be made by land or water is not yet decided. . . . . . . If by water, Admiral Farragut will co-operate. The Navy Department recommends Indianola as the point of landing. It seems to me that this point is too distant, as it will leave the expedition isolated from New Orleans. If the landing can be made at Galveston, the country between that place and New Orleans can soon be cleared out, and the enemy be prevented from operating successively upon those places. In other words, you can venture to send a larger force to Galveston than to Indianola. I merely throw out these suggestions, without deciding upon any definite plan till I receive your answer to the former dispatch" [that of July 24].

On the 6th of August Halleck sends the following dispatch to Banks, *via* Vicksburg:

"There are important reasons why our flag should be restored in some point of Texas with the least possible delay. Do this by land, at Galveston, at Indianola, or at any other point you may deem preferable. If by sea, Admiral Farragut will co-operate. There are reasons why the movement should be as prompt as possible."

On the 10th, four days later, Halleck explains this order thus:

"That order, as I understood it at the time, was of a diplomatic rather than of a military character, and resulted from some European complications, or, more properly speaking, was intended to prevent such complications."

Perhaps the following from General Banks to Halleck, August 17, 1863, will throw some light upon the nature of these "foreign" complications:

"I think it my duty to represent that among the French residents of this city [New Orleans] there is evidently an expectation of some assistance from the government of France. This comes informally from the conversation of the French residents here, but too frequently to leave room for doubt that they have some grounds upon which to ground the remarks that are commonly made. This is undoubtedly the conversation of the officers of the French frigate Catinet, which has recently arrived at this port. I do not think it is more than mere surmise on their part, but have thought it worth while to direct the provost-marshal general of the department to investigate the subject and to report the facts as they are, of which I shall give you due notice."

August 20, Halleck writes:

"Mexican and French complications render it exceedingly important that the movement ordered against Texas should be undertaken without delay."

On the 28th he writes:

"Your note in regard to reports in New Orleans respecting French intervention only confirms what we have already received from other sources. While observing every caution to give no cause of offense to that government, it will be necessary to carefully observe the movements of its fleets, and to be continually on your guard. You will readily perceive the object of our immediately occupying some part of Texas."

August 6th, and Admiral Farragut's co-operation was promised, if the attack should be upon the coast. General Banks immediately made preparations for a movement against Houston by way of Sabine Pass. Grant, in obedience to orders from Washington, now sent the Thirteenth Corps to the Department of the Gulf. Including these re-enforcements, Banks had by the first of September an army of 30,000 men.[1]

If the reader will examine the map of Texas, he will find that state intersected by rivers—the Neches, Trinidad, San Jacinto, Brazos, Colorado, Guadalupe, San Antonio, and Nueces—which run from the elevated region of Northern Texas into the Gulf. The Red River, forming the northern boundary of the state, runs through Louisiana into the Mississippi; while the Rio Grande, separating Texas from Mexico, flows into the Gulf. On the eastern or Louisiana border runs the Sabine River, emptying, as does also the Neches, into Lake Sabine, which, by a narrow pass of the same name, communicates with the Gulf. From Sabine Pass, at the eastern extremity of the Texan coast, to Brazos Santiago, near the mouth of the Rio Grande, is about 375 miles. About 70 miles west of Sabine Pass is the entrance to Galveston Bay, which receives the waters of the Trinidad. Galveston Island stretches from the entrance of the harbor some 30 miles southwesterly. Houston lies west of Galveston Bay, about 40 miles inland, and by its central position as the junction of all the roads between the bay and the Rio Brazos, commands Galveston and the large and fertile district south of Montgomery. From the entrance to Galveston Bay to Velasco, the mouth of the Rio Brazos, is about 40 miles; following down the coast from this point, we reach Cavallo Pass, the entrance to Matagorda Bay, with which Aransas Bay communicates, the inlet to the latter being distant about 50 miles from Cavallo Pass. Into Aransas Bay flows the Guadalupe ar Antonio Rivers. Corpus Christi Bay, shut out from the gulf by M Island, joins Aransas. From its inlet to Brazos Santiago is about 90 Forty miles up the Rio Grande lies Brownsville, opposite Matamoras. population and the commerce of the state is concentrated in a belt of ties along the Red and Sabine Rivers and the coast. This belt is r on the north and east as far as Shelbyville, where it widens, and fro coast stretches inland from 150 to 200 miles. It will readily be see the occupation of this coast by the Federal forces would command the valuable portion of Texas, while it would also fully meet the peculiar matic emergency which then confronted the government.]

The expedition sailed from New Orleans on the 5th of September, the command of Major General W. B. Franklin. The military forc sisted of 5000 men of the Nineteenth Corps, the number being limi suit the means of transportation at hand. The naval force consisted c light-draught gun-boats—the Clifton, Arizona, Sachem, and Granite (under the command of Lieutenant Crocker. The aim of the expeditic to secure Sabine City at the mouth of Sabine River. The Pass was s ly protected by works, and the only chance of piercing or capturing was by surprising the enemy. It was supposed that the defenses of works consisted of two 34-pounders, a battery of field-pieces, and two converted into rams. The arrangement made between the naval and tary commanders contemplated an attack at early dawn on the morni

[1] *Report on the Conduct of the War, Red River Campaign*, p. 8.

[1] "The occupation of Houston would place in our hands the control of all the railway nications with Texas; give us command of the most populous and productive part of th enable us to move at any moment into the interior in any direction, or to fall back upon th of Galveston, which could be maintained with a very small force, holding the enemy u coast of Texas, and leaving the Army of the Gulf free to move upon Mobile, in accordan my original plan, or wherever it should be required."—*Banks's Report.*

September 7th by the gun-boats, assisted by about 180 sharp-shooters from the army. After driving the enemy from the works, and repulsing the rams, the troops were to land under cover of the gun-boats, and capture the town. The gun-boats, originally lightly-built merchant vessels, were mere shells as against a well-defended fortress, and it was not expected that they would have any such encounter. If resistance was offered, General Franklin was instructed to land his troops ten or twelve miles below the Pass, and advance by land against the fortifications.[1]

The plan proposed was not carried out, and the expedition proved an utter failure. There was over a day's delay in getting into position, and for 28 hours the fleet was open to the observation of the enemy, who was thus given abundant time for preparation. Captain Crocker, with foolhardy daring, ventured upon a direct attack at 3 P.M. on the 8th. Of course the gun-boats were unable to make any impression upon the works. At 6 A.M. the Clifton stood in the bay, and opened upon the fort, which deigned no reply. The other boats soon followed, and in the afternoon the Sachem, followed by the Arizona, advanced up the eastern channel of the Pass to draw the fire of the fort, while the Clifton and Granite City moved up the western channel to cover the landing of a division under General Weitzel. The fort was silent until the gun-boats were clean abreast of it, when a fire was opened upon them from eight guns. The Clifton on one side, and the Sachem on the other, ran aground in the shallow water under the enemy's guns, and, being disabled, were compelled to surrender. The garrison of the fort consisted only of 47 men—not more than sufficient to man the guns—but it did its work as efficiently as if it had numbered a thousand. It was with great difficulty that the Arizona and Granite City escaped. With these vessels Franklin probably might still have landed the expedition below the pass, but no such attempt was made, and the troops returned on the 11th to New Orleans.[2]

The concentration of the enemy forbade any attempt to repeat the movement. Banks now directed his attention to the chances for a movement overland into Texas, either across Southern Louisiana to the Sabine, or up the Red River to Shreveport. For this purpose his troops were rapidly transferred to the Bayou Teche region. But neither of the movements in view were found practicable. That from the Teche to the Sabine proceeded over a barren country, with little water, for a distance of 300 miles from New Orleans. The route to Shreveport was 200 miles longer, through a country equally destitute of supplies, having been repeatedly overrun by both armies, and occupied by a hostile population. In either movement the army must depend entirely upon wagon transportation.

In the mean time General Herron had been sent to Morganzia, on the Mississippi, above Port Hudson, but on the opposite side. He had established a post several miles inland, garrisoned with about 700 men, under command of Major Montgomery. On the night of September 30th this force was surprised by a detachment of the enemy, who crossed the bayou, surrounded the Federal camp, and captured the artillery and 400 infantry.

The government urged the prompt occupation "of some point in Texas." If it could not be by land, it must be by sea. Accordingly, General Banks again turned to the coast, and organized a small expedition, to be under the command of Major General N. J. T. Dana, for the occupation of the lower Rio Grande. The concentration of the enemy in the southeastern part of Texas seemed to favor this movement.

Dana's expedition, consisting of 4000 men and three gun-boats—the Monongahela, Virginia, and Owasco—and accompanied by General Banks, left New Orleans October 26th. The all-important affair of raising the flag on some portion of the soil of Texas was at length accomplished on the 2d of November. On that day Brazos Santiago was occupied, and on the next the enemy was driven from his position, and the troops ordered up the Rio Grande to Brownsville, which was occupied without resistance on the 6th. The establishment of communications with the mouth of the river was assisted by the friendly offices of the Mexican government, who furnished boats for this purpose. General Dana was left in command of Brownsville, and Banks began to operate against the coast adjacent to Brazos. Point Isabel was occupied on the 8th, and by means of boats troops were transported to Mustang Island, off Corpus Christi Bay. Aransas Pass, east of this island, was occupied on the 17th by a detachment under General T. E. G. Ransom, the works defending the point having been taken by assault, with 100 prisoners and three guns. On the 19th General C. C. Washburne, of the Thirteenth Corps, moved upon Pass Cavallo, commanding the entrance to Matagorda Bay, and defended by strong works and a force of about 2000 men. Fort Esperanza was invested, and, after a brief but gallant resistance, the enemy blew up his magazines, partially dismantled the works, and evacuated the position, retreating to the main land by way of the peninsula near the mouth of Rio Brazos.

Thus, in about three weeks from the occupation of the mouth of the Rio Grande, General Banks was in possession of the whole coast of Texas, with the exception of the works at the mouth of Rio Brazos and the island of Galveston, which were still firmly held by the enemy, who would not abandon them without a desperate struggle. In order to gain possession of these remaining points on the coast—more important than all the others combined—it would be necessary to move inland, and attack them from the rear. In this case the enemy must be encountered in full force. At this point the misfortune of Franklin's failure to obtain Sabine City was painfully evident

[1] *Banks's Report.* These instructions must have been verbal. The written orders allude to no other than a direct attack.

[2] "Had a landing been effected, even after the loss of the boats, in accordance with the original plan, the success of the movement would have been complete, both as it regarded the occupation of Sabine Pass, and operations against Houston and Galveston. The enemy had at this time all his forces in that quarter, and less than a hundred men on the Sabine."—*Banks's Report.*

in its full extent, and the regret which it occasioned General Banks w tense and lasting. Still he felt confident that, by withdrawing the which he had left in the Teche region to the coast, he might succeed i cherished plans against Houston and Galveston. He asked Halleck f enforcements to secure this object, which he deemed of the utmost im ance.[1]

All the diplomatic or political measures involved in General Ba Texas campaign had been successfully carried out. Henceforth the lem was purely military. Unquestionably the best solution of this pro would have been upon the theory of a defensive trans-Mississippi camp Upon this theory General Banks would have been allowed to comple operations against Galveston, and after that would have simply hel coast of Texas with a few small garrisons, and so much of the Techo try as would suffice for the protection of New Orleans on the western The remainder of his army, with as many troops from the armies nor the Arkansas as could be spared after guarding against Kirby Smith' vance north of that river, would have been withdrawn to the east of th sissippi, where they would have been occupied in offensive operations: during the winter, in conjunction with Sherman's troops, against Mobil the railroads connecting Atlanta with Montgomery in Alabama, and Tallahassee in Florida; and, secondly, in the spring of 1864 against At co-operating with the army advancing upon that point from Chattan No greater military mistake could have been made than that which w volved in an *offensive* trans-Mississippi campaign. By such a campaig that had been gained strategically by the possession of the Mississippi er would be thrown away. For what *was* the real strategic importan this possession except in so far as it made the trans-Mississippi region, in the hands of the enemy, and also the trans-Mississippi armies of the federacy, of as little worth to the Confederacy as if they had not exis But to send large Federal armies into this region for offensive opera was to neutralize the vast advantage gained by this isolation—was to the trans-Mississippi territory all the value to the Confederacy whi could possibly have had if the great river had still remained within Co erate control.

It was precisely this mistake which the government now insisted making. While General Banks was perfecting his plans for the captu Galveston, he was diverted from that movement by the urgency with w preparations for an advance up the Red River were recommended by leck and other officers.[2] As we have seen, the political designs of the

[1] "I intended to withdraw my troops to the island of Galveston, which could have bee with perfect security by less than 1000 men, which would have left me free to resume oper suggested in August and September, against Mobile. The Rio Grande and the island of G ton could have been held with 2000 or 3000 men. This would have cut off the contr trade of the enemy at Matamoras and on the Texas coast. The forces occupying the isl Galveston could have been strengthened by sea at any moment from Berwick's Bay, conn with New Orleans by railway or by the river, compelling the enemy to maintain an army Houston, and preventing his concentrating his forces for the invasion of Louisiana, Arkans Missouri. The occupation of the Rio Grande, Galveston, and Mobile would have led to th ture or destruction of all the enemy's river and sea transportation on the Gulf coast, and le Western Gulf blockading squadron, numbering 150 vessels, and mounting 450 guns, free to p the pirates that infested our coast and preyed upon our commerce. The army would have at liberty to operate on the Mississippi, or to co-operate with the Army of the Tennessee Alabama River and Montgomery in the campaign against Atlanta. . . . . It would have bled the government to concentrate the entire forces of the Department of the Gulf, as oc might require, at any point on the river or coast, against an enemy without water transpor or other means of operation than by heavy land marches, or to move by land into the rebel east or west of the Mississippi. The winter months offered a favorable opportunity for suc terprise."—*Banks's Report.*

[2] In order to illustrate the details of the inception of the Red River campaign more fully is possible in the text, we give the substance of the correspondence submitted as evidence the Committee on the Conduct of the War. General Halleck, from the beginning, was part operations on the line of the Red River as preferable to movements on the Texan coast.

August 10, 1863, he writes:

"In my opinion, neither Indianola nor Galveston is the proper point of attack. If it is sary, as urged by Mr. Seward, that the flag be restored to *some one point* in Texas, that can b and most safely effected by a combined military and naval movement up the Red River to andria, Natchitoches, or Shreveport, and the military occupation of Northern Texas. This be merely carrying out the plan proposed by you at the beginning of the campaign [the b ning of the Louisiana campaign, in the spring of 1863], and, in my opinion, far superior in its tary character to the occupation of Galveston or Indianola. Nevertheless, your choice is le restricted. In the first place, by adopting the line of the Red River you retain your conn with your own base, and separate still more the two points of the rebel confederacy. Mor you cut Northern Louisiana and Southern Arkansas entirely off from supplies and re-enforce from Texas. They are already cut off from the rebel states east of the Mississippi. If you o Galveston or Indianola you divide your own troops, and enable the enemy to concentrate forces upon either of these points, or on New Orleans."

To this Banks replies, August 26:

"To enter Texas from Alexandria or Shreveport would bring us at the nearest point to ville, in Sabine county, or Marshall, in Harrison, due west of Alexandria and Shreveport re ively. These points are accessible only by heavy marches, for which the troops are hardly pre at this season of the year; and the points occupied would attract but little attention; and purpose was to penetrate farther into the interior, they would become exposed to sudden a of the enemy, and defensible only by a strong and permanent force of troops.

"The serious objection to moving on this line in the present condition of the forces of th partment is the distance it carries us from New Orleans—our base of operations necessarily- the great difficulty and the length of time required to return, if the exigencies of the s should demand, which is quite possible. In the event of long absence, Johnston threatens us the East. The enemy will concentrate between Alexandria and Franklin, on the Teche, unt purpose is developed. As soon as we move any distance, they will operate against the rive New Orleans. It is true we could follow up such a movement by falling on their rear, bu would compel us to abandon the position in Texas, or leave it exposed with but slender de and garrison. This view is based, as you will see, upon the impossibility of moving even to Al dria, at the present low stage of the rivers, by water, and the inability of the troops to accom extended marches."

September 30, after the failure of the Sabine Pass Expedition, General Halleck writes:

"The failure of the attempt to land at Sabine is only another of the numerous examples uncertain and unreliable character of maritime descents. The chances are against their suc

General Banks writes, October 16:

"The movement upon Shreveport and Marshall is impracticable at present. It would re a march from Brashear City of between four hundred and five hundred miles. The enem stroying all supplies in the country as he retreats, and the low stage of the water making i possible for us to avail ourselves of any water communications, except upon the Teche as f Vermillionville, it requires communication for this distance by wagon trains. Later in the s this can be done, making Alexandria the base of operations; but it could not be done now. rivers and bayous have not been so low in this state for fifty years, and Admiral Porter in me that the mouth of the Red River, and also the mouth of the Atchafalaya, are both hermeti sealed to his vessels by almost dry sand-bars, so that he can not get any vessels into any o streams. It is supposed that the first rise of the season will occur early in the next month."

The following, from General Halleck to Banks, December 7, 1863, could only be constru the latter as a censure of his coast operations:

THE ATTACK ON SABINE PASS.

LANDING OF BANKS'S EXPEDITION ON BRAZOS SANTIAGO.

CONFEDERATE EVACUATION OF BROWNSVILLE.

paign had been effected. Both General Grant and General Banks would then have preferred, after securing Galveston, that all the troops which could be spared from the Department of the Gulf should be withdraw the east side of the Mississippi for operations against Mobile. Ge

"In regard to your 'Sabine' and 'Rio Grande' expeditions, no notices of your intention to make them were received here till they were actually undertaken. The danger, however, of dividing your army, with the enemy between the two posts, ready to fall upon either with his entire force, was pointed out from the first, and I have continually urged that you must not expect any considerable re-enforcements from other departments."

To this Banks replies, December 28:

"My orders from the department were to establish the flag of the government in Texas at the earliest possible moment. I understood that the point and the means were left at my discretion. It was implied, if not stated, that time was an element of great importance in this matter, and that the object should be accomplished as speedily as possible. In addition to the instructions received from your department upon this subject, the President addressed me a letter, borne by Brigadier General Hamilton, military governor of Texas, dated September 19, 1863, in which he expressed the hope that I had already accomplished the object so much desired. In the execution of this order, my first desire was to obtain possession of Houston; and the expedition which failed to effect a landing at the Sabine was designed to secure that object. The failure of that expedition made it impossible to secure a landing at that point. I immediately concentrated all my disposable force upon the Teche, with a view to enter Texas by the way of Niblett's Bluff, on the Sabine, or by Alexandria, at some more northern point. The low stage of water in all the rivers, and the exhaustion of supplies in that country, made it apparent that this route was impracticable at this season of the year—I might say impossible within any reasonable time—and it would be accomplished by imminent peril, owing to the condition of the country, the length of marches, and the strength of the enemy, making this certain by thorough reconnoissance of the country; but, without withdrawing my troops, I concluded to make another effort to effect a landing at some point upon the coast of Texas, in the execution of what I understood to be imperative orders. For this purpose I withdrew a small force stationed at Morganzia, on the Mississippi, which had been under command of General Herron, and was then under Major General Dana, and put them in a state of preparation for this movement.

"Assisted by the commander of the naval forces, Commodore Bell, I directed a reconnoissance of the coast of Texas as far as Brazos Santiago, making my movements entirely dependent upon that report. A return from this reconnoissance was made October 16, and my troops being in readiness for movement somewhere, without the delay of a single day, except that which the state of the weather made necessary, I moved for the Brazos. You will see from these facts that it was impossible for me to give you sufficient notice of this intention to receive instructions from you upon this subject; but as soon as I had received the information necessary, or arrived at the determination to land at the Brazos, I gave you full information of all the facts in the case. It is my purpose always to keep you informed of all movements that are contemplated in this department, but it did not seem to me to be possible to do more in this instance; and, upon a review of the circumstances, I can not now see where or when I could have given you more complete and satisfactory information than my dispatches conveyed.

"I repeat my suggestion that the best line of defense for Louisiana, as well as for operations against Texas, is by Berwick's Bay and the Atchafalaya, and I also recall the suggestions made by you upon the same subject. But that line was impracticable at the time when I received your orders upon the subject of Texas. I ought to add that the line of the Atchafalaya is available for offensive or defensive purposes only when the state of the water admits the operations of a strong naval force. At the time when I made this suggestion to you it was impossible to get a boat into the Atchafalaya, either from Red River or from the Gulf, owing to the low stage of the water, and there were very few, if any, boats on the Mississippi or in this department that could have navigated these waters at that time. It was therefore impossible to avail myself of this natural line—first, for the reason that we had not sufficient naval force for this purpose, and that the navigation was impossible. As soon as the Mississippi and Red Rivers shall rise, the government can make available the advantages presented by this line of water communication."

A week later Banks again writes, urging the importance of the capture of Galveston before entering upon the Red River campaign:

"It is my desire, if possible, to get possession of Galveston. This, if effected, will give us control of the entire coast of Texas, and require but two small garrisons, one on the Rio Grande, and the other on Galveston Island, unless it be the wish of the Department of War that extensive operations should be made in the State of Texas. A sufficient number of men can probably be recruited in that state for the permanent occupation of these two posts. It will relieve a very large number of naval vessels, whose service is now indispensable to us, on the Mississippi and in the Gulf. This can occupy but a short time, and, if executed, will leave my whole force in hand to move to any other point on the Red River, or wherever the government may direct. Once possessed of Galveston, and my command ready for operation in any other direction, I shall await the orders of the government; but I trust that this may be accomplished before undertaking any other enterprise. It is impossible, at this time, to move as far north as Alexandria by water. The Red River is not open to the navigation of our gun-boats, and it is commanded by Fort De Russy, which has been remounted since our occupation of Alexandria. This position must be turned by means of a large force on land before the gun-boats can pass. To co-operate with General Steele in Arkansas, or north of the Red River, will bring nearly the whole rebel force of Texas and Louisiana between New Orleans and my command, without the possibility of dispersing or defeating them, as their movement would be directed south, and mine to the north. It is necessary that this force should first be dispersed or destroyed before I can safely operate in conjunction with General Steele. Once possessed of the coast of Texas, and the naval and land forces relieved, I can then operate against the forces in Louisiana or Texas, and I can disperse or destroy the land forces in Louisiana, and safely co-operate with General Steele, or with any other portion of the army of the United States. It was in this manner that we captured Port Hudson. It would have been impracticable to proceed against Port Hudson from the Mississippi without having first dispersed the army of Texas and Louisiana on the west of that river.

"I bear in mind the danger consequent upon the division of forces, but must suggest to you that my department is extended, and many posts must be occupied; and while I would be very glad to keep my forces concentrated, it is impossible to do so. The orders of the government seemed to be peremptory that I was to occupy a position in Texas, and those which I have in view, Brownsville and Galveston, required as little force as any other positions in that state. To this fact it may be added that there were supplies and recruits which can not be found in any other portion of this department. In all my operations you may rely upon the bulk of my forces being kept together, and prepared for any movements of the enemy. It is possible, but not probable, that they may make a successful assault upon some of the isolated positions. We shall endeavor to prevent this by all possible means. I repeat, that in any movements in which I engage I shall concentrate the available forces of my command, and peril nothing by an unnecessary division. * * * * * *

"The true line of occupation, in my judgment, offensive and defensive, for this department is the Atchafalaya and the Mississippi. The Teche country, and that between the Atchafalaya and the Mississippi, can be defended only by the assistance of the navy. It is impossible for land forces to operate on that line successfully without the assistance of gun-boats. The best position that we could occupy will be to defend this line by the aid of a strong naval force of light and heavy draught gun-boats for the different waters in which they may operate, and the disposable land forces so held as to be able to move from one point to another in a body. We should then have one complete line of water navigation from the Rio Grande to Alexandria or Shreveport during the winter and spring, and from the mouth of the Mississippi to Key West, in the Gulf, and could throw our entire force against any point of the territory occupied by the enemy, without the possibility of their anticipating our movements or purposes. I am endeavoring constantly to secure means for offensive and defensive war upon this plan, and am confident that it can be very speedily accomplished."

Halleck, in his reply to Banks, January 11, 1864, makes no allusion to Galveston. He says:

"I am assured by the Navy Department that Admiral Porter will be prepared to co-operate with you as soon as the stage of the water in the Southwest will admit of the use of his flotilla there. General Steele's command is now under the general orders of General Grant, and it is hoped that he and General Sherman may also be able to co-operate with you at an early day. General Sherman is now on the Mississippi River, and General Grant expects to soon be able to re-enforce him. . . . . It has never been expected that your troops would operate north of the Red River, unless the rebel forces in Texas should be withdrawn into Arkansas; but it was proposed that General Steele should advance to Red River if he could rely upon your co-operation, and he could be certain of receiving supplies upon that line. Being uncertain on these points, he determined not to attempt an advance, but to occupy the Arkansas River as his line of defense.

"The best military opinions of the generals in the West seem to favor operations on the Red River, provided the stage of water will enable gun-boats to co-operate. I presume General Sherman will communicate with you on this subject. If the rebels could be driven south of that river, it would serve as a shorter and better line of defense for Arkansas and Missouri than that now occupied by General Steele; moreover, it would open to us the cotton and slaves of Northeastern Louisiana and Southern Arkansas. I am inclined to think that this opens a better field of operations than any other for such troops as General Grant can spare during the winter. I have written to him and also to General Steele upon the subject."

General Banks, it will be remembered, has all along conceded that the line of the Red River was the best base of operations against Texas, but it was only practicable at high water. There were also some important difficulties connected with an advance by this route which he considered it his duty to lay before General Halleck. Hence the following correspondence. Jan. 23 he writes:

"*With the forces you propose*, I concur in your opinion, and with Generals Sherman and S 'that the Red River is the shortest and best line of defense for Louisiana and Arkansas, an base of operations against Texas,' but it would be too much for General Steele or myself dertake separately. With our united forces, and the assistance of General Sherman, the s of movements on that line will be certain and important. I shall most cordially co-operat them in executing your orders. With my own command I can operate with safety only c coast of Texas, but from the coast I could not penetrate far into the interior, nor secure c of more than the country west of San Antonio. On the other line, *with commensurate forc* whole state, as well as Arkansas and Louisiana, will be ours, and their people will gladly allegiance to the government. The occupation of Shreveport will be to the country west Mississippi what that of Chattanooga is to the east, and as soon as this can be accomplishe country west of Shreveport will be in condition for a movement into Texas. I have writ General Sherman and General Steele in accordance with these views, and shall be ready with them as soon as the Atchafalaya and Red River will admit the navigation of our gun-b Our supplies can be transported by the Red River until April, at least. In the mean tim railway from Vicksburg to Shreveport ought to be completed, which would furnish communic very comfortably for the whole of Eastern Texas. I do not mean that operations should b ferred for this purpose, but, as an ultimate advantage in the occupation of these states and t tablishment of governments, it would be of great importance.

"I inclose to you with this communication a very complete map of the Red River countr Texas, which embraces all the information we have been able to obtain up to this time. I been prepared by Major D. C. Houston, of the Engineer Corps, and will show that we have overlooked the importance of this line. Accompanying this map is a memorial which exl the difficulties that are to be overcome. To this I respectfully invite your attention. I have to General Sherman and General Steele copies of this map.

"I shall be ready to move on Alexandria as soon as the rivers are up, most probably marc by Opelousas. This will be necessary to turn the forts on the Red River and open the way fo gun-boats. From that point I can operate with General Steele, north or south of Red Rive the direction of Shreveport, or from thence await your instruction. I do not think opera will be delayed on my account. I have received a dispatch from General Sherman, in whic expresses a wish to enter upon the campaign, but had not at that time received orders upo subject. . . . . I can concentrate on Red River all my force available for active service cept the garrisons at Matagorda and Brownsville, which will be small."

He adds, January 29:

"I shall be ready to operate with General Sherman and General Steele as soon as I rec definite information of the time when they will be ready to move. I can take possession of A andria at any time, but could not maintain the position without the support of the forces on upper river. . . . . Pending information and orders in regard to the movement on River, but little change has occurred in the position of troops. . . . . Anxiously wai information and instructions in regard to operations on Red River, I have done nothing in T except provide for the security of the positions held."

The following is a copy of Major Houston's memorial, dated January 22, 1864:

"I have the honor to submit the following information concerning the routes from the Mi sippi to the interior of Texas:

"*Table of Distances.*

	Miles.		Miles
Brashear City to Alexandria	174	Little Rock to Shreveport	2.5
Brashear City to Shreveport	344	Fort Smith to Shreveport	300
Natchez to Alexandria (*via* Harrisonburg)	80	Alexandria to Shreveport	170
Natchez to Natchitoches	120	Alexandria to Houston	270
Vicksburg to Shreveport	143	Shreveport to Houston	2 5

"The water *via* Red River commences falling about the 1st of May, and the navigation of river for most of our gun-boats and transports is not reliable after that time. The months March and April are unfavorable for operations in Northern and Eastern Texas, owing to the h stage of water in the Sabine, Nueces [meant for Neches], and Trinity [Trinidad] Rivers and tributaries, and the overflow to which their banks are subject. The concentration of all the fo available for operations west of the Mississippi, in the vicinity of Shreveport, requires that the of supply with the Mississippi be kept up. It would not be practicable to abandon the base w so large a force, with a line of operations of three hundred miles through a country occupied the enemy to be overcome before communication could possibly be effected with points held by on the coast. The water communication to Alexandria can not be depended on after the 1st May, and it would be necessary to depend on the road from Natchez, a distance of eighty mil and possibly from Harrisonburg, a distance of fifty miles.

"Boats of a very light draught, say three or three and a half feet of water, may go to Alex dria during low water at ordinary seasons, but the larger majority of our boats and gun-boats of greater draught than this.

"The most reliable route would be by railroad from Vicksburg to Shreveport. The track now laid from Vicksburg to Monroe. The road is graded from Monroe to Shreveport, and nic bridged; the distance is ninety-six miles. There is a good wagon-road from Monroe to Shre port, crossing the Washita River and other streams. It would require at least three months rebuild this railroad, which is indispensable to the supply of our army in Northeastern Texas.

"To insure success and permanent results to the operations of a force to operate against Tex or rather against the rebel forces west of the Mississippi, it is essential that the forces available this purpose, viz., those now west of the Mississippi, and any additional forces that may be assi ed, *should be placed under the command of a single general*. The rebel forces west of the Mississi have a single head, and so should the force operating against them.

"*Preparations should be made to establish a line of supply independent of the water-courses*, oth wise, by the time the forces are concentrated and ready to move forward, they will be compel to halt until a new line of supply is established, thus giving the enemy a breathing spell, and opportunity to harass our communications with their mounted troops. It is of vital importance operations of this kind, where the distances traveled are so great, that there should be no dela for our main security against raids on our communications consists in keeping the enemy so occupied in taking care of himself that he will have no time or opportunity to trouble us. He the importance of thorough preparation and perfect concert of action among the different corp

"Suppose it is determined to concentrate the forces near Shreveport preliminary to a movem into Texas. This point is the principal dépôt of the enemy west of the Mississippi. There some machine-shops and dock-yards there, and the place is fortified by a line of works will radius of two or three miles. The position is a strong one, being on a bluff, and commanding eastern bank. This point suggests itself at once as the proper one for such a concentrati *The most direct and only reliable line of supply to this point would be the road from Vicksburg Monroe*—railroad as far as Monroe, fifty-two miles, and a graded road the rest of the way, nine six miles. It would be necessary to put the road in running order, and procure materials completing the road. The security of this road requires that the enemy be driven out of North Louisiana and Southern Arkansas. This line could be held more easily than the Red River, wh is very narrow and crooked, and has in many places high bluff banks, where field artillery co be placed to enfilade the channels, and have no fear of gun-boats. Such a point is Grand Eco where the bluff is one hundred and twenty feet high. This point, I have been informed by spi is fortified. Concerning the mode of uniting the forces near Shreveport, I will mention no deta as it will depend much upon the enemy's movements and the character of the routes in South Arkansas, which I have not had time to examine fully. Our forces there have doubtless the formation necessary to arrange this matter. These movements, however, should be so arranged to drive the enemy out of Arkansas and Northern Louisiana.

"I anticipate no danger from any large force moving on New Orleans, Louisiana, from Tex In case of this movement, our forces would immediately come in on the rear of this force and it off.

"The enemy will, I think, be unable to interfere seriously with our concentration of troops, will then mass his whole force, except that at Galveston, near Shreveport, where he will fight, retire on the line he may select.

"Suppose our force to be united at Shreveport, which would probably be effected during season of high water, and that arrangements have been perfected to supply the army by the ro from Vicksburg *via* Monroe, Arkansas and Louisiana clear of rebels, and the enemy in retre I assume that he will do this, as our forces should be much larger than his, and that he will co tinue to retreat, knowing that we will be weakened thereby, while he can select a defensive po tion far from our base. Whatever way he takes we must follow, and expect to have our path d puted at every point, as he will be driven to desperate efforts. The numerous streams with hi banks will afford him a favorable opportunity to retard our progress and effect a secure retreat any point he may select.

"Our subsequent movements can not well be foreseen. It does not seem probable that enemy will retire to Houston unless his force is large, and he should propose to draw us into trap. It is more probable that he will retire farther west, and use his cavalry to harass our flan and rear, a species of war peculiarly adapted to Central and Western Texas. We should *then* prepared for a most active campaign, and our force of cavalry should be especially large and ef cient.

"Again recurring to the line of supply, it will be seen that the Vicksburg and Shreveport Ra extends to Marshall, where there is an interval of 40 miles to Henderson, whence the road completed to Galveston. The road from Marshall to Henderson, however, is graded, and con

Banks was by no means averse to an offensive campaign west of the Mississippi. In his evidence before the Committee on the Conduct of the War, he says: "If you cripple or scatter the enemy's army of the James, he will take refuge first in the Appalachian range of mountains, and ultimately in the country west of the Mississippi, and there reorganize. Therefore it was wise and expedient for us first to have cleared that country and held it, so that they could not cross the Mississippi. The enemy should be held on this side of the Mississippi, between the mountains and the Atlantic and the Gulf coasts." Nor was he opposed to the line of the Red River as a base of operations against Texas. He repeatedly admitted that this was the shortest and best line for that purpose. But he did insist upon certain conditions as necessary to operations from this base.

1. In the first place, the Red River campaign could not be undertaken until the waters of the river were high enough to admit Porter's gun-boats and heavy-draught transports.

---

be completed in a short time. In case the enemy should abandon the coast, this road will fall into our possession, and supplies could be obtained from two directions. Our colored troops, who are especially qualified for fighting guerrillas, would be usefully employed in guarding the entire line of the road from Vicksburg to Galveston. Texas is said to be full of blacks, who will be a valuable auxiliary in our operations in that state.

"The campaign above sketched would, I believe, be a long one. Much preparation and labor will be required to insure the army against vexatious delays, which permit the enemy constantly to elude us.

"I should estimate roughly that it would require until some time in May to effect the union of forces and be prepared with transportation for a movement into the interior. This would be about the commencement of the season most favorable for active operations in Texas. I suppose that by that time wagon trains will be provided to haul supplies from Monroe to Shreveport, that the railroad will be in running order to Monroe, and the work of completing the road well under way. The time required for subsequent operations can not be well estimated. It is highly probable that the rebel army will suffer greatly from desertion—an easy matter in active campaigning. The Arkansians will probably leave in the greatest numbers. Should their army, however, hold together, they will be able to prolong the contest some time.

"The results of this campaign will be very great. As long as we are able to keep the enemy actively engaged in Texas, Arkansas and Louisiana will be safe, and the process of reconstruction can be carried on without interruption; and should those states establish loyal state governments, there can be no doubt that desertions would be very numerous.

"This plan of operations has these advantages over that of operations from the coast of Texas. It also has the advantage of enabling us to bring a much larger force of cavalry into the field.

"It is, however, a much more difficult plan to execute, requires much more time, and is much more uncertain as to the time it will require to accomplish any of the objects undertaken.

"The movement by the coast of Texas possesses the great advantage of enabling us to deceive the enemy as to our intentions, which is not the case with the other plan. Our troops and supplies can be quickly moved by steamers to any point on the coast, landing can be threatened at different points, and the enemy kept in ignorance of our intentions. We now hold the harbor of Matagorda, the best on the coast next to Galveston. We have a secure point for the debarkation of troops and supplies. The distance by land to Houston is 150 miles, over good roads; three in number; one *via* Texana and Wharton; one *via* Matagorda and Columbia; the third along the beach to the mouth of Brazos River. Very little baggage need be required on the march, as the point of supply can be transferred to Brazos River and Sabine Pass in succession. A much less force would be required for this operation than the other. The rebel forces now in Arkansas will remain there as long as our forces are opposed to them, and we would only have to meet the force in Lower Texas. To direct and draw off this force as much as possible, the following plan could be adopted: Every preparation should be made for debarking the troops at Matagorda and transferring them to the main land. The troops intended to be sent should be designated and collected at New Orleans, so as to go aboard at a moment's notice. The steamers should be got ready and the troops assigned. All the heavy material, artillery, horses, etc., should be placed on board the light-draught vessels, having only men and light stores to be lightened. A demonstration of gun-boats, and troops in transports, could then be made at Alexandria in moderate forces, the effect of which would be to withdraw the enemy from Lower Texas. This having been effected, the force at New Orleans should be sent with all dispatch to Texas, the forces marched to Houston without delay, and Galveston be invested, and the garrison captured unless they hurriedly evacuated. This would give us entire control of the coast of Texas in a comparatively short time.

"For subsequent operations we would not be as well prepared as we would be at Shreveport with our forces concentrated. The object we started out with would have been accomplished, viz., the possession of the coast. The object proposed by the movement *via* Shreveport is much greater than the other, and hence requires more time and means. That direct object is no less than the complete destruction or scattering of the rebel forces west of the Mississippi, and it will be impracticable to stop short of this result.

"To attempt simply to hold Shreveport as a post would subject us to continued annoyance as long as an organized force remains in Texas. They would make continued raids on our flank and rear, and our resources would be gradually frittered away. The rebel army must be pursued till it is broken up, and then we can occupy the country and restore order.

"I have written the above in some haste necessarily, and have endeavored to make my ideas clear, though they may be somewhat boldly expressed. A strict comparison between the two plans of operations can hardly be made, as their objects are different. The only question is, which can be most successfully carried out. The results provided by the first plan are much more satisfactory, and they include those of the second. I do not believe, with some, in the impossibility of long land marches *with a large force*, but I am fully aware of the difficulties to be overcome, and the uncertainty of foreseeing results."

On the receipt of this memorial, General Halleck writes February 1:

"Your dispatches of January 23, transmitting report and map of Major Houston, are received. This report and map contain very important and valuable information.

"The geographical theatre of the war west of the Mississippi indicates Shreveport as the most important objective point of the operations of a campaign for troops moving from the Teche, the Mississippi, and Arkansas Rivers.

"Of course, the strategic advantages of this point may be more than counterbalanced by disadvantages of communications and supplies. General Steele reports that he can not advance to Shreveport this month unless certain of finding supplies on the Red River, and of having there the co-operation of your forces or those of General Sherman.

"If the Red River is not navigable, and it will require months to open any other communication to Shreveport, there seems very little prospect of the requisite co-operation or transportation of supplies. It has, therefore, been left entirely to your discretion, after fully investigating the question, to adopt this line or substitute any other. It was proper, however, that you should have an understanding with Generals Steele and Sherman, as it would probably be hazardous for either of those officers to attempt the movement without the co-operation of other troops.

"If the country between the Arkansas and Red Rivers is impassable during the winter, as has been represented, it was thought that a portion of General Steele's command might be temporarily spared to operate with Sherman from the Mississippi. The Department of Arkansas was therefore made subject to the orders of General Grant.

"It is quite probable that the condition of affairs in East Tennessee, so different from what General Grant anticipated when he detached General Sherman, may have caused him to modify his plans, or, at least, to postpone their execution. This may also prevent your receiving the expected aid from Sherman. Communications by the Mississippi River are so often interrupted, and dispatches delayed, that I am not advised where General Sherman now is, or what are his present plans.

"So many delays have already occurred, and the winter is now so far advanced, that I greatly fear no important operations west of the Mississippi will be concluded in time for General Grant's proposed campaign in the spring. This is greatly to be regretted, but perhaps is unavoidable, as all our armies are greatly reduced by furloughs, and the raising of new troops progresses very slowly. Re-enforcements, however, are being sent to you as rapidly as we can possibly get them ready for the field.

"Have you not over-estimated the strength of the enemy west of the Mississippi River? All the information we can get makes the whole rebel force under Magruder, Smith, and Price much less than ours under you and General Steele. Of course you have better sources of information than we have here."

On the 11th of February General Halleck writes:

"Your dispatches of January 29 and February 2 are received. In the former you speak of awaiting "orders" and "instructions" in regard to operations on Red River. If by this is meant that you are waiting for orders from Washington, there must be some misapprehension. The substance of my dispatches to you on this subject was communicated to the President and Secretary of War, and it was understood that, while stating my own views in regard to operations, I should leave you free to adopt such lines and plans of campaign as you might, after a full consideration of the subject, deem best. Such, I am confident, is the purport of my dispatches, and it certainly was not intended that any of your movements should be delayed to await instructions from here. It was to avoid any delay of this kind that you were requested to communicate directly with Generals Sherman and Steele, and concert with them such plans of co-operation as you might deem best, under all the circumstances of the case.

"My last communication from General Sherman is dated January 29, 1864, and received here to-day. He says the stage of water in Red River is such that he can not operate in that direction earlier than March or April, and that in the mean time he would operate on the east side of the Mississippi River. I think he had not then communicated with you."

Turning now for a moment from the correspondence between Halleck and Banks, we find that the former, in his dispatches to General Grant on the subject of the trans-Mississippi campaign, clearly intimates that Banks's operations west of the river must continue during the winter, and that, while he partially recommends the Red River campaign, he leaves it to General Grant's discretion as to how far or in what manner he will allow Generals Steele and Sherman to co-operate. On January 8th he writes to Grant:

"Keeping in mind that General Banks's operations in Texas, either on the Gulf coast or by the Louisiana frontier, must be continued during the winter, it is to be considered whether it will not be better to direct our efforts, for the present, to the entire breaking up of the rebel forces west of the Mississippi River, rather than divide them by operating against Mobile and the Alabama. If the forces of Smith, Pierce, and Magruder could be so scattered or broken as to enable Steele and Banks to occupy Red River as a line of defense, a part of their armies would probably become available for operations elsewhere. General Banks reports his present force as inadequate for the defense of his position and for operations in the interior; and General Steele is of the opinion that he can not advance beyond the Arkansas or Sabine unless he can be certain of co-operation and supplies on Red River. Under these circumstances, it is worth considering whether such forces as Sherman can move down the Mississippi River should not co-operate with the armies of Steele and Banks on the west side. Of course, operations of any of your troops in that direction must be subordinate, and subsequent to those which you have proposed for East and West Tennessee. I therefore present these views at this time merely that they may receive your attention and consideration in determining upon your ulterior movements."

Again, on the 17th of January:

"General Banks represents the condition of affairs in his department to be such as to require all the re-enforcements that we can possibly send him. As soon as I found that he had divided his forces by operating upon the Gulf coast, I urged that troops should be sent him from South Carolina, and that the attack on Charleston should be abandoned. It was decided otherwise. My opinion has been, and still is, that all troops not required to hold our position in Virginia and on the Atlantic coast should be sent to you and to General Banks for operations this winter, and as preparatory to a spring campaign. I hoped that by this means Tennessee, Arkansas, Mississippi, and Louisiana would be secured, and the rebel force in Texas be so reduced and hemmed in as to give us but little trouble hereafter. Our armies in the west and south could then have been so concentrated, or at least could have so co-operated as to inflict some terrible blows upon the rebels. But I fear that the unexpected condition of affairs in East Tennessee will prevent the accomplishment of these objects, or at least a part of them, this winter, and that we must soon prepare for a spring campaign. The furloughing of so many troops has greatly reduced our forces in the North, but I hope to send some more to General Banks. There is, however, much difficulty and delay in obtaining transportation by sea. This makes it still more important that the navigation of the Mississippi should be well protected, and that Sherman and Steele should so operate as to assist General Banks as much as possible. I leave it entirely to your judgment to determine how and to what extent such assistance can be rendered."

Grant appears to have been willing that Sherman, after his Meridian campaign, should co-operate with General Banks in the movement on Shreveport, provided the time occupied in this operation would not interfere with the spring campaign against Atlanta. Sherman was himself very partial to the project. On the 31st of January he writes to General Banks:

"The Mississippi, though low for the season, is free from ice and in good boating order, but I understand Red River is still low. I had a man in from Alexandria yesterday, who reported the falls or rapids at that place impassable save to the smallest boats.

"My inland expedition is now working, and will be off for Jackson, etc., to-morrow. The only fear I have is in the weather. . . . My orders from General Grant will not, as yet, justify me in embarking for Red River, though I am very anxious to operate in that direction. The moment I learned that you were preparing for it, I sent communication to Admiral Porter, and dispatched to General Grant at Chattanooga, asking if he wanted me and Steele to co-operate with you against Shreveport, and I will have his answer in time, for you can not do any thing till Red River has twelve feet of water on the rapids of Alexandria. That will be from March to June. I have lived on Red River, and know somewhat of the phases of that stream. The expedition on Shreveport should be made rapidly, by simultaneous movements from Little Rock on Shreveport, from Opelousas on Alexandria, and a combined force of gun-boats and transports directly up Red River. Admiral Porter will be able to have a splendid fleet by March 1. I think Steele could move with 10,000 infantry and 5000 cavalry. I could take about 10,000, and you could, I suppose, the same. Your movement from Opelousas simultaneous with mine up the river would compel Dick Taylor to leave Fort De Russy, near Marksville, and the whole could appear at Shreveport about a day appointed. I doubt if the enemy would risk a siege, although they are, I am informed, fortifying, and placing many heavy guns. It would be better for us that they should stand at Shreveport, as we might make large and important captures.

"But I do not believe the enemy would fight a force of 30,000 men with gun-boats. I will be most happy to take part in the proposed expedition, and hope, before you have made up your dispositions, I will have the necessary permission. . . . . I think by March 1 I could put afloat for Shreveport 10,000 men, provided I succeed in my present plan of clearing the Mississippi, and breaking up the railroad about Meridian."

By the 1st of March it is clear that the Red River campaign had been fully decided upon, so far as Generals Grant, Sherman, and Banks, and Admiral Porter were concerned. Banks writes to Halleck March 6th:

"Major General Sherman, of General Grant's department, arrived in this city [New Orleans] on the evening of the 1st instant, having completed his expedition to Meridian to his entire satisfaction. He returned to Vicksburg on the evening of the 3d, to arrange for his co-operation in the Red River movement. Unless delayed by want of steam transportation, of which we have put every thing we have at his command, he will be ready to join me on the Red River by the 17th, where I hope to be at that date. He expects to furnish 10,000 men for that purpose.

"Captain Dunham, of my staff, returned from the headquarters of General Steele yesterday, bearing communications from him, copies of which will be forwarded to you. General Steele appears to have changed the plan entertained when he last communicated with me. Copies of his dispatches at that time have been forwarded to you. He then proposed to move by the way of Monroe for the Red River. He is now apprehensive, in consequence of the reduction of his force, that he can only enter upon a movement for the diversion of the enemy in the direction of Arkadelphia, without any expectation of joining us at Shreveport, or any other position on the river. General Sherman and myself have earnestly urged him to abandon this idea, that, in any event, the three forces in the course of thirty days would meet at Shreveport. General Steele represents that he will have about 6000 men at his command. I respectfully request that orders may be given to him to co-operate with us upon the point named, in accordance with the plans originally proposed by you. I see nothing to defeat its success. Admiral Porter is ready to move up the river in co-operation with us as soon as his vessels can be admitted. General McClernand has been assigned to the command of the troops in Texas, and will leave for an examination of the posts at Matagorda Bay and Brownsville to-morrow. Brigadier General Ransom will have command of the Thirteenth Army Corps, which participates in the movement on the Red River."

General Steele said the movement was earlier than he had anticipated. A large number of his troops were on furlough, and the presence of the remainder was necessary in order to secure the success of an election to be held March 14th. He writes to General Halleck March 12:

"General Banks with 17,000, and 10,000 of Sherman's, will be at Alexandria on the 17th instant. This is more than equal for any thing Kirby Smith can bring against them. Smith will run. By holding the line of the Arkansas secure, I can soon free this state from armed rebels. Sherman insists upon my moving upon Shreveport to co-operate with the above-mentioned forces with all my effective force. I have prepared to do so against my own judgment and that of the best-informed people here. The roads are most, if not quite impracticable; the country is destitute of provisions on the route we should be obliged to take. I made a proposition to General Banks to threaten the enemy's flank and rear with all my cavalry, and to make a feint with infantry on the Washington Road. I yielded to Sherman, so far as this plan is concerned. Blunt wished me to move by Monroe to Red River; Sherman wants me to go by Camden and Overton to Shreveport. The latter is impracticable, and the former would expose the line of the Arkansas and Missouri to cavalry raids. Holmes has a large mounted force. I agreed to move by Arkadelphia or Hot Springs and Washington to Shreveport. I can move with 7000, including the frontier. Our scouting-parties frequently have skirmishes with detached parties all over the state, and if they should form in my rear in considerable force I should be obliged to fall back to save my dépôts, etc."

On the 18th of March Halleck advised Steele to co-operate with the movement of Banks and Sherman on Shreveport. The appointment of Grant as lieutenant general rendered Sherman's presence necessary at Chattanooga, so that he did not in person direct the movements of his troops in the Red River campaign.

2. It should be undertaken with a commensurate force.

3. Time must be given sufficient for the accomplishment of its great object—the defeat of Kirby Smith's armies.

4. And as this prolongation of the campaign would compel the army, after the 1st of May at least, to depend upon some line of supply independent of the water-courses, it was necessary that the railroad from Vicksburg to Shreveport should be put in running order.

5. Finally, as forces from other departments must participate in the campaign, Banks urged the necessity that the operations of all should be under the control of a single general.

All these conditions were distinctly insisted upon by General Banks, and the importance of each was fully explained. If they had all been met; if the campaign had been in season, undertaken with adequate forces, free from any arbitrary limitations in regard to time, supported by land communication with Vicksburg, and controlled by a single head, even then the difficulties encountered would have been as great as in any other campaign of the war. The requirements of the campaign could not be answered—at least not in the spring of 1864.

1. The time at which the movement might commence could not be calculated with certainty. It would have been safe ordinarily to have predicted a sufficient rise of the Red River in March. But in 1864 it was not safe. The Mississippi and Red Rivers, during the winter, had been lower than they had been for years. It was reasonable, therefore, not only to anticipate unusual delay in the spring flood, but also to doubt whether, when it came, it would answer the purpose. And, if the river had been left out of view; if the possibility of efficient naval support had been left to depend upon circumstances, and reliance had been placed only upon the railroad from Shreveport, in that case not only must three months be occupied in putting the railroad in running order, but expeditions, which would occupy considerable time, must be undertaken to clear Southern Arkansas of all such hostile forces as might, if left there, interrupt this land line of supply. It was impossible, therefore, to count upon an *early* commencement of the campaign. And if not commenced early, it could not be undertaken at all, without interfering with the progress of the war east of the Mississippi.[1]

2. And this leads us to the second requirement—a sufficient force. No period of the war could have been more inopportune in this respect. The term of three years, for which the greater portion of the army had enlisted, was now expiring. It could not be safely asserted as certain that the majority of the veteran soldiers would re-enlist, though that was a probable event. The solution of the important problem thus arising ought to have been anticipated by proper measures on the part of the government. Such measures had been tried, but the result was exceedingly unsatisfactory. The conscription of 1863 had furnished only a meagre re-enforcement to the national armies. Thus, although General Halleck was partial to operations in the West, and especially partial in his estimate of the importance of the trans-Mississippi campaign, he found it extremely difficult to increase General Banks's command. He advised that operations in South Carolina be postponed for this purpose; but the government took a different view. In North Carolina the defensive could hardly be maintained, and no troops could be withdrawn from that state. To farther deplete the Army of the Potomac was also impossible. General Longstreet, after abandoning the siege of Knoxville, had occupied a position which seriously threatened East Tennessee, and from General Grant's department only about 10,000 men of Sherman's army could be detached for operations elsewhere. This small corps, and a few regiments, chiefly of cavalry, which, with great difficulty, had been secured from the East by General Halleck, were all that could be sent to the Department of the Gulf, and Sherman's troops could not co-operate with Banks until the conclusion of the Meridian expedition. The only other possible source of aid in the proposed Red River campaign must come from General Steele's department. At the most, Steele could not bring to bear upon the campaign more than 10,000 men, and his column must be independent of the direct movement on Shreveport. Advancing from Little Rock, his route to Shreveport was, at this season of the year, so difficult, and almost impracticable, that it might reasonably be apprehended that he would not be able to strike an effective blow. General Banks's own force, which could be made available for the campaign, amounted to 15,000 or 17,000 men.[2] Thus less than 40,000 troops could engage in the campaign, and only about 28,000 could be certainly counted upon in the event of an encounter with the enemy, should the latter determine to fight a battle below Shreveport.

3. The time allowed for the campaign was limited to thirty days. It was for this period, and no longer, that Sherman's troops were "loaned" to General Banks. This force was indispensable to the continuance of the campaign after reaching Shreveport. The difficulties incident to Steele's advance from Little Rock were so great that no absolute reliance could be placed upon *that* movement. The main dependence was upon A. J. Smith's command—that portion of Sherman's troops which was loaned to Banks for a month. If the campaign was not concluded within that time, it must evidently be abandoned, except in the very improbable event of Steele's prompt arrival at Shreveport. The uncertainty of Steele's success in advancing, and the limited time allowed for the co-operation of Sherman's troops, made General Banks's command the only one to be relied upon as a permanent force.

4. This limitation as regards time of course made it out of the question to occupy several months in the establishment of communications between Vicksburg and Shreveport. For this reason, if for no other, the campaign must be concluded before the fall of the Red River, or be then abandoned.

5. No attention whatever seems to have been given to General Banks's suggestion that all the operations of the campaign should be under a single general. Four distinct commands were thus allowed to participate in the campaign—Porter's, Steele's, A. J. Smith's, and Banks's—each independent of the others. That this was the case was, in great part, General Banks's fault. In accordance with military usage, he ought to have assumed the command of Smith's troops. But he did not do so, and there was, therefore, no unity of command.[1]

The whole affair seems rather to have happened than to have been ordered. General Halleck had been recommending the campaign for months, but he would not assume the responsibility of ordering it. He left the decision entirely with Banks, Sherman, and Steele. The two former, in spite of circumstances which made failure almost certain, while success was a bare possibility, seem to have been confident of a fortunate issue. Partly from this confidence, and probably still more from the urgency with which Halleck had formerly pressed the matter, they entered upon the campaign. It is difficult to conceive what objects they expected to attain within the space of a single month. It is conceded on all hands that, even if Shreveport were reached, nothing beyond that could be accomplished, and a speedy retreat to the Mississippi was inevitable.[2] To march to Shreveport—the Richmond of the trans-Mississippi territory—to capture that place, possibly, and destroy its manufactories, and then to march back again—*this* certainly was no object commensurate with the risk or expense of the campaign, or with the forces employed. Halleck certainly dissuaded Banks from undertaking the movement unless, within the period allowed for its accomplishment, it promised an important success.

That the campaign ought not, under the circumstances, to have been undertaken, is evident. But upon whom rests the responsibility? This must lie between Halleck and Banks. Neither of them would have assumed the responsibility of ordering the movement. Banks very clearly stated the conditions upon which he could enter upon the campaign, and, upon consideration of this statement, Halleck ought to have abandoned the affair as impracticable. But he did not. He communicated with General Sherman, and the latter seemed to favor the undertaking. He reported this opinion to Banks, and advised him to communicate with Generals Steele and Sherman upon the subject. General Banks knew that his own decision was absolute in regard to the matter. He ought to have decided promptly against the movement. But, with the re-enforcements from Sherman, and General Steele's co-operation, he seems to have thought success possible. Besides, General Halleck's scarcely disguised censure of his coast operations, and the urgency with which the latter had pressed the Red River route upon his attention from the beginning, seemed to render farther opposition on his part indecorous. The matter being left to his discretion, any such consideration ought not to have influenced him. He ought to have followed his better judgment. To do otherwise was an inexcusable exhibition of weakness. We are compelled, therefore, to assume that he either weakly yielded his consent, or that his judgment had been altered in view of the co-operation which he would receive, and by "the best military opinions of the generals in the West," which Halleck urged as favorable to operations on the Red River.[3] Whichever way we may determine, he certainly consented to the campaign, and is, in so far, responsible for its results.

---

[1] General Grant's idea of the Red River expedition is shown in the following extract from a letter, written by him to Sherman, dated Nashville, February 18, 1864:

"While I look upon such an expedition as is proposed as of the greatest importance, I regret that any force has to be taken from east of the Mississippi for it. Your troops will want rest for the purpose of preparing for a spring campaign, and all the veterans should be got off on furlough at the very earliest moment. . . .

"Unless you go in command of the proposed expedition, I fear any troops you may send with it will be entirely lost from further service in this command. This, however, is not the reason for my suggestion that you be sent. Your acquaintance with the country, and otherwise fitness, were the reasons. I can give no positive orders that you send no troops up Red River, but what I do want is their speedy return, if they do go, and that the minimum number necessary be sent. . . ."

[2] A large portion of his force, including all of his colored troops, was occupied in garrisoning posts, distributed as follows:

Rio Grande	3000	Key West	791	Plaquemine (colored)	620
Pass Cavallo	3277	New Orleans	1195	Port Hudson (colored)	6400
Pensacola	900	Baton Rouge	6665	Total	20,687

[1] General Sherman's orders, issued to General Smith March 4, 1864, certainly contemplated that the latter would be under General Banks's command. Sherman writes to Smith to join Banks at Alexandria. He says: "You will meet him there, *report to him, and act under his orders.*"—*Sherman's Report to the Committee on the Conduct of the War*, p. 7.

[2] The evidence before the Committee on the Conduct of the War is conclusive on this point. General Banks says (p. 20): "I believe, if any of our forces had taken Shreveport, they could not have held it for one month. . . . We might have gone there, destroyed the place, and then come back again; but I think if the enemy had allowed us to go up there, we should never have got back with the army to the fleet." The question was asked, "How could that have been supposed to conform to the idea of going into Texas with an army?" To which Banks replied: "That is not for me to say. It was the purpose of the expedition to occupy Shreveport, and hold it. General Steele's forces were to hold it if we occupied it. But without some communication on that line, independent of river navigation, . . . General Steele could not have got his supplies. It would have taken at least 10,000 men to hold Shreveport against the concentrated forces of the enemy. There was nothing in the country upon which he could subsist. They would have cut off his communications, and he would have been compelled to surrender. But there is another view of operations west of the Mississippi which, if I had had command of the forces, I should have been disposed to adopt. There were about 100,000 men west of the Mississippi, in Louisiana, Arkansas, and Missouri. If a campaign without limit of time had been set on foot, with the purpose of concentrating all disposable forces in these states, with means of supply independent of the river, and orders to follow up the enemy wherever he could be found, and then destroy him, we would have cleared the country west of the Mississippi of any organized force of the enemy; then, by constructing a railroad from the Mississippi River to Shreveport, fortifying that place, and getting supplies there sufficient for a year, and leaving troops enough there to hold it, we could cover Louisiana, Arkansas, and Missouri. The occupation of Shreveport at the conclusion of such a campaign would have been an important achievement."

[3] General Banks says in his report:

"Having made known my plan of operations on the Coast, and fully stated, at different times, the difficulties to be encountered in movements by land in the direction of Alexandria and Shreveport, I did not feel at liberty to decline participation in the campaign, which had been pressed upon my attention from the time I was assigned to the command of this department, and which was now supported by the concurrent opinions of the general officers in the West, on account of difficulties which might be obviated by personal conferences with commanders, or by orders from the general-in-chief. It was not, however, without well-founded apprehensions of the result of the campaign, and a clear view of the measures (which I suggested) indispensable to success, that I entered upon this new campaign. . . . In the instructions I received from government, it was left to my discretion whether or not I would join in this expedition, but I was directed to communicate with General

ADMIRAL PORTER'S FLEET ON RED RIVER.

Sherman, on the conclusion of his Mississippi expedition, went to New Orleans, and there and then the principal features of the campaign seem to have been determined upon. Returning to Vicksburg, he, on the 6th of March, instructed General A. J. Smith to report to General Banks with 7500 men of Hurlbut's (Sixteenth), and 2500 of McPherson's (Seventeenth) Corps. It was intended that Banks, Smith, and Porter should be at Alexandria by the 17th of March. General Steele was notified of this intention, and replied that he had not anticipated so early a movement; that the presence of his troops was necessary to secure the success of an election to be held at Little Rock March 14, and that he would probably only be able to make a demonstration against Shreveport.[1] After some delay, by the 13th, orders were dispatched to him to move upon Shreveport "with all his available force."

The enemy had a force nearly equal to that which was sent against him. From the official returns of the trans-Mississippi department, Kirby Smith's entire force amounted to 41,000 men, of whom 35,000 were serviceable. The greater portion of this force, probably about 20,000 men, under General Magruder, covered Galveston and Houston. General Taylor, with about 5000, held the line of the Atchafalaya and Red Rivers, while General Price, with 6000 infantry and 3000 cavalry, confronted Steele in Southern Arkansas. Probably 10,000 men could be sent from Magruder's army to re-enforce Price and Taylor. The enemy was strongly fortified at Fort De Russy, on the Red River, and at Camden, on the Washita River, in Arkansas.

Political affairs which had been set on foot by the President required General Banks's personal presence in New Orleans, and the organization of the expedition, so far as it involved his department, was intrusted to General Franklin. It was only on the 10th of March that General Franklin knew that the expedition was expected to reach Alexandria on the 17th. As Alexandria is 117 miles from Franklin, where the troops were to be concentrated for the advance, it was, of course, impossible to fulfill this expectation. Only 3000 men were then at Franklin; the remainder of the infantry, just arrived from Texas, was at Berwick's Bay, and the cavalry was still at New Orleans. On the 13th the movement commenced. General A. L. Lee, with 3300 cavalry, held the advance. Then followed two divisions of the Thirteenth Corps—Landrum's and Cameron's—under General T. E. G. Ransom, and the Nineteenth Corps under General Emory. The whole command, numbering about 18,000 men, reached Alexandria on the 25th of March.

In the mean time, Admiral Porter[2] had already arrived at Alexandria. On the 7th he had at the mouth of Red River a fleet of fifteen iron-clad and four lighter vessels.[1] On the 11th he was joined by General Smith's command, embarked on thirty transports. There was found just sufficient water to allow the larger boats to enter the river. The Eastport was ordered to take the lead, and remove the obstructions which the enemy had placed below Fort De Russy. A portion of the fleet then accompanied the transports down the Atchafalaya, and covered the landing of troops at Simmsport. Dick Taylor's force retreated to Fort De Russy, followed by General A. J. Smith's command, and the gun-boats returned to Red River. In the

Sherman, and General Steele, and Admiral Porter upon the subject. I expressed the satisfaction I should find in co-operating with them in a movement deemed of so much importance by the government, to which my own command was unequal, and my belief that, *with the forces designated*, it would be entirely successful. Having received from them similar assurances, both my discretion and my authority, so far as the organization of the expedition was concerned, were at an end."

[1] Sherman writes to Steele, March 6: "I confess I feel uneasy at your assertion that you can only move with 7000 infantry, and that you prefer to wait until after the election of the 14th. *If we have to modify military plans for civil elections, we had better go home.*"

[2] The following statement is made by Porter before the Committee on the Conduct of the War: "The Red River expedition was originally proposed by General Sherman and myself; we were to have gone up there together. But while we were making the preparations for it, General Banks notified General Sherman that he was about to ascend the Red River with 30,000 men. General Banks also requested co-operation from me, showing me certain orders from General Halleck, in which he was directed to go as far as Shreveport," etc.

In explanation of this statement, it should be said that Sherman's confidence in the success of the expedition was based upon a full supply of water in Red River. In his instructions to General A. J. Smith (March 4), he says: "Now Red River is too low for the season, and I doubt if the boats can pass the falls or rapids of Alexandria. What General Banks proposes to do in that event, I do not know; but my own judgment is that Shreveport ought not to be attacked until the gun-boats can reach it. Not that a force marching by land can not do it alone, but it would be bad economy in war to invest the place with an army so far from heavy guns, mortars, ammunition, and provisions, which can alone reach Shreveport by water." Again (March 7) he writes to Admiral Porter: "I . . . . authorize you to use my name with General Banks that a further move ought not to be attempted above Alexandria unless the Red River admits the navigation by your first-class gun-boats and large transports, viz., seven feet of water on the 'rapids' of Alexandria.'"

[1] Porter's fleet consisted of the Essex, Benton, Lafayette, Choctaw, Chillicothe, Ozark, Louisville, Carondelet, Eastport, Pittsburg, Mound City, Osage, Neosho, Ouachita, Fort Hindman, and the lighter boats Lexington, Cricket, Gazelle, and Black Hawk.

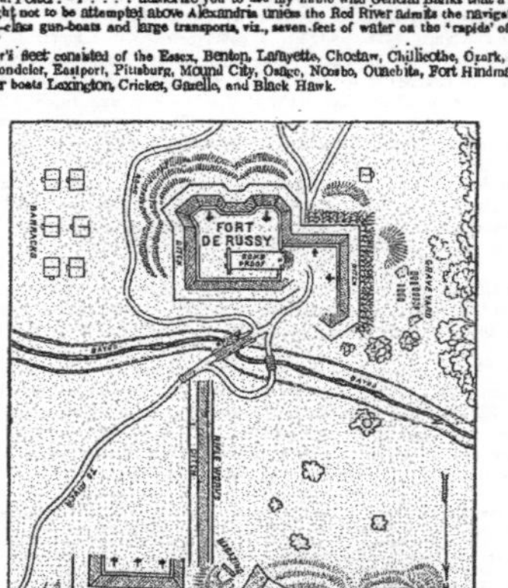

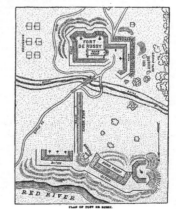

PLAN OF FORT DE RUSSY.

MAP OF THE RED RIVER CAMPAIGN.

mean time, the obstructions, consisting of heavy piles driven into the mud, clamped with iron plates and chains, had been removed. Just as the fleet, on the afternoon of the 14th, approached the fort, the latter was, at the same time, surrounded by the troops, who then assaulted and captured the work, with eight guns and 250 prisoners. General Smith had done a good day's work with his command. He had marched twenty-eight miles, being detained two hours to build a bridge, and had, after an action of two hours, captured the only fort which the enemy had on Red River below Shreveport. Two days afterward the fleet reached Alexandria.[1]

The work of getting the gun-boats over the rocky rapids at Alexandria was slow and difficult. Indeed, it was hazardous to advance farther up the river with the fleet, which, if it should ever reach Shreveport, would probably never return. General Banks arrived at Alexandria on the 24th. The delay caused by the slow progress of the fleet above the rapids rendered it necessary to establish a depôt of supplies at Alexandria, and a line of wagon transportation from the steamers below to those above the falls. To guard this point, therefore, Grover's division of the Nineteenth Corps (3000 strong) had to be left behind. Ellet's marine brigade of 3000 men, of A. J. Smith's command, was recalled to Vicksburg. It was necessary that T. K. Smith's division of the same command (2500 men) should go with the fleet for the protection of the transports. Thus, when the army left for Alexandria, April 1, its number of men available for active operations on land had been reduced by 8500.

Just after the occupation of Alexandria, the troops were in good spirits; indeed, the impression prevailed in the army that the Confederates in this region were demoralized, and that Shreveport would be reached without a battle. General Steele had the same feeling. This is shown in his dispatch to Halleck on March 12, where he says that Sherman's and Banks's troops were "more than equal for every thing Kirby Smith can bring against them." Smith, he said, would run. With this conviction, his co-operation must have been inefficient. At Alexandria there seems to have been some bad feeling between the military and naval forces on account of the seizure by the latter of cotton as a naval prize. Porter, during the period in which he was waiting for the army, and for the passage of his fleet above the falls, took possession of a considerable quantity of cotton. It would have been wiser to have refrained from the seizure at this time for two reasons. In the first place, it naturally created jealousy among the military forces. Then, again, it caused the cotton within the reach of the Federal forces to be burned by the inhabitants, who would otherwise have gladly disposed of it to the United States on terms advantageous to themselves and to the government. If, however, the cotton was to become a naval prize, there was no motive for its preservation. It would have been better if the existence of cotton had been ignored by the navy as well as the army until the territory in which the staple was found should be thoroughly subjugated. This was General Grant's policy. General Banks's theory was that the products of the country ought to be bought at a reasonable price. This policy was open to the objection that it added largely to the resources of the enemy, and in so far prolonged the war.

While the army was at Alexandria, a movement was made to Henderson's Hill, twenty-five miles up the river, resulting in a surprise of the enemy at that point, and the capture of 250 prisoners, 200 horses, and four guns. Three brigades of Smith's command, and one of Emory's, participated in this expedition.

On the 2d and 3d of April the army reached Natchitoches, eighty miles from Alexandria, and 100 below Shreveport. This place was about four miles inland from Grand Ecore. It is situated on the old channel of the Red River, while Grand Ecore is on the new. Lee's cavalry had skirmished with the enemy all the way to Natchitoches. The navy proceeded up to Grand Ecore. The difficulties of navigation had increased rather than diminished. The river was falling, and it was found impossible for the larger gun-boats to pass Grand Ecore. A. J. Smith's command was forced to abandon the transports and march by land. Here there was a delay of four days. On the 6th of April the army advanced from Natchitoches. The only practicable road to Shreveport lay through Pleasant Hill and Mansfield, through a barren, sandy country, with little water and scarcely any forage, and, for the most part, an unbroken pine forest. Notwithstanding the failure of Franklin at Sabine Pass, Banks still intrusted to him the active command and the regulation of the march, while he remained at Grand Ecore until the fleet advanced, on the 7th.

Lee's cavalry found the enemy in his front all the way to Pleasant Hill, thirty-six miles distant. Kirby Smith's design was to draw the Federal force as far as possible from its base before a general engagement. The delay of the fleet had given him time for concentration, and Green's cavalry had been withdrawn from Southern Texas.

General Banks intended that the fleet, with its six lightest boats, should reach Loggy Bayou, opposite Springfield, where communications would be established with the land forces at Sabine Cross-roads, near Mansfield, fifty-four miles from Natchitoches. The navy, with twenty transports, succeeded, though with great difficulty, in reaching Springfield. But on the way to Mansfield the army, encountering the enemy in strong force, sustained a disastrous reverse, which caused it to retreat, and finally to abandon the expedition.

On the 7th of April the advance of the Federal army reached Pleasant Hill, and there encamped for the night. General Lee had driven a small force of the enemy to Pleasant Hill and about three miles beyond, to Wilson's farm, where a fight occurred in which Lee lost sixty-two in killed, wounded, and missing. The enemy, after losing severely, was driven to St. Patrick's Bayou, nine miles from Pleasant Hill. During the action, Lee had called upon Franklin for a brigade of infantry. This was dispatched; but the firing having ceased, it was withdrawn.

As to the force of the enemy in his front, General Franklin seems to have been totally ignorant. He certainly did not expect soon to fight a battle, otherwise his order of march would not have been what it was. General Lee, with about 5000 cavalry, held the advance, skirmishing with and developing the enemy, who, whatever his force, seemed determined to retreat. Then came the train of the cavalry, consisting of over 200 wagons.[1] The size of this train is partly accounted for by the fact that it carried 20,000 rations; but even with this allowance it was very much larger than was necessary. After it came Ransom's command, consisting of two divisions of the Thirteenth Corps; then the Nineteenth Corps, Franklin's proper command, followed by A. J. Smith's troops. From the front to the rear, the line extended from twenty to thirty miles, over a single road. The cavalry train delayed the columns in the rear, and the difficulties thus experienced were increased by a rain-storm, which, lasting all day on the 7th, rendered the road next to impassable by the Nineteenth Corps and Smith's command. General Banks rode along the line that day; after having seen the fleet off from Grand Ecore, and urged on the impeded columns. He reached Franklin's headquarters, at Pleasant Hill, on the evening of the 7th, at about 9 P.M. At about the same time, Colonel Clarke, of Banks's staff, returned from the front, and reported that Lee was anxious to have infantry support, having met with strong opposition. Franklin declined to send support. If General Lee could not hold his position, he must fall back. Franklin had previously ordered Lee to crowd the enemy vigorously, and keep his train well up.[2] Lee had found his train a source of great annoyance, being obliged to detach from one third to one half of his force to guard it. He had parked about a third of his wagons, and forced the others to the rear. Franklin's order led him to keep his train close up to his column. There was evidently no proper understanding between Franklin and Lee. It ought to have been Lee's proper business to develop the enemy's force and report to his superior officer. This General Lee failed to do. All he knew of the enemy's force in his front was that it was "considerable." General Franklin's impression that the enemy would not fight interfered with the proper operations of the cavalry. Lee expected a fight near Pleasant Hill, and strongly insisted upon the probability of a battle at that point. His advice was disregarded, and the orders which he received indicated that Franklin thought him advancing too cautiously, and that the cavalry was in the way.

General Banks's arrival at Pleasant Hill on the evening of the 7th does not seem to have helped matters at all. Without being aware of the situation in the front, he ordered that a brigade of infantry should be dispatched in accordance with Lee's request. His only reason for doing this was his notion that "the advance-guard should be composed of cavalry for celerity, artillery for force, and infantry for solidity."[3] He had no idea of bringing on a general engagement. He knew what was the position of his rear columns, for he had just rode past them. Franklin's objection to moving forward the infantry was that he thought it would bring on a battle. This is clear from the conversation between him and General Banks at 11 A.M. on the 8th. At that time Franklin had moved forward with the advance of the infantry to a point about ten miles from Pleasant Hill, and was building a bridge for his train, when he was joined by Banks. He remarked to the latter that there would be no fight. Banks replied, "I will go forward and see." Lee was then five miles beyond this point. One of Ransom's brigades had been sent to him, reaching him that morning. He now reported that this brigade was much exhausted, and asked for another, which Franklin ordered forward, instructing Ransom to go with it in person. General Banks arrived

[1] Admiral Porter, at this time, does not seem to have had a very exalted idea of the enemy's pluck. Writing from Alexandria on the 16th, he says: "Colonel De Russy, from appearances, is a most excellent engineer to build forts, but don't seem to know what to do with them after they are constructed. The same remark may apply to his obstructions, which look well on paper, but don't stop our advance. The efforts of these people to keep up the war remind one very much of the antics of Chinamen, who build canvas forts, paint hideous dragons on their shields, turn somersets, and yell in the face of their enemies to frighten them, and then run away at the first sign of an engagement. It puts the sailors and soldiers out of all patience with them, after the trouble they have had in getting here. Now and then the army have a little brush with their pickets, but that don't often happen. It is not the intention of these rebels to fight." Admiral Porter probably had occasion to reverse his judgment before the campaign was over.

[1] The number of wagons is variously estimated. Banks speaks of it as 156. J. G. Wilson, Banks's aid-de-camp, makes it 180. General Lee, who certainly ought to have known, makes the number from 320 to 350. The enemy claims that he captured 320 at Sabine Cross-roads.

[2] These were verbal orders as delivered through Colonel Clarke in the afternoon. The written dispatch reads thus:

"The commanding general has received your dispatch of 2 P.M. A brigade of infantry went to the front; but the fire having ceased, it was withdrawn. The infantry is all here. The general commanding directs that you proceed to-night as far as possible with your whole train, in order to give the infantry room to advance to-morrow."

[3] *Report on the Conduct of the War*, p. 11.

at the extreme front at 1 P.M. He found there an unexpected force of the enemy. He felt, he says, instinctively that "we were in presence of the whole force of the enemy." He then saw with his own eyes the disadvantageous position of the cavalry train, which was stretched along for a distance of two or three miles in the rear. Skirmishing with the enemy had already commenced; a battle was imminent, and could not be avoided. There had been mismanagement, the injurious results of which it was now too late to avert entirely. The extent of the injury must depend upon the decision made at this critical moment by General Banks. If he fell back, declining a general battle, it was at some risk to the train; but if he determined upon a battle at that point, bringing up his infantry to Lee's support, the risk was much greater. Indeed, it was, under the circumstances, almost certain that he would be defeated if he ventured battle. General Banks determined to take the greater risk. He hurried up the infantry in the rear, and brought up fourteen pieces of artillery in addition to the twelve already with General Lee. Notwithstanding his own admission that he felt himself to be confronted by the full force of the enemy, Banks does not seem to have appreciated the risk which he was running. In his dispatch to Franklin half an hour after he reached Lee, he advises him that the enemy seems prepared to make a strong stand, and that he had better make arrangements to bring up his infantry, and concludes: "You had better send back and push up the trains, as manifestly we shall be able to rest here."

General Franklin, on receipt of this order, was at the point where Banks had passed him in the morning, where he had the remainder of the Thirteenth Corps under General Cameron, and Emory's division of the Nineteenth. The order to move forward quickly followed the dispatch above mentioned, and before 5 o'clock P.M. Franklin was on the field with Cameron's command. The battle had been going on then for half an hour. Ransom had reached the field at 1 30 P.M., and found that the enemy had been driven across an open field. Landrum, with the brigade sent in the morning, was advancing to a ridge which the Confederates had abandoned, and which be now occupied (at 2 P.M.), the other brigade brought up by Ransom going in to his support. Landrum's third brigade arrived soon afterward, making the infantry force under Ransom 2413 strong. This, with Lee's cavalry, made the entire force between 6000 and 7000 men. The position taken was about four miles from Mansfield, at a place called Sabine Cross-roads. It was about fifty miles south of Shreveport, and twenty miles west of Red River. Nims's battery, posted on a hill near the road, was near the left of the line, supported on either side by the Twenty-third Wisconsin and Sixty-seventh Indiana regiments. Then came the Seventy-seventh Illinois, reaching to a belt of timber 200 yards to the right of the hill. The right of the line consisted of the One Hundred and Thirtieth Illinois, the Forty-eighth Ohio, the Nineteenth Kentucky, the Ninety-sixth and Eighty-third Ohio, with a section of artillery. The Chicago Mercantile and the First Indiana batteries, brought up at a later period, were posted on a ridge in the rear, near Banks's headquarters. The cavalry was posted on the two flanks. The ground in front was open, and descended in the rear to a creek, from which it again ascended to a covered ridge.

The Confederate force was under the command of General Dick Taylor, and consisted of Walker's and Mouton's divisions, and Green's cavalry, in all probably amounting to 12,000 men. Taylor had been ordered to retreat steadily before the advance of the Federal army, leading it on to Shreveport. Two circumstances led him to disobey this order. In the first place, he saw that it would be giving Banks a great advantage to leave him in possession of the roads in the open country near Mansfield, since these would enable him to communicate with the advancing fleet. In the second place, the opportunity offered for defeating General Banks was too tempting to be rejected. Taylor had already retreated beyond Mansfield, when, acting upon these considerations, he directed Walker and Mouton to retrace their steps through the town, and take up a position three miles beyond. Thus Green, who had been skirmishing and retreating steadily, found himself, on the 8th, supported by two infantry divisions. Taylor was still undecided whether to fight the battle, when Mouton, occupying the left, advanced without orders, and gained such a decisive advantage that Walker also was ordered forward.

The attack commenced about 4 P.M. The Federal right maintained its position, but the left was soon turned, and Nims's battery was captured. The hill was now occupied by the enemy, and the position first taken by the Federals was no longer tenable. The routed cavalry, galloping to the rear, rushed through the infantry line, throwing it into confusion, and some of the regiments were cut off from retreat and surrounded. The arrival of Franklin with Cameron's command was too late to retrieve the misfortune. Out of 26 pieces of artillery engaged, all but eight had been captured. To make a stand with Cameron's fresh division, and so many of the routed troops as might be rallied, would have resulted in fresh disaster. The Thirteenth Corps and the cavalry abandoned the field in as good order as was possible under the circumstances, leaving the train in possession of the enemy. But for the position of this train fewer prisoners would have been taken by the enemy, and probably a much larger portion of the artillery would have been saved. General Banks's loss in this unfortunate battle was over 3000 men, killed, wounded, and prisoners.[1] The enemy lost about 1000. The disaster at Sabine Cross-roads must be attributed to several causes: 1st. The failure of the cavalry to obtain prompt and full infor-

[1] The responsibility for this disaster lies between Generals Banks and Franklin. The majority of the Committee on the Conduct of the War throw the weight of responsibility upon Banks. They claim that it was his duty to be cognizant of the details of the march; that if he did not know these details on the 7th, he certainly did on the 8th, before the affair at Sabine Cross-roads: and that with this knowledge he assumed the responsibility of the position by remaining where he was and sending for the troops in the rear to re-enforce him.

D. W. Gooch submits a separate report, in which he takes a different view of General Banks's connection with the disaster. He claims that both Lee and Ransom "regarded the position held by our forces as a good one; that, in addition to the cavalry and artillery which had composed Lee's advance, there were on the field, also, at that time, two brigades of infantry, and that the balance of the Thirteenth and Nineteenth Corps were respectively about five and seven miles in the rear, and probably at that time advancing." "Under these circumstances," says Gooch, "General Banks, when he arrived upon the field, was obliged to decide to abandon this favorable position, over which he would be compelled to pass in order to establish his proposed communication with the transports at Loggy Bayou, and to reach Shreveport; withdraw his artillery and the large baggage train of the cavalry, in the presence of a superior force of the enemy, on the narrow and difficult road which has been described, or remain upon the field and order up to his assistance the troops of the Thirteenth and Nineteenth Army Corps from the points heretofore mentioned. He decided to remain upon the field and take the chances of a battle. Had the enemy deferred the attack one hour longer, or had it been possible for our troops to reach the field one hour earlier, the result of that battle would undoubtedly have been reversed."

But the attack was not deferred, and Banks had no reason to suppose that it would be; nor could Cameron and the Nineteenth Corps have been up in time. Banks admits that he thought the enemy in full force in his front. But his dispatch to Franklin (received by the latter at 3 P.M. on the 8th) only ordered him to make arrangements to bring up the infantry, and to await instructions before advancing. He also ordered Franklin to push up his trains (over seven hundred wagons), "as manifestly," says Banks, "we shall be able to rest here." Ten minutes later the order came to move, and Franklin promptly advanced with Cameron's division, coming upon the field too late to prevent disaster. The Nineteenth Corps, which was also ordered forward, being still farther in the rear, could not have been brought up in time to effect any thing. It is plain, therefore, that in venturing a battle instead of withdrawing the train under cover of the troops already in front, General Banks made himself responsible for the consequences. There is no testimony to the effect that the cavalry could not have fallen back.

The responsibility for the order of march rests with General Franklin. General Banks testifies: "The order of march was perfectly proper, but it was not compact enough. The different parts of the column were not within supporting distance of each other; they were extended for from twenty to thirty miles. . . . It was certainly a great fault that the advance-guard, with a possible chance of meeting the enemy, should have had its train close upon its rear. That was inexcusable. . . . The order in which the divisions should move was the established order which had continued from our movement from Alexandria. The only addition was that General Smith's forces brought up the rear. Every thing in that respect was perfectly right. It was approved by me, and it may be said to have been changed by me somewhat, because, when the enemy in our front was found to be increasing in strength, I gave directions to General Franklin to send a brigade to the assistance of the cavalry. But the fact that this force was stretched out more than twenty miles was necessarily without my knowledge, and I am not responsible for it in any way. The responsibility rests with General Franklin. General Lee, who is responsible for the advance, received written instructions from General Franklin, which are stated in General Lee's report. My own staff officers took written instructions to General Lee from General Franklin to keep his trains close up, the theory probably being that they would not meet the enemy. When I passed General Franklin on the morning of the 8th of April, he said, 'There will be no battle.' Besides, in his instructions to General Lee he evidently supposes that the enemy was not there; for he says, 'General Banks and General Ransom have gone to the front; but it is not expected that they will remain there.'"

In answer to the question, "At what point in your advance were you expecting to meet the enemy?" Banks replies:

"My expectation was that we should meet the enemy between Mansfield and Shreveport; but it was never certain whether we should or not. . . . . I had information, upon which I relied implicitly, from a man who had been through that country, that we would have to fight at some point between Mansfield and Shreveport, at some point near Mansfield. My belief is that the plans of the enemy were changed as we approached Mansfield. [This belief is confirmed by the Confederate reports.] And it has been stated that the rebel General Taylor was suspended from his command for having attacked us at Sabine Cross-roads, General Kirby Smith being confident that if his orders had been complied with, and we had been allowed to reach Shreveport, we would have been unable to return. And of that I am assured myself. If General Taylor had not attacked us, I do not know what we would have done. But he was tempted by our position, knowing that we were in a condition where we could not get our forces together, and he knew he could gain an advantage over us. He was thereby induced to attack us against orders."

General Franklin testifies that he differed with Banks and Lee as to the policy of making the advance-guard include infantry. "If any fighting occurs, it is most likely that the infantry will do it, while the cavalry looks on; and if there be merely a march, the cavalry exhausts the infantry, or it must regulate its march by the infantry rate." He claims that the trains "had nothing to do with the defeating of the infantry and cavalry. But when the rout began, then the trains were in the way, and nothing could be got away, because the train was jammed up to where the infantry was driven back; and when the time came to turn the artillery back, there was no place for it to get through. . . . . I suppose that to a certain extent I am responsible thus far. The cavalry general had always been asking me to put his train behind the infantry troops, and let it march in front of the infantry train. I had always refused to do that; I told him it was his business to take care of his own train. The reasons which actuated me in this were these: I had about seven hundred wagons with me, which the infantry had to take care of. If it had taken the two hundred and fifty which the cavalry had, and put them in front of my infantry train, my infantry wagons would never have got into camp the day of my march. The consequence would have been that the cavalry would have had their wagons up, but at the expense of the infantry. I therefore told General Lee that he must take care of his own wagons. To that extent I am responsible for his wagons being where they were. But he writes me, at 7 30 A.M. on the 8th, 'I am keeping my train back in order that I may see the thing settled before I bring it up to the front.' That relieved my mind entirely about the train, and I had no idea that I would find it where I did find it. I was so anxious about the trains that I ordered them to close up during the day, finding that the wagons straggled badly as they passed my camp. I understand that General Lee has interpreted that to mean that I ordered his train forward, which I did not. I gave no orders to General Lee's train that day except to close up. There were several open places, between the point where the infantry was to encamp and the battle-ground, where a train much larger than the cavalry train could have been parked. The general in command at the front should, I think, have ordered the train in park at one of these places when he saw that a general battle was imminent. I could not, because I was with my immediate command."

But could not Franklin, when he received Lee's report that the train was a great annoyance to him, have issued this order to park the artillery? He could have done so but for his impression that there would be no battle at this stage of the march. It seems, therefore, that while General Franklin must be held exclusively responsible for the detached order of march, a large share of the blame attached to the position of the cavalry train should be attributed to Generals Lee and Banks, either of whom ought to have seen the necessity of parking the trains before engaging an enemy which Banks believed to be from 15,000 to 18,000 strong. *If they* failed to attend to this, it was the business of Brigadier General C. P. Stone, General Banks's chief of staff, to do so. He was on the field, and this was one of his especial duties.

Brigadier General Dwight, who, a week after the battle, succeeded General Stone as chief of staff, corroborates General Franklin's testimony as to the feasibility of parking the train. He testifies: "There was no objection to the train being on the road, provided the cavalry was not so heavily engaged with the enemy as to endanger it. There were a great many places on the road where the train could have been parked." He denies that the wagons in any way impeded the march of the Nineteenth Corps. General Lee, he says, "should by no means have permitted his train to be between the infantry of the army and the cavalry of the army when he was going to fight a battle. But he ought to have known whether there was danger of a battle; he ought to have known the enemy's force in front of him; for he had a very large force. But it is to be remarked here that he did not seem to know well; that he did not manage as if he knew the whole force of the enemy was in his front. The moment that he found the enemy was in his front in force, he should have parked the train where it would be safe; and if he found that he had got it too far in the front, he should have turned it to the rear. That is a matter of his own responsibility, of which he ought to be a competent judge." Dwight evidently thinks that Lee mismanaged the entire conduct of the advance-guard. He says the cavalry ought to have been still farther in advance of the infantry than it was; that Lee had too large a train; but that, large as it was, it could have been parked in three hours; that it was Lee's business to know that he was likely to be attacked, and thus have gained time for preparation; "it was the easiest country in the world in which to tell when you are going to be attacked, or when there was a liability to attack, because it was comparatively a narrow country. A strong advance-guard of cavalry, much less than the main body, of good cavalry scouts, could have always told where the main body of the enemy was, so that no battle should have occurred until the army was prepared for it." He thus describes Lee's command:

"This cavalry force, as it was called, of General Lee consisted of cavalry proper, of mounted infantry, and a very large proportion of artillery for such a force. It was really more infantry than it was cavalry. For the work of cavalry proper it was utterly unfit. The men were not good riders, and did not understand how to take care of their horses properly. They were infantry soldiers who had been put on horseback; they were not properly cavalry. General Lee's force, therefore, consisted of some of the very best infantry regiments that were ever in the Department of the Gulf, with cavalry proper, and a large amount of artillery. Considering the character of that force, it was an eminently proper disposition to place the whole of it, or so much of it as was in advance, in advance. The whole of it was not in advance; one brigade of it, at least, was in

T. E. G. RANSOM.

mation concerning the enemy. 2d. General Lee's neglect to park his trains before fighting. 3d. The detached order of march, the column of infantry with its head fronting the enemy on a field over twenty miles distant from its rear. And, 4th. The decision of General Banks to venture a battle under these unfavorable circumstances. This last was the great mistake, and gave each of the disadvantages mentioned its operative force; but for this decision there need have been no defeat, at least not at this point. It would probably have been better if Banks had staid behind at Grand Ecore, or any where else, as in that case the battle, if fought at all, would have been fought with a concentrated command. For, notwithstanding General Franklin's conviction that there would be no fighting, it is clear that on the morning of the 8th his plan was to concentrate his whole command before marching beyond St. Patrick's Bayou. Had this been done, the advance would have continued to Shreveport without fighting a battle, and there it would have confronted a force of the enemy superior in numbers—Price's command united with Dick Taylor's. Still, even in that event, a far greater disaster would have befallen General Banks's army, with its immense baggage trains, and 400 miles from its base. Most certainly, in that event, the fleet—so much of it as could wriggle its way up to Shreveport—together with the transports, would have been exposed to utter destruction.

While the Thirteenth Corps and Lee's cavalry were falling back in a disorganized mass from Sabine Cross-roads, General Emory's division of the Nineteenth Corps was advancing to the field of battle. At Pleasant Grove, three miles back of where the fighting had been, this division met the fugitives, who passed through their ranks to the rear. Following these came the pursuing enemy, who just at nightfall fell upon Emory's unbroken wall of bayonets, and were repulsed after an engagement of an hour and a half. General Mouton was killed in the first onset. "The first division of the Nineteenth Corps," says General Banks, "by its great bravery in this action, saved the army and navy." The enemy now retreated to Mansfield, so that during the night the Federal forces occupied both battle-fields.

It was then decided to fall back to Pleasant Hill. A renewal of the attack was expected on the morning of the 9th, and it was not likely that General Smith's command would be able to reach Pleasant Grove in time to participate in the action; without his presence it would be impossible for Banks, with the Nineteenth Corps and the demoralized troops who had been driven from Sabine Cross-roads, to maintain his position. The movement to Pleasant Hill began before daylight, Emory's division covering the rear, burying the dead, and bringing off the wounded. At 8 30 A.M. the retreat had been completed, and a junction effected with Smith's command.

In the mean time the enemy had been re-enforced by Churchill's division of infantry from Arkansas—there being no immediate apprehension as to Steele's advance—so that he was able to bring into the field upward of 20,000 men. Kirby Smith had ordered Taylor to follow up Banks's force. To meet this force Banks had only 15,000 men. But a battle for the safety of the fleet would have to be fought somewhere, and General Banks concluded that it might as well take place at Pleasant Hill as farther back. A strong position was taken, and this time the trains were sent to the rear under a strong cavalry guard. The forenoon passed quietly by. The Confederates, wearied by their previous battles, and—in the case of Churchill's command—by a long march, advanced slowly, and it was not until 4 o'clock P.M. that Green's cavalry encountered the Nineteenth Corps, guarding the approaches to the open ground surrounding Pleasant Hill. The army under Banks now consisted of the Nineteenth Corps and the Western troops under A. J. Smith. The remainder had been sent to the rear with the baggage and wounded. The greater part of A. J. Smith's command was held in reserve. The troops most advanced were soon driven in, and so easily that Taylor was led to believe that he was about to fight only the rear-guard of a retreating army. Walker was ordered to attack in front. Polignac—a French gentleman of aristocratic birth who had espoused the Confederate cause—having succeeded to General Mouton's command, was held in reserve. Churchill was ordered to make a detour and strike the Federal left flank. The conflict that followed was desperate, and for a long time doubtful. The Federals held rising ground, and presented a stubborn front to every attack. Churchill found the resistance so strong in his front that he had to be supported by a brigade from Walker's division. Even with this re-enforcement he was roughly handled, and driven back across the open to the cover of the woods. Walker, supported by Polignac (who was sheltered by woods), in the mean time had advanced across the valley under a galling fire, from which he suffered severe loss, against the Federal right flank. Re-enforced by Polignac, he kept advancing, and, toward night, seemed to be gaining a decisive advantage, having driven back the force in his front. But Smith's reserves were then brought up, and the Confederates were driven from the field, fairly beaten. Some guns which had been taken by the enemy in the early stage of the action were afterward recaptured. The battle had been fought by Banks for the existence of his army and of Porter's fleet, and had resulted in victory.

But what then? Should the army advance or continue its retreat? Smith, with his Western soldiers, cried out for an advance. Banks's judgment was in favor of advance; but Franklin, more wisely, advised retreat. Indeed, no folly could have been greater than to renew the attempt against Shreveport. For the army to remain where it was involved peril. A single day could add to the enemy's force sufficient re-enforcements to give him a decided advantage against Banks. With this increased force, and with proper management on Kirby Smith's part, the defeat of the Union

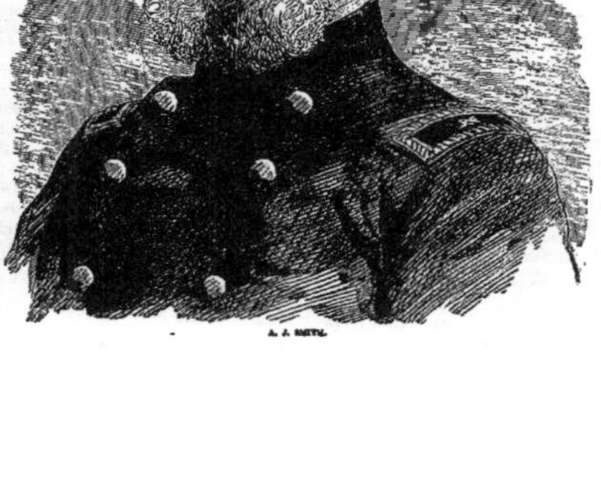

A. J. SMITH.

rear. . . . . I consider our force of cavalry, mounted infantry, etc., was badly commanded; that the officer commanding it did not well understand the manner of leading an advance, of obtaining proper information concerning the enemy, or of penetrating any little curtain of troops which the enemy might throw in front of him to prevent his obtaining information which he ought to have had. Our force, or that portion of the force which, on the 8th of April, advanced to the position in which it was attacked by the enemy, stood dormant in the presence of the enemy until the enemy completely enveloped it. There can be but one solution of such a conduct of affairs, and that is, that whoever directed that on our part was incapable."

"*Question.* Then, if I understand you, it is your opinion that that disaster occurred in consequence of the failure of the cavalry and its officers to do that which they should have done?"

"*Answer.* I consider that was the cause of our not having proper information. I consider that the cause of the disaster of that day was that the infantry of the army was in three detachments, one near the scene of action, and the other two respectively nine and twenty-four miles from it, and that a battle never ought to have occurred under those circumstances. The infantry of the army was not concentrated; it was in exactly the proper position to be beaten in detail, which, in fact, was what occurred."

General Dwight's opinion of General Lee's inefficiency seems to have been concurred in by a majority of the general officers of the army. General Banks says in his testimony: "General Lee was relieved from the command of the cavalry subsequent to this affair at Sabine Cross-roads, but it was not on account of this action. It was because the general officers expressed to me so positively their want of confidence in the organization and condition of the cavalry, and advised so earnestly a change. This was an act which I afterward regretted. It was done because of the demoralized condition in which the cavalry found itself after this affair, and the very important part it must have in subsequent movements. I have no complaint to make of General Lee's general conduct. He was active, willing, and brave, and suffered more or less unjustly, as all of us did, for being connected with that affair." General Arnold, formerly Chief of Artillery, succeeded General Lee.

CONFEDERATE LAND ATTACK ON PORTER'S FLEET.

army was inevitable, and, following this, the capture of the gun-boats, and possibly the repossession of the Mississippi by the Confederates. Besides this, there were also other reasons for a retreat. It would consume much valuable time to turn the train back again toward Shreveport and to reorganize the army. And the enemy would certainly have attacked before Banks was fully prepared to meet him. There was no water at Pleasant Hill for man or beast. All the horses with the army had been without food for 36 hours. Without rations and without water, without tidings of the fleet with which was the supply of ammunition, General Banks, reluctantly following Franklin's advice, determined to fall back to Grand Ecore, where he could reorganize his army and be sure of communication with Porter. The losses in the campaign thus far amounted to nearly 4000 men, besides artillery, mules, and wagons. Grant was now lieutenant general, and in March had ordered General Banks to send back Smith's command if the expedition could not be terminated successfully by the 1st of May, saying that if it should be continued beyond that date he would much rather it had never been begun. This was an additional reason for retreat. How General Banks or General A. J. Smith could have for a moment contemplated an advance under these circumstances it is difficult to imagine. But orders for such an advance had been given, and the train had been ordered to return, and it was only after consultation with his general officers that Banks countermanded these orders, and at midnight on the 9th directed preparations to be made for the return of the army to Grand Ecore. It was an unfortunate circumstance that, although this withdrawal was accomplished at leisure, a large number of the wounded were left behind for want of transportation.[1]

[1] The following is the testimony of Surgeon Eugene F. Sanger on this point:
Question. "What is your position in the army?"
Answer. "Surgeon of United States Volunteers."
Question. "Did you accompany the Red River expedition under General Banks?"
Answer. "I did."
Question. "Were you present at the battles of Sabine Cross-roads and Pleasant Hill?"
Answer. "I was."
Question. "What was the condition of our wounded there?"
Answer. "We brought off about half our wounded in the first battle, and in the second battle we brought off all that could walk off."
Question. "It has been said that at Pleasant Hill we won a victory; how happened it that we left our wounded in the hands of the enemy?"

The fleet had reached Loggy Bayou on the 10th, when, learning of the disaster which had happened to the army, it began to return down the narrow, snaggy channel which it had with great difficulty just ascended. Removed from the military force (except that of T. K. Smith's command, which accompanied the transports), the fleet was peculiarly exposed to attack from the bluffs on either side. Failing to destroy the army, the Confederates turned their attention to the gun-boats and transports. The river was falling, and the progress of the fleet was slow—about thirty miles per day—so that the enemy easily followed him down, continually increasing in numbers. The first attack was made at Coushutta, and a second, with 1900 of Green's cavalry and four guns, at Harrison. Both these attacks were easily met and repulsed. On the 12th of April a more determined onset was made by 2000 infantry, infuriated by Louisiana rum, from the right bank. It was a novel conflict, this, in which these reckless Texans charged upon Porter's gun-boats with the assistance of two guns! The crazy attempt was persisted in for two hours. Detachment after detachment, they were brought to the river's edge and mown down by the guns of the fleet, until at length their leader, General Tom Green, lost his head, blown off by a shell, when the enemy withdrew, leaving the river bank strewn with his killed and wounded, whose bodies, says Admiral Porter, "actually smelled" of the rum which had bedeviled them. This affair seems to have satisfied the enemy as to the chances of success in an attack by infantry upon gun-boats. On the 15th the fleet reached Grand Ecore. Here Porter found most of his larger gun-boats aground, drawing a foot more water than there was on the bar. While he was extricating them, the Eastport, eight miles below, was sunk, and was with great difficulty got afloat again.

The retreat of the army was continued on the 22d to Alexandria. The fleet followed soon, but was delayed by Porter's anxious and persistent efforts to get away the Eastport, which, finally, he was obliged to destroy. When the fleet reached Cane River, ninety miles below Grand Ecore, it was attacked by eighteen Confederate guns. Every shot from these struck the Cricket, the admiral's flag-ship, whose decks were rapidly cleared. The after gun was disabled, and every man in attendance killed or wounded. Another shell exploded her forward gun, sweeping away the crew from it, and, passing into the fire-room, left but one man there unwounded. Admiral Porter made up a crew from contrabands for the after gun, put an assistant in the place of the chief engineer, who had been killed, and ordered the vessel to run by the battery, "which was done," says the admiral, "under the heaviest fire I have ever witnessed." Driving around the point on which were posted the enemy's guns, he shelled the latter in the rear, and by this diversion the light-draught Juliet and pump-boat Champion, lashed together, escaped from under the bank where they had drifted. The Hindman from above co-operated with the Cricket by pouring an enfilading fire into the Confederate batteries, but dared not pass them. Porter therefore went down to obtain the assistance of some of the iron-clads below, but in the trip he got aground, and was delayed for three hours. After proceeding three miles he found the Osage and Lexington engaging another Confederate battery, the latter having been hulled fifteen times, with only one man killed. It was now night, and impossible to return to the Hindman, yet the latter vessel succeeded in running the battery, but, having her wheel-ropes cut away by the enemy's fire, got badly cut up in drifting down. Three of her men were killed and four wounded. The Juliet also passed, sustaining severe injuries. The Champion was disabled and set on fire. During these operations the Cricket was hulled thirty-eight times, and fifteen of her crew were killed or wounded. After such difficulties as we have described, the fleet at length arrived at Alexandria. Admiral Porter estimates that on his way down he killed and wounded at least 500 Confederates, his own loss being less than 100.

General Banks had also met with formidable resistance on his way to Alexandria, at the crossing of Cane River, where he met a Confederate force of 8000 men, with 16 guns, under General Bee. This force, flanked by the river on one side and an impenetrable swamp on the other, was confident of checking Banks until the rest of the Confederate army could come up in his rear. Banks's only safety was in rapidity of movement. Aware of the enemy's designs, he commenced his march from Grand Ecore on the morning of the 22d, and that day and night marched 40 miles, moving upon the enemy at Monet's Bluff, on Cane River, before daybreak of the 23d. General Emory, with his own division of the Nineteenth Corps, one of the Thirteenth, and Arnold's cavalry, was ordered to attack the enemy in front. The position was found too strong to be carried by a direct attack. Therefore General H. W. Birge, with a command consisting of his own brigade (the Third of Emory's division) and Cameron's division, was dispatched across the river, three miles above, to strike the enemy's flank. Birge, after a difficult march through swamps and dense woods, reached his destination late in the afternoon. Fessenden, commanding Birge's brigade, assaulted and carried two strong positions, whose occupation forced the enemy to retreat southwestwardly into Texas. Kilby Smith, covering Banks's rear, was on the next morning unsuccessfully attacked by the Confederate force which was co-operating with Bee. The Federal loss in these engagements was 250 men. General Banks, by his promptness, had prevented the enemy from concentrating his forces and fortifying his position, otherwise the Federal army would have been compelled to cross Red River above the bluff in the presence of the enemy on both sides of both Cane and Red Rivers. The army reached Alexandria on the 25th and 26th of April, precisely a month after its occupation of the town in March.

Here, also, it was impossible to remain without the support of A. J. Smith,

Answer. "That is a great mystery to me. I was at that time medical director of the Nineteenth Army Corps. I saw General Franklin immediately after our victory, as we assume it to be. I told him that in the hurry of sending off the supply trains in the morning, they had sent off my medical supply train. He said at that time that it should be ordered to return at once. To make sure of this matter, I went to see Major Drake, General Banks's adjutant general. He told me to give myself no uneasiness about the matter, as he would send off a courier at once and order up the medical supply train. I saw General Franklin, and told him that I should be busy all night, and in case the army moved off in any direction he must apprise me. I was told that I should be informed. That was the last I knew of the matter until between 6 and 7 o'clock the next morning, when, observing a little squad of cavalry drawn up in front of my hospital, I went out and inquired, and found that the army had retired during the night, and that this cavalry was the rear-guard about leaving the place. They said they had seen the enemy approaching in the distance, whereupon I left one or two assistant surgeons with instructions, mounted my horse, and rode off."

Question. "Did you see any real necessity for leaving our wounded in the hands of the enemy there?"

Answer. "Yes, sir; we had no transportation at that time of any kind. There was not a wagon of any kind there."

GENERAL BANKS CROSSING CANE RIVER.

PORTER'S FLEET PASSING THE DAM AT ALEXANDRIA.

whose time for co-operation with Banks had already expired. But, before retreating farther, it was necessary to rescue the fleet from its perilous situation by getting it below the falls. The difficulty had been foreseen by Lieutenant Colonel Joseph Bailey, engineer of the Nineteenth Corps, who, as early as the battle of Pleasant Hill, had suggested to General Franklin a plan for its removal by means of dams. Franklin approved the project. Admiral Porter does not seem to have had much faith in it. He remarked, when the plan was first proposed to him, that "if damming would get the fleet off, he would have been afloat long before."

The plan was carried out by the army under Bailey's supervision. Between two and three thousand men were engaged in the work of damming the river, which was commenced on the 2d and completed on the 8th of May. The rapids, or falls at Alexandria, are over a mile long. At the foot of these the main dam was constructed, the river at this point being 758 feet wide, and the depth of water from four to six feet, with a swift current of about ten miles per hour. Two wing-dams were also constructed at the head of the rapids. By means of these dams the depth of water was increased by 6½ feet, and eight valuable gun-boats were thus saved from destruction. Four of the gun-boats passed immediately upon the completion of the work. The rest might have passed at the same time if Porter had been prepared to avail himself of the advantage. The pressure of the water upon the dam was very great, as might have been expected, and before the admiral was ready to get down his other boats, the works gave way. Additional wing-dams were then constructed, and on the 13th the entire fleet was safe below the falls.

Before the relief of the fleet Banks had received a dispatch from Lieutenant-General Grant directing that no troops should be withdrawn from the operations against Shreveport, which were to be continued until farther orders.

But the continuance of the campaign was, of course, impracticable. As soon as the fleet had been relieved Banks evacuated Alexandria, moving from that point to Simmsport, on the Atchafalaya. On the morning of his departure a fire broke out in a building on the levee, and, under a high wind, extended to a large portion of the town.

Previous to the evacuation of Alexandria, the light gun-boats Signal and Covington, passing down the river with the transport Warner, were fired on by a large Confederate force. The Covington was burned, and the Signal, with the transport, were surrendered, with 150 soldiers. Soon afterward the transport City Belle was captured, with 225 men, who were being conveyed up to Alexandria.

The march to Simmsport was interrupted for a few hours at Mansura, near Marksville, by a Confederate cavalry force, which, after a spirited skirmish, was driven away. Simmsport was reached on the evening of May 16th. Here the army crossed the Atchafalaya by a bridge built of steam-boats on the 20th. While the wagon train was crossing the bridge, a Confederate force under Polignac attacked the rear of the army, but was repulsed by A. J. Smith's command. Having crossed the river, Banks met General E. R. S. Canby, who had been sent to relieve him of the command of the Department of the Gulf, and to whom General Banks turned over the army, proceeding himself to New Orleans. General A. J. Smith now returned to his own department. Admiral Porter descended the Red River and resumed his patrol of the Mississippi.

Before tracing the progress of Steele's co-operative column from Little Rock, let us rapidly review the military events which had taken place in Missouri and Arkansas up to the inception of the Red River campaign.

Shortly after Hindman's defeat at Prairie Grove in the latter part of 1862, a Confederate force of about 4000 men, under General Marmaduke, moved around General Blunt's command in Northern Arkansas, and marched on Springfield, in Missouri. This important station, the dépôt of munitions and supplies for the Federal troops operating in Arkansas, was partially fortified, and was held by a garrison of 1200 men under Brigadier General E. B. Brown, consisting of state militia, a small portion of the Eighteenth Iowa, and about 300 convalescent soldiers known as the "Quinine Brigade." The main body of the Federal army under General Blunt was in the vicinity of Fayetteville, on the Arkansas border, too distant to furnish assistance, and yet dependent for its own safety upon the secure possession of Springfield. Marmaduke attacked Brown on the 8th of January, 1863, and after fighting from 10 A.M. till dark, losing some 200 men, withdrew without gaining any other advantage than the capture of a single gun. The loss of the garrison was 164 men, of whom 14 were killed. Among the wounded was General Brown, who had managed the defense of his post with great skill and bravery.

At Hartsville, 40 miles east of Springfield, Marmaduke encountered on the 10th a small detachment of Federal troops under Colonel Merrill, consisting of the Twenty-first Iowa and Ninety-ninth Illinois, with portions of the Third Missouri and Third Iowa cavalry, and a battery of artillery. Here, after a sharp skirmish, he was repulsed with a loss of 300 men; Merrill's loss amounting to 78, including 7 killed. While the Federal forces were being concentrated to intercept his retreat, Marmaduke retreated into Arkansas. At Batesville, on the 4th of February, a part of his force was attacked by Colonel Waring, who, with the Fourth Missouri cavalry, drove him across the White River.

General Curtis on the 9th of March, 1863, was relieved of the command of the Missouri Department, which about a month later was assigned to General Schofield.

In the latter part of April, Marmaduke, with a considerable force, again entered Missouri, and made an attempt on Cape Girardeau, the capture of which would have very much disturbed Grant's Vicksburg campaign, but the timely appearance of the Federal gun-boats frightened him off, sending him back to Arkansas. A month later an engagement occurred at Fort Blunt, in Indian Territory, which was occupied by the Federal Colonel Phillips with 800 cavalry and an Indian regiment. A Confederate force about 3000 strong was led by Colonel Coffey against this fort. The defense was successfully maintained, and the enemy driven south of the Arkansas.

During the summer of 1863, the more important military operations in Mississippi and Tennessee reduced both the Federal and Confederate forces in the trans-Mississippi territory to such an extent that there were no hostilities in that region of any moment. Blunt had an encounter in July with a force of the enemy under General Cooper, which was menacing Fort Blunt. The fight took place on Elk River. Cooper had about 6000 men, and Blunt 3000 infantry, 250 cavalry, and 4 guns. General Blunt crossed the river, and, after a fight of two hours, drove the enemy, who left on the field 150 killed and 77 prisoners, besides 400 wounded, which were removed. The Federal loss was 17 killed and 60 wounded. Immediately after Cooper's defeat, 3000 Texans arrived under Cabell to re-enforce the enemy, but retired during the night without a battle.

In August, 1863, the Confederate partisan "Quantrell" made his notorious raid through Western Missouri into Kansas. With a force of 300 bandits gathered together in Western Missouri, he crossed the Kansas border, and on the morning of August 22 entered Lawrence and commenced a sack of that town. The citizens were murdered without discrimination. For a citizen to appear in the street with a defensive weapon of any sort, or to be a German or a negro, were deemed sufficient reasons why he should be shot. The finest dwellings and the public buildings were committed to the flames. The banks and stores were pillaged. Many private citizens, after surrendering to these merciless fiends all their money, were killed. Eighteen recruits found without arms in their hands were cowardly butchered. J. H. Lane, a United States senator, was at Lawrence, but, with Colonel Deitzler and others, managed to escape. General Collamore, taking refuge in a well, was suffocated, and two men in an attempt to rescue him suffered a similar fate. By 10 o'clock A.M. 140 men had been killed and nearly 200 buildings burned, when the savage monsters left the scene of their cruelties. As

RUINS OF LAWRENCE, KANSAS.

LITTLE ROCK, ARKANSAS.

they were leaving three of them were killed by the fire of some soldiers who had just reached the opposite bank of the Kansas River. The band was pursued by a small force of cavalry, but, with the loss of a few men, effected its escape.

The day after this event, Colonel Woodson, with 600 men from Pilot Knob, captured at Pocahontas, Arkansas, General Jeff. Thompson and about 50 of his men.

At the close of July, 1863, General Steele was sent to Helena to organize an expedition for the capture of Little Rock, Arkansas. The force assigned to him for this purpose consisted of 6000 men, including 500 cavalry and 22 guns. He was afterward re-enforced by General Davidson with nearly 6000 more men, most of them mounted, and 18 guns. He advanced from Helena on the 10th of August, crossing the White River at Clarendon, 60 miles east of Little Rock, on the 17th, with Davidson's cavalry in the advance. His sick at this time numbered about 1000. These were sent to Duvall's Bluff, which was made the dépôt of supplies. On the 25th Davidson reached Brownsville, 25 miles distant from Little Rock, driving Marmaduke before him to his intrenchments at Bayou Metea, from which he was dislodged and driven across the bayou. Meanwhile Steele had concentrated his forces—re-enforced by General True's brigade from Memphis—at Brownsville. Shut off from an advance north of Bayou Metea by the nature of the country, which, on account of swamps, was impracticable, he determined to advance to the Arkansas, and threaten with his cavalry the enemy's communications southward. Davidson crossed the Arkansas to carry out this plan. Marmaduke, sent out by General Holmes to resist him, was completely routed. General Price, the Confederate commander in Arkansas, then evacuated Little Rock, which was occupied by Steele on the 10th of September. Price, in some disorder and in great haste, fell back to Arkadelphia, eluding pursuit. Steele had started out on his campaign with 12,000 men, and entered Little Rock with only 7000. Of this loss less than one fiftieth was caused in battle, the remainder arising from sickness.

On the 4th of October we again hear from Quantrell, who, with 600 guerrillas disguised in Federal uniform, attacks General Blunt on his way to Fort Smith (captured by a Union force a month previous) with an escort of about 100 cavalry. General Blunt, with about 15 men, fortunately escaped. The remainder were captured, and then murdered in cold blood.

Pine Bluff, fifty miles below Little Rock, on the south bank of the Arkansas, was occupied early in October by Colonel Clayton with 350 men of the Fifth Kansas Cavalry and four guns. Marmaduke advanced against this point on the 25th of October with 12 guns and a cavalry force of between 2000 and 3000 men. In the mean time Clayton had been re-enforced by the First Indiana Cavalry and five guns. Marmaduke's attack failed. His loss was 150 killed and wounded, and 33 captured. Clayton lost 17 killed and 40 wounded.

The Confederate General Shelby, of Cabell's command, having failed in a series of unimportant attempts in Indian Territory, about this time undertook a raid into Missouri. Crossing the Arkansas between Fort Smith and Little Rock, he was joined in Southwestern Missouri by a force under General Coffey, their combined command numbering possibly 2500 men. This expedition advanced as far north as Booneville, on the Missouri River, when it commenced to retreat, pursued by General E. B. Brown with a detachment of State militia. The enemy was brought to a stand near Arrow Rock on the 13th of October. Here there was an engagement which lasted five hours, resulting finally in the defeat of the Confederates, who, besides all their artillery and baggage, lost 300 men, killed, wounded, and prisoners. On the 18th of December General McNeil superseded General Blunt as commander of the Army of the Frontier.

General Steele commenced his movement southward from Little Rock to co-operate with Banks's advance to Shreveport on the 23d of March, 1864, or about the time of Franklin's arrival at Alexandria. His army was 7000 strong. General Thayer at the same time marched from Fort Smith with 5000 men, intending to unite with Steele at Arkadelphia, while Colonel Clayton, with a small force, advanced from Pine Bluff on Steele's left. Steele reached Arkadelphia on the 29th of March; but Thayer, owing to heavy rains and almost impracticable roads, was delayed, and after waiting for him two days, the main column continued its advance. The Confederate cavalry under Shelby and Marmaduke had skirmished with its front all the way from the Sabine River, and farther down the Washita was a considerable force of infantry under General Price. Two days after Banks's defeat at Sabine Cross-roads this latter force was encountered at Prairie d'Anne, and a sharp fight, chiefly with artillery, followed. A charge of the enemy upon Steele's artillery was repulsed, and Price fell back to Washington, near the Upper Red River. From prisoners and spies, intelligence was now received of Banks's defeat. This report turned Steele from his pursuit of Price eastward to Camden. The Confederates then became bolder, attacking on the 23d of April a train of 240 wagons, which had arrived from Pine Bluff three days before, and was then returning, guarded by one of General Salomon's brigades. The attack was made 12 miles from Camden by Shelby's cavalry, and was easily repulsed. The train proceeded six miles farther, and was then parked for the night. The road was bad, and much of the distance had to be corduroyed: thus, on the 24th, only 22 miles had been made. The next morning, while crawling through a long swamp, the guard was again attacked at Markah Mills by General Fagan's command, reported 6000 strong. The advance being cut off from the rear after a gallant resistance, which cost the Federals 250 killed and wounded—one fourth of the entire brigade—both columns surrendered, and the wagons were either captured or destroyed. According to custom, all negroes found in the command were shot after the surrender.

On the 28th of April Steele abandoned Camden, crossed the Washita, and, continually skirmishing with the enemy's cavalry, proceeded to the Sabine. By this retreat he had just escaped disaster. Kirby Smith, having thrust back General Banks, was now prepared to strike Steele. As it was, Smith assailed the rear of the retreating column as the latter was crossing the Sabine at Jenkins's Ferry. A portion of the army was already across the river, and thus the brunt of the attack fell upon the two rear brigades until re-enforcements were brought up by General Rice. The enemy succeeded finally in turning the left, but the line was restored, and by noon the attack was repulsed, and the army crossed the bridge. No artillery could be used on account of the nature of the ground. The Federal loss was 700 killed and wounded. That of the enemy was estimated as over three times that number.

With Fagan in his front menacing Little Rock, Steele's position was one of great peril. His animals were starving, compelling the destruction of nearly all his wagons. The roads were next to impassable, and over these the exhausted and hungry troops dragged their guns. Notwithstanding these difficulties, Steele succeeded in reaching Little Rock on the 2d of May.

By Steele's reverses about two thirds of the state were recovered by the Confederates, whose cavalry and partisan rangers, avoiding the few Federal strong-holds, ravaged the country without molestation or resistance. This situation was full of discomforts to those who had previously, encouraged by the prospects of restoration, which had been so flattering at the time of the capture of Little Rock in the previous autumn, committed themselves to the Union cause. During the winter of 1863–4 measures had been taken to restore the state to the Union. A Constitutional Convention was assembled at Little Rock on the 8th of January, in which 42 out of 54 counties were represented. A new State Constitution was framed, in which slavery was forever prohibited. Dr. Isaac Murphy was inaugurated provisional governor on the 22d of January. In March the new Constitution was submitted to the people, and ratified by over 12,000 votes; and state officers, three members of Congress, and a Legislature were elected. In April the Legislature convened, and elected United States senators. But all these acts were in great measure annulled by the helplessness of Steele's military force. In the autumn of 1864 a Confederate Legislature met at Washington, in Southwestern Arkansas. A message was sent to it by the Confederate Governor Hannigan, and A. P. Garland was elected to represent the state in the Confederate Senate at Richmond.

The command of the entire trans-Mississippi military division was in 1864 given to General Canby. The garrison at Matagorda had been withdrawn. After the Red River campaign, with the exception of Price's raid into Missouri in the autumn, there was no military campaign of any importance undertaken before the close of the war in 1865. Although this raid overlaps the Atlantic campaign, this is the proper connection in which it should be placed before the reader.

CHAPTER XL.

PRICE'S MISSOURI RAID.

Rosecrans assumes Command of the Department of the Missouri January 28, 1864.—Extent and Distribution of his Command.—The "Paw-paw" Militia.—Feud between Radicals and Conservatives.—Secret Organizations in Northern Missouri.—Price advances northward in September.—Rosecrans is re-enforced by A. J. Smith's Division.—Defense of St. Louis.—Price attacks Pilot Knob; Ewing retreats upon Rolla.—Rosecrans assumes the Offensive.—Pleasonton takes command of the Cavalry.—Progress of Price westward, and Movements of the Federal Forces.—General Curtis is attacked at Marshall and driven.—A good Opportunity thrown away by the Federals.—Pleasonton's Pursuit of Price.—Fight on the Big Blue.—Price is defeated, but escapes Southward.—Fight with his Rear-guard on the Osage.—Criticism of the Campaign.

ROSECRANS, after having been superseded by Thomas as commander of the Department of the Cumberland, was, on the 28th of January, 1864, assigned to the command of the Department of the Missouri. His force consisted of about 12,000 men, mainly composed of state militia, out of ten regiments of which all but one were mounted men. To this there were added four regiments of three-years' volunteers, and a similar force of cavalry. There was also in process of organization a regiment (the Second Missouri) of heavy artillery. This command was distributed through the state at the most important posts—at Springfield, Rolla, Pilot Knob, Cape Girardeau, Jefferson City, Sedalia, Macon City, and, north of the Missouri River, at St. Joseph.

There was also a force of Missouri militia, 2800 in number, in the northwestern part of the state, "provisionally enrolled," and armed by the state government. It was composed in great proportion of disloyal citizens, a large number of whom had returned home from Price's army. Pledged to obey the laws of the state and of the general government, their especial business, as they understood it, was to take care of the peaceful sympathizers with rebellion, protecting them against the indignation of the Unionists. They were called the "Paw-paw militia," to identify them with "bushwhackers"—the paw-paw being the sort of fruit upon which this class of rebel sympathizers was supposed to subsist when it took to the bush.

This Paw-paw militia was a great element of disturbance in Missouri. There was a feud at this time between the two classes of citizens in the state known respectively as Radicals, or Abolitionists, and Conservatives—the latter class being generally understood to entertain a secret preference in favor of the Confederacy. It was confidently believed that the Paw-paws were, together with the Conservatives, in league with General Price; and that they only waited his approach to throw aside their assumed disguise. The disguise, after all, seemed only partial, especially in the great slaveholding counties on the river, where the so-called Conservatives, evidently expect
a visit shortly from Price's army, warned the Union citizens "that the L
alists had pretty nearly had their time, and that it would soon come to
end, and then the Disloyalists would have *their* time." Carefully observ
these indications, and finding that arms were plentifully coming into
northern part of the state, Rosecrans felt that the apprehensions of the
ionists were well grounded, and, determined to be on his guard, he in
mean time quietly investigated the situation. Of course Rosecrans succe
ed in detecting the whole plot. If the Confederates had been leagued w
the powers of darkness, Rosecrans's spies would in some way have ferre
out their machinations; and even if the delicate business had required a
to Hades, they would surely have accomplished it and reported to he
quarters!

Rosecrans soon found that the basis of the hopes of the Confederate sy
pathizers in Missouri was a secret society. The organization of this soci
took the shape of lodges, in Northern Missouri mainly. The leaders pro
to be Confederates. There seemed to be no limit to the organization, wh
existed even in Union settlements, and extended to the backwoods. It
apparent that its designs were military in character as well as political.
intelligent physician was employed by Rosecrans, and sent into North
Missouri with a roving commission. This man made his way into one
the lodges, and advanced in degree until finally he obtained a ritual from
grand commander of the state. A closer scrutiny detected an extension
the organization into Indiana, Kentucky, and Illinois, and finally traced
to New York. In Missouri it was designated "The Order of Americ
Knights," or "Sons of Liberty." The exiled Vallandigham was the
preme commander in the North, and General Sterling Price in the Sou
It was found that about 23,000 men were sworn to join Price on his
pearance in Missouri. Under the auspices of this secret society, Vallan
gham was to return to Ohio to attend the Democratic Convention at Chica
on the 4th of July. Simultaneously a rising was to occur in all the sta
in which the order existed, the existing officials were to be put out of t
way, and the arsenals, forts, and public property were to be seized. A ge
eral Northern invasion was to be made at the same time by the Confed
ates.

In view of these developments, Rosecrans asked for an augmentation
his force in Missouri. General Hunt was sent by General Grant to th
state on a tour of observation, and reported his belief that the inhabitan
would behave themselves, that Rosecrans was too apprehensive, and that t
force already in the department was larger than was needed.

Rosecrans went on with his investigation, and having accumulated 10
pages of testimony, wrote a note to General Garfield at Washington, askin
the latter to state to President Lincoln that he had this testimony, and o
tain permission for him to send on a staff officer to lay the whole matt
before the President.[1] President Lincoln requested Rosecrans to send h
depositions by mail or express. Rosecrans replied that that would not
safe. The President then sent one of his private secretaries, Major Hay,
Missouri. He read the testimony, and reported to the President. No esp
cial notice at this time seems to have been taken of the affair at Washingto

In the mean time, it was boldly proposed in one of the lodges of the O
der of American Knights to commence the assassination of Union officers
St. Louis, "beginning with the provost-marshal, and then wind up with
grab at department headquarters." This startling proposition was laid ov
to the next meeting. Rosecrans immediately arrested the state command
of the society—the Belgian consul at St. Louis—the deputy commande
grand secretary, lecturer, and thirty or forty leading members, and comm
ted them to prison. A dispatch was soon received from the War Depa
ment ordering the release of the Belgian consul. Rosecrans refused to co
ply with the order, knowing that it would not have been given if the go
ernment had been acquainted with all the facts of the case. A full repr
sentation of the matter having been laid before the President upon the retu
of Major Hay, the order of release was countermanded. Rosecrans was
impressed with the necessity of his action that he would have sooner r
signed his command than have released the consul.

The Democratic Convention at Chicago was postponed, bu[illegible]e Confe
crate schemes in Missouri were so fully matured that they could not be th
postponed. The hostile flag was hoisted in Platte County on the 7th
July, and these peculiar exemplars of American knighthood commenc
their operations. "From that time," says Rosecrans, "until after the exp
ration of the invasion and the expulsion of Price, there was nothing b
murder and rapine wherever they could operate."

After the Fort Pillow massacre, the four regiments of three-years' volu

[1] "Having about a thousand pages of testimony, obtained in the way I have just mentioned
wrote a note to General Garfield, in Washington, requesting him to state to the President tha
had this, and to say that, as the time for the dénouement was approaching rapidly, and that
the thing was not in a sufficiently perfect state to take action on without submitting it to hi
more particularly as it concerned not only my own department, but the whole West of the natio
I wished permission from him to send a staff officer, who understood the subject, with the fra
ments of the testimony we had collected, to lay the whole matter before him, and answer su
questions as the President desired to put; that I made this request, not because I doubted
right to send a staff officer to Washington, but because, when I had before sent a staff officer
a similar occasion, on a business of importance, he had been arrested by the Secretary of War, a
I did not wish to subject another officer unnecessarily to the same indignity."—*Testimony befo
the Committee on the Conduct of the War, Rosecrans's Campaign*, p. 52.

In regard to the arrest by the Secretary of War of one of his staff officers, General Rosecra
testified: "He [the secretary] arrested my senior aid, who brought letters to General Halleck a
General Grant respecting the condition of Missouri, and the measures which I thought imme
ately necessary there to be of advantage to the government and to the state. He was arrested
the pretense that he had no permission to come here, under an old order that no officer shou
visit Washington without permission from the Secretary of War. Major Bond returned home u
der arrest; and, considering that the shortest way to get rid of his arrest would be to have hi
tried, I ordered his trial by a court composed of the highest officers in Missouri, Major Gene
Pleasanton being president. That court unanimously and honorably acquitted him."—P. 5
ibidem.

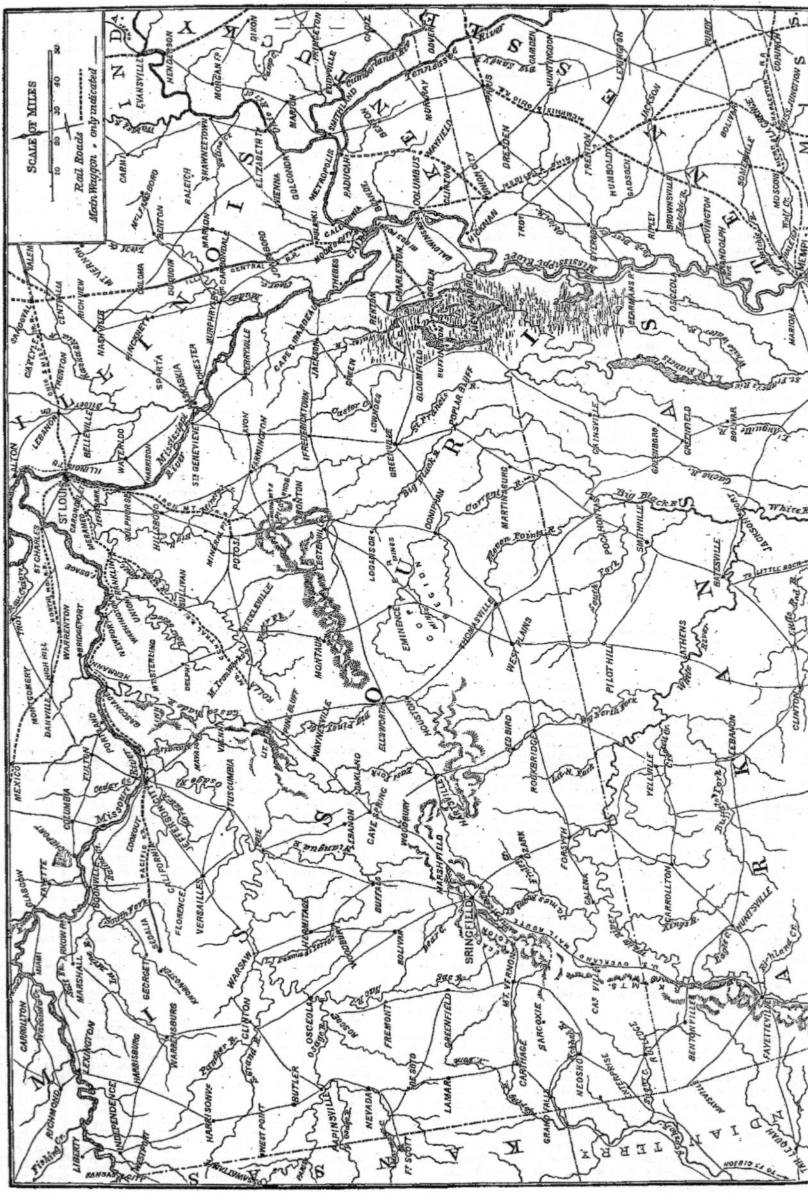

MAP OF MISSOURI.

REFUGEES FROM NORTHERN MISSOURI ENTERING ST. LOUIS.

leers which Rosecrans had at St. Louis were withdrawn from his department, as was also most of his three-years' cavalry. To supply their place, eleven regiments of twelve-months' volunteers were raised during the summer. Price's movement did not commence as early as Rosecrans had been led to anticipate. Perhaps he was deceived as to the extent and intimacy of the correspondence between the Confederate military leaders and the "Sons of Liberty;" but as to the existence of some connection between them, or as to its intent, there could be no doubt. The first sign of the invasion appeared in Arkansas early in September, 1864. On the 3d Washburn warned Rosecrans that a junction was about to be formed of Shelby's cavalry at Batesville with Price's army for the invasion of Missouri. At this time A. J. Smith's command was passing Cairo on its way to Sherman's army in Northern Georgia. At Rosecrans's request, this division was halted by order of General Halleck, and sent to St. Louis. It was decided to await Price's movements instead of advancing against him before he should cross the border.

Price by the 23d of September had crossed the Arkansas River, and was reported to be near Batesville with two divisions of mounted men, three batteries, and a large wagon train; his force probably numbered 15,000 men. He entered the southeastern portion of Missouri, and advanced northward toward Rolla, with a detachment thrown out toward Pilot Knob. General Ewing was now ordered to concentrate the troops of his district at Pilot Knob and Cape Girardeau, and two of Smith's brigades were pushed out toward the front so far as seemed consistent with the safety of St. Louis. St. Louis must be protected at all hazards, being the great dépôt of supplies for the trans-Mississippi armies. This city has three approaches by railroad south of the Missouri River: one from the east, *via* Independence and Jefferson City; another, that against which Price was marching, from the southwest, *via* Rolla; and a third from Memphis, *via* Pilot Knob. It was important to maintain Springfield, Rolla, Jefferson City, and Pilot Knob if possible, but the capture of either of these positions by the enemy must be suffered rather than that, by a general engagement at any of these points, the safety of St. Louis should be endangered. The Federal General Mower's division was daily expected from Arkansas, but, until the arrival of this re-enforcement, it was evident that Price had a free course open to him through the state.

A portion of Price's army on the 27th of September attacked Pilot Knob, which was held by one brigade under General Ewing. The fortifications at this post were rude, but sufficiently strong to enable the garrison of 1200 men to maintain an obstinate and successful stand against several times that number. But the enemy gained commanding positions, which would have finally compelled the surrender of the post. Therefore, during the night, Ewing, having blown up his magazines and spiked his heavy guns, retreated toward Rolla. In the repulse at Pilot Knob the enemy lost over 1000 men (Ewing says 1500), while the Federal loss was less than 100. Price had already a column at Potosi, little more than twenty miles north of Pilot Knob, thus compelling Ewing to retreat in the direction of Rolla, and apparently threatening St. Louis.

Perhaps it was on account of the lesson which he had learned at Pilot Knob that Price did not make an attempt to capture St. Louis. Certainly he did not continue his advance in that direction, but turned westward, and moved on Jefferson City. Ewing retreated rapidly to Webster, and there veered northward, and struck the railroad to Springfield at Harrison, having marched about sixty-six miles in thirty-nine hours, pursued by Shelby's cavalry. The latter made an attack at this point, but Ewing held his ground for thirty hours, until re-enforced by a detachment of Sanborn's cavalry, sent from Rolla to his assistance. The apparent helplessness of Rosecrans encouraged the "conservative" guerrillas in Northern Missouri, who now grew bolder in their work of murder and plunder.[1]

It was at first hard to tell whether Price would strike for St. Louis, or for Jefferson City, or for Rolla. His delay to strike a decisive blow enabled Rosecrans to accumulate a force large enough for offensive operations. Five regiments of 100-days' men were brought from Illinois before the 1st of October, and were placed in the fortifications of St. Louis, relieving General Smith's command. A cavalry force had been raised of about 1500 men. Out of the East Missouri militia about 5000 men were organized into an effective division under General Pike. Besides these, under the direction of the mayor of St. Louis, about 5000 citizen soldiers volunteered for the defense of the city. A. J. Smith's command numbered 4500 men. General Mower's veteran division, 5000 strong, arrived at Cape Girardeau on the 5th of October. Adding to these the detachments at Rolla and Jefferson City, with Ewing's force, Rosecrans must, during the first week of October, have had a veteran army full 20,000 strong, besides over 12,000 citizen soldiers.

In the mean time the enemy, moving by Potosi, had advanced across the Meramee to Richwood, only 40 miles distant from St. Louis. Between this force and the city was A. J. Smith's command and 1500 cavalry. Demonstrating against Smith with a portion of his army, Price, on the 1st of October, after burning the railroad bridge across the Meramee at Moselle, turned toward Jefferson City, having crossed the Gasconade and the Osage by the 6th, burning Herman and the railroad bridge on his way. On the 7th he appeared before Jefferson City, garrisoned by troops from Rolla under Sanborn and McNeil, and fortified by hastily-constructed intrenchments. The garrison consisted of about 7000 men, nearly three fifths of whom was cavalry. Price drew up his forces, forming a line of battle three or four miles long about the city, but did not venture to assault; for, in addition to the intrenched force in his front, Smith, and Mower, and Winslow's cavalry were rapidly following, and would soon be upon his rear. Waiting only for his train to get a fair start, he resumed his march westward. On the 8th the Federal General Pleasonton, who had distinguished himself as a cavalry leader in Virginia, arrived at Jefferson City and assumed command. He dispatched Sanborn's cavalry with instructions to harass and delay the enemy until Mower and Smith could join the forces then in the capital. Sanborn advanced, and, in accordance with these orders, attacked Price's rear-guard at Versailles, and found that the enemy was moving to Booneville, on the Missouri. Pushing his attack with vigor, he compelled the enemy to form in line of battle; but soon finding that if he remained he would probably be surrounded, Sanborn fell back a few miles to California, where he was joined by Colonel Catherwood with A. J. Smith's cavalry on the 14th. Smith's infantry in the mean time reached Jefferson City, followed on the 16th by Winslow's cavalry, and on the 17th by nearly all of Mower's division.

By this time Price had reached Marshall, 25 miles west of Booneville. A detachment of cavalry under Shelby had crossed the Missouri at Arrow Rock, about midway between the two places last mentioned, and, moving up the river to Glasgow, which he took after a fight of seven hours, captured a part of Colonel Harding's regiment—the Forty-third Missouri—with small detachments of the Ninth Missouri militia and Seventeenth Illinois Cavalry. The Federal forces were fast closing in upon the enemy's rear, and more vigorous movement on their part ought to have resulted in an important and decisive victory. Smith and Mower had reached the Lamine River, and on the 18th and 19th the former advanced westward to Dunksburg, while still farther to the left General Pleasonton, now in command of the entire cavalry force, extended to Warrensburg.

Price leisurely proceeded to Lexington, 40 miles west of Marshall, where on the 19th he attacked General Curtis, who, after a slight skirmish, retreated to Independence. The enemy pursued to the Little Blue, where he struck General Blunt's Kansas division with such force that the retreat was continued to the Big Blue. When Rosecrans learned that the enemy was at Lexington, he ordered Pleasonton, who was demonstrating toward Waverly, to push on to Lexington, and Smith to follow. Of course the enemy had left before their arrival. Supposing that Price would be unable to cross the Big Blue in the face of Curtis's force, and would therefore move southward, Rosecrans ordered Pleasonton to harass the enemy's rear with McNeil's brigade, moving the remainder of his command to Lone Jack, to which point Smith was hurrying, having returned from his mistaken chase after the enemy. This order was unfortunately conditional; and Pleasonton, instead of complying with it, supposing that the enemy would continue his flight westward, kept on in pursuit, crossing Little Blue on the 22d, and, driving Price's rear-guard to Independence, made a charge at nightfall, capturing the place and taking two guns. Dispatching McNeil's brigade to Santa Fé to intercept the enemy, he telegraphed to Rosecrans requesting him to send Smith to Lexington. Rosecrans reluctantly complied with his request. On the morning of the 23d Pleasonton moved against the enemy at the crossing of the Big Blue, where a general engagement was fought, beginning at 7 A.M., and lasting until 1 P.M., when Shelby, finding that Marmaduke and Fagan were giving way, turned on Pleasonton, and for a moment shook Sanborn's brigade; but the skillful use of artillery and a gallant charge of the cavalry decided the fortunes of the day against the enemy, who now retired, pursued by Pleasonton and Curtis. Smith, reaching Independence at 5 P.M., was ordered to move by a forced march that night to Hickman's Mill, to strike the enemy in flank while passing that point. "Had he been ordered," reports Rosecrans, "and marched for that point instead of Independence the day before, General Smith would have arrived in time to strike the enemy's compact column and train with 9000 infantry and five batteries; but it was too late. He did not reach the mill until long after not only the enemy's, but our own columns had passed there."

Pleasonton continued the pursuit, the infantry following as rapidly as possible for support. On the banks of the Osage Price's rear-guard, composed of Marmaduke's cavalry, was overtaken, after a chase of 60 miles, on the 25th. Pleasonton here, by a furious charge, routed this Confederate force, capturing eight guns, several wagons, and nearly 1000 prisoners, including Generals Marmaduke and Cabell.

This campaign had lasted 48 days. Rosecrans reports his loss as 174 killed, 336 wounded, and 171 prisoners. Price had lost 1958 prisoners and 10 guns, and had succeeded in none of the objects for which his expedition had been undertaken. Missouri remained henceforth undisturbed by the enemy, and Price's invasion was the last important event of the war west of the Mississippi River.

Strategically the campaign on Rosecrans's part was not managed with that vigor and comprehension which we should have expected. But it was so ably conducted that, while the enemy was not made to suffer the full extent of punishment to which his audacity exposed him, he did not, on the other hand, inflict any material damage upon the Federal cause.[1]

---

[1] "Rebel agents, amnesty oath-takers, recruits, 'sympathizers,' O. A. K.'s, and traitors of every hue and stripe, had warmed into life at the approach of the great invasion. 'Women's fingers were busy making clothes for rebel soldiers out of goods plundered by the guerrillas; women's tongues were busy telling Union neighbors '*their time was now coming*.' General Fisk, with all his force, had been scouring the bush for weeks in the river counties in pursuit of hostile bands, composed largely of recruits from among that class of the inhabitants who claim protection, yet decline to perform the full duties of citizens, on the ground that they 'never tuck no sides.' A few facts will convey some idea of this warfare, carried on by Confederate agents here, while the agents abroad of their bloody and hypocritical despotism—Mason, Slidell, and Maury in Europe—have the effrontery to tell the nations of Christendom our government 'carries on the war with increasing ferocity, regardless of the laws of civilized warfare.' These gangs of rebels, whose families had been living in peace among their loyal neighbors, committed the most cold-blooded and diabolical murders, such as riding up to a farm-house, asking for water, and, while receiving it, shooting down the giver, an aged, inoffensive farmer, because he was a radical 'Union man.' In the single sub-district of Mexico the commanding officer furnished a list of near 100 Union men who, in the course of six weeks, had been killed, maimed, or 'run off' because they were 'radical Union men' or d—d Abolitionists. About the 1st of September Anderson's gang attacked a railroad train on the North Missouri, took from it twenty-two unarmed soldiers—many of them were on sick-leave—and, after robbing, placed them in a row and shot them in cold blood; some of the bodies they scalped, and put others across the track and ran the engine over them. On the 27th, this gang, with numbers swollen to 300 or 400 men, attacked Major Johnson, with about 120 men of the Thirty-ninth Missouri Volunteer Infantry, raw recruits, and, after stampeding their horses, shot every man, most of them in cold blood. Anderson, a few days later, was recognized by General Price at Booneville as a Confederate captain, and, with a verbal admonition to behave himself, ordered by Colonel Maclane, chief of Price's staff, to proceed to North Missouri and destroy the railroads, which orders were found on the miscreant when killed by Lieutenant Colonel Cox, about the 27th of October."—*Rosecrans's Report.*

[1] General Grant says of this campaign:

"The impunity with which Price was enabled to roam over the State of Missouri for a long time, and the incalculable mischief done by him, shows to how little purpose a superior force may be used. There is no reason why General Rosecrans should not have concentrated his forces, and beaten and driven Price before the latter reached Pilot Knob."

In view of all the circumstances of the case, and especially considering the domestic difficulties which Rosecrans encountered in Missouri, this criticism, notwithstanding its high military authority, does not seem to us to be quite fairly sustained by facts.

GENERAL WILLIAM TECUMSEH SHERMAN. RETIRED NOVEMBER 1, 1883.

CHAPTER XLI.

THE ATLANTA CAMPAIGN.

The general Military Situation at the opening of the Spring Campaign of 1864.—Richmond and Atlanta, held by the Armies of Lee and Johnston, were the Helmet and Shield of the Confederacy.—The Progress of the National Arms thus far had been in the West.—Importance of the Victories of Vicksburg and Chattanooga.—The Exhaustion of the Confederate Strength forbids offensive Operations on a large Scale by the Confederate Armies.—Comparison of the Operations during the Last Stage of the War to those of a Siege.—President Davis's Conduct of his Western Army.—Lack of Unity in Military Operations had been a great Fault on both Sides.—U. S. Grant is made Lieutenant General of the Armies of the United States.—He is ordered to Washington to receive his Commission.—His Letter to General Sherman, and Sherman's Reply.—General Sherman succeeds to Grant's former Command, and General J. B. McPherson to Sherman's.—Sherman goes to Nashville, and accompanies Grant thence to Cincinnati.—Lieutenant General Grant's Theory of prospective Operations.—Sherman's Tour of Observation.—Composition of his Army.—His Preparations for the Atlanta Campaign.—He orders the People of Tennessee to supply their own Rations.—He is ready for movement May 6th.—Review of General Thomas's Operations during the Winter.—Difficult Task assigned to General Johnston, commanding the Confederate Army.—His Correspondence with Bragg.—Can have no Re-enforcements for a Defensive Campaign.—While Johnston and Bragg discuss, Sherman moves against Dalton.—McPherson's Movement through Snake Creek Gap, threatening Resaca.—His Attack is delayed, and Hood is sent to Resaca.—Sherman moves his entire Army against Resaca.—Johnston evacuates Dalton.—The Battles of May 14th and 15th.—Johnston, again flanked, abandons Resaca, and, crossing the Oostenaula, retreats to Cassville.—Jeff. C. Davis's Division occupies Rome, Sherman's forces, in the mean time, advancing against Cassville.—Johnston consults with his Corps Commanders; Hardee advises Battle, Hood and Polk a Retreat.—Johnston, May 20th, crosses the Etowah.—Sherman follows May 23d, and, avoiding Allatoona, moves to the right against Dallas.—He finds the Enemy in his front, May 25th, at New Hope Church.—The Battle of New Hope Church.—Sherman develops toward the Left.—Battles of May 27th and 28th.—Sherman, continuing the Movement to the Left, secures the Railroad at Ackworth, June 6th, fortifies Allatoona as a secondary Base, and is re-enforced by Blair's Corps and Long's Cavalry.—Johnston also shifts his Position, and occupies Kenesaw in Sherman's Front.—Sherman hears of Morgan's Defeat in Kentucky, and of Forrest's Victory over Sturgis in Mississippi.—Lieutenant General Polk is killed June 14, and Pine and Lost Mountains are abandoned by the Enemy.—The new Confederate Line around Kenesaw.—"Villainously bad" Weather delays Sherman.—Hooker is attacked by Hood and repulsed, June 22, near the Kulp House.—Sherman assaults the Confederate Position at Kenesaw, June 27, without success.—He extends his Right toward Marietta, and on July 2 threatens Turner's Ferry on the Chattahoochee.—The next Day Johnston abandons Kenesaw.—Sherman is foiled in the Attempt to strike the Enemy while crossing the Chattahoochee.—He secures three Crossings above Johnston's Tête de Pont, and destroys the Rosswell Factories.—Johnston crosses on the night of July 9th, and takes Position on Peach-tree Creek.—The Situation at this Stage of the Campaign.—Rousseau's Raid on the West Point Railroad.—Sherman crosses the Chattahoochee July 17th.—The same day Johnston is removed from command and succeeded by Hood.—The Battle of Peach-tree Creek, July 20.—The Battle of the 22d.—General McPherson's Death.—Stoneman's and McCook's Raids.—Sherman gives Howard command of the Army and Department of the Tennessee, and transfers that Army to the west of Atlanta.—Hooker's Resignation.—The Battle of July 28th.—Sherman extends his Lines toward East Point.—His Objective the Macon Railroad.—Hood sends Wheeler North.—Kilpatrick's Raid.—The Siege abandoned, August 25th; the Twentieth Corps guards the Chattahoochee Bridge, and the rest of Sherman's Army moves against Jonesborough and the Macon Road.—The Battles of Jonesborough, August 31st and September 1st.—Hood evacuates Atlanta on the morning of September 2d.—General Sherman occupies the City, and orders the Inhabitants to Leave.—The Exodus.—Correspondence between Generals Sherman and Hood.

IN the four last chapters we have passed round the skirts of that central field in which, during the summer and autumn of 1864, the fate of the attempted Southern Confederacy was decided. From the eastern coast of Florida to the Missouri River our survey has ranged—embracing within its scope the brief Florida campaign of General Seymour, begun February 6th, 1864, and terminating on the 20th in the disastrous battle of Olustee; General Sherman's successful expedition to Meridian, February 3-26, 1864; General Banks's operations against the coast of Texas, September 5th, 1863–January 12th, 1864; the ill-advised and mismanaged Red River expedition in the spring of 1864; the military operations in Arkansas, January 8, 1863–May 2, 1864; and Rosecrans's campaign against Price in September and

October, 1864. From a chronological stand-point this survey ought perhaps to have included the siege of Charleston in the summer of 1863, and the operations of Admiral Farragut against the forts in Mobile Bay, August, 1864. We have determined otherwise, and shall treat of these operations in other connections—those against Mobile as a preliminary part of the campaign which finally resulted in the capture of that city, and the siege of Charleston in connection with Sherman's march from Atlanta to Goldsborough.

We turn, therefore, immediately to the consideration of Sherman's campaign against Johnston, terminating, after four months of strategical manœuvring, in the capture of Atlanta.

The spring of 1864 opened a new era for the armies of the Union. The war against the rebellion had now been going on for three years. Secretary Seward's prophetic period had already been multiplied by twelve, and still two great armies protected the Confederacy—covering Richmond, its head, and Atlanta, its heart. The helmet of the rebellion was Lee's Army of Northern Virginia; the shield before its heart was Johnston's Army of the Tennessee. To crush the one or pierce the other would be a death-blow. Thus far the Army of Northern Virginia had protected Richmond against the successive approaches of McDowell, McClellan, Burnside, and Hooker, and, after the repulse of the last, had boldly reversed the order of movement and invaded Pennsylvania, almost touching the Susquehanna in its northward march. This audacity had met its rebuke at Gettysburg, but Lee's army had resumed the defensive and still defied attack. Whatever progress had been made by the national arms had been in the West. The possession of the Mississippi had severed the western from the eastern half of the Confederacy. West of that river Kirby Smith's armies were secure from attack, not so much by their own strength as by the wastes of Texas—a sort of American Russia—from which, while they could safely whisper "Moscow" to any invader, they could not advance north of the Arkansas without disaster. Between the Mississippi River and the Appalachian range of mountains the waves of conflict had fluctuated, swaying northward and southward under the varying conditions of the war. President Davis was partial to an aggressive system of warfare. At an earlier period the invasion of the Northwestern States with a large army was practicable, and disorganized the plans of the Federal generals for pushing the war southward. Bragg's invasion of Kentucky was the last of these attempts which assumed formidable proportions. Its only success had been in the delay which it occasioned in the progress of the Union army. The secure possession of Chattanooga at the close of 1863 stayed this tendency of the war to fluctuate northward. After that the Confederate invasions were undertaken only with cavalry; flying tempests they were, sometimes violent in their ravages, but the work which they accomplished was of little military importance. These petty storms were soon past, and their wreck obliterated. It is true that, even after the capture of Nashville, Hood's army advanced northward to Nashville, but it was a desperate resort, and, as we shall soon see, illustrated at the same time its danger and its folly. But, beaten back to the mountains of Northern Georgia, the Army of the Tennessee still presented a bold front, covering the central and vital portion of the Confederacy. From Richmond to Atlanta, and on the coast from Wilmington to Mobile, the outside barriers of the Confederacy stood.[1] But let this outward shell be broken, even at a single strong point, and the whole structure must crumble into ruin. For the three past years had nearly exhausted the internal resources of the rebellion. Nearly all the strength and wealth sustaining it had been drawn to the surface. Very few able-bodied men were left at home; there was no reserved force upon which to draw, in any event. Money no longer remained a standard for the valuation of property. Gardens were now the Southern treasury; those who shared the possession of these, who were producers of any thing which sustained life, were rich to the extent of their producing power, and all others lived upon them—the soldiers by a legitimate claim, and non-combatants by the claim of necessity. The theory of the war from this time was strictly that of a siege; it had been that from the beginning, but not by so strict a construction of the term. To the garrison one problem was presented, What would be the best disposition of its forces for *defense?* Offensive operations on the part of the Confederate armies were henceforth unwise: in the first place, they could result in no material advantage, and, in the second, they involved a too rapid and extensive waste of force. Early's Shenandoah campaign, and Hood's advance to Nashville, will furnish illustrations of the folly of offensive operations in these later stages of the war. They were like sallies from a besieged fort, made by a force necessary to the defense of the fort, and at the same time insufficient to raise the siege. Certainly—whatever may have been the final result—the contest would have been prolonged if, on the part of the Confederates, a wise policy, one purely defensive, had been adopted from the commencement of the Atlanta campaign. The Confederate executive does not seem to have appreciated the full importance of the situation which was now presented. No measures were taken to secure unity of operation. To no single mind was given the control of military movements. President Davis conducted the Western campaigns, as he had done for the year past, after a very whimsical manner. By the pressure of popular opinion he had been compelled to give General Johnston command of the Army of the Tennessee, but he gave him little support, and at the first opportunity relieved him of the command. Not until it was too late was the general control of all the armies given to General Lee.

But, while the Confederate government conducted the war upon its former method, adhesion to the theories of the past was no longer suffered on the part of the general government. It is not necessary, nor would it be altogether just, to criticise with a great degree of harshness the Federal conduct of the war during these three years now concluded. The United States was not at all eminent as a military nation at the commencement of the war. The graduates of the Military Academy at West Point had not been trained in the face of war, as are European students. Besides, the study of the campaigns on the Continent of Europe during the last century, while it might have prevented very many blunders which were actually committed on both sides, would, in many important respects, have been inapplicable, on account of the peculiar topographical features of the campaigns of our civil war, and the extended area over which they were conducted. For two years, at the least, the war thus became a series of costly experiments. Then came the winnowing of our generals, and much of the chaff was blown away, though not all. A few military leaders had exhibited characteristics which entitled them to the more prominent positions in the army. Pre-eminent above all others was General Grant, who had not only been most successful, but had shown rare knowledge of men, remarkable common sense, and a persistence of purpose which was unconquerable. Gradually his sphere of control had been extended, until in 1864 he commanded all the armies in the West except that of the Gulf.[1] But still the general disposition of all the armies was subject to General Halleck at Washington. Now, without criticising Halleck's generalship, it is clear that there were several reasons why it was impossible for *any* officer in his position—whatever his military capacity—to wisely control all the military movements in so extensive a conflict. In the first place, his management *must* be simply theoretical. For Halleck had no large practical experience in war. In the Mexican War, for some successful skirmishing with the enemy he had been breveted captain. He had graduated at West Point the third in his class, and for a year was an assistant professor of engineering at the Academy. He had published some important military works. In this Civil War he had not fought a single battle, and the only march he had made was that of his Western Army to the evacuated fortifications at Corinth. Without practical experience, he must resort to theory; and frequently his theories were based upon insufficient premises. In the second place, his distance from the actual fields of conflict, and his subseqent ignorance of the circumstances which must regulate the military operations of his subordinates, led him either to make great mistakes in cases where he gave positive and peremptory orders, or to fall into the exactly opposite error of letting campaigns manage themselves in such a manner that no one could be strictly and fully responsible for their being undertaken or for their results. He assumed too much when he exercised positive and responsible control; and in cases where he was negative, and left every thing to the discretion of his subordinates, as in the case of the Red River expedition, there was no unity of action, and no absolute control by any one. The only exception to this military anarchy was in General Grant's command, simply because to him was surrendered the most complete control of the armies in his vast department. Here was a partial solution of the difficulty. Why not make an entire solution by giving to General Grant control of all the armies of the United States under the President? The voice of the people was loud and universal in favor of this; and the Thirty-eighth Congress, before the close of its first session, revived, for this purpose, the grade of lieutenant general. On the 2d of March, Grant, having been assigned to this grade

[1] The following extract from Lieutenant General Grant's Official Report shows very clearly the relative situation of the Confederate and Federal forces in May, 1864:

"At the date when this report begins the situation of the contending forces was about as follows: The Mississippi River was strongly garrisoned by Federal troops from St. Louis, Missouri, to its mouth. The line of the Arkansas was also held, thus giving us armed possession of all west of the Mississippi north of that stream. A few points in Southern Louisiana, not remote from the river, were held by us, together with a small garrison at and near the mouth of the Rio Grande. All the balance of the vast territory of Arkansas, Louisiana, and Texas was in the almost undisputed possession of the enemy, with an army of probably not less than 80,000 effective men, that could have been brought into the field had there been sufficient opposition to have brought them out. The let-alone policy had demoralized this force so that probably but little more than one half of it was ever present in garrison at any one time. But the one half, or 40,000 men, with the bands of guerrillas scattered through Missouri, Arkansas, and along the Mississippi River, and the disloyal character of much of the population, compelled the use of a large number of troops to keep navigation open on the river and to protect the loyal people to the west of it. To the east of the Mississippi we held substantially with the line of the Tennessee and Holston Rivers, running eastward to include nearly all of the State of Tennessee. South of Chattanooga a small foothold had been obtained in Georgia, sufficient to protect East Tennessee from incursions from the enemy's force at Dalton, Georgia. West Virginia was substantially within our lines. Virginia, with the exception of the northern border, the Potomac River, a small area about the mouth of James River, covered by the troops at Norfolk and Fortress Monroe, and the territory covered by the Army of the Potomac lying along the Rapidan, was in the possession of the enemy. Along the sea-coast footholds had been obtained at Plymouth, Washington, and Newbern, in North Carolina; Beaufort, Folly and Morris Islands, Hilton Head, Fort Pulaski, and Port Royal, in South Carolina; Fernandina and St. Augustine, in Florida. Key West and Pensacola were also in our possession, while all the important ports were blockaded by the navy. The accompanying map, a copy of which was sent to General Sherman and other commanders in March, 1864, shows, by red lines, the territory occupied by us at the beginning of the rebellion and at the opening of the campaign of 1864, while those in blue are the lines which it was proposed to occupy.

"Behind the Union lines there were many bands of guerrillas and a large population disloyal to the government, making it necessary to guard every foot of road or river used in supplying our armies. In the South a reign of military despotism prevailed, which made every man and boy capable of bearing arms a soldier, and those who could not bear arms in the field acted as provosts for collecting deserters and returning them. This enabled the enemy to bring almost his entire strength into the field.

"The enemy had concentrated the bulk of his forces east of the Mississippi into two armies, commanded by Generals R. E. Lee and J. E. Johnston, his ablest and best generals. The army commanded by Lee occupied the south bank of the Rapidan, extending from Mine Run westward, strongly intrenched, covering and defending Richmond, the rebel capital, against the Army of the Potomac. The army under Johnston occupied a strongly intrenched position at Dalton, Georgia, covering and defending Atlanta, Georgia, a place of great importance as a railroad centre, against the armies under Major General W. T. Sherman. In addition to these armies, he had a large cavalry force, under Forrest, in Northeast Mississippi; a considerable force of all arms in the Shenandoah Valley, and in the western part of Virginia and extreme eastern part of Tennessee, and also confronting our sea-coast garrisons, and holding blockaded ports where we had no foothold upon land.

"These two armies, and the cities covered and defended by them, were the main objective points of the campaign."

[1] Sherman suggested to Grant (January 4, 1864), in connection with the Red River expedition, that he ought to have the entire command of the Mississippi Valley. In a letter of that date, he says: "There is no doubt the whole matter would be simplified if you had command of the Mississippi Valley below Cairo. I think, if you were to name the subject to General Halleck, that he would order it, for its propriety is better known to him than to any other. Admiral Porter's command extends to and below New Orleans, and ours should also."

GRANT RECEIVING HIS COMMISSION AS LIEUTENANT GENERAL.

days after, General Grant, then in Nashville, was ordered to report in person at Washington. This order was to him an assurance of his confirmation; and his first feeling upon receiving it seems to have been one of generous gratitude to his faithful subordinates who had so ably seconded the enterprise for which he was now to receive the highest reward which it was in the power of the people and the government to bestow.[1]

General Washington alone had previously been honored with the full title conferred upon General Grant. In 1798 our relations with France threatened war, and at this crisis Washington was made lieutenant general. In another year, if he had lived, he would have been made full general. After General Scott's unsuccessful campaign for the Presidency, the grade of lieutenant general *by brevet* was conferred upon him. The latter, by the provisions of the bill promoting General Grant to the full grade, was still to retain his "rank, pay, and allowances."

At one o'clock on the afternoon of the 9th of March, General Grant was received by the President in the cabinet chamber at Washington, and received his commission. There was no pomp, no gathering of the populace, no splendid celebration of the honor conferred. The President was there with his cabinet; General Halleck, the retiring general-in-chief; General Rawlins, Grant's chief of staff; Colonel Comstock, his chief engineer; the President's private secretary, Mr. Nicolay, and the Honorable Owen Lovejoy, of Illinois. The only other person forming a part of the group was General Grant's eldest son, a boy of fourteen years. President Lincoln having presented General Grant to the cabinet, addressed him thus:

"GENERAL GRANT,—The nation's appreciation of what you have done, and its reliance upon you for what remains to be done in the existing great struggle, are now presented with this commission constituting you lieutenant general in the army of the United States. With this high honor devolves upon you also a corresponding responsibility. As the country herein trusts you, so, under God, it will sustain you. I scarcely need to add, that with what I here speak for the nation goes my own hearty personal concurrence."

General Grant's response was equally brief. He replied:

"MR. PRESIDENT,—I accept the commission with gratitude for the high honor conferred. With the aid of the noble armies that have fought on so many fields for our common country, it will be my earnest endeavor not to disappoint your expectations. I feel the full weight of the responsibilities now devolving on me, and I know that if they are met it will be due to those armies, and, above all, to the favor of that Providence which leads both nations and men."[2]

General Grant's chief of staff. By the same order Sherman succeeded t General Grant's former command of the Military Division of the Mississipp and General McPherson was assigned to the command of the Departmen and Army of the Tennessee.[1]

Upon the receipt of the order placing him in command of all the armie with headquarters in the field, General Grant was at Nashville, whither She man was forthwith summoned. Arriving at Nashville on March 17th, She man accompanied the lieutenant general as far on his way to Washington Cincinnati. On this journey the two generals consulted freely together to the plan of their future campaigns. The consultation was continued i the parlor of the Burnet House, at Cincinnati, where, over their maps, w planned the simultaneous assault upon the armies covering Richmond an Atlanta. To attack these two armies at once counteracted to a great degr the advantage of interior lines which was possessed by the enemy. To a tack with vigor, and without pause, regardless of seasons, would prevent an portion of the Confederate forces from returning home on furlough durin the winter to plant crops for their own sustenance. Grant's whole theor may be summed up in two sentences. Unity of operations. The attritic to powder of the Confederate armies by a continuous series of battles.[2] Tl main objects of attack were Lee's and Johnston's armies rather than the in portant strategical points which they covered. But the details of the can paigns about to be opened would necessarily depend upon the theory of d fense adopted by these two Confederate generals.[3]

General Sherman's new command consisted of four departments, with the armies, those of the Ohio, the Cumberland, the Tennessee, and Arkansas.

The Army of the Ohio, now under the command of Major General Joh M. Schofield, consisted of the Ninth and Twenty-third Corps. Longstre having joined Lee, the Ninth Corps was sent to re-enforce the Army of tl Potomac. Two divisions of the Twenty-third Corps, those of M. S. Hasc and J. D. Cox, took the field, the other three being retained to garrison Ke tucky and East Tennessee.

The Army of the Cumberland, at Chattanooga, commanded by Gener Thomas, consisted of the Fourth, Fourteenth, and Twentieth Corps, co manded respectively by Generals O. O. Howard, John M. Palmer, and Jose Hooker. The Fourth Corps comprised three divisions, under Stanley, Jol Newton, and Wood; the Fourteenth three, under Jeff C. Davis, R. W. Joh son, and Baird; and the Twentieth three, under A. S. Williams, Geary, a Butterfield.[4]

---

[1] Before starting for Washington he writes thus to General Sherman:

"DEAR SHERMAN,—The bill reviving the grade of lieutenant general in the army has become a law, and my name has been sent to the Senate for the place. I now receive orders to report to Washington immediately *in person*, which indicates a confirmation, or a likelihood of confirmation: I start this morning to comply with the order.

"While I have been eminently successful in this war in at least gaining the confidence of the public, no one feels more than I how much of this success is due to the energy, skill, and the harmonious putting forth of that energy and skill, of those whom it has been my good fortune to have occupying subordinate positions under me.

"There are many officers to whom these remarks are applicable to a greater or less degree, proportionate to their ability as soldiers; but what I want is to express my thanks to you and McPherson as the men to whom, above all others, I feel indebted for whatever I have had of success. How far your advice and assistance have been of help to me, you know. How far your execution of whatever has been given to you to do entitles you to the reward I am receiving, you can not know as well as I.

"I feel all the gratitude this letter would express, giving it the most flattering construction.

"The word *you* I use in the plural, intending it for McPherson also. I should write to him, and will some day, but, starting in the morning, I do not know that I will find time just now.

"Your friend, U. S. GRANT, *Major General.*"

Sherman's reply, written near Memphis March 10th, is equally characteristic. He says:

"DEAR GENERAL,—I have your more than kind and characteristic letter of the 4th instant. I will send a copy to General McPherson at once.

"You do yourself injustice and us too much honor in assigning to us too large a share of the merits which have led to your advancement. I know you approve the friendship I have ever professed to you, and will permit me to continue, as heretofore, to manifest it on all proper occasions.

"You are now Washington's legitimate successor, and occupy a position of almost dangerous elevation; but if you can continue, as heretofore, to be yourself, simple, honest, and unpretending, you will enjoy through life the respect and love of friends, and the homage of millions of human beings, that will award you a large share in securing to them and their descendants a government of law and stability.

"I repeat, you do General McPherson and myself too much honor. At Belmont you manifested your traits, neither of us being near. At Donelson, also, you illustrated your whole character. I was not near, and General McPherson was in too subordinate a capacity to influence you.

"Until you had won Donelson, I confess I was almost cowed by the terrible ray of anarchical elements that presented themselves at every point; but that admitted a ray of light I have followed ever since.

"I believe you are as brave, patriotic, and just as the great prototype Washington—as unselfish, kind-hearted, and honest as a man should be—but the chief characteristic is the simple faith in success you have always manifested, which I can liken to nothing else than the faith a Christian has in the Savior.

"This faith gave you victory at Shiloh and Vicksburg. Also, when you have completed your best preparations, you go into battle without hesitation, as at Chattanooga—no doubts—no reserves; and I tell you, it was this that made us act with confidence. I knew, wherever I was, that you thought of me, and if I got in a tight place you would help me out, if alive.

"My only point of doubts was in your knowledge of grand strategy, and of books of science and history; but, I confess, your common sense seems to have supplied all these.

"Now as to the future. Don't stay in Washington. Come West: take to yourself the whole Mississippi Valley. Let us make it dead sure; and I tell you the Atlantic slopes and the Pacific shores will follow its destiny, as sure as the limbs of a tree live or die with the main trunk. We have done much, but still much remains. Time, and time's influences, are with us. We could almost afford to sit still and let these influences work.

"Here lies the seat of the coming empire; and from the West, when our task is done, we will make short work of Charleston and Richmond, and the impoverished coast of the Atlantic.

"Your sincere friend, W. T. SHERMAN."

[2] The bill for reviving the grade of lieutenant general was presented to Congress by the Hon. E. B. Washburne, of Illinois. It was slightly amended, and was passed under the following form:

"*Be it enacted by the Senate and House of Representatives of the United States of America, in Congress assembled*, That the grade of lieutenant general be, and the same is hereby revived in the Army of the United States of America; and the President is hereby authorized, whenever he shall deem it expedient, to appoint, by and with the advice and consent of the Senate, a commander of the army, to be selected during war from among those officers in the military service of the United States, not below the grade of major general, most distinguished for courage, skill, and ability; and who, being commissioned as lieutenant general, *shall be authorized, under the direction of the President, to command the armies of the United States.*

"SEC. 2. *And be it further enacted*, That the lieutenant general appointed as is hereinbefore provided shall be entitled to the pay, allowances, and staff specified in the fifth section of the act a proved May 28, 1798; and also the allowances described in the sixth section of the act appro August 28, 1842, granting additional rations to certain officers; *Provided*, That nothing in t bill contained shall be construed in any way to affect the rank, pay, or allowances of Winfield Sco lieutenant general by brevet, now on the retired list of the army."

[1] "*General Orders, No. 98.*

"War Department, Adjutant General's Office, Washington, March 12, 1864

"The President of the United States orders as follows:

"1st. Major General Halleck is, at his own request, relieved from duty as general-in-chief of army, and Lieutenant General U. S. Grant is assigned to the command of the armies of the Unit States. The headquarters of the army will be in Washington, and also with Lieutenant Gene Grant in the field.

"2d. Major General Halleck is assigned to duty in Washington as chief of staff of the army, u der the direction of the Secretary of War and the Lieutenant General commanding. His ord will be obeyed and respected accordingly.

"3d. Major General W. T. Sherman is assigned to the command of the Military Division of Mississippi, composed of the Departments of the Ohio, the Cumberland, the Tennessee, and the A kansas.

"4th. Major General John B. McPherson is assigned to the command of the Department a Army of the Tennessee.

"5th. In relieving Major General Halleck from duty as general-in-chief, the President desi to express his approbation and thanks for the zealous manner in which the arduous and respons duties of that position have been performed.

"By order of the Secretary of War. D. E. TOWNSEND, *Assistant Adj. General.*"

[2] "From an early period in the rebellion I had been impressed with the idea that active a continuous operations of all the troops that could be brought into the field, regardless of season a weather, were necessary to a speedy termination of the war. The resources of the enemy, and numerical strength, were far inferior to ours; but, as an offset to this, we had a vast territory, w a population hostile to the government, to garrison, and long lines of river and railroad commu cations to protect, to enable us to supply the operating armies.

"The armies in the East and West acted independently and without concert, like a balky tea no two ever pulling together, enabling the enemy to use to great advantage his interior lines of co munication for transporting troops from east to west, re-enforcing the army most vigorously press and to furlough large numbers, during seasons of inactivity on our part, to go to their homes, a do the work of producing for the support of their armies. It was a question whether our num ical strength and resources were not more than balanced by these disadvantages and the enem superior position.

"From the first I was firm in the conviction that no peace could be had that would be stat and conducive to the happiness of the people both North and South, until the military power of rebellion was entirely broken. I therefore determined, first, to use the greatest number of tro practicable against the armed force of the enemy; preventing him from using the same force different seasons against first one and then another of our armies, and the possibility of repose refitting and producing necessary supplies for carrying on resistance. Second, to hammer conti ously against the armed force of the enemy and his resources, until by mere attrition, if in no ot way, there should be nothing left to him but an equal submission with the loyal section of our co mon country to the Constitution and laws of the land."—*Lieut. General Grant's Official Report.*

[3] From a letter written by Lieutenant General Grant to Sherman, dated Washington, April 1864, it appears that, in conjunction with the operations of his own and Sherman's armies, he tended that an attack should be made on Mobile. We give those portions of this letter which b upon Western operations:

"It is my design, if the enemy keep quiet and allow me to take the initiative in the spring ca paign, to work all parts of the army together, and somewhat toward a common centre. . . . have sent orders to Banks by private messengers to finish up his present expedition against Shre port with all dispatch; to turn over the defense of the Red River to General Steele and the na and return your troops to you, and his own to New Orleans; to abandon all of Texas except Rio Grande, and to hold that with not to exceed 4000 men; to reduce the number of troops on Mississippi to the lowest number necessary to hold it, and to collect from his command not less th 25,000 men. To this I will add 5000 men from Missouri. With this force he is to commence erations against Mobile as soon as he can. It will be impossible for him to commence too early.

"You I propose to move against Johnston's army, to break it up, and to get into the interior the enemy's country as far as you can, inflicting all the damage you can against their war resourc I do not propose to lay down for you a plan of campaign, but simply to lay down the work it is sirable to have done, and leave you free to execute in your own way. Submit to me, however, early as you can, your plan of operations. . . . . I know you will have difficulties to encounter g ting through the mountains to where supplies are abundant, but I believe you will accomplish it."

[4] Several changes had taken place in the Army of the Cumberland since the battle of Chattan ga. The Eleventh and Twelfth Corps were consolidated, forming the Twentieth, and General S cum had, as a consequence, been displaced, and transferred to Vicksburg. Howard, who had co manded the Eleventh, relieved General Granger in command of the Fourth Corps. Phil Sherid had been relieved of his command (second division, Fourth Corps), and had been succeeded by Jo Newton.

The Army of the Tennessee, at Huntsville, Alabama, commanded by McPherson, comprised the Fifteenth, and portions of the Sixteenth and Seventeenth Corps, under Logan, G. M. Dodge, and Frank P. Blair, Jr. The remainder of the Sixteenth and Seventeenth Corps was at Memphis and Vicksburg, under Hurlbut and Slocum, or absent on the Red River expedition. The Fifteenth Corps comprised four divisions, under Osterhaus, Herron, Morgan L. Smith, and John E. Smith; the Sixteenth three, under Ransom, Corse, and T. W. Sweeny; and the Seventeenth two, under C. R. Woods and M. D. Leggett.

The cavalry in the Army of the Ohio consisted of McCook's division, in the Army of the Cumberland of Kilpatrick's and Garrard's, and in the Army of the Tennessee of Edward McCook's brigade.

The Department and Army of Arkansas, under General Steele, was in May assigned to General Canby's trans-Mississippi division. Steele's army, therefore, must be counted out of the forces engaged in the Atlanta campaign.

General Sherman immediately prepared for active operations. On the 25th of March he set out on a general tour of inspection through his department, consulting with McPherson, Thomas, and Schofield. The value of the possession of Chattanooga was now manifest. This position was the central buttress of the Federal position. On its left East Tennessee was firmly grasped by Schofield's army; on its right the Tennessee River was guarded by a line of garrisons, which permitted the access northward of cavalry only. In the rear were two good and reliable lines of railway communication from Nashville and Memphis. During the season of navigation the Tennessee River affords a third line. Having arranged with his subordinates the disposition of their several armies—how many should take the field, and how many be retained for garrison duty—Sherman returned to Nashville. At this time the citizens of Tennessee in his rear were in large measure sustained by stores which they shared with the army. Finding that this double want could not be supplied with safety to the army, he issued orders cutting off the supply of the citizens, and leaving them to other sources of relief.[1] The 1st of May was the time fixed for the completion of preparations, and by that time the store-houses of Chattanooga contained provisions for thirty days, and the ammunition trains were fully supplied. The veteran regiments, whose time had expired, and who had been released on furlough, now returned with their ranks filled by new recruits.

Sherman had intended to move against the enemy with 100,000 men of all arms, and 250 guns. His actual force on the 1st of May was 98,797 men and 254 guns. The Army of the Cumberland, numbering 60,773 men, with 130 guns, constituted three fifths of his entire command. The Army of the Tennessee numbered 24,465, with 96 guns, and that of the Ohio 13,559, with 28 guns. Sherman's whole force was distributed as follows among the three arms of the service: the infantry of the three armies numbered 88,188 men; the artillery 4450, with 254 guns; the cavalry 6149.[2]

To General Johnston, of the Confederate army, who had succeeded Bragg at the close of 1863, was assigned a difficult task. With an army half as large as that opposing him,[3] he was to resist the approach of the latter to Atlanta. His forces were concentrated at Dalton, which he had strongly fortified. President Davis having given Johnston the command of the army much against his will,[4] did not support him by any considerable re-enforcements. Yet he

called loudly for an advance into Tennessee. Of course this wo
proved immediately ruinous. Johnston, therefore, wisely declin
tempt any offensive movement, and spent the winter in preparatio
assault which he knew he must meet in the spring. During the w
sertions from his army were frequent. General Thomas reports t
averaged thirty per day, nearly all of whom desired to take the
oath, and to comply with General Grant's orders in regard to deser

Partly as a demonstration in favor of Sherman's Meridian expedi
partly to prevent Johnston from re-enforcing Longstreet in East T
Thomas had moved against Dalton in the latter part of Februa
Palmer, with Johnson's and Baird's divisions, occupied Ringgold on
That night he reported to Thomas that he had reliable informat
Johnston had dispatched Cheatham's and Cleburne's divisions to t
of Polk in Alabama. This information was not correct; but, to tes
emy's strength, the next day, Davis's division having joined the tw
at Ringgold, and Cruft's, of the Fourteenth Corps, with Matthias's
of the Fifteenth Corps, and Long's cavalry brigade, having been se
operate with Palmer, Johnston's advanced outposts beyond Tunnel
attacked and driven in. Dalton is covered on its western side b
Face Ridge, which runs north and south, and through which, at the
ed Buzzard Roost, passes the road from Ringgold. East of the
Road and in front of Rocky Face Ridge lies Tunnel Hill, which v
pied by Thomas on the 24th. On the 25th an attempt was made
Buzzard Roost Pass; but the enemy, contrary to anticipation, was
full strength, and, after becoming satisfied of this, Thomas with
forces to the vicinity of Ringgold. His loss in this reconnoissance
killed and 255 wounded.

As soon as Johnston assumed command of the Confederate Arm
Tennessee, both the President and Secretary Seddon urged an offensi
paign. "The relative forces," reports Johnston, "including the mor
of the affair of Missionary Ridge, condition of the artillery horses a
of those of the cavalry, and want of field transportation, made it im
ble to effect the wishes of the executive." Immediately after Tho
connoissance, General Johnston, on the 27th of February, suggested
ident Davis, through General Bragg, that "preparations for a forwa
ment should be made without farther delay." In reply, Bragg (M
desired him to prepare for such a movement. He then reminde
that these preparations, by the regulations of the War Department,
left to commanders of troops, but to officers receiving orders direc
Richmond. On the 18th of March Johnston received a letter from
sketching a plan of offensive operations, and enumerating the troo
used by the former. He replied to this letter, suggesting modificati
urging that the re-enforcements named should be sent immediately
ton. General Bragg on the 21st telegraphed to Johnston: "Troo
only be drawn from other points for advance. Upon your decision
point farther action must depend." Johnston believed that the enemy
be prepared for a movement sooner than he himself could. He wi
be prepared for the defensive as well as the offensive. From Brag
patch it was evident that there were troops which might be sent to the
of the Tennessee, but that these would not be sent for a defensive car
Johnston, on the 22d, explained his view of the situation to General
showing the probability of Sherman's advancing first, and urging the
sity of preparing for defensive as well as for offensive movements.
tice whatever was taken of this appeal. On the 25th Johnston renew
request for re-enforcements, "because the enemy was collecting a larg
than that of the last campaign, while ours was less than it had been
The only response which he received was the arrival of 1400 men,
Brigadier General Mercer, on the 2d of May, after Sherman's prepa
had already been completed. Considering that Johnston might hav
supported, it seems strange that, in the face of an advance, the succes

[1] "At first," he says, in his report, "my orders operated very hardly, but the prolific soil soon afforded early vegetables, and ox-wagons hauled meat and bread from Kentucky, so that no actual suffering resulted, and I trust that those who clamored at the cruelty and hardships of the day have already seen in the result a perfect justification of my course."

On May 5th Sherman writes to President Lincoln:

"We have worked hard with the best talent of the country, and it is demonstrated that the railroad can not supply the army and the people too. One or the other must quit, and the army don't intend to unless Joe Johnston makes us. The issues to citizens have been enormous, and the same weight of corn or oats would have saved thousands of the mules, whose carcasses now corduroy the roads, and which we need so much.

"We have paid back to Tennessee ten for one of provisions taken in war. I will not change my orders, and I beg of you to be satisfied that the clamor is partly humbug and for effect; and to test it, I advise you to tell the hearers of it to hurry to Kentucky, and make up a caravan of cattle and wagons, and come over the mountains by Cumberland Gap and Somerset, to relieve their suffering friends, on foot, as they used to do before a railroad was built. Tell them that they have no time to lose. We can relieve all actual suffering by each company or regiment giving of their savings. Every man who is willing to fight or work gets a full ration; and all who won't fight or work should go away, and we offer them free passage in the cars."

[2] Sherman evidently did not intend to be encumbered with baggage. April 11 he writes to Thomas: "When we move we will take no tents or baggage, but one change of clothing on our horses, or to be carried by the men, and on pack-animals by company officers. Five days' bacon, twenty days' bread, and thirty days' salt, sugar, and coffee. Nothing else but arms and ammunition in quantity proportioned to our ability. Even this will be a heavy encumbrance, but is rather the limit of our aim than what we can really accomplish. . . . . Look well to our supply of beef cattle on the hoof, and salt in large excess of the rations. Encourage drills by brigades and divisions, and let the recruits practice at the target all the time."

[3] Johnston's effective force at the commencement of the Atlanta campaign numbered about 48,000 men, one tenth cavalry. The following are the official returns from his army from December 31, 1863, to June 30, 1864:

	Present for Duty.	Aggregate Present.	Aggregate Present and Absent.
December 31, 1863	42,439	57,428	98,215
January 31, 1864	41,553	55,059	88,457
February — "	37,780	48,010	70,071
March 31, "	42,125	55,118	85,958
April 30, "	43,887	63,807	96,863
May "	Wanting.		
June 30, "	54,086	77,441	137,102

We have estimated his army at 48,000, because, in addition to the forces included in the returns for April 30, there were some 4000 cavalry scattered northward, which were afterward recalled.

[4] According to the following account of Henry S. Foote (*War of the Rebellion*, p. 356), it appears that Davis's hostility to Johnston began at an early period of the war, or, at any rate, before Benjamin, the Confederate Secretary of War, was displaced by Seddon. This author, Confederate representative from Tennessee, says:

"Just about the time I was laboring most assiduously to relieve the Department of War of Mr. Benjamin by calling forth, as far as it might be in my power to do so, co-operative responses from the people, an occurrence took place in social life in Richmond which had much effect, not only upon the fate of Mr. Benjamin, but which, in the sequel, had much influence also upon the course of public events. I chanced to be invited to a dinner-party, where some twenty of the most prominent members of the two houses of the Confederate Congress were congregated, including the speaker of the House of Representatives, Mr. Orr, of South Carolina, and others of equal rank. General

Joseph E. Johnston was also an invited guest. While the banquet was proceeding, Mr. B
gross acts of official misconduct becoming the subject of conversation, one of the compa
to General Johnston, and inquired whether he thought it even *possible* that the Confeden
could succeed with Mr. Benjamin as war minister. To this inquiry General Johnston, a
de passo, emphatically responded in the *negative*. This high authority was immediatel
both houses of Congress against Mr. Benjamin, and was in the end fatal to his hope of r
in the Department of War. Mr. Davis, after the sending in of his nominations for cabinet
ments under the permanent Constitution, for nearly four weeks, in order to have it in his
persuade the Senate to confirm Mr. Benjamin as Secretary of War, in the event of his bein
nated, ultimately relinquished this object in despair, that body, however accommodating
general to executive fancies, having been found unwilling to participate in the terrible resp
of such an act. Mr. Benjamin was finally nominated for the Department of State, and
firmed, by a very small majority, for that place, where he had it in his power, both abro
home, to perpetrate more barefaced acts of corruption and profligacy than any single i
has ever been known to commit in the same space of time in any part of Christendom. I
remark, in passing, that this frank and manly declaration of General Johnston rendered
Davis and Mr. Benjamin alike hostile to him, and he was fated to experience the effect
malevolence on more than one subsequent occasion previous to his ultimate deprivation of c

[1] This order, No. 10, was issued by General Grant at Chattanooga, December 12, 1863,
freely distributed among the Confederate soldiers. Its terms were as follow:

"I. All deserters from the enemy coming within our lines will be conducted to the co
of division or detached brigade who shall be nearest the place of surrender.

"II. If such commander is satisfied that the deserters desire to quit the Confederate se
may permit them to go to their homes, if within our lines, on taking the following oath:

"I do solemnly swear, in the presence of Almighty God, that I will henceforth faithf
port, protect, and defend the Constitution of the United States, and the union of states the
and that I will in like manner abide by and faithfully support all acts of Congress passe
the existing rebellion with reference to slaves, so far as not yet repealed, modified, or hel
Congress or by decision of the Supreme Court, and that I will in like manner abide by and
ly support all proclamations of the President made during the existing rebellion having ref
slaves, so long and so far as not modified or declared void by decision of the Supreme C
help me God.'

"III. Deserters from the enemy will at once be disarmed, and their arms turned ove
nearest ordnance officer, who will account for them.

"IV. Passes and rations may be given to deserters to carry them to their homes, and fr
over military railroads and on steam-boats in government employ.

"V. Employment at fair wages will, when practicable, be given to deserters by office
quartermaster and engineer departments.

"VI. To avoid the danger of recapture of such deserters by the enemy, they will be
from military service in the armies of the United States."

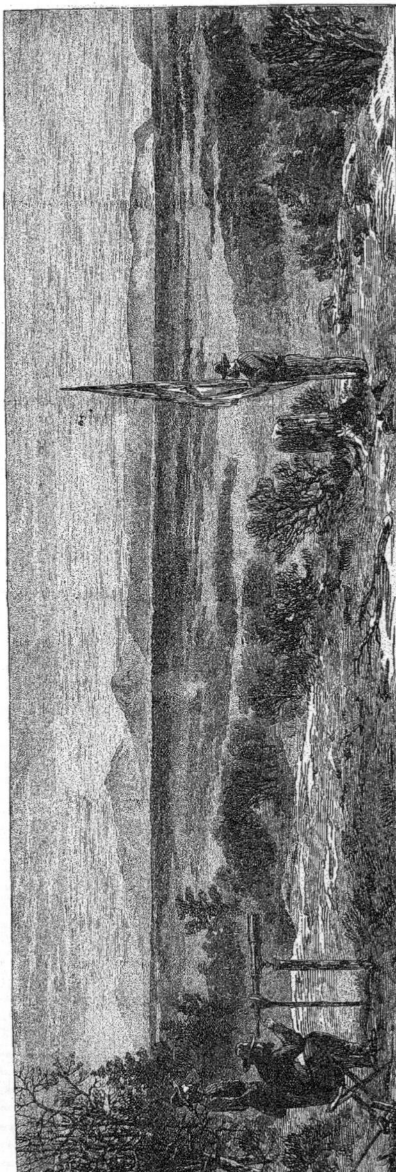

THE ADVANCE SIGNAL-STATION NEAR RINGGOLD, GEORGIA.

RINGGOLD, GEORGIA.

BUZZARD'S ROOST PASS.

pulse of which was so important to the Confederacy, he should have been left for three months with an army half as large as that which he confronted. On the 4th of May he asked for a portion of Polk's command, and was informed that this request would be granted.[1]

While the Confederate officials were disputing, Sherman had been preparing to advance. By the 1st of May, as we have before shown, he was ready to move and to strike. From Ringgold, the advanced front of the Federal army, to Atlanta was nearly one hundred miles, across a difficult country, but not so difficult as that over which Rosecrans had advanced from Murfreesborough to Chattanooga. Atlanta, the heart of Georgia, and of the Confederacy itself, was not only the principal Confederate granary, but was also the centre of a manufacturing district which supplied the Southern armies with cannon, ammunition, clothing, and equipments. To reach this point—the local objective of the campaign—three rivers had to be crossed, the Oostenaula, Etowah, and Chattahoochee. Ringgold lies amid the mountains of Taylor's Ridge, on the road from Chattanooga to Dalton. Ten miles distant, by the road from Ringgold, is Buzzard's Roost, in Rocky Face Ridge, about four miles northwest of Dalton. The enemy held Dalton, strongly fortified, the ridge covering it, and strong outposts on the road to Ringgold. His position was almost impregnable. Sherman's command on May 7th was situated thus: On the right, at Lee and Gordon's Mill, lay the Army of the Tennessee, under McPherson; the Army of the Cumberland, under Thomas, held the centre, at and near Ringgold, more directly confronting the enemy; and under Schofield, on the Georgia border, and on the road from Cleveland southward to Dalton, which runs east of Rocky Face Ridge, was the Army of the Ohio. We have said that Atlanta was the local objective of Sherman's campaign; the *vital* objective, however, was Johnston's army at Dalton. The obvious policy of the Federal commander was to force a battle upon his opponent at the earliest stage of the campaign. Johnston's equally obvious policy—a difficult one to be pursued under the circumstances—was to evade a general engagement, opposing as obstinate resistance as was possible in his front consistent with the protection of his communications with Atlanta.

[1] General Bragg, after he was relieved from the command at Chattanooga, was called to Richmond, where President Davis, whose especial favorite he was, placed him in a position very similar to that which had been occupied by the Federal General Halleck at Washington. Certainly the management of the one was only paralleled, in the annals of war, by that of the other.

GEARY'S ASSAULT ON DUG GAP.

On the 4th of May the Army of the Potomac crossed the Rapidan, and on the same day Grant telegraphed to Sherman, reminding him that the time for his advance against Johnston had come. Sherman neither intended nor did Johnston expect, an assault on the position covering Dalton—Buzzard's Roost Pass, which was obstructed by abatis, and flooded by means of dams across Mill Creek. Probably in no campaign of the war did the two opposing commanders so completely fathom each other's purposes, or so carefully estimate the possibilities, the one for attack and the other for defense. Sherman, on the 6th of May, with his largest army, that of the Cumberland, menaced Rocky Face Ridge with such vigor that it would seem as if an attempt like that made five months before against Missionary Ridge was to be repeated against the formidable position held by Johnston at Buzzard's Roost. Schofield threatened at the same time the enemy's right flank. McPherson's army, from Lee and Gordon's Mill, was thrown to the left and rear, moving by way of Ship's Gap, Villanow, and Snake Creek Gap to Resaca, eighteen miles south of Dalton, on the Atlanta Railroad. With this flanking column McPherson was ordered to break the railroad to the extent of his opportunity, and then to retire to Snake Creek Gap and there fortify himself.[1]

On the first day of the campaign Thomas occupied Tunnel Hill. Two days afterward Schofield closed upon Johnston's right, and Thomas renewed his demonstration upon Rocky Face with such vigor that Newton's division, of Howard's (Fourth) corps, carried a portion of the ridge; but, upon a farther advance, the crest was found too well protected by rock epaulements to hope for success in gaining the gorge. Geary's division, of Hooker's corps, in the mean time made a reconnoissance up a precipitous ridge south of Buzzard's Roost; but, though the men fought their way well up to the enemy's intrenchments on the crest, they could not gain possession of the Gap. But these movements were only demonstrations. Upon McPherson's flank movement through Snake Creek Gap Sherman had made the success of his plan to depend. But Johnston, who had expected this method of attack, had sent Canty's brigade to Resaca two days before the attack in his front had been developed. For weeks, also, he had been preparing roads in his rear, upon which his own troops could move more rapidly than Sherman's flanking columns. McPherson had reached Snake Creek Gap on the 8th, with Logan's and Dodge's corps, preceded by Kilpatrick's division of cavalry. Debouching from the gap, McPherson found Resaca occupied by Canty's brigade. If he had made an immediate attack his success would have been certain;[1] but he over-estimated the enemy's strength both in position and numbers. While he was waiting before Resaca, and unable to get upon the railroad above or below the town, the position in his front was strengthened. On the afternoon of the 9th, Johnston, warned by Canty of this movement on Resaca, promptly dispatched to the latter point three infantry divisions under General Hood. The orders which McPherson had received had not been so explicit, perhaps, as to cover the precise case now presented for his consideration. His discretion must supply the place of definite orders. His force, over 20,000 strong, was largely superior to that of the garrison defending Resaca. The manifest intent of his orders would have favored an attack, and the probability of success, even now, was unquestionably in his favor; but there was much to be said on the other side. He was detached from the main body of the army, and the easy approaches from Dalton toward his left and rear suggested the possibility that he might be cut off and defeated. He took the safer of the alternatives offered him, and fell back to Snake Creek Gap. In doing so he probably made a mistake. Rocky Face Ridge had perfectly covered his rear during the movement. He could now easily withstand any assault which might be made on his left if he had refused that flank toward the ridge. Even if he had taken such a position without making an attack, he could have held it until he received support. But the decisive advantage gained over the enemy by his flank movement had been thrown away by his failure to attack on the 9th. The attack would have been made if General Logan had been in command, or if he had been in the advance instead of Dodge. McPherson's wagon train, which ought never to have entered the Gap at all, offered serious obstructions to the march of columns which might be sent to his support. Sherman confesses himself "somewhat disappointed at the result"[2] of his plans, but imputes no blame to McPherson. On the 11th he withdrew his army from Johnston's front, and followed McPherson, leaving only Howard's corps and a small infantry force to keep up the demonstration against Dalton. On the night of the 12th Johnston abandoned Dalton, and moved his whole army to a position

[1] This Snake Creek Gap movement seems to have been originally suggested by General Thomas. The latter, in his report to the Committee on the Conduct of the War, says: "Shortly after his assignment to the command of the Military Division of the Mississippi, General Sherman came to see me at Chattanooga to consult about the position of affairs, and adopt a plan for a spring campaign. At that interview I proposed to General Sherman that if he would use McPherson's and Schofield's armies to demonstrate on the enemy's position at Dalton by the direct roads through Buzzard's Roost Gap, and from the direction of Cleveland, I would throw my whole force through Snake Creek Gap, which I knew to be unguarded, full upon the enemy's communications between Dalton and Resaca, thereby turning his position completely, and force him either to retreat toward the east through a difficult country, poorly supplied with provisions and forage, with a strong probability of total disorganization of his force, or attack me, in which latter event I felt confident that my army was sufficiently strong to beat him, especially as I hoped to gain a position on his communications before he could be made aware of my movement. General Sherman objected to this plan for the reason that he desired my army to form the reserve of the united armies, and to serve as a rallying-point for the two wings . . . . to operate from."

[1] The following is a part of the instructions given to McPherson: "I am in hopes that Garrard's cavalry will be at Villanow as soon as you. . . . . But, in any event, his movement will cover your right rear, and enable you to leave all encumbrances at Ship's Gap or at Villanow, as you deem best. I hope the enemy will fight at Dalton, in which case he can have no force there that can interfere with you; but should his policy be to fall back along the railroad, you will hit him in flank. Do not fail, in that event, to make the most of the opportunity, by the most vigorous attack possible, as it may save us what we have most reason to apprehend, a slow pursuit, in which he gains strength as we lose it. In either event you may be sure the forces north of you will prevent his turning on you alone."

[2] *Sherman's Report.*

SHELLING THE RAILROAD NEAR RESACA.

covering Resaca on the west. In the mean time Polk had reached J
with Loring's division. Polk, Hardee, and Hood were now the co
manders of the Confederate Army of Tennessee.

Dalton, evacuated by the enemy, was immediately occupied by
who pressed on in pursuit. Sherman's columns, following upon eac
heels through Snake Creek Gap, had the advantage of Johnston in
time. But this was counterbalanced by the more practicable and
route taken by the Confederates. On the 12th Sherman moved t
saca, McPherson on the direct road, preceded, as in his former adv
Kilpatrick's cavalry; Thomas closed in upon McPherson's left, a
field upon the left of Thomas. But it was not until the 14th that
was prepared to attack, and by that time he was confronted by t
force of the enemy, who occupied the forts of Resaca behind Cam
Polk's left resting on the Oostenaula, Hardee holding the centre, a
the right, extending northeastwardly around Resaca to the Co
Loring's division, added to those already at Resaca under Hood, ha
13th delayed Sherman's advance, thus giving time for the dispo
Hardee's and Polk's troops, then just arriving. Johnston's fores
promptness had saved his army.[1]

Sherman now repeated against Resaca the strategic movement w
forced the enemy from Dalton; but there was this difference, that
proceeded to threaten the enemy's communications with a lighter
keeping almost his entire army in the enemy's front. General S
division of the Sixteenth Corps (Dodge's) crossed the Oostenaula
toons at Lay's Ferry and threatened Calhoun, and Garrard's cava
sion moved from its position at Villanow across the same river low
to destroy the railroad between Calhoun and Kingston. While the
ments were in progress, Sherman attacked Johnston at Resaca, pres
at all points during the afternoon of May 14th. Thomas, in th
pressed through Camp Creek Valley, sending Hooker across the cre
the right and centre, however, the enemy successfully resisted Scho
Thomas; and at nightfall Hood advanced from his intrenchments,
covered a portion of the ground which the Federals had gained in t
ing. McPherson's attack on Polk was more successful, the latt
driven from his position, which, commanding the Confederate bridg
the river, was immediately occupied with Federal artillery. John
already given orders to Hood to attack the next morning, when h
formed of the movement by Sweeny menacing Calhoun, and of Po
fortune. He countermanded the orders, and sent Walker's divisio
houn. The next day there was skirmishing along the entire front,
ing on Hood's line into a severe battle in the afternoon. It app
Walker had reported no movement on Calhoun, and Hood had be
ordered to attack, but that when the latter was prepared to do s
gence was received by Johnston indicating that the Federal right w
ing the river in his rear, and the order to attack was again counter
One of Hood's divisions—A. P. Stewart's—not being aware of this,
Schofield by this time had closed down upon Hood's right, and Ho
vancing, drove the enemy from several hills, capturing four guns at
prisoners. That night Johnston abandoned Resaca, and, crossing
tenaula southward, burned the railroad bridge behind him. S
troops entered on the morning of the 16th just in time to save the
bridge, and the whole army started in pursuit, Schofield moving
roads to the left, Thomas in Johnston's immediate rear, and McPh
Lay's Ferry. In the operations around Resaca the Federal loss
tween 4000 and 5000 killed and wounded. At Resaca Sherman
to Grant that he had 1000 prisoners and eight guns.

General Sherman was now entering upon the third stage of the ca
Johnston retreated to Cassville, four miles north of Kingston.[2] At
on the 16th, Hardee, bringing up the Confederate rear, skirmish
Howard's column. At Adairsville, farther south, there was a fight
Polk's cavalry, under Jackson, and the advance of Thomas's arm
General Newton. Polk and Hood, on the 18th, took the road from
ville to Cassville, while Hardee took that to Kingston. Sherman's
centre had been delayed, Thomas having to build additional bridge
the Oostenaula, and Schofield making a detour across the two tribu
that river—the Connesauga and Coosawattie. On the 17th the thre
al armies moved southward by different roads, and the division o
Davis meanwhile marched westwardly to Rome, where, meeting n
ance, it captured eight or ten heavy guns, together with some valua
and founderies.

On the 19th it appeared as if the enemy would make a stand at C
French's division, of Polk's command, had arrived from the so
Johnston, intrenched upon a ridge in the rear of the town, confide
dered an advance against Thomas, who was moving southward from
ville. Hood, on the right, moved two miles in execution of this or
being deceived by the report that a Federal column was marchi

[1] "Nothing saved Johnston's army at Resaca but the impracticable nature of the
which made the passage of troops across the valley almost impossible. This fact c
army to reach Resaca from Dalton along the comparatively good roads constructed be
partly from the topographical nature of the country, and partly from the foresight of
chief. At all events, on the 14th of May we found the rebel army in a strong positi
Camp Creek, occupying the forts at Resaca, and his right on some Chestnut hills to
of the town."—*Sherman's Report.*

[2] Johnston thus explains his continued retreat:

"The fact that a part of Polk's troops were still in the rear, and the great numerical
ty of the Federal army, made it expedient to risk battle only when position or some blun
enemy might give us counterbalancing advantages. I therefore determined to fall ba
until circumstances should put the chances of battle in our favor, keeping so near t
States army as to prevent its sending re-enforcements to Grant; and hoping, by takir
tage of positions and opportunities, to reduce the odds against us by partial engage
also expected it to be materially reduced before the end of June by the expiration of
of service of many of the regiments which had not re-enlisted."

SHERMAN'S ARMY ENTERING RESACA.

Canton to the rear and right of Cassville, he withdrew his troops to resist the approach of this fictitious column. The Federal army in the meanwhile concentrated about Cassville, and attacked Johnston's intrenched position with artillery. On the evening of the 19th the Confederate commanders differed as to the policy which ought now to be adopted. Hood and Polk thought that the Federal artillery would render the position untenable on the morrow, and urged immediate retreat across the Etowah River. Hardee, whose position Johnston thought much weaker than Polk's or Hood's, was still confident of his ability to hold it. Johnston inclined to Hardee's opinion, but the other commanders "were so earnest and unwilling to depend upon the ability of their corps to hold the ground," that retreat was determined upon, and on the 20th the Confederate army crossed the Etowah—"a step," reports Johnston, "which I have regretted ever since." This movement, without a battle, abandoned the whole of Etowah Valley to the Federal army. Here Sherman gave his troops rest, while supplies could be brought forward for the next stage of the campaign.

But the period of rest was brief. On the 23d of May, taking supplies in its trains for twenty days, and leaving a garrison at Rome and Kingston, Sherman's army crossed the Etowah. Satisfied that Johnston would attempt to hold Allatoona Pass, just south of the river, the Federal commander did not attempt even a demonstration against that position, but leaving the railroad, moved to the right for Dallas, southwest of Allatoona. Johnston, who had not stopped at Allatoona, but continued his retreat to the range of hills north of and covering Dallas and Marietta, detected Sherman's whole plan from the start, and concentrated his army near New Hope Church, where three roads met—from Ackworth on the north, Dallas on the southwest, and Marietta on the east. Hood's corps was posted with its centre at the church, while Polk and Hardee extended the line eastward across the Atlanta Road. Sherman's army, after crossing the Etowah, moved in three columns in the accustomed order—Schofield on the left, Thomas in the centre, and McPherson on the right. McPherson, crossing the Etowah near Kingston, joined by Davis's division from Rome, was ordered to move *via* Van Wert to a point south of Dallas. Thomas advanced *via* Euharlee and Burnt Hickory, and Schofield by the road from Cassville.

Thomas's advance, under Hooker, approached New Hope Church on the 25th, and encountered the enemy's cavalry. Geary's division skirmished up to the Confederate line held by Hood, and Hooker's other divisions being well in hand by 4 P.M., Sherman ordered a bold push to be made for the cross-roads. A severe battle was fought in this position, Stewart's division by night being finally driven back to the church, but still retaining the main position. Sherman now occupied several days in deploying up to the enemy's well-intrenched lines, which extended from New Hope Church to a point north of Marietta. McPherson was pushed close up to Dallas, Thomas still confronted Hood, and Schofield was ordered to move around to the left, in order to reach and turn Johnston's right flank. Garrard's cavalry operated with McPherson, and Stoneman's with Schofield, McCook's guarding the Federal rear. The movement of the whole army was now gradually to the left, proceeding slowly over difficult, densely-wooded ground. In the course of this development there were several sharp encounters with the enemy, the results of which sometimes favored one side and sometimes the other. On the 27th Howard's corps assailed Cleburne's division, and was repulsed, Johnston reports, "with great slaughter."[1] In this action, and the battle of New Hope Church, Johnston estimates his own loss as 900, and that of Sherman as 6000. On the 28th the enemy attacked McPherson while the latter was on the point of closing up on Thomas. "Fortunately," says Sherman, "our men had erected good breastworks, and gave the enemy a terrible and bloody repulse." The enemy's loss in this attack was nearly 3000, and McPherson's not more than one tenth of that number. There were ten days of this undecisive work (May 25th–June 4th), when Sherman determined to leave Johnston in his intrenchments, and move eastward to Ackworth, on the railroad.[2] The roads leading back to Ackworth and Allatoona Pass were now in his possession, and he had rebuilt the railroad bridge across the Etowah and occupied the pass with his cavalry. When, on the 6th of June, he had established himself at Ackworth, he fortified and garrisoned Allatoona Pass, making it a secondary base of supplies.

Johnston, adapting his movements to those of Sherman, transferred his whole army to a point on the railroad north of Marietta, where Kenesaw on his right, Pine Mountain in the advanced centre, and Lost Mountain on his left, interposed a natural barrier to a direct approach from the north.[3] While the Confederate army was intrenching itself in this formidable position, Sherman repaired the railroad in his rear, and brought forward to his camp an abundant supply of provisions. He also received re-enforcements. General Blair, with two divisions of the Seventeenth Corps (10,500 men)

[1] Howard reports his loss as "very heavy, being upward of 1400 killed, wounded, and missing in General Wood's division alone." He adds, "Though the assault was repulsed, yet a position was secured near Pickett's Mills of the greatest importance to the subsequent movement of the army, and it has been subsequently ascertained that the enemy suffered immensely in the action, and regarded it as the severest attack made during the eventful campaign."

[2] Sherman writes to General Halleck, Grant's chief of staff, from "Near Dallas," May 28:

"The enemy discovered my move to turn Allatoona, and moved to meet us here. Our columns met about one mile east of Pumpkin-vine Creek, and we pushed them back about three miles, to the point [New Hope Church] where the road forks to Allatoona and Marietta. Here Johnston has chosen a strong line, and made hasty but strong parapets of timber and earth, and has thus far stopped us. My right is Dallas, centre about three miles north, and I am gradually working round by the left to approach the railroad any where in front of Ackworth. Country very densely wooded and broken; no roads of any consequence. We have had many sharp, severe encounters, but nothing decisive. Both sides duly cautious in the obscurity of the ambushed ground."

In a letter to Halleck, May 29, he thus alludes to the enemy's attack on McPherson the day before:

"With the intention of working to my left toward the railroad east of Allatoona, I ordered General McPherson . . . . . . to withdraw his army and take General Thomas's present position, while all of General Thomas's and General Schofield's armies will be moved further to the east, working round the enemy to the left. The enemy, who had observed, etc., ... massed against General McPherson and attacked him at 4½ P.M. yesterday, but was repulsed with great slaughter and at little cost to us. The enemy fled back to his breastworks on the ridge, leaving in our hands his dead and wounded. His loss, 2500, and about 300 prisoners. General McPherson's men being covered by log breastworks, like our old Corinth lines, were comparatively unhurt, his loss not being over 300 in all."

[3] "Kenesaw, the bold and striking twin mountain, lay before us; with a high range of chestnut hills trending off to the northeast, terminating to our view in another peak called Brushy Mountain. To our right was the smaller hill called Pine Mountain, and beyond it, in the distance, Lost Mountain. All these, though links in a continuous chain, present a sharp, conical appearance, prominent in the vast landscape that presents itself from any of the hills that abound in that region. Kenesaw, Pine Mountain, and Lost Mountain form a triangle—Pine Mountain the apex, and Kenesaw and Lost Mountain the base—covering perfectly the town of Marietta and the railroad back to the Chattahoochee. On each of these peaks the enemy had his signal stations. The summits were covered with batteries, and the spurs were alive with men, busy in felling trees, digging pits, and preparing for the grand struggle impending."—*Sherman's Report.*

LOST MOUNTAIN AT SUNRISE.

that had been on furlough, and Colonel Long's brigade of cavalry, arrived at Ackworth June 8th. This accession supplied the gaps which had been made in the original army by losses in battle and the detachments from garrison at Resaca, Rome, Kingston, and Allatoona Pass.[1] On the 9th the army moved to Big Shanty, a station on the railroad midway between Ackworth and Kenesaw. A triangular mountain fortress, of nature's construction, here confronted Sherman. Even war could not quench in Sherman his love of nature, nor interrupt "communion with her visible forms." "The scene," he says, "was enchanting—too beautiful to be disturbed by the harsh clamors of war; but the Chattahoochee lay beyond, and I had to reach it." Just beyond the Chattahoochee lay Atlanta—the object of the campaign.

While waiting before Kenesaw, Sherman received intelligence from General S. G. Burbridge, who had been left in command of the forces in Kentucky, that the Confederate General Morgan had entered that state through Pound Gap, June 4; that on the 9th he had been brought to battle and defeated with a loss of 600 prisoners; that on the 12th he had been again defeated, losing 500 killed and 400 prisoners, besides the wounded; and that his forces were scattered, demoralized, and being "pursued and picked up in every direction." Here also Sherman heard of Sturgis's defeat by Forrest, narrated in a previous chapter, and ordered a second expedition against Forrest to proceed immediately from Memphis.

Sherman paused for a brief moment and carefully scrutinized the Confederate position. He found that the enemy's line extended two miles in length, "more than he could hold with his force."[2] He had moved his armies close up by the 11th, McPherson on the left of the railroad toward Marietta, Schofield away to the right against Lost Mountain, and the larger army, under Thomas, confronting Pine and Kenesaw Mountains. It was Sherman's object to break the line between Pine and Kenesaw. Flank movements, at this distance from his base, were too serious affairs to be attempted until they were plainly seen to be necessary. For more than 20 days Sherman tried the enemy's lines in front by cannonade, skirmish, and assault. On the 14th of June, General Polk, commanding the Confederate centre on Pine Mountain, four miles southwest of Kenesaw, was killed by a cannon-ball,[1] and was succeeded by General Loring, who immediately withdrew from his advanced position, and on the 19th Johnston's line was contracted, abandoning Pine and Lost Mountains. Hood's right rested on the Marietta Road, Loring held the centre, now transferred to Kenesaw Mountain, and Hardee extended across the Lost Mountain and Marietta Road on the left. A division of militia had in the mean time been sent to Johnston by Governor Brown. This division, commanded by General Gustavus W. Smith, was employed to guard the crossings of the Chattahoochee, to prevent the surprise of Atlanta by Federal cavalry. "The whole country," Sherman (June 23) writes to Halleck, "is one vast fort, and Johnston must have fully 50 miles of connected trenches, with abatis and finished batteries."

Sherman pressed on through the forests and difficult ravines, and finally came upon the enemy's new position, of which Kenesaw was the salient, Hood thrown back to cover Marietta, and Hardee to cover the railroad to the Chattahoochee. During these operations the weather, according to Sherman's report, "was villainously bad." Rain fell almost without pause for three weeks, making mud gullies of the narrow roads, and preventing a gen-

[1] The losses in Sherman's Command during the month of May are not stated in his report. Thomas reports his own loss during this time as 8774.

[2] *Sherman's Report.*

[1] "It was on the afternoon of June 14th that Johnston, Hardee, and Polk rode out from their quarters to make some telescopic observations of the Federal position. At the time there was a brisk artillery fire going on between the two armies, but no engagement of the infantry. The generals, dismounting, walked to the front, where some of the enemy's artillerists, observing the party, fired. Their aim was too successful. One of the projectiles struck General Polk on the left arm, about the elbow, passed through his body, considerably mangling it, and carried off the right arm. He died on the spot, and his remains were immediately taken to Marietta, and thence to Atlanta, where funeral services were performed on the 16th."—*Southern Generals*, p. 419.

CREST OF PINE MOUNTAIN, WHERE GENERAL POLK FELL.

VIEW OF KENESAW FROM LITTLE KENESAW.

MAP OF THE ATLANTA CAMPAIGN.

eral movement; but the Federal lines with every opportunity were advanced closer to the enemy. It will be seen that Sherman had not accomplished his purpose of penetrating the Confederate line, but had only thrown it in upon itself, contracting and strengthening it. Johnston had seen the mistake of his original position, and had corrected it in time to prevent disaster. On the 21st Hood was shifted to Hardee's left, while at the same time Sherman was developing his right flank southward of Kenesaw. The next day, Hooker, having advanced his line, with Schofield on his right, was suddenly attacked by Hood near the Kulp House, southwest of Marietta. Hood appears to have gained some advantage at first, falling thus unexpectedly upon Williams's division of Hooker's corps and Hascall's of Schofield's, and driving them back; but he was checked upon reaching the main line, and himself driven back in confusion, leaving behind his dead, wounded, and many prisoners.[1]

Sherman now determined to assault Kenesaw. It was a bold and Sherman-like thing to do, and certainly failure could not have been reckoned inevitable.[1] The order was given on the 24th, and executed on the 27th. Two points were selected on the enemy's left centre—one at Little Kenesaw, in McPherson's front, the other a mile farther south, in front of Thomas. On the appointed day, after a vigorous cannonade, the armies of the Tennessee and the Cumberland leaped forward to their terrible work, their assault falling mainly on Loring's and Hardee's corps. With a loss of less than 500 men the Confederate position was maintained, and McPherson and Thomas were completely repulsed, losing altogether 3000 men, including General Harker, Colonel Dan. McCook, Colonel Rice, and other valuable officers. Success in this assault would have been decisive of the campaign; it would have cut the enemy in two, prevented his retreat, and exposed him to defeat in detail. But the assault was not a success.[2] Sherman gives the following explanation of his reasons for making this assault:

"Upon studying the ground, I had no alternative but to assault or turn the enemy's position. Either course had its difficulties and dangers. And

[1] General Thomas gives the following account of this affair:

"Williams's division of Hooker's corps skirmished itself into a position on the right of Geary's division, the right of Williams resting at Kulp's House, on the Powder Spring and Marietta Road. About 4 P. M. the enemy, in heavy force, attacked Knipe's brigade in its advanced position, before his men had time to throw up any works, and persisted in the assault until sundown, when they withdrew, their ranks hopelessly broken, each assault having been repelled with heavy loss."

[1] Perhaps the explanation of Sherman's hope of success is to be found in his dispatch to Halleck, June 25th, which says: "I shall aim to make him [Johnston] stretch his line until he weakens it; and then break through."

[2] General Harker commanded a brigade of Newton's division of Howard's (Fourth) corps. He led one column of the assault in Howard's front, and Wagner another. Palmer's (Fourteenth) corps at the same time assaulted on Howard's right. In regard to the result, Howard reports: "My experience is that a line of works thoroughly constructed, with the front well covered with abatis and other entanglements, well manned with infantry, whether with our own or that of the enemy, can not be carried by direct assault; the exceptions are when some one of the above conditions are wanting, or where the defenders are taken by surprise. The strength of such a line is of course increased by well-arranged batteries. Notwithstanding the probabilities against success, it is sometimes necessary to assault strong works, as has occurred in several instances during this campaign."

Colonels Dan. McCook and T. J. Mitchell (commanding brigades of Jeff. C. Davis's division) led the assaulting columns of Palmer's corps. McCook fell, dangerously wounded, and subsequently died at his home in Ohio.

DANIEL McCOOK.

CHARLES G. HARKER.

HOWARD'S CORPS CROSSING THE CHATTAHOOCHEE

I perceived that the enemy and our own officers had settled down into a conviction that I would *not* assault fortified lines. All looked to me to outflank. An army, to be efficient, must not settle down to one single mode of offense, but must be prepared to execute any plan that promises success. I wished, therefore, for the moral effect, to make a successful assault on the enemy behind his breastworks. . . . . Failure as it was, and for which I assume the entire responsibility, I yet claim that it produced good fruits, as it demonstrated to General Johnston that I would assault, and that boldly; and we also gained and held ground so close to the enemy's parapets that he could not show a head above them."[1]

After this repulse there was but one resource left—another flank movement. On the night of July 2d, McPherson, in front of Kenesaw, was relieved by Garrard's cavalry, and thrown around the right of the army, with instructions to advance to Nickajack Creek, and threaten Turner's Ferry, where the railroad in Johnston's rear crossed the Chattahoochee. The Confederate commander at once saw the meaning of this movement, and on the morning of the 3d Thomas found no enemy in his front. A view of the Federal skirmishers on the top of Kenesaw was the first sight which greeted Sherman's eyes at daybreak. Thomas moved forward in pursuit by the railroad; and at 8 30 A.M. Sherman in person entered Marietta just as the enemy's cavalry left the place. He hoped to strike the enemy in the confusion of crossing the Chattahoochee. Drawing Logan from McPherson's column to Marietta, the remainder of the Army of the Tennessee, with that of the Ohio, were ordered to cross the Nickajack, and attack the enemy in flank and rear.[2] Johnston, however, had covered his movement with great care, having constructed a strong *tête de pont* at the Chattahoochee, opposing also an advanced intrenched line at the Smyrna camp-meeting ground, five miles south of Marietta, his flanks resting behind Nickajack and Rottenwood Creeks. On the 5th of July this advanced position was abandoned on account of Sherman's threatening movements toward Turner's Ferry. Logan had been returned to McPherson, and Thomas was moving on Smyrna, when the enemy fell back to his *tête de pont*. The Confederate cavalry crossed the Chattahoochee, Wheeler observing the river for twenty miles above, and Jackson for the same distance below. There was skirmishing between the two armies until the 9th, Thomas's and McPherson's commands touching the river above and below the enemy, with Schofield's in reserve. While these operations were going on, Schofield had been withdrawn to Smyrna, and sent across the Chattahoochee at the mouth of Soap Creek (July 7th). This movement was successfully accomplished, Schofield surprising the Confederate guard, capturing a gun, laying a pontoon bridge across the river, and establishing himself on commanding ground on the east bank. At the same time Garrard's cavalry moved to Rosswell, farther up the river, where he destroyed the factories which had for years supplied cloth to the Confederate armies. A facetious owner of one of these mills, intent upon having his joke, even if he lost his factory, displayed a French flag above the building.[3] Having destroyed these works, Garrard secured a shallow ford, and held it until the arrival of an infantry division from Thomas's army. McPherson's whole army was soon transferred to this quarter from the Nickajack. Howard's corps, of Thomas's army, had also built a bridge at Powers's Ferry, two miles below the mouth of Soap Creek, crossed over and occupied a position on Schofield's right. These movements, securing three points of crossing the Chattahoochee above the enemy, and also a position on the east bank, from which good roads ran to Atlanta, threatened to leave Johnston at his *tête de pont* at Turner's Ferry, and turning his flank, to bring Sherman's army into Atlanta forthwith. Johnston, seeing this, followed his cavalry across the Chattahoochee on the night of the 9th, and took up a position on Peach-tree Creek and the river below,

[1] Sherman gives a similar explanation to Halleck shortly after the assault. He says: "The assault I made was no mistake; I had to do it. The enemy, and our own army and officers, had settled down into the conviction that the assault of lines formed no part of my game, and the moment the enemy was found behind any thing like a parapet, why, every body would deploy, throw up counter works, and take it easy, leaving it to the 'old man' [meaning Sherman] to turn the position. Had the assault been made with one fourth more vigor (mathematically), I would have put the head of George Thomas's whole army right through Johnston's deployed line, on the best ground for 'go ahead,' while my entire forces were well in hand on roads converging to my then object, Marietta. Had Harker and McCook not been struck so early, the assault would have succeeded, and then the battle would have all been in our favor, on account of our superiority in numbers and initiative."

As to the possibility of success if Harker and McCook had not fallen, General Thomas is the original authority. He reports to Sherman just after the assault: "Both General Harker and Colonel McCook were wounded on the enemy's breastworks, and all say had they not been wounded we would have driven the enemy from his works."

[2] "If you ever worked in your life," writes Sherman to McPherson on the evening of July 3, "work at daybreak to-morrow on the flank, crossing Nickajack somehow, and the moment you discover confusion pour in your fire. You know what a retreating mass across pontoon bridges means. Feel strong to-night, and make feints of pursuit with artillery. I know Johnston's withdrawal is not strategic, but for good reasons after he crosses the Chattahoochee; but his situation with that river behind him is not comfortable at all. . . . . I don't confine you to any crossing, but press the enemy all the time in flank till he is across the Chattahoochee."

To Thomas, at the same time, he writes:

"The more I reflect, the more I know Johnston's halt is to save time to cross his material and men. No general such as he would invite battle with the Chattahoochee behind him. I have ordered McPherson and Schofield, at any cost, and work night and day, to get the enemy started in confusion toward his bridges. I know you appreciate the situation. We will never have such a chance again, and I want you to impress on Hooker, Howard, and Palmer the importance of the most intense energy of attack to-night and in the morning, and to press with vehemence, at any cost of life and material. Every inch of his line should be felt, and the moment there is a give, pursuit should be made by day with lines, and by night with a single head of column and section of artillery to each corps following a road. Hooker should communicate with McPherson by a circuit if necessary, and act in concert. You know what loss would ensue to Johnston if he crosses his bridges at night in confusion, with artillery thundering at random on his rear."

[3] This joke might easily have cost the perpetrator his life. Sherman writes to Garrard, July 7: "I will see as to any man in America hoisting the French flag, and then devoting his labor and capital to supplying armies in open hostility to our government, and claiming the benefit of his neutral flag. Should you, under the impulse of anger, natural at contemplating such perfidy, hang the wretch, I approve the act beforehand." He adds: "I repeat my orders that you arrest all people, male and female, connected with those factories, no matter what the clamor, and let them foot it, under guard, to Marietta, whence I will send them by cars to the North. . . . . The poor women will make a howl. Let them take along their children and clothing, providing they have the means of hauling, or you can spare them. We will retain them until they can reach a country where they can live in peace and security."

VIEW OF ATLANTA FROM THE SIGNAL STATION NORTH OF THE CHATTAHOOCHEE.

covering Atlanta. Thus was abandoned to Sherman all of Georgia between the Tennessee and the Chattahoochee Rivers. In the pursuit of Johnston to the Chattahoochee, 2000 prisoners were taken.

And here let us halt to review what has already been accomplished in the two months since Sherman opened the attack upon Johnston at Buzzard's Roost. Johnston had been *driven* south of the Chattahoochee; he had not retreated from strategic motives, though his retreat had been conducted with so great skill and so little waste of force that it places him in the foremost rank of Confederate generals. No great battle had been fought in the campaign, which had been a series of sieges. Assaults there had been on both sides, and in these the loss had been severe, falling mainly upon the assailants. Johnston's losses altogether had been, according to his own report, about 10,000 in killed and wounded, and 4700 from other causes. This does not include deserters, which probably numbered 2500 at the lowest, thus bringing the total loss to about 20,000. This loss had been just about covered by re-enforcements. Sherman's losses it is difficult to estimate exactly. In the Army of the Cumberland the casualties for May and June amounted to 14,521, as reported by General Thomas. Supposing the loss in McPherson's and Schofield's commands to have been in proportion, we have a total of 25,000 for the casualties of battle. These losses, and others from sickness and detachment of troops for garrison, had been made up for by re-enforcements, so that the two armies, in respect of numbers, were now nearly the same as at the opening of the campaign. In the first stage of his advance, Sherman had it in his power to compel Johnston to fight a battle upon conditions which involved the destruction of the Confederate army. It is wonderful that Johnston should have left Snake Creek Gap unguarded, but it is still more wonderful that, once having gained access through this pass to the enemy's rear, McPherson did not appreciate his advantage, and push it to the utmost. If he had done so, and had been promptly supported, Johnston's army must have been ground to powder. No such opportunity again offered. But, notwithstanding this disappointment, the fact that Johnston could hold no position north of the Chattahoochee was really a conclusive argument that he could not hold Atlanta. Sherman's sole weakness was his long line of communications; but this was so well protected that, although Johnston, after crossing the Etowah, had sent five successive detachments of cavalry to destroy it, none of these had succeeded.

Sherman's army was now within sight of Atlanta, only eight miles intervening. Atlanta is the centre of the entire network of railroads in Georgia. From it start three railway lines of communication. The road running north to Chattanooga was occupied in its entire length by Sherman. Eastward, through Decatur, another road runs to Augusta, and thence to Charleston. The road running south divides into two branches at East Point, six miles from Atlanta; one running southeastwardly through Macon to Savannah, the other southwestwardly through West Point and Opelika to Montgomery, and thence with slight interruption to Pensacola. To destroy this latter or West Point Road, an expedition had been prepared, and General Rousseau had been assigned to its command. As early as the 10th of April, General Sherman, believing that Johnston would finally fall back beyond the Chattahoochee, had had this raid in view. The time for its operation had now come. On the 10th of July, when it was ascertained that Johnston had crossed the river, Rousseau started from Decatur, Alabama, with 2500 cavalry and two pieces of artillery.[1] No time more favorable could have been selected for the expedition. A. J. Smith was occupying Forrest's cavalry in Mississippi; expeditions were out inland from Vicksburg and Baton Rouge, and Canby was understood to be threatening Mobile. Rousseau's force consisted of the following cavalry regiments—the Fifth Indiana, Fifth Iowa, Second Kentucky, Fourth Tennessee, and Ninth Ohio. The party possessed 1000 Spencer repeating-rifles. At the crossing of Coosa River, on the 13th, a ferry-boat was captured, and a part of the command having crossed and effected a lodgment on the south bank, it was attacked by General Clanton with two regiments of Alabama cavalry. This Confederate detachment was routed after a few hours' skirmishing by an attack in flank, and Rousseau proceeded to Talladega on the railroad to Selma. Here a camp of about 700 conscripts was dispersed. The West Point Railroad was first struck at Chehaw Station, where the enemy was again encountered under Clanton, but was obliged to retire after a loss of 40 killed and a large number of

[1] The following instructions to Rousseau were dispatched by Sherman June 30th:

"The movement that I want you to study and be prepared for is contingent on the fact that General A. J. Smith defeats Forrest, or holds him well in check, and after I succeed in making Joe Johnston pass the Chattahoochee with his army, when I want you to go in person, or to send some good officer, with 2500 good cavalry well armed, and a sufficient number of pack-mules loaded with ammunition, salt, sugar, and coffee, and some bread or flour, depending on the country for forage, meat, and corn-meal. The party might take two light Rodman guns, with orders, in case of very rapid movements, to cut the wheels and burn the carriages, taking sledges along to break off trunnions and wedge them into the muzzles. The expedition should start from Decatur [Alabama], move slowly to Blountsville and Ashville, and, if the way is clear, cross the Coosa at the Ten Islands, or the railroad bridge, destroying it after their passage, then move rapidly for Talladega or Oxford, and then to the nearest ford or bridge over the Tallapoosa. That passed, the expedition should move with rapidity on the railroad between Tuskegee and Opelika, breaking up the road and twisting the bars of iron. They should work on that road night and day, doing all the damage possible toward and including Opelika. If no serious opposition offer, they should threaten Columbus, Georgia, and then turn up the Chattahoochee to join us between Marietta and Atlanta, doing all the mischief possible. No infantry in position should be attacked, and the party should avoid all fighting possible, bearing in mind, for their own safety, that Pensacola, Rome, the Etowah, and my army are all places of refuge. If compelled to make Pensacola, they should leave their horses, embark for New Orleans, and come round to Nashville. Study this well, and be prepared to act on orders when the time comes. Selma, though important, is more easily defended than the route I have named."

On July 2d the following dispatch was sent to Rousseau:

"Now is the time for the raid to Opelika. . . . . . Forrest is in Mississippi, and Roddy has also gone there. All other rebel cavalry is here."

On July 6th the order was repeated as follows:

"That cavalry expedition must now be off, and must proceed with the utmost energy and confidence. Every thing here is favorable, and I have official information that General A. J. Smith is out from Memphis with force enough to give Forrest full occupation. Expeditions inland are also out from Vicksburg and Baton Rouge, as well as against Mobile. If managed with rapidity, the expedition can not fail of success, and will accomplish much good."

wounded. At Opelika a large quantity of stores was captured, and the railroad was obliterated. From this point, on the 19th, Rousseau began to return to Marietta, where he arrived by way of Carrolton and Villa Rica on the 22d. He had destroyed 30 miles of the railroad toward Montgomery, three miles toward Columbus, and two toward West Point. His entire loss had been 12 killed and 30 wounded. He brought in 400 mules and 300 horses.

After having collected an abundant supply of stores at Allatoona, Marietta, and Vining's Station, and strengthened the railroad guards and garrisons in the rear, General Sherman, on the 17th, crossed the Chattahoochee, a matter of no small difficulty, effected, as it was, in the face of an army 60,000 strong. Schofield was already across in an impregnable position, and was ordered to New Cross Keys. Thomas crossed at Powers's and Paice's Ferries, and was to move by way of Buckhead; and McPherson was instructed to move straight from Rosswell to a point east of Decatur on the Augusta Railroad. Garrard's cavalry acted with McPherson, while Stoneman and McCook watched the rivers and roads below the railway.

At this most critical stage of the campaign, General Johnston, commanding the Confederate army, was relieved of his command. He received at 10 o'clock P.M. on the 17th a telegram from Secretary Seddon, the purport of which was that, as he had failed to arrest the Federal approach to the vicinity of Atlanta, and had expressed no confidence in his ability to defeat or repulse General Sherman, he would immediately turn the army over to General Hood.[1] Johnston, at Hood's request, continued to give orders until

[1] "Besides the causes of my removal alleged in the telegram announcing it," reports General Johnston, "various other accusations have been made against me—some published in newspapers in such a manner as to appear to have official authority, and others circulated orally in Georgia and Alabama, and imputed to General Bragg. The principal are, that I persistently disregarded the instructions of the President; that I would not fight the enemy; that I refused to defend Atlanta; that I refused to communicate with General Bragg in relation to the operations of the army; that I disregarded his entreaties to change my course and attack the enemy; and gross exaggerations of the losses of the army.

"I had not the advantage of receiving the President's instructions in relation to the manner of conducting the campaign. But as the conduct of my predecessor, in retreating before odds less than those confronting me, has apparently been approved; and as General Lee, in keeping on the defensive and retreating toward Grant's objective point, under circumstances like mine, was adding to his great fame, both in the estimation of the administration and people, I supposed that my course would not be censured. I believed then, as I do now, that it was the only one at my command which promised success.

"I think that the foregoing narrative shows that the Army of Tennessee did fight, and with at least as much effect as it has ever done before.

"The proofs that I intended to hold Atlanta are the fact that under my orders the work of strengthening its defenses was going on vigorously, the communication on the subject made by me to General Hood, and the fact that my family was in the town. That the public workshops were removed and no large supplies deposited in the town, as alleged by General Bragg, were measures of common prudence, and no more indicated the intention to abandon the place than the sending the wagons of an army to the rear on a day of battle proves a foregone determination to abandon the field.

"While General Bragg was at Atlanta, about the middle of July, we had no other conversation concerning the army there than such as I introduced. He asked me no questions regarding its operations, past or future; made no comments upon them nor suggestions, and had not the slightest reason to suppose that Atlanta would not be defended. He told me that the object of his journey was to confer with Lieutenant General Lee, and communicate with General E. K. Smith in relation to re-enforcements for me. He talked much more of affairs in Virginia than in Georgia, asserting, what I believed, that Sherman's army outnumbered Grant's, and impressed me with the belief that his visits to me were unofficial."

And here it is proper to consider General Hood's estimate of the Atlanta campaign. In the first place, he estimates General Johnston's effective force on the 6th of May, 1864, as 70,000 men. For this statement there is no authority whatsoever. "The South," he says, "had been denuded of troops to fill the strength of the Army of the Tennessee. Mississippi and Alabama were without military support, and looked for protection in decisive battle in the mountains of Georgia." Here again Hood is belied by all testimony. Forrest, whose assistance Johnston asked for, was kept in Mississippi by orders from Richmond, and not permitted to attack Sherman's communications. Besides putting Johnston's force nearly 20,000 higher than it really was, Hood says that "re-enforcements were within supporting distance." These re-enforcements were absolutely refused in a defensive campaign on Johnston's part, and no other campaign was possible.

Hood then goes on to reprimand Johnston's retreat: "In such condition," he says, "was that splendid army when the active campaign fairly opened. The enemy, but little superior in numbers, none in organization and discipline, inferior in spirit and confidence, commenced his advance. The Confederate forces, whose faces and hopes were to the north, almost simultaneously commenced to retreat. They soon reached positions favorable for resistance. Great ranges of mountains running across the line of march, and deep rivers, are stands from which a well-directed army is not easily driven or turned. At each advance of the enemy, the Confederate army, without serious resistance, fell back to the next range or river in the rear. The habit to retreat soon became a routine of the army, and was substituted for the hope and confidence with which the campaign opened. The enemy soon perceived this. With perfect security he divided his forces, using one column to menace in front and one to threaten in rear. The usual order to retreat-

the afternoon of the 18th, placi
selected near Peach-tree Creek.

not strike in detail, was issued and obe
consumed in hard labor. Daily tempo
tended to fight. The men became tr
to be soldiers by the disuse of military
army, which, if ordered to resist, no for
battle-field, continued to abandon their
waving only in retreat or in partial e
from the mountains, where the last adv
fortifications on the open plains of Geor
one third was gone, no general battle fo
and the organization and efficiency of e
diminished. These things were the ine
a large army to retreat in the face of
losses are constant and permanent. St
and are gathered by the advancing ene
wounded to the victors. The soldiers,
treat, leave many of their comrades asle
es of a single day are not large. Those
army. If a battle be fought and the fiel
will be less than to retreat in the face
are in retreat, rarely, if ever, on the fiel
soon recover, and in a few weeks the en
abled, which is not one fifth of the appar
ed, his plans deranged, territory saved,
essary, it can then be done with no ene
loses nothing but its killed and perman
ranks. It reaches the end of its mar
commanded by General Sherman and th
at the commencement of the campaign,
official report, states that his forces when
when they left Dalton. The Army of
fifty (22,750) men, nearly one third of
losses made by General Johnston in his
understates his losses some thousands;
previous official returns show more than
ont leave;' and that the returns of the
by the *records* of the army which has n
signed by me, but made up under him,
Army of Tennessee to be what I have s
army will show the losses to be more tha

Hood's own statements belie him. H
outset 70,000. This would leave 47,250
nearly 20,000; so that Hood should hav
how does Hood estimate the force which
strength was, infantry, 33,750; artillery,
making a total of 47,750 men." This is
Hood's estimates. For, by his calculatio
since the commencement of the campaig

And here let us submit the report ma
1865:

"MR. PRESIDENT,—I return the Rep
Committee on Military Affairs that it be
this recommendation would not have bee
lished. No action of the Senate can no
might be. Indeed, having been sent to
warning as to 'its tendency to induce c
in the case of General Johnston's Report,
from its contents being made known. T
ning of this Congress contained an attack
ident in open session, and published by
contained his defense against this attack
It was finally sent to us *in secret session*,
operations of the Army of Tennessee *whi*
we receive this paper *in open session as s*
character is given.

"Much of it is but a repetition of the
can be sustained, it is manifest that our p
ston's removal, but to his ever having bee
tinued in his present command. It beco
of these charges. The Senate did not a
a report of the operations of the army wh
called for, it is before us and the people,

"In reviewing the review, I shall refer
and Inspector General's Office, made an
General Johnston, and not to those with
seen. The field returns on file here are,
are made up from the returns of the corp
quaintance with Colonel Falconer, I do n
of official documents. I do know Colon
either capable of making a false or fraud

"General Hood, in his review, gives the
Dalton' to be 70,000 on the 6th of May
monthly, on the 1st, 10th, and 20th of eac
the 6th of May, on file in the Adjutant
shows his effective total to be 40,913 infa
43,887. This return shows, however, tha
eral Johnston, were in the rear recruiting
General Johnston, in his report, estimate
make the effective total of these brigades
4000. Estimating his cavalry there at 40
44,913 effective total 'at and near' Dalto
6th of that month. The official records
Johnston's forces 'at and near Dalton' by

"If General Hood, by the term 'at or
by General Johnston from General Polk,
4th of May that General Polk was order
forces at your command, to Rome, Geor
6th, the day on which General Hood say
of the enemy,' General Polk telegraphs
centrating and moving as directed.' On
first of Loring's brigade arrived and sent
arrive early to-morrow morning. * * *
ing. The others will follow in successio
morrow; Jackson's division thirty-six ho
fore this the army was 'assembled' at and
commander.' The last of these re-enfor
the 26th of May, nearly three weeks af
amounted to less than 10,000 men. If
battle, which is not probable, General Joh
on the 26th of May, instead of seventy th
sand; not very great, it is admitted, yet it
mates.

"General Hood asserts that General J
his retreat, and offers to prove that by th
sand men. The field returns of the 10t
command, shows, at Atlanta, 40,666 in
51,000. Deduct this from 64,000, and it
stead of 22,700, as alleged by General H
cavalry for want of reports. He had 40
on the 17th of May—8000. At Atlanta
2270 over and above his losses. Leaving
infantry and artillery. At New Hope he
supposing it not to have increased by recr
and artillery. At Atlanta he had, of the
shows his losses to be, in infantry and arti

.e had proposed to conduct the defense of Atlanta. In the
had proposed to attack Sherman while crossing the creek,
would be of the greatest advantage, since, in that event, both
the river would intercept the Federal retreat. If he failed in
s design had been to keep back the enemy by means of in-
onstructed between the Marietta and Decatur Roads until the
state troops which had been promised by Governor Brown at
: month. These intrenchments he would line with the state
he already had, while with his main army he would attack
ink whenever the latter should approach Atlanta.
erate army was now posted on high ground on the west bank
Creek, extending from Turner's Ferry to the Augusta Road.
the 18th, reached a point seven miles east of Decatur, and,
cavalry, broke up four miles of the road. Schofield the same
ecatur. On the 19th McPherson turned into Decatur, Schofield
d to the right leading toward Atlanta, while Thomas, by numer-
ossed Peach-tree Creek in the face of the enemy. Hood had
oops so that Cheatham's (formerly Hood's) corps on the right
Thomas from Schofield and McPherson. Hardee held the
ewart (commanding Polk's old corps) the left. These two

were ordered by Hood to attack Thomas at one P.M. on the 20th, before the latter could fortify himself. But the Federal movement threatened to flank Hood's right, and must be met by an extension of Cheatham's corps in that direction. This led to a displacement of Hardee's and Stewart's original line to close up the interval. In these manœuvres much time was consumed, and it was not till four P.M. that the attack was made. Hood's left corps, under Stewart, advanced toward Buckhead, and struck the Federal line at a point where a gap had been left between Thomas and Schofield, and which Sherman was trying to fill. The blow was sudden, and fell upon Newton's division on the road, Hooker's corps to the south, and Johnson's division of Palmer's corps. Johnson was well intrenched; Newton had hastily thrown up a line of rail breastworks in his front; but Hooker's corps was entirely uncovered, and fought on comparatively open ground. The assault was partially successful at first, Stewart gaining a temporary work in his front. But Newton's division, though exposed on the left, repelled every charge of the enemy. The battle then swayed toward the Federal right against Hooker and Johnson, who yielded not a foot of ground, and after a severe battle, which lasted until sundown, the enemy was hurled back to his works.[1] Thomas's loss was heavy, amounting to 1600 in killed and wounded, the greatest number of casualties being in Hooker's corps. The Confederate loss must have been still heavier. Five hundred dead were left upon the field, and 1000 severely wounded, and 360 Confederate prisoners were captured. Sherman estimates the loss of the enemy at 5000.[2]

A task had devolved upon General Hood to which his faculties were inadequate; it was a task which might have discouraged the most skillful general the world ever saw. Johnston had understood its difficulty, and had met the emergency in the only possible way which either military science or military experience suggested. His removal from command was a denunciation of his method of conducting the campaign. Hood, who, while a brave soldier, was no general, adopted an exactly opposite method. It was his well-known habit to fight battles and disregard strategy, and for this reason he had been assigned to the command. If Sherman could have made the appointment himself, he could not have more certainly or more completely served his own purpose. Hood was the commander, and Hood's theory of war was the policy which secured for him the opportunity for which he had been waiting, and out of which Johnston had all along been cheating him.

General Hood, having failed in his first plan, proceeded to execute the second, which involved an attack on McPherson. The movement of the latter to Hood's right, if not checked, would compel the evacuation of Atlanta. Thus, on the morning of the 22d, Sherman, to his surprise, found the Confederate works on Beach-tree Creek abandoned, and pushed his whole line up close to Atlanta. Hood in the mean time was constructing new fortifications, and, leaving Cheatham and Stewart to defend the city, had ordered Hardee to move south with his corps during the night of the 21st on the McDonough Road. This movement had for its object the turning of McPherson's flank. Wheeler's cavalry moved on Hardee's right, and both were to attack at daylight, or as soon thereafter as possible. Hardee's success would be followed by an attack of Cheatham on Thomas, and then, as the engagement became general, by a movement from the centre.

These combinations led to the battle of July 22. McPherson had the night before crossed the Augusta Railroad two miles west of Decatur, after severe skirmishing, and Blair, on the left of the road, had pushed forward and seized a commanding eminence not two miles distant from Atlanta. The general advance of Sherman's line on the morning of the 22d had been contracted and strengthened. Dodge's (Sixteenth) corps, on Logan's right, had been in this way displaced, and was sent around to Blair's left, to strengthen the commanding position which had been gained the previous night. Sherman in the morning had supposed that Atlanta was abandoned; but before noon Thomas and Schofield found the enemy well intrenched in their front, covering the city, and away to the left about eleven o'clock was heard the fire of musketry and artillery. In a moment Hood's design was fathomed; but it was already too late to completely avert the danger which threatened McPherson.

Sherman was at the Howard House at this time, on Thomas's left. Here McPherson met him and Schofield, and described the condition of affairs on his flank. Sherman had proposed to extend to the right, and was, therefore, not desirous to gain on the left. But the nature of the position gained by Blair led him to send Dodge to strengthen that point. This point having been settled, McPherson started from the Howard House to return to his army, reports having already reached him of an attempt on his left. The sound of musketry, increasing in volume and accompanied by artillery, led Sherman to order an advance from the right and centre, and to hold as large a portion of Schofield's corps as possible in reserve to await developments. About half an hour after McPherson's departure, his adjutant general, Lieutenant Colonel Clark, rode up with the sad and startling intelligence that his commander was either dead or a prisoner; that, riding from Sherman's headquarters to Dodge's column, and having dismissed his orderlies and staff officers on various errands, he had passed into a narrow path leading off from the extreme left of his line, and a few minutes later a sharp volley was heard in that direction, and McPherson's horse had come out riderless, with two wounds. "The suddenness of this calamity," says General Sherman, "would have overwhelmed me with grief, but the living demanded my whole thought."[3] General Logan, commanding the Fifteenth Corps, was ordered

---

d orders from the War Department, General Johnston had before this time sent
. Supposing them to average two hundred effective total, they would amount
h; deduct that amount from the 15,344, and it leaves but 14,744 total loss in
eserters, stragglers, and prisoners of his infantry and artillery. From this
000 killed and wounded, and we have 4744 lost from all other causes in these
tans that the cavalry had increased 2276. Deduct this from the 4744, and his
except in killed and wounded, amount to but 2468.
, a loss by desertion, and straggling, and prisoners of only some 2500 from the
ating' policy. The demoralization of the army could not have been as great
pposes, or its losses from these causes would have been greater. The 'working
ling by day' would seem, too, not to be a very bad policy where the army has
ader.
asserts that a retreating army must lose more by straggling and desertion, if it
it would in killed and wounded it it does. He attempts to show this by what
ablished principles, and not by figures. Napier differs from General Hood on
cussing the losses of *Massena* from the Torres Vedras, he says, 'It is *unques-*
ating army should fight *as little as possible.*'
also insists that the army at Atlanta was greatly demoralized by the loss of
and by constant falling back. I do not recollect any general officer, except
was killed while Johnston was in command; there may have been others, but
. What were his losses in general officers from Atlanta to Nashville? His
orough to the Tennessee line was a retreat, and from Nashville to Tupelo; yet
but 300, and left the army in fine spirits. The demoralization of Johnston's
counted for on this theory. But was it demoralized? It fought well when he
l. His disasters around Atlanta are not attributed by him to a want of spirit
incompetency in the officers. He could not have his orders executed. I in-
that he is mistaken as much as to his facts as he is in his theory.
insinuates that General Johnston attempts to dodge an acknowledgment of his
uding the idea of prisoners,' and charges that his official returns show more
e hand of 'absent without leave.' This is a very grave charge against an offi-
an. General Hood should know that the usual, if not only mode of stating
s is in a marginal note opposite the column of 'absent without leave.' It can
an approximate estimate; for no general can know how many of his 'absent
r a battle, have gone voluntarily to the enemy, and how many have been cap-
ood should know also that the absent and prisoners of an army are continued
ae to time, as the 'Field Returns' are made out, without reference to a change
l that it is very possible, therefore, that a part, or even the whole, of the 7000
been lost when the army was under the command of General Bragg. The
Ridge had occurred before General Johnston took command. This is a mat-
especially concerns General Hood. The field return of the 10th of July shows
7000 prisoners (6994). Opposite General Hood's corps is this note: '288 offi-
prisoners of war, are reported among the "absent without leave."' This shows
e 7000 prisoners of war, nearly 5000 (4835) were captured from his corps. He
were lost by him under Johnston, or by some one else under Bragg. For the
ement, he, and not General Johnston, is responsible. The returns of the army
ion of the returns of the corps commanders.
re 7000 prisoners taken during the retreat from Dalton, how does he account
by the official returns that General Johnston had, at Atlanta, on the 10th of
s killed and wounded, within 2500 men of the number put under his command
can this excess of loss in prisoners over his total loss (except in killed and
ified? Upon no other hypothesis than that his army increased by recruiting
t decreased by straggling and loss of prisoners. The *morale* of the army, then,
very bad—at least not as bad as it is supposed by General Hood to have been.
e of the territory which General Johnston was 'abandoning' have lost all con-
must have been from them that his recruits were gathered.
it at Dalton 'the enemy was but little superior in numbers, none in organiza-
and inferior in spirit and confidence.' The army which is described as 'in-
confidence' to Johnston's was the one which had lately routed it at Missionary
. An army flushed with victory is not usually wanting 'in spirit and confi-
esence of Johnston cause them to doubt their future success? What infused
ce' in the Army of Tennessee? Was it the consciousness that it, at last, had a
reless of his own blood, was careful of that of his men, who knew when to take
l how to bring them out, and whose thorough soldiership would save them from
slaughtered by being led to battle except when some good purpose was to be
oe brilliant victory achieved? If the 'discipline and organization' of the army
lescribed, who produced it? For four months it had been under the control
t evidence has General Hood to sustain his assertion that at Dalton the enemy
ior to us in numbers? He relies upon Sherman's statement that he was as
s when the campaign opened. His army at Missionary Ridge was estimated
afterward re-enforced by the army from Knoxville and the troops from North
tiers. Our scouts reported that he had been re-enforced with at least 80,000
rman told General Govan, or said in his presence, that he had commenced the
000. I have never heard it estimated at less than 90,000 infantry and artill-
eral Wheeler estimated it at between 65 and 70,000. The Northern papers,
nitted his losses to be 46,000. His cavalry was estimated by General Wheeler
000. Johnston, in the mean time, under orders of the War Department, sent
l received one.
charges that General Johnston did not intend to hold Atlanta. As evidence
no officer or soldier believed it, and that General Johnston had thrown up no
ont of his lines opposite Peach-tree Creek. If General Johnston intended, as
trike the head of Sherman's columns as soon as they appeared across Peach-
ore they were intrenched, or had time even to deploy into line of battle, what
d-works? They would have been in his way if erected, and his men would
fatigued in constructing them. Not having been present, I can not speak of
army. But, admitting the fact, I submit that the opinion of the army is not
the intentions of the general. Is it not possible, too, that General Hood may
own opinion for that of the army? The evidence that General Johnston did
place is given in his report. In addition, it may be added that he held New
, and only left it because the enemy left their intrenchments confronting it,
ad and to the rear. He then held a position in front of Kenesaw for a month,
because, by extending his intrenchments, Sherman had got nearer to Atlanta
n we were. In all the fighting we had been successful, and that in positions
for defense in a few hours. Is it probable, then, that General Johnston would
to hold a place fortified already to his hand under the direction of the Engi-
previously inspected by Major General Gilmer, the chief engineer of our army?
trengthening it from the 1st of July, with all the labor he could command, if
defend it, in the event of his failing to crush the enemy at Peach-tree Creek?
hening it at the very moment of his removal? If the position was as weak as
l Hood, why did Sherman not attempt to carry it by assault?"

[1] Thomas's Report.

[2] General Hood attributes the failure of the attack to delay, and to Hardee's failure "to push the attack as ordered."

[3] Two days after this event, it was reported as follows by General Sherman to Adjutant General Thomas:

ent being covered by dense woods. Enveloping Blair's division,
was extended to the rear until it reached Dodge's corps in mo-
e was between Blair and Dodge an interval of half a mile. The
ever given by McPherson was that Colonel Wangelin's brigade
corps, should cross the railroad and occupy this gap. The order
beyed, and its execution checked the ene-
ice. Wheeler's cavalry at the same time,
en a wider circuit, broke in upon Decatur,
portion of the trains there stationed, and
rest toward the Chattahoochee. Hardee
hecked, but Stewart's corps, on his left, at-
ront, sweeping across a portion of the hill
r was fortifying, capturing the intrenching
its tools, and bearing down upon G. A.
ision, which was driven back upon that of
o still obstinately clung to the crest. Smith's
w formed with its right touching Leggett,
t refused, facing southeast. This position
held for four hours, unmoved by the as-
enemy. On the extreme left Hardee had
guns, and Smith, in refusing his left, had
two more. Hood still persisted in the at-
n Sherman's left flank. There was a lull
, during which the enemy felt his way to
, and, suddenly breaking forth upon a regi-
, with a section of artillery, had been ad-
sort of picket, captured two more guns.

---

tinful duty to report that Brigadier General James B.
ited States Army, Major General of Volunteers, and
the Army of the Tennessee in the field, was killed by a
scade about noon yesterday. At the time of this fatal
horseback, placing his troops in position near the city of
s passing by a cross-road from a moving column toward
ops that had already been established on the line. He
but a few minutes before, and was on his way to see in
ecution of my orders. About the time of this sad event
sallied from his intrenchments of Atlanta, and by a cir-
the left and rear of this very line, and had begun an at-
ited in serious battle; so that General McPherson fell in
d spurred, as the gallant knight and gentleman should
the loss, but the country's; and this army will mourn
cherish his memory as that of one who, though compara-
d risen by his merit and ability to the command of one
as which the nation had called into existence to vindi-
d integrity.

s of but few who so blended the grace and gentleness of
he dignity, courage, faith, and manliness of the soldier.
ies, even the men who directed the fatal shot, ne'er
of him without expressions of marked respect; those
anded loved him even to idolatry; and I, his associate
fail in words adequate to express my opinion of his
feel assured that every patriot in America, on hearing
ill feel a sense of personal loss, and the country gener-
that we have lost not only an able military leader, but a
o survived, was qualified to heal the national strife which
by designing and ambitious men. His body has been
harge of Major Willard, Captains Steele and Giles, his

the Chattahoochee to a point near Rivertown, where he crossed, and, mov
on Palmetto Station, tore up a section of the West Point Road. Thence
advanced to Fayetteville, where he destroyed about 500 wagons belong
to the enemy. Pushing on to the railroad at Lovejoy's, he burned the dé
and destroyed a portion of the road. In the mean time the enemy was

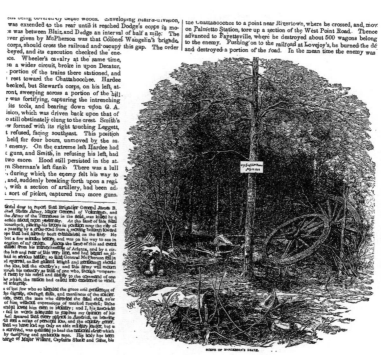

SCENE OF McPHERSON'S DEATH.

O. O. HOWARD.

'cumulating forces around him, and, receiving no tidings from Stoneman, he moved south and west to Newman, on the West Point Road, where he encountered a body of infantry on the way from Mississippi to Hood's army. This body, delayed by the break at Palmetto, together with the cavalry which had been pursuing McCook, completely surrounded the latter and compelled him to fight. McCook cut his way out with great difficulty, losing 500 men. Stoneman, disregarding all the instructions which he had received, seems never to have come near Lovejoy's. Keeping east of the Ocmulgee to Clinton, he sent detachments eastward, which succeeded in inflicting great damage upon the railroad, burning the bridges over Walnut Creek and the Oconee. With his main force he appeared before Macon. He made no attempt upon the town, however, nor did he proceed toward Andersonville, but began to retrace his steps, closely followed by various detachments of Confederate cavalry under General Iverson. He was soon hemmed in by the enemy; and giving his consent to two thirds of his command to escape, with the remainder and a section of light guns he occupied the enemy. A brigade under Colonel Adams returned to Sherman almost intact. Another, commanded by Colonel Capron, was surprised on its way back, and, being scattered, a large number were killed and captured. Stoneman surrendered himself, and the small portion of his command which remained with him. Very much was sacrificed in this expedition, and very little was gained, as the breaks made in the Macon Road were of such a character as to be easily repaired.

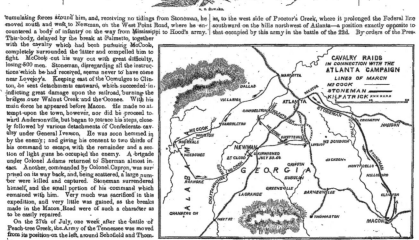

On the 27th of July, one week after the battle of Peach-tree Creek, the Army of the Tennessee was moved from its position on the left, around Schofield and Thomas, to the west side of Proctor's Creek, where it prolonged the Federal line southward on the hills northwest of Atlanta—a position exactly opposite to that occupied by this army in the battle of the 22d. By orders of the Pres-

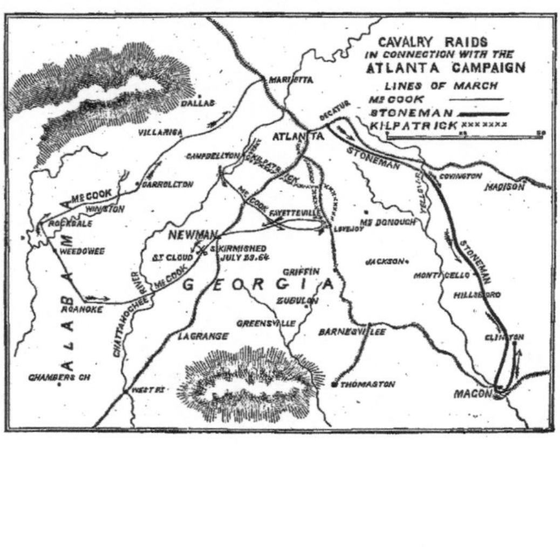

SHERMAN IN COUNCIL DECIDES TO RAISE THE SIEGE OF ATLANTA

ident, given at Sherman's suggestion, General O. O. Howard had been, on the 27th, assigned to the command of the Army of the Tennessee, General Stanley succeeding to the command of the Fourth Corps. This appointment led to General Hooker's departure from Sherman's army. Howard was a junior officer as compared with Hooker, and the latter resented his promotion on the ground that, in the natural course, he should himself have been preferred. Hooker therefore threw up his command of the Twentieth Corps, and was succeeded by General H. W. Slocum. General Sherman had very properly considered that a good department commander must be selected, and for this purpose he preferred Howard to either Logan or Hooker, whom also he wished to retain in their present positions on account of their eminent efficiency as corps commanders.[1]

Dodge, with the Sixteenth Corps, took a position just west of Proctor's Creek on the evening of the 27th. The next morning, Blair, with the Sev-

[1] The following letter, addressed by Sherman to Halleck, August 16, 1864, fully explains this affair:

"It occurs to me that, preliminary to a future report of the history of this campaign, I should record certain facts of great personal interest to officers of this command.

"General McPherson was killed by the musketry fire at the beginning of the battle of July 22. He had in person selected the ground for his troops, constituting the left wing of the army, I being in person with the centre, General Schofield. The moment the information reached me, I sent one of my staff to announce the fact to General John A. Logan, the senior officer present with the Army of the Tennessee, with general instructions to maintain the ground chosen by General McPherson if possible, but, if pressed too hard, to refuse his left flank, but, at all events, to hold the railroad and main Decatur Road; that I did not propose to move or gain ground by that flank, but rather by the right, and that I wanted the Army of the Tennessee to fight it out unaided. General Logan admirably conceived my orders and executed them; and, if he gave ground on the left of the Seventeenth Corps, it was properly done by my orders; but he held a certain hill by the right division of the Seventeenth Corps, the only ground on that line the possession of which by an enemy would have damaged us by giving a reverse fire on the remainder of the troops. General Logan fought that battle out as required, unaided save by a small brigade sent by my orders from General Schofield to the Decatur Road, well to the rear, where it was reported the enemy's cavalry had got into the town of Decatur, and was operating directly on the rear of Logan; but that brigade was not disturbed, and was replaced that night by a part of the Fifteenth Corps next to General Schofield, and General Schofield's brigade brought back so as to be kept together on its own line.

"General Logan managed the Army of the Tennessee well during his command, and it may be that an unfair inference might be drawn to his prejudice because he did not succeed to the permanent command. I am forced to choose a commander, not only for the army in the field, but of the Department of the Tennessee, covering a vast extent of country, with troops much dispersed. It was a delicate and difficult task, and I gave preference to Major General O. O. Howard, then in command of the Fourth Army Corps in the Department of the Cumberland. Instead of giving my reasons, I prefer that the wisdom of the choice be left to the test of time. The President kindly ratified my choice, and I am willing to assume the responsibility. I meant no disrespect to any officer; and hereby declare that General Logan submitted with the grace and dignity of a soldier, gentleman, and patriot, resumed the command of his corps proper (Fifteenth), and enjoys

EZRA'S CHURCH.

enteenth Corps, extended the line south and west to Ezra Church, on the Bell's Ferry or Lickskillet Road; and Logan came in on Blair's right, his own right being refused along a well-wooded ridge south of the road. By 10 A.M. on the 28th Howard's army was in position, and was rapidly fortifying itself with breastworks of rails and logs. From that time until noon there was heavy artillery firing from the Confederate position. Evidently Hood was about to repeat the tactics of the 22d. Lieutenant General S. D. Lee, who on the 25th had relieved General Cheatham of the command of Hood's former corps, was ordered to advance and attack Howard's right, and cover the Lickskillet Road. The attack about noon fell upon the corps of General Logan, who fought alone the battle which ensued. Several assaults were made by Cheatham until 4 P.M., but were each repulsed with great loss to the enemy. Logan's loss was less than 700. But when Cheatham abandoned the field he left 642 killed, which were counted and buried, besides many others buried but not counted. Sherman estimates the Confederate loss in this battle of the 28th as "not less than 5000." He had anticipated this attack, and had made dispositions which, but for his ignorance of the topography on his right rear, must have converted Cheatham's repulse into a disastrous rout. Up to this point Hood had been acting upon the plans which General Johnston had formed, but it is very doubtful whether the latter general would have executed them in the same manner. Certainly Johnston would not have attacked Howard's army on the 28th, knowing

the love and respect of his army and of his commanders. It so happened that on the 28th of July I had again thrown the same army to the extreme right, the exposed flank, where the enemy repeated the same manœuvre, striking in mass; the extreme corps deployed in line, and refused as a flank the Fifteenth, Major General Logan, and he commanded in person, General Howard and myself being near; and that corps, as heretofore reported, repulsed the rebel army completely, and next day advanced and occupied the ground fought over and the road the enemy sought to cover. General Howard, who had that very day assumed his new command, unequivocally gave General Logan all the credit possible; and I also beg to add my unqualified admiration of the bravery and skill, and, more yet, good sense that influenced him to bear a natural disappointment, and do his whole duty like a man. If I could bestow upon him substantial reward, it would afford me unalloyed satisfaction; but I do believe, in the consciousness of acts done from noble impulses, and gracefully admitted by his superiors in authority, he will be contented. He already holds the highest commission known in the army, and it is hard to say how we can better manifest our applause.

"At the time of General Howard's selection, Major General Hooker commanded the Twentieth Army Corps in the Army of the Cumberland, made up for his special accommodation out of the old Eleventh and Twelfth Corps, whereby Major General Slocum was deprived of his Corps command. Both the law and practice are and have been to fill the higher army commands by selection. Ranks or dates of Commission have not controlled, nor am I aware that any reflection can be inferred, unless the junior be placed immediately over the senior; but in this case General Hooker's Command was in no manner disturbed. General Howard was not put over him, but in charge of a distinct and separate army. No indignity was offered or intended; and I must say that General Hooker was not justified in retiring. At all events, had he spoken or written to me, I would have made every explanation and concession he could have expected, but could not have changed my course, because then, as now, I believed it right, and for the good of our country and cause.

"As a matter of justice, General Slocum, having been displaced by the consolidation, was deemed by General Thomas as entitled to the vacancy created by General Hooker's voluntary withdrawal, and has received it."

DRA[illegible] AFTER THE BATTLE OF EZRA'S CHURCH.

SHERMAN'S ARMY DESTROYING THE MACON RAILROAD BETWEEN ROUGH AND READY AND JONESBOROUGH.

ATLANTA, GEORGIA.

that the latter was intrenched. Half a dozen of such battles would have Hood without an army. At any rate, no farther attempt was made by G eral Hood to oppose Sherman's extension by flank southward. As the F eral army developed toward East Point, the enemy, without attacking, tended his intrenched line in the same direction.

By the 1st of August the Fifteenth and Seventeenth Corps had advan beyond the Lickskillet Road. On that day Schofield's army was transfer to Howard's right, Palmer's corps, of the Army of the Cumberland, foll ing. Palmer took a position below Utoy Creek, and Schofield extended line to near East Point. Here a question of rank arose between Schofi and Palmer, the former being instructed by General Sherman to give ord to the latter. This difficulty finally (on the 6th of August) led to Palm resignation, General Jeff. C. Davis succeeding him in command of the Fc teenth Corps.

By this extension of his army southward, Sherman compelled Hooc lengthen the line of defense; and while Schofield attempted to turn the C federate left, and reach the Macon Road, Thomas and Howard pressed orously on Hood's right and centre.... But, though the enemy's line was teen miles long, extending from Decatur around to below East Point, it cc easily be held by militia, and was so well masked by the shape of the gro that it was impossible for Sherman to discover its weak points. It was ginning to be evident that, in order to reach the Macon Road, the whole Sherman's army would have to be transferred to the east and south of lanta. An attempt was first made to destroy the city by means of four inch rifled guns, which on the 10th arrived from Chattanooga. These good execution, but Hood was not willing to abandon the city so long as could keep the forts, and the battering down of every building in Atla would not have altered his determination.

In the mean time Hood had dispatched Wheeler, with a cavalry fo 4500 strong, against the railroad in Sherman's rear. This, without fright ing the Federal commander, who had no immediate cause for concern a supplies, greatly enhanced his opportunity for offensive operations. It t seemed possible that, without moving the entire army, a raid might be m by Kilpatrick which should break up the Macon Road. Kilpatrick star out and broke the road to West Point, and then advanced to Jonesborou on the Macon Road, where he encountered and defeated a portion of Confederate cavalry under Ross, and held the railroad for five hours, dc it sufficient damage to give the enemy about ten days' work in repairin A brigade of Confederate infantry, with Jackson's cavalry, put a stop to work here. Moving east, he again encountered the enemy at Lovejoy's, a after defeating him and capturing four guns and a large number of pris ers, returned to Sherman's army by way of Decatur.

Not satisfied with what had been accomplished in this raid, Sherman, the night of August 25th, raised the siege of Atlanta. General A. S. W liams,[1] with the Twentieth Corps, was ordered back to hold the intrencl position at the Chattahoochee bridge, and the remainder of the army, w 15 days' rations, was set in motion toward a position on the Macon Road, or near Jonesborough. On the first night of the movement, Stanley, w the Fourth Corps, drew out from the extreme left to a position west of Pr tor's Creek, and Williams moved back, as ordered, to the Chattahoochee, b movements being effected without loss. The next night the Army of Tennessee moved south, well toward Sandtown, and the Army of the Cu berland to a position south of Utoy Creek, Schofield remaining in positi Only one casualty occurred in this second stage of the army's progress. third movement, on the 27th, brought Howard's command to the West Po Road, above Fairburn, Thomas's army to Red Oak, Schofield at the sa time closing in on the left. The 28th was spent in the destruction of West Point Road, a break being made of over 12 miles.

The railroad from Atlanta to Macon follows the ridge dividing the Fl from the Ocmulgee River, and between East Point and Jonesborough mal a wide bend to the east. It was against this ridge that the Federal ar moved on the 29th—Howard toward Jonesborough on the right; Thomas the centre, toward Couch's, on the Fayetteville Road, and Schofield on left. As soon as Hood learned of this movement of Sherman, which, if s cessful, would compel the evacuation of Atlanta, he sent (on the 30th) Le and Hardee's corps to Jonesborough. To Hardee was given the comma Hood remaining with Stewart's corps in Atlanta, intending, in case of H dee's success, to attack in flank. Hood does not seem to have been aw of the extent of the operation which Sherman was conducting, and suppo that Hardee, at Jonesborough, would encounter a force inferior to his ow

The battle of Jonesborough was fought on the 31st of August. Sherm was making dispositions to advance Schofield's and Davis's corps to Rou and Ready, between Atlanta and Jonesborough, when Hardee, coming c of the latter place, attacked Howard in his intrenched position. Hardee w well aware of the importance of this battle, and fought his troops with d perate obstinacy for two hours, when he withdrew from the field thorougl beaten, having lost 1400 killed and wounded.[2]

While the battle had been in progress, Stanley's and Schofield's, and portion of Davis's corps, had struck the railroad at several points, and we engaged in its destruction. A splendid opportunity was now offered for t destruction of Hardee's command. Sherman saw this, and ordered his thr corps to turn against Jonesborough. Howard was to occupy Hardee wh Thomas and Schofield moved down upon him from the north, destroyi the railroad on their march. What was done must be done on the 1st September. By noon of that day Davis's corps reached Howard's left, a faced southward across the railroad. Blair was then with the Seventeen

[1] Williams commanded the Twentieth Corps until Slocum should arrive from Vicksburg.
[2] Sherman estimates Hardee's loss as 2500. We have followed General Hood's report.

CONFEDERATE PRISONERS BEING CONDUCTED FROM JONESBOROUGH TO ATLANTA.

EXODUS OF CONFEDERATES FROM ATLANTA

ps, and Kilpatrick's cavalry thrown across the road south of Jonesbor-b. About 4 P.M. Davis assaulted the enemy's lines across the open, aping all before him, and capturing the greater part of Govan's brigade, uding its commander. Repeated orders were sent hurrying up Scho-l and Stanley, but, owing to the difficult nature of the country, these two s did not arrive until night rendered farther operations impossible; during the night the enemy retreated southward.

uring the same night, at 2 A.M. on the morning of September 2, the ad of heavy explosions was heard from the direction of Atlanta, 20 miles ant, indicating the evacuation of that place by General Hood. Without rding these tokens, Sherman pressed on the next morning in pursuit of dee, but found it impossible to intercept his retreat. On the 2d Slocum ered Atlanta, followed by the whole army on the 7th. In this last move-t of his army General Sherman had captured 3000 prisoners and 16 s. His loss had been 1500 men.

n the mean time Wheeler's raid on Sherman's communications had been ductive of little damage. He had broken the railroad near Calhoun, but been checked by Colonel Laibold at Dalton until Steedman could ar- from Chattanooga, when he was headed off into East Tennessee. Fi-ly, Rousseau, Steedman, and R. S. Granger, with their combined forces, ve him out of Tennessee.

"Atlanta is ours," telegraphed Sherman to Washington on the 3d of Sep-ber, "and fairly won." The loss of this position by the Confederates an irreparable misfortune. The wall which had hitherto protected the ton States was now obliterated. The victory electrified the nation; it felt to be the consummation of the triumphs won at Vicksburg and attanooga, and its political effect in the loyal states can not be too highly mated. President Lincoln wrote a letter of thanks to Sherman and his y. "The marches, battles, sieges, and other military operations that re signalized the campaign must render it famous in the annals of war, l have entitled those who have participated therein to the applause and nks of the nation." Lieutenant General Grant, before Petersburg, on the , ordered a salute to be fired in honor of the victory "with shotted guns m every battery bearing upon the enemy." On the 12th, General Sher-n received from the President a commission making him a major general the regular army.[1]

Sherman's outlook from Atlanta was magnificent. Though he had lost r 30,000 men in the numerous battles of the campaign, his army was as ge as when he set out four months before. The Confederate loss must ve been nearly equal to Sherman's.[2] G. A. Smith's militia had been sent Griffin, and Hood now confronted Sherman with an army of 40,000 men all arms. The next objective, if Hood attempted to cover Georgia, was con—103 miles east of Atlanta. But Sherman determined to give his ny a brief period of rest before another advance. The Army of the Cum-rland went into camp about Atlanta, the Army of the Tennessee about st Point, and the Army of the Ohio at Decatur.[3] At the latter point was o stationed Garrard's cavalry division, while Kilpatrick's, at Sandtown, arded the western flank. To strengthen the railroad in the rear, two di-ions—Newton's, of the Fourth, and Morgan's, of the Fourteenth Corps—re dispatched to Chattanooga, and Corse's division, of the Fifteenth Corps, Rome. A new and more compact system of fortifications was also con-acted about Atlanta, which town Sherman now proposed to make exclu-ely a military post.

To carry out this design, every thing in Atlanta, except churches and elling-houses, was burned. On the 4th of September Sherman issued an ler commanding the inhabitants of the town to leave at once. "I am not iling," said Sherman, "to have Atlanta encumbered by the families of our emies; I want it a pure Gibraltar, and will have it so by the first of Octo-r."[4] This order was a surprise to the citizens, and doubtless occasioned en much hardship. But Sherman had broken through the protecting lls of the Confederacy, and now resolved that the people of the Cotton ates should feel the heavy hand of war. He would not acknowledge the punity of treason. The city authorities and General Hood protested ainst the order as unnecessary and cruel. But Sherman's reply crushed the meaning out of their words; brought them face to face with the war mon whom they themselves had invoked, and laughed to scorn their weak d impudent claims.[5] A cessation of hostilities was agreed upon between Sherman and Hood, to continue for ten days following the 12th of September. During this time 446 families were removed south from Atlanta, comprising 1644 persons, of whom 860 were children and 79 servants. During the same period arrangements were made between Hood and Sherman for the mutual exchange of 2000 prisoners.

---

[1] Lieutenant General Grant says in his official report:
"General Sherman's movement from Chattanooga to Atlanta was prompt, skillful, and brilliant. e history of his flank movements and battles during that memorable campaign will ever be read h an interest unsurpassed by any thing in history."

[2] Hood reports his loss in battle, since he assumed the command on the 17th of July, as 5247. was probably, however, much higher than that. Indeed, in the four severe battles of July 20th, l, and 28th, and September 1st, the casualties could not have been less than 10,000. We can ce no confidence in Hood's official estimates.

[3] Several changes now took place in the army, in consequence of the expiration of the terms of rice of many of the regiments. "The Army of the Tennessee was consolidated into two corps, Fifteenth and Seventeenth, respectively commanded by Major General P. J. Osterhaus and igadier General Thomas E. G. Ransom; the former comprising the four divisions of Brigadier nerals Charles R. Woods, William B. Hazen, John E. Smith, and John M. Corse; the latter se of Major General Joseph A. Mower, and Brigadier Generals Miles D. Leggett and Giles A. ith, with the First Alabama Cavalry and the First Missouri Engineer regiment; having in charge rgo pontoon-bridge train. This organization was effected by transferring all the troops of the enteenth Corps remaining on the Mississippi to the Sixteenth Corps, breaking up the detach-nt of the latter corps in the field, and transferring Ransom's division, now commanded by Briga-r General Giles A. Smith, and Corse's division to the Seventeenth Corps. Major Generals Lo-n and Blair were temporarily absent, engaged in the important political canvass than in progress. jor General Schofield returned to the headquarters of the Department of the Ohio, at Knoxville, give his personal attention to affairs in that quarter, leaving Brigadier General Jacob D. Cox in mand of the Twenty-third Corps. The cavalry was reorganized so as to consist of two divi-ns, under Brigadier Generals Garrard and Judson Kilpatrick."—*Bowman's Sherman and his mpaigns.*

[4] *Dispatch to General Halleck, September 9, 1864.*

[5] We quote the correspondence which followed, as given in Bowman's "*Sherman and his Cam-gns:*"
"On the 11th of September, the town authorities addressed the following petition to General erman, praying the revocation of his orders:

"'SIR,—The undersigned, mayor and two members of Council for the city of Atlanta, for the time being the only legal organ of the people of the said city to express their wants and wishes, ask leave most earnestly, but respectfully, to petition you to reconsider the order requiring them to leave Atlanta.

"'At first view, it struck us that the measure would involve extraordinary hardship and loss; but since we have seen the practical execution of it, so far as it has progressed, and the individual condition of many of the people, and heard their statements as to the inconveniences, loss and suffering attending it, we are satisfied that it will involve, in the aggregate, consequences appalling and heart-rending.

"'Many poor women are in an advanced state of pregnancy; others now having young children, and whose husbands are either in the army, prisoners, or dead. Some say, "I have such a one sick at home; who will wait on them when I am gone?" Others say, "What are we to do? we have no houses to go to, and no means to buy, build, or to rent any—no parents, friends, or relatives to go to." Another says, "I will try and take this or that article of property, but such and such things I must leave behind, though I need them much." We reply to them, "General Sherman will carry your property to Rough and Ready, and General Hood will take it from there on." And they will reply to that, "But I want to leave the railway at such a point, and can not get conveyance from there on."

"'We only refer to a few facts to try to illustrate in part how this measure will operate in practice. As you advanced, the people north of us fell back, and before your arrival here a large portion of the people had retired South, so that the country south of this is already crowded, and without houses to accommodate the people, and we are informed that many are now starving in churches and other out-buildings. This being so, how is it possible for the people still here (mostly women and children) to find any shelter? And how can they live through the winter in the woods—no shelter nor subsistence—in the midst of strangers who know them not, and without the power to assist them, if they were willing to do so?

"'This is but a feeble picture of the consequences of this measure. You know the woe, the horror, and the suffering can not be described by words. Imagination can only conceive of it, and we ask you to take these things into consideration.

"'We know your mind and time are constantly occupied with the duties of your command, which almost deters us from asking your attention to this matter, but thought it might be that you had not considered the subject in all its awful consequences, and that, on more reflection, you, we hoped, would not make this people an exception to all mankind, for we know of no such instance ever having occurred—surely none such in the United States; and what has this helpless people done that they should be driven from their homes, to wander as strangers, outcasts, and exiles, and to subsist on charity?

"'We do not know, as yet, the number of people still here. Of those who are here, we are satisfied a respectable number, if allowed to remain at home, could subsist for several months without assistance, and a respectable number for a much longer time, and who might not need assistance at any time.

"'In conclusion, we most earnestly and solemnly petition you to reconsider this order, or modify it, and suffer this unfortunate people to remain at home and enjoy what little means they have.

Respectfully submitted,

JAMES M. CALHOUN, *Mayor.*
E. E. RAWSON, *Councilman.*
L. C. WELLS, *Councilman.*'

"To this General Sherman replied, in full and clear terms, on the following day:

"'GENTLEMEN,—I have your letter of the 11th, in the nature of a petition to revoke my orders removing all the inhabitants from Atlanta. I have read it carefully, and give full credit to your statements of the distress that will be occasioned by it, and yet shall not revoke my order, simply because my orders are not designed to meet the humanities of the case, but to prepare for the future struggles in which millions, yea, hundreds of millions of good people outside of Atlanta have a deep interest. We must have peace, not only at Atlanta, but in all America. To secure this, we must stop the war that now desolates our once happy and favored country. To stop the war, we must defeat the rebel armies that are arrayed against the laws and Constitution, which all must respect and obey. To defeat these armies, we must prepare the way to reach them in their recesses, provided with the arms and instruments which enable us to accomplish our purpose.

"'Now I know the vindictive nature of our enemy, and that we may have many years of military operations from this quarter, and therefore deem it wise and prudent to prepare in time. The use of Atlanta for warlike purposes is inconsistent with its character as a home for families. There will be no manufactures, commerce, or agriculture here for the maintenance of families, and sooner or later want will compel the inhabitants to go. Why not go *now*, when all the arrangements are completed for the transfer, instead of waiting until the plunging shot of contending armies will renew the scenes of the past month? Of course I do not apprehend any such thing at this moment, but you do not suppose this army will be here till the war is over. I can not discuss this subject with you fairly, because I can not impart to you what I propose to do, but I assert that my military plans make it necessary for the inhabitants to go away, and I can only renew my offer of services to make their exodus in any direction as easy and comfortable as possible. You can not qualify war in harsher terms than I will.

"'War is cruelty, and you can not refine it; and those who brought war on our country deserve all the curses and maledictions a people can pour out. I know I had no hand in making this war, and I know I will make more sacrifices to-day than any of you to secure peace. But you can not have peace and a division of our country. If the United States submit to a division now, it will not stop, but will go on till we reap the fate of Mexico, which is eternal war. The United States does and must assert its authority wherever it has power; if it relaxes one bit to pressure, it is gone, and I know that such is not the national feeling. This feeling assumes various shapes, but always comes back to that of *Union*. Once admit the Union, once more acknowledge the authority of the national government, and, instead of devoting your houses, and streets, and roads to the dread uses of war, I and this army become at once your protectors and supporters, shielding you from danger, let it come from what quarter it may. I know that a few individuals can not resist a torrent of error and passion such as has swept the South into rebellion; but you can point out, so that we may know those who desire a government and those who insist on war and its desolation.

"'You might as well appeal against the thunder-storm as against these terrible hardships of war. They are inevitable; and the only way the people of Atlanta can hope once more to live in peace and quiet at home is to stop this war, which can alone be done by admitting that it began in error and is perpetuated in pride. We don't want your negroes, or your horses, or your land, or any thing you have; but we do want, and will have, a just obedience to the laws of the United States. That we will have; and if it involves the destruction of your improvements, we can not help it.

"'You have heretofore read public sentiment in your newspapers, that live by falsehood and excitement, and the quicker you seek for truth in other quarters the better for you. I repeat, then, that by the original compact of government, the United States had certain rights in Georgia which have never been relinquished, and never will be; that the South began the war by seizing forts, arsenals, mints, custom-houses, etc., etc., long before Mr. Lincoln was installed, and before the South had one jot or tittle of provocation. I myself have seen, in Missouri, Kentucky, Tennessee, and Mississippi, hundreds and thousands of women and children fleeing from your armies and desperadoes, hungry, and with bleeding feet. In Memphis, Vicksburg, and Mississippi, we fed thousands upon thousands of the families of rebel soldiers left on our hands, and whom we could not see starve. Now that war comes home to you, you feel very differently—you deprecate its horrors, but did not feel them when you sent car-loads of soldiers and ammunition, and moulded shells and shot to carry war into Kentucky and Tennessee, and desolate the homes of hundreds and thousands of good people, who only asked to live in peace at their old homes, and under the government of their inheritance. But these comparisons are idle. I want peace, and I believe it can only be reached through Union and war, and I will ever conduct war purely with a view to perfect and early success.

"'But, my dear sirs, when that peace does come you may call upon me for any thing. Then will I share with you the last cracker, and watch with you to shield your home and families against danger from every quarter. Now you must go, and take with you the old and feeble; feed and nurse them, and build for them in more quiet places proper habitations to shield them against the weather, until the mad passions of men cool down, and allow the Union and peace once more to settle on your old homes at Atlanta.'

"As soon as his arrangements were completed, General Sherman wrote to General Hood, by a flag of truce, notifying him of his orders, and proposing a cessation of hostilities for ten days from the 12th of September, in the country included within a radius of two miles around Rough and Ready Station, to enable him to complete the removal of those families electing to go to the south. Hood immediately replied on the 9th, acceding to the proposed truce, but protesting against Sherman's order. He concluded:

"'Permit me to say, the unprecedented measure you propose transcends in studied and ingenious cruelty all acts ever before brought to my attention in the dark history of the war. In the name of God and humanity, I protest, believing you are expelling from homes and firesides wives and children of a brave people.'"

ULYSSES S. GRANT.

WORKSHOPS—ARMY OF THE POTOMAC.

CHAPTER XLII.

THE CAMPAIGN IN VIRGINIA.—FROM THE RAPIDAN TO THE JAMES.

Result of Meade's Campaign.—Action of the Committee on the Conduct of the War.—Grant appointed Lieutenant General.—Retirement of Halleck.—Arrangements for the Campaign of 1864.—The Union Forces.—Changes in Organization and Command.—Hancock, Warren, Sedgwick, Burnside.—Sykes, French, Newton.—Kilpatrick, Pleasonton, Sheridan, Sherman.—Meade retained in command of the Army of the Potomac.—Grant's Plans of Campaign.—Position and Strength of Lee's Army.—Lee's Right Flank to be turned.—Opening of the Campaign.—How conducted by Lee and Grant.—*The Battles in the Wilderness:* Passage of the Rapidan.—Positions in the Wilderness.—Military Features of the Region.—Lee moves to the Wilderness.—Grant's proposed Line of March.—Ewell encounters Warren.—Forces him down the Turnpike.—Hill checks him on the Plank Road.—Hancock ordered up.—Getty holds the Brock Road.—Sedgwick attacks on the Right.—Hancock arrives, and attacks Hill.—The Wadsworth Movement.—Hancock repulsed.—Close of the Action of May 5.—Its Results.—Preparations for the Battle of the 6th.—Simultaneous Attack by both Armies.—Slight Engagement between Ewell and Hancock.—Hancock attacks Hill, and forces him back.—Lee on the Field.—Hancock checked.—Longstreet arrives.—Hancock forced back.—Wadsworth Killed.—Longstreet moves toward Hancock's Rear.—Is Wounded.—Burnside's Movements.—Lee assails Hancock's Intrenchments.—Close of the Action on the Left.—Night Assault upon Sedgwick.—Seymour's Division captured.—Results of the Battle.—Losses.—Grant and Lee move toward Spottsylvania.—Lee arrives First.—The whole of both Armies come up.—Fighting on the 7th.—The Action of the 9th.—Death of Sedgwick.—Fighting on the 10th.—Grant's Dispatch.—Washington Bulletins.—Losses in these Actions.—The Battle of the 12th.—Hancock carries Works, and captures Johnson's Division.—The Confederates rally.—Hancock repelled.—Other Operations.—Close of the Battle.—Results and Losses.—Grant moves for the North Anna.—Lee assails and is repulsed.—Lee's Plan of defending Rivers.—Grant crosses the North Anna.—Recrosses.—Both Armies re-enforced.—Sigel defeated at New Market.—He is superseded by Hunter.—Crooke's fruitless Expedition.—Hunter advances.—Defeats Jones at Piedmont, and moves upon Lynchburg.—Retreats northwestward.—Loses his Trains.—Butler moves up the James.—Intrenches at Bermuda Hundred.—Kautz cuts the Weldon Railroad.—Beauregard in Virginia.—Grant's Plan for Butler.—Butler attacks Fort Darling.—He is assailed by Beauregard, and retreats to his Intrenchments.—Beauregard's Plans.—The "Bottling-up" at Bermuda Hundred.—Grant moves toward the Chickahominy.—Lee's corresponding Movement.—Positions assumed.—Sheridan occupies Cold Harbor.—Is assailed.—Smith brought from Bermuda Hundred.—Action of June 1.—Value of Intrenched Positions.—Grant's Purposes.—Battle of Gold Harbor, June 3.—Hancock, Wright, and Smith attack and are repulsed.—Burnside's Movement.—Defeat of the Federal Army.—Losses.—Results of the Battle.—Both armies intrench.—Skirmishing.—Grant moves to the James River.—Lee falls back to Richmond.

THE result of the ineffective campaigns at the East brought with it the conviction that the command of the armies in Virginia must be committed to other and stronger hands. The Congressional Committee on the Conduct of the War had hardly begun their investigations into the operations conducted by General Meade when the two members by whom it had been mainly conducted[1] repaired to the President and Secretary of War, and "demanded the removal of General Meade, and the appointment of some one more competent to command." They suggested the reinstatement of Hooker, but would acquiesce in that of any other general whom the President might think better fitted for the place, but declared emphatically that unless some change was made "it would become their duty to make the testimony public which they had taken, with such comments as the circumstances of the case seemed to require." But events had been so shaping themselves as to obviate the necessity of farther action. Congress, after much deliberation, had passed a bill reviving the grade of lieutenant general, which had never been held except by Washington, for Scott was such only by brevet. Congress also recommended that this appointment should be conferred upon General Grant, and that he should be placed in actual command of all the armies of the United States. The bill was passed, and approved on the 2d of March, and on the 9th Grant was formally presented with his commission. "The nation's appreciation of what you have done," said the President, "and its reliance upon you for what remains to be done in the existing great struggle, are now presented with this commission constituting you lieutenant general in the armies of the United States. With this high honor devolves upon you a corresponding responsibility. As the country herein trusts you, so, under God, it will sustain you. I need scarcely add that with what I here speak for the nation goes my own hearty personal concurrence."

No man was ever more heartily rejoiced at being relieved from an onerous task than was the President when thus enabled virtually to resign his position as commander-in-chief of the army. He had at length found a man into whose hands that trust might be confided. Halleck's occupation as general-in-chief was gone. He was relieved from active duty, and made chief of staff of the army, under the direction of the President, the Secretary of War, and the Lieutenant General. He was to remain at Washington, while Grant's headquarters were to be with the Army of the Potomac in the field, whence the operations of all the Union armies were to be directed. Henceforth the war was to be carried on by a soldier uncontrolled by civilian direction. Even the strong-willed Secretary of War ceased from interfering with operations in the field.[1]

The arrangements for the spring campaign of 1864 were made for a force of a million of men. On the first of May all the armies nominally counted within 30,000 of that number; but of these 109,000 were on detached service, 117,000 were in hospitals or unfit for duty, 66,000 were absent on furlough or prisoners of war, 15,000 were absent without leave. The entire force "available and present for duty" was 662,345. Nothing was left undone to put this immense force into a condition of the utmost efficiency. Congress made appropriations with unsparing hand. Vast amounts of arms,

[1] Senators Wade and Chandler; see *Com. Rep.*, ii., xvii.-xix.

[1] "So far as the Secretary of War and myself are concerned, he has never interfered with my duties, never thrown any obstacles in the way of any supplies I have called for. He has never dictated a course of campaign to me, and never inquired what I was going to do. He has always seemed satisfied with what I did, and has heartily co-operated with me."—Grant's Testimony, May 18, 1865, in *Com. Rep.*, ii., 524.

LIEUTENANT-GENERAL PHILIP HENRY SHERIDAN. NOVEMBER 1, 1883.

ammunition, stores, clothing, and medical supplies were provided and distributed in dépôts. The means of transportation, by land and water, were multiplied. Of this great army 310,000 men were in Virginia and upon its borders, and in the Carolinas. The Army of the Potomac numbered 140,000, including the Ninth Corps, which acted with it from the first, and was soon formally incorporated with it. In and around Washington were 42,000. In Western Virginia were 31,000. In the Department of Virginia and North Carolina were 59,000; of these, fully 25,000, known as the Army of the James, were available for active service in the field. In South Carolina and Georgia, the Department of the South, were 18,000. In the various minor departments were 20,000. To oppose these, the Confederates had in the field not more than 125,000, in Virginia and the Carolinas. The immediate struggle was to be between the Union Army of the Potomac, 140,000 strong, and the Confederate Army of Northern Virginia, of less than half that number, probably not much exceeding 60,000.[1]

Considerable changes were made in the organization of the Army of the Potomac. The five corps of which it had consisted were concentrated into three,[1] to be known as the Second, Fifth, and Sixth. The former First and Third Corps were broken up, the troops being distributed among the Second and Fifth. There was little room for hesitation as to the choice of corps commanders. Hancock, having recovered from his wound at Gettysburg, resumed the command of the Second. Warren, who had manifested great military capacity, was placed at the head of the Fifth. There was no question as to continuing Sedgwick in command of the Sixth. Hooker had indeed sharply censured his operations near Chancellorsville,[2] but when men came to learn the history of the disastrous operations at that place, they

[1] My estimates of the Confederate forces differ considerably from those generally given. I shall hereafter give the data upon which mine are based.

[1] This change was suggested by Warren on the day following Grant's formal investiture. He said: "I would consolidate the army into three corps. Then I would get the best man to command the army; then I would allow him to have the choice of his corps commanders; then I would allow these corps commanders to choose their own subordinate commanders, and hold them to a strict accountability for what they did—let them understand that their position depended upon their doing well; not merely excusing themselves, but doing something."—*Com. Rep.*, ii., 384.

[2] "By his movements [after carrying the heights at Fredericksburg] I think that no one would infer that he was confident in himself, and the enemy took advantage of it. He was a perfectly brave man, and a good one; but when it came to manœuvring troops, or judging of positions, then in my judgment, he was not able or expert."—Hooker, in *Com. Rep.*, ii., 146.

GOUVERNEUR K. WARREN.

ald not fail to perceive that, wherever lay the blame for that inexplicable uster; it did not rest upon Sedgwick. Had Hooker shown half the omptitude and energy displayed by Sedgwick, the result would have been : other than what it was. The command of the Army of the Potomac had en more than once urged upon Sedgwick, and as often declined by him. ssides these three corps, there was the Ninth, under Burnside, which had just turned from Tennessee, having lately been recruited, notably by a division colored troops. The original intention was to send it to North Carolina, d it was not until within a week of the opening of the campaign that it is decided to retain it in Virginia. Then it was proposed to hold it in serve, but the exigencies of the campaign rendered it necessary to bring it rward. It really formed, from the first, a part of the Army of the Potoac, although for three weeks it was not under the command of Meade, but ceived its orders directly from Grant. Burnside was superior in rank to eade, and could not, in military etiquette, be called upon to serve under m, but, with characteristic unselfishness, he waived his priority in rank, d served under his former subordinate.

The change in organization involved many changes in officers of high nk. Generals Sykes, French, and Newton, who had commanded corps, ere relieved from services in this army, and sent to other departments. ilpatrick was sent to Sherman to act as his chief of cavalry. Pleasonton, 10 had led the cavalry with great vigor, was sent to Missouri; for Grant d already fixed upon a leader for his cavalry. This was Philip Sheridan, young man of barely thirty, who, in command of an army division in the 'est, had manifested a dashing bravery and a genius for command which, the keen eye of the lieutenant general, pointed him out as the man to ad his cavalry. The people had before—not altogether unreasonably—mplained that the Federal cavalry had not performed service commensute with that of the Confederates. The fault rested not upon the men, nor lete upon the leaders, but rather upon the commanding generals, who iled to appreciate the true work of this arm of the service. They had en mainly employed as scouts and in guarding trains. Sheridan "took the idea that our cavalry ought to fight the enemy's cavalry, and our inotry his infantry;" and he resolved to correct "the want of appreciation the part of infantry commanders as to the power of a large and wellanaged body of horse," which led to "the established custom of wasting valry for the protection of trains, and for the establishment of cordons ound a sleeping infantry force."[1]

The general command of all the forces of the Union had been conferred pon and assumed by Grant. East of the Mississippi the bulk of these rces was concentrated into two great armies, confronting the two main mies of the Confederacy—that in Virginia under Lee, and that in Georgia ider Johnston. It was evidently necessary that each of the main Union mies, so widely separated, should be under the immediate command of e general. There was no question that all the forces operating against hnston should be confided to Sherman. No two men of great military pacity could well differ more widely in the type of their genius than did rant and Sherman. But they had planned together for months during d after the wearisome Vicksburg campaign, and each had interpenetrated e other with his own ideas, so that it would be hard for either to say how uch belonged to each other in the scheme of operations in the Southwest. hey were in perfect accord; and Sherman was left in command of the great military division of the Mississippi. "I had," says Grant, "talked over with him the plans of the campaign, and was satisfied that he understood them, and would execute them to the fullest extent possible."

[1] *Sheridan's Report.*

Grant having decided to take his position with the Army of the Potomac in the field, the choice of an immediate commander of that army involved very different considerations. By the necessity of the case, Grant must take upon himself the supreme direction of operations. What he here needed was an executive officer able and willing to carry out his designs. The choice fell upon Meade. The very defects which he had exhibited during his command—defects which showed him to be ill fitted for the actual leadership of a great army, proved him to be admirably fitted for any position short of the first. His patriotism and earnestness were beyond doubt; his bravery upon the field was unquestioned; his tactical abilities had been proved. His failures had all arisen from want of self-confidence. Instead of directing, he was ever in search of some one to direct him. In default of better authority, he was perpetually calling consultations and councils of war, and yielding to their decision instead of acting upon his own responsibility. A council of war, not the general in command, decided that the army should not abandon the heights of Gettysburg on the night before the last decisive day. A council of war decided by a bare majority that Lee should not be followed up when he retreated from that lost field. A council of war decided, against Meade's own judgment, that the Confederate army should not be assailed when brought to bay on the banks of the swollen Potomac. The lack of moral courage on the part of Meade caused the unaccountable retreat from Culpepper to Centreville. Fear of responsibili. ty led him to abandon the Mine Run expedition. If Senators Wade and Chandler, of the Congressional Committee, had waited but two days more, until General Meade's own testimony had been given, they could have made out a much stronger case for demanding his removal. But if Meade lacked the faculty of command—the first requisite of a great general, he possessed the second requisite—the faculty of comprehending and executing the orders of another. As commander of the Army of the Potomac, under the immediate direction of a higher intelligence and a stronger will, he proved himself, in the long campaign which followed, to be "the right man in the right place."[1]

Grant had, in the me an while, matured his plans for the campaign. His purpose was to attack simultaneously the two great armies of the Confederacy—"to hammer continuously against the armed force of the enemy and his resources, until by mere attrition, if in no other way," they should be destroyed. Sherman, in the West, was simply instructed to "move against Johnston's army, break it up, and go into the interior of the enemy's country as far as he could, inflicting all the damage he could upon their war resources." With what vigor and skill this order was executed will be shown hereafter. The Army of the Potomac, under Grant's own eye, was to be directed upon a principle altogether new to it. The instructions to Meade read like a covert censure upon all previous operations of the Army of the Potomac. "Lee's army is to be your objective point; wherever that goes you must go." There was to be no more of that indecisive manoeuvring whereby had been lost the fruit so ripe and ready for plucking at Antietam and Gettysburg. The Army of the Potomac was to move, not from, nor merely toward the enemy, but upon him. Butler, with the Army of the James, was to co-operate, at first indirectly, in this movement upon Lee. With at least 20,000 men he was to go up the James River, lay siege to Richmond, if possible, or, at all events, take up a position so threatening to the Confederate capital as to insure that none of the force which it was foreseen would be brought up from the Carolinas would be pushed forward to Lee. Sigel's 30,000 men were actually confronted by not a third of their number; but he had a large frontier to defend against raids and partisan adventurers. Yet this defense could be better performed by pushing forward a large part of his force than by lying idly in garrison. He was therefore to organize two columns, one to march up the Valley of the Shenandoah, the other to move down the western flank of the Alleghanies, and then, crossing that ridge, to fall upon the Virginia and Tennessee Railroad, one of the great avenues of supply for the Confederate army and capital, destroying also the salt-works whence was derived the main portion of the supply of this great necessary of life. All these movements were to commence simultaneously, as nearly as possible on the first of May.

The Confederate Army of Northern Virginia had lain in winter quarters along the bluffs which skirt the south bank of the Rapidan, the lines extending for a distance of twenty miles. The position, strong by nature, had been industriously fortified. Rifle-pits commanded every ford, and intrenchments crowned every hill-top. So little had an advance during the winter been apprehended, that after the demonstration at Mine Run a third of the soldiers had been allowed leave of absence upon furlough. In January and February the muster-rolls showed but 35,000 men present for duty. As spring opened the absentees were gradually recalled. On the 10th of March there were about 40,000; on the 10th of April, 53,000. The returns for May are wanting, but it may be assumed that on the first of the month, when the campaign opened, the numbers had increased to fully 60,000, probably somewhat more. Before these, at and around Culpepper, from ten to thirty miles distant, was the Union Army of the Potomac, 140,000 strong, Burnside's corps included.

An assault in front upon the Confederate lines was neither meditated by Grant nor apprehended by Lee. The attack would be made by turning,

[1] "Commanding, as I did, all the armies, I tried, as far as possible, to leave General Meade in independent command of the Army of the Potomac. My instructions for that army were all through him, and were general in their nature, leaving all the details and the execution to him. The campaigns that followed proved him to be the right man in the right place."—*Grant's Report,* July 22, 1865.

either upon the right or left. There were many advantages and many disadvantages in either case. If the lines were turned by the left, the Union army would still cover Washington; but if the enemy fell back, as it was assumed he would do, every step would carry the assailing force farther and farther from its base of supply. Practically it must do all that it did while the rations with which it started held out. If the turning was by the right, the distance to be marched, in case the enemy fell back to Richmond, would be much greater, and, moreover, Washington would be uncovered, and the way open for another invasion of Maryland and Pennsylvania, should Lee dare to venture it. But, on the other hand, should the enemy fall back toward Richmond, the Union base of supply could be shifted as the army moved—from Brandy Station to Acquia Creek, thence down the Rappahannock to the York, or even, as it proved, to the James. Moreover, Grant seems not to have shared in the nervous apprehension for the safety of the capital which had for two years paralyzed every fresh movement; and he had good reason to be assured that Lee, taught by Antietam and Gettysburg, would not venture to renew the experiment of crossing the border. With 60,000 men he would not attempt to perform that in which he had twice failed to succeed with 100,000. So it was decided that the turning should be made on the Confederate right, that is, to the east, not by the left, to the west. But it so happened that Lee, bearing in mind the result which had followed the movement of Burnside, and reasoning from what he presumed to be the views of the authorities at Washington—not knowing that the military power had passed from their hands—assumed that the movement would be made upon his left. He therefore massed the bulk of his force in that direction. Of the three corps of which his army was composed, those of Ewell and Hill lay behind the defenses of the Rapidan, the mass being at Orange Court-house, near the centre, while Longstreet's corps, just returned from its disastrous expedition to Tennessee, was at Gordonsville, thirteen miles farther to the southwest.

The combined operations of all the Union armies was to take place in the early days of May. On the 1st Sigel began his movement up the Valley of the Shenandoah. On the 6th, Sherman, with the combined armies of the Cumberland, the Tennessee, and the Ohio, advanced from Chattanooga. On the 4th, Butler, with the Army of the James, moved up the James River. On the night of the 3d the Army of the Potomac broke up its camps around Culpepper, and marched for the Rapidan. With this movement began the closing campaign of the war. The campaign lasted for eleven months. On the part of Lee it soon resolved itself into a purely defensive scheme, and, as such, will stand among the great defensive campaigns of history. Two of the campaigns of Frederick of Prussia may be fairly set down as its equal. That of Napoleon in 1814, when, with not more than 110,000 men, he well-nigh foiled 600,000 which the Great Alliance poured into France, is its only superior. That the one, after a hundred days, closed with the exile to Elba, and the other, after more than three hundred, with the surrender at Appomattox Court-house, detracts nothing from their merits. All that skill on the part of the Confederate commander, all that bravery on the part of his troops could do, was done to win victory in the teeth of impossibilities.

I have had occasion more than once to take exceptions to the generalship of Lee where he was successful, and where he avoided what should have been certain destruction. In this final campaign, which resulted in his total overthrow, I find little done which should have been left undone, nothing left undone which should have been done, to insure success. It has been the fashion to say that with the death of Jackson expired the dash and vigor of the Confederate Army of Virginia. Impartial history will record that its greatest achievements, whether of daring or endurance, were performed thereafter. Lee was indeed overcome, but he was overcome by forces greatly superior, wielded by generalship certainly not inferior to his own. It has sometimes been asked what would have been the result had the two commanders changed places. The careful military student will answer that the result would have been just what it was. Lee, in command of Grant's army, would have won; Grant, in command of Lee's army, would have failed. What would have been the result had each general had an equality of force and situation, no wise man will venture to say.

It has been alleged against Grant that the campaign at last assumed a shape wholly different from what he had proposed. This is only partly true. He indeed expected to fight and win a decisive battle north of Richmond; but, failing in this, he from the outset proposed to take his army to the south of the James.[1] It has also been said that after two months of marching and fighting, wherein he suffered losses far greater than he inflicted, he gained a position which he might have reached in a fortnight, without the loss of a man. But those who urge this overlook the cardinal point, that the army of Lee, not merely the geographical spot known as the capital of the Confederacy, was the thing aimed at. If that army were destroyed, the capital and all else was won. If that army remained; it mattered little where the capital of the Confederacy was placed. The army of Lee was, relatively to its opponent, far weaker when it fell back to Richmond and Petersburg than it would have been had not the great battles been fought in the Wilderness, at Spottsylvania, on the North Anna, and at Cold Harbor. War is a game in which there are two players, and it is the one who is upon the whole the stronger that wins. Looking forward, as Grant could only do, there could be little doubt as to the wisdom of his plans. Looking back, as we now can, we must still conclude that it was the wisest which could have been adopted, and brought the war to a more speedy and decisive close than any other which lay before him.

THE WILDERNESS.

Before daybreak on the morning of the 4th of May the Army of the Potomac broke up camps and commenced its march for the fords of the Rapidan. It moved in two columns—Warren's corps, followed by that of Sedgwick, on the right for Germania Ford; Hancock's, with the bulk of the trains, for Ely's Ford, six miles to the east. Burnside's corps was to remain in its position on the Alexandria Railroad, stretching as far back as Bull Run, until the passage of the Rapidan had been effected, when it was to ad-

[1] "My idea, from the start, had been to beat Lee's army north of Richmond, if possible. Then, after destroying his lines of communication north of the James River, to transfer the army to the south side, and besiege Lee in Richmond, or follow him south if he should retreat."—*Grant's Report.*

HANCOCK'S CORPS CROSSING THE RAPIDAN.

vance.[1] The march of so great an army could not be effected without being perceived by a watchful enemy, and as the columns approached the fords the Confederate signal-fires were seen blazing from hill-top to hill-top, summoning the corps to concentrate. But the crossing was to be made ten miles below the extreme of the Confederate lines, at Raccoon Ford, held by Ewell, and as much farther from Orange Court-house, where Hill's corps was lying, while Longstreet was thirteen miles farther away. It was therefore impossible for Lee, had he been so inclined, to oppose the passage of the Rapidan. The vedettes at the fords were swept back by Sheridan's cavalry, and both columns, with their great train of 4000 wagons, crossed in the afternoon. Grant believed, as Hooker had done a twelvemonth before, that with the passage of the Rapidan the great danger was overpast. That evening Warren's corps, the advance of the right column, pressed on half a dozen miles, and encamped in the very heart of the Wilderness. Sedgwick halted near the bank of the river. Hancock moved to Chancellorsville, which he reached a little after noon.

On the evening of Wednesday, the 4th, the entire Army of the Potomac was thus encamped in the very heart of the Wilderness, the two columns being about five miles apart. Grant assumed that Lee, finding his position turned by a greatly superior force, would fall back toward Richmond, and his order for the next day was based upon that assumption. But Lee had resolved upon a wholly different movement—a movement apparently perilous and even desperate. With his 60,000 men, he resolved to fling himself upon the enemy, whom he knew to have twice that number. This determination was justified by the soundest military reasons. To set these forth, it is necessary to take a survey of the region.

We have before[1] described the general features of the "Wilderness," touching mainly upon that portion of it wherein were fought the battles of Chancellorsville. The Wilderness Tavern, where Grant and Meade established their headquarters on the evening of the 4th, is at the very centre of this wild region. Six miles northward is the Rapidan; as far southward begin the cleared fields of Spottsylvania; eight miles westward is Mine Run; just as far eastward is Chancellorsville. The Wilderness, stretching from a dozen to a score of miles in either direction, is traversed north and south, west and east, by two systems of roads, which, in conjunction with the jungles and chaparrals pierced by them, constitute its military features. From north to south, or more accurately from northwest to southeast, starting from Germania Ford, runs a tolerable plank road, continued after a few miles by the "Brock Road," over which Jackson in May, 1863, marched to the attack upon Hooker's weak right. Nearly parallel to this, some six miles away, starting from Ely's Ford, and passing by Chancellorsville, goes another road. These two, after many windings and turnings, come together near Spottsylvania Court-house, eight miles southeast of Chancellorsville. These are the main roads running southwardly by which Grant's two columns were to pass through the Wilderness. Running from west to east are two good roads, the northern known as the Old Turnpike, the southern as the Orange Plank Road. These, starting from Orange Court-house, run nearly parallel at a distance of about three miles, coming together again near Chancellorsville. They strike at a right angle those by which Grant would move, and the Confederates, pressing down these roads, would strike squarely upon the flank of the long Union columns slowly defiling through the tangled mazes of the Wilderness, with every probability of cutting them in two. In these labyrinths of forests, thickets, and swamps, which no eye could penetrate for more than a few yards, and where artillery could not be brought into action, Grant's preponderance of numbers would be neutralized; and indeed Lee, having two good parallel roads, might reasonably expect to be able to throw a superior force upon the decisive point. He had, moreover, the great advantage of a thorough knowledge of the country, which was wholly unknown to his opponent.

When, therefore, on the morning of the 4th, Lee learned that the Union army was heading for the Rapidan, he put his columns in motion to intercept it on its march through the Wilderness. Ewell moved by the turnpike, and the head of his column lay that night within three miles of the camp of Warren at the Wilderness Tavern. Hill moved by the plank road, but, having a longer march, was somewhat farther away. Longstreet, a day behind, was ordered up with all speed. Grant's plan for the ensuing day contemplated a leisurely march mainly for the purpose of concentrating his somewhat scattered corps. Warren was to march by a wood path southwestward till he struck the plank road, up which he was to proceed three miles to Parker's store; Sedgwick was to follow, joining upon Warren's right; Hancock was to move from Chancellorsville southward to Shady Grove Church, and stretch his right to unite with Warren's left. Meade's whole army, none of it having marched more than ten miles, would then have cleared the Wilderness, its movements being masked in front by Sheridan's cavalry. Burnside's corps would have reached Germania Ford, ready to cross and follow in the track of Meade. Grant would then be prepared for a rapid advance toward Gordonsville, whither it was taken for granted that Lee would retire.

Warren began to move at five o'clock on the morning of Thursday, the 5th. Wilson's division of cavalry had on the preceding afternoon scouted for some distance up the turnpike without encountering any enemy, for Ewell, who was coming down the road, was yet miles away. Warren, however, by way of precaution, threw Griffin's division westward up the turnpike. Ewell at the same time moved eastward down the road, and the head of the columns came unexpectedly in collision. Even now the Union commanders were wholly unaware that the enemy were approaching in force. "They have left a division here to fool us," said Meade, "while they concentrate and prepare a position toward the North Anna, and what I want is to prevent these fellows from getting back to Mine Run." Only a single division—that of Johnson, forming the van of Ewell's corps—had as yet come up. Griffin fell furiously upon this, and drove it back for a space. Strongly re-enforced, the Confederates turned at bay, held their ground, and soon advanced in turn, and forced Griffin back over all the space which he had won. Wadsworth, endeavoring to join Griffin, missed his way through the woods, and exposed his naked flank to a fierce fire, from which his division recoiled in confusion. In the mean time, Crawford, who had struck the plank road, and was moving up it toward Parker's store, encountered the cavalry scouts dashing back with tidings that a heavy force was pouring down that road. Crawford's movement was suspended, and his division withdrawn; one brigade, however, became isolated, and lost in prisoners nearly the whole of two regiments.

It was an hour past noon. Two hours before, Grant, perceiving that the enemy were in force and bent upon delivering battle in the Wilderness, had sent orders to Hancock to suspend his southward march, and, taking the Brock Road, to hurry to the scene of conflict. He had also sent Getty, with his division of Sedgwick's corps, to the junction of this road with the Orange Plank, with orders to hold the position, at all hazards, until Hancock, who was ten miles away, should come up. Thus far the brunt of the fight had been borne by Warren's corps, opposed to that of Ewell. Warren had been pressed back to the line whence he had started in the early morning, where he stood stoutly at bay. Ewell's on-coming brigades, spreading northward, threatened to turn Warren's right. Sedgwick's corps, or, rather, two of its three divisions, for the strongest, under Getty, had been sent elsewhere, was ordered to advance through the thick woods upon Warren's right. As they pressed on through the dense undergrowth, broken here and there by a slight clearing, they would encounter a body of Confederate skirmishers, hidden in the skirts of the chaparral. These would deliver a sharp fire, and disappear in the thickets. At length they came square in front of a strong line of battle. The Confederates charged fiercely and unavailingly upon the leading brigades, and then, with equal ill success, endeavored to turn their flank. At four o'clock they suspended their offensive movements, fell back, and began to fortify their position. The confronting lines now lay upon the opposite slopes of a swampy, wooded hollow. They were but a hundred or two yards apart, and though the ring of axes felling trees to form breastworks and abatis filled the air, not a man on either side could be discerned from the other.

At four o'clock the fight had lulled upon Warren's and Sedgwick's front. But in the mean while, and thereafter, it was raging on the plank road, barely three miles to the southward. Here Getty held grimly to the vital point at the junction of the Brock and Plank Roads, which he had been ordered to maintain, toward which Hancock was advancing. Hill's corps of the Confederates was pressing strongly down the Plank Road. Getty seemed on the point of being overwhelmed, when at three o'clock the welcome sound of Hancock's approach up the Brock Road was heard. Hancock drew up his force fronting that of Hill, and began to level the woods and throw up breastworks, designing simply to receive an assault. But Meade had ordered Getty to take the offensive, and drive Hill up the plank road. Getty had but three hundred paces to go to encounter the Confederate line. He found them in superior force, lying hidden in the woods bordering the road. Hancock backed up the attack by divisions from his own corps. The assaults were hot and furious—"repeated and desperate assaults," as Lee styles them; "a fierce fight, the lines being exceedingly close, the musketry continuous and deadly along the entire line," says Hancock. It was

ALEXANDER HAYS.

[1] *Ante*, p. 488.

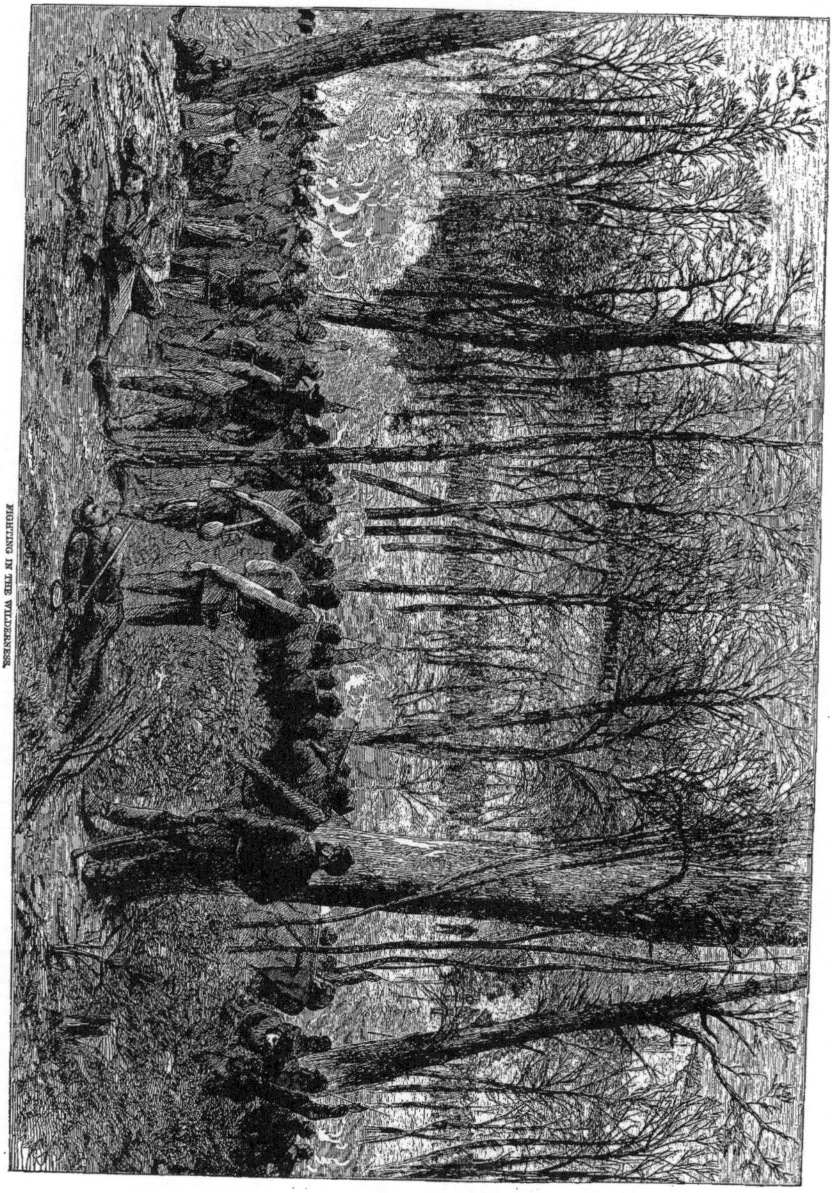

FIGHTING IN THE WILDERNESS.

all in vain. Hill could not be pushed back, and the hot volleys of musketry caused more than one of the assailing divisions to waver and break. In the effort to repair one such break, General Alexander Hays, who had won high renown at Gettysburg, was shot dead, while leading his command into the heart of the fight. So for four hours, until night closed in, the contest raged with no decisive advantage on either side.

Late in the afternoon, the fight in front of Warren and Sedgwick having been suspended, Wadsworth's division was ordered to press southward through the forest, and thus fall upon the flank and rear of Hill, who was holding his position against the hot assaults of Hancock. But, though the distance was hardly three miles, the appointed position was only reached at nightfall, when the conflict was over. Wadsworth rested on the field, in line of battle, in a position where he could strike when the fight should be opened the next morning. Hancock's and Hill's forces, who had been marching and fighting all day, lay upon their arms upon the opposite side of the Brock Road, awaiting what the next day should bring forth. But as darkness closed in, an irregular contest was opened in the woods on the extreme Union right, and the gloom of the forest was lighted up by volleys of musketry which rolled along the opposing lines. At two hours past midnight, and three hours before dawn, the noise sank away into silence.

The engagement of this day can hardly be styled a battle. It was rather a series of fierce encounters between portions of two armies, each ignorant of the position, strength, and force of the other. Neither commander had succeeded in effecting his purpose. Lee had hoped to fall upon the flank of Grant's columns while stretched out in a long, feeble line of march, cut them in two, and annihilate one portion while it was isolated from the other. If the collision had taken place two hours later, when the whole of Hill's and Ewell's divisions would have come up, while the Federals were fairly on the march, it could hardly have failed to succeed. But Grant had now been able to place his force in line of battle, opposing his front instead of his flank to the enemy. He had failed, however, to push the Confederates back upon the roads by which they had advanced. But the state of affairs was such as to warrant both in renewing the issue the next day. Grant, indeed, had no choice but to fight. He was still enmeshed in the Wilderness. He could not go southward without exposing himself to a disastrous flank assault. It would have been equally perilous to have attempted to recross the Rapidan, even had he been of a temper to give up his forward purpose. He might, indeed, have fallen back eastward toward Fredericksburg by way of the Brock Road, plank, and turnpike, and thus have got clear of the Wilderness, but there was nothing in the position of affairs to warrant such a resort. Moreover, neither general had used his whole force. Burnside's corps, 20,000 strong, had pushed on by forced marches, were crossing at Germania Ford, and could be brought into action the next day. Lee could not be aware of this accession to the numbers to be opposed to him. He also had fresh forces at hand. Longstreet's veteran corps was moving on from its cantonments forty miles away. During the afternoon he had reached a position ten miles from where the battle was raging, but in these close woods the noise of the musketry was unheard, and he was ignorant that a battle was being fought until midnight, when he received orders from Lee to advance. Two hours later he was on the march, and would come up. Anderson's division, moreover, one third of Hill's strong corps, had been left behind to watch the upper fords of the Rapidan. These were now close at hand. Longstreet and Anderson would add 20,000 fresh men to Lee's force on the field. With two thirds of his army he had gained some apparent advantage, with this addition it was not unreasonable to hope that he could win a decisive victory.

So both commanders resolved to fight; and, a rare occurrence in warfare, each proposed at daybreak to assault the lines of the other. Grant united his heretofore disjointed line by bringing forward Burnside and posting him between Warren and Hancock, so that the line from right to left ran thus: Sedgwick, as before, on the right; then Warren, who had been severely handled on the preceding day; then Burnside; then, on the left, Hancock, strengthened by detachments from Sedgwick and Warren. There was no room for the display of elaborate manœuvres or skillful combinations. Grant's plan of battle was simply a simultaneous assault along the whole line of five miles, each division attacking whatever appeared in its front. Lee, however, had two good avenues of approach. His plan was more elaborate. The main attack was to be made by Longstreet and Hill upon the Union left, while Ewell was to make an assault, or, rather, demonstration upon the right. If Longstreet succeeded, Hancock would be forced back upon the centre, and the whole Union army flung together in inextricable confusion in the almost impenetrable forests, where it could not act as an army.

Five o'clock, the hour when the gray dawn was breaking into day, was the time fixed by Grant for attack. But Ewell anticipated him by fifteen minutes, moving out of his lines upon Sedgwick's extreme right. The attack was not seriously made, and probably not seriously intended. It was easily repelled. Sedgwick and Warren then advanced, pushing the enemy back for a space until he regained the strong position from which he had sallied. Upon this no impression could be made, and the contest ceased to be a battle at this point.

Hancock, in the mean while, deploying his skirmishers, pushed half of his force through the thickets on each side of the plank road, straight westward upon Hill's front. Wadsworth, who had slept the night before hard by, advanced southward upon the Confederate flank. The attack was wholly unexpected. Longstreet, who was just coming up, was to take the position in front, relieving Hill, whose front divisions, those of Heth and Wilcox, were just preparing to retire. These divisions broke and fled back in disorder for a mile and a half, overrunning Lee's headquarters, which were in the way, and not halting until they touched the head of Longstreet's advancing column. But here they met three regiments of Kershaw's division, who briefly stayed the flight. Other troops were hurrying up; the whole line seemed wavering and on the point of again breaking. Lee, who had narrowly escaped being shot down, flung himself at the head of Gregg's Texans, and ordered them to follow him in a charge. First one soldier, and then the whole brigade, shouted out a remonstrance, and refused to advance until their commander had retired from the front. But in the fierce rush through the pathless woods the Federal troops had likewise lost all semblance of battle array—every thing which distinguishes an army from isolated groups of Indian fighters. Coming upon a line somewhat firm, it was necessary to halt and readjust their own broken formation. This, in a tangled wilderness, was a work of time. Two hours passed—from seven to nine—before the Union line was reformed. Those hours had wrought an entire change in the aspect of the field. Longstreet's whole corps had come up, Hill's entire corps was concentrated, and the Confederate line had gained such force that it was able not only to repel assault, but to give attack. The Union force was swept back over all the space which it had won, and reformed only upon the Brook Road, whence it had started. In a vain attempt to stay the retreat of his command, which had fallen into disorder, Wadsworth was mortally wounded, and his body remained in the enemy's hands. Few as noble men have ever fallen upon the field of battle. He was the largest landholder, and one of the wealthiest men of Western New York. Past the prime of life, verging closely upon threescore, his years had been devoted to peaceful pursuits. When the war broke out he offered his purse and his person to the government. At the battle of Bull Run he acted as aid-de-camp to McDowell. Appointed brigadier general, he for a time acted as Military Governor of the District of Columbia. In the dark year of 1862 he was the Republican candidate for Governor of New York, but was defeated by Horatio Seymour. Then assigned to the command of a division in the Army of the Potomac, he did good service at Fredericksburg and Chancellorsville. At Gettysburg the heaviest brunt of the first day's fighting, whereby the Confederates were prevented from occupying the heights, fell upon his division.

JAMES S. WADSWORTH.

Hancock had sallied out from his intrenchments with only half the force under his command. The reason of this was that Longstreet was said to be coming up by a way which, passing south of the plank road, would bring him upon the left of his position on the Brook Road, and so, if that point was abandoned, by an advance the enemy would be upon his rear. Longstreet was, indeed, at six o'clock, making this very movement; but so urgent was the stress caused by the unlooked-for attack upon Hill, that Lee was obliged to change the direction of Longstreet, and bring him to the front. When now Hancock's advance had been stayed, Lee reverted to his original plan, the execution of which was committed to Longstreet, who was to send a portion of his corps to make a detour beyond the extreme Union left, gain the Brock Road, and thus fall upon its rear. Not until this force was well in position was the front assault to be made. This took until noon, by which time Hancock's advanced right had been forced back to its intrenchments. Longstreet then rode down the plank road to direct the turning column. He met General Jenkins, an old comrade whom he had not seen for months. Mahone's brigade, a portion of his own flanking force, lay hidden in the bushes. They mistook Longstreet and others for Federal officers, and fired upon them. Jenkins fell dead, and Longstreet received a ball in his throat, which passed out through the shoulder. He was borne away fatally wounded, as was thought. But he survived, and months afterward was able to take part in the closing scenes of the war, the only survivor of the three lieutenants of Lee who fought in the battles of the Army of Northern

THE WILDERNESS—SCENE OF WADSWORTH'S DEATH.

Virginia, for Hill fell almost a year later, and Jackson had a year before received his death-wound hardly six miles from the spot where Longstreet fell wounded.

The fall of Longstreet checked for a space the execution of the operation which had been committed to him. Lee assumed immediate command of this part of the field, and at length, as the afternoon was wearing away, urged the whole strength of the two corps of Longstreet and Hill against Hancock's lines, then resting behind their intrenchments, but also preparing for a renewed assault. Much had been hoped from an advance of Burnside's corps through the woods between Hancock and Warren. Two of his three white divisions—for the colored one had been left behind to guard the trains—touched the fight somewhat sharply, losing a thousand men; but they failed to attain a place wherein their action seriously affected the fortunes of the day. Now the woods wherein the battle of the morning had been fought were on fire, and a strong westerly wind blew the flames right down upon the Federal intrenchments, forcing the foremost lines to abandon the works. The Confederates, following the fire, swept down, the foremost troops crowning the parapet and planting their colors upon the blazing breastworks. But they were met by a rush from Carroll's brigade, which came up first by flank and then straight forward, and driven back in wild disorder. With this sharp assault ended the fighting upon the left. Each side had advanced upon the other, and each, after winning some success, had been repelled. Both, as night again fell, occupied substantially the same positions which they had held when morning broke.

The battle of the day was over on the left of the field, where Hancock was struggling against Longstreet and Hill. But on the right, where the contest had lulled for hours, there was at dusk one more stirring episode. The Confederate left overlapped the Union right, held by some brigades of raw troops of Sedgwick's corps. They had wearily kept their post for thirty hours, in front of breastworks which had been thrown up, behind which they might retire in case of attack. None having been made, they at dusk began to retire to this sheltered line. The vigilant enemy, perceiving this movement, made a sudden rush upon their flank, and threw every thing into confusion. One of these brigades had on that very day been given to Seymour, just released from captivity, into which he had fallen at the battle of Olustee, in Florida; another was commanded by Shaler. These brigades, four thousand strong, were enveloped, and, with their commander, captured, almost to a man. For a space it seemed that the fatal rout of the Eleventh Corps at Chancellorsville was to be renewed. But the sudden assault was soon repelled, and the Confederates fell back to the lines from which they had so suddenly emerged. This brilliant feat, wherein they made three thousand prisoners, cost the Confederates, it is said, only twenty-seven men.[1]

The morning of Saturday found both armies in a mood different from that of the day before. Each, while quite willing to be assailed in its intrenchments, was indisposed to attack the other. The losses had been heavy. Those of the Federals numbered fully 20,000 men, of whom about 5000 were prisoners. The Confederate loss was hardly 10,000, of whom few were captured. The two days' action had otherwise been a fairly drawn battle. Both commanders had failed in their purpose. Grant had turned the impregnable position of the Rapidan only to find himself confronted in the Wilderness by the enemy in a new position equally unassailable. In this first blow the hammer had suffered more than the anvil. According to all precedent in the Army of the Potomac, Grant should have abandoned the enterprise, and cast about for something new. But of this he had no thought. To strike and keep striking, as he had done at Vicksburg, was his fixed purpose.

The first thing to be done was to flank the enemy from the Wilderness. The movement was to be upon Spottsylvania Court-house, fifteen miles southwest of the battle-field. The direct route was by the Brock Road; a more indirect one was by a detour eastward to Chancellorsville, then southward to the point of destination. Warren's and Hancock's corps were to follow the first route; Sedgwick's and Burnside's, with all the trains, were to take the latter. The wounded were to be sent through Chancellorsville to Fredericksburg. Warren was to commence his march at half past eight in the evening. If he met no obstruction he would soon after daylight reach the Court-house, of which possession in the mean time was to be taken by Wilson's cavalry. The other corps would not be long behind. Then the whole army would be again upon Lee's flank, ready to fling itself between him and Richmond.

SPOTTSYLVANIA.

But Warren, upon reaching Todd's Tavern, about half way, found the narrow road obstructed by Meade's cavalry escort, and it was an hour and a half before the way could be cleared. Two miles beyond that point the road was blocked by Stuart's Confederate cavalry, who had been posted there the day before, and which Merritt's troopers, who were in advance, had not succeeded in dislodging. It was now daylight. Warren, advancing, cleared the way and pressed on slowly, for barricades had been formed by felling trees, which could be removed only by the axe. Here and there, also, there was a slight show of opposition by dismounted troopers. At last, at half past eight, four hours behind time, the head of the column emerged from the woods into an open clearing, beyond which rose the wooded ridge whereon is the Court-house, still two miles away. Thus far there had been no intimation of any enemy except the few dismounted troopers. But when half way across the clearing the advancing column encountered a fierce musketry fire from infantry lying hidden in the opposite wood, and fell back across the plain. By one of those accidents which sometimes change the course of a whole campaign, the Confederates were first at Spottsylvania.

When Lee, on the afternoon and evening, saw the Federal trains moving due east toward Chancellorsville, he at once inferred that the enemy was heading for Fredericksburg; the Brock Road also at first trends in that direction; and when columns were perceived defiling down that road, the conclusion was confirmed. Lee was not undeceived until the next day; for on

[1] So Pollard, doubtful authority, says: *Lost Cause*, p. 516. If one chooses to see a Federal account, describing a hot fight, with charges and countercharges, he is referred to Stevens's *Three Years in the Sixth Corps*, p. 311-318.

JOHN SEDGWICK.

HORATIO G. WRIGHT.

the 8th he sent a dispatch to Richmond stating that "the enemy have abandoned their position, and are marching toward Fredericksburg. I am moving on their right flank"—that is, toward Spottsylvania. The march was at first leisurely, for it was not his purpose to overtake the Federal army, but simply to interpose between it and what was assumed to be its march down the Fredericksburg Railroad toward Richmond. It was, indeed, by accident that this march was commenced during the night of the 7th. At ten in the evening, Anderson, who now commanded Longstreet's corps, was ordered to withdraw his troops from the breastworks from before which the enemy had disappeared, and encamp in readiness to march next morning. Anderson, finding no good place to bivouac in the burning woods, kept on. Thus, during that night, Warren and Anderson were moving by roads nearly parallel upon Spottsylvania. Although Warren had the start by an hour or two, Anderson, meeting with no obstructions, as day broke was ahead. Then for the first time learning the approach of the enemy, he double-quicked his march and reached the Court-house some hours in advance. The Federal cavalry who held the place abandoned it, and Anderson drew up his men across the road by which Warren, ignorant of his presence, was advancing. He had time to throw up slight breastworks, behind which, and hidden in the woods, he awaited the approach of his enemy. Some sharp fighting here took place, continuing all the morning; and at last Warren began to intrench close in front of the Confederate line. Hancock's corps, which was following that of Warren, was delayed all day at Todd's Tavern in readiness to repel an attack upon the rear, which was apparently threatened by Lee, who, now perceiving the real aim of the Federal movement, was hurrying his whole force on toward Spottsylvania. Some time in the afternoon Sedgwick came up from Chancellorsville and took command of the field. Toward evening a slight attack was made upon the Confederate line, but nothing of

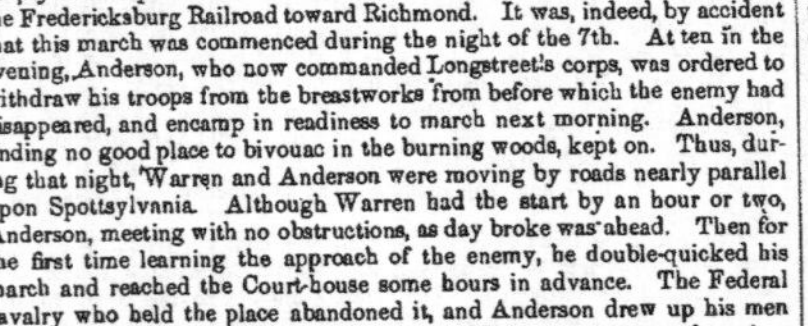

FIRE-PROOF WHERE SEDGWICK FELL.

importance was effected. Lee, with his whole force, was firmly posted upon Spottsylvania ridge, and every hour was strengthening his position, from which it was clear that he could be driven only by hard fighting. Grant, whose entire army was now well in hand, and notwithstanding its severe losses in the Wilderness, was in sound heart, resolved to try what could be effected by heavy blows.

Monday, the 9th, was mainly employed by Grant in making his dispositions, and by Lee in fortifying his lines, which mainly followed the course of a wooded ridge, from the Court-house on the east, sweeping in an irregular semicircle to the north and east. Artillery and musketry firing was kept up at points from the Confederate lines, especially upon points where batteries were being established. At one of these points Sedgwick was superintending the placing of a battery. The men seemed to wince at the fire poured in upon them. "Pooh!" said Sedgwick, drawing himself up to his full height, "they can't hit an elephant at that distance." At that moment a rifle-shot struck him fairly in the face, and he fell dead. The command of the Sixth Corps now devolved upon Wright.

The 10th was spent in tentatives upon the left of the Confederate lines. These, though fiercely made, were unsuccessful, though Grant at the close sent an encouraging dispatch to Washington, which was duly published, and, for the time, was held to announce a victory; at all events, it indicated a determination which, in view of his known superiority in numbers, was held to be a sure presage of speedy and decided success.[1] He "proposed to fight it out on that line, if it took all summer." If he had known it, he was to fight all summer, and autumn, and winter, and far into the next spring. The "indecisive actions of these three days had cost wellnigh 10,000 men, the very flower of the Army of the Potomac. The enemy, fighting almost wholly behind intrenchments, could have suffered hardly a third as much."[2]

Lee's left had been found, by bitter experience, to be impregnable. But it seemed that his centre presented a weak point through which an entrance might be forced. Here his lines were thrust forward in a sharp salient which might be carried by a sudden dash. All the day of the 11th was spent in arrangements. Toward night a heavy rain set in, and under the cover of this and the darkness, Hancock's corps was brought around from the left, and posted twelve hundred yards from this salient angle. This point seemed to be so difficult of approach that it was weakly held and carelessly guarded. In the gray dawn, and through a dense fog, Hancock's men moved softly and noiselessly, sweeping over the Confederate pickets without firing a shot; then, with a shout and a rush, they dashed through the abatis, and over the breastworks on every side. Johnson's division of

[1] Grant's Dispatch, May 11th, 8 P.M. "We have now ended the sixth day of very hard fighting. The result to this time is very much in our favor. Our losses have been heavy, as well as those of the enemy. I think the loss of the enemy must be heavier. We have taken over 5000 prisoners, while he has taken from us but few except stragglers. I propose to fight it out on this line if it takes all summer." In his report a year later, he says, "The 9th, 10th, and 11th were spent in manœuvring and fighting, without decisive results." It is worth while to recall some of the official dispatches of this period put forth by the War Department. *Sunday, May 9th:* "Lee's army commenced falling back on Friday. Our army commenced the pursuit on Saturday. The rebels were in full retreat for Richmond by the direct road. Hancock passed through Spottsylvania Court-house at daylight yesterday." *Same day:* "Dispatches have just reached here direct from General Grant. They are not fully deciphered yet; but he is on to Richmond." The President appointed a day of thanksgiving for the victories of the last five days.

[2] No returns have been rendered of the separate losses during the seven days, from May 5 to 11. The entire number is given together as follows: *killed*, 3288; *wounded*, 19,278; *missing*, 6844; *total*, 29,410. Allowing, as we have done, 20,000 for the Wilderness, there remain fully 10,000 for these three days at Spottsylvania. The Confederate loss is wholly a matter of estimate. In placing it at 15,000 during this period, we can not very greatly err.

SPOTTSYLVANIA COURT-HOUSE.

Ewell's corps, 4000 strong, were nearly all captured. Hancock sent back a hasty note to Grant, "I have finished up Johnson, and am now going into Early." But this salient was after all an outwork, adopted because the heights swelled out in that direction. Behind it, at the distance of half a mile, a second line had been laid out and partly completed. Here the Confederates rallied, Ewell in the centre, Hill rushing in from the right, and Longstreet from the left. The position was vital. If these works were carried the Confederate line would be cut in two, and their whole position forced. Hancock, struggling alone—for so rapid had been his rush that he had far outstripped Wright who was to support him—was speedily thrown back to the captured salient. The Sixth Corps now came up, and the Confederates could not gain another inch. Half of Warren's corps were sent to support Hancock and Wright, and the battle raged with hardly an interval during the whole day and far into the night. Five several assaults were made by the Confederates, and five times they were bloodily repelled. At midnight Lee withdrew to his interior line, which was still intact. During the day Burnside and Warren had demonstrated strongly upon their fronts. Burnside carried the rifle-pits, but could make no impression upon the intrenchments behind them. "The resistance," says Grant, "was so obstinate that the advantage gained did not prove decisive." The Union loss this day was probably 10,000, that of the Confederates quite as many.[1]

Grant had struck a heavy blow, but the enemy were by no means crushed. For six days longer he manœuvred in the hope of turning the lines; but, in whatever direction he moved, he found himself confronted by intrenchments which forbade assault. He was, moreover, awaiting re-enforcements which were hurried on from Washington. On the 18th, orders were given to break up the position at Spottsylvania, and move southward to the North Anna. Lee, who now seemed to divine the purposes of his opponent, saw in the preparatory movements a chance for a blow. He launched Ewell through the woods upon Grant's right flank; but the attack was easily repelled, and Ewell, after heavy loss, fell back to his intrenchments. This demonstration delayed Grant's movement until the night of the 21st. Next morning Lee saw before him no trace of the great army by which he had been confronted. Breaking up his camps, he hastened once more to fling himself athwart the line of the enemy's advance.

THE NORTH ANNA.

When, after a two days' march through a fertile region as yet untrodden by armies, Grant reached the North Anna River, he found his vigilant adversary confronting him upon the opposite bank. Lee's settled policy was never strongly to oppose the passage of a river in his front. He had not seriously contested the passage of the Chickahominy, the Rappahannock, the Antietam, or the Rapidan. He chose rather to intrench himself a little distance back, allow his adversary to cross, hoping to fight him with a stream in his rear. Here, however, he made some show of opposition to the passage, though his main line of defense was some distance beyond the stream. The opposition was speedily brushed away. Hancock and Warren crossed at two points four miles apart. But now Lee thrust his army like a sharp wedge right between the two Union columns, repelled all attempts to unite them, and was in a position to strike either. The manœuvre was a brilliant one. Grant, perceiving his peril, and the impossibility of assailing his opponent, after two days recrossed the river, and on the 26th resumed his old turning movement, which was to bring him within view of the Chickahominy.

While at Spottsylvania Grant had received re-enforcements fully equal to all his losses. Here, upon the North Anna, Lee was joined by Pickett's division and Hoke's brigade from North Carolina, and Breckinridge's command from the Valley of the Shenandoah. All told, they numbered some 15,000 men, considerably less than his losses, so that Grant was relatively stronger than at the opening of the campaign. To understand how it was possible for these re-enforcements to be given to the Army of Northern Virginia requires a rapid survey of operations in other quarters.

OPERATIONS OF SIGEL, HUNTER, AND BUTLER.

It had been a part of Grant's plan that Sigel, with 7000 men, should move up the Valley of the Shenandoah, and Crook, with 10,000, up the Kanawha. These two columns were designed to hold in check the scattered Confederate forces in that region, and destroy the salt-works in the Valley of the Kanawha, and threaten the communications between Richmond and the West by way of the Tennessee Railway. Sigel moved from Winchester on the 1st of May. On the 15th he reached Newmarket, a distance of fifty miles, having encountered no serious opposition. Here he encountered Breckinridge with a force somewhat superior.[1] Sigel suffered a severe and mortifying defeat, and fell back, leaving behind him his trains and 700 prisoners. At the instance of Grant he was superseded by Hunter. The column under Crook met with somewhat better fortune, inasmuch as it suffered no actual defeat, although Averill, who had been detached with 2000 men to destroy the lead-works at Wytheville, was foiled by Morgan; and Crook, having reached the railroad, destroyed the track for a short distance, and, on a slight encounter, defeated McCausland. But, finding the enemy gathering in his front, he retreated by the way he came. Breckinridge, thus relieved from immediate pressure, was free to join Lee with the whole of his movable force.[2] Hunter, a fortnight later, collected 20,000 men, and and moved up the valley. He encountered W. E. Jones at Piedmont on the 5th of June, defeated him, took 1500 prisoners, and, crossing the mountains, advanced upon Lynchburg. So important was the possession of this place, as the key to one of his main avenues of supply, that Lee, although Grant's whole army was in his immediate front near Cold Harbor, detached Early with a quarter of the whole Army of Northern Virginia to oppose the advance of Hunter. They reached the vicinity of Lynchburg at about the same time with Hunter. Some skirmishing ensued; but Hunter was now quite destitute of ammunition, and, not daring to seek a battle, retreated. From some unaccountable reason, instead of falling back northward down the valley, he struck northwestward down the Kanawha. His supplies were nearly exhausted, but large quantities had been collected at a point a few marches on the way. These were guarded only by a few cavalry, two regiments of hundred-days' men. Gilmor, an active partisan, dashed upon the train, destroyed the whole, and disappeared. Hunter kept up his retreat by a long detour by way of the Kanawha and Ohio, through the mountains of Western Virginia, and it was several weeks before he was able to regain the Potomac. This absence of Hunter's force gave opportunity for the annoying invasion of Maryland by Early, whereby the safety of the Federal capital was seriously endangered.

Another simultaneous co-operative movement was to be made from Yorktown by Butler. His available force consisted of the Tenth Corps under W. F. Smith, and the Eighteenth under Gillmore, which had not long before been brought from before Charleston, numbering together about 25,000 men, besides 3000 cavalry under Kautz, who were posted at Suffolk. To this force was given the name of the Army of the James. The army lay at Yorktown, apparently threatening a movement upon Richmond across the peninsula, by the route followed by McClellan two years before. Butler, on the 4th of May, embarked his infantry on board transports, passed down the

[1] The losses in the Army of the Potomac are grouped together for the period from the 12th to the 21st of May. They sum up 10,381; but after the 12th there were probably not more than 2000, leaving 8381 for the 12th. Of the Confederate losses we have no reliable statement. Pollard says (*Lost Cause*, 520), "The enemy had taken twenty-five pieces of artillery and about 2000 men in Johnson's division; he had inflicted a loss of 6000 or 7000." Whether he means to include the 2000 prisoners in the "loss" is uncertain; but the prisoners certainly numbered 3000; and, considering the character of the fighting, it can not be doubted that in the main action at the salient the Confederates lost most heavily. On the other parts of the field it is probable that the Union loss was in excess. It may be safely assumed that in a persistent assault, which is repulsed, the assailants suffer most.

[1] Breckinridge's returns for April show 6488 men; but, besides these, he collected many scattered bands, among them a company of 250 boys, cadets in the Military Academy at Lexington. These cadets were pushed to the front, and fought like veterans, losing a third of their number.

[2] According to Early, Breckinridge brought only 2500 men. Little reliance, however, can be placed upon any statement of this officer. Thus he states that the force with which he was some months later defeated by Sheridan was only 8500 men, whereas Sheridan showed that he had taken more than that number of prisoners, and Early's losses in killed and wounded were very severe.

JERICHO MILLS, NORTH ANNA.

RIFLE-PITS, NORTH ANNA.

QUARLES'S MILLS, NORTH ANNA.

York River and up the James, and next day occupied City Point, at the junction of that river and the Appomattox, and Bermuda Hundred, a narrow-necked peninsula between those rivers. Here he intrenched himself in a position which he affirmed he "could hold against the whole of Lee's army." Kautz, at the same time, made a dash upon the Weldon Railroad, by which it was known that troops from South and North Carolina were approaching Richmond.

Beauregard, who had been conducting the defense of Charleston, had not long before been placed in command of the Department of South Virginia and North Carolina. The departure of Gillmore rendered it safe to withdraw nearly all the force from South Carolina. Hoke, also, had, about the middle of April, captured Plymouth, North Carolina, almost the only point yet held by the Federals in that state, and he had been able to bring to Richmond Pickett's division, then under his command. On the 21st of April Beauregard passed through Wilmington with a considerable force, and proceeded toward Richmond. Butler supposed that most of them were still on the way, and when he found that Kautz had cut the railroad he assumed that they could not advance.[1]

Having intrenched himself at Bermuda Hundred, Butler, on the 7th, made a demonstration against the railroad from Petersburg to Richmond, and succeeded in destroying a small portion of it. Had he pushed straight to Petersburg that city would have been easily taken, for the defenses which had been begun two years before were of little account, and there were there few or no troops. But the capture of Petersburg formed no part of the plan which had been agreed upon between him and Grant. The essential part of it was that, as soon as Grant should approach Richmond from the northeast, Butler should move up southeastwardly, and the two armies would then invest Richmond on the south, west, and north, thus avoiding the almost impregnable lines of works which protected the city on the east. On the 9th he resumed his attack upon the railroad in considerable force, and with favorable results, and proposed to follow up the success next day. But that night he received the glowing dispatches from Washington announcing that Lee was in full retreat for Richmond, with Grant close upon his heels. Pausing for two days to strengthen his lines at Bermuda Hundred, on the 13th he began an attempt to carry out his part of the programme. On the 13th a portion of the outer lines near Fort Darling, which formed the extreme southern point of the defenses of Richmond, were carried. But the interior lines were strong, and their extent was unknown. Butler, after spending two days in examination and concentrating his force, determined to attack on the morning of the 16th.

[1] On the 9th he telegraphed to the Secretary of War: "Beauregard, with a large portion of his force, was left South by the cutting of the railroad by Kautz. That portion which reached Petersburg under Hill I have whipped to-day, killing and wounding many, and taking many prisoners, after a severe and well-contested fight. General Grant will not be troubled with any farther re-enforcements to Lee from Beauregard's army."

But, in the mean while, Beauregard, with all the force which he could gather, had reached the scene. What with the former garrison of Richmond of some 7000 men, and these additions, there were there some 20,000 men. Beauregard, who had studied the position from the lines at Fort Darling, conceived a bold plan for the destruction of Butler. He proposed that 15,000 men from Lee's army should be brought by rail and temporarily added to his command; with these he would overwhelm Butler's army, which lay weakly stretched over a considerable space, and then, with the whole of his victorious force, march northward. Lee was to fall back toward Richmond, Grant, of course, following. Beauregard would then fall upon Grant's left flank when on the march, while Lee, turning, should assail him in front. But Davis, who kept in his own hands the direction of all military matters, saving that he rarely interfered with Lee's operations, refused his consent, and ordered Beauregard to attack with what force he had.

The evening of the 15th was somewhat overcast, but not dark, for the moon was up. There were no indications of any movement among the Confederates. About midnight a fog arose from the river so dense that nothing could be seen at a distance of ten yards. Under this dense pall Beauregard quietly assembled his whole force, and before dawn burst upon the sleeping Federal camps. Butler, not dreaming that he would be assailed, had made the worst possible disposition of his force to resist an attack. His front was widely extended, and his right was a mile and a half from the river. Through this gap, only watched by a few cavalry, Beauregard proposed to strike this flank, cutting it off from Bermuda Hundred: this was the main assault, to be conducted by Ransom. The left was to be more lightly assaulted by Hoke, while Colquitt, held in reserve, was to act as occasion should require. But the dense fog interfered with these plans. Ransom, after gaining some ground against Smith, suffered heavy loss, and his division fell into disorder, and even with the aid of Colquitt could hardly hold its own; Gillmore, on the left, pressed severely upon Hoke; Whiting, who, with 4000 men, was to have come up from Petersburg and fall upon Butler's rear, did not make his appearance. When the fog fairly cleared away it seemed as though Beauregard had utterly failed. His elaborate plan of assault had wholly miscarried, and there was nothing to replace it. But Smith, though he had foiled every effort against him, was apprehensive that he would be cut off by a turning movement from Bermuda Hundred, and fell back a little; Gillmore, instead of swinging around and taking Beauregard in reverse, fell back to the same line with Smith; and then Butler ordered a general retreat. Beauregard began to follow, but a heavy rain came up, and he could do no more than open a distant artillery fire upon the retreating columns. And so, as night fell, Butler found himself unassailed behind his intrenchments. A more insignificant action, save for the loss which it involved, was never fought. Beauregard took 1400 prisoners. Apart from these, the Union loss was about 2500; that of the Confederates, in killed and wounded, somewhat greater; but they lost no prisoners. Butler now began to set about strengthening his intrenchments across the narrow neck of the peninsula to keep the Confederates out. Beauregard threw up parallel works, to keep

BATTERY ON THE NORTH ANNA.

CROSSING THE NY.

the Federals in. Either line could be held against double the force that could be brought against it. Butler found himself, as he phrased it, securely "bottled up"[1] at Bermuda Hundred. And thus it happened that Beauregard was enabled to send a large part of his force to the aid of Lee; but Grant was also able, as soon as he saw fit, to draw still larger re-enforcements from the Army of the James.

[1] This phrase of Butler's, repeated by Grant, who also speaks of Butler's being "hermetically sealed up," has really very little pertinence. Butler could not, indeed, get out toward Richmond; but he could at any time move his army down the James, as he had come, or cross the Appomattox toward Petersburg, or cross the James, having pontoons for these purposes. All three of these movements were actually made at different times without opposition, or, indeed, the possibility of any by the enemy. Grant, in fact, was as much "bottled up" at Spottsylvania and on the North Anna as was Butler at Bermuda Hundred. Neither could march straight upon Richmond, but either could move in any other direction.

COLD HARBOR.

Grant's turning movement from the North Anna brought him, by a wide detour, to the Pamunkey River, formed by the junction of the North and South Anna, and this, uniting with the Mattapony, forms the York. At the head of this was the White House, where Grant's base of supplies was to be established. Hitherto his great army had to be supplied from an ever-shifting base by wagons, over narrow roads through a densely wooded country. Now they could be brought by water close to his lines, wherever they should be posted. The Pamunkey was crossed, after several sharp skirmishes, on the 28th of May, and after three days Lee was found in his new position. The Union losses at the North Anna, and in the actions from the 21st

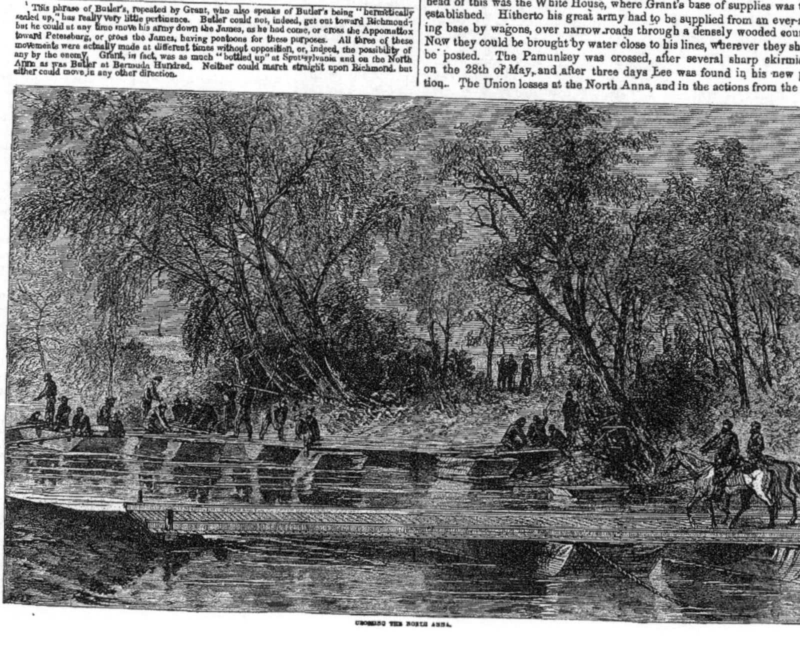

CROSSING THE NORTH ANNA.

HANOVER FERRY—CROSSING THE PAMUNKEY.

to the 31st, were 1607, of whom 327 were prisoners. The loss of the Confederates was much greater.

From the North Anna Lee had fallen back in a straight line, and assumed a position still covering Richmond. The two armies were now verging toward the scene where they had contended two years before. Since then, in anticipation of what was soon to happen, the ground had been thoroughly surveyed by the Confederates, lines of intrenchments and barricades laid out and partly constructed. The lines covered the upper fords and bridges of the Chickahominy. As finally developed, they formed a curve, the convex side turned toward the quarter from which Grant was advancing. The southern extremity, which was as yet only slightly held, was as far southward as Cold Harbor, a mere point where converge several roads from the fords of the Chickahominy to the Pamunkey and York. Here, in a quite isolated position, was a body of Confederate horse and foot, posted behind some slight breastworks. Torbert's and Custer's cavalry had scouted in this direction, and these generals had formed a plan to seize this point by a sudden dash. Sheridan, coming down, agreed to this. The attack was made on the 21st, and the place carried. Sheridan notified Meade of this, but said that he could not retain it, for the enemy was hard by in considerable force. He was directed to hold it at all hazards until relieved by infantry. Grant had some days before embarked two thirds of the Army of the James from Bermuda Hundred, and ordered them to join the Army of the Potomac; they were now on the march, but still some miles distant. On the morning of June 1st the enemy made efforts to drive out Sheridan; they were twice repulsed with severe loss. Meanwhile Wright's Sixth corps was sent by Grant, and Longstreet's corps by Lee, marching by roads almost parallel, to the point. Wright came up at 10 o'clock, arriving first, Longstreet halting behind intrenchments in a thick wood hard by. Smith came up soon after, and the two corps made an attack upon the Confederate position. An advanced line of rifle trenches was carried, and six hundred prisoners taken. But the second line was too strong to be forced. But the possession of Cold Harbor had been secured, though at a cost of two thousand men. Hancock's corps was now brought down and posted on the right of Wright's.

Grant had proposed to cross the Chickahominy here, having thus swung two thirds of his army around the Confederate left. Lee, anticipating this, moved Hill and Ewell in the same direction, so that now, on the 2d of June, he occupied almost the position which Fitz-John Porter had occupied two years before, while Grant held that from which Lee and Jackson had advanced. The fords were then covered by Lee, as they had before been by Porter, and to cross without a battle was clearly impossible. These movements had not been effected without collision. Lee sallied out upon Burnside's corps, which was moving to take post behind Warren, who was to hold the extreme right. His skirmish line was driven through a swamp, and some hundreds of prisoners taken. But the movement had no real significance.

The Confederate position, as finally assumed, was exceedingly strong; breastworks had been thrown up, which could only be reached by passing through thickets and swamps. These thickets and swamps had, indeed, opposed Lee's advance two years before; but the breastworks and intrenchments had been wanting, for officers of that day were opposed to field-works. "It made men timid," they said. Had there been in Porter's army axes with which to have felled a few trees in his front, it is believed, by those who took part in his battle, that Lee would have suffered a disastrous repulse, and the whole issue of the seven days have been changed. Porter had that morning called for re-enforcements and axes, but the messenger, being somewhat deaf, heard only half of his order, and so the axes never came. Both armies had now grown wiser; they had learned that even a slight intrenchment will stop three fourths of the bullets which would otherwise have borne wounds or death, while an abatis that will detain an attacking force under direct fire for fifteen minutes, with the present improvements in fire-arms, more than doubles the defensive power of its defend-

COLD HARBOR.

ers. There is, indeed, hardly an instance in our war in which a line of works stoutly defended by half the assailing force has been carried.

Still, things had now come to such a pass that it seemed necessary to Grant to drive the enemy from his position. There was no longer room for any turning movement which should do more than cause Lee to retire within the defenses of Richmond, and then the campaign would resolve itself into a long siege of that city. It was his last chance to hammer against Lee in the field, and a blow sufficiently weighty might shatter to fragments the Confederate army. So he resolved to assault the enemy in his lines. If he could be forced from these he would be thrown back upon the Chickahominy, or at least be driven pell-mell up its bank, pressed in the rear by the victorious columns, while Sheridan's 10,000 horsemen, flushed by a long series of success, would assail his flank, and throw themselves in his front. The catastrophe which began at Five Forks, and ended at Appomattox Court-house, would have been antedated by ten weary months. If numbers could avail against position, Grant had good reason to hope for success. Now that he had been joined by Smith's corps, he had fully 150,000 men, while Lee had barely a third as many.

The 2d of June was spent in getting the troops into position for the battle. Hancock's corps was placed on the left, next Wright's, then Smith's, closely massed opposite the Confederate right. Then came Warren's, stretched in a long thin line, continued by Burnside's, with his right flung back. The plan of attack was simple. Hancock, Wright, and Smith, at daybreak, were to make a simultaneous assault upon the lines in their front.

In the gray dawn, under a drizzling rain, these corps, already formed into line, sprang forward from their rude parapets—for now neither army rested for a moment in front of the enemy without intrenching themselves as best they might, using, in default of better implements, the tin cups slung by their haversacks. Barlow's division, formed into two lines, was the left of Hancock's corps. The first line in a few minutes came upon a sunken road in front of the Confederate intrenchments, strongly held. This was cleared with a rush, the defenders flying to their works, the assailants hard on their heels, capturing, indeed, some hundreds of prisoners; but a solid mass of lead and flame was poured into the advancing line; for a few minutes—not fifteen, it is said, they held their ground—the second line fortunately, perhaps, lingering a little behind. It was the tragedy of Fredericksburg and Gettysburg re-enacted. The division, leaving a third of its numbers behind, recoiled, but not in rout, and only some twoscore yards, where a slight swell of ground sheltered them from the fierce fire. Gibbon's division, which had won the honors on the last day of Gettysburg, supported by Birney's, dashed on simultaneously. The story of their charge reads like that of Pickett against Cemetery Hill. They had to pass a swamp; skirting this on either side, they swept clear up to the very works, breasting the torrent of musketry. Some even mounted the parapets, crowning them with their colors. But it was all in vain; they could not pass the intrenchments, but clung to them for a space. Wright and Smith assaulted with equal and equally unavailing valor, though the contest was of longer endurance. But in an hour the contest was over. It had been virtually decided by the repulse of Barlow. Warren's division was not expected to do more than hold in check the force in its front; but Burnside, his left pivoting upon Warren's right, was to swing round and strike the Confederate left flank. The movement was made, but not till the main action had been decided. The Confederate outposts were driven in, and a little before noon Burnside was in position to make an assault upon the Confederate left. He was directed to attack at one o'clock. But just before that hour the order was countermanded, Meade judging that the failure on the right had rendered it useless. The skirmish line was drawn in, and the corps began to intrench itself in its position. The enemy made a rather feeble sortie upon this point, but was repulsed. With this closed the battle of Cold Harbor.[1] Grant's blow had utterly failed. His loss had been severe—not less than 7000, mostly in less than half an hour. That of the Confederates was far less—probably not half as many.[2]

The result of the battle of Cold Harbor decided conclusively that the campaign was to take the shape of a siege of Richmond. However Grant might manœuvre, the result would be that Lee would fall back to the lines so elaborately fortified. Two courses lay open to the Union commander. He might move around Lee's left, and invest the city upon the north; or around his right, crossing the James River, and invest it from the south. Both plans had been considered by Grant in case he should fail, as he had done, to crush the enemy in the field. Then the former seemed most feasible; but, now that the Army of the James could not co-operate in it, he determined upon the latter, meanwhile sending Sheridan's cavalry to endeavor to cut the railway connections between Richmond and the Shenandoah Valley and Lynchburg, one of the main avenues of supply for the capital and the great army soon to hold it. Meanwhile, for a few days, the army was left essentially in its position, now intrenched, facing the Confederate intrenchments upon the Chickahominy. The lines lay so close together that the sharp-shooters on either side were able to pick off many men when

[1] Swinton (*Army of the Potomac*, 487) says, "Some hours after the failure of the first assault, General Meade sent instructions to each corps commander to renew the attack without reference to the troops on his right or left. The order was issued through these officers to their subordinate commanders, and from them descended through the wonted channels; but no man stirred, and the immobile lines pronounced a verdict silent, yet emphatic, against further slaughter." This statement is accepted by subsequent writers; but it is so utterly at variance with the whole conduct of the army, before and after, that I do not admit it into the text, even upon the authority of Mr. Swinton, whose statements of facts I rarely find occasion to question.

[2] "The loss on the Union side," says Mr. Swinton, p. 487, "in this sanguinary action was over 13,000, while on the part of the Confederates it is doubtful whether it reached as many hundreds." This is a singular *lapsus* of the author, for the very tables which he cites as authority give the entire loss, killed, wounded, and missing, during the ten days from June 1 to 10, at 18,168. Nearly every day during this period was marked by severe fighting.

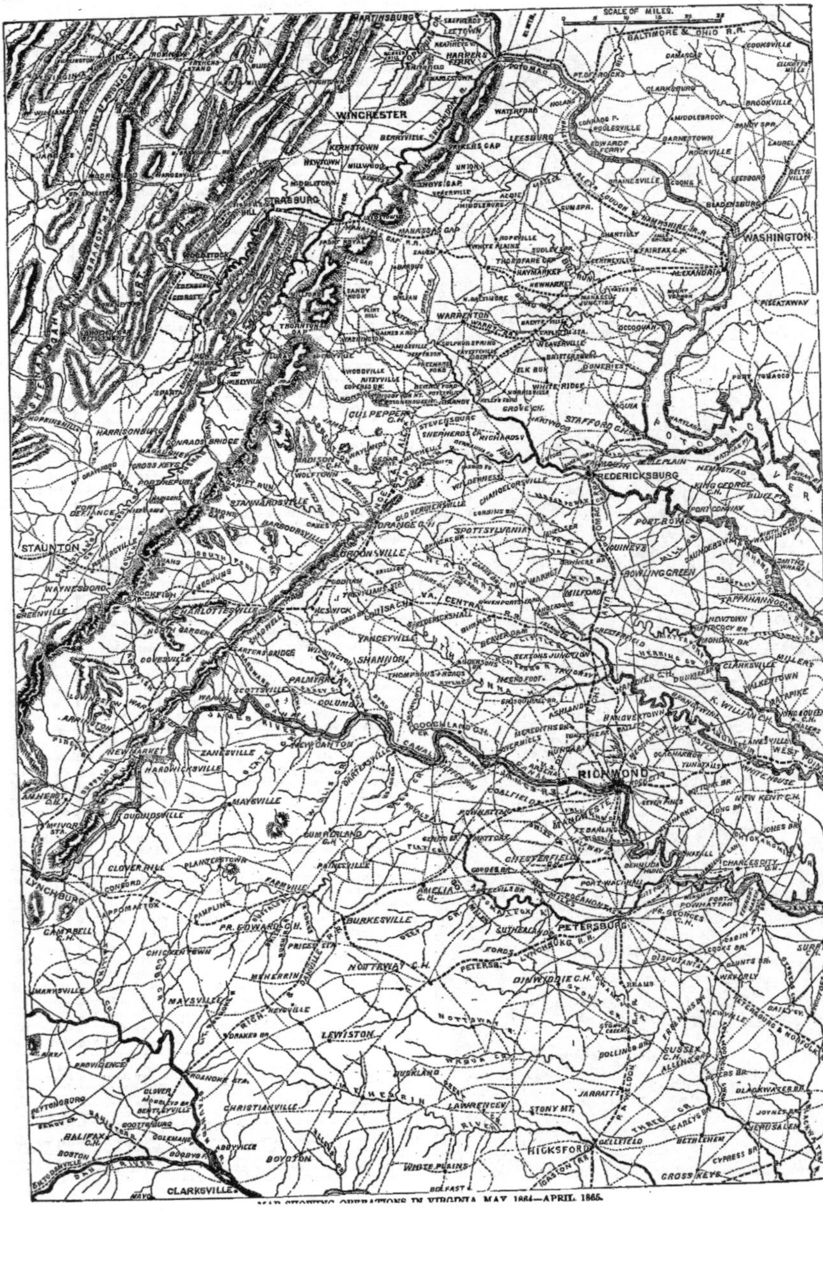

MAP SHOWING OPERATIONS IN VIRGINIA, MAY, 1864—APRIL, 1865.

they showed themselves in the trenches. For ten days the army remained nearly in the same position, only gradually extending its lines to the south, and approaching the Chickahominy, covering itself with intrenchments as it moved. Lee, presuming that the purpose of Grant was to effect a crossing at Bottom's Bridge, made correspondent movements, extending his right farther and farther down the stream, likewise intrenching at every step, so that the whole arid plain was dug over until it resembled an immense prairie-dog town. General officers had their tents pitched in deep excavations fronted by high embankments. Pickets and outposts excavated burrows, in which they lay unsheltered under the fierce sun. High breastworks were thrown up, and deep trenches dug at every conceivable angle, under shelter of which the men passed to and fro, from front to rear, without being observed. The intricate system of mounds and trenches, which still scar the plain upon the north bank of the Chickahominy, were the work of these days. The Confederates made several sallies upon portions of the line, but were invariably repulsed, and after the third day ceased from formal offensive operations; yet the lines were within rifle range, and a continual fire of sharp-shooters was kept up. Not an hour passed without its quota of dead and wounded. This was interrupted only for two hours on the 7th, when a truce was entered into for removing the wounded and burying the dead.

Grant, while making preparations to transfer his army to the south bank of the James, still hoped that the enemy would make some movement which would give a favorable opportunity for a renewed attack. But Lee remained immovable in his intrenchments, which the experience of Cold Harbor had shown to be inexpugnable. On the evening of the 12th the movement for the passage of the James began. Warren, preceded by Wilson's cavalry, marched six miles down to the Long Bridge over the Chickahominy, where he crossed, masking the movements of the other corps. Hancock followed, and then, taking the advance, marched down to the James, which it struck a little below the point where McClellan had lain after the battle of Malvern Hill. Wright and Burnside moved by an exterior and longer route, crossing the Chickahominy at Jones's Bridge, six miles below the Long Bridge. The trains, making a wide detour to the south, crossed at a ferry twelve miles below. The columns moved rapidly over the sandy road, hardly stopping for a moment until the night of the 13th, when the wearied troops bivouacked upon the high lands from which they could behold the James lying broad before them, bordered by fields now ripening for the harvest. Smith's corps had in the mean while marched to the White House, whence, embarking on transports, it sailed down the York and up the James, rejoining Butler at Bermuda Hundred on the 14th, while the Army of the Potomac was crossing the James fifteen miles below.

Lee, of course, could not be for many hours ignorant of the general movement, but he was in no position to offer any resistance. He had already extended his line so far that it was as weak as he dared make it. He evidently supposed that it was Grant's purpose to march toward Richmond by the north bank of the James instead of crossing and transferring operations to the south bank. Warren, indeed, was so posted for two days near White Oak Swamp as to give color to this supposition. Lee, therefore, hastily abandoned his position, and, crossing the Chickahominy, fell back to Richmond.

The cavalry under Sheridan, 10,000 strong, had in the mean while been active. No sooner had Grant taken his position near Spottsylvania, than, on the 9th of May, Sheridan was sent toward Richmond to operate upon the enemy's lines of communication. The design was masked by a movement eastward toward Fredericksburg, which drew Stuart's Confederate cavalry in that direction. Sheridan, then turning sharply southward, struck straight for the railroad between Lee's army and Richmond. Stuart followed for a space, and ineffectually assailed Sheridan's rear. Then, imagining that Richmond was the aim of the enemy, he urged his horsemen to their utmost speed, and gained Sheridan's front, placing himself between him and Richmond. Sheridan meanwhile moved leisurely, destroying the railroad as he advanced. At Ashland Station he fell upon Lee's provision trains, which had been brought down from Orange Court-house, and destroyed a million and a half of rations, and most of the medical stores. On the 11th a sharp encounter took place between the opposing cavalry forces at Yellow Stone Tavern, a few miles north of Richmond; the Confederates were repulsed, and in the mêlée, Stuart, their ablest cavalry leader, was mortally wounded. The loss was irreparable. The Union cavalry had by this time been raised to a higher state of efficiency than that of the enemy, and, now that their ablest commander was gone, the disparity became marked. From this time forth the Union cavalry always went into action with the prestige of success. Pursuing his advantage, Sheridan crossed the Chickahominy, passed the exterior line of the defenses of Richmond, but, reaching the inner line, he found it unassailable by a cavalry force. Turning back, he crossed the Chickahominy at Meadow Bridge, skirted down its northern bank, and recrossed at a lower passage. He had been misinformed by negroes, who told him that Butler had taken up a position on the north side of the James. Then, after communicating with Butler on the James, he again recrossed the Chickahominy, made a wide detour across the Peninsula, and at length, on the 25th of May, rejoined the Army of the Potomac, and aided in its forcing the passage of the Pamunkey, and in the earlier operations at Cold Harbor.

Hunter was now supposed to be moving down the Valley of the Shenandoah toward Lynchburg, and on the 7th of June, Sheridan, with two of his three divisions, was sent in that direction to join him, and, after breaking up the Virginia Central Railroad, to unite with Hunter, when both were to join the Army of the Potomac. Sheridan did some damage to the road, and had several sharp encounters with the Confederate cavalry, the severest being on the 12th of June, at Trevillian Station, where each side lost wellnigh a thousand men, of whom a third were prisoners. Sheridan here found that Hunter, instead of coming by way of Charlottesville, as was supposed, had turned off westward toward Lexington, and, moreover, Lee had dispatched a large force toward Lynchburg, which lay right in his way. The ammunition which he had brought with him was nearly expended; his horses were fast becoming exhausted, for the region was destitute of forage. He turned eastward, passed over the battle-field of Spottsylvania, thence down the Pamunkey to the White House. The Confederate cavalry were just then about to attack the dépôt, which had not been wholly withdrawn. Sheridan drove them off after a sharp conflict, and then, crossing the James, on the 25th of June rejoined the Army of the Potomac. In these two raids he had lost 5000 men, but had inflicted a loss quite as great.

During the thirty-seven days from the Battle of the Wilderness, May 5, to the close of the fighting on the Chickahominy, Grant had lost 54,551, of whom 7289 were killed, 37,406 wounded, 9856 missing. Of the killed, 539 were officers, and 6750 privates; of the wounded, 1764 were officers, 35,642 privates; of the missing, 262 were officers, 9594 privates. This does not include the losses of the Army of the James at Bermuda Hundred. The Confederate losses, exclusive of those of Beauregard at Bermuda Hundred, were about 32,000, of whom about 8500 were prisoners, 4000 having been captured at Spottsylvania, and 2000 by Sheridan's cavalry.

CHAPTER XLIII.

THE INVESTMENT OF PETERSBURG.

Richmond to be besieged.—Prospects for its Defense.—Napoleon on the Defense of fortified Cities.—Forces of Lee and Grant.—Character of the Fortifications.—Butler's unsuccessful Attempt upon Petersburg.—Importance of Petersburg in relation to Richmond.—Smith ordered to assail Petersburg, June 15.—Delays and Misapprehensions.—The Attack suspended.—Renewed on the 16th.—The Confederates re-enforced by Beauregard.—The Confederates driven from their Lines.—Beauregard checks the Flight.—Withdraws to an inner Line, where he intrenches.—Butler advances from Bermuda Hundred, and is driven back.—Actions of June 17 and 18.—The Confederates hold their new Line.—Forces and Losses from May 5 to June 20.

EVENTS had now so shaped themselves that it was apparent that, instead of a conflict in the open field, the campaign was to resolve itself into a siege of Richmond, held by the entire Army of Northern Virginia, with such re-enforcements as could be gathered from the Carolinas and Georgia. The Confederate authorities had good right to believe, upon the soundest military reasons, that, provided they could supply their army, Richmond could hold out against any besieging force. "Empires," said Napoleon, "frequently stand in need of soldiers, but men are never wanting for internal defense if a place be provided where their energies can be brought into action. Fifty thousand National Guards, with three thousand gunners, will defend a fortified capital against an army of three hundred thousand men. The same fifty thousand men in the open field, if they are not experienced soldiers, commanded by skilled officers, will be thrown into confusion by the charge of a few thousand horse." When Lee fell back within the lines of Richmond, he had about 70,000[1] men, nearly half more than the great master of war pronounced sufficient to hold a fortified capital against 300,000; Grant had, including the Army of the James, about 150,000, half the number which Napoleon judged could be foiled by 50,000. The fortifications, indeed, bore little resemblance to the formidable works constituting the defenses of the fortified cities of Europe, which Napoleon had probably in mind. They consisted of redoubts of low profile, with ditches, parapets, and abatis, and forts at all salient points from which the lines could be swept by artillery. But Todtleben had demonstrated at Sebastopol, and Lee was to demonstrate at Petersburg, that the defensive power of such works, resolutely held by an adequate force, is fully equal to the elaborate masonry of Vauban and Cohorn. Indeed, with modern artillery, of which Napoleon never dreamed, it is doubtful whether any system of fortifications of extent sufficient to protect a great capital can be constructed on any other plan. At all events, Lee's works were never pierced until, constrained by the menaces upon his lines of supply, he virtually abandoned them.

Strangely enough, the vital importance of Petersburg seems not to have been at all appreciated on either side. While McClellan lay at Harrison's Landing, some works had been commenced on the northern and eastern sides, but upon his retreat nothing farther was done. Again, a year later, about the time of the battle of Chancellorsville, when an advance from Suffolk was threatened by Peck, a trench, not unlike the first parallel of a siege, had been dug upon the south; but there were then no works over which even cavalry could not pass. There was now here scarcely the semblance of a garrison. Butler could easily have taken it from the east at any time up to three days before he settled himself at Bermuda Hundred. On the 10th of May he made such an attempt. He had—Smith being yet with Grant—barely 7000 men in the "bottle," which was tightly enough corked at the mouth, but had no bottom. Gillmore, with 3500 men, was sent across

[1] The Confederate muster-roll of the Army of Northern Virginia, on the 30th of June, showed 51,633 "present for duty." In the Department of Richmond, that is, the proper garrison of the city, now commanded by Ewell, who had for some time been disabled from acting in the field, were 6176. In the Department of South Virginia and North Carolina, under Beauregard, were 12,892 at Richmond and Petersburg. It will be borne in mind that Lee was at this time merely commander of the Army of Northern Virginia, Davis, with Bragg for his "military adviser," keeping in his own hands the direction of all the other forces. Some months later, Lee having been appointed general-in-chief of all the armies, all of the troops at Richmond excepting the garrison proper, which was still a separate organization, was consolidated into the Army of Northern Virginia. In November this numbered 69,290 "present for duty," about 20,000 more being returned as "present," the aggregate "present and absent" being 181,826.

PETERSBURG.

the Appomattox to attack from the north, while Kautz, with 1500 cavalry, was to dash in from the south. Gillmore advanced to within two miles of the city, driving the enemy's skirmishers before him until he came to their works. These, though feeble and feebly manned, he thought yet too strong to be assailed by his small force; so he retreated. Kautz, meanwhile, had rode straight over the ditch on the south, and penetrated the town; but the retreat of Gillmore permitted the enemy to return, and Kautz was easily forced back. The whole assailing force was too weak to effect any thing unless by sheer surprise; and even if it had succeeded, they could not have held Petersburg, and Butler could spare no more to re-enforce them.

Grant now went in person to Bermuda Hundred, and saw at a glance the vital importance of Petersburg, and the ease with which it could be taken by an adequate force, provided only the attempt were made in time. Hence it was that he directed Smith's corps to be sent by water so as to reach the scene at the earliest moment, before, it was hoped, it could be re-enforced from Richmond.

Petersburg was a quiet town of 18,000 inhabitants, on the southern bank of the Appomattox. In itself it was of little consequence to either army. Its military importance arose solely from its relations to the system of railroads which connected Richmond with the region from which its supplies were almost wholly to be drawn. Had the Confederate capital been provisioned for a siege, Petersburg might safely have been abandoned. But at no time were full rations for a fortnight in advance ever accumulated—oftener there was not three days' supply in dépôt. Northward from Richmond runs the Virginia Central Railroad, which, crossing the Orange Road at Gordonsville, penetrates the fertile region known by way of eminence as "The Valley," the granary of Virginia. The Orange Road, running southwestward through Lynchburg, merges into the Virginia and Tennessee Railroad, which, with its connections, penetrates into the extreme southwest. It is the great artery of communication between the Atlantic and the Mississippi. From Lynchburg, following the windings of the James, is the James River Canal. This place, therefore, became one of the natural dépôts of the Confederacy. Next, starting from Richmond, and running southwestward, is the Danville Road, passing through North Carolina, and uniting with all the railways branching through the Carolinas and Georgia. Next, running south, is the railway to Petersburg. From Petersburg, running southward to Lynchburg, where it connects with the Tennessee Road, is the Southside Railroad. Then, running south to Wilmington, where it joins with the southern system, is the Weldon Railroad. Now the occupation of Petersburg by the Federals would not only give them the control of the Weldon and Southside Roads, but would place them in a position to strike the Danville Road at any point south of Richmond. The possession of Petersburg would insure the capture of Richmond by giving to the assailants the absolute control of the Weldon and Southside, and rendering almost certain that of the Danville railways; two certainly, and almost inevitably a third, of the five avenues of supply for the Confederate army. Moreover, Grant hoped, by means of his cavalry, and Hunter's expedition, to destroy the Central Road and the James River Canal. But even should these latter fail, the Danville and Central roads and the canal would be inadequate to transport supplies to the army of the capital.

Smith's corps reached Bermuda Hundred on the 14th of June, crossed the Appomattox that night, and next day were pushed forward toward Petersburg, seven miles distant. By noon, having been somewhat delayed by carrying an advanced line of rifle trenches covered with a light battery, he came upon the works, two and a half miles from the town.[1] These works were not strong, and were only feebly held. In and around Petersburg, apart from a few militia, there were but two infantry and two cavalry regiments.[2] There was, however, a considerable quantity of artillery, which was briskly served, and it was assumed that there must be a strong infantry support. Smith wore away the whole afternoon in reconnoitring and making his dispositions, and then, at sundown, instead of attacking in force, threw forward a heavy line of skirmishers. Even these were successful, and the feebly-manned lines were fairly carried at every point where they were assailed, fifteen guns and three hundred prisoners being taken. Hancock, with two divisions of his corps, now came up. He had been marching since ten o'clock, but, owing to an incorrect map, in a direction quite different from that which was intended. By some strange misadventure, also, he had not even been notified that he was to assist Smith in an attack upon Petersburg; this notice only reached him between five and six o'clock. He reached Smith's position just as the attack had been suspended. Waiving his superior rank to Smith, whom he naturally supposed must be the best judge of what should be done, he placed his troops at the disposal of that officer. Smith, instead of taking these troops and pushing straight into Petersburg, merely requested Hancock to occupy a part of the captured works.[3]

Grant came on the ground next morning. Burnside's corps was advancing, and, to give them time to aid, the attack was postponed until six in the afternoon. Another unaccountable delay;[4] for, although some slight re-eu-

[1] Grant says in his Report that Smith "confronted the enemy's pickets near Petersburg before daylight." He seems to have fallen into an error as to time, for the march from the Appomattox did not begin until after daylight. He had ordered Butler to send Smith forward the night before, and probably assumed that he had marched straight on; Grant himself returned to the Army of the Potomac to hurry it on, division by division, as rapidly as possible, assuring Butler that "we could re-enforce our armies more rapidly than the enemy could bring troops against us." But this discrepancy as to time is of no real importance. There was, even after noon, as will be seen, abundant time to have assailed Petersburg with a force fourfold the number by which it was that day defended.

[2] For the details of the actions of this and the ensuing days on the Confederate side, I am indebted to Fletcher's *History of the American War*. The author, a colonel in the British service, derived his information mainly from General Beauregard, and officers of his staff.

[3] Grant's Report, and Hancock's, the latter as yet unpublished, but quoted in Swinton, *Army of the Potomac*, 502, 503.

[4] To whom this delay is to be attributed is not clear. Swinton says (p. 508, 509) that "Hancock, to whom, in the absence of Grant and Meade, the command of the field fell, was fully alive to the importance of securing all the commanding ground before heavy Confederate re-enforcements should arrive," and had the night before instructed Birney and Gibbon to attack and take all these positions before daylight, and that these instructions were not complied with. For authority he refers to, but does not quote, Hancock's Report. He also states that "Hancock was admonished by General Meade to refrain from attack until the remaining corps of the army, the Fifth and the Ninth, should arrive. Of these, the Ninth reached the front at noon, and an assault was ordered to be made about 4 P.M. by Hancock and Burnside—Smith to demonstrate merely." Grant places the time of the attack at six o'clock. From a comparison with Fletcher (p. 201), I judge the attack must have been made not later than four. Grant seems to imply that

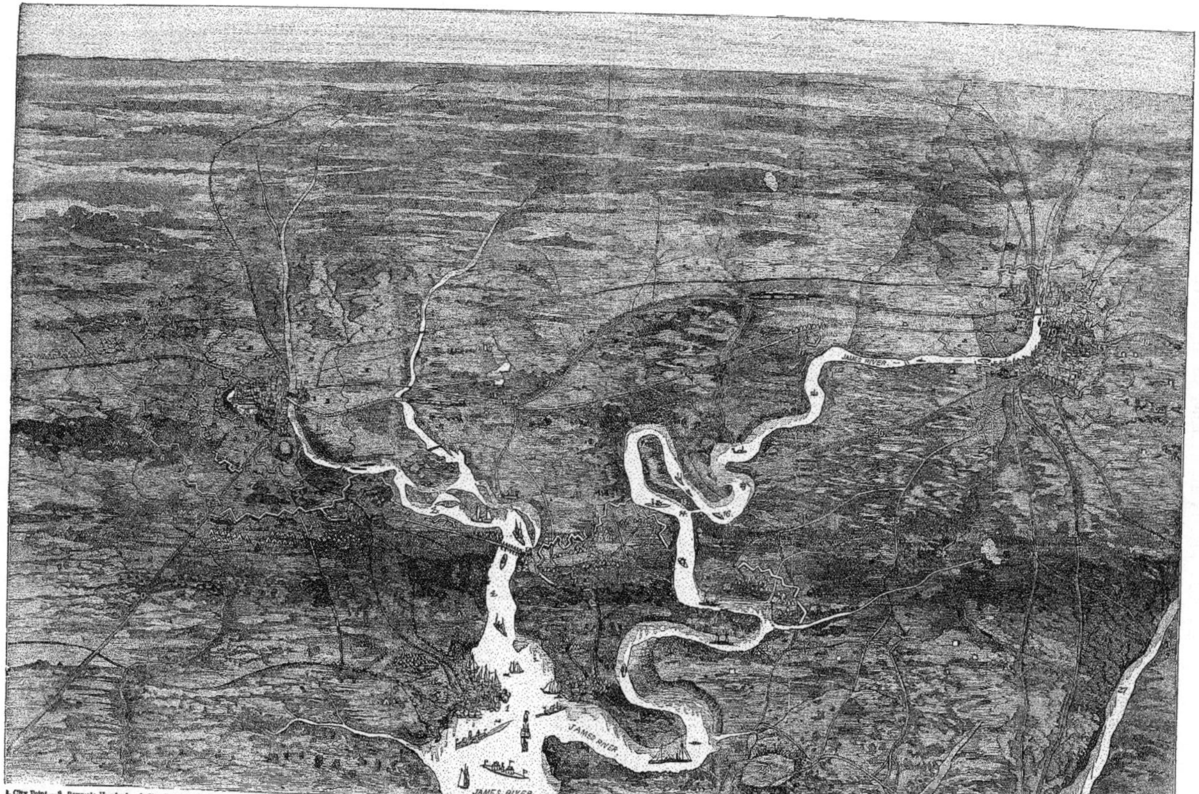

1. City Point.—2. Bermuda Hundred.—3. City Point Railroad.—4, 4. Appomattox River.—5. Port Walthal.—6, 6, 6, 6, 6, 6. Union lines.—7, 7, 7. Confederate lines.—8. Petersburg.—9. Reams Station.—10. Weldon Railroad.—11, 11, 11, 11. Richmond and Petersburg Railroad.—12. Southside Railroad.—13. Deep Bottom.—14. Canal at Dutch Gap.—15. Farrar's Island.—16. Confederate Gun-boats above this point.—17. Fort Darling.—18. Danville Railroad.—19. Richmond.—20. Richmond and Fredericksburg Railroad.—22, 23, 24, 25, 26. Roads leading out of Richmond.—27. The Chickahominy.—28. Malvern Hill.—30. Butler's lines.—31. Jones's Neck.—O. Norfolk Railroad.

ISOMETRIC VIEW OF THE VIRGINIA CAMPAIGN [LOOKING WESTWARD]

forcements had arrived, the Federals were in overwhelming force, and had full possession of all the defensive works. Beauregard had hastened down from Richmond. By withdrawing every thing from the intrenchments at Bermuda Hundred, he had gathered 8000 men at Petersburg. In vain he telegraphed to Richmond for re-enforcements, or at least for orders. Should he abandon Petersburg or Bermuda Hundred? he could not hold both. He received neither help or orders; so, acting on his own responsibility, he evacuated the intrenchments at Bermuda Hundred, leaving only a few sentries—took the cork out of the broken bottle—and during the day concentrated his command before Petersburg. The attack on the afternoon of the 16th was made with great vigor. The Confederates held their ground stoutly, but at length began to give way. Late in the day Beauregard had left the front to snatch a hasty meal. All at once a horseman, galloping at full speed, dashed through the streets, announcing that all was lost; the enemy had broken through the defenses, and were now entering the city. Beauregard, ordering the man to be arrested and shot if his report should prove false, mounted and galloped to the front. He soon met crowds of fugitives, unarmed, hatless, panic-stricken, swarming along all the roads. In vain he essayed to check the wild rout. The fugitives poured onward; and the day seemed hopelessly lost. Just then Gracie's single brigade from Bermuda Hundred came on. Beauregard formed these and his escort across the road, with orders to shoot down every man who refused to come into line. At length order was restored; the Confederates regained their abandoned line, from which, indeed, they had not been pursued. The fighting was by no means over, but continued long after dark. It died away by midnight, and under cover of the thrice-welcome darkness Beauregard withdrew his weary troops to an inner and shorter line, which he had chosen with the quick eye of an engineer. This line was as yet wholly unfortified, and must be intrenched in the brief hours before morning should most likely renew the conflict. With bayonets, split canteens, and hands—for they had no intrenching tools—the men dug in the darkness and through the hours of the early morning. By noon of the 17th the intrenchments had assumed a defensive character, and, moreover, their defenders had been largely re-enforced. These intrenchments, so hastily flung up, were the beginning of those great works which for so long a time held in check the Union army before Petersburg.[1]

Butler meanwhile, perceiving that the lines in his front were abandoned, moved out a force upon the railroad from Petersburg to Richmond. But he had hardly touched it when he was forced back by a heavy column coming down from Richmond; for Lee, fully alive to the necessity of holding Petersburg, had sent Longstreet's corps, now commanded by Anderson, to the aid of the sorely-pressed Beauregard. Butler returned to his old position. Anderson, leaving as he passed a force to hold the lines from which Gracie had been withdrawn, hurried on his remaining troops to the defense of Petersburg.

The morning of the 17th had begun to wear away before the fighting was renewed. It was fierce but undecisive. The contest was mainly for some portion of the original Confederate line, which had not as yet been abandoned, and which, as events proved, was of great value. At heavy cost, hardly less than 4000 men, Hancock and Burnside, upon whom the brunt fell, succeeded in winning and holding these points. "The advantages of position gained," says Grant, "were very great." Next day, the 18th, a general assault was to be made early in the morning; but when the skirmishers moved forward it was found that the enemy had abandoned every point which was to be assailed, and had firmly taken up their new and interior position, from which, says Grant, "they could not be dislodged."

These attempts upon Petersburg, lasting four days, had cost fully 9000 men.[2] The result was, as expressed by Grant, that while "the advantages of position gained by us were very great, yet the enemy were merely forced into an interior position from which he could not be dislodged," and, consequently, "the army proceeded to envelop Petersburg, as far as possible without attacking fortifications."

Petersburg, which on the 10th of June had been an easy prey, which, in effect, was already taken by Smith, who needed only to have pushed on to have marched straight into the town, defended by only a mere handful of men, was now garrisoned by almost the whole of the Confederate army. Two days of heavy fighting, in which Grant employed fully three fourths of his army, had demonstrated, at a cost of wellnigh 10,000 men, that Beauregard's intrenchments, hastily flung up, but growing stronger hour by hour, could not be taken by assault, and that nothing now remained but to lay regular siege to them. The siege of Petersburg, upon which was soon concentrated the interest of the war in the East, fairly began on the 19th of June.

NOTE ON FORCES AND LOSSES FROM MAY 5 TO JUNE 20.

The numbers of the Confederate Army of Northern Virginia during the whole of this campaign, down to its final close in April, 1865, have been studiously and persistently understated. The Confederate authorities after 1862 never made public their force or losses. Pollard, the only formal historian upon the Confederate side, had no accurate means of information. Writing after the close of the war, he had every motive to understate. He says:

"The Confederate Army on the Rapidan, at the beginning of the campaign, consisted of two divisions of Longstreet's corps, Ewell's corps, A. P. Hill's corps, three divisions of cavalry, and the artillery. Ewell's corps did not exceed 14,000 muskets at the beginning of the campaign. On the 8th of May the effective strength of Hill's corps was less than 13,000 muskets, and it could not have exceeded 18,000 in the beginning of the month. Longstreet's corps was the weakest of the three when all the divisions were present, and the two with him had just returned from an arduous and exhausting winter campaign in East Tennessee. His effective strength could not have exceeded 8000 muskets. General Lee's whole effective infantry, therefore, did not exceed 40,000 muskets, if it reached that number. The cavalry divisions were weak, neither of them exceeding the strength of a good brigade. General Lee's whole effective strength at the opening of the campaign was not over 50,000 men of all arms. There were no means of recruiting the ranks of the army, and no re-enforcements were received until the 23d of May."

The captured Confederate returns (cited *ante*, p. 383, as far as relate to this army) enable us to fix the number far more accurately. On the 10th of April the returns of the Army of Northern Virginia show a nominal force of 97,576, of whom 61,218 were "present," and 52,626 "present for duty." The conscription was in operation, and was still rigorously enforced. During the preceding month Lee's army was augmented by 12,000, sent in from the various camps of instruction, and, according to their judicious system, incorporated at once into regiments already in the field. It is not at all probable that these accessions during the three weeks preceding the opening of the campaign could have been less than 10,000 or 15,000, which would raise Lee's strength at the beginning of May to between 60,000 and 70,000. This continual access went on all through the summer, quite compensating for the losses in action and from sickness. Thus, on the 30th of June, his army had present for duty 51,863—within eight hundred as many as on the 10th of April—while its nominal strength was 92,686, which includes those absent from all causes—sick, disabled, and deserters. This was after a series of sharp actions, including those of June 15 to 18, and those which, from June 23 to 28, hereafter to be described, resulting from the first attempts made upon the Weldon, Southside, and Danville Railroads. On the 10th of July the nominal force, present and absent, was 135,803, so that within ten days 43,000 were added to the muster-rolls of the army; but of these only 68,844 were present, and 57,007 present for duty, showing an actual increase of effective men only about 6000, to which should be added some small losses suffered in the interval. At the close of August the nominal strength was 146,838, of whom there were present for duty but 44,247. But at this time Early, with some 15,000 of this army, was on detached service in the Valley of the Shenandoah, and this body is not counted among those "present for duty" with the Army of Northern Virginia. Owing to a clerical error in copying the returns, this number, 44,247, is given in our table (p. 383) as the force for May instead of August. This is of some importance, as it vitiates an estimate by Mr. Swinton of Confederate losses, which will presently be referred to. The considerable apparent access to the Army of Northern Virginia after October is owing to the return of the remnants of Early's force, and the incorporation of the troops heretofore formally under Beauregard at Petersburg.

Of the losses of the Confederates during this period (May 5 to June 10) there is no report even approximating to an official character. The "impression" of General Lee's adjutant general (Swinton, 492) was that it was about 18,000. Mr. Swinton finds corroboration of this estimate in a comparison of figures. He says, in substance, that Lee opened the campaign with 52,626; that he received re-enforcements (7000 under Pickett and 2000 under Breckinridge) of 9000, making in all 61,626; that on the 31st of May he had 44,248; the difference showing a loss, up to the battle of Cold Harbor, of 17,478. To this he adds less than 1000 for Cold Harbor, making 18,000. He, however, is dubious as to the correctness of these figures, and estimates the entire loss at 20,000. This estimate is worthless, from the fact that each one of the elementary data upon which it is based is erroneous. The original force (52,626), as shown by the returns which he cites, was that of April 10 instead of May 5, during which interval it must have been considerably augmented. The re-enforcements are considerably understated. Pollard says that Breckinridge brought "2000 muskets with a battalion of artillery." Certainly not less than 3000, and probably more, for in April he had present for duty 6500, and after the defeat of Sigel at Newmarket there was no immediate necessity for retaining a man of these in the Valley. The re-enforcements brought from North Carolina were certainly more than 7000. They consisted, according to Pollard (*Lost Cause*, 505), of "Pickett's division of Longstreet's corps, and one small brigade of Early's division of Ewell's corps, which had been in North Carolina with Hoke"—Pickett being ill, and not then in actual command. Now we find that in February Pickett and Whiting had in North Carolina about 18,500; at the close of April Whiting had there about 5000; Hoke must then have brought to Richmond early in May some 12,000 or 15,000. They lost considerably in the action of May 16, which resulted in the shutting up of Butler at Bermuda Hundred; but the bulk of the command, which could hardly have been less than 10,000, were thereby at liberty to join Lee, which they did during the last week in May, simultaneously with the arrival of Breckinridge from the Valley. These conjoined re-enforcements must have been fully 15,000 instead of 9000, as stated. Finally, the number (44,247) given by Mr. Swinton as Lee's effective strength on the 31st of May should be put down as the number of the army of Northern Virginia on the 31st of August, when a quarter or more of its force was with Early in the Valley of the Shenandoah. I, as well as Mr. Swinton, was misled by a clerical error in copying these returns, whereby "May" appeared in place of "August," which error will be found in the table heretofore given.

All statements of the Confederate losses, whether based upon the impressions of officers or upon assumed calculation of forces, being wholly unreliable, we are driven to a consideration of the character of the fighting for an approximate estimate of the loss. There can be no doubt that in the two days' battles in the Wilderness, and in the five days which followed (May 5 to 11), the Confederate loss was far less than the Federal. During these days the Federal loss, including wellnigh 7000 missing, was 29,410, of which 20,000—12,000 killed and wounded—were lost on the 5th and 6th; the Confederate loss was probably about 10,000, of whom not more than 1000 were prisoners. At Spottsylvania, previous to the great battle of the 12th, the Federal loss was about 10,000; that of the Confederates not more than 5000. In the battle of the 12th the Federals lost about 8000, and in the operations which followed up to the 20th about 2000, of whom not 300 were prisoners. The Confederate loss must have been quite equal, including the 3000 prisoners. At the North Anna, and in the turning operation which followed (May 21 to 31), the losses were about equal, not far from 2000 upon each side. At Cold Harbor, including the sharp engagement of June 1, the main action of June 3, and the subsequent skirmishing up to the 10th, the Federal loss was 13,000, of whom 2400 were captured. The Confederate loss during this time could hardly have exceeded 5000, including 2000 prisoners brought in by Sheridan from his cavalry raid. In the main assault on the 3d, where the Federals lost 8000 in less than an hour, the Confederates lost hardly 1000. On the 2d, when the Federals lost 2000, the Confederates suffered far less, probably not more than 1000; of whom 500 were prisoners. In the subsequent skirmishing and sharp-shooting from the 4th to the 10th, the losses were about equal. The entire Confederate loss from May 5 to June 10, thus approximately estimated, is 33,000. There is no statement of the Confederate losses in the actions before Petersburg from June 15 to 18, in which the Union loss in killed, wounded, and prisoners was 9665, there being 1600 prisoners. The Confederates, fighting mainly behind slight intrenchments, certainly suffered far less—probably not more than 5000, of whom about 1000 were prisoners.

The Union force at the opening of the campaign is officially given. The Army of the Potomac, including Burnside's corps, numbered, according to the Report of the Secretary of War, 141,164, of whom 10,000 were cavalry. While resting at Spottsylvania, re-enforcements were received from Washington fully equaling the losses which had been sustained. At Cold Harbor, the accession of Smith's command raised the Union force to fully 150,000; after the battles there, other re-enforcements arrived, so that when the crossing of the James was effected, Grant had still, including Butler's command, at least 140,000.

The losses in the Army of the Potomac during this period are accurately given. The following statement was furnished Mr. Coppée (*Grant and his Campaigns*, 399) by a member of Grant's staff, the report being subsequently officially indorsed. We place with it our approximate estimate of Confederate losses, merely attempting to discriminate between the killed and wounded and the prisoners. Meade, in his congratulatory address, issued May 13, claims 8000 prisoners—considerably in excess of the true numbers captured up to that time. The number actually reported from May 4 to 12 is 7000, of whom many were taken by Sheridan, of whom, at that time, Meade could know nothing. In the 2500 put down as taken at Cold Harbor are included the captures by the cavalry during the whole series of operations. With these explanations, we think that the summation in the following table gives very closely the respective losses during the period therein embraced.

LOSSES FROM MAY 5 TO JUNE 18.

Battles.	Union.				Confederate.		
	Killed.	Wounded.	Missing.	Total.	Killed and Wounded.	Missing.	Total.
Wilderness, May 5–11	3288	19,278	6,844	29,410	13,000	2,000	15,000
Spottsylvania, May 12–20...	2146	7,956	279	10,381	7,000	4,000	11,000
North Anna, May 21–31 ...	150	1,130	327	1,607	1,000	1,000	2,000
Cold Harbor, June 1–10 ...	1705	9,042	2,406	13,153	2,500	2,500	5,000
Petersburg, June 15–18	1198	6,853	2,217	9,665	4,000	1,000	5,000
	8487	44,259	12,073	64,216	27,500	10,500	38,000

he was on the ground, and that the delay for Burnside's arrival was by his order. His words are: "By the time I arrived next morning [the 16th] the enemy was in force. An attack was ordered to be made at six o'clock that evening by the troops under Smith and the Second and Ninth Corps. It required until that time for the Ninth Corps to get up and into position."

[1] Fletcher, p. 260–268.

[2] Losses from June 10 to 20: killed, 1198; wounded, 6853; missing, 1614—in all, 9665. Of these, all except a few hundred were during the days from the 15th to the 18th.

CHAPTER XLIV.

POLITICAL DEVELOPMENTS OF 1863.

The Reaction against the Administration in the Autumn of 1862.—The Elections show a Loss in the Republican Vote.—The President ahead of the People in his Emancipation Proclamation.—The need of decisive Military Victories.—The Elections in the Spring of 1863 show no better Result.—Meeting of the Second Regular Session of the Thirty-seventh Congress, December 1, 1862.—The President's Message.—His proposed Plan for compensated Emancipation.—The Arguments in its Favor.—It is not adopted by Congress.—The Change produced in the popular Sentiment by two Years of Civil War.—Repudiation of Compromise.—The political Problem made subservient to the Military.—The Tactics of the Opposition.—The Action of Congress in regard to Military Arrests.—The Case of Vallandigham.—He is arrested under Order No. 38 by General Burnside, May 4, 1863.—His Trial by a Military Commission.—His Application for a Writ of *Habeas Corpus* refused by Judge Leavitt.—The Sentence of Imprisonment commuted by the President, who orders Vallandigham to be transported beyond the Federal Lines, not to return during the War.—Vallandigham is nominated the Democratic Candidate for Governor of Ohio.—Indignation of the Democratic Party at his Arrest and Punishment.—Correspondence with President Lincoln.—The Conscription Act adopted by Congress.—Necessity and Justice of the Measure.—Its Constitutionality.—Debate upon its Passage.—The Features of the Bill.—Debate in the House on the Relation of the Insurgent States to the General Government.—Thaddeus Stevens states his Position.—Lovejoy repudiates Stevens's Theory of Subjugation.—Passage of the Bill to provide a National Currency.—Admission of West Virginia.—The Members from Louisiana admitted to the House.—Resolutions against Foreign Mediation.—Correspondence between Secretary Seward and M. Mercier.—Dissolution of the Thirty-seventh Congress, March 4, 1863.—The Political Situation in the following Summer.—The Efforts of the Opposition.—Fourth of July Speeches by Seymour and Pierce.—The New York Draft Riots; their Cause and Meaning.—The Influence of the Victories of Gettysburg and Vicksburg upon the National Politics.—The Autumn Elections.—Overwhelming Triumph of the Administration.

THE policy of the Federal and Confederate governments has already been followed in this history down to the close of the year 1862.[1] We purpose in this and the following chapter to continue the political history of the war down to the close of President Lincoln's administration. The United States government, while contending against the armies arrayed for its destruction, was from an early period of the contest embarrassed by a peculiar form of treason in the loyal states at the same time that it was also menaced by hostile intentions on the part of European powers.

The conflict with armed rebels was in itself sufficiently difficult, from its gigantic proportions, to overwhelm any other government, and at times its final issue appeared doubtful. In the darkest hours of the struggle was tested the patient endurance of the patriotic, and the treacherous infidelity of the disloyal was exposed. The universal enthusiasm which had glorified the few months immediately following the capture of Fort Sumter by the insurgents could not be sustained through a long war. This was not to be expected. Thousands upon thousands of those who had, in the April of 1861, been carried along by the tide of popular emotion when the first check was given to the progress of the national arms, wavered, hesitated, and fell back to their old landmarks. The reaction was natural. Men do not from momentary impulse, however strong, abandon sentiments which have become habitual. A majority of the Democratic party in the North were undoubtedly faithful adherents to the cause of loyalty; but a considerable number of that party believed that the Southern revolution was justifiable, both on the basis of state sovereignty, and because the long-continued and ever-increasing agitation on the subject of slavery had so menaced the slaveholding states that instant revolution was the only means of redress. Naturally, therefore, this portion of the Democratic party sympathized with the revolutionists. It was overawed for a season; but when it became evident that the rebellion was not to be put down in a few months, and that the war would be long and burdensome, then this faction found room and opportunity for political manœuvre, and began to throw aside its disguise. Every disaster to the Union army, every doubt as to ultimate victory for the nation, furnished these rebel sympathizers with arguments against the war. The boldest among them maintained their position by an open and direct appeal in favor of peace, even at the price of disunion. The more cautious resorted to strategy. Instead of making a direct assault, they moved by the flank, and sought to reach and destroy the base of supplies. Their political batteries were masked by various pretexts. Under that of conservatism they opposed the emancipation of slaves; in the name of liberty they cried out against conscription, and against interference with their own licentious use of speech and of the press; and the pretext of economy served them in their opposition to the appropriation of such vast sums of money as were needed for the prosecution of the war. The defeat of this cunning political strategy was a glorious national triumph, deserving to rank with the decisive victories achieved on the field of battle.

In any war politics becomes subservient. Whenever men appeal to the arbitration of arms, logic is silent, and waits upon victory or defeat. The victories of Vicksburg and Gettysburg, as we shall see, materially altered the political situation. There had been Union victories early in 1862—principal among them the capture of New Orleans—but they were not of a decisive character; they were not so positive as to counterbalance political prejudice against the action of the President on the question of slavery. Thus we find that, in the autumn elections of 1862, the administration was by no means supported by the popular vote. Even where the opposition candidates were not elected there was a noticeable falling off of the administrational support, as compared with the presidential election of 1860. By these elections Horatio Seymour was made governor of New York in place of Morton; Joel Parker, of New Jersey, in place of Olden; and in Pennsylvania, Ohio, Indiana, and Illinois there were opposition majorities.[2]

Thus it is clear that the President, in his proclamation for emancipation, instead of following, was far ahead of the majority of the voters in the loyal states. Of course, the other elements involved had much to do with the result of these state elections, but the sentiment in regard to slavery was the paramount and determining motive.

The elections in the spring of 1863, in New Hampshire, Rhode Island, and Connecticut, though resulting in a triumph for the administration, were closely contested, and showed a falling off in the Republican party vote as compared with that of 1860. The election in New Hampshire took place on the 10th of March; a governor and members of Congress were to be chosen. For the first time in several years a Democratic representative was returned to Congress from that state. For the office of governor there were three candidates. Eastman, the Democratic, polled 32,823 votes; Gilmore, the Republican, 29,035; Harriman, War Democrat, 4372. Eastman lacking 574 of a majority, the election devolved upon the state Legislature, and only by this circumstance was a Republican victory secured.

On the first of April, in Rhode Island, the Republicans carried both the state and congressional ticket, electing Governor Smith over Cozzens by a majority of a little over 3000—a decided reduction from that of previous years.

In Connecticut the election was held on the 6th of April. Here the two candidates for governor were exactly opposed to each other on the war question. The Republicans nominated the then incumbent, William A. Buckingham, a strenuous advocate of "coercion." Colonel Thomas H. Seymour, the Democratic nominee, was as distinctly recognized as an opponent of the war. Buckingham was elected by a majority of less than three thousand votes.

The second regular session of the Thirty-seventh Congress opened on the 1st of December, 1862.[1] The political complexion of Congress remained essentially the same as in the previous session. The President's message, in so far as it related to foreign affairs, contained very little of special importance. He announced that the treaty with Great Britain for the suppression of the slave-trade had been put into operation, with a good prospect of complete success. He alluded to the subject of African colonization. The Spanish-American republics had protested against the sending of negro colonies to their territories; only in Liberia and Hayti would the negro be received and adopted as a citizen. The negroes, however, did not seem so willing to migrate to these countries as to some others—not so willing, the President thought, as their interest demanded.

Turning from foreign to domestic affairs, the President alluded to the prosperity of our Territories, which had, with unimportant exceptions, been exempt from the ravages of war. He recommended to Congress measures for the rapid development of the mineral resources of these Territories as a means of increasing the national revenues. While he justified as necessary and expedient the legalization of the paper currency during the last session, he advised Congress to keep ever in view the speediest return to specie payments which would be compatible with the public interest. To meet the demand for a circulating medium, and at the same time to secure the advan-

[1] See Chapters VII., VIII., and IX.

[2] The following table shows the results of these elections, as compared with the presidential election of 1860:

	1860—Presidency.		1862—For Governor or Congress.	
	Lincoln.	All Others.	Administration.	Opposition.
New York	362,646	312,510	295,897	306,649
New Jersey	58,324	62,801	46,710	61,307
Pennsylvania	268,030	208,412	215,616	219,140
Ohio	231,610	210,831	178,755	184,332
Indiana	139,033	133,110	118,517	128,160
Illinois	172,161	160,215	120,116	136,662
Michigan	88,480	66,267	28,716	62,102
Wisconsin	86,110	60,070	66,801	67,985
Iowa	70,409	57,922	66,014	50,898
Minnesota	22,069	12,668	15,754	11,442
	1,498,872	1,290,806	1,192,896	1,228,677
1860—Lincoln's majority, 208,066. 1862—Opposition majority, 35,781.				

The following table gives the comparison in regard to Representatives in Congress elected in 1860 and 1862:

	1860.		1862.	
	Republican.	Democratic.	Administration.	Opposition.
New York	28	10	14	17
New Jersey	2	3	1	4
Pennsylvania	18	7	12	12
Ohio	13	8	5	14
Indiana	7	4	4	7
Illinois	4	5	5	9
Michigan	4	0	5	1
Wisconsin	3	0	3	3
Iowa	2	0	6	0
Minnesota	2	0	2	0
	78	37	57	67
1860—Republican majority, 41. 1862—Opposition majority, 10.				

[1] The following changes in the constitution of this session should be noticed.

In the Senate, Samuel G. Arnold, of Rhode Island, succeeded James F. Simmons, resigned. Richard S. Field had been appointed for New Jersey, in place of John R. Thompson, deceased. On the 21st of January, 1863, Field was succeeded by James W. Wall, who had been elected to fill the vacancy. January 14th, 1863, Thomas H. Hicks, of Maryland, succeeded, first by appointment and then by election, James A. Pierce, deceased. Garret Davis, of Kentucky, succeeded John C. Breckinridge, expelled December 4th, 1862. Joseph A. Wright, of Indiana, succeeded Jesse D. Bright, expelled. Wright was, on the 22d of January, 1863, superseded by David Turpie. January 30th, 1863, William A. Richardson, of Illinois, superseded by election O. H. Browning. Waldo Johnson, of Missouri, expelled, had been succeeded by R. Wilson, and Trusten Polk, of the same state, expelled, by John B. Henderson. Jacob M. Howard, of Michigan, had succeeded K. S. Bingham, deceased. Edward D. Baker, of Oregon, killed at Ball's Bluff, had been succeeded by Benjamin F. Harding.

In the House, Thomas A. D. Fessenden, of Maine, had succeeded Charles A. Walton, resigned. Amasa Walker, of Massachusetts, succeeded Goldsmith F. Bailey, deceased. Samuel Hooper, of the same state, had (December 2d, 1861) succeeded William Appleton, resigned. John D. Stiles, of Pennsylvania, June 3d, 1862, had succeeded J. B. Cooper, deceased. George H. Yeaman, of Kentucky, succeeded James S. Jackson, deceased; Samuel L. Casey had, on March 10th, 1862, succeeded Henry C. Burnett, expelled. February 25th, 1863, George W. Bridges, of Tennessee, was qualified. A. L. Knapp, of Illinois, had (December 12th, 1861) been qualified in place of J. A. McClernand, resigned; June 2d, 1862, William J. Allen had been qualified in place of John A. Logan, resigned; and on January 30th, 1863, William A. Richardson withdrew to take a seat in the Senate. Thomas L. Price, of Missouri, had succeeded John W. Reid, expelled; William A. Hall had succeeded John B. Clark, expelled. James F. Wilson, of Iowa, had succeeded Samuel R. Curtis, resigned. On the 26th of January, 1863, Walter D. McIndoe, of Wisconsin, succeeded Luther Hanchett, deceased. In February, 1863, Michael Hahn and Benjamin F. Flanders, of Louisiana, were confirmed.

-tages of a safe and uniform currency, he recommended the organization of bank associations by the act and subject to the regulation of Congress. For the year ending June 30th, 1862, the receipts from all sources, including loans and the balance from the preceding year, had been $583,885,247. The balance from the preceding year was $2,257,065. The loans of all forms had amounted to $529,692,460. From customs, direct tax, public lands, and miscellaneous sources, the receipts amounted to nearly $52,000,000. The balance left in the treasury, July 1st, 1862, was $13,053,546. Of the expenditures, $437,042,977 had been for the army and navy.

Notwithstanding the burdens laid upon the nation by the war, the President had favored the project for connecting the United States with Europe by an Atlantic telegraph, and a similar project to extend the telegraph from San Francisco, to connect by a Pacific telegraph with the line then being laid across Russian Asia. A Department of Agriculture had been established, and the President pressed upon Congress the claims of the Pacific Railroad project.

A very prominent feature of the President's message was his recommendation of a constitutional amendment providing for the compensated emancipation of slaves. This provision was to the effect that every slave state which should abolish slavery before January 1, 1900, should receive compensation from the United States; that this compensation should be extended to all loyal owners of slaves freed by the chances of the war; and that Congress might appropriate money, and otherwise provide for colonizing free negroes, with their own consent, at any place outside of the United States.[1] The President's proposition, coming in this form, indicates that he was not at this time fully convinced as to the justice of abolishing slavery in the loyal states, even by a constitutional amendment, without compensation to the slave owners. In regard to those states which were in open war against the government, he had no hesitation either as to the powers of the government to abolish slavery, or as to the justice of the measure. He still adhered to his proclamation of September 22d, and on the 1st of January, 1863, consummated the act therein contemplated. He believed that "without slavery the rebellion could never have existed; without slavery it could not continue." In the loyal slave states he was disposed to compromise, and would respect the opinions of all classes.

"Among the friends of the Union," he says, "there is great diversity of sentiment and of policy in regard to slavery and the African race among us. Some would perpetuate slavery; some would abolish it suddenly and without compensation; some would abolish it gradually and with compensation; some would remove the freed people from us, and some would retain them with us; and there are yet other minor diversities. Because of these diversities we waste much strength in struggles among ourselves. By mutual concessions we should harmonize and act together. This would be compromise; but it would be compromise among the friends, and not with the enemies of the Union."

The length of time contemplated in the proposed amendment, and the compensation of the owners of slaves, would, thought the President, weaken the opposition of those who did not favor emancipation. They would yield something by conceding emancipation as a fact to be accomplished, while those already in favor of emancipation would sustain the disappointment occasioned by the delay, and bear their portion of the financial burden imposed upon the country by compensation. Besides, he argued, immediate emancipation would lead to vagrant destitution; therefore the system of gradual abolition would be best for the generation of slaves now passing away, while it promised freedom to their posterity. While, by offering compensation, the government presented to every state a strong motive for adopting emancipation before the close of the century, it left to each state within that limit freedom to choose its own time and mode of effecting the object in view. In answer to the objection that by this plan some must pay who would receive nothing in return, he replied that the measure was both just and economical.

In the first place, it was just. "In a certain sense, the liberation of slaves is the destruction of property; property acquired by descent or by purchase, the same as any other property. It is no less true for having been often said that people of the South are not more responsible for the original introduction of this property than are the people of the North; and when it is remembered how unhesitatingly we all use cotton and sugar, and share the profits of dealing in them, it may not be quite safe to say that the South has been more responsible than the North for its continuance. If, then, for a common object, this property is to be sacrificed, is it not just that it be done at a common charge?"

[1] The following is a copy of the resolution recommended by the President:

"*Resolved by the Senate and House of Representatives of the United States of America, in Congress assembled* (two thirds of both houses concurring), That the following articles be proposed to the Legislatures (or Conventions) of the several states as amendments to the Constitution of the United States, all or any of which articles, when ratified by three fourths of the said Legislatures (or Conventions), to be valid as part or parts of the said Constitution, viz.:

"ARTICLE 1. Every state wherein slavery now exists, which shall abolish the same therein at any time or times before the first day of January, in the year of our Lord one thousand and nine hundred, shall receive compensation from the United States as follows, to wit:

"The President of the United States shall deliver to every such state bonds of the United States, bearing interest at the rate of — per cent. per annum, to an amount equal to the aggregate sum of $—— for each slave shown to have been therein by the eighth census of the United States, said bonds to be delivered to such state by installments or in one parcel, at the completion of the abolishment, accordingly as the same shall have been gradual or at one time within such state; and interest shall begin to run upon any such bond only from the proper time of its delivery as aforesaid. Any state having received bonds as aforesaid, and afterward reintroducing or tolerating slavery therein, shall refund to the United States the bonds so received, or the value thereof, and all interest paid thereon.

"ARTICLE 2. All slaves who shall have enjoyed actual freedom by the chances of the war at any time before the end of the rebellion shall be forever free; but all owners of such who shall not have been disloyal shall be compensated for them at the same rates as is provided for states adopting abolishment of slavery, but in such way that no slave shall be twice accounted for.

"ARTICLE 3. Congress may appropriate money, and otherwise provide for colonizing free colored persons, with their own consent, at any place or places without the United States."

It was also economical. The adoption of this plan, by securing an earlier termination of the war, would save more than it would cost. Besides, the expense caused by the war was an immediate burden, and must be borne all at once, whether we would or no; while the cost of compensation would be gradually incurred, and the full burden would fall upon the people thirty-seven years hence, when it would be sustained by one hundred millions instead of thirty-one millions.[1]

While the President was strongly in favor of the colonization, with their own consent, of the freed negroes, he thought the objection to their remaining in the country on the ground that they displaced white laborers was "largely imaginary, if not sometimes malicious."[2]

Even if this plan should not be adopted by the slave states, the President proclaimed his willingness that the national authority should be restored without it; also, that notwithstanding its recommendation, neither the war, nor proceedings under the proclamation of September 22d, would be stayed. It is evident, however, that in the event of the universal and immediate adoption of this plan, the President contemplated its substitution in place of sudden emancipation, except in the cases of those slaves who had been or might be freed by the chances of war, and even in these cases loyal owners would receive compensation.

"The plan is proposed," said the President, "as permanent constitutional law. It can not become such without the concurrence of, first, two thirds of Congress, and, afterward, three fourths of the states. The requisite three fourths of the states will necessarily include seven of the slave states. Their concurrence, if obtained, will give assurance of their severally adopting emancipation, at no very distant day, upon the new constitutional terms. This assurance would end the struggle now, and save the Union forever.

"I do not forget the gravity which should characterize a paper addressed to the Congress of the nation by the chief magistrate of the nation, nor do I forget that some of you are my seniors, nor that many of you have more experience than I in the conduct of public affairs; yet I trust that, in view of the great responsibility resting upon me, you will perceive no want of respect to yourselves in any undue earnestness I may seem to display.

"Is it doubted, then, that the plan I propose, if adopted, would shorten the war, and thus lessen its expenditure of money and of blood? Is it doubted that it would restore the national authority and national prosperity, and perpetuate both indefinitely? Is it doubted that we here—Congress and executive—can secure its adoption? Will not the good people respond to a united and earnest appeal from us? Can we, can they, by any other means, so certainly or so speedily assure these vital objects? We can succeed only by concert. It is not, 'Can *any* of us *imagine* better?' but, 'Can we *all* do better?' Object whatsoever is possible, still the question recurs, 'Can we do better?' The dogmas of the quiet past are inadequate to the stormy present. The occasion is piled high with difficulty, and we must rise with the occasion. As our case is new, so we must think anew, and act anew. We must disenthrall ourselves, and then we shall save our country.

"Fellow-citizens, *we* can not escape history. We, of this Congress and

[1] "Taking the nation in the aggregate, and we find its population and ratio of increase, for the several decennial periods, to be as follows:

1790	3,929,827	
1800	5,305,937	35.02 per cent. ratio of increase.
1810	7,239,814	36.45 " " "
1820	9,638,131	33.13 " " "
1830	12,866,020	33.49 " " "
1840	17,069,453	32.67 " " "
1850	23,191,876	35.87 " " "
1860	31,443,790	35.58 " " "

"This shows an annual decennial increase of 34.60 per cent. in population through the 70 years from our first to our last census yet taken. It is seen that the ratio of increase at no one of these seven periods is either 2 per cent. below or 2 per cent. above the average, thus showing how inflexible, and, consequently, how reliable the law of increase in our case is. Assuming that it will continue gives the following results:

1870	42,323,341	1910	138,918,526
1880	56,967,216	1920	186,984,335
1890	76,677,872	1930	251,680,914
1900	103,208,415		

"These figures show that our country *may* be as populous as Europe now is at some point between 1920 and 1930—say about 1925—our territory, at 73⅓ persons to the square mile, being of capacity to contain 217,186,000.

"And we *will* reach this, too, if we do not ourselves relinquish the chance by the folly and evils of disunion, or by the long and exhausting war springing from the only great element of national discord among us. While it can not be foreseen exactly how much one huge example of secession, breeding lesser ones indefinitely, would retard population, no one can doubt that the extent of it would be very great and injurious. The proposed emancipation would shorten the war, perpetuate peace, insure this increase of population, and proportionately the wealth of the country. With these, we should pay all that emancipation would cost, together with our other debt, easier than we should pay our other debt without it. If we had allowed our old national debt to run at 6 per cent. *per annum*, simple interest, from the end of our revolutionary struggle until to-day, without paying any thing on either principal or interest, each man of us would owe less upon that debt now than each man owed upon it then; and this because our increase of men through the whole period has been greater than 6 per cent.—has run faster than the interest upon the debt. Thus time alone relieves a debtor nation so long as its population increases faster than unpaid interest accumulates on its debt. . . . . . A dollar will be much harder to pay for the war than will be a dollar for emancipation on the proposed plan. And, then, the latter will cost no blood, no precious life."—*President's Message.*

[2] "*It is insisted that their presence would injure and displace white labor and white laborers.* . . . . Is it true, then, that colored people can displace any more white labor by being free than by remaining slaves? If they stay in their old places, they jostle no white laborers; if they leave their old places, they leave them open to white laborers. Logically, there is neither more nor less of it. Emancipation, even without deportation, would probably enhance the wages of white labor, and very surely would not reduce them. . . . . But it is dreaded that the freed people will swarm forth and cover the whole land. Are they not already in the land? Will liberation make them any more numerous? Equally distributed among the whites of the whole country, and there would be but one colored to seven whites. Could the one, in any way, greatly disturb the seven? There are many communities now having more than one free colored person to seven whites, and this without any apparent consciousness of evil from it. The District of Columbia, and the States of Maryland and Delaware, are all in this condition. . . . . But why should emancipation South send the freed people North? People of any color seldom run unless there be something to run from. *Heretofore* colored people, to some extent, have fled North from bondage, and now, perhaps, from both bondage and destitution. But if gradual emancipation and deportation be adopted, they will have neither to flee from. . . . . Again, as practice proves more than theory, has there been any irruption of colored people northward because of the abolishment of slavery in this district last spring?"—*President's Message.*

this administration, will be remembered in spite of ourselves. No personal significance or insignificance can spare one or another of us. The fiery trial through which we pass will light us down, in honor or dishonor, to the latest generation. We *say* we are for the Union. The world will not forget that we say this. We know how to save the Union. The world knows we do know how to save it. We—even *we here*—hold the power, and bear the responsibility. In *giving* freedom to the *slave*, we *assure* freedom to the *free*—honorable alike in what we give and what we preserve. We shall nobly save, or meanly lose, the last best hope of earth. Other means may succeed; this could not fail. The way is plain, peaceful, generous, just—a way which, if followed, the world will forever applaud, and God must forever bless."

It is clear from this proposed plan of the President, urged with such earnestness, that, notwithstanding his proclamation of September 22d, he preferred gradual and compensated to sudden and arbitrary emancipation. His reasons for this preference have already been given at some length. They may be briefly enumerated thus:

1. Gradual emancipation was better for the slave. While freedom was secured to all future generations, the present would be relieved of the destitution which it might be presumed would follow their sudden emancipation.

2. The measure proposed would reconcile differences of opinion, and therefore meet with less opposition. Undoubtedly the autumn elections of 1862 gave cogency to this argument.

3. The measure was dictated by justice, the North being no less responsible for slavery than the South.

4. By its tendency to restore peace, it would substitute for a war debt another, less in amount, and more easily borne.

The President, in a previous message to Congress (March 6, 1862), had recommended the passage of a joint resolution, declaring that the United States ought to co-operate with any state which should adopt the gradual abolition of slavery, by giving pecuniary aid to such state;[1] and this resolution had been passed by the House March 11th, 1862, and by the Senate on the 2d of April following. The President had urged the border states to embrace this opportunity, but no state had responded. It is not strange, therefore, that when the President, in the Message of December 1st, 1862, again brought the subject before Congress, it met with little consideration. On the 6th of January a bill passed the House, 83 to 50, offering compensation to Missouri in the event of that state adopting immediate emancipation. In the Senate the bill came up for consideration, and on the 14th of January Mr. Trumbull reported a substitute granting compensation to Missouri if, within twelve months, that state should adopt measures either for immediate or gradual emancipation. This substitute passed the Senate, 23 to 18, on the 12th of February; but, returning to the House, it was six days later recommitted, and never again considered. A similar bill in regard to Maryland was submitted in the House on the 19th of January, was on the 25th recommitted, and never heard of again; it did not even reach the Senate. No proposition was ever offered in Congress to incorporate into the Constitution the articles recommended by the President.

The President's proclamation of September 22d more completely met the views of Congress on the subject of slavery. This proclamation cut the Gordian knot with a single blow of the sword. By this, all the slaves within the limits of the Confederacy were henceforth and forever free. This act might be extreme; it might be arbitrary, and involve, in some measure, injustice to certain owners of slaves; it might even involve distress to the slaves thus suddenly released from bondage; but its advantage to the country was deemed so great as to outweigh such petty considerations. It was emphatically a war measure, and none but war measures, in the opinion of Congress, could hasten the termination of the war. It was bold, positive, and conclusive. It said plainly to Southern Revolutionists, "The decree of the nation has gone forth declaring absolute freedom in your fortified strongholds of slavery; only by the destruction of the nation can you nullify this decree." Clearly nothing was to be gained, as against the Confederacy, by any measure less decisive; and among Loyalists what was to be gained by a weak compromise? The offer of compensation in return for gradual emancipation had already been held out to the border states, and had been refused. Congress must choose between renewing this offer, which would certainly be again rejected, or declaring that henceforth the preservation of the nation was identified with the destruction of slavery. The moral strength thus gathered up, to be hurled against the rebellion, was as a mountain to a mole-hill when compared to the injury which could come to the nation by the repulsion of those who would identify the safety of their country with the perpetration of a monstrous wrong.

On the 15th of December, 1862, a resolution, offered by Mr. S. C. Fessenden, was adopted in the House, 78 to 52, declaring that the President's proclamation of September 22d indicated a policy of emancipation well adapted to hasten the restoration of peace, was well chosen as a war measure, and was an exercise of power with proper regard for the rights of the states and the perpetuity of free government. Two Democrats voted in favor of the resolution, and six Republicans against it.

And here it is proper to remark the change which had been effected in Congressional sentiment by two years of civil war. The burden of the conflict now began to be palpable. Every day the public debt increased by hundreds of thousands of dollars. The credit of the nation was disturbed not so much by this daily augmentation of the debt as by a prevailing disquietude as to the final success of the war. Once it had been confidently predicted that three months would conclude the struggle. But the tremendous energies which had been enlisted in the rebellion were not then appreciated. It had been hoped that compromise might neutralize and disarm treason; and in the special session of 1861, Congress had distinctly proclaimed its willingness to restore every rebellious state to its former position in the Union, with all its ancient rights and institutions undisturbed, upon the simple condition of returned allegiance. This attitude of Congress only provoked the scorn of the Revolutionists, and was interpreted by them as a sign of weakness in the national government. "We have," said these rebels, "given our challenge. We have appealed to arms. Subdue us if you can. If you can not, grant us our independence. But by no *political* overtures which you can make will we be induced either to resume our allegiance, or to abate the violence of our attempted revolution." After two years of fighting, with the exception of the capture of New Orleans, no great national victory had been won. The national reverses had been many, and were balanced only by temporary advantages and indecisive battles. One military leader and then another had been tried and set aside, but as yet no masterly generalship had been developed. The first outburst of martial enthusiasm had given place to partial discouragement. Still, the nation was not dismayed, nor did its armies shrink from the conflict because the latter had become doubtful and difficult. If the sentiment of patriotism had been in great measure exhausted, its place had been taken by patriotic good sense. As the strength and persistency of the rebellion became manifest, all attempts at political compromise were summarily set aside. The defiance of armed rebels could only be met by the confidence of the nation in its power to maintain itself by the strength of arms. In such a struggle the wisest political theories were useless, because such a struggle was, in the first instance, an appeal from the decision of statesmen to the decision of battles, in which physical and material conditions were the controlling elements—in which even moral forces could only be considered in their relations to a purely military problem. Legislation had not been able to prevent civil war, and the direct and primary authority of law was now equally powerless to procure peace. *Inter arma leges silent.* The very existence of the government was threatened, and so long as the menace endured, so long must the government stand behind its army; which was at once its representative, its shield against treason, and its uplifted arm for the punishment of traitors. The executive, the legislative, and the judicial functions of the government, in their bearing upon the war, had no significance or value except in so far as they subordinated all things else to the support of the army, and to measures which would secure its ultimate success. If this lesson had not been learned at once, two years of bitter experience had impressed it upon the popular mind. Thus the political problem which was presented for immediate solution became very simple by its subordination to military necessity. In this way there was also furnished a palpable line of separation between parties—between those who were willing to surrender every thing for national preservation, and those who preferred national dissolution to any surrender or any sacrifice whatsoever. Those who heartily supported the war did so because only by war could the nation be saved, and these were willing to legalize any method, not in itself dishonorable, which would help to secure military success, even if it involved a violation of the Constitution. In justification, no resort need be had to extraordinary statesmanship; the dictates of common sense were sufficient. The Constitution, and, *à fortiori*, all laws growing out of the Constitution, can never override the law of national existence itself. This principle needs no argument to support it, nor any amplification.

But, in fact, no great strain need be put on the Constitution, which, though not contemplating a violent civil war, yet in most respects adequately provided for the national safety in any event.

Those who opposed the war based their opposition on various grounds. Some held it to be unjust—an opinion very nearly allied to treason, and acts of opposition based upon it *were* treason. Others expected defeat, and this timidity was an insult to patriotism. Others counted the success of the war a poor recompense for its burdens; such were unworthy of their title to citizenship in the great republic. Still others, while disguising their direct opposition to the war, opposed all means proposed for its effective prosecution on the ground that they were unconstitutional. Their arguments in support of the unconstitutionality of measures thus adopted were generally baseless, and in any case were not worthy of respect.

The conflict between the two parties began early in this session of the Thirty-seventh Congress. On the first day of the session a resolution was offered by Cox, of Ohio, declaring that all arrests previously made by the United States authorities of citizens in states where there was no insurrection, were unwarranted by the Constitution, and a usurpation of power. This was laid upon the table, 80 to 40. A similar resolution offered the next day in the Senate met the same fate. A week later (December 8th), in the Senate, a resolution was offered by Saulsbury, of Delaware, calling upon the Secretary of War for information in regard to the arrest of two citizens of his state—Dr. John Laws and Whitely Meredith. In the debate which followed, Mr. Wilson, of Massachusetts, opposed the resolution on the ground that the government had been too lenient in this matter. "Instead," said he, "of the few hundred arrests we have had, we ought to have had several thousand." John Sherman, of Ohio, a leading Republican, took a different view. He thought that arrests should not be made except upon a reason which could be definitely stated to Congress. Congress ought to demand this. "The power to suspend the writ of *habeas corpus* should only be exercised with all the guards that can be thrown by wise legislation around it. Such a power, uncurbed, unregulated, and unchecked, would make this government a despotism worse than England ever saw, worse than France was in the time when *lettres de cachet* were used for the arrest of citizens, and they were confined for 40 years." Powell, of Kentucky, claimed that the right to suspend the writ of *habeas corpus* did not involve the right to make

[1] See Chapter VIII. of this History, p. 204.

CLEMENT L. VALLANDIGHAM.

arrests. The object of the writ was to relieve a man once arrested from illegal imprisonment. Neither the President nor his ministers had a right to arrest any man who was not in the military service of the United States. The claim made by Powell was not disputed by any senator. The right of the executive to make arrests in time of war, and when the public safety demanded, was too well established to admit of debate. Davis, Powell's colleague, claimed that the suspension of the writ was not within the scope of executive power. After a prolonged debate, Saulsbury's resolution was laid upon the table, 29 to 13. At the same time, a bill was passed in the House by a vote of 90 to 45, indemnifying the President and his subordinate officers for his action in making arrests, and in the suspension of *habeas corpus*.[1]

This bill went to the Senate, where it was amended. In its final shape it authorized the President to suspend the privilege of the writ of *habeas corpus* in any case throughout the United States; it directed that the Secretary of War and the Secretary of State should furnish to the judges of the Circuit and District Courts of the United States the names of all state prisoners then confined, or who should thereafter be confined, with the date of each arrest, and that those prisoners against whom the grand jury should find no indictment during the session sitting when the list was furnished should be released upon taking the oath of allegiance, either with or without recognizance or bond, as the judges of the respective courts might determine; it provided that any order of the President should be a sufficient defense in any case of prosecution for arrests made under such order, and that in any such prosecution the defendant might, by filing a petition, have it removed from the State Court to the Circuit Court of the United States. By a writ of error any case might even be transferred to the United States Supreme Court.

Not long after the close of this session Mr. Vallandigham was arrested in Ohio. The busy and persistent efforts made by domestic enemies to thwart the plans of the national government, and to prevent the enlistment of troops, led to the famous Order No. 38, issued by General Burnside from his headquarters at Cincinnati on the 13th of April. By this order, all persons found within his lines affording aid or comfort to the enemy were to be tried as spies or traitors, and upon conviction to suffer death.

[1] A fortnight after the passage of this bill, a resolution in the nature of a protest was submitted to the House, signed by 37 representatives. These protested for the following reasons:

"1. Because it purports to deprive the citizen of all existing, peaceful, legal modes of redress for admitted wrongs, and thus constrains him tamely to submit to the injury inflicted, or to seek illegal and forcible remedies.

"2. Because it purports to indemnify the President and all acting under his authority for acts admitted to be wrongful, at the expense of the citizen upon whom the wrongful acts have been perpetrated, in violation of the plainest principles of justice, and the most familiar precepts of constitutional law.

"3. Because it purports to confirm and make valid, by act of Congress, arrests and imprisonments which were not only not warranted by the Constitution of the United States, but were in palpable violation of its express prohibitions.

"4. Because it purports to authorize the President, during this rebellion, at any time, as to any person, and every where throughout the limits of the United States, to suspend the privilege of the writ of *habeas corpus*, whereas, by the Constitution, the power to suspend the privilege of that writ is confided to the discretion of Congress alone, and is limited to the places threatened by the dangers of invasion or insurrection.

"5. Because, for these and other reasons, it is unjust and unwise, an invasion of private rights, an encouragement to lawless violence, and a precedent full of hope to all who would usurp despotic power and perpetuate it by the arbitrary arrest and imprisonment of those who oppose them.

"6. And, finally, because in both its sections it is 'a deliberate, palpable, and dangerous' violation of the Constitution, 'according to the plain sense and intention of that instrument,' and is therefore utterly null and void."

It was signed by the following members: Geo. H. Pendleton, W. A. Richardson, J. C. Robinson, P. B. Fouke, Jas. R. Morris, A. L. Knapp, C. L. Vallandigham, C. A. White, Warren P. Noble, W. Allen, William J. Allen, S. S. Cox, E. H. Norton, Geo. K. Shiel, S. J. Ancona, J. Lazear, Nehemiah Perry, C. Vibbard, John Law, C. A. Wickliffe, Chas. J. Biddle, J. A. Cravens, Elijah Ward, Philip Johnson, John D. Stiles, D. W. Voorhees, G. W. Dunlap, Hendrick B. Wright, H. Grider, W. H. Wadsworth, A. Harding, Chas. B. Calvert, Jas. E. Kerrigan, Henry May, R. H. Nugent, Geo. H. Yeaman, B. F. Granger.

Within the scope and meaning of this order were included "carriers of secret mails; writers of letters sent by secret mails; secret recruiting officers within the lines; persons who have entered into an agreement to pass our lines for the purpose of joining the enemy; persons found concealed within our lines belonging to the service of the enemy, and, in fact, all persons found improperly within our lines who could give private information to the enemy; all persons within our lines who harbor, protect, conceal, feed, clothe, or in any way aid the enemies of our country." All those who declared their sympathy with the enemy were to be arrested, either to be tried as spies or to be sent beyond the lines. This order had a very beneficial influence in Kentucky. In the states north of the Ohio it was construed by the disaffected as an extraordinary instance of military despotism.

Foremost among those who bade defiance to this order was Clement L. Vallandigham, of Ohio, lately a member of the Thirty-seventh Congress, and the leader in his state of what was known as the "Copperhead" wing of the Democratic party. He had been defeated as a candidate for the Thirty-eighth Congress by General Robert C. Schenck, but was the prospective Democratic candidate for Governor of Ohio. He was opposed to the war, and bitterly reviled the administration of President Lincoln. He was not, strictly speaking, an advocate for the rebellion; but, for the sake of peace, he was in favor of surrendering to the rebels all for which they were fighting. He preferred the re-establishment of the Union to its dissolution, if such a result could be reached by a compromise reinstating the slave oligarchy with its former prestige and power; failing in that, he would have acquiesced in secession, yielding the Confederacy its independence without further struggle. That there should have been a war for the Union at all he denied; that this war should continue he held to be a national misfortune and manifest injustice. His voice, from first to last, was against the war; and in his opposition he was the most unscrupulous of demagogues. His convictions were strong—and to these he had a right. But at this critical period his open and violent opposition could not be without injury to the national cause, if maintained with impunity. No distinction could practically be made between a traitor in arms against the government and Vallandigham hurling against it his violent philippics, whatever distinction in favor of the latter might have existed in theory. For the government to have winked at his opposition while it was on the battle-field crushing those with whom he sympathized, and for whom his energetic co-operation was worth more than an additional army corps, would have been to convict itself of the most palpable folly and inconsistency.

It was in this light that Burnside looked upon Vallandigham's conduct, and accordingly, after an address made by the latter at Mount Vernon, about the 18th of May, he dispatched Captain Charles G. Hutton, his aid-de-camp, to Dayton, where Vallandigham resided, with orders for the arrest of the offender and his conveyance to Cincinnati for trial. The arrest took place on the night of May 4th, Hutton bringing his prisoner to Cincinnati without disturbance. The next day a charge was preferred against him for "publicly expressing, in violation of General Orders No. 38, from Headquarters Department of the Ohio, sympathy for those in arms against the government of the United States, and declaring disloyal sentiments and opinions with the object and purpose of weakening the power of the government in its efforts to suppress an unlawful rebellion." The specific charge was that be had declared the war to be "wicked, cruel, and unnecessary," "for the purpose of crushing out liberty and erecting a despotism," "for the freedom of the blacks and the enslavement of the whites;" had stated that "if the administration had so wished, the war could have been honorably terminated months ago;" had characterized the order No. 38 as a "base usurpation of arbitrary authority;" had invited resistance to this order by saying "the sooner the people inform the minions of usurped power that they will not submit to such restrictions upon their liberties, the better;" and had declared himself resolved at all times and upon all occasions "to do what he could to defeat the attempts now being made to build up a monarchy upon the ruins of our free government."

Vallandigham was tried by a military commission, of which General R. B. Potter was President, and which consisted of Colonel J. F. De Courcy, Lieutenant Colonel E. R. Goodrich, Major J. M. Brown, Major J. L. Van Buren, Major C. H. Fitch, Captain P. M. Lydig, with Captain J. M. Cutts, of the Eleventh United States Infantry, as judge advocate. The trial continued for two days. Vallandigham protested against the jurisdiction of the commission, declaring that no such charge could apply to him, as he belonged to neither the naval or military service of the United States, and that he was subject to arrest only by due process of law.[1] He demanded to be tried by

[1] The President had issued the proclamation of martial law on the 24th of September, 1862. The following are the important clauses of the proclamation:

1. "During the existing insurrection, and as a necessary means for suppressing the same, all rebels and insurgents, their aiders and abettors, within the United States, and all persons discouraging volunteer enlistments, resisting militia drafts, or guilty of any disloyal practice, affording aid and comfort to the rebels, against the authority of the United States, shall be subject to martial law, and liable to trial by courts-martial or military commission.

2. "That the writ of *habeas corpus* is suspended in respect to all persons arrested, or who are now, or hereafter during the rebellion shall be, imprisoned in any fort, camp, arsenal, military prison, or other place of confinement, by any military authority, or by the sentence of any court-martial or military commission."

This proclamation received the sanction both of Congress and of the judiciary. It violated neither the letter nor the spirit of the Constitution; and if the Constitution did not explicitly provide for martial law in case of war, it must be remembered that war proceeds not according to rules laid down by constitutions, but according to established usages. And under no government is any use more established than that of the proclamation and enforcement of martial law in time of rebellion. When the illustrious Lord Brougham addressed the House of Peers in support of a bill which empowered the Lord Lieutenant of Ireland to apprehend all persons *suspected* of con-a civil court, and in accordance with the ordinary usages adopted in his state. Witnesses were examined on both sides. But the case was submitted without argument. The validity of the prisoner's protest was not admitted, and Mr. Vallandigham was found guilty and sentenced to close confinement in some fortress of the United States, to be designated by General Burnside, there to be kept until the close of the war. Burnside, approving the finding of the court, ordered the prisoner to be confined in Fort Warren, in Boston Harbor.

In the mean time, Vallandigham, through the Hon. George H. Pugh, had applied to the Circuit Court of the United States for the Southern District of Ohio for a writ of *habeas corpus*. The case was argued before Judge H. H. Leavitt, who refused the writ. "It is clearly not a time," said the judge, "when any one connected with the judicial department of the government should allow himself, except from the most stringent obligations of duty, to embarrass or thwart the executive in his efforts to deliver the country from the dangers which press so heavily upon it." He argued that the legality of the arrest depended upon the necessity of making it, and that must be determined by the military commander. "Men should know," he said, "and lay the truth to heart, that there is a course of conduct not involving overt treason, and not, therefore, subject to punishment as such, which nevertheless implies moral guilt and a gross offense against the country. Those who live under the protection and enjoy the blessings of our benignant government must learn that they can not stab its vitals with impunity. If they cherish hatred and hostility to it, and desire its subversion, let them withdraw from its jurisdiction, and seek the fellowship and protection of those with whom they are in sympathy. If they remain with us while they are not of us, they must be subject to such a course of dealing as the great law of self-preservation prescribes and will enforce. And let them not complain if the stringent doctrine of military necessity should find them to be the legitimate subjects of its action. I have no fear that the recognition of this doctrine will lead to an arbitrary invasion of the personal security or personal liberty of the citizen. It is rare indeed that a charge of disloyalty will be made on insufficient grounds. But if there should be an occasional mistake, such an occurrence is not to be put into competition with the preservation of the nation; and I confess I am but little moved by the eloquent appeals of those who, while they indignantly denounce violation of personal liberty, look with no horror upon a despotism as unmitigated as the world has ever witnessed."

Burnside only awaited the President's confirmation of the sentence before carrying it out. But Mr. Lincoln decided to commute the punishment awarded by the military commission, and ordered the prisoner to be sent, "under a secure guard, to the headquarters of General Rosecrans, to be put by him beyond our military lines, and that, in case of his return within our lines, he be arrested and kept in close custody for the term specified in his sentence." This order was executed. General Bragg transferred the involuntary exile to Richmond, where he was very coldly received. He left the Confederacy as speedily as possible, and found an asylum in Canada, where he remained during the following autumn and winter. In the mean time he was made the Democratic candidate for Governor of Ohio, and sustained at the polls the most overwhelming defeat recorded in the political annals of this country. He returned home toward the close of the war, but it was not then considered worth while to molest him.[1]

Burnside did not content himself with banishing Vallandigham, but l
his hand upon such organs of the press as maintained the exile's cau

---

spiracy against the British government, he said: "A friend of liberty I have lived, and such will I die; nor care I how soon the latter event may happen if I can not be a friend of liberty without being a friend of traitors at the same time—a protector of criminals of the deepest dye—an accomplice of foul rebellion and of its concomitant, civil war, with all its atrocities and all its fearful consequences."*

The Constitution provides that "no person shall be held to answer for a capital or otherwise infamous crime unless on a presentment or indictment of a grand jury, except in cases arising in the land or naval forces, or in the militia, when in actual service in time of war or public danger." But this provision only applies in time of peace. It has no bearing upon martial law. Says Chancellor Kent: "*Military* law is a system of regulations for the government of the armies in the service of the United States, authorized by the act of Congress of April 10, 1806, known as the Articles of War; and *naval* law is a similar system for the government of the navy, under the act of Congress of April 23, 1800. But *martial* law is quite a distinct thing, and is founded upon paramount necessity, and proclaimed by a *military chief*."

[1] The arrest of Vallandigham created considerable excitement in the Democratic party, and a vain attempt was made at his canonization as a martyr to liberty. A mass meeting was held at Albany, May 16, and strong resolutions were adopted denouncing Burnside's action. The following is a record of the meeting, as transmitted by Honorable Erastus Corning, its chairman, to President Lincoln, to which we append the President's reply:

"Albany, May 19, 1863.

"To his Excellency the President of the United States:

"The undersigned, officers of a public meeting held at the city of Albany on the 16th day of May, instant, herewith transmit to your excellency a copy of the resolutions adopted at the said meeting, and respectfully request your earnest consideration of them. They deem it proper, on their personal responsibility, to state that the meeting was one of the most respectable as to numbers and character, and one of the most earnest in the support of the Union, ever held in this city.

"Yours, with great regard,

"ERASTUS CORNING, President.	WM. S. PADOCK, Vice-President.
"ELI PERRY, Vice-President.	J. B. SANDERS, Vice-President.
"PETER GANSEVOORT, Vice-President.	EDWARD MULCAHY, Vice-President.
"PETER MONTEITH, Vice-President.	D. V. N. RADCLIFFE, Vice-President.
"SAMUEL W. GIBBS, Vice-President.	WILLIAM A. RICE, Secretary.
"JOHN NIBLACK, Vice-President.	EDWARD NEWCOMB, Secretary.
"H. W. MCCLELLAN, Vice-President.	R. W. PECKHAM, Jr., Secretary.
"LEMUEL W. RODGERS, Vice-President.	M. A. NOLAN, Secretary.
"WILLIAM SEYMOUR, Vice-President.	JOHN R. NESSEL, Secretary.
"JEREMIAH OSBORN, Vice-President.	C. W. WEEKS, Secretary.

"*Resolutions adopted at the Meeting held in Albany, N. Y., on the 16th day of May*, 1863.

"*Resolved*, That the Democrats of New York point to their uniform course of action during the two years of civil war through which we have passed, to the alacrity which they have evinced in filling the ranks of the army, to their contributions and sacrifices, as the evidence of their patriotism and devotion to the cause of our imperiled country. Never, in the history of civil wars, has a government been sustained with such ample resources of means and men as the people have voluntarily placed in the hands of this administration.

"*Resolved*, That as Democrats we are determined to maintain this patriotic attitude, and, despite adverse and disheartening circumstances, to devote all our energies to sustain the cause of the Union; to secure peace through victory, and to bring back the restoration of all the states under the safeguard of the Constitution.

"*Resolved*, That while we will not consent to be misapprehended upon these points, we are determined not to be misunderstood in regard to others not less essential. We demand that the administration shall be true to the Constitution; shall recognize and maintain the rights of the states and the liberties of the citizen; shall every where, outside of the lines of necessary milit
occupation and the scenes of insurrection, exert all its powers to maintain the supremacy of
civil over military law.

"*Resolved*, That, in view of these principles, we denounce the recent assumption of a milit
commander to seize and try a citizen of Ohio, Clement L. Vallandigham, for no other reas
than words addressed to a public meeting, in criticism of the course of the administration and
condemnation of the military orders of that general.

"*Resolved*, That this assumption of power by a military tribunal, if successfully asserted, n
only abrogates the right of the people to assemble and discuss the affairs of government, the li
erty of speech and of the press, the right of trial by jury, the law of evidence, and the privilege
habeas corpus, but it strikes a fatal blow at the supremacy of law and the authority of the sta
and federal Constitutions.

"*Resolved*, That the Constitution of the United States—the supreme law of the land—has d
fined the crime of treason against the United States to consist 'only in levying war against the
or adhering to their enemies, giving them aid and comfort,' and has provided that 'no person sh
be convicted of treason unless on the testimony of two witnesses to the same overt act, or on co
fession in open court.' And it farther provides that 'no person shall be held to answer for a ca
ital or otherwise infamous crime unless on a presentment or indictment of a grand jury, except
cases arising in the land or naval forces, or in the militia, when in actual service in time of w
or public danger;' and farther, that 'in all criminal prosecutions the accused shall enjoy the rig
of a speedy and public trial by an impartial jury of the state and district wherein the crime w
committed.'

"*Resolved*, That these safeguards of the rights of the citizen against the pretensions of arbitr
ry power were intended more especially for his protection in times of civil commotion. Th
were secured substantially to the English people after years of protracted civil war, and we
adopted into our Constitution at the close of the Revolution. They have stood the test of sevent
six years of trial under our republican system, under circumstances which show that, while the
constitute the foundation of all free government, they are the elements of the enduring stabili
of the republic.

"*Resolved*, That, in adopting the language of Daniel Webster, we declare 'it is the ancient an
undoubted prerogative of this people to canvass public measures and the merits of public men
It is a 'homebred right,' a fireside privilege. It had been enjoyed in every house, cottage, and cabi
in the nation. It is as undoubted as the right of breathing the air or walking on the earth. Be
longing to private life as a right, it belongs to public life as a duty, and it is the last duty whic
those whose representatives we are shall find us to abandon. Aiming at all times to be courteou
and temperate in its use, except when the right itself is questioned, we shall place ourselves on th
extreme boundary of our own right, and bid defiance to any arm that would move us from ou
ground. 'This high constitutional privilege we shall defend and exercise in all places—in tim
of peace, in time of war, and at all times. Living, we shall assert it; and should we leave no oth
er inheritance to our children, by the blessing of God we will leave them the inheritance of fre
principles, and the example of a manly, independent, and constitutional defense of them.'

"*Resolved*, That in the election of Governor Seymour, the people of this state, by an emphati
majority, declared their condemnation of the system of arbitrary arrests and their determinatio
to stand by the Constitution. That the revival of this lawless system can have but one result—
divide and distract the North, and destroy its confidence in the purposes of the administratio
That we deprecate it as an element of confusion at home, of weakness to our armies in the fiel
and as calculated to lower the estimate of American character, and magnify the apparent peril
our cause abroad. And that, regarding the blow struck at a citizen of Ohio as aimed at th
rights of every citizen of the North, we denounce it as against the spirit of our laws and Const
tution, and most earnestly call upon the President of the United States to reverse the action of th
military tribunal which has passed 'a cruel and unusual punishment' upon the party arrest
prohibited in terms by the Constitution, and to restore him to the liberty of which he has been d
prived.

"*Resolved*, That the president, vice-presidents, and secretary of this meeting be requested
transmit a copy of these resolutions to his excellency the President of the United States, with th
assurance of this meeting of their hearty and earnest desire to support the government in eve
constitutional and lawful measure to suppress the existing rebellion."

President Lincoln's Reply.

"Executive Mansion, Washington, June 12, 1863.

"Hon. Erastus Corning, and others:

"GENTLEMEN,—Your letter of May 19, inclosing the resolutions of a public meeting held a
Albany, New York, on the 16th of the same month, was received several days ago.

"The resolutions, as I understand them, are resolvable into two propositions—first, the expression of a purpose to sustain the cause of the Union, to secure peace through victory, and to support the administration in every constitutional and lawful measure to suppress the rebellion; and, secondly, a declaration of censure upon the administration for supposed unconstitutional action, such as the making of military arrests. And, from the two propositions, a third is deduced, which is, that the gentlemen composing the meeting are resolved on doing their part to maintain our common government and country, despite the folly or wickedness, as they may conceive, of any administration. This position is eminently patriotic, and, as such, I thank the meeting and congratulate the nation for it. My own purpose is the same; so that the meeting and myself have a common object, and can have no difference, except in the choice of means or measures for effecting that object.

"And here I ought to close this paper, and would close it if there were no apprehension that more injurious consequences than any merely personal to myself might follow the censures systematically cast upon me for doing what, in my view of duty, I could not forbear. The resolutions promise to support me in every constitutional and lawful measure to suppress the rebellion, and I have not knowingly employed, nor shall knowingly employ, any other. But the meeting, by their resolutions, assert and argue that certain military arrests, and proceedings following them, for which I am ultimately responsible, are unconstitutional. I think they are not. The resolutions quote from the Constitution the definition of treason, and also the limiting safeguards and guarantees therein provided for the citizen on trials of treason, and on his being held to answer for capital or otherwise infamous crimes, and, in criminal prosecutions, his right to a speedy and public trial by an impartial jury. They proceed to resolve 'that these safeguards of the rights of the citizen against the pretensions of arbitrary power were intended more *especially* for his protection in times of civil commotion.' And, apparently to demonstrate the proposition, the resolutions proceed: 'They were secured substantially to the English people *after* years of protracted civil war, and were adopted into our Constitution at the *close* of the Revolution.' Would not the demonstration have been better if it could have been truly said that these safeguards had been adopted and applied *during* the civil wars and *during* our Revolution, instead of *after* the one and at the *close* of the other? I, too, am devotedly for them *after* civil war, and *before* civil war, and at all times 'except when, in cases of rebellion or invasion, the public safety may require' their suspension. The resolutions proceed to tell us that these safeguards 'have stood the test of seventy-six years of trial under our republican system, under circumstances which show that, while they constitute the foundation of all free government, they are elements of the enduring stability of the republic.' No one denies that they have so stood the test up to the beginning of the present rebellion, if we except a certain occurrence at New Orleans, nor does any one question that they will stand the same test much longer after the rebellion closes. But these provisions of the Constitution have no application to the case we have in hand, because the arrests complained of were not made for treason—that is, not for *the* treason defined in the Constitution, and upon conviction of which the punishment is death; nor yet were they made to hold persons to answer for any capital or otherwise infamous crimes; nor were the proceedings following, in any constitutional or legal sense, 'criminal prosecutions.' The arrests were made on totally different grounds, and the proceedings following accorded with the grounds of the arrests. Let us consider the real case with which we are dealing, and apply to it the parts of the Constitution plainly made for such cases.

"Prior to my installation here it had been inculcated that any state had a lawful right to secede from the national Union, and that it would be expedient to exercise the right whenever the devotees of the doctrine should fail to elect a President to their own liking. I was elected contrary to their liking; and, accordingly, so far as it was legally possible, they had taken seven states out of the Union, had seized many of the United States forts, and had fired upon the United States flag, all before I was inaugurated, and, of course, before I had done any official act whatever. The rebellion thus began soon ran into the present civil war; and, in certain respects, it began on very unequal terms between the parties. The insurgents had been preparing for it more than thirty years, while the government had taken no steps to resist them. The former had carefully considered all the means which could be turned to their account. It undoubtedly was a well-pondered reliance with them that, in their own unrestricted efforts to destroy Union, Constitution, and law all together, the government would, in great degree, be restrained by the same Constitution and law from arresting their progress. Their sympathizers pervaded all departments of the government, and nearly all communities of the people. From this material, under cover of 'liberty of speech,' 'liberty of the press,' and '*habeas corpus*,' they hoped to keep on foot among us a most efficient corps of spies, informers, suppliers, and aiders and abettors of their cause in a thousand ways. They knew that in times such as we were now inaugurating, by the Constitution itself the '*habeas corpus*' might be suspended; but they also knew they had friends who would make a question as to who was to suspend it; meanwhile their spies and others might remain at large to help on their cause. Or if, as has happened, the executive should suspend the writ, without ruinous

* *Hansard's Debates*, 3d Series, vol. 100, p. 635.

The Chicago *Times* was suppressed, and a military guard placed over the office; and the circulation of the New York *World* was prohibited within the lines of the department. These latter acts were soon afterward annulled by the President.

The most important measure adopted in the last session of the Thirty-seventh Congress was the act of conscription. It was one of the latest acts passed by this Congress. Almost a year had passed since the Confederate government had resorted to conscription as a means of recruiting its armies. Hitherto no such measure had been adopted by the national government. But the time had now come when both necessity and justice demanded its adoption.

The necessity of such a measure was obvious. Over a million of men had volunteered for periods varying from three months to three years.[1] Of these there remained in the service between 600,000 and 700,000. About 160,000 of those who had disappeared from the field had been enlisted for three or nine months. Over one fourth, therefore, of those who had volunteered had been killed or wounded in battle, had become the victims of disease, had been discharged for physical disability, or had deserted. The large number of men drawn from industrial pursuits had increased the demand for labor, and the price thereof. The depreciation of the national currency had still farther increased the price of labor. These circumstances, taken in connection with the diminution of martial enthusiasm, made it impossible any longer to depend upon volunteers.

But, apart from this consideration, it was not fitting that the entire burden of the battle should be borne by those alone whose patriotism was sufficient for the sacrifice. Especially in a struggle which involved national honor, and even national existence, was it the duty of the government to insist upon its claim to the military service of every able-bodied citizen. By enrolling the entire militia of the states, which would thus become the grand reserve of the army, and by drafting from the whole number as many men, and at such periods, as the exigencies of the service might demand, seemed both the most efficient and the most impartial method of obtaining recruits. There could be no question either as to the constitutional power of Congress to enroll the militia, or as to the power of the executive, with the consent of Congress, to make requisition by draft. The Constitution authorizes Congress—

"To provide for calling forth the militia to execute the laws of the Union, suppress insurrections, and repel invasions;

---

waste of time, instances of arresting innocent persons might occur, as are always likely to occur in such cases, and then a clamor could be raised in regard to this which might be, at least, of some service to the insurgent cause. It needed no very keen perception to discover this part of the enemy's programme so soon as by open hostilities their machinery was fairly put in motion. Yet, thoroughly imbued with a reverence for the guaranteed rights of individuals, I was slow to adopt the strong measures which, by degrees, I have been forced to regard as being within the exceptions of the Constitution, and as indispensable to the public safety. Nothing is better known to history than that courts of justice are utterly incompetent to such cases. Civil courts are organized chiefly for trials of individuals, or, at most, a few individuals acting in concert, and this in quiet times, and on charges of crimes well defined in the law. Even in times of peace bands of horse-thieves and robbers frequently grow too numerous and powerful for ordinary courts of justice. But what comparison, in numbers, have such bands ever borne to the insurgent sympathizers even in many of the loyal states? Again, a jury too frequently has at least one member more ready to hang the panel than to hang the traitor. And yet, again, he who dissuades one man from volunteering, or induces one soldier to desert, weakens the Union cause as much as he who kills a Union soldier in battle. Yet this dissuasion or inducement may be so conducted as to be no defined crime of which any civil court would take cognizance.

"Ours is a case of rebellion—so called by the resolutions before me—in fact, a clear, flagrant, and gigantic case of rebellion; and the provision of the Constitution that 'the privilege of the writ of *habeas corpus* shall not be suspended, unless when, in cases of rebellion or invasion, the public safety may require it, is *the* provision which specially applies to our present case. This provision plainly attests the understanding of those who made the Constitution that ordinary courts of justice are inadequate to 'cases of rebellion'—attests their purpose that, in such cases, men may be held in custody whom the courts, acting on ordinary rules, would discharge. *Habeas corpus* does not discharge men who are proved to be guilty of defined crime; and its suspension is allowed by the Constitution on purpose that men may be arrested and held who can not be proved to be guilty of defined crime, 'when, in cases of rebellion or invasion, the public safety may require it.'

"This is precisely our present case—a case of rebellion, wherein the public safety does require the suspension. Indeed, arrests by process of courts, and arrests in cases of rebellion, do not proceed altogether upon the same basis. The former is directed at the small percentage of ordinary and continuous perpetration of crime, while the latter is directed at sudden and extensive uprisings against the government, which, at most, will succeed or fail in no great length of time. In the latter case, arrests are made not so much for what has been done as for what probably would be done. The latter is more for the preventive and less for the vindictive than the former. In such cases the purposes of men are much more easily understood than in cases of ordinary crime. The man who stands by and says nothing when the peril of his government is discussed can not be misunderstood. If not hindered, he is sure to help the enemy; much more if he talks ambiguously—talks for his country with 'buts,' and 'ifs,' and 'ands.' Of how little value the constitutional provisions I have quoted will be rendered if arrests shall never be made until defined crimes shall have been committed may be illustrated by a few notable examples. General John C. Breckinridge, General Robert E. Lee, General Joseph E. Johnston, General John B. Magruder, General William B. Preston, General Simon B. Buckner, and Commodore Franklin Buchanan, now occupying the very highest places in the rebel war service, were all within the power of the government since the war began, and were nearly as well known to be traitors then as now. Unquestionably, if we had seized and held them, the insurgent cause would be much weaker. But no one of them had then committed any crime defined in the law. Every one of them, if arrested, would have been discharged on *habeas corpus*, were the writ allowed to operate. In view of these and similar cases, I think the time not unlikely to come when I shall be blamed for having made too few arrests rather than too many.

"By the third resolution the meeting indicate their opinion that military arrests may be constitutional in localities where rebellion actually exists, but that such arrests are unconstitutional in localities where rebellion or insurrection does not actually exist. They insist that such arrests shall not be made 'outside of the lines of necessary military occupation and the scenes of insurrection.' Inasmuch, however, as the Constitution itself makes no such distinction, I am unable to believe that there is any such constitutional distinction. I concede that the class of arrests complained of can be constitutional only when, in cases of rebellion or invasion, the public safety may require them; and I insist that in such cases they are constitutional *wherever* the public safety does require them, as well in places to which they may prevent the rebellion extending as in those where it may be already prevailing; as well where they may restrain mischievous interference with the raising and supplying of armies to suppress the rebellion, as where the rebellion may actually be; as well where they may restrain the enticing men out of the army, as where they would prevent mutiny in the army; equally constitutional at all places where they will conduce to the public safety, as against the dangers of rebellion or invasion. Take the peculiar case mentioned by the meeting. It is asserted, in substance, that Mr. Vallandigham was, by a military commander, seized and tried 'for no other reason than words addressed to a public meeting, in criticism of the course of the administration, and in condemnation of the military orders of the general.' Now, if there be no mistake about this; if this assertion is the truth and the whole truth; if there was no other reason for the arrest, then I concede that the arrest was wrong. But the arrest, as I understand, was made for a very different reason. Mr. Vallandigham avows his hostility to the war on the part of the Union; and his arrest was made because he was laboring, with some effect, to prevent the raising of troops, to encourage desertions from the army, and to leave the rebellion without an adequate military force to suppress it. He was not arrested because he was damaging the political prospects of the administration or the personal interests of the commanding general, but because he was damaging the army, upon the existence and vigor of which the life of the nation depends. He was warring upon the military, and this gave the military constitutional jurisdiction to lay hands upon him. If Mr. Vallandigham was not damaging the military power of the country, then his arrest was made on mistake of fact, which I would be glad to correct on reasonably satisfactory evidence.

"I understand the meeting, whose resolutions I am considering, to be in favor of suppressing the rebellion by military force—by armies. Long experience has shown that armies can not be maintained unless desertion shall be punished by the severe penalty of death. The case requires, and the law and the Constitution sanction, this punishment. Must I shoot a simple-minded soldier-boy who deserts, while I must not touch a hair of a wily agitator who induces him to desert? This is none the less injurious when effected by getting a father, or brother, or friend into a public meeting, and there working upon his feelings till he is persuaded to write the soldier-boy that he is fighting in a bad cause, for a wicked administration of a contemptible government, too weak to arrest and punish him if he shall desert. I think that, in such a case, to silence the agitator and save the boy is not only constitutional, but, withal, a great mercy.

"If I be wrong on this question of constitutional power, my error lies in believing that certain proceedings are constitutional when, in cases of rebellion or invasion, the public safety requires them, which would not be constitutional when, in absence of rebellion or invasion, the public safety does not require them; in other words, that the Constitution is not, in its application, in all respects the same in cases of rebellion or invasion involving the public safety, as it is in times of profound peace and public security. The Constitution itself makes the distinction; and I can no more be persuaded that the government can constitutionally take no strong measures in time of rebellion, because it can be shown that the same could not be lawfully taken in time of peace, than I can be persuaded that a particular drug is not good medicine for a sick man because it can be shown not to be good food for a well one. Nor am I able to appreciate the danger apprehended by the meeting, that the American people will, by means of military arrests during the rebellion, lose the right of public discussion, the liberty of speech and the press, the law of evidence, trial by jury, and *habeas corpus*, throughout the indefinite peaceful future which I trust lies before them, any more than I am able to believe that a man could contract so strong an appetite for emetics during temporary illness as to persist in feeding upon them during the remainder of his healthful life.

"In giving the resolutions that earnest consideration which you request of me, I can not overlook the fact that the meeting speak as 'Democrats.' Nor can I, with full respect for their known intelligence, and the fairly presumed deliberation with which they prepared their resolutions, be permitted to suppose that this occurred by accident, or in any way other than that they preferred to designate themselves 'Democrats' rather than 'American citizens.' In this time of national peril I would have preferred to meet you on a level one step higher than any party platform, because I am sure that, from such more elevated position, we could do better battle for the country we all love than we possibly can from those lower ones where, from the force of habit, the prejudices of the past, and selfish hopes of the future, we are sure to expend much of our ingenuity and strength in finding fault with, and aiming blows at, each other. But, since you have denied me this, I will yet be thankful, for the country's sake, that not all Democrats have done so. He on whose discretionary judgment Mr. Vallandigham was arrested and tried is a Democrat, having no old party affinity with me; and the judge who rejected the constitutional view expressed in these resolutions, by refusing to discharge Mr. Vallandigham on *habeas corpus*, is a Democrat of better days than these, having received his judicial mantle at the hands of President Jackson. And still more, of all those Democrats who are nobly exposing their lives and shedding their blood on the battle-field, I have learned that many approve the course taken with Mr. Vallandigham, while I have not heard of a single one condemning it. I can not assert that there are none such. And the name of President Jackson recalls an instance of pertinent history. After the battle of New Orleans, and while the fact that the treaty of peace had been concluded was well known in the city, but before official knowledge of it had arrived, General Jackson still maintained martial or military law. Now, that it could be said the war was over, the clamor against martial law, which had existed from the first, grew more furious. Among other things, a Mr. Louaillier published a denunciatory newspaper article. General Jackson arrested him. A lawyer by the name of Morel procured the U. S. Judge Hall to order a writ of *habeas corpus* to relieve Mr. Louaillier. General Jackson arrested both the lawyer and the judge. A Mr. Hollander ventured to say of some part of the matter that 'it was a dirty trick.' General Jackson arrested him. When the officer undertook to serve the writ of *habeas corpus*, General Jackson took it from him, and sent him away with a copy. Holding the judge in custody a few days, the general sent him beyond the limits of his encampment, and set him at liberty, with an order to remain till the ratification of peace should be regularly announced, or until the British should have left the southern coast. A day or two more elapsed, the ratification of the treaty of peace was regularly announced, and the judge and others were fully liberated. A few days more, and the judge called General Jackson into court and fined him $1000 for having arrested him and the others named. The General paid the fine, and there the matter rested for nearly thirty years, when Congress refunded principal and interest. The late Senator Douglas, then in the House of Representatives, took a leading part in the debates, in which the constitutional question was much discussed. I am not prepared to say whom the journals would show to have voted for the measure.

"It may be remarked, First, that we had the same Constitution then as now; secondly, that we then had a case of invasion, and now we have a case of rebellion; and, thirdly, that the permanent right of the people to public discussion, the liberty of speech and the press, the trial by jury, the law of evidence, and the *habeas corpus*, suffered no detriment whatever by that conduct of General Jackson, or its subsequent approval by the American Congress.

"And yet let me say that, in my own discretion, I do not know whether I should have ordered the arrest of Mr. Vallandigham. While I can not shift the responsibility from myself, I hold that, as a general rule, the commander in the field is the better judge of the necessity in any particular case. Of course, I must practice a general directory and revisory power in the matter.

"One of the resolutions expresses the opinion of the meeting that arbitrary arrests will have the effect to divide and distract those who should be united in suppressing the rebellion, and I am specifically called on to discharge Mr. Vallandigham. I regard this as, at least, a fair appeal to me on the expediency of exercising a constitutional power which I think exists. In response to such appeal, I have to say, it gave me pain when I learned that Mr. Vallandigham had been arrested—that is, I was pained that there should have seemed to be a necessity for arresting him—and that it will afford me great pleasure to discharge him so soon as I can, by any means, believe the public safety will not suffer by it.

"I farther say, that as the war progresses, it appears to me opinion and action, which were in great confusion at first, take shape and fall into more regular channels, so that the necessity for strong dealing with them gradually decreases. I have every reason to desire that it should cease altogether, and far from the least is my regard for the opinion and wishes of those who, like the meeting at Albany, declare their purpose to sustain the government in every constitutional and lawful measure to suppress the rebellion. Still, I must continue to do so much as may seem to be required for the public safety.

A. LINCOLN."

[1] It is impossible to calculate exactly the number of volunteers in 1861 and 1862, but the following table gives an approximate estimate:

STATES.	3 Months.	9 Months.	3 Years.	Total.
Maine	779	7,493	24,771	33,043
New Hampshire	800	2,023	14,915	17,738
Vermont	782	4,777	13,457	19,006
Massachusetts	3,736	16,896	50,406	71,038
Rhode Island	3,147	2,069	9,410	14,626
Connecticut	2,340	5,697	20,182	28,219
New York	15,922		176,788	192,705
New Jersey	3,105	10,714	16,395	30,214
Pennsylvania	20,979	15,100	164,257	194,558
Ohio	26,893		143,228	170,121
Indiana	4,698		93,840	104,316
Illinois	4,901		130,539	135,440
Michigan	780		44,890	45,670
Wisconsin	810	491	39,345	40,646
Minnesota	930	1,200	10,136	12,266
Iowa	959		47,855	48,814
Missouri			27,407	27,407
Kentucky		878	41,163	42,041
Delaware	No Returns.			
Maryland				
Virginia				
Tennessee				
California				
	91,561	67,335	1,068,769	1,227,758

This estimate does not include 30,131 men enlisted in New York for two years, 2589 twelve-months' men enlisted in Pennsylvania, nor 15,858 men raised for the defense of Maine, Pennsylvania, Missouri, and Kentucky. Including these, the grand total reaches 1,276,331.

. "To provide for organizing, arming, and disciplining the militia, and for governing such part of them as may be employed in the service of the United States, reserving to the states respectively the appointment of the officers, and the authority of training the militia according to the discipline prescribed by Congress."

With the exception of official appointments and the authority of training the militia, the state governments, under the Constitution, have nothing whatsoever to do with the raising of armies for the United States service.

On the 5th of February a bill for enrolling and drafting the militia was reported to the Senate by Mr. Wilson, of Massachusetts, chairman of the Committee on Military Affairs. The batteries of the opposition were immediately opened against it. As there was no valid constitutional objection to the bill, it is fair to consider the attempt on the part of certain members in the two houses to defeat it as an indication of their opposition to the war itself. Apart from this, they were also influenced by a political motive of the most contemptible sort. They knew that so long as the nation depended upon volunteers its armies would be filled from the ranks of those who heartily supported the administration, while those who were politically opposed to the war would remain at home, and support by their votes the opposition party. If, however, the government called upon all its citizens alike, in the method proposed by this bill, then the soldiers would be drawn in just proportion from among the supporters and opponents of the administration. The bill would also, if successful, defeat the purposes of the opposition leaders, who hoped to see the army dwindle away under the volunteer system, which, they knew, must prove inadequate. It is easy to understand, therefore, how these men in Congress pronounced the bill one "of doubtful propriety and doubtful constitutionality," "despotic," "conferring upon the President of the United States more power than belongs to any despot in Europe or any where else."[1] This bill passed the Senate, the yeas and nays not being called. The vote on Mr. Bayard's motion, that the measure be indefinitely postponed, shows the exact strength of the opposition. Eleven Democrats voted in favor of postponement; 35 voted against it, including every Republican present, with Messrs. McDougall, of California, and Harding and Nesmith, of Oregon.

The bill came up for consideration in the House on the 23d of February. The same objections were urged which had been offered in the Senate. Mr. Thomas, of Maryland, who was strongly opposed to emancipation, to the use of negro soldiers, and to confiscation, but who yet had no sympathy with rebellion, supported the measure as necessary.[2] Mr. Crittenden, of Kentucky, while agreeing with Mr. Thomas as to the causes of the difficulty ex enced by the government in sustaining its military strength by the v teer system, still opposed the measure.[1] The bill was finally passed, o 3d of March, by a vote of 115 to 49.

¹ In the Senate Mr. Wilson strongly urged the passage of the bill. "We are now," he said, "engaged in a gigantic struggle for the preservation of the life of the nation, menaced by the foulest and most wicked rebellion recorded in the annals of mankind. The young men of the republic for more than twenty months have been thronging to the field to uphold the cause of their periled country. They left their homes in the pride and bloom, and filled with the high hopes of young manhood. Those noble regiments of volunteers that left their homes full of lusty life, and in all the pride and strength of assured manhood, are now thinned and wasted by the diseases of the camp and the storms of battle.

"The old regiments hardly average now more than four hundred men in the field fit for the stern duties of war. Many who rallied at the call of their country, and who followed its flag with unswerving devotion, now sleep in bloody graves, or linger in hospitals, or, bending beneath disease and wounds, can no longer fill the ranks of our legions in camp or on the battle-field. If we mean to maintain the supremacy of the Constitution and the laws, if we mean to preserve the unity of the republic, if we mean that America shall live and have a position and name among the nations, we must fill the broken and thinned ranks of our wasted battalions.

"The issue is now clearly presented to the country for the acceptance or rejection of the American people—an inglorious peace, with a dismembered Union and a broken nation on the one hand, or war, fought out until the rebellion is crushed beneath its iron heel. Patriotism, as well as freedom, humanity, and religion, accepts the bloody issues of war, rather than peace purchased with the dismemberment of the republic and the death of the nation.

"If we accept peace, disunion, death, then we may speedily summon home again our armies; if we accept war until the flag of the republic waves over every foot of our united country, then we must see to it that the ranks of our armies, broken by toil, disease, and death, are filled again with the health and vigor of life. To fill the thinned ranks of our battalions we must again call upon the people. The immense numbers already summoned to the field, the scarcity and high rewards of labor, press upon all of us the conviction that the ranks of our wasted regiments can not be filled again by the old system of volunteering. If volunteers will not respond to the call of the country, than we must resort to the involuntary system."

² "The policy," said he, "inaugurated on the 1st of December, 1861, has been fruitless of good. It has changed the ostensible, if not the real issue of the war. That policy, and the want of persistent vigor in our military counsels, render any farther reliance upon voluntary enlistments futile. The nostrums have all failed. Confiscation, emancipation by Congress, emancipation by the proclamation of the President, compensated emancipation, arbitrary arrests, paper made legal tender, negro armies, will not do the mighty work. Nothing will save us now but victories in the field and on the sea, and then the proffer of the olive-branch, with the most liberal terms of reconciliation and reunion. We can get armies in no other way but by measures substantially those in the bill before us, unless the administration will retrace its steps, and return to the way of the Constitution—for us the strait and narrow way which leads unto life. At any rate, the war on paper is at an end. The people have, for a time, been deluded by it. That delusion exists no longer. If you are to suppress this rebellion, all instrumentalities will fail you but the power of your own right arm. Mr. Speaker, the measures and policy heretofore pursued have not been merely fruitless of good, they have been fruitful of evil. They have made, or largely contributed to make, a united South; they have made for you a divided North; they have alienated from the administration the confidence and affection of large portions of the people; they have paralyzed your arm, and divided your counsels. Gentlemen flatter themselves this alienation and disaffection are the work of Democrats; that the people have been misled and deceived by their wiles. Sir, the people of this country read, and keep their eyes open, and comprehend, and the plain fact is, you can not unite them upon the policy you now pursue. They do not believe in destroying the Union and the Constitution in the hope of building up better by force of arms. You may unite them on the issue of maintaining the Union and the government at every price and cost, but upon no other.

"Having distracted the public mind, having alienated to a great degree the affection and confidence of the country, what is left to you? To resort to those constitutional powers vested in you for the preservation of the government which you have in trust, and which you must use or be false to that trust. Gentleman say the people will not bear this measure. I will not believe it. I believe the people of this country are ready to do and to endure every thing for the preservation of their unity, their national life, and, through that unity and that national life, all that makes life precious to men. They will submit to it. In view of the infinite interests at stake in this great controversy; in the solemn conviction that there is to-day no hope of peace except in disintegration; that as a nation we must conquer in arms or perish, they will meet and respond to this imperative call of duty. Such is my hope and trust.

"But, Mr. Speaker, suppose they hesitate; suppose they do not submit; you can but try; you have no other hope; the negro will not save you, paper money will not save you, your infractions of personal liberty will not save you. If persisted in in the peaceful and loyal states, they will ruin you. Go firmly to the people, and present to them the issue. They will understand the terrible exigency in which the country is placed, and they will be true to that country if you show clearly to their comprehension the length, and breadth, and height, and depth of that exigency. Mr. Speaker, the issue must be met at all hazards. If the people will not support you, if they will not do this highest act of duty, the days of this republic are numbered, and the end is nigh. Satisfy them that you mean to be true to the Constitution and the Union, and they will be true to you.

"The issue, I repeat, must be met. You die without this measure; you can do no more with it, except you die, as cowards die, many times. I go, therefore, for appealing from these panaceas, and makeshifts, and paper bullets, to this highest, most solemn, and imperative duty of the c to protect the life of the state, and I believe that appeal will be answered."

¹ "The measure, it seems to me," said he, "is but the natural result of the course of which this Congress has pursued from the commencement, or very near the commencement o war.

"When this war first broke out, it was a national war, with a single national object; and that one purpose and object all hearts were united. That object was the re-establishment o great republic—our republic. Upon that great object, I repeat, we were all united. There w division; and in order to satisfy the country more effectually of the fact of our unity, but more than eighteen months ago a resolution offered by me was passed, almost unanimously, de ing that this was our sole object. We then declared that this was our only object. We ple ourselves that no interference should be made in any of the institutions of the states having s cial reference to the institution of slavery.

"Mr. Speaker, had the pledges then solemnly made by this Congress been adhered to, how ferent would be the condition of the country to-day! There was then but one sentiment pe ing the whole people of the country. The people then flocked to your standard by hundre thousands, filling the ranks of such an army as the world never saw. There was then bu sentiment in the people of the country. No coercion was then talked of. What has prod the change that now presents itself? What, as my friend from Massachusetts says, has unite South in one solid iron phalanx? What has crushed out, and destroyed to a great extent, i wholly, the confidence and enthusiasm that swelled up in the heart of the people of the na What has done all this? It is our departing from our faith. It is our departing from that c which we declared to be the only just and patriotic one. What else has done it? Have yo departed from the policy of that faith? Have you not, in a manner considered perfidious, vio pledges which you gave the country more than eighteen months ago? Was there any disco expressed at that time? I heard of none. The hearts of the loyal people North and South fired with a common purpose to preserve the integrity and honor of the republic. Every ma himself under every honorable obligation to step forward, and abandon his private affairs, and after the welfare of the Union. That was the undivided, pervading, patriotic sentiment o whole body of the people. Nowhere in the North or Northwest was heard a murmur of dis tent; and the same confidence and patriotic feeling was as strong among the Union men o border states as it was any where in the North and West. It was every where the same. were willing to suffer to the last extremity to preserve the government. That was the feelin the people then; we all know it.

"What has brought this mighty change? What has done it, Mr. Speaker? Do not w know? Can there be any doubt on the subject? It has been our infidelity to the pledges to the people. It has been because of the reckless course of the dominant power. It is bec of the impolicy of which Congress has been guilty. Is it not time to learn that the course we pursued and are pursuing has produced a state of division and dissension even in the remai states? Yes, sir, the policy that has been recently pursued has been the fruitful source of disastrous dissensions. It has been our departure from our policy of not attacking the instit of slavery, and fighting only for the government, for the Union, and the Constitution.

"What have we seen at this session? We have passed bills changing the rules and article war in order that slavery might be encroached upon. We deprive the loyal people of the S of all protection by the army for their property. You have passed a law taking the slaves any of the citizens of the country. You have passed a law for organizing an army of three h red thousand negroes. This, you know, is against the deep-rooted prejudices of at least one our people. Such a bill would have been rejected with one common voice eighteen months Even the mention of the subject created profound indignation. You have done this and m You have passed laws, in the opinion of the people, which violate the Constitution. You scorned the friends of the government. You have turned away from us the hearts of the pe by these measures. We have sown deep the seeds of future disasters to the government. I plore the House to pause before it sanctions any more measures of that kind.

"Mr. Speaker, can we carry on the war more successfully by transcending the Constitu than we can by obeying it? I have always said that the Constitution was our bulwark; th was the best defense; that our strongest defense was to keep within the clearly-defined powers that instrument. But what have we done? We have assumed powers not delegated by the C stitution. We have acted, not according to the provisions of the Constitution, but according the sentiment which actuated us at the moment. We seem to have been controlled by the p spirit of party rather than by the spirit of patriotism and a determination to obey the Constitu and the laws. You have lost the heart of the people, and you have lost it by the dogmas have inaugurated and established rather than follow the Constitution.

"The gentleman from Pennsylvania (Mr. Stevens) said the other day that we have every n in the field that we can get voluntarily. Why is that? Because the object is clearly proclaim of abolishing slavery throughout the United States. You have done this while you have had accidental majority here. Hence it is that the people have changed. This is the only time wh that party ever had a majority in the House—I mean a majority of Abolitionists. With this ac dental power, what has it done? It has declared emancipation by law. It has declared by l for the raising of negro armies. It has declared emancipation and confiscation by law. By th means, I say, you have lost the hearts of the people. Why do not the people have the same ent siasm in the war that they had at first? Then they put a million of men into the field. T country is still in peril, in more peril than at first, and why is not an army of two million n now put into the field? It is only because of the bad policy by which you have established dogmas of the Abolitionists, of emancipation of slavery throughout the country. It is that wh has induced them to lose confidence in you. It is not for the country, it is not for the white m it is for the negro this war is to be waged; and for that war I am not. The logical conclus from the impolitic course we have pursued is, that we have lost the hearts of the people.

"You say that this bill is framed on the idea that the people will no longer volunteer—that people will no longer stand a draft. Why not? Because the people will not do one thing another; they will neither volunteer nor stand a draft, and you are obliged by law to coerce the That is the condition in which we are placed, and this bill is nothing more than the logical c clusion of what we have previously done. We have created a necessity for it. The people are longer with us, and therefore we must force the people, by coercive and penal laws, by new ju dictions, provost-marshals scattered through the land, and by a new sort of military judicature which the people have not been accustomed. And knowing that you have an unwilling people deal with, you make that law as coercive as possible, and accompany it with every sort of inqu torial and compulsory power, judicial and executive, in order to insure obedience, willing or unw ling, to that law. Is not that our condition fairly considered?

"There is but one sort of consistency which deserves the respect of honest men, and that is let your acts be consistent with your convictions at the time you are called upon to vote. It is what we did yesterday that we are to consider alone. We have lived through a time of trial a of trouble. Have we learned nothing? Up to this time I fear we have learned very little. O lessons have been very severe, and the fear of more dangerous lessons hereafter ought to insin us. The life of the country is attacked, and that life is upon your hands, and its preservation pends in a great measure upon your wisdom, upon your solemn deliberations, and your sole consideration of all the mighty questions upon us.

"If we want to get back the Union, how must we do it? We must change our policy. T will not answer your purpose. You must get back what you have lost. You have lost the he of the people, and the confidence of the people. The people's affections are turned away from and will they bear more exactions and burdens laid upon them? No, sir; you are mistaken the remedy. Your only remedy is to regain the confidence and heart of the people, to substi for the distrust which now exists confidence that your object is a national one, and not a me public one; not the abolition of slavery, but the salvation of the country. Get that back, and y do not want this bill; fail to get it back, and this bill will be just as inoperative as if there was a word written upon it.

"You say a draft will not do; that a draft will not be submitted to. I know nothing abo that. Will, then, this more exacting provision be submitted to? In a country like ours, la which do not carry along with them the assent of the people are but blank paper. Have you n cause to fear that unless you win back the hearts of the people, and their confidence, this bill w do no good? You are mistaking the disease altogether. The disease of the public heart is l of confidence in us, members of Congress. It is the Abolition element here which has destroy every thing; that has clouded the great ideas of nationality—the pride of the American heart.

"That is the disease of the public heart, and you should endeavor to administer measu which will reclaim it, and that will heal discontent. And yet in the last moments of our existen you are endeavoring to consummate a policy which the people have condemned, and to put t people beyond the means of redress. The remedy, and the sole remedy, is by reversion, by retra ing our steps, and making this again a national war. Then you will not want this bill, nor w you want a draft. You will have volunteers enough. I do not speak rashly, because you had vo unteers enough, and more than you know what to do with, when you stood upon that groun But you chose to change that ground. Political abolitionists thought the time had come for the to introduce the sword and the spear into the public arena, and to make use of this war to car out the ends which they have long cherished—the abolition of slavery."

OWEN LOVEJOY.

This act, as passed by Congress, included, as a part of the national forces, all able-bodied male citizens of the United States between the ages of twenty-one and forty-five years, except such as should be rejected as physically or mentally unfit for the service. The militia thus enrolled were to be divided into two classes—the first to contain those under thirty-five and all unmarried persons under forty-five; the second, all others liable to military duty. The country was to be divided into districts, in each of which an enrollment board was to be established. Those enrolled were subject to be called into service for two years from July 1st, 1863, and to continue in service for three years. Any person drafted might furnish an acceptable substitute, or pay $300, and be discharged from farther liability under that draft. Those who, after being drafted, failed to report, were to be treated as deserters. No choice was given to those drafted as to the corps or regiment, or as to the branch of the service in which they should serve.[1]

In the House a bill had already been passed, 83 to 54, authorizing the President "to enroll, arm, and equip, and receive into the land or naval service of the United States, such numbers of volunteers of African descent as he may deem useful to suppress the present rebellion, for such term as he may prescribe, not exceeding five years." This bill was not passed by the Senate, on the ground that the authority thereby granted had already been given in the act of July 17, 1862.

Early in the session a discussion was opened in the House which brought out an expression of views as to the position of the insurgent states in their relation to the general government. On the 8th of January, the appropriation bill being under consideration, an amendment was offered to add to the clause for the compensation of thirty-three revenue commissioners and twelve clerks (with salaries amounting to $112,000) a proviso that their compensation should be collected in the insurgent states. Thaddeus Stevens, of Pennsylvania, insisted that the Constitution did not embrace a state in arms against the government. "The establishment of a blockade," he said, "admitted the Southern States, the Confederates, to be a belligerent power. Foreign nations have all admitted them as a belligerent power. Whenever that came to be admitted by us and by foreign nations, it placed the rebellious states precisely in the position of an alien enemy with regard to duties and obligations." He held, therefore, that all obligations or contracts previously existing between these states and the general government were abrogated, and that the former were to be treated simply in accordance with the laws of war. "With regard to all the Southern states in rebellion the Constitution has no binding influence and no application." In his opinion these states were not members of the Union, nor under the laws of the government. He proposed to levy the tax and collect it as a war measure.

In this expression of opinion Mr. Stevens was not sustained by his party. Abram Olin, of New York, held this doctrine in utter abhorrence—equally unsound and mischievous as that of the so-called right of secession. Mr. Thomas, of Massachusetts, favored the amendment, but would collect the tax under the provisions of the Constitution, "because to-day, as always heretofore, the authority of the national government covers every inch of the territory of the national domain; because that law which we call the

[1] The following persons were exempted: The Vice-President, the judges of United States courts, the heads of executive departments, and the governors of the several states; the only son, liable to military service, of a widow dependent upon his labor for support; the only son of aged or infirm parent or parents dependent upon his labor for support; also, where there are two or more sons of aged or infirm parents subject to draft, the father, or, if he be dead, the mother, may elect which son should be exempt; also the father of motherless children under twelve years of age, dependent upon his labor for support; also, where there were a father and sons in the same family and household, and two of them were in the military service as non-commissioned officers, mu-

Constitution is to-day the supreme law of the land.[1] Mr. Lovejoy, of Illinois, emphatically repudiated Mr. Stevens's theory.[2]

On the 18th of February the bill to provide a national currency came up for consideration in the Senate. The President, in his message, had urged the passage of this bill. It passed the Senate by a majority of two votes—23 to 21—and the House by a vote of 78 to 64.[3]

[1] Mr. Stevens did not claim to speak for his party. "I desire," he said, "to say that I know perfectly well . . . . I do not speak the sentiments of this side of the house as a party. I know more than that: that, for the last fifteen years, I have always been a step ahead of the party I have acted with in these matters; but I have never been so far ahead, with the exception of the principles I now enunciate, but that the members of the party have overtaken me and gone ahead; and they, together with the gentleman from New York (Mr. Olin), will again overtake me, and go with me, before this infamous and bloody rebellion is ended. They will find that they can not execute the Constitution in the seceding states; that it is a total nullity there, and that this war must be carried on upon principles wholly independent of it. They will come to the conclusion that the adoption of the measures I advocated at the outset of the war—the arming of the negroes, the slaves of the rebels—is the only way left on earth by which these rebels can be exterminated. They will find that they must treat those states now outside of the Union as conquered provinces, and settle them with new men, and drive the present rebels as exiles from this country; for I tell you they have the pluck and endurance for which I gave them credit a year and a half ago, in a speech which I made, but which was not relished on this side of the house, nor by the people in the free states. They have such determination, energy, and endurance, that nothing but actual extermination, or exile, or starvation will ever induce them to surrender to this government. I do not now ask gentlemen to indorse my views, nor do I speak for any body but myself; but, in order that I may have some credit for sagacity, I ask that gentlemen will write this down in their memories. It will not be two years before they will call it up, or before they will adopt my views, or adopt the other alternative of a disgraceful submission by this side of the country."

[2] "I repudiate," said he, "the theory which, if I understand the gentleman from Pennsylvania, is his theory, that, if I own a vessel, the mere fact that pirates come and take possession of it destroys the validity of my title to it. I may not be in possession; I may go and demand the possession to which I am legally and constitutionally entitled, and force may prevent my taking possession; but that does not invalidate my rightful claim.

"I hold that if one third of the citizens of Kentucky are loyal, the state belongs to that third; that if one fourth of the citizens of Tennessee are loyal, the state belongs to that fourth; and that just as soon as the government can enforce their rights, it is bound to enforce them; and the whole machinery of state government can be set going by those who remain, who are loyal, whether one half, one fourth, one tenth, or one hundredth. The right of the federal government never was invalidated, and never ceased for a moment."

[3] The provisions of the bill, the objections to it, and the arguments in its favor, will be best shown by the following speeches of Senators Collamer, of Vermont, and Sherman, of Ohio:

Mr. Collamer opposed the bill. "What," asked he, "are its great purposes and objects as aisted by those who framed, recommended, and support it? It is said to be to institute a great national paper currency through the medium of banks, to be organized under this act, who are to take United States stocks and deposit them in the Treasury, and take ninety per cent. of them in notes to circulate as money, with which to do banking business, and that they shall have twenty-five per cent. more than this circulating part as a permanent capital to work upon. They are to pay two per cent. on their circulation to the United States government annually, or one per cent. every six months, and the United States are to pay them six per cent. per annum on the bonds in gold. The United States further agree that they will take all this money in circulation, receive it for and pay it out on all public dues, and declare it to be in the act a national currency. Besides that, the United States agree that they will guarantee to the bill-holders the payment of these bills at the Treasury. If the banks do not redeem them in currency when asked for their redemption, they may be protested and presented at the Treasury, and the Treasury is to pay them, and to pay them in full, whether the stocks left upon deposit are able to meet them or not. Besides this investment, the property put into those associations is itself to be clear of taxation.

"Now, Mr. President, it is to be further understood, and is an integral part of the very system, without which it is good for nothing, that the circulation of the existing banks of the country is to be withdrawn. Measures are to be taken with those banks that shall induce or compel them to take home their circulation and put it out no more, so that this shall be a national currency. Unless this latter part of the scheme is secured, its great professed object of making a uniform national currency throughout the United States is not and can not be effected. It therefore implies all this, and we must understand that if we enter upon this proposition and entertain this plan, we are to take measures in order to perfect it to do the other thing; that is, to destroy, put out of existence, the circulation of the present state banks.

"The Supreme Court, in the case of McCullough vs. Maryland, decided that the United States had the right to make a United States Bank, with branches in different states, and they said the states could not tax that United States Bank. Why? Because the exercise of that power in the extreme would destroy it, and therefore you would make it out that the Congress had a power to establish a bank; but, after all, it was subject to the power of the states to put it down. In the case of Kentucky, the Supreme Court decided that the long-continued usage in this country in states to make banks was constitutional, and that a state had a right to make a bank of issue. There were other questions in that case which it is not necessary now to bring in here. It was decided that a state had a right, not to make a bank to issue the state paper, but a bank to issue paper currency.

"Now, sir, if a state has that right, it has that right certainly independent of the consent of Congress. Does it hold it at the will of Congress? Certainly not. The United States, in making a United States Bank, held it independent of state action, and it was so decided. If the state has this right, and has it independent of the consent of Congress, it can not have that right if the United States can tax it out of existence. Hence I say the United States has no more power to tax a state institution out of existence than a state has to tax a United States institution out of existence. I should like to see that answered. I have sometimes proposed that question, but I have never received any answer to it. In most of the states, the State of New York, for instance, almost all their banks are founded upon their own state stocks. It is a part of their financial system to make their stocks valuable, and to enable them to make internal improvements. All these state banks are more or less connected with and ramified in with the business of their several states. Can they be taxed out of existence by the United States? Why, sir, you might just as well tell me that the United States, under the power of taxation, could go on and extinguish all the schools in New England by taxing its schools, its colleges, and its academies, and their books, and their buildings, and the salaries of the professors, and in that way destroy them under the very general principle of the power of universal taxation. I shall not dwell any longer upon that point. I have stated my view upon it.

"But, Mr. President, there is another principle involved in this measure, and I am looking at it now in its great national aspects, as a national principle, without regard to the time. I say it is to establish corporations in all the states and Territories, entirely independent of any power of visitation by those states or Territories. This, to say the least of it, is an extremely questionable power. What may be the number of these institutions? As the capital is to be $300,000,000, that will make three thousand banks of $100,000 each; and the bill provides that they may be made $50,000 banks, which will make six thousand $50,000 banks. I believe we have now, in what are called the loyal states, between thirteen and fourteen hundred banks altogether; and this bill proposes to make at least three thousand, or perhaps six thousand of these bank corporations, established all over the states.

"That is not all. It is proposed that there shall be no other banks but these; the whole banking capital is to be put into these banks, and the whole of that property is removed from all state taxation. I ask gentlemen to reflect on what will be the effect in their different states of clearing up the present banks, and taking the capital belonging to the stockholders, putting it into the banks under this bill, and removing the whole of it from all the forms of state taxation—state, county, city, and town. Many of our states derive their school-fund from what they obtain from these state banks. I believe it is so in New Hampshire. They have their school-fund in that way.

"The next point to which I desire to call attention is the propriety of our undertaking as a nation to say that we will be responsible for the ultimate redemption of these bills by the securities that are deposited. I am aware that the honorable senator who is the parent of the bill here thinks he has got in it something very valuable in the provision about the liability of individual stockholders, and requiring twenty-five per cent. of the amount of their circulation to be kept on hand. All these things, to my mind, are hardly worth the paper on which they are written; they are good for nothing at all. How can you follow the responsibility of stockholders? The very stocks are assignable; they are personal property. They are bought and sold in the market every day for more or less, according to their worth. Although one of these banks may start with some very responsible men when it first sets up, the moment it becomes at all doubtful or troublesome it quickly passes off into the hands of men who have no responsibility. You can never pursue it in that way. As to the provision that they shall retain twenty-five per cent. on their circulation on hand, that is their own money; it is not United States money. The fact is just this: whenever your bonds that you hold for your security to redeem these bills depreciate essentially, the

The bill for the admission of West Virginia passed both houses during this session. It first came up before the House of Representatives on the 9th of December, 1862. The senators elected by West Virginia had alr been admitted into the Senate. The question as to the admission of Virginia as a separate state was involved in great difficulty. While it consistent to recognize the Legislature of this portion of Virginia as Legislature of the state, to the exclusion of that assembled at Richmon was still a violation of the Constitution to admit West Virginia as a sepa state. To do this was to take the ground which Mr. Stevens held—that Constitution had no longer any application to the states engaged in re lion. Probably not more than one third of the proposed new state wer favor of its separation from Virginia. But the bill passed the House 9 55, and the Senate without debate.

On the 9th of February, 1868, resolutions were adopted by the House mitting to seats in that body Benjamin F. Flanders and Michael Hahn, el ed from the first and second Congressional districts of Louisiana. The ad tion of these resolutions was a protest on the part of the House against political theories of Thaddeus Stevens.

Resolutions were adopted in both houses toward the close of the sess repudiating foreign mediation in our civil war. These were passed in Senate 31 to 5, and in the House 103 to 28.[1] The occasion for this act

---

that they are very much down; we will not redeem any more of these bills; we will leave them to be redeemed by the government; we gave them $100,000 and deposited it with them in bonds; they only allowed us $90,000; that is all we have had of them; we leave these notes in their hands to redeem; we will let them redeem them; we gave them a great deal more than they ever gave us, and let them redeem them.' When would that occur? Why, sir, in great national calamities such as those under which we already suffer by the unfortunate proceedings of this war, we know that public stocks rise and fall with the prosperity or decline of the nation.

"Again, I will take the very reverse of this state of things. Suppose we should close this unfortunate controversy and return to peace. The moment you are at peace every man wants all the money he has got to go into business. He has lent it to the United States, taken this, that, or the other sort of stock, in order to have it earn something while this public controversy and difficulty was going on. The moment that is ended he wants his money to go into business again in our cities and towns—importing and the like. He immediately cashes these bonds, and a very large portion of these bonds will at once be thrown on the market at a discount the moment you are at peace. In either of these cases, whether from public calamity or from peace, there comes a deterioration upon the value of these bonds; these banks are wound up, the bills are protested and presented to the Treasury here in bundles for payment. What will you do? It is said in the bill that they are to be paid here. You may take the stocks the bank left as security and go and sell them in the market, and thus get money to pay them. If they have deteriorated so much that the banks do not want to pay their bills, it will be a pretty hard bargain for us to pay them with those bonds. We should have to sell at as much discount as they. Besides, we do not get rid of any thing in that way. We have to anticipate our bonds. They run twenty years. We have got to pay these notes when they are presented; and if we sell our bonds at a discount in the market to get some money to redeem them with, we have got to meet that bond in the end, have we not? We do not get rid of it at all; but we are compelled to get the money about twenty years before it is due. I do not see the policy, the expediency, or the profit of such a bargain.

"The next aspect to which I will call attention is this: we once had, or twice had, a United States Bank. The history of the last one is within the recollection of most of those who hear me. That bank had a capital of $35,000,000. The proposition now is to make United States banks with a capital of $300,000,000. The United States took $7,000,000 of that stock. They paid nothing in, but put in their stock for it on time. They had directors of their own appointed to keep watch of that bank. They had the right to borrow money at that bank. The bank was bound to loan it to them at a certain rate and limitation. They went on with that bank during the whole period of its existence. They took their dividends from year to year by extinguishing the payment of interest on their bonds; and at the close of the whole they received back their stock and ten per cent. upon it of accumulated profits that had not been divided. Every body concerned in it was paid, the stock was paid back; and the United States made that money.

"Now, sir, why did that institution go down; or, rather, why was it not renewed, and enlarged, and adapted to the condition of the country? It was because it was said to be a dangerous political engine in the hands of whatever political party existed at the time; that it would be used as a great machine in the different states by the favor which the government would give it, or the control which they would exercise over it; and it was dangerous, as it was said then, and I think it was demonstrable.

"Mr. President, look at the proposition now before us in this aspect. It provides that the Secretary of the Treasury shall nominate the Comptroller of the Currency. He can be appointed by the President only on the nomination of the Secretary of the Treasury; and he is given any number (not limited at all) of clerks and agents. There are established, if you please, three thousand of these banks under this bill, of $100,000 each, scattered through all the country. They can be visited by agents appointed here under this bill, and inspected from time to time, and reported upon. The Secretary is authorized to make such of them as he thinks proper depositories of the public revenue, and he is to distribute this stock, one half of the $300,000,000 to the different states according to their representative population, and the other half according to the banking resources of the country; there is no limitation upon him whatever. If the old United States Bank furnished well-grounded apprehensions of its dangerous political tendency as a political agency, permit me to ask gentlemen to reflect for a moment on what you have got here, with $300,000,000 of capital, with three thousand banks subject to inspection, and to be troubled just as much as the head of the Treasury Department pleases, if they do not support his views; or to receive favors by way of being made depositories for the public dues; and the Secretary having the power to appoint agents and clerks *ad libitum*. I do not wish to enlarge upon this point at all, but I say this: if a Secretary of the Treasury can be furnished with these powers and chooses to use them, he must be a very bungling politician if he can not make himself President any day.

"Then, putting it in plain English, you propose to hire these people to go into these associations, take these bonds, and deposit them. They are to pay two per cent. on their circulation, and you pay them six on their bonds. I will call it four per cent.; though it is more, as the gentleman knows, because the two per cent. they pay in currency, and the six per cent. we pay in gold. The amount of it is this: we say to them, 'If you will do this to the amount of $300,000,000, and put out notes to the extent of ninety per cent. of the bonds, we will pay you $12,000,000 in gold every year for doing it.' You may talk about its being in the form of bonds, but that does not alter it at all. We are to enter into that arrangement with them. If they take their money, buy these bonds, put them on deposit, issue paper to the extent of ninety per cent. of those bonds and circulate it, and pay two per cent. on that circulation, we pay them six on the bonds; that is, we pay them four per cent. on the bonds, if they will do us this great service! There is all there is about it. You may discuss it as you please, and use a great many financial expressions and schemes; but that is the English of it; that is the simple common sense of it. Instead of circulating that amount of our own currency upon our own responsibility and paying nothing, we are to hire them to circulate that amount of our currency, and pay them $12,000,000 a year in gold for doing it; and we are to be responsible after all. That is all there is of it. Yankee as I am, I am unable to perceive how it is possible that that can be a good trade for us, or how any shrewd man would ever think of entering into an agreement of that kind.

"It is said, however, that it is a fair tax in proportion to our other war taxes. Let us look at this for a moment. My neighbor here has $100,000 saved, we will say, and having retired from business, he lives by loaning out that money, and he realizes six per cent. a year on it. How much do we tax him? One hundred and eighty dollars, three per cent. on what he gets. I am going now upon the ground that he has got $6000 income in some other way. We tax him three per cent. on his *gain*; and that is $180, although he has used $100,000. Here are three other neighbors of mine—I will not include myself, because that would make the supposition too improbable—who have $100,000, and they bank with it according to the law of their state. What do they make? Perhaps they make eight per cent. If they do make $8000 on the $100,000, they have to pay a tax of three per cent. on that now, and it goes into the Treasury. But what is the proposition here? The government says to them, 'You have got $100,000 invested in banking; you will therefore probably have about $150,000 of circulation; we will tax you on the $150,000 one per cent. every six months, or two per cent. a year.' How much will that be? Three thousand dollars. 'For the use of your $100,000 in banking you shall pay $3000 a year.' The other man, for the use of his $100,000, pays but $180 a year. Do you call that fair and equal taxation? The one pays $180, while the other, on the same amount of capital, pays $3000. It is perfectly monstrous.

"But, in the next place, I think it a mere matter of figures, and capable of mathematical certainty about this problem of whether banks will be set up in my part of the country under this bill, even if the existing banks are all destroyed. To illustrate it, I will take the plain case of a $100,000 bank, because that is the ordinary size of a country bank in my part of the country, and it is, in round numbers, easy of calculation. You are to take $100,000, go and buy bonds with it, leave them there, and take out $90,000 of circulating notes. As to exchange, that is to be the same all over the country, and that is to be no item in the profit of a bank hereafter.

"Now let us see how it will work. In the first place, I believe I am borne out by examination of experienced men in saying that you can not operate a country bank, or any bank of the amount of $100,000, with less than $2500 per year. Pay your cashier, open your office, warm it, light it, take care of it, pay your expresses, and do all your business, and it can not be done for less than $2500, and that is putting it very low. Now a $100,000 bank, under this bill, will, in the first place, get from the government of the United States $4000 a year interest, after paying the tax. We understand that. They lend the $90,000 which they receive, and they get six per cent. interest on that. That interest would amount to $5400. There is all they can make without stealing. It is all that can be made. What does it cost? It costs $2500 to operate the bank, the ordinary expenses, and they lose the use of $22,500 for that year, because they are to keep on hand twenty-five per cent. on their circulation. They have kept that on hand, and of course the use of it is lost. That is over $1300. That expense and loss makes $3800. The interest from the government and the interest on the $90,000 amounts to $9400. Deducting the one from the other, it leaves $5600. Now what did it make that on? On the $100,000 put in, and the $22,500 which was kept on hand. The investment was $122,500, and the profit is $5600; that is, about four per cent. That is all that can be made under it. They are to run the risk in their loans of all the loanings of $90,000, and getting it out and in, and can not make five per cent., if all works smoothly and there are no losses at all. I say that is not a matter of speculation; that is a matter of certainty. Those figures which I have given in this instance can not lie."

Mr. Sherman, of Ohio, followed in defense of the bill. "That bankers can make a reasonable profit under this bill I have no doubt. They have the benefit of four per cent. on the bonds deposited by them. They have the benefit of interest on the notes given them for circulation. They have the benefit of exchange; not the rates of exchange formerly paid, but that incidental exch which every bank charges in drawing a draft, probably a quarter or a half of one per cent. T have the profits they can make from deposits. They have other profits from the ordinary incid of banking. I have no doubt, from all these various profits, they will make what banks in ord ry times under specie payments could make, that is, seven or eight per cent. a year.

"But, sir, the principal point made by the honorable senator, and one most likely to influ the judgment of senators, is this: he asks what benefit the United States derives from this rangement, and he endeavors by argument to show that the United States derives no benefit would put to him this simple proposition: there are now $167,000,000 of local bank circula in the country. Suppose we can induce through their interests—I do not propose to do it by arbitrary mode—the retirement of $100,000,000 of this circulation, taking the smallest sum will probably be used in the course of a year; suppose we can induce the banks to withd $100,000,000 of their circulation, is it no benefit to the United States? Now the United St gets no benefit whatever from their circulation. The United States can not receive it in thei dinary business transactions. It fills the channels of circulation to the exclusion of the gr backs. Suppose we can induce the banks to withdraw $100,000,000 of their circulation, and vest that much money in our bonds, and receive United States circulation, does not the honor senator see that we should derive a great advantage from it? That is the object of this bill. object is, by appealing to the patriotism and the interest of the people and the banks, to induce banks to withdraw their local circulation and convert it into a national circulation. If it fail a matter of course it does no harm. But suppose it succeeds, does not the United States deri benefit from it? Certainly; because at once a demand is created for the purchase of $100,000, of United States bonds. We are anxious to sell these bonds. They are now below the par of g The creation of a demand for $100,000,000 will, as I showed yesterday, by the well-known recognized laws of trade, probably create a demand for $500,000,000. There is the benefit, th is the advantage we seek to derive. We shall make a market at once for the sale of $100,000, worth of our bonds, and the additional market which is always created by making a demand a particular commodity, which is equivalent at least to five times the amount of the real demo The government of the United States is willing to borrow money from the honorable senato six per cent. and pay the interest in gold coin. Any person who desires to loan money to United States may receive six per cent. interest on it, and we are very glad to sell our bonds that rate in this time of war; but to those who avail themselves of the privileges of this law only pay four per cent., so that we save one third of the interest on the amount of our bonds us for banking; and more than that, we get a circulation which by the laws of the United Sta may be used in the collection of our dues; and in the ordinary operations of our government th banking agencies may be made useful and beneficial as depositories. There is the answer. T benefit derived to the government is by making a market for its bonds, by having fiscal agenc throughout the United States, so that it may the more readily collect its debts, and by saving o third of the interest on the payment of its bonds, and by securing to the people of the country uniform national currency which can be passed from hand to hand in all parts of the coun without loss by exchange, or deterioration, or alteration.

"But the honorable senator says that the power granted by this bill would render the Secre ry of the Treasury a very dangerous person, or a very powerful person; probably that is the mea ing. He says that this bill would create a dangerous political power. According to all expe ence, if you invest in any particular person the power to appoint men to office, or the power manage banks or control a scheme of this kind, it rather weakens him. Sir, it will be a dang ous power in one sense; not to the American people, but it will be dangerous to the individu who exercises the power. Any man in this country who is clothed with the power of appointi men to office, or selecting certain persons to have certain privileges, loses more than he makes, the well-known law that he disappoints more than he benefits. And if you confer upon the Se retary of War or the Secretary of the Treasury the power to appoint twenty clerks, as we did t other day, there are five hundred applicants at once; and you disappoint four hundred and eigh and make them enemies, for the sake of gaining twenty friends. No, sir, the administration patronage, the power to select depositories; all the power conferred by this bill, the power of vis ation, all these are powers which tend rather to decrease the influence of the Secretary of t Treasury, because they are more likely to make him enemies than friends."

[1] The following is the text of the resolutions as offered in the Senate, March 3d, by Mr. Sumne

"*Whereas*, it appears from the diplomatic correspondence submitted to Congress that a prop sition, friendly in form, looking to pacification through foreign mediation, has been made to t United States by the Emperor of the French, and promptly declined by the President; and whe as the idea of mediation or intervention in some shape may be regarded by foreign governments practicable, and such governments, through this misunderstanding, may be led to proceedings ten ing to embarrass the friendly relations which now exist between them and the United States; a whereas, in order to remove for the future all chance of misunderstanding on this subject, and secure for the United States the full enjoyment of that freedom from foreign interference which one of the highest rights of independent states, it seems fit that Congress should declare its conv tions thereon: Therefore,

"*Resolved* (the House of Representatives concurring), That while, in times past, the Unit States have sought and accepted the friendly mediation or arbitration of foreign powers for the p cific adjustment of international questions, where the United States were the party of the one p and some other sovereign power the party of the other part; and while they are not disposed misconstrue the natural and humane desire of foreign powers to aid in arresting domestic troubl which, widening in their influence, have afflicted other countries; especially in view of the circu stance, deeply regretted by the American people, that the blow aimed by the rebellion at the nati al life has fallen heavily upon the laboring population of Europe; yet, notwithstanding these thin Congress can not hesitate to regard every proposition of foreign interference in the present cont as so far unreasonable and inadmissible, that its only explanation will be found in a misunderstan ing of the true state of the question, and of the real character of the war in which the republic engaged.

"*Resolved*, That the United States are now grappling with an unprovoked and wicked rebellio which is seeking the destruction of the republic that it may build a new power, whose corner-stor according to the confession of its chiefs, shall be slavery; that for the suppression of this rebellio and thus to save the republic and prevent the establishment of such a power, the national gove ment is now employing armies and fleets, in full faith that through these efforts all the purposes conspirators and rebels will be crushed; that while engaged in this struggle, on which so much pends, any proposition from a foreign power, whatever form it may take, having for its object t arrest of these efforts, is, just in proportion to its influence, an encouragement to the rebellion a to its declared pretensions, and, on this account, is calculated to prolong and embitter the confli to cause increased expenditure of blood and treasure, and to postpone the much-desired day of peace that, with these convictions, and not doubting that every such proposition, although made with go intent, is injurious to the national interests, Congress will be obliged to look upon any further a tempt in the same direction as an unfriendly act, which it earnestly deprecates, to the end that no ing may occur abroad to strengthen the rebellion or to weaken those relations of good-will with f eign powers which the United States are happy to cultivate.

"*Resolved*, That the rebellion from its beginning, and far back even in the conspiracy whi preceded its outbreak, was encouraged by the hope of support from foreign powers; that its chi frequently boasted that the people of Europe were so far dependent upon regular supplies of t great Southern staple, that sooner or later their governments would be constrained to take side w the rebellion in some effective form, even to the extent of forcible intervention, if the milder ta did not prevail; that the rebellion is now sustained by this hope, which every proposition of forei

understood the real temper of the government to which he made this of-
. Undoubtedly he would have been joined by the British government
his offer had not the latter been recently (November, 1862) advised by
rd Lyons that such an offer at the present crisis would be injurious to the
ice party in the North. Perhaps, also, Napoleon was deceived as to the
l import of the autumn elections of 1862, mistaking them for an indica-
n of a popular desire for peace even at the price of disunion.

Secretary Seward's reply was at once courteous and firm. It was ac-
owledged that the people of France were "faultless sharers with the
nerican nation" in the misfortunes of the war. The traditional friendship
ween France and the United States had not been forgotten. The land
l naval forces of the United States had steadily advanced, until now the
nfederates retained "only the states of Georgia, Alabama, and Texas, with
f of Virginia, half of North Carolina, two thirds of South Carolina, half of
ssissippi, and one third respectively of Arkansas and Louisiana." The
ermination to preserve the integrity of the country had not relaxed.
'his government," said the secretary, "if required, does not hesitate to sub-
; its achievements to the test of comparison; and it maintains that, in no
t of the world, and in no times, ancient or modern, has a nation, when ren-
ed all unready for combat by the enjoyment of eighty years of almost un-
ken peace, so quickly awakened at the alarm of sedition, put forth ener-
s so vigorous, and achieved successes so signal and effective as those which
re marked the progress of this contest on the part of the Union. M.
ouyn de l'Huys, I fear, has taken other light than the correspondence of
; government for his guidance in ascertaining its temper and firmness.
has probably read of divisions of sentiment among those who hold them-
ves forth as organs of public opinion here, and has given to them an un-
; importance. . . . . . While there has been much difference of popular
nion and favor concerning the agents who shall carry on the war, the
nciples on which it shall be waged, and the means with which it shall be
secuted, M. Drouyn de l'Huys has only to refer to the statute-book of
ngress, and the executive ordinances, to learn that the national activity
hitherto been, and yet is, as efficient as that of any other nation—what-
r its form of government—ever was under circumstances of equally
ve import to its peace, safety, and welfare. Not one voice has been
ed any where, out of the immediate field of the insurrection, in favor of
eign intervention, mediation, or arbitration, or of compromise, with the re-
quishment of one acre of the national domain, or the surrender of even
; constitutional franchise. At the same time, it is manifest to the world
t our resources are yet abundant, and our credit adequate to the existing
ergency." To surrender the subject to neutral arbitration amounted to
hing less than for the government, while engaged in the suppression of
urrection, to enter into diplomatic discussion with the insurgents. Either
government or the insurgents must yield the whole question in dispute,
ich neither was prepared to do; therefore the end of arbitration would
y be a recommittal of the question to the decision of battle. "It is a
at mistake," continued the secretary, "that European statesmen make if
y suppose this people are demoralized. Whatever, in the case of an in-
rection, the people of France, or of Great Britain, or of Switzerland, or the
therlands would do to save their national existence, no matter how the

the mouths and binding the hands of such opponents as, i
loyal, sought to perfect the work begun by traitors.

The spring and early summer of 1863 was the most d
the war. The Confederate armies were at their maximum
Vicksburg they held Grant at bay; in middle Tennessee
crans, and in Virginia they were preparing for an invasio
states. These were the days of sunshine in which the
made hay which they never could garner. Vallandigha
into the clutches of martial law, was arrested, sentenced
has been already related; but the others thundered at the
administration. As the national anniversary approached,
were to be a repetition of its gloomy predecessor of 186
heads"—as the peace-at-any-price party in the North wa
forward to the Fourth of July as the grand harvest-day of
when it came, their leaders were prepared for its celebrati
Franklin Pierce, a former President of the United States, in
ered to the citizens of his own state, at Concord, New Hamp
not one word to say against the sectionalism which had rais
the nation, denounced the war for the Union as section
"Nor is that all," said he; "for in those states which are
actual ravages of war, in which the roar of the cannon, an
musketry, and the groans of the dying are heard but as
other lands, even here in the loyal states the mailed hand o
tion strikes down the liberties of the people, and its foot tr
crated Constitution." Not a word had he to say about t
the Constitution by traitors. The chief grievance of whi
was that it was "made criminal for that noble martyr o
Vallandigham, to discuss public affairs in Ohio." An
Franklin Pierce, of New Hampshire, will go down to hist
with Vallandigham, who could enlist a larger share of hi
his own nation in peril.

On the same day Governor Seymour addressed a larg
bled at the Academy of Music in New York City. Th
elaborate oration was an amplification of the calamiti
These calamities, he said, had been predicted years ago by
consequence of the refusal of the people to be ruled by a
But the fears of Democrats had been laughed at. Wh
menced they had implored for compromise. Their pray
heeded. On this account the country had been brought "
of destruction." He therefore had come before them to r
and the prayer which had hitherto been scorned. There
bloody civil war, but the hostile attitude of the two par
threatened a second revolution. "Remember," he wa
"that the bloody, and treasonable, and revolutionary doct
cessity can be proclaimed by a mob as well as by a gover

But Governor Seymour and ex-President Pierce were
pression when compared to others throughout the Nort
to revolutionize the government if a Democratic success
no other way. Among the motives used to excite to viol
was that furnished by the impending conscription. The

HORATIO SEYMOUR.

been ordered to begin in the city on Saturday, July 11th, these journals pronounced the work of evil-minded men, intended to accomplish their own selfish ends. Those who had determined to strike at slavery, the chief support of the rebellion, were styled "neither more nor less than murderers." The administrators of the government were styled "weak and reckless men." The draft was declared to be "a measure which could not have been ventured upon in England, even in those dark days when the press-gang filled the English ships-of-war with slaves, and dimmed the glory of England's noblest naval heroes—a measure wholly repugnant to the habits and prejudices of our people." It was asserted that the aim of the government, in conscription, was "to lessen the number of Democratic votes at the next election." "The miscreants at the head of the government," said the *Daily News*, "are bending all their powers, as was revealed in the late speech of Wendell Phillips at Framingham, to securing a perpetuation of their ascendency for another four years; and their triple method of accomplishing this purpose is to kill off Democrats, stuff the ballot-boxes with bogus soldiers' votes, and deluge recusant districts with negro suffrage." The operation of the draft was declared to have been unfair. One out of about two and a half of our citizens was to be brought off into Lincoln's charnel-house. Governor Seymour was quoted as having openly expressed "his belief that neither the President nor Congress, without the consent of the state authorities, has any right to enforce such an act as is now being carried out under the auspices of the War Department." Every possible argument was adduced to excite violence on the part of the people against the government.

On Saturday, the 11th, after several postponements, Colonel Nagent, the provost-marshal of New York city, was directed to proceed with the draft, and the several deputies were instructed accordingly. In compliance with these instructions, Provost-marshal Jenkins, of the Ninth Congressional district, commenced operations at a building on the corner of Forty-sixth Street and Third Avenue. There was a large crowd assembled at the place of drawing, and it seemed to be in good humor, saluting well-known names with cheers. No disturbance was apprehended, and the draft was to be continued on the following Monday. But in the vicinity there were residing a large number of foreigners of Irish birth, and some of these had been drafted on Saturday. Here the turbulent element, encouraged by the utterances of a disloyal press, began to exhibit itself. Secret meetings were held, and

FIGHT WITH THE MILITARY.

NEW YORK RIOTERS HANGING A NEGRO.

it was determined to resort to force. On Monday morning organized parties proceeded from place to place, compelling workmen to desist from their accustomed labors, and join the processions already wending their way to the corner of Third Avenue and Forty-sixth Street.

Scarcely had the drawing recommenced when it was interrupted by the turbulent crowd assembled outside. Paving-stones were hurled through the windows. The crowd was in an instant transformed into a mob. The doors were broken down, and the crowd rushed in, demolishing every thing connected with the office, and taking complete possession. Only the drafting-wheel escaped destruction. Provost-marshal Jenkins escaped, and the reporters; but one of the deputies, Lieutenant Vanderpoel, was badly beaten, and taken home for dead. Having possession of the office, the rioters, regardless of the women and children residing in the stories above, poured camphene over the floor and set the place ablaze. In two hours the entire block was a smoking ruin. Officers of the Fire Department, under Chief Engineer Decker, arrived, but the hydrants were in possession of the mob, and it was only after the most persistent persuasion on the part of Decker that the firemen were allowed to prevent the farther progress of the conflagration. In the mean time, Police Superintendent Kennedy had been attacked by the mob and nearly killed.

There were no troops in the city, the militia being absent on duty in Pennsylvania. A small force of the Invalid Corps appeared on the ground soon after the disturbance commenced, armed with muskets loaded with blank cartridges. Of course these were promptly overpowered by the mob, which had now swollen to thousands. A detachment of the police was in like manner beaten and forced to retreat. The mob was composed almost entirely of Irishmen. Now it is a curious circumstance that, while no class of our foreign population is more jealous of its own liberties than the Irish, there is also none which more strongly resents every liberty accorded to the negro race. The rioters took possession of hotels and restaurants whose servants were negroes, destroyed the furniture, maltreated the guests, and sought the lives of the poor servants. These things were done deliberately, and not in the heat of passion. The writer of this chapter passed through the mob on the afternoon of the 14th, as they were burning down the Colored Orphan Asylum at the corner of Fifth Avenue and Forty-sixth Street. He saw no tumult, no exhibition of rage, but only a cruel, fiendish, and deliberate purpose to persecute to the death an innocent race, against whom they were only moved by a political prejudice. The asylum was burned to ashes, while the female friends of the rioters lugged off to their shanties the plundered furniture. At about the same hour the armory on Twenty-ninth Street and Second Avenue was burned. Another portion of the mob had made its way to the City Hall Park, and made an attack upon the *Tribune* office, but were severely handled and dispersed by the police.

It is supposed that about a dozen negroes were, on Monday, brutally murdered by the rioters. A colored man residing in Carmine Street was seized by the mob, and, after his life had been nearly beaten out, his body was suspended from a tree, a fire was kindled under him, and, in the midst of excruciating torments, he expired.

On Tuesday the spirit of the rioters was even more malignant. Governor Seymour, who had been absent in New Jersey, arrived in the city, and issued proclamations commanding the rioters to disperse, and declaring the city and county of New York to be in a state of insurrection. In the afternoon he addressed the mob from the steps of the City Hall. After their courteous acknowledgment of his leadership, he could not well address them otherwise than as his "friends." He assured them of his friendship, and informed them that he had sent his adjutant general to Washington "to con-

CHARGE OF THE POLICE AT THE TRIBUNE OFFICE.

THE RIOTERS BURNING THE COLORED ORPHAN ASYLUM, CORNER OF FIFTH AVENUE AND FORTY-SIXTH STREET, NEW YORK CITY.

ANDREW G. CURTIN.

JOHN BROUGH.

fer with the authorities there, and to have this draft suspended and stopped." He gave over to these friends of his the charge over the property and persons of all other citizens, and the good order of the city, and then advised them to retire peaceably. This step on the part of the governor had little effect. The riot continued for four days, and this day was the worst of them all. All stores were closed, and no business was transacted. A small military force had been marshaled, and, wherever it encountered the mob, the latter was dispersed. But the police were far more efficient than the military, and in every conflict subdued the rioters. But neither the police nor the small military force could be omnipresent, and the most cruel atrocities were inflicted upon negroes wherever they were found. It was on Tuesday that Colonel O'Brien was killed. Commissioned to disperse a mob in Third Avenue, he had successfully accomplished his duty with the troops in his command. He had sprained his ankle in the excitement, and, stepping into a drug-store, had become separated from his troops. Here he was surrounded by the mob, and suffered a cruel death.

On the 16th several militia regiments returned from Pennsylvania, and after that there was no farther trouble. It is estimated that during the excitement over 1000 of the rioters had been killed, while of those opposed to them less than 50 lives were lost. The property destroyed by the mob was estimated at $2,000,000. The municipal authorities had, in the mean time, passed a relief bill, to pay $300 commutation, or substitute money, to every drafted man unable to pay that sum for himself

Riots of a less serious nature occurred at the same time in Boston and other cities, but in all these foreigners were principally the disturbing element.

Governor Seymour strongly urged upon the President to postpone the draft until its constitutionality was determined upon by the courts. The President replied that he did not object to abide the decision of the courts, but he could not consent to lose the time while it was being obtained.

The subjects which had for the past few months agitated the loyal states—the emancipation proclamation, the enlistment of negro soldiers, arbitrary arrests, and the conscription—were submitted in the autumnal elections of 1863 for the decision of the people. The result was a decisive success for the administration. In Vermont, on the 1st of September, J. G. Smith, the Republican candidate for governor, was elected by a majority of nearly 18,000. In California, two days later, a Republican governor, F. F. Low, was elected by 20,000 majority. On the 14th of September Maine gave 18,000 majority to Governor Cony, Republican. In October Pennsylvania re-elected Governor Curtin by a majority of 15,000. His opponent was George W. Woodward, a peace man, whose election was regarded by General McClellan as "called for by the interests of the nation." In the same election Chief Justice Lowrie, who had declared the enrollment act unconstitutional, was defeated by over 12,000 votes. In the State of Ohio the success of the administration was most strongly marked. In 1862 the Democratic Secretary of State had received a majority of 5000 votes. But now a governor was to be elected, and the opposing candidates were the exiled "martyr" Vallandigham and Brough. Vallandigham was defeated by over 100,000 votes, of which 40,000 were polled by soldiers. The Legislature of this state, elected at the same time, stood 27 to 5 in the Senate, and 73 to 24 in the House. Iowa elected a Legislature almost entirely Republican, and a Republican governor and judge. Similar results followed in Wisconsin, Minnesota, and Michigan. In New York the Republican majority amounted to 30,000, against a Democratic majority in 1862 of over 10,000. In Massachusetts the Republican majority was over 40,000. Even Maryland supported the administration by a majority of 20,000. When we compare these results with those of the preceding year, it is clear that the people of the loyal states had not yet deserted the administration, and that their determination to sustain the war had increased rather than diminished.

CHAPTER XLV.

POLITICAL DEVELOPMENTS OF 1864.

The Spring Elections of 1864.—Meeting of the Thirty-eighth Congress, December 7, 1863.—Position of Parties.—Colfax elected Speaker.—The President's Message.—The Amnesty Proclamation.—Arbitrary Arrests.—The Test-Oath reaffirmed.—Repeal of the Fugitive Slave Law.—The Montana Bill and Negro Suffrage.—The Anti-Slavery Amendment; its Defeat in the House.—Reverdy Johnson's Argument in favor of the Amendment.—Negro Soldiers declared free.—Congress presents a Gold Medal to General Grant.—Views of the Thirty-eighth Congress in regard to Reconstruction.—The Theory of Lincoln's Amnesty Proclamation.—Stevens's Ideas as expressed in Debate on the Confiscation Act.—The Civil Code and the Laws of War.—Henry Winter Davis's Bill for the Appointment of Provisional Governors over rebel States; passed by the House May 4, 1864, by the Senate July 2d.—Lincoln refuses to Sign the Bill; his Proclamation.—The Wade and Davis Manifesto.—Debate on the Expulsion of Alexander Long.—Financial Measures.—Resolutions on the Mexican Imbroglio.—The Presidential Campaign of 1864.—Radical Convention at Cleveland; Fremont and Cochrane nominated for President and Vice-President.—The Republican Convention at Baltimore; President Lincoln renominated, and Andrew Johnson nominated for Vice-President.—The military Situation.—Peace Missions.—Meeting of the Democratic Convention at Chicago.—Character and Purposes of the Convention; its Platform and Resolutions; Nomination of McClellan and Pendleton.—McClellan's Letter of Acceptance.—Victory at Atlanta.—Other Victories in the Shenandoah Valley.—Brighter Prospects.—Democratic Defeat at the Polls.—The Vote for President.—Lincoln and Johnson elected.—Ratification of the new Constitution in Maryland.—The Peace Commission at Hampton Roads.

IN the spring elections of 1864 we can estimate the weight of General Grant's success in the battles around Chattanooga, won in November, 1863. In New Hampshire, Gilmore, the Republican candidate for governor, was elected by a majority of nearly 6000 votes over Harrington. In Connecticut, Buckingham (Republican) was elected over O. S. Seymour by a majority of 5658 votes. In Rhode Island, also, the Republican candidate for governor, J. Y. Smith, was elected over G. H. Browne by a majority of 1538.

The first session of the Thirty-ninth Congress assembled on the 7th of December, 1863.[1] The position of parties was not far different to that of the

[1] The following is a list of the members of the Thirty-eighth Congress, with their political designation. Those marked A. were adherents of the administration; its opponents are marked O. An asterisk precedes those who were members of the Thirty-seventh Congress.

SENATE.

California	John Conness, A.	*Delaware*	*James A. Bayard, O.
	*James A. McDougall, O.		*Willard Saulsbury, O.
Connecticut	*James Dixon, A.	*Illinois*	William A. Richardson, O.
	*Lafayette S. Foster, A.		*Lyman Trumbull, A.

	Nehemiah Perry, O.
New York	Henry G. Stebbins, O.
	Martin Kalbfleisch, O.
	*Moses F. Odell, O.
	*Benjamin Wood, O.
	Fernando Wood, O.
	*Elijah Ward, O.
	John W. Chanler, O.
	James Brooks, O.
	Anson Herrick, O.
	William Radford, O.
	Charles H. Winfield, O.
	Homer A. Nelson, O.
	*John B. Steele, O.
	John V. L. Pruyn, O.
	John Q. Griswold, O.
	Orlando Kellogg, A.
	Calvin T. Hulburd, A.
	James W. Marvin, A.
	Samuel F. Miller, A.
	*Ambrose W. Clark, A.
	Francis Kernan, O.
	De Witt C. Littlejohn, A.
	Thomas T. Davis, A.
	*Theodore M. Pomeroy, A.
	Daniel Morris, A.
	Giles W. Hotchkiss, A.
	*Robt. B. Van Valkenburg, A.
	Freeman Clark, A.
	*Augustus Frank, A.
	John B. Ganson, O.
	*Reuben E. Fenton, A.
Ohio	*George H. Pendleton, O.
	Alexander Long, O.
	Robert C. Schenck, A.
	J. F. McKinney, O.
	Frank C. Le Blond, O.
	*Chilton A. White, O.
	*Samuel S. Cox, O.
	William Johnson, O.
	*Warren P. Noble, O.
	*James M. Ashley, A.
	Wells A. Hutchins, O.
	William E. Finck, O.
	John O'Neill, O.
	George Bliss, O.
	*James R. Morris, O.
	Joseph W. White, O.
	Ephraim R. Eckley, A.
	Rufus P. Spaulding, A.
	James A. Garfield, A.
Oregon	John R. McBride, A.
Pennsylvania	Samuel J. Randall, O.
	Charles O'Neill, A.
	Leonard Myers, A.
	*William D. Kelley, A.
	M. Russell Thayer, A.
	*John D. Stiles, O.
	John M. Broomall, A.
	*Sydenham E. Ancona, O.
	*Thaddeus Stevens, A.
	Myer Strouse, O.
	*Philip Johnson, O.
	Charles Dennison, O.
	Henry M. Tracy, A.
	William H. Miller, O.
	*Joseph Baily, O.
	Alexander H. Coffroth, O.
	Archibald McAllister, O.
	*James T. Hale, A.
	Glenni W. Scofield, A.
	Amos Myers, A.
	John L. Dawson, O.
	*James K. Moorhead, A.
	Thomas Williams, A.
	*Jesse Lazear, O.
Rhode Island	Thomas A. Jenckes, A.
	Nathan F. Dixon, A.
Vermont	Fredk. E. Woodbridge, A.
	*Justin S. Morrill, A.
	*Portus Baxter, A.
West Virginia	*Jacob B. Blair, A.
	*William G. Brown, A.
	*Killian V. Whaley, A.
Wisconsin	James S. Brown, O.
	*Ithamar C. Sloan, A.

year ago," said he, "the war had already lasted twenty months, and there had been many conflicts on both land and sea, with varying results. The rebellion had been pressed back into reduced limits; yet the tone of public feeling and opinion, at home and abroad, was not satisfactory. With other signs, the popular election, just then past, indicated uneasiness among ourselves, while, amid much that was cold and menacing, the kindest words coming from Europe were uttered in accents of pity that we were too blind to surrender a hopeless cause. Our commerce was suffering greatly by a few armed vessels built upon and furnished from foreign shores, and we were threatened with such additions from the same quarter as would sweep our trade from the sea and raise our blockade. We had failed to elicit from European governments any thing hopeful upon this subject. The preliminary emancipation proclamation, issued in September, was running its assigned period to the beginning of the new year. A month later the final proclamation came, including the announcement that colored men of suitable condition would be received into the war service. The policy of emancipation and of employing black soldiers gave to the future a new aspect, about which hope, and fear, and doubt contended in uncertain conflict. According to our political system, as a matter of civil administration, the general government had no right to effect emancipation in any state, and for a long time it had been hoped that the rebellion could be suppressed without resorting to it as a military measure. It was all the while deemed possible that the necessity for it might come, and that, if it should, the crisis of the contest would then be presented. It came, and, as we anticipated, it was followed by dark and doubtful days.

"Eleven months having now passed, we are permitted to take another view. The rebel hordes are pressed still farther back, and, by the complete opening of the Mississippi, the country dominated by the rebellion is divided into distinct parts, with no practical communication between them; Tennessee and Arkansas have been substantially cleared of insurgent control, and influential citizens in each, owners of slaves and advocates of slavery at the beginning of the rebellion, now declare openly for emancipation in their respective states. Of those states not included in the emancipation proclamation, Maryland and Missouri, neither of which three years ago would tolerate any restraint upon the extension of slavery into new territories, only dispute now as to the best mode of removing it within their own limits. Of those who were slaves at the beginning of the rebellion, full one hundred thousand are in the United States military service, about one half of which number actually bear arms in the ranks, thus giving the double advantage of taking so much labor from the insurgent cause, and supplying the places which otherwise must be filled with so many white men. So far as tested, it is difficult to say they are not as good soldiers as any. No servile insurrection, or tendency to violence or cruelty, has marked the measures of emancipation or arming the blacks. These measures have been much discussed in foreign countries, and contemporary with such discussion the tone of public sentiment there is much improved. At home the same measures have been fully discussed, supported, criticised, and denounced, and the annual elections following are highly encouraging to those whose official duty it is to bear the country through this great trial. Thus we have the new reckoning. The crisis which threatened to divide the friends of the Union is past."

In this changed condition of public affairs the President had seen fit to put forth an amnesty proclamation. The Constitution authorized the President to grant or withhold pardon for offenses committed against the United States at his own absolute discretion, and this involved the power to grant pardon on terms. The constitutional obligation to guarantee to every state in the Union a republican form of government was explicit and full. But why tender the benefits of this provision to governments only in such states [illegible] ncluded in the oath; and it is believed the executive may lawfully claim it a return for pardon and restoration of forfeited rights, which he has clear onstitutional power to withhold altogether, or to grant upon the terms which e shall deem wisest for the public interest."

The message thus concluded:

"In the midst of other cares, however important, we must not lose sight f the fact that the war power is still our main reliance. To that power lone can we look, yet for a time, to give confidence to the people in the conested regions that the insurgent power will not again overrun them. Until that confidence shall be established, little can be done any where for what is called reconstruction. Hence our chiefest care must still be directed to the army and navy, who have thus far borne their harder part so nobly and well. And it may be esteemed fortunate that, in giving the greatest efficiency to these indispensable arms, we do also honorably recognize the gallant men, from commander to sentinel, who compose them, and to whom, more than to others, the world must stand indebted for the home of freedom disenthralled, regenerated, enlarged, and perpetuated."

It was a new Congress, and many of the contests already decided in favor of the administration had to be fought over again. The House had been in session scarcely a week when the subject of arbitrary arrests was introduced. By a vote of 90 to 67 the decision of the previous Congress was reaffirmed. This was purely a party vote, if we except the name of Brutus J. Clay, who, though nominally a Democrat, in all important matters supported the administration. On the 29th of February, Pendleton, of Ohio, offered a resolution denouncing the arrest of Vallandigham as an arbitrary act, and a violation of the Constitution, which the House rejected by 77 votes against 47. Here also Clay was the only Democrat in favor of rejection. Other resolutions of a similar character in regard to the general subject of arrests were introduced during the session, but were invariably tabled.

In the Senate, on the 17th of December, Sumner offered as a new rule for the Senate that the oath prescribed for senators by the act of July 2, 1862, should be taken and subscribed by every senator in open Senate before entering upon his duties. Thus the whole subject was again laid open to discussion, and the next day a substitute was moved by Saulsbury, of Delaware, instructing the Judiciary Committee to inquire whether members of Congress were included within the provisions of the act of July 2, 1862, and whether this act was constitutional. The substitute was rejected, and Sumner's resolution was adopted. Bayard, of Delaware, who had been reelected for the term ending March 3, 1869, was the only senator who had not taken the oath. On the 26th of January he subscribed to the oath, and then resigned his seat.[1] His place was supplied by George R. Riddle, a supporter of the administration.

It is curious and suggestive to trace the steady progress of negro emancipation in the congressional history of the war. Undoubtedly this progress was in a large degree due to a sense of moral justice on the part of the Northern people, which had been for many years repressed by the supposed necessity of sanctioning and actually upholding a system of gross injustice, in order to preserve the Constitution and the Union. But when it became evident that this system, thus nursed, was a serpent in the bosom of the people—a serpent whose fangs were now thrust into both the Union and the Constitution—this monstrous incubus was thrown off, and justice breathed unshackled. And it should also be remembered that in this case the dictates of freedom and justice were uttered in the very teeth of a prejudice against the negro race which was far stronger in the North than it was in the South. No greater tribute could be paid to the virtue of republican institutions than this victory of the moral sense over prejudice. But in this case the suppression of the prejudice against the negro was made easy by the aid of a stronger prejudice against treason. Then, again, the *military* necessity of striking at slavery in order to weaken treason, and the *political* necessity of emancipation in order to prevent a future reign of discord, were overmastering motives, helping on the great revolution in behalf of an oppressed race—a moral revolution, in comparison with which the war itself, and its immense sacrifices of blood and treasure, would become almost insignificant, were they not inseparably linked therewith in the sequences of Providence.

During this session a bill "to repeal the Fugitive Slave Law of 1850, and all acts and parts of acts for the rendition of fugitive slaves," was passed. It was reported in the Senate by Sumner on the 19th of April. An amendment offered by Sherman, of Ohio, excepting the act of 1793, was adopted 24 to 17. Among those voting in the affirmative were Senators Collamer, [illegible] repeal the law prohibiting negroes from being employed as carriers of the mail, with an amendment providing that in the courts of the United States there should be no exclusion of any witnesses on account of color. The amendment was not passed in this connection, but subsequently was attached as a provision to the Civil Appropriation Bill—a favorite device of Senator Sumner.[1] It was afterward approved in the House and became a law.

On the 31st of March the House bill, in the usual form, providing a temporary government for Montana, was considered in the Senate, and an amendment was passed ignoring any distinction based on color in the organization of the territorial government. The House refused to concur. A conference committee was appointed, and the bill was finally passed without the amendment. As there was not a negro in the territory, the subject was of no practical importance, but in any case probably the amendment would not have been adopted; for, in a joint resolution amending the charter of the District of Columbia, which passed both houses a few weeks later, Sumner's amendment providing that there should be no exclusion from the register on account of color was rejected. Congress at this time certainly was not in favor of negro suffrage even in the district over which it had legislative control. In the bill, however, incorporating the Metropolitan Railroad Company of the District of Columbia, which passed both houses, provision was incorporated that there should be no regulation excluding any person from any car on account of color. On the 24th of June Sumner succeeded in attaching to the Civil Appropriation Bill a section prohibiting the coastwise slave-trade, which passed both houses.

About the end of March a joint resolution was offered in the Senate, proposing to the Legislatures of the several states the following article as an amendment to the Constitution:

"ARTICLE XIII., *Section* 1. Neither slavery nor involuntary servitude, except as a punishment for crime, whereof the party shall have been duly convicted, shall exist within the United States; or in any place subject to their jurisdiction.

"*Section* 2. Congress shall have power to enforce this article by appropriate legislation."

"When this amendment shall be consummated," said Senator Wilson, "the shackles will fall from the limbs of the hapless bondsman, and the lash drop from the weary hand of the task-master. . . . . Then the slave-mart, pen, and auction block, with their clanking fetters for human limbs, will disappear from the land they have brutalized, and the school-house will rise to enlighten the darkened intellect of a race imbruted by long years of enforced ignorance. Then the sacred rights of human nature, the hallowed family relations of husband and wife, parent and child, will be protected by the guardian spirit of the law which makes sacred alike the proud homes and lowly cabins of freedom. Then the sacred earth, blighted by the sweat and tears of bondage, will bloom again under the quickening culture of rewarded toil. Then the wronged victim of the slave system, the poor white man, and sand-hiller, the clay-eater of the wasted fields of California, impoverished, debased, dishonored by the system that makes toil a badge of disgrace, and the instruction of the brain and soul of man a crime, will lift his abashed forehead to the skies, and begin to run the race of improvement, progress, and elevation. Then the nation, 'regenerated, and disenthralled by the genius of universal emancipation,' will run the career of development, power, and glory, animated and guided by the spirit of the Christian Democracy, that 'pulls not the highest down, but lifts the lowest up.'" The resolution was adopted by a vote of 38 to 6. In the House it failed of the necessary two thirds majority. Reverdy Johnson, of Maryland, on most subjects a member of the opposition, and himself a slaveholder, strongly advocated the passage of the amendment in the Senate. "There was a period," said he, "in our own time when there was but one opinion upon the question of right, or almost but one opinion upon that question. The men who fought through the Revolution, those who survived its peril and shared in its glory, and who were called to the Convention by which the Constitution of the United States was drafted and recommended to the adoption of the American people, almost without exception, thought that slavery was not only an evil to any people among whom it might exist, but that it was an evil of the highest character, which it was the duty of all Christian people, if possible, to remove, because it was a sin as well as an evil.

"I think the history of those times will bear me out in the statement, that if the men by whom that Constitution was framed, and the people by whom it was adopted, had anticipated the times in which we live, they would have provided by constitutional enactment that that evil and that sin should at some comparatively remote day be removed. Without recurring to authority, the writings, public or private, of the men of that day, it is sufficient for my purpose to state what the facts will justify me in saying, that every man of them who largely shared in the dangers of the revolutionary struggle, and who largely participated in the deliberations of the Convention by which the Constitution was adopted, earnestly desired, not only upon grounds of political economy, not only upon reasons material in their character, but

[1] "With a firm conviction," said he, "that your decision inflicts a vital wound upon free representative government, I can not, by continuing to hold the seat I now occupy under it, give my personal assent and sanction to its propriety. To do so, I must forfeit my own self-respect, and sacrifice my clear conviction of duty, for the sake merely of retaining a high trust and station with its emoluments. That will I never do; but, retiring into private life, shall await, I trust, with calmness and firmness, though certainly with despondency, the farther progress of a war which it is apparent to my vision will, in its continuance, subvert republican institutions, and sever this Federal Union into many arbitrary governments.

"Among these, wars for dominion will arise and continue until, from exhaustion, the different [illegible]

CHARLES SUMNER.

upon grounds of morality and religion, that sooner or later the institution should terminate. . . .

"The present incumbent of the presidential chair was elected—elected by a sectional vote—and the moment the news reached Charleston, where some of the leading conspirators were, and here in this chamber, where others were to be found, it was hailed, not with regret, but with delight. Why? Because, as they thought, it would enable them to drive the South to madness by appealing to the danger in which such an event involved this institution, which the people were made to believe was so essential to their power and to their happiness, and that will be repeated over and over again just as long as the institution is suffered to remain. Terminate it, and the wit of man will, as I think, be unable to devise any other topic upon which we can be involved in a fratricidal strife. God and nature, judging by the history of the past, intend us to be one. Our unity is written in the mountains and rivers in which we all have an interest. The very difference of climate render each important to the other and alike important. That mighty horde which from time to time have gone from the Atlantic, imbued with all the principles of human freedom which animated their fathers in running the perils of the mighty deep and seeking liberty here, are now there, and as they have said, and will continue to say until time shall be no more: 'We mean that the government in the future shall be as in the past, one, an example of human freedom for the light and example of the world, and illustrating in the blessings and the happiness it confers the truth of the principles incorporated into the Declaration of Independence, that life and liberty are man's inalienable right.'"

This able senator, on a former occasion during this session, when the section providing for the freedom of negro soldiers, their wives and their children, was under discussion, had very plainly demonstrated the wickedness of slavery. "I doubt very much," he said, "if any member of the Senate is more anxious to have the country composed of free men and free women than I am. I understand the bill to provide that upon the enlistment as a soldier of any man of African descent, his wife and children are at once to be free. No provision is made to compensate the owner of the wife and children if they happen to be slaves, and it of course only applies to such wives and children as are slaves—those who are to be set free, and not those who are now free.

"The bill provides that a slave enlisted any where, no matter where he may be, whether he be within Maryland or out of Maryland, whether he be within any of the loyal states or out of the loyal states altogether, is at once to work the emancipation of his wife and his children. He may be in South Carolina; and many a slave in South Carolina, I am sorry to say it, *can well claim to have a wife, and perhaps wives and children, within the limits of Maryland.* It is one of the vices, and the *horrible vices* of the institution—one that has shocked me from infancy to the present hour—the whole marital relation is disregarded. They are made to be, practically and by education, forgetful or ignorant of that relation. When I say they are educated, I mean to say they are kept in absolute ignorance, and out of that *immorality of every description* arises, and among the other immoralities is that the connubial relation does not exist.

"The men who were here preaching their treason from these desks, telegraphing from these desks—I saw it, though I was not a member, and my heart burned within me—for their minions, or the deluded masses at home, to seize upon the public property of the United States, its forts, its means, its treasure, its material of war, and who were seeking to seduce from their allegiance officers of the army and navy of the United States—they have done it; and they were told that such would be the result. They did not believe it. They believed that your representatives would not have the firmness to try the wager of battle. They believed—I have heard them say so—that a Southern regiment could march without resistance successfully from Washington to Boston, and challenge for themselves independence in Faneuil Hall. Sad delusion! Gross ignorance of the character of your people! You were free, and you knew its value. You are free, and you are brave because you are free; and as I have told them over and over again, let the day come when in their madness they should throw down the gage of battle to the free states of the Union, and the day of their domestic institution will have ended. They have done it. I have said it was, as against them, retributive justice. Hoping and believing that their effort will be fruitless, that their treason will fail in its object, that the authority of the government will be sustained, and the Union be preserved, I thank God that as a compensation for the blood, the treasure, and the agony which have been brought into our households, and into yours, it has stricken now and forever this institution from its place among our states."

Though the section providing for the freedom of the families of negroes engaged in the military service was not passed, yet the soldiers themselves were by another act declared free, and provision was made for their receiving the same payment as white soldiers.[1]

In legislating upon slavery, Congress did not forget the army. One of the first acts of the session was a joint resolution directing that the thanks of Congress be presented to General Grant, and to the officers and soldiers under him, and requesting the President to cause a gold medal to be struck, with suitable emblems, devices, and inscriptions, to be presented to General Grant. A copy of the joint resolutions engrossed on parchment was directed to be transmitted with the medal, to be presented to the general in the name of the people of the United States.

No act of Congress relating to the war was of so much importance as that approved by the President on the 29th of February, reviving the grade of lieutenant general. The circumstances connected with General Grant's nomination to and confirmation in this office have already been narrated in a previous chapter.

Resolutions were offered in December by Johnson, of Pennsylvania, and by Eldridge, of Wisconsin, in opposition to the Conscription Act of the previous Congress, but these were promptly laid on the table. Toward the close of the session the commutation clause was repealed, and no exemption was allowed except for alienage, previous service of two years, or physical disability.

The President's Amnesty Proclamation naturally introduced the subject of reconstruction early in the session. On the 15th of December, Henry Winter Davis, of Maryland, moved the reference of that portion of the President's message which related to reconstruction to a select committee of nine, to be named by the speaker. He objected to the use of the term reconstruction as vague and inaccurate, as there had been "no destruction of the Union, no breaking up of the government." "The fact," said he, "as well as the constitutional view of affairs in the states enveloped by rebellion, is that a force has overthrown, or the people, in a moment of madness, have abrogated the governments which existed in those states under the Constitution, and were recognized by the United States prior to the breaking out of the rebellion. The government of the United States is engaged in two operations. One is the suppression of armed resistance to the supreme authority of the United States, and which is endeavoring to suppress that opposition by arms. Another—a very delicate and perhaps as high a duty—is to see, when armed resistance shall be removed, that governments shall be restored in those states republican in their form."

Lovejoy, of Illinois, expressed very similar views of the subject. "I do not believe," said he, "strictly speaking, that there are any rebel states. I know there are states which rebels have taken possession of and overthrown the legitimate governments for the time being; and I hold, with the gentleman from Maryland, as I understood him, that those governments still remain, and that as soon as we can get possession of them we will breathe into them the spirit of republican life—a free soul once again. I am for the Constitution as it is and the Union as it was. Yes, I am for the Constitution as it is, and not as it has been falsely interpreted, and for the Union as it was before it was taken possession of by slaveholding tyrants."

The House adopted Davis's proposition[1] by a vote of 91 to 80. Thus it will be seen that even at this time there was a great difference of opinion in regard to the restoration of the insurrectionary states to their normal relations in the Union. The dividing line was already being drawn between those who were willing to base restoration upon the returning allegiance to the Constitution of the people of the South, and upon their support of the action of the government in regard to slavery, and those who, insisting upon the right and expediency of treating the Southern people as a conquered nation of aliens, would impose additional conditions of a harsher and more humiliating character. The majority of the members of Congress belonged at this time to the former class, and adopted the views of Henry Winter Davis and Lovejoy. The President's Amnesty Proclamation was a practical expression of the same views. The proclamation consists of two parts—one declaring the executive pardon upon certain conditions and with certain exceptions; the other declaring the willingness of the government to recognize state governments, republican in form, whenever re-established by loyal voters, not less than one tenth in number of the votes cast in the respective states at the presidential election of 1860.

1. The subject of pardon was purely within executive control. The Constitution expressly declares that the President "shall have power to grant reprieves and pardons for offenses against the United States, except in cases of impeachment." Of course, the power to grant pardon includes the power to grant it upon conditions and with exceptions. The condition required by the President was the taking of the following oath:

"I, —— ——, do solemnly swear, in presence of Almighty God, that I will henceforth faithfully support, protect, and defend the Constitution of the United States and the Union of the states thereunder; and that I will, in like manner, abide by and faithfully support all acts of Congress passed during the existing rebellion with reference to slaves, so long and so far as not repealed, modified, or held void by Congress, or by decision of the Supreme Court; and that I will, in like manner, abide by, and faithfully support all proclamations of the President made during the existing rebellion, having reference to slaves, so long and so far as not modified or declared void by decision of the Supreme Court. So help me God."

The following persons were excepted: "All who are or shall have been civil or diplomatic officers of the so-called Confederate government; all who have left judicial stations under the United States to aid the rebellion; all who are, or shall have been, military or naval officers of said so-called Confederate government above the rank of colonel in the army, or of lieutenant in the navy; all who left seats in the United States Congress to aid the rebellion; all who resigned commissions in the army or navy of the United States, and afterward aided the rebellion; and all who have engaged in any way in treating colored persons, or white persons in charge of such, otherwise than lawfully as prisoners of war, and which persons may have been found in the United States service as soldiers, seamen, or in any other capacity."

2. The second part of the proclamation also rested upon a constitutional basis. The Constitution provides that "the United States shall guarantee to every state in this Union a republican form of government, and shall protect each of them against invasion, and, on application of the Legislature or the executive (when the Legislature can not be convened), against domestic violence." It was only in cases like this—where loyal governments had been subverted—that such a guaranty could become necessary. It was a guaranty to loyal men as against rebels—a guaranty backed by the whole military power of the government. It was granted in good faith, and sustained by every pledge which it was in the power of the executive to give. So far as it went, it was authoritative, without the sanction of any legislative or judicial body. It was a proclamation by the executive declaring a mode by which loyal men in the disturbed states might restore the latter to their

[1] The *American Annual Cyclopædia* for 1864 thus enumerates the several acts relating to slavery which were passed by the Thirty-seventh and during the first session of the Thirty-eighth Congress: "Slaves used for military purposes by the enemy were declared to be free; an additional article of war dismissed from service all officers who should surrender escaped fugitives coming within the lines of the armies; three thousand slaves in the District of Columbia were emancipated, and slaveholding forbidden; it was enacted that colored persons in the District should be tried for the same offenses, in the same manner, and be subject to the same punishment as white persons, and that such persons should not be excluded as witnesses on account of color; and that colored schools should be provided, and the same rate of appropriation made to them as to schools for white children; and that there should be no exclusion from any railway car in the District on account of color; slavery was forever prohibited in all territory of the United States; a joint resolution was passed pledging the faith of the nation to aid non-seceding states to emancipate their slaves; all slaves of persons aiding the enemy who should take refuge within the lines of the army were declared free; it was enacted that no slave should be surrendered to any claimant until such person had made oath that he had not given aid and comfort to the rebellion; the President was authorized to receive into the military service persons of African descent, and such person, his mother, wife, and children, owing service to any person giving aid to the rebellion, were declared free; the mutual right of search was arranged within certain limits with Great Britain in order to suppress the slave-trade; the independence of Hayti and Liberia were recognized, and diplomatic relations with them authorized; colored persons, free or slave, to be enrolled and drafted the same as whites, the former to have the same pay as the latter, and the slave to be free; all fugitive slave acts were repealed; the coastwise slave-trade was declared illegal; colored persons enabled to testify in all the courts of the United States; colored persons were authorized to carry the mails of the United

[1] "That so much of the President's message as relates to the duty of the United States to guarantee a republican form of government to the states in which the governments recognized by the United States have been abrogated or overthrown, be referred to a select committee of nine, to be named by the speaker, which shall report the bills necessary and proper for carrying into execution

normal relations with the executive. The direct participation of these states in the Federal government by means of representation was left entirely to Congress. "Whether members sent to Congress from any state shall be admitted to seats constitutionally, rests exclusively *with the respective houses*, and not, to any extent, with the executive." We have said that the provisions of this proclamation were made for loyal men; yet the proclamation was by its very terms addressed to rebels, to induce them to return to their allegiance to the government, and time was given for its operation upon the minds of the people. The amnesty had no reference to the *past*, but only to *prospective* allegiance. Only those were excluded from participation in the work of restoration who refused to take this oath, and who were not qualified voters by the election laws of their respective states. This work might proceed in any of the eleven so-called Confederate States "*whenever*" (not *if now*, or *if immediately*) one tenth of the voters in the state should have taken the amnesty oath in good faith.

Thus the real burden of restoration, according to President Lincoln's method, was thrown upon the people of the disturbed states. The only conditions imposed were the modification of the new governments to suit the altered situation of the negro, and that the governments should be republican in form. That otherwise than in regard to slavery Lincoln's method did not contemplate any radical revolution in the revived state governments is evident from the fact that he saw no impropriety in maintaining "the name of the state, the boundary, the subdivisions, the Constitution, and the general code of laws, as before the rebellion." Negro suffrage was not even alluded to either as necessary or desirable. It was simply declared that any provision which might be adopted in relation to the freed people, recognizing and declaring their permanent freedom, providing for their education, or meeting their present condition as a laboring, landless, and homeless class, would "not be objected to by the executive."

It must be remembered that this plan, so liberal in its provisions, was offered while the war was yet in progress, though no longer doubtful as to its result. Perhaps there is no stronger evidence of the blindness and persistency of the rebellion, or of the want of foresight among its leaders, than the fact that this generous plan was not immediately and universally adopted. The nation would have been thus delivered not only from sixteen months of useless strife, but also from the dissensions which, after the close of the war, arose in regard to the methods of restoration. Whether, on the whole, so sudden a deliverance would have been better for the interests of freedom on this continent, there is room for doubt. If treason had thus suddenly and of its own motion been transformed into loyalty, in order to save itself from impending woes, it would not then have been utterly slain; if it had thus willingly put off its own armor, and resigned the conflict while yet in its full might of resistance, might it not then again have proudly stepped into the political arena, changed only in respect of *prudence*? The nation would have lost that complete sense of the victory of right over wrong which followed the forced surrender of the Confederate armies; and who can estimate the moral power lodged in that sublime exaltation which thrilled the whole loyal people in the spring of 1865? But in that way also lay fearful temptation and possible madness, arising out of the very completeness of a victory by which the people of an entire section were laid prostrate at the feet of that of another. But even this test, if it could be borne, it were a pity to have lost—losing, as we should have done, at the same time, so much of moral force; escaping at once inestimable good and the possibility of inestimable harm. If the war had thus concluded, slavery would have been abolished indeed; but whatever of positive liberty the negro might gain he must owe to the magnanimity or the fears of his former masters, or else to his own utility as a political dummy.

By the amnesty proclamation, property forfeited under the Confiscation Act of Congress, and not already sold, was restored to all persons taking the oath of allegiance.

In Congress the general subject of reconstruction came up in the course of a discussion relating to the Confiscation Act of 1862, and its application to the perpetual forfeiture of property. During the debate in the House on the 22d of January, Thaddeus Stevens reiterated the views upon which he had so strongly insisted in the previous session. It had been argued by some members that the Constitution permitted no forfeiture of real estate beyond the natural life of the offender, and by others that no such meaning was intended by the framers, whose design was merely to prevent the act of forfeiture from original application after the offender's decease. Stevens claimed that the Confiscation Act was not affected, either directly or indirectly, by the provisions of the Constitution; that its operation was not under the Constitution, but in accordance with the laws of war. The seizure of property operated not as against traitors, but as against alien enemies. "It is, however," said he, "essential to ascertain what relation the seceded states bear to the United States, that we may know how to deal with them in re-establishing the national government. There seems to be great confusion of ideas and diversity of opinion on that subject. Some think that those states are still in the Union, and entitled to the protection of the Constitution and laws of the United States, and that, notwithstanding all they have done, they may at any time, without any legislation, come back, send senators and representatives to Congress, and enjoy all the privileges and immunities of loyal members of the United States; that whenever those 'wayward sisters' choose to abandon their frivolities and present themselves at the door of the Union and demand admission, we must receive them with open arms, and throw over them the protecting shield of the Union, of which it is said they had never ceased to be members. Others hold that, having committed treason, renounced their allegiance to the Union, discarded its Constitution and laws, organized a distinct and hostile government, and by force of arms

having risen from the condition of
ent power *de facto*, and having bee
foreign nations and our own gove
Union are abrogated so far as the
two belligerents, they are under t
alone, and that whichever power c
quered provinces, and may impose
it may deem best.

"It is obvious that this questio
tion should be established, then the
and reduced to helplessness throu
money and the shedding of oceans
which they can no longer wield,
Union, send senators and represen
and possessions, and leave the loya
with no indemnity for their suffe
for the future.

"If the latter proposition prevail
ment on the firm basis of individu
nocent and pardon the least guilt
their lands and estates, sell them in
tional treasury to discharge the ex
vide a permanent fund for pensio
maimed and mangled survivors o
forever exclude the infernal cause
the continent of North America."

Stevens then proceeded to argu
the war was waged by the Confed
them of belligerent rights, both by
operation of the war was exactly th
two hostile nations, and that all tr
tween the same were therefore a
rights to the seceding states, he c
out of the Union. These states, a
erated together in a major corp
were waging war against the Un
townships, and counties, and paris
the states, by acknowledged major
idle was the claim that the loyal i
each of the belligerent states, const
were not at war. "This," said he
of democratic republics, which is, th
the majority, however wicked an
the minority choose to stay withi
citizens, and subject to its conditi
no protection (except in a persona
tile territory. Even the innocenc
them from the fate of their nation
tile state. "From all this," said
the people and all the territory
which, by a legitimate majority of
took their states out of the Union,
so far as they are concerned, subj
the United States government is
of nations, *both while the war con*
United States succeed, how may
Must she treat her precisely as i
then this war on the part of the
but a very wicked one. But the
the hands of the injured victor.
seize and convert to his own us
This may be done when the war i
it is ended the things seized may
and the damages caused by it. T
a punishment for an unjust war, a
The property thus taken is not co
viction for treason, but is held by
crime need be proved against the
enemy carries the forfeiture with i
to *what we have a right to do* if,
should finally conquer the Confe
may be more difficult to determi
waged the most unjust, cruel, and
ruthless murderers and pirates.
self-defense to expend billions c
guilty portion of this usurping p
burse all the costs of the war, to p
loyal men, and to create an ampl
and to the bereaved friends of th

[1] He quoted from Vattel, p. 424, 425:
"When, in a republic, the nation is divi
arms, this is called a civil war. The sove
rebels on all such of his subjects as openly r
strength to give him effectual opposition, an
ing to the established rules, he must necessa
"On earth they have no common superi
two nations who engage in a contest, and, b
arms."
Also from the same, book iii., chap. x., sc
"The conventions, the treaties made wit
between the contending parties."

will consent that his constituents and their posterity shall be burdened with an immense load caused by these bloody traitors? Their lands, if sold in fee, would produce enough for all these purposes, and leave a large surplus."

Broomall, of Pennsylvania, thought that the government should be confined absolutely neither to the position of those who would for all purposes treat those engaged in the rebellion as public enemies, nor to that of those who would for all purposes treat them as "our fellow-citizens, and entitled to the benefits of the Constitution and laws of the United States." The rebels were wrong by their own voluntary act, and, while not entitled to any of the advantages of their position, were subject to all its disadvantages. They could not claim to be treated either as subjects or as public enemies, but the government might at its own election treat them in either capacity. Sometimes, as in the case of prisoners, the more humane laws of war ought to step in in the place of civil law. But the power to enforce civil law still remained. In regard to the property of rebels either code might be applied. This property might be confiscated absolutely under the laws of war, and in this case the confiscation would not be penal in its nature, would have nothing to do with attainder for treason, and would therefore fall outside of the scope of constitutional provisions; or, under the civil code this property could be fined or forfeited as a penalty of treason, and in the latter case the effects of the attainder could not extend beyond the life of the offender.

But both Stevens and Broomall were wrong in assuming that because the general laws of war are applicable to civil wars, therefore under and by virtue of those laws private property on land belonging to the enemy might be confiscated. By modern usage, the private property of a public enemy on land is exempt from capture except when taken as a penalty for military offenses, as a forced contribution for the support of invading armies, or to pay the expenses of maintaining order and affording protection to the conquered. It was necessary, therefore, to resort to the civil code in order to reach the private property of rebels. The inhabitants of the states engaged in rebellion must, in this respect at least, be regarded as subjects, or escape the penalty of confiscation.

The House was disposed, therefore, to consider the provision of the Constitution in regard to attainder for treason as applicable to the Confiscation Act. By a vote of 83 to 74, a joint resolution was passed amending the joint resolution explanatory of the Confiscation Act, and adopted at the President's suggestion, so that no punishment or proceeding under the act might be construed to work the forfeiture of the offender's estate contrary to the Constitution. In the Senate, the clause of the joint resolution of 1862, limiting forfeiture to the life of the offender, was repealed, 23 to 15. Returning to the House, the subject was postponed to the next session, and the act of 1862 remained as it was.

The President's amnesty proclamation had only spoken for the executive. It was also deemed necessary that Congress should speak for itself in terms equally explicit, either adopting the President's plan or proposing some other. Accordingly, in the House, on the 15th of February, Henry Winter Davis, from the Select Committee, reported a bill to guarantee to certain states a republican form of government.[1] The plan thus offered differed from that proposed by the President in several important particulars. It provided for the supervision, by a provisional governor, of the work of restoration. It postponed this work in any state until the rebellion in that state should have been suppressed, and until a majority had taken the oath of allegiance. No person was allowed to vote for, or act as a delegate in the Convention who had held any civil, military, state, or Confederate office under the rebel occupation, or who had voluntarily borne arms against the United States. Three distinct articles were dictated to the Convention for insertion in the state Constitution: the first disfranchising, in elections for governor and Legislature, all citizens who had held any military or civil office (except offices merely ministerial and military offices below that of colonel) under the usurping power; the second abolished slavery, and guaranteed the freedom of all persons; and the third prohibited the recognition or payment of the Confederate debt. The assent of Congress was made a necessary condition precedent to the President's proclamation recognizing the government thus established. From the date of such recognition, and not before, could senators, representatives, and presidential electors be elected in any of the states included within the provisions of the bill. The bill also emancipated all slaves in these states, and affixed a distinct penalty to any attempt to re-enslave those who had been thus declared free. It disfranchised all those whom it required the several state Conventions to disfranchise. It agreed with the President's proclamation in ignoring negro suffrage.

This bill was passed by the House on the 4th of May, 74 to 66. Every affirmative vote was Republican, and only six Republicans voted in opposition. On the 27th, B. F. Wade, of Ohio, reported the bill in the Senate. In the course of the discussion which followed, Wade, in the most emphatic terms, repudiated as "most hazardous" the theory that the states could lose their organization, their rights as states, or their corporate capacity by rebellion.[1] The Senate passed the bill July 2d, yeas 18, and nays 14. Among those voting nay were Senators Doolittle, Lane (of Indiana), and Trumbull. The President refused to sign the bill, but on the 9th of July he issued a proclamation concerning it. It had, he said, been presented to him less than one hour previous to the close of the session, and he had not signed it. He declared that he was "unprepared, by the formal approval of this bill, to be inflexibly committed to any single plan of restoration;" to set aside the free state constitutions and governments already adopted and installed in Arkansas and Louisiana, thus discouraging loyal citizens from farther effort; or to declare the constitutional competency of Congress to abolish slavery in the states. Yet he was "fully satisfied with the system for restoration contained in the bill as one very proper for the loyal people of any state choosing to adopt it," and was prepared to give executive aid and assistance in carrying out such a method, and he would appoint military governors for this purpose so soon as military resistance to the government should have been suppressed in any state, and the people thereof sufficiently returned to their obedience to the Constitution and laws of the United States. This proclamation called forth a political manifesto from Davis and Wade, which was published in the New York *Tribune* for August 5, 1864, censuring the President, and charging him with usurpation and unworthy motives.[2]

---

[1] The bill authorized the President to appoint in each of the states declared in rebellion a provisional governor, with the pay and emoluments of a brigadier, to be charged with the civil administration until a state government therein shall be recognized. As soon as the military resistance to the United States shall have been suppressed, and the people sufficiently returned to their obedience to the Constitution and the laws, the governor shall direct the marshal of the United States to enroll all the white male citizens of the United States resident in the state, in their respective counties; and whenever a majority of them take the oath of allegiance, the loyal people of the state shall be entitled to elect delegates to a Convention to act upon the re-establishment of a state government—the proclamation to contain details prescribed. Qualified voters in the army may vote in their camps. No person who has held or exercised any civil, military, state, or Confederate office under the rebel occupation, and who has voluntarily borne arms against the United States, shall vote or be eligible as a delegate. The Convention is required to insert in the Constitution provisions—

"1. No person who has held or exercised any civil or military office (except offices merely ministerial and military offices below a colonel), state or Confederate, under the usurping power, shall vote for, or be a member of the Legislature or governor.

"2. Involuntary servitude is forever prohibited, and the freedom of all persons guaranteed in said state.

"3. No debt, state or Confederate, created by or under the sanction of the usurping power, shall be recognized or paid by the state."

Upon the adoption of the Constitution by the Convention, and its ratification by the electors of the state, the provisional government shall so certify to the President, who, after obtaining the assent of Congress, shall, by proclamation, recognize the government as established, and none other, as the constitutional government of the state; and from the date of such recognition, and not before, senators and representatives, and electors for President and Vice-President may be elected in such state. Until reorganization, the provisional governor shall enforce the laws of the Union and of the state before rebellion.

The remaining sections are as follows:

"*Sec.* 12. That all persons held to involuntary servitude or labor in the states aforesaid are hereby emancipated and discharged therefrom, and they and their posterity shall be forever free. And if any such person or their posterity shall be restrained of their liberty, under pretense of any claim to such service or labor, the courts of the United States shall on habeas corpus discharge them.

"*Sec.* 13. That if any person declared free by this act, or any law of the United States, or any proclamation of the President, be restrained of liberty, with intent to be held in or restored to involuntary labor, the person convicted before a court of competent jurisdiction of such act shall be punished by fine of not less than $1500, and be imprisoned not less than five nor more than twenty years.

"*Sec.* 14. That every person who shall hereafter hold or exercise any office, civil or military, except offices merely ministerial and military offices below the grade of colonel, in the rebel service, state or Confederate, is hereby declared not to be a citizen of the United States."

[1] The following is an extract from Mr. Wade's speech:

"It has been contended in the House of Representatives, it has been contended upon this floor, that the states may lose their organization, may lose their rights as states, may lose their corporate capacity by rebellion. I utterly deny that doctrine. I hold that once a state of this Union, always a state; that you can not by wrong and violence displace the rights of any body or disorganize the state. It would be a most hazardous principle to assert that. No, sir; the framers of your Constitution intended no such thing. They did not leave this great question untouched; and when we study that great instrument, I can hardly help but stop and contemplate the all-embracing wisdom that seemed to actuate them, for you can find hardly an exigency that may arise in the complicated affairs of government that they did not anticipate and provide for. They did foresee that in the progress of the government some of the states might go into rebellion; that they might undertake themselves to absolve their connection with the general government and set up some hostile government of their own; and they expressly provided for just such a case; and how gentlemen with this principle of the Constitution staring them in the face can fancy that states can lose their rights because more or less of the people have gone off into rebellion, is marvelous to me. The principle of law every where is that no honest man shall lose a right by wrong or usurpation. The act of rebellion is void. It may have physical force for the moment to displace rights; but the law never yields to any such power as that. The law never any where acknowledges that right can be overthrown by wrongful action. They, then, who contend that the state governments are lost, obliterated, blotted out, are contending against the face and eyes of the Constitution. Has that said any such thing? No, sir. It has said that the Federal government shall guarantee to every state a republican form of government; and if a portion of the people undertake to overthrow their government and set up another, it is the manifest duty of the general government immediately to interfere, and, if necessary, to interpose the strong arm of its power to prevent such a state of things. Precisely that state of things is upon us, and this bill proceeds upon that idea, and discards absolutely the notion that states may lose their rights, and that they may be abrogated and may be reduced to the condition of Territories. It denies any such thing as that. No sound principle can be adopted that warrants any such thing."

[2] *Protest of Senator Wade and H. Winter Davis, M. C., to the supporters of the Government.*

"We have read without surprise, but not without indignation, the proclamation of the President of the 8th of July, 1864.

"The supporters of the administration are responsible to the country for its conduct; and it is their right and duty to check the encroachments of the executive on the authority of Congress, and to require it to confine itself to its proper sphere.

"It is impossible to pass in silence this proclamation without neglecting that duty; and, having taken as much responsibility as any others in supporting the administration, we are not disposed to fail in the other duty of asserting the rights of Congress.

"The President did not sign the bill 'to guarantee to certain states whose government have been usurped, a republican form of government'—passed by the supporters of his administration in both houses of Congress after mature deliberation.

"The bill did not, therefore, become a law, and it is, therefore, nothing.

"The proclamation is neither an approval nor a veto of the bill; it is, therefore, a document unknown to the laws and Constitution of the United States.

"So far as it contains an apology for not signing the bill, it is a political manifesto against the friends of the government.

"So far as it proposes to execute the bill which is not a law, it is a grave executive usurpation.

"It is fitting that the facts necessary to enable the friends of the administration to appreciate the apology and the usurpation be spread before them.

"The proclamation says:

"'And whereas the said bill was presented to the President of the United States for his approval less than one hour before the *sine die* adjournment of said session, and was not signed by him—'

"If that be accurate, still this bill was presented with other bills which were signed.

"Within that hour the time for the *sine die* adjournment was three times postponed by the votes of both houses; and the least intimation of a desire for more time by the President to consider this bill would have secured a farther postponement.

"Yet the committee sent to ascertain if the President had any further communication for the House of Representatives reported that he had none; and the friends of the bill, who had anxiously waited on him to ascertain its fate, had already been informed that the President had resolved not to sign it.

"The time of presentation, therefore, had nothing to do with his failure to approve it.

"The bill has been discussed and considered for more than a month in the House of Representatives, which it passed on the 4th of May. It was reported to the Senate on the 27th of May, without material amendment, and passed the Senate absolutely as it came from the House on the 2d of July.

"Ignorance of its contents is out of the question.

"Indeed, at his request, a draft of a bill substantially the same in material points, and identical in the points objected to by the proclamation, had been laid before him for his consideration in the winter of 1862–3.

"There is, therefore, no reason to suppose the provisions of the bill took the President by surprise.

"On the contrary, we have reason to believe them to have been so well known that this method of preventing the bill from becoming a law without the constitutional responsibility of a veto had been resolved on long before the bill passed the Senate.

The Senate, a short time before its adjournment, declared by a vote 27 to 6 that W. M. Fishback and Elisha Baxter, claiming seats from Arkansas,

"We are informed by a gentleman entitled to entire confidence, that before the 22d of June, in New Orleans, it was stated by a member of General Banks's staff, in the presence of other gentlemen in official position, that Senator Doolittle had written a letter to the department that the House Reconstruction Bill would be staved off in the Senate to a period too late in the session to require the President to veto it in order to defeat it, and that Mr. Lincoln would retain the bill, if necessary, and thereby defeat it.

"The experience of Senator Wade, in his various efforts to get the bill considered in the Senate, was quite in accordance with that plan; and the fate of the bill was accurately predicted by letters received from New Orleans before it had passed the Senate.

"Had the proclamation stopped there, it would have been only one other defeat of the will of the people by the executive perversion of the Constitution.

"But it goes farther. The President says:

"'And whereas the said bill contains, among other things, a plan for restoring the states in rebellion to their proper practical relation in the Union, which plan expresses the sense of Congress upon that subject, and which plan it is now thought fit to lay before the people for their consideration—'

"By what authority of the Constitution? In what forms? The result to be declared by whom? With what effect when ascertained?

"Is it to be a law by the approval of the people, without the approval of Congress, at the will of the President?

"Will the President, on his opinion of the popular approval, execute it as a law?

"Or is this merely a device to avoid the serious responsibility of defeating a law on which so many loyal hearts reposed for security?

"But the reasons now assigned for not approving the bill are full of ominous significance.

"The President proceeds:

"'Now, therefore, I, Abraham Lincoln, President of the United States, do proclaim, declare, and make known that, while I am (as I was in December last, when by proclamation I propounded a plan for restoration) unprepared by a formal approval of this bill to be inflexibly committed to any single plan of restoration—'

"That is to say, the President is resolved that people shall not *by law* take *any* securities from the rebel states against a renewal of the rebellion, before restoring their power to govern us.

"His wisdom and prudence are to be our sufficient guarantees! He farther says:

"'And while I am also unprepared to declare that the free state Constitutions and governments already adopted and installed in Arkansas and Louisiana shall be set aside and held for naught, thereby repelling and discouraging the loyal citizens who have set up the same as to farther effort—'

"That is to say, the President persists in recognizing those shadows of governments in Arkansas and Louisiana which Congress formally declared should not be recognized—whose representatives and senators were repelled by formal votes of both houses of Congress—which it was declared formally should have no electoral vote for President and Vice-President.

"They are mere creatures of his will. They are mere oligarchies, imposed on the people by military orders under the form of election, at which generals, provost-marshals, soldiers, and camp-followers were the chief actors, assisted by a handful of resident citizens, and urged on to premature action by private letters from the President.

"In neither Louisiana nor Arkansas, before Banks's defeat, did the United States control half the territory or half the population. In Louisiana, General Banks's proclamation candidly declared, 'The fundamental law of the state is martial law.'

"On that foundation of freedom he erected what the President calls 'the free Constitution and government of Louisiana.'

"But of this state, whose fundamental law was martial law, only sixteen parishes out of forty-eight parishes were held by the United States; and in five of the sixteen we held only our camps.

"The eleven parishes we substantially held had 233,185 inhabitants; the residue of the state not held by us, 575,617.

"At the farce called an election, the officers of General Banks returned that 11,346 ballots were cast; but whether any or by whom the people of the United States have no legal assurance; but it is probable that 4000 were cast by soldiers or employés of the United States, military or municipal, but none according to any law, state or national, and 7000 ballots represent the State of Louisiana.

"Such is the free Constitution and government of Louisiana; and like it is that of Arkansas. Nothing but the failure of a military expedition deprived us of a like one in the swamps of Florida; and before the presidential election like ones may be organized in every rebel state where the United States have a camp.

"The President, by preventing this bill from becoming a law, holds the electoral votes of the rebel states at the dictation of his personal ambition.

"If those votes turn the balance in his favor, is it to be supposed that his competitor, defeated by such means, will acquiesce?

"If the rebel majority assert their supremacy in those states, and send votes which elect an enemy of the government, will we not repel his claims?

"And is not that civil war for the Presidency inaugurated by the votes of rebel states?

"Seriously impressed with these dangers, Congress, 'the proper constitutional authority,' formally declared that there are no state governments in the rebel states, and provided for their erection at a proper time; and both the Senate and the House of Representatives rejected the senators and representatives chosen under the authority of what the President calls the free Constitution and government of Arkansas.

"The President's proclamation 'holds for naught' this judgment, and discards the authority of the Supreme Court, and strides headlong toward the anarchy his proclamation of the 8th of December inaugurated.

"If electors for President be allowed to be chosen in either of those states, a sinister light will be cast on the motives which induced the President to 'hold for naught' the will of Congress rather than his government in Louisiana and Arkansas.

"That judgment of Congress which the President defies was the exercise of an authority exclusively vested in Congress by the Constitution, to determine what is the established government in a state, and in its own nature and by the highest judicial authority binding on all other departments of the government.

"The Supreme Court has formally declared that, under the 4th section of the IVth article of the Constitution, requiring the United States to guarantee to every state a republican form of government, 'it rests with Congress to decide what government is the established one in a state;' and 'when senators and representatives of a state are admitted into the councils of the Union, the authority of the government under which they are appointed, as well as its republican character, is recognized by the proper constitutional authority, and its decision is binding on every other department of the government, and could not be questioned in a judicial tribunal. It is true that the contest in this case did not last long enough to bring the matter to this issue; and as no senators or representatives were elected under the authority of the government of which Mr. Dorr was the head, Congress was not called upon to decide the controversy. Yet the right to decide is placed there.'

"Even the President's proclamation of the 8th of December formally declares that 'whether members sent to Congress from any state shall be admitted to seats constitutionally rests exclusively with the respective houses, and not to any extent with the executive.'

"And that is not the less true because wholly inconsistent with the President's assumption in that proclamation of a right to institute and recognize state governments in the rebel states, nor because the President is unable to perceive that his recognition is a nullity if it be not conclusive on Congress.

"Under the Constitution, the right to senators and representatives is inseparable from a state government.

"If there be a state government the right is absolute.

"If there be no state government there can be no senators or representatives chosen.

"The two houses of Congress are expressly declared to be the sole judges of their own members.

"When, therefore, senators and representatives are admitted, the state government under whose authority they were chosen is conclusively established; when they are rejected, its existence is as conclusively rejected and denied; and to this judgment the President is bound to submit.

"The President proceeds to express his unwillingness 'to declare a constitutional competency in Congress to abolish slavery in states' as another reason for not signing the bill.

"But the bill nowhere proposes to abolish slavery in states.

"The bill did provide that all *slaves* in the rebel states should be *manumitted*.

"But as the President had already signed three bills manumitting several classes of slaves in states, it is not conceived possible that he entertained any scruples touching *that* provision of the bill respecting which he is silent.

"He had already himself assumed a right by proclamation to free much the larger number of slaves in the rebel states, under the authority given him by Congress to use military power to suppress the rebellion; and it is quite inconceivable that the President should think Congress could vest in him a discretion it could not exercise itself.

"It is the more unintelligible from the fact that, except in respect to a small part of Virginia and Louisiana, the bill covered only what the proclamation covered—added a Congressional title and judicial remedies by law to the disputed title under the proclamation, and perfected the work the President professed to be so anxious to accomplish.

"Slavery, as an institution, can be abolished only by a change of the Constitution of the United States, or of the law of the states; and this is the principle of the bill.

"It required the new Constitution of the state to provide for that prohibition; and the President, in the face of his own proclamation, does not venture to object to insisting on that condition. Nor will the country tolerate its abandonment—yet he defeated the only provision imposing it.

"But when he describes himself, in spite of this great blow at emancipation, as 'sincerely hoping and expecting that a constitutional amendment abolishing slavery throughout the nation may be adopted,' we curiously inquire on what his expectation rests, after the vote of the House of Representatives at the recent session, and in the face of the political complexion of more than enough of the states to prevent the possibility of its adoption within any reasonable time; and why he did not indulge his sincere hopes with so large an instalment of the blessing as his approval of the bill would have secured?

"After this assignment of his reasons for preventing the bill from becoming a law, the President proceeds to declare his purpose to execute it as a law by his plenary dictatorial power.

"He says: 'Nevertheless, I am fully satisfied with the system for restoration contained in the bill as one very proper plan for the loyal people of any state choosing to adopt it; and that I am, and at all times shall be, prepared to give the executive aid and assistance to any such people as soon as the military resistance to the United States shall have been suppressed in any such state, and the people thereof shall have sufficiently returned to their obedience to the Constitution and the laws of the United States—in which cases military governors will be appointed, with directions to proceed according to the bill.'

"A more studied outrage on the legislative authority of the people has never been perpetrated.

"Congress passed a bill; the President refused to approve it, and then, by proclamation, puts as much of it in force as he sees fit, and proposes to execute those parts by officers unknown to the laws of the United States, and not subject to the confirmation of the Senate.

"The bill directed the appointment of provisional governors by and with the advice and consent of the Senate.

"The President, after defeating the law, proposes to appoint, without law and without the advice and consent of the Senate, military governors for the rebel states!

"He has already exercised this dictatorial usurpation in Louisiana, and defeated the bill to prevent its limitation.

"Henceforth we must regard the following precedent as the presidential law of the rebel states:

"'Executive Mansion, Washington, March 15, 1864.

"'His Excellency Michael Hahn, Governor of Louisiana:

"'Until farther orders, you are hereby invested with the powers exercised hitherto by the military governors of Louisiana. Yours, ABRAHAM LINCOLN.'

"This Michael Hahn is no officer of the United States; the President, without law, without the advice and consent of the Senate, by a private note not even countersigned by the Secretary of State, makes him dictator of Louisiana!

"The bill provided for the civil administration of the laws of the state—but it should be in a fit temper to govern itself—repealing all laws recognizing slavery, and making all men equal before the law.

"These beneficent provisions the President has annulled. People will die, and marry, and transfer property, and buy and sell; and to these acts of civil life courts and officers of the law are necessary. Congress legislated for those necessary things, and the President deprives them of the protection of the law!

"The President's purpose to instruct his military governors 'to proceed according to the bill'—a makeshift to calm the disappointment its defeat has occasioned—is not merely a grave usurpation, but a transparent delusion.

"He can not 'proceed according to the bill' after preventing it from becoming a law.

"Whatever is done will be at his will and pleasure, by persons responsible to no law, and more interested to secure the interests and execute the will of the President than of the people; and the will of Congress is to be 'held for naught,' 'unless the loyal people of the rebel states choose to adopt it.'

"If they should graciously prefer the stringent bill to the easy proclamation, still the registration will be made under no legal sanction; it will give no assurance that a majority of the people of the states have taken the oath; if administered, it will be without legal authority and void; no indictment will lie for false swearing at the election, or for admitting bad or rejecting good votes; it will be the farce of Louisiana and Arkansas acted over again, under the forms of this bill, but not by authority of law.

"But when we come to the guaranties of future peace which Congress meant to enact, the forms, as well as the substance of the bill, must yield to the President's will that none should be imposed.

"It was the solemn resolve of Congress to protect the loyal men of the nation against three great dangers: (1) the return to power of the guilty leaders of the rebellion; (2) the continuance of slavery, and (3) the burden of the rebel debt.

"Congress required assent to those provisions by the Convention of the state; and if refused, it was to be dissolved.

"The President 'holds for naught' that resolve of Congress, because he is unwilling 'to be inflexibly committed to any one plan of restoration,' and the people of the United States are not to be allowed to protect themselves unless their enemies agree to it.

"The order to proceed according to the bill is therefore merely at the will of the rebel states; and they have the option to reject it, accept the proclamation of the 8th of December, and demand the President's recognition!

"Mark the contrast! The bill requires a majority, the proclamation is satisfied with one tenth; the bill requires one oath, the proclamation another; the bill ascertains voters by registering, the proclamation by guess; the bill exacts adherence to existing territorial limits, the proclamation admits of others; the bill governs the rebel states *by law*, equalizing all before it—the proclamation commits them to the lawless discretion of military governors and provost-marshals; the bill forbids electors for President, the proclamation and defeat of the bill threaten us with civil war for the admission or exclusion of such votes; the bill exacted exclusion of dangerous enemies from power and the relief of the nation from the rebel debt, and the prohibition of slavery forever, so that the suppression of the rebellion will double our resources to bear or pay the national debt, free the masses from the old domination of the rebel leaders, and eradicate the cause of the war—the proclamation secures neither of these guaranties.

"It is silent respecting the rebel debt and the political exclusion of rebel leaders, leaving slavery exactly where it was by law at the outbreak of the rebellion, and adds no guaranty even of the freedom of the slaves he undertook to manumit.

"It is summed up in an illegal oath, without sanction, and therefore void.

"The oath is to support all proclamations of the President, during the rebellion, having reference to slaves.

"Any government is to be accepted at the hands of one tenth of the people not contravening that oath.

"Now that oath neither secures the abolition of slavery, nor adds any security to the freedom of the slaves the President declared free.

"It does not secure the abolition of slavery; for the proclamation of freedom merely professed to free certain slaves while it recognized the institution.

"Every Constitution of the rebel states at the outbreak of the rebellion may be adopted without the change of a letter; for none of them contravene that proclamation; none of them establish slavery.

"It adds no security to the freedom of the slaves, for their title is the proclamation of freedom.

"If it be unconstitutional, an oath to support it is void. Whether constitutional or not, the oath is without authority of law, and therefore void.

"If it be valid and observed, it exacts no enactment by the state, either in law or Constitution, to add a state guaranty to the proclamation title; and the right of a slave to freedom is an open question before the state courts on the relative authority of the state law and the proclamation.

"If the oath binds the one tenth who take it, it is not exacted of the other nine tenths who succeed to the control of the state government, so that it is annulled instantly by the act of recognition.

"What the state courts would say of the proclamation, who can doubt?

"But the master would not go into court—he would seize his slaves.

"What the Supreme Court would say, who can tell?

"When and how is the question to get there?

"No *habeas corpus* lies for him in a United States court; and the President defeated with this bill the extension of that writ to his case.

"Such are the fruits of this rash and fatal act of the President—a blow at the friends of his administration, at the rights of humanity, and at the principles of republican government.

"The President has greatly presumed on the forbearance which the supporters of his administration have so long practiced, in view of the arduous conflict in which we are engaged, and the reckless ferocity of our political opponents.

"But he must understand that our support is of a cause and not of a man; that the authority of Congress is paramount and must be respected; that the whole body of the Union men of Congress will not submit to be impeached by him of rash and unconstitutional legislation; and if he wishes our support, he must confine himself to his executive duties—to obey and execute, not make the laws—to suppress by arms armed rebellion, and leave political reorganization to Congress.

"If the supporters of the government fail to insist on this, they become responsible for the usurpations which they fail to rebuke, and are justly liable to the indignation of the people whose rights and security, committed to their keeping, they sacrifice.

"Let them consider the remedy of these usurpations, and, having found it, fearlessly execute it.

"B. F. WADE, Chairman Senate Committee.

"H. WINTER DAVIS, Chairman Com. House of Rep. on the Rebellious States."

were not entitled to them. This was as emphatic a rejection of the President's plan of restoration as was possible. In the House, A. C. Rogers, J. M. Johnson, and T. M. Jacks, claiming seats from Arkansas, were not admitted. In the same body the claims of A. P. Fields and Thomas Cotton, from Louisiana, were rejected by a vote of 100 to 71.

During this session several resolutions were offered concerning the object and conduct of the war. A number of these reiterated the resolutions adopted by the Thirty-seventh Congress to the effect that the war was not waged for the purpose of conquest or subjugation, or of overthrowing or interfering with the rights or established institutions of the insurgent states, "but to defend and maintain the supremacy of the Constitution, and to preserve the Union with all the dignity, equality, and rights of the several states unimpaired." Such resolutions were invariably tabled, laid over, or referred to the Select Committee never to be heard of again.

On the 8th of April, the House sitting in Committee of the Whole on the State of the Union, Alexander Long, of Ohio, rose, and in a long speech prophesied the ultimate failure of the war, and declared himself in favor of the recognition of the Confederacy. General Garfield, his patriotic colleague, as soon as Long took his seat, rose and asked that a white flag might be placed between his colleague and himself. "I recollect," said he, "that on one occasion, when two great armies stood face to face, that under a white flag just planted I approached a company of men dressed in the uniform of the rebel Confederacy, and reached out my hand to one of the number, and told him I respected him as a brave man. Though he wore the emblems of disloyalty and treason, still underneath his vestments I beheld a brave and honest soul. I would reproduce that scene here this afternoon. I say were there such a flag of truce—but God forgive me if I should do it under other circumstances!—I would reach out this right hand and ask that gentleman to take it, because I honor his bravery and honesty. . . . . He has done a brave thing. It is braver than to face cannon and musketry." Then, in a speech—the most thrilling of that session—General Garfield analyzed and developed the significance of Long's proposition. "Now," said he, "when hundreds of thousands of brave souls have gone up to God under the shadow of the flag, and when thousands more, maimed and shattered in the contest, are sadly awaiting the deliverance of death; now, when three years of terrific warfare have raged over us, when our armies have pushed the rebellion back over mountains and rivers, and crowded it into narrow limits, until a wall of fire girds it; now, when the uplifted hand of a majestic people is about to let fall the lightning of its conquering power upon the rebellion; now, in the quiet of this hall, hatched in the lowest depths of a similar dark treason, there rises a Benedict Arnold and proposes to surrender us all up, body and spirit, the nation and the flag, its genius and its honor, now and forever, to the accursed traitors to our country! And that proposition comes —God forgive and pity my beloved state!—it comes from a citizen of the honored and loyal commonwealth of Ohio. . . . . .

"For the first time in the history of this contest, it is proposed in this hall to give up the struggle, to abandon the war, and let treason run riot through the land! * * * *

"Suppose the policy of the gentleman were adopted to-day. Let the order go forth; sound the 'recall' on your bugles, and let it ring from Texas to the far Atlantic, and tell the armies to come back. Call the victorious legions back over the battle-fields of blood, forever now disgraced. Call them back over the territory they have conquered and redeemed. Call them back, and let the minions of secession chase them with derision and jeers as they come. And then tell them that that man across the aisle, from the free state of Ohio, gave birth to the monstrous proposition."

The next day Speaker Colfax took the floor, and offered a resolution for the expulsion of Long. He did this, he said, in the performance of a high public duty—a duty to his constituents and to the soldiers in the field. He believed in the freedom of speech, and had during this Congress heard nothing, save this single speech, which could have prompted him to offer such a resolution. The flag of the Confederacy had been boldly unfurled by a gentleman who had taken an oath at the opening of the session that up to that time he had not given aid, countenance, or encouragement to the enemies of the United States. If such an oath was necessary to membership, then he who could thus publicly give the encouragement which he had sworn not to have given in the past was an unworthy member, and ought not to remain. The soldiers who deserted did not more surely turn their backs upon the obligation they had assumed than had the member from Ohio. If the House allowed such sentiments to go unquestioned, they should stop shooting deserters. Could the United States go to war with a foreign nation recognizing the Confederacy, while from the halls of Congress an opinion was permitted to go forth in favor of such recognition, and unaccompanied by the highest expression of Congressional censure?

Cox, of Ohio, while opposing the resolution, and pleading for the utmost freedom of discussion, emphatically disavowed for himself and his Democratic colleagues the sentiments expressed by Long. On the other hand, Harris, of Maryland, as emphatically indorsed those sentiments, and in terms far more distinct than Long had adopted. "I am," said he, "a peace man, a radical peace man, and I am for peace by the recognition of the Confederacy. I am for acquiescence in the doctrine of secession. I thought I was alone; but now, thank God! there is another soul saved. . . . . The South asked

HENRY WINTER DAVIS.

Probably there was no man who more completely commanded the atten
tion of the House, whenever he spoke, than Henry Winter Davis. His elo
quence and impressiveness were only matched by his profound culture an
his elegance of expression. On this occasion he addressed a silent an
crowded house in support of the resolution for Long's expulsion. In th
course of his speech, he said:

"Mr. Speaker, if it be said that a time may come when the question o
recognizing the Southern Confederacy will have to be answered, I admit it
and it is answering the strongest and the extreme case that gentlemen o
the other side can present. I admit it. When a Democrat shall darken th
White House and the land; when a Democratic majority here shall proclai
that freedom of speech secures impunity to treason, and declare recognitio
better than extermination of traitors; when McClellan and Fitz John Po
ter shall have again brought the rebel armies within sight of Washingto
City, and the successor of James Buchanan shall withdraw our armies fro
the unconstitutional invasion of Virginia to the north of the Potomac; whe
exultant rebels shall sweep over the fortifications and their bomb-shells sha
crash against the dome of the Capitol; when thousands throughout Pen
sylvania shall seek refuge on the shores of Lake Erie from the rebel inv
sion, cheered and welcomed by the opponents of extermination; when Va
landigham shall be Governor of Ohio, and Bright Governor of Indiana, an
Woodward Governor of Pennsylvania, and Seymour Governor of Connect
cut, and Wall be Governor of New Jersey, and the gentleman from Ne
York city sit in Seymour's seat, and thus, possessed of power over the gre
centre of the country, they shall do what they attempted in vain before :
the midst of rebel triumphs—to array the authorities of the states again
those of the United States; to oppose the militia to the army of the Unit
States; to invoke the *habeas corpus* to discharge confined traitors; to de
to the government the benefit of the laws of war, lest it exterminate its en
mies; when the Democrats, as in the fall of 1862, shall again, with mo
permanent success, persuade the people of the country that the war shou
not be waged till the integrity of the territory of the Union is restored, c
what it might, but that such a war violates the spirit of free institutio
which those who advocate it wish to overthrow, and should stop, for t
benefit of the Democratic party, somewhere this side of absolute triump
lest there be no room for a compromise; when gentlemen of that party
New York shall again, as in November, 1862, hold illegal and criminal n
gotiations with Lord Lyons, and avow their purposes to him, the represen
tive of a foreign and unfriendly power, and urge him to arrange the ti
of proffering mediation with a view to their possession of power and th
preparation of the minds of the public to receive suggestions from abroa
and when mediation shall appear by the event to be the first step tow
foreign intervention, swiftly and surely followed by foreign armed enem
upon our shores to join the domestic enemies; when the war in the c

fore the advancing foe; when vast chasms across every state shall make apparent to every eye, when too late to remedy it, that division from the South is inauguration of anarchy at the North, and that peace without union is the end of the republic—THEN the independence of the South will be an accomplished fact, and gentlemen may, without treason to the dead republic, rise in this migratory house, wherever it may then be in America, and declare themselves for *recognizing* their masters at the South rather than exterminating them! Until that day, in the name of the American nation—in the name of every house in the land where there is one dead for the holy cause—in the name of those who stand before us in the ranks of battle—in the name of the liberty our ancestors have confided to us, I devote to eternal execration the name of him who shall propose to destroy this blessed land rather than its enemies."[1]

On the side of the opposition, Pendleton, of Ohio, one of the most popular leaders of his party, closed the debate with an able argument in favor of free discussion. It was in reply to Davis's speech of the night before. "The gentleman from Maryland," said he, "told us last night, in terms of eloquence which I can not emulate, that when Lord Chatham, aged, feeble, wrapped in flannel and suffering from disease, came, resting upon the arm of his still greater son, to address for the last time the British House of Lords, and to die upon the floor, he came to speak against the dismemberment of the British empire. It is true; and what did he say? 'I told you this war would be disastrous; I predicted its consequences; I told you you could not conquer America; I begged you to conciliate America; you would not heed my advice. You have exhausted the country; you have sacrificed its men; you have wasted its treasures; you have driven these colonies to declare their independence; you have driven them into the arms of our ancient and hated enemy, and now, without striking a blow, without firing a shot, cowardly under difficulties as you were truculent in success, you propose to yield through fear to France what you have refused as justice to America.' Did it not occur to the gentleman from Maryland that possibly at a future day, when the history of that civil strife shall have been reproduced in this land, another Chatham may come to this House, and hurl against those who are now in power these bitter denunciations because they have shown themselves unable to make an honorable peace even as they have been unable to make a victorious war? . . . .

"Sir, if there be depths of public opinion where eternal stillness reigns, there gather, even as festering death lies in those ocean depths, the decaying forms of truth, and right, and freedom. Eternal motion is the condition of their purity. Did he think this resolution would for one instant retard its progress? Did he not know that the surging waves would wash away every trace of its existence? Did he suppose this puny effort would avail him? The rocks of the eternal hills alone can stay the waves of the ever-rolling sea. Nothing but the principles of truth and right can stay the onward progress of public opinion in this our country as it swells, and sways, and surges in this mad tempest of passion, and seeks to find a secure resting-place."

The resolution was finally changed to one of censure in place of expulsion, and in that shape passed 80 to 70. If any evidence were needed of the jealous regard for freedom of debate in the American Congress, it is furnished by the fact that Harris and Long were only censured and not expelled.

During the session enabling acts were passed for the formation of state governments in Colorado, Nevada, and Nebraska. The people of Colorado voted against a Convention, preferring to remain for the present under the territorial organization. The pay of soldiers was increased to $16 per month,[2] and a Bureau of Military Justice was established. The government was authorized to borrow $400,000,000 on coupon bonds running from 5 to 30 years, at not less than 6 per cent. interest, payable in coin. These and the 5.20 bonds might be disposed of in Europe at the discretion of the Secretary of the Treasury. All United States bonds were declared exempt from taxation.[3] Provision was also made for the issue of $50,000,000 in fractional or postage currency. A separate bureau was established, to be charged with the execution of all laws respecting a national currency, secured by United States bonds.[4] At the head of this bureau the President placed Hugh McCulloch, afterward Secretary of the Treasury. A special inco[me] tax was levied at the rate of five per cent. on all sums exceeding $600 cl[ear] income, to be collected under the rules of the Internal Revenue Dep[art]ment.

At this time the relations between this government and that of Fran[ce] were exceedingly critical, and it required all the skill and prudence of S[ec]retary Seward to avert war.

Maximilian, the oldest brother of the reigning Emperor of Austria, h[ad] been proclaimed Emperor of Mexico, July 10th, 1863, by an assembly [of] "Notables" summoned by a government established under the auspices [of] the French army. The choice of Maximilian was of course made by Lo[uis] Napoleon. But the French emperor had commanded that the question between an empire and a republic should be submitted to the Mexican pe[o]ple. Accordingly, at the same time that the Mexican deputation was pr[o]ceeding to Europe with the vote of the Notables engrossed on parchment a[nd] inclosed in a golden sceptre, instructions were on their way from Paris to t[he] French commander in Mexico to carry out the emperor's instructions [to] the letter. Thus Maximilian's acceptance was delayed. An election w[as] held under the impressive authority of French bayonets, and on the 10th [of] April, 1864, the Mexican deputation was again at Miramar, and Maximili[an] was informed that the vote of the "Notables" had been ratified by an i[m]mense majority. Maximilian accepted the sceptre, which, at first the bad[ge] of empire, became in the end, to him, the wand of martyrdom. He visit[ed] the Pope, and, having received the blessing of the latter, embarked with [his] consort, the Empress Carlotta, for Mexico, where he arrived on the 28th [of] May, and entered upon his imperial career.

The French occupation of Mexico, resulting in the subversion of its repu[b]lican government, was construed as an act of hostility both by the people a[nd] the government of the United States. The full expression of this feeli[ng] on the part of the executive was held in check by the civil war. No pled[ge] was given to France that this question—now held in abeyance—would n[ot] arise for settlement, and in the mean while every honorable effort was ma[de] by the government to prevent a foreign war. That this was the wisest po[l]icy is too evident to require argument. It was the policy adopted both b[y] the President and the Senate. In the latter body, McDougall, of Californi[a,] on January 11th, introduced a series of resolutions, declaring that the Fren[ch] attempt to subvert the Mexican republic was an act hostile to the Unit[ed] States, and that it was the duty of our government to require France [to] withdraw her armed forces from Mexico. These resolutions were referr[ed] to the Committee on Foreign Relations, and not heard of again. On t[he] 14th of June McDougall sought in vain to introduce a resolution, whic[h] was in form a general expression of the Monroe doctrine.

The House took an entirely different view as to the question of an imme[diate] protest. On the 4th of April, Henry Winter Davis reported from th[e] Committee on Foreign Affairs the following joint resolution, which passe[d] without a single dissentient voice: "That the Congress of the United State[s] are unwilling, by silence, to leave the nations of the world under the impres[]sion that they are indifferent spectators of the deplorable events now trans[]piring in the republic of Mexico, and they therefore think fit to declare tha[t] it does not accord with the policy of the United States to acknowledge [a] monarchical government erected on the ruins of any republican governmen[t] in America, under the auspices of any European power." The resolutio[n]

---

[1] Mr. Davis thus illustrated the freedom of opinion and its limitations:

"Surely, sir, opinion is the life of our nation. It is the measure of every right, the guarantee of every privilege, the protection of every blessing. It is opinion which creates our rulers. It is opinion that nerves or palsies their arms. It is opinion which casts down the proud and elevates the humble. Its fluctuations are the rise and fall of parties; its currents bear the nation on to prosperity or ruin. Its free play is the condition of its purity. It is like the ocean, whose tides rise and fall day by day at the fickle bidding of the moon; yet it is the great scientific level from which every height is measured—the horizon to which astronomers refer the motion of the stars. But, like the ocean, it has depths whose eternal stillness is the condition of its stability. Those depths of opinion are not free, and it is they that are touched by the words which have so moved the House. Men must not commit treason and say its guilt is a matter of opinion, and its punishment a violation of its freedom. Men can not swear to maintain the integrity of the nation, and avow their intention to destroy it, and cover that double crime by the freedom of speech. *That* is to break up the fountains of the great deep on which all government is borne, and to pour its flood in revolutionary ruin over the land. To punish that is not a violation of the freedom of opinion or its expression. It is to protect its normal ebb and flow, its free and healthy fluctuations, that we desire to relieve it from the opprobrium of being confounded with the declarations of treasonable purposes here, in the high and solemn assemblage of the Union."

[2] Chapter cxlv.

[3] Chapter clxxii. This act also provided that in lieu of so much of this loan, the secretary might issue $200,000,000 of treasury notes redeemable within three years, bearing interest of seven and three tenths per cent., convertible into bonds. The secretary might also cancel all treasury notes heretofore issued, and issue these in their stead. These notes were not to be a legal tender. Bonds might be exchanged for seven and three tenths notes. The secretary might receive temporary loans, and issue certificates of deposit therefor, at six per cent., the certificates to be payable on ten days' notice—such deposits not to exceed $150,000,000.

[4] Chapter cvi.—*National Currency*—establishes a separate bureau, to be charged with the execution of this and all laws respecting a national currency, secured by United States bonds, and names the officers of said bureau, together with the securities conditioned by their assumption of office. Every certificate, assignment, and conveyance shall be as valid as when the comptroller's seal is stamped on the paper. Associations for carrying on the business of banking may be formed by any number of persons not less than five, who shall enter into articles of association, signed by the members of the association, a copy of which shall be forwarded to the Comptroller of the Currency. The requisite capital for the organization of associations of this kind shall be not less than two hundred thousand dollars in a city exceeding fifty thousand inhabitants, and not less than one hundred thousand dollars in a city whose population is less than fifty thousand; provided, howeve[r,] that banks may be organized, with a capital of not less than fifty thousand dollars, in any place n[ot] exceeding six thousand inhabitants, with the approval of the Secretary of the Treasury. Such a[s]sociation shall transact no business, except such as may be incidental to its own organization, unt[il] authorized by the Comptroller of the Currency. The number of directors must be not less tha[n] five, one of whom shall be president. The capital stock of any association shall be in shares of o[ne] hundred dollars each, deemed personal property, and transferable on the books of the associatio[n.] The shareholders shall be held individually responsible, equally and ratably, and not one for anoth[]er, for all contracts, debts, and engagements of their association, according to the par value of the[ir] amount of stock therein, in addition to the amount invested in such shares; except in the case o[f] shareholders in present existing state banking institutions, of not less than five millions of dolla[rs] of capital, and a surplus of twenty per centum on hand, who shall be liable only to the amount in[]vested in their shares. It shall be lawful for an association, formed under this act, to provide fo[r] an increase of its capital from time to time, subject to the limitations of this act; provided tha[t] the maximum of such increase shall be determined by the comptroller; and that no increase of cap[]ital shall be valid until the whole amount of such increase shall be paid in. And every associatio[n] shall have power, by a vote of shareholders owning two thirds of its stock, to reduce the capital o[f] such association to any amount not below the amount required by this act for its outstanding cir[]culation. Every association, preliminary to commencing business, shall deliver to the Treasure[r] of the United States United States registered bonds to an amount equal to one third of the capit[al] stock; the deposit to be increased as the capital is paid up or increased; while an association, de[]siring to diminish its capital or to close up its business, may take up its bonds, upon returning t[o] the comptroller its circulating notes. The comptroller shall examine and determine if any associ[]ation can commence business. All transfers of United States bonds shall be made to the Treasure[r] of the United States, in trust for the association, the comptroller to keep the transfer-book. As[]sociations, after the transfer and delivery of bonds to the treasurer, may receive from the comp[]troller circulating notes, in blank, equal in amount to ninety per centum of the current market val[]ue of the United States bonds so transferred; but at no time shall the total amount of such note[s] exceed the amount of its capital stock actually paid in. The entire amount of circulating note[s] to be issued under this act shall not exceed three hundred millions of dollars. Such notes shal[l] be received at par in payment of all indebtedness to the United States except for duties on im[]ports; and also for all indebtedness of the United States except interest on the public debt, an[d] in redemption of the national currency. Associations shall, annually or oftener, examine its bond[s] deposited, and execute to the treasurer a certificate, setting forth the different kinds, and th[e] amounts thereof; such examination to be made by a duly appointed officer or agent of the associ[]ation, whose certificate shall be of full force and validity. The deposited bonds shall be held exclu[]sively for the security of the association's circulating notes, the association having the benefit o[f] the interest on the bonds which it may have deposited so long as it may redeem its circulatin[g] notes. The total liabilities to any association, of any person, company, corporation, or firm, shal[l] at no time exceed one tenth part of the capital stock of such association actually paid in; provide[d] that the discount of commercial paper actually owned by the person, company, etc., negotiating th[e] same, shall not be considered as money borrowed. The established interest of the state or territo[r]y wherein the banking association is located shall govern its charge of interest on loans, notes, bills, etc., and, when there is no established interest in such state or territory, the association ma[y] take interest not exceeding seven per centum. The penalty for taking greater interest than herei[n] prescribed shall be a forfeiture of the entire interest which has been agreed to be paid; and th[e] person or persons who may have paid a greater interest may recover back from the association re[]ceiving the same twice the amount of the interest thus paid, provided that such action for recov[]ery is commenced within two years after the occurrence of the usurious transaction. The circula[]ting notes of the different associations shall be redeemed in New York at par by associations se[]lected for that purpose.

WILLIAM L. DAYTON.

was introduced into the Senate and referred, but not again reported during the session.

This torch, which the House had thrown into a magazine already almost on the point of explosion from other causes, was snatched away by the Secretary of State before it had done its destructive work. A letter of instructions was immediately forwarded to Mr. Dayton, our minister at the French court. A copy of the resolution was inclosed. It was admitted by the secretary that this resolution truly interpreted the unanimous sentiment of the people of the United States. But it had not passed the Senate, and, even if it had, the form of expression which the government might choose to adopt toward that of France on this subject depended, not upon Congress, but upon the executive. "While the President," he added, "receives the declaration of the House of Representatives with the profound respect to which it is entitled as an exposition of its sentiments on a grave and important subject, he directs that you inform the government of France that he does, not at present contemplate any departure from the policy which this government has hitherto pursued in regard to the war which exists between France and Mexico."

The passage of the resolution produced a great degree of excitement in France. When Mr. Dayton visited M. Drouyn de l'Huys on the 21st of April, the first words addressed to him by the latter were, "Do you bring us peace or bring us war?" Mr. Dayton had not then received his instructions from the secretary. When these were made known to the French government the excitement subsided, and the *Moniteur*, the official organ of the emperor, announced that satisfactory explanations had been received from the United States government.

On the 27th Mr. Davis made a long report, closing with a recommendation that a resolution be passed declaring the constitutional right of Congress to an authoritative voice in determining the foreign policy of the United States, and that a proposition in regard to such policy while pending and undetermined is not a fit topic of diplomatic explanation with any foreign power. This report was ordered to be printed, but did not again come up for action during the session.

The people of Kentucky—so strongly opposed to secession and to sympathizers with rebellion that they had (August 3, 1863) elected Bramlette, the Union candidate, over Wickliffe, the Democratic, by a majority of over 50,000—were still so bitterly opposed to emancipation and to the enrollment of negroes for military service, that their governor was compelled, when these measures were adopted, to issue a proclamation, counseling them against unlawful resistance. But the President remained firm. He had 130,000 soldiers to show as the result of a policy which had been tried for one year, and this, to him, was a sufficient argument why that policy should be maintained. The fact that the Union delegates from Kentucky would be sent to the Democratic Convention to be assembled at Chicago for the nomination of a presidential ticket was not deemed a compensatory argument to the contrary.

In the autumn of 1864 a presidential election was to be decided in the midst of war, as the one four years previous had been decided under its pro-chiefly because he was considered too slow to adopt their own revolutionary theories on the subject of emancipation and reconstruction. This faction of the party held its National Convention at Cleveland, Ohio, on the 31st of May, pursuant to a call addressed "to the Radical Men of the Nation." Of the 350 persons who answered this call, few, if any, were properly delegates representing constituencies. These men, representing their own principles rather than the people, nominated General John C. Fremont for President, and for Vice-President General John Cochrane. The distinctive articles of the platform adopted by this Convention were those declaring that the President ought to be elected for a single term and by a direct vote of the people, that the question of reconstruction belonged to Congress and not to the executive; and that justice required the confiscation of rebel property and its distribution among "the soldiers and actual settlers." This policy of general confiscation was repudiated by General Fremont in his letter accepting the nomination.

Just a week later—June 7th—the Republican Convention proper assembled at Baltimore, in response to a call issued by the Executive Committee, which had been created by the Chicago Convention of 1860. Senator Morgan, of New York, chairman of that committee, called the Convention to order, and proposed Dr. Robert J. Breckinridge, of Kentucky, as temporary president. Breckinridge and the ten other delegates from Kentucky did not claim to fairly represent that party in their state which would cast the majority of votes. Hon. William Dennison, of Ohio, was elected president in the permanent organization of the Convention.[1] The work of the Convention was soon accomplished. The platform of resolutions, as reported by H. J. Raymond, of New York, and unanimously adopted, maintained the integrity of the Union; the paramount authority of the Constitution and laws of the United States; the suppression of the rebellion and the punishment of rebels; the repudiation of compromise, and of any terms of peace except those based on the unconditional surrender of hostility on the part of the enemies arrayed against the government; the abolition of slavery by constitutional amendment; the policy and measures of the administration, especially the Emancipation Proclamation and the employment of negro soldiers; the recognition of the valor and patriotism of the soldiers and sailors, and provision—ample and permanent—for those disabled by wounds; prompt and full redress for the violation of the laws of war in the treatment by the enemy of our soldiers, without distinction of color; the encouragement of immigration; the inviolability of the public debt; and the Monroe doctrine.[2]

[1] There were 520 delegates admitted, from the following States and Territories:

From Maine, 14.	From Maryland, 14.	From Wisconsin, 16.
New Hampshire, 10.	Louisiana, 14.	Iowa, 16.
Vermont, 10.	Arkansas, 10.	Minnesota, 8.
Massachusetts, 24.	Missouri, 22.	California, 10.
Rhode Island, 8.	Tennessee, 15.	Oregon, 6.
Connecticut, 12.	Kentucky, 21.	West Virginia, 10.
New York, 66.	Ohio, 42.	Kansas, 6.
New Jersey, 14.	Indiana, 26.	Nebraska, 6.
Pennsylvania, 49.	Illinois, 32.	Colorado, 6.
Delaware, 6.	Michigan, 16.	Nevada, 6.

[2] The following is a copy of these resolutions:

Resolved, That it is the highest duty of every American citizen to maintain against all their enemies the integrity of the Union, and the paramount authority of the Constitution and laws of the United States; and that, laying aside all differences of political opinion, we pledge ourselves as Union-men, animated by a common sentiment, and aiming at a common object, to do every thing in our power to aid the government in quelling by force of arms the rebellion now raging against its authority, and in bringing to the punishment due to their crimes the rebels and traitors arrayed against it.

Resolved, That we approve the determination of the government of the United States not to compromise with rebels, nor to offer any terms of peace except such as may be based upon an "unconditional surrender" of their hostility and a return to their just allegiance to the Constitution and laws of the United States, and that we call upon the government to maintain this position and to prosecute the war with the utmost possible vigor to the complete suppression of the rebellion, in full reliance upon the self-sacrifice, the patriotism, the heroic valor, and the undying devotion of the American people to their country and its free institutions.

Resolved, That as slavery was the cause, and now constitutes the strength of this rebellion, and as it must be always and every where hostile to the principles of republican government, justice and the national safety demand its utter and complete extirpation from the soil of the republic; and that we uphold and maintain the acts and proclamations by which the government, in its own defense, has aimed a death-blow at this gigantic evil. We are in favor, furthermore, of such an amendment to the Constitution, to be made by the people in conformity with its provisions, as shall terminate and forever prohibit the existence of slavery within the limits of the jurisdiction of the United States.

Resolved, That the thanks of the American people are due to the soldiers and sailors of the army and navy, who have periled their lives in defense of their country and in vindication of the honor of the flag; that the nation owes to them some permanent recognition of their patriotism and valor, and ample and permanent provision for those of their survivors who have received disabling and honorable wounds in the service of the country; and that the memories of those who have fallen in its defense shall be held in grateful and everlasting remembrance.

Resolved, That we approve and applaud the practical wisdom, the unselfish patriotism, and unswerving fidelity to the Constitution and the principles of American liberty with which Abraham Lincoln has discharged, under circumstances of unparalleled difficulty, the great duties and responsibilities of the presidential office; that we approve and indorse, as demanded by the emergency and essential to the preservation of the nation, and as within the Constitution, the measures and acts which he has adopted to defend the nation against its open and secret foes; that we approve especially the Proclamation of Emancipation, and the employment as Union soldiers of men heretofore held in slavery; and that we have full confidence in his determination to carry these and all other constitutional measures essential to the salvation of the country into full and complete effect.

Resolved, That we deem it essential to the general welfare that harmony should prevail in the national councils, and we regard as worthy of public confidence and official trust those only who cordially indorse the principles proclaimed in these resolutions, and which should characterize the administration of the government.

Resolved, That the government owes to all men employed in its armies, without regard to distinction of color, the full protection of the laws of war; and that any violation of these laws or of the usages of civilized nations in the time of war by the rebels now in arms, should be made the subject of full and prompt redress.

Resolved, That the foreign immigration, which in the past has added so much to the wealth and development of resources and increase of power to this nation, the asylum of the oppressed of all nations, should be fostered and encouraged by a liberal and just policy.

Resolved, That we are in favor of the speedy construction of a railroad to the Pacific.

Resolved, That the national faith, pledged for the redemption of the public debt, must be kept inviolate; and that for this purpose we recommend economy and rigid responsibility in the public expenditures, and a vigorous and just system of taxation; that it is the duty of every loyal state to sustain the credit and promote the use of the national currency.

Resolved, That we approve the position taken by the government that the people of the United States never regarded with indifference the attempt of any European power to overthrow by force, or to supplant by fraud, the institutions of any republican government on the Western continent, and that they view with extreme jealousy, as menacing to the peace and independence of this our

The nomination of Mr. Lincoln for President was already a foregone conclusion when the Convention met. On the first ballot he received the vote of every delegation except that from Missouri, which had been instructed to vote for General Grant. This delegation changing its vote, the nomination was made unanimous.

For Vice-President there were three candidates—Andrew Johnson, Military Governor of Tennessee, Hannibal Hamlin, the then incumbent, and Daniel S. Dickinson. On the first ballot the vote stood, Johnson, 200; Dickinson, 108; Hamlin, 150; scattering, 59. Several delegations changed their vote in favor of Johnson, who, on the second ballot, received 494 votes, and was then declared unanimously nominated.

In his letter accepting the nomination, President Lincoln announced, to avoid misunderstanding, that the position of the government in relation to the action of France in Mexico, as assumed through the State Department, and indorsed by the Convention, would be maintained so long as it was pertinent and applicable.

When the Republican Convention met it was confidently expected that the war would soon close by the downfall of Atlanta and Richmond. But in the interval that elapsed before the meeting of the Democratic Convention, which was postponed from July 4th to August 29th, the situation was materially changed. Grant, in his march from the Rapidan to the James, inflicted great losses upon the Confederate army, but he suffered far greater losses himself, and had not captured Richmond. The progress of the Atlanta campaign seemed slow to the people who, a few weeks before, were confident of speedy victory. Since the defeat of Bragg at Chattanooga, no important and decisive triumph had been won by the Union armies. Numerous failures there had been, and, though none of them were of great magnitude or decisive in character, yet they added a sting to the disappointment of looking over a nine months' calendar barren of any palpable success. There was no doubt as to final results—it was simply a period of gloomy disappointment. There was no flinching either on the part of the army or the people. The army pushed grimly on, and met partial discomfiture with soldierly fortitude; the people afforded it a grim but determined support, though their efforts had been unrewarded by immediate success.

If there was much in the military situation which gave encouragement to the opposition party, the financial aspect of the country afforded them a still more palpable fulcrum upon which to swing their lever for the overthrow of the administration. The amount of the public debt was rapidly climbing

up to two billions.[1] In July, 1864, gold was quoted at 290, having reached that point from 195 since Grant and Sherman began their campaigns in May.

Just at this crisis, Salmon P. Chase, the Secretary of the Treasury, resigned, and there were not a few who attributed his resignation to the financial difficulties of the nation. It is probable, however, that he was influenced chiefly by political reasons, arising out of the relations which, during the presidential canvass, had grown up between himself and Mr. Lincoln. That there was no hostility toward the secretary on the part of the President is evident from the fact that, upon the death of Roger B. Taney, October 12, 1864, he appointed Mr. Chase chief justice of the United States Supreme Court.[2]

During the summer of 1864, two attempts were made by irresponsible parties, apparently having for their object the conclusion of the war through mutual accommodation, but in reality influenced solely by political motives. It is a curious fact that, at the same time, President Lincoln was sounded on the subject of peace by Confederate agents in Canada, for the express purpose of drawing out of him a distinct refusal to afford accommodation—a refusal which might be used both to incite the South to renewed efforts to gain Confederate independence, and to strengthen the cause of the opposition in the North; and President Davis was sounded upon the same subject for the purpose of drawing out from him a like refusal, to be used for a similar purpose in behalf of the supporters of the administration.

On the 5th of July, George N. Sanders, from the Clifton House, Niagara Falls, addressed a letter to Horace Greeley, stating that he himself, and Clement C. Clay, of Alabama, and James P. Holcombe, of Virginia, were willing to go to Washington if full protection were accorded them. Nothing was said in the letter as to the object of the proposed visit to Washington. But from other sources Greeley understood that Clay and Holcombe had full powers from Richmond to treat on the subject of peace. He therefore forwarded the application to President Lincoln, urging a response, and suggesting terms of accommodation. The "plan of adjustment" suggested by him proposed the restoration of the Union; the abolition of slavery, the Union paying $400,000,000 in 5 per cent. bonds as compensation to the owners of slaves, whether loyal or rebel; the representation in Congress of the slave states on the basis of their total population; and a National Convention, to be convened as soon as possible, for the ratification of these terms. He added: "I do not say that a just peace is now attainable, though I believe it to be so. But I *do* say that a frank offer by you to the insurgents of terms which the impartial must say ought to be accepted, will, at the worst, prove an immense and sorely-needed advantage to the national cause. It may save us from a Northern insurrection."

The President forthwith deputed Greeley to Niagara to communicate with the Confederate agents. Greeley went to Niagara, and on the 17th informed Messrs. Clay and Holcombe that, if they were duly accredited agents from Richmond, the President would grant them a safe-conduct to Washington. These gentlemen replied that they were not accredited agents, but thoroughly understood the views of the Confederate government on the subject of peace. Upon learning this the President sent a message, addressed "to whom it may concern," in the following terms:

"Any proposition which embraces the restoration of peace, the integrity of the whole Union, and the abandonment of slavery, and which comes by and with an authority that can control the armies now at war with the United States, will be received and considered by the executive government of the United States, and will be met by liberal terms on other substantial and collateral points, and the bearer or bearers thereof shall have safe-conduct both ways."

This, of course, was final, being all the Confederate gentlemen had waited for. They had now their text, and they issued their manifesto against the tyranny which could thus rudely spurn the offer of peace. But President Lincoln had simply been honest with them, and certainly had not been discourteous. Nor had he rejected their overtures. His design in addressing his mission "to all whom it may concern" is evident. These gentlemen had admitted that they were not accredited agents of the Confederate government, but had expressed their confidence that they could obtain the requisite power. But they might be, and probably were, indulging false hopes as to the accommodation which the government would be willing to grant. It was only fair, therefore, that both they and the Confederate government—all whom it might concern—should be made to understand the ultimatum of the government which must be met before the door could be open to ne-

[1] The public debt was thus estimated at the close of each fiscal year since 1860:

1860—June 30th	$64,769,703	1863—June 30th	$1,097,274,860
1861— "	90,867,828	1864— "	1,740,036,689
1862— "	514,211,371		

[2] JOHN JAY, the first chief justice of the United States, was born in New York, December 12, 1745. He graduated at King's (now Columbia) College in 1764, and was admitted to the bar four years later. When the Revolutionary troubles came on he took a prominent part in the contest. He was the youngest member of the first Congress which convened in 1774. In 1777 he prepared the draft of the Constitution of the State of New York, and was appointed the first chief justice of the state. In 1779 he was sent on a mission to Spain. That government demanded as a condition of recognizing the independence of the United States that the possession of Florida and the exclusive right to navigate the Mississippi should be guaranteed to Spain. Jay refused to consent that the mouth of our great river should be shut up by a foreign power. In conjunction with Adams, Franklin, and Laurens, Mr. Jay negotiated the treaty by which Great Britain recognized the independence of the United States. In 1784 he returned to his country, and was appointed Secretary for Foreign Affairs. When the Union took the place of the old Confederation, Washington requested him to select any office which he might prefer. He chose that of Chief Justice of the United States, to which he was appointed in 1789. In 1794 he was sent to Great Britain as envoy extraordinary to negotiate an important treaty. This treaty, which settled the questions in dispute between the two nations, was violently opposed by the Democratic party, especially at the South. He was absent a year, during which time he was elected Governor of New York. He then resigned the chief justiceship, was twice re-elected governor, and then, in 1801, at the age of fifty-six, resolved to retire from public life. President Adams, wishing to retain his services for the public, nominated him for his former place as chief justice, then vacant by the resignation of Oliver Ellsworth. Jay declined, on the ground that he had deliberately made up his mind to retire from public life, and duty to his country did not then require him to accept office. He retired to his farm in Bedford, New York, where he died May 17, 1829, in the eighty-fourth year of his age. Mr. Jay was one of the noblest and purest characters in our history. No man, except a few violent partisans in South Carolina, however much he might oppose his public policy, dared to asperse the perfect integrity of John Jay.

Upon the resignation of Mr. Jay, JOHN RUTLEDGE was nominated by the President as chief justice of the United States, but was not confirmed.

The President then nominated as chief justice Judge WILLIAM CUSHING, of Massachusetts; the nomination was confirmed; but Mr. Cushing, after holding the commission a few days, resigned on account of ill health. As he never acted in that capacity, his name does not properly belong to the list of chief justices.

OLIVER ELLSWORTH was then nominated and confirmed as chief justice. He was born at Windsor, Connecticut, April 29, 1745. His studies commenced at Yale, were completed at Princeton, where he graduated at the age of twenty-three. For a time he was a teacher, then commenced the study of theology, but subsequently decided on the profession of law. He had then married, and his father gave him a farm of wild land and an axe. While slowly working his way at the bar he cleared his wild farm with his own hands. His early career gave no promise of future eminence; but the first upward steps once taken, his progress was sure. He was appointed state's attorney, and yearly elected to the General Assembly. In 1777 he was chosen delegate to Congress, 1784 Judge of the Superior Court of Connecticut, and in 1789 senator in Congress. In 1796 he was appointed chief justice of the United States. His unquestioned probity and the soundness of his judicial decisions gained him the highest respect. In 1799 he was sent, against his wishes, as minister to France, though still retaining for two years his seat on the bench. His health failing, he resigned his office in 1801. He died November 26, 1807, at the age of sixty-two.

JOHN MARSHALL, the most eminent of our chief justices, was born in Fauquier County, Virginia, September 24, 1755. His father was a farmer in narrow circumstances, but of decided ability. By his own unaided exertions he subsequently became a fair classical scholar, and was intimately acquainted with English literature. He had just begun the study of law when the war of the Revolution broke out. In 1775 he was appointed lieutenant in a company of minute-men. He afterward became captain in a Virginia regiment of the Continental army, and was present at the battles of Brandywine, Germantown, and Monmouth. He pursued his legal studies at intervals during the war, and at its close commenced practice. He soon rose to eminence at the bar and in politics. He was one of the small but distinguished body of men through whose influence Virginia was induced to accept the Federal Constitution. In 1794 Washington offered him the post of attorney general, and subsequently the mission to France. Both offers were declined. The French government having refused to receive Mr. Pinckney as minister, Mr. Adams, who was then President, appointed Mr. Marshall as one of three envoys to that country. Shortly after his return he yielded to the personal solicitations of Washington, and consented to become a candidate for Congress. President Adams at the same time offered him a seat on the bench of the Supreme Court, which was declined. He was elected to Congress after a sharp contest, taking his seat in December, 1799. During the excited session which followed he was one of the ablest supporters of the administration of Mr. Adams. In May, 1800, he was nominated and confirmed as Secretary of War, but he declined to accept the appointment. Shortly after he accepted the post of Secretary of State. On the 31st of January, 1801, he was appointed chief justice of the United States, a position which he held for thirty-five years, until his death in July, 1835, at the age of eighty years. His unquestioned character, sound judgment, and felicitous diction, added to the long period during which he held his seat, and the magnitude of the questions which came before him for decision, entitle Mr. Marshall beyond all question to the first place in the noble list of our chief justices. Besides his judicial labors, he was the author of a History of the American Colonies and of a Life of Washington.

ROGER BROOKE TANEY was born in Calvert County, Maryland, March 17, 1777. In 1831 President Jackson appointed him attorney general of the United States. Two years later, Mr. Duane, then Secretary of the Treasury, refused to remove the government deposits from the United States Bank; he was removed, and Mr. Taney was appointed in his place. The Senate refused to confirm the nomination; but in the mean while Mr. Taney had obeyed the orders of the President and removed the deposits. Jackson then nominated him as associate justice of the Supreme Court, to fill a vacancy occasioned by the resignation of Judge Duval. The Senate refused to confirm the nomination. Chief Justice Marshall died in 1835, and Jackson at once nominated Mr. Taney for the place. The Democrats, having now a majority in the Senate, confirmed the nomination, and Mr. Taney became chief justice—a position he retained until his death, October 12, 1864, a period of twenty-seven years. Chief Justice Taney is best known by his famous "decision," or rather "opinion," in the Dred Scott case, in which, going beyond the question before the court, he endeavored to settle the general question of the *status* of persons of African descent in the United States. Undeserved obloquy has been attached to him on account of a sentence in this opinion which apparently affirmed that blacks had no rights which whites were bound to respect. The context shows that this was the very reverse of the meaning intended to be conveyed by Judge Taney. He says that it is now difficult to realize the state of opinion on this subject held at the formation of our government. Blacks were then regarded as beings of an inferior order, "*and so far inferior that they had no rights which the white man was bound to respect.*" This outrageous sentiment is mentioned only to be impliedly condemned. The "opinion" of the chief justice, harsh enough as he gave it, being to the effect that no person whose ancestors were imported to this country and sold as slaves had any right to sue in a court of the United States, or could become citizens of the United States. It is due to the honor of our highest judicial tribunal to state that the opinion of the chief justice did not affirm, but did by plain implication condemn, the doctrine that such persons "had *no* rights which whites were bound to respect." Mr. Taney's last notable public act was in May, 1861, when the case of John Merryman came before him. This man was arrested near Baltimore, on charge of being an officer in a company raised to aid the rebellion. He was imprisoned by the military authorities in Fort M'Henry. He prayed for a writ of *habeas corpus*, which was granted by Judge Taney. General Cadwalader, the commander, refused to obey, on the ground that the execution of the writ of *habeas corpus* had been suspended by the President in the State of Maryland. The judge issued an order for the arrest of General Cadwalader. The marshal was not allowed to serve the writ. Judge Taney thereupon prepared an opinion, denying the right of the President to suspend the writ, and affirming that it was the duty of all military officers to obey it. He added that if the officer had been brought before him he should have punished him by fine and imprisonment; but as he had no force capable of carrying his order into effect, he should report the whole case to the President, and call upon him to enforce the process of the court. No farther action was had on the case. Mr. Taney died October 12, 1864, at the age of eighty-seven, having filled the chief judicial chair of the nation for twenty-seven years. He owed his appointment to the purely partisan services which he rendered to President Jackson. As a jurist he can not be ranked with the great men who had occupied his seat before him. His judicial integrity has never been impeached, even in the case of his unfortunate opinion in the Dred Scott case, or the later and equally unfortunate course in the Merryman case, by which he will be chiefly remembered in after years.

SALMON PORTLAND CHASE, now chief justice of the United States, was born in Cornish, New Hampshire, January 13, 1808. His father having died, he was sent at the age of twelve to Ohio, and placed under the care of his uncle, Bishop Chase. After studying for a year at Cincinnati College, he entered Dartmouth College in New Hampshire, from which he graduated in 1829. He went to Washington, where he opened a school, at the same time studying law under the direction of William Wirt. Having been admitted to the bar, he went to Cincinnati, and entered upon the practice of his profession. To this for some years he applied himself exclusively, taking no prominent part in politics, although he belonged to the Democratic party. In 1841 he first took a decided part in politics. He was then a member of the Convention of those opposed to the farther extension of slavery, and was the author of the address unanimously adopted by that body. He took a prominent part in all the subsequent movements having this end in view, and was president of the Free Soil Democratic Convention at Buffalo in 1848. The Democratic party in Ohio had at this time assumed the position of hostility to slavery in the Territories. Mr. Chase was chosen United States Senator in February, 1849, receiving the votes of all the Democratic members of the Legislature, together with those of others who were in favor of free soil. Though elected as a Democrat, he declared that if the party withdrew from its position in regard to slavery he should withdraw from it. This he did formally, in consequence of the action of the Democratic Convention held at Baltimore in 1852. When the Republican party was organized, Mr. Chase took the position of one of its acknowledged leaders. Soon after the close of his senatorial term in 1855 he was elected Governor of Ohio. He was re-elected, his second term closing in 1860. In the Republican Convention at Chicago in that year, he was, next after Mr. Lincoln and Mr. Seward, the leading candidate for the presidency. He had in the mean time been again elected to the Senate of the United States, and had he taken his place would undoubtedly have been the leader in that body. But he resigned his seat in order to accept the position of Secretary of the Treasury—a position for which he was especially pointed out by the success of his financial policy while Governor of Ohio. As the presidential canvass of 1864 approached, a strong effort was made to bring forward Mr. Chase as the Union candidate; but the current of popular feeling was so unmistakably in favor of the re-election of Mr. Lincoln that Mr. Chase refused to become a candidate, and gave his cordial support to Mr. Lincoln. Meanwhile, finding that Congress hesitated to carry out the financial system which he proposed, Mr. Chase had, on the 30th of June, 1864, resigned the post of Secretary of the Treasury. Almost the first important public act of Mr. Lincoln after his re-election has been to appoint Mr. Chase to the most important position within the executive nomination. Mr. Chase enters upon the duties of his high office at the age of fifty-six, with a sound legal reputation, and with a physical vigor which gives reason to hope that he may be able to perform its duties for a period as long as that of his predecessor.

gotiation. This ultimatum was simply the integrity of the Union and the abandonment of slavery.

Undoubtedly the people of the South longed for peace. The whole people longed for peace, except a few to whom war was money. But peace was impossible until either the government or the rebels were defeated, except by the abandonment on one side or the other of the very object for which it was fighting. No proposition indicating the willingness of the Confederate government to surrender its independence upon any conditions had ever been made. That no such disposition existed in the summer of 1864 is shown by the result of a visit made to Richmond by Colonel Jacques and J. R. Gilmore while Greeley was in communication with Clay and Holcombe at Niagara. These gentlemen went to Richmond with no credentials. They were not sent by the government. They did not expect to accomplish any thing in the way of peace. Yet in a certain sense they were commissioners, not of the government, but of a party, sent to receive a distinct expression of the unwillingness of Mr. Davis to negotiate for peace except on the basis of Confederate independence. This they obtained in the most explicit terms. Davis told them that the "war must go on till the last of this generation falls in his tracks, and his children seize his musket and fight our battle, unless you acknowledge our right to self-government. We are not fighting for slavery; we are fighting for independence, and that or extermination we will have." Certainly his declaration did not improve the prospects of the opposition party in the North in the approaching elections.

On the 29th of August the National Democratic Convention assembled at Chicago. The next day it was permanently organized, with Governor Seymour, of New York, as president. Upward of 250 delegates were present. Among these, and master spirits of the Convention, were Vallandigham—recently returned from exile—Price, and Long. A large portion of the audience consisted of the most disaffected men of the Northwestern states, among whom were mingled Confederate spies from Canada, who, with their friends, were at this very moment meditating a scheme for the liberation of the 8000 Confederate prisoners at Camp Douglas, near the city, the execution of which scheme was to be followed by a general uprising of the disloyal in all the Northwestern states. This movement was only prevented by the preparations which had been made to thwart it through the vigilance of Colonel B. J. Sweet, the commander at Camp Douglas.

Governor Seymour, upon assuming the chair, addressed the delegates and the audience. Seymour, while he was thoroughly identified with the peace party, was the most astute and prudent member of that party. Not turbulent himself, he rejoiced in the turbulence of others. His style of eloquence was modeled upon that which Mark Antony (as rendered by Shakspeare) adopted over the corpse of Cæsar. His thunderbolts, like those of Wendell Phillips, always fell out of a clear sky. There was no measure of the opposition, however extreme, which he did not heartily indorse; and yet the problem to be solved in this Convention, as it seemed to him, was to at the same time apparently ignore all such measures, and adopt such as would secure their execution. The task was not an easy one. There was a great diversity of opinion among the members of the Convention. Only the utmost tact could prevent such a division as had occurred at the Charleston Convention four years ago. Seymour counseled them to select such men for their candidates as enjoyed the popular confidence. He reminded them of the Republican Convention held in that city in 1860, and that while the party which it represented had there declared that it would not interfere with the rights of states, the sentiment by which it was animated—its sectional prejudices and fanaticism—had overruled this declaration. Even now, under the shadow of impending ruin, this party would not let the shedding of blood cease even for a little, "to see if Christian charity or the wisdom of statesmanship" might not save the Union. But, even if it would, the administration could not save the country. It had, by its proclamations and vindictive legislation, placed obstacles in its own way which it could not overcome; its freedom of action was hampered by its own unconstitutional acts. Seymour then proceeded to pay a tribute to our soldiers, which falls upon our ears like mockery when we remember that he did all he could to weaken the armies in the field by his opposition to conscription. But his compliment to the soldiers was of a very doubtful sort when he intimated that they were more lenient toward traitors than was the administration.

"But if the administration can not save the Union," said he, "*we* can. . . There are no hinderances to *our* pathways to union and to peace." He forgot under what administrations disunion had blossomed and matured to ripeness. And when he added, "we have no hates, no prejudices, no passions," did he remember the fiendish, negro-hunting mob, whom a little more than a year ago he had addressed in New York city as "my friends?" Yes, this astute statesman could look down into the face of Long, who had a few weeks before, in the halls of Congress, advocated the recognition of the Confederacy, and into the faces of others who had applauded his words to the echo, and say, "the administration can not save the Union, but *we* can do it." He had complained of the lack of wise statesmanship in the Republican party to secure the fruit of victories won in the field. Was wise statesmanship in this trying hour of the nation's life confined to such men as Price, Vallandigham, and the Seymours? With remarkable coolness he alluded to the military edict which three days before had gone forth, forbidding the transportation of arms or ammunition into Ohio, Indiana, Illinois, and Michigan. Did he know of the existence of secret organizations in those states, the members of which were the sworn enemies of the national government, waiting only their opportunity to aid the Confederate armies by domestic insurrection in the North? Did he know that he was addressing men who directly controlled and sustained these organizations? So well did he understand the character of his audience, that he especially guarded those who were not delegates against an unbecoming expression of their opinion b applause or condemnation. He had noticed with chagrin that the loude cheers followed the expression of disloyal sentiments, and feared the resul of the impression which would thus be made upon the people at large. In deed, he had scarcely given this prudent bit of advice when he was inte rupted by loud calls for Vallandigham.

Seymour to a great degree succeeded in impressing his own temper upo the Convention, but he could not control the members in their conduct ou side of the wigwam. From the balconies of hotels and on street-corne sentiments were uttered which more fully represented the temper of th crowd which had naturally gathered about this Democratic Conventio Here C. Chauncey Burr, Vallandigham, and Henry C. Dean could speak ou clearly their sympathy with rebels without disguise or circumlocutio Here they could charge Lincoln with spoon-stealing and negro-stealing could declare that the South, fighting for her honor, could not honorably la down her arms, and that Lincoln's army, already the slaughter-pen of tw millions of men, could not again be filled either by enlistment or conscrip tion; and could utter their prayers for the failure of the national arms. Her they could call Lincoln a usurper, traitor, tyrant, blood-thirsty old monste or any other odious name which the Democratic vocabulary of that da readily furnished. And yet these men belonged to a party which, Seymou said, had "no hates, no prejudices, no passions." War-Democrats received their share of this wholesale vituperation and execration. Between a War-Democrat and an Abolitionist, said Judge Miller, of Ohio, there is no real difference; "they are links of one sausage, made out of the same dog," and the crowd yelled its applause. Judge Miller was a fair representative of that "insulted judiciary" which Seymour in his speech had declared "would again administer the laws of the land" when the Democratic administration should have displaced that of Mr. Lincoln.

The platform of resolutions was constructed by a committee, of which Vallandigham was a member. In the contest for the chairmanship of this committee, Vallandigham received 8 votes and Guthrie 12. This man was the master-spirit of the Convention, so far as its objects were concerned, while Seymour furnished the model for its style of utterance. In the Committee on Resolutions, James Guthrie, of Kentucky, its chairman, acted the same part which Seymour played in the conduct of the entire Convention. Vallandigham was the irrepressible soul of the resolutions, and it was the business of Guthrie to hide this wretched soul within a becoming body, to disguise sympathy with treason by sandwiching it in between a declaration of fidelity to the Union and one of pity toward unnecessarily slaughtered soldiers.[1] The resolutions as adopted pretended to speak for a party, a large and the most respectable and patriotic portion of which repudiated them; they declared as a sentiment of the Convention "unswerving fidelity to the Union under the Constitution." But how many members of this Convention had publicly declared that under the Constitution the right of secession was justifiable? They declared in behalf of the Convention and as the sense of the American people that the experiment of war, tried for four years, had proved a failure, and that "justice, humanity, liberty, and the public welfare demand that immediate efforts be made for a cessation of hostilities, with a view to an ultimate Convention of the states, or other peaceable means, to the end that at the earliest practicable moment peace may be restored on the basis of the Federal Union of the states."[2] It is in vain that one inquires after the reasons for this demand by either "justice," "humanity," "liberty," or the "public welfare." It was known—it had been the undeviating declaration of the Confederate government, one from which it had not swerved even in order to assist this peace party of the North—that no peace was practicable (except a conquered peace) on any other basis than that of Confederate independence. And this Convention knew that the peace for which they declared must result in the recognition of the Confederacy. How justice, or humanity, or liberty, or the public welfare were to be advanced by that inglorious consummation it is not easy to discover. Let us suppose for an instant that this peace party should succeed, and that the leaders who controlled its action should come into possession of the executive and legislative

[1] The following is the platform adopted by the Convention:

Resolved, That in the future, as in the past, we will adhere with unswerving fidelity to the Union under the Constitution, as the only solid foundation of our strength, security, and happiness as a people, and as a framework of government equally conducive to the welfare and prosperity of all the states, both Northern and Southern.

Resolved, That this Convention does explicitly declare, as the sense of the American people, that, after four years of failure to restore the Union by the experiment of war, during which, under the pretense of a military necessity of a war power higher than the Constitution, the Constitution itself has been disregarded in every part, and public liberty and private right alike trodden down, and the material prosperity of the country essentially impaired, justice, humanity, liberty, and the public welfare demand that immediate efforts be made for a cessation of hostilities, with a view to an ultimate Convention of all the states, or other peaceable means, to the end that at the earliest practicable moment peace may be restored on the basis of the Federal Union of the states.

Resolved, That the direct interference of the military authority of the United States in the recent elections held in Kentucky, Maryland, Missouri, and Delaware, was a shameful violation of the Constitution, and the repetition of such acts in the approaching election will be held as revolutionary, and resisted with all the means and power under our control.

Resolved, That the aim and object of the Democratic party is to preserve the Federal Union and the rights of states unimpaired; and they hereby declare that they consider the administrative usurpation of extraordinary and dangerous powers not granted by the Constitution, the subversion of the civil by military law in states not in insurrection, the arbitrary military arrest, imprisonment, trial, and sentence of American citizens in states where civil law exists in full force, the suppression of freedom of speech and of the press, the denial of the right of asylum, the open and avowed disregard of state rights, the employment of unusual test-oaths, and the interference with and denial of the right of the people to bear arms, as calculated to prevent a restoration of the Union and the perpetuation of a government deriving its just powers from the consent of the governed.

Resolved, That the shameful disregard of the administration to its duty in respect to our fellow-citizens who now and long have been prisoners of war in a suffering condition, deserves the severest reprobation, on the score alike of public interest and common humanity.

Resolved, That the sympathy of the Democratic party is heartily and earnestly extended to the soldiery of our army, who are and have been in the field under the flag of our country; and, in the event of our attaining power, they will receive all the care and protection, regard and kindness, that the brave soldiers of the republic have so nobly earned.

[2] This resolution, the second and most important one of the platform, was written by Vallandigham. So Vallandigham himself states in a letter written to the New York *Daily News* from Chicago, October 22d.

SOLDIERS VOTING FOR PRESIDENT.

powers of the nation. Suppose an armistice declared under such auspices. The armies, with ultimate victory already in sight, rest upon their arms, while these men try their boasted "statesmanship" in the interests of peace. Soldiers levied by conscription, and on their way to the field, are halted, released from obligation, and returned to their homes. Recruiting and conscription cease. Military ardor is already dead, or this peace party could not else have come into power. What would be the action of Davis and his associates, and of the Southern people? They seceded under the auspices of Buchanan's administration; but now an administration is in power which is pledged to desist from war in any event. The storming of cannon, the musketry attack, the strong hands of soldiers already about to clutch this demon of treason and strangle it to death, silently vanish from the scene, and are replaced by this nest of cooing doves, who from the national capital seek to woo traitors back to their spurned allegiance. Can there be any doubt as to the result of this innocent, amicable sport? Would the Confederacy dance to the piping of these men of peace? No, it would claim the right of secession, which these men would instantly yield; it would become a nation which these doters would forthwith recognize. The armies in the field would then slink back to their homes, cursing the people who had betrayed them. Grant, and Sherman, and Thomas, and Farragut, would hide their faces for shame, and quietly receive their reward—the brand of murder placed upon their foreheads by Peace Democrats and an unworthy people. The uncoffined, living corpse of Lincoln—more than murdered by these political assassins—would proceed from Washington to Springfield amid the jeers of faithless multitudes. And this was to be the Democratic apotheosis of justice, humanity, and liberty!

We do not wonder, after this declaration, that the Convention tendered its sympathy to the Union soldiers, who would need so much sympathy in the event of its political success.

The members of the Convention, after the adoption of this platform, named various candidates for President, and spent the remainder of the day in discussing their comparative merits. General McClellan was the only nominee who stood any fair chance of success, but there was certainly room for discussion as to the propriety of asking a major general of the United States army to stand upon the platform adopted by the Convention. On the 31st the voting commenced. On the first ballot it stood: McClellan, 174; Thomas H. Seymour, 38; Horatio Seymour, 12. This was revised so that McClellan stood 202½, and Thomas H. Seymour 28½. On the motion of Vallandigham, the nomination of McClellan was made unanimous. No less than eight candidates were offered on the first ballot for Vice-President. James Guthrie received the largest number of votes—65; George H. Pendleton stood next, receiving 55; and the third on the list was Lazarus W. Powell, who received 36. But the New York delegation, commanding 33 votes, went over to Pendleton, who was finally declared the nominee of the Convention.

McClellan's letter accepting the nomination expressed sentiments at variance with those of the Convention. "If a frank, earnest, and persistent effort," said he, "to obtain these objects [peace and union] should fail, the responsibility for ulterior consequences will fall upon those who remain in arms against the Union. But the Union must be preserved at all hazards." This idea—that of resuming the war in the event of the failure to obtain peace on the basis of the Union—came up before the Committee on Resolutions in the Convention, and was *unanimously* rejected.[1] "I could not," adds McClellan, in allusion to one of the resolutions adopted at Chicago, "look in the face of my gallant comrades of the army and navy, who have survived so many bloody battles, and tell them that their labors and the sacrifice of so many of our slain and wounded brethren had been in vain; that we had abandoned that Union for which we have so often periled our lives. A vast majority of our people, whether in the army and navy or at home, would, as I would, hail with unbounded joy the permanent restoration of peace on the basis of the Union under the Constitution, without the effusion of another drop of blood. But no peace can be permanent without the Union." He differed with the Convention also in postponing the effort to procure peace by the exhaustion of "all the resources of statesmanship" until it should become clear or probable "that our present adversaries are ready for peace upon the basis of the Union." A similar proposition coming before the Convention Committee on Resolutions in exactly the same terms used in this letter, received only three votes out of twenty-four.[2]

Pendleton very cautiously refused to commit himself except in so far as to state that he deprecated and would persistently oppose the establishment of another government over any portion of the territory within the limits of the Union. With one hand he clung to Vallandigham, and with the other to McClellan, while the latter shouldered Pendleton, Vallandigham, and the Chicago platform—protesting against the burden, but still bearing it—and with this incubus ran the race with Lincoln for the presidential chair. Even without these entanglements his prospects of success were doubtful, as his success involved the abandonment of the emancipation policy, which had already grown as dear to the American people as to President Lincoln.

Scarcely had the members of the Convention returned home, and begun to mingle with the people again, when they discovered too late that they had made a great mistake. As Gettysburg and Vicksburg had followed the harangues of Seymour, Pierce, and others on the 4th of July, 1863, so now the people got up from reading the Chicago platform to celebrate the capture of Atlanta, which was the sternest rebuke and most striking refutation of that document. Men who were disposed to split hairs with the Chicago statesmen were knocked down by Sherman's more palpable arguments. As Seward truly said at the time, "Sherman and Farragut had knocked the bottom out of the Chicago nominations."

[1] Vallandigham, in a public speech at Sidney, Ohio, September 24th, makes this statement in the most positive terms, and it has never been denied.

[2] See Vallandigham's speech alluded to in the previous note.

GEORGE H. PENDLETON.

Fremont now withdrew from the contest, and while still pronouncing Lincoln's administration "politically, militarily, and financially a failure," he abandoned the field, "not to aid the triumph of Lincoln," but to do his part to prevent the election of McClellan. The latter would establish the Union *with* slavery, while the former was pledged to re-establish it *without* slavery, and thus the great issues of the day were fairly joined, and there ought to enter into the contest no disturbing element to diminish the full strength of the victory of emancipation. Sheridan's victories over Early in the Valley of the Shenandoah, though not necessary to a Republican triumph, doubtless increased the popular majority for Lincoln.

The state elections in October and November, preceding that for presidential electors, betokened a certain victory for the administration. In Vermont the Republican candidate for governor was elected by a majority larger than that of 1863. In Maine there was a slight loss as compared with the election of 1863. In Indiana, O. P. Morton, the Republican candidate for governor, was elected by a majority of over 20,000. In Pennsylvania there was no general election for state officers, but the delegation from that state to Congress was changed from 12 against 12 to 15 against 9—a gain of three Republican Congressmen. In New York, Reuben E. Fenton was elected by 8000 majority over Seymour.

The presidential election, November 8th, resulted in an overwhelming victory for the administration. McClellan received the electoral votes of three states—Delaware, New Jersey, and Kentucky—21 in all; the remainder—212—were cast for Lincoln and Johnson. Lincoln's popular majority was 411,428.[1] In the twelve states whose vote by soldiers was counted so as to be distinguished, the success of the administration was even more signal, its majority being over 3 to 1. Such was the decision of the soldiers on the questions of peace and emancipation.[2]

An important issue in this election had been to secure a House of Representatives which would adopt the constitutional amendment abolishing slavery. The returns indicated that in the Thirty-ninth Congress the Republican majority would be so great that the members of that party, as compared with the Democrats, would number over 4 to 1. But it was not necessary to wait for another Congress.

The Thirty-eighth Congress reassembled for its second session December 5th, 1864.[1] The important act of this short session was the passage by the House of the joint resolution to amend the Constitution so as to abolish slavery. The President had in his message strongly urged this action. On the 31st of January the question was brought to a final issue. The form of the amendment remained the same as when it came from the Senate. The resolution passed by the requisite majority, receiving 119 ayes to 56 nays.[2] In this connection it is proper to mention the death of Owen Lovejoy, of Illinois, which occurred on the 25th of March, 1864. This old advocate of emancipation did not live to see the anti-slavery amendment passed, but he died in the faith that both Congress and the President would maintain justice.

In Maryland, on the 24th of June, in Constitutional Convention, the abolition of slavery in that state was declared as the twenty-third article of the Bill of Rights. In the following October this article was ratified by the people of the state. The vote stood 30,174 for, to 29,699 against the ratification. The majority was very small, and the measure would have failed but for the preponderance of the soldiers' vote in its favor. The soldiers' vote stood 2633 to 163.

Early in February, 1865, an attempt was made to open negotiations for peace. Alexander H. Stephens, the Confederate Vice-President, R. M. T. Hunter, and John A. Campbell, were permitted to pass through Grant's lines to Hampton Roads, where they were met by President Lincoln and Secretary Seward. The conference was soon concluded, President Lincoln refusing to treat on the basis of Confederate independence. Upon the return of the Confederate commissioners a great meeting was held to revive the drooping spirits of the Confederacy, and it was unanimously resolved that the conditions of peace offered by President Lincoln were a gross and premeditated insult to the Southern people. Three days later a war meeting was held, R. M. T. Hunter presiding, and it was there resolved that the Confederates would never lay down their arms until they should have achieved their independence.

The events—political and military—which from this point followed fast upon each other—the reinauguration of President Lincoln; the surrender of the Confederate armies; the attempt of a conspiracy to overthrow the government by the assassination of its principal officers; the succession of President Johnson; and the detailed history of reconstruction, belong properly to other chapters.

[1] The vote in the twenty-five loyal states stood as follows:

	Lincoln.	McClellan.		Lincoln.	McClellan.
Maine	72,278	47,736	Indiana	150,422	130,233
New Hampshire	36,595	33,034	Illinois	189,487	158,349
Vermont	42,419	13,325	Missouri	72,991	31,026
Massachusetts	126,742	48,745	Michigan	85,352	67,370
Rhode Island	14,343	8,718	Iowa	87,331	49,260
Connecticut	44,693	42,288	Wisconsin	79,564	63,875
New York	368,735	361,986	Minnesota	25,060	17,375
New Jersey	60,723	68,014	California	62,134	43,841
Pennsylvania	296,389	276,308	Oregon	9,888	8,457
Delaware	8,155	8,767	Kansas	14,228	3,871
Maryland	40,153	32,739	West Virginia	23,223	10,457
Kentucky	27,786	64,301	Nevada	9,826	6,594
Ohio	265,154	205,568	Total	2,213,665	1,802,237

[2] The army vote is shown in the following table. The soldiers of New York sent their ballots home to be deposited there, and so can not be distinguished. The vote of Minnesota soldiers, and a large portion of the Vermont soldiers' votes reached the canvassers too late to be counted:

	Lincoln.	McClellan.		Lincoln.	McClellan.
Maine	4,174	741	Michigan	9,402	2,957
New Hampshire	2,066	690	Iowa	15,178	1,364
Vermont	243	49	Wisconsin	11,372	2,458
Pennsylvania	26,712	12,349	Kansas	2,867	543
Maryland	2,800	321	California	2,600	237
Kentucky	1,194	2,823	Total	119,754	34,291
Ohio	41,146	9,757			

[1] The following changes occurred from the last session: In the Senate, Wm. Pitt Fessenden, of Maine, resigned to become Secretary of the Treasury, was succeeded by Nathan A. Farwell. On the 1st of February, 1865, William W. Stewart and James W. Nye took their seats as senators from Nevada—the former for the term expiring March 3, 1867, the latter for the term expiring March 3, 1869. On the 13th of February, Thomas H. Hicks, of Maryland. His successor, John A. Cresswell, was not qualified until March 10th, during the special executive session of the Senate.

In the House, Dwight Townsend, of New York, succeeded Henry G. Stebbins, resigned. December 21, Henry G. Worthington, of Nevada, was qualified.

[2] The vote in detail was as follows:

YEAS.

Alley	Mass.	Dixon	R. I.	King	Mo.	Rollins, E. H.	N. H.
Allison	Iowa.	Donnelly	Minn.	Knox	Mo.	Rollins, J. S.	Mo.
Ames	Mass.	Driggs	Mich.	Littlejohn	N. Y.	Schenck	Ohio.
Anderson	Ky.	Dumont	Ind.	Loan	Mo.	Schofield	Pa.
Arnold	Ill.	Eckley	Ohio.	Longyear	Mich.	Shannon	Cal.
Ashley	Ohio.	Elliot	Mass.	Marvin	N. Y.	Sloan	Wis.
Bailey	Pa.	English	Conn.	McAllister	Pa.	Smith	Ky.
Baldwin, A. C.	Mich.	Farnsworth	Ill.	McBride	Oregon.	Smithers	Del.
Baldwin, J. D.	Mass.	Frank	N. Y.	McClurg	Mo.	Spalding	Ohio.
Baxter	Vt.	Ganson	N. Y.	McIndoe	Wis.	Starr	N. J.
Beaman	Mich.	Garfield	Ohio.	Miller	N. Y.	Steele	N. Y.
Blaine	Me.	Gooch	Mass.	Moorhead	Pa.	Stevens	Pa.
Blair	W. Va.	Grinnell	Iowa.	Morrill	Vt.	Thayer	Pa.
Blow	Mo.	Griswold	N. Y.	Morris	N. Y.	Thomas	Md.
Boutwell	Mass.	Hale	Pa.	Myers, A.	Pa.	Tracy	Pa.
Boyd	Mo.	Herrick	N. Y.	Myers, L.	Pa.	Upson	Mich.
Brandagee	Conn.	Higby	Cal.	Nelson	N. Y.	Van Valkenburg	N. Y.
Broomall	Pa.	Hooper	Mass.	Norton	Ill.	Washburne	Ill.
Brown	W. Va.	Hotchkiss	N. Y.	Odell	N. Y.	Washburne	Mass.
Clarke, A. W.	N. Y.	Hubbard, A. W.	Iowa.	O'Neill, C.	Pa.	Webster	Md.
Clarke, Freeman	N. Y.	Hubbard, J. H.	Conn.	Orth	Ind.	Whaley	W. Va.
Cobb	Wis.	Hurlburd	N. Y.	Patterson	N. H.	Wheeler	Wis.
Coffroth	Pa.	Hutchins	Ohio.	Perham	Me.	Wilder	Kansas.
Cole	Cal.	Ingersoll	Ill.	Pike	Me.	Williams	Pa.
Colfax	Ind.	Jenckes	R. I.	Pomeroy	N. Y.	Wilson	Iowa.
Creswell	Md.	Julian	Ind.	Price	Iowa.	Windom	Minn.
Davis, H. W.	Md.	Kasson	Iowa.	Radford	N. Y.	Woodbridge	Vt.
Davis, T. T.	N. Y.	Kelley	Pa.	Randall	Ky.	Worthington	Nev.
Dawes	Mass.	Kellogg, F. W.	Mich.	Rice, A. H.	Mass.	Yeaman	Ky.
Deming	Conn.	Kellogg, O.	N. Y.	Rice, J. H.	Mo.		

NAYS.

Allen, J. C.	Ill.	Eldridge	Wis.	Law	Ind.	Scott	Mo.
Allen, W. H.	Ill.	Finck	Ohio.	Long	Ohio.	Steele, W. G.	N. J.
Ancona	Pa.	Grider	Ky.	Mallory	Ky.	Stiles	Pa.
Bliss	Ohio.	Hall	Mo.	Miller, W. H.	Pa.	Strouse	Pa.
Brooks	N. Y.	Harding	Ky.	Morris, J. R.	Ohio.	Stuart	Ill.
Brown, J. S.	Wis.	Harrington	Ind.	Morrison	Ill.	Sweat	Me.
Chanler	N. Y.	Harris, B. G.	Md.	Noble	Ohio.	Townsend	N. Y.
Clay	Ky.	Harris, C. M.	Ill.	O'Neill, J.	Ohio.	Wadsworth	Ky.
Cox	Ohio.	Holman	Ind.	Pendleton	Ohio.	Ward	N. Y.
Cravens	Ind.	Johnson, P.	Pa.	Perry	N. J.	White, C. A.	Ohio.
Dawson	Pa.	Johnson, W.	Ohio.	Pruyn	N. Y.	White, J. W.	Ohio.
Dennison	Pa.	Kalbfleisch	N. Y.	Randall, S. J.	Pa.	Winfield	N. Y.
Eden	Ill.	Kernan	N. Y.	Robinson	Ill.	Wood, B.	N. Y.
Edgerton	Ind.	Knapp	Ill.	Ross	Ill.	Wood, F.	N. Y.

NOT VOTING.

Lazear	Pa.	Marcy	N. H.	McKinney	Ohio.	Rogers	N. J.
Le Blond	Ohio.	McDowell	Ind.	Middleton	N. J.	Voorhees	Ind.

treats to Gadsden.—Is joined there by Beauregard.—The Confederate Plan of a Campaign against Nashville.—Sherman, tired of chasing Hood, prepares for his March to the Sea.—He sends the Fourth and Twenty-third Corps to Thomas.—His Theory of the grand March.—He puts his Plan into Operation.

THE period immediately following the campaign which had closed with the capture of Atlanta was full of contingencies and uncertainties. What shall I do next? was the question which occupied the minds both of Hood and Sherman. It was a brief period; for Hood could not wait long, and Sherman would not. The Federal commander, while he was compelling the exodus of citizens from Atlanta, reorganizing his army, protecting his rear, and making arrangements with General Hood for an exchange of prisoners, and for the relief of some of the inconveniences suffered by Union prisoners in the South,[1] was revolving great schemes in his mind. He must secure the position which he had already gained in the heart of the enemy's country. But when secured, Atlanta was of no consequence to him except as a point from which to strike. Of one thing he was well satisfied. Hood would not divide his army; it would remain, therefore, a compact organization, whether in his front or moved against his rear. Sherman's desire was to march through Georgia to the Atlantic coast. While guarding the railroad to Chattanooga, his eyes were fixed upon Savannah. But, so long as Hood's army remained in his front, no such scheme could be ventured, at least not until the Savannah River was in the possession of the Federal navy.[2] The Confederate cavalry swarmed about his army, and he could not advance far from Atlanta eastward or southward and protect the railroad in his rear without detaching forces which were necessary to his advance. If Canby should be heavily re-enforced and advance to Columbus, Georgia, and establish a new base for Sherman by way of the Alabama

[1] The relief which was proposed by General Sherman is indicated in the following letter from him to Hood, September, 1864:

"My latest information from Andersonville is to the 12th, and from what I learn, our prisoners of war confined there, and being removed to Savannah, Charleston, and Millen, need many articles which we possess in superfluity, and can easily supply with your consent and assistance, such as shirts and drawers, socks, shoes, soap, candles, combs, scissors, etc.

"If you will permit me to send a train of wagons, with a single officer to go along under a flag of truce, I will send to Lovejoy's or Palmetto a train of wagons loaded exclusively with 10,000 or 15,000 of each of these articles, and a due proportion of soap, candles, etc., under such restrictions as you may think prudent to name. I would like to have my officer go along to issue these things, but will have no hesitation in sending them if you will simply promise to have them conveyed to the places where our prisoners are, and have them fairly distributed."

Sherman expected a refusal. He writes to James G. Yeatman, President of the Western Sanitary Commission (date same as above): "I doubt if he [Hood] will consent. These Confederates are as proud as the devil, and hate to confess poverty, but I know they are unable to supply socks, drawers, undershirts, scissors, combs, etc., which our men need more than any thing else to preserve cleanliness and health."

In the same letter he says: "The condition of the prisoners at Andersonville has always been present to my mind, and, could I have released them, I would have felt more real satisfaction than to have won another battle." General Hood acceded to Sherman's request, and the articles were sent.

[2] We see clearly what Sherman's designs were from his dispatches during the month of September to Generals Halleck, Canby, and Grant. He writes to Halleck on the 4th (before he had in person entered Atlanta), evidently on the supposition that Hood would cover Macon:

"For the future I propose that of the drafted men I receive my due share, say 50,000 men; that an equal or greater number go to General Canby, who should now proceed with all energy to get Montgomery and the reach of the Alabama River above Selma; that when I know he can move on Columbus, Georgia, I move on La Grange and West Point, keeping to the coast of the Chattahoochee; that we form a junction, repair roads to Montgomery, and open up the Appalachicola and Chattahoochee Rivers to Columbus, and move from it as a base straight on Macon."

On the 10th he writes to Canby:

"We must have the Alabama River now, and also the Appalachicola at the old arsenal, and up to Columbus. My line is so long now that it is impossible to protect it against cavalry raids; but if we can get Montgomery and Columbus, Georgia, as bases in connection with Atlanta, we have Georgia and Alabama at our feet."

The same day he writes to Grant:

"I do not think we can afford to operate farther, dependent on the railroad, it takes so many men to guard it, and even then it is nightly broken by the enemy's cavalry that swarms about us. Macon is distant 103 miles, and Augusta 175 miles. If I could be sure of finding provisions and ammunition at Augusta or Columbus, Georgia, I can march to Milledgeville, and compel Hood to give up Augusta or Macon, and could then turn on the other. The country will afford forage and many supplies, but not enough in any one place to admit of delay. . . . If you can manage to take the Savannah River as high as Augusta, or the Chattahoochee as far up as Columbus, I can sweep the whole state of Georgia; otherwise I would risk the whole army by going too far from Atlanta."

The above was in reply to Grant's suggestion that Canby should operate against Savannah and Sherman against Augusta.

On the 12th he writes to Grant:

"I don't understand whether you propose to act against Savannah direct from Fort Pulaski, or by way of Florida, or from the direction of Mobile. If you take Savannah by a sudden *coup de main*, it would be valuable."

On the 20th again: "It [Savannah] once in our possession, I would not hesitate to cross the State of Georgia with 60,000 men, hauling some stores, and depending on the country for the balance. Where a million of people find subsistence my army won't starve; but, as you know, in a country like Georgia, with few roads and innumerable streams, an inferior force could so delay an army and harass it that it would not be a formidable object; but if the enemy knew that we had our boats on the Savannah, I could rapidly move to Milledgeville, where there is abundance of corn and meat, and I could so threaten Macon and Augusta that he would give up Macon for Augusta; than I would move to interpose between Augusta and Savannah, and force him to give me Augusta, with the only powder-mills and factories remaining in the South, or let us have the Savannah River. Either horn of the dilemma would be worth a battle. I would prefer his holding Augusta, as the probabilities are, for then, with the Savannah River in our possession, the taking of Augusta would be a mere matter of time. This campaign would be made in the winter. But the more I study the game, the more am I convinced that it would be wrong for me to penetrate much further into Georgia without an objective beyond. It would not be productive of much good. I can start east, and make a circuit south, and back, doing vast damage to the state, but resulting in no permanent good; but by merely threatening to do so I hold a rod over the Georgians, who are not over loyal to the South. I will therefore give my opinion that your army and Canby's should be re-enforced to the maximum; that after you get Wilmington you strike for Savannah and the river; that General Canby be instructed to hold the Mississippi River, and send a force to get Columbus, Georgia, either by way of the Alabama or Appalachicola; and that I keep Hood employed, and put my army in fine order for a march on Augusta, Columbus, and Charleston.

Davis, on the 23d of Septem
of that town. Among the
his administration, this spee
formed General Sherman o
have been discovered till the
nunciation of Governor Brow
undignified, that the reporte
the Richmond papers. Eve
thenticity. Governor Brow
contempt was thrown upon J
chee. His speech was not,
two thirds of the Confederat
He said it was impossible to
disparity of forces was just
his hearers, to Georgia, to th
eracy had been reduced. H
for the war, and informed G
route eastward to the Atla
army for protection, but tha
minding them that they had
45. But that which must b
the declaration that he was
and his subordinates. In vi
Confederacy which he had s
The burden of his prophecy
from the deserts of Russia, e

[1] Hood's explanation of this move
"A serious question was now prese
He had it in his power to continue hi
for subsistence. I could not hope to
strength, nor was there any advantag
of the army, greatly improved during
consequence of the recurrence of retr
Something was absolutely demanded
cess, would go far to restore its fighti
commanders, to turn the enemy's rig
him to retire from Atlanta. The o
Forrest in Tennessee, proved to me
service could not permanently inte
ciently to cause him to abandon his p
sary for me to move with my entire
Instead of having any hope of forc
was in doubt as to the possibility of
dispense with dependence upon his
army, he was not likely to improve it

[2] The following is a copy of Davis
LADIES AND GENTLEMEN, FRIEND
to have met you in prosperity insteа
The son of a Georgian, who fought
should forget the state in her day o
Decatur to Jonesboro', our cause is
cation, and retreat sooner or later be
of the French empire in its retreat f
harass and destroy his army as did
him, will escape with only a body-gu
santees of Hood's army returning to
ies; can they hear the wail of their s
influences they are made to stay aw
away at this hour, he is unworthy of
They are like the Spartan mothers o
eight years. She wrote that she w
able General Polk, to whom I read
tic of her; but I will not weary yo
the last son to the cause of our cou
hands of our noble women enlisted
They have one duty to perform—to
felt by Georgia at our army falling
of those who considered Atlanta lo
it should not be, and I then put a m
city, and many a Yankee's blood wa
not become us to revert to disaster.
effort, endeavor to crush Sherman.
end must be the defeat of our ene
Shame upon such falsehood. Wh
when General Stephen D. Lee were
this was a scoundrel. He was not
possess the right qualities to comma
our army was falling back from No
toons to cross it to Cuba. But we
made to take up his musket. Whe
tablish our independence—who will
ladies I would say that, when choos
home and grown rich, always take
bread. But should they know of
made to go any other way, let the
people, but have not the time to r
forty-five left. The boys—God bles
the field. The city of Macon is fil
when threatened; but when the en
old men must fight, and when the
general rejoicing. Your prisoners
their generals said that their excha
every thing to effect an exchange.
sioner of exchange would hold inte
sent to the exchange of negroes all
his to get himself whitewashed, by
effected, I don't know but I might

ite army was at West Point, in a position to move on his flank; but ıvis's Macon speech, which he had read in full in the Southern papers, left n no room for doubt that an attempt would be made by the enemy, movg in full force to his rear, to compel him to release his hold upon Georgia. could not decide at once as to his future movements. It was still a estion with him whether, while protecting Tennessee against Hood's insion, he would have men enough left for the execution of his favorite oject—the march eastward to Georgia. This question was soon settled by eneral Grant's generous co-operation and encouragement, and by the patrism of the loyal states. Every day increased Sherman's confidence. In e mean time he carefully watched the enemy's movements. Tennessee ust be protected at all hazards. The devastation of Georgia and the capre of Savannah would not compensate for the surrender of Nashville and hattanooga to the Confederates.

Hood had already sent Forrest with a cavalry force 7000 strong into Mide Tennessee as a prelude to the march of his whole army. Forrest, on the th of September, crossed the Tennessee near Waterloo, Alabama, and deoyed a portion of the railroad between Decatur and Athens. On the 23d appeared before the latter place, and drove the garrison of 600 men into eir fort. The commander of this post was Colonel Campbell, who, in a rsonal interview with Forrest on the 24th, was persuaded that it was uses to resist the odds against him, and induced to surrender. In half an ur two regiments of Michigan and Ohio troops came to his assistance, and ere driven back. Before Forrest reached Pulaski, General Rousseau had llected a force sufficient to defend that place, and the Confederate cavalry the 29th swung around upon the Nashville and Chattanooga Road, and gan to break it up between Tullahoma and Decherd. Rousseau had also oved promptly eastward, and at Tullahoma again barred the progress of orrest northward. Steadman also, with 5000 men from Chattanooga, had ossed the Tennessee, and put his force in front of the enemy, compelling e latter to fall back through Fayetteville. The injuries done to the road ere repaired in the course of a single day. Forrest now divided his force to two columns, commanded by Buford and himself, his own consisting of 00 men. Buford demanded the surrender of Huntsville on the 30th, and ing refused, proceeded against Athens, which General R. S. Granger had dered to be reoccupied by the Seventy-third Indiana, and, attacking the from Rome. The enemy had already got upon the railroad, as we have seen, by the 4th, destroying the railroad and cutting the telegraph; and on the night of that day, General Corse, with Rowett's brigade and 165,000 rounds of ammunition, reached Allatoona just in time to meet the attack made on the morning of the 5th by French's division of Stewart's corps. Sherman reached the top of Kenesaw Mountain at 10 A.M., and from that point—a distance of 18 miles—he could see the smoke of the battle and hear faintly the sound of the artillery. He could not reach the scene of conflict in time, nor was it probable that he could afford any assistance from his main army; but he sent General J. D. Cox, with the Twenty-third Corps, to attack the assailants in the rear, on the Dallas and Allatoona Road. Signals were exchanged between Sherman and General Corse, and as soon as the Federal commander learned that the latter was at the point of danger, all his anxiety vanished. Corse's arrival increased the number of the garrison to 1944 men. By 8 30 A.M. French had turned Allatoona, reaching the railroad north, and cutting off communication with Cartersville and Rome. At this time he sent a flag of truce summoning the garrison to surrender, "to avoid needless effusion of blood." Corse promptly replied that he was prepared for "the needless effusion of blood," whenever it would be agreeable to General French. The enemy then attacked with great fury, the first assault falling upon Colonel Rowett, who held the western spur of the ridge. This onset was successfully resisted, but the assault was repeated over and again, and as often repulsed. On the north side, a brigade of the enemy under General Sears made an attack in flank with better success. "The enemy's line of battle," reports General Corse, "swept us like so much chaff." But Tourtellotte from the eastern spur poured on Sears's advancing troops a fire which caught them in flank and broke their ranks. The battle thus far had been going on outside of the fort, into which, by the volume and impetuosity of the enemy's assaults, the garrison was driven before noon. But, notwith

LOVELL H. ROUSSEAU.

tarily appeals strongly to executive clemency. But suppose he stays away until the war is over, d his comrades return home, and when every man's history will be told, where will he shield himf? It is upon these reflections that I rely to make men return to their duty; but, after conferg with our generals at headquarters, if there be any other remedy it shall be applied. I love my ends and I forgive my enemies. I have been asked to send re-enforcements from Virginia to orgia. In Virginia the disparity in numbers is just as great as it is in Georgia. Then I have en asked why the army sent to the Shenandoah Valley was not sent here. It was because an ny of the enemy had penetrated that valley to the very gates of Lynchburg, and General Early s sent to drive them back. This he not only successfully did, but, crossing the Potomac, came ll-nigh capturing Washington itself, and forced Grant to send two corps of his army to protect

This the enemy denominated a raid. If so, Sherman's march into Georgia is a raid. What uld prevent them now, if Early were withdrawn from taking Lynchburg, and putting a complete rdon of men around Richmond? I counseled with that great and grave soldier, General Lee, on all these points. My mind roamed over the whole field. With this we can succeed. If e half the men now absent without leave will return to duty, we can defeat the enemy. With at hope I am going to the front. I may not realize this hope; but I know there are men there o have looked death in the face too often to despond now. Let no one despond. Let no one strust; and remember that if genius is the beau ideal, hope is the reality.

' Grant writes him September 27:

"It is evident from the tone of the Richmond press, and all other sources, that the enemy intend king a desperate effort to drive you from where you are. I have directed all new troops from e West, and from the East too, if necessary, if none are ready in the West, to be sent to you."

HOOD'S ATTACK ON ALLATOONA.

standing the odds against them, they had inflicted sufficient injury upon French's division to make it pause, and consider whether it was worth the while to attack the fort, held by men who, outside of its walls, had fought with such obstinacy. The delay gave Corse time to dispose his force in the trenches and behind the parapet. From noon till almost night the enemy closed around the fort, enfilading its trenches, and making death almost certain to those who ventured to expose themselves. The unyielding temper of the garrison baffled the enemy, who, learning that a hostile force was almost upon his rear, gave up the contest. In this action General Corse was wounded in the face.[1] The loss of the garrison was about 700 men—over one third of the entire command. Corse reports that he buried 231 of the enemy's dead and captured 411 prisoners, one of whom, Brigadier General Young, estimated the Confederate loss at 2000. In no instance during the war was the value of the Signal Corps more fully illustrated than in the affair at Allatoona. The service which it rendered here, General Sherman afterward said, more than paid its entire expense from the time of its origination.

The army with which Hood had crossed the Chattahoochee, if we include Wheeler's command which subsequently joined him, numbered about 36,000, of which one fourth was cavalry. After his failure at Allatoona, Hood moved northwestwardly across the Coosa. Sherman followed by the railroad, marching through Allatoona Pass on the 8th, and reaching Kingston on the 10th. Here he found that, making a feint on Rome, the enemy had crossed the river about 11 miles below that place. The next day, therefore, he advanced to Rome, pushing forward Garrard's cavalry and the Twenty-third Corps, with instructions to cross the Oostenaula and threaten Hood's right flank, if the latter continued his movement northward. But the Confederates, by reason of their superior cavalry force, moved more rapidly, and on the 12th Hood summoned the garrison of Resaca to surrender, threatening to take no prisoners if the surrender was refused. Colonel Weaver, the commander at Resaca, saw no cause for alarm, and bluntly refused. He had been re-enforced by Sherman, and the enemy, deeming it prudent to avoid a battle, pushed on toward Dalton, destroying the railroad in his progress. Capturing the garrison at Dalton, he moved through Tunnel Hill to Villanow.

Sherman reached Resaca on the 15th, and endeavored to force Hood to a battle by moving upon his flank and rear. Howard's army was ordered to Snake Creek Gap, where the enemy was found occupying the former Federal defenses. Here Howard tried to hold Hood until Stanley, with the Fourth Corps, could come up in his rear at Villanow. But the Confederate commander did not intend to fight Sherman's army; he was well content with being chased. Covering his rear with Wheeler's cavalry, he fell back to Gadsden, Alabama. Sherman followed as far as Gaylesville. Here there was a pause on the part of both armies. At Gadsden, General Beauregard, commanding the military division of the West, joined Hood. The latter had anticipated that Sherman would divide his forces, and give him a chance, but he had been disappointed. To venture a general engagement in the open field with an enemy whom he had been unable to oppose behind the fortifications of Atlanta was a step too reckless for even General Hood to take. To retreat utterly at this stage of affairs would be the ruin of his own not-too-well-established reputation, and would demoralize his army. It was therefore finally determined between him and General Beauregard that Sherman should be drawn north of the Tennessee.

But Sherman had long been growing weary of chasing an army that would not, and could not be made to fight. He had now a splendid position for defense, covering Bridgeport, Rome, Chattanooga, and the railroad thence to Atlanta. It was necessary that he should hold this position for a time, until his plans were matured. The strategy to which Hood was about to tempt him was not the strategy suited to his nature. If Hood would only cross the Tennessee, he would soon gratify him by a division of the Federal army. The railroads were speedily repaired, and Atlanta was being supplied with an abundance of provisions. Sherman was urging upon Grant his project of the march through Georgia to Savannah, and anxiously watching the accumulation of an army under Thomas sufficient to oppose Hood, leaving himself free to use his main army for offensive operations.[1]

[1] The day after the battle, Corse writes to Sherman: "I am short a cheek-bone and one ear, but am able to whip all hell yet."

[1] Sherman says in his report: "Hood's movements and strategy had demonstrated that he had an army capable of endangering at all times my communications, but unable to meet me in open fight. To follow him would simply amount to being decoyed away from Georgia, with little prospect of overtaking and overwhelming him. To remain on the defensive would have been bad policy for an army of so great value as I then commanded, and I was forced to adopt a course more fruitful in results than the naked one of following him to the southwest. I had previously submitted to the commander-in-chief a general plan, which amounted substantially to the destruction of Atlanta and the railroad back to Chattanooga, and sallying forth from Atlanta, through the heart of Georgia, to capture one or more of the great Atlantic sea-ports. This I renewed from Gaylesville, modified somewhat by the change of events."

Sherman's dispatches during this period contain a very complete history of the progress of his favorite scheme of the March to the Sea. They are so characteristic that we here give all of them which have a direct bearing upon the subject:

September 29, 1864. To General HALLECK: "I prefer for the future to make the movement on Milledgeville, Millen, and Savannah River."

September 30. To General COX: "I may have to make some quick counter-moves east and southeast. Keep your folks ready to send baggage into Atlanta, and to start on short notice. . . . . . There are fine corn and potato fields about Covington and the Ocmulgee bottoms. . . . . If we make a counter-move I will go out myself with a large force, and take such a route as will supply us, and at the same time make Hood recall the whole or part of his army."

September 30. To General THOMAS: "If he [Hood] moves his whole force to Blue Mountain, you watch him from the direction of Stevenson, and I will do the same from Rome; and as soon as all things are ready, I will take advantage of his opening to me all of Georgia."

October 30. To General GRANT: "Hood is evidently on the west side of Chattanooga, below Sweetwater. If he tries to get on my road this side of the Etowah, I shall attack him; but if he goes on to the Selma and Talladega Road, why would it not do for me to leave Tennessee to the forces which Thomas has, and the reserves soon to come to Nashville, and for me to destroy Atlanta, and then march across Georgia to Savannah or Charleston, breaking roads, and doing irreparable damage? We can not remain on the defensive."

There is no immediate reply to this from Grant.

October 1. To Generals HOWARD and COX: "It is well for you to bear in mind that if Hood swings over to the Alabama Road, and thence tries to get into Tennessee, I may throw back to Chattanooga all of General Thomas's men as far down as Kingston, and draw forward all else, send back all cars and locomotives, destroy Atlanta, and make for Savannah or Charleston via Milledgeville and Millen. If Hood aims at our road this side of Kingston, and in no manner threatens Tennessee, I will have to turn on him. Keep those things to yourselves. The march I propose is less by 200 miles than I made last fall, and less than I accomplished in February, and we could make Georgia a break in the Confederacy by ruining both east and west roads, and not running against a single fort until we get to the sea-shore, and in communication with our ships."

October 1. To General THOMAS: "Use your own discretion as to the matters north of the Tennessee River. If I can induce Hood to swing across to Blue Mountain, I shall feel tempted to start for Milledgeville, Millen, and Savannah or Charleston, absolutely destroying all Georgia, and taking either Savannah or Charleston. In that event, I will order back to Chattanooga every thing the other side of Kingston, and bring forward all else, destroy Atlanta and the bridge, and absolutely scour the Southern Confederacy. In that event, Hood would be puzzled, and would follow me; or, if he entered Tennessee, he could make no permanent stay. But if he attempts the road this side of Kingston or Rome, I will turn against him."

io Grant the general outlines of his scheme
ıt that time Hood was in his front, on the

me well advised, for I now think Hood will rather
ıoe Bridge than against Kingston and the Etowah
tess his movements as I could those of Johnston, who
ings. If Hood does not mind, I will catch him in a

ıs up here to relieve our road. Twentieth Corps at
e it between Big Shanty and Ackworth, and attack-
ınt to destroy all the road below Chattanooga, includ-
'e can not defend this long line of road."
be a physical impossibility to protect the road, now
ıole batch of devils, are turned loose, without home or
ıp the railroad from Chattanooga, and strike out with-
ah. Until we can repopulate Georgia it is useless to
ads, houses, and people will cripple their military re-
e will lose a thousand men monthly, and will gain no
orgia howl. We have over 8000 cattle, and 3,000,000
'nge in the interior of the state."
is now crossing the Coosa, twelve miles below Rome,
: and Ohio Road, had I not better execute the plan of
ieneral Thomas, with the troops now in Tennessee, to
o when the re-enforcements ordered reach Nashville."
: "I will not say positively that I can hold Hood with
ıents expected, because I do not know how many re-
, however, and, as you direct, will concentrate the in-
leaving a portion of the cavalry to watch the river be-

moved his army from Palmetto Station across by Dal-
ı River, south of Rome. He threw one corps on my
ow. I hold Atlanta with the Twentieth Corps, and
ıese reduce my active force to a comparatively small
efensive. With 25,000 men, and the bold cavalry
' road. I would infinitely prefer to make a wreck
ooga to Atlanta, including the latter city, send back
ny effective army move through Georgia, smashing
Tennessee and Kentucky, but I believe he will be
the defensive, I would be on the offensive. Instead
d have to guess at my plans. The difference in war
Charleston, or the mouth of the Chattahoochee (Ap-
rill not have the telegraph long."
want the first positive fact that Hood contemplates
so. Send him a free pass in."
n the statement made in a Montgomery paper that
is going to cross the Tennessee.
as to "adopt Grant's idea of turning Wilson loose
with the whole force through Georgia to the sea."
ı't want to be in command of the defense of Tennes-
gton deem it absolutely necessary."
enemy will not venture into Tennessee except around
Corps to General Thomas, and leave him with that
d the line of the Tennessee, and with the rest to push
vannah, destroying all the railroads of the state."
a report to me as soon as possible of what troops you
and how disposed. I propose, with the armies of
of yours, to sally forth, and make a hole in Georgia
ood has little or no baggage, and will escape me. He
of Huntsville. . . . . I will send back into Tennes-
', all sick and wounded, and all encumbrances what-
ınd will probably, about November, break up the rail-
e a break for Mobile, Savannah, or Charleston. I
ommand of all my division not actually present with
ı0 of all arms fit for duty; he may follow me or turn
he Tennessee in my absence of three months is all I

Q. M. at Atlanta): "Hood will escape me. I want
ovember I want nothing in Atlanta but what is neces-
have on hand thirty days' food and but little forage.
ıd back to Chattanooga, and sally forth to ruin Geor-

ı must not be on the defensive, and I now consider
roy the railroad from Chattanooga to Atlanta, includ-
e heart of Georgia, and make for Charleston, Savan-
ıneral Grant prefers the middle one, Savannah, and I
ıama. I must have alternatives, else, being confined
ıt delay and want would trouble me; but, having al-
at no general can guess at my objective. Therefore,
erris Island, South Carolina, Ossabaw Sound, Georgia,
ıp somewhere, and believe I can take Macon, Mil-
ınd wind up with closing the neck back of Charleston,
ıt is not purely military or strategic, but it will illus-
on't know what war means; but when the rich plant-
ces, and corn, and hogs, and sheep vanish before their
mean opinion of the 'Yanks.' Even now our poor
oldiers riot on chestnuts, sweet potatoes, pigs, chick-
beg us for their lives; but my customary answer is,
h supplied us bountifully, and you can not suppose our
vithin reach.'
ads, during which I will eat out this flank, and along
, was at Summerville, Georgia], and then will rapidly
time I ask that you will give General Thomas all the
e may hold the line of the Tennessee during my ab-

ral Garrard has about 2500 cavalry, General Kilpat-
be about 1000 other cavalry with my army. These
wish you would . . . . bring to me about 2500 new
ee divisions, each of 2500, for the hardest fighting of
'the Confederacy, and propose to leave a trail that will

ık I have thought over the whole field of the future.
things bent to the following general plan of action for

n I propose to organize an efficient army of 60,000 to
Macon, Augusta, and, it may be, Savannah and Charles-
s of the mouth of the Appalachicola and Mobile. By
y of the South, and make its inhabitants feel that war
To pursue Hood is folly, for he can twist and turn like
continue to occupy long lines of railroads simply ex-
ı in detail, and forces me to make countermarches to
n right in this, and shall proceed to its maturity. As
d and his army, General Schofield and his, and two

Macon Road. He was not, under these circumstance
venture unless he could be sure of some objective po

of access. We have now a good entering wedge, and should drive
time to complete these details, and I hope to hear from you in the me
a large amount of secrecy, and I may actually change the ultimate poi
object."

October 20. To General SLOCUM: "Use all your energies to send
needed for the grand march. I will take your corps along. We wi
bread, coffee, sugar, and salt, 500,000 rations of salt meat, and all c
. . . . I want to be near Atlanta and ready by November 1st."

October 22. To General GRANT: "I feel perfectly master of the
Atlanta, and the road with all bridges and vital points well guarded,
before which Hood has retreated precipitately down the Coosa. It
plans; but by abandoning Georgia, and taking position with his rea
road from Chattanooga to Atlanta, and may move up to Tennessee by
the Tennessee except at Muscle Shoals, for all other points are patrol
"I am now perfecting arrangements to put into Tennessee a force
Tennessee while I break up the railroad in front of Dalton, including
into Georgia and break up all its railroads and depôts, capture its hor
lation every where, destroy the factories at Macon, Milledgeville, and
60,000 men on the sea-shore about Savannah or Charleston. I think
ing a long line of railroad. I will leave General George H. Thomas
division behind me, and take with me only the best fighting material.
the bountiful corn-fields and potato-patches, as I am now doing, luxu

October 23. To General SLOCUM: "Go on; pile up the forage, c
your artillery horses fat; send back all unserviceable artillery, and,
count up our horses, and see what we can haul, and send back all else.
will be plenty to take along. Hood is doubtless now at Blue Moun
Corinth and Tuscumbia, hoping by threatening Tennessee to make
piling up men in Tennessee enough to attend to them, and to leave
railroad will be done in a day or two. We find abundance of corn an
enjoy them much; they cost nothing a bushel. If Georgia can affor
can afford to feed us."

October 23. To General THOMAS: "Hood is now at Blue Mountai
about Tuscumbia. No doubt they will endeavor conjointly to make
I don't want them to succeed. All Georgia is now open to me, and
best qualified to manage the affairs of Tennessee and North Mississip
"I want approximate returns of all troops subject to your orders
spare you the Fourth Corps and about 5000 men not fit for my pur
enough for garrison at Chattanooga, Murfreesborough, and Nashvill
points fortified and stocked with provisions, and a movable column o
in any direction."

October 24. To General HALLECK: "Beauregard announces his t
man out of Atlanta, which he still holds defiantly, and dares him to t
ing to chase him all over creation."

October 26. To General THOMAS: "A reconnoissance pushed dow
the fact that the rebel army is not there, and the chances are it has m
Guntersville I will be after it, but if it goes, as I believe, to Decatur
to you at present, and push for the heart of Georgia."

October 28. To General THOMAS: "I have already sent the Fourt
Wauhatchee to-morrow; use it freely, and if I see that Hood cross
Schofield. On these two corps you can ingraft all the new troops
south."

October 29. To General THOMAS: "Ingraft on Stanley and Sc
Give Schofield a division of new troops. Give General Tower all th
forts at Nashville, and urge on the navy to pile up gun-boats in the T

October 29. To General ROSECRANS: "I have pushed Beauregard
I know he is pledged to invade Tennessee and Kentucky, having his
Ohio Road. I have put Thomas in Tennessee, and given him as mac
ary, but I don't want to leave it to chance, and therefore would like
divisions up the Tennessee River as soon as possible. . . . I proj
down into the heart of Georgia, smashing things generally."

November 1. To General GRANT: "As you foresaw, and as Jeff. D
now in the full tide of execution of his grand plan to destroy my com
army. His infantry, about 30,000, with Wheeler and Roddy's caval
now in the neighborhood of Tuscumbia and Florence, and the water
at will. Forrest seems to be scattered from Eastport to Jackson, P
&c, and General Thomas reports the capture by him of a gun-boat
Thomas has near Athens and Pulaski Stanley's corps, about 15,000
10,000, *en route* by rail, and has at least 20,000 to 25,000 men, with
arriving all the time also. General Rosecrans promises the two div
belonging to me, but I doubt if they can reach Tennessee in less tha
go Atlanta and North Georgia and make for Hood, he would, as he d
west, leaving his militia, now assembling at Macon and Griffin, to oc
work of last summer would be lost. I have retained about 50,000 goo
25,000, and have instructed General Thomas to hold defensively Nas
catur, all strongly fortified and provisioned for a long siege. I will des
and do as much substantial damage as is possible, reaching the sea-
hitherto indicated, trusting that Thomas with his present troops, a
promised, will be able in a very few days to assume the offensive. H
deal of damage, and I have sent Wilson back with all dismounted
4500. This is the best I can do, and shall, therefore, when I get to
move south as soon as possible."

The same day Grant writes to Sherman: "Do you not think it a
gone so far north, to entirely ruin him before starting on your propos
army destroyed, you can go where you please with impunity. I beli
had started south while Hood was in the neighborhood of you, he v
after you. Now that he is so far away, he might look upon the chase
one direction while you are pushing the other. If you can see the c
army, attend to that first, and make the other move secondary."

November 2. To General THOMAS: "According to Wilson's accour
full 12,000 cavalry, and I estimate your infantry force, independent o
which is a force superior to the enemy."

November 2. To General GRANT: "If I could hope to overhaul Ho
with my whole force; then he would retreat to the southwest, drawing
which is his chief object. If he ventures north of the Tennessee, I m
get between him and his line of retreat, but thus far he has not gone a
will have a force strong enough to prevent his reaching any country
and he has orders, if Hood turns to follow me, to push for Selma. N
and I am convinced the best results will follow from our defeating Je
making me leave Georgia by manœuvring. Thus far I have confi
plans, and have reduced my baggage so that I can pick up and start i
regard a pursuit of Hood as useless. Still, if he attempts to invade M
Decatur, and be prepared to move in that direction; but, unless I let
be equal to his."

To this Grant replies the same day: "Your dispatch of 9 A.M. y
dispatched you the same date, advising that Hood's army, now that
ought to be looked upon more as the object. With the force, howeve
Thomas, he must be able to take care of Hood and destroy him. I r
withdraw from where you are to follow Hood, without giving up all w

November 2. To General GRANT: "General Thomas reports to-d

ready in possession of the national armies. But, as soon as Hood moved from his front, the way seemed open for an advance through Georgia to the sea-coast. He had then to consider whether he could make the march, and at the same time protect Chattanooga and Nashville. This was a question which could only be answered when it was certainly ascertained what re-enforcements would be received. By the middle of October Hood had been driven off from the Chattanooga and Atlanta Railroad. About the 1st of November he threatened to cross the Tennessee in the neighborhood of Decatur. This, indeed, was the only point at which he could effect a crossing, the rest of the river—from Muscle Shoals above and Colbert Shoals below—being guarded by gun-boats. Sherman had, by this time, dispatched Stanley's Fourth and Schofield's Twenty-third Corps—about 25,000 infantry—to General Thomas. Breve. Major General James Wilson had arrived from the Army of the Potomac, to take command of Sherman's cavalry, and it seemed probable that in the course of a few days he would be able to mount 12,000 men. New regiments of recruits were continually coming into Nashville, and Sherman ordered these to be ingrafted into the veteran corps of Stanley and Schofield. Hood would be delayed for some days in the accumulation of supplies, and in the mean time A. J. Smith's and Mower's divisions could be brought over from Missouri. With these divisions added to his other forces, Sherman thought Thomas would have a force sufficient to attend to Hood. He thought, however, that Hood, learning of his march eastward, would follow him, at least with his cavalry. In any event, he had no uneasiness in regard to Tennessee.

But Thomas was not so confident. He thought it would be better to send Wilson's cavalry through Georgia, and fight Hood with the whole of Sherman's army. Grant also urged this at first; but Sherman's arguments finally convinced him that Thomas could take care of Tennessee, and that it was better that Sherman should carry out his project. Thomas also, in the end, reached the same conclusion.

Sherman's perfect confidence in his own scheme excites our admiration. He had no doubts. He had carefully balanced the forces on both sides, and knew that Thomas would be a match for Hood. To protect his long line of railroad, garrison Atlanta, and pursue Hood "all over creation" involved, in his judgment, the waste of 60,000 men. To make a wreck of Atlanta and Rome, and of the railroad from Atlanta to Dalton, left nothing for the enemy to occupy, nothing for himself to guard. The four army corps which he still retained—60,000 strong—contained the best fighting material of his command. North of Atlanta they were not needed. If they should operate with Thomas against Hood, the latter, "turning and twisting like a fox," would slip out of their hands, and thus time, energy, and opportunity would be wasted, without any adequate results. In the strict economy of war, therefore, Sherman was justified in using this superfluous army elsewhere, striking instead of waiting, marching, and countermarching. It is true there were no armies in his front to strike, southward or eastward. Still, there were several important ends to be attained by his march.

In the first place, the march of an organized army, as strong in numbers as that with which Sherman proposed to move through the interior of the enemy's country, from its easternmost to its westernmost limit, would at the same time illustrate the inherent weakness of the Confederacy and the strength of the national armies. Such a march, with such an army, would demonstrate to the world that the ultimate triumph of the nation over the rebellion was an assured fact. In connection with President Lincoln's re-election, it would ruin the hopes of the peace party in the loyal states. It would also destroy all confidence on the part of the Southern people that their usurped government could afford them protection. Well might Sherman say that, "even without a battle, the results, operating upon the minds of sensible men, would produce fruits more than compensating for the expense, trouble, and risk."

But it would not be simply a political demonstration. The military con-

two full corps and about 8000 cavalry, besides 10,000 dismounted cavalry and all the new troops recently sent to Tennessee, with the railroad guards, with which to encounter Beauregard, should he advance farther. Besides which, General Thomas will have the active co-operation of the gun-boats both above and below the Shoals, and the two divisions of Smith and Mower, *en route* from Missouri. I therefore feel no uneasiness as to Tennessee, and have ordered General Thomas to assume the offensive in the direction of Selma, Alabama. With myself I have the Twentieth Corps at Atlanta, the Fifteenth and Seventeenth near Kenesaw, and the Fourteenth here [near Kingston]. I am sending to the rear, as fast as cars will move, the vast accumulation of stuff that, in spite of my endeavors, has been got over the road, and am sending forward just enough bread and meat to enable me to load my wagons, destroy every thing of value to the enemy, and start on my contemplated trip. I can be ready in five days, but am waiting to be more certain that Thomas will be prepared for any contingency that may arise. It is now raining, which is favorable to us and unfavorable to the enemy. Davis has utterly failed in his threat to force me to leave in thirty days, for my railroad is in good order from Nashville to Atlanta, and his army is farther from my communications now than it was twenty days ago. . . . . . I propose to adhere, as near as possible, to my original plan, and, on reaching the sea-coast, will be available for re-enforcing the army in Virginia, leaving behind a track of desolation, as well as a sufficient force to hold fast all that is of permanent value to our cause."

November 6. To General GRANT:

"DEAR GENERAL,—I have heretofore telegraphed and written you pretty fully, but I still have some thoughts in my busy brain that should be confided to you as a key to future developments.

"The taking of Atlanta broke on Jeff. Davis so suddenly as to disturb the equilibrium of his usually well-balanced temper, so that at Augusta, Macon, and Columbia, South Carolina, he let out some of his thoughts, which otherwise he would have kept to himself. As he is not only the President of the Southern Confederacy, but also its commander-in-chief, we are bound to attach more importance to his words than we would to those of a mere civil chief magistrate.

"The whole burden of his song consists in the statement that Sherman's communications *must* be broken and his army destroyed. Now it is a well-settled principle that, if we prevent his succeeding in his threat, we defeat him, and derive all the moral advantages of a victory. Thus far Hood and Beauregard conjointly have utterly failed to interrupt my supplies or communications. My railroad and telegraph are now in good order from Atlanta back to the Ohio River. His losses in men at Allatoona, Resaca, Ship's Gap, and Decatur exceed in number ours at the block-houses at Big Shanty, Allatoona Creek, and Dalton; and the rapidity of his flight from Dalton to Gadsden takes from him all the merit or advantage claimed for his skillful and rapid lodgment on my railroad. The only question in my mind is whether I ought not to have dogged him far over into Mississippi, trusting to some happy accident to bring him to bay and to battle; but I then thought that by so doing I would play into his hands, by being drawn or decoyed too far away from our original line of advance. Besides, I had left at Atlanta a corps, and guards along the railroad back to Chattanooga, which might have fallen an easy prey to his superior cavalry. I felt compelled, therefore, to do what is usually a mistake in war—divide my forces—send a part back into Tennessee, retaining the balance here.

"As I have before informed you, I sent Stanley back directly from Gaylesville, and Schofield from Rome, both of which have reached their destination; and thus far Hood, who has brought up at Florence, is farther from my communications than when he started; and I have in Tennessee a force numerically greater than his, well commanded and well organized, so that I feel no uneasiness on the score of Hood reaching my main communications.

"My last accounts from General Thomas are to 9 30 last night, when Hood's army was about Florence in great distress about provisions, as it well must be, and that devil Forrest was down about Johnsonville, making havoc among the gun-boats and transports; but Schofield's troops were arriving at Johnsonville, and a fleet of gun-boats was reported coming up from below, able to repair that trouble. You know that line of supplies was only opened for summer's use, when the Cumberland is not to be depended upon. We now have abundant supplies at Atlanta, Chattanooga, and Nashville, with the Louisville and Nashville Railroad and the Cumberland River unmolested, so that I regard Davis's threat to get his army on my rear, or on my communications, as a miserable failure.

"Now as to the second branch of my proposition. I admit that the first object should be the destruction of that army; and if Beauregard moves his infantry and artillery up into the pocket about Jackson and Paris, I will feel strongly tempted to move Thomas directly against him, and myself move rapidly by Decatur and Purdy to cut off his retreat. But this would involve the abandonment of Atlanta, and a retrograde movement, which would be very doubtful of expediency or success; for, as a matter of course, Beauregard, who watches me with his cavalry and his friendly citizens, would have timely notice, and slip out and escape, to regain what we have earned at so much cost. I am more than satisfied that Beauregard has not the nerve to attack fortifications, or it would be a great achievement for him to make me abandon Atlanta by mere threats and manoeuvres.

"These are the reasons which have determined my former movements.

"I have employed the last ten days in running to the rear the sick, wounded, and worthless, and all the vast amount of stores accumulated by our army in the advance, aiming to organize this branch of my army into four well-commanded corps, encumbered by only one gun to a thousand men, and provisions and ammunition which can be loaded up in our mule-wagons, so that we can pick up and start on the shortest notice. I reckon that by the 10th instant this end will be reached, and by that date I also will have the troops all paid; the presidential election over and out of the way; and I hope the early storms of November, now prevailing, will also give us the chance of a long period of fine healthy weather for campaigning. Then the question presents itself, 'What shall be done?' On the supposition always that Thomas can hold the line of the Tennessee, and very shortly be able to assume the offensive as against Beauregard, I propose to act in such a manner against the material resources of the South as utterly to negative Davis's boasted threat and promises of protection. If we can march a well-appointed army right through his territory, it is a demonstration to the world—foreign and domestic—that we have a power which Davis can not resist. This may not be war, but rather statesmanship; nevertheless, it is overwhelming to my mind that there are thousands of people abroad and in the South who will reason thus: If the North can march an army right through the South, it is proof positive that the North can prevail in this contest, leaving only open the question of its willingness to use that power. Now Mr. Lincoln's election (which is assured), coupled with the conclusion thus reached, makes a complete logical whole. Even without a battle, the results, operating upon the minds of sensible men, would produce fruits more than compensating for the expense, trouble, and risk.

"Admitting this reasoning to be good, that such a movement *per se* be right, still there may be reasons why one route should be better than another. There are three from Atlanta—southeast, south, and southwest—all open, with no serious enemy to oppose at present.

"*The first* would carry me across the only east and west railroad remaining to the Confederacy, which would be destroyed, and thereby the communication between the armies of Lee and Beauregard severed. Incidentally I might destroy the enemy's dépôts at Macon and Augusta, and reach the sea-shore at Charleston and Savannah, from either of which points I could re-enforce our armies in Virginia.

"*The second* and easiest route would be due south, following substantially the valley of Flint River, which is very fertile and well supplied, and fetching up on the navigable waters of the Appalachicola, destroying *en route* the same railroad, taking up the prisoners of war still at Andersonville, and destroying about 400,000 bales of cotton near Albany and Fort Gaines. This, however, would leave the army in a bad position for future movements.

"*The third*, down the Chattahoochee to Opelika and Montgomery, thence to Pensacola or Tensas Bayou, in communication with Fort Morgan. This latter route would enable me at once to co-operate with General Canby in the reduction of Mobile, and occupation of the line of the Alabama.

"In my judgment, the first would have a material effect upon your campaign in Virginia; the second would be the safest of execution; but the third would more properly fall within the sphere of my own command, and have a direct bearing upon my own enemy, 'Beauregard.' If, therefore, I should start before I hear farther from you, or before farther developments turn my course, you may take it for granted that I have moved *via* Griffin to Barnsville; that I break up the road between Columbus and Macon *good*, and then, if I feign on Columbus, will move *via* Macon and Millen to Savannah, or, if I feign on Macon, you may take it for granted I have shot off toward Opelika, Montgomery, and Mobile Bay or Pensacola.

"I will not attempt to send couriers back, but trust to the Richmond papers to keep you well advised. I will give you notice by telegraph of the exact time of my departure."

To this Grant replies, November 7: "I see no present reason for changing your plan; should any arise, you will see to it, or if I do, I will inform you. I think every thing here favorable now. Great good fortune attend you. I believe you will be eminently successful, and at worst can only make a march less fruitful of results than hoped for."

November 8. To G. W. TYLER, *Louisville, Ky.*: "Dispatch me to-morrow night and the next night a summary of all news, especially of elections, that I may report them to Governor Brown at Milledgeville, where I expect a friendly interview in a few days. Keep this very secret, for the world will lose sight of me shortly, and you will hear worse stories than when I went to Meridian. Jeff. Davis's thirty days are up for wiping us out, and we are not wiped out yet by a good deal."

November 10. To C. A. DANA, *Assistant Secretary of War*: "If indiscreet newspaper men publish information too near the truth, counteract its effect by publishing other paragraphs calculated to mislead the enemy—such as Sherman's army has been much re-enforced, especially in the cavalry, and he will soon move in several columns in a circuit, so as to catch Hood's army. Sherman's destination is not Charleston, but Selma, where he will meet an army from the Gulf," etc.

November 11. To General HALLECK: "My arrangements are now all complete. Last night we burned all founderies, mills, and shops of every kind in Rome, and to-morrow I leave Kingston, with the rear-guard, for Atlanta, which I propose to dispose of in a similar manner, and to start on the 16th on the projected grand raid. All appearances still indicate that Beauregard has gone back to his old hole at Corinth, and I hope he will enjoy it; my army prefers to enjoy the fresh sweet-potato fields of the Ocmulgee. I have balanced all the figures well, and am satisfied that General Thomas has in Tennessee a force sufficient for all probabilities, and I have urged him, the moment Beauregard turns south, to cross the Tennessee at Decatur and push straight for Selma. To-morrow our wires will be broken, and this is probably my last dispatch. I would like to have Foster break the Savannah and Charleston Road about Pocotaligo about the 1st of December. All other preparations are to my entire satisfaction."

The same day Colonel Beckwith reports to Sherman as follows: "The Army of the Tennessee have obtained and have got in their wagons all they can haul and all they want; same of the Twentieth Army Corps. There is great plenty of salt, coffee, meat, pepper, and soap here. The Fourteenth Army Corps may want a little more bread, and perhaps a little more sugar. I have about 100,000 rations of bread for the Fourteenth Army Corps; 22,000 rations sugar. I do not know how much General Davis may have on hand, but presume he has 200,000 rations of bread. Every thing is loaded in Atlanta save what is held for the Fourteenth Army Corps. There are at least 11,200,000 rations of the principal rations in hands of troops and available."

November 11. To General THOMAS: "All right. I can hardly believe Beauregard would attempt to work against Nashville from Corinth as a base at this stage of the war, but all information points that way; if he does, you will whip him out of his boots. But I rather think you will find commotion in his camp in a day or two. Last night we burned Rome, and in two days more will burn Atlanta, and he must discover that I am not retreating, but, on the contrary, fighting for the very heart of Georgia. . . . . By using detachments of recruits and dismounted cavalry in your fortifications, you will have Schofield, and Stanley, and A. J. Smith strengthened by eight or ten new regiments, and all of Wilson's cavalry; you could safely invite Beauregard across the Tennessee, and prevent his ever returning. I still believe, however, that public clamor will force him to turn and follow me, in which event you should cross at Decatur, and move directly toward Selma as far as you can transport supplies. The probabilities are the wires will be broken to-morrow, and that all communication will cease between us. . . . . You may act, however, on the certainty that I sally from Atlanta on the 16th, with about 60,000 men, well provisioned, but expecting to live liberally on the country."

Thomas replies the next day: "I have no fears that Beauregard can do us any harm now, and if he attempts to follow you I will follow him as far as possible; if he does not follow you, I will then thoroughly organize my troops, and, I believe, shall have men enough to ruin him unless he gets out of the way very rapidly. The country of Middle Alabama, I learn, is teeming with supplies this year, which will be greatly to our advantage. . . . . I am now convinced that the greater part of Beauregard's army is near Florence and Tuscumbia, and that you will at least have a clear road before you for several days, and that your success will fully equal your expectations."

This was the last dispatch received by Sherman from Thomas before starting out on the great march. Sherman replied "All right," and the wires were cut.

DESTRUCTION OF THE DEPOTS, PUBLIC BUILDINGS, AND MANUFACTORIES AT ATLANTA.

sequences of such a march must be important and decisive. The cities of the Atlantic sea-board were doomed the moment Sherman's army should reach their rear. At Savannah or Charleston this army could be transported by sea, or could march by land through the Carolinas, and, re-enforcing Grant, terminate the long-protracted conflict with Lee's army.

But what if Thomas should be conquered by Hood? Then, indeed, Sherman's march would have demonstrated only his own folly. He would have ascended like a rocket and come down a stick. But to have anticipated such an event would have been an insult to General Thomas, and to the armies of Schofield, Stanley, and Smith. Sherman had no apprehensions on that score. Not until Thomas had himself expressed his faith in his own power to ruin Hood, if the latter advanced, or to assume the offensive against him if he retreated, did Sherman move from Atlanta.

By the 14th of November, the Fourteenth, Fifteenth, Seventeenth, and Twentieth Corps were grouped about Atlanta, constituting an army 60,000 strong, with an additional force of cavalry under Brigadier General Judson Kilpatrick, numbering 5500 men. The artillery consisted of about 60 guns, or one piece to every thousand men. Every thing had been sent to the rear which could not be used in the campaign. The railroad north had been destroyed as far as Dalton. Rome and Atlanta had been burned, only the dwelling-houses and churches escaping destruction. On the 16th of November Sherman commenced his grand March to the Sea. While he is advancing eastward through the fruitful fields of Georgia, let us follow the counter-movement of Hood against Nashville.

CHAPTER XLVII.

BATTLE OF NASHVILLE.

Hood attacks Decatur and is repulsed.—Forrest's Demonstration against Johnsonville.—Hood north of the Tennessee.—Estimate of the opposing Forces.—Schofield abandons Pulaski.—Retreat from Columbia to Franklin.—Narrow Escape at Spring Hill.—Battle of Franklin.—Its Results.—Hood in front of Nashville.—Demonstration against Murfreesborough.—Preparations for Battle on both sides.—Inclement Weather.—General Thomas assumes the Defensive.—Battles of December 15th and 16th.—Defeat of Hood's Army.—The Pursuit.—Results of the Nashville Campaign.—Gillem defeated by Breckinridge.—Stoneman drives Breckinridge into North Carolina.—Destruction of the Works at Saltville.

FORREST had intended to cross the Tennessee in the vicinity of Gunter's Landing and threaten Bridgeport, thus compelling Sherman to abandon Georgia in order to protect Tennessee. Beauregard had ordered Forrest to move with his cavalry into Tennessee, Hood not having a sufficient cavalry force to protect his trains north of the river.[1] These orders did not reach Forrest in time, and Hood was therefore compelled to move down the Tennessee and await Forrest's arrival. On the 26th of October a portion of Hood's infantry appeared before Decatur, on the south side of the river, at the southern terminus of the Nashville and Decatur Railroad, and on the afternoon of that day made a feeble attack on the garrison, which was commanded by R. S. Granger. Granger was re-enforced by two regiments from Chattanooga, and instructed to hold his post at all hazards. The next day the enemy established a line of rifle-pits within 500 yards of the town. On the 28th a sortie was made by a part of the garrison, which, advancing under cover of the guns of the fort, down the river bank and around to the rear of the enemy's rifle-pits, dislodged the Confederates, capturing 120 prisoners. Forrest in the mean while had reached Corinth, and advanced from that point upon Fort Heiman, on the west bank of the Tennessee, about 75 miles from Paducah. Here he captured the gun-boat No. 55 and two transports on the 31st, having previously burned the steamer Empress. He had about 17 regiments of cavalry, probably numbering altogether 5000 men, and 9 pieces of artillery. On the 2d of November he planted batteries above and below Johnsonville, one of General Thomas's bases of supplies on the river, isolating, at that place, three gun-boats and eight transports. The gun-boats made an unsuccessful attack upon the lower batteries, but, though repulsed, they recaptured from the enemy one of the transports which he had taken, and forced him to destroy the gun-boat No. 55. On the 4th Forrest made an attack on the gun-boats and the garrison, consisting of 1000 men. The gun-boats, being disabled, were burned to prevent their falling into the enemy's hands, and the fire, spreading to the buildings of the commissary and quartermaster's departments, and to the stores on the levee, caused the government a loss estimated at $1,500,000. The next morning Forrest repeated his attack upon the garrison, and, after a furious cannonade of over an hour's duration, withdrew from Johnsonville.

Hood's army arrived at Florence on the 31st of October, one month after it had been transferred from Sherman's front. This long delay, caused partly by the difficulties attending the transportation of supplies, had thwarted the sole object of Hood's campaign. It had given Sherman and Thomas time for completing their preparations, the former for his march eastward, and the latter for the accumulation of an army large enough to protect Tennessee.

Hood's force, including all arms, on the 1st of November did not number over 40,000 effective men. Thomas had in his command a considerably larger force. After deducting the garrisons of Nashville, Decatur, and Chattanooga, however, his army available for battle numbered about 30,000 men.[2]

[1] *Hood's Report.*

[2] Thomas says in his report: "At this time (November 5th) I found myself confronted by the army which, under General J. E. Johnston, had so skillfully resisted the advance of the whole active army of the military division of the Mississippi from Dalton to the Chattahoochee, re-enforced by a well-equipped and enthusiastic cavalry command of over 12,000, led by one of the boldest and most successful commanders in the rebel army. My information from all sources confirmed the reported strength of Hood's army to be from 40,000 to 45,000 infantry, and from 12,000 to 15,000

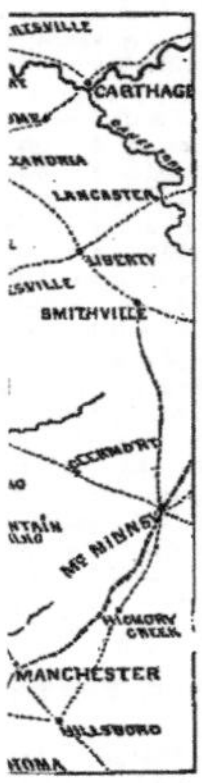

General Beaure-
ence in this matter.
not solve it. He
ither to divide his
h the other, or to
d delayed on the
er, and until Sher-
across the river,
Florence, and had
art and Cheatham
On the 21st For-
nt northward was

the disposition of
would not, be de-
tion of it than that
per course for him
having for the first
two parts to direct
re through Georgia
ed territory to the
each the enemy in
and greatly impair
ld be considered a
Sherman except
advancing against
hus far in his cam-
ranced from Jones-
which he had bast-
had taken less than
n, and had moved
y military value to
n except his design
ly, to compel Sher-
no longer existed,

out 12,000, under Major
r General John M. Scho-
and Capron's brigade of
and posted at Murfrees-
keep open our commu-
re-enforced, as up to this
nce on Nashville or turn

homas about 80,000, ex-

sture of the Confederate
men. This is exclusive

,000 strong; but, taking

.... 2,500
.... 1,200
9,700

: 84,200. It must also
oops, in addition to those
Notice whatever is taken
ce of force as compared
at Nashville; 2d, A. J.
hich in a few days would
rrison duty which would
r unfitness for the great

, one thing is worthy of
load, his army numbered
. the retreat to Gadsden,
. large proportion of this
invasion very much im-

for Sherman had defied his projected invasion in the boldest and bluntest terms. The railroad from which Hood had been driven Sherman had destroyed with his own hands. Atlanta, which Hood had hoped to recover, Sherman had made a useless possession to the enemy as well as to himself. And Georgia, which Hood was pledged to redeem, was already being trampled down under the heels of 60,000 men, whom, with his own army, he could not reach if he would, and whom, if he could have reached, he dared not encounter. As to the *morale* of his army, Hood's invasion thus far had certainly not improved *that;* for since he had started from Jonesborough he had lost 10,000 men, or one fourth of his army, though in that time he had only fought a single serious battle—that of Allatoona. Hood could have lost nothing by a judicious retreat which could be compared with what he risked by an advance against Thomas. To allow the Federal forces to assume the defensive was to give them such advantages as must be decisive. The advance was the result of the infatuation of both Hood and Davis. The threat had been uttered, the pledge given, and it was too late now to hesitate or falter.

The wager which Hood had offered Thomas was ready to accept. The latter would have preferred an encounter with the enemy south of Duck River: this would have been possible if the Confederate army had delayed its movements for a week or ten days. The Federal cavalry guarding the Tennessee about Florence had already been driven back, so that Croxton was on the east side of Shoal Creek, and Hatch occupied Lawrenceburg. Schofield, with the Twenty-third Corps, had arrived at Nashville November 5th, and was directed to join the Fourth Corps at Pulaski, take the command of the troops at that point, and, as far as possible, retard Hood's advance into Tennessee. It was obviously Thomas's policy to impede Hood's movements, gradually withdrawing Schofield and Stanley, until he could receive the re-enforcements under A. J. Smith, and organize Wilson's cavalry and the new regiments. Hood's army moved by parallel roads to Waynesborough and eastward of that place, with Forrest on the right flank. On the 22d of November Hatch's cavalry was driven from Lawrenceburg. Hood desired to push his army up between Nashville and Schofield's command; but on the 23d the Federal forces evacuated Pulaski, and fell back to Columbia, on the Duck River. The retreat was ably conducted, all the public property being removed beforehand from Pulaski, and the trains carefully guarded. Thomas had meanwhile received some 7000 men which had been sent back from Atlanta by General Sherman; his command had also been re-enforced by 20 new one-year regiments, very many of which were absorbed in the veteran corps, replacing old regiments whose term of service had expired. R. S. Granger had withdrawn the garrisons at Athens, Decatur, and Huntsville, Alabama, taking a part of the force thus collected to Stevenson, and sending back five regiments to Murfreesborough. The garrison at Johnsonville was withdrawn to Clarksville.

Hood's movement on Columbia was slow; not until the evening of November 27th had his advance reached Schofield's front. During that night Schofield crossed Duck River, taking a position on the north bank, where he was not disturbed during the 28th. General Wilson's cavalry, 4300 strong, guarded the crossings of the river above and below. On the afternoon of the 29th Wilson was pressed back and cut off from Schofield, while Hood's infantry crossed the river, and threatened to turn Schofield's flank by an advance on Spring Hill, about 15 miles north of Columbia. Schofield, therefore, sending Stanley with Wagner's division to Spring Hill to head off the enemy at that point and cover the retreat, prepared to fall back toward Franklin. Stanley reached Spring Hill just in time to check Forrest's advance and save the trains. The Confederate infantry coming up to Forrest's assistance, a doubtful battle was maintained till dark, in which the enemy nearly succeeded in dislodging Stanley from his position. Schofield, having sent back his trains, was at the same time occupied in resisting the enemy's attempts to cross Duck River in his front, and, after having several times repulsed the Confederate force opposed to him, retreated at night, his command making 25 miles under cover of the darkness, and, passing Spring Hill in safety, got into position at Franklin, 18 miles south of Nashville, on the morning of the 30th.

With Cheatham's corps supported by Stewart's, it seems that the enemy ought to have defeated Stanley at Spring Hill and cut off Schofield's retreat. But Stanley maintained his position and saved the army.[1] He was re-enforced toward night by Ruger's division of the Twenty-third Corps. But, even after this re-enforcement, the enemy had the advantage. With two

[1] General Hood, in his report, gives the following account of the affair at Spring Hill:

"When I had gotten well on his flank, the enemy discovered my intention, and began to retreat on the pike toward Spring Hill. The cavalry became engaged near that place about midday, but his trains were so strongly guarded that they were unable to break through them. About 4 P.M. our infantry forces, Major General Cheatham in the advance, commenced to come in contact with the enemy, about two miles from Spring Hill, through which place the Columbia and Franklin Pike passes. The enemy was at this time moving rapidly along the pike, with some of his troops formed on the flank of his column to protect it. Major General Cheatham was ordered to attack the enemy at once, vigorously, and get possession of this pike, and, although those orders were frequently and earnestly repeated, he made but a feeble and partial attack, failing to reach the point indicated. Had my instructions been carried out there is no doubt that we could have possessed ourselves of this road. Stewart's corps and Johnson's division were arriving upon the field to support the attack. Though the golden opportunity had passed with daylight, I did not at dark abandon the hope of dealing the enemy a heavy blow. Accordingly, Lieutenant General Stewart was furnished a guide, and ordered to move his corps beyond Cheatham's, and place it across the road beyond Spring Hill. Shortly after this General Cheatham came to my headquarters, and when I informed him of Stewart's movement, he said that Stewart ought to form on his right. I asked if that would throw Stewart across the pike. He replied that it would, and a mile beyond. Accordingly, one of Cheatham's staff officers was sent to show Stewart where his (Cheatham's) right rested. In the dark and confusion, Stewart did not succeed in getting the position desired, but about 11 P.M. went into bivouac. About 12 P.M., ascertaining that the enemy was moving in great confusion—artillery, wagons, and troops intermixed—I sent instructions to General Cheatham to advance a heavy line of skirmishers against him, and still farther impede and confuse his march. This was not accomplished. The enemy continued to move along the road in hurry and confusion, within hearing, nearly all the night. Thus was lost a great opportunity of striking the enemy, for which we had labored so long, the greatest this campaign had offered, and one of the greatest during the war."

G. D. WAGNER.

full corps of Forrest's cavalry in the vicinity of Spring Hill, Schofield ought to have been cut off at least from the direct road to Franklin. His main army did not leave Duck River, where it had been fighting Lee, until after dark, and passed Spring Hill about midnight. It certainly had a narrow escape. General Wagner's division of Stanley's corps held on to its position at Spring Hill until near daylight. Notwithstanding the superior numbers of the enemy, the only disturbances suffered in the retreat was from a slight attack made north of Thompson's by Forrest's cavalry, causing the loss of a few wagons. General Cooper, who had been left to guard the crossing at Duck River, was cut off from the direct road to Franklin, and proceeded to Nashville.

When Schofield reached Franklin he found no wagon bridge across the Harpeth River, and the fords in a bad condition. The railroad bridge was rapidly repaired and a foot-bridge was constructed, which was also available for the use of wagons. He sent his train across, and intended to cross with his army. But the enemy was in too close proximity. As the Federal troops arrived they were placed in position on the south side of the river, the Twenty-third Corps, under General Cox, on the left and centre, covering the approaches from Columbia and Lewisburg, and Kimball's division of Stanley's corps on the right; both flanks of the army resting on the river. Wood's division of Stanley's corps was sent to the north side of the river to cover the flanks, in the event of Hood's crossing above or below. Two brigades of Wagner's division—the last to reach Franklin—were left in front, to retard the advance of the enemy.

At daylight Hood had commenced the pursuit, which was pushed with great vigor. Stewart was in the advance, Cheatham following, while Lee, with the trains, brought up the rear from Columbia. Hood determined to make a direct attack with Stewart's and Cheatham's corps without waiting for Lee. No flank movement which he could now make would prevent Schofield from reaching Nashville.[1] Stewart advanced on the right, Cheatham on the left, with the cavalry on either flank, the main body of the latter, under Forrest, moving to the right. Johnson's division of Lee's corps arrived during the engagement, and went in on the left.

Fortunately for Schofield, Hood's attack was delayed until 4 o'clock on the afternoon of the 30th. In the mean time the Federal troops were constructing breastworks and protecting them by a slight abatis on the left. To them, with the river in their rear, and with the roads, by which alone retreat was possible, crowded with the wagon trains, defeat would have been a terrible disaster, affecting the safety of Nashville. On both sides the decisive nature of the contest was fully appreciated. It was a brief battle, for at this season of the year 4 P.M. was the verge of twilight.[2] Wagner's men, holding the outposts, "imprudently brave," reports Schofield, maintained the conflict outside of the intrenchments longer than was necessary, suffering heavy loss. When they fell back it was at a full run, and this movement swept back a portion of the first line in the works, allowing the enemy to

[1] "I learned from dispatches captured at Spring Hill, from Thomas to Schofield, that the latter was instructed to hold that place till the position at Franklin could be made secure, indicating the intention of Thomas to hold Franklin and his strong works at Murfreesborough. Thus I knew that it was all-important to attack Schofield before he could make himself strong, and, if he should escape at Franklin, he would gain his works about Nashville. The nature of the position was such as to render it inexpedient to attempt any farther flank movement, and I therefore determined to attack him in front, and without delay."—*Hood's Report.*

[2] On the 30th of November, 1864, the sun set at 4 39. Schofield's report makes the battle to have commenced at 3 30 P.M.

enter in large numbers. In this attempt to fight a
Wagner lost over a thousand men. The enemy had g
which, if pressed, might have resulted in success. Vic
within his grasp. The Federal line had been broken in
teries of four guns each had been captured. But at this m
manding the remaining brigade of Wagner's division,
in reserve inside the works, leading his men on, shout
lines!" rushed forward, recovered the lost batteries, and
oners. The gap had been closed; but the enemy, thou
not disheartened. He charged the works, making four
was each time hurled back with heavy loss. "So vigo
these assaults that the enemy reached the exterior slope
ments, and hand-to-hand encounters occurred between
batants across the works."[1] Between the assaults, the en
undulations of the ground, pressed his sharp-shooters clo
kept up a galling fire.

The Confederates persistently assailed Schofield's li
continuing the attack at intervals until near midnight, b
every attempt to carry the works. The Confederate los
and 6000 men. Schofield lost 2326, of which number
occurred in Wagner's division.[2] On the Federal side, C
severely wounded in the neck. The Confederate loss in
very great, including among them Major General Pat. C
dier Generals Gist, John Adams, Strahl, and Granbury;
Carter, Manigault, Quarles, Cockrell, and Scott were wou
General Gordon was captured.[3] At midnight Schofield
trenches which he had held against the repeated assau
numbers, and fell back to Nashville.

Hood's orders to his corps commanders to drive Scho
and for Forrest to advance and capture the trains, had
General Thomas's position was now secure. On the 1
had behind the fortifications of Nashville and coverin
proaches an investing force superior to General Hood's,
in process of organization at Edgefield, north of the ri
days would in numbers be at least equal to Forrest'
Smith's command of three divisions had also reached Na
placed on the right of the line, Wood, now commandin
in the centre, and Schofield on the left.

The next day, December 2d, the enemy advanced to
Nashville, and invested the town on the south side, Gen
centre of the line, Cheatham the right, and Stewart the
either flank extended to the river. The whole line
strong detached works were constructed to guard the fla
On Hood's right, Murfreesborough was held by a Federa
under General Rousseau, which cut off all communicatio
Virginia. Bates's division of Cheatham's corps attacked
Overall's Creek, four miles north of Murfreesborough, on t
The garrison maintained its position, and being soon re-e
freesborough with three infantry regiments, four compan
a section of artillery, the enemy was driven off. During t
Bates, re-enforced by the greater portion of Forrest's cav
against Fortress Rosecrans at Murfreesborough. As th
to make a direct assault, Rousseau determined to assume
self. Accordingly, on the 8th, General Milroy, with seven
(3325 men), proceeded to the Wilkinson Pike, there enc
Forrest, and drove them from their temporary breastwo
prisoners.[4] The Federal loss in killed and wounded was
vision of Forrest's cavalry entered the town of Murfree
day, but was speedily driven out by a single infantry regi
of artillery. Forrest's cavalry, retiring from before Mu
ceeded northward to Lebanon, and threatened to cros
above Nashville and cut off Thomas's communications
Road. This movement was thwarted by a division of g
tachment of Wilson's cavalry.

From the 3d to the 15th of December was spent by bo
aration for the conflict which was to decide the fate of
was furnishing his army with supplies and with shoes.
the 14th both armies were ice-bound. Thomas thus ha
Wilson's cavalry, increase the strength of his works, br
ments of new recruits and temporary volunteers, and to
operations. Nashville was well fortified when Thomas
army. The southern approaches were covered by Fort
Confiscation, Houston, and Gillem. Some of these had b
the latter part of 1862, when the city was threatened by a
army. These forts were situated on commanding hills
some distance beyond ran the line now held by Thom
Fort Morton westward an interior line of defense was also
the range of hills nearer Nashville.[5]

[1] General T. J. Wood's Report.

[2] Hood reports his own loss as 4500. Schofield, from information obt
the enemy's loss "1750 buried upon the field, 3800 disabled, and 702 pri
that he captured 1000 prisoners. This tallies well with Schofield's report, k
missing, 670 of whom were from Wagner's division.

[4] Hood reports that Bates's division behaved badly.

[5] Thomas's army at Nashville consisted of the following forces:

Schofield's Twenty-third Corps...
Wood's Fourth Corps...
A. J. Smith's Corps, say...
Steadman's Command, which arrived at Nashville from December 1..........
Wilson's Cavalry ....
Quartermaster's Troops under Brigadier General Donaldson, and other forces
der General Miller used in the immediate defense of Nashville, say.........
Total..

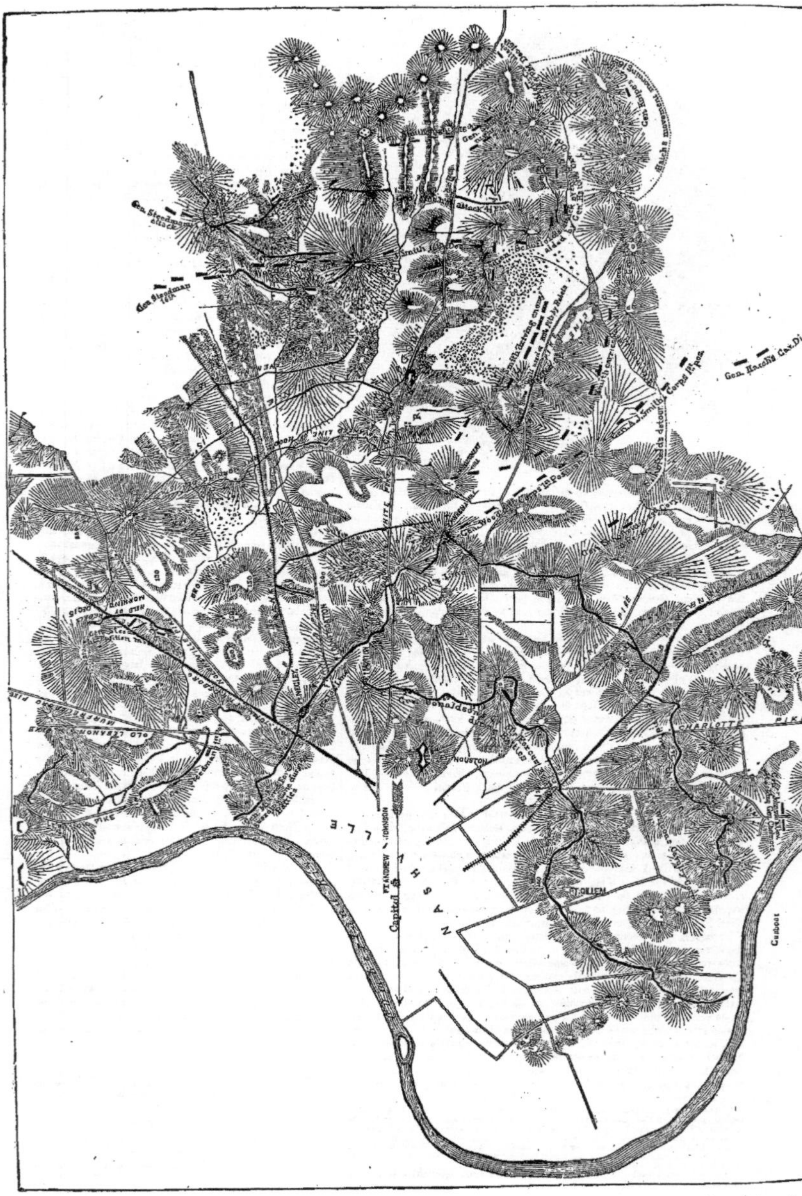

MAP OF THE BATTLE OF NASHVILLE.

The severity of the weather began to relax on the 14th, and on the afternoon of that day Thomas issued orders to his corps commanders for an advance against the enemy. His army was now 50,000 strong, and fully prepared for battle. A large portion of Forrest's cavalry was still absent from the Confederate army. Hood seems in his infatuation to have been absolutely confident of victory in the event of Thomas's assuming the offensive.[1] He even dreamed of besieging Nashville. But the swollen river, patroled by gun-boats, hindered an advance against the Louisville Road, and, even if this road had been reached and broken by Confederate cavalry, Thomas was well supplied at Nashville with all that was necessary for either a defensive or offensive campaign. The term siege would be scarcely applicable to General Hood's operations.

Upon his first approach to the city on the 2d of December, Hood had seized Montgomery Hill, within 600 yards of the Federal centre, and thrown up strong lines of earth-works on the hills south and parallel with those occupied by Thomas. His infantry stretched from the Nolensville Pike, on the right, along the high ground south and east of Brown's Creek, and across the Franklin and Granny White Pikes to the hills bordering the Hillsborough Pike. A wide interval, therefore, separated his left from the river. This—as also the corresponding interval between the Nolensville Pike and the river—was held by the cavalry, who had established batteries about eight miles below Nashville, blockading the river. The weak point of the Confederate position was its left flank, which, though strongly intrenched, was easily turned.

Thomas's long silence appeared to have increased Hood's confidence. It also led to considerable apprehension on the part of Lieutenant General Grant, who, at so great a distance from the field, was not aware of the rigorous cold which hindered Thomas's advance, and was also a serious inconvenience to the poorly-clad soldiers of Hood's army. He thought that Thomas ought to have moved upon Hood as soon as the latter had made his appearance in front of Nashville, and before he was fortified, and that by waiting to remount Wilson's cavalry he had made a great mistake. Perhaps, also, the narrow escape of Schofield's army in the retreat from Columbia to Franklin—an escape which could only be attributed to either the stupidity of the Confederate generals or to their want of confidence in their commander—led him to suspect that the campaign was not being properly conducted. At any rate, so great was his impatience that he started West with the idea of superintending matters there in person. He had only reached Washington when he received a dispatch from Thomas announcing the successful commencement of the battle of Nashville.[2]

General Thomas's plan of the battle was very simple, involving the turning of the enemy's left flank by a sudden and irresistible blow to be struck with the bulk of his army, and to be followed up until Hood's army was destroyed or dispersed in utter rout. Success was as certain as the event of a battle ever could be. The execution of this plan was so perfect in all its details that it justly conferred upon General Thomas the first rank among the Union generals as a tactician.[3] He had delayed for the purpose of organizing an efficient cavalry corps, in order that, in the event of victory, he might reap its full fruits by a relentless pursuit of the defeated army. He was prepared to attack a week before he did, but the weather, as we have said, was unfavorable. On the 12th Wilson's cavalry had crossed the Cumberland from Edgefield to the left of the Hillsborough Pike.

The morning of the 15th of December was every way favorable to the immediate execution of General Thomas's plans. The sheet of ice which had covered the earth for nearly a week was broken up; and, in addition to the undulations of the ground, a heavy mist, lasting until noon, completely

JAMES B. STEEDMAN.

masked the preparations for battle. Under these auspicious circumstances, Smith advanced immediately in front of his works, with Wilson's cavalry on his right. Wood and Schofield, leaving strong skirmish lines in their trenches, marched to the right, Wood forming in line on Smith's left, and Schofield supporting Wood, guarding the left flank against attack. Steedman, who had charge of the defenses of Nashville, leaving Donaldson's and Miller's troops to hold the interior line of defense, advanced with his main force against the enemy's right. Steedman's operations were demonstrative, and preceded the main attack. His force consisted of three brigades—Thompson's, Morgan's, and Grosvenor's, the two former being composed of disciplined negro soldiers. Though unsuccessful in his attack on the Confederate right, he succeeded in diverting the enemy's attention from the centre and left, leaving the way open for Wilson, Smith, Wood, and Schofield, 40,000 strong, to sweep around against the enemy's works on the Hillsborough Pike.

The advance of Smith and Wilson commenced as soon as Steedman's movement was completely developed on either side of the Hardin Pike. Over difficult and broken ground, their movement proceeded from the Cumberland and the hills adjoining it across and along the Hardin Pike, and then swept eastward, enveloping the Confederate left on the Hillsborough Pike, threatening to strike Brentwood, in Hood's rear, on the road to Franklin. Hood was completely surprised, and his cavalry, a great portion of which was in the vicinity of Murfreesborough and along the Cumberland, was too weak to meet the sudden blow. Hatch's cavalry division moved on Smith's right, with Croxton's brigade on his own right, and Knipe's division in support. McArthur's infantry division held the right, and therefore the advance of Smith's corps, and, with Hatch's cavalry, encountered the enemy a little after noon. On the right of the Hillsborough Pike the enemy had some advanced works protecting his left. The Confederates were driven from this position by Hatch and McArthur, who, swinging to the left, came upon a redoubt containing four guns, which was carried by a portion of Hatch's division, and the captured artillery turned upon the enemy. A second redoubt was then carried, with four guns and about 800 prisoners. McArthur justly shared the glory of these captures.

While the enemy's left was being driven back on the Granny White Pike, the Fourth Corps, under Wood, was assaulting the centre at Montgomery Hill. This position was carried by Post's brigade of Wagner's division, and several prisoners were captured. Wood now connected with Smith's left, and Schofield's corps was moved from the reserve to Smith's right, the cavalry, at the same time, being thrown still farther around against the enemy's rear. But, while Wilson, Schofield, and Smith pressed forward during the afternoon, sweeping every thing before them, Wood had still another line of works to assault on his front. This was at length carried, and 700 prisoners, 8 guns, and 5 caissons were captured. By night, Hood's army had been driven out of its original line of works, and back from the Hillsborough Road, but still held possession of two lines of retreat to Franklin by the main road through Brentwood and the Granny White Pike. Thomas had won substantial trophies of victory, his captures consisting of 1200 prisoners, 16 guns, 40 wagons, and a large number of small-arms. Owing to the unexpectedness of the attack, and the brilliant tactics of the Federal commander, these results had been gained with slight Union loss, while the Confederate loss was heavy. During the afternoon, Johnson's division of Wilson's cavalry had, with the co-operation of the gun-boats, captured the Confederate batteries blockading the river below Nashville at Bell's Landing. At 9 P.M. Thomas telegraphed to Washington: "I shall attack the enemy again to-morrow if he stands to fight, and if he retreats during the night I will pursue him, throwing a heavy cavalry force in his rear to destroy his trains, if possible."

But Hood did not yet give up the contest. During the night he withdrew

[1] "Should he attack me in position, I felt that I would defeat him, and thus gain possession of Nashville, with abundant supplies for the army. This would give me possession of Tennessee."—*Hood's Report.*

[2] In his official report, Grant says:

"Before the battle of Nashville I grew very impatient over, as it appeared to me, the unnecessary delay. This impatience was increased upon learning that the enemy had sent a force of cavalry across the Cumberland into Kentucky. I feared Hood would cross his whole army and give us great trouble there. After urging upon General Thomas the necessity of immediately assuming the offensive, I started West to superintend matters there in person. Reaching Washington City, I received General Thomas's dispatch announcing his attack upon the enemy, and the result as far as the battle had progressed. I was delighted. All fears and apprehensions were dispelled. I am not yet satisfied but that General Thomas, immediately upon the appearance of Hood before Nashville, and before he had time to fortify, should have moved out with his whole force and given him battle, instead of waiting to remount his cavalry, which delayed him until the inclemency of the weather made it impracticable to attack earlier than he did. But his final defeat of Hood was so complete that it will be accepted as a vindication of that distinguished officer's judgment."

[3] The following is a copy of Thomas's order issued to his corps commanders on the 14th:

"As soon as the state of the weather will admit of offensive operations, the troops will move against the enemy's position in the following order: Major General A. J. Smith, commanding detachment of the Army of the Tennessee, after forming his troops on and near the Hardin Pike, in front of his present position, will make a vigorous assault on the enemy's left. Major General Wilson, commanding the cavalry corps, Military Division of the Mississippi, with three divisions, will move on and support General Smith's right, assisting, as far as possible, in carrying the left of the enemy's position, and be in readiness to throw his force upon the enemy the moment a favorable opportunity occurs. Major General Wilson will also send one division on the Charlotte Pike to clear that road of the enemy, and observe in the direction of Bell's Landing, to protect our right rear until the enemy's position is fairly turned, when it will rejoin the main force. Brigadier General T. J. Wood, commanding Fourth Army Corps, after leaving a strong skirmish line in his works from Lauréns's Hill to his extreme right, will form the remainder of the Fourth Corps on the Hillsborough Pike to support General Smith's left, and operate on the left and rear of the enemy's advanced position on Montgomery Hill. Major General Schofield, commanding the Twenty-third Army Corps, will replace Brigadier General Kimball's division of the Fourth Corps with his troops, and occupy the trenches from Fort Negley to Laurens's Hill with a strong skirmish line. He will move with the remainder of his force in front of the works, and co-operate with General Wood, protecting the latter's left flank against an attack of the enemy. Major General Steedman, commanding the District of Etowah, will occupy the interior line in front of his present position, stretching from the reservoir on the Cumberland River to Fort Negley with a strong skirmish line, and mass the remainder of his force in its present position, to act according to the exigencies which may arise during these operations. Brigadier General Miller, with the troops forming the garrison of Nashville, will occupy the interior line from the battery on hill 210 to the extreme right, including the inclosed work on the Hyde's Ferry Road. The quartermaster's troops, under command of Brigadier General Donaldson, will, if necessary, be posted on the interior line from Fort Morton to the battery on hill 210. The troops occupying the interior line will be under the direction of Major General Steedman, who is charged with the immediate defense of Nashville during the operations around the city. Should the weather permit, the troops will be formed to commence operations at 6 A.M. on the 15th, or as soon thereafter as practicable."

NASHVILLE, FROM EDGEFIELD.

NASHVILLE FROM THE OPPOSITE BANK OF THE CUMBERLAND.

EASTPORT, TENNESSEE.

his right and centre to conform to the left. Cheatham's corps was transferred from right to left, leaving Stewart in the centre and Lee on the right. Thus, when Wood advanced at 6 A.M. on the morning of the 16th, he found only skirmishers in his front. He advanced, therefore, directly south from Nashville on the Franklin Pike until he developed the enemy's main line. Then Steedman came up by the Nolensville Pike on Wood's left, and Smith on his right. These troops faced southward, while Schofield, facing to the east, held the position which he had gained the evening before. Wilson extended away off to the enemy's rear, still threatening Brentwood, at the same time that he guarded the Federal right, and was ready, in case of Hood's retreat, to fall upon his flank. Hood's right rested upon Overton's Hill, four miles north of Brentwood, and his left upon the hills bordering the Granny White Pike. His centre was weaker than either flank. The whole line, about three miles long, had been hastily but strongly intrenched, with abatis thrown up in front.

Not until mid-afternoon were Thomas's preparations for attack completed. About 600 yards separated the opposing armies. On the right, Wilson had extended well to Hood's rear and across the Granny White Pike. The tactics of the day before were repeated in the attack of the 16th. Wood and Steedman proceeded to assault Overton Hill. The movement, commencing at 3 P.M., was open to the enemy's observation, and troops were hurried from the Confederate left and centre to meet the attack at this point. Post's brigade, which the day before had stormed Montgomery Hill, again formed the main column of assault, Steedman's colored troops co-operating on the left. The result is thus briefly reported by General Thomas: "The assault was made, and received by the enemy with tremendous fire of grape and canister, and musketry. Our men moved steadily onward up the hill until near the crest, when the reserve of the enemy rose and poured into the assaulting column a most destructive fire, causing the men first to waver and then to fall back, leaving their dead and wounded, black and white indiscriminately mingled, lying amid the abatis, the gallant Colonel Post among the wounded."

Wood again reformed his command in its first position, and prepared to renew the attack. Hood, in the momentary enthusiasm following his partial success, began to hope that the day was already won. But his anticipations were doomed to disappointment; for Smith and Schofield had heard of Hood's weakening his lines in their front to support Lee's corps, and rushed forward upon the enemy's right and centre, "carrying all before them, irreparably breaking his lines in a dozen places, and capturing all his artillery and thousands of prisoners."[1] Among the latter were four general officers, including Major General Edward S. Johnson, and Brigadier Generals Jackson and Smith. Wilson made a simultaneous advance in the rear, falling upon the flank of the routed enemy and cutting him off from the Granny White Pike. This was a fitting prelude to Wood's second assault on Overton Hill. Once again the slopes of that eminence were ascended in the face of the enemy's fire. The summit was gained, the enemy was swept like chaff from his works, so many, at least, as were not taken prisoners, and all the artillery was captured. Hood's army, routed as no army had been in the history of the war, with but a remnant of artillery, abandoning its wagons and flinging aside its muskets, blankets, and every thing which might impede its own flight, or, clogging the road behind, might delay the pursuit of its victorious enemy, scattered in irrecoverable confusion down the Franklin Pike through Brentwood Pass.

If the battle could have been fought in the forenoon instead of in the afternoon, nothing could now have saved Hood's army from annihilation. The Fourth Corps pursued rapidly for several miles, capturing more prisoners, until darkness kindly enveloped the enemy's retreat. As soon as Hatch's dismounted men received their horses they also pursued on the Granny White Pike, Croxton and Knipe closely following. After proceeding about a mile, Hatch encountered Chalmers's Confederate cavalry, posted across the road behind barricades. The Twelfth Tennessee, Colonel Spaulding, charged and broke the enemy's lines, scattering the Confederates, and capturing, among other prisoners, Brigadier General G. W. Rucker.

Thus ended the two days' battle of Nashville. Hood's dead and wounded were left upon the field; besides these, he had lost 4462 prisoners, including 287 officers of all grades, from major general down, 53 guns, and thousands of small-arms.

The next morning the pursuit was continued. The Fourth Corps was followed by Steedman, and Wilson's cavalry by Schofield and Smith. Johnson's cavalry division was dispatched directly across the Harpeth to menace Franklin. Upon reaching the point where the Granny White runs into the Franklin Pike, Wilson took the advance, and encountered the Confederate rear-guard, under Stevenson, four miles north of Franklin, and charging in front and flank, dispersed the enemy and captured 413 prisoners. The presence of Johnson's cavalry division near Franklin compelled Hood to abandon that town, leaving in the hospitals over 2000 Confederate wounded. Wilson's cavalry still pursued. Now, more than ever, did Hood feel his need of Forrest, whom, in an evil moment, he had sent off on a bootless errand, just as formerly he had sent off Wheeler's cavalry at the very crisis of the Atlanta campaign. Forrest had been ordered back, but, owing to the swollen streams which barred his progress, he did not join Hood until the latter had reached Duck River. About five miles south of Franklin, the rear-guard, toward nightfall, made a temporary stand in the road, posting a battery of artillery on some rising ground. But Wilson, sending Hatch to the left and Knipe to the right of the road, with their batteries, charged Stevenson with his own body-guard, the Fourth Regular Cavalry, 180 strong. Freely using their sabres, the Union horsemen broke the Confederate centre,

[1] *Thomas's Report.*

Knipe and Hatch at the same time falling upon the flanks. Stevenson was thus swept from his chosen position for the second time, leaving his artillery in the road.

The 18th, like the day before, was rainy and dismal. The pursuit was continued to Duck River, where Hood had intrenched to make a stand, but wisely repented of his rash design and continued his flight to the Tennessee, leaving some of his guns at the bottom of Duck River. On reaching Rutherford's Creek, three miles north of Columbia, that stream was found impassable by the national troops. Sherman had taken the best pontoon train along with his army, and another, which had been hurriedly constructed at Nashville, was incomplete, and did not arrive in time. The delay thus occasioned relieved Hood from instant danger. But his army was reduced—so far as organization was concerned—to a simple rear-guard. Hood was retreating from Tennessee in precisely the same condition in which Davis had three months before predicted that Sherman would retreat from Georgia. Still, Thomas, as soon as possible, continued the pursuit to the Tennessee River. The route of the flying enemy—if toilsome dragging along the miry roads could be called flight—was easily traced by ruins of baggage wagons, by small-arms and blankets, and other *débris* of a demoralized army. At Pulaski, four guns were abandoned and thrown into Richland Creek; and a mile beyond, twenty wagons loaded with ammunition, and belonging to Cheatham's corps, were destroyed. All along the road Hood's stragglers lined the wayside, where they had fallen out, tired and discouraged.[1] The Confederate army, or rather its disorganized remnant, crossed the Tennessee on the 27th of December, and fell back to Tupelo, Mississippi. Here Hood, overwhelmed by the denunciations which beat upon him heavily from all sides, resigned his command of the wreck of an army which he had brought back, and was succeeded by General Dick Taylor, who had managed to get across from the west of the Mississippi.[2] But the Confederate Army of Tennessee, as an organized force, had fought its last campaign.

Thomas, on December 30th, announced to his army the successful completion of the campaign. It was an army which had been hastily gathered together from all quarters to meet Hood's invasion. Its numbers and efficiency were indications at the same time of the prompt and unyielding patriotism of the West, and of the generalship of Thomas. He it was who had moulded its segregate parts into a mobile army. And in all military history probably no army was ever more skillfully wielded. Thomas had quietly manifested his military capacity in the early battles of 1862; he had greatly distinguished himself, in a situation more adapted to a larger display of tactical skill, on the battle-field of Chickamauga, in 1863; but the battles of Nashville were the seal and impress of his military genius. In these latter battles he saw the end from the beginning; the victorious event was as clear to him on the morning of the 15th as on the night of the next day, when Hood had been routed; with him no mistake was possible, and thus upon victory followed its full fruits. For the first time in the history of the war, a Confederate army 40,000 strong had been destroyed on the field of battle and in its flight. The numbers *directly* brought to bear upon Hood's army had not been far superior; the result is therefore to be attributed to the admirable tactics of General Thomas. The battles of Nashville deserve to rank with those of Lookout Mountain and Missionary Ridge. A very memorable feature of these battles is the slight loss of the Federals in killed and wounded.[3] The grand result had been accomplished rather by skillful manœuvre than by an enormous sacrifice of life. The Confederate loss had been heavier in killed and wounded, and, in addition, over 8000 prisoners had been captured. During the Tennessee campaign Hood lost 13,189 prisoners, and by desertion over 2000, besides 72 guns.

At the close of 1864 Thomas disposed of his army as follows: Smith's corps was stationed at Eastport, Mississippi; Wood's was concentrated at Huntsville and Athens, Alabama; Schofield's at Dalton, Georgia; and Wilson's cavalry at Eastport and Huntsville.

In the mean time the cavalry force, 800 strong, which, under General Lyon, had been sent by Hood across the Cumberland to operate against Thomas's communications in Kentucky, had been defeated and driven back into Alabama, after some 600 of its number had been scattered or captured. The small remnant was about the middle of January surprised in camp between Warrenton and Tuscaloosa, where General Lyon, with about 100 of his men, was captured. Lyon was taken in bed, and, having been permitted to dress himself, he watched his opportunity and treacherously shot his sentinel, escaping in the darkness.

To finish this chapter, it remains only for us to glance at the operations which, toward the close of the year, had been going on east of Knoxville, on the yet contested border of East Tennessee and West Virginia.

General Morgan had been captured and killed on the 4th of September, 1864, at Greenville, in East Tennessee, and his command had passed into the hands of his confederate and recent biographer, General Basil Duke. In November General Breckinridge proceeded to East Tennessee, and took command of the operations in that quarter. On the 13th of November, with about 3000 men, he attacked Brigadier General A. C. Gillem, near Morristown, routing him and capturing his artillery (6 guns), with about 500 prisoners. The remainder of Gillem's command escaped to Strawberry Plains, and thence to Knoxville. Gillem's command, 1500 strong, had formerly belonged to the Army of the Cumberland, but at the instance of Governor Andrew Johnson had been made an independent command. It was this separation, and the consequent lack of co-operation between Gillem and the officers of Thomas's army, which doubtless led to this disaster.

Breckinridge followed up his success, moving through Strawberry Plains to the immediate vicinity of Knoxville, but on the 18th of November began hastily to retrace his line of advance. For General Thomas, in all his preparations against Hood, had not weakened his rear, and the force under Breckinridge was not competent to meet that suddenly brought to his front. On the 18th—the day of Breckinridge's retreat—General Ammen's troops, re-enforced by 1500 men from Chattanooga, reoccupied Strawberry Plains.

General Schofield had left Stoneman at Louisville to take charge of the Department of the Ohio during his absence with Thomas's army. Stoneman started for Knoxville, having previously ordered Brevet Major General Burbridge to march with all his available force in Kentucky, by way of Cumberland Gap, to Gillem's relief. On his way to Knoxville, Stoneman received instructions from Thomas to concentrate as large a force as possible in East Tennessee against Breckinridge, and either destroy his force or drive it into Virginia, and destroy the salt-works at Saltville, in West Virginia, and the railroad from the Tennessee line as far into Virginia as practicable.

Having rapidly concentrated the commands of Burbridge and Gillem at Bean's Station, on the 12th of December General Stoneman advanced against the enemy. Gillem struck Duke at Kingsport, on the north fork of the Holston River, killing, capturing, or dispersing the whole command. Burbridge, at Bristol, came upon the enemy under Vaugn, and skirmished with him until Gillem's troops came up. Vaugn then retreated. Burbridge pushed on to Abingdon, to cut the railroad between Wytheville and Saltville, to prevent re-enforcements from Lynchburg. Gillem also reached Abingdon on the 15th, and the next day struck the enemy at Marion, routed him, and captured all his artillery and trains, and 198 prisoners. Wytheville, with its stores and supplies, was destroyed, as also the extensive lead-works near the town, and the railroad bridge over Reedy Creek. Stoneman, having made a demonstration on Saltville, proceeded to join Burbridge at Marion, where Breckinridge had collected the scattered remnants of his command. But the Confederates avoided battle, retreating into North Carolina. Stoneman then moved on Saltville with his entire command, capturing at that place eight guns, a large amount of ammunition, and two locomotives. The salt-works were destroyed by breaking the kettles, filling the wells with rubbish, and burning the buildings. Stoneman then returned to Knoxville, accompanied by Gillem's command, while General Burbridge, by way of Cumberland Gap, fell back into Kentucky. The country marched over by Stoneman's troops during these operations was laid waste, and all mills, factories, and bridges were destroyed.

[1] "With the exception of his rear-guard, his army had become a disheartened and disorganized rabble of half-armed and barefooted men, who sought every opportunity to fall out by the wayside and desert their cause, to put an end to their sufferings. The rear-guard, however, was undaunted and firm, and did its work bravely to the last."—*Thomas's Report.*

[2] "Here, finding so much dissatisfaction throughout the country as in my judgment to greatly impair, if not destroy, my usefulness and counteract my exertions, and with no desire but to serve my country, I asked to be relieved, with the hope that another might be assigned to the command who might do more than I could hope to accomplish. Accordingly, I was so relieved on the 23d of January by authority of the President."—*Hood's Report.*

[3] General Thomas reports his loss in killed, wounded, and missing during the entire campaign as 10,000.

THE FOURTEENTH AND TWENTIETH CORPS MOVING OUT OF ATLANTA.

CHAPTER XLVIII.

SHERMAN'S CAMPAIGN.—THE MARCH TO THE SEA.

After the Battle of Nashville the East becomes the Theatre of the War.—Estimate of General Sherman's Generalship.—He marches from Atlanta.—Constitution of his Army.—The Order of March.—The Movement not simply "a big Raid."—The Country traversed.—Occupation of Milledgeville.—Action at Griswoldville.—Crossing of the Oconee.—Sandersville occupied.—Kilpatrick's Movement on Millen.—Destruction of Railroads.—Apprehension in the North.—Crossing of the Ogeechee.—The Approaches to Savannah.—Capture of Fort McAllister, and communication with Dahlgren's Fleet.—Investment of Savannah.—Sherman demands a Surrender.—Hardee declines.—Movement against the Charleston and Savannah Railroad.—Hardee's Retreat.—Sherman enters Savannah.—Results of the March.—The Amount of Property captured or destroyed.—Character of the Defenses of Savannah.—Conduct of Sherman's Army on the March.

BY Thomas's victory at Nashville the Confederate army of Tennessee had been eliminated from the problem of the war. After this event the continuance of the struggle on the part of the Confederate government involved a useless waste of human life. The interest of the war from this point is transferred to the East. With the exception of the conflict terminating in the capture of Mobile, there were, after the battle of Nashville, no great military operations in the West. We are therefore prepared to follow Sherman's March to the Sea, and thence to Goldsborough in North Carolina.

Since General Sherman had been given an independent command in the West, he had fully illustrated his characteristic qualities as a great captain. As a subordinate he had shown these qualities only in a limited degree, because in that capacity he could only display his power to execute operations which were conceived and planned by others. No officer had so completely won the confidence of General Grant. At Shiloh his military talents were so conspicuous that Grant afterward acknowledged that the final triumph of the national arms on that occasion was chiefly due to Sherman. Of course, in this acknowledgment, we must make large allowances on the score of General Grant's natural modesty; but, if he was modest, he was also just. Sherman's prompt and unquestioning obedience to the orders of his superior officer ought not, perhaps, to be remarkable, but it was, nevertheless. He was never behind time. His comprehension of the task assigned him made misconception or mistake impossible, and he never lacked in vigor of execution. It is true that he sometimes failed in the object sought. His assault on the Confederate works at Chickasaw Bayou has been frequently adduced as proof of his indiscretion. But it must be remembered, in the first place, that he was acting in obedience of positive orders, and, secondly, that he was ignorant of the failure that had attended General Grant's movement in the rear, and it was this latter circumstance alone which made the assault indiscreet, or its success impossible. The assault on Kenesaw has also been adduced for a similar purpose. But here, too, the critics have a losing case, unless they can withstand the testimony of General Thomas and the best officers of Sherman's army, who assert that success must have followed the attempt but for the fall of Harker and McCook at a critical moment. The popular conception of General Sherman is greatly at fault. It has been the fashion to accord him brilliancy of conception—great strategic powers—and to ignore those characteristic qualities of his mind without which his strategy would have been ludicrous and useless.

In the first place, a factitious distinction has been made between *strategy* and *tactics*, and Sherman has been pronounced a great strategist, but an inferior tactician. Strategy properly includes tactics. The commander who can so determine and control the movements of his army as to, in the surest way, and with the least friction and waste, accomplish the object in view, is a great strategist.[1] If we confine these movements to the disposition of an army upon the field of battle, then we have what is properly termed tactics. Of course the original conception of the object and plan of a campaign is back of both strategy and tactics, and depends upon the speculative side of military genius—the power of ideal combination. This power of combination *may* exist without the practical knowledge or experience necessary to successful strategy or to successful tactics. But this is rarely the case, for the very practicability of the theoretical scheme must be determined by a knowledge of the material elements involved. So also it might happen that a great strategist should not be a great tactician—that a commander might be successful in large movements, and fail in his combinations on the battle-field and in the presence of the foe. But such cases must of necessity be very exceptional; for the skillful disposition of an army on a large scale would naturally involve its skillful manipulation on a limited field of operations. The exception could only occur by reason of certain elements involved in actual battle which demand peculiar qualities in the commander. Thus a general might exhibit brilliant strategic powers in bringing his army upon a well-chosen field of battle, or in forcing a battle upon his antagonist, and yet utterly fail in the battle itself through a lack either of promptness or of self-control in the presence of the enemy. Certainly Sherman lacked none of the qualities demanded upon the battle-field. In what, then, did his poor tactics consist? Was it for his strategy or his tactics that Grant commended him at Shiloh? Or upon what battle-field did he illustrate his weakness in tactics? If the battle of Chickasaw Bayou was a failure, that certainly was not Sherman's fault. No general on earth could have succeeded there, and Sherman only obeyed orders in fighting there. Under the circumstances he had no discretion, any more than he had at Tunnel Hill, in the battle of Chattanooga. But if we consider the tactics displayed by Sherman in the Atlanta campaign, where he had an independent command, do we find him deficient? It is true that, at Resaca, Sherman failed to destroy Johnston's army, where that result was possible. But why? Simply because his orders were not executed. But the order given is to decide his tactical ability, and not its execution by a subordinate. Surely all the op-

[1] This is clear from the very etymology of the term *strategy*, which is from two Greek words—*stratos*, an army, and *ago*, to move.

Howard. Kilpatrick. Logan. Hazen. Sherman. Jeff C. Davis. Slocum. Blair. Mower.

SHERMAN AND HIS GENERALS.

erations of the Atlanta campaign were tactical as well as strategic, and the success of these operations was as much due to skillful tactics as it was to skillful strategy.

It must be admitted that Johnston, by leaving open the approach to Resaca through Snake Creek Gap at the beginning of the campaign, afforded Sherman a splendid opportunity to destroy the Confederate army. And Sherman designed to accomplish this. He only failed through the excessive caution of McPherson. A similar opportunity was offered by Hood at the close of the Atlanta campaign by the division of his army. And here again, while Sherman's tactics were faultless, his subordinate officers failed him. But in both cases—at Resaca and Jonesborough—if Sherman's orders had been executed, the result would have involved the annihilation of the Confederate army.

It has also been said that Sherman could not organize and discipline an army. To this we only need reply that, so far as the purposes of war are concerned, Sherman's army was as well disciplined and efficient as any other. Beyond that it would be too curious to inquire.

General Sherman's conceptions were always bold, and his daring was only equaled by his confidence in ultimate success. No movement ever made by General Thomas or General Grant surpassed that by which Sherman transferred the bulk of his army to Jonesborough. Sherman was never vacillating or irresolute. His plans, once formed, were immutable. He was also as remarkable for discretion as for boldness. Thus his audacity never verged upon rashness. He was the Centaur general, being at once the fiery horse and the curbing rider. No pet military project could infatuate him. No better illustration of Sherman's caution can be given than his manner of undertaking the boldest movement of the war—his March to the Sea. With Hood in his front, he would not attempt the movement without an objective point on the coast already secured and awaiting his arrival. And even when Hood moved to the rear, leaving him an open path eastward, Sherman followed him, and, driving him far westward, waited and watched until he was over 200 miles west of Atlanta, and Thomas was prepared to meet his invasion.

Sherman's foresight was almost prophetic. At the beginning of the war he discerned the gigantic proportions which it would assume. He was laughed at, and thought insane, when he asserted that 200,000 men were necessary to prosecute the first great Western campaign; but time proved that he was right, and that the insanity with which he had been charged was lodged in other brains than his. He predicted Butler's failure at Fort Fisher. No military man ever had a clearer discernment between the practicable and the impracticable, or as to what might be accomplished with given means. He was as sure of the success of his grand march before he set out as when he reached its termination; he predicted the time of his arrival upon the coast, and anticipated the full effect of the movement in its bearings upon the war.

This foresight is not so strange when we consider Sherman's wonderful knowledge of the minute details of the conflict. He had been not only a careful student of military science, but also a careful observer of the country in which the war was conducted. He knew its mountains, its rivers, its railroads, its resources, and its people. His experience in regard to all these matters had been large before the war began, but since that time he had made them an especial study. What he once learned he never forgot. The movements of Cape Fear River were as well known to him as those of the Red River, upon whose banks he had lived. The whole Southern country was a grand chart before his mind; no geographical feature escaped him; he knew the natural products of each district, its population, its proportion of slaves, its cattle, its horses, its factories. This kind of knowledge his mind seemed to absorb and retain almost without effort. Yet, with all this attention to the *minutiæ* of campaigning, Sherman always based his plans upon general principles. Therefore, while he knew perfectly how to feed, march, and fight an army of a hundred thousand men, the conceptions which controlled him in the use of this army, and which formed the basis of his campaign, were calculated to accomplish the grandest results possible with the means employed. Sherman's military economy, as illustrated in the Atlanta campaign, and the operations which were its natural sequel, will hereafter be to the military student the most instructive portion of the American Civil War. The greatest results were accomplished with the smallest possible waste of force.

Perhaps the most characteristic point of Sherman's generalship was his perfect appreciation of the American soldier and of the discipline best adapted to his peculiarities. He was *par eminence* the American general, and his army was the military microcosm of the republic, for the maintenance of which it fought and marched. Both on the part of the general and his army there was perfect military subordination; but there was, at the same time, absolute freedom from conventional or arbitrary restraint in minor details. The martial enthusiasm of the soldier was not held in check by petty restrictions. Sherman scouted the idea that the American army must be made a mere machine. In the place of a purely mechanical discipline he substituted one which recognized the intelligence, not only of his subordinate officers, but of every private in the army. To inspire his soldiers with his own ideas appeared to him a more efficient means of control than the establishment over them of a military autocracy. The result fully vindicated his peculiar mode of discipline. His army moved as if by inspiration; but its movements, like that of the tides, were mathematically accurate and certain. There was no lagging from the march, there was no shrinking from battle.

It was a grand moment for Sherman when he had been, by Hood's folly, released from his dependence upon the railroad in his rear. In the event of an advance upon an army in his front, this long line of communication was a serious and unavoidable perplexity. From Atlanta to Allatoona, Sherman's sub-base was 40 miles. Thence to Chattanooga was 98 miles. But Chattanooga itself was only a dépôt, and was exposed to siege and capture, unless a large portion of the army was detached for its protection. Thus Sherman's real base of supplies is pushed back to Nashville, 290 miles from Atlanta, and, in the case of a successful Confederate attack on Nashville, back to Louisville, nearly 500 miles. This perplexity, as we have seen, was removed by Hood's invasion of Tennessee; and by giving Thomas an army sufficient to meet Hood, Sherman was permitted to ignore his connection with the North, and move eastward with from 60,000 to 70,000 men.

On the 16th of November, Sherman's army, with the smoking ruins of Atlanta in his rear, began its great march.[1] The right wing of the army, under General Howard, with Kilpatrick's cavalry, was put in motion in the direction of Jonesborough, and McDonough, with orders to make a strong feint on Macon, to cross the Ocmulgee near Planter's Mills, and rendezvous in the neighborhood of Gordon in seven days. At the same time, Slocum, with the Twelfth Corps of the left wing, moved by Decatur, with orders to tear up the railroad from Social Circle to Madison, to burn the railroad bridge across the Oconee, east of Madison, and, turning south, to reach Milledgeville on the same day that Howard should reach Gordon. General Sherman in person accompanied Jeff. C. Davis's corps—the Fourteenth—on the road through Covington, directly to Milledgeville. All the troops were provided with good wagon trains, loaded with ammunition and supplies, approximating 20 days' bread, 40 days' sugar and coffee, with a double allowance of salt, and beef-cattle sufficient for 40 days' supplies. The wagons were supplied with three days' rations in grain. Each brigade commander was instructed to organize a foraging party, to gather near the route corn, forage, meat, and vegetables, aiming at all times to keep in the wagon trains at least 10 days' provisions and three days' forage. The cavalry was to receive orders direct from General Sherman. Soldiers were forbidden to enter the dwellings of the inhabitants or to commit any trespass, but were permitted, during a halt or when in camp, to gather vegetables, and to drive in stock in their front. On the march the gathering of provisions was to be left entirely to regular foraging parties. Army commanders were permitted to destroy mills, houses, cotton-gins, etc., but such destruction must only take place in regions where the army should be molested. Horses, mules, and wagons were to be appropriated as they were needed, but discrimination must be made in these captures, the rich rather than the poor being made the victims. No family was to be deprived of any thing necessary to its maintenance. Able-bodied negroes might be taken along, in so far as this would not cause embarrassment in the matter of supplies. The troops were to start each morning at 7 o'clock, and make about 15 miles per day.[2]

[1] Major Nichols thus describes the spectacle of Atlanta in flames: "A grand and awful spectacle is presented to the beholder in this beautiful city, now in flames. By order, the chief engineer has destroyed by powder and fire all the store-houses, dépôt buildings, and machine-shops. The heaven is one expanse of lurid fire; the air is filled with flying, burning cinders; buildings covering two hundred acres are in ruins or in flames: every instant there is the sharp detonation or the smothered booming sound of exploding shells and powder concealed in the buildings, and then the sparks and flame shoot away up into the black and red roof, scattering cinders far and wide.

"These are the machine-shops where have been forged and cast the rebel cannon, shot and shell that have carried death to many a brave defender of our nation's honor. These warehouses have been the receptacle of munitions of war, stored to be used for our destruction. The city, which, next to Richmond, has furnished more material for prosecuting the war than any other in the South, exists no more as a means for injury to be used by the enemies of the Union.

"A brigade of Massachusetts soldiers are the only troops now left in the town: they will be the last to leave it. To-night I heard the really fine band of the Thirty-third Massachusetts playing 'John Brown's soul goes marching on,' by the light of the burning buildings. I have never heard that noble anthem when it was so grand, so solemn, so inspiring."

[2] The following is a copy of the general orders for the march, issued by General Sherman at Kingston, November 9th:

"I. For the purpose of military operations, this army is divided into two wings, viz., the right wing, Major General O. O. Howard commanding, the Fifteenth and Seventeenth Corps; the left wing, Major General H. W. Slocum commanding, the Fourteenth and Twentieth Corps.

"II. The habitual order of march will be, whenever practicable, by four roads, as nearly parallel

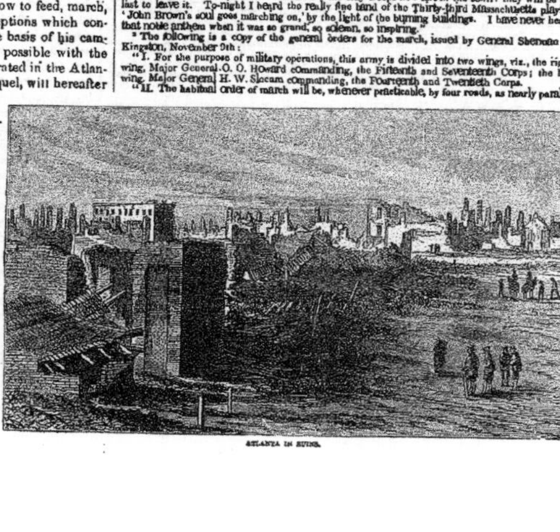

ATLANTA IN RUINS.

JUDSON G. KILPATRICK.

The line of march of the several corps of Sherman's army we shall not attempt to follow in detail, but will merely trace the general features of the movement. In the first place, it must be distinctly asserted that Sherman's march was not simply "a big raid." It accomplished all the purposes of a raid—the destruction of railroads and supplies. The large force with which Sherman marched of course more effectually accomplished these purposes than could have been done by a cavalry expedition. To destroy the railroads by which Georgia was connected with the Carolinas and with Virginia, and to consume the supplies upon which the Confederate armies depended, was a very important object. But, after all, this was only incidental. The Grand March was at once a magnificent raid and a decisive campaign. Sherman was conducting offensive operations against Lee's army, threatening his rear and flank.

Again, it was not Sherman's object to capture important strategic points upon his route to Savannah. Macon and Augusta were the main points likely to be defended by the enemy. Sherman could not afford to delay his columns in consideration of the results to be gained by the capture of either place; accordingly, he determined to demonstrate against each and avoid both. Kilpatrick, therefore, until the army was past Macon, kept on the right flank, and from that point covered the left wing, demonstrating against Augusta. Sherman's line of march followed the Georgia Central Railroad, covering a wide belt on either side, and, east of Louisville, extended over the entire tract—the most fertile in Georgia—between the Ogeechee and Savannah Rivers.

On the 23d of November Slocum occupied Milledgeville, the capital of Georgia, and Howard had reached Gordon. Slocum gained possession of

as possible, and converging at points hereafter to be indicated in orders. The cavalry, Brigadier General Kilpatrick commanding, will receive special orders from the commander-in-chief.

"III. There will be no general trains of supplies, but each corps will have its ammunition and provision train, distributed habitually as follows: Behind each regiment should follow one wagon and one ambulance; behind each brigade should follow a due proportion of ammunition wagons, provision wagons and ambulances. In case of danger, each army corps should change this order of march by having his advance and rear brigade unencumbered by wheels. The separate columns will start habitually at seven A.M., and make about fifteen miles per day, unless otherwise fixed in orders.

"IV. The army will forage liberally on the country during the march. To this end, each brigade commander will organize a good and sufficient foraging party, under the command of one or more discreet officers, who will gather near the route traveled corn or forage of any kind, meat of any kind, vegetables, corn meal, or whatever is needed by the command; aiming at all times to keep in the wagon trains at least ten days' provisions for the command and three days' forage. Soldiers must not enter the dwellings of the inhabitants or commit any trespass; during the halt or a camp they may be permitted to gather turnips, potatoes, and other vegetables, and drive in stock in front of their camps. To regular foraging parties must be intrusted the gathering of provisions and forage at any distance from the road traveled.

"V. To army corps commanders is intrusted the power to destroy mills, houses, cotton-gins, etc., and for them this general principle is laid down: In districts and neighborhoods where the army is unmolested, no destruction of such property should be permitted; but should guerrillas or bushwhackers molest our march, or should the inhabitants burn bridges, obstruct roads, or otherwise manifest local hostility, then army corps commanders should order and enforce a devastation more or less relentless, according to the measure of such hostility.

"VI. As for horses, mules, wagons, etc., belonging to the inhabitants, the cavalry and artillery may appropriate freely and without limit; discriminating, however, between the rich, who are usually hostile, and the poor or industrious, who are usually neutral or friendly. Foraging parties may also take mules or horses to replace the jaded animals of their trains, or to serve as pack mules for the regiments or brigades. In all foraging, of whatever kind, the parties engaged will refrain from abusive or threatening language, and may, when the officer in command thinks proper, give written certificates of the facts, but no receipts; and they will endeavor to leave with each family a reasonable portion for their maintenance.

"VII. Negroes who are able-bodied, and can be of service to the several columns, may be taken along: but each army commander will bear in mind that the question of supplies is a very important one, and that his first duty is to see to those who bear arms.

"VIII. The organization at once of a good pioneer battalion for each corps, composed, if possible, of negroes, should be attended to. This battalion should follow the advance-guard, should repair roads and double them if possible, so that the columns will not be delayed after reaching bad places. Also, army commanders should study the habit of giving the artillery and wagons the road, and marching their troops on one side; and also instruct their troops to assist wagons at

	Corps.	Divisions.
Right Wing, Major General O. O. Howard.	*Fifteenth*, Major General P. J. Osterhaus.	Brigadier General C. R. Wood's. " " W. B. Hazen's. " " J. E. Smith's. " " J. M. Corse's.
	Seventeenth, Major General Frank P. Blair, Jr.*	Major General T. A. Mower's. Brigadier General M. D. Leggett's. " " G. A. Smith's.
Left Wing, Major General H. W. Slocum.	*Fourteenth*, Brevet Major General Jeff. C. Davis.	Brigadier General W. P. Carlin's. " " J. D. Morgan's. " " A. Baird's.
	Twentieth, Brigadier General	Brigadier General N. T. Jackson's. " " J. W. Geary's.

EXTERIOR VIEW OF THE PRISON PEN AT MILLEN.

INTERIOR VIEW OF THE PRISON PEN AT MILLEN.

DESTRUCTION OF MILLEN JUNCTION.

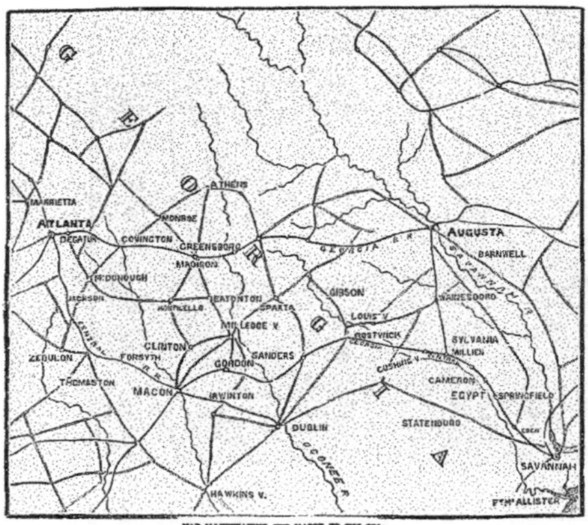

MAP ILLUSTRATING THE MARCH TO THE SEA.

the bridge across the Oconee. The day before, a force of the enemy, consisting mainly of Cobb's militia, had advanced from Macon to Griswoldville, and attacked Walcott's infantry brigade and a portion of Kilpatrick's cavalry, but was severely punished, losing over 2000 men. In this affair General Walcott was wounded. A few days before Slocum's occupation of Milledgeville, the State Legislature, then assembled at the capital, had hurriedly absconded on hearing of Sherman's approach. The panic seems to have spread to the citizens, and the trains out of Milledgeville were crowded to overflowing, and at the most extravagant prices private vehicles were also pressed into service by the fugitives. Only a few of the Union troops entered Milledgeville. The magazines, arsenals, dépôts, factories, and storehouses, containing property belonging to the Confederate government, were burned; also some 1700 bales of cotton. Private dwellings were respected, and no instances occurred of pillage or of insult to the citizens. Sherman occupied the executive mansion of Governor Brown, who had not waited to receive the compliments of his distinguished visitor, but had removed his furniture, taking good care, it is said, to ship even his cabbages.

Slocum continued his progress eastward, crossing the Oconee, when it was discovered that Wheeler, with a large body of Confederate cavalry, had also crossed, and was covering the approaches to Sandersville, to which point he was driven by the advancing Federal column. On the 26th the Fourteenth and Twentieth Corps entered the town. Howard, in the mean time, accomplished the passage of the Oconee lower down, in the face of a Confederate cavalry force under Wayne, and proceeded to Tennille Station, opposite Sandersville.

Before reaching Milledgeville, Kilpatrick had been ordered to move rapidly eastward to break the railroad from Augusta to Millen, and, turning upon the latter place, to rescue the Union prisoners there confined. He skirmished with Wheeler all the way to Waynesborough, destroying there the railroad bridge across Brier Creek, between Augusta and Millen. But at Millen he found only the empty prison pens in which the Union soldiers had been confined. For some time past the Confederates had been removing these prisoners to points far remote from Sherman's line of march. But they had left behind the traces of their cruel neglect. The corpses of several of those who had died in the prison were found yet unburied on the cold ground, while near by lay the graves of 700
by head-boards designating them by the fifties.

By the last of November Sherman's army had cr
River, still covered by Kilpatrick's cavalry—an i
to the enemy. The railroad was destroyed all
march.[1] In the mean while the Confederates ha
the ruin of Sherman's army. They do not seem
accurate knowledge of its numbers. Hood and
mated it as about 36,000 strong. In the Nort
anxiety for Sherman's fate. Both the confidence
the apprehensions of the loyal are indications
which then prevailed as to the audacity of Sherm

After Sherman crossed the Ogeechee there was
the enemy to oppose his march to the city of Sa
position from the enemy worth speaking of," sa
encountered until the heads of the columns were
of Savannah, where all the roads leading to the ci
more or less by felled timber, with earth-works a
these were easily turned and the enemy driven a
10th of December the enemy was driven within
nah." There were five approaches to the city—
and three dirt pikes—but they were narrow c
otherwise impassable swamps, and were strongly
lery. The entrance of the Ogeechee River to O
guarded by Fort McAllister. To invest the city,
fort, so as to command an outlet to the sea, we
to be accomplished. Admiral Dahlgren's fleet w
man off Tybee, Warsaw, and Ossibaw Sounds; and
ter had an abundant supply of beef-cattle and l
held it of the utmost importance that he should
fleet outside. Captain Duncan, one of Howard's best
down the Ogeechee in a canoe to Dahlgren's fleet, givi
of Sherman's present situation. But, in order to establ
munication with the sea by way of the Ogeechee River,
reduce Fort McAllister.

CAPITOL AT MILLEDGEVILLE.

To Hazen's division of the Fifteenth Corps was allott
the 13th of December this division crossed to the sout
Ogeechee. The fort was commanded by Major Anderso
son of about 200 men; it was mounted by 23 guns *en ba*
tar. As Hazen was crossing the Ogeechee, Generals Sh
went to Dr. Cheves's rice-mill on the river bank, wher
view of the fort. About noon they heard the guns of t
and Hazen's skirmishers were seen
By means of signals, Hazen was o
work that day, if possible. He soo
mission. The guns, being *en barbet*
ble for defense. With a loss of only
Union troops carried the work by as
the garrison. That very night Shern
a small boat, passed down the river to
down to a steamer which during the
up from the fleet within view of the

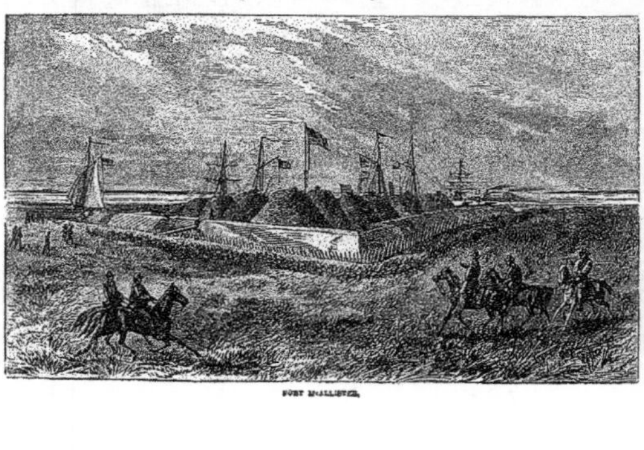

FORT McALLISTER.

[1] "The destruction of railroads in this camp
ough. The work of demolition on such long lin
quires time, but the process is performed as ex
order to prevent any serious delay of the move
method of destruction is simple, but very effec
struments have been made for this purpose.
which hooks under the rail. It has a ring in
serted a long lever, and the rail is thus ripped
sleepers are then piled in a heap, and set on fire
flames until they bend by their own weight.
each rail is taken off by wrenches fitting closel
turning in opposite directions, it is so twisted
chine could not bring it back into shape. In t
stroyed thirty miles of rail which lay in the city
Augusta and Atlanta Road from the last-named
the entire track of the Central Georgia line, from
of Macon to the station where I am now writing.
Great March.

ASSAULT ON FORT McALLISTER.

WILLIAM B. HAZEN.

By the route thus opened abundant supplies were soon brought from Hilton Head, and heavy ordnance for the reduction of Savannah. Sherman's army had already invested the city, shutting up every avenue of supply, and the only possible way of retreat left to General Hardee, who now, with about 10,000 men, mostly militia, conducted the defense of Savannah, was in the northeast toward Charleston. On the 17th General Sherman demanded the surrender of the city. He wrote to Hardee that he held all the avenues by which Savannah was supplied, and that if the city was surrendered he would grant liberal terms to the garrison, while, if he was compelled to assault, or depend upon the slower process of starvation, he should feel justified in resorting to the harshest measures, and should make little effort to restrain his army, "burning to avenge the great national wrong they attach to Savannah and other large cities, which have been so prominent in dragging our country into civil war." To this communication Sherman added: "I inclose you a copy of General Hood's demand for the surrender of the town of Resaca, to be used by you for what it is worth."

General Hardee declined to surrender on the ground that he still maintained his line of defense, and was in communication with his superior officer. In order to complete the investment of Savannah on the north, and across the plank road on the South Carolina shore, known as the "Union causeway," it would be necessary for Sherman to throw his left across the Savannah River. This would be scarcely safe, since the enemy still held the river opposite the city with gun-boats, and could easily destroy the pontoon bridge and isolate any force which might cross to that side. General Foster, with Admiral Dahlgren's co-operation, had established a division of troops on the narrow neck between the Coosawatchee and Tullifiny Creeks, at the head of Broad River, threatening the Savannah and Charleston Railroad, which was within easy range of his artillery. On the 20th Sherman started for Port Royal by water to confer with Foster and Dahlgren. He intended to increase the forces operating up Broad River, which would thus be able to break the railroad, and then turn upon the single line of retreat held by Hardee. He left instructions for his army commanders to prepare for an attack on the enemy's lines before Savannah.

But, before Sherman's arrangements were concluded, Hardee evacuated the city, retreating to Charleston, and on the morning of the 21st the Federal army took possession of the enemy's lines. The next morning Sherman, having returned up the Ogeechee, rode into the city of Savannah. Then, in a brief note to President Lincoln, Sherman thus announced the termination of his campaign:

"I beg to present you, as a Christmas gift, the city of Savannah, with 150 heavy guns and plenty of ammunition, and also about 25,000 bales of cotton."

Between the 16th of November and the 10th of December, Sherman's entire army had marched 255 miles.[1] For the greater portion of the army, the march really commenced at Rome and Kingston, and extended over 300 miles. The railroads had been rendered completely useless along the line of march, and a belt of country from Atlanta to Savannah, thirty miles wide, had been exhausted of supplies. If we include the devastation involved in the Atlanta campaign, Sherman's immense army had spread itself over more than one third of the State of Georgia. Georgia, as a feeder of the Confederacy, had been wholly annihilated. Sherman estimates the damage done to the state as fully $100,000,000, one fifth of which had been of use to his

[1] It is 190 miles in a straight line from Atlanta to Savannah. The following is a table of distances on the road followed by the Twentieth Corps:

	Miles.		Miles.
Atlanta to Decatur	7	Milledgeville to Hebron	18
Decatur to Rockbridge	14	Hebron to Sandersville	10
Rockbridge to Sheffield	13	Sandersville to Davisboro'	10
Sheffield to Social Circle	14	Davisboro' to Louisville	12
Social Circle to Rutledge	7	Louisville to Millen	28
Rutledge to Madison	9	Millen to Springfield	40
Madison to Eatonton	20	Springfield to Savannah	30
Eatonton to Milledgeville	21	Atlanta to Savannah	255

SHERMAN'S ARMY ENTERING SAVANNAH.

FORT JACKSON, SAVANNAH.

CONFEDERATES EVACUATING SAVANNAH.

own army, and the rest sheer waste and destruction. "This," he adds, "may seem a hard species of warfare, but it brings the sad realities of war home to those who have been directly or indirectly instrumental in involving us in its attendant calamities." About 7000 negroes followed the march through to the coast, and General Slocum estimates that as many more joined the Federal columns, but through weakness or old age were unable to hold out to the end. Over 10,000 horses and mules were captured on the march. A large quantity of cotton, estimated at about 20,000 bales, was destroyed before reaching Savannah. As regards the provisions captured, the estimate given is almost incredible, including 10,000,000 pounds of corn, and an equal amount of fodder. Slocum reports the capture of 1,217,527 rations of meat, 919,000 of bread, 483,000 of coffee, 581,534 of sugar, 1,146,500 of soap, and

137,000 of salt. Howard estimates the breadstuffs, beef, sugar, and coffee captured by the Fifteenth and Seventeenth corps as amounting in value, at the government cost of rations at Louisville, to $283,202.[1]

The grand prize of the campaign, however, was the city of Savannah. This was indeed a precious "Christmas gift" to the nation. It had been gained—if we count out the assault on Fort McAllister—without a battle. The whole number of casualties on the march had not amounted to 1000 in killed and wounded. With Savannah were captured 25,000 bales of cotton; and, as was found on a careful reckoning, about 200 guns. The city was almost impregnable against a purely naval attack. Both the north and the south branch of the Savannah River, at the head of Elba Island, were obstructed by a double line of cribs; to remove which, so as to allow a channel in each branch a little over 100 feet wide, occupied the navy for nearly three weeks. These obstructions were commanded by four works—Forts Lee and Jackson, Battery Lawton, and a water battery—mounted with 26 heavy guns, of which 13 were Columbiads. The river is so completely lined with marshes that the attack in front could have no co-operation from troops on either side. To guard against the approach by St. Augustine Creek there were also formidable batteries—Turner's Rocks, Thunderbolt, and Barton, with its outpost Causton's Bluff—mounting 34 heavy cannon; and obstructions were sunk in the narrow channel of the creek. But this entire net-work of defenses could be turned by troops landing on the Vernon and Ogeechee Rivers. To prevent this, the former was closed with obstructions commanded by Fort Beaulieu, 9 guns, while Big Ogeechee, in addition to the obstructions, was guarded by Fort McAllister with 23 guns. On the Little Ogeechee stood Fort Rosedew, with 6 guns. In the land works around the city there were 116 cannon of less calibre. Altogether the defensive works of Savannah mounted 229 cannon. It is clear, therefore, that, without a great sacrifice of life, Savannah could not have been captured in any other way than that adopted by General Sherman.

In justice to General Sherman and to the United States government, it is necessary that we should, in our comments upon the Great March, allude to the conduct of the army. It must be candidly admitted that many outrages were committed, or, to use the words of General Sherman, his soldiers "did some things they ought not to have done." We can safely affirm, however, that, with the same opportunities for wantonness, no European and no other American army would have accomplished the march with less violence. The only way in which outrage could have been absolutely prevented by the commander would have been the disbandment before the march of every soldier who would, under strong temptation, disobey the Decalogue. It is simply nonsense to attribute the violence of scattered foraging parties to the lack of discipline in Sherman's army. The strictest orders were given forbidding soldiers to enter the dwellings of the inhabitants, or to commit any trespass. If General Sherman could have been every where present these orders would have been obeyed. It must be remembered that whatever supplies could in any way assist the Confederates in prolonging the war were a legitimate prize. In many cases there was wanton plunder. Many of the wealthy planters had fled suddenly on the approach of Sherman's army, and had hastily concealed their treasures of gold, silver, and precious stones in the earth. Aided by the disclosures of the negroes, these places were diligently sought and rifled wherever opportunity offered. This gave color to extravagant reports, which had no other basis of credibility than the imagination of those who circulated them. But the violence actually perpetrated was far less than, under the circumstances, might have been expected. While we do not exculpate the wrong, we entirely exonerate General Sherman in the matter. No restrictions imposed by discipline would have prevented the evil done; and that there was no serious want of discipline in Sherman's army is clearly shown by the promptness with which the march was accomplished, and the perfect efficiency of the army as an organization when it reached Savannah. This would have been impossible if the army had not been held under restraint. There is universal and undisputed testimony that, in connection with the occupation of Savannah, there was no breach of good order.[1]

[1] Howard's report includes the following statistics of property captured and destroyed, negroes freed, and prisoners taken by the right wing:

Negroes set free (estimated number)		3,000
Prisoners captured.—By Fifteenth Army Corps:		
Commissioned officers	32	
Enlisted men	615	647
By Seventeenth Army Corps:		
Commissioned officers	2	
Enlisted men	117	119
Total prisoners captured		666
Escaped Federal prisoners:		
Commissioned officers	6	
Enlisted men	43	49
Bales of cotton burned		3,528
Ocmulgee Mills, 1000. Spindles and large amount of cotton cloth burned, Value not known.		
Subsistence captured; namely, breadstuffs, beef, sugar, and coffee, at government cost of ration in Louisville		$283,202
Command started from Atlanta with head cattle	1,000	
Took up as captured	10,500	11,500
Consumed on the trip	9,000	
Balance on hand December 18, 1864		2,500
Horses captured.—By the Fifteenth Army Corps	369	
By the Seventeenth Army Corps	562	931
Mules captured.—By the Fifteenth Army Corps	780	
By the Seventeenth Army Corps	1,064	1,550
Corn.—By the Fifteenth Army Corps	lbs. 2,500,000	
By the Seventeenth Army Corps	" 2,000,000	4,500,000
Fodder.—By the Fifteenth Army Corps	" 2,500,000	
By the Seventeenth Army Corps	" 2,000,000	4,500,000
Miles of railroad destroyed		191

Slocum's report gives the following estimate for the left wing:

"It was thirty-four days from the date my command left Atlanta to the day supplies were received from the fleet. The total number of rations required during this period was 1,360,000. Of this amount there were issued by the Subsistence Department 440,900 rations of bread, 142,473 rations of meat, 876,800 of coffee and tea, 778,466 of sugar, 218,500 of soap, and 1,123,000 of salt. As the troops were well supplied at all times, if we deduct the above issues from the amount actually due the soldiers, we have the approximate quantities taken from the country, namely, rations of bread, 919,000; meat, 1,217,537; coffee, 483,000; sugar, 581,534; soap, 1,146,500; salt, 137,000. The above is the actual saving to the government in issue of rations during the campaign, and it is probable that even more than the equivalent of the above supplies was obtained by the soldiers from the country. Four thousand and ninety (4090) valuable horses and mules were captured during the march, and turned over to the Quartermaster's Department. Our transportation was in far better condition on our arrival at Savannah than it was at the commencement of the campaign.

"The average number of horses and mules with my command, including those of the pontoon train and a part of the Michigan engineers, was fourteen thousand five hundred. We started from Atlanta with four days' grain in wagons. Estimating the amount fed the animals at the regulation allowance, and deducting the amount on hand on leaving Atlanta, I estimate the amount of grain taken from the country at five million pounds; fodder, six million pounds; besides the forage consumed by the immense herds of cattle that were driven with the different columns. It is very difficult to estimate the amount of damage done the enemy by the operations of the troops under my command. During the campaign one hundred and nineteen miles (119) of railroad were thoroughly and effectually destroyed, scarcely a tie or rail, a bridge or culvert, on the entire line being left in a condition to be of use again. At Rutledge, Madison, Eatonton, Milledgeville, Tennille, and Davisboro', machine-shops, turn-tables, depôts, water-tanks, and much other valuable property was destroyed. The quantity of cotton destroyed is estimated by my subordinate commanders at seventeen thousand bales." A very large number of cotton-gins and presses were also destroyed.

"Negro men, women, and children joined the column at every mile of our march, many of them bringing horses and mules, which they cheerfully turned over to the officers of the Quartermaster's Department. I think at least fourteen thousand of these people joined the two columns at different points on the march; but many of them were too old and infirm, and others too young, to endure the fatigues of the march, and were therefore left in the rear. More than one half of the above number, however, reached the coast with us. Many of the able-bodied men were transferred to the Officers of the Quartermaster and Subsistence Departments, and others were employed in the two corps as teamsters, cooks, and servants."

[1] In regard to this, General Sherman reports: "The behavior of our troops in Savannah has been so manly, so quiet, so perfect, that I take it as the best evidence of discipline and true courage. Never was a hostile city, filled with women and children, occupied by a large army with less disorder, or more system, order, and good government. The same general and generous spirit of confidence and good feeling pervades the army which it has ever afforded me especial pleasure to report on former occasions."

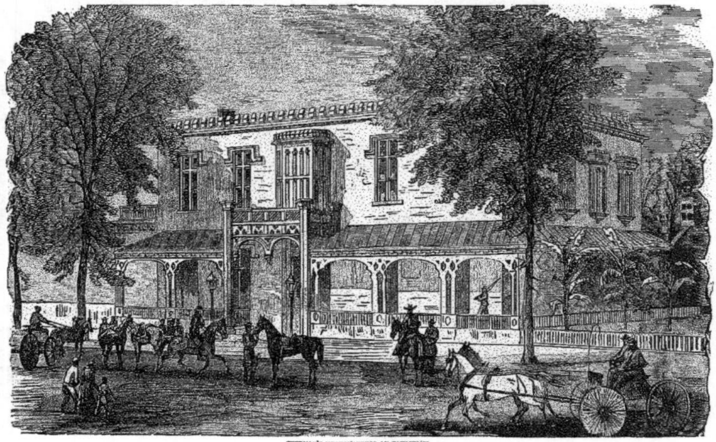

SHERMAN'S HEADQUARTERS AT SAVANNAH.

THE LINES AT PETERSBURG AND RICHMOND.

CHAPTER XLIX.

THE SIEGE OF PETERSBURG.

Opening of the Siege.—Strategic Relations of Petersburg and Richmond.—The Defenses of Richmond.—The Confederate Commissariat.—The Weldon, Southside, and Danville Railroads.—Birney and Wright's Attempt on the Weldon Road.—Character of the Region.—Hill drives back Birney, and is repulsed.—Anderson assails Wright.—Results of the Movement.—Wilson and Kautz's Cavalry Raid.—They cut the Railroads.—Are assailed, and return with Loss.—Results of the Expedition.—The Financial Effects of the Destruction of the Railroads.—Condition of the Federal Army.—Early sent to the Shenandoah.—Grant demonstrates before Richmond.—Burnside's Mine before Petersburg.—Grant resolves to assail the Confederate Works.—Condition of Burnside's Corps.—He wishes to put the Colored Division in Front.—This is refused by Meade and Grant.—The leading Division chosen by Lot.—Delay in the Explosion of the Mine.—The Explosion.—Burnside's Plan of Assault.—The Assault after the Explosion.—The Confederates paralyzed.—They rally.—Potter attempts to advance.—Meade orders a general Assault.—Advance and Repulse of the Colored Division.—Meade Orders a Withdrawal.—Losses at the Mine.—The Opinions of the Court of Inquiry.—Grant's Opinion as to the Causes of the Failure.—The Situation after the Mine Failure.—Lee re-enforces Early.—Grant again demonstrates North of the James.—The Operation fails.—Warren's Movement against the Weldon Railroad.—Warren holds the Road.—Hancock's Movement upon Reams's Station.—The Action.—Both Parties withdraw.—Prisoners and Deserters.—Period of Repose.—Assaults upon Forts Harrison and Gilmer.—Fight at Peebles's Farm.—First Movement upon Hatcher's Run.—Butler's Co-operative Movement.—The Army in Winter Quarters.—The Dutch Gap Canal.—Warren destroys the Weldon Railroad.—Raid of the Confederate Iron-clads.—Another Movement upon Hatcher's Run.

THE fatal misapprehension and delay of the 15th of June forfeited the golden opportunity when Petersburg, defended only by a mere handful, would have fallen at a touch. During the next three days it had been demonstrated, at a cost of 10,000 men, that its improvised defenses had become so strong, and were so strongly held, as to preclude all hope of carrying them by assault. This siege could be conducted only by gaining the avenues through which the defending army received its supplies. Richmond itself was even more impregnable to direct assault than Petersburg, for the elaborate system of works by which it was encircled had been the leisurely work of two years. The James River, coming in from the west, makes a sharp bend, almost a right angle, to the south. Here, on the north bank, at the head of navigation, stands Richmond. The river runs straight northward for ten miles, then turns eastward, and, after a tortuous course, alternating to every point of the compass, receives the Appomattox at City Point. The Appomattox, coming also from the west, bends northward. At this bend, upon the southern bank, stands Petersburg. The Appomattox approaches within three miles of the James, at the point where it makes its eastward turn; then bends to the east, running parallel with the James, which at length turns southwestward to meet it. The peninsula inclosed by these rivers is styled Bermuda Hundred; it is of irregular shape, from six to ten miles in either direction. Here, upon the northern bank of the Appomattox and the southern bank of the James, lay the Army of the James, shut in upon the landward side by the Confederate lines thrown up across the narrow neck of the peninsula. The Army of the Potomac lay upon the south bank of the Appomattox, over which had been thrown pontoon bridges, which, with the gun-boats, afforded ready means of connection between the two armies. Richmond and Petersburg were thus separated by the two rivers; but bridges at the two cities, and pontoons across the James ten miles below Richmond, enabled an army to pass without interruption from one to the other. The cities are connected by a railroad and highway running parallel with the James and Appomattox at the distance of a mile or two. The rivers, except for the space of three miles across the neck of the peninsula at Bermuda Hundred, effectually covered the Confederate line from any assault from either of the Federal armies. Had the Confederate works across the isthmus been taken, a way would have been opened for a direct assault upon the line of the railway. This, if successful, would have severed the connections of Richmond with the south as effectually as would have been done by the capture of Petersburg. This might easily have been done on the 16th, for during that day Beauregard had abandoned these works, and for hours they were occupied only by a few sentries. An attempt was indeed made to occupy these lines on that day; they were held for hours by a mere picket-guard, and the failure to retain them forms a conspicuous part of the first ill-judged operations around Petersburg.[1] This opportunity lost was never again presented. Thereafter no attempt was made to disturb the communications between Petersburg and Richmond.

The defenses of Richmond had long been complete. The exterior line, not in itself very strong except at one or two points, covered the city on the east at a distance varying from four to ten miles, terminating on the south at Chapin's Bluff, on the north bank of the James, opposite to which, on the south bank, is Fort Darling, which effectually bars the passage of the river. From this fort a line of works was extended westward across the railroad. This exterior line, saving at its southern extremity, was never occupied in force. Kilpatrick and Sheridan, in their raids, rode through it, back and forth, but were brought up before the inner line. This line enveloped the city, at a distance of about two miles, from the northeast to the southwest, both extremities resting upon the James, which completed the circuit. The works, extending fully ten miles, were never assailed. They were never even seen by any part of the Union army, save the cavalry, until they were finally abandoned. During the long siege, really of Richmond, though apparently of Petersburg, it is doubtful whether any Federal soldier, save as a prisoner, ever caught sight of the spires of the Confederate capital, or whether the noise of the great battles which were waged for its defense were ever heard in its streets.

Richmond, as fortified, was clearly invulnerable to assault, and could be held so long as the great army which defended it could be fed. But, as has been seen, the capture of Petersburg would involve the loss of the avenues of supply for that army, which must then, of necessity, abandon Richmond. But, as matters stood during the summer and autumn of 1864, the abandonment of Richmond involved the probability of the speedy disbandment of the Army of Northern Virginia. Not only would the abandonment of Richmond be looked upon as the virtual surrender of the cause, but there was then no point in Virginia or the Carolinas at which sufficient supplies could be concentrated. Richmond was the focus upon which converged all the lines of railway from the producing regions, which were soon practically reduced to portions of the states of Georgia, Alabama, and Mississippi. What with the ravages of both armies, the conscription of every able-bodied man, thus reducing the area planted, and finally the general failure of crops, Virginia was practically exhausted.[2] Supplies from these distant and widely spread regions, and from abroad through the port of Wilmington, could reach the army only over the Weldon, Southside, and Danville railways. These, then, were the vital and assailable points of attack; and to gain these, not the intrenchments which guarded the two cities, or rather fortified camps, was the aim of Grant. To hold these, not to waste his strength in

[1] "On the 16th the enemy, to re-enforce Petersburg, withdrew from a part of his intrenchments in front of Bermuda Hundred [that they withdrew entirely from these intrenchments is shown by Fletcher, vol. iii., 260; referred to *ante*, p. 640], expecting, no doubt, to get troops from the north of the James to take the place of those withdrawn before we could discover it. General Butler, taking advantage of this, at once moved a force on the railroad between Petersburg and Richmond. As soon as I was apprised of the advantage thus gained, to retain it I at once ordered two divisions of the Sixth Corps, General Wright commanding, to report to General Butler at Bermuda Hundred, of which General Butler was notified, and the importance of holding a position in advance of his present line urged upon him. About two o'clock in the afternoon General Butler was forced back to the line the enemy was forced from in the morning. General Wright, with his two divisions, joined General Butler on the morning of the 17th, the latter still holding with a strong picket line the enemy's works. But, instead of putting these divisions into the enemy's works to hold them, he permitted them to halt and rest some distance in the rear of his own line. Between four and five o'clock in the afternoon the enemy attacked and drove in his pickets, and reoccupied his old line."—*Grant's Report.*

[2] See Pollard, *Lost Cause*, 648.—In October, before Sherman's march had cut off the supplies from Georgia, the chief of the Bureau of Subsistence reported to President Davis: "The commissariat is in an alarming condition. Georgia, Alabama, and Mississippi are the only states where we have an accumulation, and from these all the armies of the Confederacy are now subsisting, to say nothing of the prisoners. The chief commissary of Georgia telegraphs that he can not send forward another pound. Alabama, under the most urgent call, has recently shipped 125,000 pounds, but can not ship more. Mississippi is rendering all the aid possible to the command of General Beauregard in supplying beef; she is without bacon. South Carolina is scarcely able to subsist the troops at Charleston and the prisoners in the interior of the state. During my late visit to North Carolina I visited every section of the state for the purpose of ascertaining the true condition of affairs, and under your orders to send forward every pound of meat possible to the Army of Northern Virginia, and to supply the forts at Wilmington; I was unable to ship one pound to either Virginia or Wilmington. We have on hand in the Confederate States 4,105,048 rations of fresh meat, and 3,426,518 rations of beef and pork, which will subsist 300,000 men twenty-five days. We are now compelled to subsist, independent of the armies of the Confederacy, the prisoners of war, the Navy Department, and the different bureaus of the War Department."—This statement was furnished in the autumn, after the harvests had been gathered. Before that time the state of things could not have been better in this respect. Thus Pollard says that "at the opening of the campaign Lee had urged that rations for thirty days should be kept in reserve at Richmond and Lynchburg, yet on the 2d of May there were at Richmond rations for only two days, and on the 23d of June rations for only thirteen days."

BATTERY BEFORE PETERSBURG.

the almost hopeless task of dislodging the beleaguering force from its position, was the policy of Lee. Only twice during the siege, and in both cases under extraordinary circumstances, was any real attempt made by either army upon the intrenchments of the other, and both attempts resulted in disaster.

The siege of Petersburg really began immediately after the repulse of the assault of the 18th of June. Within two days the Union army had thrown up strong lines parallel to those of the Confederates. On the 21st Grant made his first attempt to seize or destroy the railroads. Hancock's and Wright's corps, the Second and the Sixth, were moved out of their intrenchments. Hancock's wound, received at Gettysburg, had broken out afresh, and Birney was now in command of the Second Corps. The object of the movement was to capture the lines to the Weldon Road, and, while holding that, to push the investment of Petersburg farther to the west. The region to be traversed was covered by forests and swamps filled with a dense undergrowth, and cut up by small creeks and runs which fall mainly southward into the streams emptying into Albemarle Sound. These had all to be crossed by the advancing force, while between them ran several tolerable roads by which the Confederates could strike the advancing columns in the flank. The position was, on a smaller scale, not unlike that of the Wilderness. Birney, having the advance, soon came upon the enemy, posted behind earth-works three miles south of Petersburg, but beyond the line of the regular intrenchments. A slight attempt was made upon these by Barlow's division of the Second Corps; but this was soon recalled, and a position taken up for the night. Next morning Wright, who had marched in the rear of Birney, was pushed forward, with the design of taking up a position on his left, reaching to the railroad. While this movement, somewhat slowly made, was going on, Birney was ordered to swing his left around, so as to take the Confederate works in the flank. This carried him directly away from Wright, and left a wide gap between the two corps, increased every moment by Wright's movement. Hill, who had drawn to this quarter the bulk of his corps, availed himself of the opportunity thus presented, and flung a strong column into the opening, striking each Union corps upon the flank. The weightiest blow fell upon the Second. Barlow's division, on the left, was doubled upon itself, and fell back in confusion, losing heavily; Mott, the next on the right, was then struck, and retreated with loss; this uncovered Gibbon's right, from which whole regiments were swept away. But the corps was finally reformed upon its original line, where it was assailed. But the fierce Confederate swoop had exhausted its impetus. The assault was repelled; and Hill's columns withdrew as suddenly as they had advanced, carrying with them many hundreds of prisoners and several guns. Meanwhile another Confederate column had struck Wright's corps, and forced back its advanced line. But in the evening the whole line was reformed and intrenched for the night, while the Confederates intrenched themselves upon the railroad. The next morning, the 23d, Wright sent a small reconnoitring force to the railroad, which was reached at a point below the Confederate position. But hardly had they cut the telegraph wires when Anderson, at the head of Longstreet's division, fell upon their flank, drove them away, capturing many prisoners, and assailed the main line, which was withdrawn to the cover of the breastworks.

This attempt, which cost from 3300 to 4000 men in killed, wounded, and prisoners, resulted in no advantage. The line of investment was indeed somewhat extended to the left; but, as the railroad was not reached, the extension was of no use; and after it had been held without molestation for a

GERSHOM MOTT.

DAVID B. BIRNEY.

BUILDING WORKS.

few days, most of it was abandoned, and the advanced force was withdrawn to its former intrenchments in front of the Confederate lines.[1]

Simultaneously with this infantry movement, a cavalry expedition, consisting of Wilson's and Kautz's divisions, 8000 strong, was sent against the railroads. On the 22d they struck the Weldon Road at Reams's Station, ten miles below Petersburg, seven miles from the point where Birney and Smith were engaged. Having burned the dépôt and water-tank, and destroyed a considerable stretch of the road, they pushed on for the Southside Road, which they struck at a point fifteen miles from Petersburg. Kautz rode forward to Burkesville, the junction of the Southside and Danville roads, 50 miles from Petersburg, where he began to destroy the track. Wilson pushed ten miles down the Southside Road, which he destroyed in his way. Here he was met by Fitzhugh Lee's cavalry, which he defeated after a brisk fight, and thence moved on to rejoin Kautz. Both divisions then pushed down the Danville Road, damaging it for eighteen miles to Roanoke Bridge. This was found defended by a considerable body of militia, hastily gathered from the adjacent parts of Virginia and North Carolina. The whole region was now aswarm, and on the 24th the expedition, having accomplished its purpose, set out on its return. At Stony Creek, on the Weldon Road, they had a sharp but indecisive action with a force of Confederate cavalry. Finding these too strong to be dislodged, by a wide detour to the left they struck for Reams's Station, which was supposed to be in possession of the Union forces. But, instead of this, it was held by a strong force of Confederate cavalry and infantry, sent down from Petersburg after the abandonment of Birney's and Wright's attempt. Wilson was forced to fall back in every direction, losing all his artillery and trains. The two divisions became separated, and only succeeded in making their way back within the Federal lines in straggling parties and most wretched plight, having lost at least 1000 men.[1]

Although this expedition terminated so disastrously, it had accomplished much for which it was undertaken. The destruction of the railroads was so thorough, that, urgent as was the need of their repair, it required twenty-three days to accomplish this. Lee had then but thirteen days' rations for his army. To feed them the commissary general had to offer the market price for wheat still standing uncut or shocked in the field. This market price was then twenty dollars a bushel in Confederate money; for specie it could be bought for a dollar. The price rose almost at a bound to forty dollars. That is, Confederate paper, which had for months been received and paid at the rate of twenty dollars for one in specie, fell suddenly to forty, and thence steadily declined to sixty for one. For months, indeed, it would have wholly lost all recognized value had not the government steadi-

[1] It is singular that this costly attempt upon the Weldon Road is not even alluded to in Grant's otherwise comprehensive Report. For the losses we are compelled to resort mainly to conjecture. Swinton, p. 512, states that the Second Corps lost 2500 prisoners, and the Sixth several hundreds. I do not find the authority upon which the statement is made, and think it an over-estimate. The semi-official statement furnished to Coppée (*Grant and his Campaigns*, 399) gives the entire loss in the Army of the Potomac from June 20 to July 30 at 5316, of whom 605 were killed, 2494 wounded, and 2217 missing. It does not certainly appear whether this includes the losses in the cavalry expedition of Wilson and Kautz, in which Lee claims to have taken 1000 prisoners; and whether among these are to be included several hundred negroes who had followed this expedition on its return, does not appear. Although in these forty days there was no active battle, there was continued picket-firing between the lines. Burnside, whose corps was most exposed, gives (*Testimony, Battle of Petersburg*, 144) the loss in his corps during this time at 1188 men killed and wounded. The other corps undoubtedly lost many; probably the entire loss in the trenches was about 1500 (for the eighteen days following August 1 it was 865). Assuming that in the foregoing 5316 are included the losses of the cavalry expedition, and that these amounted, exclusive of captured negroes, to 1000, and that the losses in the trenches were 1500, there remain 2886 for this attempt upon the railroad, of whom probably more than 1800 were prisoners, leaving about 400 for the captures from the cavalry. From the best accessible data, I judge the foregoing estimates to be a close approximation to the truth.

[1] Lee, in his dispatch, says: "In the various conflicts with the enemy's cavalry in their late expedition against the railroads, besides their killed and wounded left on the field, 1000 prisoners, 18 pieces of artillery, and 80 wagons and ambulances were taken." As before noted, we think that among the prisoners are included some hundreds of negroes who had attached themselves to the expedition.

A MORTAR BATTERY.

RETURN OF KAUTZ'S CAVALRY.

SIGNAL STATION.

ly sold gold at nearly or quite that rate. Bankruptcy of the government had quite as much to do with the sudden collapse of the Confederacy as the defeats which it suffered in the field. For a time, indeed, under a rigid despotism, soldiers can be kept in the ranks without pay. The Confederate government succeeded in doing this for months. Indeed, it is said that "there were thousands of soldiers who had not received a cent of pay in the last two years of the war." When a "loaf of bread was worth three dollars in Richmond, and a soldier's monthly pay would hardly buy a pair of socks,"[1] it mattered little whether this nominal pay was ever received. But to feed, clothe, and equip an army requires money. Any government which has exhausted all its resources, actual and possible, must go down. The bankruptcy of the French monarchy under Louis XVI. was the immediate cause of its overthrow; for without this, the States-General, which inaugurated the Revolution, would never have been convened. This raid of Wilson hurried on the bankruptcy of the Confederacy. But for this it might have had a longer lease of life, with all the innumerable possibilities of the chapter of accidents. Grant, therefore, looking back after a year, was justified in affirming that "the damage suffered by the enemy in this expedition more than compensated for all the losses we sustained."

But for the time the attitude of the Army of Northern Virginia was more defiant, and seemingly more threatening than at any former period during the campaign. It was, after all its losses, nearly as strong as when it moved upon the Wilderness; stronger than when it foiled Grant at Spottsylvania, held him in check upon the North Anna, and defeated him upon the Chickahominy. The efficiency of the Federal army, in the mean while, had been greatly impaired. Its numbers, perhaps, had been kept up, but it had lost well-nigh half of its best officers and men; the remainder had suffered fearfully by their arduous labors under a fierce midsummer sun, through a drought of unexampled intensity, with a sky of brass overhead, and a soil of ashes underfoot. Not a few of the recruits, brought in by the enormous bounties then paid, were poor material for soldiers; and even the good material needed time to transform them into efficient soldiers. Even the tried veterans lacked much of their old determination. More than one leader of a storming-party in the fresh assaults upon the outworks of Petersburg was compelled to admit that his men did not charge as they had done a month before. But when, in the Weldon movement, the Second Corps, which had come to be recognized as the best in the army, fell back, division after division, almost routed by an inferior foe, losing twice as many in prisoners as in killed and wounded, it became clear that there must be a pause for reorganization and recuperation. Five weeks passed before another active operation was undertaken, and that also resulted in disaster.

[1] Pollard, *Lost Cause*, 647. For the effect of Wilson's raid upon Confederate finances, see *Ibid.*, 647, 652.

Lee, indeed, was now so confident of the invulnerability of his posit that he ventured to detach a quarter of his army from Petersburg and R mond to threaten once more the Federal capital. Hunter's eccentric ret from Lynchburg had left the Valley of the Shenandoah bare of troops. defenses of Washington had been stripped of almost every man to re-enf the Army of the Potomac. Lee, reasoning justly from all former experie was warranted in believing that a demonstration upon Washington w induce the recall of a large part of the force in his front, and not improb even to the entire abandonment of the siege. Early had been already with a part of his corps to check the advance of Hunter upon Lynchb Now re-enforced by a part of Longstreet's corps, he was directed to m down the Valley of the Shenandoah to the Potomac, thus separating hir a perilous distance from the main army. This movement failed in its purpose of causing Grant to detail any considerable part of his force f the lines before Petersburg. The Sixth Corps was sent thence, and to t was added the Nineteenth, under Emory, which had just arrived at Ha ton Roads from the unlucky Red River expedition of Banks, and, wit even disembarking, sailed up the Potomac to Washington. Grant's a was thus reduced by about the same number of men which Early had ta from that of Lee. Of the career of Early in this expedition, ending mo after, in the annihilation of his forces, we shall speak hereafter.

As the month of July drew toward a close, signs of movement bega appear in the Federal army upon the James. Butler had, simultaneo with the attempt on the railroads, crossed a division over to the north b of that river, which had intrenched itself securely at Deep Bottom, ten m below Richmond. This position formed a point from which a force mi upon occasion, be directed against Richmond. Grant now planned an o ation with a twofold object. The immediate purpose was by means o cavalry expedition to cut the railroads north of Richmond, and thus m Lee wary of the situation of Early, who, having failed in his demonstra upon Washington, was lying in the Valley of the Shenandoah. The ondary purpose was, by apparently threatening a movement against Ri mond, to force Lee to withdraw a considerable force from Petersburg, wh was then to be assaulted. On the night of the 26th of July, Hancoc corps, with three divisions of cavalry, crossed the James. On the two lowing days offensive movements were made in such force as to convi Lee that Richmond was to be assailed. He brought over five of his ei divisions, leaving but three at Petersburg. This force was sufficient to p vent the Union cavalry from moving to the railroad, but its withdra across the James seemed to promise success to a sudden attack upon t lines at Petersburg, to be opened by the explosion of a mine which had be excavated under a fort which formed a part of the Confederate works.

This mine had been prepared with the consent rather than the approv of Meade. Burnside's corps had held the line upon the right. At one poi his intrenchments approached within a hundred and forty yards of the Co federate works. Just in the rear of the advanced position was a deep ho low, where work could be carried on unseen by the enemy. One of Bur side's regiments was made up of miners from Pennsylvania. Some of t soldiers suggested that a mine should be dug right under this Confedera fort, perched upon the brow overhanging the hollow. The talk passed fro grade to grade, until it reached Colonel Pleasants, the commander of t regiment, by whom it was communicated to his division commander, and b him to Burnside, who at once gave permission for the commencement of t work. So little confidence had Meade in its success that only the slighte facilities were afforded for its execution. Nothing better than empty crac er-boxes were furnished to carry out the earth. In spite of all obstacl Pleasants pushed on the work. It was begun on the 25th of June, and w finished on the 23d of July. It consisted of a main shaft four or five feet diameter, five hundred and twenty feet long, terminating in lateral branch forty feet in either direction. Four days after, Grant having finally resolv upon assaulting Petersburg, orders were given to charge the mine wi 8000 pounds of powder. Burnside asked for 12,000 pounds, but the eng ueers at headquarters decided that this was too much.

Daybreak of the 30th was the time fixed upon for the attack. The mi was to be exploded at half past three. Burnside was to dash through t

CARRYING POWDER TO THE MINE.

EXPLOSION OF THE MINE.

breach, and seize a crest a few hundred yards in the rear, which was apparently unfortified. This crest, known as Cemetery Hill, commanded Petersburg. Warren, upon Burnside's right, was to mass his whole corps, except just enough to hold his intrenchments, and join in the assault. Ord, who had replaced Gillmore in the command of the Eighteenth Corps of the Army of the James, was to support Burnside on the left. Thus fully 50,000 men were appointed for the attack. Hancock, moreover, who had been secretly withdrawn from the north side of the James, was to hold himself in readiness to support the assaulting column; while Sheridan, with his whole cavalry corps, was to move against the enemy's left. It seemed that the operation could hardly fail of success, for the entire Confederate force holding the intrenchments at Petersburg was barely 15,000 men.

But in the execution of this well-conceived plan every thing went awry. Burnside had proposed to put Ferrero's division of colored troops in the front. They had not as yet been engaged, and were comparatively fresh, while the other divisions had performed arduous duty during the whole campaign, and ever since they had occupied the position before Petersburg had been so close to the enemy that no man could safely raise his head above the parapet. In forty days, without being engaged in any formal action, they had lost more than 1100 men out of 9000. They had acquired the habit of seeking shelter, and it could be hardly expected that they would at once forego the habit, and be efficient in the fierce and sudden charge upon which depended success. The colored division, on the contrary, had been for several weeks trained for just such an enterprise. Meade disapproved of the plan of putting the colored troops in the front. He averred that, should the operation prove unsuccessful, it would be said that these men had been pushed ahead because we did not care for them. Burnside was, however, so urgent that the question was referred to Grant, who agreed with Meade. Then Burnside left it to be decided by lot which of his three white divisions should lead. The chance fell upon Ledlie's, the poorest probably, certainly the worst commanded, of all. The fuse was lighted at the appointed moment. An hour passed, and no explosion followed. Two brave men, Lieutenant Douty and Sergeant Rees, volunteered to creep into the mine and ascertain the cause. They found that the fuse had parted within fifty feet of the magazine. They relighted it, and had just emerged from the mine when the explosion took place. A solid mass of earth, mingled with timbers, rose two hundred feet into the air, and fell sullenly back, leaving where the fort had stood a crater two hundred feet long, sixty feet wide, and thirty deep. At the instant the guns from all the batteries opened fire. The enemy were taken completely by surprise, and replied but feebly, and this feeble fire was soon almost silenced. Ledlie's men dashed over the lip of the crater, and plunged wildly into its depths. Between them and the commanding crest there was nothing but the rough, steep sides of the crater. A determined rush would have crowned the crest with the loss of hardly a man.

Burnside's original plan of assault, submitted to Meade four days before, was judiciously conceived. The fort occupied a re-entering angle where the Confederate intrenchments receded from the general direction of the lines. This fort being demolished, not only were the defenses pierced, but the works to the right and left were taken in reverse. Believing that his colored division might be relied upon for a vigorous charge, he proposed that it should be massed into two close columns; as soon as the heads of these had passed through the breach caused by the explosion, the two leading regiments of each were to sweep to the right and left, seizing the enemy's lines, while the remainder of the columns should dash straight forward upon Cemetery Hill, to be followed by the other divisions as rapidly as they could be thrown in. The crest gained, the colored division was to push right into the town. He seems to have supposed that his corps was sufficient for the assault, merely suggesting that the other corps should co-operate indirectly, and be in readiness to hold the crest, while he pushed forward toward Petersburg.[1] But the refusal of Meade to permit the colored divi-

[1] The sending the whole of the Ninth Corps to Cemetery Hill would, says Burnside, "involve the necessity of relieving these divisions by other troops before the movement, and of holding columns of other troops in readiness to take our place on the crest in case we gain it and sweep down

sion to take the advance materially changed Burnside's plans; and Meade's general order, issued on the evening before the assault, was so worded as apparently to ignore the movement to the right and left, or at least to leave the seizure of the lines to be performed by Warren and Ord.[1] There was one important part of the order of Meade with which Burnside failed to comply. He directed that Burnside should "prepare his parapets and abatis for the passage of the columns." Nothing of the kind was done. Burnside declares that "this part of the order was necessarily inoperative, because of the lack of time and the close proximity of the enemy, the latter of which rendered it impossible to remove the abatis from the front of our line without attracting not only a heavy fire of the enemy, but letting him know exactly what we were doing." Thus it was that the only approach to the breach was by two crooked covered ways, only wide enough to admit the passage of two to four men abreast.[2]

The explosion of the mine took the enemy completely by surprise. Hardly had the concussion ceased when the head of Ledlie's division began to move for the breach. Climbing the rim, they saw before them the deep crater, its sides of loose sand, from which protruded masses of clay, mingled with beams and timbers, the ruins of the fort. It presented an obstacle over which it was impossible to pass in military order. Into this the men pressed and huddled in inextricable confusion. The enemy abandoned their lines for a space on each side of the chasm. Into these the troops spread themselves, and, although as yet no fire was opened upon them, they sought shelter, and refused to move. Brigade after brigade poured in, until the crater was crowded with a disorganized mass. A single regiment climbed the slope, and advanced a few hundred yards toward the crest, to seize which was the first object of the assault, but, seeing no others following them, fell back into the shelter of the crater and the abandoned Confederate lines. So an hour passed, the confusion growing momentarily greater. Ledlie all this time was safely ensconced in a bomb-proof in the rear of the Union lines, which he hardly left for a moment. In the mean while the enemy, recovering from his first astonishment, began to plant batteries so as to sweep the approaches to the crater, toward and upon each side of which Burnside's divisions were now pressing. Potter, on the right, endeavored to extricate his division from the crowded gulf and gain the crest in its rear. But he found the way blocked up by Ledlie's men, lying in the shelter of the works which they had seized, and from which they made no attempt to advance. Potter at length got two or three regiments across, and had formed them into something like order. It was now six o'clock, an hour and a quarter after the explosion. Meade, who had taken his position a mile from the scene of action, imperfectly informed of what was going on, sent orders to Burnside to push his men, white and black, forward at all hazards; to lose no time in making formations, but to rush for the crest. Ferrero's colored division dashed forward gallantly toward the crater, although the approach was swept by a heavy cross-fire right and left. A part of these troops rushed straight for the chasm and plunged into it, filling it so that there was barely standing-room. Some of them pressed through the troops near the crater, partially formed, and charged toward the crest, capturing two or three hundred prisoners—the only semblance of success on this fatal day. But they were met by a counter-charge, and broke and fled in utter confusion, sweeping back in their flight many of the white troops. It was clear that all chance of success was past. Orders had been given to Warren and Ord to support Burnside; these were countermanded, and at a quarter to ten Burnside was directed to abandon the crater and withdraw to his intrenchments. Burnside was chagrined at this order. He still hoped against hope that he could carry the crest. Ord, who had advanced a brigado of his division, declared that this was impossible, and the order to cease all further efforts was reiterated.

But to withdraw now was a work of difficulty and danger. The space over which the troops must retire was now swept by a furious fire of musketry and artillery. The men within the crater were sheltered by the declivity from a direct fire; but the Confederates had planted mortars, from which shells were rained down among the densely packed masses. To remain was as perilous as to retreat, more perilous than it would have been to advance. The troops swarmed out in squads, losing fearfully on the way. The enemy charged fiercely down to the edge of the crater, and were repulsed; a second charge was made; the whole mass broke and fled. It was now past noon. For eight hours the men had been crowded, without water, under a fierce July sun, within that narrow slaughter-pen. This disastrous attempt cost 4000 men, of whom 1900 were prisoners, who surrendered rather than run the fierce gauntlet of fire. In Burnside's corps of hardly 15,000 men, the loss was 3828. With the exception of a single brigade of Ord's corps, none of the 50,000 men who had been prepared for this assault, save Burnside's corps, were put into action. Burnside had no authority to call upon Warren or Ord, and Meade delayed until too late to order them into action.

This affair of the mine was made the subject of searching investigation by a Court of Inquiry and by the Congressional Committee. Their conclusions as to the causes of the failure were somewhat different. The court found that this was owing to the injudicious formation of the troops, the movement being made by flank instead of extended front; to the halting of the troops in the crater instead of going forward to the crest when there was no fire of consequence from the enemy; that some parts of the assaulting column were not properly led; and to the want of a competent common head at the scene of assault to direct affairs as occurrences should demand. They mildly censured Burnside for all except the last of these, and sharply censured Ledlie and Ferrero for absolute inefficiency, if not cowardice in, keeping themselves habitually in a bomb-proof instead of being present at the assault. The Congressional Committee attribute the failure primarily to the refusal of Meade, sanctioned by Grant, to permit the colored division to lead the assault, and generally to the fact that "the plans and suggestions of the general who had devoted his attention for so long a time to the subject, who had carried out to a successful completion the project of mining the enemy's works, and who had carefully selected and drilled his troops for the purpose of securing whatever advantages might be attainable from the explosion of the mine, should have been so entirely disregarded by a general who had evinced no faith in the successful prosecution of that work, had aided it by no countenance or open approval, and had assumed the entire direction and control only when it was completed, and the time had come for reaping any advantages that might be derived from it." Grant, in his testimony, attributes the disaster to the utter inefficiency of the division commanders, and especially of the one who was to lead the advance of the attacking columns. Meade's order, he says, was all that was required; "if the troops had been properly commanded, and been led in accordance with this order, we should have captured Petersburg, with all the artillery, and a good portion of its support, without the loss of five hundred men. There was a full half-hour when there was no fire against our men, and they could have marched past the enemy's intrenchments just as they could in the open country; but that opportunity was lost in consequence of the division commanders not going with their men, but allowing them to go into the enemy's intrenchments and spread themselves there without going on farther, thus giving the enemy time to collect and organize against them. If they had marched through to the crest of that ridge they would have taken every thing in the rear. I do not think there would have been any opposition at all to our troops had that been done." Although Grant afterward believed that, if Burnside had been allowed to put his colored division in the advance, "it would have been a success," he still thought his own refusal and that of Meade to permit this was at the time right and proper. "We had," he says, "but one division of colored troops in the whole army about Petersburg at that time, and I do not think it would have been proper to put them in front, for nothing but success would have justified it. The cause of the disaster was simply the leaving the passage of orders from one to another down to an inefficient man. I blame his seniors, also, for not seeing that he did his duty, all the way up to myself." He thought this commander the poorest of all; he knew that he had been chosen simply by lot; yet he adds, "I did nothing in regard to it." This great effort, for which such abundant preparations had been made, was conducted without any common head. Although the lieutenant general and the second in command were all the while close at hand, neither gave any practical orders until the crisis was past. Neither even took adequate measures to know what had been done or left undone. They seem to have thought success so certain that they neglected all precaution to secure it. It is inexplicable that, out of the 50,000 men who stood drawn up in battle order for this very purpose, not a third were ordered to advance for the hours during which the operation continued. In Warren's front the fire of the enemy was silenced, and yet he was never permitted to move a man from his lines. "Thus terminated in disaster what promised to be the most successful assault of the campaign."[1] It cost more than 4000 men to the assailants, while the entire loss to the Confederates, including the regiment blown up in the fort, and the prisoners captured by the colored division, were hardly a quarter as many.

The mine enterprise had been undertaken under a conjuncture of favorable circumstances, a recurrence of which could not be looked for. It had failed utterly and disastrously. The failure had demonstrated that the works about Petersburg could not be carried by direct assault upon their strong centre. But the whole line necessary for the defense of the two cities was so extended that it seemed certain that there must be weak points somewhere, and that these points were to be found at the extremities. Grant had thrown up works opposite those of the enemy, in front of Petersburg, so strong that they could be held by a fraction of his army, leaving the bulk of it free to operate upon either flank of the Confederate lines. These lines nominally extended from the north side of Richmond around to the James, thence to and around Petersburg. As finally developed north-

it. It would, in my opinion, be advisable, if we succeed in gaining the crest, to throw the colored division right into the town. There is a necessity for the co-operation, at least in the way of artillery, by the troops on our right and left. Of the extent of this General Meade will necessarily be the judge. I think the chances of success in a plan of this kind are more than even."—Burnside, however, had good reason to avoid more than a mere suggestion as to the employment of other corps. Nearly a month before, when asked for his opinion as to the practicability of making an assault in front of his lines, he had said: "If the assault be delayed until the completion of the mine, I think we should have a more than even chance of success. If the assault be made now, I think we have a fair chance of success, provided my corps can make the attack, and it is left to me to say when and how the other two corps shall come to my support." Meade replied, somewhat curtly: "The recent operations in your front," that is, the mine, "as you are aware, though sanctioned by me, did not originate in any orders from these headquarters. Should it, however, be determined to employ the army under my command in offensive operations, I shall exercise the prerogative of my position to control and direct the same, receiving gladly, at all times, any suggestions which you may think proper to make. I consider these remarks necessary in consequence of certain suggestions which you have thought proper to attach to your opinion, acceding to which in advance would not, in my judgment, be consistent with my position as commanding general of this army."

[1] "Major General Burnside will spring his mine, and his assaulting columns will immediately move rapidly upon the breach, seize the crest in the rear, and effect a lodgment there. He will be followed by Major General Ord, who will support him on the right, directing his movement to the crest indicated, and by Major General Warren, who will support him on the left." Meade, however, says: "General Burnside submitted for my consideration a plan of attack of which I never disapproved. The only question of difference was in regard to the troops to be employed. I never objected to the handling of his troops; I only objected to the colored troops being placed in the advance. General Burnside afterward seemed to be under the impression that I objected to all of his plans. But as to his tactical formation, and what he was to do with his troops, I made no objection."

[2] Many officers attribute mainly to this neglect to remove the abatis and parapets the disastrous result of the Operation. This forms one of the four grounds upon which the Court of Inquiry censured General Burnside.

[1] Grant's Report.

IN THE TRENCHES BEFORE PETERSBURG.

CONFEDERATE WORKS AT HATCHER'S RUN.

ward to Hatcher's Run, their whole extent from the north of Richmond to the south of Petersburg was forty miles. But Grant, in placing his army on the south side of the James, had abandoned all purpose of assailing, or even menacing Richmond from the north or east. The works immediately around the Confederate capital were therefore held only by Ewell, who had been disabled from active service in the field. The garrison of Richmond was really nothing more than a body of militia, nominally numbering about 10,000; but of these there were never during the summer 5000 reported as present for duty. During the whole siege, indeed, the gay people of the Confederate capital—and Richmond was never so gay as during this period—never saw a regiment of the veteran troops who were defending it.

The real line which Lee had to hold began upon the James River, ten miles below Richmond. Here, at Chapin's Bluff, on the north bank, and Fort Darling, opposite on the south bank, strong works had been erected. Thence to Petersburg the distance is fifteen miles. But this space, as has been shown, was protected by the two rivers, and by the works across the narrow neck of Bermuda Hundred. So perfect were the natural defenses of this space of fifteen miles that it was never occupied in force. It could be assailed only by the narrow isthmus. During the whole siege this space was never even menaced. At the time of the mine affair a demonstration here was suggested, but the idea was pronounced impracticable. Lee's Army of Northern Virginia was then posted in two great divisions: the left, under Longstreet, who was slowly recovering from the wound received in the Wilderness, at Chapin's Bluff; the right, with which was Lee, at Petersburg. An attack any where upon the centre, from Petersburg to Fort Darling, being out of the question, Grant was shut up to the alternative of assailing one flank or both of the Confederate lines; that is, to move upon the left from Deep Bottom, where a part of Butler's force had a secure lodgment, up the north bank of the James, and thus threaten Richmond directly, or to operate upon the right flank, assailing, not Petersburg directly, but the railroads whereby the Confederate armies were mainly fed.[1] Grant's theory of operations was to make a strong demonstration upon one flank, and then to follow it up with a movement upon the other, each being made in such force as to be converted into a real attack should circumstances warrant. It was assumed throughout that the enemy could not strengthen one flank without greatly weakening the other. The capture of Richmond, though important, was still a secondary consideration, for the Confederate army occupying Petersburg would still remain to be destroyed before any decisive advantage was gained; whereas, if the railroads were destroyed or seized, the enemy, deprived of sustenance, must become a certain prize. Hence Grant's main efforts were always directed against the enemy's right, while Lee, equally aware of the nature of the case, massed the bulk of his force in the works around Petersburg, leaving at Chapin's Bluff hardly more than a corps of observation, yet always ready to strengthen it whenever a menace was made in that quarter.

The terrain south of Petersburg presented great natural obstacles for attack, and furnished admirable facilities for an offensive defense. The roads radiate like the sticks of an expanded fan. First running south is the Jerusalem Plank Road. This was now in the possession of the Union force. Next, parallel to it, is the Weldon Railroad; then come several minor roads, and then the Boydton Plank Road running southwest; and, lastly, the Southside Railroad, running almost west. Hatcher's Run, a small stream threading through swamps and thickets, flows eastwardly from near the Southside Railroad, crossing the Boydton Plank Road, when it bends southward, forming a sort of wet ditch to the south side of Petersburg, at a distance of six miles. The Confederate works closely encircled Petersburg until they reached the Boydton Plank Road, which they then followed to Hatcher's Run, crossing it and continuing for a space along its southern bank. They thus effectually covered the Southside Railroad for a space of many miles. To reach this vital artery the assailants must pass westward clear around the Confederate lines, and then turn northwest, involving a march of at least thirty miles by any practicable roads. A column making this march was exposed to a blow upon its flank from any one of the roads leading from Petersburg. The Confederates could sally from their intrenchments, strike any exposed part of the column, and return, in case of check, to their fortified position. The Union lines followed the general course of those of the enemy. But the complete development of both was a work of months. Early in August the Confederate intrenchments had only reached the Weldon Railroad, while the extreme left of the Federal line was on the Jerusalem Plank Road.

After the repulse of the mine assault, Lee felt his position so strong as to warrant him in detaching re-enforcements to Early, who, having given up the invasion of Maryland, was still hovering in the Valley of the Shenandoah. Only Kershaw's division was actually dispatched, although orders were ostentatiously given that Anderson, who yet commanded Longstreet's corps, should take the command. This would leave the north bank of the James only weakly defended; and Grant perceived in this a favorable occasion to menace Richmond. On the 13th of August, Hancock, with the Second Corps, and Birney, who had replaced Smith, and now commanded the Tenth, followed by Gregg's cavalry division, were sent across the James. To mask the movement, Hancock's force was embarked on transports, which were ostentatiously towed down the river as though their destination was Fortress Monroe, and thence up the Potomac to Washington. But, as soon as darkness set in, their course was reversed, and next morning, after some vexatious delays, they were landed at Deep Bottom, whence they advanced in the direction of Richmond. In the afternoon they came upon the enemy's intrenched line, upon the right of which an attack was made by Barlow with two of Hancock's divisions. This was vigorously repelled, and nothing was effected. Birney, on their left, gained some slight advantage. During the four succeeding days a series of brisk but undecisive en-

[1] It has indeed been suggested that the works in front of Petersburg might have been operated against by a system of regular approaches. "Two saps," it is said, "might have been run, and, in the course of a month, there is every likelihood that the Confederate line might have been carried." But during that month the enemy would have had ample time to fortify an inner line to which he could fall back, and so the work would have to be repeated. Lee was too accomplished an engineer to neglect such an obvious precaution. When, in the end, the line of works, having been almost stripped of troops, was carried, there was found an inner line before which the overwhelming Union force was held in check. This inner line was never actually carried. It was abandoned by the Confederates when defeats in another quarter had rendered the abandonment of Petersburg a necessity. Those who suggest this course quite overlook the essential difference between the siege of a fortress, the capture of whose works involve the loss of every thing, and operations against a line defended by a series of parallel or concentric works, which may be continued to any number, the seizure of any one of which involves only the gain of a few rods of space.

UNION WORKS ON THE WELDON ROAD.

gagements was kept up, Hancock trying in vain to discover some weak point. Lee, in the mean while, by detaining two of the three divisions ordered to the Shenandoah, and withdrawing largely from those at Petersburg, had accumulated a force too strong to be formally assaulted. He even ventured, on the 18th, to assume the offensive by an attack upon Birney; but the assault was repelled with heavy loss. In this operation the Union loss was about 1500, of which two thirds fell upon the corps of Hancock. The Confederate loss was about the same.

The operation had failed in its ostensible and perhaps its immediate purpose to secure a position more directly menacing Richmond. It had, however, accomplished two ulterior objects. It had prevented large re-enforcements being sent to Early, and had, by weakening the force at Petersburg, given a promising occasion for a movement against the Weldon Railroad. This was committed to Warren. On the 18th he moved quietly from his position on the extreme left, and struck the railroad without serious opposition at a point four miles below Petersburg. Leaving Griffin's division to hold this, he pushed Ayres's and Crawford's divisions for a mile up the road, until they found themselves confronted by the enemy drawn up in line of battle. Warren's position was a critical one. His corps was isolated, for its march had left a wide gap between itself and the troops on his right. The left of his advanced division also was approached by an obscure road of which he had no knowledge. Down this came the enemy, striking heavily upon Ayres, forcing him back for a space with heavy loss. The troops rallied, and the Confederates were repulsed in turn, Warren still holding

SENDING IN PRISONERS BY NIGHT.

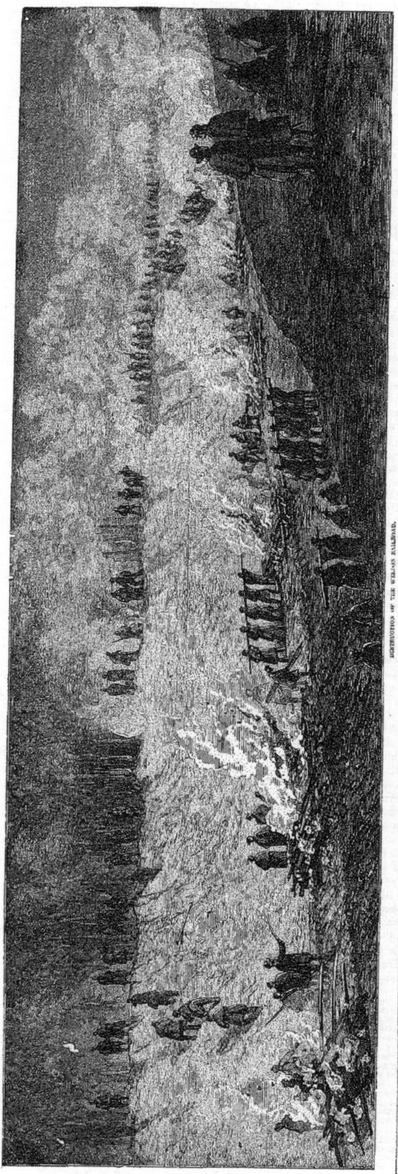
DESTRUCTION OF THE WELDON RAILROAD.

fast to and intrenching himself upon the railroad. This was of too great importance to be surrendered without a struggle. The next day Lee, having concentrated a powerful force, burst suddenly upon Warren. The wide space between Warren and Burnside had by some mischance been left uncovered. Into this broad gap Lee thrust Mahone's division, striking Warren's right, and, gaining its rear, pressed fiercely along it toward the left, throwing the whole line into confusion, and sweeping away more than 2000 prisoners, while at the same time Heth's division assailed the left. The core of Warren's troops still stood firm, and opportunely at the moment 2000 men from the Ninth Corps came upon the scene. With his whole force Warren now struck back upon his assailants right and left, and drove them back in confusion within their lines. On the 20th all was quiet along the lines, and Warren wisely passed it in strengthening the position against an attempt which he could not doubt would be made to regain it. On the morning of the 21st, Lee, having massed thirty guns, opened a fierce fire, under cover of which a heavy infantry force moved upon Warren's front, while another body endeavored to turn the left flank. The front attack was speedily repelled; the turning force met with still worse success; pushing heedlessly on, they encountered a fire so severe that they broke and fled in confusion, leaving behind 300 prisoners. So the Weldon Railroad was won, but at heavy cost. In the three days' struggle the Union loss was 4543, of whom more than two thirds were "missing."[1]

It was now resolved to destroy the railroad for a dozen of miles south of the point where it was held by Warren. For this purpose a part of Hancock's corps, which had been withdrawn from across the James, with a brigade of cavalry, 8000 men in all, was dispatched on the 21st. In the course of the next two days the work was effectually performed for four miles, as far as Reams's Station, where hasty and ill-planned breastworks were erected. On the morning of the 24th it was pursued three miles farther, and orders were given that on the next day five miles more should be destroyed. Up to this time no enemy had been encountered, and none was looked for. But Lee had in the mean while sent a strong force under Hill down the Boydton Road, which showed itself on the morning of the 25th. Hancock then withdrew his infantry behind the breastworks at Reams's Station, the cavalry having been pushed some distance to the left. Two sharp attacks were made and repulsed. Hill then, assuming a position where his artillery could take Hancock's line in reverse, opened a hot fire, throwing the Federals into some confusion. This was followed by an impetuous charge, by which the disordered lines were broken through and three batteries captured. The breastworks were carried after a feeble resistance, and all seemed lost. Miles, whose lines had been broken through, succeeded in rallying upon a new line, where the advance of the enemy was checked, and one of the lost batteries regained. Night put an end to the contest, and Hancock in the darkness withdrew. Hill, not suspecting how small was the force opposed to him, also withdrew at the same time, and when morning broke the place was vacant save of the dead. Out of his 8000 men, Hancock had lost 2400, of whom almost three fourths were missing.[2]

Five weeks of almost unbroken quiet now ensued. To all seeming the armies of Lee and Grant had come to a dead-lock. Each lay behind intrenchments which it was hopeless for the other to assail. Men's eyes were turned to other quarters—to Georgia, where Sherman at Atlanta was watching the heady manœuvres of Hood, ready to take advantage of the first false move, and meditating the great March to the Sea; to the Valley of the Shenandoah, where Sheridan was operating against Early, who had for a month menaced the Federal capital; to Mobile, where Farragut was sealing up that important port, precious to the Confederacy as the last save Wilmington hitherto open to blockade-runners. Grant, meanwhile, was steadily tightening his grasp upon what he had won, and seeking to make this a base for farther acquisitions. The extension of his lines across the Weldon Road had compelled Lee in like manner to stretch his, so that it seemed that he could have left few troops north of the James, and that there was most likely an opportunity of gaining something in the direction of Richmond. On the 28th of September, Ord and Birney, with the two divisions of the Army of the James, crossed the river, and fell fiercely upon the strong works near Chapin's Bluff. One of these, Fort Harrison, was captured, but an assault upon Fort Gilmer was repulsed with heavy loss. Fort Harrison occupied a commanding position, and was the main defense of that part of the Confederate lines. Desperate attempts were made to retake it, but they were unavailing, and Butler held a secure position from which to threaten Richmond. This compelled Lee to maintain a larger force than before upon the north bank of the James.

[1] Killed and wounded, 1367; missing, 3176. The Confederate loss in killed and wounded was probably quite as great; in prisoners, hardly a sixth as many.

[2] Killed and wounded, 663; missing, 1769. The Confederate loss is stated by Pollard (*Lost Cause*, 607) to have been "720 killed, wounded, and missing;" of prisoners there were very few, so that the respective losses in killed and wounded were about equal. When we consider the character of the fighting during the seven days from August 18 to 25, and note the inordinate ratio of Union prisoners to the killed and wounded (2000 killed and wounded, 6000 missing), we are forced to the conclusion that the greater part of the prisoners were really deserters—the scum of the army who had been brought in by the enormous bounties which had been for some months paid for recruits and substitutes, the loss of whom was really a gain to the effective strength of the army. Of the 24,000 losses in the army of the Potomac during what may be strictly considered the siege of Petersburg, from June 20 to November 1, considerably more than 12,000 were "missing;" yet during this period there was no action excepting that at the mine, in which the Union forces were really defeated. The Confederates during that period, while losing fully 10,000 in killed and wounded, lost barely 2000 prisoners. There were, indeed, some thousands of deserters who sought refuge in the Union lines, and a still larger number who managed to escape from the army and regain their homes. Pollard (*Lost Cause*, 647), speaking of the manner in which, during the last year, the Confederate ranks were recruited, says: "It was not unusual to see at the railroad station long lines of squalid men, with scraps of blankets in their hands, or small pine boxes of provisions, or whatever else they might snatch in their hurried departure from their homes, whence they had been taken almost without an hour's notice, and ticketed for the various camps of instruction in the Confederacy. In armies thus recruited, it is no wonder that desertions were numerous; but for every Confederate soldier who went over to the Federal lines, there were hundreds who dropped out from the rear and deserted to their homes."

EARTH WORKS BEFORE PETERSBURG.

The Confederates being thus strong upon their left, it was assumed that they must be weak on their right. To ascertain this, Warren was directed on the 30th to make a strong reconnoissance with two divisions of his own corps and two of the Ninth, now commanded by Parke. The reconnoissance was to be converted into an attack should the enemy prove to be in small force. Some works at Peebles Farm were taken and held; but Parke, pushing on, came upon the enemy in force, who charged upon him, threw Potter's division into rout, and swept off a thousand prisoners. Wilcox's and Griffin's divisions coming up, checked the pursuit, and the corps returned to the works which they had captured. Next day a fierce storm suspended operations. On the 2d of October a reconnoissance was pushed out, but the enemy had fallen back to his intrenchments. The loss in this operation was 2685, of whom 1756 were missing, mainly the unreliable recruits which had been added to Parke's corps. But the line had been extended three miles westward, and now reached within five miles of the Southern Railroad.

If this railroad could be seized, it would be equivalent to the capture of Petersburg. Grant, after long and careful preparation, attempted this with a force greater than he had put forth upon any one operation during the siege. The plan was to find the extremity of the Confederate intrenched line, turn it, gain the rear, and then move westward and strike the railroad. On the morning of the 27th of October the whole Army of the Potomac, leaving only sufficient men to hold the fortified line, was put in motion, both Grant and Meade accompanying the expeditionary force. Parke, who was posted at the extreme left, in the position which had been won ten days before, was to move out toward the Boydton Road, and, if possible, force the Confederate lines as far down as the crossing of Hatcher's Run. Warren was to support Parke, and, in case he was successful, was to closely press the retreating enemy; otherwise Warren was to cross the stream, march up its south side beyond the plank road, then recross, thus gaining the rear of the enemy's line, in front of which Parke would be posted. Meanwhile the main movement to the railroad was to be executed by Hancock. Marching down southwardly in the rear of Parke and Warren, he crossed the Run with slight opposition, then turning sharply to the northwest, he reached by noon the Boydton Road, whence a march of six miles would bring him to the railroad. Here he received an order from Meade to halt; for Parke, upon coming in front of the line which he was to carry, found it impenetrable. He therefore halted and intrenched himself. Hancock's corps was now wholly isolated, and the halt was ordered to give Warren time to execute his alternative movement, which would connect him with Hancock. Grant had by this time become convinced that it would be impossible to reach the railroad, and ordered the troops to be withdrawn to the fortified lines from which they had set out. Up to this time the enemy had not moved from his intrenchments, or shown any disposition to attack. Grant, having received an erroneous report that Warren had connected with Hancock, rode off to his headquarters at City Point, whence in the evening he sent a dispatch to Washington stating that there had been no serious fighting, intimating that he intended no offensive operation, but should hold his advanced position for a few hours to invite an attack from the enemy.[1]

But there was no need to invite an attack upon a force so isolated as was that of Hancock. Warren had, indeed, promptly endeavored to connect with Hancock. Crawford's division crossed Hatcher's Run, and moved up the south bank through dense woods, wherein whole regiments lost their way. But by the middle of the afternoon he reached a point opposite the enemy's intrenchments on the opposite side of the stream, and within a mile of Hancock's right, which had been extended to meet him. Yet such was the difficult character of the intervening space, that each command was unaware of the precise position of the other. Hill meanwhile, apparently unaware of the approach of Crawford, had arranged an assault upon Hancock. Heth crossed the run between Hancock and Crawford, fairly turned the right of the former, and fell upon Mott's division, which, looking for an attack from another direction, was struck in the rear. Pierce's brigade gave way for a space, losing a number of guns. But Egan promptly changed front with his division, so as to face Heth, who had now become aware that Crawford was close upon his left. The Confederates, bewildered, changed front so as to expose their flank to Egan, who, with his own regiment and one of Mott's brigade, swept on, while De Trobriand's brigade and Kerwin's dismounted cavalry struck in front. The Confederates, overborne by the fierce rush, gave way, and were driven from the field, leaving behind them nearly a thousand prisoners. Had Crawford in the mean while advanced, the whole Confederate force, isolated by the stream, must have been captured. But, though so close at hand, the noise of the musketry was not heard through the forest. Two hundred of the Confederates, bewildered in

[1] "The Army of the Potomac, leaving only sufficient men to hold its fortified lines, moved by the enemy's right flank. The Second Corps, followed by two divisions of the Fifth, with the cavalry in advance, forced a passage of Hatcher's Run, and moved up the south side of it toward the Southside Railroad, which I had hoped by this movement to reach and hold; but, finding that we had not reached the end of the enemy's fortifications, and no place presenting itself for a successful assault by which he might be doubled up and shortened, I determined to withdraw within our fortified line. Orders were given accordingly. Immediately upon receiving a report that General Warren had connected with General Hancock, I returned to my headquarters."—*Grant's Report.* "Our line now extends from its former left to Armstrong's Mill; thence by the south bank of Hatcher's Run Creek to its crossing at the Boydton Plank Road. At every point the enemy was found intrenched and his works manned. No attack was made during the day farther than to drive pickets and cavalry inside of the main work. Our casualties have been light, probably less than 200 killed, wounded, and missing; the same is probably true of the enemy. I shall keep the troops out where they are until toward noon to-morrow, in hopes of inviting an attack."—*Grant's Dispatch.* From the wording of the report, it might be inferred that the withdrawal was ordered to be made during the afternoon of the 27th, and that therefore the fighting which ensued was in consequence of a violation of orders. But the dispatch shows that the withdrawal was not to be made till next day. Grant's direction for holding on until then was subsequently modified by Meade, who left it optional with Hancock to withdraw during the night of the 27th. For this whole operation, see especially Swinton (*Army of the Potomac*, 540–546), where will be found citations from the as yet unpublished reports of Hancock and Warren.

DUTCH GAP CANAL.

the woods, strayed within Crawford's lines, and gave themselves up as prisoners. Meanwhile Hampton, with five brigades, assailed Gregg's cavalry upon the Union left and rear. But Hancock, sending thither all of his force not actually engaged with Heth, held his ground. The Confederates had met a decided repulse; but Hancock's position was still critical. He was yet isolated and in front of the enemy in unknown strength, who would undoubtedly attack next morning with increased force. His ammunition was well-nigh exhausted, and it was not likely that it could be replenished in time. So, the option having been given by Meade, he withdrew that night, and retraced his way to the lines from which he had set out. It was well that he did so, for during the night Hill had massed 18,000 infantry and cavalry, with which he proposed to renew the attack at daybreak. The entire Union loss was 1900, of whom a third were missing. Most of this fell upon Hancock's corps, Parke's losing only 150, and Warren's probably about as many. The Confederate loss was probably greater in killed and wounded, certainly twice as great in prisoners, of whom 1200 were taken.[1]

Butler's co-operative movement was feebly made and ineffectual. He pushed out two columns toward the Williamsburg Road and the York Railroad. The first column was checked at the outset, losing 400 prisoners; the second column carried a small fortified work, which it forthwith abandoned, and both returned to their former position. Thus the operation for which such ample preparation had been made, and from which so much had been expected, resulted in nothing beyond gaining some slight knowledge of the region, a knowledge which proved that the Southside Railroad could not be reached by that line. Yet the same costly experiment was made three months later, and with the like result.

The army now took up winter quarters behind its intrenchments, and during the remainder of the year no important operation was undertaken around Petersburg, although the quiet of the camps was broken by the continual picket-firing and artillery duels inevitable when two great armies lie intrenched face to face. Butler, indeed, was prosecuting a scheme from

[1] Lee's dispatch gives a very inadequate view of this affair. He says: "General A. P. Hill reports that the attack of General Heth upon the enemy upon the Boydton Plank Road was made by three brigades under General Mahone in front, and General Hampton in the rear. Mahone captured 400 prisoners, three stands of colors, and six pieces of artillery. The latter could not be brought off, the enemy having possession of the bridge. In the attack subsequently made by the enemy, General Mahone broke three lines of battle, and during the night the enemy retired from the Boydton Plank Road, leaving his wounded and more than 250 dead on the field."

RAID OF THE CONFEDERATE IRON-CLADS.

which he, and he alone, expected large results. Above Bermuda Hundred the James makes a double bend, first to the west, then south, thence east, and after a course of six miles returns to within less than half a mile of its starting-point. This tortuous bend was commanded by batteries which barred the farther ascent of the river. Butler proposed to dig a canal through the narrow isthmus, by which gun-boats could ascend the river and assail the Confederate works at Chapin's Bluff, and perhaps even force a passage to Richmond. The work, begun late in the summer, was prosecuted all through the autumn, mainly by details from the colored troops, not without considerable annoyance from the hostile batteries. At the close of the year the excavation was completed, save a narrow bulkhead at the upper end. On New-year's day this was blown up, but the earth fell back into the channel, leaving only space for a little rivulet. The Confederates forthwith established a battery opposite the mouth of the canal, which completely swept its whole length, and the scheme came to naught.

The Weldon Railroad meanwhile, though crossed by the Union intrenchments, and destroyed for some distance below, had not been rendered wholly useless to the Confederates. Cars still ran to within a few miles of the Union lines, and then freight, mainly supplies brought to Wilmington by blockade-runners, was hauled by wagons to Richmond. On the 7th of December Warren started out to destroy the road still farther down. The work was thoroughly and systematically done. The troops were formed in line of battle along the road. Each division destroyed that in its front; then each one moved down to the left, and so on in succession. In two days twenty miles of road were destroyed. At length the enemy were encountered in some force, strongly posted across the road. The expedition then returned, having marched a hundred miles in six days.

The communication with Wilmington was rendered somewhat more difficult, but was not wholly interrupted, for at this very period the supplies from hence saved the Confederate army in one of its sorest straits. On the 9th of December the commissary general reported that there were but nine days' food for Lee's army, producing also a letter from the commander stating that his men were deserting on account of short rations. On the 14th Lee telegraphed to Davis that his men were without meat. This disaster was only averted by the opportune arrival at Wilmington of several vessels loaded with supplies, which were then on their way to the army.[1]

The capture of Fort Fisher on the 15th of January effectually closed the port of Wilmington, and thus compelled Lee to rely solely upon the Southside and Danville roads. Taking advantage of the absence of the iron-clads at Wilmington, the Confederates made a bold attempt to destroy the Union shipping in the James. On the night of the 23d of January, their three iron-clads, the Virginia, Richmond, and Fredericksburg, accompanied by five steamers and three torpedo-boats, dropped silently down the river, passed Fort Brady, which covered the upper extremity of Butler's position, and broke the chain which had been stretched across the river opposite the lower end of the Dutch Gap Canal. The Fredericksburg got through the obstructions; the other iron-clads and the steamer Drewry grounded. The iron-clads returned, the Virginia being severely injured by a bolt from a monitor. The Drewry, being immovable, was abandoned and blown up.

[1] Pollard, *Lost Cause*, 649.

As spring approached, and Sherman was beginning to move northward through the Carolinas, Grant wished to prevent Lee from dispatching any part of his army to the south. The immediate problem to be solved was entirely changed. Before it had been how to drive Lee out of Petersburg; now it was to keep him there for a space, until Sherman had swept away the forces opposed to him. An offensive operation must be undertaken, and there seemed to be no one except an essential repetition of that which had been attempted in October.[1]

On the 5th of February, Warren's corps, accompanied by Gregg's cavalry, was sent to turn the Confederate lines at Hatcher's Run, while Humphreys, who now commanded the Second Corps—Hancock having been ordered north to organize a new corps—was to assail in front. Warren's route was nearly the same as that formerly taken by Hancock. Humphreys advanced to the Run, and was furiously assailed; but the attack was repelled, and at night the position was firmly held. Next morning Warren, who, having crossed the Run, had moved in the rear, came up, and the two corps were connected. Warren then pushed his left under Crawford up the west bank of the stream, through tangled woods and miry sloughs. Pushing before him a Confederate force under Pegram, Crawford went as far as he had gone in October. Here Pegram, re-enforced by Evans, made a stand, and in turn forced Crawford back. Meanwhile a Confederate force had made a detour around his left and rear. They struck Ayres's division, which was advancing to the support of Crawford, drove it in confusion upon Crawford, whose division also gave way and fell into rapid retreat. They fell back wildly to the position on Hatcher's Run, where Humphreys had hastily intrenched himself. The Confederates pursued fiercely; but, as they emerged into an open space, they encountered a sharp fire, and hastily withdrew into the shelter of the woods, whence they fell back within their lines. The Union loss in these two days was 2000; that of the Confederates less—probably not more than 1000. The only gain to the Federals was a farther extension of their line to the westward—an extension which might have been made without a battle. With this unsuccessful endeavor fell the curtain of the great drama, soon to be raised for the final short and stirring act.

[1] Thus only can we explain the movement now undertaken. Grant, in his report, refers to it only incidentally. He says: "The operations in front of Petersburg and Richmond until the spring campaign of 1865 were confined to the defense and extension of our lines, and to offensive movements for crippling the enemy's lines of communication, and to prevent his detaching any considerable force to send south. By the 7th of February our lines were extended to Hatcher's Run, and the Weldon Railroad had been destroyed to Hicksford."

CUTTING THE CHESAPEAKE AND OHIO CANAL.

CHAPTER L.

THE CAMPAIGN IN VIRGINIA.—EARLY AND SHERIDAN.

Hunter's Advance upon Lynchburg.—His Retreat through Western Virginia.—Early sent to the Valley of the Shenandoah.—Sigel driven from Martinsburg.—Early crosses the Potomac into Maryland.—Defeats Wallace on the Monocacy.—Threatens Washington.—Troops arrive for its Defense.—Early repulsed at Fort Stevens.—Recrosses the Potomac.—Is followed by Crook, who is defeated at Kernstown.—Early's Raid into Pennsylvania.—The Burning of Chambersburg.—Sheridan appointed to the command of the Middle Department.—His Instructions.—Opening Movements.—Position in September.—Sheridan to go in.—The Battle of the Opequan, or Winchester.—Early defeated.—Battle of Fisher's Hill.—Early routed.—The Pursuit.—Sheridan Returns.—Devastation of the Valley of the Shenandoah.—Early advances.—Battle of Middletown, or Cedar Creek.—The Federals surprised and driven back.—Sheridan comes upon the Field.—He attacks and routs Early.—Early's Address to his Troops.—Results of the Campaign.

EARLY in June, while, as has been narrated, Grant, after the battle of Cold Harbor, lay upon the Chickahominy, Hunter was successfully pressing down the great Valley of Virginia. Crossing the Blue Ridge, he emerged into the tide-water region, and on the 16th appeared before Lynchburg, whither Lee had already sent the small command of Breckinridge. This, joined to the few troops scattered in that region, was altogether insufficient to oppose the threatening movement of Hunter, and Early was hurried thither by railroad, reaching Lynchburg just in advance of the Union force. Hunter had expended most of his ordnance stores in the long march through a hostile country. On the 17th and 18th, while the first battles were waged before Petersburg, Hunter made some demonstrations, but, finding the enemy strong in his front, and with constantly increasing force, he hastily recrossed the Blue Mountains; then, apprehending that his return would be intercepted, and thinking himself in no condition to risk a battle, he continued his retreat westward, crossing the Alleghanies into the mountain region of West Virginia, whence he could regain his position on the Potomac only by a wide detour. This retreat left Washington and the whole northern frontier almost bare of troops, for every effective regiment had been sent to re-enforce Grant. The operations before Petersburg had convinced Lee that he could still hold his lines with a portion of the force which he had; and he reasoned, also, that the threat of a renewed invasion of the North would compel his opponent to detach largely from the force at Petersburg, and most likely compel him to raise the siege.

In the latter days of June, Early was therefore ordered to move down the Valley of the Shenandoah. The force with which this movement was made compared ill with the great armies which had twice before marched along this beaten track. Instead of the 100,000 men with which Lee had moved on the campaigns which closed at Antietam and Gettysburg, Early had not more than 20,000 men of all arms. But the force for the defense was still weaker in proportion, and it was within the limits of possibility that even the Federal capital might be seized by a sudden dash. Early moved with the rapidity which had always characterized the Confederate marches. In spite of the fierce summer heat, the troops made twenty miles a day, and on the 2d of July he was close upon Martinsburg. Sigel, who was there with a small force guarding a large quantity of stores, fell back toward Harper's Ferry, abandoning every thing which he could not carry off. Taught by the experience of the past, he was not entrapped into halting at Harper's Ferry, but, crossing the Potomac, took post upon Maryland Heights. Here he was safe from attack, but useless for obstructing the passage of the river, had his force been five times as great. Hunter was far away, making his toilsome circuit through the mountain wilds of Western Virginia. There was nothing to hinder Early from making a raid into Maryland and Pennsylvania. Crossing the Potomac, he sent scouting-parties in every direction. One destroyed the Baltimore and Ohio Railroad for miles, and cut the embankments of the Chesapeake and Ohio Canal in various places; another pushed on to Hagerstown, where they levied a heavy contribution and went off. The main body pushed on toward Frederick City by the same route over which Lee had marched two years before, threatening both Baltimore and Washington. Wallace was at Baltimore in the command of a few disjointed fragments of troops, but he knew that the veteran Sixth Corps was coming to his aid from the James. He therefore advanced and took position on the Monocacy River, where he covered the roads to both Baltimore and Washington, and hoped to hold the enemy in check until the arrival of Wright with the Sixth Corps, and Emory with the Nineteenth. This latter had been brought from Louisiana, had opportunely arrived at Fortress Monroe, and, without disembarking there, was sent up the Potomac to Washington. Ricketts's division of the Sixth Corps had joined him at Baltimore, and the other divisions were on the point of embarking at City Point; two days would bring them up.

On the morning of the 9th of July, Early, after some skirmishing, came upon Wallace at the Monocacy. The Confederates were more than two to one. Their first and second assaults were repelled; but the third, made in greater force, was successful. The Federals retreated, some in good order, toward Baltimore, but the greater part fled in utter confusion in every direction. The Union loss was 1959; of them, 1282 were "missing," of whom fully half were stragglers. The Confederate loss was vaguely reported at 600. It was apparently somewhat greater, since two days after 400 of those too severely wounded to be removed were found in the hospitals at Frederick.

The approach to Washington was now fairly opened, and Early moved the next day in that direction. He had with him about ten thousand men, for detachments had been sent in every direction to gather supplies and plunder. Had he pushed straight on with even this small force, he might, in all likelihood, have entered the capital, and, after doing what damage he pleased,

PILLAGING AT HAGERSTOWN.

SACKING A FLOUR MILL.

have retired by the way he came. A delay of a single day forfeited an opportunity for striking a blow which might have changed the current of history. On the evening of the 10th Early's whole force was within half a dozen miles of Washington. Between him and the Federal capital there were only a few isolated forts manned by militia, invalids, and convalescents from the hospitals. For one day it was not Richmond, but Washington that was in peril. Few men in the Federal capital believed that it could be saved from capture. On the afternoon of the 12th Early made demonstrations looking toward an assault. He advanced his line close up to Fort Stevens, an isolated work half a dozen miles north of the city, covering one of the roads. But during the previous night the whole aspect of things had been changed. The Nineteenth Corps, and the two remaining divisions of the Sixth, had steamed up the Potomac, and were disembarked. A great weight was lifted from the heart of the man upon whose calm courage rested more than even upon any general in the field the destiny of the nation. As the tried veterans stepped ashore, they saw upon the wharf the gaunt figure of Abraham Lincoln. He greeted them with kindly words and the winning smile which was wont to light up his homely features, munching at intervals a bit of army bread. No wonder that he had that day missed his dinner. As the foremost men filed swiftly through the streets, they were greeted with acclamation. "It is the old Sixth Corps, the men who took Marye's Heights; the danger is over." That night it was felt that the peril was overpast. Toward evening of the 12th a brigade of the Sixth Corps moved out to dislodge the Confederates, who had all day kept up annoying demonstrations in front of Fort Stevens. A hot conflict ensued, for the combatants were veterans who had encountered each other on more than one stricken field. Each side lost heavily in proportion to the numbers engaged. The Union brigade, a thousand strong, lost a quarter of its numbers. The Confederates lost more, and were driven from the field.

Early saw that his opportunity was past. The Federal capital was held by a force too strong in number and quality to be encountered by his little army. Under the cover of night he withdrew, recrossing the Potomac, and thus closing the last invasion of the North. This attempt, however, had not been an entire failure. He had won one considerable battle, and swept back with him no inconsiderable booty, not the least valuable part of which was 5000 horses and 2500 cattle.

Having placed the Potomac between himself and the enemy, Early moved leisurely up the Valley of the Shenandoah. Wright, who was now placed at the head of the Sixth and Nineteenth Corps, followed by the same route and with the same undecided steps wherewith McClellan and Meade had before gone after Lee. Passing through Snicker's Gap, he came up on the 19th of July with the retreating Confederate column at the crossing of the Shenandoah. When half way over, Early turned, repelled him, and then fell back leisurely to Winchester; while Wright, under orders from Grant, returned to Washington.

It was supposed that Early's command was returning to join Lee at Petersburg, and the Federal commander proposed to recall the Sixth Corps to the Army of the Potomac. But Lee, who was aware of the importance of maintaining a force in the Valley of the Shenandoah, and thus keeping up a constant menace of raids across the Potomac, had no thought of withdrawing Early. The Federals soon had reason to find to their cost that Early was yet close at hand. On the 23d of July, Crook, who was in command at Harper's Ferry, pushed up the Valley, which he supposed had been abandoned by the enemy. At Kernstown, four miles beyond Winchester, hard by where Jackson had suffered his only defeat in the Valley, his small force encountered Early, was defeated, and driven back in rout to Martinsburg, losing 1200 men. It then recrossed the Potomac, leaving the way open for a raid across the river. Early took prompt advantage of the opportunity. His cavalry, 3000 strong, under McCausland, passed the Potomac, and, making a wide sweep so as to conceal their real destination, reached Chambersburg on the 30th. The purpose of this raid was destruction. McCausland demanded $200,000 in gold as a ransom for the town. Compliance was out of the question, and orders were at once given to burn the town. The execution of this was committed to Gilmor, a Marylander, who had joined the Confederates, and in an hour two thirds of that flourishing town of 4000 inhabitants was in flames. This is the only instance during the war in which a town was wantonly, and by express order, destroyed, without any pretense of military advantage; for the destruction of Atlanta by Sherman was ordered as a military necessity, and the burning of Columbia was not by any order from the Union commander. The raiding party now made their way back across the Potomac, after several skirmishes, in which the losses were about equal upon either side.

These annoying occurrences upon the frontier were owing quite as much to defective military arrangements on the Federal side as to skill on the part of the Confederates. It seemed as though this region was looked upon as a hospital for incapable commanders. The departments were so divided and subdivided that no commander had any real authority or responsibility. Thus Washington, Baltimore, and the adjacent region formed one department; parts of Pennsylvania and Maryland another; West Virginia another; the region of the Shenandoah another. Grant saw clearly that the first thing to be done was to form all these into one military department. This was done, and Hunter, who had now got back from his long wandering, was placed in command. But Grant had fixed his eye upon another man for the position. Hunter intimated his willingness to be relieved. The intimation was promptly acted upon, and Sheridan, who had just been sent to Washington in anticipation of such a contingency, was placed in the command of these departments, which were constituted the Middle Military Division, the forces there being designated as the Army of the Shenandoah.

Sheridan assumed command on the 7th of August. The Army of the Shenandoah consisted of the Sixth Corps, one division of the Nineteenth, two small divisions under Crook, known as the Eighth Corps, with Averill's and Torbert's divisions of cavalry, the latter having just come up from the

RUINS OF CHAMBERSBURG.—THE MAIN STREET.

James. In all it numbered 18,000 infantry and 3500 cavalry disposable for active operations. As many more were required for garrisons and to guard the railroad. The Confederates, with the addition of Anderson's command, were in about equal force. To Sheridan were turned over the instructions just given to Hunter. He was to concentrate all his available force near Harper's Ferry, whence he was to operate against Early: pursue and fight him if he crossed the Potomac; follow him if he retreated south; first or last he would have to pursue the enemy up the Valley of the Shenandoah, where he must leave nothing which could invite the return of the Confederates. Dwellings were to be spared, but such provisions, forage, and stock as could not be used were to be destroyed. The people must be made to understand that, so long as a Confederate army could subsist among them, raids would be of continual occurrence, and these it was determinad to stop at all hazards. This stern order was soon to be sternly executed.

Sheridan at once moved up the Valley toward Winchester, where he expected to find the enemy; but they had fallen back. Then, being notified from Grant that re-enforcements had been sent to Early, raising his force to 40,000 men, he drew back and took up a strong defensive position near Harper's Ferry, to await the development of the intentions of his opponent. For a month the outposts and cavalry parties of the armies were in almost daily collision, with no important results. Early having been re-enforced by Anderson, in command of Kershaw's division of infantry and Fitzhugh Lee's cavalry, and Sheridan by Grover's division of the Nineteenth Corps and Wilson's cavalry, the respective forces were not greatly disproportionate—the Confederates numbering about 22,000, and the Federals about 27,000. There was some question as to the command between Early and Anderson. Both had been made lieutenant generals on the same day; but Anderson's commission as major general was prior to that of Early, which gave him the military seniority; but he had been sent to Early's deportment. There was thus a question of rank, and the two commanders never cordially co-operated.

At the middle of September the Confederates were concentrated around Winchester, and the Federals near Berryville, ten miles to the east, the Opequan running between. The armies were so posted that either could bring on an action; but neither commander was disposed to attack the other in a position of his choosing. Grant indeed for a while held Sheridan in check, for defeat would lay Maryland and Pennsylvania open to a renewed invasion. At length he left the James, and came to the Potomac to confer with Sheridan. At the very time of his arrival, Sheridan had learned that Kershaw's division had been recalled. Lee was meditating an offensive operation at Petersburg, and wished Kershaw to be at hand in case it should be undertaken. He was therefore directed to fall back as far as Culpepper, whence he could reach Richmond by rail in a few hours. This left Early with from 15,000 to 18,000.[1] Sheridan had resolved to attack Early, and, on submitting his plans to Grant, received the emphatic order to "go in."

Sheridan proposed to march upon Newtown, above Winchester, and thus throw himself upon the Confederate rear; but on the 18th of September, just as the movement was to have commenced, he learned that Early had sent two of his four divisions to Martinsburg, twenty-two miles from Winchester, with the purpose of destroying the Baltimore and Ohio Railroad at that point. He therefore changed his plan, and resolved to catch the two divisions left near Winchester, and, having routed them, to fall upon those sent to Martinsburg. Thus ensued the action called by him the Battle of

[1] Early indeed asserts that his effective force was only 8500 muskets—say 9000 infantry, and less than 3000 cavalry, with three battalions of artillery: not more than 13,000 men in all. But, as will be seen hereafter, this is evidently an under-statement; for, taking into account his statement of all the re-enforcements which he at any time received, Sheridan captured during this campaign nearly as many prisoners as the whole of Early's alleged force. His losses in killed and wounded were also very heavy, and a considerable remnant of his army rejoined Lee at Petersburg. Pollard (*Lost Cause*, p. 598) adopts Early's statement; but Pollard's own accounts elsewhere show that this must be erroneous.

RUINS OF CHAMBERSBURG.—THE TOWN HALL.

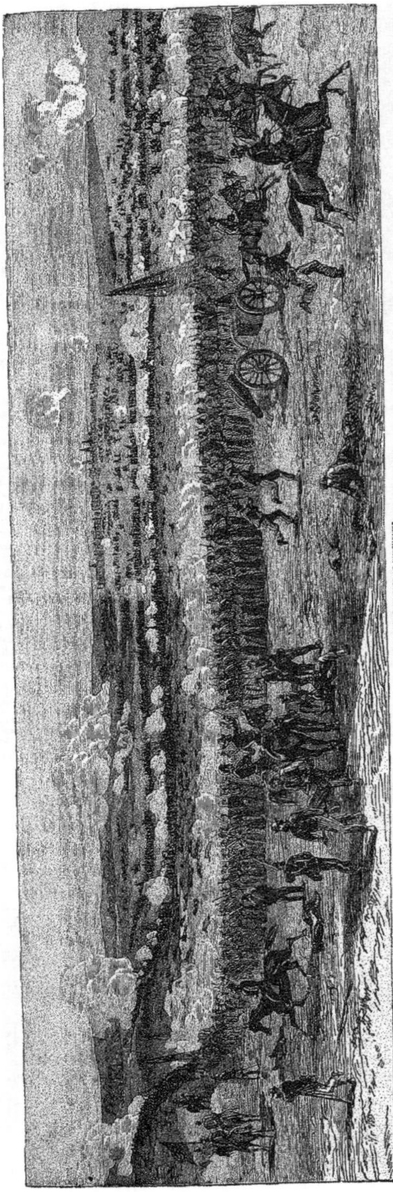

THE CONFEDERATE ROUT AT WINCHESTER.

the Opequan, by the Confederates that of Winchester. As it happened, however, Early marched only half way to Martinsburg, and was able to bring his whole force upon the field. Before dawn of the 19th Sheridan was in motion. Torbert's cavalry, in front, was to cross the Opequan, and clear the passage of the stream in one direction. Wilson, supported by the Sixth and Nineteenth Corps, was to move rapidly down the defile through which ran the direct road from Berryville, and thus fall upon the portion of the enemy lying directly in front of Winchester, Crooks's corps being held in reserve. Wilson charged into the deep gorge, drove back the enemy's pickets, and captured the earthworks at its mouth. Wright and Emory defiled through the narrow gorge, and emerged, under a heavy artillery fire, into an irregular undulating valley, dotted over with ledges of rock and patches of wood, sloping gradually up to the semicircular heights of Winchester. Time was lost in making these movements, and it was nine o'clock before the order to advance was given. The attack and defense were alike obstinate, and, neither being sheltered except by the natural cover afforded by the formation of the ground, the loss on both sides was heavy. Ramseur, upon whom the attack first fell, held his ground stoutly for two hours. But the whole of Wright's and Emory's corps having at length passed through the gorge, he began to give way. At this moment Rodes came back from the direction of Martinsburg and joined in the fight. Rodes was shot dead, the centre of Early's first line was broken, and the Federals rushed on. They now encountered Gordon, who had followed hard after Wharton. The advance was checked, and then Gordon made a countercharge, which, striking Sheridan's centre, where the Sixth and Nineteenth Corps joined, forced it back in confusion, which threatened to become a total rout. Gordon pushed on in pursuit so fiercely that his flank was exposed to Russell's brigade, of the Sixth, which was on the left. He was in turn driven back, and Sheridan's line was soon re-established, most of the two or three thousand men who had gone to the rear being brought back.

Still the battle hung in even scales. Breckinridge, with the last of the cavalry, the last of Early's absent men, now came up from the rear, and took position on the Confederate left. Now ensued the fiercest fighting of the day. Early sought to extend his left so as to outflank Sheridan's right; then, sweeping round, to seize the mouth of the narrow gorge and cut off the retreat. Sheridan's quick eye perceived that his opportunity had now come. Crook's corps had not yet been brought into action. He had kept them in reserve upon his right, intending also to turn the enemy's left and cut off his retreat. Crook was now directed to the left, turn the Confederate right, strike it in flank and rear, and, as soon as it was broken, the Federal left should swing round and strike on the other flank. Both movements were made with the utmost precision. On what was now the decisive point the Federals were in great preponderance. They fairly overlapped the Confederates, who were powerless to prevent the turning of their flank. Crook's line swept steadily on over the open fields in the face of a fierce musketry fire, under which 900 men went down in a few minutes. Emory's corps now sprung from the ground where they had been lying to shelter themselves from the artillery, by which they had for three hours been sorely pelted, poured in a fire so rapid that in five minutes their ammunition was exhausted, and then dashed straight upon a patch of woodland where was the extreme left of the Confederate line, into the other side of which Crook was already pouring. The enemy rushed out in utter rout, many of them in their flight throwing away their guns and accoutrements.

The battle was irretrievably lost. To hold this wood Early had brought in his last two divisions, those of Breckinridge. These divisions had all the morning, and until far in the afternoon, held in check Merritt's and Torbert's cavalry. These magnificent horsemen had then pressed up, sweeping before them the Confederate cavalry, and circling round to the Confederate flank and rear. They charged fiercely upon the disorganized mass, which broke and fled in confusion back to Winchester. The fragments of the routed army entered the town as night was falling. But here was no rest. In the darkness they kept on their flight, only halting until they reached Fisher's Hill, a strong position eight miles south of Winchester, and twelve from the battle-field. It had been a well-fought action, and decisive, won indeed by superior force, but with equal bravery. Sheridan's losses summed up 4990, of whom 653 were killed, 3719 wounded, and 618 missing. The heaviest loss, 1956, fell upon Emory's corps, among whom were 450 missing, captured when they were repulsed early in the day. In Wright's corps there were 1687 killed and wounded, and 48 missing. In Crook's corps, which struck the final decisive blow, out of a total loss of 953, there were but 8 missing. The cavalry lost 441, of whom 109 were missing. The Confederate loss is not stated, but in all it could not have been less than 6000. Upon the field and in the pursuit 2500 prisoners were taken; 2000 wounded were found in the hospitals at Winchester.

On the next morning Sheridan set out in pursuit, and soon came in front of the position which Early had taken up at Fisher's Hill. Here the valley is split by an intervening ridge, the main branch contracting to the breadth of three and a half miles, overhung on each side by precipitous bluffs. Early had availed himself of the brief respite to throw up breastworks across the valley. Here he thought himself secure, for it was a position which could be held against a direct assault from a fivefold force. So safe did Early think himself that his ammunition-boxes were taken from the caissons and placed behind the breastworks. Sheridan determined to drive him out of his position by turning his left. To do this, the turning force must gain the summit of the North Mountain, and, marching for a space along the crest, plunge down into the valley. The movement must be made by night, for from a signal station the enemy could observe every movement made by daylight.

GEORGE CROOK.

Crook's corps was at night placed in a mass of wood, where they lay hidden all through the 21st, while Wright's and Emory's corps were drawn up in front of the Confederate centre, ready to join in the assault. Crook made his movement without being perceived. Noon had passed before be. was in position. Sheridan then, posting Ricketts in front of the Confederate left, sent Averill, with his cavalry, to drive in the enemy's skirmish line. The movement succeeded beyond expectation. It was reported from the Confederate signal station that a turning column was moving against their left front. Early massed his force to check this. At that moment Crook burst in upon his rear. The Confederates broke and fled after some show of resistance in front, and Wright's corps, swinging round, joined with Crook's.

The victory was complete, and won at little cost—not 300 in all, of whom 237 were in Wright's corps, and 60 in Emory's. Crook, whose mere presence in position won the fight, appears not to have lost a man. The Confederate loss in killed and wounded was not much greater; but they left behind them 1100 prisoners. Complete as was the success, Sheridan had expected to render it still more decisive. He had hoped to capture Early's whole army. For this purpose he had sent Torbert down the parallel Luray Valley, whence it was to cross over into that of the Shenandoah, and intercept the enemy's retreat. But Torbert was held in check at a narrow gorge by the Confederate cavalry and a small body of infantry until the fugitives had passed the point.

It was almost dark when the fight at Fisher's Hill was begun. The remnants of Early's broken divisions fled rapidly down the Valley, hardly a company preserving its organization. Sheridan pushed on the pursuit for a day and night as rapidly as possible, but the fugitives were too fleet for the infantry, and there was present of cavalry only Devins's small division, for Torbert was in Luray Valley, on the opposite side of the dividing range, and Averill had unaccountably gone into camp immediately after the fight. On the morning of the 23d Devins came up with the enemy's rear at Mount Jackson, twenty-five miles from Fisher's Hill. Here, not in sufficient force to attack, he waited for Averill, who arrived late in the afternoon, and then fell back again. Averill was here superseded by Powell. Early's divisions kept on their flight by different routes until they reached New Market, where several roads converge. Here the shattered force got itself partly reorganized, but kept on its retreat, now presenting a line of battle too strong for the cavalry to assail. The Federal infantry pushed on in columns, but were unable to bring on an action. Torbert, in the mean time, had beaten the enemy in Luray Valley; and on the 25th Wright's and Emory's corps had reached Harrisburg, Crook's having been left a little behind until the movements of Early were ascertained. Kershaw, with his fresh division, now rejoined Early, and the Confederates, nearly as strong as they had been at the Opequan, made a show of advancing.

Sheridan was now in doubt what course to pursue—whether to again assault or to fall back. He finally decided on the latter course. He was little, if any, superior to the enemy; his transportation would not keep him in supplies for a much farther advance; and, moreover, it was by no means sure that Grant would be able to hold the entire Confederate force in the lines at Petersburg. Lee might secretly detach a sufficient number, which, moving rapidly by rail, could overwhelm him, and then return before their absence should be perceived. He had, moreover, in a week, accomplished more than he had dared to count upon. He had destroyed or captured half of Early's army, and driven the remainder so far to the south that it no longer threatened Maryland and Pennsylvania. He therefore determined to terminate the active campaign and return northward. But on the way back he was to carry out his original instructions to devastate the valley which had so long served as a granary for the Confederate army and an avenue for an invading force. This done, he could give back to Grant at Petersburg the bulk of the infantry which had been sent to check the diversion made by Lee. The plan was carried out, but not for three weeks, and after Early had once more staked all in a desperate venture and lost.

On the 6th of October Sheridan commenced his return march. The cavalry swept across the whole breadth of the valley of the Shenandoah from the Blue Ridge to the eastern slope of the Alleghanies. The order to transform the valley into a barren waste, with nothing which should tempt the enemy to return, was carried out with unsparing severity. Before the army was a fertile region filled with the stores of an abundant harvest just gathered in; behind was a desert and devastated region. Sheridan himself shall describe his work of destruction: "In moving back to Woodstock, the whole country from the Blue Ridge to the North Mountain has been rendered untenable for a rebel army. I have destroyed over two thousand barns filled with wheat, and hay, and farming implements; over seventy mills filled with flour and wheat; have driven in front of the army over four thousand head of stock, and have killed and issued to the troops not less than three thousand sheep. This destruction embraces the Luray Valley and the Little Fort Valley, as well as the main valley; a large number of horses has also been obtained." This was the work of but two days. Dwelling-houses were indeed spared save in a single retributive case. One of the Union engineer officers was murdered, and for this act all the houses within an area of five miles were burned.

It is hard, in the midst of peace, to decide where the military right of destruction and retribution begins and ends. Early, in retreating from Maryland, had seized more cattle and horses than Sheridan took in the valley. The numerous guerrilla parties who had made the Valley their lair plundered at will. "Since I came in the valley," continues Sheridan, "every train, every small party has been bushwhacked by the people, many of whom have protection papers from commanders who have hitherto been in the valley." Sheridan spared dwellings, although the ruins of Chambersburg, fired without pretence of military necessity, had hardly ceased to smoke. But this devastation only partly accomplished its purpose. The valley was not rendered untenable to a Confederate force until a fortnight later, when the army there ceased to exist.

The Confederate cavalry followed Sheridan's return at a distance, and at length came into conflict with Torbert's division, by whom they were defeated; and when, four days after the commencement of the return march, Sheridan, passing Fisher's Mountain, took up his post four miles beyond, Early, strengthened by Kershaw, was close behind. Here he suffered the final crushing defeat which put an end to the war in the valley of the Shenandoah.

On the 15th of October, Sheridan, having posted his army at Cedar Creek, set out for Washington to consult with the Secretary of War as to the route by which Wright's corps should be sent back to Petersburg. He had just started on the journey when he received a message from Wright, who was left in command, inclosing a dispatch deciphered from the enemy's signal-flag. It purported to be from Longstreet to Early, and read, "Be ready to move as soon as my forces join you, and we will crush Sheridan." Suspecting it to be, as it undoubtedly was, a ruse, Sheridan sent back word to Wright, "If Longstreet's dispatch be true, he is under the impression that we have largely detached. If the enemy should make an advance, I know that you will defeat him. Look well to your ground, and be well prepared."

On the night of the 18th of October the Federal army lay encamped in a position apparently unassailable. It was disposed upon three parallel ridges of no great height, facing southward. To the west, four miles away, lay Early in unknown force at the wooded base of Fisher's Hill. The left of the Union army—the corps farthest from the Confederate position—was occupied by Crook. At the foot of this crest ran a deep valley. Next, and half a mile in the rear, across the turnpike, and to the right, was Emory. Then, somewhat farther to the right, and considerably in the rear of all, was Wright. From the extreme right to the extreme left was a space of three miles, and still farther to the right was Torbert's cavalry. The fronts and flanks of Crook and Wright were protected by breastworks and batteries. The position, unless turned by surprise and taken in the rear, was impregnable to any force which the enemy could by any possibility have. Early resolved to turn both flanks by surprise. The march toward Emory upon the right flank presented no great natural difficulty; but to reach the left flank the assailants had to descend a rugged gorge so steep that a man must here and there support himself by holding fast upon the bushes, then wade the Shenandoah, recross it again, enter the Valley, skirting Crook's front, and go up it for three miles, moving scarcely four hundred yards from the picket-line. If we may credit Early's express averment, he had an effective force of less than 10,000 men of all arms. This was hardly half the number that was to be opposed to him; of this, however, he was not aware; for he supposed that a considerable portion of Sheridan's army was miles away, at Front Royal, where he knew them to have been a few days before, or still farther away on the way to Washington.

Early commenced his march at midnight. His left column, with the artillery and cavalry, moved over easy ground, and at dawn began to demonstrate against Emory. Meanwhile the other column, consisting of the divisions of Gordon, Ramseur, Pegram, Kershaw, and Wharton, the remnants of those who had just a month before fled in rout from the Opequan and Fish-

ALFRED TORBERT.

r's Hill, moved silently down the mountain slope, forded the Rappahannock, nd crept stealthily along Crook's front. So imperative was the necessity or silence that they had left their canteens behind, lest their rattling should etray them. Before dawn they had pursued their dark-long march of seven niles. These three divisions passed beyond Crook's left flank, and turned it rithout having been perceived, and were fairly within striking distance of is rear, while the other two crouched in his front. Once, indeed, the pickets eported that they had heard a suspicious rustling, and a part of the front ne was sent into the trenches; but, so little was danger apprehended, that nany went in with unloaded muskets. The gaps left in the line were not lled, and no reconnoissance was made. There was just then a slight stir in Emory's camp, for he was to send out a reconnoissance at daybreak toward Fisher's Hill. His aid was in the saddle, ready to report the exact time vhen the troops moved. The gray dawn was just breaking through a dense nist which shrouded mountain and valley when this impatient aid heard far o the left a sudden sharp rattle of musketry, and the fierce yell which de. oted a Confederate charge.[1] The five divisions had broken on front, flank, nd rear, through the lines of the sleeping Eighth Corps. In fifteen minutes t was perfectly routed and streaming back in confusion upon the Nineteenth, ts guns being captured and turned upon the fugitives. Simultaneously a risk artillery fire, with demonstrations of cavalry, was opened upon Emory's ight; while his front and left flank were assailed as Crook's had been, and he enemy were already sweeping around his rear. The Nineteenth Corps vas now fighting the whole Confederate force. Desperate, but brief and un. vailing efforts were made to hold their lines until the Sixth Corps could ome up; but from point to point they were driven back before the furious ush of Kershaw in front, while Gordon and Ramseur poured in a fire upon heir left flank. The camps of the Eighth and Nineteenth Corps were now n possession of the Confederates, and what remained of these corps were nushed back upon the Sixth, which alone maintained the fight. This also ell back, but slowly and in order, from one position to another, until at ength, after three miles of retreat, it had fairly outstripped Gordon, and stood vith its left flank free from his pertinacious assault. Here at last they held ast, and awaited the attack. The assailants had now exhausted their im. oulse. Most of them, weary and hungry, scattered through the captured amps, eager for food and plunder; only a distant artillery fire was kept up. Wright fell back undisturbed a little farther to a position where he could cover the high road to Winchester, and began, at nine o'clock, to form his broken lines. He had been beaten, but was not routed, and now stood pre. pared to repel any farther attack.

Sheridan, in the mean while, was on his way back from Washington. He had slept that night at Winchester. At seven in the morning a picket here reported that he had heard artillery firing; but Sheridan, supposing hat it proceeded from the reconnoissance which he had ordered that morn. ng, gave little heed. He rode leisurely on until nine o'clock, when, a mile and a half beyond the town, the head of the foremost fugitives appeared in sight—men and trains rushing to the rear with a rapidity which betokened a great disaster. There happened to be a brigade at Winchester. Stopping briefly to halt the trains and draw out this brigade to stem the flight, Sheri. dan pushed rapidly on, and soon approached the front. His very presence stayed the flight of the fugitives, who were running from they knew not what. "Face about!" he shouted; "we're going back to our camps! We're going to lick them out of their boots!" Hundreds turned and followed his black steed. He found Getty—the same who had held the road in the Wil. derness—far in front of the remainder of the line of the Sixth Corps, con. fronting the enemy, and momentarily expecting an attack. The other divi. sions of Wright and Emory were brought forward, and soon were ready for the enemy.

Two hours and more passed. Then Early pushed a column toward Em. ory. No sooner was it within range than a single volley sent it whirling back, and Sheridan was about to order an advance, when word came to him from the cavalry far off to the left that a fresh infantry column of Confeder. ates were pressing toward Winchester to gain his rear. The report was erroneous, but it delayed the order to advance. At four o'clock the order came. Early had now thrown up breastworks and taken strong positions under cover of stone fences. For a space he fought bravely, and gave way slowly and sullenly, but surely. Once, indeed, by a flank movement, he wheeled Gordon's division around Emory's right, and threw it into some confusion; but the movement was a fatal one. McMillan's brigade dashed into the angle thus formed in the Confederate line, pressed through, and cut off the turning column, upon which Custer's cavalry charged. At the same moment the whole Union line rushed forward, and swept the enemy before them. Gordon first broke, then Kershaw, then Ramseur, and all rushed in wild tumult down the turnpike which led to their position at Fisher's Hill, charged by cavalry on both flanks, and pressed by infantry in the centre. The fugitives outran their foot-pursuers, who, weary and thirsty, toiled after them. But the swift cavalry were on their heels. At the crossing of Cedar Creek Custer and Devin charged the train without provoking a shot. A lit. tle farther on was another bridge; this broke down, and the whole train, guns and wagons, was abandoned. At length, once more behind the lines at Fisher's Hill, which cavalry could not pass, Early had a brief respite; but in the darkness the whole crowd rushed on, never halting for thirty miles. There was no need for pursuit the next day. So utterly destroyed was Early's army that there was nothing worth chasing.

With this battle ended the fighting in the Valley of the Shenandoah. The remnant of Early's force rejoined Lee, by swift marches, at Petersburg, only enough of his own three divisions being left in the valley to form one small division. Early put forth a bitter address to his troops. After re. counting the brilliant success of the morning, he added: "I have the mor. tification of announcing to you that, by your subsequent misconduct, all the benefits of that victory were lost, and a serious disaster incurred. Many of you, including some commissioned officers, yielding to a disgraceful propen. sity to plunder, deserted your colors to appropriate the abandoned property of the enemy; and subsequently those who had previously remained at their posts, seeing their ranks thinned by the absence of the plunderers, when the enemy, late in the afternoon, with his shattered columns, made but a feeble effort to retrieve the failures of the day, yielded to a needless panic, and fled the field in confusion."

The defeat was indeed as total as "Lee's bad old man" represented it; but the reproach was undeserved. The troops had fought themselves out in the morning. The victory was won by surprise against superior numbers. The surprise was over in the afternoon, and the numbers were still largely against them,[1] while the advantage of position was not great. Early appears once more for a moment in the history of the war, when, four months after, a little band of 1500 men whom he had gathered was rode over and captured almost to a man by a single division of Sheridan's cavalry.

The Federal victory was complete and absolute, but it was purchased at a heavy cost. The losses numbered 5990, of whom 1890 were missing, mostly prisoners, more than a third of them from Crook's corps, captured in the surprise. This corps lost but 65 killed, while it had 654 missing. Early's loss was barely half as great. There were 1500 prisoners, and prob. ably about as many killed and wounded, nearly all in the final fight in the afternoon. He lost also 30 guns, all that he brought into action, besides 16 which he had captured in the morning.

Sheridan's decisive campaign in the Valley was comprised within just a month, counting from the time when he commenced direct offensive opera. tions. In that month he completely annihilated his opponent, capturing ful. ly 13,000 prisoners, and killing and wounding quite 10,000. His own losses in killed and wounded indeed were greater. Including the three great bat. tles and about thirty skirmishes, which mainly took place in the six weeks while he was watching the enemy, preparatory to striking, they amounted to 13,831; the missing 3121—a total loss of 16,952; of whom 11,327 were in the great battles, and 5625 in minor engagements.[2]

[1] A graphic account of this battle, by Captain De Forest, the aid in question, is given in *Harper's Magazine* for February, 1865.

[1] I accept Early's statement of his force as an approximation to the truth. I do not think it possible that his force exceeded 12,000 infantry, although many endeavor to make it twice as great. To do this, they speak of a re-enforcement of 12,000 or 16,000 of Longstreet's corps, received the day before the battle. Of these I can find no credible information. I find with Early only that half of his army which had escaped from the Opequah and Fisher's Hill—say not more than 8000 men, and Kershaw's one division of probably 4000. Pollard says definitely 2750 muskets—shy 3000 men.

[2] The following is a summary of the losses of Sheridan during his whole campaign in the Shen. andoah Valley, from August 7 to October 19:

Battle of the Opequan	5,015	Battle of Cedar Creek	5,995
Battle of Fisher's Hill	207	Minor Engagements	5,625
			16,952

. The Confederate loss in prisoners is officially given. Of the killed and wounded we can only conjecture.

APPROACHES TO SAVANNAH.

CHAPTER LI.

SHERMAN'S CAMPAIGN.—THE CAROLINA MARCH.

:o between Grant and Sherman.—The Idea of transporting Sherman's Army to Vir- a abandoned.—Sherman's Preparations for a March through the Carolinas.—Civil tion at Savannah.—Trade Regulations.—Sherman's Orders respecting Freedmen.— for the Government of Savannah.—Cotton taken as a Prize of War.—Howard's on Pocotaligo.—A Flood in the Savannah River impedes Slocum's Operations.— of the Carolina March with that from Atlanta to Savannah.—Sherman's Acquaint- he Country.—Feint Movement on Charleston.—Crossing of the Salkehatchie.—De- f the Railroad connecting Augusta with Charleston.—Crossing of the South Edisto. declines Wheeler's Cotton Compromise.—Union of the two Wings south of the Con- pture of Columbia.—Explanation of the Burning of Columbia.—Occupation of igh.—Crossing of the Catawba.—Sherman retaliates for the Murder of his Fora- :espondence with Wheeler on this Subject.—Occupation of Cheraw.—Charleston —Affair between Kilpatrick and Wade Hampton.—Sherman's Army at Fayetteville, e Fear River.—Concentration of the Enemy's Forces under Johnston.—Sherman tes with Terry and Schofield.—Crossing of the Cape Fear.—Battle of Averys- Battle of Bentonville.—Sherman, re-enforced by Terry and Schofield, concentrates t Goldsborough, and establishes Communications with Newbern and Morehead City.

N General Sherman, after the capture of Fort McAllister, passed vn the Ogeechee into Ossibaw Sound, and to the flag-ship of Ad- lgren, he found two communications waiting him from Lieutenant rant. When these were written Sherman was still marching eorgia, and had not "struck bottom." But they express no fear ultimate success of the extraordinary campaign which Sherman taken. The second of these communications, of date December ted Grant's intention to transport Sherman's army, after it had l a base on the coast, to the James River, to co-operate in the cam- inst Lee.[1]

n, although his original plan had contemplated a continuation of through the Carolinas to Virginia,[2] immediately set out to obey rant's instructions. In the delay incident to the transportation y he determined to capture Savannah. As we have seen, he ac- dict the issue of a movement which was almost universally considered too bold to rank among the legitimate ventures of war; and now, suddenly, out of this ominous silence arose a universal shout at once of triumph and of praise to the victor, who had been no less signally crowned by his own success at Savannah than by that of his subordinate at Nashville, 657 miles away.[1] General Grant, even before the capture of Savannah, congratulated General Sherman and his army upon the successful termination of his "brilliant campaign." It is true, he had heard of Hood's defeat; but he says, "I never had a doubt of the result. When apprehensions for your safety were expressed by the President, I assured him, with the army you had, and you in command of it, there was no danger but you would strike bottom on salt water some place; that I would not feel the same security, in fact would not have intrusted the expedition to any other living commander." On the 26th, in answer to Sherman's note presenting him with Savannah as a Christmas gift, President Lincoln replied:

"MY DEAR GENERAL SHERMAN,—Many, many thanks for your Christmas gift. When you were about leaving Atlanta for the Atlantic coast, I was anxious, if not fearful; but, feeling that you were the better judge, and remembering that 'nothing risked, nothing gained,' I did not interfere. Now, the undertaking being a success, the honor is all yours; for I believe none of us went farther than to acquiesce. And, taking the work of General Thomas into the count, as it should be taken, it is indeed a great success. Not only does it afford the obvious and immediate military advantages, but, in showing the world that your army could be divided, putting the stronger part to an immediate new service, and yet leaving enough to vanquish the old opposing force of the whole—Hood's army—it brings those who sat in darkness to see a great light. But what next? I suppose it will be safer to leave General Grant and yourself to decide."[2]

General Grant, after Thomas's victory at Nashville, was shaken in his determination to transport Sherman's army by sea to the James River. It would be impossible to effect this in less than two months, and in that time Sherman could make the march by land, and in doing so strike the enemy a far heavier blow. He writes on the 18th of December: "If you capture the garrison of Savannah, it will certainly compel Lee to detach from Richmond, or give us nearly the whole South. My own opinion is, Lee is averse to going out of Virginia; and, if the cause of the South is lost, he wants Richmond to be the last place surrendered. If he has such views, it may be well to indulge him until we get every thing else in our hands." General Sherman was delighted at the modification of Grant's plan, as he would thus be permitted to carry out his original scheme of a march through the Carolinas.[3]

---

owing are copies of both these letters. The first, from City Point, Virginia, Decem- thus:

e information gleaned from the Southern press indicating no great obstacle to your we directed your mails, which previously had been collected in Baltimore by Colonel ecial agent of the Post-office Department, to be sent as far as the blockading squadron , to be forwarded to you as soon as heard from on the coast. Not liking to rejoice ictory is assured, I abstain from congratulating you and those under your command has been struck. I have never had a fear, however, as to the result.

a left Atlanta no great progress has been made here. The enemy has been closely watch- nd prevented from detaching against you. I think not one man has gone from here 1200 or 1500 dismounted cavalry. Bragg has gone from Wilmington. I am trying ntage of his absence to get possession of that place. Owing to some preparations Ad- and General Butler are making to blow up Fort Fisher, and which, while I hope for not believe a particle in, there is a delay in getting this expedition off. I hope they to start by the 7th, and that Bragg will not have started back by that time.

etter I do not intend to give you any thing like directions for future action, but will al idea I have, and will get your views after you have established yourself on the sea- your veteran army I hope to get control of the only two through routes, from east to ed by the enemy, before the fall of Atlanta. This condition will be filled by holding d Augusta, or by holding any other post to the east of Savannah and Branchville. If falls, a force from there can co-operate with you.

has got back into the defenses of Nashville, with Hood close upon him. Decatur has ned, and so have all the roads, except the main one leading to Chattanooga. I hope badly crippled or destroyed. After all becomes quiet, and the roads up here are so re is likely to be a week or two that nothing can be done, I will run down the coast

he writes again:

ction, since sending my letter by Lieutenant Dunn, I have concluded that the most eration toward closing out the rebellion will be to close out Lee and his army. You

[1] That General Sherman looked upon the defeat of Hood by Thomas as necessary to justify his march is evident from the following letter, written by him to General J. D. Webster (at Nashville), December 23:

"Major Dixon arrived last night, bringing your letter of the 10th of December, for which I am very much obliged, as it gives me a clear and distinct view of the situation of affairs at Nashville up to that date. I have also from the War Department a copy of General Thomas's dispatch, giving an account of the attack on Hood on the 15th, which was successful, but not complete. I await farther accounts with anxiety, as Thomas's complete success is necessary to vindicate my plans for this campaign, and I have no doubt that my calculations that Thomas had in hand (including A. J. Smith's troops) a force large enough to whip Hood in fair fight were correct. I approve of Thomas's allowing Hood to come north far enough to enable him to concentrate his own men, though I would have preferred that Hood should have been checked about Columbia. Still, if Thomas followed up his success on the 15th, and gave Hood a good whaling, and is at this moment following him closely, the whole campaign in my division will be even more perfect than the Atlanta campaign, for at this end of the line I have realized all I had reason to hope for except in the release of our prisoners, which was simply an impossibility."

[2] General Sherman's reply to this is equally characteristic. Writing January 6th, he says: "I am gratified at the receipt of your letter of December 26th at the hands of General Logan, especially to observe that you appreciate the division I made of my army, and that each part was duly proportioned to its work.

"The motto, 'Nothing venture, nothing win,' which you refer to, is appropriate; and, should I venture too much and happen to lose, I shall bespeak your charitable inference.

"I am ready for the 'great next' as soon as I can complete certain preliminaries, and learn of General Grant his and your preferences of intermediate 'objectives.'"

[3] He replies to General Grant, December 24: "I am gratified that you have modified your former orders, as I feared that the transportation by sea would very much disturb the unity and

General Grant fully sanctioned Sherman's scheme before the close of 1864. There was nearly a month's delay at Savannah. This time was occupied in gathering supplies, in disposing of captured property, and in local administration. The march through Georgia had already led to some important political results in that state. In Liberty and Tatnall counties, south of Savannah, Union meetings were held by the citizens, and patriotic resolutions were adopted. Sherman recognized the movement, and promised his aid, encouragement, and defense to all citizens who would "stay quietly at home, and call back their sons and neighbors to resume their peaceful pursuits." He invited all such to bring their produce to Savannah, to be sold to the highest bidder or to his commissary. Merchants and attorneys in Savannah were required to acknowledge the national supremacy in order to the continuance of their avocations. But, in Sherman's judgment, all matters relating to reconstruction in Georgia were of secondary importance until the final victory of the nation should be secured.

Sherman caused a thorough examination to be made of the defenses of Savannah, which city was now to become an important dépôt of supplies. New lines of fortification were constructed, "embracing the city proper, Forts Jackson, Thunderbolt, and Pulaski, with slight modifications in their

FORT THUNDERBOLT, SAVANNAH.

armament and rear defenses." The other forts were dismantled, and their heavy ordnance transferred to Hilton Head. The obstructions in the river were with great difficulty removed, as also the torpedoes in the channels

Charleston and taking Wilmington, I would then favor a movement direct on Raleigh. The game is then up with Lee, unless he comes out of Richmond, avoids you and fights me, in which case I should reckon on your being on his heels.

"Now that Hood is used up by Thomas, I feel disposed to bring the matter to an issue as quick as possible. I feel confident that I can break up the whole railroad system of South Carolina and North Carolina, and be on the Roanoke, either at Raleigh or Weldon, by the time spring fairly opens; and if you feel confident that you can whip Lee outside of his intrenchments, I feel equally confident that I can handle him in the open country.

"One reason why I should ignore Charleston is this: That I believe they will reduce the garrison to a small force, with plenty of provisions, and I know that the neck back of Charleston can be made impregnable to assault, and we will hardly have time for siege operations.

"I will have to leave in Savannah a garrison, and, if Thomas can spare them, I would like to have all detachments, convalescents, etc., belonging to these four corps, sent forward at once. I don't want to cripple Thomas, because I regard his operations as all-important, and I have ordered him to pursue Hood down into Alabama, trusting to the country for supplies.

"I reviewed one of my corps to-day, and shall continue to review the whole army. I don't like to boast, but I believe this army has a confidence in itself that makes it almost invincible."

Grant replied on the 27th of December, giving Sherman permission to follow out his plan, and making some suggestions. He says:

"Your confidence in being able to march up and join this army pleases me, and I believe it can be done. The effect of such a campaign will be to disorganize the South, and prevent the organization of new armies from their broken fragments. Hood is now retreating, with his army broken and demoralized. His loss in men has probably not been far from 20,000, besides deserters. If time is given, the fragments may be collected together, and many of the deserters reassembled. If we can we should act to prevent this. Your spare army, as it were, moving as proposed, will do this.

"In addition to holding Savannah, it looks to me that an intrenched camp ought to be held on the railroad between Savannah and Charleston. Your movements toward Branchville will probably enable Foster to reach this with his own force. This will give us a position in the South from which we can threaten the interior without marching over long, narrow causeways, easily defended, as we have heretofore been compelled to do. Could not such a camp be established about Pocotaligo or Coosawatchie?

"I have thought that, Hood being so completely wiped out for all present harm, I might bring A. J. Smith with from 10,000 to 15,000. With this increase I could hold my lines, and move out with greater force than Lee has. It would compel him to retain all his present force in the defenses of Richmond, or abandon them entirely. The latter contingency is probably the only danger to the easy success of your expedition. In the event you should meet Lee's army, you would be compelled to beat it or find the sea-coast. Of course I shall not let Lee's army escape if I can help it, and will not let it go without following it to the best of my ability.

"Without waiting farther directions, then, you may make preparations to start on your Northern expedition without delay. Break up the railroads in South and North Carolina, and join the armies operating against Richmond as soon as you can.

"I will leave out all suggestions about the route you should take, knowing that your information, gained daily in the progress of events, will be better than any that can be obtained now. It may not be possible for you to march to the rear of Petersburg; but, failing in this, you could

below the city. General Geary
His policy, just but conciliatory, h
R. D. Arnold, continued in the ex
to yield a ready obedience to the
resentative. A public meeting w
adopted, and Governor Brown wa
toration of Georgia to the Union.
city enjoyed undisturbed tranquil
eral Sherman issued orders regula
the citizens to bring their produce
discussion of their present situati
the national army.[1]

Nor did General Sherman forg
Secretary Stanton, who visited Sa
orders devoting the abandoned
fields along the rivers of Georgia
exclusive use and management,
authority and the acts of Congr
promulgated regulations for the

[1] The following is a copy of these orders
"It being represented that the Confedera
under the authority of the Confederate go
deavoring to intimidate them in the efforts
ing, security to life and property, and the
is hereby ordered and made public:
"I. That the farmers of Georgia may bri
marketing, such as beef, pork, mutton, vege
quantities, and sell the same in open mark
the treasury agents, and may invest the pr
reasonable quantities, groceries, shoes, and
the same back to their families. No trad
goods sold for them, but families may club
and going.
"II. The people are encouraged to mee
looking to their safety and good governme
and will be protected by the national army
isfy the commanding officers that they ar
undisturbed in property and person, but m
military operations. If any farmer or peac
federate army of guerrillas, because of his
if caught, will be summarily punished, or
crime can not be traced to the actual party
cause of the rebellion. Should a Union ma
or if a Union family be persecuted on acc
foreign land. In aggravated cases, retaliat
ing officers will act promptly in such cases,

[2] The following are the orders:
"I. The islands from Charleston south
miles back from the sea, and the country b
set apart for the settlement of the negroes
of the President of the United States.
"II. At Beaufort, Hilton Head, Savan
blacks may remain in their chosen or accu
ments hereafter to be established, no whit
detailed for duty, will be permitted to resid
be left to the freed people themselves, sub
acts of Congress. By the laws of war and
is free, and must be dealt with as such.
military service, save by the written orde
under such regulations as the President
smiths, carpenters, and other mechanics w
the young and able-bodied negroes must
United States, to contribute their share to
rights as citizens of the United States.
"Negroes so enlisted will be organized
ders of the United States military authorit
The bounties paid on enlistment may, wi
settlement in procuring agricultural imple
essary for their livelihood.
"III. Whenever three respectable neg
shall have selected for that purpose an isl
designated, the inspector of settlements an
as he may appoint, give them a license to
ance as he can to enable them to establis
named will subdivide the land, under the
others as may choose to settle near them
forty acres of tillable ground, and, when
eight hundred feet water-front, in the pos
them protection until such time as they
their title.
"The quartermaster may, on the req
place at the disposal of the inspector one
tlements and one or more of the commer
tlers the opportunity to supply their nec
labor.
"IV. Whenever a negro has enlisted i
his family in any one of the settlements
and privileges of a settler as though pres
"In like manner, negroes may settle
fishing, or in the navigation of the inland
tages derived from this system. But no
absent on government service, will be ent
ment by virtue of these orders.
"V. In order to carry out this system
or of settlements and plantations, whose
police and general management, and wh
to the approval of the President of the U
as possible, the description of boundarie
arise under the same, subject to the lik
The same general officer will also be char
cruits, and protecting their interests wh
the rules and regulations prescribed by t

[3] Of which the following is a copy:
"The city of Savannah and surroundi
future military uses, but, as it contains
provided for, and as other citizens may
that all within its military jurisdiction m
"I. During war, the military is supe
must give way; yet, where there is no
posed and peaceful inhabitants to resum
little as possible in their residences, and
Churches, schools, all places of amuseme
roads made perfectly safe to persons in t
the line of outer pickets; but if any pers

ders regulating trade he had excluded cotton from ordinary commerce, holding this staple to be a legitimate prize of war, and the property of the United States.[1] These trade regulations included within their scope the whole Department of the South, which, though still under the immediate command of General Foster, was now subordinate to General Sherman.

By the 19th of January Sherman was ready to move. Grover's division of the Nineteenth Corps had been withdrawn from Sheridan's Army of the Shenandoah to Savannah, relieving Geary's division, and forming thereafter a part of General Foster's command. General Schofield, with the Twenty-third Corps, had been transferred from the West to re-enforce Generals Terry

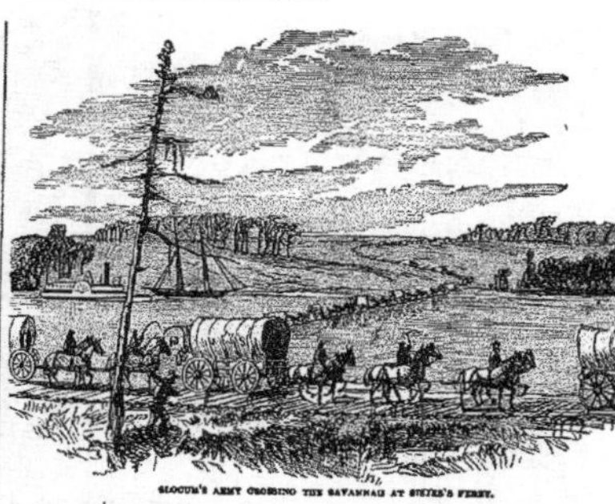

SLOCUM'S ARMY CROSSING THE SAVANNAH AT SISTER'S FERRY.

and Palmer, who were operating on the coast of North Carolina, and preparing the way for General Sherman's arrival. On the 24th of December an unsuccessful attack had been made on Fort Fisher, at the mouth of Cape Fear River, by Admiral Porter. The failure of the expedition was due to a want of proper management on the part of General Butler, the military commander. On the 15th of January the attack was renewed, General Butler being replaced by General Terry, and was successful. The remaining works of the enemy at the mouth of the Cape Fear soon followed the fate of Fort Fisher. This victory was auspicious for Sherman, who was then setting out upon his northward march.

General Howard was ordered to effect a lodgment on the Savannah and Charleston Railroad, at Pocotaligo. He embarked with the Seventeenth Corps at Thunderbolt, and proceeded to Beaufort, and there landing his troops, succeeded in reaching Pocotaligo Station. Leggett's division dislodged the enemy, and a secure dépôt for supplies was established at the mouth of Pocotaligo Creek, within easy communication by Broad River with Hilton Head. Three divisions of Logan's corps (the Fifteenth) followed Blair; but Corse's division was cut off by the freshets, and compelled to move with the left wing.

Slocum, with the left wing and Kilpatrick's cavalry, was ordered to move directly across the Savannah River up to Coosawatchie, on the Charleston Road, and to Robertsville, on the road to Columbia. He had established a good pontoon bridge across the river opposite the city, and the Union causeway, over which Hardee had retreated a month before, had been repaired and corduroyed; but before the time appointed for his march the heavy rains of January had swollen the river, swept away the bridge, and overflowed the whole bottom, so that the causeway was four feet under

be had, and may extend temporary relief in the way of provisions and vacant houses to the worthy and needy, until such time as they can help themselves. They will select, first, the buildings for the necessary uses of the army; next, a sufficient number of stores to be turned over to the treasury agent for trade-stores. All vacant store-houses or dwellings, and all buildings belonging to absent rebels, will be construed and used as belonging to the United States until such times as their titles can be settled by the courts of the United States.

"III. The mayor and city council of Savannah will continue and exercise their functions as such, and will, in concert with the commanding officer of the post and chief quartermaster, see that the fire-companies are kept in organization, the streets cleaned and lighted, and keep up a good understanding between the citizens and soldiers. They will ascertain and report to the chief commissary of subsistence, as soon as possible, the names and number of worthy families that need assistance and support.

"The mayor will forthwith give public notice that the time has come when all must choose their course, namely, to remain within our lines and conduct themselves as good citizens, or depart in peace. He will ascertain the names of all who choose to leave Savannah, and report their names and residence to the chief quartermaster, that measures may be taken to transport them beyond the lines.

"IV. Not more than two newspapers will be published in Savannah, and their editors and proprietors will be held to the strictest accountability, and will be punished severely, in person and property, for any libelous publication, mischievous matter, premature news, exaggerated statements, or any comments whatever upon the acts of the constituted authorities: they will be held accountable even for such articles though copied from other papers."

[1] This led to some dissatisfaction on the part of the citizens of Savannah and of foreign consuls. On the 2d of January Sherman writes to Secretary Stanton in regard to this matter as follows:

"I have just received from Lieutenant General Grant a copy of that part of your telegram to him of 26th December relating to cotton, a copy of which has been immediately furnished to General Eaton, my chief quartermaster, who will be strictly governed by it.

"I had already been approached by all the consuls and half the people of Savannah on this cotton question, and my invariable answer has been that all the cotton in Savannah was prize of war, and belonged to the United States, and nobody should recover a bale of it with my consent; and that as cotton had been one of the chief causes of this war, it should help pay its expenses; that all cotton became tainted with treason from the hour the first act of hostility was committed against the United States, some time in December, 1860, and that no bill of sale subsequent to that date could convey title.

"My orders were that an officer of the quartermaster's department, United States army, might furnish the holder, agent, or attorney a mere certificate of the fact of seizure, with description of the bales, marks, etc.; the cotton then to be turned over to the agent of the Treasury Department, to be shipped to New York for sale. But since the receipt of your dispatch I have ordered General Eaton to make the shipment himself to the quartermaster at New York, where you can dispose of it at pleasure. I do not think the Treasury Department ought to bother itself with the prizes or captures of war.

"Mr. Barclay, former consul at New York—representing Mr. Molyneux, former consul, but absent since a long time—called on me in person with reference to cotton claims by English subjects. He seemed amazed when I told him I should pay no respect to consular certificates, and that in no event would I treat an English subject with more favor than one of our own deluded citizens; and that, for my part, I was unwilling to fight for cotton for the benefit of Englishmen openly engaged in smuggling arms and munitions of war to kill us; that, on the contrary, it would afford me great satisfaction to conduct my army to Nassau and wipe out that nest of pirates. I explained to him, however, that I was not a diplomatic agent of the general government of the United States; but that my opinion, so frankly expressed, was that of a soldier, which it would be well for him to heed. It appeared also that he owned a plantation on the line of investment to Savannah, which, of course, is destroyed, and for which he expected me to give him some certificate entitling him to indemnification, which I declined emphatically.

"I have adopted in Savannah rules concerning property, severe but just, founded upon the laws of nations and the practice of civilized governments; and am clearly of opinion that we should claim all the belligerent rights over conquered countries, that the people may realize the truth that war is no child's play."

POCOTALIGO DEPÔT.

MARCHING THROUGH THE SWAMPS.

water. Driven thus from the route originally determined upon, Slocum, on the 26th of January, ascended the river to Sister's Ferry. But even there the river was three miles wide, and his command was prevented from crossing until the 7th of February. Two divisions of the Twentieth Corps—Jackson's and Geary's—had crossed the river at Pureysburg, and, proceeding to Hardeeville, on the Charleston Road, secured communication with Howard at Pocotaligo.

Sherman, in the mean time, on the 22d, embarked for Hilton Head, where he conferred with Admiral Dahlgren and General Foster in regard to their co-operative movements. General Foster was to follow Sherman's army inland, and occupy in succession Charleston and such other points on the seacoast as would be of any military value. Thus Sherman's army was free to move directly upon Goldsborough.

In all its general features, the march through the Carolinas was a repetition of that through Georgia, already accomplished. No important stronghold of the enemy was attacked. As Sherman in the Georgia promenade had feigned on Macon and Augusta, and passed between without striking either, so now he purposed to demonstrate against Augusta and Charleston, avoiding both, and make the quickest possible march to Goldsborough. In boldness, his present scheme exceeded the one already executed. The country to be traversed was more difficult, and the enemy had been given time to concentrate his fragmentary forces in Sherman's front. But Sherman had no doubts. "I think," he says,[1] "the time has come now when we should attempt the boldest moves, and my experience is that they are easier of execution than more timid ones, because the enemy is disconcerted by them."[2] He was as familiar with the country over which he was about to march as with Georgia. "I have hunted it over many a time," he says, "from Santee

[1] Letter to General Halleck, December 24th, 1864.

[2] He adds in the same letter: "I also doubt the wisdom of concentration beyond a certain point, as the roads of this country limit the amount of men that can be brought to bear in any one battle; and I don't believe that any one general can handle more than 60,000 men in battle. I think my campaign of the last month, as well as every step I take from this point northward, is as much a direct attack upon Lee's army as though I were operating within the sound of his artillery. . . . . I attach more importance to these deep incisions into the enemy's country, because this war differs from European wars in this particular—we are not only fighting hostile armies, but a hostile people, and must make old and young, rich and poor, feel the hard hand of war, as well as their organized armies. I know that this recent movement of mine through Georgia has had a wonderful effect in this respect. Thousands who had been deceived by their lying papers into the belief that we were being whipped all the time, realized the truth, and have no appetite for a repetition of the same experience. To be sure Jeff. Davis has his people under a pretty good shape of discipline, but I think faith in him is much shaken in Georgia, and I think before we are done South Carolina will not be so tempestuous. . . . . I felt somewhat disappointed at Hardee's escape from me. . . . Still, I know that the men that were in Savannah will be lost, in a measure, to Jeff. Davis, for the Georgia troops, under G. W. Smith, declared they would not fight in South Carolina, and they have gone north en route for Augusta; and I have reason to believe the North Carolina troops have gone to Wilmington."

ENTERING BLACKVILLE, SOUTH CAROLINA.

CROSSING THE SOUTH EDISTO.

SHERMAN'S ARMY ENTERING COLUMBIA, SOUTH CAROLINA.

to Mount Pleasant." His army did not lack enthusiasm, and the prospect of a march through South Carolina was one which it relished exceedingly. The general feeling of the North toward Charleston may be inferred from General Halleck's suggestion to Sherman: "Should you capture Charleston, I hope that by *some* accident the place may be destroyed; and if a little salt should be sown upon its site, it may prevent the growth of future crops of nullification and secession."[1] Poor South Carolina! she was sandwiched between two states who looked upon her as the original source of their past madness and their present woes.

Perhaps if Sherman had had Johnston as an antagonist in his immediate front he would not have been so confident. He calculated on the same Confederate scheme for the defense of the Carolinas which he had baffled in Georgia. He knew that they would hold on to Augusta and Charleston as they had, six weeks before, to Augusta and Macon, leaving him the route between, molested only by Wheeler's cavalry and a mob of disorganized militia, which would be swept like chaff before his march.

General Sherman accompanied the right wing of his army. On the 25th of January, with a small force, he demonstrated against the Combahee Ferry and the railroad bridge across the Salkehatchie, which river the enemy had adopted as his line of defense covering Charleston. After amusing the enemy at this point for nearly a week, the real march of Howard's army began on the 1st of February. Still keeping up the feint on Charleston, the main body of the army moved westward up the Salkehatchie. All the roads northward had been held for weeks by Wheeler's cavalry; the bridges had been burned and trees had been felled to obstruct Sherman's movements. But the pioneer battalions soon cleared the way and rebuilt the bridges. On the 2d the Fifteenth Corps was well advanced at Loper's Cross-roads, while the Seventeenth had reached River's Bridge, and was ready to cross the Salkehatchie.

Slocum's army in the mean time, as we have seen, was still struggling with the Savannah floods. Kilpatrick, however, and two of Williams's divisions, had crossed on pontoons. The latter were ordered to Beaufort's Bridge, and Kilpatrick to Blackville. Howard crossed the Salkehatchie in the face of the enemy at River's and Beaufort's bridges. The position of the enemy at River's Bridge was on the 3d carried by Mower's and G. A. Smith's divisions of the Seventeenth Corps, who crossed the swamp, nearly three miles wide, through water reaching from knee to shoulder, and in bitter cold weather, and making a lodgment below the bridge, turned on the Confederate brigade posted there, driving it in confusion toward Branchville. The Confederate killed and wounded, numbering eighty-eight, were sent back to Pocotaligo. The Fifteenth Corps, with less resistance, but with equal success, effected the crossing at Beaufort's Bridge, a short distance above.

The line of the Salkehatchie being broken, the enemy fell back behind the Edisto River to Branchville, and Sherman occupied the South Carolina Railroad connecting Augusta with Charleston. While waiting for the remainder of Slocum's army, this road was thoroughly destroyed from the Edisto to Blackville, Kilpatrick in the mean time being dispatched eastward to Aiken to threaten Augusta. Slocum reached Blackville on the 10th. The destruction of the railroad was continued to Windon. The whole army was on the 11th well concentrated about midway between Augusta and Charleston, thus dividing the forces of the enemy covering those two points.

Crossing the South Edisto, the right wing appeared in front of Orangeburg on the 12th, swept away a detachment of the enemy intrenched at that

[1] Sherman, in the letter already quoted, replies to this: "I will bear in mind your suggestion as to Charleston, and don't think "salt" will be necessary. . . . . . The whole army is burning with an insatiable desire to wreak vengeance on South Carolina. I almost tremble at her fate, but feel that she deserves all that seems in store for her. Many and many a person in Georgia asked me why we did not go to South Carolina, and when I answered that I was *en route* for that state, the invariable reply was, 'Well, if you will make those people feel the severities of war, we will pardon you for your desolation of Georgia.'"

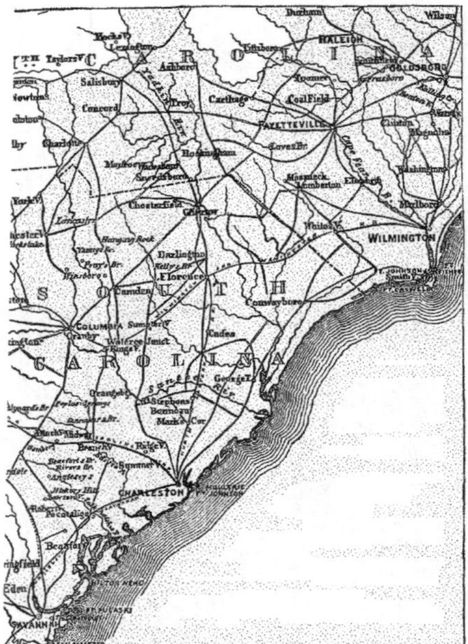

MAP OF SHERMAN'S CAROLINA MARCH.

oint, and followed, pushing him across the north branch of the Edisto, here he took refuge behind a rampart, supported by a battery, and, having artially burned the bridge, threatened to dispute the crossing. From this osition he was soon flanked, and Blair's corps, having crossed, began the destruction of the railroad to Columbia. Slocum's army moved by roads farther to the west, covered by Kilpatrick on its left. On the morning of February 16th the advance of Sherman's army beheld Columbia from the south bank of the Congaree.

In the mean time Sherman had received a communication from Wheeler, in which the latter promised not to burn cotton if Sherman would not burn houses. Sherman replied, "I hope you will burn all the cotton and save us the trouble. We don't want it, and it has proved a curse to our country. All you don't burn I will. As to private houses occupied by peaceful families, my orders are not to molest or disturb them, and I think my orders are obeyed. Vacant houses, being of no use to any body, I care little about, as the owners have thought them of no use to themselves."

On the south bank of the Congaree the two wings of the army were again united, but forthwith began to diverge again. Slocum was ordered to cross the Saluda at Zion Church, above Columbia, and proceed direct to Winnsborough, destroying the bridges and railroads about Alston. Howard crossed at the same time a little below the point selected for Slocum, and, turning the enemy's position at Columbia, moved upon the town from the north. The next morning, February 17th, under cover of Stone's brigade of Wood's division (Logan's corps), a pontoon bridge was thrown across Broad River, and, while the remainder of the corps was crossing, the Mayor of Columbia rode out and formally surrendered the city to General Stone, who marched his brigade directly into the town. Sherman, crossing the pontoon bridge accompanied by General Howard, rode into the capital of South Carolina. They found perfect quiet in the city, the citizens and soldiers mingling together in the streets. General Wade Hampton, commanding the rear guard of the Confederate cavalry, had, before leaving, ordered all the cotton in the town to be burned. The bales had been piled in the streets, the ropes and bagging cut, and tufts of cotton were thrown about by the wind, which was blowing a perfect gale, lodging in the trees and upon the houses. As this threatened the destruction of the entire town, the soldiers assisted the citizens in putting out the flames. Sherman had ordered the destruction of the arsenals, of all public property not needed for the use of the army, and of the railroads, dépôts, and such machinery as could assist the enemy in carrying on war. But, before this order began to be executed, the smouldering fires of the morning had been rekindled by the wind and communicated to the surrounding buildings. By night they had spread into a conflagration that baffled the efforts of both citizens and soldiers to allay its fury. It was not until about 4 A.M. on the 18th that the fire was got under control. It was due to the assistance of Sherman's soldiers that any portion of the city was left standing. After this matter had been attended to, during the 18th and 19th, Sherman's orders for the destruction of the arsenals, railroads, etc., were properly carried out.[1]

[1] The origin of the destructive conflagration in Columbia has been the subject of much discussion, which we can not give here in full. The statements of General Sherman, Major G. W. Nichols, a member of Sherman's staff, General Wade Hampton, and James McCarter (a Confederate citizen who was in Columbia when the event took place), form the body of evidence so far as published. The statements made in Confederate journals at the time are of no value, except in their details as to the exact time the conflagration commenced, the direction of the wind, etc. In regard to the four principal authorities above mentioned, it is assumed that each is reliable so far as he states facts within the scope of his own personal observation.

Sherman, in his official report, says: "Without hesitation, I charge General Wade Hampton with having burned his own city of Columbia, not with a malicious intent, or as the manifestation of a silly 'Roman stoicism,' but from folly and want of sense in filling it with lint, cotton, and tinder. Our officers and men on duty worked well to extinguish the flames; but others not on duty, including the officers who had long been imprisoned there, rescued by us, may

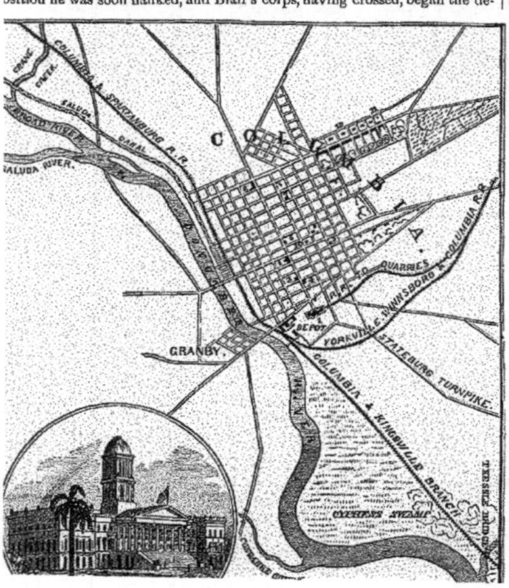

COLUMBIA ON FIRE.

Slocum reached Winnsborough on the 21st of February, and the Twentieth Corps crossed the Catawba River on the 23d, Kilpatrick following the same night, and then demonstrating agai North Carolina, to which place Beaurega federate cavalry had retreated. There . be expected Cheatham's corps, of Hood's had been cut off by Sherman's rapid m lumbia and Winnsborough. On the 26t Corps reached Hanging Rock, where it Fourteenth to cross the Catawba, now sv heavy rains. As soon as Davis came up teenth Corps, Slocum moved direct to Ch olina, nearly 70 miles south of west from

On the 22d Kilpatrick reported to S of his men had been murdered by Wade alry, and left in the road with labels upon ing a similar fate to all foragers. Shert this conduct left Kilpatrick no alternati taliate man for man. "Let it be done a Sherman. "We have a perfect war righ of the country we overrun, and may coll gers or otherwise. Let the whole peopl is now against them because their armie and do not defend their country or frontie It is pretty nonsense for Wheeler and such vain heroes, to talk of our warring and children. If they claim to be men they should defend children, and prevent us reaching their homes. Instead of n armies, let them turn their attention to their families, or we to the death; they should know that we will use the produc as we please. I want the foragers to be regulated and sy not to degenerate into common robbers; but foragers, as suc bacon, beef, and such other products as we need, are as muc protection as skirmishers and flankers. . . . . If our fora cesses, punish them yourself, but never let an enemy judge b and the law."[1]

have assisted in spreading the fire after it once had begun, and have indulged in unconcealed joy to see the ruin of the capital of South Carolina." In regard to the origin and progress of the flames he says, "Before one single public building had been fired by [my] order, the smouldering fires set by Hampton's order were rekindled by the wind, and communicated to the buildings around. About dark they began to spread, and got beyond the control of the brigade on duty within the city. The whole of Wood's division was brought in, but it was found impossible to check the flames, which by midnight had become unmanageable, and raged until about 4 A.M., when, the wind subsiding, they were got under control. I was up nearly all night, and saw Generals Howard, Logan, and Wood, and others laboring to save the houses, and to protect families thus suddenly deprived of shelter, and of bedding and wearing apparel. I disclaim on the part of my army any agency in this fire, but, on the contrary, claim that we saved what of Columbia remains unconsumed." It must be remembered in this connection that the only soldiers of Sherman's army in Columbia were those of Wood's division.

General Wade Hampton, in a letter to Hon. Reverdy Johnson, of Georgia, says: "I pledge myself to prove . . . that he [General Sherman] promised protection to the city, and that, in spite of his solemn promise, he burned the city to the ground, deliberately, systematically, and atrociously." He also asserts in the same letter, "I gave a positive order, by direction of General Beauregard, that no cotton should be fired." Of course Hampton's testimony in regard to Sherman's conduct is unreliable, as he had no means of knowing that which he affirmed. We accept his statement that he gave the order against the destruction of cotton; but the only mode of reconciling this statement with the fact that his soldiers really *did* set the cotton on fire, is to suppose either that the order against the burning came too late, and subsequent to a former order directing the cotton to be burned, or that the burning was against orders.

Major Nichols came with Sherman into Columbia about noon on the 17th. He notices the prevalence of a strong wind, and that it came from the south. It was in the southern portion of the city that the cotton was burning. "It seemed to me," he says, "I had never experienced a more powerful gale of wind." Both he and Sherman testify that the air was filled with smoking tufts of cotton, catching in trees and falling on the shingled roofs of houses. Nichols admits that, apart from the fires occasioned by the burning cotton, "there were fires which must have started independent of the above-mentioned cause. The source of these is ascribed to the desire for revenge from some 200 of our prisoners who had escaped from the cars as they were being conveyed from this city to Charlotte. Again it is said that the soldiers who first entered the town, intoxicated with bad liquor, which was freely distributed among them by designing citizens, in an insanity of exhilaration, set fire to unoccupied houses." Nichols testifies to the efforts made by officers and soldiers to put out the fire which broke out in the afternoon. He says: "I saw Sherman, Howard, Logan, Woods, and other general officers, with their staffs, working with heart and hand to stay the progress of the flames. . . . . During the progress of the fire, and afterward, while the army was in the city, every effort was made for the relief of the sufferers. They were furnished with bedding and food, and were quartered in the houses which had been deserted by their owners who had fled the city the day before. General Sherman gave up his own quarters to a family of ladies, with their children, who were fed from his table; I know from personal observation that he and the officers and men of his army could not have made greater exertions to alleviate the sufferings of these homeless ones if they had been their own kith and kin."

Mr. James McCarter entirely exonerates General Sherman from any responsibility for the conflagration, and states his belief that "Sherman intended to protect the persons and private property of the citizens." Still, he charges the burning and plundering of Columbia upon the soldiers of Sherman's army. He adduces as an argument leading to this conclusion that the wind was from the north. Here Mr. McCarter not only contradicts Major Nichols's testimony, but that of the *Columbia Daily Phœnix*, which asserts that the wind throughout the day "had steadily prevailed from southwest by west, and bore the flames eastward." This is the main argument adduced by McCarter to prove his sweeping assertion; and this, as we have seen, is based upon false premises. The only other argument presented by him is the fact that Wade Hampton's men left Columbia ten hours before the conflagration which so desolated the city. This is true; but it is also true that Sherman's soldiers, on entering the city, found the cotton burning, and assisted the soldiers in putting out the flames. But, as Sherman states in his report, the fire which had been subdued still smouldered in the cotton, and was rekindled by the wind in the afternoon, baffling every effort made by his army to resist its progress.

The above is the testimony bearing upon the case, from which it is clear,

First, that the burning of Columbia was due to two causes, the carelessness their manner of destroying the cotton, and the incendiarism of a number of p a desire to wreak vengeance upon the people whom they held responsible fo they had experienced in confinement.

Secondly, that Sherman and his army proper not only had no agency in gration, but worked heartily and persistently to subdue it, and made every ex sufferings which followed it.

We have given this matter of the burning of Columbia so much space simp presenting the facts of the case before the reader. We are making no apo business of the historian. It is worthy of note, however, that, though Sherm that South Carolina deserved destruction, after they entered that state they m an army, and not like a mob of marauders and incendiaries. Although She December 24th, 1864, had said to General Halleck, "I look upon Columbi Charleston, and I doubt if we shall spare the public buildings there as we still, upon entering Columbia, he found his pity larger than his wrath, and d the citizens against a destruction of their property for which he was in no wa at Savannah, notwithstanding his menace of punishment in case the city was he entered the city he saved it from devastation by a mob of its own citizens.

[1] Sherman writes thus to Wade Hampton in regard to this matter, Februa

"It is officially reported to me that our foraging parties are murdered and labeled 'death to all foragers;' one instance of a lieutenant and seve field, and another of twenty 'near a ravine eighty rods from the main ro from Feasterville. I have ordered a similar number of prisoners in our ha in like manner.

"I hold about 1000 prisoners captured in various ways, and can stand it but I hardly think these murders are committed with your knowledge, and w give notice to the people at large that every life taken by them results in the confederates.

"Of course you can not question my right to 'forage on the country.' I as history. The manner of exercising it varies with circumstances, and if th supply my requisitions, I will forbid all foraging. But I find no civil autho to calls for forage and provisions, therefore must collect directly from the pe this is the occasion of much misbehavior on the part of our men, but I can n judge, and punish with wholesale murder.

"Personally I regret the bitter feelings engendered by this war, but the and I simply allege that those who struck the first blow and made war i

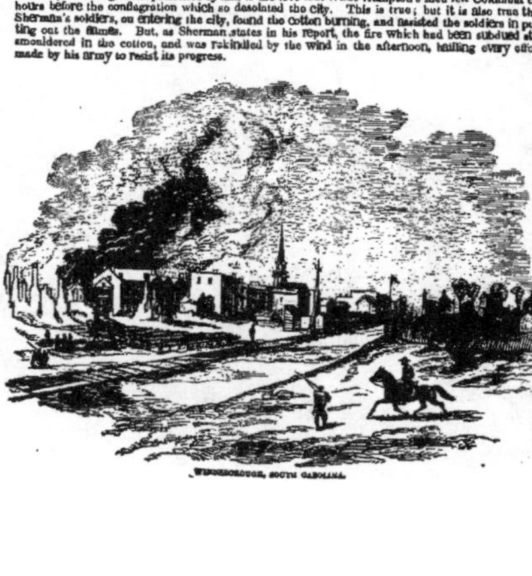

WINNSBOROUGH, SOUTH CAROLINA.

HANGING ROCK, SOUTH CAROLINA.

FORAGERS STARTING OUT.

FORAGERS RETURNING TO CAMP.

The right wing, after destroying the railroad to Winnsborough, crossed the Catawba at Peay's Ferry. Detachments were sent from the Fifteenth Corps to Camden to burn the bridge over the Wateree, a tributary of the Santee River, and to break up the railroad between Florence and Charleston. The latter object was not accomplished, as Captain Duncan, commanding the expedition, met Butler's division of Confederate cavalry, and was forced to return.

On the 3d of March Sherman's army had reached Cheraw. Charleston had in the mean time been evacuated by the Confederates, and at Cheraw were found many of the guns which had been brought from that city. From this point the weather was unfavorable and the roads bad; but, crossing the Great Pedee, the Fourteenth and Seventeenth corps entered Fayetteville on the 11th. During the night of the 9th, Kilpatrick's three brigades guarding the roads east of the Pedee were divided. General Wade Hampton, detecting this, dashed in at daylight, got possession of the camp of Colonel Spencer's brigade, and the house in which Kilpatrick and Spencer had their quarters. Nothwithstanding the completeness of the surprise and the temporary confusion which followed, Kilpatrick succeeded in rallying his

fairness to reproach us for the natural consequences. 'I merely assert our 'war right' to forage, and my resolve to protect my foragers to the extent of life for life.'"

UNITED STATES ARSENAL AT FAYETTEVILLE.

THE TUG-BOAT DONALDSON MOVING UP THE CAPE FEAR.

men, and by a prompt attack regained the artillery which he had lost and the camp from which he had been so suddenly ousted.

The 12th, 13th, and 14th of March were passed by Sherman's army at Fayetteville. The Arsenal and the machinery which had formerly belonged to the Harper's Ferry Arsenal were completely destroyed. "Every building was knocked down and burned," General Sherman reports, "and every piece of machinery utterly broken up and ruined."

Sherman's army was now on the Cape Fear River. Up to this point he had, by admirable strategy, succeeded in dividing the enemy's forces. But now Cheatham's corps had joined Beauregard, and Hardee had got across Cape Fear River in advance of Sherman; and these forces were all on their way to join the Confederate troops in North Carolina, and were under the command of General Joseph E. Johnston, Sherman's old antagonist. In cavalry Johnston's command had somewhat the advantage of Sherman's, and, taking into consideration the military genius of its leader, its artillery and infantry were sufficiently formidable to justify extreme caution on the part of the Federal commander. Before reaching Fayetteville, Sherman had dispatched from Laurel Hill to Wilmington—then in possession of the national troops—two of his best scouts. These men succeeded in their somewhat difficult adventure, and on the morning of the 12th of March Sherman beheld the army tug Donaldson approaching Fayetteville, "bringing me," he says, "full intelligence of the outer world." This tug-boat returned the same day, conveying to General Terry at Wilmington, and to General Schofield at Newbern, intelligence that on the 15th Sherman would move upon Goldsborough. Both Terry and Schofield were ordered to the same point.

In the mean time pontoon bridges had been thrown across the Cape Fear River. Kilpatrick was ordered to move to Averysborough and beyond, in advance of the left wing. Four of Slocum's divisions were to follow, while his two remaining divisions moved as an escort to the trains. Howard moved by a more eastward route to Goldsborough. The idea of this march was to feign on Raleigh and make Goldsborough. But four of Howard's divisions were to preserve communication with Slocum, ready to support the latter in the event of a battle. These movements commenced on the 15th of March. General Sherman went with Slocum's army.

Before reaching Averysborough, Slocum encountered General Hardee's force[1] on the 16th, at a point where the road branches off toward Goldsborough through Bentonville. The enemy must be dislodged both in order to gain the Goldsborough Road and to continue the feint on Raleigh. Hardee's position was difficult to carry, not by reason of its intrinsic strength, but on account of the difficult nature of the ground, which was so soft as to swamp the horses, and even the infantry could scarcely make its way over the pine barren. The Twentieth Corps had the lead, Ward's division in the advance. The latter was deployed, and a skirmish developed the position of a brigade of Charleston heavy artillery, armed as infantry, and commanded by Rhett, posted across the road behind a light parapet, enfilading the approach across a cleared field. Williams dispatched Casey's brigade to the left, turning this position, and Rhett's line was broken, and three guns were captured, with 217 prisoners. Besides these, 108 Confederate dead were afterward buried by Sherman's men.

Ward's division, advancing, developed a second and stronger line, and Jackson's came up on his right, and the Fourteenth Corps on his left, well toward Cape Fear River. Kilpatrick at the same time was ordered to mass his cavalry on the right, and to feel forward for the road to Goldsborough. A brigade of the cavalry gained this road, but was driven back by McLaws's Confederate division. Late in the afternoon the whole Federal line advanced, drove the enemy within his intrenchments, from which, during the stormy night of the 16th, he retreated over the wretched road in his rear. Ward's division followed the next day, beyond Averysborough, and found that Hardee had fallen back on Smithfield. General Slocum's loss in the action at Averysborough was 12 officers and 65 men killed, and 477 wounded.

The Goldsborough Road was now open to the left wing, which, on the night of the 18th, encamped five miles from Bentonville and 27 from Goldsborough. Howard was two miles farther south, and as no farther resistance was expected from the enemy, was directed to move to Goldsborough *via* Falling Creek Church. Sherman joined this wing of the army. But he had not got six miles away from Slocum when he heard artillery to the left. His apprehensions were aroused, but were soon quieted by information conveyed through Slocum's staff officers that the leading division (Carlin's) had encountered Dibbrell's cavalry, which he was driving easily. Shortly after this pleasant intelligence, other staff-officers from Slocum reported that the latter had developed the whole of Johnston's army near Bentonville.[1]

Turning, therefore, to the left wing, we find that it has been attacked by the enemy, who has gained a temporary advantage, capturing three of Carlin's guns and driving back his two advanced brigades. General Williams, however, is aware of the danger which threatens him in its full extent, and promptly brings up his whole force, with which, behind hastily-constructed barricades, he assumes the defensive, knowing that Sherman will bring the whole right wing, if necessary, to his assistance.

While Hardee had been fighting Sherman near Averysborough, Johnston was concentrating his medley army at Smithfield, and immediately after that action moved forward with great rapidity, intending to strike and overwhelm Slocum's army before it could be relieved by re-enforcements from Howard. "But," says Sherman, "he 'reckoned without his host.' I had expected just such a movement all the way from Fayetteville, and was prepared for it." During the night of the 19th Slocum got up his wagon train, with the two divisions guarding it, and Hazen's division of the Fifteenth Corps, and made his position impregnable. Johnston could only effect his purpose by placing his whole army between Sherman's two wings, which would, under the circumstances, have proved his ruin. His cavalry, of course, was unable to cut off communication with Howard. Logan's corps, therefore, approached Bentonville without serious resistance, compelling Johnston to refuse his left flank and intrench. Thus the Confederate army was put upon the defensive on the 20th, having three corps of Sherman's army in his front, and unassailable. Johnston's flanks were well protected by swamps, and as it was not Sherman's purpose to fight a battle here, unless forced to do so, the Federal army simply continued to hold its position in the enemy's front. The next day, March 21st, Schofield entered Goldsborough with little opposition, and Terry connected with Blair's corps at Cox's Bridge, on the Neuse, so that, stretching from Goldsborough around to Bentonville, Sherman had now under his command an army of 100,000 men in an impregnable position. Johnston very sensibly, therefore, retreated to Smithfield before his retreat could be cut off by a portion of this immense army. The Federal loss at Bentonville amounted in the aggregate to 1646. Johnston's loss must have been at least 8000 men, including the prisoners which he left to be captured when he abandoned his intrenchments.

The objects of the Carolina campaign had been accomplished in the full possession of Goldsborough, with its two railroads leading to Beaufort and Wilmington. By the 25th of March Sherman's army was concentrated at Goldsborough, and his line of communication with Newbern and Morehead City was firmly established. The co-operative movements which had been conducted while Sherman was marching, by Generals Terry, Foster, and Schofield, next invite our attention.

[1] Sherman reports this force as 20,000, but this is an exaggeration.

[1] Johnston's army had not yet been joined by Hoke's command, some 9000 strong. The Confederate force at Bentonville consisted of Stewart's and Cheatham's corps from Hood's old army, together amounting to about 10,000 men; of Hardee's force from Charleston, 9000 strong, and of Wade Hampton's cavalry, numbering about 5000. This made up an army of about 24,000 men.

A. S. WILLIAMS.

WILMINGTON AND ITS APPROACHES.

W. B. CUSHING.

CHAPTER LII.

RECOVERY OF THE ATLANTIC COAST.

I. WILMINGTON.

Capture of Plymouth.—Lieutenant Cushing's Expedition for the Destruction of the Albemarle.—Naval Actions in North Carolina Sounds.—Organization of the First Expedition for the Capture of Wilmington.—Delays.—Butler's Powder-boat Strategy.—His Connection with the Expedition.—Explosion of the Powder-boat.—Bombardment of Fort Fisher.—Re-enforcements received by the Enemy.—Landing of Butler's Forces.—Weitzel advises against an Assault.—Re-embarkation and Withdrawal of the Troops.—Causes of Failure.—Butler relieved of Command.—The Second Expedition.—Terry in Command.—Plan of Attack.—Assault and Capture of Fort Fisher.—Explosion of the Magazine.—Schofield comes East with the Twenty-third Corps.—Assumes command of the North Carolina Department.—Operations against Wilmington.—Capture of the City.

AT the beginning of 1865 only three important positions on the Atlantic and Gulf coasts east of the Mississippi were retained by the Confederates—Wilmington, Charleston, and Mobile. Of these, Wilmington alone afforded an outlet for even a partial and restricted commerce with Europe.

On the last day of October, 1864, Plymouth, near the mouth of the Roanoke River—a town which had been captured from the Federals early in the year—had been surrendered. Though the possession of this place was of no vital importance, yet the gallant exploit of Lieutenant W. B. Cushing, which led to its surrender, is so memorable as an instance both of a heroism which has never been surpassed, and of a success which, gained as it was by a single band, stands unparalleled in the annals of war, that it can not here be forgotten.

In the spring of 1864, the Federal forces had met with several reverses on the North Carolina coast. On the 1st of February, the Confederate General G. E. Pickett captured the Federal outpost at Bachelor's Creek, eight miles from Newbern, with a considerable number of prisoners. During the following night, a party of the enemy in barges captured the United States steamer Underwriter, lying in the Neuse River, and covering the Newbern fortifications. Surprising the garrison at Plymouth on the 17th of April, the Confederates, after a severe struggle, captured that town on the 20th. This was accompanied by the co-operation of the Confederate iron-clad ram Albemarle, which, descending the river, sunk the Federal gun-boat Southfield. The Miami, the only other national gun-boat off Plymouth, with-

THE CONFEDERATE RAM ALBEMARLE ATTACKING THE FEDERAL GUN-BOATS OFF PLYMOUTH.

THE SASSACUS RAMMING THE ALBEMARLE.

drew. General Wessels, thus cut off from communication with the fleet in Albemarle Sound, surrendered the town, with 1600 men and 25 guns, to General Hoke. Washington, at the head of Pamlico River, was evacuated by the Federals in the latter part of the same month, the town having been previously burned by some soldiers of the Seventeenth Massachusetts and Fifteenth Connecticut Regiments.

Albemarle Sound was still held by the national gun-boats. But besides the Albemarle, other Confederate rams were being prepared to recover the naval supremacy of the North Carolina sounds. Captain Melancthon Smith was accordingly sent to assume command in these sounds, with several double-enders. On the afternoon of May 5th the Albemarle came out of the Roanoke, followed by the Bombshell, a small armed tender, and engaged the national fleet collected together off the mouth of the river. A brisk little fight followed. The gun-boats succeeded in dodging the ram, but their guns made no impression. About five o'clock the Sassacus, watching her opportunity, struck the enemy behind her starboard beam, causing her to careen until her deck was washed by the waves. In this position the two vessels remained for some time, and prompt assistance on the part of one of the larger gun-boats might have accomplished the destruction of the Albemarle. Before this was effected the ram swung clear of the Sassacus, and, maintaining the fight until dark, retreated up the river, leaving her tender, the Bombshell, behind in the hands of the Federals. She appeared again on the 24th, but did not venture to renew the contest. The next day a bold attempt was made by a party of five volunteers from the gun-boat Wyalusing to destroy the Albemarle by means of a torpedo, but proved unsuccessful. Thus the affair rested, so far as the Albemarle was concerned, through the summer of 1864.

Notwithstanding the failure of the expedition to blow up the Albemarle in May, Lieutenant Cushing thought the thing practicable, and formed a scheme for accomplishing this object, which, having been submitted to Admiral Lee, he was permitted to carry out. He had formed his plan in June, at which time he was commanding the Monticello. Proceeding to New York, he, in conjunction with Admiral Gregory, Captain Boggs, and Chief Engineer W. W. Wood, applied to one of the new steam pickets a torpedo arrangement, which had been invented by Wood, and then returned to the Sound. The Albemarle was lying off Plymouth at its moorings, and formed the defense of that town. On the night of October 27th, with a select crew of 13 men, six of whom were officers, he proceeded up the river with his engine of destruction. The distance to Plymouth was eight miles. Passing the Confederate picket stationed on the wreck of the Southfield, a mile below the town, without causing alarm, he found the ram protected with a boom of pine logs 30 feet from her side. As the party approached, it encountered a fire from the enemy's infantry on shore, to which the howitzer from Cushing's boat replied. Almost at the same moment the boat ran its bows against the logs guarding the ram. With his own hands Lieutenant Cushing fixed the torpedo in its proper position. "The torpedo boom," says Cushing, "was then lowered, and I succeeded in diving the torpedo under the overhang, and exploding it at the same time that the Albemarle's gun was fired. A shot seemed to go crashing through my boat, and a dense mass of water rushed in from the torpedo, filling the launch and completely disabling her. The enemy then continued his fire at 15 feet range, and demanded our surrender, which I twice refused, ordering the men to save themselves, and removing my overcoat and shoes. Springing into the river, I swam, with others, into the middle of the stream, the rebels failing to hit us." The ram had been destroyed by the torpedo, but the necessity of immediate flight had prevented Cushing from observing the extent and efficiency of his work. All but one of the party accompanying him met death or capture. Cushing escaped, with a bullet in his wrist, by floating down the river, hid himself among the woods on the bank, and finally found a skiff, in which, after eight hours paddling, he reached the Valley City on the

DESTRUCTION OF THE ALBEMARLE.

BLOCKADING FLEET OFF WILMINGTON—OLD INLET.

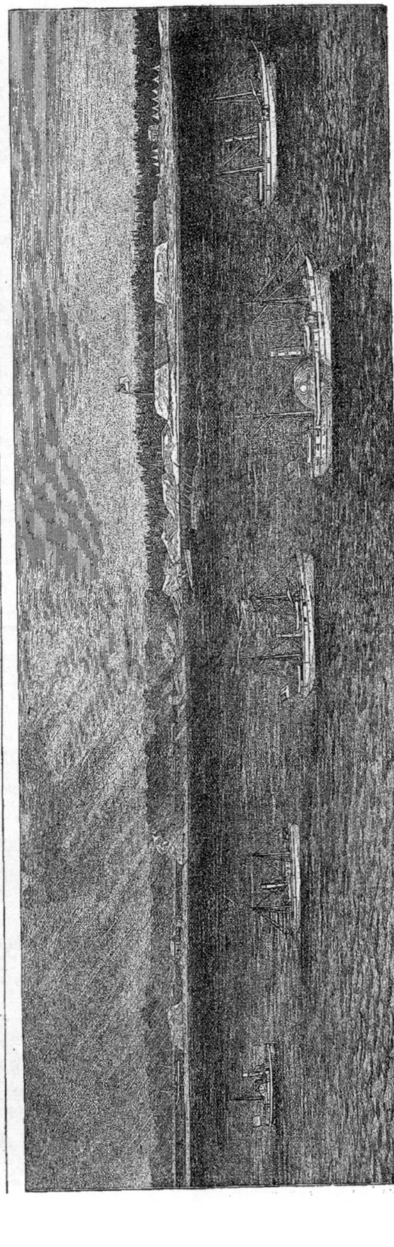

BLOCKADING FLEET OFF WILMINGTON—NEW INLET.

night of the 30th. The next day Plymouth was surrendered to the naval squadron.

The capture of Wilmington would have been undertaken in the earlier stages of the war if it could have been accomplished by a naval force alone. But military co-operation was indispensable, and the instant, ever-pressing need of the military forces on more important fields caused the expedition to be postponed until the autumn of 1864. In September—after the capture of Atlanta, and while the Federal army under Meade was besieging Petersburg, waiting its own opportunity and the accomplishment of Sherman's plans in the West—it was thought forces could be spared from Butler's Army of the James to co-operate with the Navy Department in the reduction of Fort Fisher and the capture of Wilmington.

The naval preparations were promptly made, and it was intended that Vice-Admiral Farragut, then operating on the Gulf Coast, should have command of this branch of the expedition. This was impossible on account of the impaired health of that distinguished officer, and the command was assigned to Rear Admiral Porter, who had been identified with the most important naval victories of the West. After considering the subject, Porter offered to take Fort Fisher in three days if he could have all the heaviest frigates, with 300 guns, and a co-operative military force of 13,000 men.[1] Upon consultation with Grant, the latter said he could not then detach so large a force, but could raise it within 24 hours after Porter had assembled his fleet. No definite time was fixed for the expedition, but it was expected to move by the middle of October. In the mean time Grant collected what information he could about Cape Fear River, with maps and charts, and placed this in the hands of General Weitzel, commanding the Eighteenth Corps, to whom, with General Butler's knowledge, the command of the military force was assigned. As the enemy had in some way been informed of the expedition, it was postponed, but the preparations for it were continued. The small force which Grant could detach rendered it necessary that the attack should be a surprise. The War Department had proposed General Gillmore as the military commander, but to this Grant objected on the ground that he had shown timidity on a former occasion, and appointed Weitzel.

General Butler took a great interest in this affair. It was to be carried out by his own troops, and within the limits of his own department. General Grant preferred that he should not participate in the expedition, but did not choose to interfere, though strict military propriety would have dictated Butler's remaining with the larger portion of his army instead of following a detachment which had been already assigned to an able commander. General Butler's chief interest in the affair was connected with a novel experiment which he had suggested for blowing up Fort Fisher by the explosion near it of 200 or 300 tons of powder. He had heard of the destruction caused by the explosion of a large quantity of gunpowder at Erith, England. The remarkable effect of this explosion for many miles around led him to speculate as to the possibility of destroying military fortifications by similar means. He had first proposed this matter to General Grant in connection with Charleston, which he wanted to blow up with a vessel loaded with 1000 tons of powder. But Grant was skeptical as to the effect of such an experiment. About the time the Fort Fisher expedition was ready to start, Butler again broached his gunpowder plot. Some high authorities had come to his support. Grant referred the matter to Colonel Comstock, of his staff, who reported that the explosion of 300 or 400 tons of powder out at sea would do no damage. General Delafield, Chief Engineer, said the explosion would have about the same effect on the fort that firing feathers from muskets would have on the enemy. The Navy Department and Admiral Porter looked upon the scheme with more favor. General Butler himself was perfectly confident of success. Grant therefore consented to the experiment, but would have no waiting for the powder-boat.

Sherman was at this time in the heart of Georgia, and the enemy, having nearly recovered from his apprehensions of an attack on Wilmington, had left a very small force at Fort Fisher in order to assist in impeding Sherman's march. This was the time to strike. Butler having determined to join the expedition to see that the powder-boat was properly exploded, General Grant ordered him to get off with 6500 men, General Weitzel to have the immediate command. Still Grant had no idea that Butler would go with the expedition until the latter passed his headquarters on the way to Fortress Monroe.[2] Of course, as a matter of military courtesy, all orders for Weitzel had passed through General Butler. On the 4th of D
Grant had telegraphed to the latter to get the expedition off witho
with or without the powder-boat. Instead of moving directly, Butl
ed a telegraphic correspondence with Porter about their "little expe
He issued his orders for the movement to General Weitzel on the 6t
next day thirteen of the transports were ready. Four—and those th
—were yet to arrive. On the 10th Butler had reached Fortress
and telegraphed to General Grant that he was waiting for the navy.
was waiting at Norfolk for the powder-boat. He left Hampton R
the 13th. The powder-boat had on board 200 tons of powder, an
receive 90 tons more at Beaufort. "She has delayed us a little
Porter to Butler before starting, "and our movements had to de
her." Butler's transports arrived off Masonborough Inlet, eighte
from Fort Fisher, on the 15th. The next day Porter reached Beau
off that point wrote to Butler that he would start for the rendezvous
five miles east of Cape Fear River) the next day, and, in case of fair
would be able to blow up the powder-boat on the night of the 18th.
was not ready to land, and the weather did not promise favorabl
therefore agreed to postpone the explosion. In the mean time, B
turned to Beaufort for a fresh supply of coal and provisions. P
mained with the fleet at the appointed rendezvous, and rode out
which was one of unusual violence. His vessels, however, seem to
in sight of Fort Fisher, for on the 20th their presence was reported
eral Hoke. But for the delay occasioned by the powder-boat, the th
of fine weather (the 16th, 17th, and 18th) would have been impr
troops would have been landed without difficulty, the enemy surpr
Fort Fisher captured.

THE POWDER-BOAT LOUISIANA.

Finally, the mountain gave birth to the mouse. On the night of
the powder-boat was exploded at a distance from Fort Fisher of 8[illegible]
Not a Federal gun-boat or transport dared venture an approach nea
to a point twelve miles from the scene, and even at a much greater
the steam in the boilers was lowered to prevent disaster. But, afte
effect was insignificant. It is true, the explosion was heard at the
it was there supposed that some unfortunate gun-boat had got agro
been blown up to prevent its falling into the hands of the enem
Louisiana had been chosen for this experiment, and had on boar
time of the explosion, 235 tons of powder. Commander A. C. Rh
charge of the affair, and associated with him in this perilous serv
Lieutenant Assistant Engineer A. T. Mullan, of the Agawam, Paul
acting master's mate, and seven men. Undoubtedly the effect of th
sion would have been very great if the powder had been properly c
and if the fuses could have been so arranged that the ignition of th
mass of powder would be instantaneous. As it was, there were four
explosions, and a large amount of the powder was blown away befo
nited.[1] But, in any case, the experiment ought to have been inciden
Butler and Porter, in making it so prominent a matter, disregarded
Grant's instructions.

It was designed that the troops should be ready to land as soon
sible after the powder-boat explosion. But General Butler was de
collecting water, coals, and other supplies, and did not come up t
evening of the 24th, and then with only a few of his transports.
Porter had that morning (11 30 A.M.) commenced the bombard
Fort Fisher from a fleet of naval vessels, surpassing in numbers an
ments any which had assembled during the war.[2] The attack w

[1] "I think it was about the 20th of September last that I was on my way to Cairo to resume my command of the Mississippi squadron. Secretary Welles sent me word to meet him that evening at Mr. Blair's. I had arranged to leave for the West the next morning. I went to Mr. Blair's, and found Secretary Welles and Assistant Secretary Fox, who had a number of charts of Cape Fear River, which were spread out for examination. Secretary Welles said that he thought it most important that some attempt should be made to get possession of Cape Fear River; that he had always been in favor of making the attempt, and had, time and time again, invited the co-operation of the army for that purpose, but had received no encouragement. He said he thought there was then a prospect of getting troops for that purpose, and asked me what was my opinion about the matter. I told him I had never seen Cape Fear River, and knew nothing about the defenses the rebels had erected there. He said he would put me in possession of all the papers he had from Admiral Farragut, Admiral Lee, and others who had investigated the subject, and then let me give my opinion about it. I read over carefully all the papers, and examined the charts. Admiral Lee decided most positively that the place could not be taken with 50,000 men, it was so strong; and Admiral Farragut decided that we had not ships in the navy to do any thing with it. Under these circumstances, I told the secretary that I should require time to consider this matter. I went back to the secretary the next morning, and told him that if he would give me the force I named, I would promise to take the fort in three days. That was encouraging to him, for his whole heart was bent upon the matter. . . . . I told him I wanted 300 guns on board ship, and all the heaviest frigates . . . . . that it would require 13,000 men to land with intrenching tools."—*Porter's Testimony before the Committee on the Conduct of the War: Fort Fisher*, p. 88.

[2] At City Point Butler met Grant, and explained his presence with the expedition. He said: "This expedition is a matter of very grave responsibility. (I had known Admiral Porter somewhat in the Mississippi River. General Weitzel and himself, I had understood, had some little difference upon the report as to the damage done by Admiral Porter's bombardment to Fort Jackson and St. Philip.) General Weitzel is a very able general, but a very young man. I am anxious to see this powder experiment go on and succeed, for it is a very grave one; and I think I had better go with the expedition, to take the responsibility off General Weitzel, being an older officer."—*Butler before Committee*, p. 41. This explanation would never have been given if Butl
felt its necessity to account for his presence with the expedition. It is a conclusive cor
of Grant's statement that he was surprised to see Butler on the way to Fort Fisher.

[1] See General Butler's and A. C. Rhind's testimony before the Committee.

[2] Porter's haste in exploding the powder vessel, and in commencing the bombardm
morning of the 24th, before the land force was ready to co-operate, gave rise to conside
ing. On the night of the 23d Butler sent his staff officer, Captain Clarke, to visit Port
form the latter that the transports would arrive the next day. General Weitzel, in his
says: "Captain Clarke returned just before we left the harbor, and reported that the a
said he would explode the powder vessel during the night of Friday, and commence the
soon thereafter as possible. It was a question of discussion between us, while sailing to
Inlet, whether the admiral would commence the attack before we were there to co-op
him. Several—I think General Butler among the number—doubted that he would do
not doubt it, having been with the admiral on two or three previous expeditions. . . .
the opinion expressed on board our vessel by several officers when it was found that the
made the attack as they did. There was one officer who particularly surprised me by
the opinion he did. He said that he believed Admiral Porter made the attack in the v
because he believed he could knock the fort all to pieces, and would thus get all the cre
ing it to himself. This officer is generally very quiet in the way of expressing his opini

FORT FISHER.

THE IRON-CLAD MONITOR MON-ADNOCK.

with thirty-seven vessels, five of which were iron-clads; and, besides these, there was a reserve force of nineteen vessels.[1] The main attack was made with the iron-clads and seven other vessels on the land face of the fort. The fleet had upward of 500 guns.

Fort Fisher is situated on Federal Point, on the north bank and at the mouth of Cape Fear River, 20 miles below Wilmington. The original plan of the expedition, as proposed in September, 1864, contemplated the passage of the fleet by the fort up the Cape Fear River. This had been abandoned on account of its impracticability. The channel was intricate, and was commanded by strong forts. It was also full of torpedoes. It was extremely difficult to cross the bar except at high tide, and even when this was accomplished it was unsafe for the vessels to enter without good pilots, or until the channel had been buoyed and the torpedoes removed. The only way in which the fort could be reduced was to land troops north of the work, and then either assault or lay siege to it. It was an earth-work mounting over 40 guns, and though the latter might be dismounted or silenced, the work itself could not be materially injured by a bombardment.[2] This fort, probably the strongest which had been attacked during the war, was manned on the 18th of December by a garrison of 677 men, under General W. H. C. Whiting; Colonel Lamb, who had himself erected the greater portion of the work, being second in command. Within five miles of the fort, at Sugar Loaf, was a reserve force of 800 men.[3] On the 20th the alarm had been given, and on the 22d the advance of General Hoke's division reached Wilmington, and re-enforcements were rapidly sent to Sugar Loaf. Thus, on the 23d, the garrison of the fort was increased to 1087 men.[4]

Very little damage was done to Fort Fisher by the bombardment on the 24th. Twenty-three of the garrison were wounded, all but three only slightly. Five gun-carriages were

FEDERAL FLEET AT HAMPTON ROADS.

The distance between Fort Fisher and Beaufort Harbor was about seventy miles. Porter's explanation of his prompt attack is this: "Captain Clarke said he could make fourteen miles an hour. This would bring him in five hours to Beaufort, with information to General Butler as to the precise time of the explosion of the powder-boat (1 30 A.M. on the 24th). Butler would therefore have plenty of time to reach Fort Fisher before the commencement of his attack, at 11 30 A.M." But it seems Butler, although starting from Beaufort when Clarke returned, did not reach the fleet until night. It is clear, therefore, that Admiral Porter took too much for granted. If he had waited till the night of the 24th for the explosion of the powder-boat, and given Butler prompt notice of this—as he could have done through Captain Clarke—then Butler would have been on hand with the transports, and the attack, taking place on the 25th, would have been a combined one of the navy and army. The reader, however, should understand that, as the affair turned out, this lack of combination on the 24th had nothing whatever to do with the failure of the expedition.

[1] The five iron-clads were the New Ironsides, Canonicus, Monadnock, Saugus, and Mahopac. The four last were turreted monitors.

[2] The following description of the fort is given by General Grant's engineer, Colonel Comstock:

"The land front consists of a half bastion on the left or Cape Fear River side, connected by a curtain with a bastion on the ocean side. The parapet is 25 feet thick, averages 20 feet in height, with traverses rising 10 feet above it and running back on their tops, which are from 8 to 12 feet in thickness, to a distance of from 30 to 40 feet from the interior crest. The traverses on the left half bastion are about 25 feet in length on top. The earth for this heavy parapet and the enormous traverses at their inner ends, more than 30 feet in height, was obtained partly from a shallow exterior ditch, but mainly from the interior of the work. Between each pair of traverses there was one or two guns. The traverses on the right of this front were only partially completed. A palisade, which is loop-holed and has a banquette, runs in front of this face, at a distance of 50 feet in front of the exterior slope, from the Cape Fear River to the ocean, with a position for a gun between the left of the front and the river, and another between the right of the front and the ocean. Through the middle traverse on the curtain is a bomb-proof postern, whose exterior opening is covered by a small redan for two field-pieces, to give flank-fire along the curtain. The traverses are generally bomb-proofed for men or magazines. The slopes of the work appear to have been revetted with marsh sods or covered with grass, and have an inclination of 45 degrees or a little less. . . . There were originally on this front 21 guns and three mortars. . . . The sea front consists of a series of batteries, mounting in all 24 guns, the different batteries being connected by a strong infantry parapet, so as to form a continuous line. The same system of heavy traverses for the protection of guns is used as on the land front, and these traverses are also generally bomb-proofed."

[3] The Confederate Department of North Carolina was under the command of General Bragg, as it had been since October.

[4] These facts were stated by General Whiting after his capture.

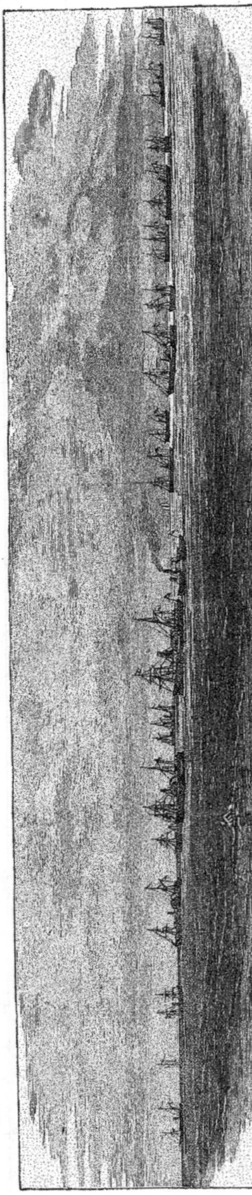

TRANSPORT FLEET OFF FEDERAL POINT.

THE MONITORS IN A GALE.

disabled, but this and every other injury done to the work was repaired during the night.

The next day, the 25th, was at once Sabbath and Christmas. The bombardment was renewed in the morning, and was more effective. The casualties in the fort were 46, three men being killed and nine mortally wounded. Four gun-carriages and one 10-inch gun were disabled. While the bombardment was going on, and under cover of the fleet, the landing of the troops began about noon. About this time Admiral Porter's flag-ship came alongside Butler's. After an exchanged greeting, the admiral hallooed through his speaking-trumpet, "There is not a rebel within five miles of the fort. You have nothing to do but to land and take possession of it."

The military force was 6500 strong, consisting of General Ames's division of the Twenty-fourth Corps, and General Paine's division of the Twenty-fifth. Paine's division consisted of colored troops. Between 2100 and 2300 men were landed. General Weitzel went with the first 500 (General Curtis's brigade of Ames's division) to reconnoitre. In advancing upon the fort about 300 prisoners were captured by the reconnoitring column. The skirmishers were pushed up by General Curtis to within 150 yards of the fort. Weitzel mounted an artificial knoll, and took a view of the fort. As a defensive work, it did not appear to be injured by the terrific bombardment which it had sustained, and which was still going on. He counted 16 guns, all in proper position, on the land face. Even the grass slopes of the traverses and parapet remained unbroken, and their regular shapes undisturbed. The row of palisades in front of the ditch presented no opening. "It was a stronger work," he says, "than I had ever seen or heard of being assailed during this war." Weitzel remembered Fort Wagner; he recalled his experience in regard to assaults upon works not nearly so strong as this, and which had all proved failures; he remembered, also, that he had been appointed by General Grant to command the expedition instead of Gillmore on the ground that the latter had once shown timidity; that he himself had just been appointed to a major generalship, and that his confirmation depended largely upon his present conduct. He had every possible motive for boldness. Yet he considered that it would be murder to assail the fort, which, if skillfully defended (as he must assume it would be, knowing nothing to the contrary), ought to repulse any attack which he could make; and he advised General Butler against an assault. In the mean time another brigade had landed, and Curtis's skirmishers advanced boldly up to the par-

ADELBERT AMES.

; which had been shot down and fallen outside the parapet. But this ·loit did not change Weitzel's opinion. He knew that a portion of an ·ulting column might even enter a fort, and yet the main body be re-·sed. Curtis's advance had not been resisted, but this might be due either ·he severity of the bombardment or to a deliberate design on the part of garrison to tempt an assault. Even if it was due to the bombardment, latter must cease at the moment of assault, and the garrison would ·ing again to its guns. General Curtis thought that, if allowed to advance, could capture the fort. But as there was no well understood and skill-·y arranged plan of attack, and no feint to cover his operations, it is very

two reasons for taking this step. In the first place, a storm was approach-ing, and he feared that it would be impossible to supply his troops on the shore. In the second place, a considerable force of the enemy was on his right flank at Sugar Loaf, and he thought that, under these circumstances, the position was untenable. There was nothing in the way of his landing the remainder of his force, and nothing prevented the landing of supplies until midnight.[1] The fleet would probably outride the gale, and would see to it that his force was supplied and protected against attack. Besides, General Butler had been ordered by General Grant to remain if he effected a landing. The question of immediate assault was left to his discretion; but,

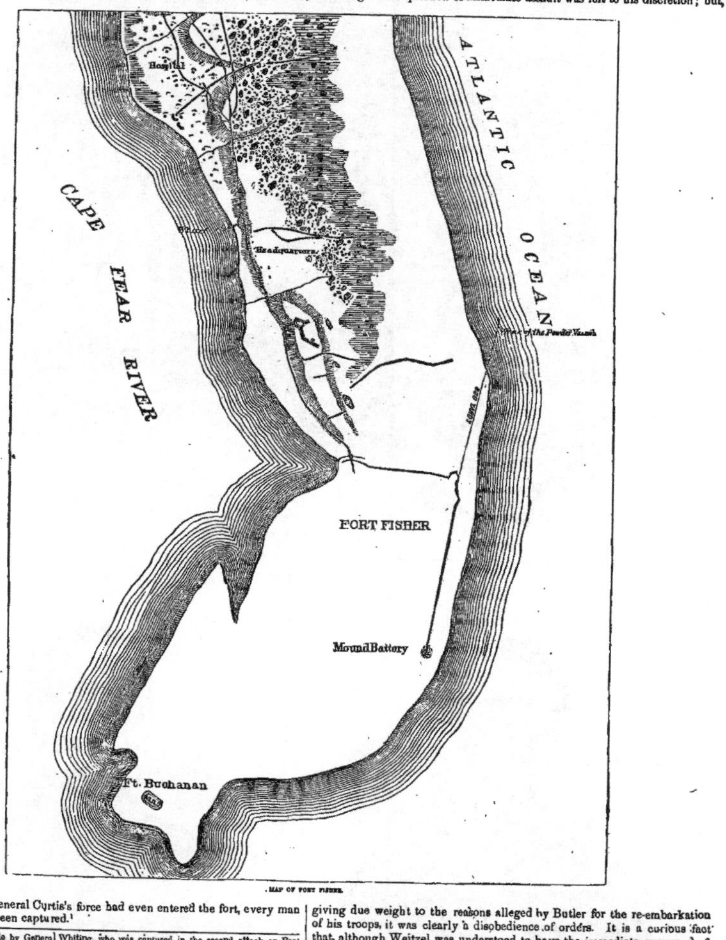

MAP OF FORT FISHER.

·robable that, if General Curtis's force had even entered the fort, every man ·f it would have been captured.[1]

giving due weight to the reasons alleged by Butler for the re-embarkation of his troops, it was clearly a disobedience of orders. It is a curious fact that, although Weitzel was understood to have the immediate command of the expedition, he never saw the orders issued by General Grant for its conduct, and was not aware, until some time afterward, of Grant's intention that the land force should maintain its position after landing.[2]

[1] The statement made by General Whiting, who was captured in the second attack on Fort ·isher, certainly confirms the wisdom of General Weitzel's opinion. He says that "the garrison ·as in no instance driven from its guns, and fired in return, according to orders, slowly and delib-·ately, 662 shot and shells;" that on the land front 17 guns were in position, and the palisade was ·perfect order; and that, while it was possible that 8000 or 6000 men might have carried the ·ork by assault, such an event was not probable. "The work," he adds, "was very strong, the ·arrison in good spirits, and ready; and the fire on the approaches (the assaulting column having ·o cover) would have been extraordinarily heavy. In addition to the heavy guns, I had a battery ·f Napoleons, on which I placed great reliance. The palisade alone would have been a most for-·midable obstacle."

same time making a concentrated and tremendous enfilading fire upon the curtain. The garrison, however, at the proper moment, when the fire slackened to allow the approach of the enemy's land force, drove them off with grape and musketry; at dark the enemy withdrew."

[1] See Captain Alden's testimony.—*Committee Report*, p. 60.

DAVID D. PORTER.

BENJAMIN H. PORTER.

SAMUEL W. PRESTON.

LANDING OF TROOPS ABOVE FORT FISHER.

Thus the expedition failed, and the failure was due to mismanagement. It had been delayed, in the first place, until the enemy had gained time for re-enforcement. There was no well-arranged plan of attack. And there was no attempt made to maintain the position secured by the military force on Federal Point.[1] The loss in life, however, had been slight. Upward of forty casualties occurred in the navy from the bursting of 100-lb. Parrott guns on several of the vessels. The loss thus caused was greater than that inflicted by the enemy.

The popular disappointment which followed the failure of an expedition from which, chiefly on account of the extent of the naval force, so much had been expected, was diversified with the mutual recriminations between the army and navy commanders. But these find no proper place in history. The Committee on the Conduct of the War (Benjamin F. Wade, chairman) investigated the affair, and acquitted General Butler of blame. But General Grant gave his own decision in another way by relieving General Butler of his command of the Army of the James.

Admiral Porter determined to remain until a more efficient military commander should be sent to co-operate with him. He even proposed to take the fort with his sailors.

While the altercation occasioned by the first attack on Fort Fisher was going on, a second expedition was organized, in which the command of the military force was assigned to Major General Alfred H. Terry, who, after the death of General D. B. Birney, stood next to Weitzel in the Army of the James. His command was the same as that with which Butler had sailed, with a single brigade added, bringing its number up to about 8000 men. General Terry, though not a graduate of West Point, had carefully studied the art of war theoretically and practically.

Porter, after experimenting on Fort Fisher for two or three days subsequent to Butler's departure, had returned to Fortress Monroe, where he was joined by Terry before the middle of January. On the 12th of that month the combined expedition reached New Inlet, and the next day the troops were landed. General Whiting and Colonel Lamb still commanded the garrison, which now numbered 2500 men, more than double the force which had confronted Butler. At 2 P.M. on the 13th the debarkation was completed, and the bombardment commenced again, and was more precise and effective than in the first attack. The garrison were driven from their guns, which were soon silenced, and many of them disabled. All night the bom-

ALFRED H. TERRY.

order—stated that in certain cases he was to intrench and hold his position, and co-operate with the navy in the reduction of the fort. General Grant said to me the other night that when he ordered the expedition to sail he knew that Wilmington and the works there were nearly devoid of troops, and he thought if we moved down there and landed quickly, the mere effect of landing the troops, together with the presence of such a fleet, would be to compel them to surrender. But in consequence of the delay the enemy got troops down there. But he said that his intention was, after we had made a landing there, finding that it was not possible to assault, that General Butler should intrench there."

Question. "What was there to prevent compliance with such an order?"

Answer. "There was nothing to prevent a compliance with it. There would have been difficulties to contend with at that season of the year. The landing of supplies would have been one difficulty; the annoyance from the rebel gun-boats in the river would have been another. But they might, and probably would have been driven off by our artillery. . . . . If I had had the instructions that General Grant gave to General Butler . . . . I would have intrenched and remained there. . . . . No matter what the difficulties were, that order would have covered him from any consequences."

General Grant testifies (*ibidem*, p. 54): "There is no question that General Butler could have remained, in obedience to my instructions; but I do not think he was guided by them; I do not think he paid any particular attention to them."

[1] The following correspondence passed between General Butler and Admiral Porter just after the re-embarkation:

General Butler writes: "Upon landing the troops and making a thorough reconnoissance of Fort Fisher, both General Weitzel and myself are fully of the opinion that the place could not be carried by assault, as it was left substantially uninjured as a defensive work by the navy fire. We found seventeen guns protected by traverses, two only of which were dismounted, bearing up the beach and covering a strip of land, the only practicable route, not more than wide enough for a thousand men in line of battle.

"Having captured Flag-pond Hill Battery, the garrison of which, sixty-five men and two commissioned officers, were taken off by the navy, we also captured Half-moon Battery and seven officers and 218 men of the Third North Carolina Junior Reserves, including its commander, from whom I learned that a portion of Hoke's division, consisting of Kirkland's and Haygood's brigades, had been sent from the lines before Richmond on Tuesday last, arriving at Wilmington Friday night.

"General Weitzel advanced his skirmish line within fifty yards of the fort, while the garrison was kept in their bomb-proofs by the fire of the navy, and so closely that three or four of the men of the picket line ventured upon the parapet and through the sally-port of the work, capturing a horse, which they brought off, killing the orderly, who was the bearer of a dispatch from the chief of artillery of General Whiting to bring a light battery within the fort, and also brought away from the parapet the flag of the fort.

"This was done while the shells of the navy were falling about the heads of the daring men who entered the work, and it was evident, as soon as the fire of the navy ceased because of the darkness, that the fort was fully manned again, and opened with grape and canister upon our picket line.

"Finding that nothing but the operations of a regular siege, which did not come within my instructions, would reduce the fort, and in view of the threatening aspect of the weather, wind rising from the southeast, rendering it impossible to make farther landing through the surf, I caused the troops, with their prisoners, to re-embark, and see nothing farther that can be done by the land forces. I shall therefore sail for Hampton Roads as soon as the transport fleet can be got in order.

"My engineers and officers report Fort Fisher to me as substantially uninjured as a defensive work."

To this Porter replies:

"I beg leave to acknowledge the receipt of your letter of this date, the substance of which was communicated to me by General Weitzel last night.

"I have ordered the largest vessels to proceed off Beaufort and fill up with ammunition, to be ready for another attack, in case it is decided to proceed with this matter by making other arrangements.

"We have not commenced firing rapidly yet, and could keep any rebels inside from showing their heads until an assaulting column was within twenty yards of the works.

"I wish some more of your gallant fellows had followed the officer who took the flag from the parapet, and the brave fellow who brought the horse out from the fort. I think they would have found it an easier conquest than is supposed.

"I do not, however, pretend to place my opinion in opposition to General Weitzel, whom I know to be an accomplished soldier and engineer, and whose opinion has great weight with me.

"I will look out that the troops are all off in safety. We will have a west wind presently, and a smooth beach about three o'clock, when sufficient boats will be sent for them.

"The prisoners now on board the Santiago de Cuba will be delivered to the provost-marshal at Fortress Monroe, unless you wish to take them on board one of the transports, which would be inconvenient just now."

bardment went on, giving the enemy no opportunity to repair injuries. On the 14th the fleet continued the battle with the silent fort, its efforts being chiefly directed to dismount the guns. In the mean time preparations were made for the assault, which was to take place on the afternoon of the 15th. Up to this time shot and shell from 500 guns had been beating upon the earth-work, doing the work itself little damage, but breaking the palisade and dismounting its guns. About 1400 sailors and marines had landed, and were to participate in the assault, the plan of which had been most skillfully arranged. The marines and sailors were to attack the sea-face of the fort, while Terry's three brigades should carry the land front. The assault by the sailors was to be covered by an intrenched party on the beach. A perfect system of signals was agreed upon between the military commander and the admiral. No precaution was neglected, no measure overlooked which would assist in securing success.

At 3 P.M. the preconcerted signal was given for the commencement of the assault, and the admiral turned his guns from the parapet and against the upper batteries (on the centre mound). The attack by the marines appears to have been mistaken by the garrison for the main assault. The intrenched party of sharp-shooters did not well cover the advance of the sailors, and the latter were repulsed, losing Lieutenants Preston and Porter, who were bravest among the brave.[1] In the mean while the soldiers had gained the northeastern rampart. The guns of the fleet were turned upon the traverses, while the brave men of Terry's command fought their way from traverse to traverse,[2] overpowering the garrison, and driving it back to the Mound Battery. Both Generals Whiting and Lamb had been wounded. Dispirited by the loss of their leaders, the Confederates were easily driven from their last refuge, and the entire command surrendered, with 75 guns. The fighting had been desperate, and had lasted from 3 o'clock till 10 P.M. The Federal loss in Terry's command was 110 killed and 536 wounded, including among the latter all three of the brigade commanders engaged in the assault—Generals Curtis, Bell, and Pennybacker. The casualties in the fleet amounted to 309, making a total loss of nearly 1000 men.

In a great degree this success had been due to surprise, or rather to an attack made in an unexpected quarter with the main column. This column, advancing out of the woods, suddenly approached the western extremity of the land front, and one brigade (Bell's) charged along a narrow causeway in the face of four guns.[1] Nothing, however, was accomplished by the second expedition which might not, under good management, have been as well accomplished by the first.

The next morning a sad event occurred, which to some extent marred the cheer of victory. By some culpable negligence, the soldiers were allowed to approach the magazine with lighted candles. In this way an explosion was occasioned, resulting in the loss of about 200 men. Among the severely wounded was Colonel Alonzo Alden, of the One Hundred-and-Sixty-ninth New York regiment.

As a result of the fall of Fort Fisher, the surrounding work—Fort Caswell, a large work at the West Inlet, mounting 29 guns, all the works on Smith's Island, those between Caswell and Smithville up to the battery on Reeves's Point, on the west side of the river, were abandoned. Including the guns taken at Fort Fisher, 169 were captured in all.

The same day that Fort Fisher was assaulted and carried by Terry's troops, Major General Schofield, with the Twenty-third Corps, 21,000 strong, left Thomas's army for the East. In February Schofield was appointed commander of the Department of North Carolina, just created. He then commenced a campaign, the ultimate object of which was the occupation of Goldsborough, in order to prepare for the arrival of Sherman's army by opening railway communication from that point with the sea-coast, and accumulating supplies. Wilmington was to be captured first, because it would be a valuable auxiliary base to Morehead City if Sherman should reach Goldsborough, and absolutely necessary in the event of Sherman's concentrating his army farther south.

Schofield, with the Third division (J. D. Cox's) of his corps, reached the mouth of Cape Fear River on the 9th of February, landing near Fort Fisher. Terry and Porter had already made the port of Wilmington useless to blockade runners. The former, still retaining his command, and having the co-operation of the North Atlantic Squadron, held a line across the peninsula two miles above Fort Fisher, and occupied Smithville and Fort Caswell. The Cape Fear had been entered by a portion of the fleet, so that both of Terry's flanks were secure. The enemy, under General Hoke, still covered Fort Anderson on the west bank, and the immediate defenses of Wilmington, in position impregnable against a direct attack. The Confederate line must be turned either on its left by the fleet passing above Masonborough Inlet, or by a march of the army around the swamp covering its right. The

[1] K. R. Breese thus alludes to the death of these gallant officers in a special report:

"North Atlantic Squadron, U. S. Flag Ship Malvern, off Fort Fisher, January 16, 1865.

"ADMIRAL,—In my report of the assault on Fort Fisher I have scarcely mentioned the names and services of Lieutenant S. W. Preston, your flag-lieutenant, and Lieutenant B. H. Porter, your flag-captain, thinking that by a little delay I might the more do justice, yet I seem to feel that impossible in me. Preston, after accomplishing most splendidly the work assigned him by you, which was both dangerous and laborious, under constant fire, came to me, as my aid, for orders, showing no flagging of spirit or body, and returning from the rear, whither he had been sent, fell among the foremost at the front, as he had lived the thorough embodiment of a United States naval officer. Porter, conspicuous by his figure and uniform, as well as by his great gallantry, claimed the right to lead the headmost column with the Malvern's men he had taken with him, carrying your flag, and fell at its very head. Two more noble spirits the world never saw, nor had the navy ever two more intrepid men. Young, talented, and handsome, the bravest of the brave, pure in their lives, surely their names deserve something more than a passing mention, and are worthy to be handed down to posterity with the greatest and best of naval heroes.

"Were you not so well acquainted with their characters I should deem it my duty to speak of their high merits; but as chief of your staff, to which they belonged, I must speak of their wonderful singleness of purpose to do their whole duty; always most cheerful and willing, desirous of undertaking any thing which might redound to the credit of the service, giving me at all times the most ready assistance in my duties, combining with their intelligence a ready perception as to the best mode of accomplishing their orders, the country has lost two such servants as could illy be spared, and your staff its brightest ornaments.

"Very respectfully, your obedient servant,

K. R. BREESE,

"Fleet Captain, North Atlantic Squadron.

"Rear-Admiral DAVID D. PORTER, Commanding North Atlantic Squadron."

[2] "These traverses," says Admiral Porter, "are immense bomb-proofs, about sixty feet long, fifty feet wide, and twenty feet high—seventeen of them in all, being on the northeast face. Between each traverse, or bomb-proof, are one or two heavy guns. The fighting lasted until ten o'clock at night, the *Ironsides* and Monitors firing through the traverses in advance of our troops, and the level strip of land called Federal Point being enfiladed by the ships to prevent re-enforcements reaching the rebels."

[1] Admiral Porter says in his report:

"I have since visited Fort Fisher and its adjoining works, and find their strength greatly beyond what I had conceived. An engineer might be excusable in saying they could not be captured except by regular siege. I wonder even now how it was done. The work, as I said before, is really stronger than the Malakoff Tower, which defied so long the combined powers of France and England; and yet it is captured by a handful of men, under the fire of the guns of the fleet, and in seven hours after the attack commenced in earnest."

PORTER'S FLEET CELEBRATING THE CAPTURE OF FORT FISHER.

latter movement was adopted. The result was successful. On the 19th of February Fort Anderson was abandoned, and the enemy retreated behind Town Creek, where he again intrenched. Terry meanwhile occupied the force on the peninsula. The next day, the 20th, General Cox crossed Town Creek, gained the enemy's flank, attacked and routed him, taking two guns and 375 prisoners. Cox continued his advance, and threatened to cross the Cape Fear above Wilmington. General Hoke then gave up the struggle, set fire to his steamers, cotton, and other stores, and abandoned Wilmington on the night of the 21st. The next morning Cox entered the town without opposition. In these operations the Federal loss was very slight, amounting to about 200 in killed and wounded. That of the enemy is estimated at 1000 men, besides 80 guns. Goldsborough was occupied by General Schofield on the 21st of March, where he effected a junction with Sherman's army.

FORT SUMTER.

CHAPTER LIII.

RECOVERY OF THE ATLANTIC COAST.

II. CHARLESTON.

Defenses of Charleston.—Its Approaches.—The Department of the South.—Hunter's Operations against Charleston.—Federal Repulse at Secessionville, May, 1862.—Attack on the Blockading Fleet by the Palmetto State and Chicora.—Beauregard's *Ruse de Guerre.*—Admiral Dupont's Bombardment, April, 1863.—The Obstructions in the Harbor defeat the Undertaking.—Results of the Bombardment.—Sinking of the Keokuk.—How the Monitors came out of the Fight.—Dupont succeeded by Dahlgren, and Hunter by Gillmore.—The Situation when Gillmore assumed Command.—Capture of Morris's Island.—Terry's co-operative Movement on James's Island.—The First Assault on Fort Wagner.—Second Assault.—Death of Strong and Shaw.—Siege of the Fort.—Operations of the Fleet.—The "Swamp Angel."—Correspondence between Gillmore and Beauregard.—Demolition of Fort Sumter.—Dahlgren's Error in not immediately advancing upon Charleston.—Fort Johnson strengthened by the Confederates during the delay.—Confederate Evacuation of Forts Wagner and Gregg.—Williams's Night Attack on Fort Sumter.—Result of the Conquest of Morris's Island.—General Foster's Operations in 1865.—He is relieved by Gillmore.—Charleston is turned by Sherman's Movement.—Capture of the City by Gillmore.—Raising of the old Flag over Fort Sumter.

FORT Sumter was captured by the Confederates on the 13th of April, 1861. The defenses of Charleston at that time consisted of the following works, which had been constructed by the United States government:

1. Fort Sumter, a strong casemated brick work of five faces, with three tiers of guns, two in embrasure and one *en barbette.* This fort is distant a little more than three miles from the city, and is on the south side of the channel, about midway between Morris's Island on the south, and Sullivan's Island on the north. Its full armament would comprise 135 guns. At the time of its capture by the Confederates the fort mounted 78 guns.

2. Fort Moultrie, 1700 yards from Fort Sumter, on Sullivan's Island. This also is a brick work, with one tier of guns *en barbette.* In 1860 it mounted 52 guns.

3. Castle Pinckney, a brick work on Shute's Folly Island, distant one mile east of the lower end of the city, and mounting, at the beginning of the war, 28 guns.

The city of Charleston is situated at the head of Charleston Harbor, on the point of the narrow peninsula formed by Ashley and Cooper Rivers. Across the entrance of the harbor—between Sullivan's and Morris's Islands—stretches a bar, seven miles below the city. The islands on either side are each about three and a half miles in length, low, narrow, and sandy, and separated from the main land by deep and impenetrable marshes, which are submerged by the spring tides. The distance from their nearest point to Charleston is between three and four miles. Charleston Harbor itself is bounded by James's Island on the south, and on the north by the main land. Its entrance is 2700 yards in width. James's Island, south of the city, is limited on the west by Stono River, which separates it from John's Island. Stono River is connected with the Ashley, south of Charleston, by Wappoo Creek. South of James's Island is Cole's Island, which is for the most part marsh, with Folly River on the south separating it from Folly Island. Lighthouse Inlet, at its mouth, separates Morris's and Folly Islands. The formation of all these islands is thin quartz sand.

The fortifications of Charleston at the opening of the war were only adapted to resist a naval attack. To these, other works were rapidly added. On Sullivan's Island were erected, in addition to Fort Moultrie, the following works: Marion, Beauregard, Marshall, and Battery Bee. On Morris's Island a battery had been constructed at Cummings's Point, and a mile farther south Fort Wagner. Forts Sumter and Moultrie were strengthened, and their armament increased. Old Fort Johnson, on James's Island, was rebuilt and armed with heavy guns, and north of it was constructed Fort Ripley. The preparations against a land attack were formidable. On the James a line of works was built fronting Stone River, with Fort Pemberton near its northern extremity. An inclosed work on Cole's Island covered the Stono Inlet and harbor. Heavy guns were mounted on the wharves of Charleston, and in the rear of the city formidable works were erected. Such and so extensive were the defenses of Charleston under the command of the Confederate General Beauregard.

On the 15th of March, 1862, the Department of the South was created, embracing South Carolina, Georgia, and Florida, and was assigned to General Hunter. Port Royal had been occupied by a military force under General T. W. Sherman and Dupont's squadron late in 1861. Edisto Island, farther north, was taken possession of by Sherman in February, 1862. The expeditionary force commanded by General Sherman in March became subject to General Hunter's control. During the month which followed, General Q. A. Gillmore captured Fort Pulaski.

In December, 1861, a Federal fleet of sixteen vessels, heavily laden with granite, was sunk on the bar in Charleston Harbor to obstruct the channel and obviate the necessity of a blockade. This operation excited a great degree of indignation on the part of foreign governments. The elements of nature expressed their dissent in a more quiet way, but with much more effect. In a few weeks the Ashley and Cooper Rivers made for themselves a new channel, better than the previous one.

Shortly after General Hunter assumed command of the Department of the South, operations were commenced against Charleston by way of Stono River and James's Island. The Confederates had made a great mistake in abandoning Cole's Island, which commanded the entrance of the Stono. Admiral Dupont, with three gun-boats—the Unadilla, Pembina, and Ottawa—entered the river on the 29th of May, 1862. At the approach of the gun-boats all the works of the enemy along the Stono up to the Wappoo were abandoned. Early in June Generals Hunter and Benham arrived with a considerable detachment of troops—too weak, however, for operations on James's Island, where the enemy was not only strongly intrenched from Secessionville to Fort Johnson, but had an easy and open communication with the rear, and could bring up re-enforcements at his pleasure. On the 16th of June an attack was made on Secessionville by General I. I. Stevens's and General H. G. Wright's divisions of General Benham's command—some 6000 strong—but was repulsed by the enemy, the Federal loss amounting to over 500 men.

After this action for nearly a year the operations against Charleston were suspended. The Charleston campaign from the beginning of 1863 till the close of the war may be treated under three heads:

I. Admiral Dupont's bombardment, April 7, 1863.

II. General Gillmore's operations on Morris's Island during the summer of 1863.

III. General Foster's and Gillmore's movements co-operative with Sherman's Carolina campaign, resulting in the occupation of Charleston, February 21, 1865.

I. Admiral Dupont's expedition was an experiment, in which the offensive and defensive power of monitors was to be put to the severest test. The original Monitor—whose name came to be applied to all iron-clads of similar construction—had been lost on her way to join Dupont's squadron (the South Atlantic) in the autumn of 1862.[1] The popular expectation as to the omnipotence of the monitors was extravagant and unfounded. The Merrimac had been beaten by the original Monitor, and the Nashville had been sunk by another vessel of the same class. Fort Pulaski had fallen, not before the gun-boats of Dupont's fleet, but from the effect of batteries on shore.[2] It is true, Dupont had at that time no monitors, but the presence of these could scarcely have affected the result. The monitors, however, had undergone a pretty fair trial in the attack on Fort McAllister. The only vessel of this class engaged in the assault was the Montauk. The result seemed to prove the invulnerability of the monitor, but its offensive power as

[1] See Chapter XIII., p. 258.

[2] Gillmore's Operations against Charleston, p. 240.

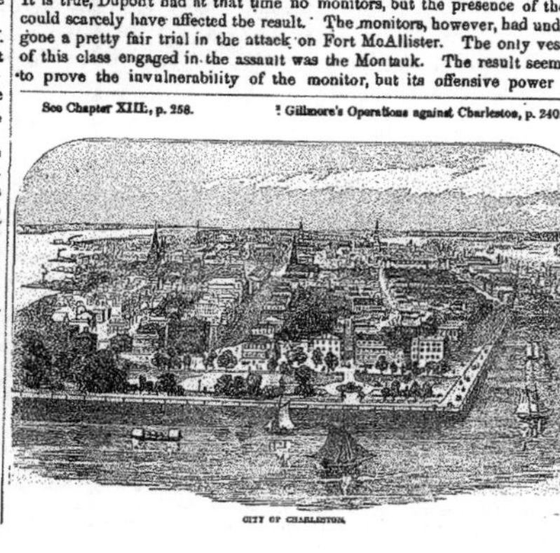
CITY OF CHARLESTON.

SAMUEL F. DUPONT.

against forts was not so well established. A visible impression was made upon McAllister, but not of such a character as to destroy either its offensive or defensive power. It was still a question whether a large number of monitors might not do what one alone had failed to accomplish. Indeed, it was confidently expected that the monitor fleet which Dupont commanded in April, 1863, would batter down Fort Fisher and ride up to Charleston, while a military force about 10,000 strong, under General Hunter, would occupy and hold that city under the guns of the fleet.

Previous to the attack on Charleston an event occurred which showed the insufficiency of blockading vessels against rams. Early on the morning of January 29th, 1863, the Princess Royal was captured while attempting to pass through the blockading squadron into Charleston Harbor. Her cargo would have been of great value to the enemy, consisting of two engines intended for iron-clads, with rifled guns, arms, ammunition, and medicines. Her loss was a severe blow to the Confederates, who, ascertaining that she was still at anchor off the harbor, organized an expedition for her recapture. Before light on the morning of the 31st two Confederate iron-clad steam rams—the Palmetto State, commanded by Lieutenant Rutledge, and the Chicora, Commander Tucker—ran out by the main ship channel from Charleston, and attacked the blockading squadron with great vigor. The latter consisted of 10 vessels—the Housatonic, Mercedita, Ottawa, Unadilla, Keystone State, Quaker City, Memphis, Augusta, Stettin, and Flag—most of them being light vessels, and incompetent to resist such an onslaught. The iron-clads and two of the heaviest men of war, the Powhatan and Canandaigua, were off at Port Royal. The Palmetto State, with Flag-officer D. N. Ingraham on board, almost immediately disabled the Mercedita with a 7-inch shell, which entered her side, exploded in one of her boilers, and in its exit killed and wounded several men. One blow from the ram settled the case of this ship, which, as it seemed to be sinking, was surrendered. Both the Palmetto and Chicora then attacked the Keystone State. The latter bore down rapidly upon the Palmetto, intending to sink her. But a shot from the ram passed through both her steam chests; 10 rifle shells struck her near and below water mark, and almost simultaneously a fire broke out in her forehold. Commander Le Roy hauled down his flag. The enemy still continued to fire, and the flag was again hoisted and the battle renewed. The Augusta, Memphis, and Quaker City came up and relieved the suffering vessel, one fourth of whose crew had been killed or wounded. Together with the Mercedita, whose leak had been stopped and who had not been secured by the enemy, the Keystone State went to Port Royal. The other vessels of the squadron kept at a prudent distance from the rams. Soon however, the Housatonic came up, and the rams, refusing battle, fled back into the harbor.

CONFEDERATE RAMS ENGAGING THE BLOCKADING FLEET OFF CHARLESTON.

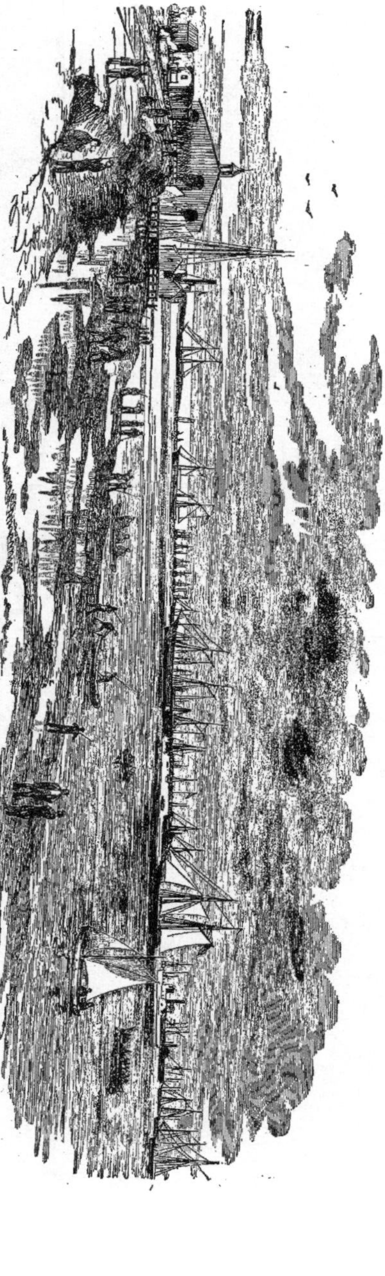

DEPARTURE OF DUPONT'S EXPEDITION FROM HAMPTON.

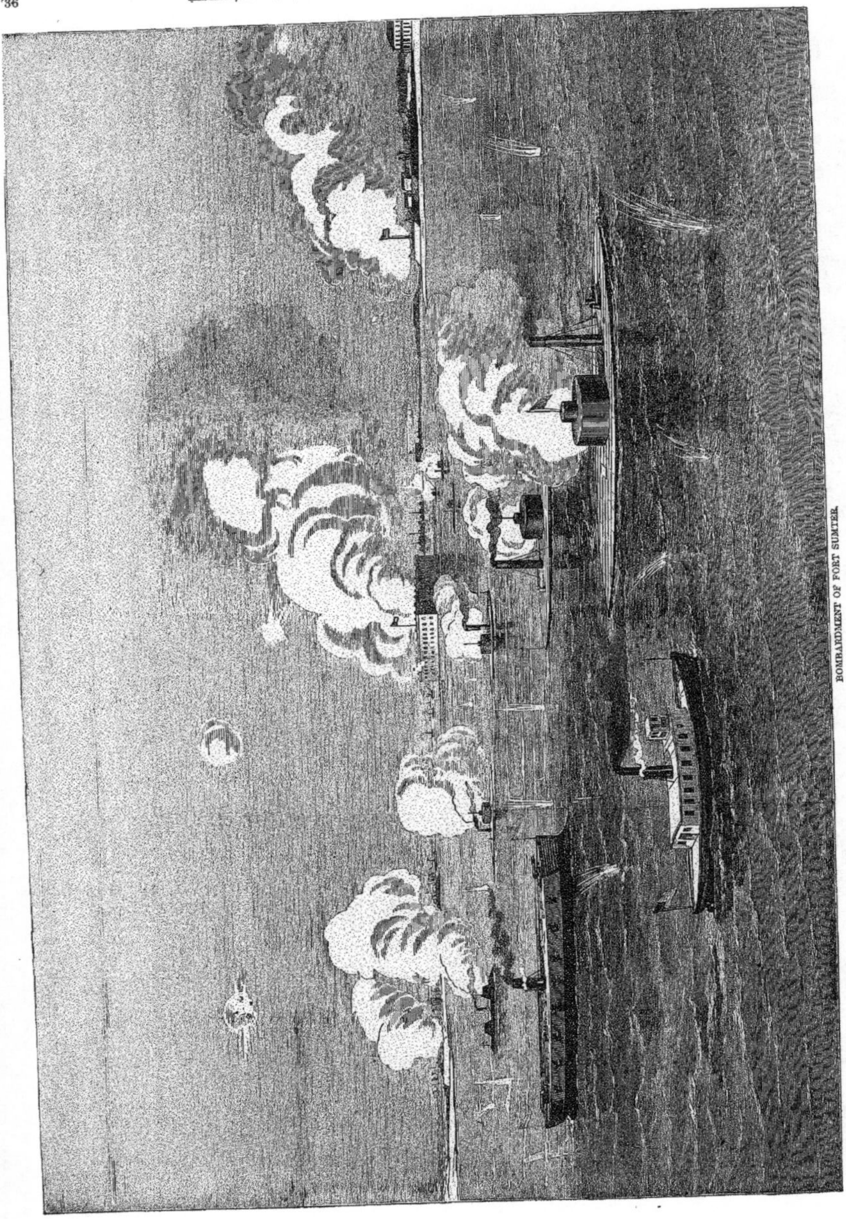

BOMBARDMENT OF FORT SUMTER.

Upon the return of his rams a bright idea occurred to Beauregard. He knew that the reports of Admiral Dupont could not reach the North for some three days at least. His own communication by telegraph with Richmond was uninterrupted, and the Richmond papers soon found their way to New York. Here, then, was a splendid opportunity for a *ruse de guerre*, which, if it involved considerable lying, might—so thought the chivalrous, honor-loving general—be excused on the maxim that "all is fair in war." Accordingly, over his own signature and that of Flag-officer Ingraham, he dispatched to Richmond an official proclamation, stating that the Confederate naval force at Charleston had attacked the blockading fleet off the harbor, and had sunk, dispersed, and drove off the same, and declaring the blockade of Charleston to be raised from and after the 31st of January, 1863. This proclamation, with Beauregard's account of the affair, asserting that, as a result of the naval engagement on the 31st, two Federal vessels were sunk, four set on fire, and the rest driven away, was published in the Richmond papers of February 2d. As if this were not enough in the way of falsification, another dispatch was added, declaring that on the afternoon of the 31st the British consul, on board the British war steamer Petrel, had gone five miles beyond the usual anchorage of the blockaders, and could see nothing of them with glasses.

Now, without characterizing these declarations by the plain English term that is applicable to them, it is sufficient to say that they are false in every particular. And they were recognized as false by every European government. The raid with the rams had not succeeded in the object for which it was undertaken—the recovery of the Princess Royal; they had retreated on the appearance of the Housatonic, and did not venture out again. Not a single Federal steamer was sunk, not one was burned, and only two were in any way disabled. The position of the blockading squadron was not shifted, and no vessel advanced from Charleston, after the affair, beyond the bar of the harbor.[1]

By the 7th of April the preparations for the bombardment of Fort Sumter were completed. At noon of that day the vessels of Dupont's fleet, having crossed the bar by the new channel formed since the sinking of the stone fleet, proceeded to the attack. The attacking fleet consisted of nine vessels, all of which were monitors except the New Ironsides and Keokuk, which were iron-clad and turreted. The five strongest vessels of the blockading squadron were held in reserve.[2] The orders issued by the admiral were that the fleet should pass up the main ship channel, open fire upon Fort Sumter when within range of that work, disregarding the batteries on Morris's Island, advance to a position northwest of Sumter in order to attack its weakest face, fire upon the work with precision rather than rapidity, and, having reduced the fort, turn against the Morris's Island batteries. The advance had been delayed till noon, waiting for the tide, and from the fleet, in the mean while, could be seen the steeples and roofs of Charleston crowded with spectators, just as they had been two years before, when Fort Sumter was attacked by its present defender. It is a novel conflict whose spectacle is now anxiously awaited—that of a fleet mounting 32 guns arrayed against forts which mount 300. The forts know little of the monitors, but stand defiant. The monitors know little of the forts, or the obstructions to their progress, but defiantly they advance.

The reserve fleet lies outside the bar, while the monitors approach Sumter. The Weehawken has the lead, and as she advances, a raft attached to her prow looks out for torpedoes. Scarcely has she started, however, before the grappling irons attached to this raft become fouled in the anchor cable, and an hour's delay is occasioned. Then the movement is resumed. The entire fleet passes Morris's Island, but no gun opens upon her. Now (3 P.M.) she rounds to enter the harbor, and comes within range of Fort Sumter and the batteries on Sullivan's Island. A broadside from the upper tier of guns (*en barbette*) greets the Weehawken, who is seeking, according to orders, to reach the left face of the fort. Suddenly she halts midway between Sumter and Moultrie. Her progress has been stopped by an unforeseen obstacle—a stout hawser stretches between the two forts, strung with torpedoes. The fleet has been proceeding along the right channel thus far, and, meeting this obstruction in the way of reaching its desired position, it changes its course, and tries the left channel, between Fort Sumter and Cummings's Point. This also is blockaded, and more effectually than the other, by a row of piles stretching across the channel. Beyond is seen another row extending between Forts Johnson and Ripley, and more careful scrutiny discloses a third row, beyond which lie three Confederate rams.

Thus the original design of reaching Fort Sumter's weakest face is frustrated at the outset. And there is no help for it. The fort could probably be reduced but for these obstructions which cover its weakness: the obstructions might be removed but for the thundering guns of the fort.

To make matters worse, the New Ironsides—the flag-ship—caught by the tide, refuses to obey her rudder, and becomes unmanageable. The Catskill and the Nantucket fall foul of her, and thus remain a full quarter of an hour. While, in the midst of these difficulties, the vessels are taking such positions as they can gain, they are in a circle of fire, which concentrates upon them from Cummings's Point Battery, Battery Bee, and Forts Beauregard, Moultrie, and Sumter. The range is less than 800 yards, and the fire is from guns of the heaviest calibré that could be obtained from the Tredegar works of Richmond or from the armories of Europe. This fire has been going on from the time of its first opening by Sumter; but now for thirty minutes it pours upon the fleet the white heat of its fury. One hundred and sixty shots are counted in a single minute; they strike the iron plates of the monitors as rapidly as the ticking of a watch. It is estimated that from all the forts, in this brief engagement, not less than 3500 rounds have been fired. In reply, only 139 shots have been delivered by the fleet.

And what is the result to the fort? What to the fleet? A few marks are visible on Fort Sumter, and the parapet near the eastern angle shows a huge crater.[1] If the monitors could remain where they are, time would solve the problem of the reduction of the fort. But they can not. Apart from the embarrassments under which they are working as regards effective offense—their confined space; their tendency to drift against the obstructions or upon submerged batteries; and the clouds of smoke which hang over the water, obscuring their range—they have sustained injuries which compel their withdrawal, and at 5 P.M. the signal is given for their retreat. Already the Keokuk, which advanced to within 570 yards of Fort Sumter, has left the field in a sinking condition, having been completely riddled with shots. It is her last fight. The Ironsides also has lost one of her port-shutters, her gun-deck is thus exposed, and her bows have been penetrated with red-hot shot. But these are not monitors. How is it with the latter? The Nahant has received thirty wounds, her turret has been jammed so that it will not turn, and her pilot-house is in such a rickety condition that every bolt in it flies about when it is struck, killing and wounding its tenants. The turret of the Passaic is broken and unmanageable. The Nantucket's turret is jarred so that the cover of the port can not be opened, and consequently her 15-inch gun can not be used. The other four monitors are essentially uninjured.[2]

After the withdrawal of the fleet, Admiral Dupont having been informed as to the conditions of his vessels, decided not to renew the conflict, and the next day returned to Port Royal. The Keokuk sank on the morning of the 8th abreast of Morris's Island, and her armament was thus left in the hands of the enemy. In the action of the 7th only one man was mortally wounded. The entire casualties were twenty-six.

Within the short space of about two hours had been decided the question of monitors against forts. The result was decisive on two points: first, that the defensive powers of these vessels was not sufficient to withstand the concentrated fire of half a dozen forts heavily armed; and, secondly, that while the reduction of brick forts might result from a long-continued bombardment, yet the limits of endurance on the part of the monitors were such as to render this impracticable.[3]

II. The War Department was not satisfied with the result of the experiment, and determined to renew the attack, but upon a somewhat different plan. Admiral Dupont was relieved of the command, and would have been succeeded by Admiral Foote but for the death of the latter on the way to Port Royal. The command of the South Atlantic squadron was therefore, on the

---

[1] Beauregard's statements are fully refuted by that subsequently made by Admiral Dupont, and signed by nearly all the commanding officers of the fleet lying off Charleston Harbor on the 31st. We make the following extract from this statement:

"We deem it our duty to state that the so-called results are false in every particular—no vessels were sunk, none were set on fire seriously. . . . . So hasty was the retreat of the rams that, although they might have perceived that the Keystone State had received serious damage, no attempt was ever made to approach her. The Stettin and Ottawa, at the extreme end of the line, did not get under way from their position till after the firing had ceased, and the Stettin merely saw the black smoke as the rams disappeared over the bar. The rams withdrew hastily toward the harbor, and on their way were fired at by the Housatonic and Augusta until both had got beyond reach of their guns. They anchored under the protection of their forts, and remained there. No vessel, iron-clad or other, passed out over the bar after the return of the rams inshore. The Unadilla was not aware of the attack until the Housatonic commenced firing, when she moved out toward that vessel from her anchorage. The Housatonic was never beyond the usual line of the blockade. We do not hesitate to state that no vessel came out beyond the bar after the return of the rams, at between 7 and 8 A.M., to the cover of the forts. We believe the statement that any vessel came any where near the usual anchorage of any of the blockaders, or up to the bar, after the withdrawal of the rams, to be deliberately and knowingly false. If the statement from the papers, as now before us, has the sanction of the captain of the Petrel and the foreign consuls, we can only deplore that foreign officers can lend their official positions to the spreading before the world, for unworthy objects, untruths patent to every officer of this squadron."

[2] The vessels of the monitor fleet, including the New Ironsides and Keokuk, advanced in the following order:

1. Weehawken, Captain John Rodgers.
2. Passaic, Captain Percival Drayton.
3. Montauk, Commander John L. Worden.
4. Patapsco, Commander Daniel Ammen.
5. New Ironsides, Commodore Thomas Turner.
6. Catskill, Commander George W. Rodgers.
7. Nantucket, Commander Daniel McN. Fairfax.
8. Nahant, Commander John Downes.
9. Keokuk, Lieutenant Commander A. C. Rhind.

The reserve squadron consisted of the Canandaigua, Unadilla, Housatonic, Wissahickon, and Huron, under the command of Captain Joseph H. Green.

[1] Mr. William Swinton gives the following graphic description of the inside of a monitor during the engagement:

"Could you look through the smoke, and through the flame-lit ports, into one of those revolving towers, a spectacle would meet your eye such as Vulcan's stithy might present. Here are the two huge guns which form the armament of each monitor—the one eleven, and the other fifteen inches in diameter of bore. The gunners, begrimed with powder and stripped to the waist, are loading the gun. The charge of powder—thirty-five pounds to each charge—is passed up rapidly from below; the shot, weighing four hundred and twenty pounds, is hoisted up by mechanical appliances to the muzzle of the gun, and rammed home, the gun is run out to the port, and tightly 'compressed;' the port is open for an instant, the captain of the gun stands behind, lanyard in hand—'Ready, fire!' and the enormous projectile rushes through its huge parabola, with the weight of 10,000 tons, home to its mark."

[2] The following estimate was made of the shots received by each vessel:

New Ironsides	65	Nantucket	51
Keokuk	90	Catskill	51
Weehawken	60	Patapsco	45
Montauk	20	Nahant	80
Passaic	53	Total	515

[3] A year after the attack on Charleston Admiral Dupont thus alludes to the affair:

"I am well aware," he says, "that the results at Charleston were not all that were wished for, and I quite agree with the department that there was, nevertheless, much in them that was gratifying, particularly that the loss of life was so small, and that the capacity of the iron-clads for enduring the hot and heavy fire brought to bear upon them, which would have destroyed any vessels of wood heretofore used in warfare, was made so evident. But I must take leave to remind the department that ability to endure is not a sufficient element wherewith to gain victories; that endurance must be accompanied with a corresponding power to inflict injury on the enemy; and I will improve the present occasion to repeat the expression of a conviction which I have already conveyed to the department in former letters, that the weakness of the monitor class of vessels, in this important particular, is fatal to their attempts against fortifications having outlying obstructions, as at the Ogeechee and at Charleston, or against other fortifications upon elevations, as at Fort Darling, or against any modern fortifications before which they must anchor or lie at rest, and receive much more than they can return. With even their dismantled surface they are not invulnerable, and their various mechanical contrivances for working their turrets and guns are so liable to immediate derangement, that, in the brief though fierce engagement at Charleston, five out of eight were disabled, and, as I mentioned in my detailed report to the department, half an hour more fighting would, in my judgment, have placed them all *hors de combat*."

SINKING OF THE KEOKUK.

6th of July, assigned to Admiral Dahlgren, and General Q. A. Gillmore succeeded Hunter in the command of the Department of the South. Toward the close of May, 1863, Gillmore had received orders to repair to Washington, to consult with General Halleck and Secretary Welles as to future operations against Charleston. No more troops could be spared for the Department of the South. Gillmore did not ask for more, although he knew that his operations must, on account of his small military force, be restricted to Morris's Island. With this force he proposed to occupy that island, capture Forts Wagner and Gregg, and demolish Fort Sumter by means of shore batteries. The way would thus be open for Dahlgren to advance with his fleet, remove the obstructions in the harbor, and command Charleston. Even if the city was not captured, the full possession of Morris's Island would effectually blockade the harbor.

General Gillmore assumed command of the department on the 12th of June. At that time the coast from Light-house Inlet to St. Augustine, Florida—a distance of 250 miles—was in possession of the national forces. The positions actually occupied by troops were Folly Island, Seabrook Island, on the North Edisto, St. Helena Island, Port Royal Island, Hilton Head Island, the Tybee Islands, Fort Pulaski, Ossibaw Island, Fort Clinch and Amelia Island, and the city of St. Augustine. Off or inside the principal inlets lay the blockading squadron.[1]

Folly Island was occupied by a brigade under General Vogdes, strongly intrenched, with heavy guns mounted on the south end of the island to control the entrance of the Stono River. Vogdes had also constructed a road, practicable for artillery, and affording a means of concealed communication between the several parts of the island. In Stono and Folly Rivers a naval force was stationed, consisting of two gun-boats and a mortar schooner, to secure Folly Island against attack, and to hold the Stono against the light-draught gun-boats of the enemy. Folly Island was necessarily the base of operations against Morris's Island.[2] The dense undergrowth with which it was covered afforded cover for batteries on the north end, within musket range of the enemy's picket on the opposite side of Light-house Inlet.

The forces in Ossibaw Sound and on the North Edisto were withdrawn. Gillmore's entire command available for offensive operations then consisted of 11,500 men and 66 guns, besides about 30 mortars.

The descent upon Morris's Island was made July 10th, 1863. It was an operation which required boldness and great skill, as it involved the storming of a fortified position, not by the regular approaches of a siege, but by an advance covered by a few batteries, and made in small boats exposed to the enemy's fire. There were two co-operative expeditions—one conducted by General A. H. Terry, with 3800 men, on James's Island, which was eminently successful, diverting a portion of the garrison from Morris's Island; and a second, sent from General Saxton's command at Beaufort to cut the Charleston and Savannah Railroad at Jacksborough, in order to delay re-enforcements from Savannah. This latter expedition proved a signal failure, involving the loss of two guns and a small steamer, which was burned to prevent its capture.

The main column engaged in the attack on Morris's Island—about 2000 men of General Strong's brigade—was embarked in Folly River, and passed by night during high tide through the shallow creeks into Light-house Inlet. This movement was first fixed for the night of the 8th of July, but had been postponed until the night of the 9th. At daybreak on the 10th the column halted, having reached Light-house Inlet, the boats keeping close to the east shore of the creek, where they were screened by the marsh grass from hostile observation. Shortly after daybreak the batteries on the north end of Folly Island—10 in number, and mounting 47 guns—opened against the opposite shore, the undergrowth having been previously cleared away in their front to give them an unobstructed view. Four monitors joined their fire to that of the batteries. For two hours this bombardment continued, and then Strong's brigade moved across the inlet to the assault.

The movement had been planned with much skill and secrecy, and was a surprise to the enemy. At Oyster Point, and on the firm land lower down, the Federal troops were landed under a hot fire of musketry and artillery. But the column never faltered, and by 9 o'clock A.M. all the hostile batteries south of Fort Wagner were overrun and captured. This success closed the operations of that day. The troops were within musket range of Fort Wagner, and were exhausted by the intense heat and three hours' hard fighting. Throughout the day the bombardment from the monitors was kept up, directed chiefly at Fort Wagner.

On the morning of the 11th an assault was made upon Fort Wagner. The advance, led by General Strong in person, reached and gained the parapet of the fort. But the supports could not be brought up in face of a fire from which they had no protection, and the attack failed. In the actions

[1] Gillmore's Operations against Charleston, p. 42.

[2] "The question has been asked why the route across James's Island from Stono River, the same that Brigadier General Benham attempted, was not selected to operate upon.

"The answer is simple. The enemy had more troops available for the defense of Charleston than we had for the attack. The general-in-chief, in the preliminary discussions of the project, had mentioned 10,000 men as the approximate number that could be collected in the Department of the South for this operation. The force actually got together there did not vary much from 11,500 men, including engineers and artillerists. Upon Morris's Island, on account of its narrowness, this force was ample, and it was not until the command had been reduced one third by sickness and casualties that re-enforcements were asked for. But James's Island presents a different case. There our progress would soon have been arrested by the concentration of a superior force in our front. Upon Morris's Island both parties had all the force that could be applied with advantage. Our superiority in artillery, ashore and afloat—particularly in the use of mortars in the trenches—the successful application of new devices, the energy and skill of our engineers, and a strictly maintained initiative, gave us the controlling elements of success. Moreover, according to the programme of joint operations, the demolition of Fort Sumter was what the land forces had to accomplish, and that could be done with more ease and certainty from Morris's Island than from any other position. James's Island was too wide to operate upon, with a fair promise of success, with our small force."—Gillmore's Operations, p. 22.

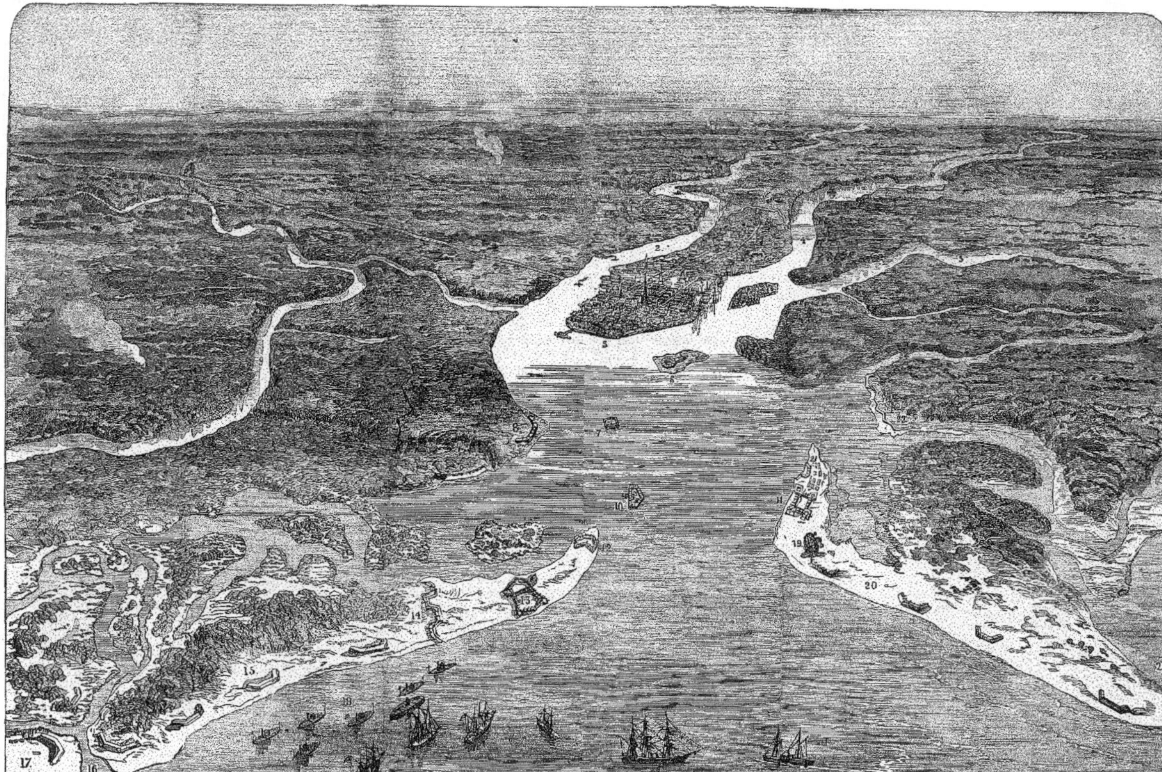

1. Charleston and Savannah Railroad.—2. Ashley River.—3. Charleston.—4. Cooper River.—5. Wando River.—6. Castle Pinckney.—7. Fort Ripley.—8. Fort Johnson (James's Island).—9. Stono River.—10. Fort Sumter.—11. Fort Moultrie.—12. Battery Gregg (Cummings's Point).—13. Fort Wagner.—14. General Gillmore's Advanced Batteries.—15. Captured Works (Morris's Island).—16. Light-house Inlet.—17. Union Battery (Folly Island).—18. Iron-clads and Wooden Ships.—19. Hotel.—20. Sullivan's Island and Rebel Batteries.—21. Moultrieville.—22. Mount Pleasant.—23. Breach Inlet.—24. Shem Creek.—0, 0. Rebel Batteries on James's Island.

CHARLESTON AND ITS ENVIRONS

Q. A. GILLMORE.

ROBERT G. SHAW.

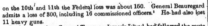

on the 10th and 11th the Federal loss was about 150. General Beauregard admits a loss of 300, including 16 commissioned officers.[1] He had also lost 11 heavy guns.

In the mean time, General Terry, on James's Island, had followed the route taken by Benham's two divisions on the 16th of June, and demonstrated against Secessionville. On the 16th of July he was attacked by a largely superior force of the enemy; but with the assistance of the gun-boat Pawnee in the Stono, and two smaller vessels, the attack was easily repulsed. Terry's command was the next day withdrawn from James's Island.

On the 18th, just one week after the failure of the first assault on Fort Wagner, a second was undertaken. In the interim, four batteries—Reynolds, Weed, Hays, and O'Rourke—mounting twenty-nine guns and fourteen mortars, had been erected on Morris's Island bearing upon Fort Wagner, and at a distance from that work of from 1330 to 1920 yards. In addition to the four monitors (the Catskill, Montauk, Nahant, and Weehawken), which were across the bar on the 10th, two other vessels—the Patapsco and the New Ironsides—now lay abreast of Morris's Island. The guns of this fleet and of the shore batteries bombarded the fort all day. At twilight, in the midst of a thunder-storm, the assaulting columns, commanded by Brigadier General T. Seymour, advanced. Strong's brigade—consisting of Colonel Shaw's Fifty-fourth Massachusetts (colored) Regiment; the Sixth Connecticut, Colonel Chatfield; a battalion of the Seventh Connecticut; the Forty-eighth New York, Colonel Barton; the Third New Hampshire, Colonel Jackson; the Ninth Maine, Colonel Emery; and the Seventy-sixth Pennsylvania, Colonel Strawbridge—was in the advance, and was supported by Colonel H. S. Putnam's brigade. The whole force engaged in the attack numbered about 6000 men. The approach of darkness, hastened by the storm, made it impossible for the fleet to discern friend from foe, so that the advance was exposed to the fire of Forts Wagner, Gregg (on Cummings's Point), and Sumter, assisted by the works on James's and Sullivan's Island. Never, during the war, was an assault made in the face of such opposition. As soon as the columns approached the fort, and the Federal guns in the batteries and on the monitors were silent, the garrison of Wagner, 1000 strong, sprang to its guns and muskets. Notwithstanding this tremendous fire from four different quarters, and although the leading regiment was thrown into such disorder that Putnam's supporting brigade had to be sent in, still the troops went forward, and the southeast bastion of Fort Wagner was gained and held for nearly three hours. The darkness was so great an advantage to the garrison that it more than compensated for the partial success of the assailants, and a retreat was ordered. The Federal loss was very

[1] Gillmore's Operations, p. 76.

GEORGE C. STRONG.

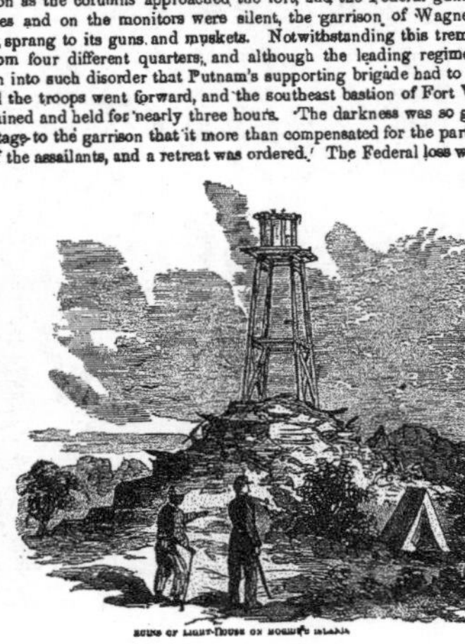

RUINS OF LIGHT-HOUSE ON MORRIS'S ISLAND.

severe, especially in officers. General Strong, and Colonels Chatfield, Putnam, and Shaw, were either killed on the spot, or died subsequently of their wounds. Colonel Shaw was killed upon the parapet of the fort. If, as was reported at the time, he was buried with the fallen negroes of his gallant regiment, it can only be said that what was intended for a disgrace will in the light of history be regarded as a monumental honor. General Seymour and several regimental commanders were severely wounded. The entire loss sustained in the assault must have amounted to 1200 killed and wounded.

SHARPSHOOTERS BEFORE WAGNER.

This repulse revived the faltering hopes of the citizens of Charleston, who regarded Fort Wagner as the key to the city. They had looked upon the conflict with anxiety and doubt. They remembered that this same General Gillmore had once demolished Fort Pulaski—which they considered in impregnability next to Sumter—as easily as if it had been a house built of cards.[1] They had trembled, therefore, for the fate of Wagner and Sumter, but now they breathed more freely.

But General Gillmore had as yet scarcely commenced operations. His principal object was the demolition of Fort Sumter, in order to allow the iron-clads an entrance to the harbor. Failing in this, there was still left a secondary object to be accomplished—namely, to secure a perfect blockade of the port. This could be effected by the reduction of Forts Wagner and Gregg.

Fort Wagner was an inclosed work, one fourth of a mile in width, extending from high-water mark on the east, to Vincent's Creek and the impassable marshes on the west. It had an excellent garrison, and was constructed of sand, upon which the heaviest bombardment could make little impression, with a ditch in front. Its bomb-proof shelter was capacious and secure; and its armament consisted of between fifteen and twenty guns, covering the solitary approach to it on the south. This approach was in many places scarcely half a company front in width, and was swept by Fort Sumter, the batteries on James's Island, and that at Cummings's Point. Its communication with the rear was secure, thus giving opportunity for the increase of its armament or garrison.[2]

[1] See the *Augusta Sentinel* of July 15, 1863.

[2] Gillmore's Operations, p. 105.

Fort Wagner was neared by regular approaches. Immediately after the repulse of the 18th, the first parallel was established about 1300 yards from Fort Wagner.[1] On the night of the 23d the second parallel was established 600 yards in advance of the first, on a line running diagonally across the island northwest and southeast. In the creek on the left two boome of floating timber were stretched across, to resist the approach of the enemy's boats. It must be remembered that these approaches to Fort Wagner were chiefly *defensive* as to that work, and were preliminary to offensive operations against Fort Sumter. The third parallel was established within less than 400 yards of Fort Wagner. The fire from the fort now became so severe that it was determined to operate against Sumter before another advance.

Breaching batteries had been constructed for this purpose in rear of the several parallels. By the 11th of August 12 of these batteries were ready

[1] "A row of inclined palisading, reaching entirely across the island, was planted about 200 yards in advance of the line, with a return of fifty yards on the right. This return was well flanked by two guns on the right of the parallel. The parallel was arranged for infantry defense; a bomb-proof magazine was constructed, and the armament of the line modified and increased; so that the parallel contained eight siege and field guns, ten siege mortars, and three Requa rifle batteries."—Gillmore's Operations, p. 114.

THE "SWAMP ANGEL."

PORTION OF CHARLESTON EXPOSED TO THE FIRE OF THE FEDERAL FLEET.

for operation, mounting 28 heavy guns and 12 mortars. Their distance from Fort Sumter ranged from 8516 to 4290 yards. The bombardment commenced on the morning of the 17th, and the guns were served steadily and deliberately for several days, until Fort Sumter was literally knocked out of all shape and deprived of its offensive power. During this time the fleet also bombarded Fort Wagner, whose fire, unless silenced, would interfere with the operations of the batteries on shore.

On the 21st of August a demand was made upon General Beauregard for the surrender of Morris's Island and Fort Sumter, accompanied by the assurance that, if the demand was not complied with during the four hours following its delivery, fire would be opened upon Charleston from batteries already established within range of the city. For three weeks Gillmore had been locating a battery, commonly known among the troops as the "Swamp Angel," mounted with an 8-inch Parrott rifle, and within range of Charleston, on the marsh between Morris's and James's Islands. He waited ten hours beyond the time specified in his notice to the Confederate general, and, receiving no reply, opened fire on the city.[1]

On the 24th of August the military force operating against Charleston had accomplished its primary object—the elimination of Fort Sumter. This fort was not obliterated, and its offensive power was only temporarily removed.[1] For at least ten or fifteen days it could oppose to the monitors no serious resistance. Fort Wagner still remained in the bands of the enemy, but could be easily avoided by the fleet. But Admiral Dahlgren did not embrace the opportunity, and in the mean time the enemy strengthened Fort Johnson, converting it into an earth-work. This work is on the north end of James's Island, and commands the channel.

Gillmore continued his parallel approaches up to within 150 yards of Fort Wagner, and on the 5th of September commenced a bombardment of that work, which was continued for forty-two consecutive hours. Seventeen siege and Coehorn mortars dropped their shells into the work, thirteen heavy Parrott rifles pounded away at the southwest angle of the bomb-proof, while by day the New Ironsides poured an uninterrupted stream of eleven-inch shells from her eight-gun broadside against the parapet. An assault would have been made on the morning of the 7th upon the now silent fort; but during the night of the 6th the Confederates, convinced of their inability to maintain their position on Morris's Island, slipped away from Forts Wagner and Gregg, and all but seventy men effected their escape. Eighteen guns were captured in Fort Wagner, and seven in Fort Gregg.

This success concluded General Gillmore's work. From Cummings's Point an irregular bombardment was commenced upon the city, and continued till the evacuation of the latter in 1865. The "Swamp Angel" battery had long discontinued its fire upon Charleston. At the thirty-sixth round its gun—a 100-lb. Parrott—had exploded, and the guns mounted afterward were directed against the James's Island batteries.

Admiral Dahlgren was unwilling to attempt the entrance to the harbor until Fort Sumter was in possession of the national forces. This possession could only be effected by an open assault, involving great sacrifice of life; and after the acquisition of the fort, Gillmore could not expect to hold it against the formidable works of the enemy which bore upon its weakest points. Gillmore, on the 27th of September, offered to remove the obstruc-

[1] The following is a copy of the correspondence which passed between Generals Gillmore and Beauregard:

No. 1.

"Headquarters Department of the South, Morris's Island, S. C., August 21, 1863.

"General G. T. Beauregard, Commanding Confederate Forces about Charleston, S. C.:

"General,—I have the honor to demand of you the immediate evacuation of Morris's Island and Fort Sumter by the Confederate forces.

"The present condition of Fort Sumter, and the rapid and progressive destruction which it is undergoing from my batteries, seem to render its complete demolition within a few hours a matter of certainty. All my heaviest guns have not yet opened. Should you refuse compliance with that demand, or should I receive no reply thereto within four hours after it is delivered into the hands of your subordinate at Fort Wagner for transmission, I shall open fire on the city of Charleston from batteries already established within easy and effective range of the heart of the city.

"I am, general, your obedient servant,

"Q. A. Gillmore, Brigadier General Commanding."

No. 2.

"Headquarters South Carolina, Georgia, and Florida, Charleston, S. C., August 22, 1863.

"Sir,—Last night, at 15 minutes before 11 o'clock, during my absence on a reconnoissance of my fortifications, a communication was received at these headquarters, dated 'Headquarters Department of the South, Morris's Island, S. C., August 21, 1863,' demanding the immediate evacuation of Morris's Island and Fort Sumter by the Confederate forces on the alleged ground that 'the present condition of Fort Sumter, and the rapid and progressive destruction which it is undergoing from my batteries, seem to render its complete demolition within a few hours a matter of certainty,' and if this letter was not complied with, or no reply was received within four hours after it was delivered into the hands of my subordinate commander at Fort Wagner for transmission, a fire would be opened on the city of Charleston from batteries already established within easy and effective range of the heart of the city. This communication to my address was without signature, and, of course, returned. About half past one o'clock one of your batteries did actually open fire and throw a number of heavy shells into the city, the inhabitants of which, of course, were asleep and unwarned.

"About 9 o'clock the next morning the communication alluded to was returned to these headquarters, bearing your recognized official signature, and it can now be noticed as your deliberate official act. Among nations not barbarous, the usages of war prescribe that when a city is about to be attacked, timely notice shall be given by the attacking commander, in order that non-combatants shall have an opportunity of withdrawing beyond its limits. Generally the time allowed is from one to three days; that is, time for the withdrawal in good faith of at least the women and children. You, sir, gave only four hours, knowing that your notice, under existing circumstances, could not reach me in less than two hours, and not less than that time would be required for an answer to be conveyed from this city to Battery Wagner.

"With this knowledge you threaten to open fire on this city, not to oblige its surrender, but to force me to evacuate those works which you, assisted by a great naval force, have been attacking in vain for more than 40 days. Batteries Wagner and Gregg and Fort Sumter are nearly due north from your batteries on Morris's Island, and in distance therefrom ranging from half a mile to two and a quarter miles. This city, on the other hand, is to the northwest, and quite five miles distant from the battery which opened against it this morning. It would appear, sir, that, despairing of reducing these works, you now resort to the novel measure of turning your guns against the old men, women, and the hospitals of a sleeping city—an act of inexcusable barbarity; from your own confessed point of sight, inasmuch as you allege that the complete demolition of Fort Sumter within a few hours by your guns seems a matter of certainty. Your omission to attach your signature to such a grave paper must show the recklessness of the course upon which you have adventured. While the facts that you knowingly fixed a limit for receiving an answer to your demand, which made it almost beyond the possibility of receiving any reply within that time, and that you actually did open one, and threw a number of the most destructive missiles ever used in war into the midst of a city taken unawares and filled with sleeping women and children, will give you a bad eminence in history—even in the history of this war. I am only surprised, sir, at the limits you have set to your demand. If, in order to obtain the abandonment of Morris's Island and Fort Sumter, you feel authorized to fire on this city, why did you not include the works on Sullivan's and James's Islands, nay, even the city of Charleston, in the same demand? Since you have felt warranted in inaugurating this method of reducing batteries in your immediate front which were otherwise found to be impregnable, and a mode of warfare which I confidently declare to be atrocious and unworthy of a soldier, I now solemnly warn you that, if you fire again on the city from your Morris's Island batteries, without giving a somewhat more reasonable time to remove the non-combatants, I shall feel impelled to employ such stringent means of retaliation as may be available during the continuance of this attack. Finally, I reply that neither the works on Morris's Island nor Fort Sumter will be evacuated on the demand you have been pleased to make. Already, however, I am taking measures to remove all non-combatants, who are now fully aware and alive to what they may expect at your hands. Respectfully, your obedient servant,

"G. T. Beauregard, General Commanding.

"To Brigadier General Q. A. Gillmore, Commanding U. S. Forces, Morris's Island."

No. 3.

"Headquarters Department of the South, Morris's Island, S. C., August 22, 1863—9 P.M.

"General G. T. Beauregard, Commanding Confederate Forces, Charleston, S. C.:

"Sir,—I have the honor to acknowledge the receipt of your communication of this date, complaining that one of my batteries has opened upon the city of Charleston, and thrown 'a number of heavy rifled shells into the city, the inhabitants of which, of course, were asleep and unwarned.'

"My letter to you demanding the surrender of Fort Sumter and Morris's Island, and threatening, in default thereof, to open fire upon Charleston, was delivered near Fort Wagner at 11 15 o'clock A.M. on the 21st instant, and should have arrived at your headquarters in time to have permitted your answer to reach me within the limit assigned, viz., four hours. The fact that you were absent from your headquarters at the time of its arrival may be regarded as an unfortunate circumstance for the city of Charleston, but one for which I clearly am not responsible. This letter bore date at my headquarters, and was officially delivered by an officer of my staff.

"The inadvertent omission of my signature doubtless affords ground for special pleading, but is not the argument of a commander solicitous only for the safety of sleeping women and children, and unarmed men. Your threats of retaliation for acts of mine, which you do not allege to be in violation of the usages of civilized warfare except as regards the length of time allowed as notice of my intentions, are passed by without comment. I will, however, call your attention to the well-established principle, that the commander of a place attacked, but not invested, having its avenues of escape open and practicable, has no right to expect any notice of an intended bombardment other than that which is given by the threatening attitude of his adversary. Even had this letter not been written, the city of Charleston has had, according to your own computation, forty days' notice of her danger.

"During that time my attack on her defenses has steadily progressed; the ultimate object of that attack has at no time been doubtful. If, under the circumstances, the life of a single non-combatant is exposed to peril by the bombardment of the city, the responsibility rests with those who have first failed to remove the non-combatants or secure the safety of the city, after having held control of all its approaches for a period of nearly two years and a half, in the presence of a threatening force, and who afterward refused to accept the terms upon which the bombardment might have been postponed.

"From various sources, official and otherwise, I am led to believe that most of the women and children of Charleston were long since removed from the city; but upon your assurance that the city is still 'full' of them, I shall suspend the bombardment until 11 o'clock P.M. to-morrow, thus giving you two days from the time you acknowledge to have received my communication of the 21st instant. Very respectfully, your obedient servant,

"Q. A. Gillmore, Brigadier General Commanding."

[1] "The barbette fire of the work was entirely destroyed. [It was this plunging fire from the barbette tier from which the monitors had most to fear.] A few unserviceable guns still remaining on their carriages were dismounted a week later. The casemates of the channel fronts were more or less thoroughly searched by our fire, and we had trustworthy information that but one serviceable gun remained in the work, and that pointed up the harbor toward the city. The fort was reduced to the condition of a mere infantry outpost, alike incapable of annoying our approaches to Fort Wagner, or of inflicting injury upon the iron-clads.

"The enemy soon after commenced removing the dismounted guns by night, and not many weeks elapsed before several of them were mounted in other parts of the harbor. The period during which the weakness of the enemy's interior defenses was most palpable was during the ten or fifteen days subsequent to the 23d of August, and that was the time when success could have been most easily achieved by the fleet. The concurrent testimony of prisoners, refugees, and deserters represented the obstacles in the way as by no means insurmountable."—Gillmore's Operations, p. 149, 150.

General Gillmore gives the following tabular statement of the firing from seven of his batteries on Fort Sumter, August 17–23:

Name of Battery.	No. and Calibre of Parrott Rifles.	Distance from Battery to centre of Gorge Wall in yards.	Whole No. of Projectiles thrown.	Total Weight of Metal thrown.	No. of Projectiles which struck Fort.	No. which struck Gorge Wall, and helped to form Breach.	Weight of Metal which formed Breach.
Strong	One 300-pr.	4290	76	19,142	46	22	5,600
Brown	Two 200-prs.	3516	543	82,970	299	108	32,670
Hays	One 200-pr.	4173	531	86,129	225	196	38,320
Reno	One 200-pr.	4272	383	115,171	480	316	38,940
	Two 100-prs.	4272	784				
Rosecrans	Three 100-prs.	3447	1173	105,867	547	303	37,240
Meade	Two 100-prs.	3428	1004	98,282	602	336	39,222
Stevens	Two 100-prs.	4278	566	46,032	340	208	43,924
Total			5009	552,683	2479	1668	[illegible]

CONFEDERATE EVACUATION OF MORRIS'S ISLAND.

E. R. S. CANBY.

tion with his soldiers, but Dahlgren would not agree to this, considering it his own "proper work." He promised to proceed as soon as his monitors were repaired, if the musketry fire from Fort Sumter should be completely silenced. Delays followed, and finally the attempt was abandoned.

The same day that Gillmore occupied the forts on the north end of Morris's Island, an expedition more gallant than judicious was undertaken by a hundred marines under Lieutenant Commander Williams. This force approached Fort Sumter in 30 boats, but was driven back before a fire of musketry and hand-grenades, which killed or wounded about 50 men.

III. No serious attack was made on the defenses of Charleston by sea. New fortifications were built on Morris's Island, and named after the brave men who had fallen in the second assault on Fort Wagner. The capture of Morris's Island secured a more perfect blockade of the port, but proved of no great value from any other point of view. After all the labor and cost involved in the defense of Charleston by the Confederates, and in offensive operations against it by the national forces—naval and military—the city was finally captured without a battle. As soon as General Sherman had reached Branchville in his march through South Carolina, and had, by his destruction of the railroad in that neighborhood, left General Hardee only a single line of retreat, the latter determined to evacuate Charleston. Beauregard, who had been in command at Charleston, was at this time on the North Carolina border, collecting forces, and awaiting Hill's troops from Augusta, and the remnants of Hood's army from the West.

General Foster had been relieved by General Gillmore shortly after Sherman's departure from Savannah. The available forces in the Department of the South had been making demonstrations against Charleston from James's Island on the south, and Bull's Bay on the north. On the 10th of February General Schemmelfennig effected a lodgment on James's Island, and, covered by a naval force on the Stono, advanced and carried the works of the enemy with a loss of 70 or 80 men. The movement from Bull's Bay was under the immediate command of General Potter, Admiral Dahlgren co-operating. Hardee evacuated Charleston on the night of the 17th of February, and moved northward so rapidly that he managed to join Johnston's forces in North Carolina before he could be intercepted by General Sherman.

The plan of defense against Sherman's march was extremely novel: Wilmington, Augusta, and Charleston were held until the latest moment. These points ought all to have been abandoned the moment General Sherman entered South Carolina, and, with the forces from the West, been concentrated in his front.

On the morning of the 21st General Gillmore's army entered Charleston. Lieutenant Colonel A. G. Bennett, with two companies of the Fifty-second Pennsylvania regiment, and about 80 men of the Third Rhode Island Artillery, had entered the city on the 18th. Fort Sumter and the works on Sullivan's Island had been abandoned, and that morning Lieutenant Colonel Bennett had hoisted over Fort Sumter the United States flag. He then moved toward the city, having then with him only 22 men, replacing the national colors on Fort Ripley and Castle Pinckney in his progress, and at 10 A.M. landed at Mills's Wharf, Charleston, where he learned that a part of the Confederate troops yet remained in the city, and that mounted patrols "were out in every direction, applying the torch and driving the inhabitants before them." He addressed a communication to Mayor Macbeth, demanding the surrender of Charleston in the name of the United States, and then awaited re-enforcements. Mayor Macbeth, probably astonished at the audacity of this meagre force, replied, addressing "the general commanding the army of the United States at Morris's Island," that the Confederate military authorities had evacuated the city, and that he himself remained to enforce order until the national forces took possession. Bennett replied, offering to move into the city with his command and assist in extinguishing the fires. Having received re-enforcements, he landed, and took measures for putting out the fires, and for the preservation of the United States Arsenal and the railroad dépôts. With Charleston were captured 450 guns. These guns, and the importance which had been attached to Charleston on account of its historic connection with the origin of the rebellion, were the only considerations which made its possession valuable to the captors.

On the 14th of April, 1865—just four years after the evacuation of Fort Sumter by Major Anderson—the old flag which had once been hauled down at the bidding of rebels was again raised above the fort by the hands of Major Anderson. On this occasion the Reverend Henry Ward Beecher delivered an oration which will be recognized by posterity as the ablest production of that orator, and worthy to hold a place by the side of the most brilliant efforts of Burke or Demosthenes.

CHAPTER LIV.

THE MOBILE CAMPAIGN.

Situation and Defenses of Mobile.—Canby assumes command of the Mississippi Department, May 11, 1864.—The proposed Campaign against Mobile frustrated by the failure of the Red River Expedition.—Attack on Fort Gaines, in Mobile Bay.—Fort Powell evacuated.—Farragut passes Forts Morgan and Gaines.—Sinking of the Tecumseh.—Naval Engagement in Mobile Bay.—Capture of the Tennessee.—Surrender of Forts Gaines and Morgan.—Suspension of Operations against Mobile.—Opening of a new Campaign in March, 1865.—The Situation.—Military and Naval Forces.—Investment of Spanish Fort.—Bombardment of April 8th.—The Enemy evacuates.—Steele's Movement against Montgomery.—Evacuation of Forts Huger and Tracy.—The Fleet again moves up in Front of Mobile.—Capture of Fort Blakely.—Surrender of Mobile.—Losses.

MOBILE—the last surrendered of the Confederate strong-holds—is the chief city and port of Alabama. It is situated on low ground at the mouth of Mobile River, and on the western shore of Mobile Bay. At the outset, the city was not in favor of secession; but the false prediction of Yancey, which promised such an extraordinary development of its com-

GORDON GRANGER.

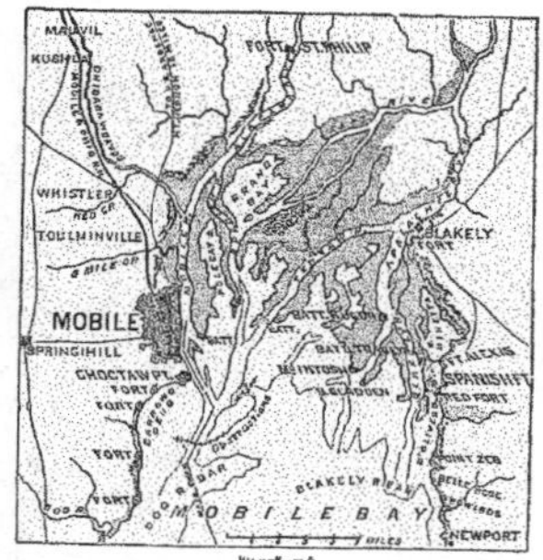

merce as a consequence of rebellion that the only peril to be dreaded would be the excess of luxury that must follow, had overcome its scruples.

Mobile had often been threatened with attack, but no blow was directed against the city until the summer of 1864. At this time it was considered the best fortified city in the Confederacy. It had three lines of defenses. The outer was constructed three miles distant from the city, upon commanding ground, and comprised fifteen redoubts. Through the suburbs of the city, after the fall of Vicksburg, a line of works was built with sixteen inclosed forts. Midway between these two lines still another was constructed in 1864, including nineteen bastioned forts and eight redoubts. Below the city ten batteries swept the channel, which was also obstructed by long rows of piles with narrow openings here and there for blockade-runners. Besides these obstacles on the Spanish River Channel, Forts Huger and Tracy had been erected on the eastern shore, close to the Appalachee River, and obstructions placed in the river to prevent the ascension of national gun-boats up that stream, and their progress thence into the Tensas River to the front of the city.

At the entrance of the bay stood two walled forts—Morgan and Gaines—four miles apart, built by the United States, but seized by the Confederates early in 1861. Fort Gaines, on Little Dauphin Island, mounted 30 guns, and had a garrison of 900 men. Fort Morgan, at the western extremity of Mobile Point, was a more formidable work, armed with 60 guns, with a water battery in its front. Fort Powell—a small work, mounting 98 guns—commanded Grant's Pass, west of Little Dauphin Island. A large number of torpedoes had been planted in the channel abreast of Fort Morgan, but the strength of the current at this point hindered their efficiency.

Behind these forts, in the bay, lay a small Confederate fleet, consisting of the ram Tennessee, and the gun-boats Gaines, Morgan, and Selma. Such were the defenses of Mobile against approach by land and sea.

In General Grant's plan of operations for 1864, a campaign against Mobile held a prominent place. But among the other unfortunate consequences of the disastrous Red River campaign was the impossibility of carrying out this part of the lieutenant general's programme. On the 11th of May, 1864, General Canby assumed command of the military division of West Mississippi. He had been instructed to make the movement on Mobile, if possible. But he found Kirby Smith's forces, encouraged by Banks's repulse and Steele's retreat, threatening both the Arkansas and Mississippi. Thus the forces under Canby, as well as those under Steele, were for a time put on the defensive. This attitude was rendered all the more necessary by the withdrawal of 6000 men of the Nineteenth Corps to Virginia.

Admiral Farragut, commanding the West Gulf Squadron, attacked Fort Gaines on the 5th of August. Fort Powell was that day blown up and evacuated by the Confederates. On the 3d, General Gordon Granger joined Farragut with 1500 men, who were landed on Dauphin Island. The military force marched up the island under cover of the fleet, and on the 4th intrenched within half a mile of Fort Gaines. The next morning, with fifteen vessels, Farragut—having promised his men that they should breakfast in Mobile Bay—steamed up to Fort Morgan, the admiral being bound to the main rigging of his flag-ship, the Hartford. Forts Morgan and Gaines sim-

FEDERAL FLEET IN MOBILE BAY.

CAPTURE OF THE TENNESSEE.

FORT MORGAN AFTER ITS SURRENDER.

ultaneously opened upon the fleet. Scarcely had the Tecumseh, the leading vessel, fired her first shot, when she struck a torpedo, and with her gallant Captain Craven and 120 of the crew, sank to the bottom of the channel. Under a galling fire from Fort Morgan, ten of the crew were rescued by a boat's crew of the Metacomet. The Hartford then took the lead, and, after an hour's engagement, passed the fort and entered the bay. The forts have been passed. Now the Confederate navy opposes a new obstacle to the advance of the fleet. But this affair is soon settled. In about an hour after entering the harbor the Metacomet has captured the Selma, with her crew—90 officers and men. The Morgan, more fortunate, has escaped, and the Gaines, disabled, has sought refuge under the protecting guns of Fort Morgan. But the ram Tennessee bids defiance to the entire Federal fleet. She makes for the Hartford, but, in the mean time, is attacked on every side. A desperate struggle follows, lasting two full hours. At length a 15-inch shot from the Manhattan penetrates her armor, and at the same time a shell from one of the monitors, reaching her steering apparatus, disables her, and she surrenders, with 20 officers and 170 men. Admiral Buchanan, her commander, has been seriously wounded, and she has lost eight or ten of her crew by death or wounds. The Federal loss in the engagement with the forts and the hostile fleet is 52 killed and 170 wounded. But the battle—so far as Mobile Bay is concerned—has been fought and won.

On the 8th, at 9 A.M., Fort Gaines was surrendered by its commander, Colonel Anderson, with 900 men. Fort Morgan still held out. Granger's land force was then transferred to Mobile Point, and siege operations were commenced. On the 22d there was a general bombardment. At night a fire broke out in the fort, compelling the garrison to throw 90,000 pounds of powder into the cisterns. The interior of the fort soon became a mass of smoking ruins. All night the bombardment was kept up at intervals, and on the morning of the 23d the Confederate General Page surrendered the fort, with its garrison.

Admiral Farragut removed the torpedoes planted in the bay. But, with the exception of some demonstrative movements made by Granger from Pascagoula, and by cavalry expeditions from Baton Rouge and Memphis, no farther attack was made on Mobile until the spring of 1865. Without doubt 8000 could have, immediately after Farragut's entrance to Mobile Bay, moved up Dog River and captured the city; but, until after General Hood's defeat in December, so large a force could not be spared for this purpose. The capture of Forts Gaines, Morgan, and Powell had secured a perfect blockade of the port, and it was the best policy of the national commanders to let the Confederates weaken themselves by detaching large garrisons for the protection of their coast cities, and then to disregard them, and rapidly concentrate against the two great armies of the Confederacy.

But after Hood's defeat, and when, by Sherman's strategic marches, the field of conflict had been limited to the states of Virginia and North Carolina, there were two motives which urged a campaign against Mobile. In the first place a portion of Hood's, now Dick Taylor's army, would be prevented from joining Johnston against Sherman; and, in the second place, forces could be thus occupied on the Federal side which were not available or necessary elsewhere.

In March, 1865, a force of 45,000 men was collected for operating against Mobile. It consisted of three commands—General Granger's Thirteenth Corps, 13,200 strong; A. J. Smith's Sixteenth Corps, 16,000 strong, to which must be added 3000 for engineers, artillery, and cavalry; and Steele's column, 13,200 strong. At this time Dick Taylor had his headquarters at Meridian, Mississippi, and Major General D. H. Maury commanded the District of the Gulf, with headquarters at Mobile. The garrison of Mobile numbered about 9000 men. The defenses near the city had been strengthened, and on the eastern shore a system of defenses, known as Spanish Fort, had been erected.

The movement against Mobile was made from the east side. On the 17th of March the Thirteenth Corps marched from Fort Morgan along the peninsula, and on the 24th reached Danley's, on Fish River. The Sixteenth Corps had already reached this point, being conveyed thither by transports from Fort Gaines. A demonstration was at the same time made by Colonel J. B. Moore, with one brigade of the Sixteenth Corps, west of Mobile.

General Steele's command arrived at Barrancas on the 28th of February, and on the 19th of March reached Pensacola. It was designed with this column to cut the railroad from Mobile to Montgomery, and, if possible, capture the latter city.

The naval force, which had been increased by several light-draught ironclads from the Mississippi, and which was now under the command of Admiral Thatcher, in the absence of Farragut, had covered the landing of the troops on Fish River.

On the 27th of March Spanish Fort was invested by the national troops—A. J. Smith's corps on the right, and Granger's on the left. This fort—or rather system of defenses—was seven miles east of Mobile, and was flanked on the one side by D'Olieve's Creek and Bay, and on the other by Minette Bay. It was held by three thousand Confederates under Generals Gibson, Holtzclaw, and Ector. The line of works was two miles in length, and was weakest on its extreme left, opposite General Carr's division. The siege lasted 13 days, during which the investing force made regular approaches to the fort. On the ninth day of the siege (April 4th) a bombardment was opened from 38 siege-guns and 37 field-pieces, but little was accomplished either in the way of injuring the fort or its garrison. At this time the advance parallels of the besiegers were within a hundred yards of the enemy's works. The Confederate General Gibson, who commanded the fort, telegraphed to Maury on the 5th: "Enemy sweeps my flanks with heavy batteries, and presses on at all points. . . . My line is extended now to the water and in it. My men are worked all the time, and I don't believe I can possibly do the work necessary in the dense flats on the flanks. Can't you take a look at the situation to-morrow? . . . My men are wider apart than they ever were under Generals Johnston and Hood. The works not so well managed nor so strong, and the enemy in larger force, more active, and closer. Can't you send me the detachment belonging to Ector and Holtz-

LIGHT-HOUSE AT FORT MORGAN.

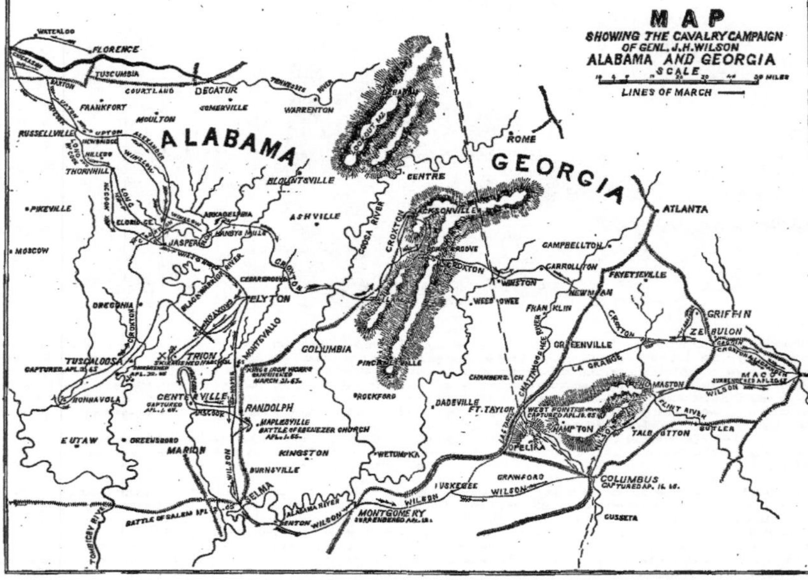

claw? Can't you send a force of negroes with axes? I can make good soldiers of the negroes."

On the 8th of April the bombardment was renewed, continuing from 5 30 to 7 30 P.M. General Canby intended to assault on the morning of the 9th, but had instructed his corps commanders in their operations on the 8th to take advantage of every opportunity for assault which promised decisive success. Such an opportunity was offered during the bombardment. General Carr, on the extreme Federal right, had advanced his works as close to the enemy's as was practicable. In his front was Ector's brigade, 659 strong. By attacking this brigade on the flank, it seemed to him possible to gain some 200 yards on the Confederate left, and secure a commanding crest well covered with pines, where a battery might be erected which would take the enemy in reverse. A little after 6 P.M., the Eighth Iowa, led by Colonel Bell, advanced boldly, and, in the face of a sharp musketry fire, gained the crest and a portion of the parapet. Then a hand-to-hand struggle ensued between the Iowans and the garrison in their immediate front. The fight was severe, but the enemy was forced to yield. The clamor of the bombardment had covered this brief combat so effectually that those of the garrison occupying the detached pits next to those who had been worsted were surprised. Advancing from pit to pit, Colonel Bell captured 300 yards of the Confederate works, and over one half of Ector's brigade. His own loss had been five killed and 20 wounded. Then supports came up, until a whole Federal brigade was inside the works and had begun to intrench.

General Gibson, hearing of the reverse on his left, determined to evacuate Spanish Fort under cover of a bold attack on Carr's division. While, therefore, some two or three hundred men maintained the unequal struggle against the Federals already in the works, the remainder of the garrison, under General Gibson, silently and barefooted, glided out by the narrow treadway leading to Fort Huger, and crossed the Appalachee in boats. Five hundred prisoners and fifty guns were captured by Canby's army, which entered the fort on the 9th—the same day that, hundreds of miles away, General Lee was surrendering to Grant the Confederate Army of Northern Virginia.

In the mean time General Steele's column had made its demonstration against Montgomery, moving with great difficulty through the swamps of Florida northward on the Pollard Road. A few miles south of Pollard the Confederate General Clanton's brigade was encountered and defeated. General Clanton was seriously wounded, and 130 prisoners captured. Steele's advance entered Pollard on the 26th of March, and destroyed a portion of the railroad. From this point he turned again southward, and joined the main army in front of Mobile at the close of the month. His command was then moved against Fort Blakely. This work is about five miles north of Spanish Fort, on the east bank of the Appalachee River, opposite its point of junction with the Tensas. The garrison occupying the defenses at this point consisted of French's division, then under General Cockrell, on the left, and General Thomas's division of Alabama reserves on the right, and numbered 3500 men. The general command of the works had been assigned to General St. John Lidell.

Fort Blakely—which, like Spanish Fort, is a name designating a system of defenses rather than the fort proper—was stronger than Spanish Fort The works were more extended, being about three miles in length, and were held by a stronger garrison, which, after the capture of Spanish Fort, might also be re-enforced by a large portion of Gibson's escaped command. On the 2d of April these works were invested by General Steele.

On the evening of the 11th of April Forts Huger and Tracy were evacuated by the enemy. Thus the way was open for the fleet to move up the river into the Tensas. Contrary to the expectation of the enemy, the iron-clads had been able to cross Blakely Bar, but in doing so the Milwaukee and Osage had both been sunk. After the evacuation of Forts Huger and Tracy, the obstructions were removed from the channel of the river, and on the 13th Admiral Thatcher, with the Octorara and iron-clads, anchored off Mobile.

But before this time the fate of Blakely had been decided. The siege of the Confederate works at this point was not essentially different from that of Spanish Fort. After the fall of the latter the entire army moved upon Blakely. The works were carried on the evening of the 9th by an assault, in which General Hawkins's negro troops especially distinguished themselves. They captured nine guns, twenty-two officers, and 200 enlisted men. The entire garrison was captured—3423 men—and forty guns. The loss of the Federals in the assault was 654 in killed and wounded.

Mobile, now left with a garrison less than 5000 strong—a force too weak to oppose resistance to nearly ten times that number of men, assisted by a powerful fleet—was evacuated on the 11th of April. The remnant of General Maury's command retreated up the Tombigbee to Meridian. On the 12th Mayor R. H. Slough surrendered the city to General Granger and Admiral Thatcher. In this Mobile campaign 5000 Confederate prisoners were captured. General Canby's entire loss in killed and wounded was 1500 men.

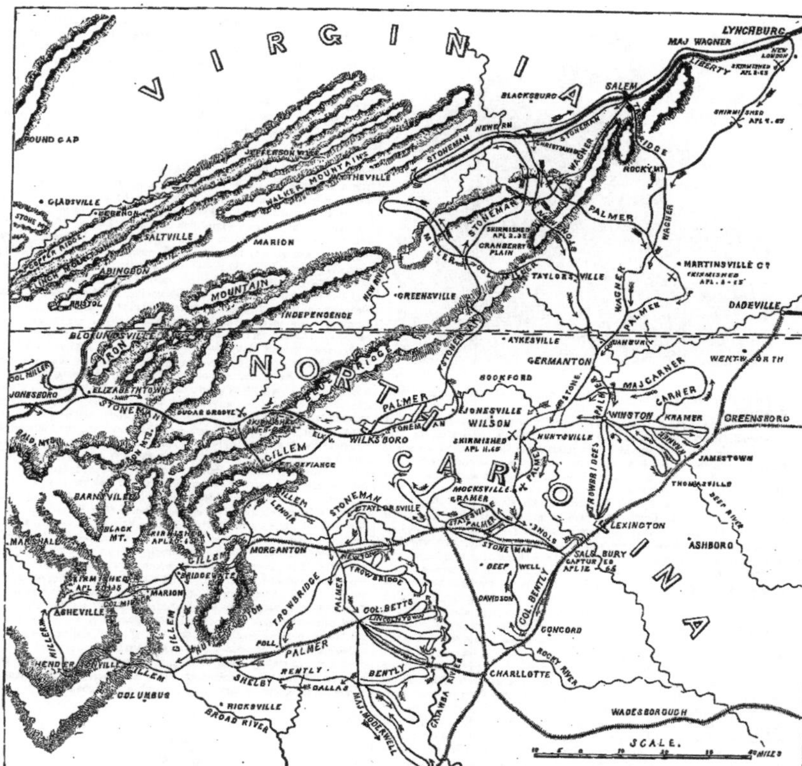

MAP OF STONEMAN'S NORTH CAROLINA RAID.

CHAPTER LV.

WILSON'S AND STONEMAN'S RAIDS.

Situation in the West at the close of January, 1865.—Organization of two Co-operative Expeditions under Wilson and Stoneman.—The Object of these Movements.—Wilson's Raid.—Intercepted Confederate Dispatches.—Capture of Selma.—Surrender of Montgomery.—Capture of Fort Taylor at West Point.—Macon surrendered under Protest.—Croxton joins Wilson at Macon.—Stoneman's Raid.—Change of Plan.—Stoneman enters Southwestern Virginia.—Capture of Towns, Destruction of Railroads, etc.—Stoneman returns to North Carolina.—Fight at Salisbury.—Gillam defeats the Confederate Detachment covering Ashville.—Is checked by the Sherman-Johnston Armistice.

AT the close of January, 1865, General Thomas's army consisted of A. J. Smith's and Stanley's corps—the Sixteenth and Fourth—and of Wilson's cavalry command, then about 22,000 strong. The only organized Confederate forces in the West this side of the Mississippi amounted to about 21,000 men, of which 12,000 were in Mississippi and the remainder at Mobile. As we have seen, A. J. Smith's corps and 5000 of Wilson's cavalry were sent in February to re-enforce General Canby. Thus Thomas retained the Fourth Corps and 17,000 of Wilson's cavalry. General Stoneman's command was also subject to his control.

Dick Taylor's army at Meridian, Mississippi, consisted of one infantry corps and 7000 cavalry under Forrest. It was not sufficiently large for an offensive campaign, and not an element of enough importance in the operations now contemplated by Thomas to justify the latter in attempting its elimination. In accordance with instructions received from the lieutenant general, Thomas determined to use the Federal forces under his control in co-operative movements. Two expeditions were organized; one to consist of Stoneman's command supported by the Fourth Corps, and the other of 12,000 cavalry under General Wilson. The former was designed to penetrate North Carolina and South Carolina toward Columbia, to co-operate with General Sherman, destroying the railroads and supplies on its march; the latter was to co-operate with Canby by an advance, conducted upon a similar plan, against Selma, Montgomery, and Macon.

Wilson's expedition, delayed by unfavorable weather and the exhausted condition of the horses, caused by the recent pursuit of Hood, did not leave Chickasaw, Alabama, until the 22d of March. It consisted of three cavalry divisions, commanded by Generals Upton,[1] Long, and McCook. The dismounted men of the three divisions, numbering 1500, acted as an escort to the supply train, which consisted of about 250 wagons. Wilson's instructions from the lieutenant general allowed him the largest discretion as an independent commander.[2] By divergent roads the command moved upon Russellville, and reached Elyton on the 30th of March, after an extremely difficult march over bad roads and swollen streams. At Jasper, on the 27th, Wilson had been informed that a part of Forrest's force, under Chalmers, was moving toward Tuscaloosa, and he knew that as soon as the direction of his movement was discovered the balance of the enemy's cavalry would move to the same point. The country so recently overrun by Hood's army was nearly destitute of supplies, and Wilson's train was consequently very large. Obviously Forrest would make every effort to destroy this train. Wilson therefore ordered his wagons to be left between the two branches of the Black Warrior, and his troops to fill their haversacks and load the pack animals with supplies, and advance as rapidly as possible to Montevallo. At Elyton, Croxton's brigade, of McCook's division, was detached, and sent to Tuscaloosa, "to burn the public stores, military school, bridges, and founderies" at that place. In the neighborhood of Montevallo,

[1] Upton commanded the Fourth Division. Wilson says in his report: "Brigadier General B. H. Grierson had been originally assigned to the command of this division, but, failing to use diligence in assembling and preparing it for the field, he was replaced by Brevet Major General E. Upton, an officer of rare merit and experience."

[2] Wilson's Report.

JAMES H. WILSON.

on the 31st, a large number of iron works, rolling-mills, and collieries were destroyed.

From this point the advance was resumed toward Selma. Just south of Montevallo there was some skirmishing with Roddy's cavalry on the 31st, and fifty prisoners were captured. At Randolph a Confederate courier was captured with two dispatches, one from General Jackson, commanding one of Forrest's divisions, and the other from Major Anderson, Forrest's chief of staff. From the first Wilson learned that Forrest was in his front with a portion of his command; that Jackson, with his division, and all the wagons and artillery of the Confederate cavalry, was marching from Tuscaloosa to Centreville; that Croxton had struck Jackson's rear, and interposed between him and the Federal train, and that Jackson, knowing this, would attack Croxton on the following morning. The other dispatch indicated that Chalmers had reached Marion, and was about to cross the Cahawba for the purpose of joining Forrest in Wilson's front, or in the works at Selma; also that the bridge across the Cahawba at Centreville was held by the Confederates. Following fast upon this intercepted intelligence came a dispatch from Croxton, dated the previous night, stating that he had struck Jackson's rear, and, instead of pushing on direct for Tuscaloosa, would follow the enemy, and bring on an engagement, if possible, to prevent Jackson's junction with Forrest. Wilson immediately ordered McCook to advance to Centreville and secure the bridge there, and continue the march to Trion, where, after breaking up Jackson's command, he was to join Croxton and return with the entire division to the main army. Long and Upton were ordered to press Forrest back to Selma. Forrest's force, about 5000 strong, was encountered at Ebenezer Church on the 1st of April, and completely routed, losing two guns and 200 prisoners. By 4 P.M. on the 2d Wilson reached the immediate vicinity of Selma, having destroyed the trestle and bridges on the railroad as far as Burnsville.

Selma is situated on the north bank of the Alabama River. A line of bastioned fortifications extended three miles distant from the city, on the north side, from the river below to the river above, flanked on the west by Valley Creek, and on the east by an almost impracticable swamp. Including the citizen militia, the garrison numbered about 7000 men. On the approach of the Federal columns, Dick Taylor left the city under the command of General Forrest. The works were carried by assault on the 2d. The loss in Long's division, which was mainly engaged in the direct assault, was 40 killed and 260 wounded. Forrest, Armstrong, Roddy, and Adams escaped with the main portion of their commands under cover of the darkness. Thirty-two guns and 2700 prisoners—including 150 officers—and a large quantity of stores were captured. Selma was the principal Confederate dépôt in the southwest. In anticipation of its capture, 25,000 bales of cotton had been burned by the enemy.

On the 5th McCook came in with the train, not having attacked Jackson or effected a junction with Croxton. After having constructed a bridge 870 feet long across the Alabama, General Wilson crossed his troops on the 10th, leaving the arsenal, founderies, and stores of Selma a complete ruin. Montgomery was on the 12th surrendered by the city authorities, the Confederate General Adams having fallen back before Wilson, after the destruction of 90,000 bales of cotton. The Federal cavalry then entered Georgia, and on the 16th General Upton, with 400 dismounted men, captured Columbus, saving the bridges over the Chattahoochee, and taking 52 field-guns and 1200 prisoners. The Confederate ram Jackson, nearly ready for sea, and carrying an armament of six 7-inch guns, was destroyed, together with the navy yard, arsenal, armory, factories, 200 cars, and an immense amount of cotton. The same day La Grange's brigade, of McCook's division, captured Fort Taylor at West Point, above Columbus, taking three guns and 300 prisoners.

On the 20th Wilson arrived at Macon, which was surrendered under protest by the municipal authorities, who claimed that, under the provisions of armistice which had been agreed upon between Sherman and Johnston, and of which Wilson now heard for the first time, the capture was contrary to the usages of war. Notwithstanding this, Wilson held as prisoners of war Major Generals Howell Cobb and G. W. Smith, and three brigadier generals.

Croxton's brigade, in the mean time, had eluded Jackson, and captured Tuscaloosa on the 3d of April, and, advancing a few miles farther southwest, had then turned back to Jasper, and thence, *via* Talladega and Newman, joined Wilson at Macon, having marched 650 miles in 30 days.

Stoneman's expedition had started from Knoxville, Tennessee, two days before Wilson's departure from Chickasaw. Its original purpose was co-operation with General Sherman; but before it set out Sherman had already captured Columbia, South Carolina, and was moving into North Carolina. The plan of Stoneman's expedition was therefore modified. About this time it was feared that General Lee might evacuate Richmond and Petersburg, and force his way through East Tennessee, *via* Lynchburg and Knoxville. To prevent this, Stoneman was sent toward Lynchburg, with orders to completely annihilate the railroad west of that point. The Fourth Corps was also ordered to advance from Huntsville, Alabama, as far up into East Tennessee as it could supply itself, repairing the railroad as it advanced, and forming, in conjunction with Tillson's infantry division, a strong support for Stoneman's cavalry in the event of the latter being driven back.

Stoneman moved with three brigades—Brown's, Miller's, and Palmer's—commanded by General Gillem, through Bull's Gap, and thence eastward up the Watauga River, and across Iron Mountain to Boone, in North Carolina, where, on the 18th of April, he had a slight skirmish with some horse-guards. Continuing his advance to Wilkesborough, he then moved into southeastern Virginia. By the main column and detachments from it, Christiansburg, Wytheville, and Salem were captured, and the railroad was destroyed from near Lynchburg to Wytheville. Concentrating his command, Stoneman returned to North Carolina through Jacksonville and Taylorsville. From Germantown Palmer's brigade was sent to Salem (North Carolina), where 7000 bales of cotton were burned and the cotton factories destroyed; also the bridges on the railroad between Greensborough and Danville, and between Greensborough and the Yadkin River. In the accomplishment of these objects there was some fighting, and 400 prisoners were captured. From Germantown Stoneman moved on Salisbury, where he charged a Confederate force 3000 strong defending the place, capturing 14 guns and 1364 prisoners. The immense dépôts of supplies in Salisbury were destroyed, and the bridges on all the railroads leading out of the town were burned for several miles. Stoneman then returned to Greenville, East Tennessee, with his prisoners and captured artillery, leaving Gillem with the three brigades east of the mountains to intercept or disperse any Confederate troops moving south. On the 23d of April, Gillem, having defeated a detachment of the enemy defending Ashville, would have captured the town, but was met by a flag of truce announcing the armistice agreed upon between Sherman and Johnston. This armistice, and the circumstances which led to it, will be considered in a subsequent chapter.

ALVAN C. GILLEM.

GRANT'S HEADQUARTERS, CITY POINT.

CHAPTER LVI.

THE CAPTURE OF PETERSBURG AND RICHMOND.

Position in the Autumn of 1864.—Davis's Macon Speech.—Political Aspect.—Presidential Election at the North.—The Democratic Convention.—How McClellan's Nomination was regarded at the South.—Views of Alexander H. Stephens.—Moral Effect of Sherman's Campaign.—Forces of Johnston.—Military Situation in the Spring of 1865.—Actual Boundaries of the Confederacy.—Forces in the Field.—Strength of Lee's Army.—Project for arming the Slaves.—Opposed by the President and Secretary of War.—Favored by Lee.—Act passed for this purpose.—Protest by Mr. Hunter.—Provisions of the Act.—Confederate Finances.—Enormous Issue of Paper Money.—Practical Repudiation.—Depreciation of the Currency.—The Confederate Commissariat.—Difficulty in Feeding the Armies in Virginia.—New Tax Laws.—Lee determines to abandon Richmond.—His Plans.—Grant's Plans.—His Orders to Sheridan.—Sheridan moves up the Valley.—Routs Early at Waynesborough.—Destroys Canal and Railroads.—Joins Grant at Petersburg.—Designs of Lee and Grant.—Changes in the Organization of the Federal Army.—Commanders and Position.—The Confederate Lines.—Strategical Position of the Five Forks.—General Confederate Position.—The Confederates assault Fort Steadman.—The Fort surprised and taken.—The Confederates checked by Hartranft.—They are cut off, and surrender.—The Confederate Picket Line assaulted and carried.—Losses on both Sides.—Grant's Plans unchanged.—The Idea of the Operations.—Special Directions to Sheridan.—Strength of Sheridan's Cavalry.—Advance of Warren's Corps.—Lee's Counter-movement.—He masses Troops against Sheridan and Warren.—Operations suspended by a Storm.—Battle of White Oak Ridge, March 31.—Sheridan reaches Five Forks, and is forced back.—Action at Dinwiddie Court-house.—Warren directed to join Sheridan.—The Orders received by him.—The Confederates fall back to the Five Forks.—Sheridan's Movements.—Sheridan and Warren.—The Battle of the Five Forks.—The Fifth Corps captures the Confederate Lines.—Cavalry Operations.—The last Confederate Stand.—Their Rout.—How Lee received the Tidings.—Warren superseded.—Sheridan's Reasons.—Bombardment of Petersburg.—The general Assault.—The Ninth Corps carries the first Lines in their Front, and is checked.—The Sixth Corps pierces the Confederate Lines.—Capture of Fort Gregg.—Movements of Sheridan and Humphreys.—Death of A. P. Hill.—Lee determines to abandon his Position.—His Strength at the Time.—He concentrates his Force, and assaults the Union Lines.—Fort Mahone captured and recaptured.—Petersburg abandoned.—Davis notified of the intended Evacuation.—Scenes in Richmond.—Davis leaves Richmond.—Riots and Pillaging.—Ewell fires the Warehouses.—The Conflagration at Richmond.—In the Lines.—Naval Interlude.—Weitzel enters Richmond.—Hoisting of the Union Flag upon the Capitol.—Shepley appointed Military Governor.—His Orders.—The Conflagration checked.—Jefferson Davis reaches Danville.—His last Proclamation.

AS the spring of 1865 drew near, all men might see that the end of the Confederacy was close at hand. Late into the autumn of the preceding year its fortunes had seemed far from desperate. Never had it borne itself to the world more defiantly than in October. The two great armies east of the Mississippi, for the destruction of which the campaign of 1864 had been planned, were in October as strong as they had been in May. In Virginia Grant had been brought to a dead stand by Lee before Petersburg. Early lay in the Valley of the Shenandoah, threatening a renewed invasion of Maryland and Pennsylvania. Sherman had indeed penetrated far into Georgia, and had won Atlanta—a heavy blow, but one lighter than others from which the Confederacy had apparently recovered. Sherman's position, indeed, seemed full of peril. He was 300 miles from his only source of supplies, with which he was connected by two slender lines, and if these should be severed his army would be starved out. So it seemed to Jefferson Davis, who had gone on a tour of inspection to the West. The army of Sherman, he declared in public speeches, "would meet the fate that befell the army of the French empire in its retreat from Moscow." "Our cavalry and our people," he said, "will harass and destroy his army as did the Cossacks that of Napoleon, and the Yankee general will, like him, escape with only a body-guard." "Be of good cheer," he said to a division of Tennessee troops; "for within a short time your faces will be turned homeward, and your feet pressing Tennessee soil."[2] All thoughts of peace which did not start with the recognition of the absolute independence of the Confederacy were scouted.

While the military operations of the campaign had not been decidedly unfavorable, and it needed only a sanguine spirit to consider them rather favorable than otherwise to the Confederate cause, there was much in the apparent political aspect of affairs to encourage the South. To all appearance the Confederacy was yet thoroughly united for the prosecution of the war to the utmost extremity. It is now known that a general feeling of dissatisfaction with the government was growing up, but hitherto it had hardly manifested itself openly. All the functions of authority had been merged in the executive. Congress was little more than a debating club. Vehement opposition speeches were indeed made, but, as the sessions were mainly held in secret, they had little influence upon public opinion. It was different in the Union. There had all along been an active party opposed to the administration and to the conduct of the war, if not, as was believed at the South, to the war itself. The presidential election was approaching; all the elements of opposition had combined in the nomination of McClellan. The Chicago Convention had embraced in its platform a proffer of thanks to the soldiery of the army and the sailors of the navy, who had fought upon land and water under the flag of the country; but it had also declared that the four years of war had been a failure, and that immediate efforts should be made for a cessation of hostilities, with a view to an ultimate Convention of the states, or other means, for the restoration of peace. It was indeed added that the restoration should be "on the basis of the Federal Union of the states." But so emphatic had been the declaration of the South against any restoration or reconstruction of the Union, that it was firmly believed that, should the opposition come into power, hostilities be suspended, and a Convention called, the North would yield this point, and consent to a separation. So the South looked with much anxiety and something of hope to the result of the coming election at the North.[1]

These hopes, political and military, were soon dispelled. Lincoln was re-elected as President; Sherman accomplished his march through Georgia, and thence traversed South Carolina, and penetrated the very heart of North Carolina, with scarcely a show of opposition. Hood's army was crushed, and in effect annihilated in Tennessee. Sherman's march demonstrated to both parties and to the world the exhaustion of the Confederacy. It was not so much that the march was effected, but that there was no force left to dispute it. Johnston, once more called to the rescue, and placed in command of all the Confederate forces east of the Mississippi up to the very lines of Petersburg, swept together all the troops left in that wide region. Saving those shut up at Mobile, he drew together almost every man from Mississippi to Alabama, from Alabama to Georgia, with all in the two Carolinas. By the Confederate muster-rolls there were still enough for a great army. But to gather them was like collecting water with a sieve. On the last day of January Hardee had in South Carolina 23,000 men present for duty. Three weeks after he evacuated Charleston with 18,000; three weeks later, when he joined Johnston in North Carolina, he had but 6000. The Governor of South Carolina had withdrawn from him 1100 state troops; the remaining 11,000 missing had deserted on the march.[2] All told, the garrisons of Savannah, Charleston, Wilmington, and Augusta, with the relics of Hood's army, Johnston could not gather more than 40,000 men.[3] Pressing hard upon these was Sherman, now re-enforced by Schofield from Thomas's victorious army, raising his force to fully 100,000.

Before the last week of March, when the active operations of the campaign were opened, the field of contest had been restricted within narrow

[1] September and October, 1864.

[2] Davis's speech at Macon, September, 1864.

[1] "The action of the Chicago Convention, so far as its platform of principles goes, presents a ray of light which, under Providence, may prove the dawn of day to this long and cheerless night—the first ray of real light I have seen from the North since the war began." (*Alexander H. Stephens, September 22, 1864.*)—"I look upon the election of McClellan as a matter of vast importance to us in every view of the case, and hence I thought it judicious, patriotic, and wise to do every thing that could properly be done to aid in his election. Whatever may be his individual opinions, he is the candidate of the State Rights party at the North, in opposition to the Centralists and Consolidationists, whose hobby now is abolitionism. . . . Some think that if what they term a Conservative man should be elected, or any on the Chicago platform even, that such terms for a restoration of the Union would be offered as our people could accept. The spectre of reconstruction rears its ghastly head at every corner, and haunts their imagination. These apprehensions, I doubt not, are sincere, but I entertain none such myself. The old Union and the old Constitution are both dead—dead forever, except so far as the Constitution has been preserved by us. There is for the Union as it was no resurrection by any power short of that which brought Lazarus from the tomb. These fears of voluntary reconstruction are but chimeras of the brain. No one need entertain any such from McClellan's election. But, on the contrary, I think that peace—and peace on the basis of a separation of the states and our independence—would be the almost certain result. . . . . So, in any and every view I can take of the subject, I regard the election of McClellan and the success of the State Rights party at the North, whose nominee he is, as of the utmost importance to us. . . . . On the question of reconstruction, I stand now just where I did in October, 1861, when I wrote to a gentleman, in answer to a letter from him stating that I was charged with such sentiments, that I looked upon such charges as no less an imputation upon my intelligence than upon my integrity. The issue of this war, in my judgment, was subjection or independence." (*Alexander H. Stephens, November 5, 1864.*)

[2] Pollard, *Lost Cause*, 676.

[3] Johnston surrendered 31,248; but in this number were included many not actually present with him in front of Sherman. By his own statement, which must pass unquestioned, he had with him near Raleigh about 24,000, of whom 18,578 were infantry and artillery, and a little more than 5000 cavalry. In the interval he had lost some thousands in battle, and it is presumable many more by desertion. Our estimate of 40,000 will unquestionably cover his force when the largest.

FIELD HOSPITAL OF NINTH CORPS.

limits. There was still a considerable Southern force beyond the Mississippi, but this was so thoroughly isolated from the remainder of the Confederacy that it could effect nothing toward the general result. The West was swept clear of Confederate troops. In Alabama they held useless and precarious possession of Mobile, with feeble garrisons at a few points in the interior. The remainder of the state, together with Georgia, South Carolina, and two thirds of North Carolina, were held by the Federals. Wilson's and Stoneman's cavalry, sent out by Thomas, rode at will, with none to molest or hinder them. If they gained no great victories, it was because there was no enemy to encounter save in trifling skirmishes. All Northern and Eastern Virginia, down to the banks of the James, had been wrested from the hands of the Confederates. As a military, and, by consequence, as a political power, the Confederacy now embraced only the southern third of Virginia and the northern third of North Carolina. Its boundaries were the James on the North and the Neuse on the south, the Atlantic on the east and the Alleghanies on the west—one hundred and fifty miles from Raleigh to Richmond, and cutting off a broad strip on the sea-board, practically in Federal hands, as far from the mountains toward the ocean—a territory of 22,500 square miles, less than one half of the area once comprised in the State of Virginia. Within these boundaries the Confederate armies numbered about 100,000, with no prospect of the addition of a single regiment; the Union forces numbered fully 250,000, with 100,000 more ready to be launched thither, and still another 100,000 in arms, which could be sent in a few weeks.[1] Lee, indeed, still held his strong lines at Petersburg with a powerful army. On paper it numbered 175,000 men; but of these more than half were absent, and only about 65,000 present for

[1] The Federal force "available and present for duty" on the 1st of March numbered 602,598, of whom about 150,000 were with Grant, and 100,000 with Sherman. There were 40,000 in the departments of Washington and West Virginia; these, with quite 60,000 from various departments of the West where hostilities had ceased, could have been sent at once to Virginia and North Carolina, leaving 252,000 for operations in the extreme South and elsewhere, from which another 100,000 could, in case of need, have been spared for operations on the actual scene of war. Besides the 602,000, there were 180,000 in hospitals or on sick leave, and 50,000 absent as prisoners of war or without leave; there were 132,000 on detached service in the different military departments, many of whom could have been brought into active service. The entire nominal force of the Union armies on the 1st of March was 965,591.—See Report of the Secretary of War for 1865.

duty.[1] With such an army, according to the dictum of Napoleon, Lee might have held Richmond against the whole Federal army, had that been the simple problem presented to him for solution. But, as we have seen, the maintenance of Richmond involved also the holding of a long line of intrenchments, designed to cover the only communications by means of which his army could be fed.

But the depletion of the army was only an external symptom of the general infirmity which had fallen upon the Confederate state. As usual, the patient tried to remove the symptom rather than heal the disease. The project began to be broached of replenishing the army by arming the slaves. A proceeding so utterly at variance with every idea upon which Southern society was based met at first with little favor. Slaves had, indeed, from the very first, been employed as laborers upon fortifications, and gradually as teamsters and pioneers in the field. In September, 1864, the Governor of Louisiana urged upon the Secretary of War that the time had come to put into the army every able-bodied negro as a soldier. "I would," he said, "free all able to bear arms, and put them into the field at once." In his message in November Mr. Davis discussed the question. It was to be viewed, he said, "solely in the light of policy and our domestic economy. When so regarded, I must dissent from those who advise a general levy and arming of the slaves for the duty of soldiers; but," he added, "should the alternative ever be presented of subjugation or the employment of the slave as a soldier, there seems no reason to doubt what should then be our decision." Mr. Seddon, then Secretary of War, took the same view. So long as there were whites who could be brought into the army, it was not safe to "risk our liberties and safety on the negro. For the present, it seems best to leave the subordinate labors of society to the negro, and to impose its highest, as now existing, on the superior class." But it became apparent that few more whites could be brought into the depleted armies. Late in February, 1865, Lee strongly urged the employment of negroes as soldiers. "I think," he said, "the measure not only important, but necessary. I do not think our white population can supply the necessities of a long war. I think those who are employed should be freed. It would not be just or wise to require them to remain as slaves." An impressment or draft he thought would not bring out the best class; he would rather call upon those who were willing to come, with the consent of their owners. "If," he wrote, "Congress would authorize their reception, and empower the President to call upon individuals or states for such as they are willing to contribute, with the condition of emancipation to all enrolled, a sufficient number would be forthcoming to enable us to try the experiment." Soon after an act was passed by Congress for this purpose. It had passed the House, and was lost in the Senate by a single vote; but the Legislature of Virginia having instructed the senators from that state to vote for it, it was reconsidered, and passed by one majority. Mr. Hunter, who had before voted against the bill, in now voting for it in obedience to the instructions of the Legislature, accompanied his vote with an emphatic protest. "When we left the old government," he said, "we thought we had got rid forever of the slavery agitation. We insisted that Congress had no right to interfere with slavery. We contended that whenever the two races were thrown together, one must be master and the other slave. We insisted that slavery was the best and happiest condition of the negro; now, if we offer slaves their freedom as a boon, we confess that we were insincere and hypocritical. Yet, if the negroes were made soldiers, they must be made freemen. There is something in the human heart that tells us that when they come out scarred from this conflict they must be free. If we can make them soldiers—the condition of the soldier being socially equal to any other—we can make them officers, perhaps to command white men. If we are right in passing this measure, we were wrong in denying to the old government the right to interfere with the institution of slavery and to emancipate slaves." The measure, he said, would also injure the Confederacy abroad. It would be regarded as a confession of despair, and an abandonment of the ground upon which secession was based. As a matter of expediency, it was, he declared, worse than as a question of principle. No considerable body of negro troops could be got together without stripping the country of the labor absolutely necessary to produce food. Moreover, the negroes abhorred the profession of a soldier. They would not volunteer, and if they were impressed they would desert to the Yankees, who could give them a better price than the Confederacy could do. The act, as passed, empowered the President to ask for and accept from owners of slaves such number of negroes as he should deem expedient, for and during the war, "to perform military service in whatever capacity he may direct." They were to be formed into companies and regiments by the general-in-chief, and commanded by such officers as the President should appoint, and to receive the same pay and rations as other troops in the same branch of the service. If a sufficient number was not thus raised, the President might call upon each state for her quota of any number not exceeding 300,000 troops, in addition to those subject to military service under existing laws, "to be raised from such classes of the population, irrespective of color, in each state as the proper authorities thereof may determine." But it was provided that "nothing in this act shall be construed to authorize a change in the relation of the said slave;" and that not more than a quarter of the male slaves between the ages of eighteen and forty-five should be called for. Whatever might have been the effect of such a law if enacted at an earlier period, it came too late. The Confederacy had now no arms to put into their hands, and no means of producing them at home or procuring them from abroad;[1] and, moreover, long before the requisition could be made and complied with, the Confederacy had ceased to exist.

The finances of the Confederacy were even in a worse condition than its armies. It had long since practically ceased to pay its soldiers. It was hardly worth the trouble even to go through the form, when a month's pay of a soldier in paper money would not buy a pair of shoes. Yet, for many purposes, the government must have something to represent money; and at last notes and bonds were put forth with a profusion limited only by the ability of the printing-press to execute them. What the total sum was no man can tell with any approach to accuracy.[2] The financial measures of the government have been made the subject of unbounded animadversion; but it is hard to see how the wisest financier could have materially changed the general results. Most of the twenty millions of specie in the Confederacy was loaned to government, or soon became absorbed in the tempting business of blockade-running; all that government could borrow or raise by the export of cotton was spent abroad for vessels, arms, munitions, and military supplies. Bank-notes, themselves in the end to become almost worthless, were carefully hoarded, and the government could only pay its home expenses in its own notes and bonds; and these, as the expenses accumulated, must be issued in larger and still larger quantities, accelerated by what was styled the universal advance in prices, but which was really the depreciation in the estimate put upon the circulating medium. The Confederate financiers had laid upon them a task more grievous than that imposed by the Egyptians upon the Hebrews. They had to make bricks not only without straw, but without clay—with nothing but sand. No wonder that their bricks crumbled at a touch. The Confederate paper depreciated until it had a real purchasing power of only a twentieth, a fortieth, and finally a sixtieth of its nominal value. It grew to be a common jest, that when one went to market he needed a basket to carry his money, and only a wallet to bring home his purchases.

A vigorous government may for a long time keep armies in the field without pay, but not without food. The Confederate commissariat was in worse plight than its treasury. The South, though essentially agricultural, and abundantly supplied with food, had yet no large accumulations. It had no great dépôts where supplies were collected in advance. The crops were consumed in the year of their harvesting, and mainly in the region of their production. The means were scanty for their transportation from place to place. Hence, when the sudden necessity arose for accumulating large amounts at Richmond, it was with the utmost difficulty that this want could be met. We have already[3] seen how sorely this difficulty pressed upon Lee in the summer and autumn of 1864. As weeks passed on, the difficulty became greater and greater. The immediate region was well-nigh exhausted. Early in the winter the state of things was thus set forth in secret session of Congress:[4] There was not meat enough in the Confederacy for the armies it had in the field. In Virginia there was not meat enough for the armies within her limits. The supply of even bread depended upon keeping open railroad connections with the South. Meat must be obtained from abroad; and bread could no longer be had by impressment, but must be paid for at market rates, and in a better currency than that in circulation.

Grave as were these difficulties, they grew rapidly graver. The capture of Fort Fisher, by closing the port of Wilmington, shut off all possibility of obtaining meat from abroad. The wharves at Nassau might be piled with meat purchased for the Confederacy, but not a barrel could reach the army. Sherman's march though Georgia and the Carolinas had severed all connection with the regions where bread was mostly to be found. Even if it was to be found, whence was to come that better currency wherewith to purchase it? Congress, near the close of its last session, made a desperate ef-

---

[1] The strength of Lee's force has been most persistently and strangely understated. Pollard (*Lost Cause*, 679) asserts that "in the first months of 1865 Lee held both Richmond and Petersburg with not more than 33,000 men." Swinton (*Army of the Potomac*, 573) says: "At the opening of the spring campaign General Lee had on paper 160,000 men, but, in reality, less than 50,000, from which, if there be deducted the 10,000 troops on detached duty, it will appear that he had 40,000 men wherewithal to defend forty miles of intrenchments." It is somewhat strange that Mr. Swinton should have failed to refer to the Confederate reports which he had in his possession. These reports give the following as the sum of Lee's force at the close of February:

	Present and Absent.	Present.	Present for Duty.
Army of Northern Virginia	160,411	73,349	59,094
Department of Richmond	9,675	5,431	4,692
Total	170,086	78,780	64,786

The troops in the Department of Richmond, under Ewell, were the actual garrison of Richmond; they marched out at the evacuation, and formed the rear-guard of the retreating army. Upon what "detached duty" any of Lee's force could have been engaged, it is hard to see. The one thing to be done was to defend his lines. It is probable that Lee's force was slightly increased during the three weeks between the date of this report and the commencement of operations; for, as will be seen hereafter, about 65,000 are definitely accounted for as killed and wounded, captured on the field, or surrendered; and it is certain that considerable numbers escaped, and were not included in the lists of paroled prisoners.

[1] At the time when "Congress was debating a bill to put 300,000 negroes into the Confederate armies, there were not five thousand spare arms in the Confederacy, and our returned prisoners could not actually find muskets with which to resume their places in the field."—Pollard, *Lost Cause*, 660.

[2] Pollard (*Lost Cause*, 420) says: "The total cost of the war to the Confederate government had reached at its close, according to the opinion of intelligent officers of the Treasury, about thirty-five hundred millions of dollars. Of this total about twenty-five hundred millions consisted of eight, six, and four per cent. bonds of long dates, of treasury notes, unsettled accounts," etc.; the remaining thousand millions being in the form of unpaid claims for property purchased or impressed and damages sustained at the hands of the enemy. He elsewhere (page 651) puts down the amount of treasury notes in circulation as money at three hundred and twenty-five millions; but, as appears, many millions had been practically repudiated by the government a year before. At that time the amount of notes was more than six hundred millions. By the law of February 17, 1864, holders of these notes above the denomination of five dollars were for a few months to be allowed to exchange them for four per cent. bonds; after that they should cease to be current, but might be exchanged for new notes at the rate of three of the old for two of the new. Old notes of one hundred dollars could not be exchanged for the new ones, but only for four per cent. bonds; all of them outstanding after April 1 were to be taxed ten per cent. a month until January, 1865, when they should be taxed one hundred per cent.—that is, repudiated wholly. Notes of the new issue, and the small ones of the old scaled down to two thirds of their value, might be exchanged for certificates bearing four per cent. interest, and payable two years after the notification of a treaty of peace with the United States. A large majority of the note-holders, it is added, exchanged the old notes for new ones under the conviction that the reduction of the amount of the currency would make the two dollars worth more than three now were. If we suppose that this large majority held two thirds of the whole six hundred millions, the scaling down was in effect a repudiation of one hundred and fifty millions of dollars.

[3] *Ante*, p. 698.

[4] Pollard (*Lost Cause*), 649.

UNION AND CONFEDERATE WORKS SOUTHWEST OF PETERSBURG, FROM SIGNAL STATION.

fort to grapple with this last difficulty. Early in March a tax-bill was passed, more stringent than any civilized people had ever endured. Agriculturists must pay in kind a tenth of their produce. All property, real and personal, not otherwise provided for, must pay eight per cent.; specie, bullion, and bills of exchange, twenty per cent.; paper money five per cent.; incomes five per cent.; all profits of above twenty-five per cent. upon sales, twenty-five per cent. Upon all prescribed taxes, of whatever kind, there was to be an addition of one eighth, to be applied toward the increased pay of soldiers. On the 17th of March another act was passed, "to raise coin for the purpose of furnishing necessaries for the army." A tax of twenty-five per cent. was imposed upon all coin held by banks or individuals in excess of two hundred dollars; not, however, to go into effect in case banks and individuals would, within a month, raise a loan of two millions to the government. The tax was also commuted in cases where the owners of coin would exchange it for cotton at the rate of fifteen cents a pound. On the 28th, the very day before Grant opened the final ten days' campaign, the State of Virginia advanced three hundred thousand dollars in coin, taking in exchange an order from the Secretary of the Treasury for two millions of pounds of cotton, "with the right to export the same free of all conditions except the payment of the export duty of seventy-five cents a pound." This duty, being payable in paper, was, at the then existing rate, equivalent to one and a quarter cents a pound in coin.

Thus threatened with starvation, imminent at the best, and certain in case either of the two railroads running southward were interrupted even for a week, Lee at last determined that his position was no longer tenable. He resolved to abandon it, and unite with Johnston somewhere near the borders of Virginia and North Carolina. If the retreat could be successfully executed, he would have a force of nearly or quite 100,000. Perhaps he might be able to crush Sherman, and thus regain possession of the Carolinas and Georgia, and then, gathering together the troops beyond the Mississippi, inaugurate a new war. At worst, the contest could be prolonged for a while, for it would be a work of months for the Federal army, with its material, to concentrate upon this new and difficult field of operations, and who could tell what changes a few months might not bring? Would the North hold out for another campaign? At all events, the army would escape immediate peril of starvation. If its food could not come to it, it would be going toward its food. This resolution was formed early in March, and the arrangements for its execution concerted with Johnston. But time was required to carry these arrangements into effect. Dépôts of provisions must be gathered at different points on the way, and the march could not begin until opening spring should make the roads practicable for an army and its trains of material.

Grant, on his part, was aware of the situation of Lee, and divined what must be the means which he would essay to extricate himself. Day after day was spent by him in anxiety lest each morning should bring the report that his opponent had retreated the night before. He had before meditated bringing Sherman, by water or land, upon the rear of Lee's position, but he became convinced that Sherman's crossing the Roanoke would be the signal for Lee to march toward Johnston. To forestall the junction of these two armies, and thus prevent a long and tedious campaign, seemed the thing nearest at hand to be done. Perhaps, also, he wished that the armies of the East, after their long and as yet not successful struggle, should have the glory of destroying their stout opponent, and thus match the achievements of their heretofore more fortunate comrades of the West. Something which seemed almost an accident now favored the execution of this design.

Early in February Grant had begun to make dispositions for the campaign. In the far South, Canby was moving upon Mobile, while Thomas was to send his cavalry to raid in different directions. Sheridan had wintered at Winchester, where he had recruited his cavalry until he had more than 10,000 in excellent condition. These, Merritt being Chief of Cavalry, had been organized into two divisions, under Devin and Custer. On the 20th Grant sent his orders, or rather suggestions, to Sheridan. As soon as the roads would permit, he would find no difficulty in going with cavalry alone up the Valley of the Shenandoah, and thence crossing the Blue Ridge still farther southward to Lynchburg. From there he was to destroy the canal and railroads in every direction, so that they would be of no farther use to the enemy. Grant was desirous to re-enforce Sherman with cavalry, in which arm he was greatly inferior to the enemy. Accordingly, when Sheridan had reached Lynchburg, and done his work in that region, he might, if circumstances should warrant, strike southward, heading the streams in Virginia, and push on to join Sherman, whom he would be likely to find somewhere near Raleigh.

Sheridan set out from Winchester on the 27th of February, his men carrying five days' rations in haversacks, and each horse bearing thirty pounds of forage; fifteen days' rations of coffee, sugar, and salt were borne in wagons. Besides the ammunition trains, a pontoon train of eight boats, eight ambulances, and one wagon for each division headquarters, no vehicle was permitted to accompany the march. Thus lightly equipped, the command moved rapidly, though the weather was bad. The mountains were covered with snow, rapidly disappearing under the heavy rains, rendering most of the streams past fording. Small parties of guerrillas hovered upon the flanks of the column; but they kept at a respectful distance, and no notice was taken of them. Once, however, Rosser, with one or two hundred cavalry, attempted to impede the march by burning a bridge over a fork of the Shenandoah, but was driven off with loss of men and material. In three days Staunton was reached, the farthest point which any Union force had hitherto attained by this route. Early, with a miscellaneous force of 2000 men, had been hovering in this region ever since his defeat at Cedar River. He retreated eastward, leaving word behind that he would figh Waynesborough, which commanded the only practicable gorge through Blue Mountains, which Sheridan must pass to debouch into the Valley the James, and reach Lynchburg. Custer's division was pushed in pur He found Early, true to his word, well posted, with two divisions of in try and Rosser's cavalry, behind breastworks. Without even pausing reconnoitre, with his troopers partly dismounted and partly in the sad Custer dashed straight at the works, drove the enemy out, pursued th until they were brought up by the river, where they threw up their ha in token of surrender, "with cheers at the suddenness with which they been captured."[1] The fruits of this brilliant dash were 1600 prison 11 guns, and 200 wagons, with ammunition and subsistence. Early caped with two of his staff. Rosser's cavalry also rode off, to appear fo moment a few days later. Herewith Early disappears from the war. the 30th of March Lee wrote, dismissing him from command, couching order in the kindest terms possible: He himself had full confidence in E ly's zeal, ability, and discretion; but he had lost public confidence, an commander must be sought for who could secure this. Lee had no oc sion to make this search; for, before Early had received the order of d missal, Lee was forced from Petersburg, and was on his disastrous retre which ten days after closed in his surrender.

Sheridan pushed through the gorge in the Blue Mountains thus open to him, and reached Charlottesville in the Valley of the James, where he w obliged to wait two days for his trains to make their slow way through t thick mud. The prisoners, meanwhile, were sent under a strong escort ward Winchester. Rosser followed this body, and at Mount Jackson ma an attack, hoping to rescue the prisoners. He was repulsed, and left b hind some of his own men. The delay at Charlottesville enabled the Co federates to gather at Lynchburg a force too strong to be assailed by cava ry. Sheridan abandoned the purpose of reaching that point, but sent h troopers in every direction to destroy the canal, railroad, and public pro erty. The James River Canal was for miles so thoroughly destroyed as be impassable, and thus one important means of supply for Lee's army w cut off. Sheridan then proposed to cross the James between Lynchbu and Richmond, and, pressing southward, to reach the Southside Railro fifty miles in the rear of Lee's lines. But the Confederates succeeded i destroying every bridge between these two points, and the pontoons woul not half span the still swollen stream.

Sheridan now, exercising the discretion which had been wisely give him, resolved, instead of endeavoring to join Sherman in North Carolin to more thoroughly destroy the railroads leading northward from Richmond and then, pressing eastward to the York River, bend southward, and, afte eight months' absence, rejoin Grant in front of Petersburg. After raidin hither and yon for a week, destroying every thing destructible down t within ten miles of Richmond, he resumed his march. Nature imposed ob stacles to this march such as had been heretofore pronounced insurmounta ble. It was the worst season of the Virginian year. There were incessan rain, deep and almost impassable streams, swamp and mud to be endure or overcome. The animals suffered much, mostly from hoof-rot. The men buoyed up by the thought that they had completed their work in the Val ley of the Shenandoah, and were now on their way to aid in what remaine to be done upon the Appomattox, bore up bravely. The whole loss on th march was not more than a hundred men, and some of these were left b the wayside, overborne by fatigue. Crossing the South and North Ann Rivers, passing hard by many famous battle-fields whereon there was nov no hostile force, this cavalry force reached the site of the memorable Whit House upon the 19th of March. Sheridan's march from Winchester ha occupied twenty days. In its course he had traversed thirteen counties i Virginia, and, by the almost utter destruction of the James River Canal an of the railroads, had effectually deprived the Confederate army at Richmon of all subsistence from the region of Virginia lying north and east of th James River. After resting and refitting for a week at the White Hous Sheridan resumed his route. Crossing the Chickahominy and the James he encamped near Petersburg on the evening of the 26th of March.

Here, at points only a few score rods apart, two men, neither of them t a casual observer notable for any thing but the rare faculty of saying little however much they might think, yet both somehow having that power o command which more showy men never cared to question, had fixed upo measures the result of which was to determine the issue of the war. Eacl of these two men, Grant and Lee, had by this time learned to value the oth er; each knew nearly the condition of the other, and so could gauge wha he should, and therefore would endeavor. Either could then play the par of his opponent almost as well as his own. Lee's main purpose toward th close of March was to withdraw his army, with its materials, from the Jame and the Appomattox, and, joining Johnston, to carry on the fight in Nort Carolina, or, events favoring, far to the southward. Grant's purpose was t prevent this orderly retreat, either by shutting up Lee within his lines, an therein forcing him to surrender by assault or famine, or to drive him ou by sheer force, in which case he would be able to follow hard on in pursuit.[2]

---

[1] Sheridan's Report.

[2] Neither Lee himself, nor any one qualified by position or knowledge to speak for him, has a yet undertaken to set forth the purpose of the Confederate commander at this period; but his op erations, soon to be described—such as bringing to Petersburg only the food needed from day t day, accumulating supplies at different points on the railroads, and the assault upon Fort Stead man—can be explained and justified only upon this theory. Grant, in a few significant sentences clearly sets forth his design. He says: "The greatest source of uneasiness to me was the fea that the enemy would leave his strong lines about Petersburg and Richmond, for the purpose o uniting with Johnston, before he was driven from them by battle or I was prepared to make an ef fectual pursuit. . . . With Johnston and him combined, a long, tedious, and expensive campaign, consuming most of the summer, might become necessary. By moving out I would put the army in better condition for pursuit, and would at least, by the destruction of the Danville Road, retar

BRIDGE ON MILITARY RAILROAD.

Important changes had within a few months taken place in the organization of the Federal armies in Virginia. Not long after the failure of the mine enterprise, and in consequence of the censure of the Court of Inquiry, Burnside, at his own request, received leave of absence. He wished to resign his commission, but the President refused to accept it, thinking that there would arise occasion to place him again in active service. The command of the Ninth Corps was in the mean time given to Parke, who happened to be the ranking general in command of a corps, and who consequently found himself at an imminent moment in command of the whole army. Hancock, never fully recovered from his wound at Gettysburg, had given up the command of the Second Corps, and gone East to recruit a new corps, to be known as the First. Humphreys, who had acted as chief of staff to Meade, was placed at the head of the Second Corps, Webb taking his place as Meade's chief of staff. Wright retained the command of the Sixth Corps, to which he had acceded upon the death of Sedgwick at Spottsylvania. This corps, having done brave service in the annihilation of Early in the Valley of the Shenandoah, had returned to the Appomattox, and to it was reserved the honor of giving two out of the three great blows which decided the issue of the war.[1] Warren still retained the command of the Fifth Corps. Butler had been, at the special request of Grant, removed from the command of the Department of Virginia and North Carolina, including what was known as the Army of the James. This army had been reorganized. The former Tenth and Eighteenth Corps had been discontinued, and the troops, to which was added the colored division formerly attached to Burnside's corps, were formed into two corps, designated as the Twenty-fourth and Twenty-fifth. Ord, having performed brilliant service in the West and Southwest, had been ordered to the North, and had replaced Smith at the head of the old Eighteenth Corps, and was at length placed in command of the department vacated by the removal of Butler, the newly-arranged Twenty-fourth and Twenty-fifth Corps, constituting the Army of the James, being confided to Gibbon and Birney. Thus it happened that, of the six generals who commanded corps in the combined armies of the East at the opening of operations in May, 1864, Warren only retained his place in March, 1865. Sheridan also, though now with his troopers upon the James, was still nominally commander of the Army of the Shenandoah. But the distinction between the armies of the Potomac, the James, and the Shenandoah had been practically set aside. The entire force around Richmond and Petersburg was directly under Grant, Meade being second in command, Sheridan coming next in grade, the corps commanders following in order of seniority in the date of their commissions. The combined force of all arms numbered about 150,000 men present for duty, of whom about two thirds were available for direct offensive operations in the field, the remainder being required for guards, camp duty, and other multifarious work.[2] As posted, Ord lay on the right, north of the James, and at Bermuda Hundred; next, and before Petersburg, Parke; then Wright; then Humphreys; and upon the extreme left, Warren.

Lee had, during the winter, continued his intrenchments two miles farther westward, bending the extremity in a sharp crotchet to the north. Farther he could not go from sheer want of men to hold the lines; otherwise there was no reason why they might not have stretched across the continent. Four miles beyond where the works ceased was a point as important as any other. Here three roads came together, the point of junction being known as the Five Forks. One, the White-oak Road, ran westward from the Boydton Plank Road, nearly parallel with the vital Southside Railroad, from which at the Five Forks it was but three miles distant, by way of the Ford Road, running north and south. An enemy, having gained the Five Forks, could in an hour strike the railroad, and in a few hours so damage it that days would be required for its repair. It was of prime importance that the Five Forks should be guarded. Intrenchments were therefore laid out here, stretching for two miles north and south behind the White-oak Road. This, between the Forks and the extremity of the regular lines, ran along a slight ridge, southward of which the region was woody and swampy. The White-oak Road thus formed practically a covered way by which troops could, in case of a menaced movement by the enemy, be hurried to the defense of the Forks. Thus, at the opening of spring, the absolute right of the Confederate line was a mile to the west of the Five Forks: this was watched by the bulk of the cavalry under Fitzhugh Lee. Thence it stretched eastward and northward, girdling Petersburg and Richmond. Ewell commanded the few thousand men which formed the proper garrison of Richmond. Longstreet commanded below the city, north of the James, and across the river to within a few miles of Petersburg. Then came Gordon at Petersburg, the bulk of his force consisting of the remnants of the three divisions reduced to the numbers of one in the disastrous campaign in the Valley of the Shenandoah. Lastly came Hill with three strong divisions, holding the long line south and west of Petersburg. Lee's headquarters were with Hill's division.

On the 24th of March Grant issued his order for a grand movement to be commenced on the 29th against the Confederate right. Lee, knowing the imminency of such a movement, and perceiving that the time had now come for the evacuation of his position, resolved to anticipate the movement of his antagonist by an offensive thrust which should facilitate his own withdrawal. The thing to be done was to prevent Grant from adding to the strength upon his left, and, if possible, to cripple for a space the forces already there, so as to leave open his own meditated line of retreat. He therefore planned a sudden assault upon the Federal right, the point farthest removed from that upon which the effect of the blow was to be felt.

The point chosen was Fort Steadman, close by the crater where Burnside's mine had so signally failed. This fort occupied a salient projected forward toward the Confederate works, the distance between being only one hundred and fifty yards. The fort itself was of no great strength. It was a small earthwork, without bastions, slightly constructed originally, and now much dilapidated by the frosts and rains of winter. So completely was it covered by the enemy's artillery that it was impossible to make any repairs except imperfectly and by stealth. This, however, was of less consequence, as the hill[1] upon which it stood was commanded in the immediate rear by a crest of nearly equal height, and covered upon each side by flanking batteries. Still it seemed to Lee that if the fort and a few of the flanking batteries could be taken by surprise, an opening could be made through which a strong column could be thrust, which should carry the

the concentration of the two armies of Lee and Johnston, and cause the enemy to abandon much material that he might otherwise save." As late as March 27, just two days before active operations commenced, Grant concerted with Sherman, who had come to City Point from North Carolina, a plan of campaign based on the supposition that Lee would continue to hold his lines at Petersburg and Richmond. Sherman, on the 20th of April, was to move northward, his army fully equipped and rationed for twenty days. He would, as circumstances should indicate, strike the Danville and Southside Railroads at their junction at Burkesville, 52 miles in the rear of Lee's lines, or join the armies operating in front of Richmond. Sherman, unless otherwise directed, was to begin this movement on the 10th of April; but, as events finally shaped themselves, on the very day before, Lee, having been forced from Richmond and Petersburg, surrendered his army at Appomattox Court-house. It may be safely assumed that, at the opening of the spring campaign of 1865, both of the opposing commanders so well understood the whole situation, that the immediate aim of each was to prevent the other from accomplishing the thing which at the moment he most desired. As, therefore, Grant's main purpose was to prevent Lee from getting safely away from his lines, it may be safely assumed that thus to get away was the main purpose of Lee. Each general, of course, was eager to avail himself of any advantage which circumstances should throw into his hands. In this view of the plans of the opponents—that is, Lee wishing to carry off his army and material, and Grant wishing to prevent him from so doing—the operations of the last fortnight of this long campaign are clearly explicable.

[1] The three great blows were: (1st) The battle of the Five Forks, won April 1 by Warren's Fifth Corps and Sheridan's Cavalry; (2d) The piercing of the Confederate lines, April 2, by the Sixth Corps; (3d) The capture of Ewell's Corps at Sailor's Creek, April 6, mainly by the Sixth Corps. These three blows cost the Confederates a loss of 20,000 prisoners, and probably 5000 in killed and wounded—nearly a half of the nominal, and more than a half of the real fighting force which Lee had left to him on the 31st of March.

[2] Force present for duty, March 1: Army of the Potomac, Meade, 103,273; Department of Virginia, Ord, 45,986, some thousands being at Fortress Monroe and elsewhere, and so not available for direct operations; cavalry of Middle Division, 12,980, of whom there were, at the close of March, about 9000 ander Sheridan, at hand on the James. The actual movable force may be estimated from the fact that when Warren moved on the 29th of March, his corps counted 15,300 men. The corps appear to have been of about equal strength, so that the six would have contained 91,800 movable men. Add to these 9000 cavalry, and there will be 100,800 at Grant's command for immediate offensive operations.

[1] Known as Hero's Hill. Confederate writers usually denominate the action which here ensued as the battle of Hare's Hill.

heights in the rear, and thus effectually pierce the Federal lines. Thence a sudden rush of less than two miles would reach the military railroad which Grant had constructed from City Point southwestward, by which the left of the Union army received its supplies. Such an attack, it was not unreasonably anticipated, would induce Grant to bring all his force from both extremities of his lines. If nothing more than this was accomplished, Longstreet and Hill, relieved from immediate pressure in front and on flank, could start southward without obstruction, while the assaulting column would be suddenly withdrawn and follow in their rear, and, before the Federal commander could reorganize his army for pursuit, would, with its material, be fairly on its way, with two full days' start, to unite with Johnston, and could so obstruct the roads behind them that they could not be overtaken until the junction already prepared for was effected. It was no wholly impossible that still greater results might be accomplished. The railroad destroyed, City Point itself might perhaps be reached, and in a brief space the great accumulation of stores there be given to the flames. The plan was a bold one; but Lee was now in such case that he must venture much. In its very audacity lay its best augury of success.

Lee left nothing undone which it was in his power to do to insure success. The initial blow was to be struck by Gordon with two of his divisions, while 20,000 more were massed to follow up the blow in case an opening was made at Fort Steadman and the crest in its rear was gained. The first blow must be given by surprise. Accident favored this. The Federal picket-line was advanced fifty yards in front of the fortifications, and within a hundred yards of the Confederate works. Across this narrow space deserters, often in squads and with arms in their hands, had been wont to make their way within the Union lines. At four o'clock on the morning of March 25 the officer on duty made his rounds along the picket-line; the men were alert, and there was no indication of any movement on the part of the enemy. Soon after, squad after squad, announcing themselves as deserters, began to drop in. The occurrence had come to be so common that no alarm was taken. Suddenly these squads dashed upon the pickets, and overpowered them with scarcely a show of resistance. At the same moment the near Confederate abatis was opened and three strong columns emerged. The central column struck straight for Fort Steadman; the others diverged to the right and left, taking in reverse small advanced batteries which flanked the fort on either hand. All these were carried with a rush, the garrison, five hundred strong, being made prisoners. A gap of a quarter of a mile wide had been made into, but not through the Union lines—an opening large enough to give passage to the 20,000 who had been massed to follow up the assault. If they had followed promptly in the gray dawn no man can say what would have been the result. They might possibly have won the commanding crest in the rear, and thence dashed upon the railroad; they might thus have won a great success, or they might have been cut off to a man, shut in by the enemy closing in behind them. By whose merit or whose fault it was that the 5000 whom Gordon pushed forward were left unsupported has been left untold.[1]

The lines, for a long distance to the right and left of Fort Steadman, were held by Parke's Ninth Corps. At half past five, when the attempt of the enemy was apparent, he sent tidings of it to headquarters. Three times within half an hour the message was repeated without an answer. Then came the reply through the telegraph operator: "General Meade is not here, and the command devolves upon you." Hurrying couriers to City Point to inform Grant and Meade of what was going on, Parke summoned Wright and Warren to move troops toward the point assailed. But before they could come up the Ninth Corps had done the work. Tidball, chief of artillery, was ordered to post his batteries upon the hill in the rear. These effectually stopped the advance of the central column. The two other assailing columns soon came to grief. The right column met Hartranft's division, which had sprung to arms; they were checked, and soon forced back. The left gained some success, capturing momently two batteries, but were in like manner checked and forced back. The three columns were now drawn together within the captured works of Fort Steadman; but these were commanded by Fort Haskell on the left, as well as by the batteries in the rear. After making a feeble attempt to take this fort, the troops of Gordon crouched in disorder behind the breastworks which they had captured, for the way of retreat was by this time closed upon them. Forts Haskell on the left, and McGilvery on the right, swept the narrow space to the Confederate lines with a fire under which no troops could live. Hartranft, upon whom the immediate direction of operations had devolved, had posted his own division and portions of others so as to cover their front and both flanks.[2] Hartranft now dashed upon the works, and carried them with hardly a show of resistance. Some of the Confederates ran the terrible cross-lines of fire and got back to their own lines, but nearly 2000 of t surrendered. Their loss in killed and wounded is unknown, but it n have exceeded that of the Federals, which amounted to 500. Of the 5 men whom Gordon led to the attack, about 3000 were killed, wounded captured.

The Confederate disasters of the day were not yet over. The confic Fort Steadman was finished before nine o'clock, only a part of the Ni Corps having taken part in it. Wright and Humphreys, whose corps w now well in hand, were anxious to follow up the advantage by an assaul their fronts; but Parke considered that his accidental and temporary c mand of the entire army would not warrant him in forcing a general gagement. Meade, who soon after came upon the field, forbade a gen attack, but later in the day pushed forward the Second and Sixth Corps feel the enemy in their respective fronts. After a fierce struggle the str Confederate picket-lines were carried, and held in spite of desperate attem to retake them. This cost the Federals 1100 men, of whom 200 were m ing. The Confederates lost 800 prisoners, and probably as many in kil and wounded. The entire Confederate loss on this day was not far fr 4500, that of the Federals 2000.[1]

There was nothing in the result of the affair on the 25th of March to duce Grant to change his order issued the day before, to be carried into fect four days later. The essential thing contemplated in this plan was t Sheridan, with all the cavalry of all the armies upon and near the Ja and the Appomattox, should, by a wide detour, pass clear beyond the most westward extension of Lee's lines, and cut the railroads by which Confederate army was fed, nearly half way to the point where Johnston w presumably awaiting the approach of the Army of Northern Virginia. T movement was rendered feasible only by what we have already styled t "accident" whereby Sheridan was in Virginia, instead of far away in No Carolina, ready to operate with Grant instead of with Sherman. Subsidi to this cavalry movement, the infantry was to make a determined effort turn the enemy out of his position around Petersburg. To effect this, eve available man of the two armies of the Potomac and the James was to brought against the Confederate right before Petersburg, and to its sou and southwest.

Ord, leaving Weitzel in command north of the Potomac, was to bri half of his two corps over, and, sweeping around in the rear of the lines b fore Petersburg, pass toward the left of the position. Parke was to hold t position which his corps had so long maintained; Wright, next to him, w to be ready to hold his lines or to move; Humphreys, and the movab part of Ord's corps, and that of Warren, were to form the great turning c umn whose movements, it was hoped, would force the abandonment of P tersburg; the general purpose of all being "not to attack the enemy in h intrenched position, but to turn him out of it if possible." But, at the sa time, all corps and division commanders were to hold themselves ready f offense should the enemy weaken himself in their front. Above all thing no commander of a corps or division, in case of attack, was to wait for sp cial orders from headquarters. The strength of the enemy was pretty we ascertained. Should he appear in great force at any one point, it coul only be by weakening himself elsewhere. Advantage should be prompt taken of every weakening, and every advantage any where gained shou be promptly followed up. For the rest, the men of the moving colu were to take four days' rations in their haversacks, twice as much followi in wagons. The artillery was to be kept within the smallest compass, si or eight guns to a division being the utmost to be taken; for in the wood and swampy region where operations were to be carried on, artillery woul be an incumbrance rather than aid. Such was the substance of the gene order of the 24th.

The order to Sheridan, given on the 28th, just as he was setting out, w to the same purport, but with some special additions: First and foremo he was to aim at the railroads; "but if the enemy should come out of h own lines and attack, or put himself in a position where he can be attacke move in your own way; the army will engage or follow, as circumstanc will dictate. Having accomplished the destruction of the two railroads," concluded the order, "which are now the only avenues of supply to Lee army, you may return to this army, selecting your road farther south, may go on into North Carolina, and join General Sherman." No wid discretion was ever given to a general than this of Grant to Sheridan. Ne day, indeed, March 29, when matters had apparently taken shape, this ord was modified: "I feel like ending this matter, if it is possible to do so, b fore going back," wrote Grant. "I do not want you, therefore, to cut loo and go after the enemy's roads at present. In the morning, push aroun the enemy's rear, if you can, and get on to his right rear. We will act together as one army here until it is seen what can be done with the en my." How nearly this last plan failed of the success which it finally a tained is now to be shown.

[1] Pollard (*Lost Cause*, 686) says: "Had this opportunity" (that is, the capture of the fort and batteries) "been taken advantage of, there is no telling the result; but the troops could not be induced to leave the breastworks they had taken from the enemy, and to advance beyond them and seize the crest in rear of the line they had occupied." But nothing can be clearer than that the force which had effected the capture was inadequate for any thing more. Swinton (*Army of the Potomac*, 597) says: "It is well known that there was great dereliction on the part of the supporting columns, for Gordon's attack was left almost wholly unsupported, notwithstanding that Lee had massed in the vicinity all his available force." He, however, fails to give his authority for this representation, and does not state upon whom rests the blame of this dereliction. The one thing certain is, that this supporting force was not pushed forward. We can hardly suppose that a movement upon which so much was staked should have been made except under the direct supervision of Lee. In the light of the account given in the text, which shows how rapidly the Union troops recovered from their momentary surprise, we think that the failure to follow up the attack was wise. Twenty thousand men could not then have carried the lines. It was better to submit to the inevitable loss of a fifth than to risk the almost certain destruction of the whole of the force assigned to the adventure.

[2] "At half past seven o'clock the position of affairs was thus: Batteries 11 and 12 had been recaptured; a cordon of troops, consisting of Hartranft's division, with regiments belonging to McLaughlin's and Ely's brigades, was formed around Fort Steadman and battery 10, into which

[1] The entire Federal loss is officially given. It was, at Fort Steadman, 68 killed, 337 wounde 506 missing—in all, 911; at the picket-lines, 52 killed, 864 wounded, 207 missing—in all, 112 a total of 2084. The number of Confederate prisoners taken is also given: these were, at Fo Steadman, 1900; at the picket-lines, 834—in all, 2734. Their loss in killed and wounded is pur ly conjectural. From the facts that at Fort Steadman they were for two or three hours under hea fire, and that at the picket-lines they were repulsed after desperate charges, it is safe to assu that it was in both cases considerably greater than that of their opponents. Grant, in his final R port, says: "Their loss in killed and wounded was far greater than ours." In his first dispatc he says: "Humphreys estimates the loss of the enemy in his front at three times his own, a Wright, in his front, as double that of ours." This would indicate the entire Confederate loss have been greater than we have estimated it. But those who have had occasion to compare the guesses, on either side, with actual facts as subsequently verified, will place little reliance up them. In the absence of authenticated reports, they will rather rely upon estimates based up the nature of the operations. Thus, in the case under consideration, the Union loss in killed a wounded [illegible]

EWELL'S HEADQUARTERS, NEAR RICHMOND.

Sheridan had a month before set out from Winchester with 10,000 horsemen. Of these, 1500 had been sent back to guard the prisoners taken from Early at Waynesborough. In his great ride up the Valley, and thence through thirteen counties, he had lost by casualty hardly a hundred men. But his animals had suffered severely, and when he joined Grant, his two divisions, under Devin and Custer, numbered 5700 men in saddle;[1] but Crook, with 3300, was ready to join him, and he thus set out with 9000. In a day or two, McKenzie, with 1000 horsemen from the Army of the James, was added to his mounted command, making 10,000 in all. The Confederate cavalry under Fitzhugh Lee could hardly have reached a third of this number. With this magnificent force Sheridan swept southward and then westward, until, after encountering a few mounted pickets, who were easily brushed away, he reached Dinwiddie Court-house. Here several roads centred, along some of which his proposed raid would be conducted. Here, on the evening of the 29th, he received the order from Grant countermanding the plan of a raid, and directing him to co-operate with the infantry in the effort to turn the right flank of Lee's army.

Warren's corps—the Fifth—consisting of the three divisions of Crawford, Griffin, and Ayres, 15,300 strong in all, with twenty guns, marched out at three o'clock on the morning of the 29th.[2] They moved southwestward until they struck the Quaker Road running straight north to the Confederate lines. Turning up this, Griffin, whose division was in the advance, encountered a force of the enemy pushed in front of their lines, and after a sharp conflict, in which some four hundred were killed and wounded on each side, forced them back within the shelter of their intrenchments. Humphreys, also moving to the right of Warren, got close up to the Confederate fortified line without meeting opposition. It seemed now that the enemy was shut up in his lines to their utmost westward reach; and now, if this could be turned by Sheridan, it was as sure as any thing can be in warfare that the matter might be ended. To secure this, Grant was prepared, if need were, to give up every thing south of the position still held by Parke, flinging upon Lee's right his cavalry, with the entire corps of Warren, Humphreys, and Wright, with the three divisions detached from Ord. It was then that the order was sent to Sheridan to abstain from his projected raid upon the railroads.

Lee had in the mean time learned something of the mighty effort to be put forth against him. He still misconceived its ultimate purport. He thought it only a more determined repetition of the old efforts to reach the railroads, for the great sweep of Sheridan's cavalry was still unknown to him. Yet this must be thwarted at all hazards, and those roads protected for a few days, or all was lost; for, these roads seized, he had no means of feeding his army for a week, and no means of escaping from his position. So, stripping his intrenchments in front of Petersburg until to guard ten miles of works there were hardly as many thousand men, he gathered a mobile force, which, added to the cavalry on his right, numbered in all some 15,000 or 20,000, to meet the endeavor of Grant.[1] This column was only sent out after nightfall, and there was a fearful probability that it would not reach the scene of operations, fifteen miles away, until it was too late. But a fortune which neither general could anticipate intervened in favor of Lee. During the night a furious rain set in, which lasted all through the next day, the 30th. The region through which Warren was working his way was a low land covered mainly with tangled woods, threaded every where with swampy brooks, which a sharp shower would render difficult of passage. The soil of mingled sand and clay, upheaved by the winter frosts, was still soft, and the rain quickly converted the ill-made roads into mortar-beds. Any thing on wheels could hardly move a rod unless the road was laboriously corduroyed. Footmen and cavalry could indeed advance slowly; so, during the 30th, Warren and Sheridan worked their way a little onward, the former toward the White-oak Road, the latter toward the Five Forks. Lee's column had much farther to go, but they had the advantage of a less intolerable road, and thus, on the morning of the 31st, had passed beyond the extremity of the intrenched line, and occupied the White-oak Road toward the Five Forks.

On the morning of Friday, March 31, Warren's corps had worked itself up in sight of the White-oak Road, clear beyond the line of the enemy's intrenchments. On account of the woods and swamps, they could not form a regular line of battle, but each division was so massed that it could fight in any direction. Humphreys's corps had connected with Warren on the right. Just before nine o'clock Warren received an order from Meade, informing him that there was firing along Humphreys's front, and directing him to be ready to support Humphreys, if necessary, adding that there would be no movement of troops that day. Warren replied that he thought it best, if possible, to drive the enemy from the road, and in two hours received permission to make the attempt. Winthrop's brigade of Ayres's division was sent to make the attempt. The Confederates, at the same time, had planned a counter-move to drive Warren off. They rushed forward from both north and west. Ayres's division was forced back in confusion upon Crawford's, which lay next behind. This also gave way, and both fell back upon Griffin, who was posted in an opening in the woods large enough to give room for all. The two divisions which had fallen back, bewildered by the fierce assault in front and flank, amidst the unknown forests and swamps, rallied with that of Griffin, and held their ground. Humphreys, in the mean while, had sent Miles's division against the enemy's left flank. Warren, at two o'clock, finding that the enemy had ceased from his onset, advanced upon him with all his force. To his surprise, he met with little resistance; only one of his brigades was seriously engaged, and this swept up nearly a whole Confederate regiment, with its flags. At half

[1] These two divisions formed Merritt's command; Sheridan directing all the cavalry, together with such infantry as were at times added to it for special operations.

[2] For the movements of March 29, 30, 31, and April 1, culminating in the battle of the Five Forks, one needs to compare Sheridan's Report with Warren's Account of Operations. For the operations of the Fifth Corps we rely upon Warren; for those of the cavalry, upon Sheridan. Grant's report of this critical period is very meagre. Confederate reports are wholly wanting.

[1] The numbers of this body are given conjecturally from the indicia afforded by its known losses. Swinton (*Army of the Potomac*, 585; *Decisive Battles*, 485) gives the number at 15,000, apparently exclusive of the cavalry, which could not then have been more than 3000. In this statement he apparently follows Pollard (*Lost Cause*, 689), whose words are: "In the night of the 29th, General Lee, having perceived Grant's manœuvre, dispatched Pickett's and Bushrod Johnson's divisions, Wise's and Ransom's brigades, Huger's battalion of infantry, and Fitzhugh Lee's division—in all about 17,000 men—to encounter the turning column of the enemy." But Fitzhugh Lee's cavalry division were already upon the right, falling back before Sheridan. Taking into account the ascertained losses in this force, we think that Pollard's statement is a very close approximation to the actual number.

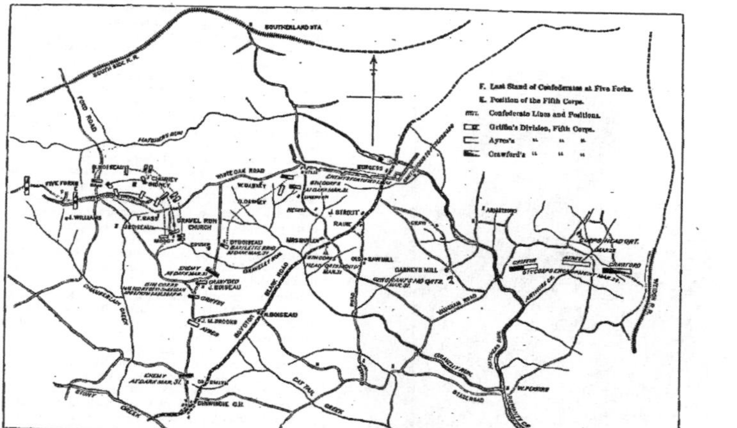

FIVE FORKS—MOVEMENTS OF THE FIFTH CORPS, MARCH 29–APRIL 1.

past three he wrote from the White-oak Road to Meade's chief of staff: "We have driven the enemy, I think, into his breastworks. The prisoners report General Lee here to-day, and also that their breastworks are filled with troops. We have prisoners from a portion of Pickett's and Johnson's divisions." He had, to appearance, won a decided victory on the White-oak Ridge, though at heavy cost, for his losses in killed and wounded numbered 1400.

Lee had, indeed, recoiled from the attack. Possibly he would in any case have given it up after having forced Warren back a space from his threatening position, for he was in no condition to run great risks, unless urged by imperative necessity. But the immediate occasion was that he was called upon to meet a still more imminent peril. To understand this, we must look to Sheridan's movements.

On the 30th, Sheridan, in spite of the rain, had pushed a part of his command toward the Five Forks, forcing the Confederate cavalry westward, and right away from the army of Lee. In the forenoon of the 31st a division of the cavalry reached the Forks. This point must be regained by Lee at all hazards, so the force which had been engaged with Warren was withdrawn and sent down the White-oak Road, and, falling upon the Union cavalry, drove them from the Forks. Then, uniting with the cavalry of Fitzhugh Lee, the whole force pressed upon Sheridan's cavalry, who were much scattered, and, in spite of strong resistance, forced them back upon Dinwiddie Court-house. The two divisions of Devin and Davies were cut off from a direct retreat, and compelled to make a wide detour to gain the main body at Dinwiddie, reaching it only after the fight which there ensued was over. But Sheridan's horsemen, dismounting, took post behind a slight breastwork of rails, where they recovered and repulsed the assault of the enemy, who at dark withdrew a little, and lay upon their arms within a hundred yards. During the evening, Sheridan was informed by a dispatch from Grant that Warren's corps were ordered to report to him, and would reach him by midnight. This dispatch was written hours before—Grant's headquarters being ten miles away—and in ignorance of what had transpired. Warren also, some time before, had begun to receive orders from Meade. At five o'clock he was told that Sheridan was pushing up the White-oak Road, and he might send down a small force to communicate with him, but must be careful not to fire into his advance. An hour and a half later, the tidings to Warren were that a portion of Pickett's force had penetrated between him and Sheridan. Warren had learned this before. An hour and a half more, and tidings came that Sheridan had been forced back to Dinwiddie by a strong force of cavalry, supported by infantry. Close upon the heels of this came an intimation from Meade that "the probability is that we shall have to contract our lines to-night." To contract the lines was equivalent to a retreat. All the indications at the moment were that this movement would be a repetition of those which had gone before. Warren urged that, instead of retreating, he might be allowed to move down to Dinwiddie, and attack the enemy on one side, while Sheridan assailed him on the other. Orders for movements were given, few of which, owing to the darkness, were capable of exact literal execution, but the general purport of all was that Warren should advance to the aid of Sheridan.[1] He obeyed the intent of his orders, and moved as rapidly as possible.

[1] The last order from Meade to Warren, written a quarter of an hour before midnight, and received an hour after, contained these sentences: "Sheridan can not maintain himself at Dinwiddie without re-enforcements, and yours are the only ones that can be sent. Time is of the utmost importance. Use every exertion to get troops to him as soon as possible. If Sheridan is not re-enforced, and is compelled to fall back, he will retire by the Vaughan Road."

But, in the mean time, the Confederates had their own difficulties to encounter. They had found it impossible to shake Sheridan away from Dinwiddie; and, knowing that re-enforcements were coming to him, they began a little after midnight to retire cautiously toward the Five Forks. Sheridan suspected that this movement was going on, and so notified Meade by verbal message; but he could not be sure, for at three o'clock he sent an order to Warren stating that he was holding on at Dinwiddie with Custer's division, where he might be attacked at daybreak. In that case, Warren, who was thought to be nearer than he was, should also attack in flank and rear. "Do not fear," added Sheridan, "my leaving here. If the enemy remain I shall fight at daylight." But just after daylight, when Ayres's division, the advance of Warren's corps, came in sight, the enemy "hastily decamped,"[1] and hurried back toward their intrenchments at the Five Forks. Merritt followed hard after with the cavalry, until he saw the enemy fairly within their works, and had even driven them from two lines of temporary works.

The whole of Warren's corps were united at seven o'clock on the morning of April 1 at a point three miles from the Forks, and somewhat to the right of the extremity of the Confederate works, which had in the mean while been much strengthened. Here they were halted for four hours by Sheridan until he could complete his arrangements for attack, for he proposed nothing less than to dispose absolutely of this body, crushing it if possible, and driving westward any who might escape, isolating them from the main army at Petersburg. There was a likelihood that Lee, comprehending the peril, might venture to send re-enforcements down the White-oak Road to the Forks. Fortunately, Sheridan had just been joined by McKenzie's fresh cavalry, a thousand strong. These were sent straight to the White-oak Road, with orders to attack any force of the enemy which they might find. The prevision was justified. McKenzie met a force coming down, and drove it back.

The day was wearing away when Sheridan had completed his preliminary dispositions. His plan was beautiful in its simplicity. Merritt was to hold the enemy in front with a part of the cavalry, while with the remainder he should demonstrate as if proposing to turn their right flank. Warren was to move the infantry up to the White-oak Road, and then, by a sharp wheel to the right, strike the enemy's left, and, doubling it up, gain their rear. This plan presupposed a great superiority of force, but that was at hand. Sheridan had of cavalry and infantry quite 20,000; the Confederates could hardly number more than 10,000 infantry, with only a few guns; and they do not appear to have brought their cavalry behind their intrenchments, where they could be of little service.

Having, as was his wont, made his plans with careful deliberation, Sheridan was eager for their prompt execution. He chafed at every thing which looked like delay. Warren, quite as earnest, strove to repress all outward manifestations of impatience, which he thought would tend to impair the confidence of his troops. "When every thing possible is being done," he argued, "it is important to have the men think it is all that success demands." So Sheridan rode off firmly impressed with the idea that Warren was not exerting himself to get his corps up as rapidly as he should have done, and that "he wished the sun to go down before the dispositions for the attack could be completed."[2]

[1] Ayres's Report.

[2] *Sheridan's Report.*—Sheridan had also been previously dissatisfied with Warren. He had, very naturally, asked that Wright's corps, which had been with him in the Valley of the Shenandoah, should be sent to him instead of that of Warren. This, owing to its position, could not be

ROMEYN B. AYRES.

But the sun was still more than two hours high when Warren advanced from the point where his corps had been formed, a thousand yards from the White-oak Road. In the operations of the three days about 2000 of his corps had been disabled, and 1000 more had fallen out from weariness, or been sent on detached duty, so that the corps went into action 12,000 strong. Ayres's division, the weakest, was on the left; next came Crawford's, with Griffin's as a support, in its rear, and a little to the right. It was supposed that upon reaching the road they would strike just upon the enemy's left; then, pivoting upon Ayres's division, the others were to wheel round, so that Crawford's would just fall upon the flank. But, on reaching the road, it was found that they were some distance from the hostile line, which was also hidden in a thick wood beyond an open space. This mistake, slight in itself, changed the whole order of the battle. The division of Ayres, forming that part of the radius nearest to the centre of the semicircle to be described in the turning movement, and thus having the shortest distance to be traversed, effected its change of front earliest, and moved across the open space toward the enemy's position. The order given to each division was to keep closed upon that to its left; and as the region where they were to move was wholly unknown, the direction to march was to be maintained by keeping the sun over their left shoulders. But now, Crawford having the larger distance to sweep, his left became disjoined from Ayres's right, which was thus thrown out into the air, in the open space over which both were advancing. At this moment, also, a sharp fire was poured from the woods upon these exposed flanks—Ayres's right and Crawford's left. The effect was that the right of Ayres became disordered, many of the men rushing back to the rear, while Crawford's left obliqued to the right, where the woods and a slight ridge gave shelter. Thus the interval between the two became still wider. The firing, however, was more noisy than destructive, owing to the dense wood through which the shot had to pass. Ayres soon rectified his line; the portions which had become unsteady "moved up and bore their part of the action in a handsome manner."[1] Pressing forward, he soon came upon the enemy's position. The Confederate line ran from west to east, but its extremity was turned at a right angle northward for a hundred yards. This crochet, fronting to the east, was that part of the line facing Ayres. It was a strong breastwork secured behind a dense undergrowth of pines. Through this undergrowth and over the breastwork Ayres's corps charged with the bayonet, and captured a thousand prisoners—more than a third of its own number.[2] Here it was halted by Sheridan, who was now on this part of the field, awaiting the result of what was transpiring elsewhere. It was soon "apparent that the enemy were giving way generally," and Ayres pushed forward rapidly, holding his men in hand, and marching steadily in line of battle.[3]

Crawford, having completed his wider circuit, moved steadily westward, urged on by both Sheridan and Warren. His way lay through bogs, tangled woods, and thickets of pines, interspersed here and there with open spaces. The Confederate skirmishers spread northward from the extremity of their intrenched line. These were steadily driven back; and so Crawford moved straight along parallel to the enemy's main line until he reached the Ford Road, running north from the Five Forks, and directly in the rear of what had been its centre. It was no longer its centre. Griffin, whose circle of movement was a little exterior to that of Crawford, moved on a little behind. Pressing westward for a mile, and finding nothing on his front except a few cavalry vedettes, he halted to reconnoitre. Heavy firing to his left and rear showed that the enemy were in that direction, and thither he directed his march. Warren had sent a messenger with orders to that effect. Moving at double-quick, he struck the rear of the enemy's left, capturing the breastworks, and securing 1500 prisoners.

The whole Confederate left almost to its centre was now driven in. Half or more of it were prisoners. The rest streamed down the White-oak Road. But Crawford had reached the Ford Road, and barred the only avenue of escape to the north. Down this pressed Crawford, with whom Warren had now taken his position. Sheridan had before directed McKenzie with his cavalry to sweep clear to the right of the infantry and gain the Ford Road. He took too wide a circuit through an unknown region, and found himself moving away from the battle; and, turning back, reached the road, not till after Crawford had won it, but in time to take part in the closing scenes of the fight and the pursuit.

Meanwhile the cavalry had borne their share in the action. Two divisions of Crook's command had been left behind at Dinwiddie to guard the trains and crossings of the streams; the other, that of Gregg, was on the left and rear, skirmishing with the Confederate cavalry. Merritt, with the divisions of Devin and Custer, charged the enemy's lines in front, the signal being the firing of Warren's infantry. They carried the lines at several points, not without enduring heavy loss. While Griffin and Ayres pressed upon the routed left flank, Crawford came down upon their rear. One brief but determined effort was made to stop him. A stiff line, supported by artillery, was formed across the road, from which Coulter's brigade suffered severely. But the effort was vain. Entrapped, assailed in front, flank, and rear, almost the whole of the force surrendered to Crawford.

Warren now rode on to the coveted Five Forks, thence westward along the White-oak Road. A mile beyond the Forks the remnant of the Confederates made one more attempt to stand. Their line was formed at a right angle, one branch facing southward toward Merritt's cavalry, the other eastward to confront Warren, whose three divisions had come up in pursuit. These were somewhat disordered by their long march and fighting through the woods. They halted, but kept up a rapid fire. Warren, with a few of his staff, dashed to the front, shouting to those at hand to follow. He was met with a single sharp fusilade; his horse was shot under him, an aid at his side was killed, and Colonel Richardson, who had sprung right between him and the enemy, fell sorely wounded. But Warren's appeal had not been in vain. All along the line officers and color-bearers sprang to the front; and the troops, advancing at a run, and without firing, captured every man in their front. Those who had been trying to make a stand against Merritt broke and fled in wild confusion by the only way open to them—that leading westward. Merritt and McKenzie dashed forward in pursuit, which was kept up for six miles, and until long after darkness had set in. The two divisions upon which Lee had counted for the salvation of his army were gone. Johnson's was utterly annihilated; of Pickett's we find, five days later, note of a remnant of a few hundred men. Whether they had been in the fight and escaped, or whether they had been kept back, is not recorded. The Union loss in the battle of the Five Forks was about 1000, of which 684 were of Warren's corps. Of the Confederate killed and wounded there is no statement. They lost in prisoners between 5000 and 6000, of whom 3244 were captured by Warren.

The blow to Lee was a crushing one. It is said that upon the receipt of the tidings of his loss, he for the only time gave utterance to any reproach in the field. The next time his troops were taken into the field he would put himself at their head; and, turning to one of his generals, he ordered him sharply to gather up and put under guard all the stragglers in the field —officers as well as men. It may be granted that the Confederates fought at Five Forks with less than their wonted vigor; but they must have felt that, after Sheridan had fairly shut them up within their lines, victory was impossible; and, moreover, could they have made their escape, now that their lines were fairly turned, it would be but to prolong for a few days a hopeless struggle.

When Warren had captured the last of the enemy opposed to him, he sent to Sheridan a report of the result, and asked for farther instructions. The reply was that his instructions had been sent. They reached him at seven o'clock. Surely no general who had just gained a victory so brilliant and decisive ever before received upon the field which he had won such a message. The order ran thus: "Major General Warren, commanding Fifth Corps, is relieved from duty, and will report at once for orders to Lieutenant General Grant, commanding armies U.S." The command of the corps was conferred upon Griffin.[1]

granted. He also believed that Warren had not joined him as promptly as he should have done; and had even received, "unsolicited," as he says, authority to remove him. But it is hardly possible that such permission would have been expressly given unless Grant, to whom Sheridan directly reported, was somehow assured that it was desired.

[1] Ayres's Report.

[2] Ayres's division marched out on the 29th not quite 4000 strong. In the interval it had lost about 1000.—*Warren's Narrative.*

[3] Ayres's Report.

[1] That the general credit of the victory of the Five Forks must be given to Sheridan is undoubted. The plans were his, and they were, as he affirms, "successfully executed." But the essential feature of these plans, without which all else would have been comparatively fruitless, was the operations of the Fifth Corps. These operations were conducted by Warren. After the movement was begun, there is record of but a single order given by Sheridan to any portion of this corps. The main allegation brought by Sheridan against Warren is that "General Warren did not exert himself to get up his corps as rapidly as he might have done, and his manner gave me the impression that he wished the sun to go down before dispositions for the attack could be completed." But the dispositions were made and the attack commenced while the sun was yet more than two hours high, and in time to win the victory before it had set. Moreover, each of Warren's division commanders—and no one more explicitly than Griffin, who succeeded him—aver that their divisions were formed without any unnecessary delay. Sheridan, indeed, makes two other specifications against Warren: (1.) "Had General Warren moved according to the expectations of the Lieutenant General, there would appear to have been but little chance for the escape of the enemy's

CHARLES GRIFFIN.

While the result of the movements of Sheridan and Warren were uncertain, active operations directly before Petersburg were suspended to await the issue upon the extreme Union left. When, at nightfall, Sheridan had utterly routed the force directly opposed to him, his position was not free from peril. His command, now numbering about 18,000 cavalry and infantry, was widely separated from the main army, and there was reason to apprehend that Lee would, during the night, abandon his lines, and, falling upon Sheridan, drive him off, and thus open the way for retreat. To guard against this, Miles's division of Humphreys's corps was sent to the support of Sheridan, while a furious bombardment was opened along the whole line, sweeping from the north of Petersburg clear around to Hatcher's Run. The Union batteries had gradually crept closer to the city, and for the first time during the siege the balls fairly crashed through the streets of Petersburg. This fierce fire was kept up until almost daybreak, when the general assault was ordered. Parke and Wright had before expressed their belief that they could carry the lines in their front.

The assault commenced just before daybreak on the morning of Sunday, April 2. Parke's Ninth Corps was in front of the strongest portion of the Confederate defenses. The general plan for this corps was that Wilcox's division should make a feint in front of Fort Steadman, while the divisions of Potter and Hartranft were to make the assault to the left, at the very points which it had been hoped would have been opened by the explosion of the mine eight months before. Each column was accompanied by pioneers with axes, and details of artillerists to work any guns that might be captured. Wilcox's feint was successful. His division carried the whole outer line in its front, causing the Confederates to concentrate a heavy force to stay their farther advance. Then, at half past four, the signal was given for the opening of the main assault. The troops, eager to avenge their former repulse, sprang forward with a rush, and in the teeth of a deadly storm of grape, canister, and musketry, plunged through the ditch, tore away the abatis, mounted the parapet, and carried the line of works. Here Hartranft's division captured 12 guns and 800 prisoners. Potter's division, next on the left, attacked with equal vigor, and, in spite of the most gallant opposition, pressed the enemy clear back to his interior cordon of works. This inner line had within the last few months been most elaborately fortified. From it the position gained by Parke was swept on the right and the left by an enfilading fire of artillery. Potter made a determined but unsuccessful effort to force this inner cordon. He fell severely wounded, and the command of his division fell upon Griffin.[1] But the assault in other quarters had met with such success that there was no need for the Ninth Corps to essay to carry the lines opposed to them. Parke was directed not to advance unless he saw the way clear to success, but to strengthen his position so as to hold it against any assailing force.

The Sixth Corps, under Wright, was next on the left to that of the Ninth. As it lay, it occupied a salient where the Union lines, after trending away from the Confederate works, again closely approached them. Here, during the darkness, this corps had been formed into a mighty wedge, which was, in the result, to be driven straight through the Confederate lines which had for so long bidden defiance to all assault. At half past four a single gun gave signal for the advance of the Sixth. It happened that the very point where the edge of the wedge was to strike had been left weakly held by the withdrawal of the force which had held it to defend a point which seemed of more pressing importance. The Confederate pickets and skirmishers were swept away in a moment, the three lines of abatis overpassed, the works crowned, the long lines which had guarded Petersburg and its railway communications pierced. The Confederate army, a quarter of which had twelve hours before been annihilated by Sheridan and Warren, was again cut in two, a quarter of what remained being to all appearance wholly severed from the main body. Wright swept leftward for a space down the line of the Confederate intrenchments, repeating Warren's movement at Five Forks, and capturing some thousands of prisoners; and then, being joined by portions of Ord's command and Humphreys's corps, who had carried every thing in their own fronts, turned to the right, and moved straight toward Petersburg, leaving that portion of the Confederate force which had been severed from the main army to be disposed of by Sheridan, whose command had in the mean while been augmented by Miles's division of Humphreys's corps.

Miles was ordered by Sheridan to move up the White-oak Road and attack the extreme right of the enemy. This, in the mean time, had been cut off from Petersburg by Wright and by Humphreys, who, with the divisions of Hays and Mott, carried a redoubt in their front, and then swept round and took up their position upon the left of Wright. The Confederates here made no opposition, and their isolated right fled northward, crossing Hatcher's Run, and took up a position at Southerland's Station, on the Southside Railroad. Miles was anxious to attack, and Sheridan gave him permission to do so; but at this moment Meade directed that Miles should be returned to the command of Humphreys, and the attack, to Sheridan's regret, was not made. Sheridan, who had been moving in the same direction with the Fifth Corps, now retraced his steps, and moved back to the Five Forks. Thence they struck the railroad, and, after destroying it for

infantry in front of Dinwiddie Court-house" on the morning of the 1st of April. Whether or not Warren could, either with or without the expectation of Grant, have made movements which would have had this result, it is certain that Sheridan, on the evening of that day, could have had no adequate means of knowing. (2.) "During this attack I again became dissatisfied with General Warren. In this engagement, portions of his line gave way when not exposed to a heavy fire, and simply from want of confidence on the part of the troops, which General Warren did not exert himself to inspire. I therefore relieved him from the command of the Fifth Corps, authority for this action having been sent to me before the battle unsolicited."—Leaving out of view Sheridan's emphatic testimony to the gallantry of the troops in this engagement, there is no mention of any part of Warren's line giving way under any fire, light or heavy, saving the very brief one of a part of Ayres's division, and this was soon rectified; and these very men, in a few minutes, "bore a part in a handsome manner in the first brilliant charge which took place." In any case, Warren could not personally inspire them with confidence, for he was in a different part of the field; and he, as commander of the corps, had a right to judge on what portion of the field his presence was most required, subject, of course, to the ultimate decision of his superiors, upon due consideration, as to the military soundness of his judgment. In any case, Sheridan, being on a still different part of the field, could have had no personal knowledge on this point; and, in the interval of less than two hours between any possible giving way and the order of supersedure, could not have had opportunity to ascertain the facts in the case with sufficient certainty to warrant such a summary procedure. The misconduct, if any had existed, could no longer produce any evil effect, for the victory had been fully won when the supersedure took place. The order was certainly over-hasty, and we think no one who examines the question will hesitate to say unjust. There is, indeed, no reason to suppose that Sheridan was moved by any unworthy personal feeling, for the two generals had never happened to serve together. Sheridan was likely somewhat annoyed that Warren's corps, instead of Wright's, was sent to him; for on the day before, in writing his plans to Grant, he said: "I believe I could, with the Sixth Corps, turn the enemy's left or break through his lines, but I would not like the Fifth Corps to make such an attempt." But the Fifth Corps, under his own dispositions, did make the attempt, and with a success which did not fall short of his most sanguine anticipations of what the Sixth would have accomplished. Warren, on reporting to Grant, was at once assigned to the command of the defenses at City Point and Bermuda Hundred. Just a month after his supersedure from the command of the Fifth Corps he was assigned to the command of the Department of the Mississippi, the only one in which there was then any prospect of farther hostilities.

[1] General S. G. Griffin, who commanded the division during the few remaining days of the campaign with such ability that he received therefor the brevet rank of major general. He is to be distinguished from General Charles Griffin, who was now in command of the Fifth Corps.

NELSON A. MILES.

a space, moved up it toward Southerland's Station, upon the flank of the Confederates who still held position there. His cavalry meanwhile had been sent westward to break up the Confederate cavalry, who had gathered in some force, but not sufficient to offer any resistance. These operations consumed the whole day. Toward evening Miles attacked the enemy at Southerland's, and, after a brief conflict, routed them, capturing 600 prisoners, and driving them in confusion to the Appomattox. It was supposed that the river was impassable, and that this body, shut in by Sheridan on the one side and Humphreys on the left, must surrender. But there happened to be a ford, over which they escaped, leaving their guns behind, and next day joined Lee in his retreat.

Two or three hundred yards behind the lines which Wright had carried a series of strong forts had been erected to guard against just such results as had ensued. In the movement which had followed, Gibbon's division of Ord's command came right upon the two strongest of these, Forts Alexander and Gregg, which were all that stood in the way of the Federal forces marching straight upon Petersburg by the rear. Gibbon dashed upon these. Fort Alexander was carried with a rush. Within Fort Gregg had been gathered a mixed garrison from the very extremities of the Confederacy. There were Virginians and Louisianians, North Carolinians and Mississippians. Its commander was Captain Chew, of Maryland. Gibbon marched straight for this fort, but was met by a fire so fierce and deadly that the troops recoiled for a moment. Then the charge was renewed; the assailants, unchecked by the fusilade which met them, swarmed up the parapet. Once, twice, and thrice they were pressed back; but at length the crest was gained, and a brief hand-to-hand conflict ensued. The fort was carried. Of its two hundred and fifty defenders, only thirty survived; of the assailants, five hundred lay dead or wounded.

It was now barely seven o'clock, hardly three hours from the time when the grand assault had been commenced; but within that time the whole outer line of defenses had been carried, and what remained of the Confederate army was shut up within the interior lines. Lee, with Hill and Mahone, was within the city, listening to the noise of battle which sounded from every side, and endeavoring from it to judge how the fight was going, and to decide upon what remained to be done. The reports grew momently nearer and nearer. "How is this, general?" exclaimed Lee to Hill; "your men are giving way!" Hill, buttoning around him a rough citizen's coat, upon the shoulders of which were only the stars of a colonel, and accompanied by a single orderly, rode out to reconnoitre. In a wooded ravine he came upon half a dozen soldiers in the blue Federal uniform. They had penetrated in advance of their comrades. He ordered them to surrender. For an instant they were confounded by the very audacity of the demand. The next instant their answer was given from their rifles, and Hill fell dead from his horse. Of all the great generals in the Confederate army, no other one had borne part in so many of the great battles in Virginia, Maryland, and Pennsylvania, from Bull Run onward. No one division of the Army of Northern Virginia had been engaged in so many fights as his. After the seven days on the Peninsula, it had formed part of Jackson's command while that daring general lived. It bore the brunt of the fight at Groveton, saved the lost day at Antietam, won the action at Chancellorsville, was foremost in the Wilderness, and to it, during this last campaign, was confided the most important task, that of holding the Confederate lines on the right, the vital point in Lee's system of defense.

Sheridan's victory at the Five Forks and Wright's piercing of the Confederate lines had in a few hours solved the long-questioned problem of the siege of Petersburg. The place was no longer tenable, for its avenues of supply were lost beyond all hope of recovery. Lee resolved upon a speedy abandonment of the lines which he had held so long. The bells were ringing for church on that Sunday morning when a dispatch was sent to President Davis, at Richmond, giving notice of what had happened, and informing him that the two besieged cities would be abandoned by the army, and advising that the authorities should make preparations to leave the capital that night.

Lee, indeed, was shut up to the alternative to surrender or to make his escape, and try the almost desperate chance of a race for life or death with a victorious army of thrice his force close upon his rear and flank. He chose the latter course, and in the execution of it manifested energy and skill not exceeded in any other portion of his career. After all the losses of the two days, he had still an army of more than 40,000 men; but they were widely scattered. Some 5000, cut off from the rest, were at Southerland's, fifteen miles west of Petersburg; as many more were in Richmond, a score of miles to the north; Longstreet, with half the remainder, was on the James; leaving 15,000 at and around Petersburg, confronting the corps of Parke, Wright, and Humphreys, with half that of Ord—in all not less than 50,000 men ready for action; while upon the flank of his line of retreat was Sheridan with well-nigh 20,000 cavalry and infantry.[1] The obstinate defense of Fort Gregg gave Lee a breathing space, and enabled him to assume a strong defensive position which could be held for a brief space. It must be held for twelve hours at all hazards; for the retreat could not be begun until darkness had come on, veiling the movement from the eyes that were keenly watching every sign of the abandonment, which all saw was speedily inevitable.

[1] The data upon which I estimate the present force of Lee will be stated hereafter. In giving that of Grant, I only include the numbers actually available for immediate pursuit from before Petersburg. Besides these 70,000, there was a considerable force at City Point, and half of the Army of the James, left under Weitzel on the north side of the James. The actual number in each corps available for instant action in the field at the commencement of operations on the 29th was about 15,000, or 90,000 in all. To these are to be added 10,000 cavalry. The losses in the interval had been not far from 10,000 in killed, wounded, and prisoners.

WORKS CAPTURED BY THE SIXTH CORPS.

THE EVACUATION OF PETERSBURG.

Lee was still ignorant that the force north of the James had been reduced to three divisions But immediately after the tidings of the disaster at Five Forks he had ordered Longstreet to send re-enforcements from the James to the Appomattox. That veteran commander, with a few brigades, arrived just in time to stay the Federal advance, and enable Lee to form his new line. This, in a narrow semicircle, girdled Petersburg, each flank resting upon the Appomattox. A show of offense was the best defensive, and at intervals, from ten o'clock until dark, blows were struck at various parts of the Federal line closely encircling his own. These attempts were mainly directed upon that part of the line held by the Ninth Corps. In one of these assaults Fort Mahone fell again into the hands of the Confederates.[1] So threatening were these assaults, that two brigades were ordered up from City Point and one from the Sixth Corps to re-enforce the Ninth. Fort Mahone was soon recaptured, and Parke wished to renew the assault which had been closed in the morning; but, finding that his men were greatly exhausted, he decided merely to make his position perfectly secure, and await the operations of the next day, but in the mean while to be in a position to take advantage of any movement which the enemy might make showing an intention of evacuating his position.

The night had almost passed before any such indications were perceived. At two o'clock in the morning the Confederate pickets were still out; but the evacuation had been commenced in the darkness hours before. By three o'clock the troops were all across the river, and the only bridge in flames, while the air was luminous with the glare of the burning warehouses. At this moment the heavily-charged magazine of the battery of siege-guns before Bermuda Hundred was blown up; then followed the explosion of that of Fort Clifton on the James. The explosion was taken up all along the line to Richmond, giving some tokens that the evacuation was accomplished, and the Confederate army in full retreat. The skirmishers of the Ninth were at once pushed forward, but found no trace of an enemy. The entire corps went forward, Ely's brigade leading. They were met by the mayor and a deputation from the Common Council, who announced that the city, having been evacuated, was formally surrendered, and asked for the protection of the persons and property of the inhabitants. At half past four the flag of the First Michigan Regiment was raised upon the Court-house of Petersburg.

The dispatch of Lee, announcing his purpose to evacuate the cities, was received by Davis while in church. Three years before, lacking a month, he had been baptized and confirmed on the same day, and had since been a devout worshiper. As nearly as such hurried moments can be noted, the message reached the church just when the Litany, with its solemn responses, "Good Lord, deliver us!" was being uttered. The Confederate President rose from his knees and left the house with his wonted stately step. But men remembered, or thought they remembered, that he seemed to have grown older by years since he had entered the sacred edifice an hour before. Evil tidings find speedy messengers. Though no announcement was made, within an hour every inhabitant knew that the Confederate capital was to be abandoned. In the leading Presbyterian Church, the minister, at the close of his sermon, announced to the congregation that there was sad news; the army had met with great reverses, and it was not likely that the congregation would ever again assemble in that house of God.

Never since when the Babylonians learned that Cyrus had penetrated their walls, or when the dwellers in New Carthage assembled in the theatre were told that the Vandals of Genseric were upon them, was there a greater surprise than at Richmond when on that bright April Sabbath it was made known that within a few hours the city was to fall into the hands of the beleaguering force. They could see no signs of siege. They knew, indeed, that for months a great hostile force was encamped not far away, but between them and it was their own invincible army under its indomitable commander, who had three years before driven off a like threatening force, and had held this at bay so that not a sound of battle had reached their ears, and who had vowed that he would die before he would abandon their defense. Richmond had been notably gay all through the winter and spring, so much so that the clergy had been constrained to institute special religious services to counteract the prevailing current of dissipation. The newspapers were allowed to give only brief scraps of tidings furnished by the War Department, and these amounted simply to nothing. But in the absence of all true accounts there was a superabundance of rumors and reports. One day it was said that a messenger was making his way overland with a treaty duly signed, whereby the French emperor, and, by consequence, the British queen, had formed an alliance with the Confederacy against the Union. Again it was reported that Johnston had crushed Sherman, and was in full march to unite with Lee, and that by the combined force the army of Grant would be swept away, as that of McClellan had been swept away not three years before. Of the great battles which had been fought not a score of miles away, not a word was told; but on the very day before they commenced, the morning train from Petersburg brought reports that Lee had made a night attack, in which he had crushed the enemy along his whole line. That day John Daniel, the editor of the leading Richmond paper, and the wielder of the most trenchant pen in the Confederacy, had died. Next morning his obituary appeared in the papers, closing with a regret that "the great Virginian" had passed away just as the decisive victory had been won which was likely to prove the turning-point to the success of the Southern Confederacy. So, of all the days in the year, this bright April Sabbath seemed the last which was to be the day of doom to the Confederacy.

[1] Fort Mahone was at a point where the two lines had approached most closely. Opposite to it was Fort Sedgwick. So fierce and continuous had been the fire from these forts that the latter was known in the army as "Fort Hell," and the former as "Fort Damnation."

THE OCCUPATION OF PETERSBURG.

St. Paul's. 2d Baptist Church. Presbyterian Church. City Hall. 1st Baptist Church. Capitol. Governor's House. Custom-house.

RICHMOND, FROM GAMBLE'S HILL.

When, therefore, the authentic tidings came that before another sun should rise the Confederate capital was to be abandoned, they were like a thunder-clap from a cloudless sky. All was confusion and dismay. Those who rushed to the government offices could learn nothing; but the hasty packing of archives, and the long lines of wagons conveying them to the railroad dépôts, told the story. A special train during the afternoon bore the President and a part of his cabinet toward Danville. This was now the only avenue for those who hoped to escape from the apprehended horrors of a sacked city. They could not forget how the Confederates had wantonly burned Cumberland; they knew what had befallen Columbia. So the great throng of those who had means of paying their fare pressed to the dépôt of the Danville Road. They found the doors guarded by lines of soldiers, with orders to allow no one to enter without a special pass from the Secretary of War. To find that functionary was hopeless. Now and then one who knew the premises, or had special means of influence, succeeded in getting within, only to find the waiting trains loaded to twice their regulated capacity with the employés and effects of the government.

In the streets the disorder grew fiercer and fiercer till it rose to tumult and riot. As night closed in all the rascality of the city seemed let loose, and surged around every spot where there was a chance of pillage. There were numerous stores and warehouses filled with goods which, having run the blockade, were rated at prices which, reckoned in Confederate currency, were worth a prince's ransom. These were broken open, and their contents borne away with scarcely a pretense of opposition. The poorest scoundrel in the city was for the moment a richer man than he had ever hoped to become. For a few hours there had been a lingering hope that Lee would be able to escape the necessity of withdrawing his army. But when at last the mayor announced that this hope was vain, and that the evacuation was a foregone conclusion, the city council proposed to get together some regiments of militia to preserve order, and to establish a regular patrol for the night. Above all, every drop of liquor in the shops and warehouses was to be destroyed. This was partially executed, and the gutters ran with a liquor freshet whose reeking fumes filled the air. But the destruction could be only partial. Not a few who were to carry out the order chose to drink rather than destroy the liquor. The militia slipped through the hands of their officers; the patrols disappeared; soldiers, half famished during the long months in the intrenchments, straggled from their commands, maddened by the thirst for liquor, which they now found it easy to satiate. The city was given up to pillage; stores were entered and stripped; the sidewalks were strewn with a mingled rubbish of costly goods, provisions, and broken glass. The early night was made hideous by the shouts of the mob, the yells of drunken men, and wild cries of distress from women and children.

But the horrors of that night had only begun. The great body of troops from the fortifications had been passing through the city, and had crossed the river. Their presence had some effect in checking the outrages. To Ewell's corps, the rear-guard, had been committed the task of destroying the bridges across the James, and blowing up the iron-clad vessels which lay in the stream, and, in general, of making way with every thing which could be of use to the enemy. In the very heart of the town were four warehouses filled from top to bottom with tobacco; close by were the great Gallego Flour-mills, the largest in the world, with all the combustible materials which gather around such establishments. To these Ewell ordered the torch to be applied. A fire breaking out here at any time would be disastrous; now, when all means of checking it were paralyzed, a general conflagration was inevitable. The mayor and a committee of citizens remonstrated against the execution of this order. The warehouses were fired, the flames spread from building to building, and from street to street, over whole acres of ground whereon was the whole business part of Richmond. Within its area were all the banks, insurance offices, auction stores, newspaper offices, and nearly all the mercantile houses. Here, too, were arsenals stored with shells and munitions of war: the successive explosion of these sounded like a continuous peal of thunder. While this great conflagration was raging, without even an effort to check it, the tumult, and riot, and ravaging, and pillaging grew madder and madder all through that long night.

When the sun rose in the morning it looked upon a strange and sorrowful scene. The streets were crowded with a motley throng—drays loaded with goods, men toilsomely rolling barrels, women and children of all colors staggering under heavy loads, their own goods or that which they had plundered. The Capitol Square, seeming to be safest from the conflagration, was covered over with piles of furniture dragged from the burning houses, among which were huddled together women and children, whose only homes were now beneath the open sky; even here the air was dim with smoke, and blinding with a snow of fiery cinders. The sun was an hour high when from the rear of the motley crowd pressing up Main Street arose the ominous cry of "The Yankees! The Yankees!"

During the three days while fighting had been going on around Petersburg there had been perfect quiet on the James. Confederates and Federals seemed aware that nothing which could be done there would influence the issue. When that Sabbath night closed in, each was aware that the result was decided. All the bands in Weitzel's lines struck up the national airs. They were answered with corresponding music from the Confederate lines. Until midnight the air was vocal with the strains of "Hail Columbia" and "Dixie," the "Star-spangled Banner" and the "Bonnie Blue Flag." Then came a brief interval of absolute repose, during which the Confederate troops were silently withdrawn, and, as morning was breaking, the glare of the flames, and the dense masses of smoke which rose over Richmond, proclaimed to Weitzel that the Confederate capital, the prize of such long endeavor,

RUINS OF RICHMOND—MAIN STREET.

was probably at his mercy. Slowly and cautiously at first he put his troops in motion. They threaded the intricate lines of works before which they had so long lain, and for the first time learned how formidable they were. Every thing showed how hasty had been the abandonment. Around Fort Field, the first approached, were three lines of abatis and one of torpedoes. The flags which marked the place of the torpedoes had not been taken down. The torpedoes were carefully removed by the advance-guard. A second and third line, each commanding that exterior to it, was passed. The camps were entered, the tents still standing, and all the furniture within. Then, when, for the first time, Richmond was fairly in view by a Federal army, Weitzel sent forward a squad of cavalry, twoscore strong, to enter the city. It was this little body whose coming aroused the cry of "The Yankees!" They proceeded at a leisurely walk up the main street and down the by-streets. The crowd fled cursing and trampling up the main street and down the by-streets. The troopers then broke into a trot for the public square, and in a few minutes their guidons were fluttering from the Capitol. Soon afterward a regular flag was raised. This was the same which had been hoisted over the headquarters of Butler at New Orleans. It had been brought there by Shepley, who hoped to raise it over the Capitol at Richmond. It had been given in charge of Johnston de Peyster, a young aid of Shepley, who had asked permission to hoist it himself when the Confederate capital should be captured. By some misapprehension, the flag was raised over the "State" end of the Capitol instead of over the "Confederate States" end. Those who believed in omens saw in this an augury that Federal authority had now triumphed over the cherished theory of "States Rights."

Soon they were followed by all the troops, marching in order, but with cheers and martial music. It was noted with bitter indignation that a regiment of colored cavalry, as if moved by an irrepressible impulse as they swept by the principal hotel, drew their sabres and broke into wild shouts. Mayo, the mayor, had gone out to surrender the city, but missed his way. Three years before he had declared that "when the citizens of Richmond demand of me to surrender the capital of Virginia and the Confederacy, they must find some other man to fill my place." But the scenes of the past night, and the flames which were still surging and spreading, were enough to convince him that there was something worse even than surrender to the Yankees. The city had been fired against his earnest remonstrance, and now the conquering army alone could put a stop to the conflagration, and prevent a general pillage which was going on.

General Shepley, the same who had been appointed military governor of New Orleans, was placed in command of Richmond. He issued orders at once. The first duty of the army was to save the city, which the Confederate army, unable to hold, had sought to destroy. The fire department of the city would report to the provost-marshal, who would aid them with a detachment of troops; all attempts at plunder, whether by soldiers or citizens, would be summarily punished; no officer or soldier should enter any private dwelling without express orders; no soldier should use offensive words or gestures toward citizens; no treasonable expressions, or insults to the national flag or cause, would be allowed; the rights and duties of the citizens were laid down in the proclamations of the President; and, finally, "with the restoration of the flag of the Union, the citizens might expect the restoration of that peace, prosperity, and happiness which they enjoyed under the Union of which that flag was the glorious symbol."

All attempts to check the conflagration seemed unavailing; but toward evening the wind changed, blowing the flames back in the direction from which they had spread, and the fire died out for lack of fuel. A third part of Richmond had been burnt. The pencil of the surveyor could not have more distinctly marked out the business portion of the city. For a night and a day the Confederate capital had undergone all the horrors of a sacked town; but they had been inflicted by its own populace, not by the victors. The bitterest enemies of the conquerors find hardly an instance of the slightest outrage committed by the Federal troops.[1] Men have wrongly, we think, in the main, charged the burning of Columbia upon the Federal troops; but no one has ventured to charge upon them the far more destructive conflagration of Richmond. The responsibility for this wanton act, palliated by no possible pretext of military necessity, rests solely upon Ewell, who had for well-nigh a year commanded the garrison of the city. Deliberately, and against all remonstrance, he applied the torch where there was no human possibility that the result could have been other than what it was.

Jefferson Davis had in the mean while reached Danville, where, on the next day, he issued a characteristic proclamation. The general-in-chief, he said, had found it necessary to make such movements of his troops as to uncover the capital. The loss of the capital was certainly a great misfortune; for months the finest army of the Confederacy had been obliged, in order to defend Richmond, to forego many promising enterprises. But now a new phase of the struggle had begun. The army, free from the necessity of guarding particular points, was free to move, and could strike the enemy in detail far from his base. Virginia, and no part of it, should be permanently abandoned. If compelled temporarily to withdraw, the army would return until the baffled and exhausted enemy should give over the contest; and no peace should ever be made with the infamous invaders. The people of Richmond only knew of this proclamation when they read it in the Northern newspapers. Before that time arrived the Confederate army had surrendered. Davis, indeed, returned to Virginia, but it was as a prisoner of state, captured in the vain attempt to escape to a foreign soil.

[1] The best account of the incidents at the capture of Richmond is that given by the Rev. Dr. Leyburn, in *Harper's Magazine* for June, 1866. From this we cite a few sentences: "The curtain had now fallen on one act of the stupendous drama. It was soon to rise on what, in its opening at least, would prove even more striking and impressive. The government and army which for years had protected us was gone; that other army, which had come so near that they could hear the sound of our church-bells, and we could see the flash and smoke of their guns—that army, probably by this time exasperated and infuriated to the last degree, was to be upon us with the dawn of the coming day, and we helplessly at their mercy. . . . . Imagine our condition, left by our own army and anticipating the enemy's; the entire business part of the city on fire—stores, warehouses, mills, depôts, and bridges, all covering acres, one sea of flame; and as an accompaniment, the thunder of exploding shells, and in the midst of it that long-threatening, hostile army entering to seize its prey. . . . . Up to this time I do not remember to have seen a fire-engine at work. I went to one of the Federals and told him that, unless they went to work to arrest the conflagration, the entire city would be swept away. Soon after, the military authorities organized the crowds of blacks as a fire corps, and this, with their own efforts and the steam-engines at length brought to play, was instrumental in checking, and at length stopping the tempest of fire. But all the forenoon, and till well on in the afternoon, flame and smoke, and burning brands, and showers of blazing sparks filled the air. Seldom has a city in proportion to its population and wealth suffered so terribly. Very agreeable was the disappointment at the behavior of the victorious army. The fact was that, with few exceptions, the troops behaved astonishingly well, and were remarkably courteous and respectful. Some cases of outrage were committed in the suburbs, but every attempt of the sort in the city of which I heard was followed by condign punishment."

McLEAN'S HOUSE.

CHAPTER LVII.

THE RETREAT AND SURRENDER OF LEE.

The Line of Retreat.—Number of Lee's Army.—The Pursuit.—Lee reaches Amelia Court-house.—Finds no Supplies.—Sheridan reaches Jettersville.—Position of Lee.—He resumes his Retreat.—Sheridan's Plan of Assault.—Engagement at Sailor's Creek.—Capture of Ewell's Corps.—Straggling from the Confederate Army.—Ord's Column reaches Farmville.—Reade attacks and is repulsed.—The Confederates recross the Appomattox, make a stand, and repulse Humphreys.—They continue their Retreat.—Sheridan's Movements.—A Scout reports Supplies at Appomattox Station.—Custer sent forward.—He captures the Trains and heads off Lee's Retreat.—Ord and Griffin urged forward.—The Confederate Retreat on the 8th of April.—Reach Appomattox Station.—Are assailed by Custer and driven back.—Situation on the 9th.—Gordon attempts to break through.—He fails.—Asks a Suspension of Hostilities.—Lee and Grant.—Their Correspondence.—Conference of Confederate Generals.—Lee seeks Grant.—Their Meeting.—Terms of Surrender.—The Correspondence between Grant and Lee.—The Paroles.—Lee's Farewell Address to his Army.—His Return to Richmond.—The formal Surrender.

WHEN Lee abandoned Richmond and Petersburg, his purpose was to retreat to Danville, where he hoped to unite with Johnston. The first necessity was to concentrate his widely-spread forces. The point of junction fixed upon was Chesterfield Court-house, midway between Petersburg and Richmond, but to the west of both cities. The forces at Petersburg thus at first headed northwestward, those at Richmond southwestward. Leaving the burning warehouses of Petersburg and the fast-spreading conflagration of Richmond behind them, the troops plunged into the thick darkness of a moonless night. When all were brought together there were about 40,000 men.[1] The men, unencumbered by rations, moved rapidly, and at dawn had put nearly a score of miles between them and Petersburg. All the next day they pressed on with no signs of an enemy on their track. To Lee it seemed that the great peril was overpast. His troubled brow lightened. He had accomplished the almost hopeless task of getting his army safely on its way, and had gained a start of many miles. One more day unmolested, and he would have passed the junction of the Southside and Danville Railroads, and then, by destroying roads and bridges behind him, he could easily keep ahead of any possible pursuit. But he had now to deal with a different opponent from the one who had suffered him after Antietam to slip quietly across the Potomac, or that other who failed to follow up the retreat from Gettysburg.

Early on Monday morning Grant put his pursuing columns in motion, not following the line of Lee's retreat, but moving so as to intercept him before he should reach the junction of the Southside and Danville roads. This is at Burkesville, fifty-two miles almost due west from Petersburg. If the Confederates passed that point, they were safely on their way to Danville, and could laugh at present pursuit. If the Federals reached that place, or any other on the railroad nearer Richmond ahead of the Confederates, Lee's purpose of joining Johnston would be frustrated.

The Appomattox River, rising in the county of the same name, runs eastward for fifty miles toward Richmond. At a distance of thirty miles from the capital it bends sharply southward for twenty miles, and then, resuming its eastward course, reaches Petersburg. The Danville Railroad, along which lay Lee's proposed line of retreat, runs southwestward, crossing the Appomattox just at its southward bend. For a rapid day's march Lee's line of retreat lay on the north side of the river, which he had then to cross in order to head toward Danville. Grant's pursuing, or rather intercepting columns, moved upon the south side of the river, which ran between, and thus it happened that for the first two days the two armies, though heading for the same point, never came in sight of each other. The Union army moved in two parallel lines. Ord, with his two half corps of the Army of the James, marched along the Southside Railroad straight for the junction at Burkesville. The other and larger column, to the north, kept close to the Appomattox. This column consisted of the cavalry and the Fifth Corps under Sheridan, followed closely by the corps of Wright and Humphreys. In the rear of this was the Ninth Corps, which was left behind to occupy Petersburg, form the rear-guard of the whole army, and cover the communications with City Point.

As the morning of Monday, April 3, broke, it was doubtful whether pursuers or pursued would first reach the Danville Road. The chances were rather in favor of Lee, for he had about the same distance, with the advantage of better roads, and was at the outset unencumbered with provision trains. So all day he marched cheerily on. Making a brief halt during the night, he crossed the Appomattox at Goode's Bridge, and early on the morning of the 4th reached Amelia Court-house, on the Danville Road. Here, according to his carefully-planned arrangements, he was to have found supplies for his troops, who had started out with only food for a single day. He had ordered that trains from the South, loaded with a quarter of a million of rations, should await him here. The trains arrived duly on the evening of Sunday. They were met by orders from Richmond to press on to the capital in order to carry off the persons and archives belonging to the government. In the hurry and confusion of the moment, no order was given for the unloading of the trains, and so, with all their stores of food, they moved on to Richmond, and when Lee reached the Court-house he found not a morsel of food for his famishing troops. Thus, at a moment when every hour was precious, Lee had no alternative but to halt, break up his force into foraging squads, and sweep the region round for such scanty supplies of food as might be picked up. This enforced delay proved fatal.

Sheridan, on the other side of the Appomattox, had kept up a neck-and-neck race with Lee. His cavalry, striking that of the enemy at Deep Creek, routed them, capturing many prisoners, and leaving Griffin, who was close behind, to pick up whatever spoils were left behind. Lee's enforced delay at Amelia Court-house enabled Sheridan's cavalry to push ahead of him, and strike the Danville Road. Up this they moved, and late in the afternoon the Fifth Corps also gained the railroad at Jettersville, seven miles south of the Court-house. Here they intrenched themselves, resolved to contest the passage until the main body could come up. Had Lee been able to move his army that afternoon, he might possibly have broken through,[1] and kept up his retreat. Such, indeed, was apparently Lee's design; for he sent on a dispatch, here intercepted, to the commissaries at Danville and Lynchburg, directing 200,000 rations to meet him at Burkesville. But the Confederate troops were in no condition to fight, much less to make a rapid march that day. They had been pushed to the utmost limits of human en-

[1] I am aware that this number is far in excess of that usually assigned. Thus Pollard (*Lost Cause*, 703) says: "With the additions made to the Petersburg section of troops from the Richmond lines and from Lee's extreme right which had crossed the Appomattox above Petersburg" [that is, those who, having been cut off by Wright, retreated before Miles], that resourceful commander had now well in hand more than 20,000 troops." There is some ambiguity in this statement, as it is not clearly said whether in this number are to be included those from the north of the James and from Richmond, 15,000 at least. Elsewhere (*Southern History of the War*, ii., 507) he says, "Lee had on the lines he had abandoned between 27,000 and 28,000." This would seem not to include that portion cut off by Wright. Swinton (*Army of the Potomac*, 605) puts the entire number at 25,000; and (*Twelve Decisive Battles*, 499) says "the army was reduced to almost 20,000 effective men." But the official returns show that Lee finally surrendered 27,805 men (*Report of the Secretary of War*, 1865, p. 45); and Pollard (*Lost Cause*, 711) says, "About 7500 men laid down their arms; but the capitulation included in addition some 18,000 stragglers, who were unarmed, and who came up to claim the benefit of surrender and accept paroles."—Besides those there were, as will be seen, not far from 10,000 prisoners captured during the retreat; and there were, moreover, considerable losses in killed and wounded. Perfect accuracy where official reports are wanting is impossible; but I think, in placing Lee's entire force when the retreat was begun at 40,000, I am rather below than above the true number.

[1] "It seems to me that this was the only chance the army of Northern Virginia had of saving itself, which might have been done had General Lee promptly attacked and driven back the comparatively small force opposed to him, and pursued his march to Burkesville Junction."—*Sheridan's Report*.

durance. Half of them were broken up into foraging parties, and all were in a state of starvation. Moreover, their long trains of ammunition, stretching for thirty miles, must at all hazards be protected, for these, if lost, could not be replaced. So Lee, sending forward a portion of his trains under a cavalry escort, was compelled to lie at Amelia Court-house all that day and until the afternoon of the next. Humphreys's corps now came up, Meade accompanying it, but, being unwell, he placed it under the charge of Sheridan. Sheridan pushed out Davies with a brigade of cavalry to strike the moving trains. Davies routed the escort, destroyed 180 wagons, and captured five guns, with many prisoners. Meade now requested that the Fifth Corps should be returned to his immediate command. Sheridan complied with reluctance. He had learned the worth of that corps, with which not a week before he had been loth to undertake an offensive operation.

Wright's corps now came up, and three fourths of the army of the Potomac were concentrated at Jettersville. On the morning of the 6th it was put in motion toward Amelia Court-house; but Lee, anticipating such a movement, had the evening before moved off. Bending a little to the north, he turned the head of the advancing force, and Sheridan, upon nearing Amelia, found that Lee had given him the slip, and had gained a full half day's march to the westward.

The faces of the pursuing force were now turned from the north to the west. To secure greater rapidity, it was divided into three columns, Humphreys in the rear of the retreating enemy, Griffin on the south, and Wright on the north of it. Lee's retreat was now painfully slow. Worn out, half famished, and encumbered by the wagons, which the half-starved animals could hardly drag over the rough roads, they could barely move half a mile an hour. The advantage of the start was soon lost. Sheridan, whose command was now reduced to the cavalry, soon came upon the left flank of the long column. The trains were the tempting objects of attack, and against these Sheridan directed his fiery energy. Crook, who was in the advance, was to attack; if he found the enemy too strong, he was to hold them in check, while another division passing was to strike farther on, and so on alternating until a weak point was at last found. Crook found the enemy too strong to be driven; he held his own, while Custer passed him and found a weak point at Sailor's Creek, a small tributary of the Appomattox. Crook and Devin coming up, the whole force charged the train, dispersed the guards, capturing hundreds of prisoners and sixteen guns, destroying four hundred wagons, and cutting off a large body of the enemy from their line of retreat.

The troops thus cut off were Ewell's corps and the remnants of Pickett's division who had escaped from the disaster of Five Forks—in all, some six or eight thousand strong. This force thus isolated was a prize so tempting that Sheridan, not for the first time, deviated from the principle that he had laid down that cavalry should not be employed to attack infantry in position, and gave Merritt permission to make a mounted charge against their lines. The charge was gallantly made by Stagg's brigade, which dashed up to, but were unable to break the hostile lines. But the charge accomplished its main purpose. It detained the enemy for a space. Sheridan, who had waited behind, sent back a message urging Wright's corps to come up with the utmost speed. He was still unaware of Custer's complete success in cutting the Confederate line two miles beyond. But information came to him in an unexpected way. A single horseman dashed up. He was one of Custer's men, who had rode right into the enemy's works, had been a prisoner for a brief space, and then, getting clear of his captors, had fairly passed through the hostile troops and brought tidings of what had been accomplished, and that Custer and Crook were pressing hard upon the opposite side. Sheridan, in the hurry of the moment, forgot the name of the trooper, but he must have kept the exploit in mind, for in a note added long after to his report he mentions that he had ascertained that it was private William Richardson, of the Ohio Veteran Cavalry. The head of Wright's division now came up, and Ewell and Pickett faced about and met them with such a hot fire that Seymour's division was checked until Wheaton's came up to its support. Pickett's remnant was overpowered and broke into rout. Ewell made a brief stand, and from a commanding position poured in a fire which broke a portion of the assailants who were advancing over a patch of open ground. But now a general charge was made. Stagg struck one flank, Custer the rear, while Wright assailed in front. Humphreys, a little to the right, also struck a body of the enemy, destroyed two hundred wagons, and made many prisoners. Ewell was outnumbered and completely surrounded. His whole corps threw down their arms. Ewell, Custis Lee, and Kershaw, with six or eight thousand men, surrendered themselves as prisoners.[1]

The straggling from Lee's army had become enormous. Quite a quarter of its remaining effective force was now lopped off at a blow. The remainder had, however, won a brief respite, and moved on. Their sufferings from hunger during the last days had been fearful. Save the single ration which they had brought with them, and the scanty scraps gathered by some foraging parties, they had been without food since they had left Petersburg. Company after company was sent out into the woods to browse upon the tender shoots of the trees just bursting into bud.[2] More pitiable even than the condition of the troops was that of the animals. At every step the jaded horses and mules sank down. At every difficult place the way was blocked up with wagons which could not be moved, and which were set on fire to save them from falling into the hands of the enemy. The exploding ammunition sounded like the continuous noise of a great battle. The spirits of the men gave way at every step. They threw away their arms by regiments, too weak to carry them. Thousands of these unarmed men wandered away, the officers finally ceasing to make any effort to restrain the straggling. Other thousands dragged themselves along mechanically by the side or at the rear of the few who yet kept their ranks, and held on to their arms; for there was yet, after the disaster at Sailor's Creek, a solid core of some ten thousand in whom was now concentrated all the vitality of the great Army of Northern Virginia. So the army struggled on, heading for Farmville, where they hoped to recross the Appomattox, and, by burning the bridges behind them, place the river once more between them and their eager pursuers.

While the Army of the Potomac thus pressed hard upon the Confederates, Ord, with his command from the Army of the James, had, on the evening of the 5th, reached Burkesville. Next morning he moved northward toward Farmville, hoping to head off the enemy there. Approaching this place, he sent Reade forward with a couple of regiments and a squadron of cavalry. He encountered the head of Lee's column and charged it vigorously. His small force was repulsed with heavy loss, he himself being among the slain. But this attack delayed the crossing until the remainder of Ord's force came up, whereupon the Confederates intrenched themselves too strongly to be assailed. During the night they began to cross the river at various points, proposing to destroy the bridges behind them. This was delayed an hour too long. The last of the stragglers had just got over, and the fuel which was to consume the bridges was just lighted, when Barlow's division of the Sixth Corps came up, drove off the Confederate rear-guard, saved the highway bridge close by the high railroad bridge, and secured the means of crossing the river. The Confederates fell back step by step to positions which had been previously selected until toward night, when their whole remaining force was seen drawn up in line of battle in a position covering the roads, their batteries sweeping a gentle slope of half a mile in their front. Humphreys, keeping Barlow in their front, sent Miles around to attack them upon their left. The assault was repelled with heavy loss; and then, under cover of night, the Confederates resumed their retreat eastward toward Appomattox Station, where supplies were awaiting them. They hoped that the start thus gained would enable them to reach Lynchburg, a score of miles beyond, where they would pass the mountains, and emerge into the great Valley of Virginia. Here they might hope for at least a temporary respite from pursuit.

Sheridan, having learned that Ord had failed to cut off the enemy at Farmville, apprehended that it might be Lee's purpose to sweep southwestwardly by rapid marches, heading the pursuing columns, and, regaining the Danville Road, follow up his original plan of joining Johnston in North Carolina. He therefore sent his cavalry in that direction. Reaching Prince Edward Court-house and discovering no traces of the enemy, he sent his divisions to reconnoitre in various directions to find the whereabouts of Lee's army. Crook, crossing the Appomattox, struck the main body near Farmville, assailed their trains, was repulsed, and recrossed the river. On the morning of the 8th the cavalry was concentrated at Prospect Station. Here Sheridan was informed by one of his scouts that at Appomattox Station, twenty-eight miles distant, were four trains of cars laden with provisions for Lee's army. The report of this scout, as the event proved, gave shape to the events of the two closing days of the campaign. It showed just whither Lee was now heading. Instead of aiming at Danville, he was moving straight for Lynchburg. The cavalry were forthwith pushed forward to seize these trains. Custer, who was in the advance, reached Appomattox Station at midnight. The Confederate van had reached the point just before, and had gone into camp. Dashing upon the rear of the trains, Custer cut them off from returning to Lynchburg, captured them, sent them to the rear, and then, without even waiting to reform, burst upon the Confederate force, and drove it pell-mell northward toward Appomattox Court-house, capturing, besides the trains, twenty-five guns and a park of wagons. Sheridan was little behind. He sent back word to Ord and Griffin, who, with their infantry corps, were behind, that if they only pressed on there was no escape for the enemy. Meanwhile he disposed of his cavalry in such a manner as to cover the roads toward Lynchburg, resolving to contest them step by step until the infantry could come up.

The Confederates having, on the evening of the 7th as it seemed, fairly shaken off the attack of Humphreys on their rear, pressed forward all that night and the next day with renewed hopes. If one from a balloon could have overlooked the region lying directly under his eye, he would have seen at a glance that the whole issue turned upon the relative speed of the pursuers and pursued for a few hours. Lee's line of retreat lay along a narrow neck of land between the Appomattox and the James, which here ran parallel at a distance of seven or eight miles. The only avenue of escape was to the west, for on the north was the James, the bridges over which had all been destroyed two months before to prevent the march of Sheridan; on the south was the Appomattox, difficult of passage, and covered on its opposite side by Ord, Griffin, and Sheridan; eastward, and pressing after in the rear, were Humphreys and Wright. For the first few hours of the day the retreating army moved slowly along by-paths running through thickets of oak and pine. At noon they struck the main road, and then moved rapidly. Every hour they appeared to be gaining upon the pursuers, for the noise of a single gun could not be heard in their rear. When, as night was falling, the head of the column came to Appomattox Station, the rear being but four miles behind, they went into camp with a feeling of security to which they had long been strangers. The wearied soldiers lay down to rest, while the bands played merrily. Just then, like a thunderbolt, Custer's cavalry burst upon them. Orders were hastily given that all the extra artillery should be cut down and the commands disbanded.

[1] No actual count of the prisoners at Sailor's Creek seems to have been made. Sheridan roughly estimates them at 10,000. Grant, probably more accurately, states the number at 6000 or 7000. Pollard gives the number of Ewell's and Pickett's men at about 5000.

[2] Fletcher, iii., 516, upon authority of one of Longstreet's staff.

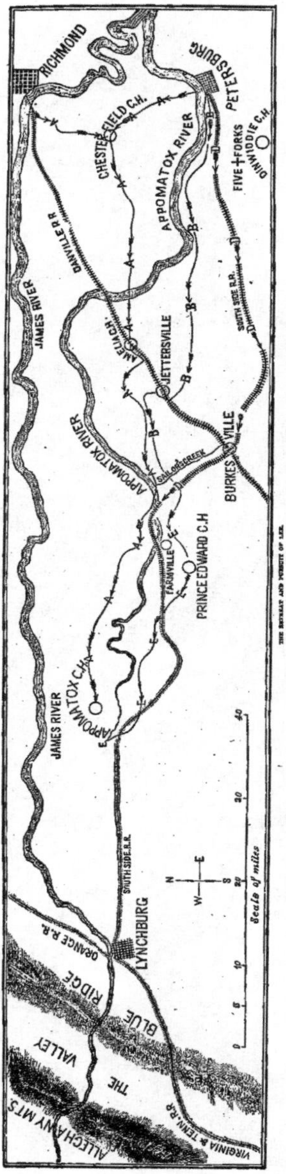

THE RETREAT AND PURSUIT OF LEE.

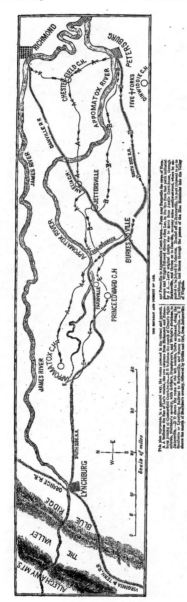

This plan represents, in a general way, the routes pursued in the retreat and pursuit. A A indicates the line of Lee's retreat, the two columns from Richmond and Petersburg joining at Chesterfield Court-house.—B B indicates the march of Grant's right column, Sheridan's cavalry, with Griffin's, Humphreys's, and Wright's divisions, to Jettersville.—D D shows the route of the left column, Ord's command, along the Southside or Lynchburg Railroad to Burkesville, and thence to Farmville.—E E shows the march of Sheridan's cavalry, followed by Griffin and Ord, from Jettersville and Farmville to Appomattox Court-house.—From near Farmville the corps of Humphreys and Wright followed directly after Lee, in the line from that point indicated by A A.—Lee's original design was to move from Amelia Court-house, through Burkesville, and thence on to Danville, seventy miles southwestward, where he expected to be joined by Johnston. Headed off at Jettersville, he next proposed to go to Lynchburg, and thence through the passes of the Blue Mountains into the Valley of Virginia.

But in the gathering darkness the extent of the peril could only be conjectured. There was certainly a Federal force right in their front; but it was apparently only cavalry, through which a way might most likely be forced. So, gathering together his army as best he might, Lee made preparations to attempt the passage at dawn. Gordon, who had brought up the rear, was sent to the front, passing the remnants of the wagon train, around which lingered thousands of men who, too weak to carry their arms, had flung them away along every mile of the road from Amelia Court-house. Early in the morning Gordon made reconnoissances in his front. He could see nothing but a line of dismounted cavalry to oppose his march. At ten o'clock his line was ordered to advance. Sheridan had directed his troops to fall back slowly, keeping a steady front, until Ord and Griffin, who had been marching all night, should come up and form in their rear. Gordon pressed on, flushed with what seemed an easy victory, when all at once Sheridan's dismounted cavalry moved to one side, like the withdrawing of a curtain, and disclosed a long line of infantry bearing straight down, while at the same moment the troopers sprang to saddle, ready to charge upon the flank of the unarmed men in the centre of the Confederate column. Had that charge been made, the whole Confederate force would have been ridden over like stubble. Gordon sent word to Lee in the rear that he was being driven back. What was to be done in such a case had already been decided. Lee mounted his horse and rode back toward the Union lines, while Gordon sent a flag of truce to the front, asking for a suspension of hostilities, for negotiations for surrender were then in progress.

Sheridan was in no mood for trifling. He had just been assailed; the smoke of the guns fired at him had hardly lifted. He had no wish to shed more blood; but, before he would order a suspension of an attack, the issue of which was patent to all, he must have positive assurance that a surrender was decided upon. Gordon came to the front and gave the required assurance. In a few moments officers of high rank upon both sides were mingling in friendly concourse, as though for four long years they had not confronted each other on a hundred battle-fields. There were men on each side who had been cadets together at West Point, and who had since fought side by side during the Mexican War, and later in the wearisome operations on the wide frontier. Now, bridging over the fatal four years, they could at last meet as friends. War has its amenities as well as its hostilities.

Lee, accompanied by two aids, was riding toward the Federal lines to meet Grant, prepared at this supreme moment to give an unconditional surrender of what remained of the remnant of the great army which had so long been under his command; for to this issue it had at last come. He hoped, indeed, to gain favorable terms, and in this hope he was encouraged by what had within a day or two occurred between himself and the commander of the Federal forces. The surrender of the Confederate Army of Northern Virginia had for some days been a foregone conclusion on both sides. On the 6th, directly after the disaster at Sailor's Creek, such of the Confederate generals as could come together met at Anderson's tent, and concluded that the end was at hand, and the surrender must soon take place. They would take upon themselves the sole responsibility of advising the surrender. Pendleton was deputed to see that this opinion was presented to Lee; if possible, Longstreet was to be induced to act as intermediary. Events following closely after rendered superfluous any direct action upon this suggestion.

On the 7th Grant took the initiative. To Lee he wrote: "The result of the last week must convince you of the hopelessness of farther resistance on the part of the Army of Northern Virginia," and so, to shift from himself the responsibility of more bloodshed, he asked that Lee should surrender the army under his immediate command. Lee replied diplomatically, and in phrases which perhaps were meant to bear a double sense. He was not entirely of the opinion that farther resistance was hopeless; but yet, hoping to avoid useless bloodshed, he asked the terms which would be offered to him on condition of surrender. Grant, understanding this to be an offer of surrender, replied that peace being his only desire, the sole terms he would insist upon were that the men surrendered should not again take up arms against the government of the United States until properly exchanged; and he was ready to arrange with Lee, either personally or by representatives, for the definite terms of surrender. Lee's answer could not well be other than a surprise to Grant. He had not intended to propose to surrender, but only to ask the terms which Grant would propose. Indeed, "to be frank," he said, "I do not think the emergency has arisen to call for surrender." He could not, therefore, meet Grant with a view to surrender his army, but would be pleased to meet him to talk over the subject of the restoration of peace, "which should be the sole object of all." To understand Lee's motive in this reply, it is only necessary to look at the operations of the day. He had flung back the assault upon his rear, and was, to all appearance, safely on his way toward Lynchburg, and at least temporary safety. This was by no means the first time in which an attempt had been made to induce Grant to transcend his authority and undertake to make peace. He, indeed, knew clearly the limits of his functions. Moreover, if more had been needed, he had the express order of the President prohibiting him from dealing with the general question of the restoration of peace. So to Lee's letter Grant responded sharply, but still with a kindly addition which left the way open for each military commander to do what he properly might. I have no authority, he said, to treat on the subject of peace, and so the meeting which you propose would do no good; but the terms upon which peace can be had are well understood: the South has only to lay down its arms.

So matters rested through the 8th of April and the night following. As day dawned on the 9th, raw and gusty, three Confederate generals sat around

POSITION OF THE CONFEDERATE ARMY WHEN THE SURRENDER WAS ANNOUNCED.

a camp-fire. They were Lee, dressed in a new uniform just donned, and contrasting with the rough garb by which he had long been best known in the army; Longstreet, his arm still in a sling, his old Wilderness wound yet unhealed; and Mahone, perhaps the best of Longstreet's surviving subordinates, who had come up from the rear to hold part in the informal council there assembled. These three were to decide upon what could be and must be done. Mahone, being junior officer, according to army rules was to speak first. His own division, he said, and one or two others, were able to fight; the rest of the army was so worn out as to be fit only for surrender. Longstreet corroborated this statement; yet both declared that the Army of Northern Virginia should surrender only upon honorable terms. Lee then, for the first time, imparted to his subordinates the substance of what had passed between himself and Grant. The terms proposed were honorable; but now, after two days' rejection, it was not certain that they would be conceded. Then—for some hours had passed in deliberation—came the message from Gordon that he was overmatched and falling back. The crisis had come and gone. Surrender on the best terms that could be obtained was all that was left. "General Longstreet," said Lee, "I leave you in charge here; I am going to hold a conference with General Grant." How that conference must result was no longer a matter of doubt. It must be surrender at all events, no matter upon what terms, for the remnant of the Confederate army, outnumbered, worn out, and surrounded, could neither fight nor fly. Its only alternative was to die or surrender. And so Gordon in front was warranted in assuring Sheridan that the surrender was now a foregone conclusion. The last shot fired by the Army of Northern Virginia was by the Richmond Howitzers, who had fired the first gun at Bethel just four years before, lacking a month and a day.

Lee rode to that part of the Union line where he expected to find Grant. Here he was met by Grant's note declining an interview to treat of the general question of peace. Grant had gone to meet Sheridan. Lee wrote a hasty note: "I received your note on the picket-line, whither I had come to meet you and ascertain definitely what terms were embraced in your proposition of yesterday with reference to the surrender of this army. I now request an interview in accordance with the offer contained in your letter of yesterday for that purpose." Two hours passed, and noon came before this request reached Grant. He returned a courteous reply, explaining the delay, and expressing his readiness to meet Lee at any point which he should select.

Appomattox Court-house, a hamlet of a half score houses, which had now become neutral ground, was the place chosen. The best house, that of Mr. McLean, was fixed upon for the interview. The owner was naturally astounded at the honor thus suddenly thrust upon him. The two great commanders, after due introduction, seated themselves at a little table in his quiet parlor to settle what each knew was in effect to end the war. The two men had certainly seen each other before, for both had served under Scott almost a score of years before at the capture of Mexico. Most likely Grant remembered Lee, but Lee could hardly be expected to remember Grant. The brilliant Virginian, the favorite of the commander, and already looked upon as the rising man of the army, could hardly be expected to have taken special note of a certain second lieutenant Grant, acting as regimental quartermaster, even though he was breveted first lieutenant for "meritorious services" at Molino del Rey; and a few days afterward, at Chapultepec, as was duly reported by General Worth and Colonel Garland, "acquitted himself most nobly" under the observation of his regimental, brigade, and division commanders.

The afternoon was wearing away when the interview began. There was really little to be said, and both men had the faculty of not spending words upon trifles. Grant's original proposition embraced all the terms that Lee could ask. The question was, were these still open to acceptance. Grant still offered them; Lee said they were lenient, and he would leave to Grant to express them in form. Lee asked a few explanations respecting certain phrases used in the formal agreement. Both commanders understood them alike. The purport of the whole was that this Confederate army surrendered, giving up all public property, the officers retaining their side-arms, baggage, and their own horses. Officers were to give their personal paroles not to take up arms against the government of the United States until properly exchanged, and also to give a like parole for the men under their command. This being done, every officer and man might return to his home, "not to be disturbed by the United States authority so long as they observe their paroles and the laws in force where they may reside." Terms so magnanimous were never before offered and accepted. So clearly were they defined, that never, amid all the complications that have ensued, has there been any question as to their import, or any serious dispute as to the exact fulfillment of the terms of surrender.[1]

The momentous interview which virtually closed the war lasted hardly an hour, for it wanted but ten minutes of noon when Grant, miles away, received the letter of Lee asking for a meeting, and at half past three the Confederate commander rode quietly back to his quarters. There was no need of inquiring what had been done. All saw at a glance that the surrender had been made. Officers and men rushed up to bid farewell to their leader. He received their greeting quietly. "We have fought through the war together," he said, "and I have done the best I could for you." The next day he issued a formal address to his army, and then rode off toward Richmond. On the afternoon of the 12th, attended by half a dozen of his staff, he rode into the smoking city which he had so long and stoutly defended. Entering his home, he disappeared from the history of the war, of which his surrender had, indeed, been the actual conclusion, though nominally it lasted a few weeks longer.

The surrender of the Army of Northern Virginia was virtually performed by the two men who sat quietly together in McLean's parlor at Appomattox Court-house. All that remained to be done was performed as quietly. There were to be none of the formal ceremonies heretofore practiced

[1] The following—mere formal terms of courtesy being omitted—is the text of the correspondence between Grant and Lee:

I. Grant to Lee, *April 7.* "The result of the last week must convince you of the hopelessness of farther resistance on the part of the Army of Northern Virginia in this struggle. I feel that it is so, and regard it as my duty to shift from myself the responsibility of any farther effusion of blood by asking of you the surrender of that portion of the Confederate States army known as the Army of Northern Virginia."

II. Lee to Grant, *April 7.* "I have received your note of this date. Though not entertaining the opinion you express on the hopelessness of farther resistance on the part of the Army of Northern Virginia, I reciprocate your desire to avoid useless effusion of blood, and therefore, before considering your proposition, ask the terms you will offer on condition of its surrender."

III. Grant to Lee, *April 8.* "Your note of last evening, in reply to mine of same date, asking the conditions on which I will accept the surrender of the Army of Northern Virginia, is just received. In reply I would say, that *peace* being my great desire, there is but one condition I would insist upon, namely, That the men and officers surrendered shall be disqualified for taking up arms again against the government of the United States until properly exchanged. I will meet you, or will designate officers to meet any officers you may name for the same purpose at any point agreeable to you, for the purpose of arranging definitely the terms upon which the surrender of the Army of Northern Virginia will be received."

IV. Lee to Grant, *April 8.* "I received at a late hour your note of to-day. In mine of yesterday I did not intend to propose the surrender of the Army of Northern Virginia, but to ask the terms of your proposition. To be frank, I do not think the emergency has arisen to call for the surrender of the army; but as the restoration of peace should be the sole object of all, I desire to know whether your proposals would lead to that end. I can not, therefore, meet you with a view to surrender the Army of Northern Virginia; but, as far as your proposal may affect the Confederate States forces under my command, and tend to the restoration of peace, I should be pleased to meet you at 10 A. M. to-morrow, on the old stage road to Richmond, between the picket-lines of the two armies."

V. Grant to Lee, *April 9.* "Your note of yesterday is received. I have no authority to treat on the subject of peace; the meeting proposed for 10 A. M. to-day could lead to no good. I will state, however, general, that I am equally anxious for peace with yourself, and the whole North entertains the same feeling. The terms upon which peace can be had are well understood. By the South laying down their arms they will hasten that most desirable event, and save thousands of human lives, and hundreds of millions of property not yet destroyed. Seriously hoping that all our difficulties may be settled without the loss of another life, I subscribe myself, etc."

VI. Lee to Grant, *April 9.* "I received your note this morning on the picket-line, whither I had come to meet you, and ascertain definitely what terms were embraced in your proposal of yesterday with reference to the surrender of this army. I now ask an interview in accordance with the offer contained in your letter of yesterday for that purpose."

VII. Grant to Lee, *April 9.* "Your note of this date is but this moment, 11 50 A. M., received. In consequence of my having passed from the Richmond and Lynchburg Road to the Farmville and Lynchburg Road, I am at this writing about four miles west of Walter's Church, and will push forward to the front for the purpose of meeting you. Notice sent to me on this road where you wish the interview to take place will meet me."

VIII. Grant to Lee, *April 9.* "In accordance with the substance of my letter to you of the 8th instant, I propose to receive the surrender of the Army of Northern Virginia upon the following terms, to wit: Rolls of all the officers and men to be made in duplicate, one copy to be given to me, the other to be retained by such officers as you may designate. The officers to give their individual paroles not to take up arms against the government of the United States until properly exchanged, and each company or regimental officer to sign a like parole for the men of their commands. The arms, artillery, and public property to be parked and stacked, and turned over to the officers appointed by me to receive them. This will not embrace the side-arms of the officers, nor their private horses or baggage. This done, each officer and man will be allowed to return to their homes, not to be disturbed by the United States authority so long as they observe their paroles and the laws where they may reside."

IX. Lee to Grant, *April 9.* "I received your letter of this date, containing the terms of the surrender of the Army of Northern Virginia as proposed by you. As they are substantially the same as those expressed in your letter of the 8th instant, they are accepted. I will proceed to designate the proper officers to carry the stipulations into effect."

The last two documents, though put in the form of letters, the former dated at "Appomattox Court-house," the letter at the "Headquarters Army of Northern Virginia," were drawn up and signed by Grant and Lee at their meeting at McLean's residence, near the Court-house.

The paroles were in the following form:

"We, the undersigned, prisoners of war belonging to the Army of Northern Virginia, having been this day surrendered by General R. A. Lee, commanding the said army, to Lieutenant General Grant, commanding the armies of the United States [in the officers' parole for the men the reading was, I, the undersigned, commanding ——, do, for the within-named prisoners of war this day surrendered, etc., give my solemn parole of honor that the within-named shall not], will not hereafter serve in the armies of the Confederate States, or in any military capacity whatever [in parole for privates, in military or any capacity whatever] against the United States of America, or render aid to the enemies of the latter, until properly exchanged in such manner as shall be mutually approved by the respective authorities."

This parole was countersigned by the provost-marshal: "The above officer or officers [in the parole for privates, the within-named] will not be disturbed by the United States authorities so long as they observe their parole and the laws in force where they may reside."

Lee's formal parting address to his army, issued on the 10th, the day following the surrender, was as follows:

"After four years of arduous service, marked by unsurpassed courage and fortitude, the Army of Northern Virginia has been compelled to yield to overwhelming numbers and resources. I need not tell the survivors of so many hard-fought battles, who have remained steadfast to the last, that I have consented to this result from no distrust of them; but feeling that valor and devotion could accomplish nothing that would compensate for the loss that would have attended the continuation of the contest, I have determined to avoid the useless sacrifice of those whose past services have endeared them to their countrymen. By the terms of the agreement, officers and men can return to their homes, and remain there until exchanged. You will take with you the satisfaction that proceeds from the consciousness of duty faithfully performed; and I earnestly pray that a merciful God will extend to you His blessing and protection. With an unceasing admiration of your constancy and devotion to your country, and a grateful remembrance of your kind and generous consideration of myself, I bid you an affectionate farewell."

THE LAST SHOT.

EDMUND RUFFIN.

when an army laid down its arms—the vanquished general courteously delivering his sword to the victor, to be as courteously returned to him. Neither Lee nor Grant even appeared on the scene. Gibbon's infantry and McKenzie's cavalry, of Ord's command, with the Fifth Corps—the victors of Five Forks, now under Griffin—remained at Appomattox Court-house to take charge of the surrendered property. The remainder of the army marched back to Burkesville, for it seemed that one more blow might have to be struck, whereby Johnston's army should share the fate of that of Lee. Sheridan with his cavalry, and an infantry corps, Wright's being chosen, was to march to aid Sherman. They had fairly started on the way when tidings came that Johnston had surrendered to Sherman.

Meanwhile the commissioners appointed by Grant and Lee had been busily at work making out the list of prisoners to be paroled. Their work was completed on the 11th, and on the next day the Confederate Army of Northern Virginia had its last formal parade. It marched to the place appointed, stacked its arms, and piled up its accoutrements. The list of paroled prisoners contained 27,805 names, but of these scarcely 8000 had arms in their hands. Thirty cannon and three hundred and fifty wagons were turned over. These comprised all the material and munitions left to this Confederate army. A week before it had set out on its retreat with fully two hundred cannon and more than a thousand wagons, bearing ammunition and material, all save food, sufficient for an army of 100,000 men.

The military history of the Confederacy covers exactly four years. On the 9th of April, 1861, the Confederate commissioners, in view of the proposed provisioning of Fort Sumter, formally announced to the government of the United States that this could not be accomplished without the effusion of blood; and that they, "in behalf of their government and their people, accept the gage of battle thus thrown down to them."[1] On the 9th of April, 1865, Lee signed the surrender to Grant. On the 12th of April, 1861, fire was opened upon Fort Sumter by Edmund Ruffin, a Virginian of threescore and ten, who asked permission thus to open the war. On the 12th of April, 1865—just four years to a day—the army of Northern Virginia laid down its arms and dispersed, thereby in effect formally closing the war. A few weeks later Ruffin committed suicide, leaving behind him a memorandum that he preferred to die rather than to live under the government of the United States.

There was to be one more formal review of Confederates in Virginia. For two years there had been a band of partisans under Mosby, operating in Northeastern Virginia. It consisted at the outset of only a few score men, but gradually accumulated to a considerable force. They received no pay, but were allowed to keep all the plunder which they could secure, and this formed an inducement for many reckless individuals to join the band. They were kept in subjection by their leader by the understanding that for any failure in obedience they would be sent to the regular army, which was "regarded in the light of a Botany Bay."[2] Even after the complete annihilation of Early's command, they managed to maintain themselves in the valley east of the Blue Ridge. Their depredations became so annoying that one of the last acts of Sheridan in the Department of Washington was to order[3] the complete devastation of the region in which they operated. All forage and subsistence was to be destroyed, all barns and mills burnt, and all stock driven off; no buildings, however, were to be burnt, and no personal violence offered to citizens. "The ultimate result of the system of guerrilla warfare," said Sheridan, "is the total destruction of all private rights in the country occupied by such parties. This destruction may as well commence at once, and the responsibility of it must rest upon the authorities at Richmond, who have acknowledged the legitimacy of guerrilla bands."[4] This band, at the time of Lee's surrender, numbered about 600 men, all well mounted. On the 15th of April, having been informed of the surrender of Lee, Mosby wrote to Hancock, then commanding this department, that, while he thought there had not arisen any emergency which would justify the surrender of his men, he was yet indisposed "to cause the useless effusion of blood, or to inflict on a war-worn population any unnecessary distress." He therefore proposed an armistice until he could communicate with his own authorities, and obtain sufficient information to determine his farther action. Hancock replied that he might have reasonable time, but that he could not communicate with Lee, who was no longer in command. Grant, having been communicated with, directed Hancock: "You may receive all rebel officers and soldiers who surrender to you on exactly the same terms that were given to General Lee, except have it distinctly understood that all who claim homes in states that never passed ordinances of secession have forfeited them, and can only return on compliance with the amnesty proclamation. Maryland, Kentucky, Delaware, and Missouri are such states. They may return to West Virginia on their parole." On the 21st of April Mosby assembled his band for their last review. "I have," he said, "summoned you together for the last time. The vision that we cherished of a free and independent country has vanished, and that country is now the spoil of the conqueror. I disband your organization in preference to surrendering to our enemies. I am no longer your commander."[5]

[1] *Ante*, p. 52. [2] Scott's *Partisan Life with Mosby*, 396. [3] November 27, 1864.
[4] *Sheridan's Report*, 47. [5] *Partisan Life with Mosby*, 476.

THE LAST REVIEW.

CHAPTER LVIII.

JOHNSTON'S SURRENDER.

Sherman's Preparations for an advance on Raleigh.—Contemporaneous Events.—Change of Plan after the Capture of Richmond.—Johnston retreats Westward.—Sherman enters Raleigh.—Johnston puzzled.—He inquires of Sherman as to Terms of Surrender.—The Reply.—Sherman's Letters to Grant.—Conference with Johnston, April 17th.—The Latter explains his Situation.—He offers, on favorable Terms, to surrender all the remaining Confederate Armies.—Conference renewed on the 18th.—Semi-political Nature of the Conversation.—Breckinridge admitted to the Conference.—Reagan's Memorandum ruled out.—Sherman pens one of his own.—"Glittering Generalities."—Substance of the Memorandum.—Sherman's Position in the Matter.—Letters to Washington.—The Cabinet Meeting.—Rejection of the Memorandum.—Grant goes to Morehead City.—His Consideration for Sherman.—Johnston's Surrender.—Secretary Stanton's Telegrams.—Injustice to Sherman.—Halleck's Interference.—Sherman's Indignation.—Surrender of Taylor and Kirby Smith.—The End of the War.

AT the close of March, 1865, Sherman's army was being reorganized at Goldsborough, and awaiting the repair of railroads and the accumulation of supplies and clothing preliminary to an advance against General Johnston, who then covered Raleigh with an army of over 40,000 men. The Twenty-third and Tenth corps were united under the designation of the Army of the Ohio. Slocum's command was now styled the Army of Georgia, while Howard's retained its former title. Wilson's and Stoneman's expeditions were in full and successful operation, and General Canby was investing the defenses of Mobile.

Sherman's preparations could not be completed before the 10th of April. In the mean time Mobile had fallen; Selma had been occupied by Wilson, who was fast approaching Montgomery; Stoneman had broken up the railroad west of Lynchburg, and had pushed down to the Catawba River, in North Carolina, destroying the railroad through Greensborough and Salisbury; Richmond and Petersburg had been abandoned, and the Confederate Army of Northern Virginia had been routed and captured.

Tidings of the battles about Petersburg reached Sherman on the 6th. Up to this time Sherman's plan was to make a feint on Raleigh, cross the Roanoke, and, securing by the Chowan River communication with Norfolk as a base of supplies, to strike for Burkesville, interposing between Johnston and Lee. But the Army of the Potomac, under General Grant's leadership, had eliminated Lee's army from the problem to be solved. This led General Sherman to change his plan. On the 5th Grant warned him that Lee would attempt to reach Danville, and urged an immediate movement against Johnston. "Rebel armies now," he writes, "are the only strategic points to strike at." Instead of making a feint on Raleigh, Sherman, on the 11th, made a real movement on that place. Hearing of Lee's surrender in the mean time, Johnston had retreated westward, and on the morning of the 13th Sherman's army entered the capital of North Carolina.

Johnston had but a single line of retreat left—that by Greensborough and Charlotte. Of course it was folly for him to venture a battle with Sherman. He could not retreat as an organized army. He had therefore to choose between the surrender and the disbandment of his forces. The consequence of the latter step would be to let loose upon the citizens of North Carolina 40,000 men with arms in their hands, who would inaugurate a reign of terror. Johnston looked upon farther opposition as criminal. But how to dispose of his army was a perplexing problem. Lee's army had been defeated on the field of battle—in effect, it had been actually surrounded and captured, and in this case no such considerations had been involved as now presented themselves to Johnston. To the army of the latter escape was possible by disorganization; it had not been defeated or surrounded. The same considerations applied with equal force to Dick Taylor's and Kirby Smith's armies. As soon as it was fully realized that farther resistance was hopeless, immediate disorganization would follow, and the Confederate armies would resolve themselves into armed bands of lawless, irresponsible marauders, scattered over the entire South, unless some motive was offered sufficient to hold these armies until they could be paroled and disarmed.

Sherman had taken measures to cut off Johnston's retreat southward when, on the 14th, he received by flag of truce a letter from the Confederate commander, asking an armistice, and information as to the best terms on which he would be permitted to surrender his army. Sherman replied that he was willing to confer with him as to the terms of surrender, and added: "That a basis of action may be had, I undertake to abide by the same terms and conditions entered into by Generals Grant and Lee at Appomattox Court-house, Virginia, on the 9th instant." Arrangements were made for a conference on the 17th.

Up to this time Sherman had entertained no other terms of surrender than those proposed by Grant in the case of Lee's army. After Lee's surrender, he wrote to the lieutenant general: "The terms you have given Lee are magnanimous and liberal. Should Johnston follow Lee's example, I shall, of course, grant the same." The very day after he had agreed to meet and confer with Johnston, he again wrote: "I will grant the same terms as General Grant gave General Lee, and be careful not to complicate any points of civil policy."

During the interval between the first correspondence between Sherman and Johnston and their meeting on the 17th, no movement was made by either army.[1] At noon of the day appointed, the two generals met at a house five miles from Durham Station under a flag of truce. They had never met before in person, though for two years they confronted each other on many battle-fields. The interview, says Sherman, was frank and soldier-like. Johnston freely acknowledged that the war was at an end, and that every sacrifice of life after Lee's surrender was simply murder. He admitted that the terms conceded to Lee were magnanimous. He had no right to ask any better conditions for himself. But the situation of his army was peculiar. The sudden revelation of the hopelessness of farther resistance was likely to operate on the fears and anxieties of his soldiers. The consequence would be to relax military restraint. He therefore asked that some general concessions might be made which would enable him to maintain his control over his troops until they could be got back to the neighborhood of their homes. He suggested, also, that the proposition agreed upon should extend to all the Confederate armies then existing. Sherman asked Johnston what authority he had as to the armies beyond his own command. Johnston admitted be had no such power, but thought he could obtain it. He did not know where Davis was, but he could find Breckinridge—the Confederate Secretary of War—whose orders would be every where respected. It was then agreed to postpone the farther consideration of the subject till noon on the next day.

Sherman returned to Raleigh and conferred with his general officers, every one of whom pronounced in favor of a conclusion of the war upon terms which seemed so favorable, and which involved no sacrifice of the national honor.

The conference with Johnston was renewed on the 18th. The territory within the immediate command of Johnston comprised the states of North and South Carolina, Georgia, and Florida. He was now able to satisfy Sherman of his power to disband also the armies in Alabama, Mississippi, Louisiana, and Texas. He then asked Sherman what he was willing to do. Sherman replied that he could only deal with belligerents—that no military man could go beyond that. He was willing to make terms for the Confederate soldiers in accordance with President Lincoln's amnesty proclamation; that is, all of the rank of colonel and under should have pardon upon condition of taking the oath of allegiance to the United States. He was also willing to go farther than this—he would grant what had been conceded to Lee's army, that *every* officer and soldier who would return home, observe his parole and obey the laws, should be free from disturbance by United States authority. But Johnston did not seem to be quite satisfied. He expressed great solicitude lest the Southern States should be dismembered, and denied representation in Congress or any separate political existence; also, lest the absolute disarming of his men might leave the South powerless, and exposed to the depredations of assassins and robbers. Sherman listened with great courtesy to all this, which both commanders equally well knew lay outside the scope of a military surrender. In reply, he simply expressed his own personal assurance that if the Southern people submitted to the lawful authority of the nation, as defined by the Constitution, the courts, and the authorities of the United States, supported by the courts, there would be no occasion for solicitude; they would "regain their position as citizens of the United States, free and equal in all respects."

While the conversation was thus drifting off from the main question, Johnston suggested that Breckinridge be allowed to come in. Sherman was never fond of politicians, and had very good reasons for not being partial to this one in particular. He reminded Johnston that it had been agreed that the negotiation must be confined to belligerents. Johnston replied that he understood that perfectly. "But," said he, "Breckinridge, whom you do not know, save by public rumor, as the secretary of state, is, in fact, a major general. Have you any objection to his being present as a major general?" Sherman then consented, and Breckinridge came in; and though it was understood that he was only present as a part of Johnston's personal staff, he joined in the conversation. Soon a courier entered and handed Johnston a package of papers, over which he and Breckinridge held a conversation, and then put the papers in their pockets. One of these was a memorandum, written, as Johnston told Sherman, by the Confederate Post-master General Reagan. It was preceded by a preamble, and concluded with some general terms. Sherman read it, and, being the court in this case, ruled it out.

The conversation then became general, touching upon slavery, which was acknowledged "to be as dead as any thing can be," and upon reconstruction. Then it occurred to General Sherman—possibly it may have been suggested by Reagan's document—to write out a memorandum consisting of some general propositions, meaning little or much, according to the construction of parties, and send them to Washington for the assent or rejection of the government. No delay would result from this, as he would be obliged to communicate with his government in any case, in order to obtain authority by which he could receive the surrender of armies beyond the limits of his proper department.

These propositions Sherman himself calls "glittering generalities." The following is the substance of the memorandum:

The contending armies were to remain as they then were, but the armistice would cease forty-eight hours after a notice to that effect should be given by either commander to the other. All the Confederate armies were to be disbanded and conducted to their several state capitals, where their arms were to be deposited in the state arsenal, subject to the control of the general government. There, also, each officer and man was to be paroled. The several state governments of the South were to be recognized by the President on their officers and Legislatures taking the oath prescribed by the Constitution of the United States. The people of these states were to be guaranteed their political rights and franchise, and their rights of person and property, as defined by federal and state Constitutions. They were not to be disturbed so long as they lived peaceably and obeyed the laws. The war was to cease, and a general amnesty to be granted, on condition of the

[1] "I was both willing and anxious thus to consume a few days, as it would enable Colonel Wright to finish our railroad to Raleigh. Two bridges had to be built, and 12 miles of new road made. We had no iron except by taking up that on the branch from Goldsborough to Weldon. Instead of losing time, I gained in every way, for every hour of delay possible was required to reconstruct the railroad to our rear, and improve the condition of our wagon roads to the front, so desirable in case the negotiations failed, and we be forced to make the race of near 200 miles to head off or catch Johnston, then retreating toward Charlotte."—Sherman's Report.

disbandment and disarmament of the Confederate armies, and the resumption by the soldiers of their peaceful pursuits.

This memorandum was signed by Generals Johnston and Sherman, who, recognizing their want of authority to carry its terms into effect, pledged themselves to promptly obtain such authority, and to endeavor to carry out the programme indicated.[1]

So far as Sherman allowed himself to take a political view of the crisis then upon the nation, this memorandum doubtless expressed, though somewhat crudely, his real sentiments. He said, some time afterward, "I stand by the memorandum." He put his signature to the document meaning thereby to give to its propositions all the sanction he could. He had hastily penned the memorandum. The act was wholly due to the suggestion of a moment; it had not been the subject of an hour's deliberation. From the beginning of the conference he had steadily resisted the encroachment of politics upon the negotiation for surrender. He would have persisted in this resistance if Johnston's army alone had been concerned. But Johnston had made a proposition for the surrender of all the Confederate armies from the Roanoke to the Rio Grande. This proposition Sherman would have rejected at once if it had not been backed by authority which seemed to him sufficient, or if it could possibly have been intended as a ruse on the part of the enemy to gain time. He had neither motive for its rejection. He was confident that the authority supporting the proposition would be respected by every Confederate soldier, and he was equally confident of its sincerity. It was, moreover, a proposition which, from its very terms, was not made to him, but through him to the United States government. Its rejection by him without reference to the government, and without a sufficient military motive, would have been as clearly a usurpation of authority as its acceptance would have been without such reference.

But why not submit the proposition to the government in the simplest terms and unaccompanied by the memorandum? Simply because the proposition was not thus submitted to him. Johnston had admitted that the terms granted to Lee's army were sufficiently magnanimous, but had begged that some official assurance might be given by the general government in regard to its future treatment of Southern citizens. Some general concessions were asked which might prevent the Confederate soldiers from resorting to a species of guerrilla warfare, from which the people of the South must suffer heavily. It must be remembered, also, that from Kentucky almost to Virginia, General Sherman was the military commander of the South, and that from the first the regulation of civil affairs had, in a large measure, been committed to military commanders within their several departments. The consideration of civil affairs—the regulation of trade, of the affairs of freedmen, of municipal government—was a part of the manifold duties of department commanders. On two previous occasions—in a letter to the mayor of Atlanta, and subsequently in a communication addressed to a citizen of Savannah—General Sherman had expressed his sentiments as to the policy which would be adopted by the government upon the return of the South to its allegiance. "Both these letters," says Sherman, "asserted my belief that, according to Mr. Lincoln's proclamations and messages, when the people of the South had laid down their arms and submitted to the lawful power of the United States, *ipso facto*, the war was over as to them; and furthermore, that if any state in rebellion would conform to the Constitution of the United States, 'cease war,' elect senators and representatives to Congress, if admitted (of which each house of Congress alone is the judge), that state becomes instanter as much in the Union as New York or Ohio. Nor was I rebuked for these expressions, though it was universally known and commented on at the time. And again, Mr. Stanton in person, at Savannah, speaking of the terrific expense of the war, and difficulty of realizing the money necessary for the daily wants of the government, impressed me most forcibly with the necessity of bringing the war to a close as soon as possible for *financial reasons*."

Some memorandum must accompany the submission of Johnston's proposition, in order that the government might understand what concessions were expected: once before the government, this basis might be modified, entirely changed, or rejected altogether. There was nothing final, nothing in the nature of an *ultimatum* about the memorandum.

In the midst of the negotiations with Johnston, Sherman had heard of the murder of the President, but saw in that event no reason to modify these negotiations. In that respect it probably had no more influence over him than did the information received from General Halleck that a man by the name of Clark had been detailed for his own assassination.[1]

Major Hitchcock, an officer on Sherman's staff, proceeded to Washington to lay the memorandum before President Johnson. No moment could have been more unfavorable for the consideration of concessions to be granted to rebels than that which witnessed Major Hitchcock's arrival at Washington. The country was buried in a sea of sorrow—a sea which, while it moaned in hopeless regret for one lost, whose need was now felt more than ever before, boiled also with indignation against the spirit of treason which had impelled the assassin's blow. It was, perhaps, too much to be expected of our poor human nature that President Johnson and his cabinet, meeting under these circumstances, would consider fairly and calmly the propositions submitted by Sherman. The document was read, and every word was listened to very much as if it had been a proclamation of pardon to Booth and his fellow-conspirators. Sherman, the scourge, with the fire and the sword, was the man for that moment, not Sherman, the liberal-minded soldier, who disdained to strike a fallen foe. No one seemed able to preserve calmness save Lieutenant General Grant, who was present at the meeting, and who, while he disapproved of the propositions submitted, was not willing to denounce his brother commander.

General Grant offered to go in person to Raleigh, and notify Sherman of the disapproval of the memorandum by the government. He arrived at Morehead City on the evening of the 23d, and from that point communicated with General Sherman. The latter gave Johnston notice of the close of the armistice, informed him of the fate of their agreement, and demanded the surrender of his army on the same terms which had been granted to General Lee. On the 26th Johnston complied with this demand.[2] So great confidence had General Grant in Sherman's ability to manage his own command, that, during these final negotiations, Johnston was not aware of his presence at Raleigh.

---

[1] The following is a copy of the memorandum in full:

"*Memorandum, or Basis of Agreement, made this, the 18th day of April, A. D. 1865, near Durham's Station, in the State of North Carolina, by and between General Joseph E. Johnston, commanding the Confederate Army, and Major General W. T. Sherman, commanding the Army of the United States, both present.*

"I. The contending armies now in the field to maintain the *status quo* until notice is given by the commanding general of any one to his opponent, and reasonable time, say forty-eight hours, allowed.

"II. The Confederate armies now in existence to be disbanded and conducted to their several state capitals, there to deposit their arms and public property in the state arsenal; and each officer and man to execute and file an agreement to cease from acts of war, and to abide the action of both state and federal authorities. The number of arms and munitions of war to be reported to the chief of ordnance at Washington City, subject to the future action of the Congress of the United States, and in the mean time to be used solely to maintain peace and order within the borders of the states respectively.

"III. The recognition by the executive of the United States of the several state governments, on their officers and Legislatures taking the oath prescribed by the Constitution of the United States; and where conflicting state governments have resulted from the war, the legitimacy of all shall be submitted to the Supreme Court of the United States.

"IV. The re-establishment of all federal courts in the several states, with powers as defined by the Constitution and laws of Congress.

"V. The people and inhabitants of all states to be guaranteed, so far as the executive can, their political rights and franchise, as well as their rights of person and property, as defined by the Constitution of the United States and of the states respectively.

"VI. The executive authority or government of the United States not to disturb any of the people by reason of the late war, so long as they live in peace and quiet, and abstain from acts of armed hostility, and obey the laws in existence at the place of their residence.

"VII. In general terms, it is announced that the war is to cease; a general amnesty, so far as the executive of the United States can command, on condition of the disbandment of the Confederate armies, the distribution of arms, and the resumption of peaceful pursuits by officers and men hitherto composing said armies.

"Not being fully empowered by our respective principals to fulfill these terms, we individually and officially pledge ourselves to promptly obtain authority, and will endeavor to carry out the above programme."

[1] The following letters were written by General Sherman on the 18th to Washington—the first to accompany the memorandum, and the second having reference to President Lincoln's assassination:

No. 1.

"Headquarters Middle Department of the Mississippi, in the Field, Raleigh, N. C., April 18, 1865.

"To Lieutenant General U. S. GRANT, or Major General HALLECK, Washington, D. C.:

"GENERAL,—I inclose herewith a copy of an agreement made this day between General Joseph E. Johnston and myself, which, if approved by the President of the United States, will produce peace from the Potomac to the Rio Grande. Mr. Breckinridge was present at the conference in the capacity of a major general, and satisfied me of the ability of General Johnston to carry out to the full extent the terms of this agreement; and if you will get the President to simply indorse the copy, and commission me to carry out the terms, I will follow them to the conclusion. You will observe that it is an absolute submission of the enemy to the lawful authorities of the United States, and disperses his armies absolutely; and the point to which I attach most importance is, that the disposition and dispersement of the armies is done in such a manner as to prevent them breaking up into a guerrilla crew. On the other hand, we can retain just as much of an army as we please. I agree to the mode and manner of the surrender of armies set forth, as it gives the states the means of suppressing guerrillas, which we could not expect them to do if we strip them of all arms.

"Both Generals Johnston and Breckinridge admitted that slavery was dead, and I could not insist on embracing it in such a paper, because it can be made with the states in detail. I know that all the men of substance South sincerely want peace, and I do not believe they will resort to war again during this century. I have no doubt but that they will in the future be perfectly subordinate to the laws of the United States. The moment my action in this matter is approved, I can spare five corps, and will ask for and leave General Schofield here with the Tenth Corps, and go myself with the Fourteenth, Fifteenth, Seventeenth, Twentieth, and Twenty-third Corps, *via* Burkesville and Gordonsville, to Frederick or Hagerstown, there to be paid and mustered out.

"The question of finance is now the chief one, and every soldier and officer not needed ought to go home at once. I would like to be able to begin the march north by May 1st.

"I urge on the part of the President speedy action, as it is important to get the Confederate armies to their homes, as well as our own. I am, with great respect, your obedient servant,

"W. T. SHERMAN, Major General Commanding."

No. 2.

"Headquarters Military Department of the Mississippi, in the Field, Raleigh, N. C., April 18, 1865.

"General H. W. HALLECK, Chief of Staff, Washington, D.C.:

"GENERAL,—I received your dispatch describing the man Clark detailed to assassinate me. He had better be in a hurry or he will be too late. The news of Mr. Lincoln's death produced a most intense effect on our troops. At first I feared it would lead to excesses, but now it has softened down, and can easily be quieted. None evince more feeling than General Johnston, who admitted that the act was calculated to stain his cause with a dark hue; and he contended that the loss was most severe on the South, who had begun to realize that Mr. Lincoln was the best friend the South had.

"I can not believe that even Mr. Davis was privy to the diabolical plot, but think it the emanation of a lot of young men of the South, who are very devils. I want to throw upon the South the care of this class of men, who will soon be as obnoxious to their industrious class as to us.

"Had I pushed Johnston's army to an extremity, it would have dispersed and done infinite mischief. Johnston informed me that General Stoneman had been at Salisbury, and was now about Statesville. I have sent him orders to come to me.

"General Johnston also informed me that General Wilson was at Columbus, Ga., and he wanted me to arrest his progress. I leave that to you. Indeed, if the President sanctions my agreement with Johnston, our interest is to cease all destruction. Please give all orders necessary, according to the views the executive may take, and inform him, if possible, not to vary the terms at all, for I have considered every thing, and believe that the Confederate armies are dispersed. We can adjust all else fairly and well.

I am yours, etc.,

"W. T. SHERMAN, Major General Commanding."

[2] "*Terms of a Military Convention entered into this twenty-sixth (26th) day of April, 1865, at Bennett's House, near Durham's Station, North Carolina, between General Joseph E. Johnston, commanding the Confederate Army, and Major General W. T. Sherman, commanding the United States Army in North Carolina.*

"All acts of war on the part of the troops under General Johnston's command to cease from this date. All arms and public property to be deposited at Greensborough, and delivered to an ordnance officer of the United States army. Rolls of all officers and men to be made in duplicate, one copy to be retained by the commander of the troops, and the other to be given to an officer to be designated by General Sherman. Each officer and man to give his individual obligation in writing not to take up arms against the government of the United States until properly released from this obligation. The side-arms of officers, and their private horses and baggage, to be retained by them.

"This being done, all the officers and men will be permitted to return to their homes, not to be disturbed by the United States authorities so long as they observe their obligations and the laws in force where they may reside.

"W. T. SHERMAN, Major General Commanding the Army of the United States in North Carolina.

"J. E. JOHNSTON, General Commanding Confederate States Army in North Carolina.

"Approved: U. S. GRANT, Lieutenant General.

"Raleigh, N. C., April 26, 1865."

JAMES BENNETT'S HOUSE, WHERE JOHNSTON SURRENDERED.

The fact that only about 30,000 men and some 10,000 small-arms were included in the surrender shows that Johnston's apprehensions as to the scattering of his command were well founded.

The conduct of the lieutenant general in this affair between the government and Sherman was noble and characteristic. Unfortunately, some of the officers in the cabinet, in their treatment of General Sherman in this connection, were neither just nor generous. It was perfectly proper for the government to reject the basis of agreement between Sherman and Johnston. But the very reasons given for this repudiation, and which must have been published by official authority, the terms of the memorandum not having yet been made public, cast reflections upon General Sherman's patriotism. These reasons were thus reported in the newspapers of April 22d:

"1st. It was an exercise of authority not vested in General Sherman, and on its face shows that both he and Johnston knew that General Sherman had no authority to enter into any such arrangement.

"2d. It was an acknowledgment of the rebel government.

"3d. It is understood to re-establish rebel state governments that had been overthrown at the sacrifice of many thousands of loyal lives and immense treasure, and placed arms and munitions of war in the hands of rebels, at their respective capitals, which might be used as soon as the armies of the United States were disbanded, and used to conquer and subdue loyal states.

"4th. By the restoration of the rebel authority in their respective states, they would be enabled to re-establish slavery.

"5th. It might furnish a ground of responsibility, by the federal government, to pay the rebel debt, and certainly subjects loyal citizens of the rebel states to debts contracted by rebels in the name of the states.

"6th. It put in dispute the existence of loyal state governments, and the new State of Western Virginia, which had been recognized by every department of the United States government.

"7th. It practically abolished the confiscation laws, and relieved rebels of every degree who had slaughtered our people from all pains and penalties for their crimes.

"8th. It gave terms that had been deliberately, repeatedly, and solemnly rejected by President Lincoln, and better terms than the rebels had ever asked in their most prosperous condition.

"9th. It formed no basis of true and lasting peace, but relieved the rebels from the pressure of our victories, and left them in condition to renew their effort to overthrow the United States government, and subdue the loyal states, whenever their strength was recruited, and any opportunity should offer."

In the first place, the people were led to suppose that Sherman had actually usurped authority, which was not the case. The assertion that the memorandum in any way recognized the Confederate government was entirely without foundation. Nor did the memorandum re-establish Confederate state governments except in the same way that President Lincoln had re-established the state government of Virginia.[1] Indeed, Sharman had introduced this feature into his memorandum on the basis of President Lincoln's action in the case of Virginia. It was not until after the rejection of his own scheme that he heard that the invitation accorded to the Virginia Legislature had been retracted.

Again, the arms to be deposited in the state capitals were subject to the control of the United States, and it could only be through the fault of the government that they could be used in another rebellion.

There was not a word or phrase in the memorandum that indicated by the remotest suggestion the liability of the United States for the Confederate debt, or any thing which might be a basis for such liability. Nor did it acknowledge the legitimacy of the obligations of that debt as binding upon the citizens of the states which had incurred it. The recognition of the state governments in no way legalized their contracts made during the rebellion any more than it sanctioned their repudiation of debts due to Northern citizens.

Instead of putting in dispute the existence of West Virginia, the memorandum left that matter to be settled by proper authority. Nor was the Confiscation Bill passed by Congress in any way touched by the guarantee of the rights of person and property to Southern citizens, so far as such guarantee could be given by the executive, for the President is bound to execute the laws of Congress. It relieved no one of the penalty of their crimes any farther than Grant's terms with Lee had done.

The assertion that the memorandum was contrary to the policy of President Lincoln was so far from being true, that it was exactly false in every particular. And President Johnston's subsequent policy of reconstruction is a curious comment on his rejection of Sherman's memorandum.

The final reason given is simply absurd. If the memorandum left the Confederate armies in a favorable situation for a renewal of the war, pray where did it find those armies? It certainly did not inorease their efficiency

[1] On the 6th of April (three days before Lee's surrender), President Lincoln wrote to General Weitzel: "It has been intimated to me that the gentlemen who have acted as the Legislature of Virginia in support of the rebellion, may now desire to assemble at Richmond and take measures to withdraw the Virginia troops and other support from resistance to the general government. If they attempt it, give them permission and protection, until, if at all, they attempt some action hostile to the United States, in which case you will notify them, give them reasonable time to leave, and at the end of which time arrest any who remain. Allow Judge Campbell to see this, but do not make it public."

Thus authorized, General Weitzel approved a call for the meeting of the Virginia Legislature. This was after Lee's surrender. The call approved by General Weitzel read thus:

"The undersigned, members of the Legislature of the State of Virginia, in connection with a number of citizens of the state, whose names are attached to this paper, in view of the evacuation of the city of Richmond by the Confederate government and its occupation by the military authorities of the United States, the surrender of the Army of Northern Virginia, and the suspension of the jurisdiction of the civil power of the state, are of the opinion that an immediate meeting of the General Assembly of the state is called for by the exigencies of the situation. The consent of the military authorities of the United States to a session of the Legislature of Richmond, in connection with the governor and lieutenant governor, to their free deliberation upon the public affairs, and to the ingress and departure of all its members under safe-conduct, has been obtained.

"The United States authorities will afford transportation from any point under their control to any of the persons before mentioned.

"The matters to be submitted to the Legislature are the restoration of peace to the State of Virginia, and the adjustment of the questions involving life, liberty, and property, that have arisen in the state as a consequence of war.

"We therefore earnestly request the governor, lieutenant governor, and members of the Legislature to repair to this city by the 26th of April, instant.

"We understand that full protection to persons and property will be afforded in the state, and we recommend to peaceful citizens to remain at their homes and pursue their usual avocations with confidence that they will not be interrupted.

"We earnestly solicit the attendance in Richmond, on or before the 25th of April, instant, of the following persons, citizens of Virginia, to confer with us as to the best means of restoring peace to the State of Virginia. We have secured safe-conduct from the military authorities of the United States for them to enter the city and depart without molestation."

JOHNSTON'S SURRENDER.

by disbanding them, sending them home, and rendering their arms subject to the disposition of the United States.

The memorandum ought to have been rejected, on the ground that the subject of reconstruction could not be settled except by the deliberate action of the executive and Congress, and should not, therefore, be introduced in connection with the surrender of the Confederate armies. But the reasons for its rejection which were published then by official sanction not only had no validity, but almost seem to have been chosen for publication because of their reflections upon General Sherman.

On the same day that these reasons were published, Secretary Stanton telegraphed to General Dix:

"Yesterday evening a bearer of dispatches arrived here from General Sherman. An agreement for a suspension of hostilities, and a memorandum of what is called 'a basis of peace,' had been entered into on the 18th instant by General Sherman with the rebel General Johnston, the rebel General Breckinridge being present at the conference.

"A cabinet meeting was held at 8 o'clock in the evening, at which the action of General Sherman was disapproved by the President, by the Secretary of War, by General Grant, and by every member of the cabinet. General Sherman was ordered to resume hostilities immediately, and he was directed that the instructions given by the late president, in the following telegram, which was penned by Mr. Lincoln himself, at the Capitol, on the night of the 3d of March, were approved by President Andrew Johnson, and were reiterated to govern the action of military commanders.

"On the night of the 3d of March, while President Lincoln and his cabinet were at the Capitol, a telegram from General Grant was brought to the Secretary of War, informing him that General Lee had asked for a conference to make arrangements for terms of peace. The letter of General Lee was published in a message of Davis to the rebel Congress. General Grant's telegram was submitted to Mr. Lincoln, who, after pondering a few minutes, took up his pen, and wrote with his own hand the following reply, which he submitted to the Secretary of State and the Secretary of War. It was then dated, addressed, and signed by the Secretary of War, and telegraphed to General Grant:

"'Washington, March 3, 1865, 12 30 P.M.'

"'Lieutenant General GRANT:

"'The President directs me to say to you that he wishes you to have no conference with General Lee, unless it be for the capitulation of General Lee's army, or some minor and purely military matters. He instructs me to say you are not to decide or confer upon any political questions. Such questions the President holds in his own hands, and will submit them to no military conference or conditions. Meantime you are to press to the utmost your military advantages. EDWIN M. STANTON, Secretary of War.'

"The orders of General Sherman to General Stoneman to withdraw from Salisbury and join him, will probably open the way for Davis to escape to Mexico or Europe with his plunder, which is reported to be very large, including not only the plunder of the Richmond banks, but previous accumulations. A dispatch received by this department from Richmond says:

"'It is stated here by respectable parties that the amount of specie taken south by Jefferson Davis and his partisans is very large, including not only the plunder of the Richmond banks, but previous accumulations. They hope, it is said, to make terms with Sherman, or some other Southern commander, by which they will be permitted, with their effects, including the gold plunder, to go to Mexico or Europe. Johnston's negotiations look to this end.'

"After the cabinet meeting last night, General Grant started for North Carolina, to direct future operations against Johnston's army."

This telegram was sent to General Dix for the purpose of publication. It would have been courteous in the secretary to have withheld this report until the circumstances under which Sherman had acted were more fully known. In the first place, it was implied, though not stated, that the same instructions had been received by Sherman which, on the 3d of March, had been addressed to the lieutenant general. This would naturally be inferred exposed, for a time at least, to a suspicion of disobedience of orders. But Sherman had not received these instructions. The statement that Grant had gone to North Carolina to direct future operations against Johnston's army was also likely to be misunderstood. Grant had gone to Raleigh to communicate to General Sherman the action of the government in regard to the memorandum. Of course, if more than that was necessary, Grant would do more. As lieutenant general, he directed the operations of all the national armies. Any instructions from Secretary Stanton could give him no power which he had not before. But he never for a moment contemplated the necessity of interference with, or personal direction of, Sherman's movements—and, in fact, did not interfere or direct. Unfortunately, Stanton's dispatch implied, and was popularly understood to imply, that Grant's presence at Raleigh was necessary.

But the matter did not end here. On the 26th of April, General Halleck, then at Richmond in command of the Military Division of the James, dispatched to Secretary Stanton that he had ordered Generals Meade, Sheridan, and Wright to move into Sherman's proper department, and pay no regard to either the orders or truce of the latter. He also advised that Sherman's own subordinates should receive similar orders. The pretext given for moving into Sherman's department was "to cut off Johnston's retreat." Now Johnston was not retreating, and could not retreat if he would, on account of the disposition which Sherman had already made of his forces.

This dispatch also was sent by Stanton to Dix for publication. A few hours later the public was informed through the same channel that the Secretary of War had instructed General Thomas, and, through him, his subcommanders, to disregard Sherman's orders. These bulletins, succeeding each other with such rapidity, excited at once serious apprehension and a tumult of indignation. Every body read and wondered. What had Sherman been doing? Had he allied himself with traitors? Could he no longer be trusted? For a time some terrible danger was supposed to hang like the sword of Damocles over the republic. It did not seem possible that the government could itself thus excite popular apprehension without good reason. Where orders were given to violate a truce—an act punishable with death by the laws of war—certainly there must be some peril impending which could only thus be averted. For a brief period a storm of denunciation was directed against General Sherman. And while all this was going on in the North, it must be remembered that Sherman was accepting Johnston's surrender, and that not one word had been said or written to him indicating the displeasure of the government.[1] He received the announcement of the rejection of the memorandum with entire good feeling. He wrote to Stanton on the 25th admitting his "folly in embracing in a military convention any civil matters." He adds: "I had flattered myself that, by four years of patient, unremitting, and successful labor, I deserved no reminder such as is contained in the last paragraph of your letter to General Grant."[2] It was not until several days afterward that Sherman saw Stanton's bulletins, and then his indignation was aroused, especially against Halleck, with whom he refused to have any friendly intercourse.[3]

[1] The following were the instructions which Grant received from Stanton when he started for Raleigh, and which were there shown to General Sherman:

"GENERAL,—The memorandum or basis agreed upon between General Sherman and General Johnston having been submitted to the President, they are disapproved. You will give notice of the disapproval to General Sherman, and direct him to resume hostilities at the earliest moment.

"The instructions given to you by the late President, Abraham Lincoln, on the 3d of March, by my telegram of that date addressed to you, express substantially the views of President Andrew Johnson, and will be observed by General Sherman. A copy is herewith appended.

"The President desires that you proceed immediately to the headquarters of General Sherman, and direct operations against the enemy."

[2] See previous note.

[3] The following extract from General Sherman's report shows the manner in which he regarded the treatment which he had received:

"On the evening of the 2d of May I returned to Hilton Head, and there, for the first time, received the New York papers of April 28th, containing Secretary Stanton's dispatch of 9 A.M. of the 27th of April to General Dix, including General Halleck's, from Richmond, of 9 P.M. of the night before, which seems to have been rushed with extreme haste before an excited public, namely, morning of the 28th. You will observe from the dates that these dispatches were running back and forth from Richmond and Washington to New York, and there published, while General Grant and I were together in Raleigh, North Carolina, adjusting, to the best of our ability, the terms of surrender of the only remaining formidable rebel army in existence at the time east of the Mississippi River. Not one word of intimation had been sent to me of the displeasure of the government with my official conduct, but only the naked disapproval of a skeleton memorandum sent properly for the action of the President of the United States.

"The most objectionable features of my memorandum had already (April 24th) been published to the world in violation of official usage, and the contents of my accompanying letters to General Halleck, General Grant, and Mr. Stanton, of even date, though at hand, were suppressed.

"In all these letters I had stated clearly and distinctly that Johnston's army would *not* fight; but, if pushed, would 'disband' and 'scatter' into small and dangerous guerrilla parties, as injurious to the interests of the United States as to the rebels themselves; that all parties admitted that the rebel cause of the South was abandoned, that the negro was free, and that the temper of all was most favorable to a lasting peace. I say all these opinions of mine were withheld from the public with a seeming purpose; and I do contend that my official experience and former services, as well as my past life and familiarity with the people and geography of the South, entitled my opinions to at least a decent respect.

"Although this dispatch (Mr. Stanton's of April 27th) was printed 'official,' it had come to me only in the questionable newspaper paragraph headed 'Sherman's Truce Disregarded.'

"I had already done what General Wilson wanted me to do, namely, had sent him supplies of clothing and food, with clear and distinct orders and instructions how to carry out in Western Georgia the terms for the surrender of arms and paroling of prisoners made by General Johnston's capitulation of April 26th, and had properly and most opportunely ordered General Gillmore to occupy Orangeburg and Augusta, strategic points of great value at all times, in peace or war; but, as the secretary had taken upon himself to order my subordinate generals to disobey my 'orders,' I explained to General Gillmore that I would no longer confuse him or General Wilson with 'orders' that might conflict with those of the secretary, which, as reported, were sent, not through me, but in open disregard of me and of my lawful authority.

"It now becomes my duty to paint in justly severe character the still more offensive and dangerous matter of General Halleck's dispatch of April 26th to the Secretary of War, embodied in his to General Dix of April 27th:

"General Halleck had been chief of staff of the army at Washington, in which capacity he must have received my official letter of April 18th, wherein I wrote clearly that if Johnston's army about Greensborough were 'pushed,' it would 'disperse,' an event I wished to prevent. About that time he seems to have been sent from Washington to Richmond to command the new Military Division of the James, in assuming charge of which, on the 22d, he defines the limits of his authority to be the 'Department of Virginia, the Army of the Potomac, and such part of North Carolina as may not be occupied by the command of Major General Sherman.' (See his General Orders, No. 1.) Four days later, April 26th, he reports to the secretary that he has ordered Generals Meade, Sheridan,

SMALL-ARMS SURRENDERED BY JOHNSTON.

ACCOUTREMENTS SURRENDERED BY JOHNSTON.

The surrender of Johnston included all the Confederate forces east of the Chattahoochee River, numbering altogether about 50,000 men. On the 4th of May Dick Taylor surrendered to General Canby all the remaining Confederate forces east of the Mississippi. On the 26th of May Kirby Smith surrendered his army. The war was concluded.

CHAPTER LIX.

FLIGHT AND CAPTURE OF DAVIS.

A memorable Sabbath.—Davis receives a startling Message.—Richmond must be abandoned.—Panic in the City.—Davis, with his Cabinet, fly by night.—Incidents of the Journey.—Danville enjoys a brief Celebrity as the Capital of the Confederacy.—Semmes's Marine Guard.—Trenholm's Treasury Department.—Davis's Proclamation to his People.—Tidings of Lee's Surrender.—Evacuation of Danville.—The Flight resumed.—Interview with Johnston at Greensborough.—The Confederacy in a Railroad Car.—Dispersion of the Cabinet.—Flight through Georgia.—General Wilson's Arrangements for the Capture of Davis.—Harnden gets upon the Track of the Fugitives.—Close Pursuit.—Pritchard anticipates Harnden, and captures the Confederate Party near Irwinsville, Georgia.—Incidents connected with the Capture.—General Wilson's Report.

WE now turn back to that memorable Sabbath—April 2, 1865—which suddenly disclosed to the Confederate capital its inevitable fate. The battle of Five Forks had been fought on Saturday, and its loss by the Confederates involved the woful necessity of evacuating Richmond. The disaster was unknown in Richmond except to Davis and his cabinet, and even these had no full knowledge of the situation, having no other intimation of what had happened than what was contained in a brief but ominous telegram received early in the morning from General Lee. The President and his cabinet, with the exception of J. P. Benjamin, who was an Israelite, were all at their respective places of worship at the usual hour of morning service. Davis was at St. Paul's, looking care-worn, but still confident. Mallory attended mass at St. Peter's. Reagan was at the Baptist church. Benjamin was probably enjoying his pipe on the veranda of his mansion in Main Street.

During the service at St. Paul's the sexton walked up to Davis's pew, and whispered a few words in the ear of the President. Another dispatch had come, and his presence was wanted immediately. The members of the cabinet received a similar call. Thus, from church to church, the note of warning was communicated, and those who were only spectators were agitated with apprehensions which were certainly not less fearful because they were based upon no definite information. The dispatch which met Mr. Davis at the door of St. Paul's conveyed to him intelligence of a startling character. That morning the outer defenses of Petersburg had been carried. A single interior line still resisted Grant's approach, but that could be held but a few hours longer. In the mean time, both Petersburg and Richmond must be evacuated. By two o'clock every body in Richmond knew that the city was to be abandoned, and a scene of dismay and confusion followed. Already the orders had been issued for the removal of the archives of the government, and for the destruction of stores for which there was no transportation. This must be completed by 7 o'clock P.M., and by 8 the military and civil authorities of the capital were to meet Davis at the Danville dépôt. By the railroad to Danville a way of escape was still open, but how long it would continue open was uncertain.

The panic in the city was almost universal. The negroes alone were jolly, and they worked with a hearty good will to help off as much of the Confederacy as they could. But, while these were placid and satisfied, nearly all others were either helpless with consternation, or were preparing to leave the city without exactly knowing where they were going. All the coaches in Richmond were waiting at the doors of private houses, and, as the afternoon wore away, the streets were filled with voluntary exiles. Of course there was transportation for a very small fraction of those who crowded toward the dépôt. The rest were compelled to return to the pandemonium from which they could not escape. The presidential party with difficulty made its way through the excited crowd which thronged and blocked the streets. At the dépôt the scramblers were concentrated in an almost impenetrable mass, which was kept back from the platform only by military force. Davis and his cabinet took their seats in a close car. Among this party were Adjutant General Samuel Cooper and a few other military officers. In an adjoining car were the heads of bureaus. A privileged few were admitted to fill up the train. In a car between the engine and that occupied by Davis was a guard of 200 picked men. The principal Confederate officers were spurred, and horses were ready for them in another car in case of an emergency. At 10 o'clock the train left the dépôt, leaving immediately behind it indescribable tumult, and further behind in the city an uncontrollable mob, which had already begun to sack the city. When Weitzel entered Richmond the next morning he found the city in flames.

Very soon the fugitive Confederacy—for it was all crowded into this train—*ubi Davis ibi Confederatio*—was beyond observation of the havoc it had left behind in the doomed city. To Davis and his fellow-conspirators the events of the last few hours must have seemed like a dream. Twenty-four hours ago Richmond was deemed an impregnable fortress. For four years it had been the Confederate capital, and had withstood five separate attempts made by large armies for its capture, and had, during a siege of nine months, repulsed every assault made upon Petersburg, its outpost. Several times its doom had been anticipated, but the fatal day had been so long postponed, it was thought that day might never come. Davis and his confederates, under as calm a sky as ever overarched Virginia, on this night of disaster vigorously rubbed their eyes, but could not escape the reality of the fate of Richmond or of their own flight. In a few hours the national flag would float over the rebel capital, and as to themselves the immediate future was misty and dark. But the dream of empire is not easily dissipated. Davis was troubled; but he did not yet despair. The hope and consolation which he had administered to his followers after the loss of Vicksburg and Atlanta he now whispered to his own agitated soul after the fall of Richmond. His capital was gone, but he said to himself, "All is not lost," and even as he fled he dreamed of newly-mustered armies that should rise at his bidding. Davis was not a matter-of-fact man. Probably no man was ever called to hold so important a position as he had held who had less appreciation of facts or knowledge of men. He did not reflect upon the actual circumstances of his present situation. He never asked himself whence these armies of his imagination were to come. He forgot that, if marshaled at all, their ranks must be filled with the old and the decrepit, beardless boys, and Southern amazons. His determination outran his judgment and transgressed common sense. He could only understand fate when he was crushed by her final blow.

any orders save those of Lieutenant General Grant, and cut off Johnston's retreat.' He knew at the time he penned that dispatch and made out those orders that Johnston was not retreating, but was halted under a forty-eight hours' truce with me, and was laboring to surrender his command and prevent its dispersion into guerrilla bands, and that I had on the spot a magnificent army at my command, amply sufficient for all purposes required by the occasion.

"The plan for cutting off a retreat from the direction of Burkesville and Danville is hardly worthy one of his military education and genius. When he contemplated an act so questionable as the violation of a 'truce' made by competent authority within his sphere of command, he should have gone himself and not sent subordinates, for he knew I was bound in honor to defend and maintain my own truce and pledge of faith, even at the cost of many lives.

"When an officer pledges the faith of his government, he is bound to defend it, and he is no soldier who would violate it knowingly.

"As to Davis and his stolen treasure, did General Halleck, as chief of staff or commanding officer of the neighboring military division, notify me of the facts contained in his dispatch to the secretary? No, he did not. If the Secretary of War wanted Davis caught, why not order it, instead of, by publishing it in the newspapers, putting him on his guard to hide away and escape? No orders or instructions to catch Davis or his stolen treasure ever came to me; but, on the contrary, I was led to believe that the Secretary of War rather preferred he should effect an escape from the country, if made 'unknown' to him. But even on this point I inclose a copy of my letter to Admiral Dahlgren, at Charleston, sent him by a fleet steamer from Wilmington, on the 25th of April, two days before the bankers of Richmond had imparted to General Halleck the important secret as to Davis's movement, designed doubtless to stimulate his troops to march their legs off to catch their treasure for their own use.

"I know now that Admiral Dahlgren did receive my letter on the 26th, and had acted on it before General Halleck had even thought of the matter; but I do not believe a word of the treasure story—it is absurd on its face—and General Halleck or any body has my full permission to chase Jeff. Davis and cabinet with their stolen treasure through any part of the country occupied by my command.

"The last and most obnoxious feature of General Halleck's dispatch is wherein he goes out of his way and advises that my subordinates, Generals Thomas, Stoneman, and Wilson, should be instructed not to obey 'Sherman's' commands.

"This is too much; and I turn from the subject with feelings too strong for words, and merely record my belief that so much mischief was never before embraced in so small a space as in the newspaper paragraph headed 'Sherman's Truce Disregarded,' authenticated as 'official' by Mr. Secretary Stanton, and published in the New York papers of April 28th."

After a ride of 23 miles the train stopped abreast of Petersburg. Here Breckinridge left the party to go to Lee's headquarters. Then the flight was resumed. Benjamin was soon asleep, and Mallory followed his example. Whether Davis slept or not there is no chronicler to tell us, but, whether asleep or awake, he still dreamed of the impossible. Burkesville was reached shortly after daybreak. As the train approached Danville, the question of destination for the first time began to be discussed. Hitherto the only concern of the party had been to get beyond the reach of Sheridan's cavalry. Where was the new capital to be established? Davis expressed his determination to cling to Virginia to the last, and, after some discussion, Danville was honored with all the glory which had departed from Richmond. It was a small town, incapable of receiving the full weight of honor which had been thrust upon it, and it was accordingly settled that the subordinate officials should proceed to Charlotte, North Carolina.

The fugitives were received with great hospitality at Danville, and on the 4th of April they began to establish the new seat of government. Trenholm opened the Treasury at one of the banks, and delighted the citizens of Danville by dispensing silver in return for Confederate notes, one dollar for seventy. In two days $40,000 in coin was disposed of in this way. Eligible structures were impressed for the other departments. Admiral Semmes organized a brigade of marines for the defense of the new capital, and mounted guns on all the hills about the town. Thousands of fugitives had followed the President from Richmond in subsequent trains, and all the able-bodied men among these were armed with muskets and pressed into the service.

On the 5th Davis issued a proclamation to his people. He announced that General Lee had been compelled to make movements which uncovered Richmond, the loss of which had, he admitted, inflicted moral and material injury upon the Confederate cause. But the energies of the people must not falter, nor their efforts be relaxed. Lee's army—"the largest and the finest in the Confederacy"—had been for months trammeled by the necessity of protecting Richmond. "It is for us, my countrymen," he urged, "to show, by our bearing under reverses, how wretched has been the self-deception of those who have believed us less able to endure misfortune with fortitude than to encounter dangers with courage. We have now entered upon a new phase of the struggle. Relieved from the necessity of guarding particular points, our army will be free to move from point to point, to strike the enemy in detail far from his base. Let us but will it, and we are free. Animated by that confidence in spirit and fortitude which never yet failed me, I announce to you, fellow-countrymen, that it is my purpose to maintain your cause with my whole heart and soul; that I will never consent to abandon to the enemy one foot of the soil of any one of the states of the Confederacy. That Virginia—noble state—whose ancient renown has been eclipsed by her still more glorious recent history; whose bosom has been bared to receive the main shock of this war; whose sons and daughters have exhibited heroism so sublime as to render her illustrious in all time to come—that Virginia, with the help of the people and by the blessing of Providence, shall be held and defended, and no peace ever be made with the infamous invaders of her territory. If by the stress of numbers we should ever be compelled to a temporary withdrawal from her limits, or those of any other border state, again and again will we return, until the baffled and exhausted enemy shall abandon in despair his endless and impossible task of making slaves of a people resolved to be free. Let us, then, not despond, my countrymen; but, relying on God, meet the foe with fresh defiance, and with unconquered and unconquerable hearts."

Brave words, but vain, uttered in the face of defeat, and falling upon the ears like the sound of the droppings of dust upon numberless graves, to be filled by a useless strife which could have no other name but murder! The words of this proclamation could not reach the ears of Davis's "countrymen" before events, already near their consummation, would expose their ludicrous insignificance. For three whole days Davis had not heard one word of tidings from General Lee or his army. This suspense continued until the 10th, and then came the startling intelligence that Lee had been defeated, and had surrendered his army. Then at Danville, on a diminished scale, was repeated the scene which had been witnessed eight days before at Richmond. The new capital was abandoned amid just such tumult as had attended the evacuation of Richmond. Narrowly escaping a raiding party, the presidential train reached Greensborough, North Carolina, on the 11th, bearing with it the disastrous tidings. Here Johnston and Beauregard met Davis. Breckinridge soon arrived with the details of Lee's surrender. The four officers then held a consultation on the slope of a hill where Nat. Green, of Revolutionary memory, had held his council of war the night before the battle of Guilford Court-house. Davis thought the struggle ought to be continued, and even ordered Johnston to fight. That general, however, did not agree with him, and refused obedience. Davis was powerless. He distrusted Johnston, and left Breckinridge with him to foil any movement which he might make to the prejudice of the Confederate cause. How Johnston acted afterward has already been told in these pages.

The people of Greensborough, unlike those of Danville, did not recognize the presence of the Confederate chief, or tender to him any offer of hospitality. The Confederacy was, therefore, now cooped up in a railroad car! On the 14th it left inhospitable Greensborough, uncertain of its destination, but too painfully conscious of the gad-fly Necessity, which urged it to "move on." A good part of the way to Charlotte was passed in wagons. At the latter place the news of Johnston's surrender and Lincoln's murder reached the fugitives. Here Breckinridge rejoined the party. From this point Davis threw off the semblance of authority which he had partially sustained thus far. The movement of the entire party was henceforth simply a flight. Davis now conceived the idea of reaching Texas. With his cabinet and staff, he left Charlotte under a cavalry escort of 2000 men. On the way to the Catawba River, Trenholm, the Secretary of the Treasury, and George Davis, attorney general, resigned their positions, and left the President to his fate. The flight was continued through Abbeville, South Carolina, Washington, Georgia, and then past Milledgeville and Macon southward, as if making for the coast of Florida. No one showed respect to the ruined President. Benjamin left the party before it reached Washington, and Mallory soon afterward. Breckinridge also broke away, and only Reagan was left of the whole cabinet.

Davis had started from Charlotte shortly after the expiration of the truce made between Johnston and Sherman. Preparations on an extensive scale were then made for his capture by General Wilson. Stoneman's three brigades—Brown's, Miller's, and Palmer's—then in Western North Carolina, were ordered to start in pursuit. These forces were commanded by General Palmer in Gillem's absence. They succeeded in crossing the Savannah River in Davis's front, and thus cut off his retreat toward the Mississippi. Wilson's cavalry was stretched over the whole country, from Kingston in Georgia to Tallahassee in Florida. In the mean time, also, a reward of $100,000 had been offered by President Johnson for the apprehension of Davis, as an accomplice of Booth in the assassination of Lincoln. Stoneman's and Wilson's cavalry now formed a network through whose meshes Davis could hardly hope to escape.

On the evening of May 7th, four days after Davis left Washington, Lieutenant Colonel Henry Harnden, of the First Wisconsin Cavalry—belonging to Wilson's command—ascertained at Dublin, on the Oconee, that during the day the fugitives had crossed the river, and were moving on the Jacksonville Road. Harnden followed close the next day, and at night reached the camp which had four hours before been occupied by Davis between the forks of Alligator Creek. He pursued the trail to Gum Swamp Creek, and there encamped for the night. On the 9th he pushed on to the Ocmulgee, crossed at Brown's Ferry, and at Abbeville learned that Davis had left that place at one o'clock that morning, and was now on the way to Irwinsville. Colonel Pritchard, of the Fourth Michigan Cavalry—also belonging to Wilson's command—had by this time reached Abbeville, and, taking a more direct route than was followed by Harnden's detachment, reached Irwinsville at two A.M. on the 10th, where he learned that Davis was encamped about a mile from the town, on another road leading to Abbeville. Sending a part of his force to the north to intercept Davis's return to Abbeville, he cautiously approached the camp from both sides, completely cutting off all escape. At daylight he surprised the encampment, and captured Davis, with his family, Postmaster General Reagan, two aid-de-camps, Davis's private secretary, four other officers, and eleven soldiers. Various details have been published in connection with the capture of the Confederate President. It was reported, soon after the event, that Davis was captured in female attire, and a recent official report by General Wilson confirms the report.[1]

---

[1] General Wilson's report here referred to is dated January 17, 1867, and gives the following details of the capture of Davis:

"The first direct information which I received of Davis's movements was on the 23d or 24th of April, from a citizen who had seen him at Charlotte, N. C., only three or four days before, and had learned that he was on his way, with a train and an escort of cavalry, to the South, intending to go to the trans-Mississippi Department. This information was regarded as entirely reliable, and hence the officers in charge of the different detachments afterward sent out were directed to dispose of their commands so as to have all roads and crossings vigilantly watched. It was thought at first that Davis would call about him a select force, and endeavor to escape by marching to the westward through the hilly country of Northern Georgia. To prevent this, Colonel Eggleston was directed to watch the country in all directions from Atlanta. Brevet Brigadier General A. J. Alexander, with the second brigade of Upton's division, having reached Atlanta in advance of the division, was directed by General Winslow to scout the country to the northward as far as Dalton, or until he should meet the troops under General Steedman in that region. On beginning his march from Macon, General Alexander was authorized to detach an officer and twenty picked men, disguised as rebel soldiers, for the purpose of trying to obtain definite information of Davis's movements. This party was placed under the command of Lieutenant Joseph O. Yoeman, First Ohio Cavalry, and at the time acting inspector general of the brigade. Verbal instructions were also given to other brigade and division commanders to make similar detachments. General Croxton was directed to send a small party toward Talladega, by the route upon which he had marched from that place, while Colonel Eggleston was directed to send a party by rail to West Point. By these means it was believed that all considerable detachments of rebels would be apprehended, and that such information might be obtained as would enable us to secure the principal rebel leaders if they should undertake to pass through the country in any other way than as individual fugitives.

"In declaring the armistice of Sherman null and void, the Secretary of War had directed that my command should resume active operations and endeavor to arrest the fugitive rebel chiefs. I accordingly notified him and General Thomas by telegraph of the dispositions I had made, and that I had no doubt of accomplishing the desired object; but having forwarded the records of my command to the Adjutant General's Department, as required by army regulations, and having been denied copies of the documents relating to these matters, I can not now fix the exact dates of these dispatches.

"After a rapid march toward the upper crossings of the Savannah River, in Northwestern Georgia, Lieutenant Yoeman's detachment met and joined Davis's party, escorted by Debrill and Ferguson's divisions of cavalry, probably under Wheeler in person, and continued with them several days, watching for an opportunity to seize and carry off the rebel chief. He was frustrated by the vigilance of the rebel escort. At Washington, Ga., the rebel authorities must have heard that Atlanta was occupied by our troops, and that they could not pass that point without a fight. They halted, and for a short time acted with irresolution in regard to their future course. The cavalry force which had remained true to Davis, estimated at five brigades, and probably numbering two thousand men, now became mutinous, and declined to go any farther. They were disbanded and partially paid off in coin which had been brought to that point in wagons. Lieutenant Yoeman lost sight of Davis at this time, but, dividing his party into three or four detachments, sought again to obtain definite information of his movements, but for twenty-four hours was unsuccessful. Persevering in his efforts, he became convinced that Davis had relinquished his idea of going into Alabama, and would probably try to reach the Gulf or South Atlantic coast and escape by sea. Couriers were sent with this information to General Alexander, and by him duly transmitted to me at Macon. The same conclusion had already been forced upon me by information derived from various other sources, and from the nature of the case it seemed quite probable. With railroad communication through most of Northern Georgia, and with a division of four thousand national cavalry operating about Atlanta, it would have been next to impossible for a party of fugitives, however small, to traverse that region by the ordinary roads. This must have been clear to the rebels. From these circumstances I became convinced that Davis would either flee in disguise and unattended, or endeavor to work his way southward into Florida. With the view of intercepting him in this attempt, I directed the crossings of the Ocmulgee River to be watched with renewed vigilance all the way from the neighborhood of Atlanta to Hawkinsville, and on the evening of May 6th I directed Brigadier General Croxton to select the best regiment in his division and send it, under its best officer, with orders to march eastward, via Jeffersonville, to Dublin, on the Oconee River, with the greatest possible speed, scouting the country well to the northward, and leaving detachments at the most important cross-roads with instructions to keep a sharp look-out for all detachments of rebels. By these means it was hoped that Davis's line of march would be intersected and his

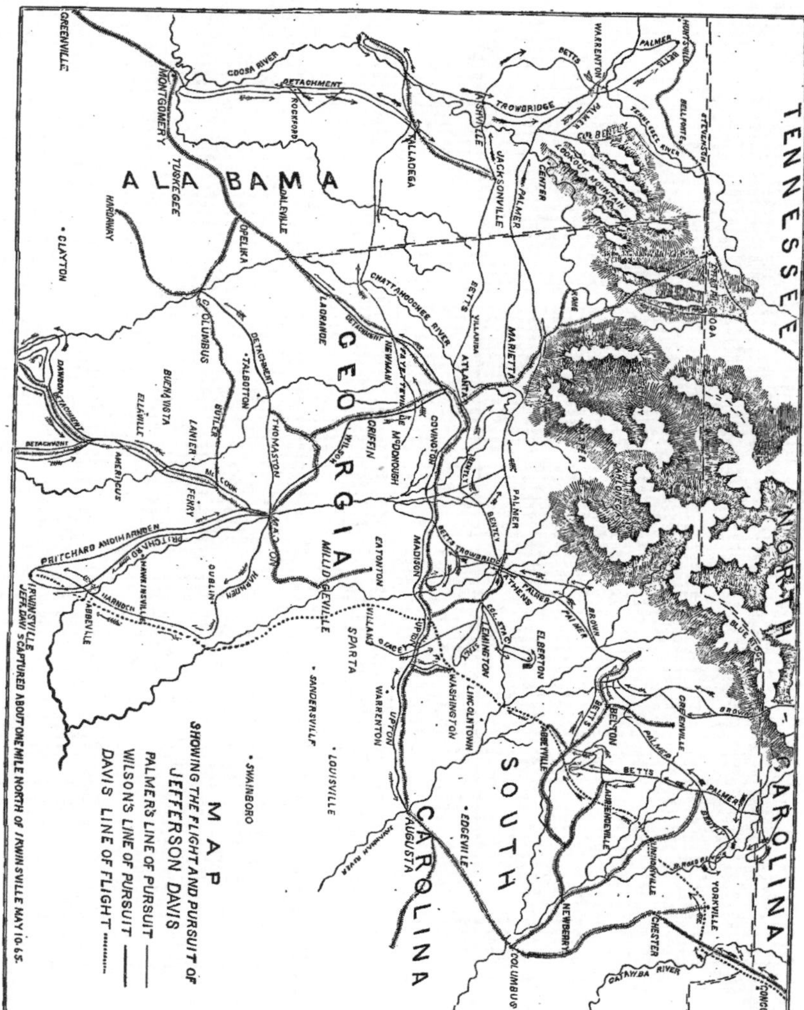
MAP
SHOWING THE FLIGHT AND PURSUIT OF
JEFFERSON DAVIS
PALMER'S LINE OF PURSUIT
WILSON'S LINE OF PURSUIT
DAVIS LINE OF FLIGHT
IRWINSVILLE
JEFF. DAVIS CAPTURED ABOUT ONE MILE NORTH OF IRWINSVILLE MAY 10-65.
TENNESSEE
NORTH CAROLINA
SOUTH CAROLINA
GEORGIA
ALABAMA

About the same time Alexander H. Stephens and Secretary Mallory were captured by other portions of General Wilson's command. Before the close of the month Davis was confined in Fortress Monroe, where he remained for two years, subject to trial. He was indicted for treason, but the trial was postponed time after time, and at length he was released upon bail of $100,000, exactly the same amount which was awarded to his captors. The Confederate Vice-President A. H. Stephens was also confined for a brief period in Fort Warren, Boston Harbor.

Thus closed at once the official and military career of the Confederacy.

movements discovered, in which event the commanding officer was instructed to follow it, wherever it might lead, until the fugitives should be overtaken and captured. General Croxton selected for this purpose the First Wisconsin Cavalry, commanded by Lieutenant Colonel Henry Harnden, an officer of spirit, experience, and resolution. During that day and the next the conviction that Davis would try to escape into Florida became so strong that I sent for General Minty, commanding the Second Division, and in person directed him to select his best regiment, and order it to march without delay to the southeastward along the right bank of the Ocmulgee River, watching all the crossings between Hawkinsville and the mouth of the Ohoopee River. In case of discovering the trail of the fugitives, they were directed to follow it to the Gulf coast, or till they should overtake and capture the party of whom they were in pursuit. General Minty selected for this purpose his own regiment, the Fourth Michigan Cavalry, commanded by Lieutenant Colonel Benjamin D. Pritchard, an excellent and dashing officer. In the mean time General Upton, at Augusta, had sent me a dispatch advising me to offer a reward of $100,000 for the capture of Davis, urging that the Secretary of War would approve my action, and that it would induce even the rebels to assist in making the capture. Not caring, however, to assume the responsibility of committing the government in this way, I authorized him to issue a proclamation offering a reward of $100,000, to be paid out of such money as might be found in the possession of Davis or his party. This was done, and copies scattered throughout the country as early as the 6th of May.

"As soon as it was known at Atlanta that Davis's cavalry escort had disbanded, General Alexander, with five hundred picked men and horses of his command, crossed to the right or northern bank of the Chattahoochee River, occupied all the fords west of the Atlanta and Chattanooga Railroad, watched the passes of the Altoona Mountains and the main crossings of the Etowah River, and with various detachments of his small command patrolled all the main roads in that region day and night, until he received news of Davis's capture in another quarter.

"The final disposition of my command may be described as follows: Major General Upton, with parts of two regiments, occupied Augusta, and kept a vigilant watch over the country in that vicinity, and informed me by telegraph of every thing important which came under his observation. General Winslow, with the larger part of that division, occupied Atlanta, and scouted the country in all directions from that place. General Alexander, with five hundred picked men, patroled the country north of the Chattahoochee, while detachments occupied Griffin and Jonesboro, closely watching the crossings of the Ocmulgee, and scouting the country to the eastward. Colonel Eggleston, commanding the post of Atlanta, had also sent a detachment to West Point, to watch the Alabama line in that quarter.

"General Croxton, with the main body of the First Division in the vicinity of Macon, had sent a detachment under my direction to the mountain region of Alabama, marching by the way of Carrolton to Talladega, and another through Northeastern Georgia toward North Carolina, and was also engaged in watching the Ocmulgee from the right of the Fourth Division to Macon, and in scouting the country to his front and rear. General Minty, commanding the Second Division, was scouring the country to the southeast, watching the lower crossings of the Ocmulgee, and had small parties at all the important points on the Southwestern Railroad, and in Western and Southwestern Georgia. Detachments of the Seventh Pennsylvania Cavalry occupied Cuthbert, Eufaula, Columbus, and Bainbridge, and kept a vigilant watch over the Lower Flint and Chattahoochee. While General McCook, with a detachment of his division at Albany, and 700 men between there and Tallahassee, Florida, was scouting the country to the north and eastward, we also had rail and telegraphic communication from my headquarters at Macon with Atlanta, Augusta, West Point, Milledgeville, Albany, and Eufaula. By inspecting the map herewith it will be seen that my force of nearly 15,000 cavalry, well mounted and vigilant, were occupying a well-defined and almost continuous line from Kingston, Georgia, to Tallahassee, Florida, with detachments and scouts well out in all directions to the front and rear. From this it will be difficult to perceive how Davis and his party could possibly have hoped to escape.

"From the time they were reported at Charlotte till their final capture I was kept informed of their general movements, and was enabled thereby to dispose of my command in such a manner as to render the capture morally certain. As reported by General Winslow, rumors came in from all directions, but by carefully weighing them, the truth became sufficiently manifest to enable me to act with confidence. It is to be regretted now, however, that the hurry of events precluded the use of written orders. In nearly every instance my instructions were given verbally to the division commanders, and by them, in turn, transmitted verbally to their subordinates. Such written dispatches and orders as were given are preserved in the records pertaining to the cavalry corps, Military Division of the Mississippi, now on file in the Adjutant General's office.

"In pursuance of my instructions to General Croxton, heretofore recited, Lieutenant Colonel Henry Harnden, with three officers and one hundred and fifty men of the First Wisconsin Cavalry, left Macon, Ga., on the evening of May 6, 1865, and marched rapidly via Jeffersonville toward Dublin, on the Oconee River. At Jeffersonville Colonel Harnden left one officer and thirty men, with orders to scout the country in all directions for reliable information as to Davis's flight. With the balance of his command he continued the march all night, and the next day, about seven P.M., reached Dublin. During the night and day he had sent out scouts and small parties on all the side roads, in the hope of finding the trail of the party for whom he was looking. Nothing of importance occurred until after he had bivouacked for the night. The white inhabitants of that place expressed entire ignorance and indifference in regard to the movement of important rebels, but were unusually profuse in their offers of hospitality to Colonel Harnden. This, together with the conduct of the colored servants, excited his suspicions, though he gained no valuable intelligence till about midnight, at which time he was informed by a negro man, who went to his camp for that purpose, that Davis, with his wife and family, had passed through Dublin that day, going south on the river road. The negro reported that the party in question had eight wagons with them, and that another party had gone southward on the other side of the Oconee River. His information seems to have been of the most explicit and circumstantial character. He had heard the lady called 'Mrs. Davis,' and a gentleman spoken of as 'President Davis,' and said that Mr. Davis had not crossed the river at the regular ferry with the rest of the party, but had gone about three miles lower down, and crossed on a small flat-boat, and rejoined the party with the wagons near the outskirts of the town, and that they had all gone toward the south together. The colored man reported Mr. Davis as mounted on a fine bay horse, and told his story so circumstantially that Colonel Harnden could not help believing it. The ferryman was called up and examined, but, either through stupidity or design, succeeded in withholding whatever he knew in regard to the case. But in view of the facts already elicited, after detailing Lieutenant Lane and sixty men to remain at Dublin, and to scout the country in all directions, Colonel Harnden, at an early hour in the morning, began the pursuit of the party just mentioned. Five miles south of Dublin he obtained information from a woman which left him no room to doubt that he was on the track of Davis in person. He dispatched a messenger to inform General Croxton of his good fortune, and pushed rapidly in pursuit. The trail led southward through a region of pine forests and cypress swamps, almost uninhabited, and therefore affording no food for either men or horses. The rain began to fall, and, as there was no road, the tracks of the wagon-wheels upon the sandy soil were soon obliterated. A citizen was pressed, and compelled to act as guide till the trail was again discovered. The pursuit was continued with renewed vigor, but as the wagon-tracks were again lost in the waters of the swamp bordering on Alligator Creek, the pursuing party were again delayed till a citizen could be found to guide them to the road upon which the trail was again visible. Colonel Harnden reports this day to have been one of great toil both to men and horses; they had marched forty miles through an almost trackless forest, much of the way under the rain, and in water up to their saddle-girths. They bivouacked after dark on the borders of Gum Swamp, and during the night were again drenched with rain. Before daylight of the 9th they renewed their march, their route leading almost southwest through swamp and wilderness to Brown's Ferry, where they crossed to the south side of the Ocmulgee River. In his anxiety to ferry his command over rapidly, Colonel Harnden allowed the boat to be overloaded; a plank near the bow was sprung loose, causing the boat to leak badly, and, as no means were at hand with which to make repairs, lighter boat-loads had to be carried. This prolonged the crossing nearly two hours. Colonel Harnden learned from the ferryman that the party he was pursuing had crossed about one o'clock that morning, and were only a few hours ahead of him on the road leading to Irwinsville. At Abbeville, a village of three families, he halted to feed, and, just as he was renewing his march, he met the advance party of the Fourth Michigan Cavalry, Lieutenant Colonel B. D. Pritchard commanding, moving on the road from Hawkinsville. Ordering his detachment to continue its march, Colonel Harnden rode to meet Colonel Pritchard, and gave him such information in regard to Davis's movements as he had been able to gather. This was about three P.M. After a conversation between these officers, the precise details of which are variously reported, they separated, Colonel Harnden to rejoin his command, already an hour or more in advance, and Colonel Pritchard continuing his march along the south side of the Ocmulgee. It will be remembered that Colonel Pritchard had began his march from the vicinity of Macon on the evening of May 7, under verbal orders given him by General Minty, in pursuance of my instructions. His attention was particularly directed to the crossings of the Ocmulgee River, between Hawkinsville and Jacksonville, near the mouth of the Ohoopee, with the object of intercepting Davis and such other rebel chiefs as might be making their way out of the country by the roads in that region. He had not gone more than three miles before he obtained such additional information in regard to the party as convinced

erwise would have been censurable for negligence and want of enterprise. Colonel Harnden having informed him that he had force enough to cope with Davis, Colonel Pritchard determined to march another road, leading to Irwinsville by a more circuitous route. Why he did not send a courier on the trail pursued by Colonel Harnden to notify the latter of his intentions has not been explained. This would probably have prevented the collision which afterward occurred between his regiment and that of Colonel Harnden, and would not have rendered the capture of Davis less certain. This is not intended to reflect upon the conduct of Colonel Pritchard, for it is believed that this omission was simply an oversight which might have occurred to any confident and zealous officer. In carrying out the plan which he had adopted, Colonel Pritchard selected from his regiment seven officers and one hundred and twenty-eight men, and at four o'clock began the march, leaving the balance of his regiment under command of Captain Hathaway, with orders to picket the river and scout the country in accordance with previous instructions. The route pursued by Colonel Pritchard led down the river nearly twelve miles to a point opposite Wilcox's Mill, and thence southwest for a distance of eighteen miles, through the pine forest to Irwinsville. He reached this place at one A.M. of the 10th, and by representing his command as the rear-guard of Davis's party, he succeeded in learning from the citizens that the party he was searching for had encamped that night at dusk about a mile and a half out on the road toward Abbeville. Having secured a negro guide, he turned the head of his column toward that place, and after moving to within half a mile of the camp, halted and dismounted twenty-five men under Lieutenant Purinton. This party were directed to move noiselessly through the woods to the north side of the camp, for the purpose of gaining a position in its rear and preventing the possibility of escape. In case of discovery by the enemy, they were directed to begin the attack from wherever they might be, while Colonel Pritchard would charge upon the camp along the main road. Lieutenant Purinton having reached the point assigned him without exciting an alarm, the attack was delayed until the first appearance of dawn, at which time Colonel Pritchard put his troops in motion, and continued his march to within a few rods of the camp undiscovered. Having assured himself of his position, he dashed upon the camp without delay, and in a few moments had secured its occupants and effects, and placed a guard of mounted men around the camp, with dismounted sentries at the tents and wagons. No resistance was offered, because the enemy had posted no sentries, and were therefore taken completely by surprise.

"Almost simultaneously with the dash of Colonel Pritchard and his detachment sharp firing began in the direction of Abbeville, and only a short distance from the camp. This turned out to be an engagement between the party under Lieutenant Purinton and the detachment of the First Wisconsin Cavalry, which, it seems, had followed the rebel trail the night before till it was no longer distinguishable in the dark, had gone into camp only two or three miles behind the party they had been pursuing so long, and had renewed the pursuit as soon as they could see to march.

"Both Colonel Pritchard and Colonel Harnden were informed that Davis had been reported as having with him a well-armed body-guard of picked men, variously estimated at from ten to fifty. They therefore expected desperate resistance, and hence, in the collision which occurred, the men of both detachments seemed inspired by the greatest courage and determination. It was several minutes before either party discovered they were fighting our own people instead of the enemy. In this unfortunate affair two men of the Fourth Michigan were killed and one officer wounded, while three men of the First Wisconsin were severely and several slightly wounded. It is difficult, under the circumstances as detailed, to perceive how the accident could have been avoided. Colonel Harnden certainly had no means of knowing, and no reason to suspect that the party whom he found in his front were any other than the rebels he had been pursuing, while Colonel Pritchard claims that he had cautioned Lieutenant Purinton particularly to keep a sharp look-out for the First Wisconsin, which he knew would approach from that direction. The hurry with which my command was subsequently mustered out of service, and the absence of the principal officers, prevented an investigation of the details of this affair, and the circumstances which led to it. At this late day nothing more can be said of them than what is contained in the official documents already submitted, except that not the slightest blame was ever intended to be cast by me upon Colonel Harnden, as seems to have been assumed by the commission convened by the Secretary of War for the purpose of awarding the prize offered for the capture of Davis.

"During the firing of the skirmish referred to, the adjutant of the Fourth Michigan, Lieutenant J. G. Dickinson, after having looked to the security of the rebel camp, and sent forward a number of the men who had straggled, was about to go to the front himself, when his attention was called by one of the men 'to three persons dressed in female attire,' who had apparently just left one of the large tents near by, and were moving toward the thick woods. He started at once toward them, and called out 'Halt!' but, not hearing him, or not caring to obey, they continued to move off. Just then they were confronted by three men under direction of Corporal Munger, coming from the opposite direction. The corporal recognized one of the persons as Davis, advanced carabine, and demanded his surrender. The three persons halted, and by the actions of the two, who afterward turned out to be women, all doubt as to the identity of the third person was removed. The individuals thus arrested were found to be Miss Howell, Mrs. Davis, and Jefferson Davis. As they walked back to the tent from which they had tried to escape, Lieutenant Dickinson observed that Davis's high top-boots were not covered by his disguise, which fact probably led to his recognition by Corporal Munger.

"As the friends of Davis have strenuously denied that he was disguised as a woman, it may not be improper to specify the exact articles of woman's apparel which he had upon him when first seen by Lieutenant Dickinson and Corporal Munger. The former states that he was one of the three persons 'dressed in woman's attire,' and had a 'black mantle wrapped about his head, through the top of which could be seen locks of his hair.' Captain G. W. Lawton, Fourth Michigan Cavalry, who publishes an account of the capture in the *Atlantic Monthly* for September, 1866, states explicitly, upon the testimony of the officers present, that Davis, in addition to his full suit of Confederate gray, had on 'a lady's waterproof (cloak), gathered at the waist, with a shawl drawn over the head, and carrying a tin pail.'

"Colonel Pritchard says in his official report that he received from Mrs. Davis, on board the steamer Clyde, off Fortress Monroe, 'a waterproof cloak or robe,' which was worn by Davis as a disguise, and which was identified by the men who saw it on him at the time of the capture. He secured the balance of the disguise the next day. It consisted of a shawl, which was identified in a similar manner by both Mrs. Davis and the men. From these circumstances there seems to be no doubt whatever that Davis sought to avoid capture by assuming the dress of a woman, or that the ladies of the party endeavored to pass him off upon his captors as one of themselves.

"In addition to Davis and his family, Colonel Pritchard's detachment captured at the same time John H. Reagan, rebel postmaster-general, Colonel B. N. Harrison, private secretary, Colonels Lubbock and Johnson, aids-de-camp to Davis, four inferior officers, and thirteen private soldiers, besides Miss Howell, two waiting-maids, and several colored servants.

"As soon as breakfast could be prepared, Colonel Pritchard, preceded by Colonel Harnden, began his march, with prisoners and wagons, for Macon, about 120 miles to the northwest of Irwinsville. The next day he met a courier with copies of the President's proclamation offering a reward of $100,000 for the capture of Davis. This proclamation had been received and promulgated by me on the 9th, and hence the officers in pursuit of Davis were in no way inspired by the promise which it contained. They performed their part from a higher sense of duty, and too much praise can not be awarded to Colonels Pritchard and Harnden, and the officers and men of their regiments who participated in the pursuit. Colonel Pritchard arrived at Macon on the afternoon of the 13th, and reported at once with his prisoners at corps headquarters. Arrangements had been already made, under instructions from the Secretary of War, for forwarding Davis to the North, *via* Atlanta, Augusta, and Savannah. Colonel Pritchard, with a detachment of his regiment, was directed to deliver his prisoner safely into the custody of the Secretary of War. I also placed in his charge the person of Clement C. Clay, Jr., for whose arrest a reward had also been offered by the President. Mr. Clay surrendered himself to me at Macon about the 11th of May, having informed me by telegraph from Western Georgia the day before that he would start for my headquarters without delay. A. H. Stephens was arrested by General Upton, at Crawfordsville, about the same time, and also placed in charge of Colonel Pritchard.

"Brevet Major General Upton was charged with making the necessary arrangements for forwarding the prisoners and escort safely to Savannah, in the department of General Gillmore. These arrangements were successfully carried out, and the prisoners delivered at Fortress Monroe for safe keeping on the 22d of May.

"My command had also arrested Mr. Mallory, the rebel Secretary of the Navy, Mr. Hill, senator, and Joseph E. Brown, governor of Georgia. Breckinridge and Toombs managed to escape by travelling alone and as rapidly as possible, the former having passed through Tallahassee, Florida, only a few hours before the arrival of General McCook at that place.

"Immediately after the capture of Davis, the small detachments and scouting parties of my command were assembled by their respective brigade and division commanders, and after paroling the bulk of the rebel forces, amounting to about 60,000 men that had been serving in Florida, Georgia, North and South Carolina, the various regiments were ordered to be mustered out.

"From the foregoing narrative, it will be seen that the first perfectly reliable information in regard to the movements of Davis was sent in by Lieutenant Joseph O. Yoeman, of General Alexander's staff; that the route actually pursued by Davis and his party after leaving Washington was first discovered by Lieutenant Colonel Harnden at Dublin, and that the capture was actually made one and a half miles north of Irwinsville, Georgia, at dawn of May 10, by Lieutenant Colonel Ben-

LINCOLN AT HOME.

CHAPTER LX.

THE DEATH OF LINCOLN.

The Mission of Abraham Lincoln.—His Conservatism.—Characteristic Peculiarities.—Charitable Disposition toward the Southern People.—Closing Days of Lincoln's Life.—His second Inaugural.—Visit to City Point.—Entrance into Richmond.—The last Day.—The Evening at Ford's Theatre.—Lincoln's Assassination.—His Death-bed.—Attempt to Assassinate Secretary Seward.—The Effect upon the Country.—The Fate of the Conspirators.—Death of John Wilkes Booth.—The Trial before the Military Commission.—Flight and final Capture of John H. Surratt.—Connection of the Conspiracy with the Confederate Government.—Burial of President Lincoln.

NEVER before, in the history of the world, was a single fortnight so thronged with events of thrilling interest, concerning not alone one continent, but commanding the attention of the world, as that which commenced on the 1st, and ended with the 14th of April, 1865. As, in the denouement of a great tragedy, events which have hitherto crept along, in light or darkness, leap forward, thronging and culminating toward their conclusion, so was it in the closing period of that antagonism in which, for four years, the republic had met, grappled, and finally put under its feet the rebellion of states against its sovereignty. This national drama had had its prelude in years of plotting and conspiracy on the part of Southern statesmen, who sought to array their states against the general government. Still its first outward act was a violent shock. The American people was raised clean off the ground; but it soon regained its footing, and saw that the crisis upon it ought not to have been a surprise. It was a long time before the intense violence of the rebellion was understood; but at length the nation put on its complete armor, and gathered up its full strength. From that moment doubt was thrust aside, and victory crowned its banners. But Gettysburg, Vicksburg, Atlanta, Nashville, and Savannah, although great national victories, had not been crushing defeats to the Confederate armies. Then within the confines of Virginia and North Carolina was marshaled the combined strength of both antagonists. The curtain uplifted to disclose the last act of the drama. It disclosed Grant's army in motion. One blow from the national arm swept away the defenses of Lee's army and uncovered the Confederate capital. A second blow crushed the finest army of the Confederacy, and its fragments were left at the mercy of the conqueror. The Confederate President was a fugitive, bearing with him to Greensborough the tidings of terrible disaster, the very weight of which crushed and crumbled Johnston's army. The rebel government, with its armies, vanished like the

LINCOLN'S HOME, SPRINGFIELD, ILLINOIS.

clouds of an April day. The winter of national discontent was passed, followed by glorious summer. The national colors floated on innumerable eminences, wafting fragrance more grateful than that of flowers. Exultation filled the whole atmosphere, and pervaded the hearts of all men. It was like a heaven from which Satan and his angels had been thrust out into the abyss. Strong men wept for joy. Inspired with awe, the people expressed their triumph, not in shouts, but in anthems.

In this sublime awe, in this inspiration of joyous triumph, Lincoln had participated not as others. He was wrapped in a cloud of glory which no man could penetrate. It was a glory which was hid from his own eyes, in which he was somehow buried, but which had not yet blossomed into the full flower. He had been chosen of God for great ends. When the Republican National Convention assembled at Chicago on the 16th of May, 1860, it was almost universally assumed that William H. Seward would be nominated for President. On the first ballot he stood far ahead of Lincoln; on the second he was three votes ahead; but on the third Lincoln stood fifty-one votes ahead of Seward, and his nomination was then made unanimous. The people were scarcely as yet familiar with the name of Lincoln. They soon learned that he was an awkward, ungainly man, one who had risen from obscurity by perseverance, a man shrewd in debate and plain in speech, and who was known simply as "Honest old Abe." But this awkward, plain man, without culture, and without that despotism of genius which commands admiration, God had taken by the hand, and had chosen as the champion of the republic at the most critical moment of its history. His very election was made the pretext for rebellion. But he accomplished nobly and wisely his great mission. Against the violence of rebellion he opposed the firmness of national authority, supported by the strong arms of patriots. The subtle machinations of those who opposed his administration were foiled by his good sense. Thus he won the confidence of the people. He had no love of arbitrary power, and indulged no radical or revolutionary theories which could tempt him to such use of power. He was a conservative in the best sense of that term: not a conservator of party, but of national integrity. Thus he was the better fitted to accomplish his divine mission. For it must be remembered that God, the great Disposer of all events, works not with the haste of man. Tares and wheat He lets grow together until the harvest, lest by rooting up the tares upon impulse He uproot the wheat also. While Lincoln never vacillated, he was never in haste. He hesitated long before he issued his proclamation of emancipation. He laid it away, and weeks passed before he signed it—and then he acted in accordance with a solemn vow which he had made to God. Even after he issued this document he doubted whether the system of gradual and compensated emancipation might not be more just and better for the slaves. He looked on every side of every question, and was therefore slow in reaching conclusions. In Lincoln thought and prayer were mingled, and thus the final word which came in answer to thought and prayer sounded solemnly in his ears like the commandment of God. Following that voice, he had no doubt as to results: it was, "This do, and thou shalt be saved."

In no life, perhaps, more than in Lincoln's, did the outward appearance contradict the inward fact and experience. A casual acquaintance with him would lead to the inference that he looked upon every subject only as the occasion of a joke or the point for an anecdote. But those who came nearer to him, or who carefully study the man, can not thus judge. Upon no man ever fell the weight of sadder care than upon him. Day by day he labored under a burden which he could not lay aside. Thus to his intimate friends he always seemed weary and sorrowful. In an equal degree his external awkwardness curiously contrasted with an inward grace and sweetness not common among men. He was as gentle as a woman. His compassion was infinite. As the hour of victory approached, when the enemies of the nation would lie prostrate at its feet, the desire nearest to his heart was to heal the wounds which the strife left open and bleeding, to pardon and restore. Thus, when the summer of triumph came, its glory wrapped him all about. He saw a nation restored, a race emancipated. He saw the seal of God set upon all which he had done. He looked upon a people inspired with solemn joy, and as their souls went up in anthems, his rose supreme above them all, crowned with an aureola such as never graced the head of Cæsar or king.

But how easily is the summer sky overcast with gloom! The serpent's head has been bruised, but his venomous fangs have not been plucked. Treason, which wears the semblance of honor on the battle-field, and whose proud crest flashing at the head of armies is an image of something glorious, is, after all, a creeping thing with a devilish instinct. And thus it is that at one moment we look upon the great leader of the people crowned with the highest honors which the hands or hearts of his countrymen can bestow, and the next are called to witness his martyrdom.

On the 4th of March Lincoln had been reinaugurated President. On that occasion he thus alluded to the war, and to the two parties engaged in it:

"Each looked for an easier triumph, and a result less fundamental and astounding. Both read the same Bible and pray to the same God, and each invokes his aid against the other. It may seem strange that any men should dare to ask a just God's assistance in wringing their bread from the sweat of other men's faces. But let us judge not that we be not judged. The prayers of both could not be answered; that of neither has been answered fully. The Almighty has his own purposes. 'Woe unto the world because of offenses, for it must needs be that offenses come, but woe to that man by whom the offense cometh.' If we shall suppose that American slavery is one of those offenses which, in the providence of God, must needs come, but which, having continued through his appointed time, he now wills to remove, and that he gives to both North and South this terrible war as the woe due to those by whom the offense came, shall we discern therein any departure from these divine attributes which the believers in a loving God always ascribe to him? Fondly do we hope, fervently do we pray that this mighty scourge of war may speedily pass away. Yet if God wills that it continue until all the wealth piled by the bondman's two hundred and fifty years of unrequited toil shall be sunk, and until every drop of blood drawn with the lash shall be paid by another drawn with the sword, as was said three thousand years ago, so still it must be said, 'The judgments of the Lord are true and righteous altogether.'

"With malice toward none, with charity for all, with firmness in the right, let us strive on to finish the work we are in, to bind up the nation's wounds, to care for him who shall have borne the battle, and for his widow and his orphan, to do all which may achieve and cherish a just and a lasting peace among ourselves and with all nations."

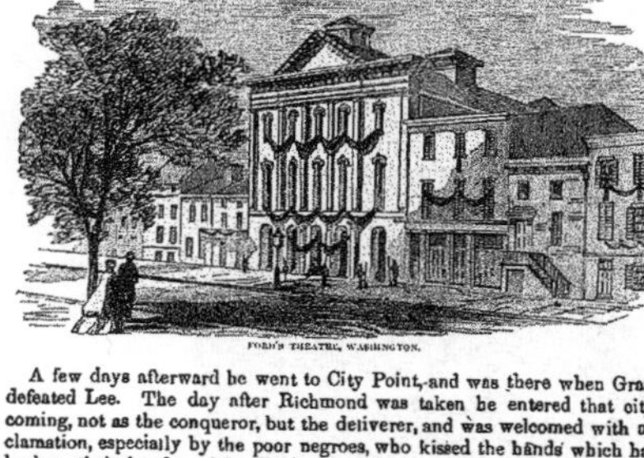

FORD'S THEATRE, WASHINGTON.

A few days afterward he went to City Point, and was there when Grant defeated Lee. The day after Richmond was taken he entered that city, coming, not as the conqueror, but the deliverer, and was welcomed with acclamation, especially by the poor negroes, who kissed the hands which had broken their bonds. After Lee's surrender he returned to Washington. Here, on the evening of the 11th, in the midst of the universal rejoicings, he addressed his fellow-citizens, calling upon them to remember Him to whom they owed the preservation of the nation, and the soldiers and sailors who, under God, had won the victory. He also, on this occasion, announced his purpose to issue another proclamation to the people of the South, in order to hasten the work of restoration.

On the morning of the 14th—the last day of Lincoln's life—his son Robert breakfasted with him, and told him all the details of Lee's surrender, from the scene of which he had just returned. The President then spent an hour with Schuyler Colfax, speaker of the House. The conversation naturally turned upon the immediate future of the nation, and every word uttered by Lincoln breathed a pardon toward repentant rebels. After a brief interview with some of his old Illinois friends, the President met his cabinet between 11 and 12 o'clock. He seemed more joyous than was his wont. The lieutenant general was also present. Then, in the afternoon, he drove out with Mrs. Lincoln, and conversed of the happier days which seemed in store for them. He seemed to be looking forward to four years of peaceful administration, and after that to retirement and a quiet conclusion of an eventful life in the midst of old and familiar scenes. But even then the weapon of death in the hands of the assassin was laden with the fatal bullet. A peace such as the world can not give was nearer to the weary heart of Lincoln than he then dreamed.

In the evening he met Colfax again, with George Ashmun, who had presided at the Chicago Convention which nominated him for the presidency. It was well understood in Washington that the President and General Grant would that evening attend Ford's Theatre, and a private box had been especially prepared and decorated for the presidential party. General Grant, owing to another engagement, could not attend. Mr. Colfax was invited to accompany the party, but declined, to his subsequent regret.[1] The President himself was reluctant, as his mind was on other things, but he was not willing to disappoint the people in this hour of public rejoicing. At nine o'clock, with his wife, Mr. Lincoln reached the theatre, and, as usual, was received with an outburst of applause. The other members of the party were Miss Harris, daughter of Senator Harris, of New York, and Major Rathbun, of the regular army. The play for the evening was "Our American Cousin." The American flag drooped over Lincoln's head, and his thoughts were occupied with a grander drama than that which was presented to the audience. Four years ago this day the flag had been hauled down from Fort Sumter, and this very day the same old flag had been restored by the hands of Major Anderson. It was natural, therefore, that the President's mind should range over the weary years which had intervened, and of which he was so great a part. His face wore a happy smile, such as had not been there since the beginning of the war.

But still another play was in progress of which neither Lincoln nor the audience knew. Shortly after the President entered the theatre three men were noticed by one Sergeant M. Dye, who was sitting in front of the theatre. They seemed to be in earnest consultation, and to be waiting for some one to come out. They went to a neighboring saloon, and in a few minutes returned. One was a well-dressed gentleman, another was a rough-looking fellow, and the third was a younger man than either of the other two. This latter stepped up and called out the time, and then started up the street. Soon he reappeared and called out "ten minutes after ten," this time louder than before. The well-dressed gentleman then entered the theatre by the door in the rear leading to the stage. He passed up the stairs and through the gallery leading to the box occupied by the President, and overlooking the stage on its right. He stood for a moment surveying the audience, and then, taking out a card, gave it to the President's messenger, and immediately followed the latter into the box. As he entered he fired, taking unerring aim at the President's head. Major Rathbun attempted to seize the assassin, but was thrust aside, receiving at the same time a wound in the breast. The assassin advanced to the front brandishing his knife, and leaped upon the stage, shouting "Sic semper tyrannis," the motto of Virginia. In a moment he was gone.

Lincoln was carried, unconscious, from the theatre to Mr. Peterson's house opposite, where he was laid upon a bed. In ten minutes all Washington was apprised of the deed which had been committed, but the extent of the injury was yet unknown. Surgeon General Barnes was hastily summoned, and the members of the cabinet were assembled in the death-chamber of the President. There also were Senator Sumner and Speaker Colfax. The wound which had been received in the back of the head was probed by the surgeon general and pronounced mortal. As the fatal word was uttered, the hearts of all present sank within them. "Oh no! general, no!" cried out Stanton, and, sinking into a chair, he wept like a child. Sumner, who held the hand of the martyred President, sobbed as if his great heart would break with sorrow. It was the night of Good Friday, and it seemed as if another had been crucified, the just for the unjust!

All night the watchers stood about the death-bed. Lincoln remained unconscious to the last. His wife and son Robert several times entered the chamber, but in their grief could not bear the scene, and they remained most of the time in an adjoining room. Lincoln lived until twenty-two minutes past seven o'clock on the morning of the 15th.

The same hour that the President was shot, a man appeared at the door of Secretary Seward and pretended that he was a messenger from the physician who was then attending upon the secretary. Being refused admittance, he forced his way to the secretary's chamber. Frederick Seward and an attendant rushed to the rescue, but were both severely wounded. The assassin—probably the rough-looking fellow observed by Sergeant Dye in front of Ford's Theatre—entered the chamber and inflicted several wounds upon the secretary, and then escaped. It had been intended by the assassins to kill Secretary Stanton, Lieutenant General Grant, and Vice-President Johnson, and thus paralyze the government. But even if all this had been accomplished the conspirators would have been disappointed. Secretary Seward survived the blows inflicted upon him, but to his dying day will wear the honorable scars which associate him in the thoughts of the people with the martyrdom of their President.

The tidings of the assassination spread rapidly over the country. In all history there was never national sorrow to be compared with this. Literally the whole people wept. Thousands there were who would willingly have received the fatal bullet in their own hearts if thereby they could have saved the precious life of their leader. Even those who had for four years reviled Lincoln, who had called him a boor and a despot, now vied with his friends in their adulation. A few rejoiced in the murder, but their lips were closed partly from fear and partly from the universal expression of sorrow which struck them dumb.

But who and where were the murderers? The assassin of the President, as he escaped across the stage, was recognized by one of the actors as John Wilkes Booth. Other evidence was soon found which fixed upon this person the guilt of the murder. But, though he left traces of his guilt behind, he was not to be found. The rendezvous of the conspirators was discovered. It was the house of Mrs. M. E. Surratt, located in the very heart of Washington. On the night of April 17th the officers of the government proceeded thither and arrested the occupants—Mrs. Surratt, her daughter Anna, Miss Fitzpatrick, and Miss Holahan. Before leaving the house a light knock was heard at the door. It was opened, and a young man appeared, evidently in disguise. He was dressed like a common laborer, and carried a pick upon his shoulder. But his hands were white and soft, apparently unused to labor, and his answers to questions put to him were unsatisfactory. During the investigation he produced the certificate of an oath of allegiance, purporting to have been taken by Lewis Payne, of Fauquier County, Virginia. He was arrested, and it was afterward proved that he was the man who had attempted to murder Secretary Seward, and that his real name was Powell. Three days later George A. Atzerott was captured

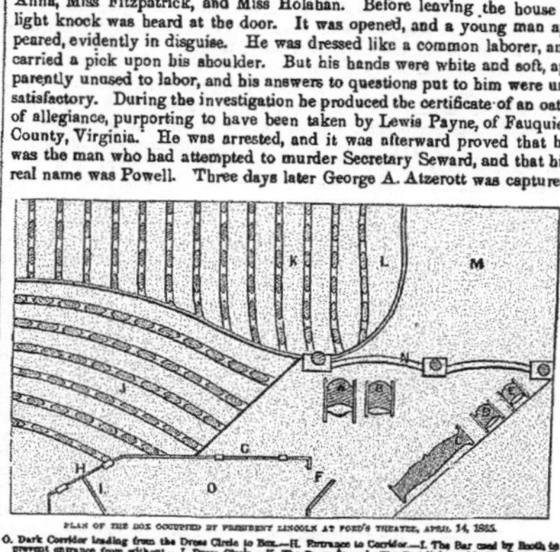

PLAN OF THE BOX OCCUPIED BY PRESIDENT LINCOLN AT FORD'S THEATRE, APRIL 14, 1865.

O. Dark Corridor leading from the Dress Circle to Box.—H. Entrance to Corridor.—I. The Bar used by Booth to prevent entrance from without.—J. Dress Circle.—K. The Parquette.—L. The Foot-lights.—M. The Stage.—F. Open door to the President's Box.—G. Closed door.—N. Place where Booth vaulted over to the Stage below.

[1] In a speech at Chicago, April 30th, Colfax said:

"* * * * My mind has since been tortured with regrets that I had not accompanied him. If the knife which the assassin had intended for Grant had not been wasted, as it possibly would not have been, on one of so much less importance in our national affairs, perhaps a sudden backward look at that eventful instant might have saved that life, so incalculably precious to wife, and children, and country; or, failing in that, might have hindered or prevented the escape of his murderer. The willingness of any man to endanger his life for another's is so much doubted that I scarcely dare to say how willingly I would have risked my own to preserve his, of such priceless value to us all. But if you can realize that it is sweet to die for one's country, as so many scores of thousands, from every state, and county, and hamlet have proved in the years that are past, you can imagine the consolation there would be to any one, even in his expiring hours, to feel that he had saved the land from a funeral gloom which, but a few days ago, settled down upon it from ocean to ocean and from Capitol to cabin, at the loss of one for whom even a hecatomb of victims could not atone."

near Middleburg, in Maryland. He had on the 14th of April occupied a room in the Kirkwood House, Washington, where Vice-President Johnson was staying. In this room a revolver was found the next day, hid under the pillow of the bed, and some bowie-knives between the mattresses. There was also found evidence of his complicity with Booth.

The principal assassin, John Wilkes Booth, was not found until eleven days after the murder. When he leaped upon the stage at Ford's Theatre, his foot became entangled in the folds of the flag decorating the box occupied by Lincoln, and his leg was broken. He had engaged one of the swiftest steeds in Washington, which was held by one of the attendants of the theatre during the accomplishment of the crime. Limping across the stage with great difficulty, he mounted his horse and was joined by one Harold, who had been on the look-out. They crossed the navy-yard bridge and rode to Surrattsville, ten miles beyond. Here they called upon a Mr. Lloyd, who occupied a hotel leased to him by Mrs. Surratt, and obtained two carbines which had been left there about six weeks before for just this emergency. That very afternoon Mrs. Surratt had driven to Mr. Lloyd's and warned him that these weapons would be called for that night. She had also brought a field-glass for Booth's use. From this point Booth and his companion hurried to the house of Dr. Mudd, on the eastern shore of the Potomac. Here Booth's leg was set, and the two criminals were concealed in the neighborhood for nearly a week. Then they crossed the Potomac into Virginia. The detectives employed by the government, under Colonel Baker's direction, and a small squad of cavalry, were already close upon them. They crossed the Potomac, and from Captain Jett, a Confederate, extorted information as to Booth's hiding-place. On the night of April 25th they found Booth and Harold secreted in a tobacco-house on Garrett's farm, a short distance from Port Royal. It was the intention of the officers to take Booth alive. The barn was surrounded, and the inmates were summoned to surrender. Colonel Baker made the demand, and suggested as an alternative "a bonfire and a shooting-match." Harold came out, but Booth wanted "fair play," and proposed that the officers stand off and give him a chance for his life. As he persisted in his refusal to surrender, the barn was fired. Booth made a desperate plunge toward the door, and at that moment was shot in the back of the head by Sergeant Boston Corbett. This act of Corbett was clearly a disobedience of orders.

Booth was taken out of the barn, and was laid upon the grass in a dying condition. The wound which he had received was in its location very similar to that which he had inflicted upon the President, but it did not deprive him of consciousness. Water was given him, and he revived. Baker put his ear close to the murmuring lips of the dying man, and heard him say, "Tell mother I die for my country." He was carried to the veranda of Garrett's house. Here he again revived, and said, "I thought I did for the best." He asked that his hands might be raised so that he could see them. As he looked upon them he muttered, "Useless! useless!" These were his last words. Ay, indeed, wretched man, how useless!

Upon Booth's body a diary was found, with some of its leaves torn out, and containing some photographs of female acquaintances. The pages removed were at the beginning of the book, and as the diary purported to be one for 1864, they probably related to events preliminary to his bloody act, and of which he did not care to leave behind him a record. What was left pertained solely to the assassination, and implicated no one else in the murder. The words written were those of a man who felt that a curse rested upon him—a mark like that which was set upon Cain. In almost the same breath he commends himself as having done well, and yet doubts if there can be pardon for him in heaven.[1]

[1] The following is a copy of the writing, which was in pencil, found in this diary:

April 13-14. Friday, the Ides.

"Te amo.

"Until to-day nothing was ever thought of sacrificing to our country's wrongs. For six months
we had worked to capture; but our cause being almost lost, something decisive and great must be
done. But its failure was owing to others, who did not strike for their country with a heart. I
struck boldly, and not as the papers say. I walked with a firm step through a thousand of his
friends, and was stopped, but pushed on. A colonel was at his side. I shouted "*Sic semper*"
before I fired. In jumping, broke my leg. I passed all his pickets, rode sixty miles that night
with the bone of my leg tearing the flesh at every jump. I can never repent it, though we hated
to kill. Our country owed all her troubles to him, and God simply made me the instrument of his
punishment. The country is not (April, 1865) what it was. This forced Union is not what I have

BOSTON CORBETT.

There was a *post-mortem* examination of the body, which was taken to Washington. This examination took place on board the Montauk, on the Potomac. On the night of the 27th of April a small row-boat received the remains of the murderer. The place and manner of his sepulture were for

loved. I care not what becomes of me. I have no desire to outlive my country. This night, before the deed, I wrote a long article and left it for one of the editors of the *National Intelligencer*, in which I fully set forth our reasons for our proceeding. He or the government—

"*Friday, 21st.* After being hunted like a dog through swamps, woods, and last night being chased by gun-boats till I was forced to return, wet, cold, and starving, with every man's hand against me, I am here in despair. And why? For doing what Brutus was honored for, what made Tell a hero. And yet I, for striking down a greater tyrant than they ever knew, am looked upon as a common cut-throat. My action was purer than either of theirs. One hoped to be great; the other had not only his country's, but his own wrongs to avenge. I hoped for no gain. I knew no private wrong. I struck for my country, and that at once; a country that groaned beneath this tyranny and prayed for this end. And yet now behold the cold hand they extend to me. God can not pardon me if I have done wrong. Yet I can not see my wrong, except in serving a degenerate people. The little, the very little I left behind to clear my name, the government will not allow to be printed. So ends all. For my country I have given up all that makes life sweet and holy; brought misery upon my family, and am sure there is no pardon in the Heaven for me, since man condemns me so. I have only heard of what has been done, except what I did myself, and it fills me with horror. God, try and forgive me, and bless my mother. To-night I will once more try the river, with the intent to cross, though I have a greater desire and almost a mind to return to Washington and in a measure clear my name, which I feel I can do. I do not repent the blow I struck. I may before my God, but not to man. I think I have done well, though I am abandoned, with the curse of *Cain upon*— *When, if the world* knew my heart, that one blow would have made me great, though I did desire no greatness. To-night I try to escape these blood-hounds once more. Who—who can read his fate? God's will be done. I have too great a soul to die like a criminal. May He spare me that and let me die bravely. I bless the entire world; have never hated or wronged any one. This last was not a wrong unless God deems it so, and it's with Him to damn or bless me. Hard for this brave boy with me, who often prays—yes, before and since, with a true and sincere heart. Was it crime in him? If so, why can he pray the same? I do not wish to shed a drop of blood, but I must fight the course. 'Tis all that's left me."

Upon a piece of paper found in the diary, and supposed to have been torn from it, is written the following:

"My dea [piece torn out.] Forgive me, but I have some little pride. I can not blame you for want of hospitality; you know your own affairs. I was sick, tired, with a broken limb, and in need of medical advice. I would not have turned a dog from my door in such a plight. However, you were kind enough to give us something to eat, for which I not only thank you, but, on account of the rebuke and manner in which to [piece torn out.] It is not the substance, but the way in which kindness is extended that makes one happy in the acceptance thereof. The sauce to meat is ceremony. *Meeting were bare* without it. Be kind enough to accept the inclosed five dollars, although hard to spare, for what we have received.

"Most respectfully, from your obedient servant."

A letter had been (November, 1864) left by Booth in the hands of his brother-in-law, J. S. Clarke. It was opened by the latter on the Monday after the assassination, and was published in the *Philadelphia Press* of April 19th. The following is a copy:

"——, ——, 1864.

"My dear Sir,—You may use this as you think best. But as some may wish to know when, who, and why, and as I know not how to direct, I give it (in the words of your master)—

"'To whom it may concern:'

"Right or wrong, God judge me, not man. For, be my motive good or bad, of one thing I am sure, the lasting condemnation of the North.

"I love peace more than life. Have loved the Union beyond expression. For four years have I waited, hoped, and prayed for the dark clouds to break, and for a restoration of our former sunshine. To wait longer would be a crime. All hope for peace is dead. My prayers have proved as idle as my hopes. God's will be done. I go to see and share the bitter end.

"I have ever held the South were right. The very nomination of Abraham Lincoln four years ago spoke plainly war—war upon Southern rights and institutions. His election proved it. 'Await an overt act.' Yes; till you are bound and plundered. What folly! The South were wise. Who thinks of argument or patience when the finger of his enemy presses on the trigger? In a foreign war, I too could say, 'Country, right or wrong.' But in a struggle such as ours (where the brother tries to pierce the brother's heart), for God's sake choose the right. When a country like this spurns justice from her side, she forfeits the allegiance of every honest freeman, and should leave him, untrammeled by any fealty soever, to act as his conscience may approve.

"People of the North, to hate tyranny, to love liberty and justice, to strike at wrong and oppression, was the teaching of our fathers. The study of our early history will not let me forget it, and may it never.

"This country was formed for the white, not for the black man. And, looking upon African slavery from the same stand-point held by the noble framers of our Constitution, I, for one, have ever considered it one of the greatest blessings (both for themselves and us) that God ever bestowed upon a favored nation. Witness heretofore our wealth and power; witness their elevation and enlightenment above their race elsewhere. I have lived among it most of my life, and have seen less harsh treatment from master to man than I have beheld in the North from father to son. Yet, Heaven knows, no one would be willing to do more for the negro race than I, could I but see a way to still better their condition.

"But Lincoln's policy is only preparing the way for their total annihilation. The South are not, nor have they been, fighting for the continuance of slavery. The first battle of Bull Run did away with that idea. Their causes since for war have been as noble and greater far than those that urged our fathers on. Even should we allow they were wrong at the beginning of this contest, cruelty and injustice have made the wrong become the right, and they stand now (before the wonder and admiration of the world) as a noble band of patriotic heroes. Hereafter, reading of their deeds, Thermopylæ will be forgotten.

"When I aided in the capture and execution of John Brown (who was a murderer on our western border, and who was fairly tried and convicted before an impartial judge and jury, of treason, and who, by the way, has since been made a god), I was proud of my little share in the transaction, for I deemed it my duty, and that I was helping our common country to perform an act of justice. But what was a crime in poor John Brown is now considered (by themselves) as the greatest and only virtue of the whole Republican party. Strange transmigration! Vice to become a virtue simply because more indulge in it!

"I thought then, as now, that the Abolitionists were the only traitors in the land, and that the entire party deserved the same fate as poor old Brown; not because they wish to abolish slavery, but on account of the means they have ever endeavored to use to effect that abolition. If Brown were living, I doubt whether he himself would set slavery against the Union. Most, or many in the North do, and openly, curse the Union, if the South are to return and retain a single right guaranteed to them by every tie which we once revered as sacred. The South can make no choice. It is either extermination or slavery for themselves (worse than death) to draw from. I know my choice.

"I have also studied hard to discover upon what grounds the right of a state to secede has been denied, when our very name, United States, and the Declaration of Independence, both provide for secession. But there is no time for words. I write in haste. I know how foolish I shall be deemed for undertaking such a step as this, where, on the one side, I have many friends and every thing to make me happy, where my profession alone has gained me an income of more than twenty thousand dollars a year, and where my great personal ambition in my profession has such a great field of labor. On the other hand, the South have never bestowed upon me one kind word; a place now where I have no friends except beneath the sod; a place where I must either become a private soldier or a beggar. To give up all of the former for the latter, besides my mother and sisters whom I love so dearly (although they so widely differ with me in opinion), seems insane; but God is my judge. I love Justice more than I do a country that disowns it; more than fame and wealth; more (Heaven pardon me if wrong)—more than a happy home. I have never been upon a battle-field; but oh! my countrymen, could you all but see the reality or effects of this horrid war as I have seen them (in every state save Virginia), I know you would think like me, and would pray the Almighty to create in the Northern mind a sense of right and justice, even should it possess no seasoning of mercy), and that he would dry up this sea of blood between us, which is daily growing wider. Alas! poor country, is she to meet her threatened doom? Four years ago I would have given a thousand lives to see her remain (as I had always known her) powerful and unbroken. And even now I would hold my life as naught to see her what she was. Oh! my friends, if the fearful scenes of the past four years had never been enacted, or if what has been had been but a frightful dream, from which we could now awake, with what overflowing hearts could we bless our God and pray for his continued favor! How I have loved the old flag can never now be known. A few years since, and the entire world could boast of none so pure and spotless. But I have of late been seeing and hearing of the bloody deeds of which she has been made the emblem, and would shudder to think how changed she had grown. Oh! how I have longed to see her break from the mist of blood and death that circles round her folds, spoiling her beauty and tarnishing her honor. But no, day by day has she been dragged deeper and deeper into cruelty and oppression, till now (in my eyes) her once bright red stripes look like bloody gashes on the face of heaven. I look now upon my early admiration of her glories as a dream. My love (as things stand to-day) is for the South alone. Nor do I deem it a dishonor in attempting to make for her a prisoner of this man, to whom she owes so much of misery. If success attend me I go penniless to her side. They say she has found that 'last ditch' which the North have so long derided and been endeavoring to force her in, forgetting they are our brothers, and that it is impolitic to goad an enemy to madness. Should I reach her in safety, and find it true, I will proudly beg permission to triumph or die in that same 'ditch' by her side.

"A Confederate doing duty upon his own responsibility. J. Wilkes Booth."

RUINS OF GARRETT'S BARN AND OUT-HOUSES NEAR PORT ROYAL, WHERE BOOTH WAS SHOT.

LEWIS PAYNE (POWELL).

a long time unknown to the world. It were better that thus it should remain forever. This man had attempted to build his fame upon the ruins of the government. There was an ancient villain—Erostratus by name—who deliberately purposed to perpetuate the memory of his name among men by shocking sacrilege, and he burned the temple of the Ephesian Diana. John Wilkes Booth once remarked to a company of his friends that this man's name had survived, while that of the builder of the temple was forgotten. It was thus that Booth sought to leave his name to posterity, preferring to be detested rather than not be remembered at all. By bringing a whole nation to tears, he would secure immortality for himself. It is not probable that either he or his fellow-conspirators in the inception of their scheme contemplated murder. But it soon came to that. It is evident that Booth attempted to poison the President in the summer of 1864, but failed. In a room of the McHenry House, Meadville, Pennsylvania, there was found on the pane of window-glass the following inscription in Booth's handwriting: "Abe Lincoln departed this life, Aug. 13th, 1864, by the effects of poison." A conspiracy long existed which contemplated the capture of Lincoln, but was at length given up. At last, when the defeat of the Confederate armies was an accomplished fact, the conspirators reverted to assassination as the surest means of destroying the government, and inaugurating a period of anarchy in which, as they confidently believed, the Confederates would, under the leadership of some master-mind, gain by murder what they had lost in battle. There is no doubt that when this scheme was adopted it was a matter of deliberation; nor can there be any question but the chief accomplices—Harold, Powell, Atzerott, Mrs. Surratt and her son John H. Surratt—were, at least for some hours previous to the murder, aware of Booth's intention, and were thus, in their several ways, participators in his guilt.

John Wilkes Booth was the third son born in America of the eminent English tragedian Junius Brutus Booth. There were three brothers, Junius Brutus Jr., Edwin, and John Wilkes, all of whom inherited a predilection for the stage. Of these three, Edwin alone has attained an eminent distinction as an actor, and he is probably unsurpassed by any living man. No suspicion rests upon his loyalty, and after the assassination, the sympathy elicited in his behalf was only equaled by the popular abhorrence of his unworthy brother. John Wilkes, the assassin, was born in 1839, and was only twenty-six years of age at the date of his crime. He had never achieved any marked success upon the stage, and but for his connection with the death of Lincoln, would never be known by even the next genera-

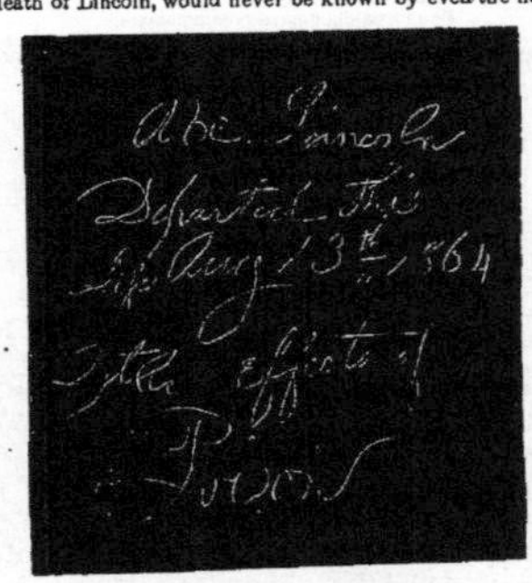

tion. In his soul inhered no nobility which could relieve his crime. He was an advocate of human slavery, and his dissolute life culminated in an act alike cowardly and despicable. Only the blank, vulgar act of murder remains as the basis of his unenviable fame. Instances there have been where brutality, allied with intellect and power, has formed the pedestal for a monument. But here the case was different: here brutality stood forth

JOHN H. SURRATT.

in its nakedness; men shrank away from the monster, and cared not to know the place of his sepulture.

The other conspirators were tried in Washington by a military commission, and on the 6th of July they received their sentence. The next day four of them—Harold, Atzerott, Powell, and Mrs. Surratt—were hung. Dr. Mudd, O'Loughlin, and Arnold were committed to a life-long imprisonment, and Spangler[1] was imprisoned for a term of six years. John H. Surratt had escaped, but he also was finally overtaken by justice, and while we write he awaits his second trial. He fled to Canada after the assassination, and there remained until September, 1865, when he started for Liverpool. In the spring of 1866 Mr. Seward was informed by Mr. King, at Rome, that Surratt had enlisted in the papal guards under the name of John Watson. He was arrested at Teroli, in Italy, but managed to escape by plunging down a ravine, making a leap of twenty-three feet. Wounded by his fall, he crawled off to a hospital, and after a few days resumed his flight. He went to Egypt, and was there again captured by our minister, Mr. Hale, and sent to this country. He every where boldly acknowledged his connection with the assassination, and seemed to think that the world had not only forgiven the crime, but admired its atrocity.

On the morning of Mr. Lincoln's death Andrew Johnson was inaugurated President. A few days afterward—on the 2d of May—he issued a proclamation offering large rewards for the capture of Jefferson Davis, Jacob Thompson, Clement C. Clay, Beverly Tucker, George N. Saunders, and William C. Cleary, on the ground that they were implicated in the assassination by evidence then in the possession of the Bureau of Military Justice.[1] It

[1] The charge against O'Loughlin was that he designed the murder of Lieutenant General Grant. Arnold was charged with having rendered assistance to Booth, Powell, Atzerott, and O'Loughlin; and Spangler with having assisted in Booth's escape.

[1] "*By the President of the United States of America:*

"A PROCLAMATION.

"Whereas, it appears from evidence in the Bureau of Military Justice that the atrocious murder of the late President, Abraham Lincoln, and the attempted assassination of the Honorable William H. Seward, Secretary of State, were incited, concerted, and procured by and between Jefferson Davis, late of Richmond, Virginia, and Jacob Thompson, Clement C. Clay, Beverly Tucker, George N. Saunders, William C. Cleary, and other rebels and traitors against the government of the United States, harbored in Canada:

"Now, therefore, to the end that justice may be done, I, Andrew Johnson, President of the United States, do offer and promise for the arrest of said persons, or either of them, within the limits of the United States, so that they can be brought to trial, the following rewards:

"One hundred thousand dollars for the arrest of Jefferson Davis.

"Twenty-five thousand dollars for the arrest of Clement C. Clay.

DAVID C. HAROLD.

MRS. SURRATT'S HOUSE, WASHINGTON.

was afterward proved that a cipher found in Booth's trunk corresponded to that used by the Confederate Secretary of State, J. P. Benjamin, and that Jefferson Davis had referred to his Secretary of War for consideration a letter from one L. W. Alston, who proposed to rid the Confederacy "of some of her deadliest enemies, by striking at the very heart's blood of those who seek to enchain her in slavery."[1]

In the mean while the people were burying their president. As soon as his death was known, business for a time ceased. Every house, from the palatial mansion to the lowest hovel, was draped with mourning. The nation was one vast funeral. From every pulpit, on the following Sabbath, there was uttered a funeral sermon. On Monday, April 17th, all the members of Congress then at Washington met at the Capitol to make arrangements for the funeral. It was finally determined that the remains of the President should be taken to his old home at Springfield, Illinois, and a Congressional Committee was appointed to accompany them, consisting of the entire Illinois delegation, and one member from each other state and each territory. The consignment of Lincoln's remains to Illinois was due to the urgent request of Governor Oglesby, Senator Yates, and others of that state. Sumner and many others desired that the body should be placed under the dome of the Capitol, at Washington, where a vault had been prepared for the Father of his Country, but had not been used for that purpose.

On Wednesday, the 19th, the funeral services were held in the east room of the White House. The coffin rested upon a canopied catafalque, and was decorated with wreaths of moss and evergreen, with white flowers and lilies. Around the catafalque at noon were gathered the late President's family, the officiating clergymen, the cabinet, the governors of several states, the Supreme Court, and the diplomatic corps. The Episcopal service for the dead was read by the Rev. Dr. Hall. Bishop Simpson, of the Methodist Episcopal Church, followed with a prayer. This portion of the service was most impressive, and, as the bishop concluded with the Lord's Prayer, the whole audience, dissolved in tears, joined as with one voice. Rev. Dr. Gurley, pastor of the church which Mr. Lincoln and his family were in the habit of attending, preached the funeral discourse. Then the concluding prayer was offered by Rev. Dr. Gray, chaplain of the Senate.

From the White House, at the close of the service, the procession passed up Pennsylvania Avenue to the Capitol, and up the steps, underneath the very spot from which, six months before, Lincoln had delivered his second inaugural; his funeral car was carried and deposited in the rotunda. Here the body remained until the 21st, when it was removed, under escort, to the dépôt of the Baltimore and Ohio Railroad. Then commenced the funeral procession of the President from Washington to Springfield—from the scene of his divinely-directed labors to his final resting-place. At each of the principal cities on the route—at Baltimore, Harrisburg, Philadelphia, New York, Albany, and Chicago—the body of the President lay for some hours in state, and hundreds of thousands of citizens were thus permitted to look upon the face which they had greeted four years before—then turned toward the national capital, now returning thence to meet the silence of the tomb. *Then* the malice of his foes had compelled Lincoln to proceed in disguise through Baltimore to Washington; now also he is in disguise, wearing the mask of death, through which all, bending over the silent features in loving reverence, discover his worthiness. His work has been all done, and this funeral procession is, after all, one of triumph. Well did Beecher say: "And now the martyr is moving in triumphal march, mightier than when alive. The nation rises up at every stage of his coming. Cities and states are his pall-bearers, and the cannon speaks the hours with solemn progression. Dead, dead, dead, he yet speaketh. Is Washington dead? Is Hampden dead? Is David dead? Is any man that was ever fit to live dead? Disenthralled of flesh, risen to the unobstructed sphere where passion never comes, he begins his illimitable work. His life is now grafted upon the infinite, and will be fruitful as no earthly life can be. Pass on, thou that hast overcome! Your sorrows, oh people, are his pæans; your bells, and bands, and muffled drums sound triumph in his ears. Wail and weep here; God makes it echo joy and triumph there. Pass on! Four years ago, oh Illinois, we took from thy midst an untried man, and from among the people; we return him to you a mighty conqueror. Not thine any more, but the nation's; not ours, but the world's. Give him place, oh ye prairies. In the midst of this great continent his dust shall rest, a sacred treasure to myriads who shall pilgrim to that great shrine to kindle anew their zeal and patriotism. Ye winds that move over the mighty places of the West, chant his requiem! Ye people, behold the martyr whose blood, as so many articulate words, pleads for fidelity, for law, for liberty!"

As the procession moved through New York on the 25th, it was witnessed by nearly a million of people. Among the most interesting of the incidents connected with the lying in state at this city was the visit to the remains of the aged soldier, General Scott, who was soon to follow the President. The funeral train reached Springfield on the 3d of May. Since his departure from that city in 1861, when he had asked his friends and neighbors to accompany him with their prayers, he had never returned till this time and in this manner. As it was beautifully expressed in one of the mottoes displayed by the citizens:

"He left us borne up by our prayers,
He returns embalmed in our tears."

Lincoln was buried at Oak Ridge Cemetery, about two miles from Springfield. The funeral oration was pronounced by Bishop Simpson.

"Here," said the bishop, "are gathered around his tomb the representatives of the army and navy, senators, judges, governors, and officers of all the branches of the government. Here, too, are members of civic processions, with men and women from the humblest as well as the highest occupations. Here and there, too, are tears as sincere and warm as any that drop, which come from the eyes of those whose kindred and whose race have been freed from their chains by him whom they mourn as their deliverer. More persons have gazed on the face of the departed than ever looked upon the face of any other departed man. More races have looked on the procession for sixteen hundred miles or more—by night and by day—by sunlight, dawn, twilight, and by torchlight, than ever before watched the progress of a procession."

He concluded with the following *Vale:*

"Chieftain, farewell! The nation mourns thee. Mothers shall teach thy name to their lisping children. The youth of our land shall emulate thy virtues. Statesmen shall study thy record and learn lessons of wisdom. Mute though thy lips be, yet they still speak. Hushed is thy voice, but its echoes of liberty are ringing through the world, and the sons of bondage listen with joy. Prisoned thou art in death, and yet thou art marching abroad, and chains and manacles are bursting at thy touch. Thou didst fall not for thyself. The assassin had no hate for thee. Our hearts were aimed at, our national life was sought. We crown thee as our martyr, and humanity enthrones thee as her triumphant son. Hero, martyr, friend, farewell!"

"Twenty-five thousand dollars for the arrest of Jacob Thompson, late of Mississippi.

"Twenty-five thousand dollars for the arrest of George N. Saunders.

"Twenty-five thousand dollars for the arrest of Beverly Tucker.

"Ten thousand dollars for the arrest of William C. Cleary, late clerk of Clement C. Clay.

"The Provost-marshal General of the United States is directed to cause a description of said persons, with notice of the above rewards, to be published.

"In testimony whereof, I have hereunto set my hand and caused the seal of the United States to be affixed.

"Done at the City of Washington, this second day of May, in the year of our Lord one thousand eight hundred and sixty-five, and of the independence of the United States of America the eighty-fifth. [L. S.]

ANDREW JOHNSON.

"By the President: W. HUNTER, Acting Secretary of State."

[1] The following is an abstract of a portion of the evidence relating to this subject, offered before the Military Commission at the trial of the conspirators:

Charles A. Dana, Assistant Secretary of War, testified that he went to Richmond April 6, and there found in Benjamin's office the key to an official cipher. It is a machine about a foot long and eight inches high, and consists of a cylinder of wood which has a paper envelope inscribed with letters; the cylinder revolves on pivot-holes at each end, and a bar across the top contains wooden indices pointing down to the letters.

Major Eckert then being sworn, testified that a cipher found in Booth's trunk corresponded with that of which Dana had spoken. Rebel dispatches of October 13th and 19th (1800) had fallen into his hand which were deciphered on the same principle. The following are the dispatches translated:

"October 13, 1864.

"We again urge the necessity of our getting immediate advantages. Strain every nerve for victory. We now look upon the re-election of Lincoln in November as almost certain, and we need to whip his hirelings to prevent it. Besides, with Lincoln re-elected, and his armies victorious, we need not hope even for recognition, much less the help mentioned in our last. Holcomb will explain this. Those figures of the Yankee armies are correct to a unit. Your friend shall be immediately set to work as you direct."

"October 19, 1864.

"Your letter of the 13th is at hand. There is yet time enough to colonize many voters before November. A blow will shortly be stricken here. It is not quite time. General Longstreet is to attack Sheridan without delay, and then move north as far as practicable toward unprotected points. This will be made instead of the movement before mentioned. He will endeavor to assist the Republicans in collecting their ballots. Be watchful and assist him."

That of the 13th passed from Canada to Richmond; that of the 19th from Richmond to Canada.

Robert A. Campbell, first teller of the Ontario Bank of Montreal, testified Jacob Thompson had kept an account with the bank from May 30, 1864. The account closed April 11, 1865. The aggregate amount of credit was $649,872 23; there was a balance due Thompson. Since March 1st he had drawn $800,000. Since the assassination Thompson had left Montreal. He said he was going overland to Halifax *en route* to Europe. This was about two weeks before navigation opened. To Mr. Campbell it seemed strange that Thompson should have gone overland, when, by waiting two weeks, he could have taken a steamer. Booth also had a small account with the Ontario Bank.

C. F. Hall testified that he had found the following paper, taken from a box marked "Adjutant General's Office. Letters received July to December, 1864."

"Montgomery, White Sulphur Springs, Va.

"To his Excellency President C. S. A.

"DEAR SIR,—I have been thinking for some time I would make this communication to you, but have been deterred from doing so on account of ill health.

"I now offer you my services, and if you will favor me in my designs, I will proceed, as soon as my health will permit, to rid my country of some of her deadliest enemies, by striking at the very heart's blood of those who seek to enchain her in slavery. I consider nothing dishonorable having such a tendency. All I want of you is to favor me by granting the necessary papers, etc., to travel on while in the jurisdiction of this government. I am perfectly familiar with the North, and feel confident that I can execute any thing I undertake. I have just returned now from within their lines. I am a lieutenant in General Duke's command. I was on a raid last June in Kentucky, under General John A. Morgan. I and all my command, except two or three commissioned officers, were taken prisoners; but, finding a good opportunity while being taken to prison, I made my escape from them. In the garb of a citizen I attempted to pass out through the mountains, but, finding that impossible, narrowly escaping two or three times being retaken, directed my course north and west through the Canadas; by the assistance of Colonel J. P. Holcombe I succeeded in making my way round through the blockade; but, having taken the yellow fever, etc., at Bermuda, I have been rendered unfit for service since my arrival. I was reared up in the State of Alabama, and educated in its University. Both the Secretary of War and his assistant, Judge Campbell, are personally acquainted with my father, William J. Alston, of the Fifth Congressional District of Alabama, having served in the time of the old Congress in 1849, 1850, and 1851. If I do any thing for you I shall expect your full confidence in return. If you can give this, I can render you and my country very important service. Let me hear from you soon. I am anxious to be doing something, and having no command at present, all or nearly all being in garrison, I desire that you favor me in this a short time. I would like to have a personal interview with you in order to perfect arrangements before starting. I am, very respectfully, your obedient servant, L. W. ALSTON.

"Address me at the Springs, in hospital."

On the above letter were the following indorsements:

"1. Brief of letter without signature.

"2. Respectfully referred by direction of the President to Honorable Secretary of War. Burton N. Harrison, Private Secretary. Received November 29, 1864. Record book A. G. O., December 6, 1864.

"3. A. G. for attention. By order, J. A. Campbell, A. S. W."

CHAPTER LXI.

CONDUCT OF THE WAR.

Grand Review at Washington.—Mustering out of the Troops.—The two Periods of the War.—Our Generals.—Connection of Negroes with the War.—The Foreign Element in our Armies.—Confederate Conscription.—The War Department and Secretary Stanton.—The Question of Supplies with the Confederates.—Sanitary Commissions.—Treatment of Prisoners.—Irregular Warfare.—Confederate Agents in Canada.—The War upon the Sea.—Anglo-Confederate Cruisers.—The Alabama Claims.—Withdrawal of the French from Mexico.—The Political Situation at the Close of the War.

UPON the surrender of the Confederate armies the war for the Union was concluded. The battles had been all fought, and the nation was victorious. It was, by reason of its victory, secure against traitors in arms. Treason might still remain, but it was a disarmed prisoner. The reward of four years of bitter strife had been grasped by a patriotic people. Peace had come, not through conciliation or compromise, but as a conquest. For a brief period the popular enthusiasm knew no bounds, until too soon it was tempered by the death of Lincoln. No one talked of political theories; all felt that such theories had no share in the glory of this triumph. The battle had been won by blood and sacrifice. With one accord the nation turned toward its armies, and showered its blessings upon them. The successful generals, the brave soldiers—these were the heroes of that time. Four years before, regiment after regiment had marched through our cities, with new banners, bright arms, and fresh, youthful faces. They were followed by hopes and prayers. Two soldiers—Ladd and Whitney—in the van of this southward march, had been slain in the streets of Baltimore, and their death so impressed the people that they received a monument, and passed into history sacredly, and by the association of time, linked with the revolutionary heroes of Lexington. These were the first victims of the war. They led that glorious march of the dead which, ere the end, numbered among its ranks over a quarter of a million of just such heroes as they, victims, by disease or mortal wounds, of this protracted struggle for a nation's life. Closing up the rear of this procession, thousands were still gathering from many hospitals.[1] But, though so large a number had disappeared by discharge, death, or wounds, their places had been filled by others. All together a million and a half of men had entered the United States service, and at the close of the war a million still remained,[2] of whom 650,000 were available for active duty. There were as many effective soldiers in the army when the Confederate forces surrendered as when, in May, 1864, Grant and Sherman entered upon their final campaigns.

Now the record of blood was all written, and the scene of four years ago was reversed. The soldiers were returning to their homes, and as they passed through our streets were welcomed back with grateful shouts. Their banners now were tattered, and their arms and uniform battle-soiled; many an absent one was mourned; and the fresh faces which went forth from us returned worn with the hardships of war. But they had served their country, and their step was proud and triumphant.

The armies of Grant and Sherman, who had shared in the latest struggle, as they passed through Washington, were marshaled in review. Over two hundred thousand soldiers made up the grand spectacle. They were assembled in one body for the first time. They were gathered together from every battle-field of the war—from the Ohio to New Orleans, from New Orleans to Olustee, and from Olustee to the Potomac. Those who looked upon that spectacle were reminded of that first stage of the war when the national capital was threatened, and when the first recruits rushed to its rescue. They looked upon a living, moving demonstration of the fact that treason in a republic *could* be subdued, though every rebel leader, from Davis and Stephens down to the most petty demagogue of the South, had prophesied to the contrary. There were some things to mar the triumph. A general who had marched and fought his army from Chattanooga through the fortifications of Atlanta to the sea, and thence to Goldsborough and Washington, still felt the wrong which had been studiously thrust upon him by some officers of the government. Sherman could not take Halleck by the hand. The soldiers also grievously missed the presence of Lincoln, who had called them to the conflict, and to whom they had always looked as father and friend. But may we not suppose that Lincoln, though withdrawn from the earth, looked down upon the sublime spectacle? Did he not, as one of our poets has imagined, marshal another host, composed of those who, like him, had been victims of this civil war, and who now participated in this grand review?[1]

---

[1] It is estimated that during the war 56,000 national soldiers were killed in battle, while about 35,000 died in hospital of wounds, and 184,000 by disease. The mortal casualties of the war, if we include those dying subsequent to their discharge, probably did not fall short of 300,000. The Confederates lost less in battle, owing to the defensive character of the struggle on their part; but they lost more from wounds and disease, on account of their inferior sanitary arrangements. The total loss of life caused by the rebellion must have been over half a million, while nearly as many more were disabled.

[2] The calls made during the war amount to nearly three millions of men. The following table shows the date of the several demands, the length of the period of service required, and the number obtained:

Date of Call.	Number called for.	Periods of Service.	Number obtained.	Date of Call.	Number called for.	Periods of Service.	Number obtained.
April 15, 1861........	75,000	3 mos.	93,326	October 17, 1863	300,000	3 yrs. }	
May and July, 1861 ..	582,748	3 yrs.	714,231	February 1, 1864......	200,000	3 yrs. }	374,807
May and June, 1862..		3 mos.	15,007	March 14, 1864.......	200,000	3 yrs.	284,021
July 2, 1862	300,000	3 yrs.	431,958	April 23, 1864.......	85,000	100 days.	83,652
August 4, 1862........	300,000	9 mos.	87,588	July 18, 1864........	500,000	1, 2, & 3 yrs.	384,882
June 15, 1863........	100,000	6 mos.	16,361	December 19, 1864...	300,000	1, 2, & 3 yrs.	204,568
				Total........	2,942,748		2,690,401

The following table shows the number of men furnished by the several states, in the aggregate, and reduced to three years' standard:

States.	Aggregate.	Aggregate reduced to Three Years' Standard.	States.	Aggregate.	Aggregate reduced to Three Years' Standard.
Maine..................	71,745	56,656	District of Columbia....	16,872	11,506
New Hampshire........	34,605	30,827	Ohio..................	317,133	239,976
Vermont...............	35,256	29,052	Indiana...............	195,147	152,283
Massachusetts.........	151,785	123,844	Illinois	258,217	212,694
Rhode Island..........	23,711	17,878	Michigan	90,119	80,865
Connecticut	57,270	50,514	Wisconsin	96,118	78,985
New York..............	455,568	380,980	Minnesota.............	25,034	19,675
New Jersey	79,511	55,785	Iowa	75,860	68,182
Pennsylvania	366,326	267,558	Missouri	108,773	86,192
Delaware	13,651	10,303	Kentucky..............	76,540	70,348
West Virginia.........	30,003	27,653	Kansas	20,097	18,654
Maryland	49,730	40,692	Total	2,653,062	2,128,941

It is impossible to give an exact estimate of the number of *different* men who entered the service. It is generally conceded, however, to have been about a million and a half. Scarcely less than three quarters of a million different men entered the Confederate armies, not including state militia. So that the number of men withdrawn from industrial pursuits by the war was over two millions.

[1] Henry Howard Brownell, in a poem originally published in the *Atlantic Monthly*—a poem which is certainly the greatest of the many called forth by the war—thus expresses this imagination:

"So, from the fields they win,
Our men are marching home—
A million are marching home!
To the cannon's thundering din,
And banners on mast and dome;
And the ships come sailing in
With all their ensigns dight,
As erst for a great sea-fight.

"Let every color fly,
Every pennon flaunt in pride;
Wave, Starry Flag, on high!
Float in the sunny sky,
Stream o'er the stormy tide!
For every stripe of stainless hue,
And every star in the field of blue,
Ten thousand of the brave and true
Have laid them down and died.

"And in all our pride to-day
We think, with a tender pain,
Of those so far away
They will not come home again.

"And our boys had fondly thought,
To-day, in marching by,
From the ground so dearly bought,
And the fields so bravely fought,
To have met their Father's eye.

"But they may not see him in place,
Nor their ranks be seen of him;
We look for the well-known face,
And the splendor is strangely dim.

"Perished?—who was it said
Our Leader had passed away?
Dead? Our President dead?
He has not died for a day!

"We mourn for a little breath
Such as, late or soon, dust yields;
But the dark flower of death
Blooms in the fadeless fields.

"We looked on a cold, still brow,
But Lincoln could yet survive;
He never was more alive,
Never nearer than now.

"For the pleasant season found him,
Guarded by faithful hands,
In the fairest of Summer Lands:
With his own brave staff around him,
There our President stands.

"There they are all at his side,
The noble hearts and true,
That did all men might do—
Then slept, with their swords, and died.

"Of little the storm has reft us
But the brave and kindly clay—
('Tis but dust where Lander left us,
And but turf where Lyon lay).

"There's Winthrop, true to the end,
And Ellsworth of long ago
(First fair young head laid low!);
There's Baker, the brave old friend,
And Douglas, the friendly foe.

"(Baker, that still stood up
When 'twas death on either hand:
'Tis a soldier's part to stoop,
But the senator must stand.')

"The heroes gather and form—
There's Cameron, with his scars,
Sedgwick, of siege and storm,
And Mitchell, that joined his stars.

"Winthrop, of sword and pen,
Wadsworth, with silver hair,
Mansfield, ruler of men,
And brave McPherson are there.

"Birney, who led so long,
Abbott, born to command,
Elliott the bold, and Strong,
Who fell on the hard-fought strand.

"Lytle, soldier and bard,
And the Ellets, sire and son;
Ransom, all grandly scarred,
And Redfield, no more on guard
(But Allatoona is won!).

"Reno, of pure desert,
Kearney, with heart of flame,
And Russell, that hid his hurt
Till the final death-bolt came;

"Terrill, dead where he fought,
Wallace, that would not yield,
And Sumner, who vainly sought
A grave on the foughten field

"(But died ere the end he saw,
With years and battles outworn).
There's Harker of Kenesaw,
And Ulric Dahlgren, and Shaw,
That slept with his hope forlorn.

"Bayard, that knew not fear
(True as the knight of yore),
And Putnam, and Paul Revere,
Worthy the names they bore.

"Allen, who died for others,
Bryan, of gentle fame,
And the brave New England brothers
That have left us Lowell's name.

"Home, at last, from the wars—
Stedman, the stanch and mild,
And Janeway, our hero-child,
Home, with his fifteen scars!

"There's Porter, ever in front,
True son of a sea-king sire,
And Christian Foote, and Dupont
(Dupont, who led his ships
Rounding the first ellipse
Of thunder and of fire).

"There's Ward, with his brave death-wounds,
And Cummings, of spotless name,
And Smith, who hurtled his rounds
When deck and hatch were aflame;

"Wainwright, steadfast and true,
Rodgers, of brave sea-blood,
And Craven, with ship and crew
Sunk in the salt sea flood.

"And, a little later to part,
Our captain, noble and dear—
(Did they deem thee, then, austere?
Drayton! O pure and kindly heart!
Thine is the seaman's tear).

"All such, and many another
(Ah, list how long to name!),
That stood like brother by brother,
And died on the field of fame.

"And around—(for there can cease
This earthly trouble)—they throng,
The friends that had passed in peace,
The foes that have seen their wrong.

"(But, a little from the rest,
With sad eyes looking down,
And brows of softened frown,
With stern arms on the crest,
Are two, standing abreast—
Stonewall and Old John Brown.)

"But the stainless and the true,
These by their President stand,
To look on his last review,
Or march with the old command.

"And lo, from a thousand fields,
From all the old battle-haunts,
A greater army than Sherman wields,
A grander review than Grant's!

"Gathered home from the grave,
Risen from sun and rain—
Rescued from wind and wave
Out of the stormy main—
The legions of our brave
Are all in their lines again!

"Many a stout corps that went,
Full-ranked, from camp and tent,
And brought back a brigade;
Many a brave regiment,
That mustered only a squad.

"The lost battalions,
That, when the fight went wrong,
Stood and died at their guns—
The stormers steady and strong,

"With their best blood that bought
Scarp, and ravelin, and wall—
The companies that fought
Till a corporal's guard was all.

"Many a valiant crew,
That passed in battle and wreck—
Ah, so faithful and true!
They died on the bloody deck,
They sank in the soundless blue.

"All the loyal and bold
That lay on a soldier's bier—
The stretchers borne to the rear,
The hammocks lowered to the hold.

"The shattered wreck we hurried,
In death-fight, from deck and port—
The Blacks that Wagner buried—
That died in the Bloody Fort!

"Comrades of camp and mess,
Left, as they lay, to die,
In the battle's sorest stress,
When the storm of fight swept by;
They lay in the Wilderness—
Ah! where did they not lie?

"In the tangled swamp they lay,
They lay so still on the sward!—
They rotted in the sick-bay,
Moaning their lives away—
They flushed in the fevered ward.

"They rotted in Libby yonder,
They starved in the foul stockade—
Hearing afar the thunder
Of the Union cannonade!

"But the old wounds all are healed,
And the dungeoned limbs are free—
The Blue Frocks rise from the field,
The Blue Jackets out of the sea.

"They've 'scaped from the torture-den,
They've broken the bloody sod,
They're all come to life again!—
The third of a million men
That died for thee and for God!

"A tenderer green than May
The Eternal Season wears—
The blue of our summer's day
Is dim and pallid to theirs—
The horror faded away,
And 'twas heaven all unawares!

"Tents on the Infinite Shore!
Flags in the azuline sky,
Sails on the seas once more!
To-day, in the heaven on high,
All under arms once more!

"The troops are all in their lines,
The guidons flutter and play;
But every bayonet shines,
For all must march to-day.

"What lofty pennons flaunt?
What mighty echoes haunt,
As of great guns, o'er the main?
Hark to the sound again—
The Congress is all afloat!
The Cumberland's manned again!

"All the ships and their men
Are in line of battle to-day—
All at quarters, as when
Their last roll thundered away—
All at their guns, as then,
For the fleet salutes to-day.

"The armies have broken camp
On the vast and sunny plain,
The drums are rolling again;
With steady, measured tramp,
They're marching all again.

"With alignment firm and solemn,
Once again they form
In mighty square and column—
But never for charge and storm.

"The old flag they died under
Floats above them on the shore,
And on the great ships yonder
The ensigns dip once more—
And once again the thunder
Of the thirty guns and four!

"In solid platoons of steel,
Under heaven's triumphal arch,
The long lines break and wheel,
And the word is 'Forward, march!'

"The colors ripple o'erhead,
The drums roll up to the sky,
And with martial time and tread
The regiments all pass by—
The ranks of our faithful Dead,
Meeting their President's eye.

"With a soldier's quiet pride
They smile o'er the perished pain,
For their anguish was not vain—
'For thee, O Father, we died!
And we did not die in vain.'

"March on, your last brave mile!
Salute him, Star and Lace!
Form round him, rank and file,
And look on the kind, rough face;
But the quaint and homely smile
Has a glory and a grace
It never had known erewhile—
Never, in time and space.

"Close round him, hearts of pride!
Press near him, side by side—
Our Father is not alone!
For the Holy Right ye died,
And Christ, the Crucified,
Waits to welcome his own."

GRAND REVIEW AT WASHINGTON.—SHERMAN'S VETERANS MARCHING THROUGH PENNSYLVANIA AVENUE.

Immediately after Lee's surrender the government began to return to a peace establishment. Four days after this surrender Secretary Stanton issued orders stopping all drafting and recruiting, curtailing purchases of arms and supplies, and reducing the number of general and staff officers. Before the close of April, 1865, preparations were made for mustering out the volunteers. On November 15th, 900,000 soldiers had been discharged.[1] The stability of the republic was not more surely demonstrated by the success of the war for the Union than by the speedy and quiet return of its defenders to civil pursuits after the suspension of hostilities.

The course of the war has been traced in the pages of this history. Of the minor actions, many have been omitted because they had no bearing upon the result; but the principal campaigns have been developed as accurately and elaborately as has been possible. We who have written, while aware of the fact that many events might have been more fully developed and illustrated by private and unofficial intelligence, still feel confident that the general outlines of the war, as we have delineated them, will thus remain forever. It is unnecessary for us here to enter into a minute review of the contest. Two eras of the war are distinctly marked. The first ended in the summer of 1863, in the victories at Gettysburg and Vicksburg. In this first period no distinction can be made between the martial enthusiasm or military skill displayed on the two sides of the struggle. In the peninsular campaign of 1862, it is difficult to say which general committed the most serious blunders—Lee or McClellan. At Shiloh we are no more astonished by Grant's negligence as to any preparation for the conflict which he knew was sure to come, than by the panic which two gun-boats created among the Confederates, depriving them of the victory of which they were already assured by their preponderance of numbers. If we wonder why Hooker, at Chancellorsville, outnumbering the enemy almost two to one, was compelled to recross the Rappahannock, we are not less surprised that Johnston and Pemberton did not prevent Grant from reaching the rear of Vicksburg after the latter general had placed his army at the mercy of his antagonists. But after the defeat of the Confederates at Gettysburg, involving severe losses on their side, and after the surrender of Vicksburg and Port Hudson, involving a loss of nearly 50,000 more, we find the conflict not only contracted to smaller proportions, but proceeding upon far more favorable conditions for the national armies. After this time the Confederate forces dwindle away by discouragement and desertion, and never again reach their former numbers. The decisive victories won by Grant at Missionary Ridge and Lookout Mountain, in November, 1863, began to illustrate the new conditions of this second era of the war. At the same time, Meade was hesitating in the East; but in May, 1864, Grant was at the head of the Army of the Potomac. Then simultaneously began the campaigns against Richmond and Atlanta, and in both the Union armies were twice as large as those which confronted them. The exhaustion of the enemy now went on rapidly, and the memorable blunder of Hood's invasion hastened the final crisis. Sherman proceeded upon his two bold marches, and in the spring of 1865 the war was terminated in Virginia and North Carolina. The crushing political defeat of the peace party in the North, while it did not create military victories, insured the ultimate success of our armies, and took away from the insurgents their last hope.

Upon a careful study of the campaigns of this war, and comparing them with those of the Old World in other times, although we find much that excites admiration, we do not find upon either side a general who could rank with the first-class generals of the world. The comparison of Lee, of Johnston, or Grant, or even of Sherman, with Napoleon or Frederick, is unwarranted, while either of the American generals named might be fitly matched with the Duke of Wellington. Republics do not, in the ordinary course of events, naturally beget Cæsars, Napoleons, nor Fredericks. Few of our generals entered the war to satisfy a personal ambition, and those who did failed utterly. Whatever success was attained was the result of a desire to faithfully serve the country. It is fortunate, on the whole, that such was the case, and that the people might claim for themselves the victory.

The fact that over one eighth of the population of the country consisted of slaves, and the relation of this servile race to the war, demands our attention. The negroes of the South expected that the war would result in their emancipation, and they were not surprised when the government broke their fetters. They waited for their freedom, but not one blow of their own motion did they strike for it. When they came within our lines, their poverty and dependence made them willing conscripts. Their sympathy with the national cause is evident from the many instances in which they furnished valuable information to our officers, and assisted our fugitive prisoners in escaping northward. Their assistance, however valuable, was not absolutely necessary, and had no important bearing upon the final result of the war. About 175,000 negroes entered the United States service, and a large portion of these were employed in garrison duty. It is a very suggestive fact, and speaks well for the peaceful disposition of the Southern negro, that while thousands of opportunities were afforded, no case of servile insurrection occurred during the war. In the early part of 1865, when every other resource had apparently been exhausted, the question of enrolling the negro as a soldier, and giving him his freedom, was quite generally discussed in the South, but it did not meet with the favor of the Confederate President. If this measure had been adopted by the Confederate government at an early stage of the war, there is no reason to doubt that the slaves would have fought for the enemies of the national government as willingly as they built their fortifications or performed other offices. The disposi by the nation of the emancipated slave after the war closed did not much upon the basis of gratitude as upon general considerations affec the common welfare.

It has been frequently asserted that the foreign element of our popula was indispensable to victory, but this assertion is contradicted by the that over nine tenths of our soldiers were native-born citizens. The umph of the nation would have been certain if neither foreigners nor sl had engaged in the contest. But this fact ought not to diminish the nati gratitude toward the negroes and foreigners who fought in its behalf, who acquitted themselves well on the field of battle.

The two ideas upon which the Confederacy rested were those of s sovereignty and the untrammeled development of negro slavery. Scarc however, had the Southern States been, for these purposes, launched u their novel voyage—scarcely had they entered upon the conflict for i pendence, when the necessities of war threatened the ruin of both s sovereignty and slavery. The concentration of power in the Confede executive—more formidable and despotic than had ever before been e cised over the states of the republic—left scarcely a vestige of liberty ei to states or individuals. And, on the other hand, the progress of the tional arms—slow, but steady and sure—threatened the destruction of sl ery. The people of the South, therefore, could not, without apprehensi look forward to either success or defeat. They had espoused a cause whi if won, placed them at the mercy of the despotism to which they had co mitted themselves, and the loss of which would lay them prostrate at the f of a power whose just claim to their allegiance they had defied and resist To one of these evils they had committed themselves so absolutely that release from that lay within their power; to the other evil they *would* yield but by compulsion. They were embarked upon a ship whose pil would surely deliver it into the jaws of Scylla, unless Fate should deliver over to the opposite Charybdis. Fate was rapidly deciding in favor Charybdis; but, in the mean time, they, without heart, and in their despe tion, shouted their pilots on Scylla-ward. It was a pitiable situation, b they had brought it upon themselves by weakly yielding their property a their lives at the bidding of ambitious traitors. In a moment of enthusias believing that no power could withstand "Southern chivalry," and th Northern enterprise, industry, and intelligence were but synonyms for co ardice, and would easily be driven from every battle-field by an effete sla aristocracy, they had dared every thing, had invoked war by an outrage up the national flag, had pledged their estates, their honor, and their lives treason. A few months of war exposed their mistake, both as to the cha acter of their leaders and of the struggle in which they were engaged; bu then there was no escape for a people already demoralized by rebellion.

It was only by the most arbitrary exercise of power that the Confederat armies were recruited after the first year of the war. Those who volun teered at the beginning were forcibly retained after the expiration of thei terms of service. On the 16th of April, 1862, a Conscription Bill passed th Confederate Congress which placed in the service for three years all whit men between the ages of 18 and 35 not legally exempted. On the 15th o July, 1863, Davis issued a proclamation which included in the service al between 18 and 45. But even this act was not sufficient. The Confederat armies did not reach their former standard. This was due largely to dese tion. In February, 1864, a Conscription Bill was passed by the Confederat Congress declaring all white men between the ages of 17 and 50 "in th military service for the war." By this law, the exemption of those who ha furnished substitutes was revoked. The only persons exempted were minis ters of the Gospel who were in the actual performance of their duties; supe intendents of deaf, dumb, and blind or insane asylums; one editor for eac newspaper, and such employés as he might upon oath declare indispens able; public printers and their necessary assistants; one apothecary to eac drug-store; physicians over 30 years of age of seven years' practice; presi dents and teachers of colleges, academies, and schools, who had 30 or mor pupils; the superintendents of public hospitals, with such physicians an nurses as were indispensable for the management of the same; and one ag riculturist on each farm where there was no white male adult not liable t military duty, and which employed 15 able-bodied slaves. This act left n resource untouched. Only those were excluded from service who were ab solutely necessary to the production of supplies and for the execution of th functions of government. According to an estimate published at Richmon at the close of 1864, there were in the Confederacy in 1860, between th ages of 17 and 50, 1,299,700 white men. Since that time it was estimate that 331,650 had arrived at the age of 17. And this addition would prob ably be balanced by the ordinary mortality added to the number of thos who had advanced beyond the age of 50. But, deducting the populatio within the Federal lines, the losses in battle and by unusual disease, exemp tions for disability, prisoners held by the Federals, and those who had lef the country, there were less than half a million of soldiers left to the Con federacy, and of these full 250,000 were already in the Confederate armies From this estimate it appears that by the close of 1864 the Confederacy wa nearly exhausted of its fighting men.

The Conscription Act passed by the United States Congress did not di rectly increase the army to any considerable extent. But the number o substitutes obtained, and the high bounties offered under the influence o the act, increased the Federal armies to the full measure required.

It would be unjust to leave unnoticed Secretary Stanton's admirabl and efficient administration of the War Department. By this departmen a million of men were fed, clothed, armed, and supplied with ammunition and with all the war material necessary to organized armies; an immens

[1] Troops mustered out to August 7... 640,806 | Troops mustered out to October 15... 785,205
" " " August 22.. 719,338 | " " " November 15 800,963
" " " Sept. 14.... 741,107

fleet of transports moved at its bidding, laden with supplies; and under its orders thousands of miles of railroad were constructed and put in operation. Upon its prompt and efficient efforts our armies depended not only for subsistence, but also, to a great degree, for the successful issue of their marches and battles. At the head of this vast organization stood the secretary, untiring, conscientious, kind-hearted, but often brusque, as men are apt to be upon whom rest weighty responsibilities. His character was irreproachable, and his management was characterized by scrupulous economy. He had his failings, doubtless, and made many enemies; but no man probably could have been more wisely selected to move, adjust, and keep in harmonious operation the intricate machinery of a great war.

The task of supplying the national armies involved only a financial problem; with the Confederates it was a question of possibilities, and in 1863 it became a difficult and embarrassing question. The Confederate currency had depreciated until a dollar in paper was only worth six cents in coin. There were not in the South, as in the North, large capitalists to buy up the government bonds, and the banks were rapidly exhausted. The agriculturists were willing to sell their produce only at the highest market price in currency, and many refused to sell at all. The most fertile portion of the soil was devoted to the production of cotton, tobacco, and rice, and the substitution of other crops was a measure very reluctantly adopted. To add to the embarrassment of the situation, the year 1863 was remarkable for scarcity in every crop. The possession of the Mississippi cut off all supplies from the fertile states west of that river, and the occupation of East Tennessee deprived the Confederate armies of bacon. The stringency of the blockade made any extensive importation of supplies or exportation of cotton impossible; and an important consequence was the absorption of a large proportion of labor in the production of war material. The conscription of all the able-bodied men in the Confederacy between 18 and 45 left a small laboring population, if we except women, children, and slaves. It is easily seen, therefore, that the slaves of the South were already become an indispensable support of a war for the perpetuation of their own bondage. If at this crisis the Confederate government had proclaimed the emancipation of slaves, it would have stood on a high vantage-ground both as regarded foreign powers and the conduct of its struggle for independence. But such an act was, under the circumstances, a moral impossibility.

The Confederate government met the difficulty of obtaining supplies just as it had met that of obtaining soldiers. As it had forced the latter by conscription, so now it began to impress the former. If its despotic will could demand the lives of men, it could certainly demand their property. Thus the government obtained supplies at its own price. But this action created great popular discontent and much distress. The natural desire on the part of agriculturists to evade impressment led them to refuse their products to the public markets. Besides this, the extent to which impressment was carried on in the vicinity of the principal dépôts left a scanty supply of provisions for the people, and especially for women and children whose natural protectors were in the army. Famine cursed the large cities, and the instances were not a few in which women marched through the streets with arms in their hands, and compelled the satisfaction of their hunger which they had no money to appease.

What food there was in the Confederacy was not made fully available for the supply of the army or of the principal towns. The railroads were giving way, and there were no means at hand for their repair. The wooden ties rotted, the machinery was almost exhausted, the rails were worn out, and thus the speed and capacity of the trains were greatly reduced. This embarrassment in regard to supplies weakened and discouraged the Confederate armies, and produced disaffection among the people.

In another respect a great contrast is presented upon a comparison of the National and Confederate armies. We allude to sanitary arrangements. No nation ever took such care of its armies in the field as did the United States in this war. Scarcely had the President issued his first call for 75,000 men before, in our cities and rural districts, hundreds of soldiers and societies sprang up to furnish lint, bandages, hospital clothing, nurses, and delicacies for the sick and the wounded. It was at this time that the Women's American Association of Relief was organized in New York City. Associated with this organization were a number of eminent medical men, prominent among whom was Rev. Henry W. Bellows, D.D. This society united with the advisory committee of the Board of Physicians and Surgeons of New York, and the New York Medical Association for furnishing supplies in aid of the army, in sending a delegation to Washington to offer their co-operation with the medical bureau of the government. Accordingly, H. W. Bellows, and Drs. W. H. Van Buren, Elisha Harris, and Jacob Harsen, on the 18th of May, 1861, addressed a communication to the Secretary of War recommending the organization of a commission of civilians, medical men, and military officers, having for its object the regulation and development of the active benevolence of the people toward the army. With some reluctance the organization was permitted to exist under the name of a "Commission of Inquiry and Advice in respect of the Sanitary Interests of the United States Forces." Subsequently it was styled simply the United States Sanitary Commission.[1] From duties which at first were simply advisory, the commission soon advanced to such as were executive. Its representatives were found upon every transport, at every camp and every fort, in every hospital and on every battle-field. It carefully investigated the character of the original *material* of the army from a sanitary point of view. The diet and clothing of the recruits, the cleanliness of their persons, their camping-grounds, were all subjects of its care. Disease was thus, to a great degree, prevented in the incipient stages of the soldier's career. Every provision was made for the relief of the sick and the wounded. The ambulances of the commission followed the army into battle, took the soldier almost as he fell, and prompt and sufficient relief was applied where relief was possible, and the most tender care taken of the dead. When the soldiers of the hostile army fell into our hands, they also shared in these beneficent provisions.

The officers and agents of the commission received no compensation for their labors. The people generously supplied them with the necessary means for carrying out their designs, both by the contribution of money and supplies. There were other organizations formed for similar objects, prominent among which were the Christian and the Western Sanitary Commissions. It is estimated that through these channels, and other means used for the benefit of the soldier, not less than $500,000,000 were expended. At a single fair in New York City over a million of dollars was realized by the United States Sanitary Commission.

It must not be supposed that the Confederates at home did not make sacrifices for their soldiers in the field, but from the lack of extensive and well-regulated organizations like those which we have described, their armies suffered far heavier losses both from diseases in the camp, which might have been largely prevented, and from casualties in the field, which proved fatal for want of prompt relief.

In this general review of the war there is one page upon which the historian is loth to enter. Whatever instances of barbarity may have occurred in the heat of battle or in the excitement of the march on either side, and although in some sections of the West there was a prevailing disregard of the usages of civilized war, still, to the soldiers of both armies, history must yield the honor always due to bravery. But the treatment of national prisoners by the Confederate government, especially in the later stages of the war, is a disgrace which the conscientious historian can neither palliate nor gloss over, though his cheek burn with shame for his own countrymen.

The question of the exchange of prisoners was at the outset one beset with a legal difficulty. At first the prevailing opinion was in favor of hanging as traitors every prisoner captured by the government. The rebellion was regarded as an insurrection which could soon be put down by energy and severity, and it seemed derogatory to the national dignity to recognize the belligerent rights of rebels by negotiations with them of any sort. But it was soon found necessary to adopt a different view of the whole question.

The first prisoners captured by the government were the captain and crew of the privateer Savannah, who fell into the hands of the United States brig Perry on the 3d of June, 1861. These men were tried as pirates; but, while their trial was pending, the Confederate government threatened to visit upon the prisoners captured at Bull Run the precise punishment which should be inflicted upon the privateersmen. By this threat of retaliation, the national government was induced to abandon its position. There still remained an unwillingness on its part to directly sanction exchanges, and the whole matter was for a time submitted to the various commanders, to be arranged under flags of truce. But in this way only a few exchanges took place. Without instructions from the general government, our generals declined to receive communications on the subject from the other side. Thus, after the battle of Belmont, in November, 1861, General

HENRY W. BELLOWS.

[1] The commission was composed of the following gentlemen: Rev. H. W. Bellows, D.D., New York; Professor A. D. Bache, Vice-President, Washington; Elisha Harris, M.D., Corresponding Secretary, New York; George W. Cullum, U. S. A., Washington; Alexander E. Shiras, U. S. A., Washington; Robert C. Wood, M.D., U. S. A., Washington; W. H. Van Buren, M.D., New York; Wolcott Gibbs, M.D., New York; Cornelius R. Agnew, M.D., New York; George T. Strong, New York; Frederick Law Olmstead, New York; Samuel G. Howe, M.D., Boston; J. S. Newberry, M.D., Cleveland, Ohio. Others were afterward included, and there were nearly 600 associate members in all parts of the country.

GRAND REVIEW AT WASHINGTON—SHERIDAN'S CAVALRY PASSING THROUGH PENNSYLVANIA AVENUE, MAY 23, 1865.

CAMP OF CONFEDERATE PRISONERS AT ELMIRA, NEW YORK.

Grant refused to treat with General Polk for a general exchange of prisoners captured in that action. The shyness of the national government in this matter was as ridiculous as it was unnecessary. The existence of the blockade was a recognition of belligerent rights as full as that involved in a cartel for the exchange of prisoners. In neither case did the recognition of belligerent rights involve a recognition of sovereignty. If the necessities of war justified the blockade, the necessities of humanity justified and demanded an arrangement in regard to prisoners.

In the latter part of December, 1861, a joint resolution was adopted by Congress, requesting the President to take immediate measures to effect a general exchange. During the following January Secretary Stanton appointed two commissioners, the Rev. Bishop Ames and the Hon. Hamilton Fish, "to visit the prisoners belonging to the army of the United States now in captivity at Richmond, in Virginia, and elsewhere, and under such regulations as may be prescribed by the authorities having custody of such prisoners, relieve their necessities and provide for their comfort at the expense of the United States." The authorities at Richmond refused to admit the commissioners, but declared their readiness to negotiate for a general exchange of prisoners. Negotiations for this purpose were accordingly opened at Norfolk, Virginia. These resulted in an agreement for an equal exchange. The Confederates at this time held 300 prisoners in excess of those captured by the national troops. These they proposed to release on parole, provided the United States would release the same number of those who might afterward be captured by them. The exchanges were commenced in the latter part of February, 1862, but were interrupted on the 18th of March by a message from President Davis to the Confederate Congress, recommending that all the Confederate prisoners who had been paroled by the United States government be released from the obligations of their parole. In the mean time, the captures made at Roanoke Island and Fort Donelson left an excess of many thousands of prisoners in the hands of the national government.

On the 22d of July a cartel was agreed upon for a general exchange, based upon that established between the United States and Great Britain in 1812. According to the provisions of this cartel, an equal exchange was to be made. All prisoners taken on either side were to be released in ten days after their capture; and those for whom no exchange could be rendered were to be bound by parole not to perform military duty until exchanged.[1]

The provisions of this cartel were carried out generally in good faith on both sides; but in some instances its perfect execution was interrupted.

[1] The following is the text of this cartel:

"Haxall's Landing, on James River, Va., July 22, 1862.

"The undersigned, having been commissioned by the authorities they respectively represent to make arrangements for a general exchange of prisoners of war, have agreed to the following articles:

"ARTICLE 1. It is hereby agreed and stipulated that all prisoners of war held by either party, including those taken on private armed vessels, known as privateers, shall be discharged upon the conditions and terms following:

"Prisoners to be exchanged man for man and officer for officer; privates to be placed on the footing of officers and men of the navy.

"Men and officers of lower grades may be exchanged for officers of a higher grade, and men and officers of different services may be exchanged according to the following scale of equivalents:

"A general commander-in-chief or an admiral shall be exchanged for officers of equal rank, or forty-six privates or common seamen.

"A flag-officer or major general shall be exchanged for officers of equal rank, or for forty privates or common seamen.

"A commodore carrying a broad pennant, or a brigadier general, shall be exchanged for officers of equal rank, or twenty privates or common seamen.

"A captain in the navy, or a colonel, shall be exchanged for officers of equal rank, or for fifteen privates or common seamen.

"A lieutenant colonel, or a commander in the navy, shall be exchanged for officers of equal rank, or for ten privates or common seamen.

"A lieutenant commander or a major shall be exchanged for officers of equal rank, or eight privates or common seamen.

"A lieutenant or a master in the navy, or a captain in the army or marines, shall be exchanged for officers of equal rank, or six privates or common seamen.

"Masters' mates in the navy, or lieutenants and ensigns in the army, shall be exchanged for officers of equal rank, or four privates or common seamen.

"Midshipmen, warrant officers in the navy, masters of merchant vessels, and commanders of privateers, shall be exchanged for officers of equal rank, or three privates or common seamen; second captains, lieutenants, or mates of merchant vessels or privateers, and all petty officers in the navy, and all non-commissioned officers in the army or marines, shall be severally exchanged for persons of equal rank, or for two privates or common seamen; and private soldiers and common seamen shall be exchanged for each other, man for man.

"ART. 2. Local, state, civil, and militia rank held by persons not in actual military service will not be recognized, the basis of exchange being of a grade actually held in the naval and military service of the respective parties.

"ART. 3. If citizens held by either party on charge of disloyalty or any alleged civil offense are exchanged, it shall only be for citizens, captured sutlers, teamsters, and all civilians in the actual service of either party, to be exchanged for persons in similar position.

"ART. 4. All prisoners of war to be discharged on parole in ten days after their capture, and the prisoners now held and those hereafter taken to be transported to the points mutually agreed upon at the expense of the capturing party. The surplus prisoners not exchanged shall not be permitted to take up arms again, nor to serve as military police or constabulary force in any fort, garrison, or field-work held by either of the respective parties, nor as guards of prisoners, dépôts, or stores, nor to discharge any duty usually performed by soldiers, until exchanged under the provisions of this cartel. The exchange is not to be considered complete until the officer or soldier exchanged for has been actually restored to the lines to which he belongs.

"ART. 5. Each party, upon the discharge of prisoners of the other party, is authorized to discharge an equal number of their own officers or men from parole, furnishing at the same time to the other party a list of their prisoners discharged and of their own officers and men relieved from parole, enabling each party to relieve from parole such of their own officers and men as the party may choose. The lists thus mutually furnished will keep both parties advised of the true condition of the exchanges of prisoners.

"ART. 6. The stipulations and provisions above mentioned to be of binding obligation during the continuance of the war, it matters not which party may have the surplus of prisoners, the great principle involved being,

"1. An equitable exchange of prisoners, man for man, officer for officer, or officers of higher grade exchanged for officers of lower grade or for privates, according to the scale of equivalents.

"2. That privates and officers and men of different services may be exchanged according to the same rule of equivalents.

"3. That all prisoners, of whatsoever arm of service, are to be exchanged or paroled in ten days from the time of their capture, if it be practicable to transfer them to their own lines in that time; if not, as soon thereafter as practicable.

"4. That no officer, soldier, or employé in the service of either party is to be considered as exchanged and absolved from his parole until his equivalent has actually reached the line of his friends.

"5. That the parole forbids the performance of field, garrison, police, or guard or constabulary duty.

JOHN A. DIX, Major General.

"D. H. HILL, Major General C. S. Army"

Supplementary Articles.

"ART. 7. All prisoners of war now held on either side, and all prisoners hereafter taken, shall be sent with all reasonable dispatch to A. H. Aikens, below Dutch Gap, on the James River, in Virginia, or to Vicksburg, on the Mississippi River, in the State of Mississippi, and there exchanged, or paroled until such exchange can be effected, notice being previously given by each party of the number of prisoners it will send, and the time when they will be delivered at those points respectively; and in case the vicissitudes of war shall change the military relations of the places designated in this article to the contending parties, so as to render the same inconvenient for the delivery and exchange of prisoners, other places, bearing as nearly as may be the present local relations of said places to the lines of said parties, shall be, by mutual agreement, substituted. But nothing

The execution of William B. Mumford by order of General Butler at New Orleans; the measures taken by Federal generals to prevent private citizens not in the regular service of the Confederates from engaging in acts of war; the orders of General Pope for the impressment of property required for the use of his army in Virginia; and the action of Generals Hunter and Phelps in regard to slaves, led to a series of retaliatory orders from Richmond, issued partly for popular effect, but which were only partially executed. They contributed, however, to exaggerate the animosity of the war. Still the exchanges went on regularly at City Point during the year, and the excess of prisoners on either side was not sufficient to occasion apprehension as to the good faith of the other.

But, in the mean time, President Lincoln had issued his Emancipation Proclamation, and measures had been taken by the United States government for the employment of negroes in its military service. These measures produced consternation and fear in the minds of the Southern people. President Davis, in his message (January 14, 1863), declared his determination to deliver over to the state authorities all commissioned officers of the United States thereafter captured in any of the states embraced in the Emancipation Proclamation, to be punished as criminals engaged in exciting servile insurrection. This determination was supported by the Confederate Congress.[1]

The cartel remained in operation until July, 1863. On the third of that month, an order was issued by the Adjutant General at Washington requiring all prisoners to be delivered at City Point and Vicksburg, there to be exchanged, or paroled until exchange could be effected. The only exception allowed was in the case of the two opposing commanders, who were authorized to exchange prisoners or to release them on parole at other points agreed upon. This order was issued to prevent unauthorized paroles, and in order that the balance of exchanges might be accurately kept. The very next day General Lee was defeated at Gettysburg, and released a number of prisoners which he was unable to take with him into Virginia. He therefore paroled them, and the parole was not recognized by the United States, as it had not been made in strict accordance with the cartel, nor by the mutual agreement of the opposing commanders. At the same time, a large number of Confederate prisoners fell into the hands of the Federals by the captures of Vicksburg and Port Hudson. These were paroled by mutual agreement between the Federal and Confederate commanders. The Confederate government, without any plausible reason, declared these prisoners released from their parole, and thousands of them fought under Bragg in the battles about Chattanooga in November. But this violation of good faith did not permanently interrupt the exchange of prisoners.

The real difficulty, however, soon presented itself in the refusal of the Confederate government to recognize negro soldiers captured as prisoners of war. That government refused to exchange negro prisoners or the commissioned officers of negro regiments. The United States could not honorably make any distinction between its soldiers on the ground of color. When, therefore, the Confederate government adopted the policy of reducing to slavery all negro prisoners, and of delivering over to the state governments for punishment the commissioned officers of negro regiments, President Lincoln issued a proclamation ordering that for every national soldier killed a Confederate soldier should be executed, and for every negro in the national service sold into slavery, a Confederate prisoner should be placed at hard labor on the public works.[1] This proclamation prevented the Confederate government from carrying out its inhuman policy; but it persisted in refusing to exchange negro prisoners. This refusal interrupted the execution of the cartel of exchange. At the close of 1863 there had been captured from the Confederates one hundred and fifty thousand prisoners, of whom about 30,000 remained in the hands of the government.

In 1864 the situation in regard to prisoners remained unchanged. The positions occupied by the two governments were so antagonistic that agreement was impossible. The national government refused to exchange white for white, because the enemy would thus be relieved of the burden of maintaining his white prisoners, and, getting back his soldiers, he would dispose of the negro as he chose, since there would be left no means of retaliation. Finally, the excess of prisoners in the hands of the government became so large that the discussion ceased. It was certainly the policy of the Confederate government to yield the point in dispute. The prisoners which it held, if returned, would not, in most cases, resume their places in the field, their terms of service having expired. The Confederate prisoners, on the other hand, were soldiers for the war, and could be made immediately available. Their presence in the field was, moreover, a necessity which became every day more pressing.

What it could not accomplish by negotiation the Confederate government sought to extort by cruelty. The prison camps at Belle Isle, Andersonville, Milieu, and Salisbury were each transformed into human shambles. Thousands of men were huddled together within narrow limits. In the midst of a country abounding in timber, they were deprived of all means of shelter. Exposure to rains, dews, and frost generated disease, and there was neither medical relief at hand nor suitable food. No opportunities were afforded for cleanliness, and the prisoners were covered with vermin, which, in many cases, they were too weak to remove. They were shot by those guarding them for offenses the most trivial; they were plundered of every thing which was deemed valuable by their captors; supplies sent for their relief were in many cases appropriated by Confederate officers in charge; and the charities of Southern citizens excited in their behalf were repelled. Thousands died in those prison Golgothas, and many, from weakness induced by starvation, became idiots.[2] These barbarities were not only known to the Confederate authorities, but seem to have been encouraged by them. The officers placed over the prison appear to have been selected for their brutal capacity to carry out this system of cruelty. Among these was the notorious Captain Henry Wirz, the Anderson jailer, who was after the war tried by a military commission, and executed on the 10th of November, 1865.[3]

in this article contained shall prevent the commanders of two opposing armies from exchanging prisoners or releasing them on parole at other points mutually agreed on by said commanders.

"ART. 8. For the purpose of carrying into effect the foregoing articles of agreement, each party will appoint two agents, to be called Agents for the Exchange of Prisoners of War, whose duty it shall be to communicate with each other by correspondence and otherwise, to prepare the list of prisoners, to attend to the delivery of the prisoners at the places agreed on, and to carry out promptly, effectually, and in good faith, all the details and provisions of the said articles of agreement.

"ART. 9. And in case any misunderstanding shall arise in regard to any clause or stipulation in the foregoing articles, it is mutually agreed that such misunderstanding shall not interrupt the release of prisoners on parole, as herein provided, but shall be made the subject of friendly explanations, in order that the object of this agreement may neither be defeated nor postponed.

"JOHN A. DIX, Major General.

"D. H. HILL, Major General C. S. A."

[1] The following joint resolutions were adopted by the Confederate Congress:

"*Resolved*, by the Congress of the Confederate States of America, in response to the message of the President, transmitted to Congress at the commencement of the present session, That, in the opinion of Congress, the commissioned officers of the enemy ought not to be delivered to the authorities of the respective states, as suggested in the said message; but all captives taken by the Confederate forces ought to be dealt with and disposed of by the Confederate government.

"*Sec.* 2. That, in the judgment of Congress, the proclamations of the President of the United States, dated respectively September 22d, 1862, and January 1st, 1863, and the other measures of the government of the United States and of its authorities, commanders, and forces, designed or tending to emancipate slaves in the Confederate States, or to abduct such slaves, or to incite them to insurrection, or to employ negroes in war against the Confederate States, or to overthrow the institution of African slavery and bring on a servile war in these states, would, if successful, produce atrocious consequences, and they are inconsistent with the spirit of those usages which in modern warfare prevail among civilized nations; they may, therefore, be properly and lawfully repressed by retaliation.

"*Sec.* 3. That in every case wherein, during the present war, any violation of the laws and usages of war among civilized nations shall be, or has been, done and perpetrated by those acting under the authority of the government of the United States, on the persons or property of the citizens of the Confederate States, or of those under the protection of the land or naval service of the Confederate States, or of any state of the Confederacy, the President of the Confederate States is hereby authorized to cause full and complete retaliation to be made for every such violation, in such manner and to such extent as he may think proper.

"*Sec.* 4. That every white person, being a commissioned officer, or acting as such, who, during the present war, shall command negroes or mulattoes in arms against the Confederate States, or who shall arm, train, organize, or prepare negroes or mulattoes for military service against the Confederate States, or who shall voluntarily aid negroes or mulattoes in any military enterprise, attack, or conflict in such service, shall be deemed as inciting servile insurrection, and shall, if captured, be put to death, or be otherwise punished at the discretion of the court.

"*Sec.* 5. Every person, being a commissioned officer, or acting as such in the service of the enemy, who shall, during the present war, excite, attempt to excite, or cause to be excited servile insurrection, or who shall incite or cause to be incited a slave to rebel, shall, if captured, be put to death, or be otherwise punished, at the discretion of the court.

"*Sec.* 6. Every person charged with an offense punishable under the preceding resolutions shall, during the present war, be tried before the military court attached to the army or corps by the troops of which he shall have been captured, or by such other military court as the President may direct, and in such manner and under such regulations as the President shall prescribe, and, after conviction, the President may commute the punishment in such manner and on such terms as he may deem proper.

"*Sec.* 7. All negroes or mulattoes who shall be engaged in war or be taken in arms against the Confederate States, or shall give aid or comfort to the enemies of the Confederate States, shall, when captured in the Confederate States, be delivered to the authorities of the state or states in which they shall be captured, to be dealt with according to the present or future laws of such state or states."

"Executive Mansion, Washington, July 30th.

[1] "It is the duty of every government to give protection to its citizens, of whatever class, color, or condition, and especially to those who are duly organized as soldiers in the public service. The law of nations, and the usages and customs of war, as carried on by civilized powers, permit no distinction as to color in the treatment of prisoners of war as public enemies. To sell or enslave any captured person on account of his color, and for no offense against the laws of war, is a relapse into barbarism and a crime against the civilization of the age. The government of the United States will give the same protection to all its soldiers; and if the enemy shall sell or enslave any one because of his color, the offense shall be punished by retaliation upon the enemy's prisoners in our hands.

"It is therefore ordered that for every soldier of the United States killed in violation of the laws of war, a rebel soldier shall be executed, and for every one enslaved by the enemy or sold into slavery, a rebel soldier shall be placed at hard labor on the public works, and continue at such labor until the other shall be released and receive the treatment due a prisoner of war.

"ABRAHAM LINCOLN."

[2] A letter of the Confederate Inspector General Chandler, dated July 5, 1864, and addressed to Colonel Chilton, of Richmond, thus describes Andersonville:

"No shelter whatever, nor materials for constructing any, had been provided by the prison authorities, and the ground being entirely bare of trees, none is within reach of the prisoners, nor has it been possible, from the overcrowded state of the inclosure, to arrange the camp with any system. Each man has been permitted to protect himself as best he can by stretching his blanket, or whatever he may have about him, on such sticks as he can procure. Of other shelter there has been none. There is no medical attendance within the stockade. Many (twenty yesterday) are carted out daily who have died from unknown causes, and whom the medical officers have never seen. The dead are hauled out daily by the wagon-load, being first mutilated with an axe in the removal of any finger-rings they may have. Raw rations have to be issued to a very large portion, who are entirely unprovided with proper utensils, and furnished with so limited a supply of fuel that they are compelled to dig with their hands in the filthy marsh before mentioned for roots, etc. No soap or clothing has ever been issued. After inquiry, the writer is confident that, with slight exertions, green corn and other antiscorbutics could readily be obtained. The present hospital arrangements were only intended for the accommodation of ten thousand men, and are totally insufficient, both in character and extent, for the present needs, the number of prisoners being now more than three times as great. The number of cases requiring medical treatment is in an increased ratio. It is impossible to state the numbers of sick, many dying within the stockade whom the medical officers have never seen or heard of till their remains are brought out for interment. The transportation of the post is also represented to be entirely insufficient, and authority is needed by the quartermaster to impress wagons and teams, and saw-mills when not employed by the government, and kept diligently occupied, and instructions given to the quartermaster in charge of transportation to afford every facility practicable for transporting lumber and supplies necessary for prisoners."

[3] The following testimony, given before the Committee on the Conduct of the War, January 30, 1865, by Albert D. Richardson, a *Tribune* correspondent, describes the situation of our prisoners at Salisbury, North Carolina:

"'I am a *Tribune* correspondent, and was captured by the rebels May 3, 1863, at midnight, on a hay-bale in the Mississippi River, opposite Vicksburg. After confinement in six different prisons I was sent to Salisbury, N. C., February 3, 1864, and kept there until December 18, when I escaped. For several months Salisbury was the most endurable rebel prison I had seen. The six hundred inmates exercised in the open air were comparatively well fed and kindly treated. But early in October 10,000 regular prisoners of war arrived there, and it immediately changed into a scene of cruelty and horrors. It was densely crowded; rations were cut down and issued very irregularly; friends outside could not even send in a plate of food. The prisoners suffered constantly and often intensely for want of water, bread, and shelter. The rebel authorities placed all the prison hospitals under charge of my two journalistic comrades (Messrs. Brown and Davis) and myself. Our positions enabled us to obtain exact and minute information. Those who had to live or die on the prison rations always suffered from hunger. Very frequently one or more divisions of a thousand men would receive no rations for twenty-four hours; sometimes they were without a morsel of food for forty-eight hours. The few who had money would pay from five to twenty dollars, rebel currency, for a little loaf of bread. Most of the prisoners traded the buttons from their blouses for food. Many, though the weather was very inclement and snows frequent, sold coats from their backs and shoes from their feet. Yet I was assured, on authority entirely trustworthy, that the great commissary warehouse near the prison was filled with provisions; that the commissary found it difficult to obtain storage for his flour and meal; that when a subordinate asked the post commandant, Major John H. Gee, 'Shall I give the prisoners full rations?' he replied, 'No, God damn them, give them quarter rations.' I know, from personal observation, that

THE ANDERSONVILLE BURIAL-GROUNDS WHERE WERE INTERRED 14,000 UNION PRISONERS.

In the latter part of 1864, Lieutenant General Grant made an arrangement for an exchange of prisoners man for man, according to the old cartel, until on one side or the other the number of prisoners held was exhausted. The war seemed so near its close that the exchange could afford no substantial aid to the Confederacy, and every motive on the score of humanity demanded that the government, under these circumstances, should waive the old dispute respecting negro prisoners.[1]

During the last few months of the war, when the prospects of Confederate success through regularly conducted warfare seemed desperate, a series of attempts were made to paralyze and subvert the national government by means which desperation naturally suggested to bold and unscrupulous men. The capture of the Confederate archives at the close of the war disclosed letters which showed that propositions for the destruction of officers connected with the government had not only, at various stages of the war, been received by the Confederate executive, but had been subjects of consideration. As early as June 19th, 1861, one C. L. v. De Kalb, representing himself to be the grandson of Baron De Kalb, of Revolutionary fame, addressed a letter to L. P. Walker, the Confederate Secretary of War, reminding the latter that the Federal Congress would assemble on the 4th of July, and that the Capitol and public buildings at Washington were undermined. In regard to this matter, he begged "the honor of a few moments' private audience." letter is indorsed "About blowing up the Capitol at Washington." other letter, dated the next day, was also found, from which it appears De Kalb had been granted an audience on the 19th, but that Walker hesitated to consent to the diabolical scheme proposed, not on account nature, but because De Kalb was a stranger to him. In this letter o 20th De Kalb discloses his antecedents, his relation to Baron De Kal service in the Crimean War as second lieutenant of Engineers, his ar at Quebec in November, 1860, and at Washington three weeks ago. " the Southern Confederacy," he adds, "consider the explosion of the Fe Capitol, at a time when Abe, his myrmidons, and the Northern Con members are all assembled together, of sufficient importance as to grant in case of success, a commission as colonel of Topographical Engineers, the sum of one million of dollars?" Walker, instead of spurning the p osition, indorsed the letter with the following phrase: "See this man Benjamin." He proposed to make the matter a subject of consideratio an interview between himself, this murderous villain, and the Confede Secretary of State. In the Confederate archives was also found a le addressed to Jefferson Davis, September 12th, 1861, by J. S. Parramor which the writer offers "to dispose of the leading characters of the Nor and upon the letter was Davis's indorsement indicating the object of communication, and referring it to the Secretary of War. After due sideration, both De Kalb's and Parramore's schemes appear to have beer jected as unadvisable.

On the 17th of August, 1863, we find another letter written to Davis H. C. Dunham, of Georgia, a volunteer in the Confederate service, in wl the writer states that the evidences of Davis's Christian humility enc age him to propose the organization of from 300 to 500 men, "to go the United States, and assassinate the most prominent leaders of our mies—for instance, Seward, Lincoln, Greeley, Prentice, etc." This com nication was also referred to the Secretary of War.

Still later, Lieutenant W. Alston, in November, 1864, offered to rid Confederacy "of some of her deadliest enemies," and his communicatio referred to the Confederate Secretary of War. These various propositi for the assassination of the prominent officers of the Federal governn appear to have been considered and rejected for prudential reasons. time for such desperate measures had not yet arrived. But still they w matters of deliberate consideration.

Other schemes also were proposed. In February, 1865, W. S. Oldh of Texas, in company with Senator Johnson, of Missouri, conferred w Davis "in relation to the prospect of annoying and harassing the enemy burning their shipping, towns, etc." The Confederate President interpo objections as to the practicability of the scheme proposed. These obj tions were subsequently rebutted by Oldham. "I have seen enough," sa the latter, "of the effects that can be produced to satisfy me that in mo cases, without any danger to the parties engaged; and in others but ve slight, we can, first, burn every vessel that leaves a foreign port for the Unit States; second, we can burn every transport that leaves the harbor of N York, or other Northern port, with supplies for the armies of the enemy the South; third, burn every transport or gun-boat on the Mississippi Riv as well as devastate the country of the enemy, and fill his people with te ror and consternation. I am not alone of this opinion, but many other ge tlemen are as fully and thoroughly impressed with the conviction as I a I believe we have the means at our command, if promptly appropriated a energetically applied, to demoralize the Northern people in a very short tin For the purpose of satisfying your mind upon the subject, I respectfully b earnestly request that you will have an interview with General Harris, fo merly a member of Congress from Missouri, who, I think, is able, from co clusive proof, to convince you that what I have suggested is perfectly fea ble and practicable." Davis requested the Secretary of War to confer wi Harris, "and learn what plan he has for overcoming the difficulty herei fore experienced."

What was the "difficulty heretofore experienced?" A number of Co federates—George N. Sanders, Beverly Tucker, Jacob Thompson, Willia C. Cleary, and Clement C. Clay—had been sent to Canada as agents of th Confederate government. Jacob Thompson appears to have been the tres urer of this special organization, the objects of which were the terror ar consternation of the North through the destruction of shipping, the burnin of hotels, the introduction of pestilence, and the assassination of the prom nent officers of the national government. In the latter part of 1864 th attempt at arson had been tried without success, and the principals engage were executed. John Y. Beall, detected in the act of destroying Feder vessels in the Northwest, was tried and condemned as a spy, and suffere death. One Kennedy, on the night of November 25th, 1864, with his co federates, attempted to set fire to four hotels in New York City. The a tempt did not succeed, but Kennedy was apprehended and hung on the 19t of October. Three days later, Lieutenant Bennet H. Young, with from 30 t 40 Confederate associates, made a raid upon St. Albans, Vermont, 15 mile from the Canadian border. Over $200,000 was captured from the bank horses were seized, and several citizens were wantonly murdered. An un successful attempt was also made to fire the town. The raiders were pur sued, but escaped into Canada. Here they were arrested and brought befor the Court of Quarter Sessions at Montreal. The judge, Mr. Coursol, re leased them from custody on the ground that the court had no jurisdictio over the case. Judge Coursol was afterward suspended for this action, an the raiders were rearrested, but the prisoners finally were again release without punishment.

These expeditions all originated in Canada, and proceeded under Confed

corn and pork are very abundant in the region about Salisbury. For several weeks the prisoners had no shelter whatever. They were all thinly clad; thousands were barefooted; not one in twenty had either overcoat or blanket; many hundreds were without shirts, and hundreds were without blouses. At last one Sibley tent and one 'A' tent were furnished to each squad of one hundred. With the closest crowding these sheltered about one half the prisoners. The rest burrowed in the ground, crept under buildings, or shivered through the nights in the open air upon the frozen, muddy, or snowy soil. If the rebels, at the time of their capture, had not stolen their shelter-tents, blankets, clothing, and money, they would have suffered little from cold. If the prison authorities had permitted a few hundred of them, either upon parole or under guard, to cut logs within two miles of the garrison, the prisoners would gladly have built comfortable and ample barracks in one week. But the commandant would never, in a densely wooded region, with the cars which brought it passing by the wall of the prison, even furnish half the fuel which was needed.

"'The hospitals were in a horrible condition. By crowding the patients thick as they could lie upon the floor they would contain six hundred inmates. They were always full to overflowing, with thousands seeking admission in vain. In the two largest wards, containing jointly about two hundred and fifty patients, there was no fire whatever. The others had small fireplaces, but were always cold. One ward, which held forty patients, was comparatively well furnished. In the other eight the sick and dying men lay upon the cold and usually naked floor, for the scanty straw furnished us soon became too filthy and full of vermin for use. The authorities never supplied a single blanket, or quilt, or pillow, or bed, for those eight wards. We could not procure even brooms to keep them clean, or cold water to wash the faces of the inmates. Pneumonia, catarrh, and diarrhœa were the prevailing diseases, but they were directly the result of hunger and exposure. More than half who entered the hospitals died in a very few days. The deceased, always without coffins, were loaded in a dead-cart, piled upon each other like logs of wood, and so driven out to be thrown into a trench and covered with earth.

"'The rebel surgeons were generally humane and attentive. They endeavored to improve the shocking condition of the hospitals, but the Salisbury and Richmond authorities both disregarded their complaints and protests.

"On November 26 many of the prisoners had been without food for forty-eight hours. Desperate from hunger, without any matured plan, a few of them said, 'We may as well die in one way as another; let us break out of this horrible place.' Some of them wrested the guns from a relief of fifteen rebel soldiers just entering the yard, killing two who resisted and wounding five or six. Others attempted to open the fence, but they had neither adequate tools nor concert of action. Before they could effect a breach every gun in the garrison was turned upon them, two field-pieces operated with grape and canister, and they dispersed to their quarters. Five minutes from the beginning the attempt was quelled, and hardly a prisoner was to be seen in the yard. My own quarters were a hundred and fifty yards from the scene of the insurrection. In our vicinity there had been no participation at all in it, and yet for twenty minutes after it was ended the guards upon the fence on each side of us, with deliberate aim, fired into the tents upon helpless and innocent men. They killed, in all, fifteen, and wounded about sixty, not one tenth of whom had taken part in the attempt, many of whom were ignorant of it until they heard the guns.

"Deliberate cold-blooded murders of peaceable men, where there was no pretense that they were breaking any prison regulation, were very frequent. On October 16, Lieutenant Davis, of the 155th New York Infantry, was thus shot dead by a guard, who the day before had been openly swearing that he would 'kill some damned Yankee yet.' November 6, Luther Conrod, of the 45th Pennsylvania Infantry, a delirious patient from one of the hospitals, was similarly murdered. November 30, a chimney in one of the hospitals fell down, crushing several men under it. Orders were immediately given to the guard to let no one approach the building, on the pretext that there might be another insurrection. Two patients from that hospital had not heard the order, and were returning to their quarters, when I saw a sentinel on the fence, within twenty feet of them, without challenging them, raise his piece and fire, killing one and wounding the other. Major Gee, at the time, was standing immediately beside the sentinel, who must have acted under his direct orders. December 16, Moses Smith, of 7th Maryland (colored) Infantry, while standing beside my quarters, searching for scraps of food from the sweepings of the cook-house, was shot through the head. There were very many similar murders. I never knew any pretense, even, made of investigation or punishing them. Our lives were never safe for one moment; any sentinel, at any hour of the day or night, could deliberately shoot down any prisoner, or into any group of prisoners, black or white, and he would not even be taken off his post for it.

"Nearly every week an officer came into the prison to recruit for the rebel army. Sometimes he offered bounties; always he promised good clothing and abundant food. Between 1200 and 1800 of our men enlisted in two months. I was repeatedly asked by prisoners, sometimes with tears in their eyes, 'What shall I do? I don't want to starve to death. I am growing weaker daily; if I stay here I shall follow my comrades to the hospital and dead-house; if I enlist I may live until I can escape.'

"'I had charge of the clothing left by the dead, and reissued it to the living. I distributed articles of clothing to more than 2000 prisoners; but when I escaped there were fully 500 without a shoe or a stocking, and more yet with no garment above the waist except one blouse or one shirt. Men came to me frequently upon whom the rebels, when they captured them, had left nothing whatever except a light cotton shirt and a pair of light ragged cotton pantaloons.

"'The books of all the hospitals were kept, and the daily consolidated reports made up, under my supervision. During the two months between October 16 and December 18, the average number of prisoners was about 7500. The deaths for that period were fully 1500, or twenty per cent. of the whole. I brought away the names of more than 1200 of the dead; some of the remainder were never reported; the others I could not procure on the day of my escape without exciting suspicion. As the men grew more and more debilitated, the percentage of deaths increased. I left 6500 remaining in the garrison, December 18, and they were dying then at the average rate of 28 a day, or thirteen per cent. a month.

"'The simple truth is, that the rebel authorities are murdering our soldiers at Salisbury by cold and hunger, while they might easily supply them with ample food and fuel. They are doing this systematically, and, I believe, intentionally, for the purpose of either forcing our government to an exchange, or forcing our prisoners into the rebel army."

[1] General Grant's testimony (February 11, 1865) before the Committee on the Conduct of the War fully answers the charge which has been made against the government that it refused to consent to an exchange of prisoners because we found ours starved, diseased, and unserviceable when we received them. "There never," testifies General Grant, "has been any such reason as that for making exchanges. I will confess that if our men who are prisoners in the South were really well taken care of, suffering nothing except a little privation of liberty, then, in a military point of view, it would not be good policy for us to exchange, because every man they get back is forced right into the army at once, while that is not the case with our prisoners when we receive them. In fact, the half of our returned prisoners will never go into the army again, and none of them will until after they have had a furlough of thirty or sixty days. Still, the fact of their suffering as they do is a reason for making this exchange as rapidly as possible. . . . . Exchanges having been suspended by reason of disagreement on the part of agents of exchange on both sides before I came in command of the armies of the United States, and it then being near the opening of the spring campaign, I did not deem it advisable or just to the men who had to fight our battles to reinforce the enemy with thirty or forty thousand disciplined troops at that time. An immediate resumption of exchanges would have had that effect, without giving us corresponding benefits. The suffering said to exist among our prisoners South was a powerful argument against the course pursued, and I so felt it."

erate authority. None of them had succeeded in accomplishing what they had attempted. Some difficulties had been experienced, and the Confederate government was now considering how these difficulties might be overcome. Soon, however, other and more desperate plans were found necessary. The old scheme of assassination, formerly laid aside, was reconsidered. Ready agents were found for its accomplishment. President Lincoln was murdered, but the conspirators did not succeed in subverting the government.

The war carried on by sea against the United States by the Confederates presents many novel features. Over 200 of the officers registered in 1864 as belonging to the Confederate navy were formerly United States naval officers. Although President Davis at the outset had issued letters of marque, a Confederate navy was impossible. There were many iron-clads and rams on the Southern rivers; the defenses of the Southern harbors by means of forts, ships, torpedoes, and obstructions were very formidable; but upon the sea the Confederacy had no chance, in so far as it depended upon its own resources. But what the Confederates lacked the people of Great Britain furnished, and thus it happened that while the United States was threatened with dissolution by intestine civil war, it was compelled also, at the same time, to contend on the ocean against a British fleet—British in every sense except that it did not receive its commissions from the English government—built at Liverpool and Glasgow, sailing from those ports by the connivance of the British government, armed with British guns, and manned, for the most part, with British crews.

In the early part of the war a number of strictly Confederate privateers were fitted out. Most of these, however, did not venture far from the coast. The Sumter and Nashville, who were bolder, had a short career, which has already been traced in these pages. The only vessels which materially injured the commerce of the United States were those built in British ports, and some of which were never in a port belonging to the Confederacy.

The history of the Alabama and the Florida has already been given. In 1864, three new British vessels—the Tallahassee, Olustee, and Chickamauga—were furnished to the Confederates by the British ship-builders, and contributed each its full share in the work of destruction and plunder. By their depredations American merchantmen were almost entirely driven from the seas.

The Georgia commenced her career in 1863. She was built at Glasgow, and left Greenock as the Japan. Off the French coast she received her armament and set out upon her cruise. After a short raid upon our commerce she was sold to a Liverpool merchant. Setting out again for Lisbon, she was captured twenty miles out from that port by Captain Craven, of the Niagara, who landed her crew at Dover, in England.

Early in 1865 two new vessels—the Stonewall and Shenandoah—were added to this British tribe of corsairs. The iron-clad ram Stonewall, Captain Page, was originally built for the Danish government, and afterward purchased by the Confederates. She arrived at Ferrol, in Spain, February 4th, closely followed by the United States steamers Niagara and Sacramento. The Stonewall shifted quarters to Lisbon in March, and the Federal vessels again followed her. The Portuguese government ordered the privateer to leave, and by maritime law the national vessels were required to remain for 24 hours before entering upon the pursuit. While changing their anchorage in the Tagus, these vessels were fired upon from Belem Tower under the supposition that they were about to leave the port. No injury was done, and ample apology was rendered by the Portuguese government. On the 11th of May the Stonewall arrived at Havana. Here she was closely blockaded by Admiral Godon, with several iron-clads, and soon surrendered herself to the Spanish authorities, by whom she was given over to the United States.

The Shenandoah was built at Glasgow in 1863, and was called the Sea King. In September, 1864, she was sold to Richard Wright, of Liverpool, and thus passed into the hands of the Confederacy. She cleared at London for Bombay ostensibly as a merchant vessel. On the same day that she left London, another vessel, the Laurel, left Liverpool with armament, stores, Confederate officers, and several men enlisted in the Confederate service. At Madeira the two vessels met; the Laurel fitted out the Sea King, which then became the Shenandoah, and set forth on her piratical cruise. She destroyed a few vessels in the neighborhood of St. Helena, and on February 8th, 1865, sailed for the North Pacific from Melbourne, Australia. Between April 1st and July 1st she destroyed or bonded 29 vessels, thus breaking up the whaling season in that locality. Waddell, her captain, although aware of the surrender of the Confederate armies, continued his cruise until four months after the fall of Richmond. He then returned to England, never having been in a Confederate port, and surrendered his vessel to the English government, and by the latter was given up to the American consul at Liverpool.

It is estimated that during the war 30 vessels of all descriptions were employed by the enemy as privateers. Only seven of these were very formidable, and of these seven five were British vessels. 275 vessels were captured, comprising four steamers, 78 ships, 43 brigs, 82 barks, and 68 schooners. On the other hand, 1143 vessels were captured by blockading squadrons, valued at $24,500,000, and 355 destroyed, worth about $7,000,000.[1]

In regard to one at least of the privateers issuing from British ports, the circumstances appeared to justify the United States in claiming redress by way of compensation for the injurious consequences to American commerce. This was the case of the Alabama. The facts of the case were briefly these: The Oreto had already been permitted to sail from a British port, notwithstanding the protest of Mr. Francis Adams, the United States minister in England. Afterward Mr. Adams and the American consul at Liverpool were satisfied, upon competent evidence, that a vessel known as the 290 had been built for the Confederate service in the dock-yard of persons, one of whom was then sitting as a member of the House of Commons. This evidence was laid before the Lords Commissioners of Her Majesty's Treasury, but the latter decided that nothing had yet transpired which appeared to demand a special report. Farther evidence was procured and submitted, which, in the opinion of the queen's solicitor, was sufficient to justify the Liverpool collector in seizing the vessel. But, while the Lords Commissioners were deliberating upon the matter, the 290 sailed from Liverpool without register or clearance. Earl Russell explained to Mr. Adams that the delay in determining upon the case had been caused by the sudden illness of Sir John D. Harding, the Queen's Advocate.

It was apparent, therefore, that the fault, with its responsibility, rested upon the British government. Mr. Adams was therefore directed "to solicit redress for the national and private injuries already thus sustained, as well as a more effective prevention of any repetition of such lawless and injurious proceedings in her majesty's ports hereafter." Earl Russell replied to this demand that her majesty's government could not admit that they were under any obligation to render compensation to United States citizens for the depredations of the Alabama. There has since been a voluminous correspondence upon the subject, but the matter still stands just where it stood in 1863. Certainly it is a case in which the interests of the British government are more jeopardized by its refusal to grant compensation than its treasury could suffer by payment; and it is equally true that the United States government can well afford to waive its claim, and let the whole matter rest just as it lies.

The foreign complications with the French government arising out of the ill-advised Mexican expedition, and which at one period of the war threatened serious danger to the United States, were, soon after the suspension of hostilities, removed by the withdrawal of the French troops from Mexico. From that moment the Mexican empire which had been established rapidly waned until early in 1867, when it fell, and the Emperor Maximilian became a martyr to the cause of imperialism, which he had fought out to the bitter end.

At the close of the civil war our political sky was bright with promise. The defeated Confederates seemed disposed to accept the situation in good faith, and, on the other hand, the victorious party exhibited signs of noble magnanimity. It is true that there were in the South those who still retained the spirit which had brought on the war. Such a one was that old man Edmund Ruffin, of South Carolina, who fired the first gun against his country's flag, and who, when the national triumph was fully consummated, committed suicide. So also, on the other side, there were those who nursed a vindictive spirit against a conquered people. But, notwithstanding these exceptions, a glorious future seemed about to dawn upon the republic. How this situation was changed, and a political strife engendered which agitated the country for a series of years, and postponed the restoration and harmony which ought to have followed immediately upon the close of the war, will form the subject of the concluding chapter of this history.

[1] The number of vessels captured and sent to the United States Admiralty Courts for adjudication from May 1, 1861, to the close of the war, was 1143, of which there were—steamers, 210; schooners, 569; sloops, 139; ships, 13; brigs and brigantines, 29; barks, 25; yachts, 2; small boats, 139; rams and iron-clads, 6; gun-boats, torpedo-boats, and armed schooners and sloops, 10; class unknown, 7—making a total of 1149. The number of vessels burned, wrecked, sunk, and otherwise destroyed during the same time were—steamers, 85; schooners, 114; sloops, 32; ships, 2; brigs, 3; barks, 4; small boats, 96; rams, 6; iron-clads, 4; gun-boats, torpedo-boats, and armed schooners and sloops, 11; total, 355—making the whole number of vessels captured and destroyed 1504. During the war of 1812, the naval vessels, of which there were 301 in service at the close, made 291 captures. There were 517 commissioned privateers, and their captures numbered 1428. Nearly all the captures of value in the recent war were vessels built in so-called neutral ports, and fitted out and freighted for the purpose of running the blockade. The gross proceeds of property captured since the blockade was instituted, and condemned as prize prior to the 1st of November, 1865, amount to $21,829,543 96; costs and expenses, $1,616,228 96; net proceeds for distribution, $20,501,927 69. At the close of the year there were a number of important cases still before the courts, which will largely increase these amounts. The Secretary of the Navy estimates that the value of the 1149 captured vessels will not be less than $24,500,000, and of the 355 vessels destroyed at least $7,000,000, making a total valuation of not less than $31,500,000, much of which was British property.—*American Cyclopædia*, 1865.

ANDREW JOHNSON.

CHAPTER LXII.

RECONSTRUCTION.—1865–1867.

Difficulties incident to Restoration from the sudden Termination of the War.—The prevailing Sentiment of the North after Lee's Surrender one of Magnanimity.—Effect of Lincoln's Assassination.—Andrew Johnson's Accession to the Presidency.—Biographical Sketch.—Johnson's Inaugural Speech.—"Treason is a Crime, and must be punished as a Crime."—His View of the Situation.—His Cabinet.—Reconstruction under Lincoln's Administration.—Johnson follows the Policy of his Predecessor.—The Constitutional Provision guaranteeing to the States "a Republican Form of Government."—Meaning of this Provision.—What was involved in a Return to Allegiance on the Part of the South.—The popular Demand.—Johnson's Amnesty Proclamation.—Establishment of Provisional Governments.—The Blockade rescinded.—Release of Stephens and Trenholm.—Martial Law suspended in Kentucky.—Partial Restoration of the Writ of *Habeas Corpus*.—Southern State Conventions.—Nullification of Secession Ordinances.—Prohibition of Slavery.—Repudiation of the Rebel Debt.—Legislation in regard to Freedmen.—Its oppressive Features.—The Temper of the Southern People.—Johnson's Disappointment.—Official Announcement of the Ratification of the Anti-Slavery Amendment.—Meeting of the Thirty-ninth Congress.—Composition of the two Houses.—The new Vice-President, L. S. Foster.—The Clerk of the House, Edward McPherson, and his Disposition of the Call-roll.—Colfax re-elected Speaker of the House.—His Speech.—President Johnson's Message.—Johnson's Mistake.—He establishes a Basis for Conflict between himself and Congress.—Ought to have convened Congress in special Session at the Outset.—The Select Congressional Committee of Fifteen on Reconstruction.—Debate in the Senate.—Reports by President Johnson, Carl Schurz, and General Grant on the Southern Situation.—Unnecessary Delay of the Reconstruction Committee.—Report of the Committee by Bill, January 22, 1866.—Joint Resolution for the Amendment of the Constitution.—Its Provisions.—The President's Views on the Readjustment of the Basis of Representation.—Debate in the House.—Roscoe Conkling's Statement.—Position of Henry J. Raymond.—The Resolution referred back to the Committee, amended, and again reported.—Stevens's Speech.—Resolution passed in the House.—Debate on the Resolution in Congress.—It fails of a two-thirds Vote.—Senator Sumner's Opposition.—Second Report of the Committee, April 30, 1866.—Features of the new Amendment proposed.—Its Passage in the House and Senate.—The President's Protest.—The Prospects of the Amendment.—Full Reports of the Reconstruction Committee, June 18, 1866.—Resolution passed to exclude Southern Representatives until both Houses should consent to their Admission.—Fessenden's Support of the Resolution.—Sherman's Opposition.—His Defense of President Johnson.—Tennessee ratifies the Amendment, and her Representatives are admitted in both Houses.—The Freedmen's Bureau Bill.—The President's Veto.—The Bill fails of a two-thirds Vote.—A new Bill passed over the President's Veto.—Bill for the admission of Colorado, vetoed by the President, fails of a two-thirds Vote.—Passage of the Bill for Negro Suffrage in the District of Columbia over the Veto.—Close of the Congressional Session.—History of the Conflict between Congress and the President.—Johnson's Speech denouncing Congress, February 22, 1866.—Division in the Republican Party.—The National Union Executive Committee of Washington.—Serenade of the President and Cabinet, May 23, 1866.—Views of the Cabinet.—Resignation of Harlan and Speed.—The Political Situation in the Summer of 1866.—The Appeal to the People, and the Issues presented.—The conflicting Arguments.—The National Union Convention at Philadelphia.—Its Character and Proceedings.—The Southern Loyalists' Convention at Philadelphia.—Cleveland Convention of Soldiers and Sailors in support of the President.—Similar Convention at Pittsburg in support of Congress.—The New Orleans Riots.—Johnson's Tour to the Tomb of Douglas.—Address of the Republican National Executive Committee in support of Congress.—The Autumn Elections of 1866.—Decisive Victory of Congress.—Passage of the Military Bill.—Provisions of the Bill.—Supplementary Act of the Fortieth Congress.—Universal Suffrage in the South.—Operation of this Act.—Southern Conventions.—Reaction in the North.—Autumn Elections of 1867.—Their Significance.—A Glance at the Future.—Conclusion.

IT is always difficult to write a fair and impartial history of contemporaneous events—almost impossible for one to write such a history who has been a prominent actor in the events which he records. The position of the actor is not that of the spectator. The field which the former occupies is executive, that held by the latter is judicial. The historian is a judicial spectator, whose business it is to reproduce before his readers not simply the facts, the bare plot of a drama, but also the ideas involved in the connections between facts, the moral and physical powers by which the drama is evolved. The strength of action depends upon concentration, which precludes extensive generalization. Strong impressions upon the world are made with clenched fists, while many-sided thought tends to relax the muscles, and leads to weak and random blows, "beating the air." Especially is this true in politics, where progress is usually marked by the fluctuations of a conflict between parties. Each of the conflicting parties lives through its own distinctive ideas, and undergoes dissolution or modification only by the destruction or change of these ideas. Neither party monopolizes either all the right or all the wrong of the contest. The political actor is generally strong in the proportion that he avails himself, and becomes the representative of the one or the other class of ideas involved in the struggle. His action does not assimilate all the good of both parties, and exclude all the evil. He is, therefore, of necessity, partial, one-sided. He who will fight under neither banner, who is unwilling to identify himself with either of the great party organizations of his time, by this isolation weakens his power to strike. But with the historian it is different. The necessity of partisanship does not exist for him. Partisan history is not history, but special pleading. The historian must generalize, must be many-sided, must be impartial. His standard of truth and justice is not a party standard.

In the present case, where the writer is about to enter upon the history of the political struggle which immediately followed the Civil War, it is peculiarly appropriate that this distinction between the necessities which obligate party leaders and those which obligate the historian should be clearly drawn. If the reader, however partisan, will remember that the historian, in his judgment of men and events, is bound by a more absolute criterion of truth than is possible in party conflict, the writer will also bear in remembrance that many political acts which involved or threatened serious evils, were rendered necessary by the inevitable political conditions which controlled the development of the time of which he writes.

The manner in which the war closed, and some of the accidents of its conclusion, largely influenced subsequent political movements. If the collapse of the Confederacy had not been sudden, but gradual, the problem of reconstruction would, indeed, have been the same in its essential elements, but much of the difficulty attending its development would have been obvinted. If state after state had been brought back to its allegiance, while the war still went on in others, restoration would have been immediate and thorough in each particular case, and would not have been beset with legal doubts and difficulties. The vastness of the problem was increased by the sudden cessation of hostilities, and many of its complications arose from the universal peace which all at once settled upon the country, and seemed to demand the immediate revival of constitutional civil law. Under these circumstances, there was great danger lest restoration might come in the form of reaction, by which the country would be swept along without mature de-

WILLIAM PITT FESSENDEN.

liberation, or a prudent regard for future security. The disturbance by war of the relations between the states and the central government had been violent, and their readjustment demanded the deepest thought and the most prudent caution. The domestic revolution produced in the South by the war, giving freedom to nearly four millions of slaves, added fresh and obvious reasons for such deliberation.

The prevailing feeling in the North after the surrender of Lee's army was one of magnanimity. That was generous and proper. But there might easily grow out of this such hasty action as must afterward occasion vain regret. The murder of Lincoln—the natural result of the personal abuse which had been heaped upon him by the Southern press and by Northern Copperheads—served to temper and restrain this sentiment of generosity. It recalled to mind the malevolence of those who had sought to overthrow the government; it generated distrust. The apprehensions entertained by prudent men at that time may have been extravagant, but in the light of the past they could not be deemed baseless. Certainly they were safer than the sentiment which they displaced.

Another result of Lincoln's death was a memorable change in the national administration. Andrew Johnson succeeded Abraham Lincoln.

Johnson, by the circumstance of his birth, occupied a position similar to that of Lincoln. He was born a poor Southern white. The difference between the two men arose from their different natures rather than from the outward conditions of their lives. Both were self-educated men. Neither of them knew of any school but that of experience, and thus from the first they were kept near to the people, and in close contact with the practical facts and conditions of the popular life in America. From such a relation they might have been removed by a more scholastic education and more classic culture. They knew nothing but America. Two circumstances gave Lincoln an immense superiority. The first was his moral and mental constitution, which made him a statesman of deep and unwavering convictions, and of great reasoning powers; the second was his connection with the young, free, and enterprising West. Johnson, on the other hand, by mental constitution and by the circumstances of his political career, became a demagogue rather than a statesman.

The biography of Andrew Johnson up to the time of his accession to the presidency may be condensed into a single paragraph. He was born at Raleigh, North Carolina, December 29, 1808. While a mere child he lost his father, and at the age of ten years was apprenticed as a tailor. He worked at his trade in South Carolina for seven years, and during this time acquired the rudiments of a plain English education. Removing to Greenville, Tennessee, in 1825, he was five years later elected mayor of that town. He was elected to the State Legislature in 1835, and to the State Senate in 1841. From 1843 to 1853 he was a representative in Congress from Tennessee, and during the latter year was elected governor of that state. In 1857 he was chosen United States senator for the long term, expiring in 1863. But in 1862 he was appointed by President Lincoln military governor of Tennessee. In politics he had always been identified with the Democratic party, accepting Andrew Jackson, of whose name his own was a parody, as his model. He was prominently connected with the passage of the Homestead Law. In the Thirty-sixth Congress, he alone, of all the senators from the South, remained faithful to the Union. His bold denunciation of treason created the wildest sort of popular enthusiasm in the North, and as military governor of Tennessee his action was wise and firm, strengthening the hands of the loyal men of that state, and favoring the emancipation of slavery. In 1864 the Union Convention met at Baltimore to nominate candidates for President and Vice-President. President Lincoln was renominated by acclamation, but it was not considered advisable to renominate Mr. Hamlin. The Convention was styled a "Union" Convention, and many of its delegates were not strictly Republicans. To renominate the Chicago ticket of 1860 would appear too partisan. In Andrew Johnson, however, Providence kindly, as it then seemed, furnished a candidate who had been always a Democrat, but who had been conspicuous for loyalty during the war. His nomination was effected by the friends of Mr. Seward as a conservative movement, and Andrew Johnson was elected Vice-President,

HUGH McCULLOCH.

In the Presidential campaign of 1864 Johnson was repudiated by the opposition party in the North. His inauguration as Vice-President in the following March was an occasion of humiliation to himself, and afforded an opportunity for the most vehement and scurrilous abuse on the part of his political enemies. Evidently Johnson was at this time under the influence of liquor. He was unwell, and had, at the request of some of his friends, taken stimulants previous to entering the Senate Chamber. The closeness of the room exaggerated the effect of the artificial stimulant, and under these circumstances Johnson very unwisely allowed himself to make a speech, the incoherency of which was only too evident. It was an unfortunate affair, and his enemies made the most of it, and even some Republican journals described it as a national disgrace. Others, who knew the circumstances, were charitably silent.

Six weeks later, by the death of Lincoln, Johnson became President of the United States. The oath of office was quietly administered to him at his rooms in the Kirkwood Hotel, by Chief Justice Chase, in presence of the cabinet and several members of Congress. He felt incompetent, he said, to perform the important and responsible duties which had so suddenly devolved upon him. His policy must be left for development, as the administration progressed. The only assurance he could give as to the future was by a reference to the past. He believed that the government, in passing through its present trials, would settle down upon principles consonant with popular rights, more permanent and enduring than heretofore. "Toil," said he, "and an honest advocacy of the great principles of free government, have been my lot. The duties have been mine—the consequences are God's." In conclusion, he asked the gentlemen present for their encouragement and countenance. In the addresses made at this time by President Johnson, he carefully avoided self-committal as to his future policy. He expressed, however, a strong determination to punish conscious traitors. "The American people," said he, "must be taught to know that treason is a crime. Arson and murder are crimes, the punishment of which is the loss of liberty and life. . . . . Treason is a crime, and must be punished as a crime. It must not be regarded as a mere difference of political opinion. It must not be excused as an unsuccessful rebellion, to be overlooked and forgiven. It is a crime before which all other crimes sink into insignificance; and in saying this, it must not be considered that I am influenced by angry or revengeful feelings. Of course a careful discrimination must be observed, for thousands have been involved in this rebellion who are only technically guilty of the crime of treason. They have been deluded and deceived, and have been made the victims of the more intelligent, artful, and designing men, the instigators of this monstrous rebellion. The number of this latter class is comparatively small. The former may stand acquitted of the crime of treason—the latter never; the full penalty of their crimes should be visited upon them. To the others I would accord amnesty, leniency, and mercy."[1] There is no question but that Johnson, following his own inclination, would have doomed to the scaffold every traitor of the class which he deemed guilty of crime, had not the whole people united in unanimous protest against such an extreme and unnecessary measure.

In regard to the situation in which the Southern States were left by the rebellion, he was explicit. "Some," he said, "are satisfied with the idea that states are to be lost in territorial and other divisions—are to lose their character as states. But their life-breath has only been suspended, and it is a high constitutional obligation we have to secure each of these states in the enjoyment of a republican form of government. A state may be in the government with a peculiar institution, and by the operation of rebellion lose that feature. But it was a state when it went into rebellion, and when it comes out without the institution, it is still a state. . . . . Then, in adjusting and putting the government upon its legs again, I think the progress of this work must pass into the hands of its friends. If a state is to be nursed until it again gets strength, it must be nursed by its friends, and not *smothered* by its enemies."[2]

President Johnson retained the entire cabinet of his predecessor. William Pitt Fessenden had resigned his position as Secretary of the Treasury March 4th, 1865, to take the position of senator from Maine, and Hugh

[1] Address to the New Hampshire delegation.
[2] Address to the Indiana delegation, April 21, 1865.

McCulloch had been appointed in his stead. Hon. William Dennison, of Ohio, had succeeded Montgomery Blair, October 1, 1864, as Postmaster General, the latter having resigned at Lincoln's request. In December, 1864, Edward Bates, of Missouri, Attorney General, had been succeeded by James Speed, of Kentucky. John P. Usher, Secretary of the Interior, had succeeded Caleb B. Smith, January 8th, 1863.

The subject of reconstruction did not come into President Johnson's hands as a new affair which had never before been handled or discussed. His predecessor had not been entirely silent upon this important question, and the matter had been somewhat discussed in Congress. Lincoln's Amnesty Proclamation is the best indication as to his convictions in this matter, and as to the general principles which would have characterized his administration if he had lived. In the previous pages of this history we have considered the provisions of this proclamation. Certain prominent officers of the Confederate government were excepted from the privileges which it granted. The ultimatum, as presented by Lincoln to the insurgent states, was allegiance to the government and the emancipation of slaves. Lincoln believed that the abolition of slavery would "remove all cause of disturbance in the future." Congress had incorporated in the Constitution an amendment prohibiting slavery; he only asked that this amendment should be ratified by the requisite number of states. On the 6th of April he ordered General Weitzel to permit the Virginia Legislature to assemble, and this body was to be broken up only in the event of its attempting some action hostile to the United States. Three days before his assassination President Lincoln gave his views as to the government established in Louisiana in accordance with his Amnesty Proclamation. Every member of his cabinet, he said, had approved of the plan. As to sustaining the Louisiana government he had given his promise, and had not yet been convinced that the keeping of this promise was adverse to the public interest. The question as to whether the seceded states were in the Union or out of it he regarded as not practically material, and that its discussion "could have no effect other than the mischievous one of dividing our friends." "As yet," he added, "that question is bad as the basis of a controversy, and good for nothing at all—a merely pernicious abstraction. We all agree that the seceded states, so called, are out of their proper practical relation with the Union, and that the sole object of the government, civil and military, in regard to those states, is to again get them into that proper practical relation I believe it is not only possible, but, in fact, easier to do this without deciding or even considering whether these states have ever been out of the Union, than with it. Finding themselves safely at home, it would be utterly immaterial whether they had ever been abroad. Let us all join in doing the acts necessary to restoring the proper practical relations between these states and the Union, and each forever after innocently indulge his own opinion whether, in doing the acts, he brought the states from without into the Union, or only gave them proper assistance, they never having been out of it."

The simple question with Lincoln was how best to bring the insurgent states back to their proper relation with the Union. To him this question appeared to have a solution in his amnesty proclamation.

Congress had not accepted Lincoln's plan of restoration, nor had it, except in the "Wade and Davis Bill," which had been virtually vetoed, announced any other. The only members of Congress who seemed to have any definite ideas of reconstruction were Senator Sumner and Thaddeus Stevens, who proposed to treat the Southern States as subjugated provinces. These two men stood alone, and without substantial support in either house. But, for all that, they held a high vantage-ground from the very fact that they alone presented any positive and definite method of reconstruction. Probably there had never before been a time in the history of the republic when Congress was so utterly barren of a high order of statesmanship as during and immediately after the war. The Thirty-ninth Congress was certainly not superior in this respect to its immediate predecessors. It first regular session would commence in December, and thus for eight months President Johnson was left alone in the work of reconstruction. As we have said, no fixed principles had been furnished by previous Congresses for his guidance, and he would have been confused beyond redemption if he had attempted to frame a policy in accordance with the crude and random expressions of opinion which had from time to time been made by our statesmen. He could not and ought not have accepted the sweeping theories of Sumner and Stevens.

Johnson appears at first to have followed closely the general features of the plan adopted by Lincoln. He was compelled to act. The dissolution of the Confederacy left the Southern States without any government which could be recognized by national authority. Certain movements had already been inaugurated by President Lincoln in Arkansas and Louisiana. Johnson saw no objection to the continuance of the work after the manner in which it had been begun by his predecessor. Nor was the Constitution entirely silent and inapplicable to the pressing questions of the moment. Although its framers never contemplated the existence of such a crisis, yet it contained at least one provision which in its general meaning was fully adequate to the emergency. It provides (Art. IV., Sec. 4) that "the United States shall guarantee to every state in this Union a republican form of government, and shall protect each of them against invasion; and, on application of the Legislature, or of the executive (when the Legislature can not be convened), against domestic violence."

The latter clause of this constitutional provision evidently applies to cases where the government of a state is not wholly subverted or paralyzed by riously understood. Some have declared it to mean nothing definitely, and therefore every thing in an indefinite way; that it was a constitutional sanction for the establishment in a disturbed state of any government which the President and Congress might prescribe. Others have supposed that the term "republican" was simply opposed to the term "monarchical." It is clearly evident, however, that any state in the Union has a republican form of government so long and in so far as its government has not been so disturbed by any agency as to be out of harmony with the republic, *i.e.*, with the general government of the United States. The Constitution being the organic law of the United States government, it follows that the guaranty of a republican form of government to any state presupposes a case in which by some disturbing agency the government of such state has assumed a form inconsistent or out of harmony with the Constitution. It is immaterial what the nature of such disturbing agency may have been, whether it was usurpation from within or from without.

The question, therefore, naturally arises, How far had the rebellion been such a disturbing agency? The Confederate Constitution, under which the Southern state governments had been organized during the rebellion, was not materially different from the Constitution of the United States. Comparing the situation of the Southern States in 1865 with their situation in 1860, the chief difference which we find was the fact of a transferred allegiance. The simple return of these states to their allegiance to the United States would be also a resumption of a form of government which in 1860 was deemed "republican." But such a government of the Southern States as was in harmony with the Constitution in 1860 was not in harmony with the Constitution after the war. By the war all slaves had been emancipated. The Congress of the United States had passed a resolution proposing the anti-slavery constitutional amendment. It was eminently proper that the ratification of this amendment should be insisted upon as a condition of reconstruction. It was a measure rendered necessary by the war, and the acceptance of the situation by the Southern States in good faith involved the ratification. This general condition gave rise to others as incidental. The freedom of the negro race in the South involved also the equality of that race with white men before the law. It did not involve the enfranchisement of the negro, because the Constitution, even after the war, contained no provision to that effect. But in every other respect the negro must be placed upon an equality with the white man.

There was another important feature to be insisted upon by the government, and which was also a result of the national victory. This was a repudiation by the Southern States of the debt which they had incurred for treasonable purposes. The possibility of a repudiation of the national debt must also be obviated.

The emancipation of slaves introduced still another element. Before the war representation was apportioned among the several states "according to their respective numbers, which shall be determined by adding to the whole number of free persons, including those bound to service for a term of years, and excluding Indians not taxed, three fifths of all other persons." But after the war all persons were declared free. The "other persons" no longer existed. Thus the entire negro population of the South would be counted in the basis of representation, and the Southern States would, by emancipation, gain a political advantage which they did not have before the war. It was therefore proper that a new adjustment of the basis of representation should be insisted upon as an incidental condition of the situation arising out of emancipation. It ought also have been distinctly and permanently settled that there should be no compensation for emancipation.

Thus the allegiance demanded of the insurgent states was not simply that from which they had departed. They had made war upon the nation, and this conflict had not been without consequences, the principal of which were a Confederate debt, a National debt, and Emancipation. If the Confederacy had been victorious, it would have gained its independence—its recognition as a separate nation. Its defeat was not simply a forfeiture of this independence, but it involved submission to several important conditions, imposed, not as terms to a vanquished foe, not as penalties for treason, but for the security of the nation. Under these circumstances, a republican form of government in the disturbed states involved the acceptance by the latter of the following conditions:

1. Nullification of the theory of secession.
2. Repudiation of the Confederate debt.
3. Security of the national debt.
4. Ratification of emancipation, waiving all claim to pecuniary compensation.
5. Readjustment of the basis of representation.
6. Concession of civil rights to the colored race.
7. Disfranchisement of leading traitors for such time as Congress might deem expedient.

When it is considered that the nation could in justice demand indemnity for the national debt caused by the war, and the punishment of leading traitors, these conditions could not be considered harsh or unreasonable. Every one of them ought to have been embodied by Congress in the form of a constitutional amendment. Many of them demanded congressional sanction, and could not be imposed by the President alone. It was therefore Johnson's duty to have called the Thirty-ninth Congress together in special session to meet this new emergency. His failure to do this was a blunder from which his administration never recovered.

The President proceeded to his work alone. On the 29th of May 1865

of the United States providing for the confiscation of property. From the benefits of this proclamation the following classes were excepted:

1. All who are or shall have been pretended civil or diplomatic officers, or otherwise domestic or foreign agents of the pretended Confederate government.

2. All who left judicial stations under the United States to aid the rebellion.

3. All who shall have been military or naval officers of said pretended Confederate government above the rank of colonel in the army or lieutenant in the navy.

4. All who left seats in the Congress of the United States to aid the rebellion.

5. All who resigned or tendered resignations of their commissions in the army or navy of the United States to evade duty in resisting the rebellion.

6. All who have engaged in any way in treating otherwise than lawfully as prisoners of war persons found in the United States service as officers, soldiers, seamen, or in other capacities.

7. All persons who have been or are absentees from the United States for the purpose of aiding the rebellion.

8. All military and naval officers in the rebel service who were educated by the government in the Military Academy at West Point or the United States Naval Academy.

9. All persons who held the pretended offices of governors of states in insurrection against the United States.

10. All persons who left their homes within the jurisdiction and protection of the United States, and passed beyond the Federal military lines into the so-called Confederate States, for the purpose of aiding the rebellion.

11. All persons who have been engaged in the destruction of the commerce of the United States upon the high seas, and all persons who have made raids into the United States from Canada, or been engaged in destroying the commerce of the United States upon the lakes and rivers that separate the British Provinces from the United States.

12. All persons who, at the time when they seek to obtain the benefits hereof by taking the oath herein prescribed, are in military, naval, or civil confinement or custody, or under bonds of the civil, military, or naval authorities or agents of the United States as prisoners of war, or persons detained for offenses of any kind either before or after conviction.

13. All persons who have voluntarily participated in said rebellion, and the estimated value of whose taxable property is over twenty thousand dollars.

14. All persons who have taken the oath of amnesty as prescribed in the President's proclamation of December 8, A.D. 1863, or an oath of allegiance to the government of the United States since the date of said proclamation, and who have not thenceforward kept and maintained the same inviolate—provided that special application may be made to the President for pardon by any person belonging to the excepted classes, and such clemency will be liberally extended as may be consistent with the facts of the case and the peace and dignity of the United States.

Johnson had, on the 9th of May, re-established by an executive order the authority of the United States in the State of Virginia. The Secretary of the Treasury was instructed to nominate for appointment assessors of taxes, and collectors of customs and internal revenue, and all other officers necessary to put in execution the revenue laws; the Postmaster General was directed to establish post-offices and post-routes, and put in execution the postal laws; the Federal Courts were re-established; the Secretary of War was ordered to assign the necessary provost-marshal generals and provost-marshals, and the Secretary of the Navy to take possession of all public property belonging to the Navy Department. The acts of the political, military, and civil organizations of the state during the war were declared null and void, and Francis H. Pierpont was recognized as the lawful governor.[1]

On the same day that he issued his Amnesty Proclamation, Johnson appointed William W. Holden Provisional Governor of North Carolina. He declared it to be the duty of the provisional governor to prescribe at the earliest practicable period the rules and regulations for the assembling of a Convention, to be chosen by the loyal people of North Carolina, for the purpose of amending the state Constitution. No person could be an elector or member of such Convention unless he should have previously taken the amnesty oath, and should be a qualified voter by the laws of the state. The heads of departments were directed to resume their respective relations with the state, and the Federal Courts were re-established as in Virginia.[1]

The instructions to the heads of departments, and for the re-establishment of Federal Courts, were the same as in the case of Virginia.

During the months of June and July, similar provisional governments were established in all the other insurgent states except Louisiana, Arkansas, and Tennessee. On the 13th of June William L. Sharkey was appointed Provisional Governor of Mississippi; on the 19th, James Johnson, of Georgia, and Andrew J. Hamilton, of Texas; on the 21st, Lewis E. Parsons, of Alabama; on the 30th, Benjamin F. Perry, of South Carolina; and on July 13th, William Marvin, of Florida.

In all these cases only loyal men were allowed to become electors or members of the several Conventions, and the heads of departments were instructed to give the preference to qualified loyal men in the distribution of offices, and where such were not to be obtained in the several states they were to be appointed from other states. Neither in the Amnesty Proclamation, nor in those establishing provisional governments, was any intimation given as to what actions would be required of the several states in order to insure the recognition of their governments by the United States as republican in form.

In Louisiana, J. Madison Wells, who had succeeded Michael Hahn, March 4th, 1865, was recognized and sustained by President Johnson as the lawful governor of the state. In like manner, William G. Brownlow, elected March 4th, 1865, was recognized as Governor of Tennessee; and Isaac Murphy, elected March 14, 1864, as Governor of Arkansas. In these three states, movements toward reconstruction were already at an advanced stage under President Lincoln's administration. In each of them loyal state governments existed, with a Constitution abolishing slavery; but these governments did not rest upon a popular majority. They were instituted and put in operation during the war, at a time when large portions of the territory over which they had jurisdiction were within the control of the Confederacy, and they had not as yet received the sanction of the United States Congress.

On the 23d of June the President rescinded the blockade, and on the 29th of August removed all restrictions upon internal, domestic, and coastwise commerce, so that articles declared by previous proclamations to be contraband of war might be imported into or sold in the insurgent states, "subject only to such regulations as the Secretary of the Treasury may prescribe." On the 11th of October he released John A. Campbell, of Alabama; John H. Reagan, of Texas; Alexander H. Stephens, of Georgia; George A. Trenholm, of South Carolina, and Charles Clark, of Mississippi, from confinement, upon their parole to answer any charge which might be preferred against them, and to abide in their respective states until farther orders. On the 12th of October martial law was suspended in Kentucky, and on the 1st of December the suspension of *habeas corpus* was annulled except in the states of Virginia, Kentucky, Tennessee, North Carolina, Georgia, Florida, Alabama, Mississippi, Lousiana, Arkansas, and Texas, the District of Columbia, and the Territories of New Mexico and Arizona.

Before the assembling of the Thirty-ninth Congress, each of the states in

---

1 "Executive Chamber, Washington City, May 9, 1865.

"ORDERED—*First.* That all acts and proceedings of the political, military, and civil organizations which have been in a state of insurrection and rebellion within the State of Virginia against the authority and laws of the United States, and of which Jefferson Davis, John Letcher, and William Smith were late the respective chiefs, are declared null and void. All persons who shall exercise, claim, pretend, or attempt to exercise any political, military, or civil power, authority, jurisdiction, or right by, through, or under Jefferson Davis, late of the city of Richmond, and his confederates, or under John Letcher or William Smith and their confederates, or under any pretended political, military, or civil commission or authority issued by them, or either of them, since the 17th day of April, 1861, shall be deemed and taken as in rebellion against the United States, and shall be dealt with accordingly.

"*Second.* That the Secretary of State proceed to put in force all laws of the United States, the administration whereof belongs to the Department of State, applicable to the geographical limits aforesaid.

"*Third.* That the Secretary of the Treasury proceed without delay to nominate for appointment assessors of taxes, and collectors of customs and internal revenue, and such other officers of the Treasury Department as are authorized by law, and shall put into execution the revenue laws of the United States within the geographical limits aforesaid. In making appointments, the preference shall be given to qualified loyal persons residing within the districts where their respective duties are to be performed. But if suitable persons shall not be found residents of the districts, then persons residing in other states or districts shall be appointed.

"*Fourth.* That the Postmaster General shall proceed to establish post-offices and post-routes, and put into execution the postal laws of the United States within the said state, giving to loyal residents the preference of appointment. But if suitable persons are not found, then to appoint agents, etc., from other states.

"*Fifth.* That the district judge of said district proceed to hold courts within said state, in accordance with the provisions of the acts of Congress. The Attorney General will instruct the proper officers to libel and bring to judgment, confiscation, and sale property subject to confiscation, and enforce the administration of justice within said state in all matters civil and criminal within the cognizance and jurisdiction of the Federal Courts.

"*Sixth.* That the Secretary of War assign such assistant provost-marshal general, and such provost-marshals in each district of said state as he may deem necessary.

"*Seventh.* The Secretary of the Navy will take possession of all public property belonging to the Navy Department within said geographical limits, and put in operation all acts of Congress in relation to naval affairs having application to the said state.

"*Eighth.* The Secretary of the Interior will also put in force the laws relating to the Department of the Interior.

"*Ninth.* That to carry into effect the guarantee of the Federal Constitution of a republican form of state government, and afford the advantage and security of domestic laws, as well as to complete the re-establishment of the authority of the laws of the United States, and the full and complete restoration of peace within the limits aforesaid, Francis H. Pierpont, Governor of the State of Virginia, will be aided by the Federal government, so far as may be necessary, in the lawful measures which he may take for the extension and administration of the state government throughout the geographical limits of said state.

[L. S.] "In testimony whereof, I have hereunto set my hand and caused the seal of the United States to be affixed.

ANDREW JOHNSON.

"By the President: W. HUNTER, Acting Secretary of State."

1 "*Whereas,* The fourth section of the fourth article of the Constitution of the United States declares that the United States shall guarantee to every state in the Union a republican form of government, and shall protect each of them against invasion and domestic violence; *and whereas* the President of the United States is, by the Constitution, made commander-in-chief of the army and navy, as well as chief civil executive officer of the United States, and is bound by solemn oath faithfully to execute the office of President of the United States, and to take care that the laws be faithfully executed; *and whereas* the rebellion which has been waged by a portion of the people of the United States against the properly constituted authorities of the government thereof in the most violent and revolting form, but whose organized and armed forces have now been almost entirely overcome, has, in its revolutionary progress, deprived the people of the State of North Carolina of all civil government; *and whereas* it becomes necessary and proper to carry out and enforce the obligations of the United States to the people of North Carolina in securing them in the enjoyment of a republican form of government:

"Now, therefore, in obedience to the high and solemn duties imposed upon me by the Constitution of the United States, and for the purpose of enabling the loyal people of said state to organize a state government, whereby justice may be established, domestic tranquillity restored, and loyal citizens protected in all their rights of life, liberty, and property, I, Andrew Johnson, President of the United States and Commander-in-chief of the Army and Navy of the United States, do hereby appoint William W. Holden Provisional Governor of the State of North Carolina, whose duty it shall be, at the earliest practicable period, to prescribe such rules and regulations as may be necessary and proper for convening a Convention composed of delegates to be chosen by that portion of the people of said state who are loyal to the United States, and no others, for the purpose of altering and amending the Constitution thereof; and with authority to exercise within the limits of said state all the powers necessary and proper to enable such loyal people of the State of North Carolina to restore said state to its constitutional relations to the Federal government, and to present such a republican form of state government as will entitle the state to the guarantee of the United States therefor, and its people to protection by the United States against invasion, insurrection, and domestic violence. Provided that in any election that may be held hereafter for choosing delegates to any state Convention as aforesaid, no person shall be qualified as an elector or shall be eligible as a member of such Convention unless he shall have previously taken and subscribed the oath of amnesty as set forth in the President's proclamation of May 29, A.D. 1865, and is a voter qualified as prescribed by the Constitution and laws of the State of North Carolina in force immediately before the 20th day of May, 1861, the date of the so-called Ordinance of Secession. And the said Convention, when convened, or the Legislature that may be thereafter assembled, will prescribe the qualification of electors and the eligibility of persons to hold office under the Constitution and laws of the state—a power the people of the several states composing the Federal Union have rightfully exercised from the origin of the government to the present time."

which provisional governments had been established had elected and held its Convention and had also inaugurated a permanent government, displacing the provisional, under the auspices of President Johnson. In all cases the Ordinance of Secession was either annulled or repealed by the state Conventions, and slavery was forever prohibited. In the Georgia Convention, there was incorporated in the ordinance abolishing slavery a provision that this acquiescence in the action of the government of the United States was not intended to operate as a relinquishment of any claim made by the citizens of that state for compensation. The constitutional amendment was also ratified by the new Legislatures except in the case of Mississippi. In Alabama, South Carolina, and Florida, the ratification was made with the understanding that the clause giving Congress the power to carry out the provisions of the amendment by appropriate legislation did not give that body the right to legislate as to the political status of the freedmen.[1] The Confederate debt was also repudiated in every state save South Carolina, whose Legislature adjourned before taking final action on this subject.

The legislation in regard to freedmen seemed to have for its object the perpetuation of the spirit of slavery after its body had been decently buried. Some of the enactments passed by the various Legislatures were judicious and benevolent, but most of them were expressly designed to establish a distinction of caste between the white and the colored race. While, on the one hand, the right to sue and be sued, and to give testimony in all cases where their own interests were involved, was granted to the negroes, and marriage was legalized among them, on the other the penal code in nearly all the states abounded with oppressive distinctions against the colored race. By emancipation a very large proportion of the freedmen were left in a dependent condition, which demanded instant relief through a generous and well-considered system for the reorganization of the Southern system of labor on the principles of freedom. But, instead of the establishment of such a system, a deliberate scheme was planned to take advantage of the unfavorable condition of the negro by an enactment that all freedmen having no visible means of support should be regarded as vagrants and bound to apprenticeship. Every effort was also made to prevent any organization of the freedmen for their own relief, and making it a misdemeanor for whites to assemble or associate with them.[2] Some of this legislation was so oppressive to the freedmen that it was annulled by the order of military commanders.

It was evident that the late Confederate States misunderstood their situation. President Johnson had thrown upon them the burden of reconstruction, and properly it belonged to them. They, in turn, ought to have shown their good faith by the prompt and voluntary fulfillment of all the con-

---

[1] The following persons were elected permanent governors of the several states: Jonathan Worth, of North Carolina; Benjamin G. Humphreys, of Mississippi; Charles J. Jenkins, of Georgia; R. M. Patton, of Alabama; James L. Orr, of South Carolina; Andrew J. Hamilton, of Texas; and D. S. Walker, of Florida.

[2] The legislation in regard to freedmen may be briefly epitomized in a few paragraphs.

North Carolina.—March 10, 1866, an act was passed declaring that one eighth part of African blood constituted a person a negro. It provided that, so soon as jurisdiction in matters relating to freedmen should be committed to the courts of the state, negroes should have all the privileges of white men in the prosecution of suits, and be eligible as witnesses in cases involving their own interests. It extended the criminal laws to all persons, making no distinction in punishment except for rape, which, if committed upon a white female, was made a capital crime for a black. It legalized marriages contracted during slavery. All contracts, to which one of the parties was a colored person, for the sale or purchase of any horse, mule, jennet, ass, neat cattle, hog, sheep, or goat, whatever the value, and in the case of other articles contracts involving the value of ten dollars, were declared void, except when made in writing, and witnessed by a white person who could read and write. Marriages between whites and blacks were forbidden.

Mississippi.—November 22, 1865, an act was passed to regulate the relation of master and apprentice relative to freedmen. It provided for the apprenticeship to suitable persons, former masters being preferred, of all freedmen under the age of 18 who are orphans, or who are not supported by their parents, to be bound in the case of males till the age of 21, and to the age of 18 in case of females. Power was given to the masters to inflict moderate corporal punishment. Where the age of the freedman was uncertain, it could be fixed by the judge of the county clerk.

November 24, 1865, the vagrant act was passed.

Section 2 provides that all freedmen, free negroes, and mulattoes in this state, over the age of 18 years, found on the second Monday in January, 1866, or thereafter, with no lawful employment or business, or found unlawfully assembling themselves together, either in the day or night time, and all white persons so assembling with freedmen, free negroes, or mulattoes, or usually associating with freedmen, free negroes, or mulattoes on terms of equality, or living in adultery or fornication with a freedwoman, free negro, or mulatto, shall be deemed vagrants, and on conviction thereof shall be fined in the sum of not exceeding, in the case of a freedman, free negro, or mulatto, fifty dollars, and a white man two hundred dollars, and imprisoned at the discretion of the court, the free negro not exceeding ten days, and the white man not exceeding six months.

Section 5 provided that all negroes failing to pay any fine or forfeiture imposed should be hired out, or, if that were impossible, should be treated as paupers.

Section 6 provided that a tax not exceeding one dollar should be levied upon every negro between the ages of 18 and 60 to make up a "freedmen's pauper fund."

November 25, 1865, an act was passed to confer civil rights upon freedmen.

Section 1 provided that negroes might sue and be sued, and acquire personal property, but should not be allowed to rent or lease any lands or tenements except in incorporated towns and cities, in which places the corporate authorities should be the controlling powers.

Section 2 provided for the intermarriage of negroes, the clerk of probate to keep separate records of the same.

Section 3 declared intermarriage between whites and negroes a felony, to be punished by imprisonment for life.

Section 4 gave negroes the right to give testimony in cases where negroes were plaintiffs or defendants.

Section 5 provided that on the second Monday of January, 1866, every negro must have a lawful home or employment, and must have either a license to do irregular and job work, or a written contract for regular labor.

Section 6 provided that negroes quitting the service of employers without good cause before the expiration of their written contract should forfeit their wages.

November 29, 1865, an act was passed prohibiting negroes not in the military service of the United States to "keep or carry arms of any kind, or any ammunition, dirk, or bowie knife." Upon conviction for this event, the penalty was a fine of ten dollars and forfeiture of the weapons. Section 4 of this act provided that all the penal and criminal laws in force in that state "defining offenses and prescribing the mode of punishment for crimes and misdemeanors committed by slaves, free negroes, or mulattoes," were thereby re-enacted, and declared in full force as against freedmen.

Georgia.—December 15, 1865, negroes were made competent witnesses in cases to which freedmen were parties, and marriages between persons of color were legalized.

March 12, 1866, all vagrants or persons leading an immoral or profligate life were made subject to fine, imprisonment, or forced labor for one year, or to be bound out for one year in apprenticeship.

March 17, 1865, it was enacted that persons of color should have the right to make and enforce contracts, to sue and be sued, to give evidence, to inherit, purchase, lease, sell, hold, and convey real and personal property, and that they should not be subjected to any other or different punishment for the commission of any offense than such as were prescribed for white persons committing the same.

Alabama.—December, 1865, a bill was passed "making it unlawful for any freedman, mulatto, or free person of color to own fire-arms, or carry about his person a pistol or other deadly weapon," under a penalty of one hundred dollars fine or three months' imprisonment.

December 9, 1865, it was enacted that negroes and mulattoes should have the right to sue and be sued, and to testify in cases in which negroes were parties.

Early in 1866 Governor Patton vetoed three bills. One of these provided for the regulation of contracts with freedmen, for which the governor thought no special law was necessary. "Information," said he, "from various parts of the state shows that negroes are every where making contracts for the present year upon terms that are entirely satisfactory to the employers. They are also entering faithfully upon the discharge of the obligations contracted. There is every prospect that the engagement formed will be observed with perfect good faith. I therefore think that special laws for regulating contracts between whites and freedmen would accomplish no good, and might result in much harm." He also vetoed a bill extending the criminal laws of the state (which were applicable to free persons of color) to freedmen. The bill applied to the freedmen a system of laws enacted for free negroes in a community where slavery existed. "I have," said the governor, "carefully examined the laws which, under this bill, would be applied to the freedmen, and I think that a mere recital of some of their provisions will show the impolicy and injustice of enforcing them upon the negroes in their new condition." Governor Patton also vetoed "a bill entitled an act to regulate the relations of master and apprentice as relate to freedmen, free negroes, and mulattoes," because he deemed the present laws amply sufficient for all purposes of apprenticeship, without operating upon a particular class of persons.

South Carolina.—October 19, 1865, an act was passed providing that the statutes and regulations concerning slaves were now inapplicable to persons of color. Negroes, though not entitled to social or political equality with white persons, were allowed the right to acquire, own, and dispose of property, to make contracts, to enjoy the fruits of their labor, and to sue and be sued.

December 19, 1865, an act was passed amending the criminal law.

Section 1 provided "that either of the crimes specified in this first section shall be felony, without benefit of clergy, to wit: For a person of color to commit any willful homicide, unless in self-defense; for a person of color to commit an assault upon a white woman with manifest intent to ravish her; for a person of color to have sexual intercourse with a white woman by personating her husband; for any person to raise an insurrection or rebellion in this state; for any person to furnish arms or ammunition to other persons who are in a state of actual insurrection or rebellion, or permit them to resort to his house for advancement of their evil purpose; for any person to administer, or cause to be taken by any other person, any poison, chloroform, soporific, or other destructive thing, or to shoot at, stab, cut, or wound any other person, or by any means whatsoever to cause bodily injury to any other person, whereby, in any of these cases, a bodily injury dangerous to the life of any other person is caused, with intent, in any of these cases, to commit the crime of murder, or the crime of rape, or the crime of robbery, burglary, or larceny; for any person who had been transported under sentence to return to the state within the period of prohibition contained in the sentence; or for a person to steal a horse or mule, or cotton packed in a bale ready for market."

Section 10 provided "that a person of color who is in the employment of a master engaged in husbandry shall not have the right to sell any corn, rice, peas, wheat, or other grain, any flour, cotton, fodder, hay, bacon, fresh meat of any kind, poultry of any kind, animal of any kind, or any other product of a farm, without having written evidence from such master, or some person authorized by him, or from the district judge or a magistrate, that he has the right to sell such product; and if any person shall, directly or indirectly, purchase any such product from such person of color without such written evidence, the purchaser and seller shall each be guilty of a misdemeanor."

Section 18 declared that negroes should constitute no part of the state militia, and that they should not be permitted to keep fire-arms, except in the case of farm owners, who were allowed to keep a shot-gun or rifle.

Section 22 provided that no person of color should migrate into and reside in South Carolina unless within 20 days after his arrival he should enter into a bond in a penalty of $1000 dollars, with two good freeholders as security, for his good behavior and support.

December 21. "*An act to establish and regulate the domestic relations of persons of color, and to amend the law in relation to paupers and vagrancy,*" establishes the relation of husband and wife, declares those now living as such to be husband and wife, and provides that persons of color desirous hereafter to marry shall have the contract duly solemnized. A parent may bind his child over two years of age as an apprentice to serve till 21 if a male, 18 if a female. All persons of color who make contracts for service or labor shall be known as servants, and those with whom they contract as masters.

"Colored children between 18 and 21, who have neither father nor mother *living in the district in which they are found*, or whose parents are paupers, or unable to afford them a comfortable maintenance, *or whose parents are not teaching them habits of industry and honesty*, or are persons of notoriously bad character, or are vagrants, or have been convicted of infamous offenses, and colored children, *in all cases where they are in danger of moral contamination*, may be bound as apprentices by the district judge or one of the magistrates for the aforesaid term."

It "provides that no person of color shall pursue or practice the art, trade, or business of an artisan, mechanic, or shopkeeper, or any other trade, employment, or business (besides that of husbandry, or that of a servant under a contract for service or labor), on his own account and for his own benefit, or in partnership with a white person, or as agent or servant of any person, until he shall have obtained a license therefor from the judge of the District Court, which license shall be good for one year only. This license the judge may grant upon petition of the applicant, and upon being satisfied of his skill and fitness, and of his good moral character, and upon payment by the applicant to the clerk of the District Court of one hundred dollars if a shopkeeper or peddler, to be paid annually, and ten dollars if a mechanic, artisan, or to engage in any other trade, also to be paid annually.

Florida.—January 11, 1866, an act was passed providing that the judicial tribunals of the state should be accessible to all persons without distinction of color, and repealing all laws heretofore passed with reference to slaves, free negroes, and mulattoes, except the acts to prevent their migration into the state and the sale to them of fire-arms.

January 11, 1866, an act was passed legalizing the marriage relation among persons of color.

January 12, 1866, an act was passed in relation to contracts, similar in its provisions to those enacted by the other states.

January 15, 1866, it was enacted "that if any negro, mulatto, or other person of color shall intrude himself into any religious or other public assembly of white persons, or into any railroad car or other public vehicle set apart for the exclusive accommodation of white people, he shall be deemed to be guilty of a misdemeanor, and upon conviction shall be sentenced to stand in the pillory for one hour, or be whipped not exceeding thirty-nine stripes, or both, at the discretion of the jury; nor shall it be lawful for any white person to intrude himself into any religious or other public assembly of colored persons, or into any railroad car or other public vehicle set apart for the exclusive accommodation of persons of color, under the same penalties."

Virginia.—Early in 1866 a vagrant act was passed providing that vagrants should be hired out for a period of three months.

Tennessee.—1866, January 25, this bill became a law:

"That persons of African and Indian descent are hereby declared to be competent witnesses in all the courts of this state, in as full a manner as such persons are by an act of Congress competent witnesses in all the courts of the United States, and all laws and parts of laws of the state excluding such persons from competency are hereby repealed: *Provided, however*, That this act shall not be so construed as to give colored persons the right to vote, hold office, or sit on juries in this state; and that this provision is inserted by virtue of the provision of the 9th section of the amended Constitution, ratified February 22, 1865."

May 26, this bill became a law:

"An act to define the term 'persons of color,' and to declare the rights of such persons.

"SEC. 1. That all negroes, mulattoes, mestizoes, and their descendants, having any African blood in their veins, shall be known in this state as 'persons of color.'

"SEC. 2. That persons of color shall have the right to make and enforce contracts, to sue and be sued, to be parties and give evidence, to inherit, and to have full and equal benefits of all laws and proceedings for the security of person and estate, and shall not be subject to any other or different punishment, pains, or penalty for the commission of any act or offense than such as are prescribed for white persons committing like acts or offenses.

"SEC. 3. That all persons of color, being blind, deaf and dumb, lunatics, paupers, or apprentices, shall have the full and perfect benefit and application of all laws regulating and providing for white persons, being blind, or deaf and dumb, or lunatics or paupers, or either (in asylums for their benefit), and apprentices.

"SEC. 4. That all acts, or parts of acts or laws inconsistent herewith, are hereby repealed: *Provided*, That nothing in this act shall be so construed as to admit persons of color to serve on a jury: *And provided further*, That the provisions of this act shall not be so construed as to require the education of colored and white children in the same school.

"SEC. 5. That all free persons of color who were living together as husband and wife in this state while in a state of slavery are hereby declared to be man and wife, and their children legitimately entitled to an inheritance in any property heretofore acquired, or that may be hereafter acquired by said parents, to as full an extent as the children of white citizens are now entitled by the existing laws of this state."

May 26, all the freedmen's courts in Tennessee were abolished by the assistant commander, the law of the state making colored persons competent witnesses in all civil courts.

Louisiana.—An act was passed in relation to vagrants, providing that the latter, failing to obtain security for good behavior and industry, should be hired out for a period of twelve months.

ditions necessary to restoration. It was not expected that their military defeat would result in their conversion from secession to loyalty, but it seemed certain that the war must at least have convinced them of their folly. It did so to some extent, but it did not bring them wisdom. They appeared determined to do as little as possible to show their appreciation of the significance of the conflict which had gone against them. It was only at the earnest solicitation of the President that certain states repudiated their rebel debt. The manner in which they abolished slavery, with "inasmuches," "ifs," and "buts," showed their reluctance and their desire to find some possible chance of evasion.

Johnson was disappointed. He had calculated upon very different action. He knew that the people would not be satisfied with this half-hearted, evasive sort of allegiance. In his correspondence with the provisional governors he had scarcely been able to conceal his impatience on account of the manner in which the Southern States were moving. Some features of the criminal code adopted by these states seemed to him exceedingly unsatisfactory. He almost begged them to be sensible, and not to neglect the opportunity which had been so generously offered them; but he pleaded in vain. He knew that every mistake made by these states in the movement which he had inaugurated would give force and plausibility to the theories which such men as Stevens, Sumner, and Wendell Phillips were urging upon the country. It is probable that the Southern States still retained a vivid remembrance of the persistent efforts made in their behalf, even while they were in armed rebellion, by the Northern faction led by Seymour, Vallandigham, Pendleton, Long, Bayard, and a host of others, and that, exaggerating the power of this faction, they hoped by union and co-operation with it to obtain in the political arena what they had lost on the field of battle. It is difficult upon any other hypothesis to understand the attitude which they now so defiantly assumed.

The constitutional amendment abolishing slavery had been ratified by the requisite number of states, and on the 18th of December, 1865, Secretary Seward publicly announced this fact, certifying the validity of the amendment "to all intents and purposes as a part of the Constitution of the United States."[1]

The Thirty-ninth Congress was convened at Washington December 4, 1865.[2] The Senate was organized with Lafayette S. Foster as President *pro tempore*. He had been chosen for this position in the extra session of the Senate, and thus became acting Vice-President of the United States. He had been a senator from Connecticut since 1855, and was eminently fitted both by natural qualities and by experience for the duties of a presiding officer. In the House, the members were called to order by the clerk, Edward McPherson, of Pennsylvania. The office of clerk of the House at this time was beset with difficulties of the most delicate nature. By law, his decision as to the members who might be properly placed upon the call roll and take part in the organization of the House was absolute. By one party it was claimed that for him to exclude the names of Southern members was an assumption on his part of the right to reject members before they had been rejected by the House. By another party it was claimed that, by including those names, McPherson would equally anticipate the action of Congress by presuming to accept members before the House had acted in the matter. McPherson very wisely concluded to let the matter rest exactly where he found it. The members from the Southern States had not been admitted, and there were peculiar circumstances incident to their election which did not usually exist in ordinary cases. He determined, therefore, to leave the whole subject to Congress. It is evident, also,

---

[1] "*To all to whom these presents may come, greeting:*

"Know ye, that whereas the Congress of the United States, on the 1st of February last, passed a resolution which is in the words following, namely: 'A resolution submitting to the Legislatures of the several states a proposition to amend the Constitution of the United States.

"'*Resolved by the Senate and House of Representatives of the United States of America, in Congress assembled* (*two thirds of both houses concurring*), That the following article be proposed to the Legislatures of the several states as an amendment to the Constitution of the United States, which, when ratified by three fourths of said Legislatures, shall be valid, to all intents and purposes, as a part of the said Constitution, namely:

"'ARTICLE XIII.

"'SEC. 1. Neither slavery nor involuntary servitude, except as a punishment for crime, whereof the party shall have been duly convicted, shall exist within the United States, or any place subject to their jurisdiction.

"'SEC. 2. Congress shall have power to enforce this article by appropriate legislation.'

"*And whereas* it appears from official documents on file in this department that the amendment to the Constitution of the United States, proposed as aforesaid, has been ratified by the Legislatures of the states of Illinois, Rhode Island, Michigan, Maryland, New York, West Virginia, Maine, Kansas, Massachusetts, Pennsylvania, Virginia, Ohio, Missouri, Nevada, Indiana, Louisiana, Minnesota, Wisconsin, Vermont, Tennessee, Arkansas, Connecticut, New Hampshire, South Carolina, Alabama, North Carolina, and Georgia—in all, twenty-seven states;

"*And whereas* the whole number of states in the United States is thirty-six; *and whereas* the before specially-named states, whose Legislatures have ratified the said proposed amendment, constitute three fourths of the whole number of states in the United States:

"Now, therefore, be it known that I, William H. Seward, Secretary of State of the United States, by virtue and in pursuance of the second section of the act of Congress approved the twentieth of April, eighteen hundred and eighteen, entitled 'An Act to provide for the publication of the Laws of the United States and for other purposes,' do hereby certify that the amendment aforesaid has become valid, to all intents and purposes, as part of the Constitution of the United States.

"In testimony whereof I have hereunto set my hand and caused the seal of the Department of State to be affixed.

"Done at the City of Washington, this eighteenth day of December, in the year of our Lord one thousand eight hundred and sixty-five, and of the Independence of the United States of America the ninetieth. [L. S.] WILLIAM H. SEWARD, Secretary of State."

[New Jersey, Oregon, California, and Iowa ratified subsequently to the date of this certificate, as did Florida in the same form as South Carolina and Alabama.]

[2] The following is a list of the members of this Congress. Those marked with an asterisk were new members:

SENATE.

California—James A. McDougall, John Conness.
Connecticut—Lafayette S. Foster, James Dixon.
Delaware—George Read Riddle, Willard Saulsbury.
Illinois—Lyman Trumbull, Richard Yates.*
Indiana—Henry S. Lane, Thomas A. Hendricks.
Iowa—James W. Grimes, Samuel J. Kirkwood.*
Kansas—Samuel C. Pomeroy, James H. Lane.
Kentucky—Garret Davis, James Guthrie.*
Maine—Lot M. Morrill, William Pitt Fessenden.*
Massachusetts—Charles Sumner, Henry Wilson.
Maryland—John A. J. Creswell,* Reverdy Johnson.
Michigan—Zachariah Chandler, Jacob M. Howard.
Minnesota—Alexander Ramsay, Daniel S. Norton.*
Missouri—B. Gratz Brown, John B. Henderson.
Nevada—William M. Stewart,* James W. Nye.*
New Hampshire—Daniel Clark, Aaron H. Cragin.*
New Jersey—William Wright, John P. Stockton.*
New York—Ira Harris, Edwin D. Morgan.
Ohio—John Sherman, Benjamin F. Wade.
Oregon—James W. Nesmith, George B. Williams.*
Pennsylvania—Edgar Cowan, Charles R. Buckalew.
Rhode Island—William Sprague, Henry B. Anthony.
Tennessee—David D. Patterson,* J. S. Fowler.*
Vermont—Luke P. Poland,* Solomon Foot.
West Virginia—Peter G. Van Winkle, Waitman T. Willey.
Wisconsin—Timothy O. Howe, James R. Doolittle.

HOUSE.

California—Donald C. McRuer,* William Higby, John Bidwell.*
Connecticut—Henry C. Deming, Samuel L. Warner,* Augustus Brandegee, John H. Hubbard.
Delaware—John A. Nicholson.*
Illinois—John Wentworth,* John F. Farnsworth, Elihu B. Washburne, Abner C. Harding, Eben C. Ingersoll, Burton C. Cook,* H. P. H. Bromwell,* Shelby M. Cullom,* Lewis W. Ross, Anthony Thornton,* Samuel S. Marshall,* Jehu Baker,* Andrew J. Kuykendall,* at large, S. W. Moulton.*
Indiana—William E. Niblack,* Michael C. Kerr,* Ralph Hill,* John H. Farquhar,* George W. Julian, Ebenezer Dumont, Daniel W. Voorhees,* Godlove S. Orth, Schuyler Colfax, Joseph H. Defrees,* Thomas N. Stillwell.*
Iowa—James F. Wilson, Hiram Price, William B. Allison, Josiah B. Grinnell, John A. Kasson, Asahel W. Hubbard.
Kansas—Sidney Clarke.*
Kentucky—L. S. Trimble,* Burwell C. Ritter,* Henry Grider, Aaron Harding, Lovell H. Rousseau,* Green Clay Smith, George S. Shanklin,* William H. Randall, Samuel McKee.*
Maine—John Lynch,* Sidney Perham, James G. Blaine, John H. Rice, Frederick A. Pike.
Maryland—Hiram McCullough, John L. Thomas, Jr.,* Charles E. Phelps,* Francis Thomas, Benjamin G. Harris.
Massachusetts—Thomas D. Eliot, Oakes Ames, Alexander H. Rice, Samuel Hooper, John B. Alley, Nathaniel P. Banks,* George S. Boutwell,* John D. Baldwin, William B. Washburn, Henry L. Dawes.
Michigan—Fernando C Beaman, Charles Upson, John W. Longyear, Thomas W. Ferry,* Rowland E. Trowbridge,* John F. Driggs.
Minnesota—William Windom, Ignatius Donnelly.
Missouri—John Hogan,* Henry T. Blow, Thomas E. Noell,* John R. Kelso,* Joseph W. McClurg, Robert T. Van Horn,* Benjamin F. Loan, John F. Benjamin,* George W. Anderson.*
Nevada—Delos R. Ashley.*
New Hampshire—Gilman Marston,* Edward H. Rollins, James W. Patterson.
New Jersey—John F. Starr, William A. Newell,* Charles Sitgreaves,* Andrew J. Rogers, Edwin R. V. Wright.*
New York—Stephen Taber,* Tunis G. Bergen,* James Humphrey,* Morgan Jones,* Nelson Taylor,* Henry J. Raymond,* John W. Chanler, James Brooks, William A. Darling,* William Radford, Charles H. Winfield, John H. Ketcham,* Edwin N. Hubbell,* Charles Goodyear,* John A. Griswold,* Robert S. Hale,* Calvin T. Hulburd, James M. Marvin, Demas Hubbard, Jr.,* Addison H. Laflin,* Roscoe Conkling,* Sidney T. Holmes,* Thomas T. Davis, Theodore M. Pomeroy, Daniel Morris, Giles W. Hotchkiss, Hamilton Ward,* Roswell Hart,* Burt Van Horn,* James M. Humphrey, Henry Van Aernam.*
Ohio—Benjamin Eggleston, Rutherford B. Hayes,* Robert C. Schenck, William Lawrence,* F. C. Le Blond, Reader W. Clark,* Samuel Shellabarger,* James H. Hubbell,* Ralph P. Buckland,* James M. Ashley, Hezekiah S. Bundy,* William E. Finck, Columbus Delano,* Martin Welker,* Tobias E. Plants,* John A. Bingham,* Ephraim R. Eckley, Rufus P. Spalding, James A. Garfield.
Oregon—John H. D. Henderson.*
Pennsylvania—Samuel J. Randall, Charles O'Neill, Leonard Myers, William D. Kelley, M. Russell Thayer, B. Markley Boyer,* John M. Broomall, Sydenham E. Ancona, Thaddeus Stevens, Myer Strouse, Philip Johnson, Charles Denison, Ulysses Mercur,* George F. Miller,* Adam J. Glossbrenner,* William H. Koontz,* Abraham A. Barker,* Stephen F. Wilson,* Glenni W. Scofield, Charles Vernon Culver,* John L. Dawson, James K. Moorhead, Thomas Williams, George V. Lawrence.*
Rhode Island—Thomas A. Jenckes, Nathan F. Dixon.
Tennessee—Nathaniel G. Taylor,* Horace Maynard,* William B. Stokes,* Edmund Cooper,* William B. Campbell,* S. M. Arnell,* Isaac R. Hawkins, John W. Leftwich.*
Vermont—Frederick E. Woodbridge, Justin S. Morrill, Portus Baxter.
West Virginia—Chester D. Hubbard,* George R. Latham,* Killian V. Whaley.
Wisconsin—Halbert E. Paine,* Ithamar C. Sloan, Amasa Cobb, Charles A. Eldridge, Philetus Sawyer,* Walter D. McIndoe.

The members from Tennessee were not admitted to either house until near the close of the session. Henry P. Stockton's seat in the Senate was declared vacant. Solomon Foote, of Vermont, died March 28, and was succeeded by George F. Edmunds. In the House the seat of D. W. Voorhees was given to Henry D. Washburne. That of James Brooks was given to William E. Dodge.

The following members were elected to Congress from the Southern States, but were not admitted:

SENATE.

Alabama—George S. Houston, Lewis E. Parsons.
Arkansas—E. Baxter, William D. Snow.
Louisiana—R. King Cutler, Michael Hahn.
Mississippi—William L. Sharkey, J. L. Alcorn.
North Carolina—John Pool, William A. Graham.
South Carolina—John L. Manning, Benjamin F. Perry.
Virginia—John C. Underwood, Joseph Segar.
Florida—William Marvin, Wilkerson Call.
Georgia—Alexander H. Stephens, Herschel V. Johnson.

HOUSE.

Alabama—C. C. Langdon, George C. Freeman, Cullen A. Battle, Joseph W. Taylor, B. T. Pope, T. J. Foster.
Arkansas—William Byers, George H. Kyle, J. M. Johnson.
Florida—F. McLeod.
Georgia—Solomon Cohen, Philip Cook, Hugh Buchanan, E. G. Cabaniss, J. D. Matthews, J. H. Christy, W. T. Wofford.
Louisiana—Louis St. Martin, Jacob Barker, Robert C. Wickliffe, John E. King, John S. Young.
Mississippi—A. E. Reynolds, R. A. Pinson, James T. Harrison, A. M. West, E. G. Peyton.
North Carolina—Jesse R. Stubbs, Charles C. Clark, Thomas C. Fuller, Josiah Turner, Jr., Bedford Brown, S. H. Walkup, A. H. Jones.
South Carolina—John D. Kennedy, William Aiken, Samuel McGowan, James Farrow.
Virginia—W. H. B. Custis, Lucius H. Chandler, B. Johnson Barbour, Robert Ridgway, Beverly A. Davis, Alexander H. H. Stuart, Robert Y. Conrad, Daniel H. Hoge.

Of those elected to the Senate, Mr. A. H. Stephens was a delegate from Georgia to the Convention which framed the "Confederate" Constitution, and was Vice-President of the "Confederacy" until its downfall. Mr. H. V. Johnson was a senator in the rebel Congress in the first and second Congresses, as was Mr. Graham from North Carolina. Mr. Pool was a senator in the Legislature of North Carolina. Mr. Perry was a "Confederate States" judge. Mr. Manning was a volunteer aid to General Beauregard at Fort Sumter and Manassas. Mr. Alcorn was in the Mississippi militia.

Among those elected to the House, of the *Alabama* delegation, Mr. Battle was a general in the rebel army, and Mr. Foster a representative in the first and second rebel Congresses.

Of the *Georgia* delegation, Messrs. Cook and Wofford were generals in the rebel service.

Of the *Mississippi* delegation, Messrs. Reynolds and Pinson were colonels in the rebel service; Mr. Harrison was a member of the rebel Provisional Congress.

Of the *North Carolina* delegation, Mr. Fuller was a representative in the first rebel Congress, and Mr. Turner was a colonel in the rebel army, and a representative in the second rebel Congress; Mr. Brown was a member of the State Convention which passed the Secession Ordinance in 1861, and voted for it.

Of the *South Carolina* delegation, Mr. Kennedy was colonel and Mr. McGowan brigadier general in the rebel army; Mr. Farrow was a representative in the first and second rebel Congresses.

Of the *Virginia* delegation, Messrs. Stuart and Conrad were members of the Secession Convention of Virginia in 1861, and continued to participate after the passage of the ordinance and the beginning of hostilities.

LAFAYETTE S. FOSTER.

that President Johnson did not expect McPherson to come to any different conclusion in the matter, from his letter to Provisional Governor Perry, November 27, a week before the assembling of Congress. In this letter he said it was not necessary for the members elect from South Carolina to be present at the organization of Congress. On the contrary, he thought it would be better policy to present their certificates of election after the organization of the two houses, and then it would be "a simple question under the Constitution of the members taking their seats." "Each house," he added, "must judge for itself the election, returns, and qualifications of its own members."

An attempt was made by Brooks, of New York, to bring up the question as to the credentials of members previous to organization, but it proved unsuccessful. In the vote for speaker the House divided by a strictly party separation between Brooks and Colfax; 175 votes being cast, of which the former received 36, and the latter 139. Thus Schuyler Colfax was re-elected speaker. Being conducted to the chair, he addressed the House. He alluded to the circumstances under which this new Congress was assembled. The Thirty-eighth Congress had closed its existence while the war was still in progress, but now there was peace from shore to shore. The duties of this Congress, he said, "are as obvious as the sun's pathway in the heavens. Representing, in its two branches, the states and the people, its first and highest obligation is to guarantee to every state a republican form of government. The rebellion having overthrown constitutional state governments in many states, it is yours to mature and enact legislation, which, with the concurrence of the executive, shall establish them anew on such a basis of enduring justice as will guarantee all necessary safeguards to the people, and afford what our Magna Charta, the Declaration of Independence, proclaims is the chief object of government—protection to all men in their inalienable rights. The world should witness in this great work the most inflexible fidelity, the most earnest devotion to the principles of liberty and humanity, the truest patriotism, and the wisest statesmanship. Heroic men, by hundreds of thousands, have died that the republic might live. The emblems of mourning have darkened White House and cabin alike; but the fires of civil war have melted every fetter in the land, and proved the funeral-pyre of slavery. It is for you, representatives, to do your work as faithfully and as well as did the fearless saviors of the Union on their more dangerous arena of duty. Then we may hope to see the vacant and once abandoned seats around us gradually filling up, until this hall shall contain representatives from every state and district, their hearts devoted to the Union for which they are to legislate, jealous of its honor, proud of its glory, watchful of its rights, and hostile to its enemies; and the stars on our banner, that paled when the states they represented arrayed themselves in arms against the nation, will shine with a more brilliant light of loyalty than ever before."

The speaker then took the test oath, which still remained in operation.

In the Senate, excluding Tennessee, there were 10 new members out of 50; in the House, excluding Tennessee, 93 out of 184, or fully one half, were new members. The political complexion of the Senate remained unchanged; but in the House the change was very great. In the Thirty-eighth Congress about four ninths of the members were Democrats, now they numbered less than one fourth. This change simply indicated the popular opposition to the schemes of the peace party in 1864. The Thirty-ninth Congress had been elected, not on the special issues of reconstruction, but on issues directly connected with the prosecution of the war.

President Johnson's message was anxiously awaited by the people. The President of the United States holds a peculiar position. He is, *par excellence*, the representative of the republic. He is directly elected by the whole people, while the legislative officers are elected either by states, as in the case of the Senate, or by local districts, as in the case of the House; therefore the people naturally look to him as to one whom they have expressly chosen as the exponent of their own views. He is elected by the majority of the whole people, and is therefore supposed to represent the nation rather than any section. To him is intrusted more power than resides in the head of a constitutional monarchy, because he is the choice of the people, and not a hereditary imposition. If Johnson's present position was different from that of a President elected as such, and not as Vice-President, that was the fault of the party which had elected him.

Johnson was a Democrat elected by the Republican party as Vice-President, and who, by accident, had become President. He had been a supporter of Breckinridge in the presidential contest of 1860. Although he was an ardent advocate of the Union, his political principles had not changed. He could scarcely find a name harsh enough by which to designate the rebellion. Following his own inclinations, he would have hanged the leading men engaged in it. In his view traitors should be "punished and impoverished." He knew that slavery was dead, but he was no mourner over its corpse. As military governor of Tennessee, he had been deemed one of the most radical members of the Republican party; and such indeed he had been, so far as war measures were concerned. Yet, now that the war was over, he was satisfied with what had been accomplished, and desired the immediate restoration of the Southern States to the Union upon the basis of the Constitution as it then stood, without farther modification. He would have preferred that the Southern Conventions should have extended the elective franchise to all negroes who could "read the Constitution of the United States in English and write their names," or who owned real estate to the value of $250. He even went so far as to urge such a measure upon the Mississippi Convention. He foresaw, or thought he did, that the Republican party would demand universal negro suffrage as a condition of restoration, and thought that the adoption of partial suffrage for the colored race would satisfy the people, and, as he expressed it, "disarm the adversary." But what was the "adversary" which Johnson wished to disarm? The party which had elected him. From the extremists of this party he feared more danger to the country than from the just subdued rebellious states. The very fact that these states had not appreciated the opportunity which he had given them, and had not heartily co-operated with him in his efforts in their behalf, only increased his apprehension; for he knew that their reluctant, half-hearted submission, and their ill-considered attempts to evade the consequences of the war, would give power to the faction of whose future action he had the most serious apprehension. With all their mistakes, he preferred to trust the Southern States rather than extreme Republicans. If

SCHUYLER COLFAX.

he was dissatisfied with the former, he was more apprehensive of the latter. He would sooner forgive rebels who had laid down their arms, however sullen their submission, than support those who desired to make the victory of the nation an occasion for the aggrandizement of their party. The former were powerless for injury; the danger threatened by the latter he deemed imminent and formidable.

During the few months preceding the assembling of Congress the speculations as to Johnson's position were numerous. He was every day pardoning rebels belonging to the classes excepted from his Amnesty Proclamation of May 29th. Of course the applications for pardon were many, but the exceptions had been made to exclude a few, and there was no impropriety in the President's pardoning all others. In some cases, however, where there was a special reason for refusal, pardon was not refused.

During this period, also, the Democratic press had undergone a somewhat remarkable change. Those journals which had hitherto been foremost in abusing Johnson now altered their tone. The Democratic party had been shamefully defeated in the election of 1864, but now there seemed to be a chance for its recovery. Somewhat curiously, this party supposed that Johnson was coming over to it, while Johnson, on the other hand, supposed that this party was coming over to him. And here we are reminded of the interview between George L. Stearns and the President, October 3d, 1865. "The Democratic party," said Johnson at this interview, "finds its old position is untenable, and is coming over to ours; if it has come up to our position, I am glad of it." At the same time the President expressed his views in detail. He said the states were in the Union, "which was whole and indivisible." "We must not," he remarked, "be too much in a hurry; it is better to let them reconstruct themselves than to force them to it; for if they go wrong, the power is in our hands, and we can check them in any stage to the end, and oblige them to correct their error; we must be patient with them." He expressed his opposition both to giving too much power to the states, and also to a great consolidation of power in the central government. "Our only safety," he said, "lies in allowing each state to control the right of voting by its own laws, and we have the power to control the rebel states if they go wrong. . . . . If the general government controls the right to vote in the states, it may establish such rules as will restrict the vote to a small number of persons, and thus create a central despotism." Universal negro suffrage now he thought would breed a war of races; but he was in favor of a gradual introduction of the black race to participation in political power. He said the negro would rather vote with his master whom he did not hate, than with the non-slaveholding population of the South, against whom he had an hereditary prejudice. This prejudice was shown by the fact that outrages committed originated either from non-slaveholding whites against negroes, or from negroes against non-slaveholding whites.

To understand Johnson's position at this time we must call to mind the considerations which influenced him. In the first place, there was his theory of the situation, according to which he believed that the burden of reconstruction rested upon the South, and not upon the executive or legislative departments of the government. The rebellion had ceased, and, whatever might be the decision of government as to the punishment of individual traitors, the states in which the rebellion had existed were still states, with all their powers unimpaired, and with all their social institutions intact save that of slavery. Allegiance, as it seemed to him, consisted in the performance of constitutional obligations. It is true that by the Constitution every man who had borne arms against the government might be hung for treason, or be punished in any other way, at the option of the government; but, even after that had been done, it would still remain true that the only claim which the government had upon the Southern people was a claim to their allegiance—not their allegiance to the Republican party, but to the Constitution. The ratification of the anti-slavery amendment he deemed necessary as a recognition of what had been accomplished by the war. The nullification of secession ordinances and the repudiation of the rebel debt were, in his view, directly involved in the abandonment of the struggle by the South. His views had not changed from what they had been in 1862, when in the Senate he introduced the resolution declaring that the object of the war was simply the suppression of the rebellion, and that, so soon as this should be accomplished, the war ought to cease, leaving the Southern States with all their original powers under the Constitution. Since then slavery had been abolished, and thus far the views expressed in this resolution had been changed, but no farther. Johnson did not regard the resumption of their former functions by the late Confederate States as a privilege granted them, but as a duty—a constitutional obligation which even the existence of civil war had no power to relax. Whatever farther changes in the organic law of the nation might seem necessary in the new situation consequent upon restoration ought, in his opinion, to be made in the ordinary way, and by all the states acting in common, and upon terms of equality.

But, apart from his theory as to the basis of restoration, there were certain practical considerations which influenced the President. So long as the Southern States were prevented from resuming their normal relations to the government, the balance of political power would remain disturbed. By the very election which had given him his present position a Congress also had been chosen which was more than three fourths Republican. He foresaw, or at least feared, that this Congress, in which there was so heavy a preponderance of power on the Republican side, would be partisan in its legislation, and would use its advantages for the concentration and perpetuation of party power. The immediate representation of the South in Congress, while it would counteract this tendency, could not, it seemed to him, be productive of evil, inasmuch as each house, by its power to decide upon the qualification of its members, had a safeguard against the admission of the disloyal, and inasmuch, moreover, as, even after the admission of every Southern member, the Republicans would still maintain a majority in both houses.

These principles constituted the basis of President Johnson's policy of reconstruction as laid before Congress in his first annual message. The first question, he said, which had presented itself for decision was whether the territory of the South should be held as conquered territory under military authority emanating from the President as commander-in-chief of the army. He had decided the question in the negative. Military governments, while they would not alleviate, would, on the other hand, exaggerate existing discontent; they would envenom hatred rather than restore affection; once established, no precise limit to their continuance was conceivable; the expense occasioned by them would be incalculable and exhausting; they would operate unfavorably against emigration from the Northern to the Southern States—one of the best means for the restoration of harmony; the powers of patronage and rule thus exercised under the President over a vast, populous, and naturally wealthy region, were greater than he would, unless under extreme necessity, intrust to any one man—greater than he would consent to exercise himself except on occasions of great emergency; and the willful use of such powers for a series of years would endanger not only the purity of the general administration, but also the liberties of the states which remained loyal.

But, argued the President, there was another and more vital objection to the establishment of military governments over the Southern States. Such a policy would imply that the states whose inhabitants had participated in the rebellion had, by the act of those inhabitants, ceased to exist. The true theory, on the other hand, was "that all pretended acts of secession were from the beginning null and void." States could not commit treason, nor screen individual traitors, any more than they could make treaties with foreign powers. The vitality of the seceding states had been by the rebellion impaired, but not extinguished, and their functions suspended, but not destroyed.

"But," proceeds the argument, "if any state neglects or refuses to perform its offices, there is the more need that the general government should maintain all its authority, and, as soon as practicable, resume the exercise of all its functions. On this principle I have acted, and have gradually and quietly, and by almost imperceptible steps, sought to restore the rightful energy of the general government and of the states. To that end provisional governors have been appointed for the states, Conventions called, governors elected, Legislatures assembled, and senators and representatives chosen to the Congress of the United States. At the same time, the courts of the United States, as far as could be done, have been reopened, so that the laws of the United States may be enforced through their agency. The blockade has been removed, and the custom-houses re-established in ports of entry, so that the revenue of the United States may be collected. The Post-office Department renews its ceaseless activity, and the general government is thereby enabled to communicate promptly with its officers and agents. The courts bring security to persons and property; the opening of the ports invites the restoration of industry and commerce; the post-office renews the facilities of social intercourse and of business. And is it not happy for us all that the restoration of each one of these functions of the general government brings with it a blessing to the states over which they are extended? Is it not a sure promise of harmony and renewed attachment to the Union that, after all that has happened, the return of the general government is known only as a beneficence?"

This policy was attended with some risk; its success involved the acquiescence of the states concerned. But the risk must be taken, and in the choice of difficulties it was the smallest risk. To diminish the danger involved in his policy he had asserted his power to pardon.

"The next step which I have taken," said the President, "to restore the constitutional relations of the states has been an invitation to them to participate in the high office of amending the Constitution. Every patriot must wish for a general amnesty at the earliest epoch consistent with public safety. For this great end there is need of a concurrence of all opinions, and the spirit of mutual conciliation. All parties in the late terrible conflict must work together in harmony. It is not too much to ask, in the name of the whole people, that, on the one side, the plan of restoration shall proceed in conformity with a willingness to cast the disorders of the past into oblivion; and that, on the other, the evidence of sincerity in the future maintenance of the Union shall be put beyond any doubt by the ratification of the proposed amendment to the Constitution, which provides for the abolition of slavery forever within the limits of our country. So long as the adoption of this amendment is delayed, so long will doubt, and jealousy, and uncertainty prevail. This is the measure which will efface the sad memory of the past; this is the measure which will most certainly call population, and capital, and security to those parts of the Union that need them most. Indeed, it is not too much to ask of the states which are now resuming their places in the family of the Union to give this pledge of perpetual loyalty and peace. Until it is done, the past, however much we may desire it, will not be forgotten. The adoption of the amendment reunites us beyond all power of disruption. It heals the wound that is still imperfectly closed; it removes slavery, the element which has so long perplexed and divided the country; it makes of us once more a united people, renewed and strengthened, bound more than ever to mutual affection and support."

Thus President Johnson explained the policy which he had thus far pursued. The completion of the work of restoration would be accomplished by the resumption on the part of the states of their places in the two branches of the national Legislature. "Here," he added, "it is for you, fellow-citizens of the Senate, and for you, fellow-citizens of the House of Representatives, to judge, each of you for yourselves, of the elections, returns, and qualifications of your own members."

After advocating the speedy restoration by Congress of the Circuit Courts in the late rebel states, in order that those charged with the commission of treason might have fair and impartial trials, the President proceeded thus to consider the situation of the freedmen in those states:

"The relations of the general government toward the four millions of inhabitants whom the war has called into freedom have engaged my most serious consideration. On the propriety of attempting to make the freedmen electors by the proclamation of the executive, I took for my counsel the Constitution itself, the interpretations of that instrument by its authors and their contemporaries, and recent legislation by Congress. When, at the first movement toward independence, the Congress of the United States instructed the several states to institute governments of their own, they left each state to decide for itself the conditions for the enjoyment of the elective franchise. During the period of the Confederacy, there continued to exist a very great diversity in the qualifications of electors in the several states; and even within a state a distinction of qualifications prevailed with regard to the officers who were to be chosen. The Constitution of the United States recognizes these diversities when it enjoins that in the choice of members of the House of Representatives of the United States 'the electors in each state shall have the qualifications requisite for electors of the most numerous branch of the state Legislature.'

"After the formation of the Constitution, it remained, as before, the uniform usage for each state to enlarge the body of its electors according to its own judgment; and, under this system, one state after another has proceeded to increase the number of its electors, until now universal suffrage, or something very near it, is the general rule. So fixed was this reservation of power in the habits of the people, and so unquestioned has been the interpretation of the Constitution, that during the civil war the late President never harbored the purpose—certainly never avowed the purpose—of disregarding it; and in the acts of Congress, during that period, nothing can be found which during the continuance of hostilities, much less after their close, would have sanctioned any departure by the executive from a policy which has so uniformly obtained. Moreover, a concession of the elective franchise to the freedmen, by act of the President of the United States, must have been extended to all colored men, wherever found, and so must have established a change of suffrage in the Northern, Middle, and Western States, not less than in the Southern and Southwestern. Such an act would have created a new class of voters, and would have been an assumption of power by the President which nothing in the Constitution or laws of the United States would have warranted.

"On the other hand, every danger of conflict is avoided when the settlement of the question is referred to the several states. They can, each for itself, decide on the measure, and whether it is to be adopted at once and absolutely, or introduced gradually and with conditions. In my judgment, the freedmen, if they show patience and manly virtues, will sooner obtain a participation in the elective franchise through the states than through the general government, even if it had power to intervene. When the tumult of emotions that have been raised by the suddenness of the social change shall have subsided, it may prove that they will receive the kindliest usage from some of those on whom they have heretofore most closely depended."

But, while the President thought it was not competent for the general government to extend the elective franchise in the several states, it seemed equally clear to him that good faith required the security of the freedmen in their liberty and property, their right to labor, and to just compensation therefor. "It is," said he, "one of the greatest acts on record to have brought four millions of people into freedom. The career of free industry must be fairly opened to them; and then their future prosperity and condition must, after all, rest mainly on themselves. If they fail, and so perish away, let us be careful that the failure shall not be attributable to any denial of justice. In all that relates to the destiny of the freedmen we need not be too anxious to read the future; many incidents which, from a speculative point of view, might raise alarm, will quietly settle themselves."

This message was as able a political document as had ever been laid before the American Congress. But, for all that, the President, as we have said already, had committed a terrible blunder. He had assumed that the executive might *independently* determine the conditions necessary to restoration, and that to Congress was only left the consideration on the part of the two houses respectively of the qualifications of their members, and such action as might be deemed necessary to secure the freedmen against oppression. His mistake was not that he had not established military governments over the Southern States; it was not that he had usurped any power in re-establishing the relations between those states and the executive, which it was clearly his duty to do; but he had created an impression among the people of the South that simply by nullifying secession, repudiating the rebel debt, and ratifying the anti-slavery amendment, they had done all which was necessary to satisfy the people that the security of the country was fully established. Here was his mistake. The people were not satisfied by what had been done. They did not feel secure as to the future. On the contrary, they were greatly agitated with apprehension lest Southern politicians, combining with Northern Democrats, and assisted by the increased numerical representation resulting from the abolition of slavery, might imperil the security of the national debt, demand compensation for their freed slaves, inaugurate a system of legislation injurious to freedmen, and neutralize the results of the war. Congress also was dissatisfied, not only for the reasons which had occasioned popular discontent, but because it had not been admitted to participation in the first stages of reconstruction. In this work there were some things demanded by the people which belonged alone to the national Legislature, and could not be touched by the President. Thus, for instance, he had no right to demand the readjustment of the basis of representation.

All this difficulty might have been avoided if the President had called an extra session of Congress in July, 1865. There were two urgent reasons for such a session:

1. The perfection of the preliminary steps toward restoration in such features as required the supplementary action of Congress could only thus be secured.

2. It was an emergency which demanded harmonious action on the part of the government. This harmony implied no usurpation by the executive of the functions of Congress, or by Congress of executive powers. The President would still be perfectly independent in his own sphere, and a like independence would belong to the national Legislature. The very fact of the President's consulting with Congress would have conduced to harmony. And if, after all, there should arise a difference, and the President should deem it his duty to do his share of the work upon one plan, while Congress, after mature deliberation, should decide upon a different policy in regard to its own action, each would have shown a proper respect for the other, and thus the antagonism which might have been inevitable, however unfortunate, would have been free from bitterness. Each department of the government, moreover, would at the outset have given a full expression of its policy, and the Southern States would have been prevented from entertaining false hopes as to the result of their own action. The questions involved in the two different policies—if there must be two—would have thus been brought immediately before the people for calm discussion, and not in such a way as to lead on to an angry and acrimonious dispute.

But Johnson, as we have said, preferred another course, and proceeded to his work alone. Thus he laid the basis for a conflict between himself and Congress, for popular dissatisfaction, and for unreasonable expectations on the part of the Southern people. Whether these results followed with or without the President's design, they were equally unfortunate. It was certainly in his power to prevent them, but he did not use the power. Whatever might afterward be done by Congress to deepen and exacerbate the conflict between the executive and legislative departments of the government, it would still remain true that the President had taken the first steps toward such a conflict. Did he distrust Congress, and therefore attempt to forestall its action? Then it must be answered, first, that his distrust had no good foundation, as there was no indication that Congress was disposed to act unreasonably toward the South; and, secondly, that if Congress had been thus disposed, its action *could* not be forestalled by the President. It was the Congress of the United States; its action was as independent within its own sphere as was that of the President; so long as it remained in power, its decision as to the representation of the Southern States was irrevocable by any power on earth. And, moreover, the President could, by his distrust of Congress, or by an attempt to anticipate its action in the preliminary stages of restoration, only put that body upon its guard, and generate in it a corresponding distrust of himself, thus rendering future harmony between the executive and legislative departments almost impossible.

Previous to the organization of Congress, it had been determined in a caucus of Republicans to reject all delegations from the Southern States until both houses had agreed upon some plan of action respecting them. On the first day of the session, Thaddeus Stevens offered a resolution, which was adopted by the House, 133 to 36, "that a joint committee of fifteen members shall be appointed, nine of whom shall be members of the House and six members of the Senate, who shall inquire into the condition of the states which formed the so-called Confederate States of America, and report whether they, or any of them, are entitled to be represented in either house of Congress, with leave to report at any time by bill or otherwise; and until such report shall have been made and finally acted upon by Congress, no member shall be received into either house from any of the so-called Confederate States; and all papers relating to the representation of said states shall be referred to the said committee without debate." The previous question was demanded by Stevens, and all debate was forestalled. This resolution came before the Senate for action on the 12th of December, and was amended on motion of Senator Anthony, of Rhode Island, so as to become a concurrent instead of a joint resolution, thus making the signature of the President unnecessary. Anthony then moved another amendment, to strike out the provision preventing either house from admitting any of the members concerned until the committee should have reported and Congress should have taken final action upon the subject. This led to debate. Senator Howard, of Michigan, opposed the amendment. He held that the late Confederate States were conquered communities, without the right of self-government; we held them, not by their free will, but by the exercise of military power. Under these circumstances, he considered either house incompetent to admit members from those states without the consent of both. Senator Anthony replied that it was intended that both houses should act in concert, and it was also desirable that the executive and Congress should act in concert; "that all branches of the government shall approach this great question in a spirit of comprehensive patriotism, with confidence in each other, and that each branch of the government, and all persons in each branch of the government, will be ready, if necessary, to concede something of their own views in order to meet the views of those who are equally charged with the responsibility of public affairs." The Constitution confided to each house separately its own independent right of judgment of the elections, returns, and qualifications of its members.

Under the resolution as it came from the House, it would be necessary to refer the credentials of those claiming seats in the Senate to a committee, the majority of which was from the House. Besides, the resolution provided that papers should be referred to the committee without debate. This was contrary to the practice of the Senate.

Senator Doolittle, of Wisconsin, objected to the preponderance given to the House in the proposed committee, and said the injurious result of this could only be obviated by the amendment under consideration. He alluded to the restriction upon debate, and said the Senate was "to be led like a lamb to the slaughter, bound hand and foot, shorn of its constitutional power, and gagged." Again, the resolution, as it stood, would exclude 11 states from representation in the Union, thus accomplishing what rebellion had failed to accomplish—it was the "dissolution of the Union by act of Congress." The doctrine of Senator Howard, involving the theory of state destruction, was, he claimed, opposed to the ground taken by the Union party from the first, which was that states could not withdraw from the Union. They could not do it peacefully; they had undertaken to do it by arms; "we crushed the attempt; we trampled their armies under our feet; we captured the rebellion; the states are ours; and we entered them to save, and not to destroy." He alluded to the fact that the resolution originated in a secret caucus dominated by Thaddeus Stevens, the zealous advocate of confiscation, and to the hot haste with which this shrewd leader had pressed it through the House in the short space of 10 minutes, without debate, and before the President's message had been communicated. In conclusion, Doolittle urged upon the Senate the duty of that body to act in harmony with the President. We claim, he said, to be here acting as the friends of the late lamented President, and the friends of him upon whom had lately fallen the responsibilities of executive power. We aided in the election of both. When they were nominated, the experiment of reconstruction had already begun. For nearly a year Lincoln had been pursuing substantially the same policy which had been since followed by his successor. Their election, he claimed, was a popular support of this policy, and he predicted that Johnson would be sustained by the people. This was as certain, he said, as the revolutions of the earth.

Senator Fessenden then arose. He had at first favored the resolution as it came from the House because he sympathized with its object. The Senate ought not to adopt the convictions of the President without examination. This was a subject of infinite importance, involving the integrity and welfare of the republic in all future time, and it was the duty of senators to examine the subject with care and fidelity, and act upon their own convictions and not upon those of others. The resolution looked toward calm and deliberate consideration before action, and so far he approved it. But, upon a more careful reading, he had come to the conclusion, for the reasons already given by Senator Anthony, that the resolution perhaps went a little too far. It was important that the committee should be appointed, to secure harmony of action between the two houses. The subject would thus be carefully considered, and the delay necessary to secure deliberation was not so great an evil as party action. He concurred, however, in the objections made by Senator Anthony. From the passage of the amendment moved by that senator, the inference was not deducible, as Senator Howard thought it was, that the Senate was in favor of the immediate or hasty admission of any of the Southern members. He was himself certainly not in favor of such action, and yet he should vote for the amendment. Neither did he agree with Senator Doolittle that the appointment of this committee was any intimation with regard to the opinion entertained by the Senate of the President's policy. The Senate simply chose to consider the whole subject for itself before acting upon it.

Anthony's amendment was agreed to, and on the next day the House concurred in the amendments of the Senate, and the resolution was adopted. The House subsequently adopted for its own guidance the provisions which had been stricken out by the Senate. On the 14th the speaker announced as members of the joint committee on the part of the House, Thaddeus Stevens, of Pennsylvania; Elihu B. Washburne, of Illinois; Justin S. Morrill, of Vermont; Henry Grider, of Kentucky; John A. Bingham, of Ohio; Roscoe Conkling, of New York; George S. Boutwell, of Massachusetts; Henry T. Blow, of Missouri; and Andrew J. Rogers, of New Jersey. In the Senate, on December 21st, the following members were announced by the President *pro tem.*: Fessenden, Grimes, Harris, Howard, Johnson, Williams.

On the 12th the Senate adopted a resolution requesting the President to furnish information as to the condition of that portion of the Union lately in rebellion. The President replied on the 18th that the rebellion had been suppressed; that, so far as possible, United States courts had been restored, the post-offices re-established, and steps taken to put in operation the revenue laws. The late Confederate States, he said, had reorganized their governments, and were yielding obedience to the laws and government of the United States with more willingness and greater promptitude than under the circumstances could reasonably have been anticipated." The anti-slavery amendment had been ratified except in the case of Mississippi, and in nearly all the states measures had either been adopted or were now pending to confer upon freedmen the rights and privileges essential to their comfort, protection, and security. The aspect of affairs, in the President's opinion, was more promising than could have been anticipated. "The people," he said, "throughout the entire South evince a laudable desire to renew their allegiance to the government, and to repair the devastations of war by a prompt and cheerful return to peaceful pursuits. An abiding faith is entertained that their actions will conform to their professions, and that, in acknowledging the supremacy of the Constitution and laws of the United States, their loyalty will be unreservedly given to the government, whose leniency they can not fail to appreciate, and whose fostering care will soon restore them to a condition of prosperity. It is true that in some of the states the demoralizing effects of the war are to be seen in occasional disorders; but these are local in character, not frequent in occurrence, and are rapidly disappearing as the authority of civil law is extended and sustained. Perplexing questions were naturally to be expected from the great and sudden change in the relations between the two races; the systems are gradually developing themselves under which the freedman will receive the protection to which he is justly entitled, and by means of his labor make himself a useful and independent member of the community in which he has his home. From all the information in my possession, and from that which I have recently derived from the most reliable authority, I am induced to cherish the belief that sectional animosity is surely and rapidly merging itself into a spirit of nationality, and that representation, connected with a properly adjusted system of taxation, will result in a harmonious restoration of the relations of the states to the national Union."

With this brief message, which was somewhat rose-colored in its construction of Southern loyalty, and evidently designed to hasten the admission of Southern representatives to Congress, two reports were transmitted—from Major General Carl Schurz and Lieutenant General Grant, who had each recently made a tour of inspection through the Southern States. Schurz's report was more consonant with what was termed the "radical" sentiment, but was so prolix that, notwithstanding Senator Sumner's urgent request that it should be read by the secretary, the majority of the Senate preferred to see it in print. The lieutenant general was concise in his statements, which, though eminently conservative, were to the point. He had left Washington on the 27th of November, and his tour had only occupied little more than one week. His mission had been principally military in its nature, regarding the necessary distribution of the United States forces in the several states. He expressed himself satisfied that the "mass of thinking men of the South accepted the present situation of affairs in good faith, and that they regarded the questions of slavery and state rights as having been finally settled by the war, regarding this decision not only as final, but as a fortunate one for the whole country, 'they receiving like benefits from it with those who opposed them in the field and in council.'" But, adds the lieutenant general, "four years of war, during which law was executed only at the point of the bayonet throughout the states in rebellion, have left the people possibly in a condition not to yield that ready obedience to civil authority the American people have generally been in the habit of yielding." Therefore he thought small garrisons throughout those states necessary "until such time as labor returns to its proper channels, and civil authority is fully established." Neither the officers under the government nor the Southern citizens thought the present withdrawal of the military practicable. "The white and the black mutually require the protection of the general government." The military force needed was small. "There is," said the lieutenant general, "such universal acquiescence in the authority of the general government throughout the portions of country visited by me, that the mere presence of a military force, without regard to numbers, is sufficient to maintain order." He thought the good of the country and economy required that the force kept in the interior where there were many freedmen should consist of white troops. The presence of black troops demoralized labor not only by its direct influence, but as furnishing a resort for the freedmen for long distances around. No violence would be offered to black troops by thinking men, but it might by the ignorant; and, adds the lieutenant general, "the late slave seems to be imbued by the idea that the property of his late master should by right belong to him, or at least should have no protection from the colored soldier." He thought it was to be regretted that at this time there could not be a commingling of the two sections, especially in Congress.

In regard to the operations of the Freedmen's Bureau, there appeared to the general to have been in some of the states a lack of good judgment and economy. The agents of the Bureau had caused an idea to prevail among the freedmen that the lands of their former masters would be divided among them, and this belief had seriously interfered with the willingness of the freedmen to make contracts for the coming year. In some form the continuance of the Bureau was a necessity, and many of the disorders and much of the expense might, he thought, be removed by making every officer on duty in the Southern States an agent of the Bureau.

The Select Committee on Reconstruction, instead of being an organ of progress, proved one of obstruction. Its object had been sufficiently definite, namely, to inquire into the condition of the Southern States in respect of their fitness for representation. The elements involved in this investigation were very simple. If the entire committee had resolved itself into a board of inspectors, and had traveled over every one of the Southern States, it would have discovered no new aspect of the case presented. The primary question which they were expected to answer was, Does the security of the nation require other measures than those already included in the President's policy before Southern representatives ought to be admitted? The answer was just as plain when the committee was appointed as it was six months later. Other measures were necessary, not only in the view of Congress, but in that of the people. Then came the secondary question, What were these measures? And it was for conference concerning this question that the committee had been appointed. But here again the answer was clear, demanding the removal of no obscurity, for there was none to remove; requiring no great delay, but only careful deliberation as to details. The necessary measures to be insisted upon had been subjects of popular discussion for months, and among those whose past had proved their steadfast loyalty and patriotism there was no expression of doubt as to what these measures were. By a constitutional amendment, said the popular voice, must it be declared that the rebel debt is repudiated, the adoption of the national debt secured, the basis of representation so readjusted as to give the South no advantage on account of rebellion, the civil rights of the freedmen firmly established, and the leaders of the late rebellion disfranchised until they can be safely admitted to a share in the government which they did their best to destroy. If these conditions had been written upon the sky in letters of fire they could not have been plainer. They were not conditions dependent upon any decision which might be rendered as to the present state of the South, or as to dangers clearly in prospect; they were necessary in any case for absolute security. Delay is not deliberation; and there were no good reasons why the committee should not have been ready to report in full within a fortnight from the time of its appointment. There was no necessity for long delay; and, on the other hand, the necessity was urgent that Congress should soon and fully declare its policy. Nothing could be done before the committee reported, and several of its members boldly expressed their idea that the South was not to be represented, nor to participate in the election of President for a series of years; and some of them went so far as to confess that this exclusion was designed to perpetuate the Republican party. Thus there was occasioned popular distrust of Congress, and within that body opposition began to be shown by members, who, while they did not object to a single one of the conditions demanded by the people, grew dissatisfied with the manner and spirit in which the development of the congressional policy was proceeding.

The committee did not report in full until six months after its appointment. It did not even report by bill until January 22d, 1866. On that day Thaddeus Stevens reported a joint resolution to amend the Constitution in regard to the basis of representation. This amendment declared that representatives and direct taxes should be apportioned among all the states according to their respective numbers, excluding Indians not taxed, *provided* that whenever the elective franchise should be denied or abridged in any state on account of race or color, all persons of such race and color should be excluded from the basis of representation. In this connection Stevens said that there were twenty-two states whose Legislatures were then in session, some of which would adjourn within two or three weeks. It was therefore desirable, he said, that this amendment, if adopted, should be adopted promptly. "It does not," he added, "deny to the states the right to regulate the elective franchise as they please; but it does say to a state, 'if you exclude from the right of suffrage Frenchmen, Irishmen, or any particular class of people, none of that class of people shall be counted in fixing your representation in this House.'"

This amendment was necessary, just, and impartial. It did not meet with any strong objection from the President, who, while he doubted the propriety of making farther amendments to the Constitution, was not opposed to the readjustment of the basis of representation. In an interview with Senator Dixon, of Connecticut, January 28th, 1866, he expressed his preference for a proposition making the number of qualified voters the basis of representation. The President's proposition offered the Southern States a motive for the partial extension of suffrage to negroes, while that reported by the Reconstruction Committee made it impossible for those states to gain in representation in any other way than by establishing impartial negro suffrage. The congressional proposition did not necessarily invite to universal suffrage; it excluded the entire colored race from representation only in the event of the elective franchise being denied to any of that race *because of color*. The exclusion would not result from any restriction upon the franchise which was applicable to white and black alike. The amendment thus favored impartial suffrage in the Southern States.

The whole case was fully stated by Roscoe Conkling, of New York, a member of the Reconstruction Committee. He began his argument by alluding to the constitutional provision which had hitherto regulated the apportionment of taxes and representation. These had been apportioned among the several states according to numbers, to be determined by adding to free persons three fifths of the slaves. This provision was one of the compromises of the Constitution; but, like the present amendment, it owed its existence to the principle that political representation belongs only to those who have political existence. The slaves of the South formed no part of the political society which framed the Constitution. They were without either natural or political rights. From this it naturally followed that they should not be represented. But direct taxes and representation ought to be distributed uniformly among the members of a free government. All alike should bear the burdens—all alike should share the benefits. The exception of aliens or unnaturalized foreigners from representation was not permanent or fixed. Slaves alone were forever excluded from the political community. He was a man and not a man; in flesh and blood alive, but politically dead—the representative of nothing but value. It could not be maintained by the slaveholding states that slaves were persons to be represented; it could neither be claimed that they were persons to be taxed. For these purposes slaves were excluded altogether by the principle on which the government was built. Without some special provision, therefore, they would have been altogether ignored. Taxes, however, were desirable on the one side, and representation on the other, and, for mere convenience, a compromise was invented for the sake of both. Thus a purely arbitrary agreement was inserted in the Constitution, supported by nothing but the consent of the parties, based upon the facts as they then stood. It was agreed in substance that the free people of all the states should be counted alike, and that the people of the slaveholding states should have as much power besides as would be measured by counting every slave as three fifths of one person; direct taxes to follow the same rule. The power thus agreed upon was not exercised by the slaves, but by their masters. This covenant was operative so long as there was any thing to operate upon. That time was now past. The provision had become impotent. The fall of slavery had superseded it. To continue the compromise now that the thing upon which it rested had passed from under it would lead to results which, when the Constitution was made, were condemned by the judgment of all. An anomaly had been introduced. Four millions were suddenly among us not bound to any one, and yet not clothed with any political rights—not slaves, and not, in a political sense, "persons." No figment of slavery remained with which to spell out a right in somebody else to wield for them a power which they might not wield themselves. Their masters had a fraction of power, on their account, while they were slaves, but now there were no masters and no slaves. Did this fraction of power still survive? If so, to whom did it belong? The blacks were pronounced unfit to wield even a fraction of power, and must not have it. That answered the question. If the answer was true, it was an end of controversy. If the blacks were unfit to have the power, then the power had no belonging whatsoever, and was at once resumed by the nation. This fractional power, then, was extinct. A moral earthquake had turned fractions to units, and units to ciphers. If a black man counted at all now, he was a whole man, not three fifths of one. Revolutions had no such fractions in their arithmetic; war and humanity joined hands to wipe them out. Four millions were to be reckoned, and these four millions, we were told, were unfit for political existence. The framers of the Constitution never dreamed of reckoning in the basis of representation those who were denied all political rights. Our fathers trusted to gradual and voluntary emancipation, which would go hand in hand with education and enfranchisement. They never peered into the bloody epoch when four million fetters would be at once melted off in the fires of war—four millions, each a Caspar Hauser, long shut up in darkness, and suddenly led out into the full flash of noon, and each, it was said, too blind to walk politically. No one foresaw such an event, and no provision was made for it. The three-fifths rule gave the slaveholding states over and above their just representation as a political community eighteen representatives. The new situation would enable these states to claim 28 representatives besides their just proportion. These 28 votes were to be controlled by those who once betrayed the government, and for those so destitute, it was claimed, of intelligence as not to be fit to vote for themselves. The result of this would be that while 127,000 white people in New York cast but one vote in the House, the same number of white men in Mississippi would cast three votes. Thus the death of slavery would add two fifths to the power which slavery exercised while it lived. Should one white man have as much share in the government as three other white men merely because he lived where blacks outnumbered whites two to one? Should this inequality exist, and exist only in favor of those who, without cause, drenched the land with blood, and covered it with mourning? Should such be the reward of those who did the foulest and guiltiest act which crimsons the annals of recorded time? To prevent this, three modes had been proposed:

1. To make the basis of representation in Congress and the Electoral College consist of sufficiently qualified voters alone.

ROSCOE CONKLING.

2. To deprive the states of the power to disqualify or discriminate politically on account of race or color.

3. To leave every state free to decide who should belong to its political community, and who should vote. Those decided unworthy to vote to be excluded from the basis of representation.

The last of these methods had been adopted by the committee. If voters alone were made the foundation of representation, the actual ratio would differ infinitely among different states. In the strife of unbridled suffrage, a state might give the franchise to women, minors, and aliens. In the second method, a great objection was encountered on the very threshold, because this plan denied to states the right to regulate their own affairs. The plan adopted by the committee had several advantages over the others.

1. It provided for representation going hand in hand with taxation.

2. It brought into the basis both sexes and all ages, and thus counteracted casual and geographical inequalities of population.

3. It put every state on an equal footing in the requirement prescribed.

4. It left every state free to enumerate all its people for representation or not, as it might choose.

If the amendment was adopted, and suffrage remained confined, as it was now, upon the census of 1860, the gains and losses would be these: Wisconsin, Indiana, Illinois, Ohio, Pennsylvania, Massachusetts, New Jersey, and Maine would gain one representative each, and New York would gain three; Alabama, Kentucky, North Carolina, South Carolina, and Tennessee would each lose one; Georgia, Louisiana, and Virginia would each lose two, and Mississippi three.[1]

Such was the argument of Roscoe Conkling—a statement so full and so conclusive in its reasoning that it is unnecessary to introduce the other arguments presented in favor of the proposition. When Stevens introduced the proposition, he demanded its adoption or rejection before the going down of the sun. The committee, of which he was so prominent a member, might be allowed weeks for deliberation, but the moment any of its measures were brought before the House, he deemed a few hours sufficient for their disposition. The House, however, did not seem inclined to amend the Constitution of the United States with such haste, and Stevens yielded.

The debate in the House was continued for several days. The proposition of the committee was opposed by those who desired to prevent the Southern States from disfranchising races, and also by those who, for political purposes, objected both to the enfranchisement of the negro race and to the equalization of representation, one or the other of which results would necessarily follow the adoption of the amendment. There was also a large number of Republicans who preferred that representation should be based upon the number of voters.[*] This, it will be remembered, was the preference of the President. The objections to this basis (that of voters) which had been offered by Roscoe Conkling could easily be obviated, it was argued, by restrictions excluding women, minors, and aliens. But still it would remain true that such restrictions would limit the power of the states to regulate the franchise of their citizens—a power which they would not willingly abdicate, and thus the amendment might be defeated. The basis furnished by the committee's amendment was open to the somewhat serious objection that it left room for evasion on the part of the Southern States. Negroes or other races were excluded from representation only in case they were denied "franchise on account of race and color." But might not the Southern States prescribe as a qualification that no one should vote who had ever been a slave, and thus secure at once the exclusion of negroes from the franchise, and their inclusion in the basis of representation? Or might they not secure the same results by establishing a property qualification and then making negroes incompetent to own real estate? But, it was answered, these were evasions so evident that the courts would prevent their success. The object of the amendment was not to invite to negro suffrage, but simply to equalize representation upon a just and impartial basis, and the arguments brought forward in the course of the debate as to the probable effect of the amendment upon negro suffrage were of secondary importance, and foreign to the object which was meant to be accomplished. The amendment, if passed, would leave the subject of suffrage just where it was before.

There were a few gentlemen on the Republican side of the House who opposed the amendment of the committee because they agreed with the President that there was no good reason why Southern representatives should not be immediately admitted, if loyal, and who opposed any farther amendments to the Constitution as conditions to complete restoration. The most prominent of these was Henry J. Raymond, of New York, whose argument may stand as an exemplification of the views of those members of the House who adopted the President's policy. This argument was presented on the 28th of January, toward the close of the debate. Raymond was a man 46 years of age. He had graduated at the University of Vermont in 1840. The next year after his graduation he became managing editor of the New York *Tribune*. Subsequently he became leading editor of the New York *Courier and Enquirer*, performing at the same time the duties of reader for the firm of Harper & Brothers. In 1849 he was elected to the New York State Assembly; was re-elected and made Speaker. In 1851 he established the New York *Times*. Five years afterward he became a leader in the Republican party, and was subsequently chosen Lieutenant Governor of New York. He had been a delegate to the Chicago Convention of 1860, and, after having again served in the New York Legislature, was in 1864 elected representative from New York to the Thirty-ninth Congress. He was one of the most influential members of that Congress, and his opinions were always worthy of consideration. His speech on the 29th of January, 1866, was his first elaborate effort in Congress. He began his argument by stating that he looked upon all propositions for the amendment of the Constitution with hesitation and distrust. The Constitution had proved itself adequate to all the emergencies of peace and war. It had not been made for days or for years, but for all time. Yet he recognized the wisdom and necessity of amendments to meet changed circumstances and an altered condition of facts. In the fact that slavery was destroyed, he recognized the propriety of so amending the Constitution as to make the re-establishment of that institution impossible. The specific evil which the amendment of the Reconstruction Committee was intended to remedy properly demanded attention. By emancipation, 1,600,000 had been added to the representative population of the South. Thus arose an inequality which demanded attention and remedy. The committee had reported this amendment as a remedy. He did not suppose it would be possible to propose any remedy which would not be open to some objections. He thought, however, that this amendment was open to objections of a very serious nature. It changed the basis of representation from population to something else, and the same objection applied to the other remedies which had been proposed. It was a fundamental principle of free government that the population, the inhabitants, all who were subjects of law, should be represented in the enactment of law, "and in the election of men by whom the law is to be executed, either directly by their own votes, or through the votes of others, so connected with them as to afford a fair presumption that their wishes, their rights, and their interests will be consulted." This proposition departed from that principle, and thus disturbed the corner-stone of our Democratic institutions. Another objection was that it deprived of representation the whole of any race in a state if the state should extend to a portion only of that race the elective franchise. Thus the anomaly was introduced of having voters for representatives who were not themselves entitled to representation. It held out to the states no encouragement to enfranchise any portion of the colored race without enfranchising all. The effect of this would be most disastrous upon the relations of the Union to the Southern States, and upon the welfare of the states themselves and of the colored people within their borders. But he could not regard this as a distinct proposition standing upon its own merits alone, but as one of a series of amendments which, as the House had been given to understand, were yet to be proposed as preliminary to the admission of Southern representatives. He thought the House was entitled to know the whole programme before it acted upon specific features of it. It should know the relation of this proposition to those which were to follow. It should know "whether the powers of the general government of the United States are to be so enlarged as to destroy the rights which those states now hold under the Constitution." He was not willing to act on this proposition till he knew the rest of the schedule. He could not help believing that this was part of a scheme for reconstructing the government and the Constitution upon a distinct principle which had been announced over and over again in the House—that by the rebellion certain states had ceased to exist as states, the people of which were to be treated as vanquished enemies, subject to no law but our own discretion. He denied *in toto* the fact of such subjugation. Of defeated rebels we had a right to demand the surrender of their arms and of the principles on which their rebellion had been based. This surrender had been made and accepted. But the states still remained with all their constitutional powers. Raymond went on to illustrate the present situation of the Southern States by comparing it with that of a state whose government had been disturbed by a foreign power. The only conquest which had been made of the Southern States was their subjugation to the Constitution and the laws. He showed conclusively that every department of the government had recognized the late Confederate States as in the Union. It was possible that

[1] The following is the estimate for the several states:

FREE STATES.	Apportionment under Census of 1860.	Based on Three-fifths Slave Population.	Based on Population including Blacks.	Based on White Suffrage.	Based on Equal Suffrage.	According to proposed Amendment.
California	3	—	3	3	*3	3
Connecticut	4	—	4	5	4	4
Illinois	14	—	15	15	13	15
Indiana	11	—	10	11	10	12
Iowa	6	—	5	6	5	6
Kansas	1	—	1	1	1	1
Maine	5	—	5	6	5	5
Massachusetts	10	—	9	12	10	11
Michigan	6	—	6	7	6	7
Minnesota	2	—	2	2	2	2
New Hampshire	3	—	3	3	3	3
New Jersey	5	—	5	6	5	6
New York	31	—	29	35	31	34
Ohio	19	—	18	19	17	20
Oregon	1	—	1	1	1	1
Pennsylvania	24	—	23	24	22	25
Rhode Island	2	—	2	2	2	2
Vermont	3	—	3	3	3	3
Wisconsin	6	—	6	7	6	7
Total	156	—	147	170	153	163

SLAVE STATES.	Apportionment under Census of 1860.	Based on Three-fifths Slave Population.	Based on Population including Blacks.	Based on White Suffrage.	Based on Equal Suffrage.	According to proposed Amendment.
Alabama	6	1	7	4	7	5
Arkansas	3	1	3	3	3	3
Delaware	1	—	1	1	1	1
Florida	1	—	1	1	1	1
Georgia	7	2	8	5	7	6
Kentucky	9	1	9	8	8	8
Louisiana	5	2	6	4	6	5
Maryland	5	—	5	5	5	5
Mississippi	5	2	6	3	6	3
Missouri	9	1	9	9	9	10
North Carolina	7	2	8	5	7	6
South Carolina	4	2	5	3	5	3
Tennessee	8	1	9	7	8	7
Texas	4	1	5	4	5	4
Virginia	11	2	12	9	11	9
Total	85	18	94	71	89	73

* Not including Chinamen.

"NOTE.—In these several plans of apportionment the results are arrived at in the mode practiced under the present law, namely, the total representative population of all the states is first ascertained; this number is divided by 288, the number of representatives provided by law at the time of the taking of the last census. This gives the requisite ratio to a member. The representative population of each state is then divided by the ratio, and the result, rejecting fractions, shows the number of representatives to each state. The number unapportioned, in consequence of the fractions, is then added to the eight additional members provided by the law of 1862, and these are apportioned to the states having the largest fractions.

The ratio under the present apportionment is........ 127,000
The ratio on the basis of population, including the negroes, is........ 138,700
The ratio on the basis of white suffrage is........ 29,300
The ratio on the basis of equal suffrage, white and black, is........ 33,500
The ratio on the basis of the proposed amendment is........ 114,800

"Entirely accurate data of the number of voters in the several states can not be obtained from any recorded statistics. It is not shown by the presidential vote of 1860, for the reason that in some of the states where there was little real contest the vote was far from full. The number of males above the age of twenty years, aliens included, as given by the census of 1860, is taken as the nearest approximate to the number of voters. The proportion of aliens will not hold alike in all the states, there being a larger ratio in the northern than in the southern section of the Union; but it is believed the results indicated in the table will be sufficiently accurate for present purposes."—*Congressional Globe*, 39th Session, p. 357 8.

THADDEUS STEVENS.

Congress might attempt to expel them, but he did not think it would. He traced the various stages of the President's action since the close of the war, and added that it only remained for Congress to complete the work of restoration by the admission of the Southern representatives. If these representatives were loyal men, and each house was judge of that, then their action could not be disloyal, and there was no occasion for apprehension. We needed just the information which such loyal representatives could bring us. But Congress had given the whole subject over to a committee "which sits with closed doors, which deliberates in secret, which shuts itself out from the knowledge and observation of Congress, and which does not even deign to give us the information it was appointed to collect, and on which we are to base our action—but which sends its rescripts into this house, and demands their ratification, and without reasons and without facts, before the going down of the sun!" He thought the House ought to emancipate itself from the domination of this committee, and take the subjects assigned to it into its own keeping. There was too great reliance, he thought, placed in constitutional amendments as guarantees of the national safety. The Constitution had not prevented rebellion; was it probable that amendments could be more efficient? We must depend upon the patriotism of the American people—upon the national will and conscience. When these ceased to be efficient, what dependence was to be placed upon "paper Constitutions?" In conclusion, Raymond thus expressed his views as to what the government ought to do:

"In the first place, I think we ought to accept the present *status* of the Southern States, and regard them as having resumed, under the President's guidance and action, their functions of self-government in the Union. In the second place, I think this house should decide on the admission of representatives by districts, admitting none but loyal men who can take the oath we may prescribe, and holding all others as disqualified; the Senate acting, at its discretion, in the same way in regard to representatives of states. I think, in the third place, we should provide by law for giving to the freedmen of the South all the rights of citizens in courts of law and elsewhere. In the fourth place, I would exclude from federal office the leading actors in the conspiracy which led to the rebellion in every state. In the fifth place, I would make such amendments to the Constitution as may seem wise to Congress and the states, acting freely and without coercion. And, sixth, I would take such measures and precautions, by the disposition of military forces, as will preserve order and prevent the overthrow, by usurpation or otherwise, in any state, of its republican form of government. . . . . Above all, I beg this house to bear in mind, as the sentiment that should control and guide its action, that we of the North and they of the South are at war no longer. The gigantic contest is at an end. The courage and devotion on either side which made it so terrible and so long, no longer owe a divided duty, but have become the common property of the American name, the priceless possession of the American republic through all time to come. The dead of the contending hosts sleep beneath the soil of a common country and under one common flag. Their hostilities are hushed, and they are the dead of the nation forever more. The victor may well exult in the victory he has achieved. Let it be our task, as it will be our highest glory, to make the vanquished, and their posterity to the latest generation, rejoice in their defeat."

Raymond's argument may be fairly called a statement of the views entertained by the President, and it was open to precisely the same objections. It overlooked the necessity not only of the proposed amendment, but of others equally important. It underrated the value of constitutional provisions for national security. It is true that in extraordinary emergencies, like that presented at the opening of the rebellion, a section of the country might, in the madness of treason, throw the Constitution to the winds; but that was an appeal to arms. Congress was now considering the motives which regulate and restrain men in times of peace, and when obedience is universally yielded to law. In such a time, certainly, an amendment to the Constitution would be more efficient than a resolution or a sentiment.

The proposition was referred back to the committee for amendment, and was again reported in the House, January 31, so altered as to leave out the matter of taxation, but in no other respect. Thaddeus Stevens called the previous question, but yielded ten minutes of his time to other gentlemen. His address to the House on this occasion was characteristic. He had been informed, he said, by high authority "at the other end of the avenue," introduced through an unusual conduit (the "unusual conduit" being intended to designate Raymond), that no amendment to the Constitution was necessary. He then proceeded to consider the present amendment. He denied that it contained an implied permission to the general government to regulate the franchise of states. It left the rights of states just where they were. But it punished the abuse of this right. In making this statement Stevens committed a blunder. The object of the amendment was to remove an inequality which had hitherto existed in the basis of representation. If New York or South Carolina has the admitted right to exclude negroes from the franchise, then their exercise of that right could not be called an abuse, subject to legal penalty. Under the operation of the amendment, each state had to choose between impartial suffrage and a diminution of its representation, and its choice was not controlled. If the Southern States, continued Stevens, adopt the colored population as a part of their political community, they will have 83 votes in the House; if not, they will only have from 45 to 48, and with this diminution of their power all the Copperhead assistance they might receive could not enable them to do injury. He preferred that to an immediate declaration that all should be represented; "for, if you make them all voters, and let them into this hall, not one beneficial act for the benefit of the freedmen or for the benefit of the country would ever be passed. Their 83 votes, with the representatives from the Five Points and other dark corners, would be sufficient to overrule the friends of progress here, and this nation would be in the hands of secessionists at the very next congressional election, and at the very next presidential election. I do not, therefore, want to grant them this privilege, at least for some years. I want, in the mean time, our Christian men to go among them—the philanthropists of the North, the honest Methodists, my friends the Hardshell Baptists, and all others; and then, four or five years hence, when these freedmen shall have been made free indeed—when they shall have become intelligent enough, and there are sufficient loyal men there to control the representation from those states, I shall be glad to see them admitted here; but I do not want them to have representation—I say it plainly—I do not want them to have the right of suffrage before this Congress has done the great work of regenerating the Constitution and laws of this country according to the principles of the Declaration of Independence."

Stevens did not disguise his opinion that this amendment would result in the exclusion of Southern representatives for a period of years. It was for this reason that he preferred it to that which had been proposed fixing the representation upon voters. The latter would be more readily acceded to. An encouragement would thus be offered to extend the suffrage to the colored race. That, said Stevens, is the very objection. The Southern States would admit those whose political action they could control, and then, on this basis, enter Congress and make our laws for us; but they would not accede now to the present amendment—he did not expect to see that during his lifetime. In the mean time the freedmen would be educated, and finally receive universal suffrage (how many years hence Stevens did not conjecture), and then the Southern representatives might be admitted.

Stevens went on to say that he had a proposition which was the genuine one for the present situation—one which he loved, and which he hoped Congress would educate itself to the idea of adopting: "That all national and state laws shall be equally applicable to every citizen, and that no discrimination shall be made on account of race or color." But he was content to take what was practicable—what would be carried by the states. He then alluded to Raymond's argument, which he pronounced not pertinent to the question, but proceeded to controvert by an argument equally impertinent. He endeavored to prove, by Vattel, that the late Confederate States were out of the Union.

Stevens had already, on the 18th of December, announced his theory of the situation. He had then insisted upon two things as of vital importance:

1. That the principle should be established that none of the late Confederate states should be counted in any of the amendments to the Constitution before they were "duly admitted into the family of states by the law-making power of their conqueror." "I take no account," said he, "of the aggregation of whitewashed rebels who, without any legal authority, have assembled in the capitals of the late rebel states and simulated legislative bodies; nor do I regard with any respect the cunning by-play into which they deluded the Secretary of State by frequent telegraphic announcements that 'South Carolina has adopted the amendment,' 'Alabama has adopted the amendment, being the twenty-seventh state,' etc. This was intended to delude the people, and accustom Congress to hear repeated the names of these extinct states as if they were alive; when, in truth, they have now no more existence than the revolted cities of Latium, two thirds of whose people were colonized, and their property confiscated, and their right of citizenship withdrawn by conquering and avenging Rome."

2. It was also important that it should then be solemnly decided what power could revive, recreate, and reinstate these provinces into the family of states, and invest them with the rights of American citizens. It was time that Congress should assert its sovereignty, and assume something of the dignity of the Roman Senate.

The doctrine, added Stevens on that occasion, "of a white man's government is as atrocious as the infamous sentiment that damned the late chief justice to everlasting fame, and, I fear, to everlasting fire."

Stevens's argument upon the present proposition regarding the basis of representation did not improve its prospect of adoption. He adroitly managed to connect it with his own peculiar theories. In his entire argument, he assumed that its ratification by three fourths of the states then represented in Congress was sufficient. He distinctly advocated a postponement of restoration until it could be accomplished upon the principles asserted by the extremists of the Republican party. This connection of the proposed amendment with Stevens's peculiar theories was not necessary, and tended to misrepresent its object to Congress and the people. It furnished more arguments for the enemies than for the friends of the amendment. Notwithstanding this speech, however, the joint resolution passed the House 120 to 46. Eleven Republicans voted in the negative.[1]

In the Senate the resolution failed to receive a two-thirds vote. Indeed, it only passed by a bare majority.[2] One of its principal opponents was Senator Sumner. Charles Sumner differed from Thaddeus Stevens. Both were theorists on a grand scale, but the latter could let slip his splendid theory for a moment in order to grasp tangible objects in his way, while the former would accept nothing which did not to him seem true when tested by the plummet of absolute truth and eternal justice.[3] Of the 22 votes cast against the resolution in the Senate, one half were Republican. This opposition arose from motives so various that we find in the list of Nays the names of Democrats, and of the most extreme as well as of the most moderate Republicans.

The Reconstruction Committee after this defeat—which was due to the dissensions that divided the Republican party—again proceeded to deliberate, and on the 30th of April Thaddeus Stevens offered another resolution for the amendment of the Constitution. This new proposition covered a great deal of ground. It contemplated four results:

1. The equal protection of all citizens under the laws;
2. The equalization of representation;
3. The exclusion of all who had engaged in rebellion from the right to vote for representatives in Congress and presidential electors until July 4, 1870; and,
4. The repudiation of the rebel debt, and of any claim for compensation on account of the loss of slaves.[1]

In explaining the provisions of this amendment,[2] Stevens said they were not all that he desired, but all that he expected he could obtain, by the ratification of nineteen of even the loyal states. The idea that the ratification of amendments by the other states were to be counted he considered absurd. He would take all he could get in the cause of humanity, and leave it to be perfected by better men in better times. It might be that he would not be here to enjoy that glorious triumph, but it was as certain to come as that there is a just God. He animadverted with some bitterness to the manner in which the amendment formerly offered by the committee had been slaughtered in the Senate—in the house of its friends—by "puerile and pedantic criticism." The present amendment was, he thought, less efficient, but some way had to be devised "to overcome the united forces of self-righteous Republicans and unrighteous Copperheads." Evidently Thaddeus Stevens was disgusted with his brethren; but, said he, "it will not do for those who for thirty years have fought the beasts at Ephesus to be frightened by the fangs of modern catamounts." He wanted to secure more than was secured by this amendment. We should not approach the measure of justice until we gave every adult freedman a homestead on the land where he had toiled and suffered. Forty acres of land and a hut would be more valuable to the negro than the right to vote. Unless we gave this we should receive the censure of mankind and the curse of Heaven. The section excluding rebels from voting for a period of years he considered the mildest of all punishments ever inflicted on traitors. He might not consent to the extreme severity denounced upon them by a provisional governor of Tennessee—"the late lamented Andrew Johnson of blessed memory"—but he would have increased the severity of this section. On the 10th of March, the resolution, as presented by the committee, was passed 128 to 37.[3] Baldwin, Hale, Eliot, Jenckes, W. H. Randall, and Raymond—Republicans who had voted against the former amendment, gave their support to this one.

The resolution passed the Senate, after numerous amendments, on the 8th of June, by a two-thirds vote (33 to 11),[4] and went back to the House, where the Senate amendments were adopted, June 13th. The following is the text of the proposed amendment as finally passed:

"ARTICLE XIV. *Sec.* 1. All persons born or naturalized in the United States, and subject to the jurisdiction thereof, are citizens of the United States and of the state wherein they reside. No state shall make or enforce any law which shall abridge the privileges or immunities of citizens of the United States, nor shall any state deprive any person of life, liberty, or property without due process of law, nor deny to any person within its jurisdiction the equal protection of the laws.

"*Sec.* 2. Representatives shall be apportioned among the several states according to their respective numbers, counting the whole number of persons

---

[1] Baldwin, Eliot, Hale, Jenckes, Latham, Phelps, W. H. Randall, Raymond, Rousseau, Smith, and Whaley.

The following is the vote in detail:

YEAS.—Messrs. Alley, Allison, Ames, Anderson, James M. Ashley, Baker, Banks, Barker, Baxter, Beaman, Benjamin, Bidwell, Bingham, Blaine, Blow, Boutwell, Brandegee, Bromwell, Broomall, Buckland, Bundy, Reader W. Clarke, Sidney Clarke, Cobb, Conkling, Cook, Cullom, Darling, Davis, Dawes, Defrees, Delano, Deming, Dixon, Donnelly, Eckley, Eggleston, Farnsworth, Farquhar, Ferry, Garfield, Grinnell, Griswold, Abner C. Harding, Hart, Hayes, Hill, Holmes, Hooper, Hotchkiss, Asahel W. Hubbard, Chester D. Hubbard, Demas Hubbard, John H. Hubbard, James H. Hubbell, Hulburd, James Humphrey, Ingersoll, Julian, Kasson, Kelley, Kelso, Ketcham, Kuykendall, Laflin, George V. Lawrence, William Lawrence, Longyear, Lynch, Marston, Marvin, McClurg, McIndoe, McKee, Mercur, Miller, Moorhead, Morrill, Morris, Moulton, Myers, O'Neill, Orth, Paine, Patterson, Perham, Pike, Plants, Pomeroy, Price, Alexander H. Rice, John H. Rice, Rollins, Sawyer, Schenck, Schofield, Shellabarger, Sloan, Spalding, Starr, Stevens, Stilwell, Thayer, Francis Thomas, John L. Thomas, Upson, Van Aernam, Burt Van Horn, Robert T. Van Horn, Ward, Warner, Elihu B. Washburne, William B. Washburn, Welker, Wentworth, Williams, James F. Wilson, Stephen F. Wilson, Windom, and Woodbridge—120.

NAYS.—Messrs. Baldwin, Bergen, Boyer, Brooks, Chanler, Dawson, Denison, Eldridge, Eliot, Finck, Grider, Hale, Aaron Harding, Harris, Hogan, Edwin N. Hubbell, James M. Humphrey, Jenckes, Johnson, Kerr, Latham, Le Blond, Marshall, McCullough, Niblack, Nicholson, Noell, Phelps, Samuel J. Randall, William H. Randall, Raymond, Ritter, Rogers, Ross, Rousseau, Shanklin, Sitgreaves, Smith, Strouse, Taber, Taylor, Thornton, Trimble, Voorhees, Whaley, and Wright—46.

NOT VOTING.—Messrs. Ancona, Delos R. Ashley, Culver, Driggs, Dumont, Glossbrenner, Goodyear, Henderson, Higby, Jones, Loan, McRuer, Newell, Radford, Trowbridge, and Winfield—16.

[2] March 9, 1866. The following is the vote in detail:

YEAS.—Messrs. Anthony, Chandler, Clark, Conness, Cragin, Creswell, Fessenden, Foster, Grimes, Harris, Howe, Kirkwood, Lane of Indiana, McDougall, Morgan, Morrill, Nye, Poland, Ramsey, Sherman, Sprague, Trumbull, Wade, Williams, and Wilson—25.

NAYS.—Messrs. Brown, Buckalew, Cowan, Davis, Dixon, Doolittle, Guthrie, Henderson, Hendricks, Johnson, Lane of Kansas, Nesmith, Norton, Pomeroy, Riddle, Saulsbury, Stewart, Stockton, Sumner, Van Winkle, Willey, and Yates—22.

ABSENT.—Messrs. Foot, Howard, and Wright—3.

[3] The following is a recapitulation of Sumner's argument against the amendment:

"Following it from the beginning, you have seen, first, how this proposition carries into the Constitution itself the idea of inequality of rights, thus defiling that unspotted text; secondly, how it is an express sanction of the acknowledged tyranny of taxation without representation; thirdly, how it is a concession to State Rights at a moment when we are recovering from a terrible war waged against us in the name of State Rights; fourthly, how it is the constitutional recognition of an oligarchy, aristocracy, caste, and monopoly founded on color; fifthly, how it petrifies in the Constitution the wretched pretension of a white man's government; sixthly, how it assumes what is false in constitutional law, that color can be a 'qualification' for an elector; seventhly, how it positively ties the hands of Congress in fixing the meaning of a republican government, so that under the guaranty clause it will be constrained to recognize an oligarchy, aristocracy, caste, and monopoly founded on color, together with the tyranny of taxation without representation, as not inconsistent with such a government; eighthly, how it positively ties the hands of Congress in completing and consummating the abolition of slavery according to the second clause of the constitutional amendment, so that it can not for this purpose interfere with the denial of the elective franchise on account of color; ninthly, how it installs recent rebels in permanent power over loyal citizens; and, tenthly, how it shows forth in unmistakable character as a compromise of human rights, the most immoral, indecent, and utterly shameful of any in our history."

[1] The following is the text of the proposed amendment as first presented by Stevens:

"ARTICLE —. *Sec.* 1. No state shall make or enforce any law which shall abridge the privileges or immunities of citizens of the United States; nor shall any state deprive any person of life, liberty, or property without due process of law, nor deny to any person within its jurisdiction the equal protection of the laws.

"*Sec.* 2. Representatives shall be apportioned among the several states which may be included within this Union according to their respective numbers, counting the whole number of persons in each state, excluding Indians not taxed. But whenever in any state the elective franchise shall be denied to any portion of its male citizens not less than twenty-one years of age, or in any way abridged, except for participation in rebellion or other crime, the basis of representation in such state shall be reduced in the proportion which the number of male citizens shall bear to the whole number of such male citizens not less than twenty-one years of age.

"*Sec.* 3. Until the 4th day of July, in the year 1870, all persons who voluntarily adhered to the late insurrection, giving it aid and comfort, shall be excluded from the right to vote for representatives in Congress, and for electors for President and Vice-President of the United States.

"*Sec.* 4. Neither the United States nor any state shall assume or pay any debt or obligation already incurred, or which may hereafter be incurred, in aid of insurrection or war against the United States, or any claim for compensation for loss of involuntary service or labor.

"*Sec.* 5. The Congress shall have power to enforce by appropriate legislation the provisions of this article."

[2] March 8.

[3] YEAS.—Messrs. Alley, Allison, Ames, Anderson, Delos R. Ashley, James M. Ashley, Baker, Baldwin, Banks, Barker, Baxter, Beaman, Benjamin, Bidwell, Bingham, Blaine, Blow, Boutwell, Bromwell, Broomall, Buckland, Bundy, Reader W. Clark, Sidney Clarke, Cobb, Conkling, Cook, Cullom, Darling, Davis, Dawes, Defrees, Delano, Deming, Dixon, Dodge, Donnelly, Driggs, Dumont, Eckley, Eggleston, Eliot, Farnsworth, Ferry, Garfield, Grinnell, Griswold, Abner C. Harding, Hart, Hayes, Henderson, Higby, Holmes, Hooper, Hotchkiss, Asahel W. Hubbard, Chester D. Hubbard, Demas Hubbard, James R. Hubbell, Hulburd, James Humphrey, Ingersoll, Jenckes, Julian, Kasson, Kelley, Kelso, Ketcham, Kuykendall, Laflin, George V. Lawrence, William Lawrence, Loan, Longyear, Lynch, Marston, McClurg, McIndoe, McKee, McRuer, Mercur, Miller, Moorhead, Morrill, Morris, Moulton, Myers, Newell, O'Neill, Orth, Paine, Patterson, Perham, Pike, Plants, Price, William H. Randall, Raymond, Alexander H. Rice, John H. Rice, Rollins, Sawyer, Schenck, Schofield, Shellabarger, Spalding, Stevens, Stillwell, Thayer, Francis Thomas, John L. Thomas, Trowbridge, Upson, Van Aernam, Burt Van Horn, Robert T. Van Horn, Ward, Warner, Elihu B. Washburne, Henry D. Washburn, William B. Washburn, Welker, Williams, James F. Wilson, Stephen F. Wilson, Windom, Woodbridge, and the Speaker—128.

NAYS.—Messrs. Ancona, Bergen, Boyer, Chanler, Coffroth, Dawson, Eldridge, Finck, Glossbrenner, Goodyear, Grider, Aaron Harding, Harris, Kerr, Latham, Le Blond, Marshall, McCullough, Niblack, Phelps, Radford, Samuel J. Randall, Ritter, Rogers, Ross, Rousseau, Shanklin, Sitgreaves, Smith, Stronse, Tabor, Taylor, Thornton, Trimble, Whaley, Winfield, and Wright—37.

NOT VOTING.—Messrs. Brandegee, Culver, Denison, Farquhar, Hale, Hill, Hogan, John H. Hubbard, Edwin N. Hubbell, James M. Humphrey, Johnson, Jones, Marvin, Nicholson, Noell, Pomeroy, Sloan, Starr, and Wentworth—19.

[4] YEAS.—Messrs. Anthony, Chandler, Clark, Conness, Cragin, Creswell, Edmunds, Fessenden, Foster, Grimes, Harris, Henderson, Howard, Howe, Kirkwood, Lane of Indiana, Lane of Kansas, Morgan, Morrill, Nye, Poland, Pomeroy, Ramsey, Sherman, Sprague, Stewart, Sumner, Trumbull, Wade, Willey, Williams, Wilson, and Yates—33.

NAYS.—Messrs. Cowan, Davis, Doolittle, Guthrie, Hendricks, Johnson, McDougall, Norton, Riddle, Saulsbury, and Van Winkle—11.

ABSENT.—Messrs. Brown, Buckalew, Dixon, Nesmith, and Wright—5.

in each state, excluding Indians not taxed. But when the right to vote at any election for the choice of electors for President and Vice-President of the United States, representatives in Congress, the executive and judicial officers of a state, or the members of the Legislature thereof, is denied to any of the male inhabitants of such state, being twenty-one years of age and citizens of the United States, or in any way abridged except for participation in rebellion or other crime, the basis of representation therein shall be reduced in proportion which the number of such male citizens shall bear to the whole number of male citizens twenty-one years of age in such state.

"*Sec.* 3. No person shall be a senator or representative in Congress, or elector of President and Vice-President, or hold any office, civil or military, under the United States or under any state, who, having previously taken an oath, as a member of Congress, or as an officer of the United States, or as a member of any state Legislature, or as an executive or judicial officer of any state, to support the Constitution of the United States, shall have engaged in insurrection or rebellion against the same, or given aid and comfort to the enemies thereof. But Congress may, by a vote of two thirds of each house, remove such disability.

"*Sec.* 4. The validity of the public debt of the United States authorized by law, including debts incurred for payment of pensions and bounties for services in suppressing insurrection and rebellion, shall not be questioned. But neither the United States nor any state shall assume or pay any debt or obligation incurred in aid of insurrection or rebellion against the United States, or any claim for the loss or emancipation of any slave, but all such debts, obligations, or claims shall be held illegal and void.

"*Sec.* 5. The Congress shall have power to enforce, by appropriate legislation, the provisions of this article."

The joint resolution did not require the assent of the President. But a resolution having been passed by the House requesting the President to transmit the proposed amendment to the several state Legislatures, he took occasion to reply, expressing his opinion, and protesting that the ministerial act of transmitting the amendment to the state Legislatures did not commit the executive to an approval or recommendation of it.[1]

The amendment covered the whole ground of reconstruction, so far as Congress was concerned. There was no reason why its ratification might not be properly required of every Southern State as an evidence of its good faith, which would not also apply to the amendment abolishing slavery. Just after the war closed its ratification would have been readily acceded; but it was certain to be refused now by almost every Southern State on account of the encouragement afforded by President Johnson's policy, and the hope that this might prevail sooner or later with the Northern people. No other attitude could have been expected of the South under the circumstances. It was in the condition of an army which acknowledges its defeat, but insists upon the best terms of accommodation which there is the slightest ground to hope the conqueror will grant.

The Reconstruction Committee submitted its full report to Congress on the 18th of June, 1866—or rather it submitted two reports, one representing the views of the majority of its members, and the other those of the minority, consisting of Reverdy Johnson, A. J. Rogers, and Henry Grider. The latter report almost entirely ignores the fact of the war, and the nature of the situation immediately consequent. It refuses the right of the government to deny even temporarily, and for its own safety, to states which have been in rebellion, the resumption of all their rights and privileges; whereas, if there is any political principle clearly established and beyond dispute, it is, that the security of government lies back of even its written Constitution, and is the supreme law of national existence.

The report of the majority we shall consider more in detail. It contains many false constructions of the Constitution, based upon the erroneous theories of some members of the committee, and to which exception might be taken. Its denial to the President of any other powers, outside of his position as commander-in-chief of the army and navy, except those involved in the execution of the laws of Congress, is inconsistent with the whole spirit of the Constitution, according to which the executive is a *co-ordinate* branch of the government, and not vested merely with *subordinate* and *ministerial* functions. It is inconsistent also with the President's oath of office, by which he is bound not simply to execute the laws, but to protect the Constitution. The assumption made in the report that upon Congress alone devolves the duty to guarantee to every state a republican form of government, is contradicted by the very words of the constitutional provision making this guaranty the duty of the United States; and, as if with the very purpose of not confining it to either the President or to Congress exclusively, this provision occurs in neither of the articles defining respectively the powers of the executive and of Congress. This assumption that Congress is, in an exclusive sense, the government of the United States, pervades the whole report.

But, laying aside all matters which might be made the subject of criticism, we must regard this report as a conclusive argument in justification of the action of Congress in refusing representation to the Southern States until certain measures necessary to the national safety should be secured beyond the possibility of doubt through constitutional amendment. The nature and extent of the outrage which had been committed against the government, argues the committee, gave the government the right to exact indemnity for the injuries done, and security against their recurrence. The decision as to what that security should be, as to what proof should be required of returned allegiance, must depend upon grave considerations of the public safety and the general welfare. If it were true that, the moment when rebels lay down their arms and actual hostilities cease, all political rights of the rebellious communities are at once restored—if their right to participate in the government of the country must be allowed under these circumstances—then the government would be powerless for its own protection, "and flagrant rebellion, carried to the extreme of civil war, is a pastime which any state can play at, not only certain that it can lose nothing in any event, but may even be the gainer by defeat. If rebellion succeeds, it accomplishes its purpose and destroys the government. If it fails, the war has been barren of results, and the battle may still be fought out in the legislative halls of the country. Treason, defeated in the field, has only to take possession of Congress and the cabinet."

"It is desirable," continues the report, "that the Union of all the states should become perfect at the earliest moment consistent with the peace and welfare of the nation; that all these states should become fully represented in the national councils, and take their share in the legislation of the country. The possession and exercise of more than the just share of power by any section is injurious, as well to that section as to all others. Its tendency is distracting and demoralizing, and such a state of affairs is only to be tolerated on the ground of a necessary regard to the public safety. As soon as that safety is secured it should terminate."

Before the restoration of the states to their original privileges, the rights, as free men and citizens, of millions belonging to the colored race must be secured, and the basis of representation must be altered to prevent some states from exercising a disproportionate share in the government. Accordingly, the committee had submitted the constitutional amendment embracing these provisions, together with others, "after a long and careful comparison of conflicting opinions."[1]

[1] "Even in ordinary times," said the President, "any question of amending the Constitution must be justly regarded as of paramount importance. This importance is at the present time enhanced by the fact that the joint resolution was not submitted by the two houses for the approval of the President, and that, of the thirty-six states which constitute the Union, eleven are excluded from representation in either house of Congress, although, with the single exception of Texas, they have been entirely restored to all their functions as states in conformity with the organic law of the land, and have appeared at the national capital by senators and representatives, who have applied for and have been refused admission to the vacant seats. Nor have the sovereign people of the nation been afforded an opportunity of expressing their views upon the important questions which the amendment involves. Grave doubts, therefore, may naturally and justly arise as to whether the action of Congress is in harmony with the sentiments of the people, and whether state Legislatures elected without reference to such an issue should be called upon by Congress to decide respecting the ratification of the proposed amendment."

[1] We subjoin the concluding portion of this report:

"Your committee have been unable to find, in the evidence submitted to Congress by the President, under date of March 6, 1866, in compliance with the resolutions of January 5 and February 27, 1866, any satisfactory proof that either of the insurrectionary states, except perhaps the State of Tennessee, has placed itself in a condition to resume its political relations to the United States. The first step toward that end would necessarily be the establishment of a republican form of government by the people. It has been before remarked that the provisional governors, appointed by the President in the exercise of his military authority, could do nothing by virtue of the power thus conferred toward the establishment of a state government. They were acting under the War Department, and paid out of its funds. They were simply bridging over the chasm between rebellion and restoration. And yet we find them calling Conventions and convening Legislatures. Not only this, but we find the Conventions and Legislatures thus convened acting under executive direction as to the provisions required to be adopted in their Constitutions and ordinances as conditions precedent to their recognition by the President. The inducement held out by the President for compliance with the conditions imposed was, directly in one instance, and presumably, therefore, in others, the immediate admission of senators and representatives to Congress. The character of the Conventions and Legislatures thus assembled was not such as to inspire confidence in the good faith of their members. Governor Perry, of South Carolina, dissolved the Convention assembled in that state before the suggestion had reached Columbia from Washington that the rebel war debt should be repudiated, and gave as his reason that it was a 'revolutionary body.' There is no evidence of the loyalty or disloyalty of the members of those Conventions and Legislatures except the fact of pardons being asked for on their account. Some of these states now claiming representation refused to adopt the conditions imposed. No reliable information is found in these papers as to the constitutional provisions of several of these states, while in not one of them is there the slightest evidence to show that these 'amended Constitutions,' as they are called, have ever been submitted to the people for their adoption. In North Carolina alone an ordinance was passed to that effect, but it does not appear to have been acted on. Not one of them, therefore, has been ratified. Whether, with President Johnson, we adopt the theory that the old Constitutions were abrogated and destroyed, and the people 'deprived of all civil government,' or whether we adopt the alternative doctrine that they were only suspended, and were revived by the suppression of the rebellion, the new provisions must be considered as equally destitute of validity before adoption by the people. If the Conventions were called for the sole purpose of putting the state government into operation, they had no power either to adopt a new Constitution or to amend an old one without the consent of the people. Nor could either a Convention or a Legislature change the fundamental law without power previously conferred. In the view of your committee, it follows, therefore, that the people of a state where the Constitution has been thus amended might feel themselves justified in repudiating altogether all such unauthorized assumptions of power, and might be expected to do so at pleasure.

"So far as the disposition of the people of the insurrectionary states, and the probability of their adopting measures conforming to the changed condition of affairs can be inferred from the papers submitted by the President as the basis of his action, the prospects are far from encouraging. It appears quite clear that the anti-slavery amendments, both to the State and Federal Constitutions, were adopted with reluctance by the bodies which did adopt them, while in some states they have been either passed by in silence or rejected. The language of all the provisions and ordinances of these states on the subject amounts to nothing more than an unwilling admission of an unwelcome truth. As to the Ordinance of Secession, it is in some cases declared 'null and void,' and in others simply 'repealed;' and in no instance is a refutation of this deadly heresy considered worthy of a place in the new Constitution.

"If, as the President assumes, these insurrectionary states were, at the close of the war, wholly without state governments, it would seem that, before being admitted to participation in the direction of public affairs, such governments should be regularly organized. Long usage has established, and numerous statutes have pointed out the mode in which this should be done. A Convention to frame a form of government should be assembled under competent authority. Ordinarily this authority emanates from Congress; but, under the peculiar circumstances, your committee is not disposed to criticise the President's action in assuming the power exercised by him in this regard. The Convention, when assembled, should frame a Constitution of government, which should be submitted to the people for adoption. If adopted, a Legislature should be convened to pass the laws necessary to carry it into effect. When a state thus organized claims representation in Congress, the election of representatives should be provided for by law, in accordance with the laws of Congress regulating representation, and the proof that the action taken has been in conformity to law should be submitted to Congress.

"In no case have these essential preliminary steps been taken. The Conventions assembled seem to have assumed that the Constitutions which had been repudiated and overthrown were still in existence, and operative to constitute the states members of the Union, and to have contented themselves with such amendments as they were informed were requisite in order to insure their return to an immediate participation in the government of the United States. Not waiting to ascertain whether the people they represented would adopt even the proposed amendments, they at once ordered elections of representatives to Congress, in nearly all instances before an executive had been chosen to issue writs of election under the state laws, and such elections as were held were ordered by the Conventions. In one instance, at least, the writs of election were signed by the provisional governor. Glaring irregularities and unwarranted assumptions of power are manifest in several cases, particularly in South Carolina, where the Convention, although disbanded by the provisional governor on the ground that it was a revolutionary body, assumed to redistrict the state.

"It is quite evident from all these facts, and indeed from the whole mass of testimony submitted by the President to the Senate, that in no instance was regard paid to any other consideration than obtaining immediate admission to Congress under the barren form of an election in which

The committee had been working hard for six months, and with the results of its deliberations no reasonable ground of complaint can be found. But the necessity of every measure which it had submitted to Congress was just as clear at the beginning of the session as at the close. It had accu-

no precautions were taken to secure regularity of proceedings or the assent of the people. No Constitution has been legally adopted except perhaps in the State of Tennessee, and such elections as have been held were without authority of law. Your committee are accordingly forced to the conclusion that the states referred to have not placed themselves in a condition to claim representation in Congress, unless all the rules which have, since the foundation of the government, been deemed essential in such cases should be disregarded.

"It would, undoubtedly, be competent for Congress to waive all formalities, and to admit these Confederate States to representation at once, trusting that time and experience would set all things right. Whether it would be advisable to do so, however, must depend upon other considerations of which it remains to treat. But it may well be observed that the inducements to such a step should be of the very highest character. It seems to your committee not unreasonable to require satisfactory evidence that the ordinances and constitutional provisions which the President deemed essential in the first instance will be permanently adhered to by the people of the states seeking restoration after being admitted to full participation in the government, and will not be repudiated when that object shall have been accomplished. And here the burden of proof rests upon the late insurgents who are seeking restoration to the rights and privileges which they willingly abandoned, and not upon the people of the United States who have never undertaken, directly or indirectly, to deprive them thereof. It should appear affirmatively that they are prepared and disposed in good faith to accept the results of the war, to abandon their hostility to the government, and to live in peace and amity with the people of the loyal states, extending to all classes of citizens equal rights and privileges, and conforming to the republican idea of liberty and equality. They should exhibit in their acts something more than an unwilling submission to an unavoidable necessity—a feeling, if not cheerful, certainly not offensive and defiant; and they should evince an entire repudiation of all hostility to the general government by an acceptance of such just and reasonable conditions as that government should think the public safety demands. Has this been done? Let us look at the facts shown by the evidence taken by the committee.

"Hardly is the war closed before the people of these insurrectionary states come forward and claim as a right the privilege of participating at once in that government which they had for four years been fighting to overthrow. Allowed and encouraged by the executive to organize state governments, they at once placed in power leading rebels, unrepentant and unpardoned, excluding with contempt those who had manifested an attachment to the Union, and preferring, in many instances, those who had rendered themselves the most obnoxious. In the face of the law requiring an oath which would necessarily exclude all such men from federal offices, they elect, with very few exceptions, as senators and representatives in Congress, men who had actively participated in the rebellion, insultingly denouncing the law as unconstitutional. It is only necessary to instance the election to the Senate of the late Vice-President of the Confederacy, a man who, against his own declared convictions, had lent all the weight of his acknowledged ability and of his influence as a most prominent public man to the cause of the rebellion, and who, unpardoned rebel as he is, with that oath staring him in the face, had the assurance to lay his credentials on the table of the Senate. Other rebels of scarcely less note or notoriety were selected from other quarters. Professing no repentance; glorying apparently in the crime they had committed; avowing still, as the uncontradicted testimony of Mr. Stephens and many others proves, an adherence to the pernicious doctrine of secession, and declaring that they yielded only to necessity, they insist, with unanimous voice, upon their rights as states, and proclaim that they will submit to no conditions whatever as preliminary to their resumption of power under that Constitution which they still claim the right to repudiate.

"Examining the evidence taken by your committee still farther, in connection with facts too notorious to be disputed, it appears that the Southern press, with few exceptions, and those mostly of newspapers recently established by Northern men, abound with weekly and daily abuse of the institutions and people of the loyal states; defends the men who led, and the principles which incited the rebellion; denounces and reviles Southern men who adhered to the Union; and strives, constantly and unscrupulously, by every means in its power, to keep alive the fire of hate and discord between the sections, calling upon the President to violate his oath of office, overturn the government by force of arms, and drive the representatives of the people from their seats in Congress. The national banner is openly insulted, and the national airs scoffed at, not only by an ignorant populace, but at public meetings, and once, among other notable instances, at a dinner given in honor of a notorious rebel who had violated his oath and abandoned his flag. The same individual is elected to an important office in the leading city of his state, although an unpardoned rebel, and so offensive that the President refuses to allow him to enter upon his official duties. In another state the leading general of the rebel armies is openly nominated for governor by the speaker of the House of Delegates, and the nomination is hailed by the people with shouts of satisfaction, and openly indorsed by the press.

"Looking still farther at the evidence taken by your committee, it is found to be clearly shown, by witnesses of the highest character, and having the best means of observation, that the Freedmen's Bureau, instituted for the relief and protection of freedmen and refugees, is almost universally opposed by the mass of the population, and exists in an efficient condition only under military protection, while the Union men at the South are earnest in its defense, declaring with one voice that without its protection the colored people would not be permitted to labor at fair prices, and could hardly live in safety. They also testify that without the protection of United States troops, Union men, whether of Northern or Southern origin, would be obliged to abandon their homes. The feeling in many portions of the country toward the emancipated slaves, especially among the uneducated and ignorant, is one of vindictive and malicious hatred. This deep-seated prejudice against color is assiduously cultivated by the public journals, and leads to acts of cruelty, oppression, and murder, which the local authorities are at no pains to prevent or punish. There is no general disposition to place the colored race, constituting at least two fifths of the population, upon terms even of civil equality. While many instances may be found where large planters and men of the better class accept the situation, and honestly strive to bring about a better order of things by employing the freedmen at fair wages and treating them kindly, the general feeling and disposition among all classes are yet totally averse to the toleration of any class of people friendly to the Union, be they black or white; and this aversion is not unfrequently manifested in an insulting and offensive manner.

"The witnesses examined as to the willingness of the people of the South to contribute, under existing laws, to the payment of the national debt, prove that the taxes levied by the United States will be paid only on compulsion and with great reluctance, while there prevails, to a considerable extent, an expectation that compensation will be made for slaves emancipated and property destroyed during the war. The testimony on this point comes from officers of the Union army, officers of the late rebel army, Union men of the Southern States, and avowed secessionists, almost all of whom state that, in their opinion, the people of the rebellious states would, if they should see a prospect of success, repudiate the national debt.

"While there is scarcely any hope or desire among leading men to renew the attempt at secession at any future time, there is still, according to a large number of witnesses, including A. H. Stephens, who may be regarded as good authority on that point, a generally prevailing opinion which defends the legal right of secession, and upholds the doctrine that the first allegiance of the people is due to the states, and not to the United States. This belief evidently prevails among leading and prominent men, as well as among the masses every where, except in some of the northern counties of Alabama and the eastern counties of Tennessee.

"The evidence of an intense hostility to the Federal Union, and an equally intense love of the late Confederacy, nurtured by the war, is decisive. While it appears that nearly all are willing to submit, at least for the time being, to the federal authority, it is equally clear that the ruling motive is a desire to obtain the advantages which will be derived from a representation in Congress. Officers of the Union army on duty, and Northern men who go South to engage in business, are generally detested and proscribed. Southern men who adhered to the Union are bitterly hated and relentlessly persecuted. In some localities prosecutions have been instituted in state courts against Union officers for acts done in the line of official duty, and similar prosecutions are threatened elsewhere as soon as the United States troops are removed. All such demonstrations show a state of feeling against which it is unmistakably necessary to guard.

"The testimony is conclusive that, after the collapse of the Confederacy, the feeling of the people of the rebellious states was that of abject submission. Having appealed to the tribunal of arms, they had no hope except that by the magnanimity of the conquerors their lives, and possibly their property, might be preserved. Unfortunately, the general issue of pardons to persons who had been prominent in the rebellion, and the feeling of kindness and conciliation manifested by the executive, and very generally indicated through the Northern press, had the effect to render whole communities forgetful of the crime they had committed, defiant toward the federal government, and regardless of their duties as citizens. The conciliatory measures of the government do not seem to have been met even half way. The bitterness and defiance exhibited toward the United States under such circumstances is without a parallel in the history of the world. In return for our leniency we receive only an insulting denial of our authority. In return for our kind desire for the resumption of fraternal relations we receive only an insolent assumption of rights and privileges long since forfeited. The crime we have punished is paraded as a virtue, and the principles of republican government which we have vindicated at so terrible a cost are denounced as unjust and oppressive.

protection of loyal and well-disposed people in the South, the proof of a condition of feeling hostile to the Union and dangerous to the government throughout the insurrectionary states would seem to be overwhelming.

"With such evidence before them, it is the opinion of your committee—

"I. That the states lately in rebellion were, at the close of the war, disorganized communities, without civil government, and without Constitutions or other forms by virtue of which political relations could legally exist between them and the federal government.

"II. That Congress can not be expected to recognize as valid the election of representatives from disorganized communities which, from the very nature of the case, were unable to present their claim to representation under those established rules the observance of which has been hitherto required.

"III. That Congress would not be justified in admitting such communities to a participation in the government of the country without first providing such constitutional or other guarantees as will tend to secure the civil rights of all citizens of the republic; a just equality of representation; protection against claims founded in rebellion and crime; a temporary restoration of the right of suffrage to those who have not actively participated in the efforts to destroy the Union and overthrow the government; and the exclusion from positions of public trust of at least a portion of those whose crimes have proved them to be enemies to the Union, and unworthy of public confidence.

"Your committee will, perhaps, hardly be deemed excusable for extending this report farther; but inasmuch as immediate and unconditional representation of the states lately in rebellion is demanded as a matter of right, and delay, and even hesitation, is denounced as grossly oppressive and unjust, as well as unwise and impolitic, it may not be amiss again to call attention to a few undisputed and notorious facts, and the principles of public law applicable thereto, in order that the propriety of that claim may be fully considered and well understood.

"The State of Tennessee occupies a position distinct from all the other insurrectionary states, and has been the subject of a separate report, which your committee have not thought it expedient to disturb. Whether Congress shall see fit to make that state the subject of separate action, or to include it in the same category with all others, so far as concerns the imposition of preliminary conditions, it is not within the province of this committee either to determine or advise.

"To ascertain whether any of the so-called Confederate States 'are entitled to be represented in either house of Congress,' the essential inquiry is whether there is, in any one of them, a constituency qualified to be represented in Congress. The question how far persons claiming seats in either house possess the credentials necessary to enable them to represent a duly qualified constituency is one for the consideration of each house separately, after the preliminary question shall have been finally determined.

"We now propose to restate, as briefly as possible, the general facts and principles applicable to all the states recently in rebellion.

"1st. The seats of the senators and representatives from the so-called Confederate States became vacant in the year 1861, during the second session of the Thirty-sixth Congress, by the voluntary withdrawal of their incumbents, with the sanction and by direction of the Legislatures or Conventions of their respective states. This was done as a hostile act against the Constitution and government of the United States, with a declared intent to overthrow the same by forming a Southern Confederation. This act of declared hostility was speedily followed by an organization of the same states into a confederacy, which levied and waged war by sea and land against the United States. This war continued four years, within which period the rebel armies besieged the national capital, invaded the loyal states, burned their towns and cities, robbed their citizens, destroyed more than 250,000 loyal soldiers, and imposed an increased national burden of not less than $3,500,000,000, of which seven or eight hundred millions have already been met and paid. From the time these confederated states thus withdrew their representation in Congress and levied war against the United States, the great mass of their people became and were insurgents, rebels, traitors, and all of them assumed and occupied the political, legal, and practical relation of enemies of the United States. This position is established by acts of Congress and judicial decisions, and is recognized repeatedly by the President in public proclamations, documents, and speeches.

"2d. The states thus confederated prosecuted their war against the United States to final arbitrament, and did not cease until all their armies were captured, their military power destroyed, their civil officers, state and confederate, taken prisoners or put to flight, every vestige of state and confederate government obliterated, their territory overrun and occupied by the federal armies, and their people reduced to the condition of enemies conquered in war, entitled only by public law to such rights, privileges, and conditions as might be vouchsafed by the conqueror. This position is also established by judicial decisions, and is recognized by the President in public proclamations, documents, and speeches.

"3d. Having voluntarily deprived themselves of representation in Congress for the criminal purpose of destroying the Federal Union, and having reduced themselves, by the act of levying war, to the condition of public enemies, they have no right to complain of temporary exclusion from Congress; but, on the contrary, having voluntarily renounced the right to representation, and disqualified themselves by crime from participating in the government, the burden now rests upon them, before claiming to be reinstated in their former condition, to show that they are qualified to resume federal relations. In order to do this, they must prove that they have established, with the consent of the people, republican forms of government in harmony with the Constitution and laws of the United States, that all hostile purposes have ceased, and should give adequate guarantees against future treason and rebellion—guarantees which shall prove satisfactory to the government against which they rebelled, and by whose arms they were subdued.

"4th. Having, by this treasonable withdrawal from Congress, and by flagrant rebellion and war, forfeited all civil and political rights and privileges under the Constitution, they can only be restored thereto by the permission and authority of that constitutional power against which they rebelled and by which they were subdued.

"5th. These rebellious enemies were conquered by the people of the United States, acting through all the co-ordinate branches of the government, and not by the executive department alone. The powers of conqueror are not so vested in the President that he can fix and regulate the terms of settlement, and confer congressional representation on conquered rebels and traitors. Nor can he in any way qualify enemies of the government to exercise its law-making power. The authority to restore rebels to political power in the federal government can be exercised only with the concurrence of all the departments in which political power is vested; and hence the several proclamations of the President to the people of the Confederate States can not be considered as extending beyond the purposes declared, and can only be regarded as provisional permission by the commander-in-chief of the army to do certain acts, the effect and validity whereof is to be determined by the constitutional government, and not solely by the executive power.

"6th. The question before Congress is, then, whether conquered enemies have the right, and shall be permitted, at their own pleasure and on their own terms, to participate in making laws for their conquerors; whether conquered rebels may change their theatre of operations from the battle-field, where they were defeated and overthrown, to the halls of Congress, and, through their representatives, seize upon the government which they fought to destroy; whether the national treasury, the army of the nation, its navy, its forts and arsenals, its whole civil administration, its credit, its pensioners, the widows and orphans of those who perished in the war, the public honor, peace, and safety, shall all be turned over to the keeping of its recent enemies without delay, and without imposing such conditions as, in the opinion of Congress, the security of the country and its institutions may demand.

"7th. The history of mankind exhibits no examples of such madness and folly. The instinct of self-preservation protests against it. The surrender by Grant to Lee, and by Sherman to Johnston, would have been disasters of less magnitude, for new armies could have been raised, new battles fought, and the government saved. The anti-coercive policy, which, under pretext of avoiding bloodshed, allowed the rebellion to take form and gather force, would be surpassed in infamy by the matchless wickedness that would now surrender the halls of Congress to those so recently in rebellion, until proper precautions shall have been taken to secure the national faith and the national safety.

"8th. As has been shown in this report, and in the evidence submitted, no proof has been afforded by Congress of a constituency in any one of the so-called Confederate States, unless we except the State of Tennessee, qualified to elect senators and representatives in Congress. No state Constitution, or amendment to a state Constitution, has had the sanction of the people. All the so-called legislation of state Conventions and Legislatures has been had under military dictation. If the President may, at his will, and under his own authority, whether as military commander or chief executive, qualify persons to appoint senators and elect representatives, and empower others to appoint and elect them, he thereby practically controls the organization of the legislative department. The constitutional form of government is thereby practically destroyed, and its powers absorbed in the executive. And while your committee do not for a moment impute to the President any such design, but cheerfully concede to him the most patriotic motives, they can not but look with alarm upon a precedent so fraught with danger to the republic

mulated volumes of testimony in regard to the condition of the Southern States. That was proper enough, but it was not necessary to wait for the development of all this evidence before submitting to Congress the measures which it finally proposed. By the delay of Congress to declare its policy, its measures did not come before the country until after the conflict between the President and Congress had produced dissensions in the Republican party, increased agitation throughout the country, and exaggerated the contumacious spirit of the Southern people to such an extent as to greatly diminish the prospect that the latter would accede to the conditions offered for its acceptance. Early in the session the resistance to the Congressional plan of restoration would not have been formidable; now it was plain that it would be resisted by the executive, by the Southern States, and by a large portion of the Republican party. This delay was only less unfortunate in its consequences than the President's hasty action and his failure to convene Congress at the beginning of his administration.

Some time before the full report of the Reconstruction Committee, the latter had presented a concurrent resolution declaring "that, in order to close agitation upon a question which seems likely to disturb the action of the government, as well as to quiet the uncertainty which is agitating the minds of the people of the eleven states which have been declared to be in insurrection, no senator or representative shall be admitted into either branch of Congress from any of the said states until Congress shall have declared such state entitled to such representation." As usual, Stevens cut off debate in the House by demanding the previous question, and the resolution was adopted in that body without discussion, 109 to 40.[1]

It was a strange measure, when considered in reference to its declared purpose, "to close agitation" and "to quiet the uncertainty" of the unrepresented section! The reasons which induced the committee to introduce this resolution were more clearly stated by Fessenden in the Senate, where the measure was debated at length, than in the resolution itself. In his speech upon the resolution, Senator Fessenden confessed that the committee introduced the resolution because President Johnson had denounced it as "an irrepressible central directory" in which was lodged the concentrated power of a few, and because in his veto (February 19th) of the Freedman's Bureau Bill he had indicated "that no legislation affecting the states which have recently been in rebellion would meet with the approval of the President while those states were not represented." Under these circumstances, he thought the resolution necessary "in order that Congress may assert distinctly its own rights and its own powers; in order that there may be no mistake any where, in the mind of the executive or in the minds of the people of this country, that Congress, under the circumstances of this case, with this attempted limitation of its powers with regard to its own organization, is prepared to say to the executive and to the country, respectfully but firmly, over this subject they have, and they mean to exercise, the most plenary jurisdiction; they will be limited with regard to it by no considerations arising from the views of others than themselves, except so far as those considerations may affect the minds of individuals; we will judge for ourselves not only upon credentials, and the character of men and the position of men, but upon the position of the states which sent those men here. In other words, to use the language of the President again, when the question is to be decided whether they obey the Constitution, whether they have a fitting Constitution of their own, whether they are loyal, whether they are prepared to obey the laws as a preliminary, as the President says it is, to their admission, we will say whether those preliminary requirements have been complied with, and not he, and nobody but ourselves." The war, admitted the senator, was not commenced with the idea of subjugation; "but if subjugation must come in order to accomplish what we desire to accomplish and what we must accomplish, it is not our fault." We could not, he added, consider the country safe when the President himself does not withdraw his suspension of the writ of *habeas corpus*.

Senator Sherman, of Ohio, followed in opposition to the resolution. He did not differ from Fessenden as to the power of Congress or as to the propriety of the two houses acting in concert upon this subject of admitting Southern representatives. He considered the adoption of the resolution, therefore, as unnecessary, and as calculated to increase rather than to close agitation. The true way to assert the proper powers of Congress was to exercise them. He held that the real difficulty in this whole matter had been the unfortunate failure of the executive and legislative branches of the government to agree upon the plan of reconstruction. The blame on this account did not rest wholly with the President. If Congress had, at its last session, provided a law by which these states might be guided in their efforts toward restoration, the controversy would have been at an end. He alluded to the Wade and Davis bill, which had been passed at the first session of the Thirty-eighth Congress,[1] but which failed to receive the signature of President Lincoln. Here Senator Sumner remarked that President Lincoln, in an interview with him, had expressed his regret that he had not accepted that bill. Sherman thought every patriotic citizen would express his regret not so much that the President did not approve that bill, but that Congress did not, in connection with the President, agree upon some plan for reconstruction. Why, he asked, now arraign Andrew Johnson for following out the plan which he deemed best, especially when it was the same plan which had been adopted by Lincoln, and which had the apparent ratification of the people in Lincoln's re-election? "One whole session intervened after this vote, as I may call it, of President Lincoln, and no effort was made by Congress to reconcile this conflict of views; and when President Johnson came suddenly, by the hand of an assassin, into the presidential chair, what did he have before him to guide his steps? The forces of the rebellion had been subdued; all physical resistance was soon after subdued. . . . . Who doubts, then, that if there had been a law upon the statute-book by which the people of the Southern States could have been guided in their efforts to come back into the Union, they would have cheerfully followed it, although the conditions had been hard?" Lincoln and Johnson had both been obliged to follow out a plan of their own. We might find fault with the conditions imposed by them, but Lincoln's plan had been substantially sanctioned by the people in his re-election. At the very time Johnson was nominated for Vice-President he was, as military governor of Tennessee, executing the very plan which he subsequently adopted as President. There was now no difference between the President and Congress as to the condition of the Southern States. By both they were treated as states in insurrection, but still as states. It only remained for Congress to provide a method by which the condition of states might be tested, and they might come back, one by one, each upon its own merits, upon complying with such conditions as the public safety demands. Senator Sherman then proceeded to explain the policy which Johnson had adopted. He had retained Lincoln's cabinet, and had thus far received its full support. He had executed every law passed by Congress. He had in his proclamations adopted almost the precise words used by Lincoln in like cases, only that he had extended and made more severe the policy of the latter. In carrying out his plans he had adopted all the main features of the Wade and Davis bill—the only law bearing upon the subject ever passed by Congress. In his amnesty proclamation of May 29th he had excepted from pardon some fourteen classes of persons, "more than quadrupling the exceptions of the previous proclamation of Mr. Lincoln; so that, if there was any departure in this connection from the policy adopted by Mr. Lincoln, it was a departure against the rebels, and especially against those wealthy rebels who gave life, and soul, and power to the rebellion." He had required of the Southern States the adoption of the constitutional amendment abolishing slavery, had enforced the test oath in the case of every officer receiving his commission under the law, and had insisted upon the full protection of the freedmen. Now what were the objections to this policy? It was said that the pardoning power had been abused; but this power had been sanctioned by Congressional enactment. It was also objected that Johnson had not extended the suffrage to negroes; but there were only six of the Northern States in which negroes had the right to vote, and until the present session the proposition to give negroes this right in the District of Columbia had never been seriously considered, although Congress had complete jurisdiction over the district. Even in the Territories, also under the unrestricted jurisdiction of Congress, the franchise had never been extended to the colored race. In the Wade and Davis bill Congress expressly refused to make negro suffrage a part of their plan.

We have given Senator Sherman's arguments so much space not only on account of his recognized position as one of the most eminent statesmen of the country, but because they furnish the fullest possible defense of President Johnson's policy. This defense was just, so far as it went, but still it must be remembered that the senator's argument entirely ignored the peculiar features of the political situation at the time he spoke. The President's policy could not be separated from the President's conduct of that policy. Johnson had not confined himself to issuing proclamations and to vetoes of Congressional enactments. He had in an unbecoming manner entered into a bitter antagonism with Congress in occasional harangues before the people. Perhaps Sherman paid less regard to the objectionable features of the President's conduct because these features had not as yet assumed their peculiarly offensive character. Sherman defended the President in

---

only be found in such changes of the organic law as shall determine the civil rights and privileges of all citizens in all parts of the republic, shall place representation on an equitable basis, shall fix a stigma upon treason, and protect the loyal people against future claims for the expenses incurred in support of rebellion and for manumitted slaves, together with an express grant of power in Congress to enforce those provisions. To this end they offer a joint resolution for amending the Constitution of the United States, and the two several bills designed to carry the same into effect, before referred to.

"Before closing this report, your committee beg leave to state that the specific recommendations submitted by them are the result of mutual concession, after a long and careful comparison of conflicting opinions. Upon a question of such magnitude, infinitely important as it is to the future of the republic, it was not to be expected that all should think alike. Sensible of the imperfections of the scheme, your committee submit it to Congress as the best they could agree upon, in the hope that its imperfections may be cured, and its deficiencies supplied by legislative wisdom; and that, when finally adopted, it may tend to restore peace and harmony to the whole country, and to place our republican institutions on a more stable foundation.

"W. P. FESSENDEN, ELIHU B. WASHBURNE,
"JAMES W. GRIMES, JUSTIN S. MORRILL,
"IRA HARRIS, JOHN A. BINGHAM,
"J. M. HOWARD, ROSCOE CONKLING,
"GEORGE H. WILLIAMS, GEORGE S. BOUTWELL."
"THADDEUS STEVENS,

[1] YEAS.—Messrs. Allison, Anderson, James M. Ashley, Baker, Baldwin, Banks, Baxter, Beaman, Benjamin, Bidwell, Bingham, Blaine, Boutwell, Brandegee, Bromwell, Broomall, Buckland, Sidney Clarke, Cobb, Conkling, Cook, Cullom, Dawes, Defrees, Deming, Donnelly, Driggs, Eckley, Eggleston, Eliot, Farnsworth, Farquhar, Ferry, Garfield, Grinnell, Griswold, Abner C. Harding, Hart, Hays, Henderson, Higby, Holmes, Hooper, Hotchkiss, Asahel W. Hubbard, Chester D. Hubbard, Demas Hubbard, John H. Hubbard, James R. Hubbell, Hulburd, Ingersoll, Jenckes, Julian, Kelley, Kelso, Ketcham, Laflin, George V. Lawrence, William Lawrence, Loan, Longyear, Lynch, Marston, McClurg, McIndoe, McKee, McRuer, Mercur, Moorhead, Morrill, Morris, Moulton, Myers, O'Neill, Orth, Paine, Patterson, Perham, Pike, Plants, Pomeroy, Price, William H. Randall, John H. Rice, Sawyer, Schenck, Scofield, Shellabarger, Sloan, Spalding, Starr, Stevens, Thayer, John L. Thomas, Trowbridge, Upson, Van Aernam, Burt Van Horn, Ward, Warner, Elihu B. Washburne, William B. Washburn, Welker, Wentworth, Williams, James F. Wilson, Stephen F. Wilson, Windom, and Woodbridge—109.

NAYS.—Messrs. Bergen, Boyer, Brooks, Chanler, Coffroth, Dawson, Eldridge, Finck, Glossbrenner, Goodyear, Grider, Hale, Aaron Harding, Hogan, James M. Humphrey, Kerr, Latham, Marshall, McCullough, Newell, Niblack, Nicholson, Phelps, Radford, Samuel J. Randall, Raymond, Ritter, Rogers, Ross, Rousseau, Shanklin, Sitgreaves, Smith, Taber, Taylor, Thornton, Trimble, Voorhees, Whaley, and Wright—40.

NOT VOTING.—Messrs. Alley, Ames, Ancona, Delos R. Ashley, Barker, Blow, Bundy, Reader W. Clarke, Culver, Darling, Davis, Delano, Denison, Dixon, Dumont, Harris, Hill, Edwin N. Hubbell, James Humphrey, Johnson, Jones, Kasson, Kuykendall, Le Blond, Marvin, Miller, Noell, Alexander H. Rice, Rollins, Stillwell, Strouse, Francis Thomas, Robert T. Van Horn, and Winfield—34.

[1] See page 660 of this History.

February, 1866—what his judgment would have been five months later is another question.

Notwithstanding his speech, Sherman voted in favor of the resolution, which was passed 29 to 18.[1]

The House on the 19th, and the Senate on the 21st of July, passed a resolution declaring the State of Tennessee entitled to representation in Congress, that state having ratified the constitutional amendment proposed by the Thirty-ninth Congress. The President signed the resolution on the 24th, and at the same time sent a message to the House, scolding Congress for its previous contumacy, and denying its right to pass laws preliminary to the admission of duly qualified members from any of the states. The members elected from Tennessee were then duly qualified.

Two important bills were passed during this session, having for their principal object the protection of freedmen, both of which were vetoed by the President, but afterward became laws by a two-thirds vote.

The first of these was a bill to enlarge the powers of the Freedmen's Bureau. This bureau had been established by the previous Congress, while the war was still in progress, and was styled "a Bureau of Refugees, Freedmen, and Abandoned Lands."[2] It passed Congress March 3d, 1867, and received within the week following the approval of President Lincoln, who appointed Major General O. O. Howard as commissioner. This choice was very judicious, as General Howard was not only an able military officer, but had also a thorough knowledge of the South, and of the special duties of the office to which he was assigned. He was, moreover, a conscientious Christian gentleman. He was retained at the head of the bureau by President Johnson. The abandoned lands consisted of some 770,000 acres of lands scattered over the Southern States, the most valuable portion of which were the sea islands off the South Carolina coast, which had been given to the freedmen by General Sherman, acting in consultation with the Secretary of War.

By President Johnson's amnesty proclamation the most valuable lands were restored to their original owners, and this circumstance seriously embarrassed the operations of the bureau. Notwithstanding this obstacle, however, the bureau proved a beneficent institution to the freed slave and refugee. It secured them many educational privileges hitherto denied, stood between them and the avarice of their employers, and provided medical relief to their sick, and assistance to the old and decrepit. Great opposition was manifested to the education of freedmen. The educational statistics of October 31, 1865, show that there were at that time 560 schools in operation, with 1135 teachers, and 68,241 pupils. Toward the close of the year, General Howard estimated the number of persons receiving rations from the bureau at 45,035, which he thought would be increased during the ensuing winter to 100,000. The expenses of the bureau for 1865 amounted to nearly $12,000,000.

The bill enlarging the powers of the Freedmen's Bureau passed the Senate January 24, 1866, by a party vote. A substitute for this bill passed the House, which was subsequently accepted by the Senate. This bill continued in force the bureau until otherwise ordered by law, and provided for its extension to freedmen and refugees in all parts of the United States, the entire section containing such persons to be divided into twelve districts, over each of which an assistant commissioner should preside. These districts, in turn, were to be subdivided, so that there should be one for each county or parish, each of which was to be controlled by an agent. It provided for the issue by the Secretary of War of provisions, clothing, fuel, and other supplies, including medical stores and transportation; and that the secretary might afford such aid as was necessary for the temporary shelter and supply of destitute freedmen and refugees, with their wives and children. The President was authorized to reserve from sale and set apart unoccupied public lands in the South for the use of freedmen and loyal refugees, the amount thus appropriated not to exceed three millions of acres of good land, to be allotted in parcels of not more than forty acres each, the tenants to be protected in the use thereof for such time and at such rental as should be agreed upon between the commissioners and freedmen. This land might ultimately be purchased by the occupants. Those occupying land under General Sherman's special order of January 16, 1865, were confirmed in possession for three years. This act also provided for the erection of asylums and schools. It also contained provisions for the protection of the civil rights of freedmen.[1]

This bill was vetoed by the President February 19th, 1866. His objections may be briefly stated thus:

1. The act was unnecessary, the original act not having yet expired. That act was considered sufficiently stringent in time of war. Before its expiration, farther experience may lead to a wise policy for a time of peace.

2. The act contained provisions not warranted by the Constitution. It substituted military for civil tribunals, and military law for civil law in time of peace.

3. The exercise of such arbitrary power by so vast a number of agents must be attended by acts of caprice, injustice, and passion. From these officers of the bureau there was no appeal.

4. The continuance of this military establishment was not limited to any definite period of time.

5. While it was intended to protect the negro, it deprived other citizens of constitutional rights. "I can not," said the President, "reconcile a system of military jurisdiction of this kind with the words of the Constitution, which declare that 'no person shall be held to answer for a capital or otherwise infamous crime unless upon a presentment or indictment of a grand jury, except in cases arising in the land and naval forces, or in the militia when in actual service in time of war or public danger;' and that 'in all criminal prosecutions the accused shall enjoy the right to a speedy and public trial by an impartial jury of the state or district wherein the crime shall have been committed.'"

6. It placed too much power in the hands of the President. It would enable him to control four millions of people for his own political ends.

7. A system for the support of indigent persons in the United States was never contemplated by the framers of the Constitution, nor could any good reason be given why it should be founded for one class of our people more than another. The idea on which the slaves were assisted to freedom was that, on becoming free, they would be a self-sustaining population.

8. It was an expensive system.

9. It deprived the rightful owners of certain lands of their property without due process of law.

10. It was injurious to the freedman, encouraging him to entertain idle and vague expectations.

11. Eleven states were still unrepresented, and these were the very states most nearly concerned in the operations of the bill.

The House passed the bill over the President's veto, but it failed to receive a two-thirds vote in the Senate, and thus failed to become a law. Before the end of May a new bill was presented in the House by Thomas D. Eliot, of Massachusetts, apparently obviating many of the objections which had been urged by the President against the former enactment. This new bill simply sought to supplement the act already in operation by provisions applicable to the altered situation since that act had been passed. It continued that act in force for two years; appropriated one million instead of three millions of acres for the use of the freedmen, and embodied the provisions of the Civil Rights Bill. This bill, after various amendments, passed both houses, and was presented to the President for his approval. On the 16th of July Johnson returned the bill with objections similar to those urged against the previous act. It was again passed in both houses by a two-thirds vote, and became a law.

In the mean time Congress had passed the Civil Rights Bill. This act was supported in both houses by the entire Republican party.[2] It was

[1] YEAS.—Messrs. Anthony, Brown, Chandler, Clark, Conness, Cragin, Creswell, Fessenden, Foster, Grimes, Harris, Henderson, Howe, Kirkwood, Lane of Indiana, Morrill, Nye, Poland, Pomeroy, Ramsey, Sherman, Sprague, Sumner, Trumbull, Wade, Willey, Williams, Wilson, and Yates—29.

NAYS.—Messrs. Buckalew, Cowan, Davis, Dixon, Doolittle, Guthrie, Hendricks, Johnson, Lane of Kansas, McDougall, Morgan, Nesmith, Norton, Riddle, Saulsbury, Stewart, Stockton, and Van Winkle—18.

ABSENT.—Messrs. Foot, Howard, and Wright—3.

[2] The bill established in the War Department for the war and one year thereafter a Bureau of Refugees, Freedmen, and Abandoned Lands, for the supervision and management of all abandoned lands, and the control of all subjects relating to refugees and freedmen from rebel states, or from any district of the country within the territory embraced in the operations of the army, under rules to be approved by the President. The bureau to have a commissioner at $3000 year, and $50,000 bonds, with an assistant commissioner for each rebel state, not exceeding ten, at $2500 a year, and $20,000 bonds. The assistants to make quarterly reports to the commissioner, and he a report at each session of Congress.

Section 2 authorizes the Secretary of War to direct such issues of provisions, clothing, and fuel as he may deem needful for the immediate and temporary shelter and supply of destitute and suffering refugees and freedmen, and their wives and children, under such rules and regulations as he may direct.

The bill also gives the commissioner, under the direction of the President, authority to set apart for the use of loyal refugees and freedmen such tracts of land within the insurrectionary states as shall have been abandoned, or to which the United States shall have acquired title by confiscation, or sale, or otherwise. And to every male citizen, whether refugee or freedman, as aforesaid, there shall be assigned not more than forty acres of such land, and the persons to whom it is so assigned shall be protected in the use and enjoyment of the land for the term of three years, at an annual rent not exceeding six per cent. upon the value of said land as it was appraised by the state authorities in 1860 for the purpose of taxation, and in case no such appraisal can be found, then the rental shall be based upon the estimated value of the land in said year, to be ascertained in such manner as the commissioner may, by regulation, prescribe. At the end of said term, or at any time during said term, the occupants of any parcels so assigned may purchase the land and receive such title thereto as the United States can convey upon paying therefor the value of the land, as ascertained and fixed for the purpose of determining the annual rent as aforesaid.

[1] "*Sec.* 7. That whenever in any state or district in which the ordinary course of judicial proceedings has been interrupted by the rebellion, and wherein, in consequence of any state or local law, ordinance, police or other regulation, custom, or prejudice, any of the civil rights or immunities belonging to white persons, including the right to make and enforce contracts, to sue, be parties, and give evidence, to inherit, purchase, lease, sell, hold, and convey real and personal property, and to have full and equal benefit of all laws and proceedings for the security of person and estate, including the constitutional right of bearing arms, are refused or denied to negroes, mulattoes, freedmen, refugees, or any other persons, on account of race, color, or any previous condition of slavery or involuntary servitude, or wherein they or any of them are subjected to any other or different punishment, pains, or penalties for the commission of any act or offense than are prescribed for white persons committing like acts or offenses, it shall be the duty of the President of the United States, through the commissioner, to extend military protection and jurisdiction over all cases affecting such persons so discriminated against.

"*Sec.* 8. That any person who, under color of any state or local law, ordinance, police, or other regulation or custom, shall, in any state or district in which the ordinary course of judicial proceedings has been interrupted by the rebellion, subject, or cause to be subjected, any negro, mulatto, freedman, refugee, or other person, on account of race or color, or any previous condition of slavery or involuntary servitude, or for any other cause, to the deprivation of any civil right secured to white persons, or to any other or different punishment than white persons are subject to for the commission of like acts or offenses, shall be deemed guilty of a misdemeanor, and be punished by fine not exceeding one thousand dollars, or imprisonment not exceeding one year, or both; and it shall be the duty of the officers and agents of this bureau to take jurisdiction of, and hear and determine all offenses committed against the provisions of this section, and also of all cases affecting negroes, mulattoes, freedmen, refugees, or other persons who are discriminated against in any of the particulars mentioned in the preceding section of this act, under such rules and regulations as the President of the United States, through the War Department, shall prescribe. The jurisdiction conferred by this and the preceding section on the officers and agents of this bureau shall cease and determine whenever the discrimination on account of which it is conferred ceases, and in no event to be exercised in any state in which the ordinary course of judicial proceedings has not been interrupted by the rebellion, nor in any such state after said state shall have been fully restored in all its constitutional relations to the United States, and the courts of the state and of the United States within the same are not disturbed or stopped in the peaceable course of justice."

[2] The following is the text of the bill:

"*Be it enacted, etc.*, That all persons born in the United States and not subject to any foreign power, excluding Indians not taxed, are hereby declared to be citizens of the United States; and such citizens of every race and color, without regard to any previous condition of slavery or involuntary servitude, except as a punishment for crime whereof the party shall have been duly convicted, shall have the same right in every state and territory in the United States to make and enforce contracts; to sue, be parties, and give evidence; to inherit, purchase, lease, sell, hold, and convey real estate and personal property; and to full and equal benefit of all laws and proceedings for the security of person and property as is enjoyed by white citizens, and shall be subject to like punishment, pains, and penalties; and to none other, any law, statute, ordinance, regulation, or custom to the contrary notwithstanding.

"*Sec.* 2. That any person who, under color of any law, statute, ordinance, regulation, or custom, shall subject, or cause to be subjected, any inhabitant of any state or territory to the deprivation of any right secured or protected by this act, or to different punishment, pains, or penalties on account of such person having at any time been held in a condition of slavery or involuntary servitude, except as a punishment for crime whereof the party shall have been duly convicted, or by

vetoed by the President March 27, 1866. This veto was not based upon sound reasoning, and the message of the President totally disregarded the obvious necessity of the Congressional enactment. The bill was again passed by both houses over the executive veto.

A bill was passed early in May admitting Colorado as a state, but it was vetoed by the President on the ground that it was doubtful whether the majority of the people of that Territory desired a state government, that the population was insufficient, and that, until the Southern section of the country was represented in Congress, it was undesirable to admit new states. The bill was not repassed.

A bill was introduced early in the session to extend the right of suffrage to negroes in the District of Columbia. It passed the House, after an unsuccessful attempt on the part of a Republican member to obtain its postponement, by a vote of 116 to 54. It was not brought to a vote in the Senate until the next session, when it passed, was vetoed by the President, and on the 7th and 8th of January, 1867, was repassed by a two-thirds vote in the Senate and House.[1]

The first session of the Thirty-ninth Congress closed on the 28th of July, after a continuance of nearly eight months. During this period the political situation had been radically changed. When the Thirty-ninth Congress assembled, there was no strongly-marked popular dissatisfaction on account of the measures adopted by President Johnson in the early stages of reconstruction. Now the people murmured against the administration; the President had lost his hold upon the popular confidence. Radical Republicans now as vehemently denounced him as Copperheads had at the time of his inauguration. The latter, from calling him a boor, had come to grant him a place among the gods; the former, who had once shouted his praises to the echo, now not only took the scoffers' place, but boldly proclaimed him a traitor.

There had been in the ranks of the dominant party some apprehension of Johnson's policy at the outset, but it scarcely found a voice before the meeting of Congress. There was a feeling of insecurity, caused by the prospect of a too hasty admission of the Southern representatives to Congress, and enhanced by the half-hearted expression of loyalty on the part of the Southern Conventions and Legislatures; but this was to a great degree counteracted by the hope that Congress and the President would unite upon some plan by which harmony would soon be restored, the wounds occasioned by civil strife healed, and the national safety secured. No conflict between the executive and Congress—at least none which would prove irreconcilable—was apprehended. The war record of President Johnson, his vehement denunciation of treason, his oft-repeated expressions of deference to the popular will, and the fact that thus far he had been carrying out the policy of restoration which Lincoln had inaugurated, and had only modified that policy by severer features as against rebels—all these were taken as assurances that he, at least, would not be a ready party to such a conflict. And, on the other hand, the popular confidence in the wisdom of Congress was a source of encouragement. It was well known that there were in that body certain members who would push their extreme and impracticable theories to the utmost; but, if Sumner, and Stevens, and Boutwell, and Ashley were there, there also were Fessenden, Sherman, Trumbull, Colfax, Conkling, Doolittle, and Raymond. The factious disposition and the partisan fury of the few, it was thought, would be controlled and overruled by the unsectional patriotism of wiser and better-tempered statesmen.

But scarcely had Congress assembled before this feeling of assurance, this anticipation of harmony, began to be disturbed. We regret that we must attribute to President Johnson's policy so much of the responsibility for the discord—the more shameful because it was unnecessary—which now began to develop into the most violent antagonism. He had already established a basis for this conflict by not convening and consulting Congress at the outset. Undoubtedly he thought that the policy which he had adopted was supported by the people, and that nothing more than that was necessary. He had good reasons for judging thus. But, in carrying out this policy, some circumstances presented themselves to which he did not pay

reason of his color or race, than is prescribed for the punishment of white persons, shall be deemed guilty of a misdemeanor, and on conviction shall be punished by fine not exceeding one thousand dollars, or imprisonment not exceeding one year, or both, in the discretion of the Court.

"*Sec.* 3. That the District Courts of the United States, within their respective districts, shall have, exclusively of the courts of the several states, cognizance of all crimes and offenses committed against the provisions of this act, and also, concurrently with the Circuit Courts of the United States, of all causes, civil and criminal, affecting persons who are denied or can not enforce in the courts or judicial tribunals of the state or locality where there may be any of the rights secured to them by the first section of this act; and if any suit or prosecution, civil or criminal, has been or shall be commenced in any state court against any such person, for any cause whatsoever, or against any officer, civil or military, or other person, for any arrest or imprisonment, trespasses, or wrongs done or committed by virtue or under color of authority derived from this act, or the act establishing a bureau for the relief of freedmen and refugees, and all acts amendatory thereof, or for refusing to do any act upon the ground that it would be inconsistent with this act, such defendant shall have the right to remove such cause for trial to the proper District or Circuit Court in the manner prescribed by the 'Act relating to *Habeas Corpus* and regulating Judicial Proceedings in certain Cases,' approved March 3, 1863, and all acts amendatory thereof. The jurisdiction in civil and criminal matters hereby conferred on the District and Circuit Courts of the United States shall be exercised and enforced in conformity with the laws of the United States so far as such laws are suitable to carry the same into effect; but in all cases where such laws are not adapted to the object, or are deficient in the provisions necessary to furnish suitable remedies and punish offenses against law, the common law, as modified and changed by the Constitution and statutes of the state wherein the court having jurisdiction of the cause, civil or criminal, is held, so far as the same is not inconsistent with the Constitution and laws of the United States, shall be extended to and govern said courts in the trial and disposition of such cause, and, if of a criminal nature, in the infliction of punishment on the party found guilty.

"*Sec.* 4. That the district attorneys, marshals, and deputy marshals of the United States, the commissioners appointed by the Circuit Court and territorial Courts of the United States, with powers of arresting, imprisoning, or bailing offenders against the laws of the United States, the officers and agents of the Freedmen's Bureau, and every other officer who may be specially empowered by the President of the United States, shall be, and they are hereby specially authorized and required, at the expense of the United States, to institute proceedings against all and every person who shall violate the provisions of this act, and cause him or them to be arrested and imprisoned, or bailed, as the case may be, for trial before such court of the United States or territorial court as by this act has cognizance of the offense. And with a view to affording reasonable protection to all persons in their constitutional rights of equality before the law, without distinction of race or color, or previous condition of slavery or involuntary servitude, except as a punishment for crime, whereof the party shall have been duly convicted, and to the prompt discharge of the duties of this act, it shall be the duty of the Circuit Courts of the United States and the Superior Courts of the Territories of the United States, from time to time to increase the number of commissioners, so as to afford a speedy and convenient means for the arrest and examination of persons charged with a violation of this act. And such commissioners are hereby authorized and required to exercise and discharge all the powers and duties conferred on them by this act, and the same duties with regard to offenses created by this act, as they are authorized by law to exercise with regard to other offenses against the laws of the United States.

"*Sec.* 5. That it shall be the duty of all marshals and deputy marshals to obey and execute all warrants and precepts issued under the provisions of this act when to them directed; and should any marshal or deputy marshal refuse to receive such warrant or other process when tendered, or to use all proper means diligently to execute the same, he shall, on conviction thereof, be fined in the sum of one thousand dollars, to the use of the person upon whom the accused is alleged to have committed the offense. And the better to enable the said commissioners to execute their duties faithfully and efficiently, in conformity with the Constitution of the United States and the requirements of this act, they are hereby authorized and empowered, within their counties respectively, to appoint, in writing, under their hands, any one or more suitable persons, from time to time, to execute all such warrants and other process that may be issued by them in the lawful performance of their respective duties; and the persons so appointed to execute any warrant or process as aforesaid shall have authority to summon and call to their aid the by-standers or the *posse comitatus* of the proper county, or such portion of the land and naval forces of the United States, or of the militia, as may be necessary to the performance of the duty with which they are charged, and to insure a faithful observance of the clause of the Constitution which prohibits slavery, in conformity with the provisions of this act; and said warrants shall run and be executed by said officers any where in the state or territory within which they are issued.

"*Sec.* 6. That any person who shall knowingly and willfully obstruct, hinder, or prevent any officer, or other person charged with the execution of any warrant or process issued under the provisions of this act, or any person or persons lawfully assisting him or them, from arresting any person for whose apprehension such warrant or process may have been issued, or shall rescue or attempt to rescue such person from the custody of the officer, other person or persons, or those lawfully assisting as aforesaid, when so arrested pursuant to the authority herein given and declared, or shall aid, abet, or assist any person so arrested as aforesaid, directly or indirectly, to escape from the custody of the officer or other person legally authorized as aforesaid, or shall harbor or conceal any person for whose arrest a warrant or process shall have been issued as aforesaid, so as to prevent his discovery and arrest after notice or knowledge of the fact that a warrant has been issued for the apprehension of such person, shall, for either of said offenses, be subject to a fine not exceeding one thousand dollars, and imprisonment not exceeding six months, by indictment and conviction before the District Court of the United States for the district in which said offense may have been committed, or before the proper court of criminal jurisdiction, if committed within any one of the organized territories of the United States.

"*Sec.* 7. That the district attorneys, the marshals, their deputies, and the clerks of the said District and Territorial Courts shall be paid for their services the like fees as may be allowed to them for similar services in other cases; and in all cases where the proceedings are before a commissioner, he shall be entitled to a fee of ten dollars in full for his services in each case, inclusive of all services incident to such arrest and examination. The person or persons authorized to execute the process to be issued by such commissioners for the arrest of offenders against the provisions of this act shall be entitled to a fee of five dollars for each person he or they may arrest and take before any such commissioner as aforesaid, with such other fees as may be deemed reasonable by such commissioner for such other additional services as may be necessarily performed by him or them, such as attending at the examination, keeping the prisoner in custody, and providing him with food and lodging during his detention, and until the final determination of such commissioner, and in general for performing such other duties as may be required in the premises; such fees to be made up in conformity with the fees usually charged by the officers of the courts of justice within the proper district or county, as near as may be practicable, and paid out of the treasury of the United States on the certificate of the judge of the district within which the arrest is made, and to be recoverable from the defendant as part of the judgment in case of conviction.

"*Sec.* 8. That whenever the President of the United States shall have reason to believe that offenses have been, or are likely to be committed against the provisions of this act within any judicial district, it shall be lawful for him, in his discretion, to direct the judge, marshal, and district attorney of such district to attend at such place within the district, and for such time as he may designate, for the purpose of the more speedy arrest and trial of persons charged with a violation of this act; and it shall be the duty of every judge or other officer, when any such requisition shall be received by him, to attend at the place and for the time therein designated.

"*Sec.* 9. That it shall be lawful for the President of the United States, or such person as he may empower for that purpose, to employ such part of the land or naval forces of the United States, or of the militia, as shall be necessary to prevent the violation and enforce the due execution of this act.

[1] The following is the text of this enactment:

"*Be it enacted by the Senate and House of Representatives of the United States of America, in Congress assembled,* That from and after the passage of this act, each and every male person, excepting paupers and persons under guardianship, of the age of twenty-one years and upward, who has not been convicted of any infamous crime or offense, and excepting persons who may have voluntarily given aid and comfort to the rebels in the late rebellion, and who shall have been born or naturalized in the United States, and who shall have resided in the said District for the period of one year, and three months in the ward or election precinct in which he shall offer to vote next preceding any election therein, shall be entitled to the elective franchise, and shall be deemed an elector, and entitled to vote at any election in said District, without any distinction on account of color or race.

"SEC. 2. *And be it further enacted,* That any person whose duty it shall be to receive votes at any election within the District of Columbia, who shall willfully refuse to receive, or who shall willfully reject, the vote of any person entitled to such right under this act, shall be liable to an action of tort by the person injured, and shall be liable, on indictment and conviction, if such act was done knowingly, to a fine not exceeding five thousand dollars, or to imprisonment for a term not exceeding one year in the jail of said District, or to both.

"SEC. 3. *And be it further enacted,* That if any person or persons shall willfully interrupt or disturb any such elector in the exercise of such franchise, he or they shall be deemed guilty of a misdemeanor, and, on conviction thereof, shall be fined in any sum not to exceed one thousand dollars, or be imprisoned in the jail in said District for a period not to exceed thirty days, or both, at the discretion of the court.

"SEC. 4. *And be it further enacted,* That it shall be the duty of the several courts having criminal jurisdiction in said District to give this act in special charge to the grand jury at the commencement of each term of the court next preceding the holding of any general or city election in said District.

"SEC. 5. *And be it further enacted,* That the mayors and aldermen of the cities of Washington and Georgetown respectively, on or before the first day of March in each year, shall prepare a list of the persons they judge to be qualified to vote in the several wards of said cities in any election: and said mayors and aldermen shall be in open session to receive evidence of the qualification of persons claiming the right to vote in any election therein, and for correcting said list, on two days in each year, not exceeding five days prior to the annual election for the choice of city officers, giving previous notice of the time and place of each session in some newspaper printed in said District.

"SEC. 6. *And be it further enacted,* That on or before the first day of March, the mayors and aldermen of said cities shall post up a list of voters thus prepared in one or more public places in said cities respectively, at least ten days prior to said annual election.

"SEC. 7. *And be it further enacted,* That the officers presiding at any election shall keep and use the check-list herein required at the polls during the election of all officers, and no vote shall be received unless delivered by the voter in person, and not until the presiding officer has had opportunity to be satisfied of his identity, and shall find his name on the list, and mark it, and ascertain that his vote is single.

"SEC. 8. *And be it further enacted,* That it is hereby declared unlawful for any person, directly or indirectly, to promise, offer, or give, or procure, or cause to be promised, offered, or given, any money, goods, right in action, bribe, present, or reward, or any promise, understanding, obligation, or security for the payment or delivery of any money, goods, right in action, bribe, present, or reward, or any other valuable thing whatever, to any person with intent to influence his vote to be given at any election hereafter to be held within the District of Columbia; and every person so offending shall, on conviction thereof, be fined in any sum not exceeding two thousand dollars, or imprisoned not exceeding two years, or both, at the discretion of the court.

"SEC. 9. *And be it further enacted,* That any person who shall accept, directly or indirectly, any money, goods, right in action, bribe, present, or reward, or any promise, understanding, obligation, or security, for the payment or delivery of any money, goods, right in action, bribe, present, or reward, or any other valuable thing whatever, to influence his vote at any election hereafter to be held in the District of Columbia, shall, on conviction, be imprisoned not less than one year, and be forever disfranchised.

sufficient regard. He had thrown the burden of reconstruction upon the Southern people, which was right. But they had not taken up this burden in the proper spirit; he was himself dissatisfied, and he must have known that the loyal people would not be less so; yet, although he had expressed his disappointment, he had shown a lack of firmness and of judgment in allowing this spirit to have full sway; in finally sanctioning it by his assent, however reluctant, and without consultation with Congress; in encouraging the idea that the Southern States might hope for representation in that body on the basis of their imperfectly expressed allegiance. Congress, with good reason, felt aggrieved by this action of the President.

Congress, upon its meeting, did exactly what it would have done if Lincoln had been President. It appointed a joint committee to investigate the whole subject. Upon mature consideration, it felt that it could not, with a proper regard to the national safety, respond to the expectations which the President had encouraged the Southern people to entertain. Thus the divergence between the executive and Congress began. On the part of the majority there was no misconstruction of the motives of the President and no ill temper; but there were some members who could not refrain from denouncing "the man at the other end of the avenue." Stevens went so far as to say that the President's usurpation of authority was no less heinous a crime than that which had cost Charles the First his head.

And just here it was that President Johnson began to show his most extraordinary lack of judgment. Harmony of action was still possible between the two branches of government. The only necessity on the President's part was that he should keep his temper. Whether he ought to have kept or abandoned his policy may be a debatable question, about which much might be said on both sides; but certainly he ought not to have lost his temper and self-control, since that loss would prove fatal alike to his own good fame and to his policy. Unfortunately, Johnson belonged to that class of politicians who can never refuse a challenge to antagonism, and foolishly took up the gauntlet which Stevens had so adroitly flung. The challenge did not come from Congress. It did come from a man who, without self-conceit, could boast that he had the power arbitrarily to control the debates of the House, but that was no excuse for such an acceptance of the challenge by the President of the United States as that into which Johnson was betrayed in his speech at Washington on the 22d of February, 1866. He then and there publicly declared that, after one rebellion had been subdued, another had just begun. An attempt, he said, was being made "to concentrate all power in the hands of a few at the federal head, and thereby bring about a consolidation of the republic, which is equally objectionable with its dissolution. We find a power assumed and attempted to be exercised of a most extraordinary character. We see now that governments can be revolutionized without going into the battle-field, and sometimes the revolutions most distressing to a people are effected without the shedding of blood; that is, the substance of your government may be taken away, while there is held out to you the form and the shadow. And now, what are the attempts, and what is being proposed? We find that by an irresponsible central directory nearly all the powers of Congress are assumed, without even consulting the legislative and executive departments of the government. By a resolution reported by a committee, upon whom and in whom the legislative power of the government has been lodged, that great principle in the Constitution which authorizes and empowers the legislative department, the Senate and House of Representatives, to be the judges of elections, returns, and qualifications of its own members, has been virtually taken away from the two respective branches of the national Legislature, and conferred upon a committee, who must report before the body can act on the question of the admission of members to their seats. By this rule they assume a state is out of the Union, and to have its practical relations restored by that rule before the House can judge of the qualifications of its own members. What position is that? You have been struggling for four years to put down a rebellion. You contended at the beginning of that struggle that a state had not a right to go out. You said it had neither the right nor the power, and it has been settled that the states had neither the right nor the power to go out of the Union. And when you determine by the executive, by the military, and by the public judgment that these states can not have any right to go out, this committee turns around and assumes that they are out, and that they shall not come in." In this strain the President continued. Not satisfied with denouncing a proceeding of Congress which was evidently proper, and the purport of which he wholly misconstrued, he, in answer to a call from the crowd, went so far as to mention the names of Thaddeus Stevens, Charles Sumner, and Wendell Phillips as men "opposed to the fundamental principles of the government, and now laboring to destroy them." He called the Secretary of the Senate a "dead duck." He said he did not intend to be governed by real or pretended friends, nor to be bullied by his enemies. When he was beheaded, like Charles the First, he wanted the American people to be the witness. He foolishly attached serious importance to Stevens's equally foolish insinuation about his deserving execution. "I do not want," he said, "by innuendoes of an indirect character in high places, to have one say to a man who has assassination broiling in his heart, 'there is a fit subject,' and also exclaim that the 'presidential obstacle' must be got out of the way, when possibly the intention was to institute assassination. Are those who want to destroy our institutions and change the character of the government not satisfied with the blood that has been shed? Are they not satisfied with one martyr? Does not the blood of Lincoln appease the vengeance and wrath of the opponents of this government? Is their thirst still unslaked? Do they want more blood? Have they not honor and courage enough to effect the removal of the presidential obstacle otherwise than through the hands of the assassin? I am not afraid of assassins; but if it m would wish to be encountered where one brave man can oppose I hold him in dread only who strikes cowardly. But if they have enough to strike like men (I know they are willing to wound, but afraid to strike)—if my blood is to be shed because I vindicate th and the preservation of this government in its original purity and ter, let it be so; but when it is done, let an altar of the Union be and then, if necessary, lay me upon it, and the blood that now war animates my frame shall be poured out in a last libation as a tribut Union; and let the opponents of this government remember that wl poured out the blood of the martyr will be the seed of the Churcl Union will grow. It will continue to increase in strength and power, it may be cemented and cleansed with blood."

Nothing could have been more unwise than this speech of Johnsor showed himself too ready to answer vituperation with vituperation. the speech of a demagogue and not of a statesman. It manifested h pacity to become a popular leader, whatever might be the merits of l icy.

Thus the conflict progressed and continually increased in bitt Johnson committed himself to it with gladiatorial eagerness. He no fit temper to listen to the wisest and most potent arguments whic gress might suggest. All hope of reconciliation soon disappeared. veto messages he plumply denied the right of Congress to adopt legi measures preliminary to the admission of duly qualified members fr Southern States, and Congress, in its turn, denied his right to adc measures which he had adopted preliminary to his recognition of states. The appeal, therefore, was to the people.

The Republican party was divided. The people were divided, and peared for a long time difficult to decide whether its verdict would the executive or for Congress. In the mean time, a decision had bee dered by the Supreme Court of the United States against the constit ality of test oaths. Certain Republicans in Washington, coinciding the views of the President, formed an organization known as the "Na Union Club." This organization was subsequently united with anoth similar character in Washington, and a National Union executive co tee was appointed. On the 23d of May the members of this league naded the President and the officers of his cabinet to elicit an expr of views on the existing crisis. In most cases, and especially in th Secretary McCulloch, the ministerial advisers of the President sustain policy of restoration. Secretary Stanton did not commit himself. H that "no one better than Johnson understood the solemn duty im upon the national executive to maintain the national authority, vindi at so great a sacrifice, and the obligation not to suffer the just fruits many battles and victories to slip away or turn to ashes." After a and full discussion, he said that he had yielded to the President's op against negro suffrage. He distinctly declared that the plan report the Congressional Committee on Reconstruction did not receive his s Postmaster General Dennison regretted the difference between the dent and Congress. He did not believe it rested upon any good re and thought that time and discussion would bring reconciliation. S tary Seward was absent at Auburn, New York, but he there indulged frank expression of his views. He was hopeful—"hopeful of the Presi hopeful of Congress, hopeful of the National Union party, hopeful of th represented states—above all, hopeful of the favor of Almighty God." ought ever afterward to be styled "Secretary Hopeful."

On the 25th of June a call was issued for a National Union Conver to be composed of at least two delegates from each Congressional Distr every state, two from each Territory, two from the District of Columbia four delegates at large from each of the states, to meet at Philadelphia gust 14. This call was signed by A. W. Randall, J. R. Doolittle, O. H. Br ing, Edgar Cowan, Charles Knapp, and Samuel Fowler, members of th ecutive committee of the National Union Club. The delegates, how were to agree upon the following principles: That the Union could n dissolved even by Congressional action; that each state has the undo right to prescribe the qualifications of its own electors, and no ext power rightfully can or ought to dictate, control, or influence the fre voluntary action of the states in the exercise of that right; that the n tenance inviolate of the rights of the states, and especially of the rig each state to order and control its own domestic concerns, according own judgment exclusively, subject only to the Constitution of the U States, is essential to the balance of power on which the perfection an durance of our political fabric depend, and the overthrow of that syste the usurpation and centralization of power in Congress would be a re tion dangerous to republican government and destructive of liberty; that each house of Congress is made, by the Constitution, the sole judg the elections, returns, and qualifications of its members; but the excl of loyal senators and representatives, properly chosen and qualified the Constitution and laws, is unjust and revolutionary.

This call was followed on the 4th of July by an address to the pe signed by 41 Democratic members of Congress, who approved the cal the principles therein set forth. The executive committee addressed l to each member of the cabinet, to obtain, in reply, an expression of views as to the propriety of such a Convention, and as to the principles which the call had been based. Seward replied that he considered re tion the most vital interest of the country. Nothing could complete but the admission of loyal members from the Southern States. Every delay increased our domestic and foreign embarrassment. It seeme only proper, but expedient, therefore, that all parties should unite in re strance against the Congressional policy. Secretary Welles was not less strong and explicit in the position taken by him in favor of the Convention. Attorney General Speed expressed far different views. Many of the principles set forth in the call for the Convention he deemed unobjectionable. But the formation of this new party would dissolve the old Union party, which had, in face of the prophecies of half the New and all the Old world, saved the government from demoralization and utter ruin. The scheme of this new party was, in his view, a distraction from the real and all-absorbing question of the moment—the acceptance or rejection by the people of the Congressional amendment. Being himself decidedly in favor of the amendment, he could not identify himself with an organization which ignored its importance and smothered its discussion. Postmaster General Dennison replied on July 11th by tendering his resignation, which was accepted by the President, who appointed A. W. Randall, of Wisconsin, to act as his successor. The causes given by Dennison for his resignation were his difference of opinion with the President in regard to the proposed amendment and the movement for the Philadelphia Convention. The attorney general soon after resigned, and was succeeded by Henry Stansberry, of Ohio. The Secretary of the Interior, Mr. Harlan, of Iowa, having been elected senator, resigned, and Orville H. Browning, of Ohio, was appointed in his stead.

And here let us pause for a moment to look at the various phases of the political situation which presented itself in the summer of 1866, just before the meeting of the Philadelphia Convention. In this connection the mistakes of the President or of Congress are not to be considered; for, even if we admit that Congress had erred as well as the President, these errors belonged to the past, and could not be reversed. It was evident that the conflict between the two departments of the government now admitted of no reconciliation. We are not now to consider how previously reconciliation could have been effected; it was not now possible. We must also concede both to the President and to Congress the constitutional right to act precisely as they had acted. Whatever want of tact there may have been on the part of either is not here a subject for consideration. Neither party to the conflict had been in the slightest degree guilty of any usurpation. We are to forget all extraneous and incidental considerations, and confine ourselves to the precise issue presented to the people. For the moment we are to banish both the President and Congress from a place in our thoughts, and weigh the two policies between which the people must decide. We must not forget, however, that the people had not been all this while a silent party to the contract. The President believed that his policy was supported by the people, and Congress had been restrained from the adoption of more radical measures by the fear that these would not obtain the popular assent. Both the President and Congress appealed to the people. And the issue presented was a very plain one: it was simply a question whether it should ignore the President and accept the Congressional amendment as a preliminary to the admission of Southern representatives, or ignore Congress and decide in favor of immediate representation on the President's plan.

It was a plain question. Either the policy of the President or that of Congress must receive the popular sanction. But, although the line drawn between the two policies was so clearly defined, the motives influencing the popular judgment were various and complex. The question resolved itself into one of expediency. Which plan, under the circumstances, ought to be adopted? Thus all mere theories were swept out of the arena of discussion. The issue was intensely practical, and pressed instantly for decision—neither time nor room was left for speculation. There were dangers to be avoided, there were benefits to be maintained and secured. Which plan most surely averted danger? Which secured the most lasting good?

The plea put in for each policy was strong, and urgently demanded careful and calm consideration. The advocates of the executive plan for restoration claimed that the war had a distinct purpose which had already been accomplished—the extinction of armed rebellion. Slavery also had been extinguished with rebellion. Thus the root and seed of all our strife had been removed. But, although the slave had departed, the negro remained. In many of the states the negro population at the close of the war exceeded the white. The two races would naturally abide together, for each needed the other. The white race needed the black for labor, not because it would not itself labor, but because of the extraordinary resources of the southern section of the country, which demanded for their full development not only all the white and black inhabitants already occupying it, but thousands upon thousands more who would come from the Northern States as immigrants, and from all the nations of Europe. The black race stood in no less need of the white, because the latter had intelligence in a greater degree, was used to the exercise of political power, and must therefore, of necessity, be the regulative and controlling race. Not regulative in the despotic sense, in which it had been hitherto as the task-masters over the black, but, because of its greater civilization, it was more competent to carry out the ends of civilization. To change this relation, to give the black race all the political mastery to which it might be entitled merely on the basis of numbers, would be to fight Nature, who gives sovereignty not to numbers, but to developed capacity. Such a revolution against Nature would necessarily put back the civilization of one half of the nation by a foolish surrender of power to ignorance or incompetency. We must trust to Nature, whose movements, if they are large in their cycles and slow of accomplishment, are nevertheless efficient. Before the war, Nature had already decreed the death of slavery, and the war itself had grown out of an attempt on the part of slaveholders to defy Nature; for they saw that slavery, restricted as it must be by the nation under the pressure of moral opinion, would surely die. They said, therefore, we will resist the pressure; we will make a new nation, with slavery for the corner-stone; there shall be no restriction, and this peculiar institution shall live forever! They defied Nature, and were defeated; and the very institution which by revolution they hoped to save, was by revolution destroyed. By this revolution the society of the South was reduced back to first principles—to a new beginning. A new era was opened to labor, now emancipated. A period of transition was now commenced. Might we not trust to Nature, and to the new influences in operation, and to time for results? Labor, free, must have a destiny of its own. Intelligence must follow, and the development of political capacity in the masses. The revolution had been radical. All things were new, and must grow out of a new beginning. Might we not trust to this new growth? Would we not best help it on by an era of mutual trust and good feeling? Might not the North say to the South, "Work out your destiny for yourself under these new and better influences, and we will await with patience the result, and will not interfere?" Would not legislative interference, defying Nature, defeat its own purpose? Was it necessary to add to the changes produced by the war any change in the organic law beyond the declaration of the death of slavery? That dead, would not the new life of the South, under the new circumstances, develop satisfactory results?

Thus questioned and reasoned those, who, without partisan motives and from simple patriotism, supported the President's policy. Among the best representatives of this class was Rev. Henry Ward Beecher.

But to all this reasoning Congress, and the supporters of Congress, had a reply. It is true, said they, that we are to begin anew, and that we must largely trust to the working of Nature and the influences of time. But the South does not begin anew as a separate section, but as a part of a great nation. The responsibilities of the moment do not rest upon a part alone, but upon the whole. The whole nation is beginning anew, and not one section alone. The South does not stand by itself in this new era. The national Legislature, acting under the organic law—the Constitution—is the regulative power. The revolution which has taken place must be recognized here, in this Legislature, in this organic law. It is true that Nature is large in movement, slow, and in the end efficient. But Nature is sometimes diseased, abnormal in its action, and may be helped by remedies. The diseases of the past, the result of slavery, still cling to the ruling, regulative race in the South, and will injuriously affect not only Southern development, but the national growth. Labor in the South is emancipated, but, in those who control labor there, the oppressive spirit developed by slavery still remains. With this oppressive class, whose political power in the national councils is rather increased than diminished by the death of slavery, there is a party in the North at this moment ready to strike hands and unite in a treaty, offensive and defensive, for the control of the country. It is within our power, and is therefore a duty for which we are responsible, to avert this possible evil. So far as possible, we must start aright and upon correct principles on this new era upon which the nation is entering. We can not act arbitrarily, we can not exercise the power of despotism, but we can submit to the people such changes in the organic law of the nation as, if the people will ratify them, will establish the new nation upon a secure basis. We therefore submit to the people an amendment to the Constitution which will give to all citizens equal rights and equal representation, secure the repudiation of the rebel debt and the adoption of the national debt in good faith, and disable leading traitors for such time as we may deem expedient.

Such were the pleas in behalf of the Presidential and Congressional policies. And the appeal was to the people.

On the 14th of August the National Union Convention assembled at Philadelphia. Every state and Territory was represented excepting Arizona, Montana, and Utah. General John A. Dix was chosen temporary Chairman, and Senator Doolittle President. At the opening of the Convention quite a sensation was created by the entrance of the delegates from Massachusetts and South Carolina arm in arm. The Convention did its work rapidly. On the third day an address was read by Henry J. Raymond, and approved by the Convention, and resolutions were adopted, declaring that the rights, dignity, and authority of the states were perfect and unimpaired; that Congress had no right to deny representation to any state; that the right to regulate the elective franchise was reserved to the states; that amendments to the Constitution might be made in the usual way, and that in rectifying the same all the states of the Union had an equal and indefeasible right to a voice and a vote thereon; that slavery was abolished, and the enfranchised slaves should receive equal protection with other citizens in every right of person or property; that any debt incurred in the execution of rebellion was invalid, and that the national debt was sacred and inviolable; and that President Johnson was a chief magistrate worthy of the nation, and equal to the great crisis upon which his lot was cast.[1]

[1] "The National Union Convention now assembled in the city of Philadelphia, composed of delegates from every state and territory in the Union, admonished by the solemn lessons which, for the last five years, it has pleased the Supreme Ruler of the Universe to give to the American people; profoundly grateful for the return of peace; desirous, as are a large majority of their countrymen, in all sincerity, to forget and forgive the past; revering the Constitution as it comes to us from our ancestors; regarding the Union in its restoration as more sacred than ever; looking with deep anxiety into the future, as of instant and continuing trials, hereby issues and proclaims the following declaration of principles and purposes, on which they have, with perfect unanimity, agreed:

"1. We hail with gratitude to Almighty God the end of the war and the return of peace to our afflicted and beloved land.

"2. The war just closed has maintained the authority of the Constitution, with all the powers which it confers, and all the restrictions which it imposes upon the general government, unabridged and unaltered, and it has preserved the Union, with the equal rights, dignity, and authority of the states perfect and unimpaired.

"3. Representation in the Congress of the United States and in the electoral college is a right recognized by the Constitution as abiding in every state, and as a duty imposed upon the people, fundamental in its nature, and essential to the existence of our republican institutions, and neither

A committee was appointed to present to the President a copy of the proceedings of the Convention. Senator Reverdy Johnson acted as the representative of this committee. The President, in his reply, spoke of Congress as a body which was preventing the restoration of peace and harmony,—a body which, pretending to be a Congress of the United States, but which was, in fact, a Congress of only part of the states—a body "hanging upon the verge of the government."

Other Conventions also were held. The Southern Loyalists' Convention met at Philadelphia on the 1st of September, and adopted resolutions in favor of the Congressional policy. On the 17th of September, the Convention of soldiers and sailors assembled at Cleveland, Ohio, and adopted resolutions of a similar character with those adopted by the Philadelphia Convention of August 14th. Of this Convention Major General Gordon Granger was President. On the 25th of September, a Convention of soldiers and sailors sustaining the action of Congress assembled at Pittsburg, Pennsylvania, and Major General J. D. Cox was elected President. A series of resolutions was reported by Major General B. F. Butler, of which the two following were the most characteristic:

"*Resolved*, That the President, as an executive officer, has no right to a policy as against the legislative department of the government. That his attempt to fasten his scheme of reconstruction upon the country is as dangerous as it is unwise; his acts in sustaining it have retarded the restoration of peace and unity; they have converted conquered rebels into impudent claimants to rights which they have desecrated. If consummated, it would render the sacrifices of the nation useless, the loss of the lives of our buried comrades vain, and the war in which we have so gloriously triumphed what his present friends at Chicago, in 1864, declared it to be, a failure.

"*Resolved*, That the right of the conqueror to legislate for the conquered has been recognized by the public law of all civilized nations. By the operation of that law for the conservation of the good of the whole country, Congress had the undoubted right to establish measures for the conduct of the revolted states, and to pass all acts of legislation that are necessary for the complete restoration of the Union."

In the mean time, an event had occurred which had created the most intense excitement throughout the country. In 1864, the Louisiana State Convention had made a new Constitution, and submitted it to the people of that state. This Constitution had been ratified. Among its provisions was one for its amendment, requiring that the proposition for amendment should proceed from the state Legislature. Two years had passed, and the Convention was dissatisfied with its own work, and had grown rabid for negro suffrage. It was no longer a legitimate organization after the ratification of its Constitution. It attempted, however, to revive itself; it obtained the support of Governor Wells, who appointed an election to secure delegates from the parishes not represented in the original Convention, and the 30th of July was appointed for the revival of the Convention. The plan proposed by this Convention involved the overturning of its own Constitution, which had already been sanctioned by the people. It was a revolutionary body. It is not wonderful that its scheme occasioned excitement. As if for the purpose of revolution and tumult, this Convention held a preliminary meeting in New Orleans, at which speeches were made appealing to the negroes to come forth in force for the protection of the Convention. The mayor of New Orleans at this time was John T. Monroe. His antecedents were not of a favorable character. In company with Lieutenant Governor Voorhees, he had waited upon General Absalom Baird, who, in the absence of Major General Sheridan, commanded the United States military force at New Orleans, to ascertain whether, if the members of the Convention were arrested, the military would interfere. General Baird's answer was, that the sheriff, attempting such an arrest, would himself be arrested; that the Convention, meeting peaceably, could not be interfered with by the officers of the law. But the Convention could not be said to have met peaceably, having directly provoked tumult. A telegram was sent to
the President inquiring whether the process of the court to arrest the :
bers could be thwarted by the military. The President replied tha
military would sustain, and not interfere with the proceedings of the c
The Convention met on the 30th, but there was not a quorum. Plain
ther the majority of the members were timid, or were satisfied of the ir
larity of the Convention. The negroes whom Dr. Dostie, a member of
body, had called forth in prospect of a conflict, were ready at the tim
pointed. The citizens of New Orleans were, on the other hand, also r
The collision was inevitable. Just how the riot began is uncertain.
there is no question of the fact that both the negroes and the citizens
gathered together for no other purposes than those of strife. The r
was disgraceful to the negroes, to the citizens, to the Convention, and t
New Orleans police, whose brutality can scarcely be distinguished
murder.[1]

This occurrence was made use of by both parties as political capital.
supporters of Congress pointed to it as an indication of the disloyalty o
Southern people, and the Democrats, on the other hand, held up the :
lutionary Convention as an example of radical violence. The preva
popular impression acquitted the negroes of any desire to disturb the p
and threw the blame partly upon the Convention, which, by the incent
speech of at least one of its members, had incited tumult; but chiefly :
the white citizens of New Orleans, who had been organized for a riot,
who had met at a preconcerted signal for the purpose of violently dis
ing the Convention. The mayor, John T. Monroe, was supposed to b
the side of the rioters, and was held by General Sheridan to be largel
sponsible for their action. President Johnson suffered much loss in
people's estimation from his support of Mayor Monroe hitherto, but he
not be held consciously responsible for the violence of July 30th.

On the 28th of August President Johnson left Washington for Chic
to be present at the laying of the corner-stone of a monument to be erc
to the memory of Stephen A. Douglas. He was accompanied by Sec
ries Seward and Welles, by General Grant and Admiral Farragut. I
the cities through which the President passed, he was accorded that co
ous welcome which the people are always ready to extend to their c
magistrate. His speeches on the route were full of the most bitter de
ciation of Congress, which he described as a body hanging upon the v
of the government. In some cases he descended to bandy words wi
crowd, and to answer ill-tempered jeers at himself by an echo of their
temper. His utter lack of tact disgusted even his friends. He too cle
proved that, whatever might be the merits of his policy, he could not be :
ly trusted as leader with any policy. As Henry Ward Beecher soon a
ward aptly said, "The greatest obstacle to the success of Andrew Johns
policy is Andrew Johnson."

The autumn elections of 1866 were now at hand. The President,
of Democratic support, desired also to retain a good portion of the Re
lican vote. His especial favorites—those who received the largest shar
his patronage, were Republicans of the Philadelphia Convention scl
But the defection from the Republican ranks caused by the Philadel
Convention movement was not large. The old Union party still main
ed its ranks unbroken, and refused to be distracted from the main iss
the Congressional amendment to the Constitution. The national exect
committee, which had been appointed in 1864, held its regular meetin
Philadelphia. Governor Marcus L. Wood, of New Jersey, was elected c
man. The places on that committee of Henry J. Raymond, and others
had participated in the Philadelphia Convention, were filled, and an adc
was issued to the people calling upon them to support the Congressi
plan of restoration.

The late riots in New Orleans, the President's tour to the tomb of D
las, the attempt of the President to influence the prospective election
the distribution of patronage to his special adherents, and his evident d
mination to use Democrats, pardoned rebels, and every possible avail
element to carry out his policy, tended to consolidate the Republican p
in opposition. Another circumstance which conduced to this result
the fact that the nominees of the so-called Conservatives were in most c
men in whom the Union party of the country had no confidence.

The popular vote was decidedly in favor of the Congressional policy.
Maine, Chamberlain, the Republican candidate, was elected over Pillsl

---

Congress nor the general government has any authority or power to deny this right to any state, or to withhold its enjoyment under the Constitution from the people thereof.

"4. We call upon the people of the United States to elect to Congress as members thereof none but men who admit this fundamental right of representation, and who will receive to seats therein loyal representatives from every state in allegiance to the United States, subject to the constitutional right of each house to judge of the elections, returns, and qualification of its own members.

"5. The Constitution of the United States, and the laws made in pursuance thereof, are the supreme law of the land, any thing in the Constitution or laws of any state to the contrary notwithstanding. All the powers not conferred by the Constitution upon the general government, nor prohibited by it to the states, are reserved to the states, or to the people thereof; and among the rights thus reserved to the states is the right to prescribe qualifications for the elective franchise therein, with which right Congress can not interfere. No state or combination of states has the right to withdraw from the Union, or to exclude, through their action in Congress or otherwise, any other state or states from the Union. The Union of these states is perpetual.

"6. Such amendments to the Constitution of the United States may be made by the people thereof as they may deem expedient, but only in the mode pointed out by its provisions; and in proposing such amendments, whether by Congress or by a Convention, and in ratifying the same, all the states of the Union have an equal and indefeasible right to a voice and a vote thereon.

"7. Slavery is abolished and forever prohibited, and there is neither desire nor purpose on the part of the Southern States that it should ever be re-established upon the soil, or within the jurisdiction of the United States; and the enfranchised slaves in all the states of the Union should receive, in common with all their inhabitants, equal protection in every right of person and property.

"8. While we regard as utterly invalid, and never to be assumed or made of binding force, any obligations incurred or undertaken in making war against the United States, we hold the debt of the nation to be sacred and inviolable; and we proclaim our purpose in discharging this, as in performing all other national obligations, to maintain unimpaired and unimpeached the honor and faith of the republic.

"9. It is the duty of the national government to recognize the services of the Federal soldiers and sailors in the contest just closed, by meeting promptly and fully all their just and rightful claims for the services they have rendered the nation, and by extending to those of them who have survived, and to the widows and orphans of those who have fallen, the most generous and considerate care.

"10. In Andrew Johnson, President of the United States, who, in his great office, has proved steadfast in his devotion to the Constitution, the laws, and interests of his country, unmoved by persecution and undeserved reproach, having faith unassailable in the people and in the principles of free government, we recognize a chief magistrate worthy of the nation, and equal to the great crisis upon which his lot is cast; and we tender to him, in the discharge of his high and responsible duties, our profound respect, and assurance of our cordial and sincere support."

[1] The views of General Sheridan, in military command of the Department, are expressed i
following dispatches:

"New Orleans, August 1, 1

"U. S. GRANT, General:
"You are doubtless aware of the serious riot which occurred in this city on the 30th. A
ical body, styling itself the Convention of 1864, met on the 30th, for, as it is alleged, the purpo
remodeling the present Constitution of the state. The leaders were political agitators and r
tionary men, and the action of the Convention was liable to produce breaches of the public p
I had made up my mind to arrest the head men if the proceedings of the Convention were calc
to disturb the tranquillity of the Department, but I had no cause for action until they committe
overt act. In the mean time official duty called me to Texas, and the mayor of the city, durir
absence, suppressed the Convention by the use of the police force, and, in doing so, attacke
members of the Convention and a party of two hundred negroes with fire-arms, clubs, and k
in a manner so unnecessary and atrocious as to compel me to say that it was murder. About
whites and blacks were thus killed, and about one hundred and sixty wounded. Every thing i
quiet, but I deem it best to maintain a military supremacy in the city for a few days, until the
is fully investigated. I believe the sentiment of the general community is great regret at thi
necessary cruelty, and that the police could have made any arrest they saw fit without sacri
lives.
P. H. SHERIDAN, Major General Commandin

"New Orleans, Louisiana, August 2, 1

"U. S. GRANT, General, Washington, D. C.:
"The more information I obtain of the affair of the 30th in this city, the more revolting i
comes. It was no riot; it was an absolute massacre by the police, which was not excelled in
derous cruelty by that of Fort Pillow. It was a murder which the mayor and police of the
perpetrated without the shadow of a necessity. Furthermore, I believe it was premeditated
every indication points to this. I recommend the removing of this bad man. I believe it wou
hailed with the sincerest gratification by two thirds of the population of the city. There has
a feeling of insecurity on the part of the people here on account of this man, which is now so
increased that the safety of life and property does not rest with the civil authorities, but wit
military.
P. H. SHERIDAN, Major General Commandin

by twenty-seven thousand votes, and every Republican delegate to Congress was chosen by a considerable majority. In New Hampshire, the Republican majority for Governor Smyth over Sinclair was nearly 5000. In Connecticut, the Republican candidate, General Joseph R. Hawley, was elected over English by a few hundred votes. General Burnside was chosen Governor of Rhode Island by a majority of over 5000. Alexander H. Bullock, in Massachusetts, received a majority over Sweetser of over 65,000. Among the members elected to the state Legislature were two colored men. In Vermont, Paul Dillingham received a majority of nearly 23,000 over Davenport, the Democratic candidate for governor. In New Jersey, out of five members elected to the Fortieth Congress, three were Republican. In New York, Governor Fenton was elected over Hoffman, the Democratic candidate, by a majority of nearly 14,000. In Delaware, Saulsbury, the Democratic candidate for governor, was elected by some 1200 votes. In Kentucky, the election was not for the principal officers, but the Democratic majority was about 38,000. In California, a judge of the Supreme Court was elected by the Republican party by a majority of 7000. In Oregon, the Republican majority for Woods as governor was 327. In Ohio, the Republican majority for secretary of state was nearly 43,000. In Indiana also a Republican secretary was elected by 14,000 majority. Kansas gave a Republican majority for Crawford, as governor, of over 11,000. In Iowa, the Republican majority for secretary of state was over 35,000. In Pennsylvania, Major General Geary, the Republican candidate, was elected governor over Heister Clymer by 17,000 majority. In Michigan, Crapo, Republican candidate for governor, was elected over Williams by a majority of 29,000. Minnesota elected Republican representatives to Congress by about 10,000 majority. In Illinois, General John A. Logan was elected Congressman at large over Dickey by nearly 56,000. Wisconsin gave a Republican majority of 24,000 for Congressmen.

From this estimate, it is clear that the people repudiated the President's policy, and by overwhelming majorities in nearly all the states supported Congress. This was not more decisively shown in the election of state officers than in the vote for members of the Fortieth Congress.

From this point a new stage in the reconstruction movement commenced. The antagonism of the President was still continued against Congress, notwithstanding the popular decision in favor of the Congressional amendment. The Southern States still refused to accept the conditions submitted by Congress and supported by the loyal people. Thus there was a dead-lock in the process of restoration. There were then two methods of procedure. Either Congress and the whole country could wait until the Southern States should accept the amendment, or they could take the whole affair into their own hands, and decide arbitrarily that the movement should go on, and upon what conditions. Congress adopted the latter method. Just before the close of its second session, the Thirty-ninth Congress passed an act known as the Military Bill. This act declared that no legal state governments existed in the late rebel states (excluding Tennessee), and that in these states there was no adequate protection for life or property. These states were therefore distributed into military districts, subject to the military authority of the United States, as follows:

I. Virginia.
II. North Carolina and South Carolina.
III. Georgia, Alabama, and Florida.
IV. Mississippi and Arkansas.
V. Louisiana and Texas.

The President was to appoint as a commander of each district an officer of the army not below the rank of brigadier general, and to detail a sufficient military force to enable such officer to perform his duties and enforce his authority.

The duties of these commanders were—to protect all persons in their rights of person and property, to suppress insurrection, disorder, and violence, and to punish, or cause to be punished, all disturbers of the public peace and criminals. To this end they might allow local civil tribunals to take jurisdiction of and try offenders, or, at their discretion, might organize military commissions for the trial of offenders, and this exercise of military authority should exclude interference on the part of the state government. No sentence of death should be carried into effect without the approval of the President.

The fifth section of this act provided that when the people of any of these states should have formed a Constitution in conformity with the Constitution of the United States in all respects, and which should be framed by delegates elected by the male citizens of said state 21 years old and upward, "of whatever race, color, or previous condition, resident in the state for one year, excepting those disfranchised for participation in rebellion," and when such Constitution should provide for universal suffrage, with the exception of those disfranchised for participation in rebellion, and be ratified by the people and approved by Congress, and the Congressional amendment should have been adopted, the said state should be admitted to representation in Congress.

The sixth section of the bill provided that until this admission of representatives to Congress the civil government of each state should be considered as provisional only.

The President vetoed this bill, and it was passed over his veto by both houses March 2, 1867. He then, in obedience to the act thus passed against his remonstrance, appointed Brevet Major General John M. Schofield com-

The Fortieth Congress assembled on the 4th of March, 1867, immediately succeeding and receiving the mantle of the Thirty-ninth. Soon after its assembling it passed an act supplementary to the Military Bill adopted at the previous session. This supplementary act provided in detail for the registration of voters.[1] It was vetoed by the President, and then passed over the veto by each house.

The supplementary act was vetoed as the original act had been, but was on the 23d of March passed, notwithstanding the President's objections.[2]

[1] *An Act supplementary to an Act entitled "An Act to Provide for the more efficient Government of the Rebel States," passed March 2d, 1867, and to facilitate Restoration.*

"*Be it enacted by the Senate and House of Representatives of the United States of America, in Congress assembled*, That before the first day of September, 1867, the commanding general in each district defined by an act entitled 'An Act to Provide for the more efficient Government of the Rebel States,' passed March 2d, 1867, shall cause a registration to be made of the male citizens of the United States, twenty-one years of age and upward, resident in each county or parish in the state or states included in his district, which registration shall include only those persons who are qualified to vote for delegates by the act aforesaid, and who shall have taken and subscribed the following oath or affirmation: 'I, ——, do solemnly swear (or affirm), in the presence of Almighty God, that I am a citizen of the State of ——; that I have resided in said state for — months next preceding this day, and now reside in the county of ——, or the parish of ——, in said state (as the case may be); that I am twenty-one years old; that I have not been disfranchised for participation in any rebellion or civil war against the United States, nor for felony committed against the laws of any state or of the United States; that I have never been a member of any state Legislature, nor held any executive or judicial office in any state, and afterward engaged in insurrection or rebellion against the United States, or given aid or comfort to the enemies thereof; that I have never taken an oath as a member of Congress of the United States, or as an officer of the United States, or as a member of any state Legislature, or as an executive or judicial officer of any state, to support the Constitution of the United States, and afterward engaged in insurrection or rebellion against the United States, or given aid or comfort to the enemies thereof; that I will faithfully support the Constitution and obey the laws of the United States, and will, to the best of my ability, encourage others so to do: so help me God;' which oath or affirmation may be administered by any registering officer.

"SEC. 2. *And be it further enacted*, That after the completion of the registration hereby provided for in any state, at such time and places therein as the commanding general shall appoint and direct, of which at least thirty days' public notice shall be given, an election shall be held of delegates to a Convention for the purpose of establishing a Constitution and civil government for such state loyal to the Union, said Convention in each state, except Virginia, to consist of the same number of members as the most numerous branch of the state Legislature of such state in the year 1860, to be apportioned among the several districts, counties, or parishes of such state by the commanding general, giving each representation in the ratio of voters registered as aforesaid as nearly as may be. The Convention in Virginia shall consist of the same number of members as represented the territory now constituting Virginia in the most numerous branch of the Legislature of said state in the year 1860, to be apportioned as aforesaid.

"SEC. 3. *And be it further enacted*, That at said election the registered voters of each state shall vote for or against a Convention to form a Constitution therefor under this act. Those voting in favor of such a Convention shall have written or printed on the ballots by which they vote for delegates as aforesaid the words 'For a Convention,' and those voting against such a Convention shall have written or printed on such ballot the words 'Against a Convention.' The persons appointed to superintend said election, and to make return of the votes given thereat, as herein provided, shall count and make return of the votes given for and against a Convention; and the commanding general to whom the same shall have been returned shall ascertain and declare the total vote in each state for and against a Convention. If a majority of the votes given on that question shall be for a Convention, then such Convention shall be held as hereinafter provided; but if a majority of said votes shall be against a Convention, then no such Convention shall be held under this act: *Provided*, That such Convention shall not be held unless a majority of all such registered voters shall have voted on the question of holding such Convention.

"SEC. 4. *And be it further enacted*, That the commanding general of each district shall appoint as many boards of registration as may be necessary, consisting of three loyal officers or persons, to make and complete the registration, superintend the election, and make return to him of the votes, list of voters, and of the persons elected as delegates by a plurality of the votes cast at said election; and upon receiving said returns he shall open the same, ascertain the persons elected as delegates, according to the returns of the officers who conducted said election, and make proclamation thereof; and if a majority of the votes given on that question shall be for a Convention, the commanding general, within sixty days from the date of election, shall notify the delegates to assemble in Convention, at a time and place to be mentioned in the notification, and said Convention, when organized, shall proceed to frame a Constitution and civil government according to the provisions of this act, and the act to which it is supplementary; and when the same shall have been so framed, said Constitution shall be submitted by the Convention for ratification to the persons registered under the provisions of this act at an election to be conducted by the officers or persons appointed or to be appointed by the commanding general, as hereinbefore provided, and to be held after the expiration of thirty days from the date of notice thereof, to be given by said Convention; and the returns thereof shall be made to the commanding general of the district.

"SEC. 5. *And be it further enacted*, That if, according to said returns, the Constitution shall be ratified by a majority of the votes of the registered electors qualified as herein specified, cast at said election, at least one half of all the registered voters voting upon the question of such ratification, the president of the Convention shall transmit a copy of the same, duly certified, to the President of the United States, who shall forthwith transmit the same to Congress, if then in session, and if not in session, then immediately upon its next assembling; and if it shall moreover appear to Congress that the election was one at which all the registered and qualified electors in the state had an opportunity to vote freely, and without restraint, fear, or the influence of fraud, and if the Congress shall be satisfied that such Constitution meets the approval of a majority of all the qualified electors in the state, and if the said Constitution shall be declared by Congress to be in conformity with the provisions of the act to which this is supplementary, and the other provisions of said act shall have been complied with, and the said Constitution shall be approved by Congress, the state shall be declared entitled to representation, and senators and representatives shall be admitted therefrom as therein provided.

"SEC. 6. *And be it further enacted*, That all elections in the states mentioned in the said 'Act to Provide for the more efficient Government of the Rebel States' shall, during the operation of said act, be by ballot; and all officers making the said registration of voters and conducting said elections shall, before entering upon the discharge of their duties, take and subscribe the oath prescribed by the act approved July 2d, 1862, entitled 'An Act to prescribe an Oath of Office:' *Provided*, That if any person shall knowingly and falsely take and subscribe any oath in this act prescribed, such person so offending and being thereof duly convicted shall be subject to the pains, penalties, and disabilities which by law are provided for the punishment of the crime of willful and corrupt perjury.

"SEC. 7. *And be it further enacted*, That all expenses incurred by the several commanding generals, or by virtue of any orders issued, or appointments made by them, under or by virtue of this act, shall be paid out of any moneys in the treasury not otherwise appropriated.

"SEC. 8. *And be it further enacted*, That the Convention for each state shall prescribe the fees, salary, and compensation to be paid to all delegates and other officers and agents herein authorized or necessary to carry into effect the purposes of this act not herein otherwise provided for, and shall provide for the levy and collection of such taxes on the property in such state as may be necessary to pay the same.

"SEC. 9. *And be it further enacted*, That the word 'article,' in the sixth section of the act to which this is supplementary, shall be construed to mean 'section.'"

[2] To the original bill President Johnson objected on the following grounds:

1. That "the mass of the Southern people, while they entertain diverse opinions on questions of federal policy, are completely united in the effort to reorganize their society on the basis of peace, and to restore their mutual prosperity as rapidly and completely as the circumstances of the case will permit."

2. The military rule established by the bill is "to be used, not for any purpose of order or for the prevention of crime, but solely as a means of coercing the people into the adoption of principles and measures to which it is known that they are opposed, and upon which they have an undeniable right to exercise their own judgment." Thus it was in "palpable conflict with the plainest provisions of the Constitution."

3. The power given by the bill "is that of an absolute monarch, his mere will taking the place of all law; it places at his free disposal all the lands and goods in his district; and he may dis-

The President's objections to both the original and the supplementary acts were theoretically just; but, for all that, they did not touch the question as it offered itself to Congress. He could see in the establishment of military power and the suffrage given to the blacks only three things: a design on the part of the Republican party to perpetuate its own power; an absolute despotism; and a violation of the Constitution. There may have been, and probably were, a few members in both houses of Congress who were partisans in the sense that they preferred the success of their party to the interests of their country; there may have been those who lightly regarded constitutional liberty and constitutional law; but this was not the light in which Congress, as a body, looked upon the situation which confronted it. An appeal had been made to the people of the Northern States, and the result had been a Congressional victory. An opportunity had already been afforded to the Southern States to regain their representation in Congress by doing exactly what Tennessee had done—*i. e.*, by accepting a Constitutional amendment, which involved no imposition upon them of negro suffrage, nor indeed any conditions not really demanded by the situation at the close of the war. But they had rejected the advances of Congress, and stood defiantly upon "their rights" as interpreted for them by Andrew Johnson. The work of restoration could not, then, proceed upon the plan originally proposed by Congress. But the work must go on upon some plan. Either the people must surrender to the President against their own good sense, by reverting to his plan, now that their own had failed, or they must adopt still another. And what other was possible? Only one; and that was to appeal from the whites of the South to the whole people, white and black. In order to do this, it was necessary to give the negroes of the South the privilege of voting for Conventions in the several states. This plan evidently could not be carried into execution except under the supervision of military commanders. We are not, however, in vindicating the necessity of the Military Bill, defending every feature of that bill. Undoubtedly it would have been better if Congress had omitted that provision by which so large a portion of Southern whites were disfranchised. This provision was not essential in order to secure the objects sought.

It must indeed be admitted that the Military Bill was unconstitutional. But so in a greater or less degree had been every measure in the entire process of reconstruction, whether adopted by the President or by Congress. Lincoln's Emancipation Proclamation was unconstitutional, and was only defensible on the plea of military necessity. But the necessities of war are no more binding than those of peace. The object of the war was to conquer peace; and after the war there still remained the no less difficult work of securing the peace which had been conquered. Was the security of the conquest any less important than the conquest itself? Lincoln issued his proclamation after long hesitation and with evident reluctance: But he stood face to face with a great necessity, and was compelled to act. The deliberations of the Thirty-ninth Congress in 1866 show that that body was equally reluctant to interfere directly with the right of states to regulate their own system of franchise. But the necessity came, and came as the result of the attitude assumed by the Southern people. Congress yielded, as Mr. Lincoln had done.

At first the bill did not strike the South unfavorably. This is probably to be accounted for by the fact that the political leaders of the South anticipated that the votes of the freedmen could easily be regulated by their former masters. Every attempt was made to influence the freedmen in this direction. Thus General Wade Hampton said to them,[1] "Give your friends at the South a fair trial; when they fail you will be time enough to go abroad for sympathy; it is for your interest to build up the South, for as the country prospers you will prosper." Similar arguments were used in every Southern state. Disfranchised white men addressed assemblages mainly composed of enfranchised blacks. But they did not hold the field alone, else their success might have been assured. Several Northern men traversed the South, and urged the freedmen to act with the Republican party. Prominent among these were Senator Wilson, of Massachusetts, and Mr. Kelley, representative from Pennsylvania. Their speeches were moderate in tone, but very effective. White men attended these meetings, apparently willing that both parties should have a fair chance in this contest for the negro vote. There was a slight disturbance in Mobile, in which Mr. Kelley was placed in some peril; but in New Orleans, at a meeting addressed by Senator Wilson, the Confederate General Longstreet was one of the vice-Presidents. Whatever may have been the hopes entertained by the Southern whites as to the possibility of securing the support by the freedmen of what was termed the Conservative policy, they were not realized. So soon as it became evident that the negroes would support Congress, there began to be developed a bitter opposition to the Military Bill, both in the South and among those in the North who supported Mr. Johnson. Very many, also, who were opposed to Johnson's policy, thought that the disfranchisement of so many whites in the South, and the evident purpose shown by those who controlled registration to give political supremacy to the blacks, were not only unnecessary, but also injurious to the Republican party.

Although President Johnson had protested so strongly against the establishment of military governments, yet after the passage of the Congressional acts he proceeded promptly to their execution. Even in the appointment of the military commanders he seems to have sought just those officers in the army which would be most likely to meet the approbation of Congress. In the case of General Sheridan particularly, the President feared that the conduct of that officer might be needlessly arbitrary. Still he yielded to the popular sentiment in favor of the general, and gave him the most difficult of the five military districts. The President sought, however, in every possible way, to regulate the operations of the military government in such a manner as to relieve those features which were most obnoxious. But the legislation of Congress left him a very limited sphere of action. He could not prevent the subordination of the civil governments of the South to the military commanders; the provisions of the original Military Bill were explicit on that point, and could not be avoided. On the same day that this bill was finally passed, the Tenure of Office Bill was also passed over the President's veto. The provisions of this bill, by limiting his authority in making official appointments, almost entirely deprived him of the power to check any proceedings, however arbitrary, on the part of the military commanders; it took from him the power of removing even the members of his cabinet except by and with the consent of the Senate. Indeed, more executive power was delegated to each of the military commanders than was left to the executive head of the government.

Thus cramped and fettered by Congress, the President had recourse to Mr. Stansberry, his attorney general. Was there no way in which the executive might lay his hand upon the registration of voters in the South, and prevent the sweeping disfranchisement contemplated by Congress? Stansberry thought there was. Surely the legal opinion of the highest legal officer in the nation ought to avail somewhat. So the attorney general gave an opinion—and a very ingenious and elaborate opinion it was, we must admit.[1] The most important point in this opinion is the statement that the

sons, of every color, sex, and condition, and every stranger within their limits—to the most abject and degrading slavery. No master ever had a control over his slaves so absolute as this bill gives to the military officers over both white and colored persons."

4. The bill is unconstitutional in conferring the right of suffrage upon the freedmen. "The negroes have not asked for the privilege of voting; the vast majority of them have no idea what it means. This bill not only thrusts it into their hands, but compels them, as well as the whites, to use it in a particular way. If they do not form a Constitution with prescribed articles in it, and afterward elect a Legislature which will act upon certain measures in a prescribed way, neither blacks nor whites can be relieved from the slavery which the bill imposes upon them. Without pausing here to consider the policy or impolicy of Africanizing the southern part of our territory, I would simply ask the attention of Congress to that manifest, well-known, and universally-acknowledged rule of constitutional law which declares that the federal government has no jurisdiction, authority, or power to regulate such subjects for any state. To force the right of suffrage out of the hands of the white people and into the hands of the negroes is an arbitrary violation of this principle."

5. "We should remember that all men are entitled to at least a hearing in the councils which decide upon the destiny of themselves and their children. At present ten states are denied representation; and when the Fortieth Congress assembles on the 4th day of the present month, sixteen states will be without a voice in the House of Representatives. This grave fact, with the important question before us, should induce us to pause in a course of legislation which, looking solely to the attainment of political ends, fails to consider the rights which it transgresses, the law which it violates, or the institutions which it imperils."

The veto to the supplementary act reiterates the objections to the original bill, and adds some others. "By the oath required at registration," says the President, "every elector must decide for himself, under peril of military punishment if he makes a mistake, whether he has been disfranchised for participation in rebellion. . . . . Almost every man—the negro as well as the white—above 21 years of age, who was resident in the ten states during the rebellion, voluntarily or involuntarily, at some time and in some way, did participate in resistance to the lawful authority of the general government." Besides, urges the President, as the people themselves have no voice in conducting the registration and the subsequent election, the Conventions elected can not be considered as representing the citizens of those states.

[1] At Columbia, South Carolina, March 18.

[1] The principal points are as follows: 1. All who are registered, and none others, have the right to vote. 2. No one who is not a citizen of the United States, and of the special state, can properly take the oath; but if an alien not naturalized chooses, he can take it, and must be registered; but "he takes it at his peril, and is liable to prosecution for perjury." 3. The person who applies for registry must be of the age of twenty-one years when he applies; but the requirement for a residence of one year applies to the time of voting, not of registration.

He next proceeds to consider the various grounds of disfranchisement provided for in the bills. In his opinion, (4), the sections which "deny the right to vote to such as may be disfranchised for participation in the rebellion or felony at common law," must be interpreted to mean that "the mere fact of such participation, or the commission of the felonious act, does not of itself work as a disfranchisement. It must be ascertained by the judgment of a court, or by a legislative act, passed by competent authority." But the applicant for registration must swear that "I have never been a member of any state Legislature, nor held any executive or judicial office, and afterward engaged in insurrection or rebellion against the United States; that I have never taken an oath as a member of the Congress of the United States, or as an officer of the United States, or as a member of any state Legislature, or as an executive or judicial officer of any state, to support the Constitution of the United States, and afterward engaged in insurrection or rebellion against the United States." This provision, in the opinion of the attorney general, certainly excludes (5) members of Congress, of state Legislatures, and of Conventions which passed ordinances of secession. Then as to who are to be considered as intended by executive and judicial officers of the state, he gives his opinion that (6) officers of the militia of a state are not as such intended; that (7) governors, state treasurers, and others, commonly designated as "state officers," who "exercise executive functions at the seat of government," and also judicial officers whose jurisdiction extends through the state, are included; but that (8) those functionaries commonly known as "county, township, and precinct officers," sheriffs, county judges, commissioners of public works and improvements, and the like, are not included.

Under the provision working disfranchisement on account of the person having taken an oath to support the Constitution, and afterward engaged in insurrection, he holds that (9) the two things must concur, and "in the order of time mentioned: First, the office and the oath; and afterward engaging in the rebellion or giving aid and comfort." Hence (10) "a person who has held an office within the meaning of this law, and taken the official oath, and who has not afterward participated in the rebellion; and so too the person who has fully participated in the rebellion, but has not prior thereto held an office and taken the official oath, may with safety take the oath" required for registration.

The attorney general then proceeds to consider "what acts, within the meaning of the law, make a party guilty of engaging in insurrection or rebellion against the United States, or of giving aid or comfort to the enemies thereof?" As to official acts, he thinks that the phrase "enemies," to whom "aid and comfort" has been given, should in strict law be limited to mean only "foreign enemies;" but he adds, (11), "I am not quite prepared to say that Congress may not have used it as applicable to the late rebellion," and therefore he goes on to inquire "what is meant by engaging in insurrection or rebellion against the United States?" It implies, he thinks, (12), "active rather than passive conduct, voluntary rather than compulsory action." Hence it does not include (13) such cases as that of a person who has been forced into the ranks by conscription, or a slave who, by command of his master, or by military order, has been engaged upon military works or served in the ranks of the army. But (14) it does include many who, without having actually been in arms, were engaged in the furtherance of the common unlawful purpose, such as "members of Congress and rebel Conventions, diplomatic agents of the rebel Confederacy, or such other officials whose duties more especially appertained to the support of the rebel cause." Yet, on the other hand, it does not (15) include "officers in the rebel states who, during the rebellion, discharged duties not incident to the war. The interests of humanity," the attorney general argues, "require such officers for the performance of such official duties in time of war or insurrection as well as in time of peace, and the performance of such duties can never be considered as criminal."

From official participation the attorney general goes on to discuss what constitutes, in the view of this law, individual participation in the rebellion, premising that in the case of a great insurrection, which for a time excluded the people from the protection of the lawful government, the "obligations of allegiance are necessarily modified," and that many things should be considered as "rightfully done which in the case of a mere local insurrection would have no color of legality." He concludes, therefore, (16), that "some direct overt act, done with the intent to further the rebellion, is necessary to bring the party within the purview and meaning of the law." The expression of disloyal sentiments, the performance of acts of ordinary charity and humanity, the payment of taxes or forced contributions and the like, are not sufficient. But (17) "voluntary contributions in furtherance of the rebellion, or subscriptions to the rebel loan, and even organized contributions of food and clothing or necessary supplies, except of a strictly sanitary character, are to be classed with acts which disqualify."

mere fact of participation in the rebellion does not of itself work disfranchisement, except as it had been declared to have that effect by the judgment of a court or by a legislative act passed by competent authority. The attorney general also construed the Military Bill as not intending the disfranchisement of those who had held minor executive offices of a local nature under the Confederate government, nor those who had not *voluntarily* engaged in rebellion. He declared also that, under the law, registering officers could not refuse to permit every applicant to take the oath required; and that the oath once taken, and the applicant's name once registered, the privilege of voting could not be withdrawn.

Invested with this legal authority, President Johnson issued an order to each of the military commanders, directing them to conform to the opinion of the attorney general. The value of a legal opinion had such an impression upon the President that he shortly afterward obtained another from the same source, the purport of which was that the military commanders had no right to remove civil officers, and that therefore Mr. Wells, whom Sheridan had removed, was still the rightful governor of Louisiana, and John T. Monroe (also removed by the same officer) was mayor of New Orleans.

Congress met again July 4, and continued in session for sixteen days. In this brief period a new bill was matured and passed, defining the military acts of the two previous sessions.[1] This explanatory act completely annulled the attorney general's opinions, and left no room for doubt as to the intentions of Congress in its plan of Southern reconstruction. The President returned the bill with his objections July 19. In this veto message he denounced with equal bitterness the despotic powers conferred upon military commanders, and the limitations imposed, against the manifest intent of the Constitution, upon the executive.[2] The bill was passed over Johnson's veto.

In respect to the functions of the Boards of Registration and Election, the attorney general holds (18) that they can impose no oath other than that prescribed by this law; that (19) they must administer the oath to all who will take it, "the oath being the only and sole test of the qualification of the applicant;" that (20) if a person takes the oath his name must go upon the register; and that (21) his name being on the register, he must be allowed to vote. "There is no provision," adds the attorney general, "to surcharge or falsify, or add a single name to the registration, or erase a single name that appears upon it."

[1] The following are in brief the provisions of this explanatory act:

Sec. 1. "That it is hereby declared to have been the true intent and meaning of the act of the 2d day of March, 1867, entitled an Act to Provide for the more efficient Government of the Rebel States, thereto passed the 23d of March, 1867, that the governments then existing in the rebel states of Virginia, North Carolina, South Carolina, Georgia, Mississippi, Alabama, Louisiana, Florida, Texas, and Arkansas were not legal state governments, and that thereafter said governments, if continued, shall be subject in all respects to the military commanders of the respective districts, and to the paramount authority of Congress."

Sec. 2. "That the commander of any district named in said act shall have power, subject to the disapproval of the general of the army of the United States, and to have effect till disapproved, whenever, in the opinion of such commander, the proper administration of said act shall require it, to suspend or remove from office, or from the performance of official duties and the exercise of official powers, any officer or person holding or exercising, or professing to hold or exercise, any civil or military office or duty in such district, under any power, election, appointment, or authority, derived from, or granted by, or claimed under any so-called state or, the government thereof, or municipal or other division thereof; and upon such suspension or removal such commander, subject to the disapproval of the general as aforesaid, shall have power to provide from time to time for the performance of the said duties of such officer or person so suspended or removed by the detail of some competent officer or soldier of the army, or by the appointment of some other person to perform the same, and to fill the vacancies occasioned by death, resignation, or otherwise."

Sec. 3. "That the general of the army of the United States be invested with all the powers of suspension, removal, appointment, and detail granted in the preceding section to district commanders."

Sec. 4. "That the acts of the officers of the army already done in removing, in said districts, persons exercising the functions of civil officers, and appointing others in their stead, are hereby confirmed, provided that any person heretofore or hereafter appointed by any district commander to exercise the functions of any civil office may be removed, either by the military officer in command of the district or by the general of the army, and it shall be the duty of such commander to remove from office as aforesaid all persons who are disloyal to the government of the United States, or who use their official influence in any manner to hinder, delay, prevent, or obstruct the due and proper administration of this act and the acts to which it is supplementary."

Sec. 5 makes it the duty of the Boards of Registration, before allowing any person to be registered, to ascertain whether he is entitled to registration; and the oath of the person is not to be conclusive evidence; and no person shall be registered unless the board decides that he is entitled thereto; and "no person shall be disqualified as member of any Board of Registration by reason of race or color."

Sec. 6 declares that the true intent and meaning of the oath prescribed in the supplementary act is, among other things, "that no person who has been a member of the Legislature of any state, or who has held any executive or judicial office in any state, whether he has taken an oath to support the Constitution or not, and whether he was holding such office at the commencement of the rebellion, or had held it before and who has afterward engaged in rebellion against the United States, or given aid and comfort to the enemies thereof, is entitled to be registered or vote; and the words 'executive or judicial office in any state,' in said oath mentioned, shall be construed to include all civil officers created by law for the administration of any general law of a state, or for the administration of justice."

Sec. 7 authorizes the commander of any district to extend the period for registration until the 1st of October, 1867. Makes it their duty, commencing fourteen days previous to any election under the act, and for a period of five days, to revise the registration list, strike off the names of all persons not entitled thereto, and add any names of persons so entitled which have not been registered; "and no person shall at any time be entitled to be registered or to vote by reason of any executive pardon or amnesty for any act or thing which, without such pardon or amnesty, would disqualify him from registration or voting."

Sec. 8. "That all members of said Boards of Registration, and all persons hereafter elected or appointed to office in said military districts, under any so-called state or municipal authority, or by detail, or appointment of the district commanders, shall be required to take and subscribe to the oath of office prescribed by law for the officers of the United States."

Sec. 9. "That no district commander or member of the Board of Registration, or any officers or appointees acting under them, shall be bound in his action by any opinion of any civil officer of the United States."

Sec. 10. "That section 4 of said last-named act shall be construed to authorize the commanding general named therein, whenever he shall deem it needful, to remove any member of a Board of Registration, and to appoint another in his stead, and to fill any vacancy in such board."

Sec. 11. "That all the provisions of this act, and of the acts to which this is supplementary, shall be construed liberally, to the end that all the intents thereof may be fully and perfectly carried out."

[2] The President thus concludes his message:

"Within a period less than a year the legislation of Congress has attempted to strip the executive department of the government of some of its essential powers. The Constitution, and the oath provided in it, devolve upon the President the power and duty to see that the laws are faithfully executed. The Constitution, in order to carry out this power, gives him the choice of the agents, and makes them subject to his control and supervision; but, in the execution of these laws, the constitutional obligation upon the President remains, but the power to exercise that constitutional duty is effectually taken away. The military commander is, as to the power of appointment, made to take the place of the President, and the general of the army the place of the Senate, and any attempt on the part of the President to assert his own constitutional power may, under pretense of law, be met by official insubordination. It is to be feared that these military officers, looking to the authority given by these laws rather than to the letter of the Constitution, will re-

But the President did not relinquish his claim to the authority which he conceived rightfully belonged to him as the executive head of the nation. Scarcely had Congress adjourned when he addressed a note[1] to Secretary Stanton, stating that "grave public considerations" constrained him to request the secretary's resignation. Mr. Stanton replied, "Grave public considerations constrain me to continue in the office of Secretary of War until the next meeting of Congress." The secretary had originally co-operated with the President's plan of Southern restoration, but after the elections of 1866 he went over to Congress. His position in the cabinet thus became very embarrassing. He could not resign his position without disappointing Congress, and, as he believed, the people: nor could he retain the secretaryship without violating the hitherto well understood principles of official courtesy. But Johnson relieved him of his embarrassment on the 12th of August by removing him, ordering General Grant to assume the duties of acting Secretary of War. Stanton then submitted, "under protest," as he said, "to the superior force of the President." The general satisfaction of the people with the administration of the war office by General Grant soon reconciled them to the change, and the President's palpable defiance of the Tenure of Office Bill was for a time substantially ignored.

Five days after the removal of Secretary Stanton, the President drew up an order removing General Sheridan from the command of the Fifth Military District, and appointing General Thomas in his stead. This did not meet with General Grant's approbation. The general boldly defended Sheridan on the ground that the military district was the most difficult one in the South to manage; that this difficulty had grown out of the prevailing impression among the people of that district that the President was about to remove Sheridan; and that, under these circumstances, General Sheridan had been compelled to resort to the arbitrary measures which the President disapproved. General Grant also objected to the change as being an impolitic one at the time. But the President insisted; Grant submitted, and the order was issued on the 26th. General Thomas declined the appointment, and General Hancock finally assumed the important office from which Sheridan had been removed.

Almost simultaneously, General Sickles was removed from the command of the Second District, embracing North and South Carolina, and General Canby was appointed in his stead. The removals of Stanton, Sheridan, and Sickles, following each other in quick succession, excited considerable apprehension in the North, which was exaggerated by flying rumors that the President was now prepared to resist Congress by force, that Maryland militia were being trained for his support, and that the country was on the verge of a *coup d'etat*. Indeed, it was impossible to say what thunderbolts the President was *not* prepared to fulminate against the legislative department of the government. The autumn elections were at hand, in which a second appeal was to be made to the people, and these popular fears were used by Republican orators as an argument for the support of Congress and its military reconstruction enactments.

The results of the autumn elections of 1867 were a surprise to the Republican party. In California, on the 4th of September, the Democratic candidate for governor was elected by a majority of 7466 over both the opposing Republican candidates; a Democratic Legislature was also elected, involving the loss of a Republican United States senator. Five days later, the Maine election resulted in a falling off from Republican majority of 14,000 votes. On the 8th of October elections took place in Pennsylvania, Ohio, Indiana, Iowa, and West Virginia. In Pennsylvania there was a Republican loss of 18,000 as compared with the previous year. Ohio elected a Republican governor, but lost so largely in the Legislature as to secure a Democratic United States senator at the expiration of Benjamin F. Wade's term. There was a Republican loss in that state of 40,000 votes. In Indiana only local officers were elected. In Iowa there was a Republican loss of over 10,000. On the 5th of November, elections were held in New York, New Jersey, Massachusetts, Maryland, Illinois, Wisconsin, Minnesota, and Kansas, and with similar results. In New York, a Democratic secretary of state was elected by a majority of 48,922. There was in that state a Republican loss of over 62,000 votes. In Massachusetts, Governor Bullock, Republican, was re-elected by 25,000 majority, showing a falling off of 32,000 from the majority of 1866. In New Jersey there was a Democratic majority of about 15,000, the Republican loss being about 18,000. Maryland went Democratic by a majority of 40,000, against 13,000 in 1866. In Illinois the elections were local. Wisconsin elected a Republican governor by 4000, a loss from the previous year of 20,000. In Minnesota there was a falling off of over 6000 from the Republican majority of 1866. Estimating by majorities, the Republican loss indicated in all the elections was over 250,000.

In Kansas, Minnesota, Ohio, and Pennsylvania, the people voted upon a constitutional amendment, allowing negroes to vote in these states. The amendment was defeated by heavy majorities in all except Minnesota.

chief executive authority of the United States, while the obligation rests upon me to see that all the laws are faithfully executed, I can never willingly surrender that trust or the powers given for its execution. I can never give my assent to be made responsible for the faithful execution of laws, and at the same time surrender that trust and the powers which accompany it to any other executive officer, high or low, or to any number of executive officers. If this executive trust, vested by the Constitution in the President, is to be taken from him and vested in a subordinate officer, the responsibility will be with Congress in clothing the subordinates with unconstitutional power, and with the officer who assumes its exercise. This interference with the constitutional authority of the executive department is an evil that will inevitably sap the foundations of our federal system; but it is not the worst evil of this legislation. It is a great public wrong to take from the President powers conferred on him alone by the Constitution; but the wrong is more flagrant and more dangerous when the powers so taken from the President are conferred upon subordinate executive officers, and especially upon military officers. Over nearly one third of the states of the Union military power, regulated by no fixed law, rules supreme. Each of the five district commanders, though not chosen by the people, or responsible to them, exercises at this hour more ex-

It is evident from these estimates that there had been a popular reaction. In 1866, the people had decided against President Johnson—now they appeared to mutter against Congress. It must be remembered, however, that in most of the states the elections were of such a character as not to draw out the full strength of the Republican party. Still, even making this allowance, the people evidently disapproved of the temper and spirit which characterized the proceedings of Congress in this matter of reconstruction. It would hardly be fair to infer from the elections that the people were opposed to *what* Congress had done; but the manner in which Congress proceeded, apparently assuming that any measures, however extreme, would receive popular support, indicated that some check must be put upon that body. There was another consideration of the utmost importance, and which largely affected the popular vote. Before another general election could take place, the party Conventions would meet for the nomination of presidential candidates. The prominent leaders of the Republican party were evidently determined to select some one representing the extreme views of that party. It was important that this should not be done, and yet quite certain that it would be attempted, if in the elections the Republican party should receive the same support as in 1866. This consideration materially affected the result of the elections. Thousands of Republicans staid away from the polls, wishing neither to support Democratic candidates, nor to give their sanction to the extreme views of their own party leaders. As to the vote in four of the states upon negro suffrage, the result had no special significance, for the issue presented had none. The refusal of Ohio to allow colored citizens to vote did not by any means imply opposition to negro suffrage as a feature of the military reconstruction bill. In Ohio, as in all the Northern States, the only question involved in this matter was one between an abstract principle and the prejudice of race; but not so in the Southern States, one third of whose entire population was colored. Here there were questions of expediency as well as of abstract justice to be considered. The exclusion of the vast colored population of the South from negro suffrage involved dangers not only to the future tranquillity of the states themselves, but to the peace of the nation. The perils which many feared from this universal or impartial suffrage were mainly imaginary. President Johnson predicted that it would bring on a war of races; but it would seem far more reasonable to expect such a war to follow the exclusion of a very large class from all political power. The moment the negro becomes invested with political rights, the very basis for the antagonism of races is removed.

When Congress again assembled on the 21st of November, its proceedings were characterized by greater moderation, but it steadfastly adhered to its policy of restoration. The President's message was for the most part a reiteration of the arguments upon which he had insisted from the beginning of his administration. He urged the repeal of those "acts of Congress which place ten of the states under the domination of military masters:" He denounced the policy of negro suffrage and white disfranchisement as the "subjugation of these states to negro domination, and worse than military despotism." He alluded to certain cases in which it would become the President's duty to resist Congressional enactments by force, "regardless of consequences." "If, for instance," said he, "the legislative department should pass an act, even through all the forms of law, to abolish a co-ordinate branch of the government, in such a case the President must take the high responsibility of his office, and save the nation at all hazards."

In January, the Thirty-ninth Congress had passed a resolution looking toward the impeachment of President Johnson, and directing the judiciary committee to investigate his official conduct. This committee, at the close of the session on March 4th, had delivered over its duties and the results of its inquiry to its natural successor. In June, the judiciary committee of the Fortieth Congress, after a careful sifting of the testimony offered, stood four for and five against impeachment. But one of the members, who in June had been opposed to impeachment—Mr. John C. Churchill—changed his mind before the beginning of the November session, and thus the measure came before the House on the 25th supported by a majority report.[1] Two minority reports were also submitted. It is clear that the President had been guilty of no offense indictable by law; and both the American and British law on this subject determine that impeachment can not rest except upon offenses of this character. Besides, the impeachment of President Johnson, simply because his policy was opposed to that of the legislative department of the government, would establish a dangerous precedent, which could be used against any president by any dominant political party opposed to him. The House wisely, therefore, refused to adopt the report of the majority.

President Johnson, after having once entered into the conflict against Congress, fought obstinately for the success of his own policy of reconstruction. His legal arguments, however wise in theory, were almost always practically false. His angry denunciation of his opponents weakened the popular confidence in his wisdom and capacity for the successful leadership of any party. His subsidizing of all the subordinate offices of the government for his own purposes promised to reinaugurate the system of official corruption under which the national politics had degenerated through a long series of administrations previous to the election of Mr. Lincoln. This excited greater fear and distrust, because an enormous national debt, involving a most intricate system of internal revenue, had infinitely increased the opportunities for corruption. Johnson's administration completely disappointed the American people. It was notoriously corrupt. It misled the Southern people, sharpening continually the edge of their defiance. It drove Congress and the loyal people to the alternative of a surrender to what they believed a mistaken policy, or of adopting extreme measures, which otherwise they would have reluctantly sanctioned. It was a failure as regarded its own purposes, and an obstruction to the national development.

As we write (December, 1867) the Congressional plan of reconstruction is still in its preliminary stages. Registrations have been completed in all the ten states under military rule, and in most of them show a majority of colored voters. Elections have been held in several of these states, and in some the Conventions are now in session. The delegates of these Conventions are almost all supporters of the Congressional policy; and it is probable that the Constitutions framed by them will be ratified by the several states, and that they will include provisions for impartial or universal suffrage. Whether in other respects—for example, in the disfranchisement of a large number of whites—they will meet the approbation of Congress after the recent elections in the North, we can not predict. It seems certain, however, that, whatever else may fail, the principle of "equal rights for all men, without distinction of color," will be maintained in the next presidential election and in the election of a new Congress. But prophecy belongs not to the historian. We will not seek to lift the veil of our future. With the recital of the events of the last seven years our proper work concludes. What remains to be written we leave to other hands; what we have written we now submit to the charitable but impartial judgment of our readers.

---

[1] The charges brought in this report against the President were the following:

"1st. That the President of the United States, assuming it to be his duty to execute the constitutional guarantee, has undertaken to provide new governments for the rebellious states without the consent or co-operation of the legislative power, and upon such terms as were agreeable to his own pleasure, and then to force them into the Union against the will of Congress and the people of the loyal states, by the authority and patronage of his high office.

"2d. That to effect this object he has created offices unknown to the law, and appointed to them, without the advice or consent of the Senate, men who were notoriously disqualified to take the test oath, at salaries fixed by his own mere will, and paid those salaries, along with the expenses of his work, out of the funds of the War Department, in clear violation of law.

"3d. That, to pay the expenses of the said organizations, he has also authorized his pretended officers to appropriate the property of the government, and to levy taxes from the conquered people.

"4th. That he has surrendered, without equivalent, to the rebel stockholders of Southern railroads captured by our arms, not only the roads themselves, but the rolling-stock and machinery captured along with them, and even roads constructed or renovated at an enormous outlay by the government of the United States itself.

"5th. That he has undertaken, without authority of law, to sell and transfer to the same parties, at a private valuation and on a long credit, without any security whatever, an enormous amount of rolling-stock and machinery, purchased by and belonging to the United States, and after repeated defaults on the part of the purchasers, has postponed the debt due to the government in order to enable them to pay the claims of other creditors, along with arrears of interest on a large amount of bonds of the companies, guaranteed by the State of Tennessee, of which he was himself a large holder at the time.

"6th. That he has not only restored to rebel owners large amounts of cotton and other abandoned property that had been seized by the agents of the treasury, but has presumed to pay back the proceeds of actual sales made thereof, at his own will and pleasure, in utter contempt of the law directing the same to be paid into the treasury, and the parties aggrieved to seek their remedy in the courts, and in manifest violation of the true spirit and meaning of that clause of the Constitution of the United States which declares that no 'money shall be drawn from the treasury but in consequence of appropriations made by law.'

"7th. That he has abused the pardoning power conferred on him by the Constitution, to the great detriment of the public, in releasing, pending the condition of war, the most active and formidable of the leaders of the rebellion, with a view to the restoration of their property and means of influence, and to secure their services in the furtherance of his policy; and, further, in substantially delegating that power for the same objects to his provisional governors.

"8th. That he has further abused this power in the wholesale pardon, in a single instance, of 193 deserters, with restoration of their justly forfeited claims upon the government for arrears of pay, without proper inquiry or sufficient evidence.

"9th. That he has not only refused to enforce the laws passed by Congress for the suppression of the rebellion, and the punishment of those who gave it comfort and support, by directing proceedings against the delinquents and their property, but has absolutely obstructed the course of public justice, by either prohibiting the initiation of legal proceedings for that purpose, or, where already commenced, by staying the same indefinitely, or ordering absolutely the discontinuance thereof.

"10th. That he has further obstructed the course of justice by not only releasing from imprisonment an important state prisoner, in the person of Clement C. Clay, charged, among other things, as asserted by himself in answer to a resolution of the Senate (Ex. Doc., 39th Congress, No. 7), 'with treason, with complicity in the murder of Mr. Lincoln, and with organizing bands of pirates, robbers, and murderers in Canada, to burn the cities and ravage the commercial coasts of the United States on the British frontier,' but has even forbidden his arrest on proceedings instituted against him for treason and conspiracy in the State of Alabama, and ordered his property, when seized for confiscation by the district attorney of the United States, to be restored.

"11th. That he has abused the appointing power lodged with him by the Constitution:

"1. In the removal, on system, and to the great prejudice of the public service, of large numbers of meritorious public officers, for no other reason than because they refused to indorse his claim of the right to reorganize and restore the rebel states on conditions of his own, and because they favored the jurisdiction and authority of Congress in the premises.

"2. In reappointing, in repeated instances, after the adjournment of the Senate, persons who had been nominated by him and rejected by that body as unfit for the place for which they had been so recommended.

"12th. That he has exercised a dispensing power over the laws by commissioning revenue officers and others unknown to the law, who were notoriously disqualified by their participation in the rebellion from taking the oath of office required by the act of Congress of July 2, 1862, allowing them to enter upon and exercise the duties appertaining to their respective offices, and paying to them salaries for their services therein.

"13th. That he has exercised the veto power conferred on him by the Constitution in its systematic application to all the important measures of Congress looking to the reorganization and restoration of the rebel states, in accordance with a public declaration that 'he would veto all its measures whenever they came to him,' and without other reasons than a determination to prevent the exercise of the undoubted power and jurisdiction of Congress over a question that was cognizable exclusively by them.

"14th. That he has brought the patronage of his office into conflict with the freedom of elections by allowing and encouraging his official retainers to travel over the country, attending political conventions and addressing the people, instead of attending to the duties they were paid to perform, while they were receiving high salaries in consideration thereof

"15th. That he has exerted all the influence of his position to prevent the people of the rebellious states from accepting the terms offered to them by Congress, and neutralized, to a large extent, the effects of the national victory by impressing them with the opinion that the Congress of the United States was bloodthirsty and implacable, and that their only hope was in adhering to him.

"16th. That, in addition to the oppression and bloodshed that have every where resulted from his undue tenderness and transparent partiality for traitors, he has encouraged the murder of loyal citizens in New Orleans by a Confederate mob pretending to act as a police, by holding correspondence with its leaders, denouncing the exercise of the constitutional right of a political Convention to assemble peacefully in that city as an act of treason proper to be suppressed by violence, and commanding the military to assist instead of preventing the execution of the avowed purpose of dispersing them.

"17th. That he has been guilty of acts calculated, if not intended, to subvert the government of the United States by denying that the Thirty-ninth Congress was a constitutional body, and fostering a spirit of disaffection and disobedience to the law and rebellion against its authority, by endeavoring, in public speeches, to bring it into odium and contempt."

INDEX.

THE END.

9781333726768

ND - #0092 - 130123 - C0 - 229/152/24 - PB - 9781333726768 - Gloss Lamination